An Exegetical Bibliography of the New Testament

ROMANS AND GALATIANS

MERCER UNIVERSITY PRESS • MACON, GEORGIA

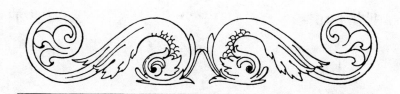

An
Exegetical
Bibliography
of the
New Testament

EDITED BY

GÜNTER WAGNER

ISBN 0-86554-468-9

MUP/H376

An Exegetical Bibliography of the New Testament.
Romans and Galatians.
Copyright ©1996
Mercer University Press, Macon, Georgia 31210-3960
All rights reserved
Printed in the United States of America
First printing May 1996

Library of Congress Cataloging-in-Publication Data

Main entry under title.
An exegetical bibliography of the New Testament.
    6 vols. 1983–
    1. Bible, N.T.—Bibliography. I. Wagner, Günter, 1928–
Z7772. L1E93 1995 [BS2361.2] 016.225   83-969
Isbn 0-86554-013-6 [vol. 1, Matthew–Mark]
Isbn 0-86554-140-X [vol. 2, Luke–Acts]
Isbn 0-86554-157-4 [vol. 3, John and 1, 2, 3 John]
Isbn 0-86554-468-9 [vol. 4, Romans and Galatians]

Contents

To Virginia Howard

Preface

This *Exegetical Bibliography of the New Testament* is an unwanted child, but it may well deserve its place. When I began teaching in 1958, I devised a detailed system for the collection of bibliographical information relevant to New Testament studies, ranging from the Old Testament background to the theology of the Early Church. Year after year I used—or misused—all available student help and secretarial assistance to work through our library holdings and current additions in order to glean references to all sorts of materials and to type each individual reference that was considered useful on a separate card. The card was then filed under its proper heading so it would take me—or any student who wished to use the file—no more than a minute to pick up a sizable pile of cards representing a basic bibliography on any topic in the entire New Testament field. The purpose of the whole undertaking was to enable the student to get down to research as quickly as possible without wasting days, even weeks, on the search for literature.

The students who helped me represented more than a dozen nationalities and spoke as many different mother tongues. Knowing or not knowing French, German, Spanish, Danish, Dutch, Italian, Norwegian, Swedish, Polish, and so forth, naturally proved to be both an asset and a liability; however, we did our best to achieve accuracy and consistency of form and of journal abbreviations. Postgraduate students who majored in the field of New Testament studies and later started teaching in various parts of the world got homesick for that monstrous steel cabinet in my office and wondered how they could still have access to it. We decided to type up the data of the exegetical section and to photocopy a reduced size of the condensed text, again on separate cards, so that everyone could add further references to his or her own card file. Between 1973 and 1979—in the good old precomputer age—we made *Bibliographical Aids* available on all New Testament writings. In 1981 we started editing the second series, copied by offset printing, again in a postcard size, looseleaf edition; upon reguest, we added the place of publication in the second series and we hope users of the bibliography will not mind this inconsistency.

I am most grateful to Mercer University Press for undertaking the time-consuming task of conflating series one and two and publishing them together in book form in one text. The first volume of *An Exegetical Bibliography of the New Testament: Matthew and Mark* appeared in 1983; *Luke and Acts* was published in 1985; and *John and 1,2,3 John* in 1987. While the file in my office continued to grow, various responsibilities kept me from editing the second series bibliographies on the letters of Paul. This was a blessing in disguise, however, since publications on Paul and his writings mushroomed in the late 1980s and early 1990s. We have therefore included significant references up to the year 1994. The combination of bibliographies on *Romans and Galatians* does not call for any justification, neither does their publication in the computer age.

Profound thanks are due to the many students who have assisted in the production of this volume, especially to Jeanette Mathews and David Hunter (Australia), Lidija and Ivica Novakovic (Croatia), and my wife Doris, who helped with the editing, typing, and proofreading. I want to express my sincere gratitude also to my friends Margaret and Floyd Patterson (Washington, D.C.) and Virginia Howard (Pineville, Louisana) whose encouragement and support have been invaluable throughout the years.

Corrales, New Mexico   *Günter Wagner*, Professor Emeritus
Thanksgiving 1995   Baptist Theological Seminary, Rüschlikon

List of Abbreviations

ABenR	American Benedictine Review (Atchison, Kansas)
ACR	Australasian Catholic Record (Sydney)
AER	American Ecclesiastical Review (Washington)
AfrER	African Ecclesiastical Review (Kampala)
AJA	American Journal of Archaelogy (New York)
AJBA	Australian Journal of Biblical Archaelogy (Sydney)
AJBI	Annual of the Japanese Biblical Institute (Tokyo)
ALUOS	Annual of Leeds University Oriental Society (Leeds)
AnBib	Analecta Biblica (Rome)
ANQ	Andover Newton Quarterly (Newton Centre, Massachusetts)
ANRW	Aufstieg und Niedergang der römischen Welt (Berlin 1972ff.)
Anton.	Antonianum (Rome)
AsiaJT	Asia Journal of Theology (Signapore)
AssS	Assemblées du Seigneur (Paris)
ASThI	Annual of the Swedish Theological Institute (Jerusalem)
AThR	Anglican Theological Review (Evanston, Illinois)
ATJ	African Theological Journal (Makumira)
AusBR	Australian Biblical Review (Melbourne)
AUSS	Andrews University Seminary Studies (Berrien Springs, Michigan)
BA	Biblical Archaelogist (Cambridge, Massachusetts)
BASOR	Bulletin of the American Schools of Oriental Research (Cambridge MA)
BCPE	Bulletin du Centre Protestant d'Études (Geneva)
BeO	Bibbia e Oriente (Genoa)
Biblica	Biblica (Rome)
BiblOr	Bibliotheca Orientalis (Leiden)
BiblSa	Bibliotheca Sacra (Dallas)
BibW	Biblical World (Chicago)
Bijdr	Bijdragen (Nijmegen)
BiLe	Bibel und Leben (Düsseldorf)
BiRe	Bible Revue (Ravenna)
BiTod	Bible Today (Collegeville/Minn.)
BJRL	Bulletin of the John Rylands Library (Manchester)
BLE	Bulletin de Littérature Ecclésiastique (Toulouse)
BLT	Brethren Life and Thought (Oak Brook/IL)
BR	Biblical Research (Chicago)
BTh	Biblical Theology (Belfast)
BThB	Biblical Theology Bulletin (Rome)
BTr	Bible Translator (London)
BTS	Bible et Terre Sainte (Paris)
BuK	Bibel und Kirche (Stuttgart)
BuL	Bibel und Liturgie (Klosterneuburg)
Burg.	Burgense (Burgos)
BVieC	Bible et Vie Chrétienne (Bruges)

BZ	Biblische Zeitschrift (Paderborn)
CahCER	Cahiers du Cercle Ernest-Renan (Paris)
CahJos	Cahiers de Joséphologie (Montreal)
CBQ	Catholic Biblical Quarterly (Washington)
ChM	Churchman (London)
ChrC	Christian Century (Chicago)
ChrTo	Christianity Today (Washington)
ChSt	Chicago Studies (Mundelein, Illinois)
CiCa	Civiltà Cattolica (Rome)
CiDi	Ciudad de Dios (Madrid)
CIM	Clergy Monthly (Ranchi)
CIR	Clergy Review (London)
ClB	Classical Bulletin (St. Louis,Mo.)
Conc	Concordia Journal (St. Louis,Mo.)
CoTh	Collectanea Theologica (Warsaw)
CrCu	Cross Currents (West Nyack, New Jersey)
CrQ	Crozer Quarterly (Chester, Pennsylvania)
CSR	Christian Scholar's Review (St. Paul, Minnesota)
CThJ	Calvin Theological Journal (Grand Rapids, Michigan)
CThM	Concordia Theological Monthly (St. Lous, Missouri)
CThMi	Currents in Theology and Mission (St. Louis,Mo.)
CV	Communio Viatorum (Prague)
DBM	Deltion Biblikon Meleton (Athens)
DDSR	Duke Divinity School Review (Durham, North Carolina)
DiThom	Divus Thomas (Poscenza)
DoLi	Dostrine and Life (Dublin)
DRev	Downside Review (Bath)
DTT	Dansk Teologisk Tidsskrift (Copenhagen)
DuRev	Dunwoodie Review (New York)
EFr	Estudios Fransiscanos (Madrid)
EphC	Ephemerides Carmeliticae (Rome)
EphL	Ephemerides Liturgicae (Rome)
EphM	Ephemerides Mariologicae (Madrid)
EphT	Ephemerides Theologicae Lovanienses (Louvain)
EQ	Evangelical Quarterly (London)
ER	Ecumenical Review (Geneva)
EstBi	Estudios Biblicos (Madrid)
EstEc	Estudios Eslesiásticos (Madrid)
EsVe	Escritos del Vedat (Torrente)
EsVie	Espirit et Vie (Langres)
ET	Expository Times (Birmingham)
EtEv	Études Évangeliques (Aix-en-Provence)
ETh	Église et Théologie (Ottawa)
EThR	Études Théologiques et Religieuses (Montpellier)
EuA	Erbe und Auftrag (Beuren)
EuD	Euntes Docete (Rome)
EvKomm	Evangelische Kommentare (Stuttgart)
EvTh	Evangelische Theologie (München)
Exp	The Expositor (London)
FilolNeot	Filologia Neotestamentaria (Cordoba/Spain)
FrR	Frieburger Rundbrief (Frieburg)
FSt	Franziskanische Studien (Münster)

FV	Foi et Vie (Paris)
FZPhTh	Freiburger Zeitschrift für Philosophie und Theologie (Fribourg)
GOThR	Greek Orthodox Theological Review (Brookline, Massachusetts)
GPM	Göttinger Predigtmeditationen (Göttingen)
GRBS	Greek, Roman and Byzantine Studies (Durham, North Carolina)
GThJ	Grace Theological Journal (Winona Lake,IN)
GThT	Gereformeerd Theologisch Tijdschrift (Amsterdam)
GuL	Geist und Leben (München)
HBTh	Horizons in Biblical Theology (Pittsburgh,PA)
HerKor	Herder Korrespondenz (Freiburg)
Herm	Hermathena (Dublin)
HeyJ	Heythrop Journal (London)
HPR	Homiletic and Pastoral Review (New York)
HR	History of Religion (Chicago)
HThR	Harvard Theological Review (Cambridge, Massachusetts)
HTS	Hervormde Teologiese Studies (Pretoria)
HUCA	Hebrew Union College Annual (Cincinnati)
IEJ	Israel Exploration Journal (Jerusalem)
IES	Indian Ecclesiastical Studies (Bangalore)
IJTh	Indian Journal of Theology (Serampore)
IKiZ	Internationale Kirchliche Zeitschrift (Bern)
IKZ	Internationale Katholische Zeitschrift (Rodenkirchen)
IndTheol	Stu Indian Theological Studies (Bangalore)
Interp	Interpretation (Richmond, Virginia)
IrBS	Irish Biblical Studies (Belfast)
IThQ	Irish Theological Quarterly (Marynooth)
JAAR	Journal of the American Academy of Religion (Atlanta, Georgia)
JAC	Jahrbuch für Antike und Christentum (Münster)
JAOS	Journal of the American Oriental Society (Baltimore)
JBL	Journal of Biblical Literature (Atlanta, Georgia)
JBTh	Jahrbuch für Biblische Theologie (Neukirchen)
JChS	Journal of Church and State (Waco/TX)
JEH	Journal of Ecclesiastical History (London)
JES	Journal of Ecumenical Studies (Philadelphia)
JEThS	Journal of the Evangelical Theological Society (Wheaton)
JHebS	Journal of Hebraic Studies (New York)
JHS	Journal of Hellenic Studies (London)
JJS	Journal of Jewish Studies (London)
JR	Journal of Religion (Chicago)
JRomS	Journal of Roman Studies (London)
JRTh	Journal of Religious Thought (Washington)
JSHRZ	Jüdische Schriften aus hellenistisch-römischer Zeit
JSJ	Journal for the Study of Judaism (Leiden)
JSNT	Journal for the Study of the New Testament (Sheffield,UK)
JSP	Journal for the Study of the Pseudepigrapha (Sheffield,UK)
JSS	Journal of Semitic Studies (Manchester)
JThS	Journal of Theological Studies (Oxford)
JTSA	Journal of Theology for Southern Africa (Braamfontein)
KG	Katholische Gedanke (Bonn)
KrR	Krest'anská revue (Praha)
KuD	Kerygma und Dogma (Göttingen)
LiBi	Linguistica Biblica (Bonn)

LM	Lutherische Monatshefte (Hamburg)
LQ	Lutheran Quarterly (Gettysburg)
LR	Lutherische Rundschau (Geneva)
LSt	Louvian Studies (Louvain)
LThJ	Lutheran Theological Journal (North Adelaide, S.Australia)
LThPh	Laval Théologique et Philosophique (Quebec)
LThQ	Lexington Theological Quarterly (Lexington, Kentucky)
LuVie	Lumière et Vie (Lyons)
LuVit	Lumen Vitae (Brussels)
LW	Lutheran World (Geneva)
MCh	Modern Churchman (Ludlow)
MisC	Miscelánea Comillas (Madrid)
MSR	Mélanges de Science Religieuse (Lille)
MTh	Melita Theologica (La Valetta)
MThZ	Münchener Theologische Zeitschrift (München)
NEAJTh	North East Asia Journal of Theology (Tokyo)
NedThT	Nederlands Theologisch Tijdschrift (The Hague)
NGTT	Nederuits Gereformeerde Teologiese Tydskrif (Stellenbosch)
NKZ	Neue kirchliche Zeitschrift (Erlangen)
NovT	Novum Testamentum (Leiden)
NRTh	Nouvelle Revue Théologique (Louvain)
NTS	New Testament Studies (Cambridge)
NTT	Norsk Teologisk Tidsskrift (Oslo)
NV	Nova et Vetera (Geneva)
NW	Neue Weg (Zürich)
NZSTh	Neue Zeitschrift für systematische Theologie (Berlin)
OCP	Orientalia Christiana Periodica (Rome)
OKS	Ostkirchliche Studien (Würzburg)
OLZ	Orientalistische Literaturzeitung (Berlin)
PaCl	Palestra del Clero (Rovigo)
PEQ	Palestine Exploration Quarterly (London)
Protest.	Protestantesimo (Rome)
PRSt	Perspectives in Religious Studies (Murfreesboro,N.C.)
PSB	Princeton Seminary Bulletin
PSThJ	Perkins School of Theology Journal (Dallas)
PThR	Princeton Theological Review (Princeton)
QR	Quarterly Review (Nashville)
RAM	Rassegna di Ascetica y Mistica (Florence)
RATh	Revue Africaine de Théologie (Kinshasa)
RB	Revue Biblique (Jerusalem)
RBen	Revue Bénédictine (Maredsous)
RBL	Ruch Biblijny i Liturgiczny (Cracow)
RBR	Ricerche Bibliche e Religiose (Milan)
RCB	Revista de Cultura Biblica (São Paulo)
RCIA	Revue de Clerge Африcian (Inkisi, Zaire)
RCT	Revista de Cultura Teologica (São Paulo)
REA	Revue des Études Augustiniennes (Paris)
REB	Revista Eclesiástica Brasileira (Petropolis)
RechSR	Recherches de Science Religieuse (Paris)
RefR(H)	Reformed Review (Holland/Mich.)
ReL	Religion in Life (Nashville)
REsp	Revista de Espiritualidad (Madrid)

RestQ	Restoration Quarterly (Abilene, Texas)
RET	Revista Española de Teología (Madrid)
RevBi	Revista Biblica (Buenos Aires)
RevEx	Review and Expositor (Louisville)
RevQ	Revue de Qumran (Paris)
RevR	Revue Réformée (Saint-German-en-Laye)
RevSR	Revue des Science Religieuses (Strasbourg)
RHE	Revue d'Histoire Ecclésiastique (Strasbourg)
RHPR	Revue d'Histoire et de Philosophie Religieuses (Strasbourg)
RHR	Revue de l'Histoire des Religions (Paris)
RHSp	Revue d'Histoire de la Spiritualité (Paris)
RivAC	Rivista di Archeologia Cristiana (Rome)
RivB	Rivista Biblica (Brescia)
RQ	Römische Quartalschrift (Freiburg)
RSLR	Rivista di Storia e Letteratura Religiosa (Turin)
RSPhTh	Revue des Sciences Philosophiques et Théologiques (Paris)
RSt	Religious Studies (London)
RT	Rassegna di Teologia (Naples)
RThAM	Recherches de Théologie Ancienne et Médiévale (Louvain)
RThL	Revue Théologique de Louvain (Louvain)
RThom	Revue Thomiste (Toulouse)
RThPh	Revue de Théologie et de Philosophie (Lausanne)
RThR	Reformed Theological Review (Hawthorn, Victoria)
RTK	Roczniki Teologiczno-Kanoniczne (Lublin)
RUO	Revue de l'Université d'Ottawa (Ottawa)
SaDo	Sacra Dottrina (Bologna)
SaDoBB	Sacra Dottrina Bolletino Bibliografico (Bologna)
Sal.	Salesianum (Torino)
SBFLA	Studii Biblici Franciscani Liber Annuus (Jerusalem)
SBTh	Studia Biblica et Theologica (Pasadena/CA)
SciE	Science et Esprit (Montreal)
ScrB	Scripture Bulletin (London)
ScrTh	Scripta Theologica (Pamplona)
ScuC	Scuola Cattolica (Milan)
SEA	Svensk Exegetisk Arsbok (Uppsala)
SEAJTh	South East Asia Journal of Theology (Singapore)
SJTh	Scottish Journal of Theology (Edinburgh)
SO	Symbolae Osloenses
SouJTh	Southwestern Journal of Theology (Fort Worth)
SThV	Studia Theologica Varsaviensia (Warsaw)
StLit	Studia Liturgica (Rotterdam)
StPa	Studia Patavina (Padua)
StPh	Studia Philonica (Chicago)
StR/SciR	Studies in Religion/Sciences Religieuses (Toronto)
StTh	Studia Theologica (Lund)
StZ	Stimmen der Zeit (München)
SVThQ	St. Vladimir's Theological Quarterly (Crestwood, New York)
SvTK	Svensk Teologisk Kvartalskrift (Lund)
TAik	Teologinin Aikakauskirja (Helsinki)
TB	Tyndale Bulletin (Cambridge)
Th	Theology: A Journal of Historic Christianity (London)
ThBeitr	Theologische Beiträge (Wuppertal)

Theok	Theokratia (Leiden)
ThEv	Theologia Evangelica (Praha)
ThG	Theologie und Glaube (Paderborn)
ThLZ	Theologische Literaturzeitung (Leipzig)
ThPh	Theologie und Philosophie (Frankfurt)
ThQ	Theologische Quartalschrift (Tübingen)
ThR	Theologische Rundschau (Tübingen)
ThRv	Theologische Revue (Münster)
ThSK	Theologische Studien und Kritiken (Hamburg)
ThSt	Theological Studies (New York)
ThT	Theology Today (Princeton)
ThViat	Theologia Viatorum (Berlin)
ThZ	Theologische Zeitschrift (Basel)
TK	Texte und Kommentare (Berlin)
TRE	Theologische Realenzyklopädie (Berlin/New York: Walter de Gruyter)
TsTK	Tidsskrift for Teologi og Kirke (Oslo)
TT	Theologisch Tidschrift (Amsterdam)
TThZ	Trierer Theologische Zeitschrift (Trier)
TvTh	Tijdschrift voor Theologie (Nijmegen)
TyV	Teología y vida (Santiago de Chile)
US	Una Sancta (Niederaltaich)
USQR	Union Seminary Quarterly Review (New York)
VChr	Vetera Christianorum (Bari)
VD	Verbum Domini (Rome)
VE	Vox Evangelica (London)
VF	Verkündigung und Forschung (München)
VieS	Vie Spirituelle (Paris)
VigChr	Vigiliae Christianae (Amsterdam)
VR	Vox Reformata (Geelong, Victoria)
VT	Vetus Testamentum (Leiden)
WaW	Word and World (St. Paul/MN)
WThJ	Westminster Theological Journal (Philadelphia)
WuW	Wissenschaft und Weisheit (Düsseldorf)
ZAW	Zeitschrift für die Alttestamentliche Wissenschaft (Berlin)
ZDMG	Zeitschrift der Deutschen Morgenländischen Gesellschaft
(Wiesbaden)	ZKG Zeitschrift für Kirchengeschichte (Stuttgart)
ZKTh	Zeitschrift für Katholische Theologie (Innsbruck)
ZNW	Zeitschrift für die Neutestamentliche Wissenschaft (Berlin)
ZRGG	Zeitschrift für Religions und Geistesgeschichte (Erlangen)
ZThK	Zeitschrift für Theologie und Kirche (Tübingen)
ZyMy	Zycie i Mysl (Warsaw)

Notations

ET	English Translation	GT	German Translation
FS	Festschrift	n.	footnote or note

In case of doubt consult: S. Schwertner, *Internationales Abkürzungsverzeichnis für Theologie und Grenzgebiete* = IATG (1974) 3-343. This is identical with *Theologische Realenzyklopädie* = TRE, *Abkürzungsverzeichnis* (1976) 3-343, with supplements.

Romans

ΠΡΟΣ ΡΩΜΑΙΟΥΣ

1-16 GAMBLE, H. The Textual History of the Letter to the Romans (Grand Rapids 1977) 35.

1:1–16:24 GAMBLE, H. The Textual History of the Letter to the Romans (Grand Rapids 1977) 141, passim.

1-15 GAMBLE, H. The Textual History of the Letter to the Romans (Grand Rapids 1977) 33-34, 124-26, 141. LAMPE, P. Die stadtrömischen Christen in den ersten beiden Jahrhunderten (Tübingen ²1989) 125-35.

1-14 BORSE, U. Der Standort des Galaterbriefes (Köln 1972) 10-11.

1:1–14:23 GAMBLE, H. The Textual History of the Letter to the Romans (Grand Rapids 1977) 16-29, 96-124, 141.

1-11 SCHELKLE, Paulus, Lehrer der Väter (1956), Rev. B. Schnackenburger, Biblica 42 (1, '61) 99-100. MUNCK, J. Paul and the Salvation of Mankind 1959) 197f. DESCAMP, L. "La structure de Rom 1–11" Studiorum Paulinorum Congressus Internationalis Catholicus 1961 vol. I (1963) 3-14. LEONDUFOUR, X. "Juif et gentil selon Romain 1–11" Studiorum Paulinorum Congressus Internationalis Catholicus 1961 vol. I (1963) 309-15. PRÜMM, K. "Röm 1-11 und 2. Kor 3," Biblica 31 (1950) 164-203. KÜMMEL, W. G. Römer 7 und das Bild des Menschen im Neuen Testament (München 1974) 5-6. SCROGGS, R. "Paul as Rhetorician: Two Homilies in Romans 1-11" in Jews, Greeks and Christians: Essays in Honor of W. D. Davies (Leiden 1976) 271-98. RAMAZ-ZOTTI, B. "Etica cristiana e peccati nelle lettere ai Romani e ai Galati," ScuC 106 (1978) 290-342. WILLIAMS, SAM K. "The 'Righteousness of God' in Romans," JBL 99 (1980) 245, 247-48, 250, 254, 290. GORDAY, P. Principles of Patristic Exegesis: Romans 9-11 in Origen, John Chrysostom, and Augustine (New York/Toronto 1983) 43-242. WATSON, F. Paul, Judaism and the Gentiles (Cambridge 1986)106-109. SCHMELLER, Th. Paulus und die "Diatribe" (Münster 1987) 226, 282. ROSSI, B. "Struttura letteraria e articolazione teologica di Rom 1, 1-11, 36," Studii Biblici Franciscani Liber Annus 38 (Jerusalem, 1988) 59-133. WEDDERBURN, A. J. M. The Reasons for Romans (Edinburgh 1988) 66, 112, 123-40. LONGENECKER, B. W. Eschatology and the Covenant. A Comparison of 4 Ezra and Romans 1-11 (Sheffield 1991) 160-282. BINDEMANN, W. Theologie im Dialog. Ein traditionsgeschichtlicher Kommentar zu Römer 1-11 (Leipzig 1992) passim.

1:1–11:36 RICHARDS, E. R. The Secretary in the Letters of Paul (Tübingen 1991) 177.

1-8 MANSON, W. "Notes on the argument of Romans (chapters 1–8)" New Testament Essays, Studies in Memory of T. W. Manson, ed. A. J. B. Higgins (1959) 150-164. FEUILLET, A. "La Citation D'Habacuc II.4 et les Huit Premiers Chapitres de l'Epître Aux Romains" NTS 6 (1959/60) 52f. MANSON, W. "The Argument of the Epistle to the Romans (Chapters I–VIII)" In Jesus and the Christian (1967) 135-40. GÄUMANN, N. "Die zwei Redeweissen vom Heil in Röm 1–8" in Taufe und Ethik (1967) 32. PERETTO, E. "De citationi-bus ex Rom 1–8 in Adversus Haereses Sancti Irenaei" VerbDom 46 (2, '68) 105-8. LUZ, U. "Zum Aufbau von Röm. 1–8" ThZ 25(3, 69) 161-81. GIBLIN, C.H. In Hope of God's Glory (1970) 311-98. MORENO, J. "La salvacion en la historia (Rom. 1–8)" TheolVida 12 (1, '71) 3-14. McARTHUR, H. K. Understanding the Sermon on the Mount (New York 1960) 63, 67, 70, 71, 75, 79. ALLEN, L. G. "The Old Testament in Romans 1-8" VE 3 (1964) 1-41. FEUILLET, A. "Les attaches bibliques des antithèses pauliniennes dans la première partie de l'épitre" in Descamps, A. et al., eds., Mélanges Bibliques en hommage au R. P. Béda Rigaux (Gembloux 1970) 323-49. PERETTO, E. La lettera ai Romani cc. 1-8 nell'Adversus Haereses d'Ireneo (Quaderni di "Vetera

Christianorum" 6: Bari 1971). SELBY, D. J. Introduction to the New Testament
(New York 1971) 394-400. GIBLIN, C. H. "A Summary Look at Paul's
Gospel: Romans Chapters 1-8" in M. J. Taylor, ed., A Companion to Paul (New
York 1975) 225-36. BOUWMAN, G. Paulus aan de Romeinen. Een retorische
analyse van Rom 1-8 (Cahiers voor levensverdieping 32: Abdij Averbode
1980). FEUILLET, A. "Ressemblances structurales et doctrinales entre Ga
3,1–6,10 et Rm 1–8. La triple référence de l'épitre aux Romains aux origines
de l'histoire humaine," NV 57 (1982) 30-64. ELORRIAGA, C. "La vida
cristiana como camino progresivo según Rom 1-8," Anales Valentinos
[Valencia] 9 (17, 1983) 1-21. FEUILLET, A. "La vie nouvelle du chrétien et
les trois Personnes divines d'après Rom. I-VIII," RThom 83 (1, 1983) 5-39.
SEGUNDO, J. L. The Humanist Christology of Paul [trans. J. Drury] (Jesus of
Nazareth Yesterday and Today 3; Maryknoll, N.Y. 1986). BECKER, J. Paulus.
Der Apostel der Völker (Tübingen 1989) 370-76, 376ff. JOHNSON, E. E. The
Function of Apocalyptic and Wisdom Traditions in Romans 9-11 (Atlanta,GA
1989) 110, 112, 114, 115, 116, 120, 121, 143. ELLIOT, N. The Rhetoric of
Romans (Sheffield 1990) 13, 20, 38-39, 41n. 42, 59, 95, 253-58. GREENE, J.
T. "Christ in Paul's Thought: Romans 1-8," JRTh 49 (1992) 44-58. GETTY,
M. A. "Sin and Salvation in Romans," BiTod 31 (1993) 89-93.

1:1–7:1   SCHMITHALS, W. "Zur Herkunft der gnostischen Elemente in der Sprache des
Paulus" in B. Aland et al., eds., Gnosis. (FS. H. Jonas; Göttingen 1978) 393.

1–5   PARKER, T. H. L. Calvin's New Testament Commen- taries (London 1971)
105-109. HAYS, R. B. The Faith of Jesus Christ (Chico, CA 1983) 2.

1:1–5:21   REID, M. L. "A Rhetorical Analysis of Romans 1:1-5:21 with Attention Given
to the Rhetorical Function of 5:1-21," PRSt 19 (1992) 255-72.

1–4   JÜNGEL, E. Paulus und Jesus (1966) 26. MADDALENA, A. La lettera ai
Romani, vol. 1: La miseria dell'uomo (Bologna 1974). BRYAN, C. Way of
Freedom: An Introduction to the Epistle of the Romans (New York 1975).
MOXNES, H. Theology in Conflict (Leiden 1980) 28-29, 32-55, 275, 279.
BEKER, J. C. "Paul's Letter to the Romans as Model for a Biblical Theology:
Some Preliminary Observations" in J. T. Butler et al., eds., Understanding the
Word. (FS. B. W. Anderson; Sheffield 1985) 359-67,esp.362ff. SCHMELLER,
TH. Paulus und die "Diatribe" (Münster 1987) 287n.6. DUGANDZIC, I. Das
"Ja" Gottes in Christus (Würzburg 1977) 257-71. WEDDERBURN, A. J. M.
The Reasons for Romans (Edinburgh 1988) 25, 125-31. DAVIES, G. N. Faith
and Obedience in Romans. A Study in Romans 1-4 (Sheffield 1990) passim.
ELLIOT, N. The Rhetoric of Romans (Sheffield 1990) 65n., 67, 165, 167-223,
226, 233, 234, 277-78, 283, 293.

1–3   MORENO, J. "Pecado e historia de la salvación (Rom. 1-3)" TyV 13 (1-2,
1972) 39-54. WILSON, S. G. The Gentiles and the Gentile Mission in Luke-
Acts (Cambridge 1973) 214, 215, 253. RICHARDSON, P. Paul's Ethic of
Freedom (Philadelphia 1979) 28-33. MALINA, B. J. Christian Origins and
Cultural Anthropology (Atlanta 1986) 137. OSTEN-SACKEN, P. VON DER,
Evangelium und Tora: Aufsätze zu Paulus (München 1987) 69, 175-79, 224.

1:1–3:31   HAYS, R. B. Echoes of Scripture in the Letters of Paul (New Haven/London
1989) 49-50.

1:1–3:26   DAVIES, G. N. Faith and Obedience in Romans. A Study in Romans 1-4
(Sheffield 1990) 113-5.

1:1–3:20   VAN DüLMEN, A. Die Theologie des Gestzes bei Paulus (1968) 72-84.

1:1–3:8   GARLINGTON, D. B. "The Obedience of Faith in the Letter to the Romans. Part II: The Obedience of Faith and Judgment by Works," WThJ 53 (1991) 47-72.

1–2   BOUZARD, W. C. "The Theology of Wisdom in Romans 1 and 2. A Proposal," Word World 7 (3, 1987) 281-91. SANDERS, E. P. Jewish Law from Jesus to the Mishnah (London/Philadelphia 1990) 287. SEGAL, A. F. Paul the Convert (New Haven/ London 1990) 255ff.

1:1–2:15   BUJARD, W. Stilanalytische Untersuchungen zum Kolosserbrief (Göttingen 1973) 168-71.

1   BONHOEFFER, A. Epiktet und das Neue Testament (1911) 149ff. DAVIES, W. D. Paul and the Rabbinic Judaism (1955) 325ff. MUNCK, J. Paul and the Salvation of Mankind 1959) 297f. HOOKER, M. D. "Adam in Romans i" NTS 6 (4, 60) 297-306. CASTELLINO, G. R. II Pgaesimo Di Romani 1, Sapienza 13-14 E. La Storia Delle religioni Studiorum Paulinorum Congressus Internationalis Catholicus 1961 (1963) II 255-63. HOOKER, M. D. "A Further Note on Rm 1," NTS 13 (1966/67) 181-83. ROON, A. VAN, The Authenticity of Ephesians (Leiden 1974) 197ff. WILLIAMS, S. K. "The 'Righteousness of God' in Romans," JBL 99 (1980) 255-63. OSTEN-SACKEN, P. VON DER, Evangelium und Tora: Aufsätze zu Paulus (München 1987) 127-31, 213, 222. WEDDERBURN, A.J.M. The Reasons for Romans (Edinburgh 1988) 26-27, 97-98. HOOKER, M. D. From Adam to Christ. Essays on Paul (Cambridge 1990) 34, 57, 73-87, 168, 170.

1:1ff.   RATHKE, H. Ignatius von Antiochien und die Paulusbriefe (1967) 43f., 47f.

1:1-17   MINEAR, P.S. The Obedience of Faith (1971) 36-43. SCHMITHALS, W. Der Römerbrief als historisches Problem (Gütersloh 1975) 51. MANSON, T. W. "St. Paul's letter to the Romans—and Others" in K. P. Donfried, ed., The Romans Debate (Minneapolis 1977) 3-5. WATSON, F. Paul, Judaism and the Gentiles (Cambridge 1986) 102-105. TOIT, A. B. DU, "Persuasion in Romans 1:1-17," BZ 33 (2, 1989) 192-209. ELLIOT, N. The Rhetoric of Romans (Sheffield 1990) 34, 60, 66, 70-86, 96, 105, 257. SIMONIS, W. Der gefangene Paulus. Die Entstehung des sogenannten Römerbriefs und anderer urchristlicher Schriften in Rom (Frankfurt/Bern/New York/Paris 1990) 21-43.

1:1-15   SHEPARD, J. W. The Life and Letters of St. Paul (Grand Rapids,Mich. 1950) 367-70. ROBINSON, J. A. T. Wrestling with Romans (London 1979) 13-15. McDONALD, J. I. H. Kerygma and Didache (Cambridge 1980) 55. FRAIKIN, D. "The Rhetorical Function of the Jews in Romans" in P. Richardson, ed., Anti-Judaism in Early Christianity, Vol 1: Paul and the Gospels (Waterloo,Ont. 1986) 94-95. AUNE, D. E. The New Testament in Its Literary Environment (Philadelphia 1987) 220. OSTEN-SACKEN, P. VON DER, Evangelium und Tora: Aufsätze zu Paulus (München 1987) 124-25. SEIFRID, M. A. Justification by Faith (Leiden/New York/Köln 1992) 188-90.

1:1-10   ROON, A. VAN, The Authenticity of Ephesians (Leiden 1974) 198.

1:1-7   DEISSMANN, A. Licht vom Osten (1923) 203f. CAMBIER, J. L'Evangile de Dieu selon l'Epître aux Romains I (1967) 177-84. STUHLMACHER, P. "Theologische Probleme des Römer-briefpräskripts" EvTh 27 (7, '67) 374-89. KASTING, H. Die Anfänge der Urchristlichen Mission (1969) 136f. GIBLIN, C.H. In Hope of God's Glory (1970) 321-26. JOHNSON, S.L. "The Jesus That Paul Preaches" BiblSa 128 (510, '71) 120-34. BJÖRCK, S. et al. Valda Texter ur Nya Testamentet (Stockholm 1972) 23-24. ZELLER, D. Juden und Heiden in der Mission des Paulus. Studien zum Römerbrief (Stuttgart 1973) 46ff., 80. ROON, A. VAN, The Authenticity of Ephesians (Leiden 1974) 140, 143-45,

161-62, 164. SCHMITHALS, W. Der Römerbrief als historisches Problem (Gütersloh 1975) 39, 145. ROLOFF, J. "Apostel I" in TRE III (1978) 439. JOSUTTIS, M. GPM 34 (1979) 27-32. MOXNES, H. Theology in Conflict (Leiden 1980) 217-19, 221-22. SCHLIER, H. "'Evangelium' im Römerbrief" in V. Kubina et al., eds., Der Geist und die Kirche (FS. H. Schlier; Freiburg/Basel/Wien 1980) 74-83. KIRCHSCHLÄGER, W. "Von Christus geprägt. Das paulinische Selbstverständnis als Zeugnis des Osterglaubens," BuK 36 (1981) 165-70. SABOURIN, L. "Formulations of Christian Beliefs in Recent Exposition on Paul's Epistles to the Romans and Galatians," Religious Studies Bulletin 1 (Sudbury,Ont. 1981) 120-36. TILSON, E. "Homiletical Resources: Exegesis of Isaiah Passages for Advent," QR 1 (Nashville,TN 1981) 29, 35. GORDAY, P. Principles of Patristic Exegesis: Romans 9-11 in Origen, John Chrysostom, and Augustine (New York/Toronto 1983) 50-52, 110, 151-52. JEUB, M. in GPM 40 (1985-86) 44-52. ZMIJEWSKI, J. Paulus— Knecht und Apostel Christi (Stuttgart 1986) 33-63. DUNN, J. D. G. "Paul's Epistle to the Romans: An Analysis of Structure and Argument" in ANRW II.25.4 (1987) 2845-46. WEDDERBURN, A.J.M. The Reasons for Romans (Edinburgh 1988) 49, 93-96.

1:1-6   FORELL, G. W. The Christian Lifestyle (Philadelphia 1975) 1-3. FRIEDRICH, G. "Lohmeyers These über das paulinische Briefpräskript kritisch beleuchetet" in Auf das Wort kommt es an. Gesammelte Aufsätze (Göttingen 1978) 103-106. ROLOFF, J. "Amt" in TRE 2 (1978) 520. WOLTER, M. Die Pastoralbriefe als Paulustradition (Göttingen 1988) 84. DAVIES, G. N. Faith and Obedience in Romans. A Study in Romans 1-4 (Sheffield 1990) 21-30.

1:1-5   GIBLET, J. "'Evangelium' S. Pauli juxta Rom. I, 1-5" Collectanea Mechliniensia T. XXIII/LLL (1953) 331-35. HERMANN, I. Kyrios und Pneuma (1961) 59-61. KRAMER, W. Christos Kyrios Gottessohn (1963) §12b. BORMANN, P. Die Heilswirksamkeit der Verkündigung nach dem Apostel Paulus (1964) 19-21, 42-46. BADENAS, R. Christ the End of the Law (Sheffield 1985) 139, 141-42, 150-51, 229n.29. SANDNES, K. O. Paul—One of the Prophets? (Tübingen 1991) 146-53. ANDERSON, C. "Romans 1:1-5 and the Occasion of the Letter: The Solution to the Two-Congregation Problem in Rome," Trinity Journal 14 (1993) 25-40.

1:1-4   SUGGES, M.J. "The Use of Patristic Evidence in the Search for a Primitive New Testament Text" NTS 4 (1957/58) 142ff. STANLEY, D.M. Christ's Resurrection in Pauline Soteriology (1961) 161-66. EGGER, W. Frohbotschaft und Lehre. Die Sammel-berichte des Wirkens Jesu im Markusevangelium (Frankfurt a. M. 1976) 48. VAN DER MINDE, H.-J. Schrift und Tradition bei Paulus (München/Pader-born/Wien 1976) 38-47. DUGANDZIC, I. Das "Ja" Gottes in Christus (Würzburg 1977) 128-54.

1:1-3   DEMKE, C. "Gott IV" in TRE XIII (1984) 645.

1:1-2   GOPPELT, L. Theologie des Neuen Testaments II: Vielfalt und Einheit des apostolischen Christus-zeugnisses (Göttingen 1976) 439. FARKASFALVY, D. M. "'Prophets and Apostels': The Conjunction of the Two Terms before Irenaeus" in W. E. March, ed., Texts and Testaments (FS. S.D. Currie; San Antonio 1980) 117-18.

1:1   SCHRAGE, W. Die kon kreten Einzelgebote in der paulinischen Paränese (1961) 133. KRAMER, W. Christos Kyrios Gottessohn (1963) § 54b. REDICK, G. "Ausgesondert für Gottes Frohbotschaft (Röm 1, 1): US 18 (1, 63) 13-28. WIEDERKEHR, D. Die Theologie der Berufung in den Paulusbriefen (1963) 99-106. RENGSTORF, K. H. "Paulus und die älteste römische Christenheit"

Studia Evangelica 2 (1964) 447-64. BORSE, U. Der Standort des Galaterbriefes (Köln 1972) 82, 120-21, 177. HAINZ, J. Ekklesia (Regensburg 1972) 112-13, 172-73, 174-77, 269-70. CONZELMANN, H. und LINDEMANN, A., Arbeitsbuch zum Neuen Testament (Tübingen 1975) 16. PAGELS, E. H. The Gnostic Paul. Gnostic Exegesis of the Pauline Letters (Philadelphia 1975) 13, 103n.14, 121. SCHÜTZ, J. H. Paul and the Anatomy of Apostolic Authority (Cambridge 1975) 35-36, 40, 206-207. FRIEDRICH, G. "Freiheit und Liebe im ersten Korintherbrief" in Auf das Wort kommt es an. Gesammelte Aufsätze (Göttingen 1978) 181. ROLOFF, J. "Amt" in TRE 2 (1978) 518. STAAB, K. Pauluskommentare aus der griechischen Kirche (Münster ²1984) 46,1-7 EusE; 113, 1-6ThM; 213, 1-10 Sev; 470, 1-10 Phot; 470, 11-14 Phot. MALHERBE, A. J. Moral Exhortation. A Greco-Roman Sourcebook (Philadelphia 1986) 36. ZMIJEWSKI, J. Paulus— Knecht und Apostel Christi (Stuttgart 1986) 85, 98-99, 119-20, 122, 145, 192. SCHNIDER, F. und STENGER, W. Studien zum neutestamentlichen Briefformular (Leiden 1987) 5 and passim. CONZEL-MANN, H. and LINDEMANN, A. Interpreting the New Testament (Peabody MA 1988) 14. JONGE, M. DE, Christology in Context. The Earliest Christian Response to Jesus (Philadelphia 1988) 54, 184, 217n.12. JERVIS, L. A. The Purpose of Romans (Sheffield 1991) 72, 78-79, 158.

1:2ff.   WREGE, H.-T. Die Ueberlieferungsgeschichte der Bergpredigt (Tübingen 1968) 36, 170, 180. FENEBERG, W. SJ. Der Markusprolog. Studien zur Formbestimmung des Evangeliums (München 1974) 36, 85, 87, 92. VIELHAUER, P. "Paulus und das Alte Testament" in Oikodome [G. Klein, ed.] (München 1979) 196-97. PLÜMACHER, E. "Bibel" in TRE 6 (1980) 15. ZMIJEWSKI, J. Paulus—Knecht und Apostel Christi (Stuttgart 1986) 145-50, 187.

1:2-4   HAYS, R. B. Echoes of Scripture in the Letters of Paul (New Haven/ London 1989) 85.

1:2-3   SCHRAGE, W. Die kondreten Einzelgebote in der paulinischen Paränese (1961) 229. LÜBKING, H.-M. Paulus und Israel im Römerbrief (Frankfurt/Bern/ New York 1986) 21-23.

1:2   PORUBCAN, S. "The Pauline Message and the Prophets" Studiorum Paulinorum Congressus Internationalis Catholicus 1961 I (1963) 256f. LUZ, U. Das Geschichtsverständnis des Paulus (1968) 111. ZELLER, D. Juden und Heiden in der Mission des Paulus. Studien zum Römerbrief (Stuttgart 1973) 46-47, 80, 287. LADD, G. E. A Theology of the New Testament (Grand Rapids 1974) 363, 394, 409. SCHMITHALS, W. Der Römerbrief als historisches Problem (Gütersloh 1975) 122. STAAB, K. Pauluskommentare aus der griechischen Kirche (Münster ²1984) 57:1-3 Apoll; 213:11-16 Sev. KOCH, D.-A. Die Schrift als Zeuge des Evangeliums (Tübingen 1986) 328-31, 342-43. JERVIS, L. A. The Purpose of Romans (Sheffield 1991) 74. LOHSE, E. Die Entstehung des Neuen Testaments (Stuttgart/Berlin/Köln ⁵1991) 12.

1:3-5   STAAB, K. Pauluskommentare aus der griechischen Kirche (Münster ²1984) 470,15–471,11 Phot. HAYS, R. B. Echoes of Scripture in the Letters of Paul (New Haven/London 1989) 72.

1:3-4   BRUNNER, Dogmatik II (1950) 404, 418. SCHWEIZER, E. "Röm 1, 3f. und der Gegensatz von Fleisch und Geist bei Paulus" EvTh 15/12 (1955) 563-571. CERFAUX, L. Christ in the Theology of St. Paul (1959) 277, 161, 17, 18, 436. ROBINSON, J.M. Kerygma und historischer Jesus (1960) 68f, 175, 179. WILCKENS, U. Die Missionsreden der Apostelgeschichte (1961) 124, 172, 177, 189, 192. WEGENAST, K. Das Verständnis der Tradition bei Paulus und in den Deuteropaulinen (1962) 70-76. SCHWEIZER, E. Erniedrigung und

Erhöhung bei Jesus und seinen Nachfolgern (1962) §8e, 16e. HAHN, F. Christologische Hoheitstitel (1963) 106, 191f, 251-59, 291. KRAMER, W. Christos Kyrios Gottessohn (1963) §§ 24a, b, 25b, 27f, 54a, 55f. SCHWEIZER, E. Ne testamentica (1963) 180-89. KÄSEMANN, E. Exegetische Versuche und Besinnungen (1964) I 49. BULTMANN, R. Theologie des Neuen Testaments (1965) 28, 52, 473. FLENDER, H. Heil und Geschichte in der Theologie des Lukas (1965) 41. BRAUN, H. Qumran und NT II (1966) 79, 177, 189, 252, 255. SEEBERG, A. Der Katechismus der Urchristenheit (1966) 61ff, 75, 120, 151. ZIMMERMANN, H. Neutestamentliche Methodenlehre (1967) 192-202. BARTSCH, H.-W. "Zur vorpaulinischen Bekenntnisformel im Eingang des Römerbriefes" ThZ 23 (5, 67) 329-39. LANGEVIN, P.E. Jésus Seigneur et l'Eschatologie (1967) 18, 23, 37, 39, 56, 91, 308. [1] CONZELMANN, H. "Auslegung von Markus 4, 35-41 par; Markus 8, 31-37 par; Römer 1, 3f" EvangErzieher 20 (7, '68) 249-60. (STROBEL, A. Erkenntnis und Bekenntnis der Sünde in neutestamentlicher Zeit (1968) 52, 38.) LEHMANN, K. Auferweckt am Dritten Tag nach der Schrift (1968) 33, 45, 49, 73, 103A, 173, 174, 254. RUGGIERI, G. Il Figlio di Deo davidico, (1968). [BLANK, J. Paulus und Jesus (1968) 250-55.] (2) SCHWEIZER, E. Neues Testament und heutige Verkündigung (1969) 39ff. ALLEN, L.C. "Old Testament Background" NTS 17 (1970-71) 104f. BURGER, Chr. Jesus als Davidssohn (1970) 25-33. GUETTGEMANNS, E. Offene Fragen zur Formgeschichte des Evangeliums (1970) 209. LINNEMANN, E. "Tradition und Interpretation in Röm. 1, 3f" EvTh 31 (5, '71) 264-75. SCHLIER, H. "Zu Röm. 1:3f" Neues Testament und Geschichte (1972) 207-18. EICHHOLZ, G. Die Theologie des Paulus im Umriss (1972) passim. DUPONT, J. Essais sur la Christologie de Saint Jean (Bruges 1951) 284, 285, 290. DALTON, W. J. Christ's Proclamation to the Spirits. A Study of 1 Peter 3:18-4:6 (Rome 1965) 129-30, 132-33, 134. HARMAN, A. M. Paul's Use of the Psalms (Ann Arbor 1968) 175-76. LUZ, U. Das Geschichtsverständnis bei Paulus (München 1968) 121-23. RUPPERT, L. Jesus als der leidende Gerechte? (Stuttgart 1972) 44. OLSSON, B. "Rom 1:3f. enligt Paulus," SEA 37-38 (1972-73) 255-73. DULING, D. C. "The Promises to David and their Entrance into Christianity—Nailing down a Likely Hypothesis," NTS 20 (1973) 55-77. DUNN, J. D. G. "Jesus—Flesh and Spirit: An Exposition of Romans i.3-4," JThS 24 (1973) 40-68. HAY, D. M. Glory at the Right Hand (Nashville 1973) 107, 112-14, 118. VAWTER, B. This Man Jesus (New York 1973) 121ff., 131ff. VÖGTLE, A. "Zum Problem der Herkunft von 'Mt 16,17-19'" in P. Hoffmann, ed., Orientierung an Jesus. Zur Theologie der Synoptiker (FS. J. Schmid; Freiburg/Basel/Wien 1973) 379=80. ZELLER, D. Juden und Heiden in der Mission des Paulus. Studien zum Römerbrief (Stuttgart 1973) 46, 47-48. LOHSE, E. Grundriss der neutestamentlichen Theologie (Stuttgart 1974) 16, 24, 54-55, 80-81, 115. ROON, A. VAN, The Authenticity of Ephesians (Leiden 1974) 131-32. CONZELMANN, H. und LINDEMANN, A., Arbeitsbuch zum Neuen Testament (Tübingen 1975) 106, 336, 367. DUNN, J. D. G. Jesus and the Spirit. A Study of the Religious and Charismatic Experience of Jesus and the First Christians as Reflected in the New Testament (London 1975) 62, 154, 159, 322, 325, 332. GOPPELT, L. Theologie des Neuen Testaments I: Jesu Wirken in seiner theologischen Bedeutung [J. Roloff, ed.] (Göttingen 1976) 73, 209, 216, 218, 285. HENGEL, M. Der Sohn Gottes. Die Entstehung der Christologie und die jüdisch-hellenistische Religionsgeschichte (Tübingen 1975) 93-104. PAGELS, E. H. The Gnostic Paul. Gnostic Exegesis of the Pauline Letters (Philadelphia 1975) 13,

14. STRECKER, G., ed., Jesus Christus in Historie und Theologie (FS. H. Conzelmann; Tübingen 1975) 14, 88, 401-402, 523, 529, 535. BECKER, J. Auferstehung der Toten im Urchristentum (Stuttgart 1976) 18-31. GOPPELT, L. Theologie des Neuen Testaments II: Vielfalt und Einheit des apostolischen Christuszeugnisses (Göttingen 1976) 347. LANGEVIN, P.-E. "Une confession prépaulienne de la 'Seigneurie' du Christ. Exégese de Romains 1:3-4" in R. Laflamme et al., eds., Le Christ hier, aujourd'hui et demain (Laval 1976) 277-327. POYTHRESS, V. S. "Is Romans 1:3-4 a *Pauline* Confession After All?" ET 87 (1976) 180-83. VAN DER MINDE, H.-J. Schrift und Tradition bei Paulus (München/Paderborn/ Wien 1976) 40-45. DUNN, J. D. G. Unity and Diversity in the New Testament: An Inquiry into the Character of Earliest Christianity (London 1977) 46. LANGEVIN, P.-É. "Quel est le 'Fils de Dieu' de Romains 1,3-4?" SciE 29 (1977) 145-77. ELLIS, E. E. Prophecy and Hermeneutic in Early Christianity (Tübingen 1978) 64. FRIEDRICH, G. "Die Auferweckung Jesu, eine Tat Gottes oder ein Interpretament der Jünger" in Auf das Wort kommt es an. Gesammelte Aufsätze (Göttingen 1978) 347-48. GAFFIN, R. B. The Centrality of the Resurrection (Grand Rapids 1978) 98-113, 119-22. SCHMITHALS, W. "Zur Herkunft der gnostischen Elemente in der Sprache des Paulus" in B. Aland et al., eds., Gnosis. (FS. H. Jonas; Göttingen 1978) 391-93, 403-404. SCHWEIZER, E. Heiliger Geist (Stuttgart 1978) 79-80. BYRNE, B. "Sons of God"—"Seed of Abraham" (Rome 1979) 6, 89, 193, 205-206. FROITZHEIM, F. Christologie und Eschatologie bei Paulus (Würzburg 1979) 101ff. HOFFMANN, P. "Auferstehung" in TRE 4 (1979) 488. BEAS-LEY-MURRAY, P. "Romans 1:3f: An Early Confession of Faith in the Lordship of Jesus," TB 31 (1980) 147-54. BERGMEIER, R. Glaube als Gabe nach Johannes (Stuttgart 1980) 255n.333. DUNN, J. D. G. Christology in the Making (London 1980) 33-36, 38, 45, 51, 62, 138-39, 144, 208, 235, 237, 285n.173, 286n.179. VAN DER MINDE, H. J. "Theologia crucis und Pneumaaussagen bei Paulus," Cath (M) 34 (1980) 143. SCHLIER, H. "Eine christologische Credo-Formel der römischen Gemeinde. Zu Röm. 1,3f" in V. Kubina and K. Lehmann, eds., Der Geist und die Kirche (FS. H. Schlier; Freiburg/Basel/Wien 1980) 56-69. BISER, E. Der Zeuge (Graz/Wien/Köln 1981) 112, 218, 241. LANGKAMMER, H. "Zum Ursprung der kosmologischen Christologie im Neuen Testament" BN 16 (1981) 35-36. SCHADE, H.-H. Apokalyptische Christologie bei Paulus (Göttingen 1981) 84-85. KLEIN, G. "Eschatologie" in TRE 10 (1982) 276. BINDEMANN, W. Die Hoffnung der Schöpfung (Neukirchen 1983) 63-64. SCHNELLE, U. Gerechtigkeit und Christusgegenwart (Göttingen 1983) 127. BERGER, K. "Geist" in TRE 12 (1984) 179. LINDARS, B. Jesus Son of Man (Grand Rapids 1984) 9. PERKINS, P. Resurrection. New Testament Witness and Contemporary Reflection (London 1984) 217-9, 234. RICHARDSON, P. and J. C. HURD, eds., From Jesus to Paul (FS. F. W. Beare; Waterloo 1984) 68, 155, 158-59. RITTER, A. M. "Glaubensbekenntnis(se) V" in TRE 13 (1984) 401. WENGST, K. "Glaubensbekenntnis(se) IV" in TRE 13 (1984) 393, 394. STAAB, K. Pauluskommentare aus der griechischen Kirche (Münster ²1984) 57:4-8 Apoll. ALLISON, D. C. The End of the Ages Has Come. An Early Interpretation of the Passion and Resurrection of Jesus (Philadelphia 1985) 67-68, 73, 80, 82. FISCHER, K. M. Das Urchristentum (Berlin,DDR 1985) 67, 81, 160. JEWETT, R. "The Redaction and Use of an Early Christian Confession in Romans 1:3-4" in D. E. Groh and R. Jewett, eds., The Living Text (FS. E. W. Saunders; Lanham/London/New York 1985) 99-122. POKORNY, P. Die Entstehung der

Christologie (Berlin 1985) 54, 58, 67, 75, 81, 85, 119, 132, 138, 153, 164.
RAU, G. "Das Markusevangelium. Komposition und Intention der ersten
Darstellung christlicher Mission" in ANRW II.25.3 (1985) 2057-63, 2234.
SCHIMANOWSKI, G. Weisheit und Messias (Tübingen 1985) 326. HARRIS,
M. J. Raised Immortal (London 1986) 74-75, 147. KOCH, D.-A. Die Schrift als
Zeuge des Evangeliums (Tübingen 1986) 156A, 232-33, 328-31. ZMIJEWSKI,
J. Paulus—Knecht und Apostel Christi (Stuttgart 1986) 100, 211. BETZ, O.
Jesus. Der Messias Israels (Tübingen 1987) 136, 142, 147, 148, 265, 268, 275,
327, 404. BOCK, D. L. Proclamation from Prophecy and Pattern: Lucan Old
Testament Christology (Sheffield 1987) 61, 67-68. CRANFIELD, C. E. B.
"Some Comments on Professor J. D. G. Dunn's *Christology in the Making* with
Special Reference to the Evidence of the Epistle to the Romans" in L. D. Hurst
and N. T. Wright, eds., The Glory of Christ in the New Testament (FS. G. B.
Caird; Oxford 1987) 269-70. EGGER, W. Methodenlehre zum Neuen Testament
(Freiburg/Basel/Wien 1987) 181-83. MERKLEIN, H. Studien zu Jesus und
Paulus (Tübingen 1987) 229, 233-35, 240, 247, 253-54, 255, 284, 286, 287,
412n.14. OSTEN-SACKEN, P. VON DER, Evangelium und Tora: Aufsätze zu
Paulus (München 1987) 59, 83, 148. SCHWEIZER, E. Jesus Christ: The Man
from Nazareth and the Exalted Lord (Macon,GA 1987) 15, 17. STUHL-
MACHER, P. "Jesus von Nazareth und die neutestamentliche Christologie im
Lichte der Heiligen Schrift" in M. Klopfenstein et al., eds., Mitte der Schrift?
Ein jüdisch-christliches Gespräch. Texte des Berner Symposions vom 6.-12.
Januar 1985 (Bern etc. 1987) 82. CONZELMANN, H. and LINDEMANN, A.
Interpreting the New Testament (Peabody MA 1988) 93-94, 193, 323. JONGE,
M. DE, Christology in Context. The Earliest Christian Response to Jesus
(Philadelphia 1988) 33, 48, 50, 68, 105, 110, 114, 128, 135, 168, 208, 211.
BECKER, J. Paulus. Der Apostel der Völker (Tübingen 1989) 117-18, 126.
LAMPE, P. Die stadtrömischen Christen in den ersten beiden Jahrhunderten
(Tübingen ²1989) 54. LOHFINK, G. Studien zum Neuen Testament (Stuttgart
1989) 15. SCHWEIZER, E. Theologische Einleitung in das Neue Testament
(Göttingen 1989) para. 5.3; 23.4. DUNN, J. D. G. Jesus, Paul and the Law
(London 1990) 205n.39, 233n.30. FOWL, S. E. The Story of Christ in the
Ethics of Paul (Sheffield 1990) 159-60, 162-63. HOOKER, M. D. From Adam
to Christ. Essays on Paul (Cambridge 1990) 34-35, 37-38, 99. OLIVEIRA, A.
DE, Die Diakonie der Gerechtigkeit und der Versöhnung in der Apologie des
2. Korintherbriefes. Analyse und Auslegung von 2 Kor 2,14–4,6; 5,11–6,10
(Münster 1990) 224. BLACKBURN, B. Theios Aner and the Markan Miracle
Traditions (Tübingen 1991) 106-107, 109. GEORGI, D. Theocracy in Paul's
Praxis and Theology (Minneapolis 1991) 85-8. JERVIS, L. A. The Purpose of
Romans (Sheffield 1991) 74, 77, 85, 158. LOHSE, E. Die Entstehung des
Neuen Testaments (Stuttgart/Berlin/Köln ⁵1991) 21, 73.

1:3   KNOX, W.L. The Sources of the Synoptic Gospels II (1957) 140. ROBINSON,
J.M. Kerygma und historischer Jesus (1960) 69, 107, 177f. HAHN, F.
Christologische Hoheitstitel (19-63) 244f, 273, 307. LANGEVIN, P.E. Jésus
Seigneur et l'Eschatologie (1967) 57, 101, 217, 294, 314. NELLESSEN, E. Das
Kind und seine Mutter (1969) 91f. LADD, G. E. A Theology of the New
Testament (Grand Rapids 1974) 143, 167, 412, 467. SCHÜTZ, J. H. Paul and
the Anatomy of Apostolic Authority (Cambridge 1975) 66-67, 114. HAACKER,
K. "Exegetische Probleme des Römerbriefs," NovT 20 (1, 1978) 1-21.
VINCENT CERNUDA, A. "La génesis humana de Jesucristo segun San Pablo,"
EstBi 37 (1978) 267-89. THISELTON, A. C. The Two Horizons (Grand Rapids

1980) 409. POKORNY, P. "Christologie et Bapteme à l'Epoque du Christianisme Primitif," NTS 27 (1980-81) 368-69. KRAFT, H. Die Entstehung des Christentums (Darmstadt 1981) 71. MÜLLER, M. Der Ausdruck "Menschensohn" in den Evangelien (Leiden 1984) 116. ZMIJEWSKI, J. Paulus—Knecht und Apostel Christi (Stuttgart 1986) 136. BERGER, K. und COLPE, C., eds., Religionsgeschichtliches Textbuch zum Neuen Testament (Göttingen/Zürich 1987) 195-96. KUHN, H.-J. Christologie und Wunder. Untersuchungen zu Joh 1,35-51 (Regensburg 1988) 356, 361, 368, 382-83, 527. WOLTER, M. Die Pastoralbriefe als Paulustradition (Göttingen 1988) 216.

1:3b-4   MELL, U. Neue Schöpfung (Berlin/New York 1989) 375ff., 387.

1:4-5   DELLING, G. Die Zueignung des Heils in der Taufe (1961) 57.

1:4   SOKOLOWSKI, E. Die Begriffe Geist und Leben bei Paulus (1903) 56ff. VOLZ, P. Die Eschatologie der Jüdischen Gemeinde (1934) 207. ROBINSON, J.M. Kerygma und historischer Jesus (1960) 69, 139. SCHWEIZER, E. erniedrigung und Erhöhung bei Jesus und seinen Nachfolgern (1962) §4g, 5c, 15k. HOOKE, S.H. "The Translation of Romans 1:4" NTS 9 (1962-63) 370f. HAHN, F. Christologische Hoheitstitel (1963) 110, 191. LJUNGMAN, H. Pistis (1964) 56f. O'ROURKE, J.J. "'Dalla risurrezione dei morti' (Rom.1, 4)" BiblOr 6 (2, '64) 59. KÄSEMANN, E. Exegetische Versuche und Besinnungen I (1964) 215. THUESING, W. Per Christum in Deum (1965) 153f. SCHNEIDER, B. "Kata Pneuma Hagiosynes (Romans 1, 4)" Biblica 48 (3, '67) 359-87. GIBBS, J.G. Creation and Redemption (1971) 36, 50, 70, 85, 108, 142, 150. RICHTER, H.-F. Auferstehung und Wirklichkeit (Berlin/Augsburg 1969) 177-78. FITZMYER, J. A. "'To Know Him and the Power of His Resurrection'" in A. Descamps et al., eds., Mélanges Bibliques en hommage au R. P. Béda Rigaux (Gembloux 1970) 417-18. DUPONT, J. "Ascension du Christ et don de l'Esprit d'après Actes 2:33" in B. Lindars et al., eds., Christ and the Spirit in the New Testament (FS. C. F. D. Moule; Cambridge 1973) 220-21, 227-28. CAVALLIN, H. C. C. Life After Death. Paul's Argument for the Resurrection of the Dead in I Cor 15. Part I: An Enquiry into the Jewish Background (Lund 1974) 4,In3I. BAUMGARTEN, J. Paulus und die Apokalyptik (Neukirchen-Vluyn 1975) 126-27. DUNN, J. D. G. Jesus and the Spirit. A Study of the Religious and Charismatic Experience of Jesus and the First Christians as Reflected in the New Testament (London 1975) 111, 435. RAYAN, S. The Holy Spirit: Heart of the Gospel and Christian Hope (New York 1978) 129. BAIRD, W. "Ascension and Resurrection: An Intersection of Luke and Paul" in W. E. March, ed., Texts and Testaments (FS. S.D. Currie; San Antonio,TX 1980) 3ff. BARTSCH, H. W. "Inhalt und Function des urchristlichen Osterglaubens" in ANRW II.25.1 (1982) 826. DETTLOFF, W. "Duns Scotus" in TRE 9 (1982) 226. KLEIN, G. "Eschatologie" in TRE 10 (1982) 274. LINDARS, B. Jesus Son of Man (Grand Rapids 1984) 206. RIESENFELD, H. "Kristi andes helighet, Rom 1:4" [Christ's Spirit's Holiness, Rom 1:4], SEA 50 (1985) 105-15. HARRIS, M. J. Raised Immortal (London 1986) 111. KUHN, H.-J. Christologie und Wunder. Untersuchungen zu Joh 1,35-51 (Regensburg 1988) 356, 360-61, 374-75, 382-83, 388.

1:5-8   LAMPE, P. Die stadtrömischen Christen in den ersten beiden Jahrhunderten (Tübingen ²1989) 9, 55, 127, 131, 133, 301.

1:5-7   PAGELS, E. H. The Gnostic Paul. Gnostic Exegesis of the Pauline Letters (Philadelphia 1975) 14-15. STAAB, K. Pauluskommentare aus der griechischen Kirche (Münster ²1984) 57, 9-11 Apoll; 352, 1-16 Genn; 471, 12-31 Phot.

1:5-6   ROLOFF, J. Apostolat—Verkündigung—Kirche (1965) 104f. WENGST, K.
Christologische Formeln und Lieder des Urchristentums (1972) 112-16.
SCHMELLER, TH. Paulus und die "Diatribe" (Münster 1987) 231. JERVIS,
L. A. The Purpose of Romans (Sheffield 1991) 76-77., 108, 158-59, 160.

1:5   SCHRAGE, W. Die konkreten Einzelgebote in der paulinischen Paränese (1961)
117, 173. HAHN, F. Das Verständnis der Mission im Neuen Testament
(1965)82. BOUSSET, W. Die Religion des Judentums im Späthellenistischen
Zeitalter (1962) 375. KERTELGE, K. "Rechtfertigung" bei Paulus (1967) 169,
175. MERK, O. Handeln aus Glauben (1968) 13, 31, 38, 183. KASTING, H.
Die Anfänge der Urchristlichen Missio (1969) 56f, 77, 137, 142. WIEFEL, W.
"Glaubensgehorsam. Erwägungen zu Römer 1:5" in H. Benckert et al., eds.,
Wort und Gemeinde (FS. E. Schott; Berlin 1967) 137-44. BORSE, U. Der
Standort des Galaterbriefes (Köln 1972) 120-21, 124. HAINZ, J. Ekklesia
(Regensburg 1972) 174-75, 176-82, 269-70, 334-35. ZELLER, D. Juden und
Heiden in der Mission des Paulus. Studien zum Römerbrief (Stuttgart 1973) 48-
49, 53, 199-200, 270. WILES, G. P. Paul's Intercessory Prayers (Cambridge
1974) 87, 110, 193, 220n., 251n. SCHMITHALS, W. Der Römerbrief als
historisches Problem (Gütersloh 1975) 10, 25, 27-28. FRIEDRICH, G. "Das
Amt im Neuen Testament" in Auf das Wort kommt es an. Gesammelte
Aufsätze (Göttingen 1978) 423-24. ROLOFF, J. "Amt" in TRE 2 (1978) 519.
ROLOFF, J. "Apostel" in TRE 3 (1978) 437. SCHMITHALS, W. "Zur
Herkunft der gnostischen Elemente in der Sprache des Paulus" in B. Aland et
al., eds., Gnosis. (FS. H. Jonas; Göttingen 1978) 399-400. THISELTON, A. C.
The Two Horizons (Grand Rapids 1980) 408. WILLIAMS, S. K. "The
'Righteousness of God' in Romans," JBL 99 (1980) 256. FRIEDRICH, G.
"Muss hypakoe pisteos Röm 1:5 mit 'Glaubensgehorsam' übersetzt werden?"
ZNW 72 (1981) 118-23. CRANFIELD, C. E. B. "Changes of Person and
Number in Paul's Epistles" in M. D. Hooker and S. G. Wilson, eds., Paul and
Paulinism (FS. C.K. Barrett; London 1982) 145, 167. ZMIJEWSKI, J.
Paulus—Knecht und Apostel Christi (Stuttgart 1986) 47, 72, 82, 98-99, 101,
114, 119-20, 122, 135, 208. DUNN, J. D. G. "'A Light to the Gentiles': the
Significance of the Damascus Road Christophany for Paul" in L. D. Hurst and
N. T. Wright, eds., The Glory of Christ in the New Testament (FS. G.B. Caird;
Oxford 1987) 251-66,esp.252. GASTON, L. Paul and the Torah (Vancouver
1987) 57, 116, 118. OSTEN-SACKEN, P. VON DER, Evangelium und Tora:
Aufsätze zu Paulus (München 1987) 116, 119, 123-24, 128, 148, 154.
SEGALLA, G. "L'obbedienza di fede' (Rm 1,5; 16, 26) tema della Lettera ai
romani?" RivB 36 (3, 1988) 329-42. GARLINGTON, D. B. "The Obedience
of Faith in the Letter to the Romans. Part I: The Meaning of ὑπακοή
πίστεως (Rom 1:5; 16:26)," WThJ 52 (2, 1990) 201-24. GARLINGTON, D.
B. "The Obedience of Faith in the Letter to the Romans. Part II: The Obedience
of Faith and Judgment by Works," WThJ 53 (1991) 47-72. GARLINGTON, D.
B. 'The Obedience of Faith' (Tübingen 1991) passim.

1:6-7   STRECKER, G. Der Weg der Gerechtigkeit (1962) 219. SCHMITHALS, W.
"Zur Herkunft der gnostischen Elemente in der Sprache des Paulus" in B. Aland
et al., eds., Gnosis. (FS. H. Jonas; Göttingen 1978) 390-93. WEDDERBURN,
A. J. M. The Reasons for Romans (Edinburgh 1988) 48f.

1:6   WIEDERKEHR, D. Die Theologie der Berufung in den Paulusbriefen (1963)
146-48. BINDEMANN, W. Die Hoffnung der Schöpfung (Neukirchen 1983)
63f. MERKLEIN, H. Studien zu Jesus und Paulus (Tübingen 1987) 5, 36, 64,

289, 291, 426n.63. JERVIS, L. A. The Purpose of Romans (Sheffield 1991) 77-79, 104, 162.

1:7-15   DAVIES, G. N. Faith and Obedience in Romans. A Study in Romans 1-4 (Sheffield 1990) 30-34.

1:7   HARNACK, A. "Zu Röm 1, 7" ZNW 3 (1902) 83-86. FLEW, R.N. Jesus and His Church (1956) 156. KUSS, O. "Sohn Gottes" Der Römerbrief (1957) 12-15. SCHWEIZER, E. "The Church as the Missionary Body of Christ" NTS 8 (1961-62) 2f. SCHRAGE, W. Die konkreten Einzelgebote in der paulinschen Paränese (1961) 188. STRECKER, G. Der Weg der Gerechtigkeit (1962) 217. WIEDERKEHR, D. Die Theologie der Berufung in den Paulusbriefen (1963) 107-14. KRAMER, W. Christos Kyrios Gottessohn (1963) §42b. STEINMETZ, R. "Textkritik Untersuchung zu Rm 1:7" ZNW 9 (1908) 177-89. SCHMITHALS, W. Der Römerbrief als historisches Problem (Gütersloh 1975) 112, 145, 175. KLIJN, A. F. J. "Die syrische Baruch-Apokalypse" in JSHRZ V/2 (1976) 175n.2a. GAMBLE, H. The Textual History of the Letter to the Romans (Grand Rapids 1977) 29-33. DEICHGRÄBER, R. "Benediktionen" in TRE 5 (1980) 563. DEIDUN, T. J. New Covenant Morality in Paul (Rome 1981) 3-10, 13f., 126f. DEICHGRÄBER, R. "Formeln, Liturgische" in TRE 11 (1983) 258. MEEKS, W. A. The First Urban Christians (New Haven/London 1983) 85, 170, 235n.16. MOHRLANG, R. Matthew and Paul (Cambridge 1984) 87f. STAAB, K. Pauluskommentare aus der griechischen Kirche (Münster ²1984) 113:7-13 ThM; 213:7-17 Sev; 214:1-11 Sev; 352:17-353:3 Genn. AUNE, D. E. The New Testament in Its Literary Environment (Philadelphia 1987) 220. CLABEAUX, J. J. The Lost Edition of the Letters of Paul (CBQ.MS; Washington 1989) 95, 97, 98. THORNTON, C.-J. Der Zeuge des Zeugen. Lukas als Historiker der Paulusreisen (Tübingen 1991) 217n.31.

1:8ff.   GÄRTNER, B. The Areopagus Speech and Natural Revelation (Uppsala 1955) 74, 80, 82, 133, 135, 139, 143f., 159, 234f., 239. WEDDERBURN, A. J. M. The Reasons for Romans (Edinburgh 1988) 69f., 75. JERVIS, L. A. The Purpose of Romans (Sheffield 1991) 51, 88.

1:8-32   CLARK, S. B. Man and Woman in Christ (Ann Arbor MI 1980) 277.

1:8-17   SCHMITHALS, W. Der Römerbrief als historisches Problem (Gütersloh 1975) 88, 129. BAIRD, W. "Romans 1:8-17" Interp 33 (4, 1979) 398-403. GORDAY, P. Principles of Patristic Exegesis: Romans 9-11 in Origen, John Chrysostom, and Augustine (New York/Toronto 1983) 52f., 110f., 152f. AUNE, D. E. The New Testament in Its Literary Environment (Philadelphia 1987) 185. LOHFINK, G. Studien zum Neuen Testament (Stuttgart 1989) 217-23, 286, 288.

1:8-15   EICHHOLZ, G. "Der ökumenische und missionarische Horizont der Kirche. Eine exegetische Studie zu Röm. 1, 8-15" EvTh 21 (1, '61) 15-27. GIBLIN, C.H. In Hope of God's Glory (1970) 326f. SCHMITHALS, W. Der Römerbrief als historisches Problem (Gütersloh 1975) 53ff., 62, 65, 67, 165, 167, 169, 176, 180f. O'BRIEN, P. Th. Introductory Thanksgivings in the Letters of Paul (Leiden 1977) 191-230. MOXNES, H. Theology in Conflict (Leiden 1980) 217f. DUNN, J.D.G. "Paul's Epistle to the Romans: An Analysis of Structure and Argument" in ANRW II.25.4 (1987) 2846. OSTEN-SACKEN, P. VON DER, Evangelium und Tora: Aufsätze zu Paulus (München 1987) 122-25. LAMPE, P. Die stadtrömischen Christen in den ersten beiden Jahrhunderten (Tübingen ²1989) 127f., 131, 133.

1:8-12   ZELLER, D. Juden und Heiden in der Mission des Paulus. Studien zum Römerbrief (Stuttgart 1973) 50ff. AUNE, D. E. The New Testament in Its Literary Environment (Philadelphia 1987) 220.

1:8-11   WOLTER, M. Die Pastoralbriefe als Paulustradition (Göttingen 1988) 205.
1:8   DELLING, G. Zueignung des Heils in der Taufe (1961) 53. THUESING, W.
           Per Christum in Deum (1965) 174-77. HAHN, F. Das Verständnis der Mission
           im Neuen Testament (1965) 60. MERK, O. Handeln aus Glauben (1968) 13,
           177. JERVELL, J. "The Problem of Traditions in Acts" in Luke and the People
           of God (Minneapolis 1972) 23f., 27. WILES, G. P. Paul's Intercessory Prayers
           (Cambridge 1974) 76, 85, 94, 187, 188, 205n., 207n. SCHMITHALS, W. Der
           Römerbrief als historisches Problem (Gütersloh 1975) 28, 53. O'BRIEN, P. Th.
           Introductory Thanksgivings in the Letters of Paul (Leiden 1977) 202-10.
           STAAB, K. Pauluskommentare aus der griechischen Kirche (Münster ²1984)
           57:12-58:2 Apoll; 113:14-114:10 ThM; 353:4-19 Genn. OSTEN-SACKEN, P.
           VON DER, Evangelium und Tora: Aufsätze zu Paulus (München 1987) 52, 120,
           125. GEBAUER, R. Das Gebet bei Paulus (Giessen/Basel 1989) 10, 87, 139,
           159, 203f., 208f., 220, 225, 252, 254f., 304, 336. OLIVEIRA, A. DE, Die Dia-
           konie der Gerechtigkeit und der Versöhnung in der Apologie des 2. Korinther-
           briefes. Analyse und Auslegung von 2 Kor 2, 14-4, 6; 5, 11-6, 10 (Münster
           1990) 29.
1:9-14   PAGELS, E. H. The Gnostic Paul. Gnostic Exegesis of the Pauline Letters
           (Philadelphia 1975) 15.
1:9-10   WILES, G. P. Paul's Intercessory Prayers (Cambridge 1974) 7, 20, 76, 86n., 90,
           155, 156n., 158, 163, 186, 188, 165, 290n.
1:9   LYONNET, S. "'Deus cui servio in spiritu meo' (Rom 1, 9)" VerbDom 41 (1-
           2, '63) 52-59. KRAMER, W. Christos Kyrios Gottessohn (1963) § 54ab.
           KÜMMEL, W. G. Römer 7 und das Bild des Menschen im Neuen Testament
           (München 1974) 32f. WILES, G. P. Paul's Intercessory Prayers (Cambridge
           1974) 4n., 157, 164n., 181n., 187, 193, 205n., 269n. KLIJN, A. F. J. "Die
           syrische Baruch-Apokalypse" in JSHRZ V/2 (1976) 184n.3a. O'BRIEN, P. Th.
           Introductory Thanksgivings in the Letters of Paul (Leiden 1977) 210-15.
           STAAB, K. Pauluskommentare aus der griechischen Kirche (Münster ²1984)
           114, 11-15 ThM; 353, 20-23 Genn. ZMIJEWSKI, J. Paulus - Knecht und
           Apostel Christi (Stuttgart 1986) 56, 61, 132, 136.
1:10ff.   FEINE, D. P. et al. Einleitung in das Neue Testament (Heidelberg 1950) 174f.
1:10-15   OLLROG, W.-H. Paulus und seine Mitarbeiter (Neukirchen-Vluyn 1979) 117.
           AUNE, D. E. The New Testament in Its Literary Environment (Philadelphia
           1987) 219, 220.
1:10-13   OLLROG, W.-H. Paulus und seine Mitarbeiter (Neukirchen-Vluyn 1979) 61,
           179.
1:10-11   SCHMELLER, TH. Paulus und die "Diatribe" (Münster 1987) 231.
1:10   HAHN, F. Das Verständnis der Mission im Neuen Testament (1965) 81.
           SCHRAGE, W. Die konkreten Einzelgebote in der paulinischen Paränese (1961)
           168. ROBINSON, J. A. Pelagius's Exposition of Thirteen Epistles of St. Paul
           (Cambridge 1922) 260. BAUMERT, N. Täglich Sterben und Auferstehen
           (München 1973) 392f. WILES, G. P. Paul's Intercessory Prayers (Cambridge
           1974) 19, 54n., 187, 188, 191, 192, 268n., 277n. O'BRIEN, P. Th. Introductory
           Thanksgivings in the Letters of Paul (Leiden 1977) 216-21. STAAB, K. Paulus-
           kommentare aus der griechischen Kirche (Münster ²1984) 114:16-17 ThM.
           FURNISH, V. P. "Der 'Wille Gottes' in paulinischer Sicht" in Koch, D.-A. et
           al., eds., Jesu Rede von Gott und ihre Nachgeschichte im frühen Christentum
           (FS. Willi Marxsen; Gütersloh 1989) 208-11, esp. 218.

1:11-16	ROBERTS, J. H. "Transitional techniques to the letter body in the *Corpus Paulinum*" in Petzer, J. H. and Hartin, P. J., eds., A South African Perspective on the New Testament (FS. B.M. Metzger; Leiden 1986) 195, 198.
1:11-15	STOLLE, V. Der Zeuge als Angeklagter. Untersuchungen zum Paulus-Bild des Lukas (Stuttgart 1973) 268, 269, 270. O'BRIEN, P. Th. Introductory Thanksgivings in the Letters of Paul (Leiden 1977) 221-4. AUNE, D. E. The New Testament in Its Literary Environment (Philadelphia 1987) 220. ELLIOT, N. The Rhetoric of Romans (Sheffield 1990) 9, 25, 83, 86.
1:11-12	ELLIS, E. E. Prophecy and Hermeneutic in Early Christianity (Tübingen 1978) 26, 50. FRIEDRICH, G. "Das Problem der Autorität im Neuen Testament" in Auf das Wort kommt es an. Gesammelte Aufsätze (Göttingen 1978) 393. STAAB, K. Pauluskommentare aus der griechischen Kirche (Münster ²1984) 58:3-13 Apoll; 471:32-472:38 Phot.
1:1-11	DUNN, J. D. G. Jesus and the Spirit. A Study of the Religious and Charismatic Experience of Jesus and the First Christians as Reflected in the New Testament (London 1975) 207f., 250, 253, 279. SCHÜTZ, J. H. "Charisma" in TRE 7 (1981) 689. STAAB, K. Pauluskommentare aus der griechischen Kirche (Münster ²1984) 114:18-23 ThM. SCHATZMANN, S. S. A Pauline Theology of Charismata (Peabody MA 1987) 4f., 14f. WEDDERBURN, A. J. M. The Reasons for Romans (Edinburgh 1988) 97-9. WOLTER, M. Die Pastoralbriefe als Paulustradition (Göttingen 1988) 209.
1:11	KÄSEMANN, E. Exegetische Versuche und Besinnungen (1964) I 113. CHEVALLIER, M.-A. Esprit de Dieu, Paroles D'Hommes (1966) 143-45. PARRATT, J.K. "Romans i. 11 and Galatians iii.5 — Pauline evidence for the Laying on of Hands" ET 79 5, '68) 151-52.
1:12	WILES, G. P. Paul's Intercessory Prayers (Cambridge 1974) 81, 163n., 187, 193. SCHMITHALS, W. Der Römerbrief als historisches Problem (Gütersloh 1975) 28, 174f. SCHMELLER, Th. Paulus und die "Diatribe" (Münster 1987) 231.
1:13-4:25	ELLIOT, N. The Rhetoric of Romans (Sheffield 1990) 105-65.
1:13-25	BARTH, M. GPM 7 47-51
1:13-20	SCHMITZ, O. in G. Eichholz, ed. Herr, tue meine Lippen auf (1965) 116ff.
1:13-17	ZELLER, D. Juden und Heiden in der Mission des Paulus. Studien zum Römerbrief (Stuttgart 1973) 54ff.
1:13-15	PARKIN, H. "Romans i. 13-15" ET 79 (3, '67) 95. WILES, G. P. Paul's Intercessory Prayers (Cambridge 1974) 3n., 185, 164n. SCHMITHALS, W. Der Römerbrief als historisches Problem (Gütersloh 1975) 10, 171. JEWETT, R. "Romans as an Ambassadorial Letter, " Interp 36 (1982) 7, 14. STAAB, K. Pauluskommentare aus der griechischen Kirche (Münster ²1984) 354:12-27 Genn.
1:13-14	STAAB, K. Pauluskommentare aus der griechischen Kirche (Münster ²1984) 473:1-474:12 Phot.
1:13	SCHRAGE, W. Die konkreten Einselgebote in der paulinischen Paränese (1961) 60. BAUMERT, N. Täglich Sterben und Auferstehen (München 1973) 201. KÜMMEL, W. G. Einleitung in das Neue Testament (Heidelberg 1973) 269f. ZELLER, D. Juden und Heiden in der Mission des Paulus. Studien zum Römerbrief (Stuttgart 1973) 50, 55ff. WILES, G. P. Paul's Intercessory Prayers (Cambridge 1974) 8n., 73, 187, 192, 193, 266. SCHMITHALS, W. Der Römerbrief als historisches Problem (Gütersloh 1975) 25, 28. OLLROG, W.-H. Paulus und seine Mitarbeiter (Neukirchen-Vluyn 1979) 32, 55, 176f. CLARK, K. W. "The Making of the Twentieth Century New Testament" in The Gentile Bias

and other Essays [selected by J. L. Sharpe III] (Leiden 1980) 154. STAAB, K. Pauluskommentare aus der griechischen Kirche (Münster ²1984) 58:14-17 Phot; 114:24:115:4 ThM; 214:12-15 Sev. KRUGER, M. A. *"TINA KARPON*, 'Some Fruit' in Romans 1:13, " WThJ 49 (1, 1987) 167-73. SCHMELLER, TH. Paulus und die "Diatribe" (Münster 1987) 231. WEDDERBURN, A. J. M. The Reasons for Romans (Edinburgh 1988) 5, 11, 15, 27, 29, 102. SCHÄFER, K. Gemeinde als "Bruderschaft" (Frankfurt/Bern/New York/Paris 1989) 349f. JERVIS, L. A. The Purpose of Romans (Sheffield 1991) 103, 105f., 108, 109, 160.

1:14-17   GLOMBITZA, O. "Von der Scham des Gläubigen. Erwägungen zu Rom. i 14-17" NovTest 4 (1, '60) 74-80. BENCKERT, GPM 1965/1966 85ff. KRECK, W. GPM 14 67-72. JANKOWSKI, G. "Macht Gottes zur Befreiung. Paulus an die Römer 1:14-17, " Texte und Kontexte 5 (1979) 24-38. KLAIBER, W. Rechtfertigung und Gemeinde (Göttingen 1982) 77-81.

1:14-15   GENSICHEN, H.-W. "Heidentum I" in TRE 14 (1985) 592.

1:14   MINEAR, P.S. "Gratitude and Mission in the Epistle to the Romans" Basileia, Walter Freytag zum 60. GEBURTSTAG (1961) 42-48. HAHN, F. Das Verständnis der Mission im Neuen Testament (1965) 83. KASTING, H. Die Anfänge der Urchristlichen Mission (1969) 56f. ZELLER, D. Juden und Heiden in der Mission des Paulus. Studien zum Römerbrief (Stuttgart 1973) 58, 270, 273. KIM, S. The Origin of Paul's Gospel (Tübingen 1981) 290-92. LIPS, H. VON, Weis-heitliche Traditionen im Neuen Testament (Neukirchen-Vluyn 1990) 123, 136.

1:15   ZELLER, D. Juden und Heiden in der Mission des Paulus. Studien zum Römerbrief (Stuttgart 1973) 55ff. SCHMITHALS, W. Der Römerbrief als historisches Problem (Gütersloh 1975) 112. GAMBLE, H. The Textual History of the Letter to the Romans (Grand Rapids MI 1977) 29-33. WILLIAMS, S. K. "The 'Righteousness of God' in Romans, " JBL 99 (1980) 255. STAAB, K. Pauluskommentare aus der griechischen Kirche (Münster ²1984) 115:5-7 ThM. AUNE, D. E. The New Testament in Its Literary Environment (Philadelphia 1987) 219. SCHMELLER, TH. Paulus und die "Diatribe" (Münster 1987) 231. WEDDERBURN, A. J. M. The Reasons for Romans (Edinburgh 1988) 13, 26, 29, 97, 102f., 124, 138, 149f. CLABEAUX, J. J. The Lost Edition of the Letters of Paul (CBQ.MS; Washington 1989) 98.

1:16–11:36 RAMAROSON, L. "Un 'nouveau plan' de Rm 1, 16-11, 36, " NRTh 94 (9, 1972) 943-58.

1:16–8:39 SEGUNDO, J. L. "Christ and the Human Being, " CrCu 36 (1, 1986) 50-67.

1:16–4:25 SCHMITHALS, W. "Zur Herkunft der gnostischen Elemente in der Sprache des Paulus" in B. Aland et al., eds., Gnosis. (FS. H. Jonas; Göttingen 1978) 392f. KOCH, D.-A. Die Schrift als Zeuge des Evangeliums (Tübingen 1986) 227A, 275ff., 289f., 343. DABOURNE, W. The Faithfulness of God and the Doctrine of Justification in Romans 1:16-4:25 (unpublished dissertation; Cambridge 1988).

1:16–3:26 BONNEAU, N. "Stages of Salvation History in Romans 1:16-3:26, " ÉglThéol 23 (1992) 177-94.

1:16-2:29 BASSLER, J. M. Divine Impartiality. Paul and a Theological Axiom, SBL Dissertation Series 59 (Chico, CA 1982).

1:16-2:11 BASSLER, J. M. Divine Impartiality (Chico, CA 1982) 123-37. BASSLER, JOUETTE M. "Divine Impartiality in Paul's Letter to the Romans, " NovT 26 (1984) 43-58. DAVIES, G. N. Faith and Obedience in Romans. A Study in Romans 1-4 (Sheffield 1990) 49-52.

1:16-2:10 BASSLER, J. M. Divine Impartiality (Chico, CA 1982) 199.

1:16ff   KÄSEMANN, E. Exegetische Versuche und Besinnungen II (1964) 33. JÜNGEL, E. Paulus und Jesus (1966) 30f, 43, 46, 54, 67. KÄSEMANN, E. New Testament Questions of Today (1969) 25. ZELLER, D. Juden und Heiden in der Mission des Paulus. Studien zum Römerbrief (Stuttgart 1973) 60ff., 145ff.

1:16-32   SEGUNDO, J. L. The Humanist Christology of Paul (New York/ London 1986) 13-27. ELLIOT, N. The Rhetoric of Romans (Sheffield 1990) 97, 108-19, 225.

1:16-18   HEROLD, G. Zorn und Gerechtigkeit Gottes bei Paulus. Eine Untersuchung zu Röm 1, 16-18, Europäische Hochschulschriften, Reihe XXIII, Bd. 14 (Bern/ Frankfurt 1973) passim. GRUNDMANN, W. Wandlungen im Verständnis des Heils (Berlin, DDR 1980) 25. STAAB, K. Pauluskommentare aus der griechischen Kirche (Münster ²1984) 474:13-477:6 Phot. BOCKMUEHL, M. N. A. Revelation and Mystery (Tübingen 1990) 138, 142, 206. DAVIES, G. N. Faith and Obedience in Romans. A Study in Romans 1-4 (Sheffield 1990) 35-46.

1:16-17   SOKOLOWSKI, E. Die Begriffe Geist und Leben bei Paulus (1903) 8ff. BRUNNER, E. Dogmatik I (1946) 321. LESQUIVIT, C. "Qui a la justice de la foi vivra" Témoignages (1954) 3-14. CERFAUX, L. "De Saint Paul á L'Evangile de la Vérité" NTS 5 (2, '59) 103-12. STROBEL, A. Untersuchungen zum Eschatologischen Verzögerungsproblem (1961) 174-88, 196-98. BRAUMANN, G. Vorpaulinische christliche Taufverkündigung bei Paulus (1962) 10f, 35. LEON-DUFOUR, X. Studiorum Paulinorum Congressus Internationalis Catholicus 1961 (1963) I 309-11. CAMBIER, J. "Péchés des Hommes et Péché D'Adam en Rom V.12" NTS 11 (1964-65) 228F. CAMBIER, J. "Justice de Dieu, salut de tous les hommes et foi" RevBi 71 (4, '64) 537-83. CAMBIER, J. L'Evangile de Dieu selon l'Epître aux Romains I (1967) 11-59. KERTELGE, K. "Rechtfertigung" bei Paulus (1967) 85-89, 297. MERK, O. Handeln aus Glauben (1968) 6, 11, 23. BLANK, J. Schriftauslegung in Theorie und Praxis (1969) 153. GIBLIN, C.H. In Hope of God's Glory (1970) 327-30. JOHNSON, S.L. "The Gospel That Paul Preached" BiblSac 128 (512, '71) 327-40. EICHHOLZ, G. Die Theologie des Paulus im Umriss (1972) passim. SHEPARD, J. W. The Life and Letters of St. Paul (Grand Rapids 1950) 370f. AALEN, S. "En eksegese av Rom 1:16-17, " TsTK 39 (3, 1968) 161-76. HARMAN, A. M. Paul's Use of the Psalms (Ann Arbor MI 1968) 176-78. CONZELMANN, H. Theologie als Schriftauslegung (München 1974) 189f., 198, 201. SCHMITHALS, W. Der Römerbrief als historisches Problem (Gütersloh 1975) 11, 20, 56, 91ff. MIRANDA, J. P. Marx and the Bible (London 1977) 244f. WUELLNER, W. "Paul's Rhetoric of Argumentation in Romans: An Alternative to the Donfried-Karris Debate over Romans" in K. P. Donfried, ed., The Romans Debate (Minneapolis 1977) 168-73. LAYMAN, F. D. Paul's Use of Abraham (Ann Arbor MI 1972). BYRNE, B. 'Sons of God' - 'Seed of Abraham'. A Study of the Idea of the Sonship of God of All Christians in Paul against the Jewish Background (Rome 1979) 88, 126, 128. OLLROG, W.-H. Paulus und seine Mitarbeiter (Neukirchen-Vluyn 1979) 134f. ROBINSON, J. A. T. Wrestling with Romans (London 1979) 15f. MOXNES, H. Theology in Conflict (Leiden 1980) 30, 33, 41, 63, 83, 89, 97, 218, 279. BISER, E. Der Zeuge (Graz/Wien/Köln 1981) 20, 73, 90, 222, 228. BASSLER, J. M. Divine Impartiality (Chico, CA 1982) 203f. RUCKSTUHL, E. "Gnade III" TRE 13 (1984) 468. STAAB, K. Paulus-kommentare aus der griechischen Kirche (Münster ²1984) 58:18-59:4 Apoll; 354:28-356:22 Genn. BEKER, J. C. "Paul's Letter to the Romans as Model for a Biblical Theology: Some Preliminary Observations" in J. T. Butler et al., eds., Understanding the Word. (FS. B. W.

Anderson; Sheffield 1985) 359-67. BEKER, J. C. "The Faithfulness of God and the Priority of Israel in Paul's Letter to the Romans" in G. W. E. Nickelsburg and G. W. MacRae, eds., Christians among Jews and Gentiles (FS. Krister Stendahl; Philadelphia 1986) 13f. FRAIKIN, D. "The Rhetorical Function of the Jews in Romans" in P. Richardson, ed., Anti-Judaism in Early Christianity, Vol 1: Paul and the Gospels (Waterloo, Ont. 1986) 275ff., 289ff. ZMIJEWSKI, J. Paulus - Knecht und Apostel Christi (Stuttgart 1986) 168-72. AUNE, D. E. The New Testament in Its Literary Environment (Philadelphia 1987) 220. DUNN, J. D. G. "Paul's Epistle to the Romans: An Analysis of Structure and Argument" in ANRW II.25.4 (1987) 2847. GASTON, L. Paul and the Torah (Vancouver 1987) 117, 118f., 133. TRILLING, W. Studien zur Jesusüberlieferung (Stuttgart 1988) 321, 328. WEDDERBURN, A. J. M. The Reasons for Romans (Edinburgh 1988) 102f., 107, 112, 122. BECKER, J. Paulus. Der Apostel der Völker (Tübingen 1989) 55, 203, 396, 441. HAYS, R. B. Echoes of Scripture in the Letters of Paul (New Haven/London 1989) 36-41. HOFIUS, O. Paulusstudien (Tübingen 1989) 82, 126, 150, 158f., 177. LIMBECK, M. Mit Paulus Christ sein. Sachbuch zur Person und Theologie des Apostels Paulus (Stuttgart 1989) 105. STUHLMACHER, P. "The Theme of Romans" in K. P. Donfried, ed., The Romans Debate. Revised and Expanded Edition (Peabody MA 1991) 333-45. ALETTI, J.-N. "Comment Paul voit la justice de Dieu em Rm. Enjeux d'une absence de définition, " Biblica 73 (1992) 359-75. SEIFRID, M. A. Justification by Faith (Leiden/New York/Köln 1992) 211-19.

1:16   SCHRAGE, W. Die konkreten Einzelgebote in der paulinischen Paränese (1961) 117. STRECKER, G. Der Weg der Gerechtigkeit (1962) 108. GRAYSTON, K. "'Not ashamed of the Gospel' Romans 1, 16a and the Sturcture of the Epistle" Studia Evangelica II, ed. F.L. Cross (1964) 569-73. KÄSEMANN, E. Exegetische Versuche und Besinnungen (1964) II 185, 187, 190. JÜNGEL, E. Paulus und Jesus (1966) 29, 44, 259. VAN DÜLMEN, A. Die Theologie des Gesetzes bei Paulus (1968) 72, 89, 93, 102, 215, 218, 222. KÄSEMANN, E. New Testament Questions of Today (1969) 173, 174, 178. BARRETT, C.K. "I as not Ashamed of the Gospel" New Testament Essays (1972) 116-43. WILSON, S. G. The Gentiles and the Gentile Mission in Luke-Acts (Cambridge 1973) 10, 30, 95, 222. ZELLER, D. Juden und Heiden in der Mission des Paulus. Studien zum Römerbrief (Stuttgart 1973) 58f., 141ff., 187. ZINGG, P. Das Wachsen der Kirche (Freiburg, Schweiz 1974) 264-68. PRETE, B. "La formula *dynamis theou* in Rom. 1, 16 e sue motivazioni, " RivB 23 (3, 1975) 299-328. KRUIJF, T. C. de "Antisemitismus" in TRE 3 (1978) 125. ROLOFF, J. "Amt" in TRE 2 (1978) 519. WIRSCHING, J. "Bekenntnisschriften" in TRE 5 (1980) 487. MOXNES, H. Theology in Conflict (Leiden 1980) 21, 29, 52, 78, 83f., 201. WILLIAMS, S. K. "The 'Righteousness of God' in Romans, " JBL 99 (1980) 255-57, 259, 262-64. HAYS, R. B. The Faith of Jesus Christ (Chico CA 1983) 148. FRANKEMÖLLE, H. "Evangelium als theologischer Begriff und sein Bezug zur literarischen Gattung 'Evangelium'" in ANRW II.25.2 (1984) 1635-1704 (Bibl.:1695-1704). HELDERMANN, J. Die Anapausis im Evangelium Veritatis (Leiden 1984) 255n.414. HÜBNER, H. Gottes Ich und Israel (Göttingen 1984) 15, 86, 117. KLEINKNECHT, K. T. Der leidende Gerechtfertigte (Tübingen 1984) 361. LINDARS, B. Jesus Son of Man (Grand Rapids 1984) 58, 202, 203. PATTE, D. Preaching Paul (Philadelphia 1984) 23f. RICHARDSON, P. and HURD, J. C., eds., From Jesus to Paul (FS. F.W. Beare; Waterloo 1984) 131f., 155. STAAB, K. Pauluskommentare aus der griechischen Kirche

(Münster [2]1984) 653:1-3 Areth. BADENAS, R. Christ the End of the Law (Sheffield 1985) 111, 116, 139, 141f., 236n.99, 258n.348. GRÄSSER, E. Der Alte Bund im Neuen (Tübingen 1985) 17, 40, 227, 228, 282. CORRIGAN, G. M. "Paul's Shame for the Gospel, " BThB 16 (1, 1986) 23-27. LÜBKING, H.-M. Paulus und Israel im Römerbrief (Frankfurt/ Bern/ New York 1986) 23-26. BERGER, K. und COLPE, C., eds., Religionsgeschichtliches Textbuch zum Neuen Testament (Göttingen/Zürich 1987) 196. GASTON, L. Paul and the Torah (Vancouver 1987) 57, 67, 95, 118, 131. HÜBNER, H. "Paulusforschung seit 1945. Ein kritischer Literaturbericht" in ANRW II.25.4 (1987) 2702. SANDERS, E. P. "Jesus and the Kingdom: The Restoration of Israel and the New People of God" in Sanders, E. P., ed., Jesus, the Gospels, and the Church (Macon GA 1987) 225-39, esp. 229. WEDDERBURN, A. J. M. The Reasons for Romans (Edinburgh 1988) 89, 104-108, 124, 126f., 132, 136, 138. JOHNSON, E. E. The Function of Apocalyptic and Wisdom Traditions in Romans 9-11 (Atlanta GA 1989) 118, 120, 122, 127, 128, 136, 138, 146, 149, 153, 154, 158, 174, 190, 202, 208. MARTIN, B. L. Christ and the Law in Paul (Leiden 1989) 11-13, 96, 124, 126, 127, 141. OLIVEIRA, A. DE, Die Diakonie der Gerechtigkeit und der Versöhnung in der Apologie des 2. Korintherbriefes. Analyse und Auslegung von 2 Kor 2, 14-4, 6; 5, 11-6, 10 (Münster 1990) 231. ROLOFF, J. Exegetische Verantwortung in der Kirche (Göttingen 1990) 26, 84f., 318. SEGAL, A. F. Paul the Convert (New Haven/ London 1990) 12, 65, 258.

1:16b   HVALVIK, R. "'For jøde først og så for greker.' Til betydningen av Rom 1, 16b ('To the Jew First and Also to the Greek.' The Meaning of Romans 1, 16b)" TidsTeolKirk 60 (3, 1989) 189-96.

1:17-4:25   ELLIS, E. E. Prophecy and Hermeneutic in Early Christianity (Tübingen 1978) 155, 162, 217.

1:17-18   SCHWEIZER, A. Die Mystik des Apostels Paulus (1954) 67, 204. STUHLMACHER, P. Gerechtigkeit Gottes bei Paulus (1965) 13-15, 23f, 26-28, 30f, 37-39, 60-66, 78-87. KERTELGE, K. "Rechtfertigung" bei Paulus (1967) 70, 87f, 123. ZIESLER, J.A. The Meaning of Righteousness in Paul (1972) 187-9, 191, 194, 201, 206.

1:17   BRUNNER, E. Dogmatik I (1946) 48, 298. OEPKE, A. "Δικαιοσύνη Θεοῦ bei Paulus in neuer Beleuchtung" ThLZ 78 (1953) 257-264. MAGNUSSON, M. Der Begriff "Verstenhen" in Exegetischern Zusammenhang (1954) 62f, 70f, 72f, 80f. ELLIS, E.E. Paul's Use of the Old Testament (1957) 116ff, 125, 187. FEUILLET, A. "La Citation d'Habacuc ii.4 et les huit premiers Chapitres de l'Epître aux Romains" NTS 6 (1, '59) 52-80. SCHRAGE, W. Die konkreten Einzelgebote in der paulinischen Paränese (1961) 229. DELLING, G. Die Taufe im Neuen Testament (1963) 120. LJUNGMAN, H. Pistis (1964) 107f. MUELLER, C. Gottes Gerechtigkeit und Gottes Volk (1964) 65ff. KÄSEMANN, E. Exegetische Versuche und Besinnungen (1964) II 182. LÜHRMANN, D. Das Offenbarungsverständnis bei Paulus und in Paulinischen Gemeinden (1965) 145f, 157f. JOEST, W. "Ex fide vita — allein aus Glauben Gerechtfertigte werden leben," Schlink, Ed, & Peters, A., eds., Zur Auferbauung des Leibes' Christi (1965) 153-65. BRAUN, H. Qumran und NT II (1966) 67, 72, 128, 169, 171f, 308f, 321f. JÜNGEL, E. Paulus und Jesus (1966) 25f, 28-31, 33, 43–45, 51, 65. KERTELGE, K. "Rechtfertigung" bei Paulus (1967) 85-95, 98, 108, 150, 288. SMITH, D.M. "ὁ δὲ δίκαιος ἐκ πίστεως ζήσεται," Studies in the History and Text of the New Testament, ed. Daniels & Suggs in honor of K.W. Clark (1967) 13–25. MERK, O. Handeln aus

Glauben (1968) 6, 11f. LUZ, U. Das Geschichtsverständnis des Paulus (1968) 90, 191. VAN DÜLMEN, A. Die Theologie des Gesetzes bei Paulus (1968) 34, 72, 89, 93, 140, 194, 195, 215, 226. KÄSEMANN, E. New Testament Questions of Today (1969) 169. MAUSER, U. Gottesbild und Menschwerdung (1971) 144-46, 164. HEROLD, G. Zorn und Gerechtigkeit Gottes bei Paulus. Eine Untersuchung zu Röm. 1, 16-18 (Frankfurt 1973) 142-87. WALLIS, W. B. "A Translation of Romans 1:17 -- A Basic Motif in Paulinism, " JEThS 16 (1, 1973) 17-23. HANSON, A. T. Studies in Paul's Technique and Theology (London 1974) 22, 40f., 153, 179, 283. LADD, G. E. A Theology of the New Testament (Grand Rapids 1974) 386, 394, 524. RIDDERBOS, H. Paul. An Outline of His Theology (Grand Rapids 1975) 162-72. KLIJN, A. F. J. "Die syrische Baruch-Apokalypse" in JSHRZ V/2 (1976) 160n.16a. DUGANDZIC, I. Das "Ja" Gottes in Christus (Würzburg 1977) 257-61. CAVALLIN, H. C. C. "'The Righteous Shall Live by Faith.' A Decisive Argument for the Traditional Interpretation, " StTh 32 (1, 1978) 33-43. ELLIS, E. E. Prophecy and Hermeneutic in Early Christianity (Tübingen 1978) 174, 177, 193, 204, 217. BYRNE, B. 'Sons of God' - 'Seed of Abraham'. A Study of the Idea of the Sonship of God of All Christians in Paul against the Jewish Background (Rome 1979) 88-90. VIELHAUER, P. "Paulus und das Alte Testament" in Oikodome [G. Klein, ed.] (München 1979) 213f. DAALEN, D. H. VAN, "The Revelation of God's Righteousness in Romans 1:17" in Livingstone, E. A., ed., Studia Biblica 1978, III: Papers on Paul and Other New Testament Authors (Sheffield 1980) 383-89. THISELTON, A. C. The Two Horizons (Grand Rapids 1980) 127, 225. WILLIAMS, SAM K. "The 'Righteousness of God' in Romans, " JBL 99 (1980) 241f., 257-59, 262-64, 271. MOODY, R. M. "The Habakkuk Quotation in Romans 1:17, " ET 92 (7, 1981) 205-8. JOHNSON, L. T. "Romans 3:21-26 and the Faith of Jesus, " CBQ 44 (1982) 78-80, 90. HAYS, R. B. The Faith of Jesus Christ (Chico, CA 1983) 150, 155, 182. BEINTKER, H. "Gott VII" in TRE 13 (1984) 664. HÄGGLUND, B. "Gerechtigkeit" in TRE 12 (1984) 432f. HÖDLI, L. "Gerechtigkeit" in TRE 12 (1984) 430. STAAB, K. Pauluskommentare aus der griechischen Kirche (Münster ²1984) 53:1-7 Akazc. HULTGREN, A. J. Paul's Gospel and Mission (Philadelphia 1985) 12, 13, 17, 22, 27, 30-31, 33, 37, 96, 102, 120. KOCH, D.-A. "Der Text von Hab 2:4b in der Septuaginta und im Neuen Testament, " ZNW 76 (1-2, 1985) 68-85. KOCH, D.-A. Die Schrift als Zeuge des Evangeliums (Tübingen 1986) 127-29, 243f., 275ff., 290f., 344. BERGER, K. und COLPE, C., eds., Religionsgeschichtliches Textbuch zum Neuen Testament (Göttingen/Zürich 1987) 196f. DOBBELER, A. VON, Glaube als Teilhabe (Tübingen 1987) 152-55. LUZ, U. "Paulinische Theologie als Biblische Theologie" in M. Klopfenstein et al., eds., Mitte der Schrift? Ein jüdisch-christliches Gespräch. Texte des Berner Symposions vom 6.-12. Januar 1985 (Bern etc. 1987) 119-47, esp. 135f. WEDDERBURN, A. J. M. The Reasons for Romans (Edinburgh 1988) 105, 108, 116, 122, 124, 130, 138. HAYS, R. B. "'The Righteous One' as Eschatological Deliverer: A Case Study in Paul's Apocalyptic Hermeneutics" in Marcus, J. and Soards, M. L., eds., Apocalyptic and the New Testament (FS. J.L. Martyn; Sheffield 1989) 191-215, esp. 206-09. MARTIN, B. L. Christ and the Law in Paul (Leiden 1989) 11, 13, 14, 81, 118, 121, 124-27, 134, 141. MERKLEIN, H. Studien zu Jesus und Paulus (Tübingen 1987) 5, 23, 34, 37, 43, 47, 292. HOFIUS, O. Paulusstudien (Tübingen 1989) 35, 125, 149f., 159, 172. LAMPE, P. Die stadtrömischen Christen in den ersten beiden Jahrhunderten (Tübingen ²1989) 54. MARTIN, B. L. Christ and the Law in Paul (Leiden 1989) 11, 13f., 81, 118, 121, 124-27,

134, 141. SCHNELLE, U. Wandlungen im paulinischen Denken (Stuttgart 1989) 63, 64. OLIVEIRA, A. DE, Die Diakonie der Gerechtigkeit und der Versöhnung in der Apologie des 2. Korintherbriefes. Analyse und Auslegung von 2 Kor 2, 14-4, 6; 5, 11-6, 10 (Münster 1990) 44, 235.

1:18ff. THACKERAY, H. The Relation of St. Paul to Contemporary Jewish Thought (1900) 224ff. POHLENZ, M. "Paulus und die Stoa" ZNW 42 (1949) 60-104. NORDEN, E. Agnostos Theos (1956) 1912 128, 130f. ELTESTER, W. "Schöpfungsoffenbarung und Natürliche Theologie im Frühen Christentum" NTS 3 (1957). OWEN, H.P. "The Scope of Natural Revelation in Romans i and Acts xvii" NTS 5 (2, '59) 133-43. SCHRAGE, W. Die konkreten Einzelgebote in der paulinischen Paränese (1961) 65, 191, 213. KNOX, W.L. St. Paul and the Church of the Gentiles (1961) 182ff. STALDER, K. Das Werk des Geistes in der Heiligung bei Paulus (1962) 260f, 277, 312, 393. KÄSEMANN, E. Exegetische Versuche und Besinnungen II (1964) 72, 191. HAHN, F. Das Verständnis der Mission im Neuen Testament (1965) 86, 87. HOOKER, M.D. "A Further Note on Romans i" NTS 13 (2, '67) 181-83. MERK, O. Handeln aus Glauben (1968) 32, 213. KÄSEMANN, E. New Testament Questions of Today (1969) 69.

1:18-15:13 WUELLNER, W. "Paul's Rhetoric of Argumentation in Romans: An Alternative to the Donfried-Karris Debate over Romans" in K. P. Donfried, ed., The Romans Debate (Minneapolis 1977) 168-73.

1:18-5:21 SCHMELLER, TH. Paulus und die "Diatribe" (Münster 1987) 233, 287.

1:18-5:11 JACQUES, X. "Colère de Dieu. Romains 1, 18-5, 11, " Christus 25 (97, 1978) 100-10. MINEAR, P. S. The Obedience of Faith (London 1971) 46-56.

1:18-4:25 MINEAR, P.S. The Obedience of Faith (1971) 46-56. MacDONALD, J. I. H. Kerygma and Didache (Cambridge 1980) 55-57. NEBE, G. 'Hoffnung' bei Paulus (Göttingen 1983) 124ff., 135. FRAIKIN, D. "The Rhetorical Function of the Jews in Romans" in P. Richardson, ed., Anti-Judaism in Early Christianity, Vol 1: Paul and the Gospels (Waterloo, Ont. 1986) 98f. SCHMELLER, TH. Paulus und die "Diatribe" (Münster 1987) 233n.4. BEKER, J. C. "Paul's Theology: Consistent or Inconsistent?" NTS 34 (1988) 374-77. LINCOLN, A. T. "From Wrath to Justification: Tradition, Gospel and Audience in the Theology of Romans 1:18-4:25" in E. H. Lovering, ed., Society of Biblical Literature 1993 Seminar Papers (Atlanta 1993) 194-227.

1:18-3:31 WEBER, E. Die Beziehung von Röm 1-3 zur Missionspraxis des Paulus (Beiträge zur Förderung Christl. Theologie IX, Heft 4) 1905.

1:18-3:20 OLTMANN, K. "Das Verhältnis von RöM 1, 18-3:20 ZU 3, 21FF" Theologische Blätter (1929) 110ff. KUHLMANN, G. Theologia naturalis bei Philon und bei Paulus (1930) 38-73. BORNKAMM, G. "Die Offenbarung des Zornes Gottes" Das Ende des Gesetzes (1952) 9-33. BARTH, M. "Speaking of Sin. Some interpretative notes on Romans 1, 18-3:20" SJTh 8/3 (1955) 288-96. LEON-DUFOUR, X. "Juif et Gentile Selon Romains I-XI" Studiorum Paulinorum Congressus Internationalis Catholicus 1961 (1963) I 311-13. BULTMANN, R. Theologie des Neuen Testaments (1965) 250f, 263. CAMBIER, J. "Péchés des Hommes et Péché d'Adam en Rom. V.12," NTS 11 ('64-65) 222f. JÜNGEL, E. Paulus und Jesus (1966) 25-30. KERTELGE, K. "Rechtfertigung" bei Paulus (1967) 51, 63, 70-72, 144, 256, 300. VAN DÜLMEN, A. Die Theologie des Gesetzes bei Paulus (1968) 73, 74, 76, 82, 85, 216. WILCKENS, U. "Was heisst bei Paulus: 'Aus Werken des Gesetzes wird kein Mensch gerecht'?" Evangelisch—Katholischer Kommetar zum Neuen Testament I (1969) 51-77. KÄSEMANN, E. New Testament Questions of Today (1969)

179. MAUSER, U. Gottesbild und Mensch-werdung (1971) 144-51, 161f. SHEPARD, J. W. The Life and Letters of St. Paul (Grand Rapids 1950) 371-82. BRANDENBURGER, E. Adam und Christus (Neukirchen-Vluyn 1962) 175, 184, 186, 214-219, 244, 255, 266. VOS, J. S. Traditions-geschichtliche Untersuchungen zur Paulinischen Pneumatologie (Assen 1973) 107-12. SCHMITHALS, W. Der Römerbrief als historisches Problem (Gütersloh 1975) 13ff. STAGG, F. "The Plight of Jew and Gentile in Sin Romans 1:18-3:20, " RevEx 73 (1976) 401-13. MIRANDA, J. P. Marx and the Bible (London 1977) 160-81. SYNOFZIK, E. Die Gerichts- und Vergeltungsaussagen bei Paulus (Göttingen 1977) 78-90. CROATTO, J. S. "Conocimiento y salvación en Romanos 1, 18-3, 20. Intento de 'relectura, '" RevBi 41 (1979) 39-55. ROLOFF, J. Neues Testament (Neukirchen-Vluyn 1979) 157f. HARTMANN, L. "Bundesideologie in und hinter einigen paulinischen Texten" in S. Pedersen, ed., Die Paulinische Literatur und Theologie (Arhus/Göttingen 1980) 112-16. SCHILLEBEECKX, E. Christ: The Christian Experience in the Modern World (London 1980) 128-32; GT: Christus und die Christen (Freiburg/ Basel/Wien 1977) 119-22. WILSON, S. G. "Paul and Religion" in M. D. Hooker and S. G. Wilson, eds., Paul and Paulinism (FS. C. K. Barret; London 1982) 339-54. RÄISÄNEN, H. Paul and the Law (Tübingen 1983) 95f., 97-109, 110, 132f., 151, 153. THEISSEN, G. Psychologische Aspekte paulinischer Theologie (Göttingen 1983) 74-82, 102, 187n.9, 242. BEKER, J. C. "Suffering and Triumph in Paul's Letter to the Romans, " HBTh 7 (2, 1985) 105-19. FRAIKIN, D. "The Rhetorical Function of the Jews in Romans" in P. Richardson, ed., Anti-Judaism in Early Christianity, Vol 1: Paul and the Gospels (Waterloo, Ont. 1986) 96f. KARRER, M. Die Johannesoffenbarung als Brief (Göttingen 1986) 281n. RÄISÄNEN, H. The Torah and Christ (Helsinki 1986) 14-18, 151, 190f., 290. GASTON, L. Paul and the Torah (Vancouver 1987) 31, 69, 119-21, 224. HOFIUS, O. "'Rechtfertigung des Gottlosen' als Thema biblischer Theologie, " JBTh 2 (1987) 79-105, esp. 80-82, 89. MERKLEIN, H. Studien zu Jesus und Paulus (Tübingen 1987) 2, 5, 15, 64, 93, 213, 292, 380. SCHMELLER, T. Paulus und die "Diatribe" (Münster 1987) 233, 280f, n.155. THEISSEN, G. Psychological Aspects of Pauline Theology (Edinburgh 1987) 66-74, 96, 183n., 241. VOUGA, F. "Römer 1, 18-3, 20 als narratio, " ThG 77 (2, 1987) 225-36. ALETTI, J.-N. "Rm 1, 18-3, 20. Incohérence ou cohérence de l'argumentation paulinienne?" Biblica 69 (1, 1988) 47-62. CONZELMANN, H. and LINDEMANN, A. Interpreting the New Testament (Peabody MA 1988) 193f. BECKER, J. Paulus. Der Apostel der Völker (Tübingen 1989) 43, 376ff., 421. HAYS, R. B. Echoes of Scripture in the Letters of Paul (New Haven/ London 1989) 46f. LIMBECK, M. Mit Paulus Christ sein. Sachbuch zur Person und Theologie des Apostels Paulus (Stuttgart 1989) 70. THEOBALD, M. "Glaube und Vernunft. Zur Argumentation des Paulus im Römerbrief, " ThQ 169 (4, 1989) 287-301. THIELMAN, F. From Plight to Solution (Leiden 1989) 87, 92-7. COUSAR, C. B. A Theology of the Cross (Minneapolis 1990) 57-64. HAMERTON-KELLY, R. "Sacred Violence and Sinful Desire. Paul's Interpretation of Adam's Sin in the Letter to the Romans" in R. T. Fortna and B. R. Gaventa, eds., The Conversation Continues. Studies in Paul and John (FS J. L. Martyn; Nashville 1990) 35-54, esp.41-47. GEORGI, D. Theocracy in Paul's Praxis and Theology (Minneapolis 1991) 21, 88f., 91, 97, 97n.36, 101n.46. LONGENECKER, B. W. Eschatology and the Covenant. A Comparison of 4 Ezra and Romans 1-11 (Sheffield 1991) 169f., 172, 202f. WAY, D. The

	Lordship of Christ. Ernst Käsemann's Interpretation of Paul's Theology (Oxford 1991) 182-88.
1:18-3:9	KOCH, D.-A. Die Schrift als Zeuge des Evangeliums (Tübingen 1986) 182f.
1:18-2:29	SANDERS, E. P. Paul, the Law, and the Jewish People (London 1985) 35ff., 78, 82, 123-25, 128f., 131, 133n.14, 135n.45, 146, 148, 150, 151. LAFONTAINE, R. "Pour une nouvelle évangélisation. L'emprise universelle de la justice de Dieu selon l'épitre aux Romains 1, 18-2, 29," NRTh 108 (5, 1986) 641-65.
1:18-2:28	WETTER, G.P. Der Vergeltungsgedanke bei Paulus (1912) 18ff., 186ff.
1:18-2:24	STROBEL, A. Erkenntnis und Bekenntnis der Sünde in neutestamentlicher Zeit (1968) 49.
1:18-2:16	HANSON, S. The Unity of the Church in the New Testament (1946) 59f. REICKE, B. "Natürliche Theologie nach Paulus" SEA 22-23 ('57-'58) 154-67.
1:18-2:16	ELLIOT, N. The Rhetoric of Romans (Sheffield 1990) 123, 173-90, 203.
1:18-2:11	SCHMELLER, TH. Paulus und die "Diatribe" (Münster 1987) 232, 286, 304, 359, 389-406, 418. SANDERS, J. T. Ethics in the New Testament (Philadelphia 1975) 48. 1:18ff. BRANDENBURGER, E. Adam und Christus (Neukirchen-Vluyn 1962) 204f., 214-19, 251-52, 255f. BAIRD, W. The Corinthian Church— A Biblical Approach to Urban Culture (Nashville/New York 1964) 37, 102, 186. RICHTER, H.-F. Auferstehung und Wirklichkeit (Berlin 1969) 76, 141, 287. STROBEL, A. "Apokalyptik" in TRE 3 (1978) 252. NIXON, R. "The Universality of the Concept of Law" in B. Kaye and G. Wenham, eds., Law, Morality and the Bible (Downers Grove IL 1978) 117-20. FROITZHEIM, F. Christologie und Eschatologie bei Paulus (Würzburg 1979) 178. GEORGI, D. "Weisheit Salomos" in JSHRZ III/4 (1980) 13n.6a. WEDDERBURN, A. J. M. "Adam in Paul's Letter to the Romans" in E. A. Livingstone, ed., Studia Biblica 1978, III: Papers on Paul and Other New Testament Authors (Sheffield 1980) 413-30. FRITZSCHE, H.-G. "Dekalog" in TRE 8 (1981) 427. BASSLER, J. M. Divine Impartiality (Chico CA 1982) 203f. THEISSEN, G. Psychologische Aspekte paulinischer Theologie (Göttingen 1983) 74, 334n.111, 338n.119, 349n.15, 355. GESTRICH, C. "Glaube und Denken" in TRE 13 (1984) 366. KLEINKNECHT, K. T. Der leidende Gerechtfertigte (Tübingen 1984) 325. LONNING, I. "Gott VIII" in TRE 13 (1984) 691, 694. SCHENKE, G. Die Dreige-staltige Protennoia (Berlin 1984) 143. BETZ, H. D. "Hellenismus III" in TRE 15 (1986) 29. BECKER, J. Paulus. Der Apostel der Völker (Tübingen 1989) 45, 58, 113f., 120, 403. JOHNSON, E. E. The Function of Apocalyptic and Wisdom Traditions in Romans 9-11 (Atlanta GA 1989) 34, 35, 173. HOOKER, M. D. From Adam to Christ. Essays on Paul (Cambridge 1990) 6. LIPS, H. VON, Weisheitliche Traditionen im Neuen Testament (Neukirchen-Vluyn 1990) 148, 167, 190, 329f.
1:18-2:10	DAXER, H. Röm 1, 18-2, 20 im Verhältnis zur Spätjüdischen Lehrauffassung (1914).
1:18-2:3	FLÜCKIGER, F. "Zur Unterscheidung von Heiden und Juden in Röm 1:18-2, 2" ThZ 10 ('54) 154-58.
1:18-2:2	CASTELLINO, G.R. "Il Paganesimo di Romani 1, Sapienza 13-14 e la Storia Della Religioni" Studiorum Paulinorum Congressus Internationalis Catholicus 1961 II (1963) 225-63.
1:18-32	SCHLIER, H. "Ueber die Erkenntnis Gottes bei den Heiden nach dem Neuen Testament" EvTh (1935). SCHLIER, H. "Von den Heiden. Römerbrief 1, 18-32" Die Zeit der Kirche (1956) 29-37. SCHULZ, S. "Die Anklage in Röm. 1:18-32" ThZ 14 (3, '58) 161-73. BIEDER, W. "Zum Problem Religion-christ-

licher Glaube" ThZ 15(6, '59) 431-45. JERVELL, J. Imago Dei (1960) 282f, 255f, 289ff. LILLIE, W. Studies in New Testament Ethics (1961) 15f. BARRETT, C.K. From First Adam to Last (1962) 17ff. KAMLAH, E. Die Form der katalogischen Paränese im Neuen Testament (1964) 18-20. HOOKER, M.D. "A Further Note on Romans I" NTS 13 (1966-67) 181ff. MANSUS, H. The Wrath of God in the Pauline Homolegoumena (Rüschlikon 1960). 34-46. GIBLIN, C.H. In Hope of God's Glory (1970) 330-36. COFFEY, D.M. "Natural Knowledge of God: Reflections on Romans 1:18-32" ThSt 31 (4, '70) 674-91. WALLS, A.F. "The First Chapter of the Epistle to the Romans and the Modern Missionary Movement" Apostolic History and the Gospel, eds. W.W. Gasque and R.P. Martin (1970) 346-57. BUSSMANN, C. Themen der paulinischen Missionspredigt auf dem Hintergrund der Spät-jüdisch-hellenistischen Missionsliteratur (1971) 108-22. EICHHOLZ, G. Die Theologie des Paulus im Umriss (1972) 63, 67f, 76ff, 82f. RIEDL, J. Das Heil der Heiden nach Röm 2, 14-16.26.27 (Mödling bei Wien 1965) 185-90. LAUB, F. Eschatologische Verkündigung und Lebensgestaltung nach Paulus (Regensburg 1973) 37, 42, 173, 180, 182, 185, 186. VANDERMARCK, W. "Natural Knowledge of God in Romans: Patristic and Medieval Interpretation," ThSt 34 (1, 1973) 36-52. ROON, A. VAN, The Authenticity of Ephesians (Leiden 1974) 148f., 157f., 191f. DUBARLE, A.-M., O. P. La manifestation naturalle de Dieu d'après l'Ecriture (Paris 1976). HERR, T. Naturrecht aus der kritischen Sicht des Neuen Testaments (München 1976) 111. MIRANDA, J. P. Marx and the Bible (London 1977) 40-42. ROMANIUK, K. "Zagadnienie naturalnego poznania Boga wedlug Rz 1, 18-32 (Le probléme de la connaissance naturelle de Dieu en Rm 1, 18-32)," RTK 24 (1, 1977) 59-68. SYNOFZIK, E. Die Gerichts- und Vergeltungs-aussagen bei Paulus (Göttingen 1977) 78-80. FURNISH, V. P. The Moral Teaching of Paul (Nashville 1979) 74-78, 81f., 120. MON, R. "Etyka objawiona a naturalna w Rz 1, 18-32 (Christian Morality and Natural Ethics in Ro 1. 18-32)," SThV 17 (2, 1979) 65-80. ROBINSON, J. A. T. Wrestling with Romans (London 1979) 16-25. MCDONALD, J. I. H. Kerygma and Didache. Society for New Testament Studies (Cambridge 1980) 55. MILNE, D. J. W. "Genesis 3 in the Letter to the Romans," RThR 39 (1980) 10-18. THISELTON, A. C. The Two Horizons (Grand Rapids 1980) 388. DEIDUN, T. J. New Covenant Morality in Paul (Rome 1981) 92f. POPKES, W. "Zum Aufbau und Charakter von Römer 1.18-32," NTS 28 (4, 1982) 490-501. BINDEMANN, W. Die Hoffnung der Schöpfung (Neukirchen 1983) 61. GORDAY, P. Principles of Patristic Exegesis: Romans 9-11 in Origen, John Chrysostom, and Augustine (New York/Toronto 1983) 53, 111f., 153f. ECKSTEIN, H.-J. Der Begriff Syneidesis bei Paulus (Tübingen 1983) 138ff., 314f. PATTE, D. Paul's Faith and the Power of the Gospel (Philadelphia 1983) 257-63. RÄISÄNEN, H. Paul and the Law (Tübingen 1983) 7, 97, 101f., 106, 110, 112f., 149. BRANDENBURGER, E. "Gericht Gottes" in TRE 12 (1984) 471. PATTE, D. Preaching Paul (Philadelphia 1984) 51. DOWNING, F. G. Christ and the Cynics (Sheffield 1988) 188. ZIESLER, J. Pauline Christianity (Oxford 1990) 18, 75f., 82. SANDERS, E. P. Paul, the Law, and the Jewish People (London 1985) 115n.5, 123f., 128f., 135n.45. DUNN, J. D. G. "Paul's Epistle to the Romans: An Analysis of Structure and Argument" in ANRW II.25.4 (1987) 2849. OSTEN-SACKEN, P. VON DER, Evangelium und Tora: Aufsätze zu Paulus (München 1987) 210, 213, 219-22. DAVIES, G. N. Faith and Obedience in Romans. A Study in Romans 1-4 (Sheffield 1990) 47ff. ELLIOT, N. The Rhetoric of Romans (Sheffield 1990) 37, 58, 67, 81, 85, 98, 107-19, 123-7, 133-5, 148, 150n., 173-6, 182-4,

186n., 223, 245, 272, 277, 289. HOOKER, M. D. From Adam to Christ. Essays on Paul (Cambridge 1990) 85. LONGENECKER, B. W. Eschatology and the Covenant. A Comparison of 4 Ezra and Romans 1-11 (Sheffield 1991) 173-5, 192, 200, 239. PAK, J. Y.-S. Paul as Missionary (Frankfurt/Bern/New York/Paris 1991) 27-9. WYRWA, D. "Über die Begegnung des biblischen Glaubens mit dem griechischen Geist," ZThK 88 (1991) 29-67. ARZT, P. Bedrohtes Christsein. Zu Eigenart und Funktion eschatologisch bedrohlicher Propositionen in den echten Paulusbriefen (Frankfurt/Berlin/Bern 1992) passim. WILLIAMS, M. "Romans 1: Entropy, Sexuality and Politics," Anvil 10 (1993) 105-10. WOLTERS, A. "Hart's Exegetical Proposal on Romans 1," CThJ 28 (1993) 166-70. PORTER, C. L. "Romans 1.18-32: Its Role in the Developing Argument," NTS 40 (1994) 210-28.

1:18-31   KLOSTERMANN, E. "Die adäquate Vergeltung in RÖM. 1:22-31" ZNW 32 (1933) 1-6. MALHERBE, A. J. Moral Exhortation. A Greco-Roman Sourcebook (Philadelphia 1986) 42.

1:18-30   BETZ, H.D. Lukian von Samosata und das Neue Testament (1961) passim.

1:18-29   SEVENSTER, J.N. Paul and Seneca (1961) passim.

1:18-28   SEGALLA, G. "L'empietà come rifiuto della verità di Dio in *Romani* 1, 18-28," StPa 34 (2, 1987) 275-96.

1:18-25   SALVONI, F. Ateismo e Paolo (*Romani* 1, 18-25)," RBR 11 (1, 1976)7-41. WALT, B. J. VAN DER, "Handelinge 17:15-34 en Romeine 1:18-25: bewyse vir aansluitingspunte in die sending of vir 'n natuurlike teologie?" In die Skriflig 10 (1976) 47-51. DUNN, J. D. Christology in the Making (London 1980) 101f.

1:18-23   LACKMANN, M. Von Geheimnis der Schöpfung (1952), 34-94, 176-211. FEUILLET, A. "La connaissance naturelle de Dieu par les hommes" LuVie 14 ('54) 63-80. SHIELDS, B. E. "The Areopagus Sermon and Rom 1:18-23: A Study in Cretaion Theology," Rest Q 20 (1977) 23-40. GEORGI, D. "Weisheit Salomos" in JSHRZ III/4 (1980) 12n.27b. PARKER, T. H. L. Commentaries on the Epistle to the Romans 1532-1542 (Edinburgh 1986) 84-124.

1:18-22   LARSSON, E. Christus als Vorbild (Uppsala 1962) passim.

1:18-21   HOOKER, M.D. "Adam in Romans I" NTS 6 (1959-60) 298f. HASENSTAB, R. Modell paulinischer Ethik (Mainz 1977) 143. CIPRIANI, S. "Il 'cognoscere Deum' è anche un 'quaerere Deum' in S. Paolo?" in Quaerere Deum. Atti della XXV Settimana Biblica Italiana (Brescia 1980) 353-67. TURNER, D. L. "Cornelius Van Til and Romans 1:18-21. A Study in the Epistemology of Presuppositional Apologetics," GThJ 2 (1, 1981) 45-58. PAK, J. Y.-S. Paul as Missionary (Frankfurt/Bern/New York/Paris 1991) 27-49, 181.

1:18-20   SCHJÖTT, P.O. ZNW 4 (1903) 75-78. CERFAUX, L. Christ in the Theology of St. Paul (1959) passim.

1:18-20a   BRANDENBURGER, E. Das Böse (Zürich 1986) 54.

1:18-19   FRIEDRICH, G. "'Αμαρτία οὐκ ἐλλογεῖται Rom. 5, 13" in Auf das Wort kommt es an. Gesammelte Aufsätze (Göttingen 1978) 126. STAAB, K. Pauluskommentare aus der griechischen Kirche (Münster ²1984) 356:32-357:7 Genn.

1:18   SCHRAGE, W. Die konkreten Einzelgebote in der paulinischen Paränese (1961) 66, 188. DA S. MARCO, P. EMMANUELE, "L'ira di Dio si manifesta in ogni genere di empieta e di ingiustizia" Studiorum Paulinorum Congressus Internationalis Catholicus 1961 (1963) I 259-69. KÄSEMANN, E. Exegetische Versuche und Besinnungen (1964) I 97. LJUNGMAN, H. Pistis (1964) 107f. LÜHRMANN, D. Das Offenbarungsverständnis bei Paulus und in Paulinischen Gemeinden (1965) 146-48. KERTELGE, K. "Rechtfertigung" bei Paulus (1967) 69f. GIBLIN, C.H. The Threat to Faith (1967) 98, 131, 185-86, 188. CRAN-

FIELD, C.E.B. "Romans 1.18" SJTh 21 (3, '68) 330-35. GÄRTNER, B. The Areopagus Speech and Natural Revelation (Uppsala 1955) 74f. MORRIS, L. The Apostolic Preaching of the Cross (Grand Rapids 1955) 166f. BOHREN, R. Predigtlehre (München 1971) 256, 259f. BAUMERT, N. Täglich Sterben und Auferstehen (München 1973) 359. LADD, G. E. A Theology of the New Testament (Grand Rapids 1974) 405, 407, 425, 430, 516. SCHMITHALS, W. Der Römerbrief als historisches Problem (Gütersloh 1975) 13. AONO, T. Die Entwicklung des paulinischen Gerichtsgedankens bei den Apostolischen Vätern (Bern/Frankfurt/Las Vegas 1979) 4ff. BERGER, K. "Hellenistisch-heidnische Prodigien und die Vorzeichen in der jüdischen und christlichen Apokalyptik" in ANRW II.23.2 (1980) 1436. THISELTON, A. C. The Two Horizons (Grand Rapids 1980) 127, 225. SCHADE, H.-H. Apokalyptische Christologie bei Paulus (Göttingen 1981) 47-49. STAAB, K. Pauluskommentare aus der griechischen Kirche (Münster ²1984) 58:5-9 Apoll; 115:8-14 ThM; 356:23-31 Genn; 653:4-16 Areth. GENSICHEN, H.-W. "Heidentum I" in TRE 14 (1985) 599. PARKER, T. H. L. Commentaries on the Epistle to the Romans 1532-1542 (Edinburgh 1986) 84-87. ECKSTEIN, H.-J. "'Denn Gottes Zorn wird vom Himmel her offenbar werden.' Exegetische Erwägungen zu Röm 1:18," ZNW 78 (1-2, 1987) 74-89. BOCKMUEHL, M. N. A. Revelation and Mystery (Tübingen 1990) 138ff. KRAUS, W. Der Tod Jesu als Heiligtumsweihe. Eine Untersuchung zum Umfeld der Sühnevorstellung in Römer 3, 25-26a (Neukirchen-Vluyn 1991) 10, 12, 108f. PAK, J. Y.-S. Paul as Missionary (Frankfurt/Bern/New York/Paris 1991) 29-33.

1:19-2:11   SCHMITHALS, W. Der Römerbrief als historisches Problem (Gütersloh 1975) 13f.

1:19-2:1   HARRISON, P. N. Paulines and Pastorals (London 1964) 79-85. MUNRO, W. Authority in Paul and Peter (Cambridge 1983) 155-60.

1:19ff   BRUNNER, E. Dogmatik II (1950) 105. OTT, H. "Röm.1, 19ff. als dogmatisches Problem" ThZ 15 (1, '59) 40-50. LÜHRMANN, D. Das Offenbarungsverständnis bei Paulus und in Paulinischen Gemeinden (1965) 21-26. SCHULZ, S. Neutestamentliche Ethik (Zürich 1987) 387.

1:19-32   FEINE, D.P. Das gesetzfreie Evangelium des Paulus (1899) 104-9. P. EMMANUELE DA S. MARCO "L'ira di Dio si Manifesta in ogni genere di Empieta E di Ingiustizia (Rom. 1, 18)" Studiorum Paulinorum Congressus Internationalis Catholicus 1961 I (1963) 261-5.

1:19-26   STAAB, K. Pauluskommentare aus der griechischen Kirche (Münster ²1984) 477:7-479: 38 Phot.

1:19-23   LOHSE, E. Grundriss der neutestamentlichen Theologie (Stuttgart 1974) 87f.

1:19-22   Studiorum Paulinorum Congressus Internationalis Catholicus 1961/I (1963) 261f.

1:19-21   BERGER, K. und COLPE, C., eds., Religionsgeschichtliches Textbuch zum Neuen Testament (Göttingen/Zürich 1987) 197f. NOVAK, D. "Before Revelation. The Rabbis, Paul, and Karl Barth," JR 71 (1991) 50-66. PAK, J. Y.-S. Paul as Missionary (Frankfurt/Bern/New York/Paris 1991) 33-7.

1:19-20   VOLZ, P. Die Eschatologie der jüdischen Gemeinde (1934) 300. BULTMANN, R. Theologie des Neuen Testaments (1965) 228f. FRIDRICHSEN, A. "Zur Auslegung von Rm 1:19f" ZNW 17 (1916) 159. GÄRTNER, B. The Areopagus Speech and Natural Revelation (Uppsala 1955) 137f., 142. GRÜNLER, R. G. New Approaches to Jesus and the Gospels (Grand Rapids 1982) 224, 239.

1:19   BRUNNER, E. Dogmatik I (1946) 83, 126, 138, 184; Dogmatik II (1950) 7; Mensch im Widerspruch (1937) 62, 178. ROSIN, H. "To gnoston tou Theou"

ThZ 17 (3, '61_161-65. ROMANIUK, C. "Le Livre de la Sagesse dans le Nouveau Testament" NTS 14 (1968) 498-514. MACK, B. L. Logos und Sophia (Göttingen 1973) 128. THISELTON, A. C. The Two Horizons (Grand Rapids 1980) 127, 225. STAAB, K. Pauluskommentare aus der griechischen Kirche (Münster ²1984) 59:10-13 Apoll; 653:17-21 Areth. PARKER, T. H. L. Commentaries on the Epistle to the Romans 1532-1542 (Edinburgh 1986) 87f. SCHNELLE, U. Wandlungen im paulinischen Denken (Stuttgart 1989) 16.

1:20-21   STACEY, W.D. The Pauline View of Man (1956) 33, 36, 200f, 195f. ELLIS, E.E. Paul's Use of the Old Testament (1957) 78f, 153. KLIJN, A. F. J. "Die syrische Baruch-Apokalypse" in JSHRZ V/2 (1976) 16on.18a.

1:20   BRUNNER, E. Dogmatik I (1946) 141, II (1950) 178, 191. STÄHELIN, E. Die Verkündigung des Reiches Gottes in der Kirche Jesu Christi I (1951) 255, 349. O'ROURKE, J.J. "Romans 1, 20 and Natural Revelation" CBQ 23 (3, '61) 301-6. SCHRAGE, W. Die konkreten Einzelgebote in der paulinischen Paränese (1961) 193, 210. GRIJS, DE F.J.A. "Theologische aantekeningen over enige wijzen waarop Romeinen 1, 20 is verstaan in de traditie van de rooms katholieke kerk" (Theological Remarks about Rom. 1, 20 in the Tradition of the Roman Catholic Church) Bijdragen 30 (1, '69) 66-83. LINDESKOG, G. Studien zum Neutestamentlichen Schöpfungsgedanken I (Uppsala 1952) 181, 182, 205. KÜMMEL, W. G. Römer 7 und das Bild des Menschen im Neuen Testament (München 1974) 28f., 181, 184, 192. GEORGI, D. "Weisheit Salomos" in JSHRZ III/4 (1980) 13n.6a. GRÜNLER, R. G. New Approaches to Jesus and the Gospels (Grand Rapids 1982) 222. DEMKE, C. "Gott IV" in TRE 13 (1984) 645. STAAB, K. Paulus-kommentare aus der griechischen Kirche (Münster ²1984) 357:8-24 Genn; 357:25-35 Genn. PARKER, T. H. L. Commentaries on the Epistle to the Romans 1532- 1542 (Edinburgh 1986) 88-91. LAYTON, B. The Gnostic Scriptures (Garden City NY 1987) 237.

1:21ff.   SCHRAGE, W. Die konkreten Einzelgebote in der paulinischen Paränese (1961) 190, 192f, 208.

1:21-32   BOUWMAN, G. "Noch einmal Römer 1, 21-32," Biblica 54 (3, 1973) 411-14.

1:21-25   PAGELS, E. H. The Gnostic Paul. Gnostic Exegesis of the Pauline Letters (Philadelphia 1975) 16, 17.

1:21-23   STAAB, K. Pauluskommentare aus der griechischen Kirche (Münster ²1984) 358:1-31 Genn. PAK, J. Y.-S. Paul as Missionary (Frankfurt/ Bern/New York/ Paris 1991) 51-61, 182.

1:21-22   JÜNGEL, E. Paulus und Jesus (1966) 31.

1:21   BRUNNER, E. Dogmatik II (1950) 7, 109. SCHRAGE, W. Die konkreten Einzelgebote in der paulinischen Paränese (1961) 164. EICHHOLZ, G. Die Theologie des Paulus im Umriss (1972) 68ff. ROBINSON, J. A. Pelagius's Exposition of Thirteen Epistles of St. Paul I (Cambridge 1922) 241, 243, 263, 327. GÄRTNER, B. The Areopagus Speech and Natural Revelation (Uppsala 1955) 74f., 79f. LADD, G. E. A Theology of the New Testament (Grand Rapids 1974) 397, 403, 475, 476. DETTLOFF, W. "Bonaventura" in TRE 7 (1981) 52. STAAB, K. Pauluskommentare aus der griechischen Kirche (Münster ²1984) 46:8-12 EusE; 59:14-17 Apoll. PARKER, T. H. L. Commentaries on the Epistle to the Romans 1532-1542 (Edinburgh 1986) 91f. LAYTON, B. The Gnostic Scriptures (Garden City NY 1987) 253. PAK, J. Y.-S. Paul as Missionary (Frankfurt/Bern/New York/Paris 1991) 37-40.

1:21a   BRANDENBURGER, E. Das Böse (Zürich 1986) 54.

1:22-32   JEREMIAS, J. "Ze Rm 1, 22-32" ZNW 45 ('54) 119-21. LYONNET, S. "La structure littéraire de Rom 1, 22-32" Biblica 38 ('57) 35-40. LYONNET, S.

"Notes sur l'exégè de l'Epître aux Romains" Biblica 38 (1, '57) 35-61. JEREMIAS, J. Abba (1966) 290-92.

1:22-31   KLOSTERMANN, E. "Die adäquate Vergeltung in Rm 1:22-31" ZNW 32 (1933) 1. BASSLER, J. M. Divine Impartiality (Chico CA 1982) 201f.

1:22-28a   BRANDENBURGER, E. Das Böse (Zürich 1986) 54.

1:22-24   EICHHOLZ, G. Die Theologie des Paulus im Umriss (1972) 69f, 76f.

1:22-23   GEORGI, D. "Weisheit Salomos" in JSHRZ III/4 (1980) 12n.24a.

1:22   PARKER, T. H. L. Commentaries on the Epistle to the Romans 1532-1542 (Edinburgh 1986) 92f.

1:23ff.   HARMAN, A. M. Paul's Use of the Psalms (Ann Arbor MI 1968) 178-82.

1:23-31   P. EMMANUELE DA S. MARCO "L'ira di Dio si Manifesta in ogni Genere di Empieta e di Ingiustizia" Studiorum Paulinorum Congressus Internationalis Catholicus 1961 I (1963) 262-5).

1:23   BRUNNER, E. Mensch in Widerspruch (1937) 178. HYLDAHL, N. "A Reminiscence of the Old Testament at Romans 1:23" NTS 2 ('56) 285-88. VOEGTLE, A. Das Neue Testament und die Zukunft des Kosmos (1970) 218-220. HOOKER, M.D. "Adam in Romans I" NTS 6 ('59/60) 297f. JERVELL, J. Imago Dei (1960) 174, 180, 187, 312-31, 335. GÄRTNER, B. The Areopagus Speech and Natural Revelation (Uppsala 1955) 141f. VANNI, U. "Homoioma in Paolo (Rm 1, 23: 5, 14: 6, 5: 8, 3: Fil 2, 7). Un' interpretazione esegetico-teologica alla luce dell'uso dei LXX—I. Parte," Gr 58 (1977) 321-45. HAACKER, K. "Exegetische Probleme des Römerbriefs" NT 20 (1, 1978) 1-21. GEORGI, D. "Weisheit Salomos" in JSHRZ III/4 (1980) 11n.15b. BASSLER, J. M. Divine Impartiality (Chico CA 1982) 195-97. DEMKE, C. "Gott IV" in TRE 13 (1984) 645. PARKER, T. H. L. Commentaries on the Epistle to the Romans 1532-1542 (Edinburgh 1986) 93f. HAYS, R. B. Echoes of Scripture in the Letters of Paul (New Haven/London 1989) 93f. HOOKER, M. D. From Adam to Christ. Essays on Paul (Cambridge 1990) 5, 73f., 76f., 80f. WAY, D. The Lordship of Christ. Ernst Käsemann's Interpretation of Paul's Theology (Oxford 1991) 203.

1:24ff.   KÄSEMANN, E. Exegetische Versuche und Besinnungen (1964) II 191. POPKES, W. Christus Traditus (1967) 134f, 236, 259, 276, 287. KÄSEMANN, E. New Testament Questions of Today (1969) 180. GEORGI, D. "Weisheit Salomos" in JSHRZ III/4 (1980) 14n.12a. FREUND, G. und STEGEMANN, E., eds., Theologische Brosamen für Lothar Steiger (DBAT 5; Heidelberg 1985) 404.

1:24-32   JOHNSON, S. L. JR. "'God gave them up'. A Study in Divine Retribution," BS 129 (1972) 124-33. GEORGI, D. "Weisheit Salomos" in JSHRZ III/4 (1980) 14n.22a.

1:24-31   LONGENECKER, B. W. Eschatology and the Covenant. A Comparison of 4 Ezra and Romans 1-11 (Sheffield 1991) 175-81.

1:24-28   JOHNSON, S.L.Jr. "'God Gave Them Up': A Study in Divine Retribution" BiblSa 129 (514, '72) 124-33. RÖHSER, G. Metaphorik und Personifikation der Sünde (Tübingen 1987) 148, 164, 180f.

1:24-27   STAAB, K. Pauluskommentare aus der griechischen Kirche (Münster ²1984) 358:32-359:14 Genn. HENRIKSEN, J.-O. "Naturen som norm? En drøfting av naturbegrepet i tilknytning til Rom 1, 24-27," TsTK 62 (1991) 95-112. PAK, J. Y.-S. Paul as Missionary (Frankfurt/Bern/New York/Paris 1991) 63-78, 182.

1:24-25   WEDER, H. Neutestamentliche Hermeneutik (Zürich 1986) 250f.

1:24   ROBINSON, J.A.T. The Body, A Study in Pauline Theology (1952) 28f. BEST, E. One Body in Christ (1955) 217. STACEY, W.D. The Pauline View of Man

(1956) 183, 194. SCHRAGE, W. Die konkreten Einzelgebote in der paulinischen Paränese (1961) 226. JÜNGEL, E. Paulus und Jesus (1966) 57. BERGER, K. "Das Buch der Jubiläen" in JSHRZ II/3 (1981) 433n.22d. STAAB, K. Pauluskommentare aus der griechischen Kirche (Münster ²1984) 423:1-2 Oek. RÄISÄNEN, H. The Torah and Christ (Helsinki 1986) 160ff.

1:25-27   SCHRAGE, W. Die konkreten Einzelgebote in der paulinischen Paränese (1961) 53, 195, 208, 210, 213.

1:25   HOOKER, M.D. "Adam in Romans I" NTS 6 (1959'60) 298f. SCHENK, W. Der Segen im Neuen Testament (1967) 97. MERK, O. Handeln aus Glauben (1968) 207. EICHHOLZ, G. Die Theologie des Paulus im Umriss (1972) 70ff. GÄRTNER, B. The Areopagus Speech and Natural Revelation (Uppsala 1955) 74f. DEICHGRÄBER, R. "Benediktionen" in TRE 5 (1980) 562. STAAB, K. Pauluskommentare aus der griechischen Kirche (Münster ²1984) 115:15-20 ThM; 214:16-17 Sev. GRÄSSER, E. Der Alte Bund im Neuen (Tübingen 1985) 235, 236, 241. SCHIMANOWSKI, G. Weisheit und Messias (Tübingen 1985) 318. AUNE, D. E. The New Testament in Its Literary Environment (Philadelphia 1987) 193. LAMPE, P. Die stadtrömischen Christen in den ersten beiden Jahrhunderten (Tübingen ²1989) 126. HOOKER, M. D. From Adam to Christ. Essays on Paul (Cambridge 1990) 74f., 78-80, 85.

1:25c   SIMONIS, W. Der gefangene Paulus. Die Entstehung des sogenannten Römerbriefs und anderer urchristlicher Schriften in Rom (Frankfurt/ Bern/New York/Paris 1990) 44, 47f.

1:26-32   "Formgeschichte" in TRE 11 (1983) 298.

1:26-27   PAGELS, E. H. The Gnostic Paul. Gnostic Exegesis of the Pauline Letters (Philadelphia 1975) 17f. FURNISH, V. P. The Moral Teaching of Paul (Nashville 1979) 58, 68, 73-78, 79-81. SWIDLER, L. Biblical Affirmations of Woman (Philadelphia 1979) 330. HÜBNER, H. "Dekalog" in TRE 8 (1981) 417. PHILONENKO-SAYAR, B. and PHILONENKO, M. "Die Apokalypse Abrahams" in JSHRZ V/5 (1982) 447n.7. MEHL, R. "Freiheit" in TRE 11 (1983) 523. SCROGGS, R. The New Testament and Homosexuality (Philadelphia 1983) 9f., 14f., 109-18. HAYS, R. B. "Relations Natural and Unnatural: A Response to John Boswell's Exegesis of Romans 1," JRE 14 (1, 1986) 184-215. OSTEN-SACKEN, P. VON DER, Evangelium und Tora: Aufsätze zu Paulus (München 1987) 211f., 215-19, 224, 232, 280. DeYOUNG, J. B. "The Meaning of 'Nature' in Romans 1 and Its Implications for Biblical Proscriptions of Homosexual Behavior," JEThS 31 (4, 1988) 429-41. WRIGHT, D. F. "Homosexuality: The Relevance of the Bible," EQ 61 (4, 1989) 291-300. IDE, A. F. Battling with Beasts. Sex in the Life and Letters of St. Paul: The Issue of Homosexuality, Heterosexuality and Bisexuality (Garland, TX 1991) passim. MALICK, D. E. "The Condemnation of Homosexuality in Romans 1:26-27," BiblSa 150 (1993) 327-40.

1:26   KNOX, W.L. The Sources of the Synoptic Gospels II (1957) 116. SCHRAGE, W. Die konkreten Einzelgebote in der paulinischen Paränese (1961) 226. MERK, O. Handeln aus Glauben (1968) 135, 244. GÄRTNER, B. The Areopagus Speech and Natural Revelation (Uppsala 1955) 80f. BERGER, K. "Das Buch der Jubiläen" in JSHRZ II/3 (1981) 433n.22d. STENDAHL, K. "Ancient Scripture in the Modern World" in F. E. Greenspahn, ed., Scripture in the Jewish and Christian Traditions (Nashville 1982) 212. STAAB, K. Pauluskommentare aus der griechischen Kirche (Münster ²1984) 115:21-25 ThM. OSTEN-SACKEN, P. VON DER, Evangelium und Tora: Aufsätze zu Paulus (München 1987) 211f., 217, 221.

1:27   STAAB, K. Pauluskommentare aus der griechischen Kirche (Münster [2]1984) 214:18-19 Sev. OSTEN-SACKEN, P. VON DER, "Paulinisches Evangelium und Homo-sexualität" in Evangelium und Tora: Aufsätze zu Paulus (München 1987) 210-36. ROBINSON, J. A. Pelagius's Exposition of Thirteen Epistles of St. Paul I (Cambridge 1922) 142f. BERGER, K. "Hellenistisch-heidnische Prodigien und die Vorzeichen in der jüdischen und christlichen Apokalyptik" in ANRW II.23.2 (1980) 1436. GÄRTNER, B. The Areopagus Speech and Natural Revelation (Uppsala 1955) 80f. LADD, G. E. A Theology of the New Testament (Grand Rapids 1974) 476, 516, 525. GEORGI, D. "Weisheit Salomos" in JSHRZ III/4 (1980) 15n.11a. BERGER, K. "Das Buch der Jubiläen" in JSHRZ II/3 (1981) 433n.22d. STAAB, K. Pauluskommentare aus der griechischen Kirche (Münster [2]1984) 359:15-25 Genn.

1:28   DEWITT, N.W. St. Paul and Epicurus (1954) 161-62. SCHRAGE, W. Die konkreten Einzelgebote in der paulinischen Paränese (1961) 53, 164, 193, 198, 226.

1:29ff.   BOUSSET, W. Die Religion des Judentums im Späthellenistischen Zeitalter (1926) 426.

1:29-32   STAAB, K. Pauluskommentare aus der griechischen Kirche (Münster [2]1984) 359:26-360:18 Genn; 480:4-5 Phot.

1:29-31   SCHRAGE, W. Die konkreten Einzelgebote in der paulinischen Paränese (1961) 44, 66, 195. HAGE, W. "Die griechische Baruch-Apokalypse" in JSHRZ V/1 (1974) 27n.17d. SCHWEIZER, E. "Gottes-gerechtigkeit und Lasterkataloge bei Paulus (inkl. Kol und Eph)" in J. Friedrich et al., eds., Rechtfertigung (FS. E. Käsemann; Tübingen/Göttingen 1976) 469-71. SCHWEIZER, E. "Traditional ethical patterns in the Pauline and post-Pauline letters and their development (list of vices and house-tables)" in E. Best and R. McL. Wilson, eds., Text and Interpretation (FS. Matthew Black; Cambridge 1979) 199, 201f. REINMUTH, E. Geist und Gesetz (Berlin/DDR 1985) 16f. MALHERBE, A. J. Moral Exhortation. A Greco-Roman Sourcebook (Philadelphia 1986) 130. JEFFORD, C. N. The Sayings of Jesus in the Teaching of the Twelve Apostles (Leiden 1989) 83f.

1:29-30   BORSE, U. Der Standort des Galaterbriefes (Köln 1972) 103f.

1:29   MASSAUX, E. Influence de l'Evangile de saint Matthieu sur la littérature chrétienne avant saint Irénée (1950) 620-24. ROBINSON, J. A. Pelagius's Exposition of Thirteen Epistles of St. Paul I (Cambridge 1922) 263, 340n.4, 341. ROON, A. VAN, The Authenticity of Ephesians (Leiden 1974) 166. LOHSE, E. Die Entstehung des Neuen Testaments (Stuttgart/Berlin/Köln [5]1991) 26.

1:31   MALHERBE, A. J. Moral Exhortation. A Greco-Roman Sourcebook (Philadelphia 1986) 138.

1:32-2:1   STAAB, K. Pauluskommentare aus der griechischen Kirche (Münster [2]1984) 215:1-12 Sev.

1:32   BORNKAMM, G. "Gesetz und Natur. Röm. 2, 14-16" Studien zu Antike und Urchristentum. Ges. Aufs. II (1959) 93-118. SCHRAGE, W. Die konkreten Einzelgebote in der paulinischen Paränese (1961) 53, 128, 193, 196, 231. VAN DÜLMEN, A. Die Theologie des Gesetzes bei Paulus (1968) 62, 73, 77, 81, 133, 135, 140. MERK, O. Handeln aus Glauben (1968) 48, 73. BRANDENBURGER, E. Adam und Christus (Neukirchen-Vluyn 1962) 164, 166, 183, 197, 204, 233, 252. MIRANDA, J. P. Marx and the Bible (London 1977) 172-75. AONO, T. Die Entwicklung des paulinischen Gerichtsgedankens bei den Apostolischen Vätern (Bern/Frankfurt/Las Vegas 1979) 4ff. STAAB, K. Pauluskommentare aus der griechischen Kirche (Münster [2]1984) 59:18-60:6 Apoll. OSTEN-SACKEN, P. VON DER, Evangelium und Tora: Aufsätze zu Paulus

(München 1987) 175, 219, 221f. MARTIN, B. L. Christ and the Law in Paul (Leiden 1989) 70, 72, 74, 81-83, 101, 152.

2:1–3:20   P. Emmanuelle da S. Marco, "L'ira di Dio si Manifesta in ogni genere di empieta e di Ingiustizia" Studiorum Paulinorum Congressus Internationalis Catholicus 1961 (1963) I 265-67. GIBLIN, C.H. In Hope of God's Glory (1970) 336-48. CAMBIER, J.-M. "Le jugement de tous les hommes par Dieu seul, selon la vérité, dans Rom 2:1-3:20," ZNW 67 (3-4, 1976) 187-213. BRANDEN-BURGER, E. "Gericht Gottes" in TRE 12 (1984) 741.

2:1-3:8   RIEDL, J. Das Heil der Heiden nach Röm 2; 14-16.26.27 (Mödling bei Wien 1965) 190-214.

2   WETTER, G.P. Der Vergeltungsgedanke dei Paulus (1912) 74ff. VOLZ, P. Die Eschatologie der jüdischen Gemeinde (1934) 288. DAVIES, W.D. Paul and Rabbinic Judaism (1955) 325ff. RIEDL, J. "Salus paganorum secundum Rom 2" VerbDom 42 (2, '64) 61-70. BOUSSET, W. Die Religion des Judentums im Späthellenistischen Zeitalter (1966) 392. ZIESLER, J.A. The Meaning of Righteousness in Paul (1972) 189f. GROVEL, K. "A Chiastic Retribution" in E. Dinkler, ed., Zeit und Geschichte (FS. R. Bultmann; Tübingen 1964) 255-261. SYNOFZIK, E. Die Gerichts- und Vergeltungsaussagen bei Paulus (Göttingen 1977) 80-83. RÄISÄNEN, H. Paul and the Law (Tübingen 1983) 16, 96-98, 107, 193. KLEIN, G. "Gesetz" in TRE 13 (1984) 68. SANDERS, E. P. Paul, the Law, and the Jewish People (London 1985) 117n.24, 126-35, 132n.11, 133n.12, 134nn.43, 44, 147, 156f. LÜBKING, H.-M. Paulus und Israel im Römerbrief (Frankfurt/Bern/New York 1986) 26-30. RÄISÄNEN, H. The Torah and Christ (Helsinki 1986) 80, 290, 293. SNODGRASS, K. R. "Justification by Grace—to the Doers: an Analysis of the Place of Romans 2 in the Theology of Paul," NTS 32 (1, 1986) 72-93. WATSON, F. Paul, Judaism and the Gentiles (Cambridge 1986) 109-22. DUNN, J. D. G. "Paul's Epistle to the Romans: An Analysis of Structure and Argument" in ANRW II.25.4 (1987) 2850f. DUNN, J. D. G. Jesus, Paul and the Law (London 1990) 7, 212, 215, 224, 234n.39, 237, 238.

2:1ff.   HAHN, F. Das Verständnis der Mission im Neuen Testament (1965) 87. JÜNGEL, E. Paulus und Jesus (1966) 26. ZELLER, D. Juden und Heiden in der Mission des Paulus. Studien zum Römerbrief (Stuttgart 1973) 149. AONO, T. Die Entwicklung des paulinischen Gerichtsgedankens bei den Apostolischen Vätern (Bern/ Frankfurt/Las Vegas 1979) 4ff. THEISSEN, G. Psychological Aspects of Pauline Theology (Edinburgh 1987) 74, 78, 82, 196. BECKER, J. Paulus. Der Apostel der Völker (Tübingen 1989) 49ff., 297f., 398.

2:1-29   SCHLIER, H. "Von den Juden. Römerbrief 2, 1-29" Die Zeit der Kirche (1956) 38-47. DAVIES, G. N. Faith and Obedience in Romans. A Study in Romans 1-4 (Sheffield 1990) 47ff. LONGENECKER, B. W. Eschatology and the Covenant. A Comparison of 4 Ezra and Romans 1-11 (Sheffield 1991) 186n.1, 194-6, 199, 245. CARRAS, G. P. "Romans 2, 1-29: A Dialogue on Jewish Ideals," Biblica 73 (1992) 183-207.

2:1-28   SEGUNDO, J. L. The Humanist Christology of Paul [trans. J. Drury], Jesus of Nazareth Yesterday and Today 3 (Maryknoll, N.Y. 1986) 28-41.

2:1-16   JOHNSON, S. L. JR. "Studies in Romans. Part V: The Judgment of God," BiblSa 130 (1973) 24-34. ROBINSON, J. A. T. Wrestling with Romans (London 1979) 25-29. MOXNES, H., Theology in Conflict (Leiden 1980) 50f. ECK-STEIN, H.-J. Der Begriff Syneidesis bei Paulus (Tübingen 1983) 137-79, 313. GORDAY, P. Principles of Patristic Exegesis: Romans 9-11 in Origen, John

Chrysostom, and Augustine (New York/Toronto 1983) 54-56, 112f., 154f. ELLIOT, N. The Rhetoric of Romans (Sheffield 1990) 85, 118, 119-27, 152, 174, 176, 187, 226.

2:1-11   STECK, K.G. 16 (61-62) 338-43. IWAND, H.-J. Predigt-Meditationen (1964) 276-83. MÜLLER—SCHWEFE GPM 10 273-77. STECK, K.G. Herr, tue meine Lippen auf II, ed. G.Eichholz (1966) 518-29. DOERNE, M. Die alten Episteln (1967) 261. KRAUSE, O. GPM 22 (1967/68) 450-56. EICHHOLZ, G. Die Theologie des Paulus im Umriss (1972) 87ff. SURKAU, H.-W. in GPM 34 (1980) 429-437. WILL, K. and WILL, I. in D. Krusche et al., eds., Predigtstudien für das Kirchenjahr 1980, II/2 (Stuttgart 1980) 278-83. HEILIGENTHAL, R. Werke als Zeichen (Tübingen 1983) 165-97. BRAUNSCHWEIGER, H. in GPM 40 (1985-86) 501-8. LONGENECKER, B. W. Eschatology and the Covenant. A Comparison of 4 Ezra and Romans 1-11 (Sheffield 1991) 169, 174f., 189f., 192, 198, 270.

2:1-10   PAGELS, E. H. The Gnostic Paul. Gnostic Exegesis of the Pauline Letters (Philadelphia 1975) 18f.

2:1-6   BOUSSET, W. Die Religion des Judentums im Späthellenistischen Zeitalter (1966) 197, 381, 391, 414. =(1926). MOXNES, H. Theology in Conflict (Leiden 1980) 35-37.

2:1-5   STOWERS, S. K. The Diatribe and Paul's Letter to the Romans (Chico CA 1981) 79, 93-96, 110-12. STAAB, K. Pauluskommentare aus der griechischen Kirche (Münster ²1984) 480:6-11 Phot.

2:1-3   DOWNING, F. G. Christ and the Cynics (Sheffield 1988) 188, 189. MALHERBE, A. J. Moral Exhortation. A Greco-Roman Sourcebook (Philadelphia 1986) 130.

2:1   KNOX, W.L. The Sources of the Synoptic Gospels II (1957) 30. SCHRAGE, W. Die konkreten Einzelgebote in der paulinischen Paränese (1961) 196, 243. EICHHOLZ, G. Die Theologie des Paulus im Umriss (1972) 82ff. SCHMITHALS, W. Der Römerbrief als historisches Problem (Gütersloh 1975) 204. BERGER, K. Exegese des Neuen Testaments (Heidelberg 1977) 25f. METZGER, B. M. The Early Versions of the New Testament. Their Origin, Transmission, and Limitations (Oxford 1977) 173. THEISSEN, G. Psychologische Aspekte paulinischer Theologie (Göttingen 1983) 74, 143n.38, 243, 243n.95. STAAB, K. Pauluskommentare aus der griechischen Kirche (Münster ²1984) 60:7-11 Apoll; 360:19-22 Genn. MALHERBE, A. J. Moral Exhortation. A Greco-Roman Sourcebook (Philadelphia 1986) 38. ELLIOT, N. The Rhetoric of Romans (Sheffield 1990) 107, 119-22, 125, 127, 134, 157, 171, 174-6, 179, 180n., 182-5, 280-2, 286. SEGAL, A. F. Paul the Convert (New Haven/ London 1990) 259. SIMONIS, W. Der gefangene Paulus. Die Entstehung des sogenannten Römerbriefs und anderer urchristlicher Schriften in Rom (Frankfurt/Bern/ New York/Paris 1990) 44f. LONGENECKER, B. W. Eschatology and the Covenant. A Comparison of 4 Ezra and Romans 1-11 (Sheffield 1991) 175-77, 180, 190, 193, 234.

2:2-11   JÜNGEL, E. Unterwegs zur Sache (1972) 173-78.

2:2-5   STAAB, K. Pauluskommentare aus der griechischen Kirche (Münster ²1984) 360:23-361:25 Genn.

2:2-3   SCHRAGE, W. Die konkreten Einzelgebote in der paulinischen Paränese (1961) 128.

2:2   STAAB, K. Pauluskommentare aus der griechischen Kirche (Münster ²1984) 115:26-28 ThM.

2:3-4   BERGER, K. "Hellenistisch-heidnische Prodigien und die Vorzeichen in der jüdischen und christlichen Apokalyptik" in ANRW II.23.2 (1980) 1436.

2:3   JÜNGEL, E. Paulus und Jesus (1966) 26.

2:4   BRUNNER, Dogmatik I (1946) 296. SANDMEL, S. The Genius of Paul (1958) 58-59. ROMANIUK, C. "Le Livre de la Sagresse dans le Nouveau Testament" NTS 14 (1967-68) 506f. NICKELS, P. Targum and New Testament (1967) 68. ROBINSON, J. A. Pelagius's Exposition of Thirteen Epistles of St. Paul I (Cambridge 1922) 292, 309, 315. GEORGI, D. "Weisheit Salomos" in JSHRZ III (4, 1980) 11n.23a. NEYREY, J. H. "The Form and Background of the Polemic in 2 Peter," JBL 99 (1980) 425. MALHERBE, A. J. Moral Exhortation. A Greco-Roman Sourcebook (Philadelphia 1986) 86. OLIVEIRA, A. DE, Die Diakonie der Gerechtigkeit und der Versöhnung in der Apologie des 2. Korintherbriefes. Analyse und Auslegung von 2 Kor 2, 14-4, 6; 5, 11-6, 10 (Münster 1990) 54n.16. KRAUS, W. Der Tod Jesu als Heiligtumsweihe. Eine Untersuchung zum Umfeld der Sühnevorstellung in Römer 3, 25-26a (Neukirchen-Vluyn 1991) 95n., 112n., 113, 117f., 120, 146n.

2:5ff.   SCHRAGE, W. Die konkreten Einzelgebote in der paulinischen Paränese (1961) 21. MATTERN, L. Das Verständnis des Gerichtes bei Paulus (1966) 123ff, 213. LUZ, U. Das Geschichtsverständnis des Paulus (1968) 305.

2:5-12   MIRANDA, J. P. Marx and the Bible (London 1977)117f. 2:5-11 BRANDENBURGER, E. "Gericht Gottes" in TRE 12 (1984) 476. HAYS, R. B. Echoes of Scripture in the Letters of Paul (New Haven/ London 1989) 41f.

2:5-9   RIDDERBOS, H. Paul. An Outline of His Theology (Grand Rapids 1975) 108f.

2:5-8   MANSUS, H. The Wrath of God in the Pauline Homolegoumena (Rüschlikon 1969) 46-55.

2:5-6   STROBEL, A. Erkenntnis und Bekenntnis der Sünde in neutestamentlicher Zeit (1968) 49. FROITZHEIM, F. Christologie und Eschatologie bei Paulus (Würzburg 1979) 9f.

2:5   BRUNNER, E. Dogmatik I (1946) 24. SCHRAGE, W. Die konkreten Einzelgebote in der paulinischen Paränese (1961) 191. SHIRES, H.M. The Eschatology of Paul (1966) 106ff. HEROLD, G. Zorn und Gerechtigkeit Gottes bei Paulus. Eine Untersuchung zu Röm. 1, 16-18 (Frankfurt 1973) 287ff. LADD, G. E. A Theology of the New Testament (Grand Rapids 1974) 386, 407, 430, 475, 476, 565, 568. SCHRAGE, W. "Die Elia-Apokalypse" in JSHRZ V (3, 1980) 236n.23e. BERGER, K. "Das Buch der Jubiläen" in JSHRZ II/3 (1981) 450n.30a. STAAB, K. Pauluskommentare aus der griechischen Kirche (Münster ²1984) 215:13-27 Sev; 423:3 Oek. REISER, M. Die Gerichtspredigt Jesu (Münster 1990) 158.

2:6ff.   LONGENECKER, R.N. Paul Apostle of Liberty (1964) 116, 117-8, 120-121. SCHULZ, S. Neutestamentliche Ethik (Zürich 1987) 379.

2:6-29   STALDER, K. Das Werk des Geistes in der Heiligung bei Paulus (1962) 258-64.

2:6-16   MOHRLANG, R. Matthew and Paul (Cambridge 1984) 59, 162f. CHARLESWORTH, J. H. The Old Testament Pseudepigrapha and the New Testament (Cambridge 1985) 124.

2:6-11   GROBEL, K. "A Chiastic Retribution—Formula in Romans 2" in Zeit und Geschichte (1964) 255-61. SALAS, A. "Dios premia segun las obras. Estudio exegétio-theologico de Rom. 2, 6-11" CiDi 182 (1, '60) 5-29. HEILIGENTHAL, R. Werke als Zeichen (Tübingen 1983) 170-72. DAVIES, G. N. Faith and Obedience in Romans. A Study in Romans 1-4 (Sheffield 1990) 53-7.

2:6-8   STAAB, K. Pauluskommentare aus der griechischen Kirche (Münster ²1984)
             480:12-19 Phot.
2:6   MERK, O. Handeln aus Glauben (1968) 14, 150. HARMAN, A. M. Paul's Use
             of the Psalms (Ann Arbor MI 1968) 182f. BERGER, K. "Das Buch der
             Jubiläen" in JSHRZ II/3 (1981) 352n.16b. HEILIGENTHAL, R. Werke als
             Zeichen (Tübingen 1983) 172-75. KOCH, D.-A. Die Schrift als Zeuge des
             Evangeliums (Tübingen 1986) 23f., 111. DAVIES, G. N. Faith and Obedience
             in Romans. A Study in Romans 1-4 (Sheffield 1990) 117.
2:7-11   MOXNES, H. Theology in Conflict (Leiden 1980) 35-37. 2:7-10 HARRIS, M.
             J. Raised Immortal (London 1986) 197f.
2:7-10   FEINE, D.P. Das gesetzesfreie Evangelium des Paulus (1899) 111-13.
             SCHRAGE, W. Die konkreten Einzelgebote in der paulinischen Paränese (1961)
             20, 22, 195. JEREMIAS, J. Abba (1966) 282. LIEBERS, R. Das Gesetz als
             Evangelium (Zürich 1989) 26.
2:7-9   FROITZHEIM, F. Christologie und Eschatologie bei Paulus (Würzburg 1979)
             180.
2:7   SIBER, P. Mit Christus leben (Zürich 1971) 20. STAAB, K. Pauluskommentare
             aus der griechischen Kirche (Münster ²1984) 653:22-654:4 Areth.
2:8-9   STAAB, K. Pauluskommentare aus der griechischen Kirche (Münster ²1984)
             215:28-31 Sev.
2:8   BERGMEIER, R. Glaube als Gabe nach Johannes (Stutt-gart 1980) 222.
             STAAB, K. Pauluskommentare aus der griechischen Kirche (Münster ²1984)
             423:4 Oek.
2:9ff.   BECKER, J. Paulus. Der Apostel der Völker (Tübingen 1989) 50, 55, 58.
2:9-10   STRECKER, G. Der Weg der Gerechtigkeit (1962) 108. ZELLER, D. Juden
             und Heiden in der Mission des Paulus. Studien zum Römerbrief (Stuttgart 1973)
             149ff. ZINGG, P. Das Wachsen der Kirche (Freiburg, Schweiz 1974) 267f.
             SCHMITHALS, W. Der Römerbrief als historisches Problem (Gütersloh 1975)
             12, 20, 56. BRANDENBURGER, E. Das Böse (Zürich 1986) 98f.
2:10   STAAB, K. Pauluskommentare aus der griechischen Kirche (Münster ²1984)
             60:12-15 Apoll; 215:32-216:6 Sev; 423:5 Oek.
2:11-16   DOWNING, F. G. Christ and the Cynics (Sheffield 1988) 188.
2:11   STÄHELIN, E. Die Verkündigung des Reiches Gottes in der Kirche Jesu
             Christi I (1951) 184. BETZ, H.D. Lukian von Samosata und das Neue
             Testament (1961) 86, 9, 96, 5. MONRO, W. "Col III. 18- IV.1 and Eph. V.21-
             VI.9: Evidences of a late Literary Stratum?" NTS 18 (1971-72) 435f.
             SHIMADA, K. The Formulary Material in First Peter: A Study According to
             the Method of Traditionsge-schichte (ThD. Diss; Ann Arbor MI 1966) 212-19,
             223-29. BASSLER, J. M. "Divine Impartiality in Paul's Letter to the Romans,"
             NovT 26 (1, 1984) 43-58. DOWNING, F. G. Christ and the Cynics (Sheffield
             1988) 159.
2:12-4:8   HEILIGENTHAL, R. Werke als Zeichen (Tübingen 1983) 279-311.
2:12-3:20   HEILIGENTHAL, R. Werke als Zeichen (Tübingen 1983) 281-88.
2:12ff.   JÜNGEL, E. Paulus und Jesus (1966) 26f. BRANDENBURGER, E. Adam und
             Christus (Neukirchen-Vluyn 1962) 184, 197, 203f., 251f., 266. THEISSEN, G.
             Psychological Aspects of Pauline Theology (Edinburgh 1987) 76, 76n.18,
             77n.21, 80, 82, 102f.
2:12-29   SCHMITHALS, W. Der Römerbrief als historisches Problem (Gütersloh 1975)
             14. MCDONALD, J. I. H. Kerygma and Didache (Cambridge 1980) 55f.
             BASSLER, J. M. Divine Impartiality (Chico CA 1982) 137-54. BASSLER, J.
             M. "Divine Impartiality in Paul's Letter to the Romans," NovT 26 (1, 1984) 43-

58. OLIVEIRA, A. DE, Die Diakonie der Gerechtigkeit und der Versöhnung in der Apologie des 2. Korintherbriefes. Analyse und Auslegung von 2 Kor 2, 14-4, 6; 5, 11-6, 10 (Münster 1990) 162-5.

2:12-27   LAFON, G. "La production de la loi. La pensée de la loi in *Romains* 2, 12-27," RechSR 74 (3, 1986) 321-40. LAFON, G. "Les poètes de la loi. Un commentaire de *Romains* 2, 12-27," Christus 134 (Paris 1987) 205-14.

2:12-13,   SANDERS, E. P. "On the Question of Fulfilling the Law in Paul and Rabbinic
17-27   Judaism" in E. Bammel et al., eds., New Testament Studies in Honour of D. Daube (Oxford 1978) 104.

2:12-16   WALKER, R. "Die Deiden und das Gericht" EvTh 20 (7, '60) 302-14. PAGELS, E. H. The Gnostic Paul. Gnostic Exegesis of the Pauline Letters (Philadelphia 1975) 19. HERR, T. Naturrecht aus der kritischen Sicht des Neuen Testament (München 1976) 155-64. KÖNIG, A. "Gentiles or Gentile Christians? On the Meaning of Romans 2:12-16," JTSA 15 (1976) 53-60. HASENSTAB, R. Modelle paulinischer Ethik (Mainz 1977) 143. RÄISÄNEN, H. Paul and the Law (Tübingen 1983) 19, 25f., 112, 145f. YATES, J. C. "The Judgment of the Heathen: The Interpretation of Article XVIII and Romans 2:12-16," ChM 100 (3, 1986) 220-30. DAVIES, G. N. Faith and Obedience in Romans. A Study in Romans 1-4 (Sheffield 1990) 57-67. LONGENECKER, B. W. Eschatology and the Covenant. A Comparison of 4 Ezra and Romans 1-11 (Sheffield 1991) 185, 190, 192.

2:12-15   SANDERS, E. P. Paul, the Law, and the Jewish People (London 1985) 123f., 130f.

2:12-13   SCHRAGE, W. Die konkreten Einzelgebote in der paulinischen Paränese (1961) 47, 85, 232. BOUSSET, W. Die Religion des Judentums im Späthellenistischen Zeitalter (1926) 198, 414. BAMMEL, C. P. H. "Philocalia IX, Jerome, Epistle 121, and Origen's Exposition of Romans VII," JThS 32 (1981) 55.

2:12   KÄSEMANN, E. Exegetische Versuche und Besinnungen (1964) II 75. VAN DÜLMEN, A. Die Theologie des Gesetzes bei Paulus (1968) 74f, 85, 86, 119, 125, 135, 160, 167, 170. KÄSEMANN, E. New Testament Questions of Today (1969) 73. EICHHOLZ, G. Die Theologie des Paulus im Umriss (1972) 95f. LADD, G. E. A Theology of the New Testament (Grand Rapids 1974) 406, 430, 565, 568. BERGER, K. Exegese des Neuen Testaments (Heidelberg 1977) 24. FRIEDRICH, G. "'Αμαρτία οὐκ ἐλλογεῖται Rom. 5, 13" in Auf das Wort kommt es an. Gesammelte Aufsätze (Göttingen 1978) 129. MOHRLANG, R. Matthew and Paul (Cambridge 1984) 35, 57, 152, 155. SCHREY, H. H. "Goldene Regel III" in TRE 13 (1984) 576. STAAB, K. Pauluskommentare aus der griechischen Kirche (Münster ²1984) 116:1-3 ThM.

2:13-16   PARKER, T. H. L. Commentaries on the Epistle to the Romans 1532-1542 (Edinburgh 1986) 125-41.

2:13-15   PIXLEY, J. V. "El evangelio paulino de la justificación por la fe. Conversación con José Porfirio Miranda," RevBi 41 (1979) 57-74.

2:13-14   LIEBERS, R. Das Gesetz als Evangelium (Zürich 1989) 82f.

2:13   KÄSEMANN, E. Exegetische Versuche und Besinnungen (1964) II 182. JÜNGEL, E. Paulus und Jesus (1966) 47f, 57. KERTELGE, K. "Rechtfertigung" bei Paulus (1967) 72, 115, 126, 128, 143f. VAN DÜLMEN, A. Die Theologie des Gesetzes bei Paulus (1968) 74, 75, 76f, 81, 83, 114, 132, 134, 135, 136, 141, 253. KÄSEMANN, E. New Testament Questions of Today (1969) 169. LADD, G. E. A Theology of the New Testament (Grand Rapids 1974) 366, 442, 447, 495, 500. SCHMITHALS, W. Der Römerbrief als historisches Problem (Gütersloh 1975) 204. SANDERS, E. P. "Jesus, Paul and

Judaism" in ANRW II.25.1 (1982) 438. STAAB, K. Paulus-kommentare aus der griechischen Kirche (Münster ²1984) 60:16-18 Apoll; 654:5-7 Areth. SANDERS, E. P. Paul, the Law, and the Jewish People (London 1985) 14n.18, 17, 125f., 129f., 134nn.29, 32. SCHNABEL, E. J. Law and Wisdom from Ben Sira to Paul (Tübingen 1985) 280, 286, 290. PARKER, T. H. L. Commentaries on the Epistle to the Romans 1532-1542 (Edinburgh 1986) 125f. MERKLEIN, H. Studien zu Jesus und Paulus (Tübingen 1987) 2, 3, 10, 14, 41, 48, 72, 94. DOWNING, F. G. Christ and the Cynics (Sheffield 1988) 188. HOFIUS, O. Paulusstudien (Tübingen 1989) 54, 127. GARLINGTON, D. B. "The Obedience of Faith in the Letter to the Romans. Part II: The Obedience of Faith and Judgment by Works," WThJ 53 (1, 1991) 47-72. BOERS, H. "We Who Are by Inheritance Jews; Not from the Gentiles, Sinners," JBL 111 (1992) 273-81.

2:14ff.   BONHOEFFER, A. Epiktet und das Neue Testament (1911) 148ff. SOUCEK, J.B. "Zur Exeges von Röm 2, 14ff" Antwort (Festschrift K. Barth 1956) 99-113. GÄRTNER, B. The Areopagus Speech and Natural Revelation (Uppsala 1955) 84f. THEISSEN, G. Psychologische Aspekte paulinischer Theologie (Göttingen 1983) 75f.

2:14-16,   RIEDL, J. Das Heil der Heiden nach Röm 2, 14-16.26.27 (Mödling/Wien 1965).
26-27
2:14-16   RIEDL, J. Das Heil der Heiden nach R 2, 14-16.26.27 (1965). FEINE, D.P. Das Gesetzesfreie Evangelium des Paulus (1899) 113-126. JUNCKER, A. Die Ethik des Apostels Paulus (1919) 223-26. FLÜCKIGER, F. "Die Werke des Gesetzes bei den Heiden (Röm. 2, 14ff)" ThZ 8 ('52) 17-42. LACKMANN, M. Vom Geheimnis der Schöpfung (1952). KUSS, O. "Die Heiden und die Werke des Gesetzes (nach Röm. 2, 14-16)" MThZ 5/2 ('54) 77-98. BORNKAMM, G. "Gesetz und Natur. Röm 2, 14-16" Studien za Antike und Urchristentum. Ges. Aufs. II (1959) 93-118. LILLIE, W. Studies in New Testament Ethics (1961) 13f. SEVENSTER, J. N. Paul and Seneca (1961) 94, 95, 96, 138, 110, 101. RIEDL, J. "Die Auslegung von Röm 2, 14-16 in Vergangenheit und Gegenwart," AnBib 17-18 (1, 1963) 271-81. Studiorum Paulinorum Congressus Internationalis Catholicus 1961 (Vol. I, 1963) 271-81. GREENWOOD, D. "Saint Paul and Natural Law," BThB 1 (3, 1971) 262-79. DUBARLE, A.-M. La manifestation naturelle de Dieu d'aprés l'Écriture (Paris 1976). BAMMEL, C. P. H. "Philocalia IX, Jerome, Epistle 121, and Origen's Exposition of Romans VII," JThS 32 (1981) 65, 68, 70. HEILIGENTHAL, R. Werke als Zeichen (Tübingen 1983) 282-84. RÄISÄNEN, H. Paul and the Law (Tübingen 1983) 11, 98, 105f., 187.

2:14-15   STACEY, W.D. The Pauline View of Man (1956) 36, 195, 209, 209f. SCHRAGE, W. Die konkreten Einzelgebote in der paulinischen Paränese (1961) 100, 117, 190, 191f, 193f, 212, 231, 232. LYONNET, S. "Lex naturalis et iustificatio Gentilium" Verb-Dom 41 (5, '63) 238-42. KUHR, F. "Römer 2:14f und die Verheissung bei Jeremia 31:31ff" ZNW 55 (3-4v'64) 243-61. JÜNGEL, E. Paulus und Jesus (1966) 27f. ROBINSON, J. A. Pelagius's Exposition of Thirteen Epistles of St. Paul I (Cambridge 1922) 140f. HENGEL, M. Judentum und Hellenismus (Tübingen 1969)315; ET: Judaism and Hellenism II (London 1974) 114. KLIJN, A. F. J. "Die syrische Baruch-Apokalypse" in JSHRZ V/2 (1976) 154n.4oa. HASENSTAB, R. Modelle paulinischer Ethik (Mainz 1977) 141. TRITES, A. A. The New Testament Concept of Witness (Cambridge 1977) 200f. FRIEDRICH, G. "Das Gesetz des Glaubens Römer 3, 27" in Auf das Wort kommt es an. Gesammelte Aufsätze (Göttingen 1978) 111. WINGREN, G. "Billigkeit" in TRE 6 (1980) 643. DEIDUN, T. J. New Covenant Morality in Paul (Rome 1981) 162-68. FRITZSCHE, H.-G. "Dekalog" in TRE 8 (1981) 418. HÜBNER, H. "Dekalog" in TRE 8 (1981) 417. GRÜNDEL, J. "Ethik" in TRE 10 (1982) 477. RÄISÄNEN, H. Paul and the Law (Tübingen 1983) 7, 28, 64, 101-04, 110, 118, 124. THEISSEN, G. Psycho-logical Aspects of Pauline Theology (Edinburgh 1987) 76n.19, 77, 150, 244, 259. KRÜGER, F. "Gewissen III" in TRE 13 (1984) 219. HEYMEL, M. "Lehre als Erfahrung. Was der Jude Paulus uns Heiden über das Gesetz zu lernen aufgibt" in G. Freund und E. Stegemann, eds., Theologische Brosamen für Lothar Steiger (DBAT 5; Heidelberg 1985) 183. RÄISÄNEN, H. The Torah and Christ (Helsinki 1986) 15, 293. JONES, F. S. "Freiheit" in den Briefen des Apostels Paulus (Göttingen 1987) 93f., 208 A 161. LIMBECK, M. Mit Paulus Christ sein. Sachbuch zur Person und Theologie des Apostels Paulus (Stuttgart 1989) 73. VOLLENWEIDER, S. Freiheit als neue Schöpfung (Göttingen 1989) 266, 401. OLIVEIRA, A. DE, Die Diakonie der Gerechtigkeit und der Versöhnung in der Apologie des 2. Korintherbriefes. Analyse und Auslegung von 2 Kor 2, 14-4, 6; 5, 11-6, 10 (Münster 1990) 164f. LONGENECKER, B. W. Eschatology and the Covenant. A Comparison of 4 Ezra and Romans 1-11 (Sheffield 1991) 186, 186n.1, 187, 187n.2, 188, 190, 192-5.

2:14   BRUNNER, E. Mensch im Widerspruch (1937) 149. BEYSCHLAG, K. Clemens Romanus und der Frühkatholizismus (1966) 87. MERK, O. Handeln aus Glauben (1968) 135, 244. LADD, G. E. A Theology of the New Testament (Grand Rapids 1974) 361, 476, 513. KÜMMEL, W. G. Römer 7 und das Bild des Menschen im Neuen Testament (München 1974) 28, 55, 184. MEHL, R. "Freiheit" in TRE 11 (1983) 520. THEISSEN, G. Psychologische Aspekte paulinischer Theologie (Göttingen 1983) 76n.20, 78n.23, 79, 80. ACHTEMEIER, P. J. "Some Things in them Hard to Understand: Reflections on an Approach to Paul," Interp 38 (1984) 254-67, esp. 255-59. STAAB, K. Pauluskommentare aus der griechischen Kirche (Münster ²1984) 60:19-21 Apoll. SANDERS, E. P. Paul, the Law, and the Jewish People (London 1985) 51n.17, 124-27, 130, 135n.45. VALGIGLIO, E. "ΠΟΙΗΤΗΣ (ΠΟΙΕΙΝ) nella Bibbia," Orpheus [Naples] 6 (2, 1985) 396-403. SCHNACKENBURG, R. Die sittliche Botschaft des Neuen Testaments I (Freiburg/Basel/ Wien 1986) 18f. PARKER, T. H. L. Commentaries on the Epistle to the Romans 1532-1542 (Edinburgh 1986) 126. BERGER, K. und COLPE, C., eds., Religions-geschichtliches Textbuch zum Neuen Testament (Göttingen/Zürich 1987) 198. MARTIN, B. L. Christ and the Law in Paul (Leiden 1989) 14, 22, 25, 39, 42, 44, 86, 90, 100, 146, 147.

2:15-16   THEISSEN, G. Psychologische Aspekte paulinischer Theologie (Göttingen 1983) 66, 80n.29, 81n.31, 116. STAAB, K. Pauluskommentare aus der griechischen Kirche (Münster ²1984) 480:20-482:12 Phot.

2:15   REICKE, B. "Syneidesis in Rom. 2, 15" ThZ XII/2 ('56) 157-61. KUSS, O. "Naturgesetz" und "Naturrecht" Der Römerbrief (1957) 72-76. JÜNGEL, E. Paulus und Jesus (1966) 28. VAN DÜLMEN, A. Die Theologie des Gesetzes bei Paulus (1968) 23, 50, 73, 77f, 81, 132, 135, 136, 141, 167. BEUTLER, J. Martyria (Frankfurt 1972) 174f., 199. KÜMMEL, W. G. Römer 7 und das Bild des Menschen im Neuen Testament (München 1974) 29, 183f., 189, 192. LADD, G. E. A Theology of the New Testament (Grand Rapids 1974) 361, 469, 477f., 487. BISER, E. Der Zeuge (Graz/Wien/Köln 1981) 99, 110, 122, 230. THEISSEN, G. Psychologische Aspekte paulinischer Theologie (Göttingen 1983) 75, 78n.23, 79, 80, 81, 204n.39, 263, 369n.39. KRÜGER, F. "Gewissen III" in TRE 13 (1984) 221. STAAB, K. Pauluskommentare aus der griechischen Kirche (Münster ²1984) 654:8-9 Areth. WOLTER, M. "Gewissen II" in TRE

13 (1984) 216f. SCHNABEL, E. J. Law and Wisdom from Ben Sira to Paul (Tübingen 1985) 333-35. PARKER, T. H. L. Commentaries on the Epistle to the Romans 1532-1542 (Edinburgh 1986) 127. BERGER, K. und COLPE, C., eds., Religionsgeschichtliches Textbuch zum Neuen Testament (Göttingen/ Zürich 1987) 198f. LAYTON, B. The Gnostic Scriptures (Garden City NY 1987) 243. LIEBERS, R. Das Gesetz als Evangelium (Zürich 1989) 41-44. MARTIN, B. L. Christ and the Law in Paul (Leiden 1989) 14, 39, 42, 44, 74, 81, 86, 90-92, 98, 100, 103, 144.

2:16   SCHRAGE, W. Die konkreten Einzelgebote in der paulinischen Paränese (1961) 21, 133. THUESING, W. Per Christum in Deum (1965) 201f. SEEBERG, A. Der Katechismus der Urchristenheit (1966) 7, 82, 152, 157, 199, 201. SHIRES, H. M. The Eschatology of Paul (1966) 115f. MERK, O. Handeln aus Glauben (1968) 6, 14, 150, 175, 238. GUETTGEMANNS, E. Offene Fragen zur Formgeschichte des Evangeliums (1970) 203, 209. DRIESSEN, E. "'Secundum Evangelium meum' (Rom 2, 16; 16, 25; 2 Tim 2, 8)," VD 24 (1944) 25-32. SIBER, P. Mit Christus leben (Zürich 1971) 27. SAAKE, H. "Echtheitskritische Überlegungen zur Interpola-tionshypothese von Römer ii.16," NTS 19 (4, 1973) 486-89. LADD, G. E. A Theology of the New Testament (Grand Rapids 1974) 417, 565, 566. SCHMITHALS, W. Der Römerbrief als historisches Problem (Gütersloh 1975) 204. SCHÜTZ, J. H. Paul and the Anatomy of Apostolic Authority (Cambridge 1975) 71f., 74, 75ff. HAACKER, K. "Exegetische Probleme des Römerbriefes," NovT 20 (1978) 1-21. ROLOFF, J. "Apostel" in TRE 3 (1978) 438. SCHMITHALS, W. "Zur Herkunft der gnostischen Elemente in der Sprache des Paulus" in B. Aland et al., eds., Gnosis. (FS. H. Jonas; Göttingen 1978) 390-93. FROITZHEIM, F. Christologie und Eschatologie bei Paulus (Würzburg 1979) 9f. OLLROG, W.-H. Paulus und seine Mitarbeiter (Neukirchen-Vluyn 1979) 70, 102. SCHADE, H.-H. Apokalyptische Christologie bei Paulus (Göttingen 1981) 40. THEISSEN, G. Psychologische Aspekte paulinischer Theologie (Göttingen 1983) 74-82, 92, 108. MOHRLANG, R. Matthew and Paul (Cambridge 1984) 57, 119, 162. STAAB, K. Pauluskommentare aus der griechischen Kirche (Münster [2]1984) 60:22-25 Apoll; 116:4-8 ThM. PARKER, T. H. L. Commentaries on the Epistle to the Romans 1532-1542 (Edinburgh 1986) 127f. THEISSEN, G. Psychological Aspects of Pauline Theology (Edinburgh 1987) 59, 66-73, 85, 103. TOWNER, Ph. H. The Goal of Our Instruction. The Structure of Theology and Ethics in the Pastoral Epistles (Sheffield 1989) 275n.7, 287n.145, 288n.153. SIMONIS, W. Der gefangene Paulus. Die Entstehung des sogenannten Römerbriefs und anderer urchristlicher Schriften in Rom (Frankfurt/Bern/New York/Paris 1990) 45.

2:17-3:20   THISELTON, A. C. The Two Horizons (Grand Rapids 1980) 318. ELLIOT, N. The Rhetoric of Romans (Sheffield 1990) 148, 154, 155n., 191-8, 227, 283, 297.

2:17-3:8   HEILIGENTHAL, R. Werke als Zeichen (Tübingen 1983) 284-88.

2:17-3:4   JOHNSON, S. L., JR. "Studies in Romans. Part VI: Rite Versus Righteousness; Part VII: The Jews and the Oracles of God," BiblSa 130 (518, 1973) 151-63, (519, 1973) 235-49.

2:17ff.   BOUSSET, W. Die Religion des Judentums im Späthellenistischen Zeitalter (1926) 75, 119, 198. ECKERT, J. Die Urchristliche Verkündigung im Streit zwischen Paulus und seinen Gegnern nach dem Galater-brief (Regensburg 1971) 25, 35, 41, 108. HENGEL, M. Judentum und Hellenismus (Tübingen 1969) 317ff.; ET: Judaism and Hellenism II (London 1974) 115. THEISSEN, G. Psychologische Aspekte paulinischer Theologie (Göttingen 1983) 75, 77, 78, 82,

241, 241n.93. OLIVEIRA, A. DE, Die Diakonie der Gerechtigkeit und der Versöhnung in der Apologie des 2. Korintherbriefes. Analyse und Auslegung von 2 Kor 2, 14-4, 6; 5, 11-6, 10 (Münster 1990) 144f.

2:17-29   RICHARDSON, P. Israel in the Apostolic Church (1969) 94, 115, 138-39, 198. EICHHOLZ, G. Die Theologie des Paulus im Umriss (1972) 96f, 84f. ROBINSON, J. A. T. Wrestling with Romans (London 1979) 29-31. GORDAY, P. Principles of Patristic Exegesis: Romans 9-11 in Origen, John Chrysostom, and Augustine (New York/Toronto 1983) 56-58, 113, 155f., 229. RÄISÄNEN, H. The Torah and Christ (Helsinki 1986) 186f. GASTON, L. Paul and the Torah (Vancouver 1987) 14, 122, 138f., 226. ELLIOT, N. The Rhetoric of Romans (Sheffield 1990) 37, 127-35, 139, 145n., 149n., 152, 162, 171, 187, 191, 194, 196, 285. KRENTZ, E. "The Name of God in Disrepute. Romans 2:17-29 [22-23]," CThMi 17 (6, 1990) 429-39. GASTON, L. "Israel's Misstep in the Eyes of Paul" in K. P. Donfried, ed., The Romans Debate. Revised and Expanded Edition (Peabody MA 1991) 312.

2:17-24   VAN DÜLMEN, A. Die Theologie des Gesetzes bei Paulus (1968) 72, 74, 79, 101, 102, 131, 179, 216. OLIVIERI, O. "Sintassi, seno e rapporto col contesto di Rom 2, 17-24," Biblica 11 (1930) 188-215. ZELLER, D. Juden und Heiden in der Mission des Paulus. Studien zum Römerbrief (Stuttgart 1973) 155ff. STOWERS, S. K. The Diatribe and Paul's Letter to the Romans (Chico CA 1981) 80, 96-98, 112f. SANDERS, E. P. Paul, the Law, and the Jewish People (London 1985) 124f., 128. KOCH, D.-A. Die Schrift als Zeuge des Evangeliums (Tübingen 1986) 260f. RÄISÄNEN, H. The Torah and Christ (Helsinki 1986) 14, 18. BERGER, K. und COLPE, C., eds., Religionsgeschichtliches Textbuch zum Neuen Testament (Göttingen/Zürich 1987) 199f. LONGENECKER, B. W. Eschatology and the Covenant. A Comparison of 4 Ezra and Romans 1-11 (Sheffield 1991) 190, 192, 259.

2:17-23   THEISSEN, G. Psychological Aspects of Pauline Theology (Edinburgh 1987) 240f.

2:17-20   HAHN, F. Das Verständnis der Mission im Neuen Testament (1965) 16. SCHNABEL, E. J. Law and Wisdom from Ben Sira to Paul (Tübingen 1985) 232-35. LIEBERS, R. Das Gesetz als Evangelium (Zürich 1989) 220-26. DUNN, J. D. G. Jesus, Paul and the Law (London 1990) 4, 68, 221, 238.

2:17-18   BERGER, K. und COLPE, C., eds., Religionsgeschicht-liches Textbuch zum Neuen Testament (Göttingen/ Zürich 1987) 199.

2:17.23   LIEBERS, R. Das Gesetz als Evangelium (Zürich 1989) 64-69.

2:17   BEST, E. One Body in Christ (1955) 22. SCHMITHALS, W. Der Römerbrief als historisches Problem (Gütersloh 1975) 24. STAAB, K. Paulus-kommentare aus der griechischen Kirche (Münster ²1984) 116:9-11 ThM. SANDERS, E. P. Paul, the Law, and the Jewish People (London 1985) 32f., 130, 134 n.31, 156, 183. LAMPE, P. Die stadtrömischen Christen in den ersten beiden Jahrhunderten (Tübingen ²1989) 54.

2:18-21   STAAB, K. Pauluskommentare aus der griechischen Kirche (Münster ²1984) 482:13-25 Phot.

2:18   SCHRAGE, W. Die konkreten Einzelgebote in der paulinischen Paränese (1961) 113, 167f, 171f, 198. DUNN, J. D. G. Jesus and the Spirit (London 1975) 223. OLLROG, W.-H. Paulus und seine Mitarbeiter (Neukirchen-Vluyn 1979) 21, 85. SCHNABEL, E. J. Law and Wisdom from Ben Sira to Paul (Tübingen 1985) 233, 326, 330f. FURNISH, V. P. "Der 'Wille Gottes' in paulinischer Sicht" in D.-A. Koch et al., eds., Jesu Rede von Gott und ihre Nachgeschichte im frühen Christentum (FS. Willi Marxsen; Gütersloh 1989) 208-21, esp. 214f.

	BEERNAERT, P. M. "Le verbe grec *katechein* dans le N.T.," LuVit 44 (1989) 377-87.
2:19-20	MALMEDE, H. H. Die Lichtsymbolik im Neuen Testament (Wiesbaden 1986) 122f.
2:19	BORNKAMM—BARTH—HELD, Ueberlieferung und Auslegung im Matthäus-Evangelium (1961) 82. STRECKER, G. Der Weg der Gerechtigkeit (1962) 139.
2:20-24	SCHRAGE, W. Die konkreten Einzelgebote in der paulinischen Paränese (1961) 94, 131, 133, 167, 231.
2:20	STAAB, K. Pauluskommentare aus der griechischen Kirche (Münster ²1984) 116:12-14 ThM. ZIMMERMANN, A. F. Die urchristlichen Lehrer (Tübingen 1984) 85, 91, 108, 110, 204.
2:21-24	RÄISÄNEN, H. Paul and the Law (Tübingen 1983) 98-101.
2:21-23	EICHHOLZ, G. Die Theologie des Paulus im Umriss (1972) 97f. MALHERBE, A. J. Moral Exhortation. A Greco-Roman Sourcebook (Philadelphia 1986) 38, 130.
2:21-22	GOPPELT, L. "Der Missionar des Gesetzes" Basileia, Walter Freytag zum 60. Geburtstag (1961) 199-207. REINMUTH, E. Geist und Gesetz (Berlin/DDR 1985) 17. NIEBUHR, K.-W. Gesetz und Paränese (Tübingen 1987) 63.
2:22-26	STAAB, K. Pauluskommentare aus der griechischen Kirche (Münster ²1984) 482:26-483:32 Phot.
2:22	NICKELS, P. Targum and New Testament (1967) 68. GARLINGTON, D. B. "'ΙΕΡΟΣΥΛΕΙΝ and the Idolatry of Israel (Romans 2.22)," NTS 36 (1, 1990) 142-51.
2:23-24	MOXNES, H. Theology in Conflict (Leiden 1980) 60f., 64, 70f., 74. BERGER, K. "Das Buch der Jubiläen" in JSHRZ II/3 (1981) 427n.6c. BERGER, K. und COLPE, C., eds., Religionsgeschichtliches Textbuch zum Neuen Testament (Göttingen/Zürich 1987) 200.
2:23	JÜNGEL, E. Paulus und Jesus (1966) 29. VAN DÜLMEN, A. Die Theologie des Gesetzes bei Paulus (1968) 80, 132, 166, 167, 179, 216. LADD, G. E. A Theology of the New Testament (Grand Rapids 1974) 366, 405, 500, 504. SANDERS, E. P. Paul, the Law, and the Jewish People (London 1985) 32f., 130. DUNN, J. D. G. Jesus, Paul and the Law (London 1990) 4, 68, 221, 222, 238.
2:24	BAUMERT, N. Täglich Sterben und Auferstehen (München 1973) 102. VIELHAUER, P. "Paulus und das Alte Testament" in Oikodome [G. Klein, ed.] (München 1979) 204. KOCH, D.-A. Die Schrift als Zeuge des Evangeliums (Tübingen 1986) 105, 143, 260f.
2:25-3:20	ELLIOT, N. The Rhetoric of Romans (Sheffield 1990) 198-204.
2:25-29	ECKERT, J. Die Urchristliche Verkündigung im Streit zwischen Paulus und seinen Gegnern nach dem Galater-brief (Regensburg 1971) 64, 70, 77, 108, 135. ZELLER, D. Juden und Heiden in der Mission des Paulus. Studien zum Römerbrief (Stuttgart 1973) 117. HÜBNER, H. Das Gesetz bei Paulus (Göttingen 1978) 93f. OLLROG, W.-H. Paulus und seine Mitarbeiter (Neukirchen-Vluyn 1979) 21, 134. BAMMEL, C. P. H. "Philocalia IX, Jerome, Epistle 121, and Origen's Exposition of Romans VII," JThS 32 (1981) 73. THEISSEN, G. Psychologische Aspekte paulinischer Theologie (Göttingen 1983) 74, 75, 76n.19. SANDERS, E. P. Paul, the Law, and the Jewish People (London 1985) 117n.24, 130f. EHLER, B. Die Herrschaft des Gekreuzigten (Berlin/ New York 1986) 80-86. RÄISÄNEN, H. The Torah and Christ (Helsinki 1986) 288ff. BERGER, K. Einführung in die Formgeschichte (Tübingen 1987) 123-5. DAVIES, G. N. Faith and Obedience in Romans. A Study in Romans 1-4 (Sheffield 1990) 67-

70. LONGENECKER, B. W. Eschatology and the Covenant. A Comparison of 4 Ezra and Romans 1-11 (Sheffield 1991) 192, 201, 201n.3, 246.

2:25-27   LIEBERS, R. Das Gesetz als Evangelium (Zürich 1989) 83-85.

2:25-26   DELLING, G. Die Taufe im Neuen Testament (1963) 124. ZIESLER, J. Pauline Christianity (Oxford 1990) 106-07.

2:25   JÜNGEL, E. Paulus und Jesus (1966) 57. VAN DÜLMEN, A. Die Theologie des Gesetzes bei Paulus (1968) 74, 81, 82, 134, 222. BAUMERT, N. Täglich Sterben und Auferstehen (München 1973) 361. JEWETT, P. K. Infant Baptism and the Covenant of Grace (Grand Rapids 1978) 87, 234. BETZ, O. "Beschneidung" in TRE 5 (1980) 719.

2:26-29   FEINE, D.P. Das gesetzesfreie Evangelium des Paulus (1899) 126f., 190f. PAGELS, E. H. The Gnostic Paul. Gnostic Exegesis of the Pauline Letters (Philadelphia 1975) 19f. MIRANDA, J. P. Marx and the Bible (London 1977) 176-80. SANDERS, E. P. Paul, the Law, and the Jewish People (London 1985) 126f. CLARK, K. W. "The Israel of God" in The Gentile Bias and other Essays [selected by J. L. Sharpe III] (Leiden 1980) 22, 29.

2:26-27   RIEDL, J. Das Heil der Heiden nach Röm 2:14-16.26.27 (Mödling bei Wien 1965) passim, 209-11. RÄISÄNEN, H. Paul and the Law (Tübingen 1983) 101-09, 110, 112, 118. RÄISÄNEN, H. The Torah and Christ (Helsinki 1986) 15. DUNN, J. D. G. Jesus, Paul and the Law (London 1990) 215, 224, 228. LONGENECKER, B. W. Eschatology and the Covenant. A Comparison of 4 Ezra and Romans 1-11 (Sheffield 1991) 193-5, 246.

2:26   JÜNGEL, E. Paulus und Jesus (1966) 57. VAN DÜLMEN, A. Die Theologie des Gesetzes bei Paulus (1968) 74, 81, 82, 133, 136, 252. KÜMMEL, W. G. Römer 7 und das Bild des Menschen im Neuen Testament (München 1974) 17, 28, 194. SCHMITHALS, W. Der Römerbrief als historisches Problem (Gütersloh 1975) 74. SANDERS, E. P. Paul, the Law, and the Jewish People (London 1985) 123f., 130. MARTIN, B. L. Christ and the Law in Paul (Leiden 1989) 15, 21, 42, 44, 90, 92f., 146f.

2:27ff.   LUZ, U. Das Geschichtsverständnis des Paulus (1968) 125f.

2:27-29   ELLIS, E.E. Paul's Use of the Old Testament (1957) 12, 26, 72, 137. KÄSEMANN, E. "Geist und Buchstabe" Paulinische Perspektiven (1969) 237-85. PROVENCE, T. E. "'Who is Sufficient for These Things?' An Exegesis of 2 Corinthians ii 15–iii 18," NovT 24 (1982) 66.

2:27-28   SCHRAGE, W. Die konkreten Einzelgebote in der paulinischen Paränese (1961) 212, 231.

2:27   VAN DÜLMEN, A. Die Theologie des Gesetzes bei Paulus (1968) 33, 81, 82, 102, 106, 134, 136, 167, 222, 252. BAUMERT, N. Täglich Sterben und Auferstehen (München 1973) 230f., 379. TRITES, A. A. The New Testament Concept of Witness (Cambridge 1977) 201. STAAB, K. Pauluskommentare aus der griechischen Kirche (Münster [2]1984) 483:33-484:5 Phot; 654:10-13 Areth.

2:28-29   HAHN, F. Das Verständnis der Mission im Neuen Testament (1965) 91. DUNN, J.D.G. Baptism in the Holy Spirit (1970) 129f., 146f., 151, 156, 212. SCHWEIZER, E. "'Der Jude im Verborgenen . . . , dessen Lob nicht von Menschen, sondern von Gott kommt'" in J. Gnilka, ed., Neues Testament und Kirche (FS. R. Schnackenburg; Freiburg/Basel/Wien 1974) 115-24. RIDDERBOS, H. Paul. An Outline of His Theology (Grand Rapids 1975) 334-36. RUDOLPH, K. Die Gnosis (Göttingen 1978) 266. THEISSEN, G. Psychologische Aspekte paulinischer Theologie (Göttingen 1983) 76 n.19, 77, 77n.21, 78n.23. MOHRLANG, R. Matthew and Paul (Cambridge 1984) 188f. BERGER, K. und COLPE, C., eds., Religionsgeschichtliches Textbuch zum Neuen Testament (Göttingen/Zürich 1987) 200f. HILHORST, A. "Biblical Metaphors Taken Literally" in T. Baarda et al., eds., Text and Testimony (FS. A. F. J. Klijn; Kampen 1988) 131. HAYS, R. B. Echoes of Scripture in the Letters of Paul (New Haven/London 1989) 44f. VOLLENWEIDER, S. Freiheit als neue Schöpfung (Göttingen 1989) 240n., 265, 267, 401. OLIVEIRA, A. DE, Die Diakonie der Gerechtigkeit und der Versöhnung in der Apologie des 2. Korintherbriefes. Analyse und Auslegung von 2 Kor 2, 14-4, 6; 5, 11-6, 10 (Münster 1990) 162-5. LONGENECKER, B. W. Eschatology and the Covenant. A Comparison of 4 Ezra and Romans 1-11 (Sheffield 1991) 185, 193-5, 240.

2:28   VAN DÜLMEN, A. Die Theologie des Gesetzes bei Paulus (1968) 74, 144, 217, 221, 222. THISELTON, A. C. The Two Horizons (Grand Rapids 1980) 277, 401, 409.

2:29   ROBINSON, J.A.T. The Body (1952) 18f. MORREALE DE CASTRO, "La antitesis paulina entre la letra y el espiritu en la traduccion y comentario de Juan de Valdes (Rom 2, 29 y 7, 6)" EstBi XIII/2 ('54) 167-83. BEST, E. One Body in Christ (1955) 11. DELLING, Die Taufe im Neuen Testament (1963) 123. VAN DÜLMEN, A. Die Theologie des Gesetzes bei Paulus (1968) 33, 74, 134, 224. SUMMERS, R. The Secret Sayings of the Living Jesus (1968) 68. KÄSEMANN, E. New Testament Questions of Today (1969) 270. SCHNEIDER, N. Die rhetorische Eigenart der paulinischen Antithese (1970) 79-89. WILLIAMS, J. A. A Conceptual History of Deuteronomism in the Old Testament, Judaism, and the New Testament (Ph.D. Diss Southern Baptist Theological Seminary; Louisville, KY 1976) 281. FRIEDRICH, G. "Das Gesetz des Glaubens Römer 3, 27" in Auf das Wort kommt es an. Gesammelte Aufsätze (Göttingen 1978) 119. JEWETT, P. K. Infant Baptism and the Covenant of Grace (Grand Rapids 1978) 88. SCHMITHALS, W. "Zur Herkunft der gnostischen Elemente in der Sprache des Paulus" in B. Aland et al., eds., Gnosis. (FS. H. Jonas; Göttingen 1978) 388-90. THISELTON, A. C. The Two Horizons (Grand Rapids 1980) 401. DEIDUN, T. J. New Covenant Morality in Paul (Rome 1981) 203-7. DAVIES, S. L. The Gospel of Thomas and Christian Wisdom (New York 1983) 133. THEISSEN, G. Psychologische Aspekte paulinischer Theologie (Göttingen 1983) 75, 76, 212. MOHRLANG, R. Matthew and Paul (Cambridge 1984) 30, 119ff., 190. STAAB, K. Pauluskommentare aus der griechischen Kirche (Münster ²1984) 116:15-27 ThM; 423:6 Oek. SANDERS, E. P. Paul, the Law, and the Jewish People (London 1985) 101f., 126f., 133n.29. LAYTON, B. The Gnostic Scriptures (Garden City NY 1987) 312. OSTEN-SACKEN, P. VON DER Die Heiligkeit der Tora (München 1989) 48f. VOLLENWEIDER, S. Freiheit als neue Schöpfung (Göttingen 1989) 401.

3-11   STOWERS, S. K. The Diatribe and Paul's Letter to the Romans (Chico CA 1981) 119-54.

3-8   DIEZINGER, W. "Unter Toten freigeworden. Eine Untersuchung zu Röm. iii-viii" NovTest 5 (4, '62) 268-98. WINDISCH, H. The Meaning of the Sermon on the Mount (Philadelphia 1937) 107, 122, 173. MYERS, C. D. "Chiastic Inversion in the Argument of Romans 3-8," NovT 35 (1993) 30-47.

3-4   SANDERS, J. T. Ethics in the New Testament (Philadelphia 1975) 116-28. McDONALD, J. I. H. Kerygma and Didache (Cambridge 1980) 56. WILLIAMS, SAM K. "The 'Righteousness of God' in Romans," JBL 99 (1980) 265-80. SANDERS, E. P. Paul, the Law, and the Jewish People (London 1985) 28-35, 37f., 42f., 46, 97, 131, 159f. WATSON, F. Paul, Judaism and the Gentiles (Cambridge 1986) 123-35.

3   HAYS, R. B. "Psalm 143 and the Logic of Romans 3," JBL 99 (1980) 107-15. CAMPBELL, W. S. "Romans iii as a Key to the Structure and Thought of the Letter," NovT 23 (1981) 22-40. HÜBNER, H. "Der 'Messias Israels' und der Christus des Neuen Testaments," KuD 27 (1981) 234-36. BASSLER, J. M. Divine Impartiality (Chico CA 1982) 156-58. HAYS, R. B. The Faith of Jesus Christ (Chico CA 1983) 81, 172-74, 191. SANDERS, E. P. Paul, the Law, and the Jewish People (London 1985) 78, 129, 134f.n.44. SEGUNDO, J. L. The Humanist Christology of Paul [trans. J. Drury], Jesus of Nazareth Yesterday and Today 3 (Maryknoll, N.Y. 1986) 42-58. CAMPBELL, W. S. "Romans III as a Key to the Structure and Thought of the Letter" in K. P. Donfried, ed., The Romans Debate. Revised and Expanded Edition (Peabody MA 1991) 251-64. CAMPBELL, W. S. Paul's Gospel in an Intercultural Context. Jew and Gentile in the Letter to the Romans (Frankfurt/ Berlin/Bern etc. 1992) 25-42.

3:1ff.   HAHN, F. Das Verständnis der Mission im Neuen Testamant (1965) 86, 90. THYEN, H. Studien zur Sündenvergebung (1970) 165f. THEISSEN, G. Psychologische Aspekte paulinischer Theologie (Göttingen 1983) 74, 75, 196, 198.

3:1-31   HAYS, R. B. Echoes of Scripture in the Letters of Paul (New Haven/London 1989) 52f.

3:1-26   VAN DER MINDE, H.-J. Schrift und Tradition bei Paulus (München/Paderborn/Wien 1976) 48-67. HÜBNER, H. Das Gesetz bei Paulus (Göttingen 1978) 94f.

3:1-22   MUELLER, C. Gottes Gerechtigkeit und Gottes Volk (1964) 65ff., 108ff.

3:1-20   STALDER, K. Das Werk des Geistes in der Heiligung bei Paulus (1962) 264-67. BAUMERT, N. Täglich Sterben und Auferstehen (München 1973) 302-10. VAN DER MINDE, H.-J. Schrift und Tradition bei Paulus (München/Paderborn/Wien 1976) 48-52. SYNOFZIK, E. Die Gerichts- und Vergeltungsaussagen bei Paulus (Göttingen 1977) 83-85. ROBINSON, J. A. T. Wrestling with Romans (London 1979) 32-37. GORDAY, P. Principles of Patristic Exegesis: Romans 9-11 in Origen, John Chrysostom, and Augustine (New York/Toronto 1983) 58-60, 113f., 156f. WATSON, F. Paul, Judaism and the Gentiles (Cambridge 1986) 124-31. GASTON, L. Paul and the Torah (Vancouver 1987) 122f. HAYS, R. B. Echoes of Scripture in the Letters of Paul (New Haven/London 1989) 47-51.

3:1-9   BORNKAMM, G. Geschichte und Glaube (2.Teil) (1971) 140-48. LUZ, U. Das Geschichtsverständnis des Paulus (1968) 20. DREJERGAARD, K. "Jødernes fortrin. En undersøgelse af Rom 3, 1-9" [The Privilege of the Jews according to Rom 3:1-9], DTT 36 (1973) 81-101. ZELLER, D. Juden und Heiden in der Mission des Paulus. Studien zum Römerbrief (Stuttgart 1973) 187. STOWERS, S. K. "Paul's Dialogue with a Fellow Jew in Romans 3:1-9," CBQ 46 (1984) 707-22. LÜBKING, H.-M. Paulus und Israel im Römerbrief (Frankfurt/Bern/ New York 1986) 30-34. ELLIOT, N. The Rhetoric of Romans (Sheffield 1990) 132-41, 147, 156n., 158n., 197n.

3:1-8   KERTELGE, K. "Rechtfertigung" bei Paulus (1967) 126. OLIVIERI, O. "Quid ergo amplius Iudaeo est? etc.," Biblica 10 (1929) 31-52. JOHNSON, S. L. JR. "Studies in Romans, Part VIII: Divine Faithfulness, Divine Judgment, and the Problem of Antinomianism," BiblSa 130 (1973) 329-37. SCHMITHALS, W. Der Römerbrief als historisches Problem (Gütersloh 1975) 14. MOXNES, H. Theology in Conflict (Leiden 1980) 27, 30, 34, 37-39, 45, 57, 63, 80, 219. PIPER, J. "The Righteousness of God in Romans 3, 1-8," ThZ 36 (1980) 3-16. THEOBALD, M. Die überströmende Gnade (Würzburg 1982) 133-39. HALL, D. R. "Romans 3.1-8 Reconsidered," NTS 29 (1983) 183-97. ACHTEMEIER,

P. J. "Some Things in them Hard to Understand: Reflections on an Approach to Paul," Interp 38 (1984) 254-67, esp.259-63. SCHMITT, R. Gottesgerechtigkeit—Heilsgeschichte—Israel in der Theologie des Paulus (Frankfurt/Bern/New York/Nancy 1984) 19-23. RÄISÄNEN, H. "Zum Verständnis von Röm 3, 1-8," SNTU 10 (1985) 93-108. MALHERBE, A. J. Moral Exhortation. A Greco-Roman Sourcebook (Philadelphia 1986) 130. RÄISÄNEN, H. "Zum Verständnis von Röm 3, 1-8" in The Torah and Christ (Helsinki 1986) 185-203. COSGROVE, C. H. "What If Some Have Not Believed? The Occasion and Thrust of Romans 3:1-8," ZNW 78 (1987) 90-105. DUNN, J. D. G. "Paul's Epistle to the Romans: An Analysis of Structure and Argument" in ANRW II.25.4 (1987) 2851f. SCHMELLER, TH. Paulus und die "Diatribe" (Münster 1987) 287. PENNA, R. "La funzione strutturale di 3, 1-8 nella lettera ai Romani," Biblica 69 (1988) 507-42. WEDDERBURN, A. J. M. The Reasons for Romans (Edinburgh 1988) 112-17, 151f. HAYS, R. B. Echoes of Scripture in the Letters of Paul (New Haven/London 1989) 52f. LOHFINK, G. Studien zum Neuen Testament (Stuttgart 1989) 14. SCHNELLE, U. Wandlungen im paulinischen Denken (Stuttgart 1989) 81. ACHTEMEIER, P. J. "Romans 3:1-8: Structure and Argument," AThR suppl. 11 (1990) 77-87. DAVIES, G. N. Faith and Obedience in Romans. A Study in Romans 1-4 (Sheffield 1990) 73-80, 100. ELLIOT, N. The Rhetoric of Romans (Sheffield 1990) 134-6, 178, 196, 198, 200-2, 220, 278. LONGENECKER, B. W. Eschatology and the Covenant. A Comparison of 4 Ezra and Romans 1-11 (Sheffield 1991) 168, 195f., 251, 275.

3:1-7   WILLIAMS, SAM K. "The 'Righteousness of God' in Romans," JBL 99 (1980) 265, 268-70, 280, 289.

3:1-4   GOPPELT, L. Christologie und Ethik (1968) 184f. WEDER, H. Neutestamentliche Hermeneutik (Zürich 1986) 252f. SCHMELLER, TH. Paulus und die "Diatribe" (Münster 1987) 327.

3:1-3   BETZ, O. "Beschneidung" in TRE 5 (1980) 719.

3:1-2   ZELLER, D. Juden und Heiden in der Mission des Paulus. Studien zum Römerbrief (Stuttgart 1973) 86f. PAGELS, E. H. The Gnostic Paul. Gnostic Exegesis of the Pauline Letters (Philadelphia 1975) 20. SCHMITHALS, W. Der Römerbrief als historisches Problem (Gütersloh 1975) 45, 56, 89. BETZ, O. "Beschneidung" in TRE 5 (1980) 719.

3:1   VAN DÜLMEN, A. Die Theologie des Gesetzes bei Paulus (1968) 20, 81, 141, 179, 216, 217, 218. ZINGG, P. Das Wachsen der Kirche (Freiburg, Schweiz 1974) 265. KLIJN, A. F. J. "Die syrische Baruch-Apokalypse" in JSHRZ V/2 (1976) 131n.5a.

3:2-4   SCHMITHALS, W. "Zur Herkunft der gnostischen Elemente in der Sprache des Paulus" in B. Aland et al., eds., Gnosis. (FS. H. Jonas; Göttingen 1978) 392f.

3:2-3   ZELLER, D. Juden und Heiden in der Mission des Paulus. Studien zum Römerbrief (Stuttgart 1973) 112f.

3:2   DOEVE, J.W. "Some notes with reference to τὰ λόγια τοῦ θεοῦ in Romans III 2" Studia Paulina (1953) 11-123. VAN DÜLMEN, A. Die Theologie des Gesetzes bei Paulus (1968) 20, 141, 216. WILLIAMS, S. K. "The 'Righteousness of God' in Romans," JBL 99 (1980) 266f. STAAB, K. Pauluskommentare aus der griechischen Kirche (Münster ²1984) 46:13-15 EusE.

3:3ff.   OLLROG, W.-H. Paulus und seine Mitarbeiter (Neukirchen-Vluyn 1979) 135.

3:3-8   MOXNES, H. Theology in Conflict (Leiden 1980) 56-60.

3:3-7   HAYS, R. B. The Faith of Jesus Christ (Chico CA 1983) 191.

3:3-5   LJUNGMAN, H. Pistis (1964) 13-36, 37-47. KÄSEMANN, E. Exegetische Versuche und Besinnungen (1964) II 192. KÄSEMANN, E. New Testament

Questions of Today (1969) 180. ZELLER, D. Juden und Heiden in der Mission des Paulus. Studien zum Römerbrief (Stuttgart 1973) 180ff. WILLIAMS, S. K. "The 'Righteousness of God' in Romans," JBL 99 (1980) 243. WAY, D. The Lordship of Christ. Ernst Käsemann's Interpretation of Paul's Theology (Oxford 1991) 203-5.

3:3-4   KERTELGE, K. "Rechtfertigung" bei Paulus (1967) 65-67, 126.

3:3   MUNCK, J. Paul and the Salvation of Mankind (1959) 45f. LJUNGMAN, H. Pistis (1964) 13f, 38f. THEYSSEN, G.W. "Unbelief" in the New Testament (Rüschlikon 1965) 5-7. BAUMERT, N. Täglich Sterben und Auferstehen (München 1973) 91. HAYS, R. B. "Psalm 143 and the Logic of Romans 3," JBL 99 (1980) 110f. MOXNES, H. Theology in Conflict (Leiden 1980) 22, 27, 37f., 220. WILLIAMS, S. K. "The 'Righteousness of God' in Romans," JBL 99 (1980) 266, 268, 273, 275. HAYS, R. B. The Faith of Jesus Christ (Chico CA 1983) 155, 163, 171f., 187, 190. STAAB, K. Pauluskommentare aus der griechischen Kirche (Münster [2]1984) 61:1-7 Apoll; 484:6-33 Phot.

3:4-9   HANSON, A. T. Studies in Paul's Technique and Theology (London 1974) 20f.

3:4-8   JEREMIAS, J. Abba (1966) 287-89. FROITZHEIM, F. Christologie und Eschatologie bei Paulus (Würzburg 1979) 173.

3:4-5   SCHRAGE, W. Die konkreten Einzelgebote in der paulinischen Paränese (1961) 74, 117. STUHLMACHER, P. Gerechtigkeit Gottes bei Paulus (1965) 84-86.

3:4   BEST, E. One Body in Christ (1955) 37. LJUNGMAN, H. Pistis (1964) 36f. STROBEL, A. Erkenntnis und Bekenntnis der Sünde in neutestamentlicher Zeit (1968) 49. HARMAN, A. M. Paul's Use of the Psalms (Ann Arbor MI 1968) 45-53, 183f. BLACK, M. "Some Greek Words with 'Hebrew' Meanings in the Epistles and Apokalypse" in J. R. McKay et al., eds., Biblical Studies (FS. W. Barclay; London 1976) 139f. TRITES, A. A. The New Testament Concept of Witness (Cambridge 1977) 201. HAYS, R. B. "Psalm 143 and the Logic of Romans 3," JBL 99 (1980) 110. THISELTON, A. C. The Two Horizons (Grand Rapids 1980) 393. WILLIAMS, S. K. "The 'Righteousness of God' in Romans," JBL 99 (1980) 268f., 289. RHYNE, C. T. Faith Establishes the Law (Chico CA 1981) 41-44. STAAB, K. Pauluskommentare aus der griechischen Kirche (Münster [2]1984) 46:16-21 EusE; 423:7 Oek; 484:34-485:12 Phot. FREUND, G. und STEGEMANN, E., eds., Theologische Brosamen für Lothar Steiger (DBAT 5; Heidelberg 1985) 77. BERGER, K. und COLPE, C., eds., Religionsgeschichtliches Textbuch zum Neuen Testament (Göttingen/ Zürich 1987) 201. SCHMELLER, TH. Paulus und die "Diatribe" (Münster 1987) 327. LÖFSTEDT, B. "Notes on St Paul's Letter to the Romans," FilolNeot (1988) 209f. LONGENECKER, B. W. Eschatology and the Covenant. A Comparison of 4 Ezra and Romans 1-11 (Sheffield 1991) 196-8, 198n.1.

3:5-8:31   BETZ, H. D. "Hellenismus III" in TRE 15 (1986) 29.

3:5-8   AONO, T. Die Entwicklung des paulinischen Gerichts-gedankens bei den Apostolischen Vätern (Bern/ Frankfurt/Las Vegas 1979) 4ff. STAAB, K. Pauluskommentare aus der griechischen Kirche (Münster [2]1984) 485:13-486:6 Phot.

3:5-6   MANSUS, H. The Wrath of God in the Pauline Homolegoumena (1969) 55-58. PAGELS, E. H. The Gnostic Paul. Gnostic Exegesis of the Pauline Letters (Philadelphia 1975) 21. SCHMITHALS, W. "Zur Herkunft der gnostischen Elemente in der Sprache des Paulus" in B. Aland et al., eds., Gnosis. (FS. H. Jonas; Göttingen 1978) 392f.

3:5   KÄSEMANN, E. Exegetische Versuche und Besinnungen (1964) II 182. JÜNGEL, E. Paulus und Jesus (1966) 33. KERTELGE, K. "Rechtfertigung" bei Paulus (1967) 13, 14, 63-70, 107. METZGER, B.M. "Explicit references in the works of Origen to variant readings in New Testament manuscripts" Historical and Literary Studies (1968) 96f. KÄSEMANN, E. New Testament Questions of Today (1969) 169. LYONNET, S. "La notion de justice de Dieu en Rom., III, 5, et L'exégèse paulinienne du 'Miserere'" in J. Coppens et al., eds., Sacra Pagina. Miscellanea biblica congressus internationalis catholici de re biblica II (Gembloux 1959) 342-56. BAUMERT, N. Täglich Sterben und Auferstehen (München 1973) 404-06. HEROLD, G. Zorn und Gerechtigkeit Gottes bei Paulus. Eine Untersuchung zu Röm. 1, 16-18 (Frankfurt 1973) 293ff. PLUTTA-MESSERSCHMIDT, E. Gerechtigkeit Gottes bei Paulus. Eine Studie zu Luthers Auslegung von Römer 3, 5 (Tübingen 1973). HAYS, R. B. "Psalm 143 and the Logic of Romans 3," JBL 99 (1980) 109-11, 115. THISELTON, A. C. The Two Horizons (Grand Rapids 1980) 267, 393. WILLIAMS, S. K. "The 'Righteousness of God' in Romans," JBL 99 (1980) 243, 270. BAMMEL, C. P. H. "Philocalia IX, Jerome, Epistle 121, and Origen's Exposition of Romans VII," JThS 32 (1981) 64. HAYS, R. B. The Faith of Jesus Christ (Chico CA 1983) 172. HÄRING, H. Das Problem des Bösen in der Theologie (Darmstadt 1985) 130. THOMPSON, S. The Apocalypse and Semitic Syntax (Cambridge 1985) 117. KRAUS, W. Der Tod Jesu als Heiligtumsweihe. Eine Untersuchung zum Umfeld der Sühnevorstellung in Römer 3, 25-26a (Neukirchen-Vluyn 1991) 19, 108f., 169f., 172n.

3:6   SCHRAGE, W. Die konkreten Einzelgebote in der paulinischen Paränese (1961) 210. ZELLER, D. Juden und Heiden in der Mission des Paulus. Studien zum Römerbrief (Stuttgart 1973) 151f. THISELTON, A. C. The Two Horizons (Grand Rapids 1980) 393. RHYNE, C. T. Faith Establishes the Law (Chico CA 1981) 41-44. SCHMELLER, TH. Paulus und die "Diatribe" (Münster 1987) 327.

3:7-8   LJUNGVIK, H. "Zu Rm 3:7-8," ZNW 32 (1933) 207. FRIDRICHSEN, A. "Nochmals Römer 3:7-8," ZNW 34 (1935) 306. SCHMITHALS, W. Der Römerbrief als historisches Problem (Gütersloh 1975) 42, 44, 89f.

3:7   BAUMERT, N. Täglich Sterben und Auferstehen (München 1973) 302-09. KÜMMEL, W. G. Römer 7 und das Bild des Menschen im Neuen Testament (München 1974) 121f. HAYS, R. B. "Psalm 143 and the Logic of Romans 3," JBL 99 (1980) 110f. THEISSEN, G. Psychologische Aspekte paulinischer Theologie (Göttingen 1983) 182, 195-98, 198n.24, 202, 203n.36.

3:8ff. SCHRAGE, W. Die konkreten Einzelgebote in der paulinischen Paränese (1961) 53, 64, 117, 195, 196.

3:8-14 TILSON, E. "Homiletical Resources: Exegesis of Isaiah Passages for Advent," QR 1 (1980) 12-14.

3:8-9   SCHNACKENBURG, R. Die sittliche Botschaft des Neuen Testaments I (Freiburg/Basel/Wien 1986) 215.

3:8   KERTELGE, K. "Rechtfertigung" bei Paulus (1967) 74. BAUMERT, N. Täglich Sterben und Auferstehen (München 1973) 254. ZELLER, D. Juden und Heiden in der Mission des Paulus. Studien zum Römerbrief (Stuttgart 1973) 41. KÜMMEL, W. G. Römer 7 und das Bild des Menschen im Neuen Testament (München 1974) 121f. SYNOFZIK, E. Die Gerichts- und Vergeltungsaussagen bei Paulus (Göttingen 1977) 34f. ELLIS, E. E. Prophecy and Hermeneutic in Early Christianity (Tübingen 1978) 121, 125, 218, 234. OLLROG, W.-H. Paulus und seine Mitarbeiter (Neukirchen-Vluyn 1979) 211, 215. HAYS, R. B. "Psalm 143 and the Logic of Romans 3," JBL 99 (1980) 112. LÜDEMANN, G. Paulus, der Heiden-apostel, Bd. II (Göttingen 1983) 110 A 23, 128 A 84, 159-61, 201. THEISSEN, G. Psychologische Aspekte paulinischer Theologie

(Göttingen 1983) 107n.65, 183, 195f., 198, 202. CANALES, I. J. "Paul's
Accusers in Romans 3:8 and 6:1," EQ 57 (1985) 237-45. JONES, F. S.
"Freiheit" in den Briefen des Apostels Paulus (Göttingen 1987) 123, 135, 152
A 64, 213 A 6.10, 216 A 34.36. WEDDERBURN, A. J. M. The Reasons for
Romans (Edinburgh 1988) 2, 114f., 126, 134. LAMPE, P. Die stadtrömischen
Christen in den ersten beiden Jahrhunderten (Tübingen ²1989) 55.

3:9-20   SCHMIDT, H.W. Der Brief des Paulus an die Römer (1962) 63. RIEDL, J. Das
Heil der Heiden nach Röm 2:14-16.26.27 (Mödling bei Wien 1965) 214-17.
JOHNSON, S. L., JR. "Studies in Romans. Part IX: The Universality of Sin,"
BiblSa 131 (1974) 163-72. PAGELS, E. H. The Gnostic Paul. Gnostic Exegesis
of the Pauline Letters (Philadelphia 1975) 21f. SCHMITHALS, W. Der
Römerbrief als historisches Problem (Gütersloh 1975) 14f., 161. HAYS, R. B.
"Psalm 143 and the Logic of Romans 3," JBL 99 (1980) 112f., 115. HAYS, R.
B. The Faith of Jesus Christ (Chico CA 1983) 172. DUNN, J. D. G. "Paul's
Epistle to the Romans: An Analysis of Structure and Argument" in ANRW
II.25.4 (1987) 2852f. LONGENECKER, B. W. Eschatology and the Covenant.
A Comparison of 4 Ezra and Romans 1-11 (Sheffield 1991) 231.

3:9-18   RÖHSER, G. Metaphorik und Personifikation der Sünde (Tübingen 1987) 15f.,
17f., 142, 156, 167ff. DAVIES, G. N. Faith and Obedience in Romans. A Study
in Romans 1-4 (Sheffield 1990) 80-100.

3:9,19   FREUND, G. und STEGEMANN, E., eds., Theologische Brosamen für Lothar
Steiger (DBAT 5; Heidelberg 1985) 186.

3:9,10ff.   ELLIS, E.E. Paul's Use of the Old Testament (1957) 10ff, 14, 102, 116, 118,
186.

3:9   LJUNGMAN, H. Pistis (1964) 44f. JÜNGEL, E. Paulus und Jesus (1966) 26f.
STROBEL, A. Erkenntnis und Bekenntnis der Sünde in neutestamentlicher Zeit
(1968) 49. VAN DÜLMEN, A. Die Theologie des Gesetzes bei Paulus (1968)
74, 75, 82, 85, 202, 218. RICHARDSON, Israel in the Apostolic Church (1969)
140f. SYNGE, F.C. "The Meaning of *proerchometha* in Romans 3:9" ET 81
(11, '70) 351. EICHHOLZ, G. Die Theologie des Paulus im Umriss (1972) 82f.
BRANDENBURGER, E. Adam und Christus (Neukirchen-Vluyn 1962) 175,
178, 187f., 218, 244. KÜMMEL, W. G. Römer 7 und das Bild des Menschen
im Neuen Testa-ment (München 1974) 28, 124, 193. HÜBNER, H. Das Gesetz
bei Paulus (Göttingen 1978) 63. HAYS, R. B. "Psalm 143 and the Logic of
Romans 3," JBL 99 (1980) 112. DAHL, N. A. "Romans 3.9: Text and
Meaning" in M. D. Hooker and S. G. Wilson, eds., Paul and Paulinism (FS. C.
K. Barrett; London 1982) 184-204. FEUILLET, A. "La situation privilégiée des
Juifs d'après *Rm 3*, 9. Comparaison avec *Rm I*, 16 et *3*, 1-2," NRTh 105 (1983)
33-46. RÄISÄNEN, H. Paul and the Law (Tübingen 1983) 97-99, 106. STAAB,
K. Pauluskommentare aus der griechischen Kirche (Münster ²1984) 117:1-2
ThM; 216:7-24 Sev; 486:7-487:8 Phot; 654:14-28 Areth. SANDERS, E. P. Paul,
the Law, and the Jewish People (London 1985) 30, 35, 43, 46, 82, 106, 123f.,
128, 129, 131, 148, 151, 160, 173. BRANDENBURGER, E. Das Böse (Zürich
1986) 89f. RÄISÄNEN, H. The Torah and Christ (Helsinki 1986) 15, 191.
OSTEN-SACKEN, P. VON DER, Evangelium und Tora: Aufsätze zu Paulus
(München 1987) 175-77, 224. JOHNSON, E. E. The Function of Apocalyptic
and Wisdom Traditions in Romans 9-11 (Atlanta GA 1989) 118f., 149, 186.
MARTIN, B. L. Christ and the Law in Paul (Leiden 1989) 13, 15, 70, 72, 80,
82, 92, 99-101, 103, 124. DAVIES, G. N. Faith and Obedience in Romans. A
Study in Romans 1-4 (Sheffield 1990) 80-2, 97-100. ELLIOT, N. The Rhetoric

of Romans (Sheffield 1990) 106f., 132-4, 137-42, 144, 147, 152, 158n., 162, 193, 194-7, 202-4, 227f., 253, 285, 287, 289.

3:9a   DE KRUIJF, T. C. "Is anybody any better off? (Rom 3, 9a)," Bijdragen 46 (1985) 234-44.

3:10ff.   THACKERAY, H. The Relation of St. Paul to Contemporary Jewish Thought (1900) 183ff.

3:10-31   ZIESKER, J.A. The Meaning of Righteousness in Paul (1972) 190-5.

3:10-20   BRAUN, H. Qumran und NT II (1966) 167, 172, 176, 304f. HANSON, A. T. Studies in Paul's Technique and Theology (London 1974) 16f., 153, 157, 171, 192. ELLIOT, N. The Rhetoric of Romans (Sheffield 1990) 142-6, 152, 157.

3:10-18   KERTELGE, K. "Rechtfertigung" bei Paulus (1967) 71. LUZ, U. Das Geschichtsverständnis des Paulus (1968) 98. HARMAN, A. M. Paul's Use of the Psalms (Ann Arbor MI 1968) 53-72. VAN DER MINDE, H.-J. Schrift und Tradition bei Paulus (München/Paderborn/Wien 1976) 54-58, 120. KECK, L. E. "The Function of Romans 3:10-18. Observations and suggestions" in J. Jervell and W. A. Meeks, eds., God's Christ and His People (FS. N. A. Dahl; New York 1977) 141-57. ELLIS, E. E. Prophecy and Hermeneutic in Early Christianity (Tübingen 1978) 150, 217f., 234. VIELHAUER, P. "Paulus und das Alte Testament" in Oikodome [G. Klein, ed.] (München 1979) 204. KOCH, D.-A. Die Schrift als Zeuge des Evangeliums (Tübingen 1986) 118f., 179-84, 250f., 278f. ELLIS, E. E. The Old Testament in Early Christianity (Tübingen 1991) 91, 95, 99, 130.

3:10-12   ELLIS, E. E. Paul's Use of the Old Testament (Edinburgh/London 1957) 150, 156. DAVIES, G. N. Faith and Obedience in Romans. A Study in Romans 1-4 (Sheffield 1990) 82-5.

3:10-11   KOCH, D.-A. Die Schrift als Zeuge des Evangeliums (Tübingen 1986) 145.

3:10-11   KOCH, D.-A. Die Schrift als Zeuge des Evangeliums (Tübingen 1986) 132.

3:10   JÜNGEL, E. Paulus und Jesus (1966) 44. STROBEL, A. Erkenntnis und Bekenntnis der Sünde in neutestamentlicher Zeit (1968) 49.

3:12   HYHEN, J. B. "Böse" in TRE 7 (1981) 9.

3:13-18   METZGER, B.M. "Lucian and the Lucianic Recension of the Greek Bible" NTS 8 ('61-62) 199f.

3:13-17   GERSTENBERGER, G. und SCHRAGE, W. Leiden (Stuttgart 1977) 213; ET: J. E. Steely (trans.) Suffering (Nashville 1980) 246.

3:13   ELLIS, E. E. Paul's Use of the Old Testament (Edinburgh/London 1957) 150, 156.

3:14   NICKELS, P. Targum and New Testament (1967) 61. ELLIS, E. E. Paul's Use of the Old Testament (Edinburgh/London 1957) 150, 158. SCHRAGE, W. "Die Elia-Apokalypse" in JSHRZ V (3, 1980) 244n.26c. KOCH, D.-A. Die Schrift als Zeuge des Evangeliums (Tübingen 1986) 109.

3:15-19   KOCH, D.-A. Die Schrift als Zeuge des Evangeliums (Tübingen 1986) 119, 143f.

3:15-17   ELLIS, E. E. Paul's Use of the Old Testament (Edinburgh/London 1957) 20, 150, 158.

3:15   KOCH, D.-A. Die Schrift als Zeuge des Evangeliums (Tübingen 1986) 106.

3:18   ELLIS, E. E. Paul's Use of the Old Testament (Edinburgh/London 1957) 11, 144, 150, 158. KOCH, D.-A. Die Schrift als Zeuge des Evangeliums (Tübingen 1986) 112.

3:19-31   BRAUN, H. GPM 7 52-54. FRIEDRICH, G. "Das Gesetz des Glaubens Römer 3, 27" in Auf das Wort kommt es an. Gesammelte Aufsätze (Göttingen 1978) 110f. ROBERTS, J. H. "Righteous-ness in Romans with Special Reference to

Romans 3:19-31," Neotestamentica 15 (1981) 12-33. LAFON, G. "Une loi de foi. La pensée de la loi en *Romains* 3, 19-31," RevSR 61 (1987) 32-53.

3:19-28 STECK, K.G. GPM 14 (1960) 305-311. Arbeitskreis "Theologia applicata" GPM 20 (1965/66) 404-11. SCHROER, u.a. GPM 20 (1965/66) 404ff. BRANDENBURGER, E. GPM 26 (1972) 428-39. FORCK, G. in GPM 32 (1977/78) 412-17.

3:19-22 FRIEDRICH, G. "Das Gesetz des Glaubens Römer 3, 27" in Auf das Wort kommt es an. Gesammelte Aufsätze (Göttingen 1978) 115f.

3:19-20 KERTELGE, K. "Rechtfertigung" bei Paulus (1967) 71-73, 115. BAMMEL, C. P. H. "Philocalia IX, Jerome, Epistle 121, and Origen's Exposition of Romans VII," JThS 32 (1981) 54, 64. STAAB, K. Pauluskommentare aus der griechischen Kirche (Münster ²1984) 361:26-32 Genn; 487:9-21 Phot. RÄISÄNEN, H. The Torah and Christ (Helsinki 1986) 111. DAVIES, G. N. Faith and Obedience in Romans. A Study in Romans 1-4 (Sheffield 1990) 102-4.

3:19 BRUNNER, E. Dogmatik I (1946) 300. BEST, E. One Body in Christ (1955) 12n. SCHRAGE, W. Die konkreten Einzelgebote in der paulinischen Paränese (1961) 65, 196, 230, 231. STALDER, K. Das Werk des Geistes in der Heiligung bei Paulus (1962) 166, 269f. PAX, E. "Ein Beitrag zur biblischen Toposforschung (Röm 3, 19)" StudBibFrancLibAnn 15 ('64-65) 302-17. JEREMIAS, J. Abba (1966) 283. JÜNGEL, E. Paulus und Jesus (1966) 56, 61. VAN DÜLMEN, A. Die Theologie des Gesetzes bei Paulus (1968) 40, 54, 74, 75, 82f, 91, 112, 119, 134, 160, 170, 188.203, 256. STROBEL, A. Erkenntnis und Bekenntnis der Sünde in neutestamentlicher Zeit (1968) 49. LADD, G. E. A Theology of the New Testament (Grand Rapids 1974) 398, 507, 630. HAYS, R. B. "Psalm 143 and the Logic of Romans 3," JBL 99 (1980) 112f.

3:20-4:25 ELLIOT, N. The Rhetoric of Romans (Sheffield 1990) 205-23.

3:20-4:8 HEILIGENTHAL, R. Werke als Zeichen (Tübingen 1983) 296-311.

3:20-28 PARKER, T. H. L. Commentaries on the Epistle to the Romans 1532-1542 (Edinburgh 1986) 142-200.

3:20-27 LONGENECKER, R.N. Paul Apostle of Liberty (1964) passim.

3:20,28 FREUND, G. und STEGEMANN, E., eds., Theologische Brosamen für Lothar Steiger (DBAT 5; Heidelberg 1985) 187. BEINTKER, H. "Gott VII" in TRE 13 (1984) 664.

3:20 FEINE, D.P. Das gesetzesfreie Evangelium des Paulus (1899) 127-29. JÜNGEL, E. Paulus und Jesus (1966) 17, 48, 57, 59. HAHN, F. Das Verständnis der Mission im Neuen Testament (1965) 86. LUZ, U. Das Geschichtsverständnis des Paulus (1968) 90, 187. MERK, O. Handeln aus Glauben (1968) 8f, 14. STROBEL, A. Erkenntnis und Bekenntnis der Sünde in neutestamentlicher Zeit (1968) 49. VAN DÜLMEN, A. Die Theologie des Gesetzes bei Paulus (1968) 22, 23, 42, 76, 83f, 91, 92, 194. BLANK, J. "Warum sagt Paulus: 'Aus Werken des Gesetzes wird niemand gerecht'?" Evangelisch—Katholischer Kommentar zum Neuen Testament I (1969) 79-95. SCHWEIZER, E. u.a., eds., Evangelisch-Katholischer Kommentar zum Neuen Testament (1969) I 79ff. EICHHOLZ, G. Die Theologie des Paulus im Umriss (1972) passim. BRANDENBURGER, E. Adam und Christus (Neukirchen-Vluyn 1962) 248f., 251. HARMAN, A. M. Paul's Use of the Psalms (Ann Arbor MI 1968) 72ff. BRANDENBURGER, E. "Gericht Gottes" in TRE 12 (1984) 122f., A 490. BAUMERT, N. Täglich Sterben und Auferstehen (München 1973) 246. KÜMMEL, W. G. Römer 7 und das Bild des Menschen im Neuen Testament (München 1974) 7f., 16, 70, 160, 180, 194. LADD, G. E. A Theology of the New Testament (Grand Rapids 1974) 430, 447, 495, 507, 592. SCHMITHALS, W. Der

Römerbrief als historisches Problem (Gütersloh 1975) 15. HÜBNER, H. Das Gesetz bei Paulus (Göttingen 1978) 62-71. STUIBER, A. "Ambrosiaster" in TRE 2 (1978) 359. OLLROG, W.-H. Paulus und seine Mitarbeiter (Neukirchen-Vluyn 1979) 21, 214. VIELHAUER, P. "Paulus und das Alte Testament" in Oikodome [G. Klein, ed.] (München 1979) 214. BARTH, G. "Bergpredigt" in TRE 5 (1980) 610. WILLIAMS, S. K. "The 'Righteousness of God' in Romans," JBL 99 (1980) 270f., 276, 284. DEIDUN, T. J. New Covenant Morality in Paul (Rome 1981) 194f., 198f. BLANK, J. Paulus. Von Jesus zum Christentum (München 1982) 42-68. RÄISÄNEN, H. Paul and the Law (Tübingen 1983) 97, 99, 102, 106, 140f., 145, 148, 161, 163, 170. HÜBNER, H. Gottes Ich und Israel (Göttingen 1984) 13, 73f., 94. KLEIN, G. "Gesetz III" in TRE 13 (1984) 71. FREUND, G. und STEGEMANN, E., eds., Theologische Brosamen für Lothar Steiger (DBAT 5; Heidelberg 1985) 392. SANDERS, E. P. Paul, the Law, and the Jewish People (London 1985) 65, 70f., 75, 86n.2, 88n.25, 93, 123f., 128f. KOCH, D.-A. Die Schrift als Zeuge des Evangeliums (Tübingen 1986) 275f. PARKER, T. H. L. Commentaries on the Epistle to the Romans 1532-1542 (Edinburgh 1986) 142-44. COSGROVE, C. H. "Justification in Paul: A Linguistic and Theological Reflection," JBL 106 (1987) 653-70. GASTON, L. Paul and the Torah (Vancouver 1987) 17, 31, 66, 69, 103, 105. MERKLEIN, H. Studien zu Jesus und Paulus (Tübingen 1987) 2f., 10, 12, 40, 69. JOHNSON, E. E. The Function of Apocalyptic and Wisdom Traditions in Romans 9-11 (Atlanta GA 1989) 120, 187, 190. LIEBERS, R. Das Gesetz als Evangelium (Zürich 1989) 44-46. MARTIN, B. L. Christ and the Law in Paul (Leiden 1989) 10, 13, 15f., 20, 25, 27f., 37, 42, 47, 85, 92, 95, 105, 116, 127, 138. THIELMAN, F. From Plight to Solution (Leiden 1989) 24, 74, 92, 95f., 108, 113, 115, 120, 127. DAVIES, G. N. Faith and Obedience in Romans. A Study in Romans 1-4 (Sheffield 1990) 118. DUNN, J. D. G. Jesus, Paul and the Law (London 1990) 158, 205n.37-38, 208. KRAUS, W. Der Tod Jesu als Heiligtumsweihe. Eine Untersuchung zum Umfeld der Sühnevorstellung in Römer 3, 25-26a (Neukirchen-Vluyn 1991) 11f., 153, 171f. WALTER, N. "Gottes Erbarmen mit 'allem Fleisch' (Röm 3, 20/Gal 2, 16)," BZ 35 (1991) 99-102.

3:21–6:23   VAN DÜLMEN, A. Die Theologie des Gesetzes bei Paulus (1968) 84-100.
3:21–5:21   MERK, O. Handeln aus Glauben (1968) 22f., 35, 157. VAN DÜLMEN, A. Die Theologie des Gesetzes bei Paulus (1968) 100. SHEPARD, J. W. The Life and Letters of St. Paul (Grand Rapids 1950) 382-96. SONGER, H. S. "New Standing Before God: Romans 3:21-5:21," RevEx 73 (1976) 415-24. SCHILLEBEECKX, E. Christ: The Christian Experience in the Modern World (London 1980) 146-54; GT: Christus und die Christen (Freiburg/Basel/Wien 1977) 137-45. SCHMELLER, TH. Paulus und die "Diatribe" (Münster 1987) 233. BECKER, J. Paulus. Der Apostel der Völker (Tübingen 1989) 382ff., 396. SEIFRID, M. A. Justification by Faith (Leiden/New York/Köln 1992) 219-26.

3:21-5:11   VOS, J. S. Traditionsgeschichtliche Untersuchungen zur Paulinischen Pneumatologie (Assen 1973) 112-18.

3:21–4:25   WILCKENS, U. "Zu Römer 3, 21-4, 25. Antwort an G. Klein" EvTh 24 (11, '64) 586-610. KLEIN, G. "Exegetische Probleme in Römer 3, 21-4, 25. Antwort an U. Wilckens" EvTh 24 (12, '64) 676-83. CAMBIER, J. L'Evangile de Dieu selon l'Epitre aux Romains I (1967) 61-175. SCHREINER, J. Gestalt und Anspruch des Neuen Testaments (1969) 69f. PERRIN, N. The New Testament (New York 1974) 108-10. SCHMITHALS, W. Der Römerbrief als historisches Problem (Gütersloh 1975) 15f. RHYNE, C. T. Faith Establishes the Law (Chico CA 1981) 63-93. SCHMITT, R. Gottesgerechtigkeit—Heilsgeschichte—Israel in der Theologie des Paulus (Frankfurt/Bern/ New York/Nancy 1984) 14-38. FRAIKIN, D. "The Rhetorical Function of the Jews in Romans" in P. Richardson, ed., Anti-Judaism in Early Christianity, Vol 1: Paul and the Gospels (Waterloo, Ont. 1986) 97f. KOCH, D.-A. Die Schrift als Zeuge des Evangeliums (Tübingen 1986) 289f. BECKER, J. Paulus. Der Apostel der Völker (Tübingen 1989) 385ff., 436.

3:21-4:22   DUGANDZIC, I. Das "Ja" Gottes in Christus (Würzburg 1977) 155-97.

3:21-4:9   BERGER, K. und COLPE, C., eds., Religionsgeschicht-liches Textbuch zum Neuen Testament (Göttingen/ Zürich 1987) 201-03.

3:21-4:8   HEILIGENTHAL, R. Werke als Zeichen (Tübingen 1983) 288-311.

3:21ff.   BRUNNER, E. Dogmatik I 294, 298, 321. II (1946) 362. JUNGMAN, H. Pistis (1964) 37-47. LÜHRMANN, D. Das Offen-barungsverständnis bei Paulus und in Paulinischen Gemeinden (1965) 148-53. STUHLMACHER, P. Gerechtigkeit Gottes bei Paulus (1965) 15-17, 24f., 61-66, 86-91. BRANDENBURGER, E. Fleisch und Geist (1968) 56, 82. LUZ, U. Das Geschichtsverständnis des Paulus (1968) 168ff. MERK, Otto, Handeln aus Glauben (1968)9, 23, 40. HEROLD, G. Zorn und Gerechtigkeit Gottes bei Paulus. Eine Untersuchung zu Röm. 1, 16-18 (Frankfurt 1973) 250ff. CONZELMANN, H. Theologie als Schriftauslegung (München 1974) 178, 189, 199f., 201. SCHMITHALS, W. "Zur Herkunft der gnostischen Elemente in der Sprache des Paulus" in B. Aland et al., eds., Gnosis. (FS. H. Jonas; Göttingen 1978) 391-93. OLLROG, W.-H. Paulus und seine Mitarbeiter (Neukirchen-Vluyn 1979) 136. SCHMELLER, TH. Paulus und die "Diatribe" (Münster 1987) 285, 418. CONZELMANN, H. and LINDEMANN, A. Interpreting the New Testament (Peabody MA 1988) 194. SCHNELLE, U. Wandlungen im paulinischen Denken (Stuttgart 1989) 63, 65. BOCKMUEHL, M. N. A. Revelation and Mystery (Tübingen 1990) 133, 138. KRAUS, W. Der Tod Jesu als Heiligtumsweihe. Eine Untersuchung zum Umfeld der Sühnevorstellung in Römer 3, 25-26a (Neukirchen-Vluyn 1991) 2, 4n., 6, 11n., 13, 18n., 21, 69, 159n., 188f.

3:21-31   BORNKAMM, G. GPM 10 (1956) 255-59. STALDER, K. Das Werk des Geistes in den Heiligung bei Paulus (1962) 267-69. LJUNGMAN, H. Pistis (1964) 35f. REUMANN, J. "The Gospel of the Righteousness of God. Pauline Reinterpretation in Romans 3:21-31" Interpretation 20 (4, '66) 432-52. RENSHAW, J.R. "A Study of Romans iii:21-31" ABR 15 (1-4, '67) 21-27. LUZ, U. Das Geschichtsverständnis des Paulus (1968) 168-73. VAN DÜLMEN, A. Die Theologie des Gesetzes bei Paulus (1968) 73, 84, 85, 216. HOWARD, G. "Romans 3:21-31 and the Inclusion of the Gentiles" HThR 63 (2, '70) 223-33. MUELLER-BARDORFF, J. Paulus (1970) 156-68. EICHHOLZ, G. Die Theologie des Paulus im Umriss (1972) 66, 157, 221f. ZIESLER, J.A. The Meaning of Righteousness in Paul (1972) 196, 209f, 191f, 210f, 193f. MAIER, W. A. "Paul's Concept of Justification, and Some Recent Interpretations of Romans 3:21-31," Springfielder 37 (1974) 248-64. PRICE, J. L. "God's Righteousness Shall Prevail," Interp 28 (1974) 259-80. KIM, S. The Origin of Paul's Gospel (Tübingen 1981) 296f. GORDAY, P. Principles of Patristic Exegesis: Romans 9-11 in Origen, John Chrysostom, and Augustine (New York/Toronto 1983) 60f., 114., 157f. HAYS, R. B. The Faith of Jesus Christ (Chico CA 1983) 186. KOCH, D.-A. Die Schrift als Zeuge des Evangeliums (Tübingen 1986) 275f. LÜBKING, H.-M. Paulus und Israel im Römerbrief (Frankfurt/ Bern/New York 1986) 34-36. WATSON, F. Paul, Judaism and the Gentiles (Cambridge 1986) 131-35. DUNN, J. D. G. "Paul's Epistle to the Romans: An Analysis of Structure and Argument" in ANRW II.25.4 (1987) 2853f. GASTON, L. Paul and the Torah (Vancouver 1987) 60, 65, 71f., 95, 122f., 198. RAMAROSON, L. "La justification par la foi *du* Christ Jésus," SciE 39 (1987) 81-92. ELLIOT, N. The Rhetoric of Romans (Sheffield 1990) 146-57, 162, 227. SEGAL, A. F. Paul the Convert (New Haven/London 1990) 128ff. LONGENECKER, B. W. Eschatology and the Covenant. A Comparison of 4 Ezra and Romans 1-11 (Sheffield 1991) 170, 203, 207, 210f., 213-5, 218, 224, 246.

3:21-30   ZELLER, D. Juden und Heiden in der Mission des Paulus. Studien zum Römerbrief (Stuttgart 1973) 158ff. RHYNE, C. T. Faith Establishes the Law (Chico CA 1981) 27-30, 63-71.

3:21-28   SCHWEITZER, A. Die Mystik des Apostels Paulus (1954) 124, 201-203, 213, 215, 217. FAUSEL, H. in Herr, tue meine Lippen auf II (1966) 414-20. JONKER, W.D. "Grace and Justification" NGTT 9 (3, '68) 132-43. BÜCHSEL, D. F. Der Geist Gottes im Neuen Testament (Gütersloh 1926) 305-07. DONFRIED, K. P. "Romans 3:21-28," Interp 34 (1980) 59-64. KLEIN, G. in GPM 34 (1980) 409-19. HILL, D. "Liberation through God's Righteousness," IrBS 4 (1982) 31-44. SCHMIDT, H. in GPM 40 (1985/86) 470-78.

3:21-26   DENNEY, J. The Death of Christ (1956) 96ff. STANLEY, D.M. Christ's Resurrection in Pauline Soteriology (1961) 166-71. BANDSTRA, A.J. The Law and the Elements of the World. An Exegetical Study in Aspects of Paul's Teaching (1964) 97ff. CADMAN, W.H. "Δικαιοσύνη in Romans 3, 21-26" Studia Evangelica II, ed. F.L. Cross (1964) 532-34. ROTH, R.P. and LINTON, C. D. "Justification by Faith—God's Free Gift to All Who Beleive" ChristToday 9 (Nov.20, '64) 164-67. BRAUN, H. Qumran und NT II (1966) 128f., 146, 171. FITZER, G. "Der Ort der Versöhnung nach Paulus. Zu der Frage des "Sühnopfers Jesu'" ThZ 22 (3, '66) 161-83. HOFFMANN, P. Die Toten in Christus (1966) 340. CAMBIER, J. L'Evangile de Dieu selon l'Epître aux Romains I (1967) 66-146. GIBLIN, C.H. The Threat to Faith (1967) 271-72, 282, n.3. KERTELGE, K. "Rechtfertigung" bei Paulus (1967) 49, 71-84, 108. MERK, O. Handeln aus Glauben (1968) 7f, 19. SCHRAGE, W. "Römer 3, 21-26 und die Bedeutung des Todes Jesu Christi bei Paulus" Das Kreuz Jesu ed. P. Rieger (1969) 65-88. GIBLIN, C.H. In Jope of God's Glory (1970) 348-53. LEE, E. K. A Study in Romans (London 1962). LAYMAN, F. D. Paul's Use of Abraham (diss. Ann Arbor MI 1972) 55-60, 193-95. PERRIN, N. The New Testament. An Introduction. Proclamation and Parenesis, Myth and History (New York 1974) 108-110. ROON, A. VAN, The Authenticity of Ephesians (Leiden 1974) 140f., 145, 162, 198. VAN DER MINDE, H.-J. Schrift und Tradition bei Paulus (München/Paderborn/Wien 1976) 53f. FROITZHEIM, F. Christologie und Eschatologie bei Paulus (Würzburg 1979) 39. ROBINSON, J. A. T. Wrestling with Romans (London 1979) 37-48. HAYS, R. B. "Psalm 143 and the Logic of Romans 3," JBL 99 (1980) 113, 115. THISELTON, A. C. The Two Horizons (Grand Rapids 1980) 399. KIM, S. The Origin of Paul's Gospel (Tübingen 1981) 278-80. JOHNSON, L. T. "Tom 3:21-26 and the Faith of Jesus," CBQ 44 (1982) 77-90. ZIESLER, J. A. "Salvation Proclaimed: IX. Romans 3:21-26," ET 93 (1982) 356-59. FINDEIS, H.-J. Versöhnung-Apostolat-Kirche (Würzburg 1983) 280-86. HAYS, R. B. The Faith of Jesus Christ (Chico CA 1983) 142, 170-74, 247. HÜBNER, H. Gottes Ich und Israel (Göttingen 1984) 72f. SCHMITT, R. Gottesgerechtigkeit—Heilsgeschichte—Israel in der Theologie des Paulus (Frankfurt/Bern/New York/Nancy 1984) 15-19, 23. BADENAS, R. Christ the End of the Law (Sheffield 1985) 140f., 149, 262n.388. HERMAN, Z. I. "Giustificazione e perdono in Romani 3, 21-26," Anton. 60 (1985) 240-78. HULTGREN, A. J. Paul's Gospel and Mission (Philadelphia 1985) 6, 30, 32f., 47, 60, 66. KERTELGE, K. "Die paulinische Recht-fertigungsthese nach Röm 3, 21-26" in K. Kertelge, ed., Die Autorität der Schrift im ökumenischen Gespräch (Frankfurt a.M. 1985) 70-76. KLAIBER, W. "Exegetisch-hermeneutische Anmerkungen zu Röm 3, 21-26 aus der Sicht eines evangelisch-methodistischen Theologen" in K. Kertelge, ed., Die Autorität der Schrift im ökumenischen Gespräch (Frankfurt a.M. 1985) 77-82. DOBBELER, A. VON Glaube als Teilhabe (Tübingen 1987) 158f. TRILLING, W. Studien zur Jesusüberlieferung (Stuttgart 1988) 328. CARTER, W. C. "Rome (and Jeru-salem): The Contingency of Romans 3:21-26," IrBibStud 11 (1989) 54-68. HAYS, R. B. Echoes of Scripture in the Letters of Paul (New Haven/London 1989) 52f. COUSAR, C. B. A Theology of the Cross (Minneapolis 1990) 27, 36-43, 63n., 187n. DAVIES, G. N. Faith and Obedience in Romans. A Study in Romans 1-4 (Sheffield 1990) 104-10. ELLIOT, N. The Rhetoric of Romans (Sheffield 1990) 146, 152, 154, 156n., 158n., 205, 214f., 219f., 222f., 226n., 228, 233, 235n., 292. GEORGI, D. Theocracy in Paul's Praxis and Theology (Minneapolis 1991) 93-6. KRAUS, W. Der Tod Jesu als Heiligtumsweihe. Eine Untersuchung zum Umfeld der Sühnevorstellung in Römer 3, 25-26a (Neukir-chen-Vluyn 1991) 1, 10-20, 92, 96n., 168, 187, 189f., 260, 280. CAMPBELL, W. S. "Romans III as a Key to the Structure and Thought of the Letter" in K. P. Donfried, ed., The Romans Debate. Revised and Expanded Edition (Peabody MA 1991) 251-64, esp. 252-57. CAMPBELL, D. C. The Rhetoric of Righteous-ness in Romans 3.21-26 (Sheffield 1992). CAMPBELL, W. S. Paul's Gospel in an Intercultural Context. Jew and Gentile in the Letter to the Romans (Frank-furt/Berlin/Bern etc. 1992) 26-29.

3:21-25,28   SCHNACKENBURG, R. "Notre justification par la foi en Jésus Christ sans les oeuvres de la Loi. Rm 3, 21-25a.28," AssS 40 (1972) 10-15.

3:21-25   BAMMEL, C. P. H. "Philocalia IX, Jerome, Epistle 121, and Origen's Expo-sition of Romans VII," JThS 32 (1981) 54. HENGEL, M. The Atonement (London 1981) 45. LIMBECK, M. Mit Paulus Christ sein. Sachbuch zur Person und Theologie des Apostels Paulus (Stuttgart 1989) 70f.

3:21-24   PAGELS, E. H. The Gnostic Paul. Gnostic Exegesis of the Pauline Letters (Philadelphia 1975) 22. BAMMEL, C. P. H. "Philocalia IX, Jerome, Epistle 121, and Origen's Exposition of Romans VII," JThS 32 (1981) 54f.

3:21-24a   BERGER, K. und COLPE, C., eds., Religionsge-schichtliches Textbuch zum Neuen Testament (Göttingen/Zürich 1987) 203.

3:21-22   SCHRAGE, W. Die konkreten Einzelgebote in der paulinischen Paränese (1961) 15, 177, 232. JÜNGEL, E. Paulus und Jesus (1966) 17, 29. KERTELGE, K. "Rechtfertigung" bei Paulus (1967) 73-79, 86, 88, 98, 136, 161. MERK, O. Handeln aus Glauben (1968) 6ff, 10, 11, 17, 32. MERKLEIN, H. Das Kirchliche Amt nach dem Epheser-brief (München 1973) 27f., 42, 194. RIDDERBOS, H. Paul. An Outline of His Theology (Grand Rapids 1975) 162-72. VIELHAUER, P. "Paulus und das Alte Testament" in Oikodome [G. Klein, ed.] (München 1979) 197. PLÜMACHER, E. "Bibel" in TRE 6 (1980) 16f. BADENAS, R. Christ the End of the Law (Sheffield 1985) 85, 105, 135, 139, 141f., 251n.282, 252n.284. FREUND, G. und STEGEMANN, E., eds., Theolo-gische Brosamen für Lothar Steiger (DBAT 5; Heidelberg 1985) 393. RÄISÄNEN, H. The Torah and Christ (Helsinki 1986) 104-06. SCHMELLER, TH. Paulus und die "Diatribe" (Münster 1987) 254. ZIESLER, J. Pauline Christianity (Oxford 1990) 89, 92f.

3:21   BOUSSET, W. Die Religion des Judentums im Späthellenistischen Zeitalter (1966 =1926) 144. BRUNNER, E. Dogmatik I (1946) 223, 296. II (1950) 192,

240. KÄSEMANN, E. Exegetische Versuche und Besinnungen (1964) II 185, 190. LJUNGMAN, H. Pistis (1964) 35-37. JÜNGEL, E. Paulus und Jesus (1966) 17, 25f., 28f., 31, 33, 43, 45, 48. SEEBERG, A. Der Katechismus der Urchristenheit (1966) 156, 166. VAN DÜLMEN, A. Die Theologie des Gesetzes bei Paulus (1968) 23, 83, 85f., 101, 132, 134, 140, 171, 213. KÄSE-MANN, E. New Testament Questions of Today (1969) 173, 178. BERGER, K. Die Gesetzesauslegung Jesu (1972) 209, 224-6. BEUTLER, J. Martyria (Frankfurt 1972) 171, 174, 204, 287. ZELLER, D. Juden und Heiden in der Mission des Paulus. Studien zum Römerbrief (Stuttgart 1973) 80f., 287. FRIEDRICH, G. "Das Gesetz des Glaubens Römer 3, 27" in Auf das Wort kommt es an. Gesammelte Aufsätze (Göttingen 1978) 115-19. HAYS, R. B. "Psalm 143 and the Logic of Romans 3," JBL 99 (1980) 107, 114f. VAN DER MINDE, H.-J. "Theologia crucis und Pneumaaussagen bei Paulus," Catholica 34 (1980) 133. THISELTON, A. C. The Two Horizons (Grand Rapids 1980) 420. WILLIAMS, S. K. "The 'Righteousness of God' in Romans," JBL 99 (1980) 242, 270f., 276, 284. HÖDL, L. "Gerechtigkeit" in TRE 12 (1984) 430. HÜBNER, H. Gottes Ich und Israel (Göttingen 1984) 63, 75f., 92f. STAAB, K. Pauluskommentare aus der griechischen Kirche (Münster ²1984) 61:8-12 Apoll; 487:22-23 Phot. DIETZFELBINGER, C. Die Berufung des Paulus als Ursprung seiner Theologie (Neukirchen 1985) 117f. KOCH, D.-A. Die Schrift als Zeuge des Evangeliums (Tübingen 1986) 342-44. PARKER, T. H. L. Commentaries on the Epistle to the Romans 1532-1542 (Edinburgh 1986) 144-46. BETZ, O. Jesus. Der Messias Israels (Tübingen 1987) 47, 342f. MERKLEIN, H. Studien zu Jesus und Paulus (Tübingen 1987) 5, 12, 23, 36f., 41, 63, 93f. OSTEN-SACKEN, P. VON DER, Evangelium und Tora: Aufsätze zu Paulus (München 1987) 9, 22, 95f., 199. SCHMELLER, TH. Paulus und die "Diatribe" (Münster 1987) 283. WERBICK, J. "Die Soteriologie zwischen 'christologischem Triumphalismus' und apokalyptischem Radikalismus" in I. Broer und J. Werbick, eds., "Auf Hoffnung hin sind wir erlöst" (Röm 8, 14) (Stuttgart 1987) 182-84. WEDDERBURN, A. J. M. The Reasons for Romans (Edinburgh 1988) 105, 116, 127-29. HOFIUS, O. Paulusstudien (Tübingen 1989) 68, 113, 126f., 150. LOHFINK, G. Studien zum Neuen Testament (Stuttgart 1989) 15. MARTIN, B. L. Christ and the Law in Paul (Leiden 1989) 15, 19, 22, 26f., 60, 64f., 95f., 124f., 127, 135f., 143, 146. BOCKMUEHL, M. N. A. Revelation and Mystery (Tübingen 1990) 135, 141f., 149, 152, 207, 229. ELLIOT, N. The Rhetoric of Romans (Sheffield 1990) 106, 147f., 151-5, 163, 205, 215, 227. OLIVEIRA, A. DE, Die Diakonie der Gerechtigkeit und der Versöhnung in der Apologie des 2. Korintherbriefes. Analyse und Auslegung von 2 Kor 2, 14-4, 6; 5, 11-6, 10 (Münster 1990) 44, 235. KRAUS, W. Der Tod Jesu als Heiligtumsweihe. Eine Untersuchung zum Umfeld der Sühnevorstellung in Römer 3, 25-26a (Neukirchen-Vluyn 1991) 12, 157, 168ff., 171n., 172, 184, 186. LONGENECKER, B. W. Eschatology and the Covenant. A Comparison of 4 Ezra and Romans 1-11 (Sheffield 1991) 195, 205-7, 223, 224.

3:21b-22a   SIMONIS, W. Der gefangene Paulus. Die Entstehung des sogenannten Römerbriefs und anderer urchristlicher Schriften in Rom (Frankfurt/ Bern/New York/ Paris 1990) 45f.

3:22-26   BOGUSLAWSKI, S. R. "Implicit Faith in Karl Rahner: A Pauline View," IThQ 51 (1985) 300-08.

3:22-24   OLIVEIRA, A. DE, Die Diakonie der Gerechtigkeit und der Versöhnung in der Apologie des 2. Korintherbriefes. Analyse und Auslegung von 2 Kor 2, 14-4, 6; 5, 11-6, 10 (Münster 1990) 159.

3:22-23   FURNISH, V. P. The Moral Teaching of Paul (Nashville 1979) 74.
3:22,26   HOWARD, G. "The 'Faith of Christ'," ET 85 (1974) 212-15.
3:22   BRUNNER, E. Dogmatik I (1946) 334. KÄSEMANN, E. Exegetische Versuche
          und Besinnungen (1964) II 191. LJUNGMAN, H. Pistis (1964) 38f. HAHN, F.
          Das Verständnis der Mission im Neuen Testament (1965) 92. JÜNGEL, E.
          Paulus und Jesus (1966) 17, 33, 43, 49. VAN DÜLMEN, A. Die Theologie des
          Gesetzes bei Paulus (1968) 23, 93, 140, 190, 194. KÄSEMANN, E. New Testa-
          ment Questions of Today (1969) 179. HAYS, R. B. "Psalm 143 and the Logic
          of Romans 3," JBL 99 (1980) 109, 114. WILLIAMS, S. K. "The 'Righteous-
          ness of God' in Romans," JBL 99 (1980) 271f., 274-76. JOHNSON, L. T.
          "Romans 3:21-26 and the Faith of Jesus," CBQ 44 (1982) 78f., 88. HAYS, R.
          B. The Faith of Jesus Christ (Chico CA 1983) 158, 160f., 171f., 175. STAAB,
          K. Pauluskommentare aus der griechischen Kirche (Münster ²1984) 362:1-6
          Genn. PARKER, T. H. L. Commentaries on the Epistle to the Romans 1532-
          1542 (Edinburgh 1986) 146f. GASTON, L. Paul and the Torah (Vancouver
          1987) 58, 118, 131, 226. RAMARONSON, L. "Trois études récentes sur 'la foi
          de Jésus' dans saint Paul," SciE 40 (1988) 365-77. HOOKER, M. D. "ΠΙΣ-
          ΤΙΣ ΧΡΙΣΤΟΥ," NTS 35 (1989) 321-42. JOHNSON, E. E. The Function of
          Apocalyptic and Wisdom Traditions in Romans 9-11 (Atlanta GA 1989) 118,
          149, 153, 186, 190, 199. MARTIN, B. L. Christ and the Law in Paul (Leiden
          1989) 65, 95, 115f., 124f., 127, 136. HOOKER, M. D. From Adam to Christ.
          Essays on Paul (Cambridge 1990) 166, 168.
3:22a   KRAUS, W. Der Tod Jesu als Heiligtumsweihe. Eine Untersuchung zum
          Umfeld der Sühnevorstellung in Römer 3, 25-26a (Neukirchen-Vluyn 1991)
          168, 172.
3:22b-23 KRAUS, W. Der Tod Jesu als Heiligtumsweihe. Eine Untersuchung zum Um-
          feld der Sühnevorstellung in Römer 3, 25-26a (Neukirchen-Vluyn 1991) 172.
3:23-26   DERRETT, J.D.M. Law in the New Testament (1970) 406n.3. FRIEDRICH, G.
          Die Verkündigung des Todes Jesu im Neuen Testament (Neukirchen-Vluyn
          1982) 57-67. ZIESLER, J. Pauline Christianity (Oxford 1990) 92-95.
3:23-26a HULTGREN, A. J. Paul's Gospel and Mission (Philadelphia 1985) 60-69.
3:23-25   SCHILLE, G. Frühchristliche Hymnen (1965) 60f. JERVELL, J. Imago Die
          (1960) 174, 180, 182, 205, 211, 298. SCHRAGE, W. Die konkreten Einzelge-
          bote in der paulinischen Paränese (1961) 95, 117, 193.
3:23-24   SANDERS, E. P. "On the Question of Fulfilling the Law in Paul and Rabbinic
          Judaism" in E. Bammel et al., eds., New Testament Studies in Honour of D.
          Daube (Oxford 1978) 105. STAAB, K. Pauluskommentare aus der griechischen
          Kirche (Münster ²1984) 487:24-33 Phot. SANDERS, E. P. Paul, the Law, and
          the Jewish People (London 1985) 23f.
3:23   VOLZ, P. Die Eschatologie der jüdischen Gemeinde (1934) 397. BRUNNER,
          E. Dogmatik II (1950) 143. Mensch im Widerspruch (1937) 148. HOOKER,
          M.D. "Adam in Romans I" NTS 6 (1959-60) 304f. KÄSEMANN, E. Exege-
          tische Versuche und Besinnungen I (1964) 96, 118. KERTELGE, K. "Rechtfer-
          tigung" bei Paulus (1967) 79. BRANDENBURGER, E. Fleisch und Geist
          (1968) 82, 83, 176. MERK, O. Handeln aus Glauben (1968) 6ff. VAN DÜL-
          MEN, A. Die Theologie des Gesetzes bei Paulus (1968) 85, 93, 160, 162, 198,
          216. BRANDENBURGER, E. Adam und Christus (Neukirchen-Vluyn 1962)
          175, 186f. METZGER, B. M. The Early Versions of the New Testament. Their
          Origin, Transmission, and Limitations (Oxford 1977) 81. DUNN, J. D. G.
          Christology in the Making (London 1980) 102f., 106, 109. STAAB, K. Paulus-
          kommentare aus der griechischen Kirche (Münster ²1984) 216:25-217:2 Sev.

3:24ff.

POBEE, J. S. Persecution and Martyrdom in the Theology of Paul (Sheffield 1985) 54, 74, 76. PARKER, T. H. L. Commentaries on the Epistle to the Romans 1532-1542 (Edinburgh 1986) 147f. BERGER, K. und COLPE, C., eds., Religionsgeschichtliches Textbuch zum Neuen Testament (Göttingen/Zürich 1987) 204. LAYTON, B. The Gnostic Scriptures (Garden City NY 1987) 264. OSTEN-SACKEN, P. VON DER, Evangelium und Tora: Aufsätze zu Paulus (München 1987) 19, 31, 224. VOIGT, S. "'Estao Faltos da Glória de Deus' (Rm 3, 23)—Ambivalencia no Pensar e Linguajar de Paulo," REB 47 (1987) 243-69. HOFIUS, O. Paulusstudien (Tübingen 1989) 6, 20, 85, 123, 131, 171. WEGENAST, K. Das Verständnis der Tradition bei Paulus und in den Deuteropaulien (1962) 76-80. MUELLER, C. Gottes Gerechtigkeit und Gottes Volk (1964) 108ff. BULTMANN, R. Theologie des Neuen Testaments (1965) 49. THYEN, H. Studien zer Sündenvergebung (1970) 95, 163ff., 189ff. PATSCH, H. Abendmahl und historischer Jesus (Stuttgart 1972) 322f. CONZELMANN, H. und LINDEMANN, A., Arbeitsbuch zum Neuen Testament (Tübingen 1975) 213.

3:24-26

KÄSEMANN, E. "Zum Verständnis von Römer 3, 24-26" ZNW 43 (19-50/51) 150-54. CERFAUX, L. Christ in the Theology of St. Paul (1959) passim. KÄSEMANN, E. Exegetische Versuche und Besinnungen (1964) I 96-100. SCHATTENMANN, J. "Das hymnische Fragment Römer 3 Vers 24-26" Studien Zum Neutestamentlichen Prosahymnus (1965) 22. KERTELGE, K. "Rechtfertigung" bei Paulus (1967) 48-62, 80-84, 302. VAN DÜLMEN, A. Die Theologie des Gesetzes bei Paulus (1968) 216. ZELLER, D. "Sühne und Langmut. Zur Traditions-geschichte von Röm 3, 24-26" ThPh 43 (1, '68) 51-75. THYEN, H. Studien zur Sündenvergebung (1970) 163-172. EICHHOLZ, G. Die Theologie des Paulus im Umriss (1972) 189ff., 191ff. SCHELKLE, K. H. Die Passion Jesu in der Verkündigung des Neuen Testaments (Heidelberg 1949) 57f., 143f., 155f., 185f., 192f. TALBERT, C. "A Non-Pauline Fragment at Romans 3, 24-26?" JBL 85 (1966) 287-96. LOHSE, E. Die Einheit des Neuen Testaments (Göttingen 1973) 115, 121, 220-23, 281. STUHLMACHER, P. "Zur neueren Exegese von Röm 3:24-26" in E. E. Ellis et al., eds., Jesus und Paulus (FS. W. G. Kümmel; Göttingen 1975) 315-33. WILLIAMS, S. K. Jesus' Death as Saving Event. The Background and Origin of a Concept (Missoula, Montana 1975) 5-56. FRIEDRICH, J. et al., eds., Rechtfertigung (FS. E. Käsemann; Tübingen/Göttingen 1976) 99, 104, 112-15, 116-18, 359, 371, 434. LANGKAMMER, H. "Ekspiacyjna formula wiary w Rz 3, 24-26 (Die Sühneformel in Röm 3, 24-26)," RTK 23 (1976) 29-38. FROITZHEIM, F. Christologie und Eschatologie bei Paulus (Würzburg 1979) 36f. FULLER, R. H. "Jesus Christ as Savior in the New Testament," Interp 35 (1981) 149. KLEINKNECHT, K. T. Der leidende Gerechtfertigte (Tübingen 1984) 182-88, 353. LÜHRMANN, D. "Gerechtigkeit" in TRE 12 (1984) 416. CRANFIELD, C. E. B. "Some Comments on Professosr J. D. G. Dunn's Christology in the Making with Special Reference to the Evidence of the Epistle to the Romans" in L. D. Hurst and N. T. Wright, eds., The Glory of Christ in the New Testament (FS. G. B. Caird; Oxford 1987) 277f. BECKER, J. Paulus. Der Apostel der Völker (Tübingen 1989) 300, 413, 425f. HOFIUS, O. Paulusstudien (Tübingen 1989) 36, 150. MARTIN, R. P. Reconciliation: A Study of Paul's Theology (Grand Rapids 1989) 81-89. COUSAR, C. B. A Theology of the Cross (Minneapolis 1990) 2, 54, 56-66, 79n. OLIVEIRA, A. DE, Die Diakonie der Gerechtigkeit und der Versöhnung in der Apologie des 2. Korintherbriefes. Analyse und Auslegung von 2 Kor 2, 14-4, 6; 5, 11-6, 10 (Münster 1990) 373. LOHSE, E. Die

Entstehung des Neuen Testaments (Stuttgart/Berlin/Köln ⁵1991) 24f. WAY, D. The Lordship of Christ. Ernst Käsemann's Interpretation of Paul's Theology (Oxford 1991) 205-7.

3:24-26a BOFF, L. Passion of Christ, Passion of the World (Maryknoll NY 1988) 75f.

3:24-25 SEIDENSTICKER, Ph. Lebendiges Opfer (1954) 160, 193, 167ff, 170ff, 215f. SANDMEL, S. The Genius of Paul (1958) 92-93. JÜNGEL, E. Paulus und Jesus (1966) 41, 45. WENNEMER, K. "Ἀπολύτρωσις in Romans 3, 24-25" Studiorum Paulinorum Congressus Internationalis Catholicus 1961 I (1963) 283-88. BRANDENBURGER, E. Adam und Christus (Neukirchen-Vluyn 1962) 233, 235, 237, 243ff., 255. SHIMADA, K. The Formulary Material in First Peter: A Study According to the Method of Traditionsgeschichte (ThD. Diss; Ann Arbor MI 1966) 245-49. LADD, G. E. A Theology of the New Testament (Grand Rapids 1974) 429, 448f. YOUNG, N. H. "Did St. Paul Compose Romans iii:24f.?" AusBR 22 (1974) 23-32. LINDEMANN, A. Die Aufhebung der Zeit. Geschichtsverständnis und Eschatologie im Epheserbrief (Gütersloh 1975) 144, 196f. DALY, R. J. Christian Sacrifice (Washington, D.C. 1978) 238-40. STRECKER, G. "'Biblische Theologie'? . . . " in D. Lührmann und G. Strecker, eds., Kirche (FS. G. Bornkamm; Tübingen 1980) 430f. RUCKSTUHL, E. "Gnade III" in TRE 13 (1984) 468. HULTGREN, A. J. Paul's Gospel and Mission (Philadelphia 1985) 56, 83. NEWTON, M. The Concept of Purity at Qumran and in the Letters of Paul (Cambridge 1985) 75-77. LAMPE, P. Die stadtrömischen Christen in den ersten beiden Jahrhunderten (Tübingen ²1989) 54.

3:24 BEST, E. One Body in Christ (1955) 6, 13n. DELLING, G. Die Taufe im Neuen Testament (1963) 99. KÄSEMANN, E. Exegetische Versuche und Besinnungen (1964) I 45, 299. THUESING, W. Per Christum in Deum (1965) 193f. JÜNGEL, E. Paulus und Jesus (1966) 49f. NICKELS, P. Targum and New Testament (1967) 68. MERK, O. Handeln aus Glauebn (1968) 6f, 11, 16f, 25, 27, 237. VAN DÜLMEN, A. Die Theologie des Gesetzes bei Paulus (1968) 85, 86, 191, 194, 197, 198, 213. MIKALSEN, T. The Traditio-Historical Place of 1 Peter in Light of 1:18-21" (Rüschlikon 1971) 33-36. LADD, G. E. A Theology of the New Testament (Grand Rapids 1974) 409, 433, 482. Ellis, E. E. und Grässer, E., eds., Jesus und Paulus (FS. W. G. Kümmel; Göttingen 1975) 268f., 315ff. HAYS, R. B. The Faith of Jesus Christ (Chico CA 1983) 173. PARKER, T. H. L. Commentaries on the Epistle to the Romans 1532-1542 (Edinburgh 1986) 149f. DAUTZENBERG, G. "Reich Gottes und Erlösung" in I. Broer und J. Werbick, eds., Auf Hoffnung hin sind wir erlöst (Röm 8, 14) (Stuttgart 1987) 59-61. MERKLEIN, H. Studien zu Jesus und Paulus (Tübingen 1987) 23, 33n.97, 36, 40, 52, 432. OLIVEIRA, A. DE, Die Diakonie der Gerechtigkeit und der Versöhnung in der Apologie des 2. Korintherbriefes. Analyse und Auslegung von 2 Kor 2, 14-4, 6; 5, 11-6, 10 (Münster 1990) 228, 393. ZIESLER, J. Pauline Christianity (Oxford 1990) 84, 86f., 91f. KRAUS, W. Der Tod Jesu als Heiligtumsweihe. Eine Untersuchung zum Umfeld der Sühne-vorstellung in Römer 3, 25-26a (Neukirchen-Vluyn 1991) 1, 159n., 174ff., 177, 183, 186.

3:25-28 PAGELS, E. H. The Gnostic Paul. Gnostic Exegesis of the Pauline Letters (Philadelphia 1975) 23.

3:25-26 MORRIS, L. The Apostolic Preaching of the Cross (Grand Rapids 1955) 170ff., 252f. DELLING, G. Studien zum Neuen Testament und zum hellenistischen Judentum. Gesammelte Aufsätze 1950-1968 (Göttingen 1970) 339-41. ZELLER, D. Juden und Heiden in der Mission des Paulus. Studien zum Römerbrief (Stutt-

gart 1973) 182ff. LOHSE, E. Grundriss der neutestamentlichen Theologie
(Stuttgart 1974) 54, 80f. RIDDERBOS, H. Paul. An Outline of His Theology
(Grand Rapids 1975) 186-92. VAN DER MINDE, H.-J. Schrift und Tradition
bei Paulus (München/Paderborn/Wien 1976) 58-64. SCHMITHALS, W. "Zur
Herkunft der gnostischen Elemente in der Sprache des Paulus" in B. Aland et
al., eds., Gnosis. (FS. H. Jonas; Göttingen 1978) 391-93. PIPER, J. "The
Demonstration of the Righteousness of God in Romans 3:25, 26," JSNT
7(1980) 2-32. WILLIAMS, S. K. "The 'Righteousness of God' in Romans,"
JBL 99 (1980) 243, 277. MEYER, B. F. "The Pre-Pauline Formula in Rom.
3.25-26a," NTS 29 (1983) 198-208. STAAB, K. Pauluskommentare aus der
griechischen Kirche (Münster ²1984) 423:8-11 Oek; 488:1-30 Phot. HULT-
GREN, A. J. Paul's Gospel and Mission (Philadelphia 1985) 21. RÄISÄNEN,
H. The Torah and Christ (Helsinki 1986) 278-81, 294. HÜBNER, H. "Paulusforschung seit 1945. Ein kritischer Literaturbericht" in ANRW II.25.4 (1987)
2709-2721. STUHLMACHER, P. "Jesus von Nazareth und die neutestamentliche Christologie im Lichte der Heiligen Schrift" in M. Klopfenstein et al.,
eds., Mitte der Schrift? Ein jüdischchristliches Gespräch. Texte des Berner
Symposions vom 6.-12. Januar 1985 (Bern etc. 1987) 82. MERKLEIN, H.
Studien zu Jesus und Paulus (Tübingen 1987) 31 n.90, 33-35, 39, 52, 73, 81,
83f., 94, 185f., 187f., 291. MACK, B. L. A Myth of Innocence (Philadelphia
1988) 106, 106n.6, 107, 109, 110n.9. STUHLMACHER, P. Jesus von Nazareth—Christus des Glaubens (Stuttgart 1988) 57. WEDDERBURN, A. J. M.
The Reasons for Romans (Edinburgh 1988) 109f., 117, 152. BREYTENBACH,
C. Versöhnung (Neukirchen-Vlyun 1989) 137, 166, 168f., 171, 187, 195.
SCHNELLE, U. Wandlungen im paulinischen Denken (Stuttgart 1989) 63.
WALTER, N. "Paul and the Early Christian Jesus-Tradition" in A. J. M. Wedderburn, ed., Paul and Jesus. Collected Essays (Sheffield 1989) 51-80, esp. 58f.,
64. BOCKMUEHL, M. N. A. Revelation and Mystery (Tübingen 1990) 130,
134. KRAUS, W. Der Tod Jesu als Heiligtumsweihe. Eine Untersuchung zum
Umfeld der Sühnevorstellung in Römer 3, 25-26a (Neukirchen-Vluyn 1991) 4n.,
5n., 8, 21, 31, 33, 40n., 42f., 45f., 55, 59, 69f., 91f., 96n., 97, 99, 105, 112,
149, 159n., 161, 163, 167, 170, 179, 184, 192n., 193ff., 197f., 228-35, 245,
259-62, 271, 276, 280ff. KLUMBIES, P.-G. Die Rede von Gott bei Paulus in
ihrem zeitgeschichtlichen Kontext (Göttingen 1992) passim.

3:25-26a   KRAUS, W. Der Tod Jesu als Heiligtumsweihe. Eine Untersuchung zum Umfeld der Sühnevorstellung in Römer 3, 25-26a (Neukirchen-Vluyn 1991).

3:25,26   WETTER, G.P. Der Vergeltungsgedanke bei Paulus (1912) 168ff. BRUNNER,
E. Dogmatik II (1950) 305, 342. FAHY, T. "Exegesis of Romans 3, 25f" IThQ
XXIII/1 (1956) 69-73. SCHRAGE, W. Die konkreten Einzelgebote in der
paulinischen Paränese (1961) 15, 64, 94, 99. KÄSEMANN, E. Exegetische Versuche und Besinnungen (1964) II 182, 189f. KÜMMEL, W.G. "*Paresis* and
endeixis. A Contribution to the Understanding of the Pauline Doctrine of Justification" JournTheolChurch 3 ('67) 1-13. GOPPELT, L. Christologie und Ethik
(1968) 155f. KÄSEMANN, E. New Testament Quesitons of Today ('69) 169,
177. GUETTGEMANNS, E. Offene Fragen zur Formgeschichte des Evangeliums (1970) 85. KESSLER, H. Die Theologische Bedeutung des Todes Jesu
(1970) 265-68. TAYLOR, V. New Testament Essays (1970) 127-39.

3:25   BRUNNER, E. Dogmatik I (1946), 203, 297, II (1950) 349. BUSCH, W.
Spuren zum Kreuz (1952) 168-72. DAVIES, W.D. Paul and Rabbinic Judaism
(1955) 232, 237-42. HEUSCHEN, J. "Rom 3, 25 in het licht van de Oudtesta-
mentlische Zoenvoorstelling" Revue ecclésiatique de liège 44 ('57) 65-79.

SCHOEPS, H.-J. Paulus (19-59) 133f. DALTON, W.J. "Expiation or Propitiation? (Rom. iii.25)" ABR 8 (1-4, '60) 3-18. DEAUT, R. "La Presentation Targuminque du Sacrifice D'Isaac et La Soteriologie Paulienne" Studiorum Paulinorum Congressus Internationalis Catholicus 1961 (1963) II 571-72. HAHN, F. Christologische Hoheitstitel (1963) 234. JÜNGEL, E. Paulus und Jesus ('66) 33, 41f. MCNAMARA, M. The New Testament and the Palestinian Targum to the Pentateuch (1966) 184 fn 95a. NICKELS, P. Targum and New Testament (1967) 68. MERK, O. Handeln aus Glauben (1968) 7, 10f., 22. ROMANIUK, C. "Le Livre de la Sagesse dans le Nouveau Testament" NTS 14 (1968) 498-514. THORNTON, T.C.G. "Propitiation or Expiation? *Hilasterion* and *Hilasmos* in Romans and 1 John" ET 80(2, '68) 53-55. VAN DÜLMEN, A. Die Theologie des Gesetzes bei Paulus (1968) 140, 157, 205, 216. KÄSEMANN, E. New Testament Questions of Today (1969) 178. Stuttgarter Bibelstudien, ed. H. Haag et al (1969). PLUTA, A. Gottes Bundestreue. Ein Schlüsselbegriff in Röm 3, 25a.LYONNET, S. Sin, Redemption and Sacrifice (1970) 155-59. WENGST, K. Christologische Formeln und Lieder des Urchristentums (1972) 87-90. SCHWEIZER, E. Erniedrigung und Erhöhung bei Jesus und seinen Nachfolgern (1962) §6e. MORRIS, L. "The Meaning of ἱλαστήριον in Romans III.25," NTS 2 (1955/56) 33ff. GREENWOOD, D. "Jesus as Hilasterion in Romans 3:25," BThB 3 (1973) 316-22. LADD, G. E. A Theology of the New Testament (Grand Rapids 1974) 423, 425, 431. ROBECK, C. M. "What is the Meaning of ἱλαστήριον in Romans 3:25?" Studies in Biblical Theology IV/1 (1974) 21-36. Ellis, E. E. und Grässer, E., eds., Jesus und Paulus (FS. W. G. Kümmel; Göttingen 1975) 315ff., 323ff. STRECKER, G. "Befreiung und Rechtfertigung. Zur Stellung der Rechtfertigungslehre in der Theologie des Paulus" in J. Friedrich et al., eds., Rechtfertigung (FS. E. Käsemann; Tübingen/Göttingen 1976) 501f. BERGER, K. "Hellenistisch-heidnische Prodigien und die Vorzeichen in der jüdischen und christlichen Apokalyptik" in ANRW II.23.2 (1980) 1436. HENGEL, M. The Atonement (London 1981) 45, 51, 91n.16. JOHNSON, L. T. "Romans 3:21-26 and the Faith of Jesus," CBQ 44 (1982) 78f., 88. HAYS, R. B. The Faith of Jesus Christ (Chico CA 1983) 172f. SCHNELLE, U. Gerechtigkeit und Christusgegenwart (Göttingen 1983) 67-72. STUHLMACHER, P. "Sühne oder Versöhnung? Randbemerkungen zu Gerhard Friedrichs Studie: 'Die Verkündigung des Todes Jesu im Neuen Testament'," in U. Luz und H. Weder, eds., Die Mitte des Neuen Testaments (FS. E. Schweizer; Göttingen 1983) 300-04. STAAB, K. Pauluskommentare aus der griechischen Kirche (Münster ²1984) 217:3-10 Sev. WENGST, K. "Glaubensbekenntnis(se) IV" in TRE 13 (1984) 395. HULTGREN, A. J. Paul's Gospel and Mission (Philadelphia 1985) 47-72. POBEE, J. S. Persecution and Martyrdom in the Theology of Paul (Sheffield 1985) 58, 61, 75f. BREYTENBACH, C. "Probleme rondom die interpretasie van die 'versoeningsuitsprake' by Paulus (Problems on the interpretation of reconciliation dictions in Paul)," HTS 42 (1986) 696-704. PARKER, T. H. L. Commentaries on the Epistle to the Romans 1532-1542 (Edinburgh 1986) 150-54. OBIJOLE, B. "St. Paul's Understanding of the Death of Christ in Romans 3:25: The Yoruba Hermeneutical Perspective," ATJ 15 (1986) 196-201. SEEBASS, H. "Gerechtigkeit Gottes," JBTh 1 (1986) 123. DOBBELER, A. VON, Glaube als Teilhabe (Tübingen 1987) 77-84. BERGER, K. und COLPE, C., eds., Religionsgeschichtliches Textbuch zum Neuen Testament (Göttingen/ Zürich 1987) 204f. FRYER, N. S. L. "The Meaning and Translation of *Hilasterion* in Romans 3:25," EQ 59 (1987) 99-116. GUNTON, C. "Christ the Sacrifice: Aspects of the Language and Imagery of the Bible" in

L. D. Hurst and N. T. Wright, eds., The Glory of Christ in the New Testament
(FS. G. B. Caird; Oxford 1987) 229-38, esp. 237. LUZ, U. "Paulinische Theologie als Biblische Theologie" in M. Klopfenstein et al., eds., Mitte der
Schrift? Ein jüdisch-christliches Gespräch. Texte des Berner Symposions vom
6.-12. Januar 1985 (Bern etc. 1987) 119-47, esp. 138f. MERKLEIN, H. Studien
zu Jesus und Paulus (Tübingen 1987) 36, 51n.129, 188, 191, 440n.121. CON-
ZELMANN, H. and LINDEMANN, A. Interpreting the New Testament
(Peabody MA 1988) 93f. FULLER, R. H. "Scripture, Tradition and Priesthood"
in R. Bauckham and B. Drewery, eds., Scripture, Tradition and Reason (FS. R.
P. C. Hanson; Edinburgh 1988) 110f. JONGE, M. DE, Christology in Context.
The Earliest Christian Response to Jesus (Philadelphia 1988) 133, 150, 227n.13,
240n.27, 241n.35. BREYTENBACH, C. Versöhnung (Neukirchen-Vlyun 1989)
7f., 16, 18, 21, 24, 27, 33f., 97-99, 157n., 158, 165-170, 190, 195, 202f.
KLAUCK, H.-J. Gemeinde, Amt, Sakrament (Würzburg 1989) 353. LOHFINK,
G. Studien zum Neuen Testament (Stuttgart 1989) 15. MARTIN, B. L. Christ
and the Law in Paul (Leiden 1989) 15f., 26, 60, 89, 95, 124-27. KOLLMANN,
B. Ursprung und Gestalten der frühchristlichen Mahlfeier (Göttingen 1990)
65n.132, 182. OLIVEIRA, A. DE, Die Diakonie der Gerechtigkeit und der
Versöhnung in der Apologie des 2. Korintherbriefes. Analyse und Auslegung
von 2 Kor 2, 14-4, 6; 5, 11-6, 10 (Münster 1990) 377, 392f. KRAUS, W. Der
Tod Jesu als Heiligtumsweihe. Eine Untersuchung zum Umfeld der Sühnevorstellung in Römer 3, 25-26a (Neukirchen-Vluyn 1991) 1n., 2, 17n., 21, 31f.,
95ff., 99, 102, 104, 107f., 110, 112f., 151f., 154n., 156, 159ff., 166, 179n.,
187n., 189, 193, 233n., 275n., 277, 281f. LONGENECKER, B. W. "*Pistis* in
Romans 3.25. Neglected Evidence for the 'Faithfulness of Christ'?" NTS 39
(1993) 478-80.

3:25a   KRAUS, W. Der Tod Jesu als Heiligtumsweihe. Eine Untersuchung zum Umfeld der Sühnevorstellung in Römer 3, 25-26a (Neukirchen-Vluyn 1991) 91,
152f., 261.

3:26   BRUNNER, E. Dogmatik I (1946) 334, II (1950) 332. LJUNGMAN, H. Pistis
(1964) 38-40. JÜNGEL, E. Paulus und Jesus (1966) 33, 41f, 44. KERTELGE,
K. "Rechtfertigung" bei Paulus (1967) 136, 161. BLACKMAN, C. "Romans
3:26b: A Question of Translation" JBL 87 (2, '68) 203-4. VAN DÜLMEN, A.
Die Theologie des Gesetzes bei Paulus (1968) 85, 140, 190, 194, 212. KÄSE-
MANN, E. New Testament Questions of Today (1969) 177. MAUSER, U.
Gottesbild und Menschwerdung (1971) 131, 133, 146f. WILLIAMS, S. K. "The
'Righteousness of God' in Romans," JBL 99 (1980) 277f. JOHNSON, L. T.
"Romans 3:21-26 and the Faith of Jesus," CBQ 44 (1982) 78, 80, 88. HAYS,
R. B. The Faith of Jesus Christ (Chico CA 1983) 158, 160, 164, 171, 175, 191,
238. PRYOR, J. W. "Paul's Use of Iesous—A Clue for the Translation of
Romans 3:26?" Colloquium 16 (1983) 31-45. STUHLMACHER, P. "Paulus und
Luther" in E. Grässer und O. Merk, eds., Glaube und Eschatologie (FS. W. G.
Kümmel; Tübingen 1985) 285-302, esp. 293ff. PARKER, T. H. L. Commentar-
ies on the Epistle to the Romans 1532-1542 (Edinburgh 1986) 154f. MERK-
LEIN, H. Studien zu Jesus und Paulus (Tübingen 1987) 36-38, 42, 61, 188,
378. RAMARONSON, L. "Trois études récentes sur 'la foi de Jésus' dans saint
Paul," SciE 40 (1988) 365-77. HOFIUS, O. Paulusstudien (Tübingen 1989) 126,
147, 150, 154, 172. HOOKER, M. D. "ΠΙΣΤΙΣ ΧΡΙΣΤΟΥ," NTS 35 (1989)
321-42. MARTIN, B. L. Christ and the Law in Paul (Leiden 1989) 115, 124-27.
HOOKER, M. D. From Adam to Christ. Essays on Paul (Cambridge 1990)
168f.

3:26b KRAUS, W. Der Tod Jesu als Heiligtumsweihe. Eine Untersuchung zum Umfeld der Sühnevorstellung in Römer 3, 25-26a (Neukirchen-Vluyn 1991) 171, 185f.

3:27–4:25 GIBLIN, C.H. In Hope of God's Glory (1970) 353-64. STOWERS, S. K. The Diatribe and Paul's Letter to the Romans (Chico CA 1981) 155-74. SANDERS, E. P. Paul, the Law, and the Jewish People (London 1985) 32-36.

3:27ff. HAHN, F. Das Verständnis der Mission im Neuen Testament (1965) 88.

3:27-31 HÜBNER, H. Das Gesetz bei Paulus (Göttingen 1978) 118-29. LAYMAN, F. D. Paul's Use of Abraham. An Approach to Paul's Understanding of History (diss. Ann Arbor MI 1978) 61f. ROBINSON, J. A. T. Wrestling with Romans (London 1979) 49-52. SCHMITT, R. Gottesgerechtigkeit—Heilsgeschichte—Israel in der Theologie des Paulus (Frankfurt/Bern/ New York/Nancy 1984) 24-26. SNODGRASS, K. "Spheres of Influence. A Possible Solution to the Problem of Paul and the Law," JSNT 32 (1988) 93-113. LAMBRECHT, J. and THOMPSON, R. W. Justification by Faith. The Implications of Romans 3:27-31 (Wilmington DE 1989). OSTEN-SACKEN, P. VON DER, Die Heiligkeit der Tora (München 1989) 23-33.

3:27-30 KOCH, D.-A. Die Schrift als Zeuge des Evangeliums (Tübingen 1986) 343f. THOMPSON, R. W. "The Inclusion of the Gentiles in Rom 3, 27-30," Biblica 69 (1988) 543-46.

3:27-28 HÜBNER, H. Das Gesetz bei Paulus (Göttingen 1978) 95-98. THISELTON, A. C. The Two Horizons (Grand Rapids 1980) 422f. LIEBERS, R. Das Gesetz als Evangelium (Zürich 1989) 46-49. OSTEN-SACKEN, P. VON DER, Römer 8 als Beispiel paulinischer Soteriologie (Göttingen 1975) 245ff.

3:27 BRUNNER, E. Mensch im Widerspruch (1937) 150. FRIEDRICH, G. "Das Gesetz des Glaubens Röm. 3, 27" THZ 10 ('54) 401-17. JÜNGEL, E. Paulus und Jesus (1966) 29, 55, 57, 270. VAN DÜLMEN, A. Die Theologie des Gesetzes bei Paulus (1968) 25.52, 216. SCHNEIDER, N. Die rhetorische Eigenart der paulinischen Antithese (1970) 95-100. FRIEDRICH, G. "Das Gesetz des Glaubens Römer 3, 27" in Auf das Wort kommt es an. Gesammelte Aufsätze (Göttingen 1978) 107-22. RÄISÄNEN, H. "Das 'Gesetz des Glaubens' (Röm. 3.27) und das 'Gesetz des Geistes' (Röm. 8.2)," NTS 26 (1979) 101-17. BLANK, J. Paulus. Von Jesus zum Christentum (München 1982) 115. HAYS, R. B. The Faith of Jesus Christ (Chico CA 1983) 180. RÄISÄNEN, H. Paul and the Law (Tübingen 1983) 16, 42, 50-53, 78, 80, 169-71, 238. HÜBNER, H. Gottes Ich und Israel (Göttingen 1984) 62, 72f. STAAB, K. Pauluskommentare aus der griechischen Kirche (Münster ²1984) 117:13-22 ThM. HÜBNER, H. "Was heisst bei Paulus 'Werke des Gesetzes'?" in E. Grässer und O. Merk, eds., Glaube und Eschatologie (FS. W. G. Kümmel; Tübingen 1985) 131f. LAMBRECHT, J. "Why is Boasting Excluded? A Note on Rom 3, 27 and 4, 2," EphT 61 (1985) 365-69. SANDERS, E. P. Paul, the Law, and the Jewish People (London 1985) 15n.26, 32, 44, 57 n.66, 59n.80, 62n.130, 116n.14, 146, 164n.25. SCHNABEL, E. J. Law and Wisdom from Ben Sira to Paul (Tübingen 1985) 266, 268, 285-87, 293f., 314, 341. PARKER, T. H. L. Commentaries on the Epistle to the Romans 1532-1542 (Edinburgh 1986) 155f. RÄISÄNEN, H. The Torah and Christ (Helsinki 1986) 13, 34, 95-118, 119-21, 143-47, 363. THOMPSON, R. W. "Paul's Double Critique of Jewish Boasting: A Study of Rom 3, 27 in Its Context," Biblica 67 (1986) 520-31. HÜBNER, H. "Paulusforschung seit 1945. Ein kritischer Literaturbericht" in ANRW II.25.4 (1987) 2679, 2682, 2684, 2688. DOWNING, F. G. Christ and the Cynics (Sheffield 1988) 188. HOFIUS, O. Paulusstudien (Tübingen 1989) 50, 68. LIEBERS, R. Das

Gesetz als Evangelium (Zürich 1989) 69-71. MARTIN, B. L. Christ and the Law in Paul (Leiden 1989) 15, 26f., 64, 67, 93, 114, 116, 127, 136. OSTEN-SACKEN, P. VON DER, Die Heiligkeit der Tora (München 1989) 13-19. SCHNELLE, U. Wandlungen im paulinischen Denken (Stuttgart 1989) 65. CALLAN, T. Psychological Perspectives on the Life of Paul (Lewiston/Queenston/Lampeter 1990) 25. DAVIES, G. N. Faith and Obedience in Romans. A Study in Romans 1-4 (Sheffield 1990) 115-39. DUNN, J. D. G. Jesus, Paul and the Law (London 1990) 200, 211, 224, 235n.52, 238. LONGENECKER, B. W. Eschatology and the Covenant. A Comparison of 4 Ezra and Romans 1-11 (Sheffield 1991) 207-9, 209nn.3, 4, 210-2, 216f., 224, 229, 231, 233, 241, 259, 272, 274.

3:28   JÜNGEL, E. Paulus und Jesus (1966) 17, 30, 43f, 48, 57. KERT-ELGE, K. "Rechtfertigung" bei Paulus (1967) 126, 161. VAN DÜLMEN, A. Die Theologie des Gesetzes bei Paulus (1968) 23, 87f., 101, 174, 191. EICHHOLZ, G. Die Theologie des Paulus im Umriss (1972) 196f, 211f. BORSE, U. Der Standort des Galaterbriefes (Köln 1972) 122f, A490. THISELTON, A. C. The Two Horizons (Grand Rapids 1980) 409. STAAB, K. Pauluskommentare aus der griechischen Kirche (Münster [2]1984) 117:23-28 ThM. BEKER, J. C. "Paul's Letter to the Romans as Model for a Biblical Theology: Some Preliminary Observations" in J. T. Butler et al., eds., Understanding the Word. (FS. B. W. Anderson; Sheffield 1985) 359-67. SCHNABEL, E. J. Law and Wisdom from Ben Sira to Paul (Tübingen 1985) 285-87, 293. PARKER, T. H. L. Commentaries on the Epistle to the Romans 1532-1542 (Edinburgh 1986) 156. RÄISÄNEN, H. The Torah and Christ (Helsinki 1986) 111f. GASTON, L. Paul and the Torah (Vancouver 1987) 13, 69, 103. HOFIUS, O. "'Rechtfertigung des Gottlosen' als Thema biblischer Theologie," JBTh 2 (1987) 79-105, esp. 85f. MERKLEIN, H. Studien zu Jesus und Paulus (Tübingen 1987) 37, 40-42, 44. JOHNSON, E. E. The Function of Apocalyptic and Wisdom Traditions in Romans 9-11 (Atlanta GA 1989) 120, 187, 190. MARTIN, B. L. Christ and the Law in Paul (Leiden 1989) 15, 26f., 116, 127, 138, 143, 146. MARXSEN, W. "Christliche" und christliche Ethik im Neuen Testament (Gütersloh 1989) 30. SCHNELLE, U. Wandlungen im paulinischen Denken (Stuttgart 1989) 65. DAVIES, G. N. Faith and Obedience in Romans. A Study in Romans 1-4 (Sheffield 1990) 119-21. CRANFIELD, C. E. B. "'The Works of the Law' in the Epistle to the Romans," JSNT 43 (1991) 89-101.

3:29-31   PAGELS, E. H. The Gnostic Paul. Gnostic Exegesis of the Pauline Letters (Philadelphia 1975) 23f.

3:29-30   BOUSSET, W. Die Religion des Judentums im Spöthellenistischen Zeitalter (1966 =1926) 319. KÄSEMANN, E. Exegetsiche Versuche und Besinnungen (1964) II 197. KÄSEMANN, E. New Testament Questions of Today (1969) 189. DEMKE, C. "'Ein Gott und viele Herren.' Die Verkündigung des einen Gottes in den Briefen des Paulus," EvTh 36 (1976) 473-84. GRÄSSER, E. Der Alte Bund im Neuen (Tübingen 1985) 65, 254ff. FREUND, G. und STEGE-MANN, E., eds., Theologische Brosamen für Lothar Steiger (DBAT 5; Heidelberg 1985) 393. DOWNING, F. G. Christ and the Cynics (Sheffield 1988) 188.

3:29   VAN DÜLMEN, A. Die Theologie des Gesetzes bei Paulus (1968) 84.85, 88, 93, 102, 124, 217, 222.

3:30   TURNER, N. Grammatical Insights into the New Testament (1965) 107ff. MAUSER, U. "Galater III.20: Die Universalität des Heils" NTS 13 (1966-67) 267ff. KERTELGE, K. "Rechtfertigung" bei Paulus (1967) 124, 161, 189. VAN DÜLMEN, A. Die Theologie des Gesetzes bei Paulus (1968) 23, 36, 84, 85, 88,

195, 217, 226. GIBLIN, C. H. "Three Monotheistic Texts in Paul," CBQ 37 (1975) 527-47. FRIEDRICH, G. "Das Gesetz des Glaubens Römer 3, 27" in Auf das Wort kommt es an. Gesammelte Aufsätze (Göttingen 1978) 120f. GRÄSSER, E. "'Ein einziger ist Gott' (Röm 3, 30). Zum christologischen Gottesverständnis bei Paulus" in N. Lohfink et al., eds., "Ich will euer Gott werden." Beispiele biblischen Redens von Gott (Stuttgart ²1982) 177-205. GRÄSSER, E. Der Alte Bund im Neuen (Tübingen 1985) 231-58. MAUSER, U. "Εἷς θεός und Μόνος θεός in Biblischer Theologie," JBTh 1 (1986) 80f. STOWERS, S. K. "'Εκ πίστεως and διὰ τῆς πίστεως in Romans 3:30," JBL 108 (1989) 665-74. LOHSE, E. Die Entstehung des Neuen Testaments (Stuttgart/Berlin/Köln ⁵1991) 20.

3:31   BANDSTRA, A.J. The Law and the Elements of the World. An Exegetical Study in Aspects of Paul's Teaching (1964) 99f. JÜNGEL, E. Paulus und Jesus (1966) 61, 271. KERTELGE, K. "Rechtfertigung" bei Paulus (1967) 202. VAN DÜLMEN, A. Die Theologie des Gesetzes bei Paulus (1968) 20, 72, 84, 88, 100, 101. LUZ, U. Das Geschichtsverständnis des Paulus (1968) 171ff. ZELLER, D. Juden und Heiden in der Mission des Paulus. Studien zum Römerbrief (Stuttgart 1973) 99. KÜMMEL, W. G. Römer 7 und das Bild des Menschen im Neuen Testament (München 1974) 5f. LOHSE, E. "'Wir richten das Gesetz auf!' Glaube und Thora im Römerbrief" in Treue zur Thora (FS. G. Harder; Berlin 1977) 65-71. FRIEDRICH, G. "Das Gesetz des Glaubens Römer 3, 27" in Auf das Wort kommt es an. Gesammelte Aufsätze (Göttingen 1978) 121. RHYNE, C. T. Faith Establishes the Law (Chico CA 1981). HAYS, R. B. The Faith of Jesus Christ (Chico CA 1983) 245. RÄISÄNEN, H. Paul and the Law (Tübingen 1983) 28, 63, 69-72, 86, 88, 201, 213, 221, 223. SCHULZ, S. "Zur Gesetzestheologie des Paulus im Blick auf Gerhard Ebelings Galaterbrief-Auslegung" in H. F. Geisser und W. Mostert, eds., Wirkungen hermeneutischer Theologie (FS. G. Ebeling; Zürich 1983) 88. MOHRLANG, R. Matthew and Paul (Cambridge 1984) 26, 29, 42. SCHNABEL, E. J. Law and Wisdom from Ben Sira to Paul (Tübingen 1985) 269f., 281, 288, 294, 297. RÄISÄNEN, H. The Torah and Christ (Helsinki 1986) 106, 181. MERKLEIN, H. Studien zu Jesus und Paulus (Tübingen 1987) 12, 93, 106, 443n.132. SCHMELLER, TH. Paulus und die "Diatribe" (Münster 1987) 287, 327. THOMPSON, R. W. "The Alleged Rabbinic Background of Rom 3, 31," EphT 63 (1987) 136-48. HOFIUS, O. Paulusstudien (Tübingen 1989) 66-8, 98, 172. LAMPE, P. Die stadtrömischen Christen in den ersten beiden Jahrhunderten (Tübingen ²1989) 55. DAVIES, G. N. Faith and Obedience in Romans. A Study in Romans 1-4 (Sheffield 1990) 139-41. DUNN, J. D. G. Jesus, Paul and the Law (London 1990) 106, 209, 211, 224, 238, 240, 241 n.7. LOHSE, E. Die Entstehung des Neuen Testaments (Stuttgart/Berlin/Köln ⁵1991) 12. LONGENECKER, B. W. Eschatology and the Covenant. A Comparison of 4 Ezra and Romans 1-11 (Sheffield 1991) 207-11, 223, 229, 248, 271f., 274.

4   SANDAY & HEADLAM "The History of Abraham as treated by St. Paul and by St. James" The Epistle to the Romans (1902) 102-6. FAHY, T. "Faith and the Law. Epistle to the Romans, Ch.4" IThQ 28 (3, '61) 207-14. JACOB, E. "Abraham et sa signification pour la foi chrétienne" RHPhR 42 (2-3, '62) 148-56. DEAUT, R. "La Presentation Targumique du Sacrifice D'Isaac et La Soteriologie Paulienne" Studiorum Paulinorum Congressus Internationalis Catholicus 1961 II (1963) 572-73. HAHN, F. Christologische Hoheitstitel (1963) 243. KLEIN, G. "Römer 4 und die Idee der Heilsgeschichte" EvTh 23 (8, '63) 424-

47. KÄSEMANN, E. Exegetische Versuche und Besinnungen II (1964) 183f. GOPPELT, L. "Paulus und die Heilsgeschichte: Schlussfolgerungen aus Röm. IV and I. Kor. X. 1-13" NTS 13 (1, '66) 31-42. KLEIN, G. "Heil und Geschichte nach Römer IV" NTS 13 (1, '66) 43-47. GOPPELT, L. Christologie und Ethik (1968) 220f. LUZ, U. Das Geschichtsverständnis des Paulus (1968) 168-86. VAN DÜLMEN, A. Die Theologie des Gesetzes bei Paulus (1968) 84, 86, 88, 185. KLEIN, G. "Römer 4 und die Idee der Heilsgeschichte" Reconstrucktion und Interpretation (1969) 145-69. KÄSEMANN, E. "Der Glaube Abrahams in Römer 4" Paulinische Perspektiven (1969) 140-77. KÄSEMANN, E. New Testament Questions of Today (1969) 70, 171. SANDMEL, S. Philo's Place in Judaism (1971). HAHN, F. "Genesis 15:6 im Neuen Testament" Probleme biblischer Theologie (1971) 90-107. MAYER, G. "Aspekte des Abrahambildes in der hellenistisch–jüdischen Literatur" EvTh XXXII (1972) 118-27. ZIESLER, J.A. The Meaning of Righteousness in Paul (1972) 195f. WILCKENS, U. "Die Rechtfertigung Abrahams nach Römer 4" in R. Rendtorff et al., eds., Studien zur Theologie der alttestamentlichen Überlieferungen (Neukirchen 1961) 111-27. BURCHARD, C. Unter-suchungen zu Joseph und Aseneth (Tübingen 1965) 121. ZELLER, D. Juden und Heiden in der Mission des Paulus. Studien zum Römerbrief (Stuttgart 1973) 99ff. CAVALLIN, H. C. C. Life After Death. Paul's Argument for the Resurrection of the Dead in I Cor 15. Part I: An Enquiry into the Jewish Background (Lund 1974) 3, 11, 5. CONZELMANN, H. und LINDEMANN, A., Arbeitsbuch zum Neuen Testament (Tübingen 1975) 24. SANDERS, J. T. Ethics in the New Testament (Philadelphia 1975) 117-19. SCHMITHALS, W. Der Römerbrief als historisches Problem (Gütersloh 1975) 15f. VIA, D. O. Kerygma and Comedy in the New Testament (Philadelphia 1975) 51, 57-59, 69. FRIEDRICH, J. et al., eds., Rechtfertigung (FS. E. Käsemann; Tübingen/Göttingen 1976) 13, 53, 84, 219f., 221, 226, 234, 236, 493. GOPPELT, L. Theologie des Neuen Testaments II: Vielfalt und Einheit des apostolischen Christuszeugnisses (Göttingen 1976) 383. VAN DER MINDE, H.-J. Schrift und Tradition bei Paulus (München/Paderborn/ Wien 1976) 68-106. SCHILLEBEECKX, E. Christus und die Christen (Freiburg/Basel/Wien 1977) 138-40; Christ: The Christian Experience in the Modern World (London 1980) 147-50. BLOCH, R. "Midrash" in W. S. Green, ed., Approaches to Ancient Judaism: Theory and Practice (Missoula 1978) 48. BRUCE, F. F. The Time is Fulfilled (Exeter 1978) 68-70. ELLIS, E. E. Prophecy and Hermeneutic in Early Christianity (Tübingen 1978) 217f. HÜBNER, H. Das Gesetz bei Paulus (Göttingen 1978) 44-50, 98-103. LAYMAN, F. D. Paul's Use of Abraham. An Approach to Paul's Understanding of History (diss. Ann Arbor MI 1978). BYRNE, B. 'Sons of God'—'Seed of Abraham'. A Study of the Idea of the Sonship of God of All Christians in Paul against the Jewish Background (Rome 1979) 88, 91, 102, 148f., 188. LARSSON, E. "Theology in Conflict," NTT 80 (1979) 65-88. OLLROG, W.-H. Paulus und seine Mitarbeiter (Neukirchen-Vluyn 1979) 136, 214. ROBINSON, J. A. T. Wrestling with Romans (London 1979) 52-56. ROLOFF, J. Neues Testament (Neukirchen-Vluyn 1979) 174-76. VIELHAUER, P. "Paulus und das Alte Testament" in Oikodome [G. Klein, ed.] (München 1979) 204, 207-09. CLARK, K. W. "The Israel of God" in The Gentile Bias and other Essays [selected by J. L. Sharpe III] (Leiden 1980) 22f., 24f., 28. GASTON, L. "Abraham and the Righteousness of God," HBTh 2 (1980) 39-68. HARRINGTON, D. J. God's People in Christ (Philadelphia 1980) 52-55. LIKENG, P. BITJICK. "La paternité d'Abraham selon Rom. 4, 1-25," RATh 4 (1980) 153-

86. MEILE, E. "Isaaks Opferung. Eine Note an Nils Alstrup Dahl," StTh 34 (1980) 111-28. RHYNE, C. T. Faith Establishes the Law (Chico CA 1981) 30-32, 75-89. STOWERS, S. K. The Diatribe and Paul's Letter to the Romans (Chico CA 1981) 168-174. BASSLER, J. M. Divine Impartiality (Chico CA 1982) 158-160. KLAIBER, W. Rechtfertigung und Gemeinde (Göttingen 1982) 154-58. GORDAY, P. Principles of Patristic Exegesis: Romans 9-11 in Origen, John Chrysostom, and Augustine (New York/Toronto 1983) 61-64, 115f., 158f. HAYS, R. B. The Faith of Jesus Christ (Chico CA 1983) 188, 198-200. PATTE, D. Paul's Faith and the Power of the Gospel (Philadelphia 1983) xxi, 190, 194, 208, 214-22, 243, 287, 379n.18. HÜBNER, H. Gottes Ich und Israel (Göttingen 1984) 13, 25, 89, 93, 99, 133. DIETZFELBINGER, C. Die Berufung des Paulus als Ursprung seiner Theologie (Neukirchen 1985) 54, 116, 130, 142. PETERSEN, N. R. Rediscovering Paul. Philemon and the Sociology of Paul's Narrative World (Philadelphia 1985) 223ff. SANDERS, E. P. Paul, the Law, and the Jewish People (London 1985) 24f., 62nn.121, 125;64n.147, 76, 102, 127, 154, 163n.18, 174. KOCH, D.-A. Die Schrift als Zeuge des Evangeliums (Tübingen 1986) 97f., 224-26, 272f., 288f., 304f., 307ff., 312-15, 323f., 343ff., 351f. LÜBKING, H.-M. Paulus und Israel im Römerbrief (Frankfurt/Bern/New York 1986) 36-40. RÄISÄNEN, H. The Torah and Christ (Helsinki 1986) 80ff. SEGUNDO, J. L. The Humanist Christology of Paul [trans. J. Drury], Jesus of Nazareth Yesterday and Today 3 (Maryknoll, N.Y. 1986) 59-75. WATSON, F. Paul, Judaism and the Gentiles (Cambridge 1986) 135-42. DOBBELER, A. VON, Glaube als Teilhabe (Tübingen 1987) 133-45, 157-70. DUNN, J. D. G. "Paul's Epistle to the Romans: An Analysis of Structure and Argument" in ANRW II.25.4 (1987) 2854f. GASTON, L. Paul and the Torah (Vancouver 1987) 14, 60-62, 123-26, 127. HOFIUS, O. "'Rechtfer-tigung des Gottlosen' als Thema biblischer Theologie," JBTh 2 (1987) 79-105. OSTEN-SACKEN, P. VON DER, Evangelium und Tora: Aufsätze zu Paulus (München 1987) 9f., 84, 241. WIESER, F. E. Die Abrahamvorstellungen im Neuen Testament (Bern/Frankfurt/New York 1987) 56-67, 79-81. CONZELMANN, H. and LINDE-MANN, A. Interpreting the New Testament (Peabody MA 1988) 20, 132. GUERRA, A. J. "Romans 4 as Apologetic Theology," HThR 81 (1988) 251-70. MARTIN, B. L. Christ and the Law in Paul (Leiden 1989) 13, 15, 27, 46, 62, 93, 136, 143f. THIELMAN, F. From Plight to Solution (Leiden 1989) 91, 97-99. DAVIES, G. N. Faith and Obedience in Romans. A Study in Romans 1-4 (Sheffield 1990) 143-72. ELLIOT, N. The Rhetoric of Romans (Sheffield 1990) 112, 157-65, 216-22, 226f., 278, 287. HOOKER, M. D. From Adam to Christ. Essays on Paul (Cambridge 1990) 83, 168-72. HEIDE, A. VAN DER. "The Call of Abraham as Read by Jews and Christians," Concilium (1991) 13-26. SILBERMAN, L. H. "Paul's Midrash: Reflections on Romans 4" in J. T. Carroll et al., eds., Faith and History (FS. P. W. Meyer; Atlanta 1991) 99ff. HARRISVILLE, R. A. The Figure of Abraham in the Epistles of St. Paul. In the Footsteps of Abraham (San Francisco 1992) passim.

4:1ff.   HAHN, F. Das Verständnid der Mission im Neuen Testament ('65) 88. JÜNGEL, E. Paulus und Jesus (1966) 52. ROKÉAH, D. "A Note on the Philo-logical Aspect of Paul's Theory of Faith," ThZ 47 (1991) 299-306.

4:1-25   YUBERO, D. "Presencia secular de Abraham" CultBibl ('55) 128/129 8-15. BARRETT, C.K. From First Adam to Last (1962) 30-33, 35f, 41f. HAYS, R. B. Echoes of Scripture in the Letters of Paul (New Haven/ London 1989) 54-7. ROLOFF, J. Exegetische Verantwortung in der Kirche (Göttingen 1990) 243-8. ELLIS, E. E. The Old Testament in Early Christianity (Tübingen 1991) 90, 98f.

4:1-22   VAN DER MINDE, H.-J. Schrift und Tradition bei Paulus (München/Paderborn/Wien 1976) 78-89.

4:1-12   JEREMIAS, J. Abba (1966) 271-72. MÜLLER, H. Die Auslegung alttestamentlichen Geschichtsstoffs bei Paulus (Diss; Halle-Wittenberg 1960) 96-104. VAN DER MINDE, H.-J. Schrift und Tradition bei Paulus (München/Paderborn/Wien 1976) 68-72. HOFIUS, O. Paulusstudien (Tübingen 1989) 67f., 128.

4:1-8   SCHWEIZER, E. u.a., eds., Evangelisch—Katholischer Kommentar zum Neuen Testament I (1969) 65-67. WILCKENS, U. "Was heisst bei Paulus: 'Aus Werken des Gesetzes wird kein Mensch gerecht'?" Evangelisch—Katholischer Kommentar zum Neuen Testament I (1969) 51-77. LONA, H. E. Abraham in Johannes 8 (Bern/Frankfurt 1976) 349-53. LAYMAN, F. D. Paul's Use of Abraham. An Approach to Paul's Understanding of History (diss. Ann Arbor MI 1978) 64-70, 137f., 197f. MOXNES, H. Theology in Conflict (Leiden 1980) 41f., 109-11, 228. THISELTON, A. C. The Two Horizons (Grand Rapids 1980) 399. RUCKSTUHL, E. "Gnade III" in TRE 13 (1984) 468. SCHMITT, R. Gottesgerechtigkeit—Heilsgeschichte—Israel in der Theologie des Paulus (Frankfurt/Bern/New York/Nancy 1984) 26-31. DOBBELER, A. VON, Glaube als Teilhabe (Tübingen 1987) 133-35. HOFIUS, O. Paulusstudien (Tübingen 1989) 68, 128-31, 197.

4:1-5   HOFIUS, O. Paulusstudien (Tübingen 1989) 68, 129-31. LONGENECKER, B. W. Eschatology and the Covenant. A Comparison of 4 Ezra and Romans 1-11 (Sheffield 1991) 211-4.

4:1-3   PAGELS, E. H. The Gnostic Paul. Gnostic Exegesis of the Pauline Letters (Philadelphia 1975) 24. STAAB, K. Pauluskommentare aus der griechischen Kirche (Münster ²1984) 488:31-489:33 Phot.

4:1-2   STAAB, K. Pauluskommentare aus der griechischen Kirche (Münster ²1984) 61:13-22 Apoll.

4:1   KÜMMEL, W. G. Römer 7 und das Bild des Menschen im Neuen Testament (München 1974) 16, 42, 124. SCHMITHALS, W. Der Römerbrief als historisches Problem (Gütersloh 1975) 24, 89. BRUCE, F. F. The Time is Fulfilled (Exeter 1978) 57-74. LAYMAN, F. D. Paul's Use of Abraham. An Approach to Paul's Understanding of History (diss. Ann Arbor MI 1978) 220-23. STAAB, K. Pauluskommentare aus der griechischen Kirche (Münster ²1984) 362:7-12 Genn. HAYS, R. B. "'Have we found Abraham to be our forefather according to the flesh?' A Reconsidera-tion of Rom 4:1," NovT 27 (1985) 76-98. MALHERBE, A. J. Moral Exhortation. A Greco-Roman Sourcebook (Philadelphia 1986) 129. LAMPE, P. Die stadtrömischen Christen in den ersten beiden Jahrhunderten (Tübingen ²1989) 56.

4:2ff.   JÜNGEL, E. Paulus und Jesus (1966) 68.

4:2-25   THISELTON, A. C. The Two Horizons (Grand Rapids 1980) 422f.

4:2-6   AMIOT, F. Les Idées Maitresses de Saint Paul (1959) 50, 63-65, 71. LIEBERS, R. Das Gesetz als Evangelium (Zürich 1989) 31-40.

4:2-5   STALDER, K. Das Werk des Geistes in der Heiligung bei Paulus (1962) 177f.

4:2   SCHRAGE, W. Die konkreten Einzelgebote in der paulinischen Paränese (1961) 85, 95, 229. HÜBNER, H. Das Gesetz bei Paulus (Göttingen 1978) 99-103. LÜDEMANN, G. Paulus, der Heidenapostel, Bd. II (Göttingen 1983) 197f. RÄISÄNEN, H. The Torah and Christ (Helsinki 1986) 35. LIEBERS, R. Das Gesetz als Evangelium (Zürich 1989) 71-73. DAVIES, G. N. Faith and Obedience in Romans. A Study in Romans 1-4 (Sheffield 1990) 121f.

4:3ff.   RIDDERBOS, H. Paul. An Outline of His Theology (Grand Rapids 1975) 170-76. LUZ, U. "Paulinische Theologie als Biblische Theologie" in M. Klopfen-

	stein et al., eds., Mitte der Schrift? Ein jüdisch-christliches Gespräch. Texte des Berner Symposions vom 6.-12. Januar 1985 (Bern etc. 1987) 119-47, esp. 136f.

4:3-15   BANDSTRA, A.J. The Law and the Elements of the World (1964) 121f.

4:3-8   VIELHAUER, P. "Paulus und das Alte Testament" in Oikodome [G. Klein, ed.] (München 1979) 199f.

4:3-5,9-12 LIMBECK, M. Mit Paulus Christ sein. Sachbuch zur Person und Theologie des Apostels Paulus (Stuttgart 1989) 92f.

4:3-5   KERTELGE, K. "Rechtfertigung" bei Paulus (1967) 120, 122, 185-95, 225. FULLER, D. P. Gospel and Law: Contrast or Continuum? (Grand Rapids 1980) 105f.

4:3   ELLIS, E.E. Paul's Use of the Old Testament (1957) 20f, 48, 56, 125, 150, 187. JÜNGEL, E. Paulus und Jesus (1966) 39. LUZ, U. Das Geschichtsverständnis des Paulus (1968) 89. BAUMERT, N. Täglich Sterben und Auferstehen (München 1973) 361. LADD, G. E. A Theology of the New Testament (Grand Rapids 1974) 363, 394, 450. VAN DER MINDE, H.-J. Schrift und Tradition bei Paulus (München/Paderborn/Wien 1976) 81. THISELTON, A. C. The Two Horizons (Grand Rapids 1980) 423. KOCH, D.-A. Die Schrift als Zeuge des Evangeliums (Tübingen 1986) 21f., 132f., 243f. BERGER, K. und COLPE, C., eds., Religionsgeschichtliches Textbuch zum Neuen Testament (Göttingen/Zürich 1987) 205. MERKLEIN, H. Studien zu Jesus und Paulus (Tübingen 1987) 36, 42, 47, 62, 67.

4:4-8   PAGELS, E. H. The Gnostic Paul. Gnostic Exegesis of the Pauline Letters (Philadelphia 1975) 24f.

4:4-5   MOXNES, H. Theology in Conflict (Leiden 1980) 43f. RÄISÄNEN, H. Paul and the Law (Tübingen 1983) 171. RÄISÄNEN, H. The Torah and Christ (Helsinki 1986) 35.

4:4   VAN DÜLMEN, A. Die Theologie des Gesetzes bei Paulus (1968) 125, 126, 171, 172, 213, 226. MOXNES, H. Theology in Conflict (Leiden 1980) 50, 114, 256. THISELTON, A. C. The Two Horizons (Grand Rapids 1980) 389.

4:5ff.   JÜNGEL, E. Paulus and Jesus (1966) 39, 44f., 48, 53, 63.

4:5-8   SCHRAGE, W. Die konkreten Einzelgebote in der paulinischen Paränese (1961) 64, 94, 229, 230.

4:5   STUHLMACHER, P. Gerechtigkeit Gottes bei Paulus (1965) 226f. KERTELGE, K. "Rechtfertigung" bei Paulus (1967) 124, 161. KOLENKOW, A. "The Ascription of Romans 4:5" HThR 60 (2, '67) 228-30. KÄSEMANN, E. "Justice for the Unjust," Colloquium 11 (1978) 10-16. VAN DER MINDE, H.-J. "Theologia crucis und Pneumaaussagen bei Paulus," Catholica 34 (1980) 133. MOXNES, H. Theology in Conflict (Leiden 1980) 22, 43f., 110, 269, 284. THISELTON, A. C. The Two Horizons (Grand Rapids 1980) 409. HAYS, R. B. The Faith of Jesus Christ (Chico CA 1983) 163. GRÄSSER, E. "Rechtfertigung des Einzelnen—Rechtfertigung der Welt: Neutestamentliche Erwägungen" in W. C. Weinrich, ed., The New Testament Age (FS. Bo Reicke; Macon GA 1984) I, 221. STAAB, K. Pauluskommentare aus der griechischen Kirche (Münster ²1984) 489:34-36 Phot. LATTKE, M. "Heiligkeit III" in TRE 14 (1985) 705. RÄISÄNEN, H. The Torah and Christ (Helsinki 1986) 86. HOFIUS, O. "'Rechtfertigung des Gottlosen' als Thema biblischer Theologie," JBTh 2 (1987) 79-105, esp. 79f., 83f., 86, 94, 103, 105. MERKLEIN, H. Studien zu Jesus und Paulus (Tübingen 1987) 36, 42, 54, 61f., 64, 191, 292. MOORE, R. K. "Romans 4.5 in TEV: A Plea for Consistency," BTr 39 (1988) 126-29. HOFIUS, O. Paulusstudien (Tübingen 1989) 68, 121-9, 131f., 136, 145, 147, 156, 171, 177, 180.

4:6-12   FULLER, R. H. "Jesus Christ as Savior in the New Testament," Interp 35
            (1981) 153.
4:6-10   STAAB, K. Pauluskommentare aus der griechischen Kirche (Münster ²1984)
            490:1-13 Phot.
4:6-8.17   LAMPE, P. Die stadtrömischen Christen in den ersten beiden Jahrhunderten
            (Tübingen ²1989) 54.
4:6-8   HARMAN, A. M. Paul's Use of the Psalms (Ann Arbor MI 1968) 79-88.
4:6   LUZ, U. Das Geschichtsverständnis des Paulus (1968) 90. DAVIES, G. N. Faith
            and Obedience in Romans. A Study in Romans 1-4 (Sheffield 1990) 122.
4:7-8   KOCH, D.-A. Die Schrift als Zeuge des Evangeliums (Tübingen 1986) 221ff.
            OLIVEIRA, A. DE, Die Diakonie der Gerechtigkeit und der Versöhnung in der
            Apologie des 2. Korintherbriefes. Analyse und Auslegung von 2 Kor 2, 14-4,
            6; 5, 11-6, 10 (Münster 1990) 377.
4:7   HANSON, A. T. Studies in Paul's Technique and Theology (London 1974) 55f.
4:8   STAAB, K. Pauluskommentare aus der griechischen Kirche (Münster ²1984)
            118:5-10 ThM.
4:9ff.   SCHRAGE, W. Die konkreten Einzelgebote in der paulinischen Paränese (1961)
            231.
4:9-25   THISELTON, A. C. The Two Horizons (Grand Rapids 1980) 406.
4:9-22   BETZ, O. "Beschneidung" in TRE 5 (1980) 719.
4:9-17   LAYMAN, F. D. Paul's Use of Abraham. An Approach to Paul's Under-
            standing of History (diss. Ann Arbor MI 1978) 70-79, 138-40, 144, 199.
4:9-12   DELLING, G. Die Taufe im Neuen Testament (1963) 141. ZELLER, D. Juden
            und Heiden in der Mission des Paulus. Studien zum Römerbrief (Stuttgart 1973)
            101f. LONA, H. E. Abraham in Johannes 8 (Bern/Frankfurt 1976) 354-56.
            LAYMAN, F. D. Paul's Use of Abraham. An Approach to Paul's Understand-
            ing of History (diss. Ann Arbor MI 1978) 71-75. FLUSSER, D. and SAFRAI,
            S. "Who Sanctified the Beloved in the Womb," Immanuel 11 (1980) 46-55.
            MOXNES, H. Theology in Conflict (Leiden 1980) 111f., 228. SCHMITT, R.
            Gottesgerechtigkeit—Heilsgeschichte—Israel in der Theologie des Paulus
            (Frankfurt/Bern/New York/Nancy 1984) 31-33. DOBBELER, A. VON, Glaube
            als Teilhabe (Tübingen 1987) 135f.
4:9-10   MÜLLER, H. Die Auslegung alttestamentlichen Geschichtsstoffs bei Paulus
            (diss. Halle-Wittenberg 1960) 42-48.
4:9   KERTELGE, K. "Rechtfertigung" bei Paulus (1967) 161. BAUMERT, N.
            Täglich Sterben und Auferstehen (München 1973) 361. THISELTON, A. C.
            The Two Horizons (Grand Rapids 1980) 423. KOCH, D.-A. Die Schrift als
            Zeuge des Evangeliums (Tübingen 1986) 15f. MERKLEIN, H. Studien zu Jesus
            und Paulus (Tübingen 1987) 36, 42, 46f., 62, 67. JOHNSON, E. E. The
            Function of Apocalyptic and Wisdom Traditions in Romans 9-11 (Atlanta GA
            1989) 119, 141, 192.
4:10-12   ELLIS, E. E. et al., eds., Neotestamentica et Semitica (Edinburgh 1969) 16f.,
            25f.
4:10-11   WOLTER, M. Die Pastoralbriefe als Paulustradition (Göttingen 1988) 55.
4:11-12:16 CHANCE, J. B. "The Seed of Abraham and the People of God. A Study of
            Two Pauls" in E. H. Lovering, ed., Society of Biblical Literature 1993 Seminar
            Papers (Atlanta 1993) 384-411.
4:11-5:21   ROON, A. VAN, The Authenticity of Ephesians (Leiden 1974) 198f.
4:11-13   VAN DER MINDE, H.-J. Schrift und Tradition bei Paulus (München/Pader-
            born/Wien 1976) 81.

4:11-12   BOURKE, M.M. "St. Paul and the Justification of Abraham" Bible Today 1 (10, '64) 643-49. LUZ, U. Das Geschichtsver-ständnis des Paulus (1968) 175f. MÜLLER, H. Die Auslegung alttestamentlichen Geschichtsstoffs bei Paulus (Diss; Halle-Wittenberg 1960) 42-48. STAAB, K. Pauluskommentare aus der griechischen Kirche (Münster ²1984) 490:14-491:4 Phot. MARQUARDT, F.-W. Die Juden und ihr Land (Gütersloh ³1986) 150. MERKLEIN, H. Studien zu Jesus und Paulus (Tübingen 1987) 47, 62, 67, 68n.167.

4:11   BARRETT, C.K. From First Adam to Last (1962) 37ff. DELLING, G. Die Taufe im Neuen Testament (1963) 105. JÜNGEL, E. Paulus und Jesus (1966) 17. KERTELGE, K. "Rechtfertigung" bei Paulus (1967) 161. ELLIS, E. E. Paul's Use of the Old Testament (Edinburgh/London 1957) 107f., 124f., 150f. FRIEDRICH, G. "Das Gesetz des Glaubens Römer 3, 27" in Auf das Wort kommt es an. Gesammelte Aufsätze (Göttingen 1978) 118. JEWETT, P. K. Infant Baptism and the Covenant of Grace (Grand Rapids 1978) 87. THISELTON, A. C. The Two Horizons (Grand Rapids 1980) 402. HAYS, R. B. The Faith of Jesus Christ (Chico CA 1983) 194. STAAB, K. Pauluskommentare aus der griechischen Kirche (Münster ²1984) 118:11-15 ThM; 217:11-15 Sev. GASTON, L. Paul and the Torah (Vancouver 1987) 118, 131. MERKLEIN, H. Studien zu Jesus und Paulus (Tübingen 1987) 42f., 46, 68n.167, 99f., 102. KLAUCK, H.-J. Gemeinde, Amt, Sakrament (Würzburg 1989) 356.

4:12   SCHRAGE, W. Die konkreten Einzelgebote in der paulinischen Paränese (1961) 59. KÄSEMANN, E. Exegetische Versuche und Besinnungen (1964) II 197. KÄSEMANN, E. New Testament Questions of Today (1969) 186. ELLIS, E. E. Prophecy and Hermeneutic in Early Christianity (Tübingen 1978) 111, 116f., 121. SWETNAM, J. "The Curious Crux at Romans 4, 12," Biblica 61 (1980) 110-15. THISELTON, A. C. The Two Horizons (Grand Rapids 1980) 402. HAYS, R. B. The Faith of Jesus Christ (Chico CA 1983) 163, 171, 190, 194. ZIMMERMANN, A. F. Die urchristlichen Lehrer (Tübingen 1984) 167, 181.

4:13ff.   FRIEDRICH, G. "Das Gesetz des Glaubens Römer 3, 27" in Auf das Wort kommt es an. Gesammelte Aufsätze (Göttingen 1978) 117.

4:13-25   MOXNES, H. Theology in Conflict (Leiden 1980) 231-82. DU TOIT, A. B. "Gesetzesgerechtigkeit und Glaubensgerechtigkeit in Rom 4:13-25: In Gespräch mit E P Sanders," HTS 44 (1988) 71-80.

4:13-22   MOXNES, H. Theology in Conflict (Leiden 1980) 42f., 113-15, 195-206, 229f.

4:13-17   LAYMAN, F. D. Paul's Use of Abraham. An Approach to Paul's Understanding of History (diss. Ann Arbor MI 1978) 75-79. ZELLER, D. Juden und Heiden in der Mission des Paulus. Studien zum Römerbrief Stuttgart 1973) 102ff. LONA, H. E. Abraham in Johannes 8 (Bern/Frankfurt 1976) 356-59. DOBBELER, A. VON, Glaube als Teilhabe (Tübingen 1987) 136-38.

4:13-17a   VAN DER MINDE, H.-J. Schrift und Tradition bei Paulus (München/Paderborn/Wien 1976) 73-75. SCHMITT, R. Gottesgerechtigkeit—Heilsgeschichte—Israel in der Theologie des Paulus (Frankfurt/ Bern/New York/Nancy 1984) 33-35.

4:13-16   LUZ, U. Das Geschichtsverständnis des Paulus (1968) 176, 183f. MOXNES, H. Theology in Conflict (Leiden 1980) 253-61. HELDERMANN, J. Die Anapausis im Evangelium Veritatis (Leiden 1984) 325n.61. LAFON, G. "La pensée du social et la théologie. Loi et grace en Romains 4, 13-16," RechSR 75 (1987) 9-38. SNODGRASS, K. "Spheres of Influence. A Possible Solution to the Problem of Paul and the Law," JSNT 32 (1988) 93-113.

4:13-15   PAGELS, E. H. The Gnostic Paul. Gnostic Exegesis of the Pauline Letters (Philadelphia 1975) 25.

4:13	BRUNNER, E. Dogmatik I (1946) 296. JÜNGEL, E. Paulus und Jesus (1966) 17. KERTELGE, K. "Rechtfertigung" bei Paulus (1967) 161. VAN DÜLMEN, A. Die Theologie des Gesetzes bei Paulus (1968) 37, 89f, 91, 101, 222. BYRNE, B. "Sons of God"—"Seed of Abraham" (Rome 1979) 128, 133, 157, 160f. MOXNES, H. Theology in Conflict (Leiden 1980) 113f., 203f., 247-49, 253-56. STAAB, K. Pauluskommentare aus der griechischen Kirche (Münster ²1984) 61:23-62:5 Apoll; 217:16-19 Sev. MARQUARDT, F.-W. Die Juden und ihr Land (Gütersloh ³1986) 24. MARTIN, B. L. Christ and the Law in Paul (Leiden 1989) 15, 20, 52, 118, 125, 127, 146.
4:14-16	STAAB, K. Pauluskommentare aus der griechischen Kirche (Münster ²1984) 491:5-492:10 Phot.
4:14-15	MOXNES, H. Theology in Conflict (Leiden 1980) 261-69. BAMMEL, C. P. H. "Philocalia IX, Jerome, Epistle 121, and Origen's Exposition of Romans VII," JThS 32 (1981) 55f.
4:14	BJERKELUND, C. J. "'Vergeblich' als Missionsergebnis bei Paulus" in J. Jervell et al., eds., God's Christ and His People (FS. N. A. Dahl; New York 1977) 175-91.
4:15	SCHRAGE, W. Die konkreten Einzelgebote in der paulinischen Paränese (1961) 65, 195f. BANDSTRA, A.J. The Law and the Elements of the World (1964) 128f. JÜNGEL, E. Paulus und Jesus (1966) 28, 58f, 68. LUZ, U. Das Geschichtsverständnis des Paulus (1968) 187f, 199f. VAN DÜLMEN, A. Die Theologie des Gesetzes bei Paulus (1968) 42, 84, 90, 91ff, 96, 97, 101, 109, 238. MAUSER, U. Gottesbild und Menschwerdung (1971) 152, 154, 162. BRANDENBURGER, E. Adam und Christus (Neukirchen-Vluyn 1962) 183f., 188, 191f., 194ff., 200f., 203, 206, 208, 210f., 237, 248f., 251. BAUMERT, N. Täglich Sterben und Auferstehen (München 1973) 346. KÜMMEL, W. G. Römer 7 und das Bild des Menschen im Neuen Testament (München 1974) 6, 8, 49f. KLIJN, A F. J. "Die syrische Baruch-Apokalypse" in JSHRZ V/2 (1976) 133n.5a. HÜBNER, H. Das Gesetz bei Paulus (Göttingen 1978) 72f. RÄISÄNEN, H. Paul and the Law (Tübingen 1983) 25, 141, 143, 146-48, 260. DIETZFELBINGER, C. Die Berufung des Paulus als Ursprung seiner Theologie (Neukirchen 1985) 101, 105f., 111. FREUND, G. und STEGEMANN, E., eds., Theologische Brosamen für Lothar Steiger (DBAT 5; Heidelberg 1985) 392. SANDERS, E. P. Paul, the Law, and the Jewish People (London 1985) 65, 70f., 75, 82, 86n.2, 93, 137. MÜLLER, H. M. "Homiletik" in TRE 15 (1986) 557. LÖFSTEDT, B. "Notes on St Paul's Letter to the Romans," FilolNeot 1 (1988) 209f. SCHNELLE, U. Wandlungen im paulinischen Denken (Stuttgart 1989) 69. THIELMAN, F. From Plight to Solution (Leiden 1989) 87, 91, 97, 100f., 108, 115.
4:16-25	GOPPELT, L. Theologie des Neuen Testaments II: Vielfalt und Einheit des apostolischen Christus-zeugnisses (Göttingen 1976) 457f.
4:16-18	BRAUN, H. Qumran und NT II (1966) 320. DAVIES, W. D. The Gospel and the Land (London 1974) 176. VAN DER MINDE, H.-J. Schrift und Tradition bei Paulus (München/Paderborn/Wien 1976) 82. MOXNES, H. Theology in Conflict (Leiden 1980) 43, 241-53.
4:16-17	DELLING, G. Die Taufe im Neuen Testament (1963) 99. PAGELS, E. H. The Gnostic Paul. Gnostic Exegesis of the Pauline Letters (Philadelphia 1975) 25f. BAMMEL, C. P. H. "Philocalia IX, Jerome, Epistle 121, and Origen's Exposition of Romans VII," JThS 32 (1981) 55. MERKLEIN, H. Studien zu Jesus und Paulus (Tübingen 1987) 62, 64, 67, 292.

4:16   MERK, O. Handeln aus Glauben (1968) 6-10, 16. VAN DÜLMEN, A. Die Theologie des Gesetzes bei Paulus (1968) 37, 93f., 170, 214. BORSE, U. Der Standort des Galaterbriefes (Köln 1972) 123f. MOXNES, H. Theology in Conflict (Leiden 1980) 114, 255f. MUSSNER, F. "Wer ist 'der ganze Samen' in Röm 4, 16?" in J. Zmijewski und E. Nellessen, eds., Begegnung mit dem Wort (FS. H. Zimmermann; Bonn 1980) 213-17. HAYS, R. B. The Faith of Jesus Christ (Chico CA 1983) 154, 163, 171, 190, 194, 237f. RÄISÄNEN, H. The Torah and Christ (Helsinki 1986) 35. MUSSNER, F. Die Kraft der Wurzel (Freiburg/Basel/Wien 1987) 160-63. JOHNSON, E. E. The Function of Apocalyptic and Wisdom Traditions in Romans 9-11 (Atlanta GA 1989) 141, 149, 178, 191. RIDDERBOS, H. Paul. An Outline of His Theology (Grand Rapids 1975) 250f. KLAIBER, W. "Aus Glauben, damit aus Gnade. Der Grundsatz paulinischer Soteriologie und die Gnadenlehre John Wesleys," ZThK 88 (1991) 313-38.

4:17-25   NICKELS, P. Targum and New Testament (1967) 68. LUZ, U. Das Geschichtsverständnis des Paulus (1968) 176f. MÜLLER, H. Die Auslegung alttestamentlichen Geschichtsstoffs bei Paulus (diss. Halle-Wittenberg 1960) 104-16. ZELLER, D. Juden und Heiden in der Mission des Paulus. Studien zum Römerbrief (Stuttgart 1973) 104f. LAYMAN, F. D. Paul's Use of Abraham. An Approach to Paul's Understanding of History (diss. Ann Arbor MI 1978) 79-81, 199-203. SCHMITT, R. Gottesgerechtigkeit—Heilsgeschichte—Israel in der Theologie des Paulus (Frankfurt/Bern/ New York/Nancy 1984) 35-38.

4:17-22   MIRANDA, J. P. Marx and the Bible (London 1977) 215-18. LAYMAN, F. D. Paul's Use of Abraham. An Approach to Paul's Understanding of History (diss. Ann Arbor MI 1978) 144f. MOXNES, H. Theology in Conflict (Leiden 1980) 104-06. VAN DER MINDE, H.-J. Schrift und Tradition bei Paulus (München/Pader-born/Wien 1976) 75f.

4:17-21   HOFFMANN, P. Die Toten in Christus (1966) 340. BYRNE, B. "Sons of God"—"Seed of Abraham" (Rome 1979) 160f. MOXNES, H. Theology in Conflict (Leiden 1980) 202-5, 274f.

4:17-18   JEWETT, P. K. Infant Baptism and the Covenant of Grace (Grand Rapids 1978) 95. BERGER, K. "Das Buch der Jubiläen" in JSHRZ II/3 (1981) 410. WEDER, H. "Hoffnung II" in TRE 15 (1986) 488.

4:17   BRUNNER, Dogmatik I (1946) 328, II (1950) 13, 24; Mensch in Widerspruch (1937) 87A2. WIEDERKEHR, D. Die Theologie der Berufung in den Paulusbriefen (1963) 148-52. KÄSEMANN, E. Exegetische Versuche und Besinnungen (1964) II 192. STUHLMACHER, P. Gerechtigkeit Gottes bei Paulus (1965) 226f. BOUSSET, W. Die Religion des Judentums im Späthellenistischen Zeitalter (1926=1966) 361. JÜNGEL, E. Paulus und Jesus (1966) 31, 47f. KERTELGE, K. "Rechtfertigung" bei Paulus (1967) 193f. MERK, O. Handeln aus Glauben (1968) 5f, 9f, 12, 240. VAN DÜLMEN, A. Die Theologie des Gesetzes bei Paulus (1968) 190, 191, 222, 238. BLANK, J. Schriftauslegung in Theorie und Praxis (1969) 28. HOFIUS, O. "Eine altjüdische Parallele zu Röm. iv.17b" NTS 18 (1, '71) 93-94. MAUSER, U. Gottesbild und Menschwerdung (1971) 126, 131, 188. BURCHARD, C. Untersuchungen zu Joseph und Aseneth (Tübingen 1965) 104. SIBER, P. Mit Christus leben (Zürich 1971) 25, 120. BAUMERT, N. Täglich Sterben und Auferstehen (München 1973) 66, 409. CAVALLIN, H. C. C. Life After Death (Lund 1974)4, 3n34, 4, 6, 4, I. KLIJN, A F. J. "Die syrische Baruch-Apokalypse" in JSHRZ V/2 (1976) 136n.4c. HASENSTAB, R. Modelle paulinischer Ethik (Mainz 1977) 151, 153-55, 185, 187, 189. FISCHER, U. Eschatologie und Jen-seitserwartung im hellenistischen Diasporajudentum (Berlin 1978) 108. FRIEDRICH, G. "'Αμαρτία οὐκ ἐλλογεῖται Rom. 5, 13" in Auf das Wort kommt es an. Gesammelte Aufsätze (Göttingen 1978) 125. LAYMAN, F. D. Paul's Use of Abraham. An Approach to Paul's Understanding of History (diss. Ann Arbor MI 1978) 201f. FROITZHEIM, F. Christologie und Eschatologie bei Paulus (Würzburg 1979) 108ff., 214. HOFFMANN, P. "Auferstehung" in TRE 4 (1979) 486. GEORGI, D. "Weisheit Salomos" in JSHRZ III/4 (1980) 11n.17c. MOXNES, H. Theology in Conflict (Leiden 1980) 41-44, 103-07, 113f., 200, 231-82. SÄNGER, D. Antikes Judentum und die Mysterien (Tübingen 1980) 153. WAGNER, F. "Berufung" in TRE 5 (1980) 686. ROCHAIS, G. Les récits de résurrection des morts dans le Nouveau Testament (Cambridge 1981) 201, 206, 208. HAYS, R. B. The Faith of Jesus Christ (Chico CA 1983) 203. LONNING, I. "Gott VIII" in TRE 13 (1984) 702. STAAB, K. Pauluskommentare aus der griechischen Kirche (Münster ²1984) 217:20-21 Sev; 492:11-25 Phot. SAUTER, G. "Hoffnung III" in TRE 15 (1986) 492. SELLIN, G. Der Streit um die Auferstehung der Toten (Göttingen 1986) 26n., 73, 80f., 85, 86n., 148n., 215. HOFIUS, O. "'Rechtfertigung des Gottlosen' als Thema biblischer Theologie," JBTh 2 (1987) 79-105, esp. 79, 86, 94, 105. MERKLEIN, H. Studien zu Jesus und Paulus (Tübingen 1987) 23, 47, 55, 59, 61, 67, 153, 191, 200, 293, 382. BECKER, J. Paulus. Der Apostel der Völker (Tübingen 1989) 82, 346, 401, 403. JOHNSON, E. E. The Function of Apocalyptic and Wisdom Traditions in Romans 9-11 (Atlanta GA 1989) 118, 128, 172. VOLLENWEIDER, S. Freiheit als neue Schöpfung (Göttingen 1989) 386.

4:18ff. RÄISÄNEN, H. The Torah and Christ (Helsinki 1986) 81.

4:18-25 LONA, H. E. Abraham in Johannes 8 (Bern/Frankfurt 1976) 359-63.

4:18-22 DAVIES, W. D. The Gospel and the Land (London 1974) 174. DOBBELER, A. VON, Glaube als Teilhabe (Tübingen 1987) 138-40.

4:18-21 HAACKER, K. "Glaube II" in TRE 13 (1984) 298. REBELL, W. Alles ist möglich dem, der glaubt (München 1989) 122.

4:18 KÄSEMANN, E. Exegetische Versuche und Besinnungen (1964) II 189, 197; New Testament Questions of Today (1969) 177, 187. NEBE, G. 'Hoffnung' bei Paulus (Göttingen 1983) 19, 21, 31, 33ff., 44, 64, 66f., 70ff., 74, 151, 233, 254. STAAB, K. Pauluskommentare aus der griechischen Kirche (Münster ²1984) 218:1-3 Sev; 492:26-28 Phot. KOCH, D.-A. Die Schrift als Zeuge des Evangeliums (Tübingen 1986) 15f., 21. SAUTER, G. "Hoffnung III" in TRE 15 (1986) 495. WEDER, H. "Hoffnung II" in TRE 15 (1986) 490. DOBBELER, A. VON, Glaube als Teilhabe (Tübingen 1987) 203f.

4:19-21 DOBBELER, A. VON, Glaube als Teilhabe (Tübingen 1987) 235f.

4:19 BEST, E. One Body in Christ (1955) 217n. GUNDRY, R. H. Soma in Biblical Theology with Emphasis on Pauline Anthropology (Cambridge 1976) 49f. MOXNES, H. Theology in Conflict (Leiden 1980) 197f., 239-41. STAAB, K. Pauluskommentare aus der griechischen Kirche (Münster ²1984) 424:1-2 Oek. MERKLEIN, H. Studien zu Jesus und Paulus (Tübingen 1987) 54f., 67.

4:20-21 SCHROGGS, R. Paul for a New Day (Philadelphia 1977) 27f.

4:20 THEYSSEN, G.W. "Unbelief" in the New Testament (1965) 5-7. JÜNGEL, E. Paulus und Jesus (1966) 56. STAAB, K. Pauluskommentare aus der griechischen Kirche (Münster ²1984) 218:4-7 Sev. WOLTER, M. Die Pastoralbriefe als Paulustradition (Göttingen 1988) 37.

4:21 NEIL, W. "Paul's Certanities. I God's Promises are Sure—Rom iv.21" ET 69 (5, '58) 146-48. MOXNES, H. Theology in Conflict (Leiden 1980) 114, 199f.

4:22-24 HAYS, R. B. The Faith of Jesus Christ (Chico CA 1983) 199. LÖFSTEDT, B. "Notes on St Paul's Letter to the Romans," FilolNeot 1 (1988) 209f.

4:22   JÜNGEL, E. Paulus und Jesus (1966) 39. KOCH, D.-A. Die Schrift als Zeuge des Evangeliums (Tübingen 1986) 22f. GASTON, L. Paul and the Torah (Vancouver 1987) 45-63.

4:23ff.   LUZ, U. Das Geschichtsverständnis des Paulus (1968) 113-16. DUGANDZIC, I. Das "Ja" Gottes in Christus (Würzburg 1977) 224-33.

4:23-25   KERTELGE, K. "Rechtfertigung" bei Paulus (1967) 195. LUZ, U. Das Geschichtsverständnis des Paulus (1968) 113ff. MUSSNER, F. Die Auferstehung Jesu (1969) 196f. VAN DER MINDE, H.-J. Schrift und Tradition bei Paulus (München/Paderborn/Wien 1976) 76f., 89-102. URSUA, F. SERRANO. "Historia de la Salvación a la Luz de Rom 4, 23-25," Estudios Teológicos 4 (1977) 117-44. LAYMAN, F. D. Paul's Use of Abraham. An Approach to Paul's Understanding of History (diss. Ann Arbor MI 1978) 145-47. MOXNES, H. Theology in Conflict (Leiden 1980) 115, 201, 272f. DOBBELER, A. VON, Glaube als Teilhabe (Tübingen 1987) 140-42. LUZ, U. "Paulinische Theologie als Biblische Theologie" in M. Klopfenstein et al., eds., Mitte der Schrift? Ein jüdisch-christliches Gespräch. Texte des Berner Symposions vom 6.-12. Januar 1985 (Bern etc. 1987) 119-47, esp. 124f.

4:23-24   SCHRAGE, W. Die konkreten Einzelgebote in der paulinischen Paränese (1961) 229. KOCH, D.-A. Die Schrift als Zeuge des Evangeliums (Tübingen 1986) 322-24. BOCKMUEHL, M. N. A. Revelation and Mystery (Tübingen 1990) 154.

4:23   KNOX, W.L. The Sources of the Synoptic Gospels II (1957) 104. GOPPELT, L. Christologie und Ethik (1968) 227f. MALHERBE, A. J. Moral Exhortation. A Greco-Roman Sourcebook (Philadelphia 1986) 65.

4:24-5:5   STAAB, K. Pauluskommentare aus der griechischen Kirche (Münster ²1984) 492:29-494:28 Phot.

4:24ff.   STUHLMACHER, P. Gerechtigkeit Gottes bei Paulus (1965) 13-15, 24f, 27-31, 33f., 36., 63-66, 185f., 199f., 207f.

4:24-25   STUHLMACHER, P. Gerechtigkeit Gottes bei Paulus (1965) 226f. JÜNGEL, E. Paulus und Jesus (1966) 2. SCHRAGE, W. Die Konkreten Einzelgebotein der paulinischen Paränese (1961) 54, 66, 236, 239. MERK, O. Handeln aus Glauben (1968) 10f. SCHELKLE, K. H. Die Passion Jesu in der Verkündigung des Neuen Testaments (Heidelberg 1949) 71, 95, 132, 155, 173, 193, 197, 249, 258. PERKINS, P. Resurrection. New Testament Witness and Contemporary Reflection (London 1984) 219-20. STUHLMACHER, P. Jesus von Nazareth—Christus des Glaubens (Stuttgart 1988) 49, 57. BECKER, J. Paulus. Der Apostel der Völker (Tübingen 1989) 300, 401, 426. COUSAR, C. B. A Theology of the Cross (Minneapolis 1990) 54, 66-70, 98.

4:24   HAHN, F. Christologische Hoheitstitel (1963) 110, 204. KRAMER, W. Christol Kyrios Gottessohn (1963) §3h. LANGEVIN, P.E. Jésus Seigneur et L'Eschatologie (1967) 32, 51, 86, 87. MAUSER, U. Gottesbild und Menschwerdung (1971) 126, 131, 134, 142. MIKALSEN, T. The Traditio—Historical Place of the Christology of 1 Peter in light of 1:18-21 (Rüschlikon 1971) 86-88. FROITZHEIM, F. Christologie und Eschatologie bei Paulus (Würzburg 1979) 79ff., 108ff. HOFFMANN, P. "Auferstehung" in TRE 4 (1979) 479, 486. SÄNGER, D. Antikes Judentum und die Mysterien (Tübingen 1980) 153. HAYS, R. B. The Faith of Jesus Christ (Chico CA 1983) 171. KLEINK-NECHT, K. T. Der leidende Gerechtfertigte (Tübingen 1984) 362. STAAB, K. Pauluskommentare aus der griechischen Kirche (Münster ²1984) 62:6-8 Apoll. GRÄSSER, E. Der Alte Bund im Neuen (Tübingen 1985) 224, 246f. KOCH,

4:25

D.-A. Die Schrift als Zeuge des Evangeliums (Tübingen 1986) 308f. MALINA,
B. J. Christian Origins and Cultural Anthropology (Atlanta 1986) 135.
PEINADOR, M. "Un texto de San Pablo a la luz del paralelismo" CultBib 16
(169, '59) 339-349. GONZALEZ RUIZ, J.M. "'Muerto por nuestros pecados
y resucitado por nuestra justificacion' Rom 4, 25)" Biblica 40 (3, '59) 837-58.
STANLEY, D.M. Christ's Resurrection in Pauline Soteriology (1961) 171-74.
BARRETT, C.K. From First Adam to Last (1962) 28f. SCHWEIZER, E.
Erniedrigung und Erhöhung bei Jesus und seinen Nachfolgern (1962) §6c.
WEGENAST, K. Das Verständnis der Tradition bei Paulus und in den
Deuteropaulinen (1962) 80-83. DELLING, G. Die Taufe im Neuen Testament
(1963) 132. HAHN, F. Christologische Hoheitstitel (1963) 62, 63, 204.
KRAMER, W. Christos Kyrios Gottessohn (1963) §§52, 26d, 27d. BULT-
MANN, R. Theologie des Neuen Testaments (1965) 49, 85. LJUNGMAN, H.
Pistis (1964) 71f. JÜNGEL, E. Paulus und Jesus (1966) 49. KLAPPERT, B.
"Zur Frage des Semitischen oder Griechischen Urtextes. Von I. Kor. XV. 3-5"
NTS 13 (1966-67) 170ff. LANGEVIN, P.E. Jésus Seigneur et l'Eschatologie
(1967) 23, 87, 289. POPKES, W. Christus Traditus (1967) 35, 96, 151, 158,
164, 193ff., 200ff., 208ff., 221ff., 238, 242, 247, 251, 253f., 276. LEHMANN,
K. Auferweckt am Dritten Tag nach der Schrift (1968) 35A, 45, 51, 58, 73, 91,
102, 104, 128, 129A, 139, 168, 249, 269A. MERK, O. Handeln aus Glauben
(1968) 5, 8, 16, 36. STROBEL, A. Erkenntnis und Bekenntnis der Sünde in neutestamentlicher Zeit (1968) 54. VAN DÜLMEN, A. Die Theologie des Gesetzes
bei Paulus (1968) 84, 90, 157, 160, 167, 183, 204, 205. BLANK, J. Schriftauslegung in Theorie und Praxis (1969) 154. Guettgemanns, E. Offene Fragen
zur Formgeschichte des Evangeliums (1970) 85. KESSLER, H. Die Theologische Bedeutung des Todes Jesu (1970) 268-70. LOHSE, E. et al, eds., Der
Ruf Jesu und die Antwort der Gemeinde (1970) 137, 204-212. JEREMIAS, J.
Neutestamentliche Theologie I (1971) 268, 281f. NEW Testament Theology I
(1971) 282, 296f. WENGST, K. Christologische Formeln und Lieder des Urchristentums (1972) 101-103. DALTON, W. J. Christ's Proclamation to the
Spirits. A Study of 1 Peter 3:18-4:6 (Rome 1965) 118. PATSCH, H. "Zum alttestamentlichen Hintergrund von Römer 4:25 und I. Petrus 2:24," ZNW 60
(1969) 273-79. PATSCH, H. Abendmahl und historischer Jesus (Stuttgart 1972)
160f. CONZELMANN, H. Theologie als Schriftauslegung (München 1974)
129n.27, 135n. 23-25.28. CHARBEL, A. "Rom 4, 25: Morte e Ressureicao, um
único Mistério alvífico," RCB 12 (1975) 17-28. CONZELMANN, H. und
LINDEMANN, A. Arbeitsbuch zum Neuen Testament (Tübingen 1975) 107.
McNEIL, B. "Raised for our Justification," IThQ 42 (1975) 97-105.
STRECKER, G., ed., Jesus Christus in Historie und Theologie (FS. H. Conzelmann; Tübingen 1975) 92-94, 400, 521. CHARBEL, A. "Ancora su Rom 4, 25:
Costruzione semitica?" BiOr 18 (1976) 28. STRECKER, G. "Befreiung und
Rechtfertigung. Zur Stellung der Rechtfertigungslehre in der Theologie des
Paulus" in J. Friedrich et al., eds., Rechtfertigung (FS. E. Käsemann; Tübing-
en/Göttingen 1976) 502f. VAN DER MINDE, H.-J. Schrift und Tradition bei
Paulus (München/Paderborn/Wien 1976) 90-99. CHARBEL, A. "Cruz y Resur-
rección único Misterio Salvífico," Estudios Teológicos 4 (1977) 103-15.
GAFFIN, R. B. The Centrality of the Resurrection (Grand Rapids 1978) 122-24.
SCHMITHALS, W. "Zur Herkunft der gnostischen Elemente in der Sprache des
Paulus" in B. Aland et al., eds., Gnosis (FS. H. Jonas; Göttingen 1978) 391-93.
FROITZHEIM, F. Christologie und Eschatologie bei Paulus (Würzburg 1979)
92f., 118. HOFFMANN, P. "Auferstehung" in TRE 4 (1979) 482. FULLER, R.

H. "Jesus Christ as Savior in the New Testament," Interp 35 (1981) 152. HENGEL, M. The Atonement (London 1981) 35, 37, 70. ASENDORF, U. "Eschatologie" in TRE 10 (1982) 310. SCHNELLE, U. Gerechtigkeit und Christusgegenwart (Göttingen 1983) 72-74. STUHLMACHER, P. "Sühne oder Versöhnung? Randbemerkungen zu Gerhard Friedrichs Studie: 'Die Verkündigung des Todes Jesu im Neuen Testament'," in U. Luz und H. Weder, eds., Die Mitte des Neuen Testaments (FS. E. Schweizer; Göttingen 1983) 298. KLEIN-KNECHT, K. T. Der leidende Gerechtfertigte (Tübingen 1984) 182, 344. LIN-DARS, B. Jesus Son of Man (Grand Rapids 1984) 68, 79, 82, 204, 208. RICHARDSON, P. and HURD, J. C., eds., From Jesus to Paul (FS. F. W. Beare; Waterloo 1984) 67f., 71. WENGST, K. "Glaubensbekenntnis(se) IV" in TRE 13 (1984) 396. HULTGREN, A. J. Paul's Gospel and Mission (Philadelphia 1985) 83f. HARRIS, M. J. Raised Immortal (London 1986) 75. MERKLEIN, H. Studien zu Jesus und Paulus (Tübingen 1987) 8, 24, 43, 46, 51, 185, 187. SCHMELLER, Th. Paulus und die "Diatribe" (Münster 1987) 241n.39. STUHLMACHER, P. "Jesus von Nazareth und die neutestamentliche Christologie im Lichte der Heiligen Schrift" in M. Klopfenstein et al., eds., Mitte der Schrift? Ein jüdisch-christliches Gespräch. Texte des Berner Symposions vom 6.-12. Januar 1985 (Bern etc. 1987) 82, 84, 90. CONZELMANN, H. und LINDEMANN, A. Interpreting the New Testament (Peabody MA 1988) 93. JONGE, M. DE. "Jesus' Death for Others and the Death of the Maccabean Martyrs" in T. Baarda et al., eds., Text and Testimony (FS. A. F. J. Klijn; Kampen 1988) 142-51, esp. 145. BREYTENBACH, C. Versöhnung (Neukirchen/Vluyn 1989) 119n., 138, 140f., 150, 153, 159, 197f., 208-10. LAMPE, P. Die stadtrömischen Christen in den ersten beiden Jahrhunderten (Tübingen ²1989) 54. MARTIN, B. L. Christ and the Law in Paul (Leiden 1989) 14f., 53, 64, 120, 122f., 156. SCHWEIZER, E. Theologische Einleitung in das Neue Testament (Göttingen 1989) ß4.4;5.4-5. WALTER, N. "Paul and the Early Christian Jesus-Tradition" in A. J. M. Wedderburn, ed., Paul and Jesus. Collected Essays (Sheffield 1989) 51-80, esp. 58f., 64. OLIVEIRA, A. DE, Die Diakonie der Gerechtigkeit und der Versöhnung in der Apologie des 2. Korintherbriefes. Analyse und Auslegung von 2 Kor 2, 14-4, 6; 5, 11-6, 10 (Münster 1990) 250, 377. KRAUS, W. Der Tod Jesu als Heiligtumsweihe. Eine Untersuchung zum Umfeld der Sühnevorstellung in Römer 3, 25-26a (Neukirchen-Vluyn 1991) 8n., 18n., 92, 94f., 108, 151, 197, 198n., 230f., 247n. LOHSE, E. Die Entstehung des Neuen Testaments (Stuttgart/Berlin/Köln ⁵1991) 21.

5–11
5–8

ELLIOT, N. The Rhetoric of Romans (Sheffield 1990) 67, 104, 225-75, 278. HANSON, S. The Unity of the Church in the New Testament (1946) 61f, 71f. LEIVESTAD, R. Christ the Conqueror (1954) 115ff, 260ff. MINEAR, P.S. Images of the Church in the New Testament (1960) 114f, 174f. KNOX, J. Life in Christ Jesus. Reflections on Romans 5–8 (1961). CAMBIER, J. "Péché des Hommes et Péché d'Adam en Rom. V.12" NTS 11 (1964-65) 236f. JÜNGEL, E. Paulus und Jesus (1966) 26. EHRLICH, E. "Paulus und das Schuldproblem, erläutert an Römer 5 und 8" Antifudaismus im Neuen Testament, eds. W.P. Eckert, N.P. Levinson and M.Stöhr (1967) 44-49. LUZ, U. Das Geschichtsverständnis des Paulus (1968) 209. MINEAR, P.S. The Obedience of Faith (1971) 57-71. BRANDENBURGER, E. Adam und Christus (Neukirchen-Vluyn 1962) 165, 178, 186, 255-64. PERRIN, N. The New Testament (New York 1974) 110-12. CRESSEY, M. H. "The Meaning of the Nairobi Theme: A Pauline Perspective," ER 27 (1975) 193-200. OSTEN-SACKEN, P. VON DER, Römer 8 als

Beispiel paulinischer Soteriologie (Göttingen 1975) 245ff. BYRNE, B. "Sons of God"—"Seed of Abraham" (Rome 1979) 86-88, 91, 120. LAMARCHE, P. and LE DU, C. Épitre aux Romains V-VIII. Structure littéraire et sens (Paris 1980). MOXNES, H. Theology in Conflict (Leiden 1980) 28f., 245, 275-77. NEBE, G. 'Hoffnung' bei Paulus (Göttingen 1983) 124ff., 135. BLACK, C. C. "Pauline Perspectives on Death in Romans 5-8," JBL 103 (1984) 413-33. LÜB-KING, H.-M. Paulus und Israel im Römerbrief (Frankfurt/Bern/New York 1986) 40-43. OLSON, S. N. "Romans 5-8 as Pastoral Theology," WordWorld 6 (1986) 390-97. RÖHSER, G. Metaphorik und Personifikation der Sünde (Tübingen 1987) 8, 15, 124, 129, 131f., 134, 136, 141ff., 156, 170. SCHMELL-ER, Th. Paulus und die "Diatribe" (Münster 1987) 287n.6. BEKER, J. C. "Paul's Theology: Consistent or Inconsistent?" NTS 34 (1988) 374-77. LIN-DARS, B. "Paul and the Law in Romans 5-8: An Actantial Analysis" in B. Lindars, ed., Law and Religion (Cambridge 1988) 126-40. MacDONALD, M. Y. The Pauline Churches (Cambridge 1988) 77f. ROLLAND, P. "L'antithèse de Rm 5-8," Biblica 69 (1988) 396-400. STUART, G. H. COHEN, Tweestrijd. Strijd tussen goed en kwaad bij Paulus en zijn tijdgenoten (Kampen 1988). WEDDERBURN, A. J. M. The Reasons for Romans (Edinburgh 1988) 130-36, 138. THIELMAN, F. "The Story of Israel and the Theology of Romans 5-8" in E. H. Lovering, ed., Society of Biblical Literature 1993 Seminar Papers (Atlanta 1993) 227-49.

5:1-8:30   FRAIKIN, D. "The Rhetorical Function of the Jews in Romans" in P. Richardson, ed., Anti-Judaism in Early Christianity, Vol. I: Paul and the Gospels (Waterloo, Ont. 1986) 99.

5:1-8:11   LORENZI, L. DE, ed., Battesimo e giustizia in Rom 6 e 8 (Rome 1974).

5-7   CROATTO, J. S. "'Hombre Nuevo' y 'Liberación' en la Carta a los Romanos," RevBi 36 (1974) 37-45. OSTEN-SACKEN, P. VON DER, Römer 8 als Beispiel paulinischer Soteriologie (Göttingen 1975) 160ff., 221ff. FORSYTH, J. J. "Faith and Eros: Paul's Answer to Freud," ReL 46 (1977) 476-87. LINDEMANN, A. "Herrscahft Gottes/Reich Gottes IV" in TRE 15 (1986) 213. RÖHSER, G. Metaphorik und Personifikation der Sünde (Tübingen 1987) 103ff., 117f., 128, 131, 177, 179f.

5-6   CONZELMANN, H. and LINDEMANN, A. Interpreting the New Testament (Peabody MA 1988) 194f.

5   BEST, E. One Body in Christ (1955) 17, 56. BARTH, K. Christ and Adam: Man and Humanity in Romans 5 (1957).BARTH, K. Christus und Adam nach Röm. 5 (1952). Christ et Adam d'après Romains 5 Contribution à l'étude ud problème de l'homme et de l'humanité (1959). BULTMANN, R. "Adam und Christus nach Rm 5" ZNW 50 (1959) 145-65; Current Issues in New Testament Interpretation (1962) 143-65, Festschrift f. A.O. Piper. STALDER, K. Das Werk des Geistes in der Heiligung bei Paulus (1962) 187, 190, 271f, 272–78, 369, 445. FONDEVILA, J.M. "La Gracia Capital de Adan y el Capitulo Quinto de la Carta a Los Romanos" Studiorum Paulinorum Congressus Internationalis Catholicus 1961 (1963) I 289-300. LEONDUFOUR, X. "Situation littéraire de Rom. V" RechSR 51 (1, '63) 83-95. LENGSFELD, P. Adam und Christus (1965) 65-110. MUELLER, H. "Der rabbinische Qau-Wachomer-Schluss in paulinischer Typologie (Zur Adam-Christus-Typologie in Rm 5)" ZNW 58 (1-2, '67) 73-92. NICKELS, P. Targum and New Testament (1967) 68. REWAK, W.J. "Adam, Immortality and Human Death" SciEccl 19 (1, '67) 67-79. SCHU-NACK, G. Das hermeneutische Problem des Todes. Im Horizont von Römer 5 untersucht (1967). BULTMANN, R. The Old and New Man (1967); Rev. T.

Stylianopoulos, GOThR 13 (1, '68) 112-14. GOPPELT, L. Christologie und Ethik (1968) 249f. VAN DÜLMAN, A. Die Theologie des Gesetzes bei Paulus (1968) 95, 163, 164, 165, 167. MUSSNER, F. Die Auferstehung Jesus (1969) 81-88. SCHUNACK, G. Das hermeneutische Problem des Todes. Im Horizont von Römer 5 untersucht, Rev. U. Luz ThLA 94 (1, '69) 37-39. WANSBROUGH, "Corporate Personality in the Bible. Adam and Christ—biblical use of the concept of personality" New Blackfriars 59 (595, '60) 798-804. ZIESLER, J.A. The Meaning of Righteousness in Paul (1972) 3, 187, 197, 197-200. RIDDERBOS, H. Paul. An Outline of His Theology (Grand Rapids 1975) 32-38, 71, 75, 95f. SCROGGS, R. Paul for a New Day (Philadelphia 1977) 7. HAYS, R. B. The Faith of Jesus Christ (Chico CA 1983) 166, 188, 244, 248. PATTE, D. Paul's Faith and the Power of the Gospel (Philadelphia 1983) 204-06. SANDERS, E. P. Paul, the Law, and the Jewish People (London 1985) 23f., 35f. WATSON, F. Paul, Judaism and the Gentiles (Cambridge 1986) 143-47. DUNN, J. D. G. "Paul's Epistle to the Romans: An Analysis of Structure and Argument" in ANRW II.25.4 (1987) 2855-58. DE BOER, M. C. The Defeat of Death: Apocalyptic Eschatology in 1 Corinthians 15 and Romans 5 (Sheffield 1988) 141-80, 181-88. KREITZER, L. "Adam as Analogy: Help or Hindrance?" KingTheol Rev 11 (1988) 59-62. BREYTENBACH, C. Versöhnung (Neukirchen-Vluyn 1989) 8, 21, 28, 30, 142f., 153, 155, 157f., 171n., 177, 180-83, 210. ELLIOT, N. The Rhetoric of Romans (Sheffield 1990) 67, 164f., 222, 225-37, 247n., 272, 278. HOOKER, M. D. From Adam to Christ. Essays on Paul (Cambridge 1990) 19, 27-32, 38f., 46, 58, 83, 98, 136, 168f., 184. COSBY, M. R. "Paul's Persuasive Language in Romans 5" in D. F. Watson, ed., Persuasive Artistry (FS G. A. Kennedy; Sheffield 1991) 209-26. PORTER, S. E. "The Argument of Romans 5: Can a Rhetorical Question Make a Difference?" JBL 110 (1991) 655-77. GARLINGTON, D. B. "The Obedience of Faith in the Letter to the Romans. Part III: The Obedience of Christ and the Obedience of the Christians," WThJ 55 (1993) 87-112.

5:1ff. BECKER, J. Paulus. Der Apostel der Völker (Tübingen 1989) 430ff.

5:1-21 GIBLIN, C.H. In Hope of God's Glory (1970) 365-77.

5:1-20 SEGUNDO, J. L. The Humanist Christology of Paul (Maryknoll NY and London 1986) 76-98.

5:1-11 KRECK, W. GPM 5 (1951) 83-86. BEST, E. One Body in Christ (1955) 34. GOLLWITZER, H. GPM 10 (1956) 78-82. KÜMMEL, W.G. Einführung in die exegetischen Methoden (1963) 49-57. SCHNEIDER, G. Der Herr unser Gott (1965) 173-76. MATTERN, L. Das Verständnis des Gerichtes bei Paulus (1966) 86f. STECK, K.G. in Herr, tue meine Lippen auf II (1965) 208-18. DOERNE, M. Die alten Episteln (1967) 90-94. RISTOW, H. "Latare" in Wandelt in der Liebe (1968) 39-51. GIBBS, J.G. Creation and Redemption (1971) 48f, 56, 152. EICHHOLZ, G. Die Theologie des Paulus im Umriss (1972) 173f. BRANDENBURGER, E. Adam und Christus (Neukirchen-Vluyn 1962) 231, 233, 235, 244, 256ff., 263f., 267ff. WENDLAND, G./ SCHÖNHALS, K.-M./ AHLHEIM, K. in E. Lange, ed., Predigtstudien für das Kirchenjahr 1973/1974 (Berlin/Stuttgart 1973) 188-94. FÜRST, T./ LENZ, D./ FÜRST, W. in GPM 28 (1974) 163-72. ELLIS, E. E. and GRÄSSER, E., eds., Jesus und Paulus (FS W. G. Kümmel; Göttingen 1975) 286ff., 332. SCHMITHALS, W. Der Römerbrief als historisches Problem (Gütersloh 1975) 16, 41, 197ff. FROITZHEIM, F. Christologie und Eschatologie bei Paulus (Würzburg 1979) 61ff. PANIKULAM, G. Koinōnia in the New Testament: A Dynamic Expression of Christian Life (Rome 1979) 67. ROBINSON, J. A. T. Wrestling with Romans (London 1979) 56-59. KIM,

S. The Origin of Paul's Gospel (Tübingen 1981) 313f. FRYER, N. S. L. "Reconciliation in Paul's Epistle to the Romans," Neotestamentica 15 (1981) 34-68. KLAIBER, W. Rechtfertigung und Gemeinde (Göttingen 1982) 115-17. KLEIN, G. "Eschatologie" in TRE 10 (1982) 283. RATSCHOW, C. H. "Eschatologie" in TRE 10 (1982) 350. FINDEIS, H.-J. Versöhnung-Apostolat-Kirche (Würzburg 1983) 253-67. DELLING, G. "Frieden" in TRE 11 (1983) 616. GORDAY, P. Principles of Patristic Exegesis: Romans 9-11 in Origen, John Chrysostom, and Augustine (New York/ Toronto 1983) 64f., 159f. HELEWA, G. "'Riconciliazione' divina e 'speranza della gloria' secondo Rom 5, 1-11," Teresianum 34 (1983) 275-306. NEBE, G. 'Hoffnung' bei Paulus (Göttingen 1983) 124, 134ff., 290.295. STUHLMACHER, P. "Sühne oder Versöhnung? Randbemerkungen zu Gerhard Friedrichs Studie: 'Die Verkündigung des Todes Jesu im Neuen Testament'," in U. Luz und H. Weder, eds., Die Mitte des Neuen Testaments (FS. E. Schweizer; Göttingen 1983) 295f. KLEINKNECHT, K. T. Der leidende Gerechtfertigte (Tübingen 1984) 182, 199, 324-37, 347-50, 354, 362f. RUCKSTUHL, E. "Gnade III" in TRE 13 (1984) 469f. HELEWA, G. "'Fedele à Dio.' Una lettura di Rom 5, 1-11," Teresianum 36 (1985) 25-57. DRYSDALE, D. "Justification by Grace through Faith," IrBS 10 (1988) 114-22. WEDDERBURN, A. J. M. The Reasons for Romans (Edinburgh 1988) 106, 130-32. BREYTENBACH, C. Versöhnung (Neukirchen-Vluyn 1989) 2n., 21, 26f., 66, 143, 153, 144-59, 157n., 158, 165f., 168-72, 168n., 178, 223. HOFIUS, O. Paulusstudien (Tübingen 1989) 6, 149, 166. MARTIN, R. P. Reconciliation: A Study of Paul's Theology (Grand Rapids 1989) 135-54. McDONALD, P. M. "Romans 5.1-11 as a Rhetorical Bridge," JSNT 40 (1990) 81-96. VOLF, J. M. G. Paul and Perseverance (Tübingen 1990) 49-56. COSBY, M. R. "Paul's Persuasive Language in Romans 5" in D. F. Watson, ed., Persuasive Artistry (FS G. A. Kennedy; Sheffield 1991) 209-26, esp.212-8. WAY, D. The Lordship of Christ. Ernst Käsemann's Interpretation of Paul's Theology (Oxford 1991) 145-8. OLIVEIRA, A. DE, Die Diakonie der Gerechtigkeit und der Versöhnung in der Apologie des 2. Korintherbriefes. Analyse und Auslegung von 2 Kor 2, 14-4, 6; 5, 11-6, 10 (Münster 1990) 370. PULCINI, T. "In Right Relationship with God. Present Experience and Future Fulfillment. An Exegesis of Romans 5:1-11," SVThQ 36 (1992) 61-85. PICKETT, R. W. "The Death of Christ as Divine Patronage in Romans 5:1-11" in E. H. Lovering, ed., Society of Biblical Literature 1993 Seminar Papers (Atlanta 1993) 726-39.

5:1-10   KÄSEMANN, E. Exegetische Versuche und Besinnungen II (1964) 183; New Testament Questions of Today (1969) 170. BERGER, K. und COLPE, C., eds., Religions-geschichtliches Textbuch zum Neuen Testament (Göttingen/Zürich 1987) 205f.

5:1-6   STAAB, K. Pauluskommentare aus der griechischen Kirche (Münster ²1984) 62:9-63:14 Apoll.

5:1-5   HEIM, K. "Nun wir denn sind gerecht geworden durch den Glauben, so haben wir Frieden mit Gott . . . " Der unerschuetterliche Grund (1946) 76. KLEIN, G.GPM 16 (1961/62) 135-40. JACOB, R. "Dieu, notre Joie. Rm 5, 1-5," AssS 31 (1973) 36-39. OSTEN-SACKEN, P. VON DER, Römer 8 als Beispiel paulinischer Soteriologie (Göttingen 1975) 124ff. MONTAGUE, G. T. The Holy Spirit (New York 1976) 204-06. MIRANDA, J. P. Marx and the Bible (London 1977) 229-322. DAHINTEN, G. in GPM 34 (1979) 123-29. KRIEGSTEIN, M. VON und DIETRICH, W. in P. Krusche et al., eds., Predigtstudien für das Kirchenjahr 1979/80. Perikopenreihe II/1 (Berlin/ Stuttgart 1979) 151-59. NEBE, G. 'Hoffnung' bei Paulus (Göttingen 1983) 81, 123ff., 134ff., 173.

	RICHES, J. "Heiligung" in TRE 14 (1985) 730. KRÖTKE, W. in GPM 40 (1985-86) 161-69. SAUTER, G. "Hoffnung III" in TRE 15 (1986) 497.
5:1-3	SCHRAGE, W. Die konkreten Einzelgebote in der paulinischen Paränese (1961) 15, 195.
5:1-2,8-11	BREYTENBACH, C. Versöhnung (Neukirchen-Vluyn 1989) 180-83.
5:1-2	KÄSEMANN, E. Exegetische Versuche und Besinnungen (1964) II 189. THUESING, W. Per Christun in Deum (1965) 184-87ff. JÜNGEL, E. Paulus und Jesus (1966) 70. SHIMADA, K. The Formulary Material in First Peter: A Study According to the Method of Traditions-geschichte (Diss; Ann Arbor MI 1969) 347-51. DINKLER, E. Eirene: Der urchristliche Friedens-gedanke (Heidelberg 1973) 32-35. BARR, J. Escaping from Fundamentalism (London 1984) 51, 144. BRANDENBURGER, E. "Gericht Gottes" in TRE 12 (1984) 477. DOBBELER, A. VON, Glaube als Teilhabe (Tübingen 1987) 183f. BREYTENBACH, C. Versöhnung (Neukirchen-Vluyn 1989) 143f., 148, 150, 155, 157, 159, 165, 170n.
5:1	BRUNNER, E. Dogmatik I (1946) 208. KOEHLER, L. Eine Handvoll Neues Testament. Ehrfurcht vor dem Leben (1954) 71-81. JÜNGEL, E. Paulus und Jesus (1966) 46. KERTELGE, K. "Rechtfertigung" bei Paulus (1967) 126, 128, 132, 161, 257, 298. KÄSEMANN, E. New Testament Questions of Today (1969) 177. THYEN, H. Studien zur Sündenvergebung (1970) 60, 171, 194f, 203. TAYLOR, V. The Text of the New Testament (London 1961) 100f. DEVITO, J. "The Leopards of Ignatius of Antioch (Romans 5, 1)," CIB 50 (1974) 63. LADD, G. E. A Theology of the New Testament (Grand Rapids 1974) 442, 456, 492, 521. CONZELMANN, H. und LINDEMANN, A. Arbeitsbuch zum Neuen Testament (Tübingen 1975) 26, 213f. BERGER, K. "Hellenistisch-heidnische Prodigien und die Vorzeichen in der jüdischen und christlichen Apokalyptik" in ANRW II.23.2 (1980) 1436. SCHLIER, H. "Der Friede nach dem Apostel Paulus" in V. Kubina und K. Lehmann, eds., Der Geist und die Kirche (FS H. Schlier; Freiburg/Basel/Wien 1980) 119f., 125, 128. THISELTON, A. C. The Two Horizons (Grand Rapids 1980) 419. MOIR, I. A. "Orthography and Theology: The Omicron-Omega Interchange in Romans 5:1 and Elsewhere" in E. J. Epp and G. D. Fee, eds., New Testament Textual Criticism (FS B. M. Metzger; Oxford 1981) 179-83. DELLING, G. "Frieden" in TRE 11 (1983) 616. FINDEIS, H.-J. Versöhnung Apostolat-Kirche (Würzburg 1983) 21. SCHMID, H. H. "Frieden" in TRE 11 (1983) 609. CONZELMANN, H. and LINDEMANN, A. Interpreting the New Testament (Peabody MA 1988) 22, 195. BREYTENBACH, C. Versöhnung (Neukirchen-Vluyn 1989) 18, 144-46, 149f., 152, 154, 157, 169f., 172, 180f., 223f.
5:2ff.	DUNN, J. D. G. Jesus and the Spirit. A Study of the Religious and Charismatic Experience of Jesus and the First Christians as Reflected in the New Testament (London 1975) 328.
5:2-3	BERGER, K. "Das Buch der Jubiläen" in JSHRZ II/3 (1981) 422n.8d.
5:2	HAHN, F. Christologische Hoheitstitel (1963) 234. BRAUN, H. Qumran und NT II (1966) 168. KERTELGE, K. "Rechtfertigung" bei Paulus (1967) 79, 149. BOVER, J. M. "'Gloriamur In Spe' (Rom. 5, 2)," Biblica 22 (1941) 41-45. BERGMEIER, R. Glaube als Gabe nach Johannes (Stuttgart 1980) 263n.465. HENGEL, M. The Atonement (London 1981) 46, 52. JOHNSON, E. E. The Function of Apocalyptic and Wisdom Traditions in Romans 9-11 (Atlanta GA 1989) 20, 120, 127, 137.
5:2a.b	BREYTENBACH, C. Versöhnung (Neukirchen-Vluyn 1989) 144n., 145, 146-50, 158, 172, 182.

5:2c,3a,11   BREYTENBACH, C. Versöhnung (Neukirchen-Vluyn 1989) 150-53.
5:2c   DE LORENZI, L. "La speranza nostro vanto. Rom 5, 2c" in E. Grässer und O.
              Merk, eds., Glaube und Escha-tologie (FS W. G. Kümmel; Tübingen 1985)
              165-88. BREYTENBACH, C. Versöhnung (Neukirchen-Vluyn 1989) 151.
5:3-5   THOMAS, J. "Anfechtung und Vorfreude. Ein biblischer Thema nach Jakobus
              1, 2-18, im Zusammenhang mit Psalm 126, Röm. 5, 3-5 und 1 Peter 1, 5-7,
              formkritisch untersucht und parakletisch ausgelegt" KuD 14 ('68) 183-206.
              LÜDEMANN, G. Paulus, der Heidenapostel, Band II (Göttingen 1983) 195f.
              LOHSE, E. Die Entstehung des Neuen Testaments (Stuttgart/Berlin/Köln [5]1991)
              129.
5:3-4   SIBER, P. Mit Christus leben (Zürich 1971) 162. GERSTENBERGER, G. und
              SCHRAGE, W. Leiden (Stuttgart 1977) 188f.; ET: J. E. Steely (trans.) Suffering
              (Nashville 1980) 218.
5:3   VOLZ, P. Die Eschatologie der Jüdischen Gemeinde (1934) 130. KLIJN, A F.
              J. "Die syrische Baruch-Apokalypse" in JSHRZ V/2 (1976) 157n.6a. NEBE, G.
              'Hoffnung' bei Paulus (Göttingen 1983) 126ff., 244.
5:3a   BREYTENBACH, C. Versöhnung (Neukirchen-Vluyn 1989) 151f.
5:4-5   KERTELGE, K. "Rechtfertigung" bei Paulus (1967) 149, 248f, 298.
5:4   DENTON, D. R. "Hope and Perseverance," SJTh 34 (1981) 313-20. WEDER,
              H. "Hoffnung II" in TRE 15 (1986) 486.
5:5ff.   SCHRAGE, W. Die konkreten Einzelgebote in der paulinischen Paränese (1961)
              56, 71, 73, 142, 239, 249, 252.
5:5-11   EICHHOLZ, G. Die Theologie des Paulus im Umriss (1972) passim.
5:5-8   OLIVEIRA, A. DE, Die Diakonie der Gerechtigkeit und der Versöhnung in der
              Apologie des 2. Korintherbriefes. Analyse und Auslegung von 2 Kor 2, 14-4,
              6; 5, 11-6, 10 (Münster 1990) 346.
5:5-6   BECKER, J. Paulus. Der Apostel der Völker (Tübingen 1989) 127, 445.
5:5   SOKOLOWSKI, E. Die Begriffe Geist und Leben bei Paulus (1903) 88ff.
              JUNCKER, A. Die Ethik des Apostels Paulus (1919) 13-15. BRUNNER, E.
              Dogmatik I (1946) 208, 226, 334. Mensch in Widerspruch (1937) 65. HER-
              MANN, I. Kyrios und Pneuma (1961) 109f. FLEW, R.N. Jesus and His Church
              (1956) 152. DELLING, G. Die Taufe im Neuen Testament (1963) 144, 152.
              KÄSEMANN, E. Exegetische Versuche und Bessinungen (1964) II 187; I 299.
              THUESING, W. Per Christum in Deum (1965) 161f. JÜNGEL, E. Paulus und
              Jesus (1966) 70. MERK, O. Handeln aus Glauben (1968) 12, 18, 60, 145.
              KÄSEMANN, E. New Testament Questions of Today (1969) 174. DUNN,
              J. D. G. Baptism in the Holy Spirit (1970) 105n, 130, 132, 139, 147, 151, 225.
              DIBELIUS, M. "Vier Worte des Römerbriefes" in Symbolae Biblicae Upsalien-
              ses 3 (Upsala 1944) 3-17. HARMAN, A. M. Paul's Use of the Psalms (Ann
              Arbor MI 1968) 184f. FEREE, N. F. S. The Extreme Center (Waco, TX 1973)
              150-55, 179-84. HEROLD, G. Zorn und Gerechtigkeit Gottes bei Paulus. Eine
              Untersuchung zu Röm. 1, 16-18 (Frankfurt 1973) 129ff. LADD, G. E. A Theol-
              ogy of the New Testament (Grand Rapids 1974) 476, 488, 518, 522. LULL, D.
              J. The Spirit in Galatia (Chico CA 1980) 64f. DEIDUN, T. J. New Covenant
              Morality in Paul (Rome 1981) 103-06, 126-30. NEBE, G. 'Hoffnung' bei
              Paulus (Göttingen 1983) 55f., 62, 66, 70, 126, 129, 131, 233. HAUSCHILD,
              W.-D. "Geist" in TRE 12 (1984) 202, 205. HAUSCHILD, W.-D. "Gnade IV"
              in TRE 13 (1984) 482, 486. HÖDL, L. "Gerechtigkeit" in TRE 12 (1984) 430.
              MOHRLANG, R. Matthew and Paul (Cambridge 1984) 102, 115, 119, 121.
              STAAB, K. Pauluskommentare aus der griechischen Kirche (Münster [2]1984)

655:1-3 Areth. WEDER, H. "Hoffnung II" in TRE 15 (1986) 488. LAYTON, B. The Gnostic Scriptures (Garden City NY 1987) 264.

5:5ff.   BAUMERT, N. Täglich Sterben und Auferstehen (München 1973) 382. MELL, U. Neue Schöpfung (Berlin/New York 1989) 344ff.

5:5-6   STAAB, K. Pauluskommentare aus der griechischen Kirche (Münster ²1984) 424:3-7 Oek.

5:5a   NEBE, G. 'Hoffnung' bei Paulus (Göttingen 1983) 131f., 293.

5:5b   NEBE, G. 'Hoffnung' bei Paulus (Göttingen 1983) 132ff.

5:6-11   SCHELKLE, K. H. Die Passion Jesu in der Verkündigung des Neuen Testaments (Heidelberg 1949) 173f., 192f. DALY, R. J. Christian Sacrifice (Washington DC 1978) 240. FURNISH, V. P. The Moral Teaching of Paul (Nashville 1979) 26, 82, 125. STAAB, K. Pauluskommentare aus der griechischen Kirche (Münster ²1984) 494:29-495:29 Phot. JONGE, M. DE. "Jesus' Death for Others and the Death of the Maccabean Martyrs" in T. Baarda et al., eds., Text and Testimony (FS. A. F. J. Klijn; Kampen 1988) 142-51, esp. 145, 151n.32.

5:6-10   FATUM, L. "Die menschliche Schwäche im Römerbrief," StTh 29 (1975) 31-52. FINDEIS, H.-J. Versöhnung-Apostolat-Kirche (Würzburg 1983) 267-75.

5:6-9   PAGELS, E. H. The Gnostic Paul. Gnostic Exegesis of the Pauline Letters (Philadelphia 1975) 26f.

5:6-8   DAVIES, W. D. The Sermon on the Mount (Cambridge 1966) 119. SHIMADA, K. The Formulary Material in First Peter: A Study According to the Method of Traditionsgeschichte (Diss; Ann Arbor MI 1969) 337-41, 342. BERGER, K. Exegese des Neuen Testaments (Heidelberg 1977) 55. BREYTENBACH, C. Versöhnung (Neukirchen-Vluyn 1989) 36, 126, 144, 150, 153, 157n., 221. COUSAR, C. B. A Theology of the Cross (Minneapolis 1990) 27, 43-5, 48. GEORGI, D. Theocracy in Paul's Praxis and Theology (Minneapolis 1991) 97-100, 97n.36. KLAUCK, H.-J. "Kirche als Freundesgemeinschaft? Auf Spurensuche im Neuen Testament," MThZ 42 (1, 1991) 1-14.

5:6-7   HAHN, F. Christologische Hoheitstitel (1963) 57, 202, 210. SCHMITHALS, W. Der Römerbrief als historisches Problem (Gütersloh 1975) 199, 205. KECK, L. E. "The Post-Pauline Interpretation of Jesus' Death in Rom 5:6-7" in Theologia crucis—signum crucis (FS E. Dinkler; Tübingen 1979) 237-48.

5:6,8   BEST, E. One Body in Christ (1955) 57. ROBINSON, J.M. Kerygman und historischer Jesus (1960) 66. DELLING, G. Die Taufe im Neuen Testament (1963) 117. BREYTENBACH, C. Versöhnung (Neukirchen-Vluyn 1989) 4, 155f., 169, 181, 198, 207, 210.

5:6   BRUNNER, E. Dogmatik I (1946) 194. KRAMER, W. Christos Kyrios Gottessohn (1963) §4b. LJUNGMAN, H. Pistis (1964) 49f. EICHHOLZ, G. Die Theologie des Paulus im Umriss (1972) 165f. DALTON, W. J. Christ's Proclamation to the Spirits. A Study of 1 Peter 3:18-4:6 (Rome 1965) 118. FROITZHEIM, F. Christologie und Eschatologie bei Paulus (Würzburg 1979) 31ff. HENGEL, M. The Atonement (London 1981) 13, 36f. MERKLEIN, H. Studien zu Jesus und Paulus (Tübingen 1987) 29n. 85, 51n.129, 52n.135, 54, 187. KOLLMANN, B. Ursprung und Gestalten der frühchristlichen Mahlfeier (Göttingen 1990) 175f.

5:7-8   LIMBECK, M. Mit Paulus Christ sein. Sachbuch zur Person und Theologie des Apostels Paulus (Stuttgart 1989) 106.

5:7,8   DENNEY, J. The Death of Christ (1956) 74.

5:7   WISSE, F. "The Righteous Man and the Good Man in Romans v.7," NTS 19 (1972) 91-93. BAUMERT, N. Täglich Sterben und Auferstehen (München 1973) 361. LANDAU, Y. "Martyrdom in Paul's Religious Ethics: An Exegetical Commentary on Romans 5:7," Immanuel 15 (1982/1983) 24-38. BERGER, K. und COLPE, C., eds., Religionsgeschichtliches Textbuch zum Neuen Testament (Göttingen/Zürich 1987) 206. DOWNING, F. G. Christ and the Cynics (Sheffield 1988) 188. BREYTENBACH, C. Versöhnung (Neukirchen-Vluyn 1989) 155f., 188, 198, 210. CLARKE, A. D. "The Good and the Just in Romans 5:7," TB 41 (1990) 128-42.

5:8ff.   BRUNNER, E. Dogmatik I (1946) 194. BARRETT, C.K. From First Adam to the Last (1962) 28f. BRAUMANN, G. Vorpaulinische christliche Taufverkündigung bei Paulus (1962) 36, 39, 41, 65f, 67, 74. MORRIS, L. The Apostolic Preaching of the Cross (London 1955) 198ff. BRANDENBURGER, E. "Gericht Gottes" in TRE 12 (1984) 477.

5:8-11   STANLEY, D.M. Christ's Resurrection in Pauline Soteriology (1961) 174-76. TACHAU, P. "Einst" und "Jetzt" im Neuen Testament (1972) 81-2. RIDDERBOS, H. Paul. An Outline of His Theology (Grand Rapids 1975) 182-91. BREYTENBACH, C. Versöhnung (Neukirchen-Vluyn 1989) 153f.

5:8-10   DENNEY, J. The Death of Christ (1956) 104. MANSUS, H. The Wrath of God in the Pauline Homologoumena (1969) 32-34. BRANDENBURGER, E. Adam und Christus (Neukirchen-Vluyn 1962) 166f., 222, 228, 234f., 237, 277. HOFIUS, O. Paulusstudien (Tübingen 1989) 33.

5:8,10   KOBAYASHI, N. "The Meaning of Jesus' Death in the 'Last Supper' Traditions," Toronto Journal of Theology 8 (1992) 95-105.

5:8-9   MÜNCHOW, C. Ethik und Eschatologie (Göttingen 1981) 150, 153f., 159. MERKLEIN, H. Studien zu Jesus und Paulus (Tübingen 1987) 187.

5:8,10   FREUND, G. und STEGEMANN, E., eds., Theologische Brosamen für Lothar Steiger (DBAT 5; Heidelberg 1985) 188.

5:8,9   DAVIES, W.D. Paul and Rabbinic Judaism (1955) 232-34. SCHRAGE, W. Die konkreten Einzelgebote in der paulinischen Paränese (1961) 21, 249.

5:8   BRUNNER, E. Dogmatik I (1946) 194, II (1950) 339. HAHN, F. Christologische Hoheitstitel (1963) 57, 210. KRAMER, W. Christol Kyrios Gottessohn (1963) §§4a, 6b. LADD, G. E. A Theology of the New Testament (Grand Rapids 1974) 424, 426, 451f. ABBING, P. J. R. "Diakonie" in TRE 8 (1981) 652. HENGEL, M. The Atonement (London 1981) 36f., 46, 74. KAHLEFELD, H. Die Gestalt Jesu in den Synoptischen Evangelien (Frankfurt 1981) 199. MEEKS, W. A. The First Urban Christians (New Haven/ London 1983) 85, 170, 239n.78. CRANFIELD, C. E. B. "Some Comments on Professor J. D. G. Dunn's 'Christology in the Making' with Special Reference to the Evidence of the Epistle to the Romans" in L. D. Hurst and N. T. Wright, eds., The Glory of Christ in the New Testament (FS G. B. Caird; Oxford 1987) 277f. MERKLEIN, H. Studien zu Jesus und Paulus (Tübingen 1987) 24n.60, 29n.85, 43, 51n.129, 52n.135, 54, 104, 187. BREYTENBACH, C. Versöhnung (Neukirchen-Vluyn 1989) 14, 33, 125, 143f., 153f., 155-59, 165, 169, 171, 194, 197f., 223. MELL, U. Neue Schöpfung (Berlin/New York 1989) 358.

5:9-11   THUESING, W. Per Christum in Deum (1965) 190-97, 205ff. FINDEIS, H.-J. Versöhnung-Apostolat-Kirche (Würzburg 1983) 280-86. VIELHAUER, P. "Paulus und das Alte Testament" in Oikodome [G. Klein, ed.] (München 1979) 199. CONZELMANN, H. and LINDEMANN, A. Interpreting the New Testament (Peabody MA 1988) 132. BREYTENBACH, C. Versöhnung (Neukirchen-Vluyn 1989) 8, 16, 34, 144, 146, 154f., 158f., 165f., 168f., 170-72, 176n., 182, 194, 222n.

5:9-10   WILCKENS, U. Die Missionsreden der Apostelgeschichte (1961) 156, 176, 184. MATTERN, L. Das Verständnis des Gerichtes bei Paulus (1966) 84, 86ff,

213. MERK, O. Handln aus Glauben (1968) 11, 12f, 15f. DERRETT, J.D.M. Law in the New Testament (1970) 399n6.

5:9   BRUNNER, Dogmatik I (1946) 245. SEIDENSTICKER, Ph. Lebendiges Opfer (1954) 152ff., 161f. DELLING, G. Fie Zueignung des Heils in der Taufe (1961) 56. KÄSEMANN, E. Exegetische Versuche und Besinnungen (1964) I 96. LJUNGMAN, H. Pistis (1964) 45f. JÜNGEL, E. Paulus und Jesus (1966) 29, 45, 49. KERTELGE, K. "Rechtfertigung" bei Paulus (1967) 52, 87, 126, 128, 150. LADD, G. E. A Theology of the New Testament (Grand Rapids 1974) 406, 423, 425, 442f., 566, 568. SYNOFZIK, E. Die Gerichts- und Vergeltungsaussagen bei Paulus (Göttingen 1977) 97-99. HOLTZ, T. "Euer Glaube an Gott'. Zu Form und Inhalt von 1 Thess. 1:9f" in R. Schnackenburg et al., eds., Die Kirche des Anfangs (FS H. Schürmann; Freiburg/Basel/Wien 1978) 465f., 480, 482. SCHMITHALS, W. "Zur Herkunft der gnostischen Elemente in der Sprache des Paulus" in B. Aland et al., eds., Gnosis (FS. H. Jonas; Göttingen 1978) 390-93. THISELTON, A. C. The Two Horizons (Grand Rapids 1980) 270, 419. HULTGREN, A. J. Paul's Gospel and Mission (Philadelphia 1985) 83. POBEE, J. S. Persecution and Martyrdom in the Theology of Paul (Sheffield 1985) 58, 76, 90. DOWNING, F. G. Christ and the Cynics (Sheffield 1988) 9. BREYTENBACH, C. Versöhnung (Neukirchen-Vluyn 1989) 157-59, 166, 168f., 172n. ZIESLER, J. Pauline Christianity (Oxford 1990) 73f., 81-83, 94.

5:10-11   BREYTENBACH, C. "Probleme rondom die interpretasie van die 'versoeningsuitsprake' by Paulus," HTS 42 (1986) 696-704. OLIVEIRA, A. DE, Die Diakonie der Gerechtigkeit und der Versöhnung in der Apologie des 2. Korintherbriefes. Analyse und Auslegung von 2 Kor 2, 14-4, 6; 5, 11-6, 10 (Münster 1990) 367. ZIESLER, J. Pauline Christianity (Oxford 1990) 42, 74, 85f, 91.

5:10   BRUNNER, Dogmatik I (1946) 194. DENNEY, J. The Death of Christ (1956) 85. DENNEY. KRAMER, W. Christol Kyrios Gottessohn (1963) §54b. BLANK, J. Paulus und Jesus (1968) 279-87. GOPPELT, L. Christologie und Ethik (1968) 153f, 157f. LADD, G. E. A Theology of the New Testament (Grand Rapids 1974) 406, 451-53. SALAS, A. "Reconciliados con Dios por la muerte de Cristo, (Rom 5, 10). La penitencia, hoy, vista desde la Biblia," BibFe 5 (1979) 47-71. SCHRAGE, W. "Die Elia-Apokalypse" in JSHRZ V/3 (1980) 269n.40c. KAHLEFELD, H. Die Gestalt Jesu in den synoptischen Evangelien (Frankfurt 1981) 199. RÄISÄNEN, H. The Torah and Christ (Helsinki 1986) 87. BREYTENBACH, C. Versöhnung (Neukirchen-Vluyn 1989) 16, 21, 24, 33, 74, 79, 80, 144, 146n., 151n.f., 156-59, 169, 172, 176, 181-83, 187, 189f., 223f. OLIVEIRA, A. DE, Die Diakonie der Gerechtigkeit und der Versöhnung in der Apologie des 2. Korintherbriefes. Analyse und Auslegung von 2 Kor 2, 14-4, 6; 5, 11-6, 10 (Münster 1990) 370.

5:11   BEST, E. One Body in Christ (1955) 22. DENNEY, J. The Death of Christ (1956) 72. 219-24. SCHRAGE, W. Die konkreten Einzelgebote in der paulinischen Paränese (1961) 15. KRAMER, W. Christol Kyrios Gottessohn (1963) §31a. BRAUN, H. Qumran und NT II (1966) 168. BRANDENBURGER, E. Adam und Christus (Neukirchen-Vluyn 1962) 230, 258f., 263. BERGER, K. Exegese des Neuen Testaments (Heidelberg 1977) 23f. FINDEIS, H.-J. Versöhnung-Apostolat-Kirche (Würzburg 1983) 276-79. STAAB, K. Pauluskommentare aus der griechischen Kirche (Münster ²1984) 63:15-19 Apoll. THOMPSON, S. The Apocalypse and Semitic Syntax (Cambridge 1985) 127. BREYTENBACH, C. Versöhnung (Neukirchen-Vluyn 1989) 9, 79, 144, 146, 150-52,

154f., 172, 177, 180-82, 223. MELL, U. Neue Schöpfung (Berlin/New York 1989) 294f., 294f.n.48.

5:12-8:39   VOS, J. S. Traditionsgeschichtliche Untersuchungen zur Paulinischen Pneumatologie (Assen 1973) 118-31.

5:12-6:1   STALDER, K. Das Werk des Geistes in der Heiligung bei Paulus (1962) 364-76.

5:12ff.   THACKERAY, H. The Relation of St. Paul to Contemporary Jewish Thought (1900) 30ff, 40ff. BOUSSET, W. Die Religion des Judentums im Späthellenistischen Zeitalter (1966=1926) 335, 408. BRUNNER, E. Dogmatik II (1950) 104, 114, 120; Mensch im Widerspruch (1937) 111, 114. BEST, E. One Body in Christ (1955) 207. CULLMANN, O. Die Christologie des Neuen Testaments (1957) 174ff. ELLIS, E.E. Paul's Use of the Old Testament (1957) 58f, 62, 116, 122. LYONNET, S. "Le sens de peirazein en Sap. 2, 24 et la doctrine du péché originel" Biblica 39 (1, '58) 27-36. RUDOLPH, K. Die Mandäer I (1960) 153, 3. SCHWEIZER, E. Erniedrigung und Erhöhung bei Jesus und seinen Nachfolgern (19-62) §6g. VANNESTE, A. "Saint Paul et La Doctrine Augustienne du péché originel" Studiorum Paulinorum Congressus Internationalis Catholicus 1961 (1963) II 517-19. DELLING, G. Die Taufe im Neuen Testament (1963) 123, 142. KÄSEMANN, E. Exegetische Versuche und Besinnungen (1964) I 80. BANDSTRA, A.J. The Law and the Elements of the World (1964) 125f. BULTMANN, R. Theologie des Neuen Testaments (1965) 251ff., 343f. HAHN, F. Das Verständnis der Mission im Neuen Testament ('65) 84. BULTMANN, R. "Adam und Christus nach Römer 5" Exegetica, ed. E. Dinkler (1967) 424-45. CAMBIER, J. L'Evangile de Dieu selon l'Epître aux Romains I (1967) 279-81. DEROSA, P. Christ and Original Sin (1967). LUZ, U. Das Geschichtsverständnis des Paulus (1968) 193-211. SCHOTTROFF, L. Der Glaubende und die feindliche Welt (1970) 115, 118, 124-6. THYEN, H. Studien zur Sünden-vergebung ((1970) 170, 197f, 203. WEISER, A. Glaube und Geschichte im Alten Testament (Göttingen 1961) 150, 257, 272. ROON, A. VAN, The Authenticity of Ephesians (Leiden 1974) 312f. RIDDERBOS, H. Paul. An Outline of His Theology (Grand Rapids 1975) 169. BÜHNER, J.-A. Der Gesandte und sein Weg im 4. Evangelium (Tübingen 1977) 79f. RUDOLPH, K. Die Gnosis (Göttingen 1978) 320. FRITZSCHE, H.-G. "Dekalog" in TRE 8 (1981) 421. SCHADE, H.-H. Apokalyptische Christologie bei Paulus (Göttingen 1981) 69-87. KÄSEMANN, E. "Zur ekklesiologischen Verwendung der Stichworte 'Sakrament' und 'Zeichen'" in Kirchliche Konflikte, Band 1 (Göttingen 1982) 58ff. THEISSEN, G. Psycholo-gische Aspekte paulinischer Theologie (Göttingen 1983) 151, 205, 210n.53, 232n.79, 266, 338n.119. DIETZFELBINGER, C. Die Berufung des Paulus als Ursprung seiner Theologie (Neukirchen 1985) 86, 117, 121, 126. SCHULZ, S. Neutestamentliche Ethik (Zürich 1987) 370f. WOLTER, M. Die Pastoralbriefe als Paulustradition (Göttingen 1988) 61. BECKER, J. Paulus. Der Apostel der Völker (Tübingen 1989) 404, 408, 477. MELL, U. Neue Schöpfung (Berlin/New York 1989) 360f., 395. VOLLENWEIDER, S. Freiheit als neue Schöpfung (Göttingen 1989) 273.

5:12-21   HANSON, S. The Unity of the Church in the New Testament (1946) 65-70. STECK, K.G. GPM 7 (1952) 14-18. LEIVESTAD, R. Christ the Conqueror (1954) 122ff. BEST, E. One Body in Christ (1955) 34ff, 38. GONZALEZ RUIZ, J.M. "El pecado original segun San Pablo" EstBi 17 (2, '58) 147-88. FERREIRA, P. Adam and Christ (1958). AMIOT, F. Les Idées Maitresses de Saint Paul (1959) 30, 42, 59-62, 70, 76, 222, 233, 248, 253. BARCLAY, W. "Great Themes of the New Testament—III Romans v.12-21" ET 70 (5, '59)

132-35; 6, '59) 172-75. JERVELL, J. Imago Dei (1960) 211, 215, 228, 242f., 267, 323. HULSBOSCH, A. "Zonde en dood in Rom. 5, 12-21" (Sin and Death in Rom 5:12-21) TvTh 1 (3, '61) 194-204. BARRETT, C.K. From First Adam to Last (1962) 15f., 70ff. BRANDENBURGER, E. Adam und Christus (1962). FONDEVILA, J.M. "La gracia capital de Adan y la carta a los romanos" EstEcl 37 (141, '62) 147-58. JÜNGEL, E. "Das Gesetz zwischen Adam und Christus. Eine theologische Studie ze Röm. 5, 12-21" ZThK 60 (1, '63) 42-74. KRECK, W. GPM 18 (1963/64) 25-30. IWAND, H.-J. Predigtmeditationen (1964) 592-99. LJUNGMAN, H. Pistis (1964) 56f. ALSZEGHY, Z. and M. Flick, "Il peccato originale inprospettiva personalistica" Gregorianum 46 (4, '65) 705-32. FLICK, M. "Riflessiono teologiche su un saggio esegetico" Biblica 46 (3, '65) 362-364.LENGSFELD, P. Adam und Christus (1965) 249-51, 73-99. SMULDERS, P. "Evolution and original sin" TheolDig 13 (3, '65) 172-76. BRAUN, H. Qumran und NT II (1966) 137, 174, 177, 228. FEUILLET, A. Le Christ sagesse de Dieu (1966) 333-39. HOFFMANN, P. Die Toten in Christus (1966) 310, 34. SCROGGS, R. The Last Adam (1966) 76ff. SIMONIS, W. "Erbsünde und Monogenismus" Catholica 20 (4, '66) 281-301. ALSZEGHY, Z. and M. FLICK, "Il peccato originale in prospettiva evoluzionistica" Gregorianum 47 (2, '66) 201-25. MICHEL, A. "Péché originel et monogénisme. A l'écoute de S.S. Paul IV" AmiCler 76 ('66) 506-10. ANON, "New Thinking on Original Sin" HerKorr 4 5, '67) 135-41. DE LETTER, P. "Rethinking Original Sin" ClerMon 31 (3, '67) 81-93. LYONNET, S. "Das Problem der Erbsünde im Neuen Testament" StZ 180 (7, '67) 33-39. KERTELGE, K. "Rechtfertigung" bei Paulus (1967) 141-46, 264. MICHEL, A. "Péché originel er polygénisme. Nouvelles questions—Nouvelles résponses" AmiCler 7 (16'67) 247-50. NICKELS, P. Targum and New Testament (1967) 68. GOPPELT, L. Christologie und Ethik (1968) 242f. LUZ, U. Das Geschichtsverständnis des Paulus (1968) 193ff., 209ff. VAN DÜLMEN, A. Die Theologie des Gesetzes bei Paulus (1968) 94f., 165, 166, 167, 211. KLEIN, G. GPM 24 (1968/69) 21-31. VOIGT, G. Der zerrissene Vorhang I (1969) 27-33. KRUSE, H. "Vorstufen der Erbschuldlehre. Vorpaulinische Schrift-grundlagen der Erbschuld-Lehre" MünchTheolZeit 20 (4, '69) 288-314. LILAND, P.P. The Function and the Scope of the Adam-Christ Parallel in Romans 5:12-21 (Rüschlikon 1969). SCHREINER, J. Gestalt und Anspruch des Neuen Testaments (1969) 60f. CRAGHAN, J.F. "Original Sin The Biblical Account" HPR 70 (4, '70) 274-282, 286. FEUILLET, A. "Le règne de la vie (Rom. v 12-21) Quelques observations sur la structure de l'Epître aux Romains" RevBi 77 (4, '70) 481-521. WERBLOWSKI, R.J.Z. and BLEEKER, C. J. Types of Redemption (1970) 62-71. BALTZER, D. Ezechiel und Deuterojesaja (1971) 125, 208, 214. GIBBS, J.G. Creation and Redemption (1971) 48-58, 83, 91f., 135f., 140f., 143-45, 147, 152. MAUSER, U. Gottesbild und Menschwerdung (1971) 177-79. EICHHOLZ, G. Die Theologie des Paulus im Umriss (1972) 144f., 172f., 175f., 181ff. JÜNGEL, E. Unterwegs zur Sache (1972) 145-72. SOIRON, T. Die Kirche als der Leib Christi (Düsseldorf 1951) 83ff. BARNHOUSE, D. G. God's Grace (Grand Rapids 1959) passim. MÜLLER, H. Die Auslegung alttestamentlichen Geschichts-stoffs bei Paulus (diss. Halle-Wittenberg 1960) 165-80. JOHNSON, H. The Humanity of the Saviour (London 1962) 75-78. KUSS, O. Paulus (Regensburg 1971) 169, 297-99, 354, 400-02. PETERS, G. W. A Biblical Theology of Missions (Chicago 1972) 72f., 148f. LOSADA, D. "El Texto de Rom. 5, 12-21. Un alálisis estructural," RevBi 36 (1974) 27-36. OSTEN-SACKEN, P. VON DER, Römer 8 als Beispiel paulinischer Soteriologie (Göttingen 1975) 160ff. PEISKER, C. H. in

GPM 30 (1975) 21-28. RIDDERBOS, H. Paul. An Outline of His Theology
(Grand Rapids 1975) 95-100. SCHMITHALS, W. Der Römerbrief als historisches Problem (Gütersloh 1975) 16f., 197. SCHWEIZER, E. "Menschensohn
und eschatologischer Mensch im Frühjudentum" in R. Pesch et al., eds., Jesus
und der Menschensohn (FS A. Vögtle; Freiburg/Basel/Wien 1975) 112f.
SZLAGA, J. "Chrystus jako nowy Adam w Listach Pawla Apostola (Christus
als der neue Adam in den Briefen des Apostels Paulus)," RTK 22 (1975) 85-96.
VENETZ, H. J. Der Glaube Weiss um die Zeit. Zum paulinischen Verständnis
der "Letzten Dinge" (Fribourg 1975) 47-52. WIEDEMANN, H.-G. und
SEIDEL, U. in P. Krusche et al., eds., Predigtstudien für das Kirchenjahr
1975/1976. IV/1 (Stuttgart 1975) 32-38. GUNDRY, R. H. Sōma in Biblical
Theology with Emphasis on Pauline Anthropology (Cambridge 1976) 45f. SAN-
DELIN, K.-G. Die Auseinandersetzung mit der Weisheit in 1 Korin-ther 15
(Abo 1976) 105f., 111. HAULOTTE, E. "Péché/ justice: par 'un seul homme'.
Romains 5:12-21," LuVie 131 (1977) 91-115. SCHILLEBEECKX, E. Christus
und die Christen (Freiburg/Basel/ Wien 1977) 140-43; ET: Christ: the Christian
Experience in the Modern World (London 1980) 150-52. SYNOFZIK, E. Die
Gerichts- und Vergeltungsaussagen bei Paulus (Göttingen 1977) 99-101. BECK,
H. W. "Der ur- und endgeschichtliche Universalismus der Schrift als hermeneu-
tischer Schlüssel für eine gesamtbiblische Theologie," ThBeitr 9 (1978) 182-94.
LAYMAN, F. D. Paul's Use of Abraham. An Approach to Paul's Understand-
ing of History (diss. Ann Arbor MI 1978) 209-12. BARCLAY, W. Great
Themes of the New Testament (Philadelphia 1979). BYRNE, B. "Sons of
God"—"Seed of Abraham" (Rome 1979) 85f. FROITZHEIM, F. Christologie
und Eschatologie bei Paulus (Würzburg 1979) 232f. HOFFMANN, P. "Auferstehung" in TRE 4 (1979) 489. ROBINSON, J. A. T. Wrestling with Romans
(London 1979) 60-66. ROLOFF, J. Neues Testament (Neukirchen-Vluyn 1979)
173. QUEK, S.-H. "Adam and Christ According to Paul" in D. A. Hagner and
M. J. Harris, eds., Pauline Studies (FS F. F. Bruce; Exeter 1980) 67-79.
BYRNE, B. "Living out the Righteousness of God: The Contribution of Rom
6:1-8:13 to an Understanding of Paul's Ethical Presuppositions," CBQ 43
(1981) 560-62. KIM, S. The Origin of Paul's Gospel (Tübingen 1981) 162-93,
264f. LOMBARD, H. A. "The Adam-Christ 'Typology' in Romans 5:12-21,"
Neotestamentica 15 (1981) 69-100. PRIEUR, J. M. "La Figure de l'apotre dans
les Actes apocryphes d'André" in F. Bovon et al., eds., Les Actes Apocryphes
des Apotres (Geneva 1981) 133. SEGALLA, G. "La struttura circolare di
Romani 5, 12-21 e il suo significato teologico," StPa 28 (1981) 377-80. JOHN-
SON, L. T. "Romans 3:21-26 and the Faith of Jesus," CBQ 44 (1982) 88f.
KLAIBER, W. Rechtfertigung und Gemeinde (Göttingen 1982) 117-21. LEI-
VESTAD, R. "Jesus—Messias—Menschensohn: Die jüdischen Heilandserwar-
tungen zur Zeit der ersten römischen Kaiser und die Frage nach dem messiani-
schen Selbstbewusstsein Jesu" in ANRW II.25.1 (1982) 251. THEOBALD, M.
Die überströmende Gnade (Würzburg 1982) 63-127. GORDAY, P. Principles
of Patristic Exegesis: Romans 9-11 in Origen, John Chrysostom, and Augustine
(New York/ Toronto 1983) 65-67, 166, 160f. HAYS, R. B. The Faith of Jesus
Christ (Chico CA 1983) 247. RUCKSTUHL, E. "Gnade III" in TRE 13 (1984)
469. SCHMITT, R. Gottesgerechtigkeit—Heilsgeschichte—Israel in der Theologie des Paulus (Frankfurt/Bern/ New York/Nancy 1984) 58-64. CARAGOUNIS,
C. C. "Romans 5.15-16 in the Context of 5:12-21: Contrast or Comparison?"
NTS 31 (1985) 142-48. HENRY, D. P. The Early Development of the Herme-
neutic of Karl Barth as Evidenced by His Appropriation of Romans 5:12-21

(Maccn GA 1985). HULTGREN, A. J. Paul's Gospel and Mission (Philadelphia 1985) 86-93. PETERSEN, N. R. Rediscovering Paul: Philemon and the Sociology of Paul's Narrative World (Philadelphia 1985) 218f., 235f. WEDER, H. "Gesetz und Sünde: Gedanken zu einem qualitativen Sprung im Denken des Paulus," NTS 31 (1985) 357-76. BENETOLLO, O. "Il peccato originale nella Bibbia," SaDo 31 (1986) 472-89. KOCH, D.-A. Die Schrift als Zeuge des Evangeliums (Tübingen 1986) 218f. RÄISÄNEN, H. The Torah and Christ (Helsinki 1986) 19. WEDER, H. Neutestamentliche Hermeneutik (Zürich 1986) 150. BETZ, O. "Der gekreuzigte Christus, unsere Weisheit und Gerechtigkeit (Der alttestamentliche Hintergrund von 1.Korinther 1-2)" in G. F. Hawthorne and O. Betz, eds., Tradition and Interpretation in the New Testament (FS E.E. Ellis; Grand Rapids/Tübingen 1987) 203f. OSTEN-SACKEN, P. VON DER, Evangelium und Tora: Aufsätze zu Paulus (München 1987) 13, 68f., 84, 89, 171, 175, 187. REBELL, W. Gemeinde als Gegenwelt (Frankfurt am Main/Bern/New York/Paris 1987) 54n.5. BYRNE, B. "'The Type of the One to Come' (Rom 5:14): Fate and Responsibility in Romans 5:12-21," AusBR 36 (1988) 19-30. DE BOER, M. C. The Defeat of Death: Apocalyptic Eschatology in 1 Corinthians 15 and Romans 5 (Sheffield 1988) 157-80. LINDARS, B. "Paul and the Law in Romans 5-8: An Actantial Analysis" in B. Lindars, ed., Law and Religion (Cambridge 1988) 130f. MacDONALD, M. Y. The Pauline Churches (Cambridge 1988) 81. BREYTENBACH, C. Versöhnung (Neukirchen-Vluyn 1989) 126f., 143, 157, 213. MARTIN, B. L. Christ and the Law in Paul (Leiden 1989) 14, 16, 39, 41, 55, 72f., 80f., 98, 112, 121f., 127. MASCELLANI, E. Prudens dispensator verbi. Romani 5, 12-21 nell'esegesi di Clemente Alessandrino e Origene (Firenze 1990). ZIESLER, J. Pauline Christianity (Oxford 1990) 52, 54-56, 60, 65, 77, 95. COSBY, M. R. "Paul's Persuasive Language in Romans 5" in D. F. Watson, ed., Persuasive Artistry (FS G. A. Kennedy; Sheffield 1991) 209-26, esp.218-25. GEORGI, D. Theocracy in Paul's Praxis and Theology (Minneapolis 1991) 98f. KERTELGE, K. "Adam und Christus: Die Sünde Adams im Lichte der Erlösungstat Christi nach Röm 5, 12-21" in C. Breytenbach et al., eds., Anfänge der Christologie (FS F. Hahn; Göttingen 1991) 141ff. KERTELGE, K. "Die Sünde Adams im Lichte der Erlösungstat Christi nach Röm 5, 12-21," IKZ/Communio 20 (1991) 305-14. KERTELGE, K. "The sin of Adam in the light of Christ's redemptive act according to Romans 5:12-21," Communio/International Catholic Review 18 (1991) 502-13. KERTELGE, K. "Adam und Christus. Die Sünde Adams im Lichte der Erlösungstat Christi nach Röm 5, 12-21" in C. Breytenbach and H. Paulsen, eds., Anfänge der Christologie (FS F. Hahn; Göttingen 1991) 141-53. WAY, D. The Lordship of Christ. Ernst Käsemann's Interpretation of Paul's Theology (Oxford 1991) 164-7. DAVIDSEN, O. "Den strukturelle Adam/ Kristus-typologi. Om Romerbrevets grundfortaelling (The Structural Adam/ Christ-typology. On the Basic Narrative of the Letter to the Romans)," DTT 55 (1992) 241-61.

5:12-19   BEST, E. One Body in Christ (1955) 26, 39, 40. DAVIES, W.D. Paul and Rabbinic Judaism (1955) 23, 31f., 34, 41, 52, 265, 268. DUBARLE, A.M. "Le péchè originel dans les livres sapientiaux" RThom 56 (4, '56) 597-619. MURRAY, J. The Imputation of Adam's Sin (1959). MICHEL, A. "Monogénisme et péché originel. Sokutions acquises et tendances nouvelles" AmiCler 75 ('66) 353-62, 376-81. DE FRAINE, J. The Bible and the Origin of Man (1967). GRISPINO, J.A. "Polygenesis and Original Sin" HPR 68 "1, '67) 17-22. JACOB, R. "La nouvelle solidarité humaine. Rm 5, 12-19," AssS 14 (1973) 32-38. DUNN, J. D. Christology in the Making (London 1980) 103, 111, 306n.16.

MILNE, D. J. W. "Genesis 3 in the Letter to the Romans," RThR 39 (1980) 10-18. OLIVEIRA, A. DE, Die Diakonie der Gerechtigkeit und der Versöhnung in der Apologie des 2. Korintherbriefes. Analyse und Auslegung von 2 Kor 2, 14-4, 6; 5, 11-6, 10 (Münster 1990) 351.

5:12-18   HAYS, R. B. The Faith of Jesus Christ (Chico CA 1983) 69, 83.

5:12-17   RENWART, L. "Péché d'Adam, péché du monde," NRTh 113 (4, 1991) 535-42.

5:12-15   ROBINSON, J. A. Pelagius's Exposition of Thirteen Epistles of St Paul (Cambridge 1922) 41ff. ENGLEZAKIS, B. "Rom 5, 12-15 and the Pauline Teaching on the Lord's Death: Some Observations," Biblica 58 (1977) 231-36. BERGER, K. "Das Buch der Jubiläen" in JSHRZ II/3 (1981) 438n.21a. BACQ, P. "Le péché originel," LuVit 45 (4, 1990) 377-93.

5:12-14   LYONNET, S. "Le péchè originel et l'exégese de Rom 5, 12-14" RSR 44 ('56) 63-84; "Le sens de' *eph ho* en Rom. 5:12 et l'exégese des pères grecs" Biblica 36 ('55) 436-56. VANNI, U. "L'analisi letteraria del contesto di Rom. 5, 12-24" RivBi 11 (2, '63) 115-44; "Rom. 5:12-14 alla luce del contesto" (4, 63) 337-66. PAGELS, E. H. The Gnostic Paul. Gnostic Exegesis of the Pauline Letters (Philadelphia 1975) 27f. BOUWMAN, G. "'Zonde wordt niet aangerekend, wanneer er geen wet is.' Een onderzoek naar de structuur van Rom. 5, 12-14," TvTh 17 (1977) 131-44. SWIDLER, L. Biblical Affirmations of Woman (Philadelphia 1979) 323f. STAAB, K. Pauluskommentare aus der griechischen Kirche (Münster ²1984) 362:13-364:13 Genn. BIJU-DUVAL, D. "La traduzione di Rm 5, 12-14," RivB 38 (3, 1990) 353-73.

5:12-13   SCHRAGE, W. Die konkreten Einzelgebote in der paulinischen Paränese (1961) 64, 65. FRIEDRICH, G. "Freiheit und Liebe im ersten Korintherbrief" in Auf das Wort kommt es an. Gesammelte Aufsätze (Göttingen 1978) 180.

5:12   BRUNNER, E. Dogmatik II (1950) 96, 112, 124, 150. ROBINSON, J.A.T. The Body (1952) 35f. BEST, E. One Body in Christ (1955) 34, 37. LYONNET, S. "Le sens de ἐφ' ᾧ en Rom 5, 12 et l'exégèse des Pères grecs" Biblica 36/4 (1955) 436-56. LACH, J. "'Poniewaz wszyscy zgrezeszyli . . . ' (Rzym 5, 12) ('In quo omnes peccaverunt . . . ' ad Rom 5, 12)" RBL 12 (6, '59) 559-72. LIGIER, L. "'In quo omnes peccaverunt' Actes ou état?" NRTh 82 (4, '60) 337-48. LYONNET, S. "Le péché originel en Rom 5, 12. l'Exégèse des Pères grecs et les décrets du Concile de Trente" Biblica 41 (4, '60) 325-55. SPADAFORA, F. "Rom. 5, 12 esegesi e riflessi dogmatici" Divinitas (2, '60) 289-98. MEYENDORFF, J. "Ἐφ' ᾧ (Rom. 5, 12) chez Cyrille d'Alexandrie or Théodoret" in Studia Patristica IV ed. F.L. Cross (1961) 157-61. LYONNET, S. "A propos de Raomains 5, 12 dans l'oeuvre de S. Augustin Note complémentaire" Biblica 45 (4, '64) 541-42. CAMBIER, J. "Péchè des Hommes et Péchè d'Adam en Rom, V.12, " NTS 11 (1964)65) 217f. O'ROURKE, J.J. "Some Considerations about Polygenism" ThSt 26 (3, '65) 407-16. TURNER, N. Grammatical Insights into the New Testament (1965) 116ff. JÜNGEL, E. Paulus und Jesus (1966) 58. RICHARDS, J.R. "Romans and I Corinthians: Their Chronological Relationship and Comparative Dates" NTS 13 (1966/67) 20ff. NICKELS, P. Targum and New Tesatment (1967) 68. DANKER, F.W. "Romans V.12. Sin Under Law" NTS 14 (1967/68)424f. CAMBIER, J. L'Evangile de Dieu selon l'Epître aux Romains, Rev. L. Dequeker, CollMech 53 (4, '68) 555-57. KNAUER, P. "Erbsünde als Todersverfallenheit. Eine Deutung von Röm. 5, 12 aus dem Vergleich mit Hebr. 2, 14f" ThuG 58 (2, '68) 153-58. ROMANIUK, C. "Le livre de la Sagesse dans le Nouveau Testament" NTS 14 (1968) 498-514. SCULLION, J.J. "An Interpretation of Romans v:12"

ABR 16 (1-4, '68) 31-36. STROBEL, A. Erkenntnis und Bekenntnis der Sünde in neutestamentlicher Zeit (1968) 49. LUZ, U. Das Geschichts-verständnis des Paulus (1968) 209f. VAN DÜLMEN, A. Die Theologie des Gesetzes bei Paulus (1968) 95, 96, 97, 160, 210, 216. CRANFIELD, C.E.B. "On Some of the Problems in the Interpretation of Romans 5, 12" SJTh 22 (3, '69) 324-41. ROMANIUK, K. "Nota su Rom. 5, 12 (A proposito del problema de male) "RivBi 19 (3, '71) 327-34. DIBELIUS, M. "Vier Worte des Römerbriefs" in Symbolae Biblicae Upsalienses 3 (Uppsala 1944) 3-17. BRANDENBURGER, E. Adam und Christus (Neukirchen-Vluyn 1962) 9f., 158-80, 181ff., 187f., 190f., 193f., 201ff., 214-19, 232, 234, 236, 238, 242-44, 253, 260, 263, 265, 268. BAUMERT, N. Täglich Sterben und Auferstehen (München 1973) 386f., 390. MIGUENS, E. "A Particular Notion of Sin," AER 167 (1973) 30-40. WEDDERBURN, A. J. M. "The Theological Structure of Romans v. 12," NTS 19 (1973) 339-54. KÜMMEL, W. G. Römer 7 und das Bild des Menschen im Neuen Testament (München 1974) 70, 86, 194, 196. LADD, G. E. A Theology of the New Testament (Grand Rapids 1974) 403, 406, 568. SCHMITHALS, W. Der Römerbrief als historisches Problem (Gütersloh 1975) 197. KLIJN, A F. J. "Die syrische Baruch-Apokalypse" in JSHRZ V/2 (1976) 134fn.XVII.3a, 160n.15a. FRIEDRICH, G. "'Αμαρτία οὐκ ἐλλογεῖται Rom. 5, 13" in Auf das Wort kommt es an. Gesammelte Aufsätze (Göttingen 1978) 126. HÜBNER, H. Das Gesetz bei Paulus (Göttingen 1978) 66f. STUIBER, A. "Ambrosiaster" in TRE 2 (1978) 360. GEORGI, D. "Weisheit Salomos" in JSHRZ III/4 (1980) 2n.24b. THEOBALD, M. Die überströmende Gnade (Würzburg 1982) 80-84. GORDAY, P. Principles of Patristic Exegesis: Romans 9-11 in Origen, John Chrysostom, and Augustine (New York/Toronto 1983) 175. HAYS, R. B. The Faith of Jesus Christ (Chico CA 1983) 203. KLEINKNECHT, K. T. Der leidende Gerechtfertigte (Tübingen 1984) 325f. STAAB, K. Pauluskommentare aus der griechischen Kirche (Münster ²1984) 424:8-11 Oek; 495:30-496:13 Phot. HÄRING, H. Das Problem des Bösen in der Theologie (Darmstadt 1985) 94, 96. SANDERS, E. P. Paul, the Law, and the Jewish People (London 1985) 23f., 35. LEON-DUFOUR, X. Life and Death in the New Testament (San Francisco 1986) 207f., 210. BERGER, K. und COLPE, C., eds., Religionsge-schichtliches Textbuch zum Neuen Testament (Göttingen/Zürich 1987) 206f. KIRBY, J. T. "The Syntax of Romans 5.12: a Rhetorical Approach," NTS 33 (1987) 283-86. RÖHSER, G. Metaphorik und Personifikation der Sünde (Tübingen 1987) 4, 14, 17, 117f., 140, 142, 157, 158ff., 162. WEDDERBURN, A. J. M. Baptism and Resurrection (Tübingen 1987) 355f. MARTIN, B. L. Christ and the Law in Paul (Leiden 1989) 44, 69f., 72f., 81, 83, 85, 98, 108, 121. SCHNELLE, U. Wandlungen im paulinischen Denken (Stuttgart 1989) 69. BEKER, J. C. "The Relationship Between Sin and Death in Romans" in R. T. Fortna and B. R. Gaventa, eds., The Conversation Continues. Studies in Paul and John (FS J. L. Martyn; Nashville 1990) 55-61, esp.57. FITZMYER, J. A. "The Consecutive Meaning of *eph ho* in Romans 5.12," NTS 39 (1993) 321-39.

5:12b   FREUND, G. und STEGEMANN, E., eds., Theologische Brosamen für Lothar Steiger (DBAT 5; Heidelberg 1985) 186.

5:13-14   LUZ, U. Das Geschichtsverständnis des Paulus (1968) 198f. BRANDENBUR-GER, E. Adam und Christus (Neukirchen-Vluyn 1962) 179f., 180-214, 218f., 242f., 250ff. SCHMITHALS, W. "Zur Herkunft der gnostischen Elemente in der Sprache des Paulus" in B. Aland et al., eds., Gnosis (FS. H. Jonas; Göttingen 1978) 392f. THEOBALD, M. Die überströmende Gnade (Würzburg 1982) 85-90. STAAB, K. Pauluskommentare aus der griechischen Kirche (Münster ²1984) 83:1-26 Diod; 118:16-119:26 ThM; 424:12-425:3 Oek; 496:14-498:11 Phot. FREUND, G. und STEGEMANN, E., eds., Theologische Brosamen für Lothar Steiger (DBAT 5; Heidelberg 1985) 392. LEON-DUFOUR, X. Life and Death in the New Testament (San Francisco 1986) 207f., 212. DE BOER, M. C. The Defeat of Death: Apocalyptic Eschatology in 1 Corinthians 15 and Romans 5 (Sheffield 1988) 165-69. GIBLIN, Ch. H. "A Qualifying Parenthesis (Rom 5:13-14) and Its Context" in M. P. Horgan and P. J. Kobelski, eds., To Touch the Text (FS J. A. Fitzmyer; New York 1989) 305-15. KLINE, M. G. "Gospel until the Law. Rom 5:13-14 and the Old Covenant," JEThS 34 (1991) 433-46.

5:13,20   SCHREINER, J. Gestalt und Anspruch des Neuen Testaments (1969) 62f.
5:13   FRIEDRICH, G. "'Αμαρτία οὐκ ἐλλογεῖται. Röm. 5, 13" ThLZ 77 ('52) 523-28. JUNGEL, E. Paulus und Jesus (1966) 51, 56, 58. STROBEL, A. Erkenntnis und Bekenntnis der Sünde in neutestament-licher Zeit (1968) 49. VAN DEULMEN, A. Die Theologie des Gesetzes bei Paulus (1968) 42, 84, 92, 101, 155, 170, 171. KÜMMEL, W. G. Römer 7 und das Bild des Menschen im Neuen Testament (München 1974) 48-50. FRIEDRICH, G. "'Αμαρτία οὐκ ἐλλογεῖται Rom. 5, 13" in Auf das Wort kommt es an. Gesammelte Aufsätze (Göttingen 1978) 123-31. BAMMEL, C. P. H. "Philocalia IX, Jerome, Epistle 121, and Origen's Exposition of Romans VII," JThS 32 (1981) 52, 55, 57, 66. RÄISÄNEN, H. Paul and the Law (Tübingen 1983) 11, 141, 145-48. DU TOIT, A. B. "Hyperbolical contrasts: a neglected aspect of Paul's style" in J. H. Petzer and P. J. Hartin, eds., A South African Perspective on the New Testament (FS B. M. Metzger; Leiden 1986) 186. RÖHSER, G. Metaphorik und Personifikation der Sünde (Tübingen 1987) 10, 55f., 103, 142, 157. MARTIN, B. L. Christ and the Law in Paul (Leiden 1989) 19, 22, 25, 42, 44, 69, 73f., 97.

5:14-19   STAAB, K. Pauluskommentare aus der griechischen Kirche (Münster ²1984) 498:12-499:13 Phot.

5:14-16   SPICQ, C. Dieu et l'Homme (1961) 207.
5:14   VOLZ, P. Die Eschatologie der Jüdischen Gemeinde (1934) 190. ROBINSON, J.A.T. The Body (1952) 35f. CAMPEAU, L. "Regnavit mors ab Adam usque ad Moysen" Sciences Eccl. V ('53) 57-65. BEST, E. One Body in Christ ('55) 34. SCHRAGE, W. Die konkreten Einzelgebote in der paulinischen Paränese (1961) 236. BARRETT, C.K. From First Adam to Last (1962) 23f, 68f. DELLING, G. Die Taufe im Neuen Testament (1963) 130. KÄSEMANN, E. Exegetische Versuche und Besinnungen (1964) I 74f. THUESING, W. Per Christun in Deum (1965) 135f. SCROGGS, R. The Last Adam, Rev. J. Bligh, HeyJ 8 (4, '67) 417-19. GOPPELT, L. Christologie und Ethik (1968) 247f. METZGER, B.M. "Explicit reference in the works of Origen to variant readings in New Testament manuscripts" Historical and Literary Studies ('68) 98. VAN DÜLMEN, A. Die Theologie des Gesetzes bei Paulus (1968) 110, 159, 160, 164, 167, 186, 187. MAUSER, U. Gottesbild und Menschwerdugn (1971) 147, 169f. ROBINSON, J. A. Pelagius's Exposition of Thirteen Epistles of St Paul (Cambridge 1922) 62, 271, 309, 314f., 317. BRANDENBURGER, E. Adam und Christus (Neukirchen-Vluyn 1962) 219f., 240f. VANNI, U. "Homoioma in Paolo (Rm 1, 23; 5, 14; 6, 5; 8, 3; Fil 2, 7). un'interpretazione esegetico-teologica alla luce dell'uso dei LXX—IᵃParte," Gregorianum 58 (1977) 321-45. FRIEDRICH, G. "'Αμαρτία οὐκ ἐλλογεῖται Rom. 5, 13" in Auf das Wort kommt es an. Gesammelte Aufsätze (Göttingen 1978) 130f. HAACKER, K. "Exegetische Probleme des Römerbriefs," NovT 20 (1978) 1-21. STUIBER, A. "Ambrosiaster" in TRE 2 (1978) 360. DUNN, J. D. Christology in the Making

(London 1980) 111, 119, 127, 307n.18. VOIGT, S. "Homoioma (Rm 5, 14) e Pecado Original: Uma Releitura Exegética," REB 41 (1981) 5-18. MUDDI-MAN, J. "'Adam, the Type of the One to Come'," Theology 87 (1984) 101-10. STAAB, K. Pauluskommentare aus der griechischen Kirche (Münster ²1984) 53:8-17 Akazc; 425:4-7 Oek; 655:4-16 Areth. MARTIN, B. L. Christ and the Law in Paul (Leiden 1989) 34, 39, 42, 44, 70, 73-75, 77f., 81-83.

5:15ff. KÄSEMANN, E. Exegetische Versuche und Besinnungen (1964) I 110.
5:15-21 LAFONT, G. "Sur l'Interpretation de Raomains V. 15-21" RechSR 45 (4, '57) 481-513. PAGELS, E. H. The Gnostic Paul. Gnostic Exegesis of the Pauline Letters (Philadelphia 1975) 28.
5:15-19 DUNN, J. D. Christology in the Making (London 1980) 126f.
5:15-17 BRANDENBURGER, E. Adam und Christus (Neukirchen-Vluyn 1962) 219-31, 242f., 273ff. VIELHAUER, P. "Paulus und das Alte Testament" in Oikodome [G. Klein, ed.] (München 1979) 199. DE BOER, M. C. The Defeat of Death: Apocalyptic Eschatology in 1 Corinthians 15 and Romans 5 (Sheffield 1988) 170ff.
5:15-16 DUNN, J. D. G. Jesus and the Spirit. A Study of the Religious and Charismatic Experience of Jesus and the First Christians as Reflected in the New Testament (London 1975) 206. SCHATZMANN, S. S. A Pauline Theology of Charismata (Peabody MA 1987) 4-6, 15-18.
5:15 BEST, E. One Body in Christ (1955) 34, 37, 133n. DELGADO VARELA, J.M. "Sentido literal mariologico de Rom. 5, 15" EphM 13 (2, '63) 253-66. DELLING, G. Die Taufe im Neuen Testament (1963) 117. MERK, O. Handeln aus Glauben (1968) 6, 16, 33. VAN DÜLMEN, A. Die Theologie des Gesetzes bei Paulus (1968) 95, 167, 197, 199, 201, 213. ROBINSON, J. A. Pelagius's Exposition of Thirteen Epistles of St Paul (Cambridge 1922) 35ff., 242. BRANDENBURGER, E. Adam und Christus (Neukirchen-Vluyn 1962) 68f., 158f., 161f., 219-224, 276f. BAUMERT, N. Täglich Sterben und Auferstehen (München 1973) 300f. ROON, A. VAN, The Authenticity of Ephesians (Leiden 1974) 114ff. SCHWEIZER, E. "Menschensohn und eschatologischer Mensch im Frühjudentum" in R. Pesch et al., eds., Jesus und der Menschensohn (FS A. Vögtle; Freiburg/Basel/Wien 1975) 117. THEOBALD, M. Die überströmende Gnade (Würzburg 1982) 90-99. HAYS, R. B. The Faith of Jesus Christ (Chico CA 1983) 168, 174. STAAB, K. Pauluskommentare aus der griechischen Kirche (Münster ²1984) 83:27-84:14 Diod; 119:27-35 ThM; 425:8-27 Oek; 426:1-3 Oek. CONZELMANN, H. and LINDEMANN, A. Interpreting the New Testament (Peabody MA 1988) 132. OLIVEIRA, A. DE, Die Diakonie der Gerechtigkeit und der Versöhnung in der Apologie des 2. Korintherbriefes. Analyse und Auslegung von 2 Kor 2, 14-4, 6; 5, 11-6, 10 (Münster 1990) 126.
5:16-17 THEOBALD, M. Die überströmende Gnade (Würzburg 1982) 99-106. STAAB, K. Pauluskommentare aus der griechischen Kirche (Münster ²1984) 84:15-25 Diod.
5:16 WETTER, G.P. Der Vergeltungsgedanke bei Paulus (1912) 62ff. SCHRAGE, W. Die konkreten Einzelgebote in der paulinischen Paränese (1961) 65. BRANDENBURGER, E. Adam und Christus (Neukirchen-Vluyn 1962) 158f., 164f., 224-27, 233f. KLEINKNECHT, K. T. Der leidende Gerechtfertigte (Tübingen 1984) 337. STAAB, K. Pauluskommentare aus der griechischen Kirche (Münster ²1984) 119:36-120:6 ThM; 364:14-18 Genn. HOOKER, M. D. From Adam to Christ. Essays on Paul (Cambridge 1990) 29f., 32. OLIVEIRA, A. DE, Die Diakonie der Gerechtigkeit und der Versöhnung in der Apologie des 2. Korintherbriefes. Analyse und Auslegung von 2 Kor 2, 14-4, 6; 5, 11-6, 10 (Münster

1990) 189. KRAUS, W. Der Tod Jesu als Heiligtumsweihe. Eine Untersuchung zum Umfeld der Sühnevorstellung in Römer 3, 25-26a (Neukirchen-Vluyn 1991) 16n., 104, 108ff., 111.

5:17-21   THUESING, W. Per Christum in Deum (1965) 191f., 210-18f. SIBER, P. Mit Christus leben (Zürich 1971) 236.

5:17   BEST, E. One Body in Christ (1955) 37. KÄSEMANN, E. Exegetische Versuche und Besinnungen (1964) II 182. JÜNGEL, E. Paulus und Jesus (1966) 39, 41. KERTELGE, K. "Rechtfertigung" bei Paulus (1967) 128, 133. VAN DÜLMEN, A. Die Theologie des Gesetzes bei Paulus (1968) 95, 97, 167, 180, 181, 197, 199. MERK, O. Handeln aus Glauben (1968) 6, 11, 13, 16. KÄSEMANN, E. New Testament Questions of Today (1969) 169. BRANDEN-BURGER, E. Adam und Christus (Neukirchen-Vluyn 1962) 158f., 161f., 164f., 227-31, 233f., 243f. ELLIS, E. E. and GRÄSSER, E., eds., Jesus und Paulus (FS W. G. Kümmel; Göttingen 1975) 267ff., 290. SCHÜTZ, J. H. "Charisma" in TRE 7 (1981) 689. STAAB, K. Pauluskommentare aus der griechischen Kirche (Münster ²1984) 120:7-12 ThM; 364: 19-26 Genn. MARTIN, B. L. Christ and the Law in Paul (Leiden 1989) 70, 74f., 81-83, 109, 118, 121-23, 125, 134. OLIVEIRA, A. DE, Die Diakonie der Gerechtigkeit und der Versöhnung in der Apologie des 2. Korintherbriefes. Analyse und Auslegung von 2 Kor 2, 14-4, 6; 5, 11-6, 10 (Münster 1990) 126.

5:18-19   BARRETT, C.K. From First Adam to Last (1962) 113f. BRANDENBURGER, E. Adam und Christus (Neukirchen-Vluyn 1962) 158f., 220f., 232-47, 269ff. SCHMITHALS, W. "Zur Herkunft der gnostischen Elemente in der Sprache des Paulus" in B. Aland et al., eds., Gnosis (FS. H. Jonas; Göttingen 1978) 391-93. JOHNSON, L. T. "Romans 3:21-26 and the Faith of Jesus," CBQ 44 (1982) 80f., 88-90. THEOBALD, M. Die überströmende Gnade (Würzburg 1982) 108-14. HAYS, R. B. The Faith of Jesus Christ (Chico CA 1983) 173. STAAB, K. Pauluskommentare aus der griechischen Kirche (Münster ²1984) 84:26-36 Diod; 120:13-29 ThM. BREYTENBACH, C. Versöhnung (Neukirchen-Vluyn 1989) 139, 141, 157f., 204, 207, 210.

5:18   BEST, E. One Body in Christ (1955) 37, 124n. DELLING, G. Die Taufe im Neuen Testament (1963) 132. LJUNGMAN, H. Pistis (1964) 72f. HAHN, F. Das Verständnis der Mission im Neuen Testament (1965) 91. MORRIS, L. The Apostolic Preaching of the Cross (1965) 287ff. KERTELGE, K. "Rechtfertigung" bei Paulus (1967) 146, 154, 263. CLARK, K. W. "The Meaning of APA" in The Gentile Bias and other Essays [J. L. Sharpe III, ed.] (Leiden 1980) 201. CLARK, S. B. Man and Woman in Christ (Ann Arbor MI 1980) 17, 37. KLEINKNECHT, K. T. Der leidende Gerechtfertigte (Tübingen 1984) 337. STAAB, K. Pauluskommentare aus der griechischen Kirche (Münster ²1984) 53:18-22 Akazc. HULTGREN, A. J. Paul's Gospel and Mission (Philadelphia 1985) 83. LEON-DUFOUR, X. Life and Death in the New Testament (San Francisco 1986) 165. MARTYN, D. W. "A Child and Adam: A Parable of the Two Ages" in J. Marcus and M. L. Soards, eds., Apocalyptic and the New Testament (FS J. L. Martyn; Sheffield 1989) 317-33. OLIVEIRA, A. DE, Die Diakonie der Gerechtigkeit und der Versöhnung in der Apologie des 2. Korintherbriefes. Analyse und Auslegung von 2 Kor 2, 14-4, 6; 5, 11-6, 10 (Münster 1990) 189, 352.

5:19   BEST.E. One Body in Christ (1955) 34, 37. ROMANIUK, K. L'Amour de Pere er du Fils dans la Soteriologie de Saint Paul (1961) 105, 110f., 139f., 149f. STANLEY, D.M. Christ's Resurrection in Pauline Soteriology (1961) 176-81. SCHWEIZER, E. Erniedrigung und Erhöhung bei Jesus und seinen Nachfolgern

(1962) §9b. DELLING, G. Die Taufe im Neuen Testament (1963) 117. KÄSE-
MANN, E. Exegetische Versuche und Besinnungen II (1964) 184. LJUNG-
MAN, H. Pistis (1964) 45f. KERTELGE, K. "Rechtfertigung" bei Paulus (1967)
132, 144-47. KÄSEMANN, E. New Testament Questions of Today (1969) 171.
BRANDENBURGER, E. Adam und Christus (Neukirchen-Vluyn 1962) 214-19.
ROCHAIS, G. Les récits de résurrection des morts dans le Nouveau Testament
(Cambridge 1981) 61. KLAIBER, W. Rechtfertigung und Gemeinde (Göttingen
1982) 118. HAYS, R. B. The Faith of Jesus Christ (Chico CA 1983) 166f.,
188f. STAAB, K. Pauluskommentare aus der griechischen Kirche (Münster
²1984) 218:8-12 Sev; 426:4-6 Oek. KOROSAK, B. J. "'Costituti peccatori'
(Rom 5, 19)," EuD 40 (1987) 157-66. MARTIN, B. L. Christ and the Law in
Paul (Leiden 1989) 59, 73f., 113, 115, 121f. HOOKER, M. D. From Adam to
Christ. Essays on Paul (Cambridge 1990) 30f., 181f.

5:20-7:6   HERMAN, Z. I. "La novità cristiana secondo Romani 5, 20-7, 6. Alcune osser-
vazioni esegetiche," Anton-ianum 61 (1986) 225-73.

5:20-21   SCHRAGE, W. Die konkreten Einzelgebote in der paulinischen Paränese (1961)
64, 83, 95, 261. BANDSTRA, A.J. The Law and the Elements of the World
(1964) 127ff. JÜNGEL, E. Paulus und Jesus (1966) 39, 41, 60, 51f. KER-
TELGE, K. "Rechtfertigung" bei Paulus (1967) 81. GOPPELT, L. Christologie
und Ethik (1968) 229f. MERK, O. Handeln aus Glauben (1968) 9, 22f., 31, 34,
37. THYEN, H. Studien zur Sündenvergebung (1970) 62, 197f. BRANDEN-
BURGER, E. Adam und Christus (Neukirchen-Vluyn 1962) 247-55, 260f.
KÜMMEL, W. G. Römer 7 und das Bild des Menschen im Neuen Testament
(München 1974) 6f. SCHMITHALS, W. "Zur Herkunft der gnostischen Ele-
mente in der Sprache des Paulus" in B. Aland et al., eds., Gnosis (FS. H. Jonas;
Göttingen 1978) 392f. THEOBALD, M. Die überströmende Gnade (Würzburg
1982) 114-20. STAAB, K. Pauluskommentare aus der griechischen Kirche
(Münster ²1984) 85:1-10 Diod. SANDERS, E. P. Paul, the Law, and the Jewish
People (London 1985) 39, 70f., 75, 88n.25, 144.

5:20   BRUNNER, E. Mensch im Widerspruch (1937) 151; Dogmatik I (1946) 206;
Dogmatik II (1950) 263. STÄHELIN, E. Die Verkündigung des Reiches Gottes
in der Kirche Jesu Christi I (1951) 283, 357. STROBEL, A. Erkenntnis und
Bekenntnis der Sünde in neutestamentlicher Zeit (1968) 49. LUZ, U. Das Ge-
schichtsverständnis des Paulus (1968) 187, 201ff. VAN DÜLMEN, A. Die The-
ologie des Gesetzes bei Paulus (1968) 42, 84, 92, 95, 97f., 100, 101, 103, 212.
MAUSER, U. Gottesbild und Menschwerdung (1972) 150, 154. ROBINSON,
J. A. Pelagius's Exposition of Thirteen Epistles of St Paul (Cambridge 1922)
122, 309, 315-17. BRANDENBURGER, E. Adam und Christus (Neukirchen-
Vluyn 1962) 205-14, 238f. HENSS, W. Das Verhältnis zwischen Diatessaron,
Christlicher Gnosis und "Western Text" (Berlin 1967) 27f., 32-34, 50, 53n.27.
KÜMMEL, W. G. Römer 7 und das Bild des Menschen im Neuen Testament
(München 1974) 7f. PHILIPOSE, J. "Romans 5.20: Did God have a bad motive
in giving the Law?" BTr 28 (1977) 445. HÜBNER, H. Das Gesetz bei Paulus
(Göttingen 1978) 73f. RÄISÄNEN, H. Paul and the Law (Tübingen 1983) 9,
100, 129, 134, 140f., 143f., 148, 153, 158. MOHRLANG, R. Matthew and Paul
(Cambridge 1984) 27-29, 38. STAAB, K. Pauluskommentare aus der griech-
ischen Kirche (Münster ²1984) 364:27-365:4 Genn; 499:14-25 Phot; 655:17-25
Areth. RÄISÄNEN, H. The Torah and Christ (Helsinki 1986) 5. SCHWEIZER,
E. Jesus Christ: The Man from Nazareth and the Exalted Lord (Macon GA
1987) 27. DE BOER, M. C. The Defeat of Death: Apocalyptic Eschatology in
1 Corinthians 15 and Romans 5 (Sheffield 1988) 165-69. DOWNING, F. G.

Christ and the Cynics (Sheffield 1988) 169. SNODGRASS, K. "Spheres of Influence. A Possible Solution to the Problem of Paul and the Law," JSNT 32 (1988) 93-113. LIMBECK, M. Mit Paulus Christ sein. Sachbuch zur Person und Theologie des Apostels Paulus (Stuttgart 1989) 107. MARTIN, B. L. Christ and the Law in Paul (Leiden 1989) 16, 19, 22, 25, 38, 42, 46f., 54f., 74f., 77, 97, 109, 134, 155. SCHNELLE, U. Wandlungen im paulinischen Denken (Stuttgart 1989) 69. SCHWEIZER, E. Theologische Einleitung in das Neue Testament (Göttingen 1989) ß14.5. THIELMAN, F. From Plight to Solution (Leiden 1989) 18, 74, 87, 89, 91f., 99-101, 103, 108, 115f. VOLLENWEIDER, S. Freiheit als neue Schöpfung (Göttingen 1989) 274, 324n., 361.

5:21-7:25 LARSSON, E. "Heil und Erlösung III" in TRE 14 (1985) 619.

5:21 DELLING, G. Die Taufe im Neuen Testament (1963) 99, 132. KRAMER, W. Christos Kyrios Gottessohn (1963) § 19c. KÄSEMANN, E. Exegetische Versuche und Besinnungen (1964) II 186. KERTELGE, K. "Rechtfertigung" bei Paulus (1967) 235, 268, 271. VAN DÜLMEN, A. Die Theologie des Gesetzes bei Paulus (1968) 95, 97, 98, 100, 162, 181, 191, 197, 212. KÄSEMANN, E. New Testament Questions of Today (1969) 173. BRANDENBURGER, E. Adam und Christus (Neukirchen-Vluyn 1962) 233f., 262f. BAUMERT, N. Täglich Sterben und Auferstehen (München 1973) 139f. STAAB, K. Pauluskommentare aus der griechischen Kirche (Münster ²1984) 120:30-121:14 ThM; 365:5-8 Genn; 499:26-28 Phot. RÖHSER, G. Metaphorik und Personifikation der Sünde (Tübingen 1987) 112, 125, 132, 140ff., 150, 158, 165. MARTIN, B. L. Christ and the Law in Paul (Leiden 1989) 14, 46, 70, 74f., 80-83, 97, 109, 119, 121-23, 125, 134. BEKER, J. C. "The Relationship Between Sin and Death in Romans" in R. T. Fortna and B. R. Gaventa, eds., The Conversation Continues. Studies in Paul and John (FS J. L. Martyn; Nashville 1990) 55-61, esp.57.

6-8 SHEPARD, J. W. The Life and Letters of St. Paul (Grand Rapids 1950) 396-414. POLHILL, J. B. "New Life in Christ: Romans 6-8," RevEx 73 (1976) 425-36. BYRNE, B. "Sons of God"—"Seed of Abraham" (Rome 1979) 86, 91. DUNN, J. D. G. "Paul's Epistle to the Romans: An Analysis of Structure and Argument" in ANRW II.25.4 (1987) 2858-66. SCHMELLER, TH. Paulus und die "Diatribe" (Münster 1987) 287.

6:1-8:30 Christian History and Interpretation: Studies presented to John Knox (1967) 381, 382-7.

6:1-8:13 BYRNE, B. "Living out the Righteousness of God: The Contribution of Rom 6:1-8:13 to an Understanding of Paul's Ethical Presuppositions," CBQ 43 (1981) 557-581. ELLIOT, N. The Rhetoric of Romans (Sheffield 1990) 164, 233, 235-53, 271f.

6-7 SCHILLEBEECKX, E. Christus und die Christen (Freiburg/Basel/Wien 1977) 145-48; ET: Christ: the Christian Experience in the Modern World (London 1980) 154-57. BYRNE, B. "Sons of God"—"Seed of Abraham" (Rome 1979) 86.

6:1-7:25 GIBLIN, C.H. In Hope of God's Glory (1970) 377-88.

6:1-7:13 SEGUNDO, J. L. The Humanist Christology of Paul (Maryknoll NY and London 1986) 99-112.

6:1-7:6 OSTEN-SACKEN, P. VON DER, Römer 8 als Beispiel paulinischer Soteriologie (Göttingen 1975) 175ff. BYRNE, B. "Living out the Righteousness of God: The Contribution of Rom 6:1-8:13 to an Understanding of Paul's Ethical Presuppositions," CBQ 43 (1981) 562-65. MacDONALD, M. Y. The Pauline Churches (Cambridge 1988) 33.

6   SEIDENSTICKER, Ph. Lebendiges Opfer (1954) 237ff. BEST, E. One Gody
in Christ (1955) 17, 46n. DENNEY, J. The Death of Christ (1956) 80, 107f.,
111f., 117. SCHLIER, H. Die Zeit der Kirche (1956) 47-56. WUEST, K.S.
"Victory over Indwelling Sin in Romans Six" BibSac 116 (461, '59) 43-50.
RUDOLPH, K. Die Mandäer I (1960). KNOX, W.L. St. Paul and the Church
of the Gentiles (1961) 97ff. SCHRAGE, W. Die konkreten Einzelgebote in der
paulinischen Paränese (1961) 32, 45, 61, 187. BRAUN, H. "Das 'Stirb und
werde' in der Antike und im Neuen Testament" Gesammelte Studien zum
Neuen Testament und Seiner Umwelt (1962) 136-59. DELLING, G. Die Taufe
im Neue Testament (1963) 132. KÄSEMANN, E. Exegetische Versuche und
Besinnungen (1964) I 45. Braun, H. Qumran und NT II (1966) 27, 174, 177,
228. GUETTGEMANNS, E. Der leidende Apostel und sein Herr (1966) 210-25.
TANNEHILL, R.C. Dying and Rising With Christ (1966) 7-39. NICKELS, P.
Targum and New Testament (1967) 68. GAUMANN, Taufe und Ethik. Studien
zu Römer 6; Rev. R.C. Tannehill, JBL 87 (4, '68) 470-72. MERK, O. Handeln
aus Glauben (1968) 23, 34f. STROBEL, A. Erkenntnis und Bekenntnis der
Sünde in neutestamentlicher Zeit (1968) 48, 54. VAN DÜLMEN, A. Die The-
ologie des Gesetzes bei Paulus (1968) 163, 207. KÄSEMANN, E. New Testa-
ment Questions of Today (1969) 125. WEISS, H.-F. "Paulus und die Häretiker.
Zum Paulusverständnis in der Gnosis" Christentum und Gnosis (1969) 116-28.
FRANKEMOELLE, H. Das Taufverständnis des Paulus. (1970) 6-20. THYEN,
H. Studien zur Sündenvergebung (1970) 194-217. CLEMEN, C. Primitive
Christianity and Its Non-Jewish Sources (Edinburgh 1912) 219ff. SCHWARZ-
MANN, H. Zur Tauftheologie des hl. Paulus in Röm 6 (Heidelberg 1950)
passim. BRANDENBURGER, E. Adam und Christus (Neukirchen-Vluyn 1962)
236, 259ff. JOHNSON, H. The Humanity of the Saviour (London 1962) 89-92.
BIEDER, W. Die Verheissung der Taufe im Neuen Testament (Zürich 1966)
187-204. HUBERT, H. Der Streit um die Kindertaufe (Bern/ Frankfurt 1972)
70-76. WENDLAND, H.-D. Vom Leben und Handeln der Christen. Eine
Betrachtung zu Römer 6 (Stuttgart 1972). KAYE, B. N. "Βαπτίζειν εἰς
with special Reference to Romans 6," Studia Evangelica VI (1973) 281-86.
KÜMMEL, W. G. Römer 7 und das Bild des Menschen im Neuen Testament
(München 1974) 7f., 10f., 12f., 41, 125. VICENTINI, J. I. "Una afirmación
paradójica: 'Ya está todo hecho; pero queda todo per hacer.' Comentario a
Romanos 6," RevBi 36 (1974) 289-98. CONZELMANN, H. und LINDE-
MANN, A. Arbeitsbuch zum Neuen Testament (Tübingen 1975) 229, 420.
SCHNACKENBURG, R. Römer 7 im Zusammenhang des Römerbriefes" in E.
E. Ellis und E. Grässer, eds., Jesus und Paulus (FS W.G. Kümmel; Göttingen
1975) 287ff. LINDEMANN, A. Die Aufhebung der Zeit. Geschichtsverständnis
und Eschatologie im Epheserbrief (Gütersloh 1975) 22, 30-34, 42, 107, 119,
125, 140f., 143, 249. OSTEN-SACKEN, P. VON DER, Römer 8 als Beispiel
paulinischer Soteriologie (Göttingen 1975) 177ff. RIDDERBOS, H. Paul. An
Outline of His Theology (Grand Rapids 1975) 206-14, 259-63, 401f. SCHMI-
THALS, W. Der Römerbrief als historisches Problem (Gütersloh 1975) 17, 35f.,
42, 44, 89f. GUNDRY, R. H. Soma in Biblical Theology with Emphasis on
Pauline Anthropology (Cambridge 1976) 239f. FRIEDRICH, G. "Freiheit und
Liebe im ersten Korintherbrief" in Auf das Wort kommt es an. Gesammelte
Aufsätze (Göttingen 1978) 182. SCHMITHALS, W. "Zur Herkunft der gnosti-
schen Elemente in der Sprache des Paulus" in B. Aland et al., eds., Gnosis (FS.
H. Jonas; Göttingen 1978) 391-93. FROITZHEIM, F. Christologie und
Eschatologie bei Paulus (Würzburg 1979) 119. HOFFMANN, P. "Auferstehung"

in TRE 4 (1979) 484. KAYE, B. N. The Thought Structure of Romans with Special Reference to Chapter 6 (Fort Worth, TX 1979). DU TOIT, A. B. "Dikaiosyne in Röm 6. Beobachtungen zur ethischen Dimension der paulinischen Gerechtigkeitsauffassung," ZThK 76 (1979) 261-91. WILCKENS, U. "Zu Römer 6" in W. Popkes, ed., Theologisches Gespräch (FS R. Thaut; Kassel 1979) 11-22. VERDES, L. ALVAREZ El imperativo cristiano en San Pablo. La tensión indicativo-imperativo en Rom 6. Análisis estructural. Institución San Jerónimo 11 (Valencia 1980). POKORNY, P. "Christologie et Bapteme à l'Epoque du Christianisme Primitif," NTS 27 (1980-81) 377. HYGEN, J. B. "Böse" in TRE 7 (1981) 17. LYALL, F. "Legal Metaphors in the Epistles," TB 32 (1981) 81-95. GORDAY, P. Principles of Patristic Exegesis: Romans 9-11 in Origen, John Chrysostom, and Augustine (New York/Toronto 1983) 68-70, 117, 161f. SCHNELLE, U. Gerechtigkeit und Christusgegenwart (Göttingen 1983) 74-88. WEDDERBURN, A. J. M. "Hellenistic Christian Traditions in Romans 6?" NTS 29 (1983) 337-55. POKORNY, P. Die Entstehung der Christologie (Berlin 1985) 154f. RICHES, J. "Heiligung" in TRE 14 (1985) 721, 729. SANDERS, E. P. Paul, the Law, and the Jewish People (London 1985) 71-73, 79, 86. WATSON, F. Paul, Judaism and the Gentiles (Cambridge 1986) 147f. DUNN, J. D. G. "Paul's Epistle to the Romans: An Analysis of Structure and Argument" in ANRW II.25.4 (1987) 2860f. RÖHSER, G. Metaphorik und Personifikation der Sünde (Tübingen 1987) 107f., 110, 121ff., 116, 127, 166. WEDDERBURN, A. J. M. Baptism and Resurrection (Tübingen 1987) 1, 3-6, 36-69, 71f., 74f., 78, 81-7, 232, 296, 305, 310, 345, 348-50, 352, 372, 382, 386, 388, 393. CONZELMANN, H. and LINDEMANN, A. Interpreting the New Testament (Peabody MA 1988) 202f., 355. MacDONALD, M. Y. The Pauline Churches (Cambridge 1988) 81. VOLLENWEIDER, S. Freiheit als neue Schöpfung (Göttingen 1989) 323ff. ELLIOT, N. The Rhetoric of Romans (Sheffield 1990) 70, 98, 104, 225, 236-8, 241n., 242, 246, 277. HOOKER, M. D. From Adam to Christ. Essays on Paul (Cambridge 1990) 19, 34, 39, 45, 57f., 60.

6:1ff.   MINEAR, P.S. Images of the Church in the New Testament (1960) 155f. ROBINSON, J.M. Kerygma und historischer Jesus (1960) 178. BEASLEY—MURRAY, G.R. Baptism in the New Testament (1962) 126ff. SCHWEIZER, E. Erniedrigung und Erhöhung bei Jesus und seinen Nachfolgern (1962) §11su. OLLROG, W.-H. Paulus und seine Mitarbeiter (Neu-kirchen-Vluyn 1979) 89. GRUNDMANN, W. Wandlungen im Verständnis des Heils (Berlin, DDR 1980) 49. SCHULZ, S. Neutestamentliche Ethik (Zürich 1987) 371ff. BECKER, J. Paulus. Der Apostel der Völker (Tübingen 1989) 127, 300, 364, 414, 446, 458, 463.

6:1-23   GRELOT, P. "Une homélie de saint Paul sur le bapteme. Epitre aux Romains, ch. 6, 1-23," EspVie 99 (1989) 154-58.

6:1-14   WARNACH, V. "Taufe und Christusgeschenhen nach Röm 6" Archiv für Liturgiewissenschaft III/2 ('54) 284-366. BEST, E. One Body in Christ (1955) 52, 56, 66f., 73. DAVIES, W.D. Paul and Rabbinic Judaism (1955) 36, 87f., 122, 233, f., 291, 319. DUNN, J.D.G. Baptism in the Holy Spirit (1970) 139ff., 155. FRANKEMOELLE, Das Taufverständnis des Paulus (1970). DINKLER, E. "Die Taufaussagen des Neuen Testaments. New untersucht im Hinblick auf Karl Barths Tauflehre" Zu Karl Barths Lehre von der Taufe, ed. Fritz Viering (1971) 70-79. SIBER, P. Mit Christus Leben (1971) 191-247. EICHHOLZ, G. Die Theologie des Paulus im Umriss (1972) 202, 204, 269f. BOHREN, R. Predigtlehre (München 1971) 182f. ROLOFF, J. Neues Testament (Neukirchen-

Vluyn 1979) 240-42. PRICE, J. L. "Romans 6:1-14," Interp 34 (1980) 65-69.
MOO, D. J. "Romans 6:1-14," TrinJourn 3 (1982) 215-20. CLERC, D. "Notes
à propos de Romains 6, 1-14," BullCentProtEtud 37 (1985) 5-10. SELLIN, G.
Der Streit um die Auferstehung der Toten (Göttingen 1986) 24A, 27A, 37A,
46A, 61, 63A, 215f., 254, 257, 263, 284, 293. ZMIJEWSKI, J. "Ueberlegungen
zum Verhältnis von Theologie und christlicher Glaubenspraxis anhand des
Neuen Testaments" in Das Neue Testament—Quelle christlicher Theologie und
Glaubenspraxis (Stuttgart 1986) 256f. VOLLENWEIDER, S. Freiheit als neue
Schöpfung (Göttingen 1989) 333. CUVILLIER, E. "Evangile et traditions chez
Paul. Lecture de Romains 6, 1-14," Hokhma 45 (1990) 3-16. LÉGASSE, S.
"Être baptisé dans la mort du Christ. Étude de Romains 6, 1-14," RB 98 (1991)
544-59.

6:1-12   HOFFMANN, P. Die Toten in Christus (1966) 303, 305-306.
6:1-11   SCHELKLE, K. Taufe und Tod. Zur Auslegung von Römer 6, 1-11: Vom
Christlichen Mysterium (1951) 9-21. SCHNACKENBURG, R. "Todes- und
Lebensgemeinschaft mit Christus. Neue Studien zu Röm. 6:1-11" Münchn.The-
ol. Zeit. 6 (1955) 32-53. NIEDER, L. Die Motive der Religiös-Sittlichen
Paränese in den Paulinischen Gemeindebriefen (1956) 23-27, 127. PRUEMM,
K. "I cosidetti 'dei morti e risorti' nel ellenismo" Gregorianum 39 (2, '58) 411-
39. FEUILLET, A. "Mort du Christ et mort du chrétien d'apres les itres paulini-
ennes" RevBi 66 (4, '59) 481-513. GILMORE, A. Christian Baptism (1959)
130ff., 146, 149. LARSSON, E. Christus als Vorbild (1962) 79f., 92ff., 105f.
WAGNER, G. Das religionsgeschichtliche Problem von Römer 6, 1-22 (1962);
Rev. G.Delling, ThLZ 88 (4, '63) 271-73; Gruenler, R.G. JBL 31 (3, '63) 251-
2. DELLING, G. Die Taufe im Neuen Testament (1963) 135, 126, 131.
THUESING, W. Per Christum in Deum (1965) 68-71ff., 78-84, 88-92, 134-44,
156f., 192f. BRAUN, H. Qumran und NT II (1966) 27, 29, 162, 213, 254, 260.
KERTELGE, K. "Rechtfertigung" bei Paulus (1967) 232-36. WAGNER, G.
Pauline Baptism and the Pagan Mysteries. The Problem of the Pauline Doctrine
of Baptism in Romans VI. 1-11 in the Light of its Religio-Historical "Parallels"
(1967). MERK, O. Handeln aus Glauben (1968) 21, 23, 235. SCHREINER, J.
Gestalt und Anspruch des Neuen Testaments (1969) 67f. JEWETT, R. Paul's
Anthropological Terms (1971) 291-93. SCHNACKENBURG, R. Schriften zum
Neuen Testament (1971) 361-91. ZIESLER, J.A. The Meaning of Righteousness
in Paul (1972) 201f, 203. SCHNACKENBURG, R. Das Heilsgeschehen bei der
Taufe nach dem Apostel Paulus (München 1950) 26-56. FORCK, G. Wie soll
es bei uns weitergehen? Tauflehre und Taufpraxis (Berlin 1969) 48f.
SCHNACKENBURG, R. Aufsätze und Studien zum Neuen Testament (Leipzig
1973) 101-29. MARTIN, R. P. Worship in the Early Church (Grand Rapids
1976 =1974) 103-6. CONZELMANN, H. und LINDEMANN, A. Arbeitsbuch
zum Neuen Testament (Tübingen 1975) 228. VENETZ, H. J. Der Glaube weiss
um die Zeit. Zum paulinischen Verständnis der "Letzten Dinge" (Fribourg
1975) 55-62. GAFFIN, R. B. The Centrality of the Resurrection (Grand Rapids
1978) 53-55, 124f. BYRNE, B. "Sons of God"—"Seed of Abraham" (Rome
1979) 170. ROBINSON, J. A. T. Wrestling with Romans (London 1979) 67-72.
HANSON, A. T. The New Testament Interpretation of Scripture (London 1980)
122-35. SCHLIER, H. "Fragment über die Taufe" in V. Kubina und K. Lehmann, eds., Der Geist und die Kirche (FS H. Schlier; Freiburg/ Basel/Wien
1980) 136f., 141f. TRACK, J. und OEFFNER, E. in P. Krusche et al., eds.,
Predigtstudien für das Kirchenjahr 1980, II/2 (Stuttgart 1980) 142-49. BARTH,
G. Die Taufe in frühchristlicher Zeit (Neukirchen-Vluyn 1981) 94-103, 117,

119. KIM, S. The Origin of Paul's Gospel (Tübingen 1981) 301f. PELSER, G. M. M. "The Objective Reality of the Renewal of Life in Romans 6:1-11," Neotestamentica 15 (1981) 101-17. DUNN, J. D. G. "Salvation Proclaimed: VI. Romans 6:1-11: Dead and Alive," ET 93 (1982) 259-64. PERKINS, P. Resurrection. New Testament Witness and Contemporary Reflection (London 1984) 273f. BURNISH, R. The Meaning of Baptism. A Comparison of the Teaching and Practice of the Fourth Century with the Present Day (London 1985) 7, 12, 29f., 50, 52, 68, 93f., 119, 127, 130, 134, 149, 156f., 161, 169f., 189. FORCK, G. Im Blickpunkt: Taufe (Berlin, DDR 1985) 40-42. DIRSCHAUER, K. "Das eschatologische Potential der Kirche und der Theologie" in G. FREUND und E. STEGEMANN, eds., Theologische Brosamen für Lothar Steiger (DBAT 5; Heidelberg 1985) 75f. POKORNY, P. Die Entstehung der Christologie (Berlin 1985) 57, 75. HARRIS, M. J. Raised Immortal (London 1986) 103f., 231. ECKERT, J. "Die Taufe und das neue Leben. Röm 6, 1-11 im Kontext der paulinischen Theologie," MThZ 38 (1987) 203-222. FOWL, S. "Some Uses of Story in Moral Discourse: Reflections on Paul's Moral Discourse and Our Own," Modern Theology 4 (1988) 293-308. LINDARS, B. "Paul and the Law in Romans 5-8: An Actantial Analysis" in B. Lindars, ed., Law and Religion (Cambridge 1988) 131f. SCHLARB, R. "Röm 6:1-11 in der Auslegung der frühen Kirchenväter," BZ 33 (1989) 104-13. COUSAR, C. B. A Theology of the Cross (Minneapolis 1990) 2, 54, 70-6, 77, 81, 102. KOLLMANN, B. Ursprung und Gestalten der frühchristlichen Mahlfeier (Göttingen 1990) 62f. SCHLARB, R. Wir sind mit Christus begraben. Die Auslegung von Römer 6, 1-11 im Frühchristentum bis Origenes (Tübingen 1990). ZIESLER, J. Pauline Christianity (Oxford 1990) 30, 95-97. WAY, D. The Lordship of Christ. Ernst Käsemann's Interpretation of Paul's Theology (Oxford 1991) 148-50.

6:1-10   BERGER, K. und COLPE, C., eds., Religions-geschichtliches Textbuch zum Neuen Testament (Göttingen/Zürich 1987) 207-11. SEGAL, A. F. Paul the Convert (New Haven/London 1990) 135.

6:1-8   McDONALD, P. M. "Romans 5.1-11 as a Rhetorical Bridge," JSNT 40 (1990) 81-96.

6:1-7   SOIRON, T. Die Kirche als der Leib Christi (Düssel-dorf 1951) 91ff.

6:1-6   MUSSNER, F. "Zusammenwachsen durch die Aehnlichkeit mit seinem Tode" TThZ 63 ('54) 257-65. MUSSNER, F. "Zur paulinischen Tauflehre in Röm. 6, 1-6. Versuch einer Auslegung" Praesentia Salutis (1967) 189.

6:1-5   LANGEVIN, P.E. "Le Baptême dans la Mort-Résurrection. Exégèse de Rm 6, 1-5" SciEccl 17 (1, '65) 29-65. SCHWARZMANN, H. Zur Tauftheologie des hl. Paulus in Röm 6 (Heidelberg 1950) 11-48.

6:1-4   PIET, J. H. "Exegetical Study on Romans 6:1-4," RefR (H) 31 (1977) 65-67. STAAB, K. Pauluskommentare aus der griechischen Kirche (Münster ²1984) 85:11-18 Diod.

6:1-3   KENNEDY, H.A.A. St. Paul and the Mystery-Religions (1913) 233, 245, 237, 297.

6:1-2   BRANDENBURGER, E. Fleisch und Geist (1968) 53. BRANDENBURGER, E. Adam und Christus (Neukirchen-Vluyn 1962) 160, 186f., 253. STAAB, K. Pauluskommentare aus der griechischen Kirche (Münster ²1984) 365:9-24 Genn. RÖHSER, G. Metaphorik und Personifikation der Sünde (Tübingen 1987) 104, 123, 141, 157, 166f. WEDDERBURN, A. J. M. Baptism and Resurrection (Tübingen 1987) 47.

6:1,15   LAMPE, P. Die stadtrömischen Christen in den ersten beiden Jahrhunderten (Tübingen ²1989) 55. KÜMMEL, W. G. Römer 7 und das Bild des Menschen im Neuen Testament (München 1974) 7f., 42, 69, 121f. OLLROG, W.-H. Paulus und seine Mitarbeiter (Neukirchen-Vluyn 1979) 211, 215. CANALES, I. J. "Paul's Accusers in Romans 3:8 and 6:1," EQ 57 (1985) 237-45. MAL-HERBE, A. J. Moral Exhortation. A Greco-Roman Sourcebook (Philadelphia 1986) 129. JONES, F. S. "Freiheit" in den Briefen des Apostels Paulus (Göttingen 1987) 110f., 116, 123, 135, 213 A 10, 216 A 34. LIMBECK, M. Mit Paulus Christ sein. Sachbuch zur Person und Theologie des Apostels Paulus (Stuttgart 1989) 107. WEDDERBURN, A. J. M. Baptism and Resurrection (Tübingen 1987) 40f., 50.

6:1   BRUNNER, E. Dogmatik I (1946) 355. MERK, O. Handeln aus Glauben (1968) 22f., 25, 30, 34, 37. VAN DÜLMEN, A. Die Theologie des Gesetzes bei Paulus (1968) 20, 72, 100, 202. ELLIOT, N. The Rhetoric of Romans (Sheffield 1990) 138, 225, 236-9, 248, 249n., 250.

6:2ff.   SOKOLOWSKI, E. Die Begriffe Geist und Leben bei Paulus (1903) 17f., 31f. FEINE, P. Der Apostel Paulus (1927) 348ff., 577f. KÄSEMANN, E. Exegetische Versuche und Besinnungen I (1964) 91. BULTMANN, R. Theologie des Neuen Testaments (1965) 143f. SEEBERG, A. Der Katechismus der Urchristenheit (1966) 169. FENEBERG, W. Der Markusprolog. Studien zur Formbestimmung des Evangeliums (München 1974) 33, 54, 85, 87f., 119. MOHR-LANG, R. Matthew and Paul (Cambridge 1984) 61, 88, 118. MacDONALD, M. Y. The Pauline Churches (Cambridge 1988) 66.

6:2-14 WIKENHAUSER, A. Die Christusmystik des Apostels Paulus (1956) 24, 71-79, 95, 104. DACQUINO, P. "La nostra morte e la nostra risurrezione con Cristo seconds San Paulo" RivB 14 (3, '66) 227-59.

6:2-11 ROBINSON, J.A.T. The Body (1952) Passim. SCHWEITZER, A. Die Mystik des Apostels Paulus (1954) passim. RUCKSTUHL, E. "Gnade III" in TRE 13 (1984) 469.

6:2-10 MERK, O. Handeln aus Glauben (1968) 25, 27, 29f., 34, 239f. MINDE, H. J. VAN DER. "Theologia crucis und Pneumaaussagen bei Paulus," Catholica 34 (1980) 136f.

6:2-7   WIKENHAUSER, A. Die Christusmystik des Apostels Paulus (1956) 163f. BARTH, M. Die Taufe—ein Sakrament (Zürich 1951) 221-318.

6:2-6   LIMBECK, M. Mit Paulus Christ sein. Sachbuch zur Person und Theologie des Apostels Paulus (Stuttgart 1989) 107-12.

6:2-4   TOWNER, P. H. The Goal of Our Instruction. The Structure of Theology and Ethics in the Pastoral Epistles (Sheffield 1989) 105.

6:2   BEST, E. One Body in Christ (1955) 49. DENNEY, J. The Death of Christ (1956) 106. BRANDENBURGER, E. Fleisch und Geist (1968) 56. VAN DÜLMEN, A. Die Theologie des Gesetzes bei Paulus (1968) 20, 25, 98, 162, 208. MERK, O. Handeln aus Glauben (1968) 23-25, 29. SIBER, P. Mit Christus leben (Zürich 1971) 185f. RIDDERBOS, H. Paul. An Outline of His Theology (Grand Rapids 1975) 206-08. SCHRAGE, W. "Ist die Kirche das 'Abbild seines Todes'?" in D. Lührmann und G. Strecker, eds., Kirche (FS G. Bornkamm; Tübingen 1980) 205. HAGEN, W. H. "Two Deutero-Pauline Glosses in Rom 6," ET 92 (1981) 364-67. RHYNE, C. T. Faith Establishes the Law (Chico CA 1981) 44f. SCHMELLER, TH. Paulus und die "Diatribe" (Münster 1987) 327. MARTIN, B. L. Christ and the Law in Paul (Leiden 1989) 11, 16, 51, 71, 80-2, 110, 113.

6:3ff.   BIEDER, W. Die Vorstellung von der Höllenfahrt Jesu Christi (1949) 70f. BRAUMANN, G. Vorpaulinische christliche Taufverkündigung bei Paulus (1962) 11, 13, 14ff., 31, 47, 50ff., 54, 73. DELLING, G. Die Taufe im Neuen

Testament (1963) 109, 118, 123, 125-32, 147, 149. SEEBERG, A. Der Katechismus der Urchristenheit (1966) 122f. EICHHOLZ, G. Die Theologie des Paulus im Umriss (1972) 152, 206f., 209. BÜCHSEL, D. F. Der Geist Gottes im Neuen Testament (Gütersloh 1926) 295ff. FAZEKAS, L. "Taufe als Tod," ThZ 22 (1966) 307-18. SIBER, P. Mit Christus leben (Zürich 1971) 182. SMITH, M. Clement of Alexandria and a secret Gospel of Mark (Cambridge MA 1973) 214f. FRIEDRICH, J. et al., eds., Rechtfertigung (FS E. Käsemann; Tübingen/Göttingen 1976) 101, 109-11, 116, 118, 496, 503. MÜNCHOW, C. Ethik und Eschatologie (Göttingen 1981) 153f., 169. SCHADE, H.-H. Apokalyptische Christologie bei Paulus (Göttingen 1981) 146. STENDAHL, K. "The New Testament Background for the Doctrine of the Sacraments" in Meanings (Philadelphia 1984) 180f.

6:3-11   HANSON, S. The Unity of the Church in the New Testament (1946) 82-85. BORNKAMM, G. GPM 5 (1951) 156-61. BEST, E. One Body in Christ (1955) 44. WEBER, O. GPM 10 (1956) 181-84. CERFAUX, L. Christ in the Theology of St. Paul (1959) passim. DELLING, G. Die Zueignung des Heils in der Taufe (1961) 74f., 78. SOUCEK, GPM 1961/62 249ff. STANLEY, D.M. Christ's Resurrection in Pauline Soteriology (1961) 181-86. STALDER, K. Das Werk des Geistes in der Heiligung bei Paulus (1962) 144-47, 215. CLAVIER, H. "Le drame de la mort er de la vie dans le Nouveau Testament" Studia Evangelica, ed. F.L. Cross (1964) 166-77. SCHNACKENBURG, R. Baptism in the Thought of St. Paul (1964) 23ff., 136, 159. STECK, K.G. in Herr, tue meine Lippen auf II (1966) 373-84. DOERNE, M. Die alten Episteln (1967) 172-76. HAHN, F. GPM 22/3 (1967/68) 313-24. WEBER, O. Predigtmeditationen (1967) 238-41. DALTON, W. J. Christ's Proclamation to the Spirits. A Study of 1 Peter 3:18-4:6 (Rome 1965) 244-49. SISTI, A. "Simbolismo e realità nel battesimo," BeO 11 (1969) 77-86. CAVALLIN, H. C. C. Life After Death (Lund 1974) 3, 5n.39. PAGELS, E. H. The Gnostic Paul. Gnostic Exegesis of the Pauline Letters (Philadelphia 1975) 28ff. MOHRLANG, R. Matthew and Paul (Cambridge 1984) 84f.

6:3-10   VIA, D. O. Kerygma and Comedy in the New Testament (Philadelphia 1975) 39, 42f., 66, 159. GOPPELT, L. Theologie des Neuen Testaments II: Vielfalt und Einheit des apostolischen Christuszeugnisses (Göttingen 1976) 430. HAYS, R. B. The Faith of Jesus Christ (Chico CA 1983) 83. CROWLEY, J. "Baptism as Eschatological Event," Worship 62 (1988) 290-98.

6:3-9   KRAMER, W. Christos Kyrios Gottessohn (1963) §§ 5a, 14, 33b, 59b. SCHWEIZER, E. Theologische Einleitung in das Neue Testament (Göttingen 1989) ß5.4; 17.6. VOLLENWEIDER, S. Freiheit als neue Schöpfung (Göttingen 1989) 328.

6:3-8   DELLING, G. Die Zueignung des Heils in der Tauge (1961) 71. GAFFIN, R. B. The Centrality of the Resurrection (Grand Rapids 1978) 44-52. STECK, K. G. in GPM 34 (1980) 291-98. HEINTZE, G. in GPM 40 (1985-86) 360-66.

6:3-6   TANNEHILL, R.C. Dying and Rising With Christ (1966) 21-39. ORTKEMPER, F.J. Das Kreuz in der Verkündigung des Apostels Paulus (1967) 68-83. DELLING, G. Studien zum Neuen Testament und zum hellenistischen Judentum (Göttingen 1970) 308f., 367f.

6:3-5   RIDDERBOS, H. Paul. An Outline of His Theology (Grand Rapids 1975) 400-14. HAHN, F. "Gottesdienst III" in TRE 14 (1985) 35. POKORNY, P. Die Entstehung der Christologie (Berlin 1985) 75, 78, 141, 154.

6:3-4   RENGSTORF, K. H. "Paulus und die älteste römische Christenheit," Studia Evangelica 2 (1963) 447-64. NÖTSCHER, F. Altorientalischer und alttestamentlicher Auferstehungsglaube (Darmstadt 1970=1926) 309. PATSCH, H. Abendmahl und historischer Jesus (Stuttgart 1972) 207f. SCHNACKENBURG, R. Aufsätze und Studien zum Neuen Testament (Leipzig 1973) 113-16, 196. RUDOLPH, K. Die Gnosis (Göttingen 1978) 206. HOFFMANN, P. "Auferstehung" in TRE 4 (1979) 483. PREEZ, J. DU. "Rom 6:3-4 in die diskussie oor die vorm van die Christelike doop" [Rom 6:3-4 in the Discussion concerning the Form of Christian Baptism], NGTT 25 (1984) 270-76). STAAB, K. Pauluskommentare aus der griechischen Kirche (Münster ²1984) 365:25-32 Genn; 499:27-500:15 Phot. PETERSEN, N. R. "Pauline Baptism and 'Secondary Burial'" in G. W. E. Nickelsburg with G. W. MacRae, eds., Christians among Jews and Gentiles (FS K. Stendahl; Philadelphia 1986) 217-26. WEDDERBURN, A. J. M. Baptism and Resurrection (Tübingen 1987) 4, 48, 60. LÉGASSE, S. "Être baptisé dans la mort du Christ. Étude de Romains 6, 1-14," RB 98 (1991) 544-59.

6:3,4   BEST, E. One Body in Christ (1955) 66f, 69. MERCURIO, R. "A Baptismal Motif in the Gospel Narratives of the Burial" CBQ 21 (1, '59) 39-54. SCHOEPS, H.-J. Paulus (1959) 54ff. QUESNELL, Q. This Good News (1964) 147f. KERTELGE, K. "Rechtfertigung" bei Paulus (1967) 274-84. CREMER, F.G. "Der Heilstod Jesu im paulinischen Verständnis von Taufe und Eucharistie. Eine Zusammenschau von Röm 6, 3f und 1 Kor 11, 26" BZ 14 (2, '70) 227-39. DUNN, J.D.G. Baptism in the Holy Spirit (1970) 118, 128, 140f, 144.

6:3   BEST, E. One Body in Christ (1955) 51. DENNEY, J. The Death of Christ (1956) 52. ELLIS, E.E. Paul's Use of the Old Testament (1957) 131, 133f. DELLING, G. Die zueignung des Heils in der Taufe (1961) 41, 73-75, 77-79, 81, 91. SCHRAGE, W. Die konkreten Einzelgebote in der paulinischen Paränese (1961) 81f. BEASLEY-MURRAY, G.R. Baptism in the New Testament (1962) 126ff., 129f. DELLING, G. Die Taufe im Neuen Testament (1963) 108, 111, 143, 148. HAHN, F. Christologische Hoheitstitel (1963) 209. FASEKAS, L. "Taufe als Tod in Röm. 6, 3ff" ThZ 22 (5, '66) 305-18. JEREMIAS, J. Abba (1966) 279. SEEBERG, A. Der Katechismus der Urchristenheit (1966) 176, 184, 236. NICKELS, P. Targum and New Testament (1967) 69. MERK, 0. Handeln aus Glauben (1968) 32. VAN DÜLMEN, A. Die Theologie des Gesetzes bei Paulus (1968) 98, 104, 207, 209. THYEN, H. Studien zur Sündenvergebung (1970) 147, 196ff. SCHNACKENBURG, R. Das Heilsgeschehen bei der Taufe nach dem Apostel Paulus (München 1950) 18-23. DELLING, G. Der Kreuzestod Jesu in der urchrist-lichen Verkündigung (1972) 27-30. LOHSE, E. Die Einheit des Neuen Testaments (Göttingen 1973) 230f. JEWETT, P. K. Infant Baptism and the Covenant of Grace (Grand Rapids 1978) 140. HENGEL, M. Zur urchristlichen Geschichtsschreibung (Stuttgart 1979) 43; ET: J. Bowden (trans.) Acts and the History of Earliest Christianity (London 1979) 44. SCHRAGE, W. "Ist die Kirche das 'Abbild seines Todes'?" in D. Lührmann und G. Strecker, eds., Kirche (FS G. Bornkamm; Tübingen 1980) 205f., 213f. BARTH, G. Die Taufe in frühchristlicher Zeit (Neukirchen-Vluyn 1981) 12, 38, 44, 46, 48, 55, 92, 145. STAAB, K. Pauluskommentare aus der griechischen Kirche (Münster ²1984) 121:15-21 ThM; 218:13-14 Sev. MERKLEIN, H. Studien zu Jesus und Paulus (Tübingen 1987) 53, 58, 59n.148. WEDDERBURN, A. J. M. Baptism and Resurrection (Tübingen 1987) 40f., 46f., 51, 57-59, 67. BADKE, W. B. "Baptised into Moses—Bap-tised into Christ: A Study in Doctrinal Development," EQ 60 (1988) 23-29.

6:4ff.   OLIVEIRA, A. DE, Die Diakonie der Gerechtigkeit und der Versöhnung in der Apologie des 2. Korintherbriefes. Analyse und Auslegung von 2 Kor 2, 14-4, 6; 5, 11-6, 10 (Münster 1990) 361.

6:4-14   GOLLWITZER, H. Veränderung im Diesseits (München 1973) 17.

6:4-10   CRUZ, H. Christological Motives and Motivated Actions in Pauline Paraenesis (Frankfurt/Bern/New York/Paris 1990) 155-62.

6:4-8   KOCH, R. "L'aspect Eschatologique de l'esprit du Seigneur D'Après Saint Paul" Studiorum Paulinorum Congressus Internationalis Catholicus 1961 (1963) I 134-35. GUNKEL, H. The Influence of the Holy Spirit (Philadelphia 1979) 108-11.

6:4-5   SCHOEPS, H.-J. Paulus (1959) 218f. SCHRAGE, W. Die konkreten Einzelgebote in der paulinischen Paränese (1961) 49. KÄSEMANN, Exegetische Versuche und Besinnungen (1964) II 126. New Testament Questions of Today (1969) 132. JEWETT, P. K. Infant Baptism and the Covenant of Grace (Grand Rapids 1978) 140. POKORNY, P. Die Entstehung der Christologie (Berlin 1985) 143, 150. FRID, B. "Römer 6, 4-5. *Eis ton thanaton und tq homoiomati tou thanatou autou* als Schlüssel zu Duktus und Gedankengang in Röm 6, 1-11," BZ 30 (1986) 188-203. KARRER, M. Die Johannesoffenbarung als Brief (Göttingen 1986) 276n., 294. LAMPE, P. Die stadtrömischen Christen in den ersten beiden Jahrhunderten (Tübingen ²1989) 43.

6:4   BEST, E. One Body in Christ (1955) 45. HARRISVILLE, R.A. The Concept of Newness in the New Testament (1960) 62ff. DELLING, G. Die Zueignung des Heils in der Taufe (1961) 77-79, 91. SCHRAGE, W. Die konkreten Einzelgebote in der paulinischen Paränese (1961) 16, 72. DELLING, G. Die Taufe im Neuen Testament (1963) 98, 124. HAHN, F. Christologische Hoheitstitel (1963) 204, 210. KERTELGE, K. "Rechtfertigung" bei Paulus (1967) 135, 250, 263-65. NICKELS, P. Targum and New Testament 91967) 69. MERK, O. Handeln aus Glauben (1968) 24, 12, 25, 39, 206, 239. VAN DÜLMEN, A. Die Theologie des Gesetzes bei Paulus (1968) 25, 98, 106, 181, 195, 209. DUNN, J.D.G. Baptism in the Holy Spirit (1970) 75, 77n, 97, 104, 139, 227. MAUSER, U. Gottesbild und Menschwerdung (1971) 127, 134, 142. DELLING, G. Studien zum Neuen Testament und zum hellenistischen Judentum (Göttingen 1970) 342f., 418f. SIBER, P. Mit Christus leben (Zürich 1971) 185f. LOHSE, E. Die Einheit des Neuen Testaments (Göttingen 1973) 234, 237, 241, 278. KÜMMEL, W. G. Römer 7 und das Bild des Menschen im Neuen Testament (München 1974) 25, 39, 71. LADD, G. E. A Theology of the New Testament (Grand Rapids 1974) 290, 492, 494, 516, 552. DUNN, J. Unity and Diversity in the New Testament (London 1977) 158f. MIRANDA, J. P. Marx and the Bible (London 1977) 239-41. DAVIES, J. G. "Baptisterium" in TRE 5 (1980) 199. DUNN, J. D. Christology in the Making (London 1980) 144. SCHRAGE, W. "Ist die Kirche das 'Abbild seines Todes'?" in D. Lührmann und G. Strecker, eds., Kirche (FS G. Bornkamm; Tübingen 1980) 206f. POUPON, G. "L'accusation de magie dans les Actes apocryphes" in F. Bovon et al., eds., Les Actes Apocryphes des Apotres (Geneva 1981) 92. KLEIN, G. "Eschatologie" in TRE 10 (1982) 287, 283. MEEKS, W. A. The First Urban Christians (New Haven/London 1983) 93, 150, 155. HEILIGENTHAL, R. "Gebot" in TRE 12 (1984) 128. STAAB, K. Pauluskommentare aus der griechischen Kirche (Münster ²1984) 218:15-17 Sev. POBEE, J. S. Persecution and Martyrdom in the Theology of Paul (Sheffield 1985) 67, 83f. MALMEDE, H. H. Die Lichtsymbolik im Neuen Testament (Wiesbaden 1986) 12. WEDDERBURN, A. J. M. Baptism and Resurrection (Tübingen 1987) 2, 43, 65, 69, 73f., 83, 200, 294,

	358, 363, 368, 382, 386, 391, 393. HOOKER, M. D. From Adam to Christ. Essays on Paul (Cambridge 1990) 43-5. SEGAL, A. F. Paul the Convert (New Haven/London 1990) 10, 137.
6:5ff.	BRUNNER, Dogmatik I (1946) 335.
6:5-23	DOWNING, F. G. Christ and the Cynics (Sheffield 1988) 188.
6:5-11	LEON-DUFOUR, X. Life and Death in the New Testament (San Francisco 1986) 167.
6:5-10	MERK, O. Handeln aus Glauben (1968) 24.
6:5-9	MERK, O. Handeln aus Glauben (1968) 239f.
6:5-8	SCHWEIZER, E. Heiliger Geist (Stuttgart 1978) 154f. ROCHAIS, G. Les récits de résurrection des morts dans le Nouveau Testament (Cambridge 1981) 188.
6:5-7	SCHRAGE, W. "Ist die Kirche das 'Abbild seines Todes'?" in D. Lührmann und G. Strecker, eds., Kirche (FS G. Bornkamm; Tübingen 1980) 207.
6:5	BEST, E. One Body in Christ (1955) 45, 51f., 54, 56, 61. DELLING, G. Die Zueignung des Heils in der Taufe (1961) 79, 91. KUSS, O. "Zu Röm 6, 5a" Auslegung und Verkündigung I (1963) 151-61. KÄSEMANN, E. Exegetische Versuche und Besinnungen I (1964) 74f. MUSSNER, F. Christus das All und die Kirche (2nd ed. 1968) 127, 223. MERK, O. Handeln aus Glauben (1968) 13, 24f., 38. HAGEMEYER, O. "Eingepflanzt dem Gleichbild seine Todes. Ein immer noch dunkles Schriftwort" EuA 45 (3, '69) 179-85. DUNN, J.D.G. Baptism in the Holy Spirit (1970) 131, 140, 141ff. MAUSER, U. Gottesbild und Menschwerdung (1971) 141, 169f. SCHNACKENBURG, R. Schriften zum Neuen Testament (1971) 363-70. SCHNACKENBURG, R. Das Heilsgeschehen bei der Taufe nach dem Apostel Paulus (München 1950) 39-48. SCHWARZMANN, H. Zur Tauftheologie des hl. Paulus in Röm 6 (Heidelberg 1950) 27-48, 94-105. SIBER, P. Mit Christus leben (Zürich 1971) 10, 185f. BAUMERT, N. Täglich Sterben und Auferstehen (München 1973) 52, 91. DUNN, J. D. G. Jesus and the Spirit. A Study of the Religious and Charismatic Experience of Jesus and the First Christians as Reflected in the New Testament (London 1975) 310, 331f. VANNI, U. "Homoioma in Paolo (Rm 1, 23; 5, 14; 6, 5; 8, 3; Fil 2, 7). Un' interpretazione esegetico-teologica alla luce dell'uso dei LXX—Iᵃ Parte," Gregorianum 58 (1977) 321-345. HAACKER, K. "Exegetische Probleme des Römerbriefs," NovT 20/1 (1978) 1-21. STEWART, R. A. "Engrafting: A Study in New Testament Symbolism and Baptismal Application," EQ 50 (1978) 8-22. SCHRAGE, W. "Ist die Kirche das 'Abbild seines Todes'?" in D. Lührmann und G. Strecker, eds., Kirche (FS G. Bornkamm; Tübingen 1980) 205-19. WIENS, D. H. "Mystery Concepts in Primitive Christianity and in its Environment" in ANRW II.23.2 (1980) 1277. BARTH, G. Die Taufe in frühchristlicher Zeit (Neukirchen-Vluyn 1981) 96, 101f. MORGAN, F. A. "Romans 6, 5a: United to a Death like Christ's," EphT 59 (1983) 267-302. STAAB, K. Pauluskommentare aus der griechischen Kirche (Münster ²1984) 85:19-22 Diod; 121:22-30 ThM; 366:1-8 Genn; 426:7-8 Oek; 500: 16-28 Phot. POKORNY, P. Die Entstehung der Christologie (Berlin 1985) 154. WEDDERBURN, A. J. M. Baptism and Resurrection (Tübingen 1987) 44-47, 84, 343, 350. SEGAL, A. F. Paul the Convert (New Haven/London 1990) 335n.38.
6:5a	GILLMAN, F. M. A Study of Romans 6:5a: United to a Death Like Christ's (San Francisco 1992) passim.
6:6ff.	OLLROG, W.-H. Paulus und seine Mitarbeiter (Neukirchen-Vluyn 1979) 146.
6:6-23	SCHWARZMANN, H. Zur Tauftheologie des hl. Paulus in Röm 6 (Heidelberg 1950) 49-67.

6:6-11   SCHELKLE, K. H. Die Passion Jesu in der Verkündigung des Neuen Testaments (Heidelberg 1949) 155f., 160f., 212f., 262, 265f.

6:6-10   GOPPELT, L. Theologie des Neuen Testaments II: Vielfalt und Einheit des apostolischen Christuszeugnisses (Göttingen 1976) 431.

6:6-8   GUNDRY, R. H. Soma in Biblical Theology with Emphasis on Pauline Anthropology (Cambridge 1976) 56f.

6:6-7   MERK, O. Handeln aus Glauben (1968) 24, 28f. MOULE, C. F. D. "Death 'to Sin', 'to Law', and 'to the World': a Note on certain Datives" in A Descamps and A. de Halleux, eds., Mélanges Bibliques en hommage au R. P. Béda Rigaux (Gembloux 1970) 368, 370f., 374. MOHRLANG, R. Matthew and Paul (Cambridge 1984) 84, 88, 93, 116. STAAB, K. Pauluskommentare aus der griechischen Kirche (Münster [2]1984) 218:18-219:7 Sev; 366:9-25 Genn.

6:6   BEST, E. One Body in Christ (1955) 45, 51, 217n. KNOX, W.L. The Sources of the Synoptic Gospels II (1957) 116. DELLING, G. Die Zueignung des Heils in der Taufe (1961) 78f. SCHRAGE, W. Die konkreten Einzelgebote in der paulinischen Paränese (1961) 21, 49, 64, 66, 164. DELLING, G. Die Taufe im Neuen Testament (1963) 122, 142. JÜNGEL, E. Paulus und Jesus (1966) 54, 57f., 60. BRANDENBURGER, E. Fleisch und Geist (1968) 51, 55, 172, 183, 216, 217. CAMBIER, J. "La Chair et l'Esprit en I Cor. V.5" NTS 15 (1968-69) 231ff. MERK, O. Handeln aus Glauben (1968) 25, 29, 204, 206. VAN DÜLMEN, A. Die Theologie des Gesetzes bei Paulus (1968) 98, 117, 144, 154, 156, 157, 158, 162, 169, 193, 208, 219. DAUER, K.A. Leiblichkeit das Ende aller Werke Gottes (1971) 148-152. EICHHOLZ, G. Die Theologie des Paulus im Umriss (1972) 103, 208f., 269. ROBINSON, J. A. Pelagius's Exposition of Thirteen Epistles of St Paul (Cambridge 1922) 77, 309, 315. PALLIS, A. Notes on St. John and the Apocalypse (London 1928) 52f. SCHNACKENBURG, R. Das Heilsgeschehen bei der Taufe nach dem Apostel Paulus (München 1950) 48-56. SIBER, P. Mit Christus leben (Zürich 1971) 185f. BAUMERT, N. Täglich Sterben und Auferstehen (München 1973) 57. KÜMMEL, W. G. Römer 7 und das Bild des Menschen im Neuen Testament (München 1974) 23, 63f., 86, 190. LADD, G. E. A Theology of the New Testament (Grand Rapids 1974) 465, 474, 486, 493. ROON, A. VAN, The Authenticity of Ephesians (Leiden 1974) 339f. GUNDRY, R. H. Soma in Biblical Theology with Emphasis on Pauline Anthropology (Cambridge 1976) 57f., 135f. BÖHLIG, A. Die Gnosis III: Der Manichäismus (Zürich/München 1980) 332n.73. SCHRAGE, W. "Ist die Kirche das 'Abbild seines Todes'?" in D. Lührmann und G. Strecker, eds., Kirche (FS G. Bornkamm; Tübingen 1980) 212f. THISELTON, A. C. The Two Horizons (Grand Rapids 1980) 269. BRÜNING, W. "Das Erbsündenverständnis der Confessio Augustana: noch ungenützte Einsichten und Möglichkeiten?" Catholica 35 (1981) 128. WEDER, H. Das Kreuz Jesu bei Paulus (Göttingen 1981) 175-82. STAAB, K. Pauluskommentare aus der griechischen Kirche (Münster [2]1984) 121:31-122:5 ThM; 500:29-501:16 Phot. POKORNY, P. Die Entstehung der Christologie (Berlin 1985) 154. MERKLEIN, H. Studien zu Jesus und Paulus (Tübingen 1987) 58, 59, 444n.134. WEDDERBURN, A. J. M. Baptism and Resurrection (Tübingen 1987) 46f., 65, 350. BECKER, J. Paulus. Der Apostel der Völker (Tübingen 1989) 218, 227, 443. MARTIN, B. L. Christ and the Law in Paul (Leiden 1989) 70f., 80-82, 108, 110, 113f., 119.

6:7-8   MÜNCHOW, C. Ethik und Eschatologie (Göttingen 1981) 154, 169f.

6:7   KEARNS, C. "The Interpretation of Romans 6, 7" Studiorum Paulinorum Congressus Internationalis Catholicus 1961 (1963) I 301-7. SCROGGS, R. "Romans vi. 7 *ho gar apothanōn dedikaiōtai apo tēs hamartias*" NTS 10 (1, '63) 104-8.

LYONNET, S. "'Qui enim mortuus est, justificatus est a peccato' (Rom 6, 7)" VerbDom 42 (1, '64) 17-21. KLAAR, E. "Rm 6:7: *ho gar apothanōn dedikaiōtai apo tēs hamartias*" ZNW 59 (1-2, '68) 131-34. MERK, O. Handeln aus Glauben (1968) 24f. KUHN, K. G. "Römer 6:7," ZNW 30 (1931) 305. DALTON, W. J. Christ's Proclamation to the Spirits. A Study of 1 Peter 3:18-4:6 (Rome 1965) 244-48. SIBER, P. Mit Christus leben (Zürich 1971) 185. BAUMERT, N. Täglich Sterben und Auferstehen (München 1973) 66.HAYS, R. B. The Faith of Jesus Christ (Chico CA 1983) 267. RÖHSER, G. Metaphorik und Personifikation der Sünde (Tübingen 1987) 8, 141, 166f. WEDDERBURN, A. J. M. Baptism and Resurrection (Tübingen 1987) 64, 350. MARTIN, B. L. Christ and the Law in Paul (Leiden 1989) 70f., 80-82. VOLLENWEIDER, S. Freiheit als neue Schöpfung (Göttingen 1989) 340.

6:8ff. DELLING, G. Die Zueignung des Heils in der Taufe (1961) 79.

6:8-11 STAAB, K. Pauluskommentare aus der griechischen Kirche (Münster [2]1984) 366:26-32 Genn.

6:8-10 MERK, O. Handeln aus Glauben (1968) 24f. BAMMEL, C. P. H. "Philocalia IX, Jerome, Epistle 121, and Origen's Exposition of Romans VII," JThS 32 (1981) 55.

6:8-9 SCHRAGE, W. Die konkreten Einzelgebote in der paulinischen paränese (1961) 16, 66. STAAB, K. Pauluskommentare aus der griechischen Kirche (Münster [2]1984) 501:17-24 Phot.

6:8 BEST, E. One Body in Christ (1955) 45, 51, 61. KERTELGE, K. "Rechtfertigung" bei Paulus (1967) 150, 180. MERK, O. Handeln aus Glauben (1968) 12f, 25, 28f, 38, 40. SIBER, P. Mit Christus leben (Zürich 1971) 10, 26, 29, 182, 185f. METZGER, B. M. The Early Versions of the New Testament. Their Origin, Transmission, and Limitations (Oxford 1977) 81. FROITZHEIM, F. Christologie und Eschatologie bei Paulus (Würzburg 1979) 209. THISELTON, A. C. The Two Horizons (Grand Rapids 1980) 248, 274. POKORNY, P. Die Entstehung der Christologie (Berlin 1985) 141, 154. LOHFINK, G. Studien zum Neuen Testament (Stuttgart 1989) 276-80, 288. TOWNER, P. H. The Goal of Our Instruction. The Structure of Theology and Ethics in the Pastoral Epistles (Sheffield 1989) 31, 104f., 287n.146.

6:9-11 STAAB, K. Pauluskommentare aus der griechischen Kirche (Münster [2]1984) 85:23-86:3 Diod.

6:9-10 DELLING, G. Die Zueignung des Heils in der Taufe (1961) 73. MOULE, C. F. D. "Death 'to Sin', 'to Law', and 'to the World': A note on certain Datives" in A Descamps and A. de Halleux, eds., Mélanges Bibliques en hommage au R. P. Béda Rigaux (Gembloux 1970) 367f. MINDE, H. J. VAN DER. "Theologia crucis und Pneumaaussagen bei Paulus," Catholica 34 (1980) 134f. BISER, E. Der Zeuge (Graz/Wien/ Köln 1981) 29, 34, 89, 102, 120, 136.

6:9 HAHN, F. Christologische Hoheitstitel (1963) 204, 209f. VAN DÜLMEN, A. Die Theologie des Gesetzes bei Paulus (1968) 98, 103, 121, 180, 208, 219. RICHTER, H.-F. "Auferstehung und Wirklichkeit (Berlin 1969) 76f. CLARK, K. W. "The Meaning of (KATA) KYRIEYEIN" in The Gentile Bias and other Essays [Selected by J. L. Sharpe III] (Leiden 1980) 207-12. STAAB, K. Pauluskommentare aus der griechischen Kirche (Münster [2]1984) 426:9-10 Oek. HÄRING, H. Das Problem des Bösen in der Theologie (Darmstadt 1985) 42. POKORNY, P. Die Entstehung der Christologie (Berlin 1985) 154. HARRIS, M. J. Raised Immortal (London 1986) 231. WEDDERBURN, A. J. M. Baptism and Resurrection (Tübingen 1987) 44, 47f., 65, 347.

6:10-12	SCHRAGE, W. Die konkreten Einzelgebote in der paulinischen Paränese (1961) 50, 61, 239.
6:10-11	SCHNACKENBURG, R. Baptism in the Thought of St. Paul (Oxford 1964) 157f., 163f., 167.FISCHER, U. Eschatologie und Jenseitserwartung im hellenistischen Diasporajudentum (Berlin 1978) 96. SANDERS, E. P. Paul, the Law, and the Jewish People (London 1985) 71f. BERGER, K. und COLPE, C., eds., Religionsgeschichtliches Textbuch zum Neuen Testa-ment (Göttingen/Zürich 1987) 211. RÖHSER, G. Metaphorik und Personifikation der Sünde (Tübingen 1987) 104, 141, 166f. OLIVEIRA, A. DE, Die Diakonie der Gerechtigkeit und der Versöhnung in der Apologie des 2. Korintherbriefes. Analyse und Auslegung von 2 Kor 2, 14-4, 6; 5, 11-6, 10 (Münster 1990) 352.
6:10	LARSSON, E. Christus als Vorbild (1962) 53f., 72f., 94f. BRANDEN-BURGER, E. Adam und Christus (Neukirchen-Vluyn 1962) 160, 186f. DALTON, W. J. Christ's Proclamation to the Spirits. A Study of 1 Peter 3:18-4:6 (Rome 1965) 115-17. STAAB, K. Paulus-kommentare aus der griechischen Kirche (Münster ²1984) 426:11-14 Oek; 655:26-656:13 Areth. HARRIS, M. J. Raised Immortal (London 1986) 231. HOOKER, M. D. From Adam to Christ. Essays on Paul (Cambridge 1990) 44f.
6:11ff.	KÄSEMANN, E. Exegetische Versuche und Besinnungen II
6:11-23	(1964) 184. New Testament Questions of Today (1969) 171.STALDER K. Das Werk des Geistes in der Heiligung bei Paulus (1962) 215-32. GRABNER-HAIDER, A. Paraklese und Eschatologie bei Paulus (1968) 129f.
6:11-14	BARRETT, C.K. From First Adam to Last (1962) 104f.
6:11-13	KERTELGE, K, "Rechtfertigung" bei Paulus (1967) 253. LYONNET, S. Ouaestiones in epistulam ad Romanos (Rome 1975) 93f. CRUZ, H. Christological Motives and Motivated Actions in Pauline Paraenesis (Frankfurt/Bern/New York/Paris 1990) 164-9.
6:11-12	ROLOFF, J. "Amt" in TRE 2 (1978) 526.
6:11,12	BEST, E. One Body in Christ (1955) 49.
6:11	BEST, E. One Body in Christ (1955) 1n, 60, 61, 69. SCHRAGE, W. Die konkreten Einzelgebote in der paulinischen Paränese (1961) 50. DELLING, G. Die Taufe im Neuen Testament (1963) 118, 124. KAMLAH, E. Die Form der katalogischen Paränese im Neuen Testament (1964) 16, 193, 202, 3. MERK, O. Handeln aus Glauben (1968) 5, 12, 25-29, 39, 235, 239. SIBER, P. Mit Christus leben (Zürich 1971) 185. LOHSE, E. Grundriss der neutestamentlichen Theologie (Stuttgart 1974) 98f. ELLIS, E. E. Prophecy and Hermeneutic in Early Christianity (Tübingen 1978) 67, 77, 98. HAGEN, W. H. "Two Deutero-Pauline Glosses in Rom 6," ET 92 (1981) 364-67. SCHNELLE, U. Gerechtigkeit und Christusgegenwart (Göttingen 1983) 110f. MOHRLANG, R. Matthew and Paul (Cambridge 1984) 84, 118, 174. STAAB, K. Pauluskommentare aus der griechischen Kirche (Münster ²1984) 656:14-16 Areth. WEDDERBURN, A. J. M. Baptism and Resurrection (Tübingen 1987) 43, 73f., 363.
6:12ff.	KÄSEMANN, E. Exegetische Versuche und Besinnungen (1964) I 29, 113, 276. MERK, O. Handeln aus Glauben (1968) 23, 25, 34, 157. RIDDERBOS, H. Paul. An Outline of His Theology (Grand Rapids 1975) 112-17, 255-66. TOWNER, P. H. The Goal of Our Instruction. The Structure of Theology and Ethics in the Pastoral Epistles (Sheffield 1989) 105.
6:12-23	ROBINSON, J.A.T. The Body (1952) passim. THUESING, W. Per Christum in Deum (1965) 93-96. KERTELGE, K. "Rechtfertigung" bei Paulus (1967) 233, 263-75, 282. MERK, O. Handeln aus Glauben (1968) 28, 40, 157, 235. SIBER, P. Mit Christus leben (Zürich 1971) 187. ROBINSON, J. A. T.

Wrestling with Romans (London 1979) 72-76. TOIT, A. B. DU. "Dikaiosyne in Röm 6. Beobachtungen zur ethischen Dimension der pauli-nischen Gerechtig-keitsauffassung," ZThK 76 (1979) 261-91. MALAN, F. S. "Bound to Do Right," Neotes-tamentica 15 (1981) 118-38. BERGER, K. und COLPE, C., eds., Religionsgeschichtliches Textbuch zum Neuen Testament (Göttingen/Zürich 1987) 211-13.

6:12-19   PAGELS, E. H. The Gnostic Paul. Gnostic Exegesis of the Pauline Letters (Philadelphia 1975) 30f.

6:12-14   BEST, E. One Body in Christ (1955) 191n, 217n. FRANKEMOELLE, H. Das Taufverständnis des Paulus (1970) 95-97, 114-116. GUNDRY, R. H. Soma in Biblical Theology with Emphasis on Pauline Anthropology (Cambridge 1976) 29-31. THISELTON, A. C. The Two Horizons (Grand Rapids 1980) 281. STAAB, K. Pauluskommentare aus der griechischen Kirche (Münster [2]1984) 86:4-10 Diod; 122:6-32 ThM; 367:1-28 Genn; 501:25-502:10 Phot. MALINA, B. J. Christian Origins and Cultural Anthropology (Atlanta 1986) 137. LINDARS, B. "Paul and the Law in Romans 5-8: An Actantial Analysis" in B. Lindars, ed., Law and Religion (Cambridge 1988) 132. MARCUS, J. "'Let God Arise and End the Reign of Sin!' A Contribution to the Study of Pauline Parenesis," Biblica 69 (1988) 386-95.

6:12-13   SCHRAGE, W. Die konkreten Einzelgebote in der paulinischen Paränese (1961) 31, 64, 66, 82, 130. BAUER, K.A. Leiblichkeit das Ende aller Werke Gottes (1971) 152-58. GOPPELT, L. Theologie des Neuen Testaments II: Vielfalt und Einheit des apostolischen Christus-zeugnisses (Göttingen 1976) 431.

6:12   DELLING, G. Die Taufe im Neuen Testament (1963) 148. MERK, O. Handeln aus Glauben (1968) 29f, 32, 34-37. STROBEL, A. Erkenntnis und Bekenntnis der Sünde in neutestamentlicher Zeit (1968) 53. VAN DÜLMEN, A. Die The-ologie des Gesetzes bei Paulus (1968) 108, 119, 149, 154, 156, 158, 162, 196. SIBER, P. Mit Christus leben (Zürich 1971) 125, 127f. BAUMERT, N. Täglich Sterben und Auferstehen (München 1973) 257. KÜMMEL, W. G. Römer 7 und das Bild des Menschen im Neuen Testament (München 1974) 19, 23, 86, 100. LADD, G. E. A Theology of the New Testament (Grand Rapids 1974) 465, 486, 525, 615. AGERSNAP, S. "Rom 6, 12 og det paulinske imperativ" [Rom 6:12 and the Pauline Imperative], DTT 43 (1980) 36-47. THISELTON, A. C. The Two Horizons (Grand Rapids 1980) 278. BRUENING, W. "Das Erb-sündenverständnis der Confessio Augustana: noch ungenützte Einsichten und Möglichkeiten?" Catholica 35 (1981) 128. STAAB, K. Pauluskommentare aus der griechischen Kirche (Münster [2]1984) 656:17-19 Areth. RÄISÄNEN, H. The Torah and Christ (Helsinki 1986) 162f. RÖHSER, G. Metaphorik und Personifi-kation der Sünde (Tübingen 1987) 4, 104, 107f., 111ff., 124, 126f., 158, 160.

6:13,19   SCHWEIZER, E. "Die Sünde in den Gliedern" Abraham unser Vater Festschrift f. Otto Michel (1963) 437-39. KÄSEMANN, E. New Testament Questions of Today (1969) 173. KERTELGE, K. "Rechtfertigung" bei Paulus (1967) 156, 304.

6:13   STACEY, W.D. The Pauline View of Man (1956) 171, 183, 202. SCHRAGE, W. Die konkreten Einzelgebote in der paulinischen Paränese (1961) 31, 49, 53. KAMLAH, E. Die Form der katalogischen Paränese im Neuen Testament (1964) 189, 193, 5.9; 202, 3. KÄSEMANN, E. Exegetische Versuche und Besinnungen (1964) I 294: II 186. JÜNGEL, E. Paulus und Jesus (1966) 33. MERK, O. Handeln aus Glauben (1968) 12f., 23, 29, 31, 37f., 158, 239f. STROBEL, A. Erkenntnis und Bekenntnis der Sünde in neutestamentlicher Zeit (1968) 52. VAN DÜLMEN, A. Die Theologie des Gesetzes bei Paulus (1968)

98, 100, 108, 148, 154, 156, 159, 162, 220. FEUILLET, A. "Morale Ancienne et Morale Chrétienne d'après Mt 5 17-20; Comparaison avec la Doctrine de l'Epître aux Romains" NTS 17 (1970-71) 134f. THYEN, H. Studien zur Sündenvergebung (1970) 187, 212f. BAUER, K.-A. Leiblichkeit das Ende aller Werke Gottes (1971) 167-170. ZIESLER, J.A. The Meaning of Righteousness in Paul (1972) 167, 201, 202, 213. BAUMERT, N. Täglich Sterben und Aufer-stehen (München 1973) 256f., 285f. HÜBNER, H. Das Gesetz bei Paulus. Ein Beitrag zum Werden der paulinischen Theologie (Göttingen 1978) 110-13. HAGEN, W. H. "Two Deutero-Pauline Glosses in Romans 6," ET 92 (1981) 364-67. MOHRLANG, R. Matthew and Paul (Cambridge 1984) 84, 118, 174, 186. RÖHSER, G. Metaphorik und Personifikation der Sünde (Tübingen 1987) 104, 109, 111ff., 126f., 141, 163, 166f. WEDDERBURN, A. J. M. Baptism and Resurrection (Tübingen 1987) 43-46, 81, 166, 386, 393. CLABEAUX, J. J. The Lost Edition of the Letters of Paul (CBQ.MS; Washington 1989) 61. MARTIN, B. L. Christ and the Law in Paul (Leiden 1989) 70, 71, 80-83, 109, 119, 121, 124, 148. OLIVEIRA, A. DE, Die Diakonie der Gerechtigkeit und der Versöhn-ung in der Apologie des 2. Korintherbriefes. Analyse und Auslegung von 2 Kor 2, 14-4, 6; 5, 11-6, 10 (Münster 1990) 413.

6:14-15   SCHRAGE, W. Die konkreten Einzelgebote in der paulinischen Paränese (1961) 65, 94, 98, 232. POTTERIE, I. DE LA," paulinienne et johannique" in E. E. Ellis und E. Grässer, eds., Jesus und Paulus (FS W.G. Kümmel; Göttingen 1975) 264. SCHNACKENBURG, R. Römer 7 im Zusammenhang des Römer-briefes" in E. E. Ellis und E. Grässer, eds., Jesus und Paulus (FS W. G. Kümmel; Göttingen 1975) 289ff.

6:14   JÜNGEL, E. Paulus und Jesus (1966) 26, 40, 42, 59, 62, 67f. MERK, O. Handeln aus Glauben (1968) 6, 30-32, 34, 157, 235, 240. VAN DÜLMEN, A. Die Theologie des Gesetzes bei Paulus (1968) 20, 63, 98, 99, 113, 201, 208, 220. SCHNEIDER, N. Die rhetorische Eigenart der paulinischen Antithese (1970) 72-76. BRANDENBURGER, E. Adam und Christus (Neukirchen-Vluyn 1962) 160, 206, 248, 252, 260f. BAUMERT, N. Täglich Sterben und Aufer-stehen (München 1973) 90. KÜMMEL, W. G. Römer 7 und das Bild des Menschen im Neuen Testament (München 1974) 7f., 13, 36, 69, 97. CONZEL-MANN, H. und LINDEMANN, A. Arbeitsbuch zum Neuen Testament (Tübingen 1975) 17. HÜBNER, H. Das Gesetz bei Paulus. Ein Beitrag zum Werden der paulinischen Theologie (Göttingen 1978) 114f. CLARK, K. W. "The Meaning of (KATA) KYRIEYEIN" in The Gentile Bias and other Essays [Selected by J. L. Sharpe III] (Leiden 1980) 207-12. MÜHLEN, K.-H. ZUR. "Demut" in TRE 8 (1981) 474. RÄISÄNEN, H. Paul and the Law (Tübingen 1983) 47, 114, 141, 148, 150, 162. MOHRLANG, R. Matthew and Paul (Cambridge 1984) 32f., 47, 61, 84, 116, 118. RUCKSTUHL, E. "Gnade III" in TRE 13 (1984) 469. SANDERS, E. P. Paul, the Law, and the Jewish People (London 1985) 71f., 84, 91n.50, 93. RÖHSER, G. Metaphorik und Personifika-tion der Sünde (Tübingen 1987) 10, 112, 120, 141, 165f., 170. CONZEL-MANN, H. and LINDEMANN, A. Interpreting the New Testament (Peabody MA 1988) 14f. MARTIN, B. L. Christ and the Law in Paul (Leiden 1989) 16, 19f., 30, 60, 70-72, 80-83, 100, 109f., 121, 127, 132, 145.

6:14b   SCHNELLE, U. Wandlungen im paulinischen Denken (Stuttgart 1989) 64.
6:15ff.   KAYE, B. "Law and Morality in the Epistles of the New Testament" in B. Kaye and G. Wenham, eds., Law, Morality and the Bible (Downers Grove IL 1978) 82-84.

6:15-23   EICHHOLZ, G. Die Theologie de Paulus im Umriss (1972) 5, 202, 204, 206, 268f., 269f. SIBER, P. Mit Christus leben (Zürich 1971) 230ff. PASTOR, F. "Libertad o esclavitud cristiana en Pablo? Rom 6:15-23" in Homenaje a Juan Prado (Madrid 1975) 443-63. SYNOFZIK, E. Die Gerichts- und Vergeltungsaussagen bei Paulus (Göttingen 1977) 69-71. MALHERBE, A. J. Moral Exhortation. A Greco-Roman Sourcebook (Philadelphia 1986) 159. LINDARS, B. "Paul and the Law in Romans 5-8: An Actantial Analysis" in B. Lindars, ed., Law and Religion (Cambridge 1988) 132f.

6:15-16   STAAB, K. Pauluskommentare aus der griechischen Kirche (Münster ²1984) 367:29-34 Genn. SCHMELLER, TH. Paulus und die "Diatribe" (Münster 1987) 327n. 126.

6:15   VAN DÜLMEN, A. Die Theologie des Gesetzes bei Paulus (1968) 20, 63, 72, 99f., 160, 201, 220. RHYNE, C. T. Faith Establishes the Law (Chico CA 1981) 45f. STAAB, K. Pauluskommentare aus der griechischen Kirche (Münster ²1984) 122:33-123:11 ThM. JONES, F. S. "Freiheit" in den Briefen des Apostels Paulus (Göttingen 1987) 110f., 112, 115-17, 123, 135, 213 A 10, 215 A 30, 216 A 34. SCHMELLER, TH. Paulus und die "Diatribe" (Münster 1987) 327. VOLLENWEIDER, S. Freiheit als neue Schöpfung (Göttingen 1989) 324. McDONALD, P. M. "Romans 5.1-11 as a Rhetorical Bridge," JSNT 40 (1990) 81-96.

6:16ff.   FEINE, D. P. und BEHM, D. J. Einleitung in das Neue Testament (Heidelberg 1950) 167ff. WALTHER, C. "Gehorsam" in TRE 12 (1984) 150.

6:16-23   SEVENSTER, J.N. Paul and Seneca (1961) 20-22, 121, 157, 162. VOLLENWEIDER, S. Freiheit als neue Schöpfung (Göttingen 1989) 331.

6:16.19   MALINA, B. J. Christian Origins and Cultural Anthropology (Atlanta 1986) 137.

6:16-17   HAINZ, J. Ekklesia (Regensburg 1972) 176f.

6:16   BOUSSET, W. Die Religion des Judentums im Späthellenistischen Zeitalter (1966 =1926) 375. BRUNNER, E. Dogmatik II (1950) 124. SCHRAGE, W. Die konkreten Einzelgebote in der paulinischen Paränese (1961)64. JÜNGEL, E. Paulus und Jesus (1966) 33. MERK, O. Handeln aus Glauben (1968) 9, 13, 23, 29-31, 33f., 38. FEUILLET, A. "Morale Ancienne et Morale Chrétienne d'après Mt 5. 17-20. Comparaison avec la Doctrine de l'Epitre aux Romains" NTS 17 (1970/71) 134f. ROBINSON, J. A. Pelagius's Exposition of Thirteen Epistles of St Paul (Cambridge 1922) 142, 148, 260. BRANDENBURGER, E. Adam und Christus (Neukirchen-Vluyn 1962) 164f. GUNDRY, R. H. Soma in Biblical Theology with Emphasis on Pauline Anthropology (Cambridge 1976) 29-31. HÜBNER, H. Das Gesetz bei Paulus. Ein Beitrag zum Werden der paulinischen Theologie (Göttingen 1978) 111-13. THISELTON, A. C. The Two Horizons (Grand Rapids 1980) 391. HAGEN, W. H. "Two Deutero-Pauline Glosses in Rom 6," ET 92 (1981) 365f. OLIVEIRA, A. DE, Die Diakonie der Gerechtigkeit und der Versöhnung in der Apologie des 2. Korintherbriefes. Analyse und Auslegung von 2 Kor 2, 14-4, 6; 5, 11-6, 10 (Münster 1990) 353n.483.

6:17ff.   SCHMITHALS, W. Der Römerbrief als historisches Problem (Gütersloh 1975) 10, 67.

6:17-19   STAAB, K. Pauluskommentare aus der griechischen Kirche (Münster ²1984) 656:20-657:15 Areth.

6:17-18   KÜRZINGER, J. "Typos didaches und der Sinn von Rom 6, 17f' Biblica 39 (2, '58) 156-76. HÜBNER, H. Das Gesetz bei Paulus. Ein Beitrag zum Werden der paulinischen Theologie (Göttingen 1978) 111-3. STAAB, K. Pauluskommentare aus der griechischen Kirche (Münster ²1984) 368:1-7 Genn. OLIVEIRA, A. DE,

Die Diakonie der Gerechtigkeit und der Versöhnung in der Apologie des 2. Korintherbriefes. Analyse und Auslegung von 2 Kor 2, 14-4, 6; 5, 11-6, 10 (Münster 1990) 28.

6:17   BEARE, F.W. "On the Interpretation of Romans vi.17" NTS 5 (3, '59) 206-10. LEE, E.K. Words denoting "Pattern" in the New Testament NTS 8 (1961-62) 169f. SCHRAGE, W. Die konkreten Einzelgebote in der paulinischen Paränese (1961) 50, 79, 11, 130, 135-37. DELLING, G. Die Taufe im Neuen Testament (1963) 79. ROLOFF, J. Apostolat-Verkündigung-Kirche (1965) 131ff. SEEBERG, A. Der Katechismus der Urchristenheit (1966) 1ff, 6, 40, 41, 42, 43. BORSE, U. "'Abbild der Lehre' (Röm 6, 17) im Kontext" BZ 12 (1, '68) 95-103. HAINZ, J. Ekklesia (Regensburg 1972) 180f. LAUB, F. Eschatologische Verkündigung und Lebensgestaltung nach Paulus. (Regensburg 1973) 2f., 29, 60, 180. SCHMITHALS, W. Der Römerbrief als historisches Problem (Gütersloh 1975) 209. GUNDRY, R. H. Soma in Biblical Theology with Emphasis on Pauline Anthropology (Cambridge 1976) 30f. SCHULZ, S. Die Mitte der Schrift (Stuttgart 1976) 128f. DUNN, J. D. G. Unity and Diversity in the New Testament. An Inquiry into the Character of Earliest Christianity (London 1977) 144f. HAACKER, K. "Exegetische Probleme des Römerbriefs," NovT 20 (1978) 1-21. JEWETT, P. K. Infant Baptism and the Covenant of Grace (Grand Rapids 1978) 54. DEICHGRÄBER, R. "Benediktionen" in TRE 5 (1980) 563. HAGEN, W. H. "Two Deutero-Pauline Glosses in Romans 6," ET 92 (1981) 365f. MÜLLER, P.-G. Der Traditionsprozess im Neuen Testament (Freiburg 1982) 226f. DEICHGRÄBER, R. "Formeln, Liturgische" in TRE 11 (1983) 259. RICHARDSON, P. and HURD, J. C., eds., From Jesus to Paul (FS F. W. Beare; Waterloo 1984) 122f. STAAB, K. Pauluskommentare aus der griechischen Kirche (Münster ²1984) 123:12-24 ThM. ZIMMERMANN, A. F. Die urchristlichen Lehrer (Tübingen 1984) 64f., 109f. BERGER, K. und COLPE, C., eds., Religionsgeschichtliches Textbuch zum Neuen Testament (Göttingen/ Zürich 1987) 213. LOHFINK, G. Studien zum Neuen Testament (Stuttgart 1989) 321-4.

6:17b   SIMONIS, W. Der gefangene Paulus. Die Entstehung des sogenannten Römerbriefs und anderer urchristlicher Schriften in Rom (Frankfurt/ Bern/New York/ Paris 1990) 46. GAGNON, R. A. J. "Hart of Wax and a Teaching that Stamps: *TYPOS DIDACHES* (Rom 6:17b) Once More," JBL 112 (1993) 667-87.

6:18-22 STAAB, K. Pauluskommentare aus der griechischen Kirche (Münster ²1984) 502:20-503:16 Phot. JONES, F. S. "Freiheit" in den Briefen des Apostels Paulus (Göttingen 1987) 29, 110-7, 123, 125, 129, 135f., 139, 141, 161A18.

6:18   SCHRAGE, W. Die konkreten Einzelgebote in der paulinischen Paränese (1961) 49, 65, 83. JÜNGEL, E. Paulus und Jesus (1966) 33. KERTELGE, K. "Rechtfertigung" bei Paulus (1967) 156. HAGEN, W. H. "Two Deutero-Pauline Glosses in Rom 6," ET 92 (1981) 364-7. MOHRLANG, R. Matthew and Paul (Cambridge 1984) 116, 118, 186. SCHNABEL, E. J. Law and Wisdom from Ben Sira to Paul (Tübingen 1985) 322, 340f. JONES, F. S. "Freiheit" in den Briefen des Apostels Paulus (Göttingen 1987) 13, 28, 110, 112f., 147A3, 214A22.

6:19ff. SCHRAGE, W. Die konkreten Einzelgebote in der paulinischen Paränese (1961) 189, 49, 50, 61, 64.

6:19-23 FUCHS, GPM (1961/62) 254ff. KÄSEMANN, E. Exegetische Versuche und Besinnungen (1964) I 263-66. SISTI, A. "Dal servizio des peccato al servizio di Dio Rom (6, 19-23)" BiblOr 6 (3, '64) 119-127. IWAND, H.-J. Predigt-Meditationen (1964) 262-67. NIESEL, W. in Herr, tue meine Lippen aug II, ed.

G. Eichholz (1965) 384-88. DOERNE, M. Die alten Episteln (1967) 176-80. FROR, K. GPM 22 (1967/68) 324-30. SCHELLONG, D. in GPM 38 (1983/1984) 321-7.

6:19-20 KÄSEMANN, E. Exegetische Versuche und Besinnungen (1964) II 186. STAAB, K. Pauluskommentare aus der griechischen Kirche (Münster ²1984) 568:8-16 Genn.

6:19 STACEY, W.D. The Pauline View of Man (1956) 159f. KERTELGE, K. "Rechtfertigung" bei Paulus (1967) 156, 275. MERK, O. Handeln aus Glauben (1968) 13, 29, 31f., 49. STROBEL, A. Erkenntnis und Bekenntnis der Sünde in neutestamentlicher Zeit (1968) 52. FEUILLET, A. "Morale Ancienne et Morale Chrétienne d'après Mt. 5, 17-20; Comparison avec la Doctrine de l'Epître aux Romains" NTS 17 (1970-71) 134f. SCHNEIDER, N. Die rhetorische Eigenart der paulinischen Antithese (1970) 114-15. LAUB, F. Eschatologische Verkündigung und Lebensgestaltung nach Paulus. (Regensburg 1973) 56, 58-60. LADD, G. E. A Theology of the New Testament (Grand Rapids 1974) 405, 469, 486, 520. GUNDRY, R. H. Soma in Biblical Theology with Emphasis on Pauline Anthropology (Cambridge 1976) 29-31. HÜBNER, H. Das Gesetz bei Paulus. Ein Beitrag zum Werden der paulinischen Theologie (Göttingen 1978) 112. HAGEN, W. H. "Two Deutero-Pauline Glosses in Rom 6," ET 92 (1981) 364, 367. STAAB, K. Pauluskommentare aus der griechischen Kirche (Münster ²1984) 86:11-3 Diod; 123:25-9 ThM. RÖHSER, G. Metaphorik und Personifikation der Sünde (Tübingen 1987) 2, 43, 107f., 110f., 113, 126f., 148, 166. MARTIN, B. L. Christ and the Law in Paul (Leiden 1989) 13, 81-3, 105, 121, 148.

6:19b CLABEAUX, J. J. The Lost Edition of the Letters of Paul (CBQ.MS; Washington 1989) 59-61.

6:20-23 MINEAR, P.S. Images of the Church in the New Testament (1960) 175f.

6:20 MEHL, R. "Freiheit" in TRE 11 (1983) 519.

6:21ff. BANDSTRA, A.J. The Law and the Elements of the World (1964) 129f.

6:21-23 STAAB, K. Pauluskommentare aus der griechischen Kirche (Münster ²1984) 368:17-25 Genn.

6:21-22 SCHRAGE, W. Die konkreten Einzelgebote in der paulinischen Paränese (1961) 49, 54, 55, 60f., 73, 83, 188. REED, J. T. "Indicative and Imperative in Rom 6, 21-22," Biblica 74 (1993) 244-57.

6:21 BRAUMANN, G. Vorpaulinische christliche Taufverkündigung bei Paulus (1962) 45f. DANKER, F.W. "Romans V 12. Sin under Law" NTS 14 (1967/68) 432f. STAAB, K. Pauluskommentare aus der griechischen Kirche (Münster ²1984) 123:30-3 ThM.

6:22-23 KÜMMEL, W. G. Römer 7 und das Bild des Menschen im Neuen Testament (München 1974) 7f., 36.

6:22 KERTELGE, K. "Rechtfertigung" bei Paulus (1967) 275. MERK, O. Handeln aus Glauben (1968) 15, 32-34, 38f., 49, 68f., 240. HAGEN, W. H. "Two Deutero-Pauline Glosses in Rom 6," ET 92 (1981) 364-7. MOHRLANG, R. Matthew and Paul (Cambridge 1984) 61, 65, 116, 118. SCHNABEL, E. J. Law and Wisdom from Ben Sira to Paul (Tübingen 1985) 322, 340f. JONES, F. S. "Freiheit" in den Briefen des Apostels Paulus (Göttingen 1987) 28f., 110, 112, 114, 125, 147A3, 161A17, 214A22. MARTIN, B. L. Christ and the Law in Paul (Leiden 1989) 13, 70f., 80, 82, 110, 119, 131, 147f.

6:23 BRUNNER, E. Mensch im Widerspruch (937) 159, A.2. DOGMATIK II (1950) 150. BEST, E. One Body in Christ (1955) 5, 11, 24, 43n. KRAMER, W. Christos Kyrios Gottessohn (1963) § 19c. KÄSEMANN, E. Exegetische

Versuche und Besinnungen (1964) I 110. JÜNGEL, E. Paulus und Jesus (1966)
59. BAUER, K.-A. Leiblichkeit das Ende aller Werke Gottes (1971) 170-76.
BRANDENBURGER, E. Adam und Christus (Neukirchen-Vluyn 1962) 72, 160,
164ff., 259. KÜMMEL, W. G. Römer 7 und das Bild des Menschen im Neuen
Testament (München 1974) 7f., 12, 18, 53, 86, 195. LADD, G. E. A Theology
of the New Testament (Grand Rapids 1974) 405, 430, 522, 568. BROCKHAUS,
U. Charisma und Amt. Die paulinische Charismenlehre auf dem Hintergrund der
frühchristlichen Gemeindefunktionen (Wuppertal ²1975) 48f., 51, 92, 130-3,
139ff. SCHMITHALS, W. "Zur Herkunft der gnostischen Elemente in der
Sprache des Paulus" in B. Aland et al., eds., Gnosis (FS H. Jonas; Göttingen
1978) 388-90. AONO, T. Die Entwicklung des paulinischen Gerichtsgedankens
bei den Apostolischen Vätern (Bern/Frankfurt/Las Vegas 1979) 4ff. GEORGI,
D. "Weisheit Salomos" in JSHRZ 3 (4, 1980) 2n.24b. KOCH, E. "Fegfeuer" in
TRE 11 (1983) 76. MOHRLANG, R. Matthew and Paul (Cambridge 1984) 27,
60, 65, 117. STAAB, K. Pauluskommentare aus der griechischen Kirche (Münster ²1984) 86:14-9 Diod; 503:17-8 Phot; 657:16-9 Areth. NATHO, E. in GPM
41 (1986/1987) 66-70. RÖHSER, G. Metaphorik und Personifikation der Sünde
(Tübingen 1987) 112, 141f., 165ff. SCHATZMANN, S. S. A Pauline Theology
of Charismata (Peabody MA 1987) 4f., 17f. BROWN, C. E. "'The Last Enemy
Is Death.' Paul and the Pastoral Task," Interp 43 (1989) 380-92. MARTIN, B.
L. Christ and the Law in Paul (Leiden 1989) 69f., 72, 80, 82f., 109, 119.

7–8   DE LORENZI, L., ed., The Law of the Spirit in Rom 7 and 8 (Rome 1976).
             LANGEVIN, P.-É. "Exégèse et psychanalyse. Lecture psychanalytique de
             Romains VII et VIII," LThPh 36 (1980) 129-37. BLANK, J. Paulus. Von Jesus
             zum Christentum (München 1982) 86-123. GRELOT, P. "La vie dans l'Esprit
             (d'après Romains 7-8)," Christus 29 (113, 1982) 83-98. BERGER, K.
             "Gnosis/Gnostizismus" in TRE 13 (1984) 529. STEPIEN, J. "Przybrane
             synostwo Boze w Rz 7-8. Z duchowosci sw. Pawla (La filiation adoptive dans
             Rm 7-8. Etude sur la spiritualité de saint Paul)," CoTh 55 (1985) 19-27.
             THEISSEN, G. Psychological Aspects of Pauline Theology (Edinburgh 1987)
             222-65. TROCMÉ, E. "From 'I' to 'We'. Christian Life according to Romans,
             Chapters 7 and 8," AusBR 35 (1987) 73-6. VOLLENWEIDER, S. Freiheit als
             neue Schöpfung (Göttingen 1989) 339ff. LAMBRECHT, J. The Wretched "I"
             and Its Liberation. Paul in Romans 7 and 8. Louvain Theological & Pastoral
             Monographs 14 (Louvain 1992) passim.
7:1-8:17   WATSON, F. Paul, Judaism and the Gentiles (Cambridge 1986) 149-58.
7:1-8:13   BAUMERT, N. Täglich Sterben und Auferstehen. Der Literalsinn von 2 Kor 4,
             12-5, 10 (München 1973) 28f. 7:1-8:8 MORRISON, B. and WOODHOUSE, J.
             "The Coherence of Romans 7:1-8:8," RThR 47 (1988) 8-16.
7:1–8:7   VAN DÜLMEN, A. Die Theologie des Gesetzes bei Paulus (1968) 100-23.
7:1-8:1   KLEINKNECHT, K. T. Der leidende Gerechtfertigte (Tübingen 1984) 333.
7   LEKKERKERKER, A. F. N. Römer 7 und Römer 9 bei Augustin (1942). MIT-
             TON, C. L. "Romans VII Reconsidered" ET 65 ('53/54) 78-81, 99-103, 132-35.
             BEST, E. One Body in Christ (1955) 35, 49. ELLWEIN, E. "Das Rätsel von
             Römer VII" KuD 1 ('55) 247-68. GOGARTEN, F. Die Wirklichkeit des
             Glaubens (1957) 72, 99f., 164ff. SANDMEL, S The Genius of Paul (1958) 27-
             33, 56. SCHOEPS, H.-J. Paulus (1959) 200ff. KOHLBRUEGGE, H.F. Das
             siebte Kapitel des Römerbriefes. In ausführlicher Umschreibung (1960). ROBIN-
             SON, J. M. Kerygma und historischer Jesus (1960) 101. KNOX, W.L. St. Paul
             and the Church of the Gentiles (1961) 96, 98ff., 182, 187. LYONNET, S.

"L'histoire du salut selon le chapitre VII de l'epître aux Romains" Biblica 43 (2, '62) 117-151. JONAS, H. "Philosophische Meditation über Paulus, Römerbrief, Kapitel 7" Zeit und Geschichte. Dankesgabe an R. Bultmann zum 80 Geburtstage, ed. E. Dinkler (1964) 557-70. LONGENECKER, R.N. Paul Apostle of Liberty (1964) 50, 88-90, 111, 116. PACKER, J. I. "The 'Wretched Man' in Romans 7" Studia Evangelica II, ed. F. L. Cross (1964) 621/627. BOUSSET, W. Die Religion des Judentums im Späthellenistischen Zeitalter (1966 =1926) 388. BRAUN, H. Qumran und NT II (1966) 167, 174, 248. TOUSSAINT, S.D. "The Contrast between the Spiritual Conflict in Romans 7 and Galatians 5" BiblSa 123 (492, '66) 310-14. BULTMANN, R. "Römer 7 und die Anthropologie des Paulus" Exegetica, ed. E. Kinkler (1967) 198-210. KERTELGE, K. "Rechtfertigugn" bei Paulus (1967) 215, 219-22. MANSON, W. "A Reading of Romans VII" in Jesus and the Christian (1967) 149-62. NICKELS, P. Targum and New Testament (1967) 69. LUZ, U. Das Geschichtsverständnis des Paulus (1968) 218. VAN DÜLMEN, A. Die Theologie des Gesetzes bei Paulus (1968) 62, 72, 83, 100ff., 114, 131, 158, 233. BLANK, J. Schriftauslegung in Theorie und Praxis (1969) 165, 172, 153, 158, 161-65. ZIESLER, J.A. The Meaning of Righteousness in Paul (1972) 203f., 206. WINDISCH, H. The Meaning of the Sermon on the Mount (Philadelphia 1937) 121f., 174. HOMMEL, H. "Das 7. Kapitel des Römerbriefes im Licht antiker Überlieferung," ThViat 8 (1961/1962) 90-116. KÜRZINGER, J. "Der Slchlüssel zum Verständnis von Röm. 7," BZ 7 (1963) 270-4. LÉON-DUFOUR, X., ed., Exegese im Methodenkonflikt (München 1971) 69ff. VERGOTE, A. "Der Beitrag des Psychoanalyse zur Exegese. Leben, Gesetz und Ich-Spaltung im 7. Kapitel des Römerbriefs" in X. Léon-Dufour, ed., Exegese im Methodenkonflikt (München 1971) 73ff. HIRSCHBERGER, H. H. "Die rabbinische Reaktion auf des Paulus Grundgedanken in Kapitel 7 des Römerbriefes," Horizonte 7 (5-6, 1972) 367-73. HEROLD, G. Zorn und Gerechtigkeit Gottes bei Paulus. Eine Untersuchung zu Röm. 1, 16-18 (Bern/Frankfurt 1973) 239ff. WATSON, N. M. "The Interpretation of Romans VII," AusBR 21 (1973) 27-39. KÜMMEL, W. G. Römer 7 und das Bild des Menschen im Neuen Testament (München 1974). RIDDERBOS, H. Paul. An Outline of His Theology (Grand Rapids 1975) 125-30, 143-7, 228f. SCHNACKENBURG, R. "Römer 7 im Zusammenhang des Römerbriefes" in E. Ellis und E. Grässer, eds., Jesus und Paulus (FS W. G. Kümmel; Göttingen 1975) 283-300. MAULTSBY, H. D. "Paul, Black Theology and Hermeneutics," JIThC 3 (1976) 49-64. MacGORMAN, J. W. "Romans 7 Once More," SouJTh 19 (1976) 31-41. YAGI, S. "Weder persönlich noch generell—zum neutestamentlichen Denken anhand Röm vii," AJBI 2 (1976) 159-73. MIRANDA, J. P. Marx and the Bible. A Critique of the Philosophy of Oppression (London 1977) 176. KRUYF, T. DE. "The Perspective of Romans VII" in T. Baarda et al., eds., Miscellanea Neotestamentica. NTS XLVIII (1978) 127-41. PIXLEY, J. V. "El evangelio paulino de la justificación por la fe. Conversación con José Porfirio Miranda," RevBi 41 (1979) 57-74. YAGI, S. "Das Ich bei Paulus und Jesus—zum neutestamentlichen Denken," AJBI 5 (1979) 133, 146. BADER, G. "Römer 7 als Skopus einer theologischen Handlungstheorie," ZThK 78 (1981) 31-56. BLANK, J. Paulus. Von Jesus zum Christentum (München 1982) 86-123. GORDAY, P. Principles of Patristic Exegesis: Romans 9-11 in Origen, John Chrysostom, and Augustine (New York/Toronto 1983) 70-2, 118f., 162-4, 174f. RÄISÄNEN, H. Paul and the Law (Tübingen 1983) 18, 65, 100, 152f., 202, 229, 232f., 264. THEISSEN, G. Psychologische Aspekte paulinischer Theologie (Göttingen 1983) 56f., 181-268. ACHTEMEIER, P. J.

"Some Things in Them Hard to Understand. Reflection on an Approach to Paul," Interp 38 (1984) 254-67, esp.263-7. STAAB, K. Pauluskommentare aus der griechischen Kirche (Münster [2]1984) 1:1-6:4 Did. SANDERS, E. P. Paul, the Law, and the Jewish People (London 1985) 23, 48n.2, 53n.23, 60n.98, 71-81, 85f., 89n.28, 90n.33, 93, 98, 132nn.9.11, 138, 197-9. SEGAL, A. F. "Romans 7 and Jewish dietary law," StR/SciR 15 (1986) 361-74. DUNN, J. D. G. "Paul's Epistle to the Romans: An Analysis of Structure and Argument" in ANRW II.25.4 (1987) 2861-3. OSTEN-SACKEN, P. VON DER, Evangelium und Tora: Aufsätze zu Paulus (München 1987) 69, 89, 97, 100, 179, 220. THEISSEN, G. Psychological Aspects of Pauline Theology (Edinburgh 1987) 47f., 179-221, 230-3. CONZELMANN, H. and LINDEMANN, A. Interpreting the New Testament (Peabody MA 1988) 195f. MacDONALD, M. Y. The Pauline Churches (Cambridge 1988) 37, 78. ZIESLER, J. A. "The Role of the Tenth Commandment in Romans 7," JSNT 33 (1988) 41-56. LUCK, U. "Das Gute und das Böse in Römer 7" in H. Merklein, ed., Neues Testament und Ethik (FS R. Schnackenburg; Freiburg/ Basel/Wien 1989) 220-37. SCHNELLE, U. Wandlungen im paulinischen Denken (Stuttgart 1989) 68f. THIELMAN, F. From Plight to Solution (Leiden 1989) 11, 90f., 101-11. VOLLENWEIDER, S. Freiheit als neue Schöpfung (Göttingen 1989) 361, 402. SEGAL, A. F. Paul the Convert (New Haven/London 1990) 139, 224-53, 261. ZIESLER, J. Pauline Christianity (Oxford 1990) 24, 108, 112-4. LONGENECKER, B. W. Eschatology and the Covenant. A Comparison of 4 Ezra and Romans 1-11 (Sheffield 1991) 225-8, 241, 249. SCHWARZ, R. C. "Not Complaining of Obscurity. Romans 7 and the Identity of 'I'," Sewanee Theological Review 36 (1992) 123-35.

7:1ff   SCHRAGE, W. Die konkreten Einzelgebote in der paulinischen Paränese (1961) 94, 200. THYEN, H. Studien zur Sündenvergebung (1970) 203ff. THEISSEN, G. Psychologische Aspekte paulinischer Theologie (Göttingen 1983) 183-5, 247-50, 380. SCHULZ, S. "Neutestamentliche Ethik (Zürich 1987) 346.

7:1-25   CERFAUX, L. Christ in the Theology of St. Paul (1959) passim. STALDER, K. Das Werk des Geistes in der Heiligung bei Paulus (1962) 284-307.

7:1-24   OLLROG, W.-H. Paulus und seine Mitarbeiter (Neukirchen-Vluyn 1979) 211, 214f.

7:1-16   SCHMITHALS, W. Der Römerbrief als historisches Problem (Gütersloh 1975) 17f. SCHMITHALS, W. "Zur Herkunft der gnostischen Elemente in der Sprache des Paulus" in B. Aland et al., eds., Gnosis (FS H. Jonas; Göttingen 1978) 392f. SCHMITHALS, W. Die theologiche Anthropologie des Paulus (Stuttgart 1980) 20-34.

7:1-12   STEYN, J. "Enkele retoriese maneuvers in Romeine 7:1-12 [Some Rhetorical Maneuvers in Romans 7:1-12]," ThEv 9 (1976) 11-20.

7:1-9   BAUMERT, N. Täglich Sterben und Auferstehen. Der Literalsinn von 2 Kor 4, 12-5, 10 (München 1973) 272f.

7:1-6   ROBINSON, J.A.T. The Body (1952) 43f., 46f., 36f., DELLING, G. Die Taufe im Neuen Testament (1963) 130. THUESING, W. Per Christum in Deum (1965) 38f., 86f., 93-101. TANNEHILL, R.C. Dying and Rising with Christ (1966) 43-47. BATEY, R.A. New Testament Nuptial Imagery (1971) 17-19. BRANDENBURGER, E. Adam und Christus (Neukirchen-Vluyn 1962) 206, 252, 255, 260f. SCHNACKENBURG, R. "Römer 7 im Zusammenhang des Römerbriefes" in E. Ellis und E. Grässer, eds., Jesus und Paulus (FS W. G. Kümmel; Göttingen 1975) 285, 288ff. OSTEN-SACKEN, P. VON DER, Römer 8 als Beispiel paulinischer Soteriologie (Göttingen 1975) 188ff. SCHMITHALS,

W. Der Römerbrief als historisches Problem (Gütersloh 1975) 59, 87. STAGG, E. and F. Women in the World of Jesus (Philadelphia 1978) 180. BYRNE, B. "Sons of God"—"Seed of Abraham" (Rome 1979) 86, 97, 146f., 154, 155f., 165. ROBINSON, J. A. T. Wrestling with Romans (London 1979) 76-80. SCHMITHALS, W. Die theologische Anthropologie des Paulus (Stuttgart 1980) 23-5. BAMMEL, C. P. H. "Philocalia IX, Jerome, Epistle 121, and Origen's Exposition of Romans VII," JThS 32 (1981) 56. RÄISÄNEN, H. Paul and the Law (Tübingen 1983) 46f., 50, 58f., 61f., 66, 239, 245, 256. LITTLE, J. A. "Paul's Use of Analogy. A Structural Analysis of Romans 7:1-6," CBQ 46 (1984) 82-90. SANDERS, E. P. Paul, the Law, and the Jewish People (London 1985) 72f. MacCOBY, H. The Mythmaker: Paul and the Invention of Christianity (New York 1986) 68f. RÄISÄNEN, H. The Torah and Christ (Helsinki 1986) 10. THEISSEN, G. Psychological Aspects of Pauline Theology (Edinburgh 1987) 246-8. LINDARS, B. "Paul and the Law in Romans 5-8. An Actantial Analysis" in B. Lindars, ed., Law and Religion (Cambridge 1988) 133f. SNODGRASS, K. "Spheres of Influence. A Possible Solution to the Problem of Paul and the Law," JSNT 32 (1988) 93-113. VOLLENWEIDER, S. Freiheit als neue Schöpfung (Göttingen 1989) 335, 339ff. MEYER, P. W. "The Worm at the Core of the Apple. Exegetical Reflections on Romans 7" in R. T. Fortna and B. R. Gaventa, eds., The Conversation Continues. Studies in Paul and John (FS J. L. Martyn; Nashville 1990) 62-84, esp.71f. LONGENECKER, B. W. Eschatology and the Covenant. A Comparison of 4 Ezra and Romans 1-11 (Sheffield 1991) 229, 229n.2, 230-2, 234, 237, 241, 244n.1, 270, 274.

7:1-4   DELLING, G. Die Zueignung des Heils in der Taufe (1961) 79. DERRETT, J.D.M. Law in the New Testament (1970) xvi, 461-71. DERRETT, J. D. M. "Fresh Light on Rm 7:1-4," JJS 15 (3-4, 1964) 97-108. STAAB, K. Pauluskommentare aus der griechischen Kirche (Münster ²1984) 368:26-369:3 Genn.

7:1-3   BEST, E. One Body in Christ (1955) 52. STALDER, K. Das Werk des Geistes in der Heiligung bei Paulus (1962) 304, 388f., 391. STAAB, K. Pauluskommentare aus der griechischen Kirche (Münster ²1984) 86:20-28 Diod.

7:1-2   STAAB, K. Pauluskommentare aus der griechischen Kirche (Münster ²1984) 503:19-23 Phot.

7:1   DELLING, G. Die Taufe im Neuen Testament (1963) 126. DAVIES, W. D. Torah in the Messianic Age and/or the Age to come (Philadelphia 1952) 83. SCHMITHALS, W. Der Römerbrief als historisches Problem (Gütersloh 1975) 23. CLARK, K. W. "The Meaning of (KATA)KYRIEYEIN" in The Gentile Bias and other Essays [selected by J. L. Sharpe III] (Leiden 1980) 207-12. THEISSEN, G. Psychologische Aspekte paulinischer Theologie (Göttingen 1983) 183n5, 249, 364. SANDERS, E. P. Paul, the Law, and the Jewish People (London 1985) 59n75, 82, 161, 183f. JONES, F. S. "Freiheit" in den Briefen des Apostels Paulus (Göttingen 1987) 118f. WEDDERBURN, A. J. M. Baptism and Resurrection (Tübingen 1987) 40f. LAMPE, P. Die stadtrömischen Christen in den ersten beiden Jahrhunderten (Tübingen ²1989) 54.

7:2-4   MUSSNER, F. Christus das All und die Kirche (1968) 158, 385.

7:2-3   BROER, I. Freiheit vom Gesetz und Radikalisierung des Gesetzes (Stuttgart 1980) 73. HETH, W. A. and WENHAM, G. J. Jesus and Divorce (Nashville/Camden/Kansas City 1984) 14, 78, 83-5, 95, 97, 123, 139f., 142. JONES, F. S. "Freiheit" in den Briefen des Apostels Paulus (Göttingen 1987) 118-22, 129, 136, 217n.44, 218nn.46.53.

7:3-4   SCHELKLE, K. H. Die Passion Jesu in der Verkündigung des Neuen Testament (Heidelberg 1949) 256f.

7:3   BEST, E. One Body in Christ (1955) 53. BAUMERT, N. Täglich Sterben und
           Auferstehen. Der Literalsinn von 2 Kor 4, 12-5, 10 (München 1973) 159.
           HETH, W. A. and WENHAM, G. J. Jesus and Divorce (Nashville/Camden/
           Kansas City 1984) 34f., 43. JONES, F. S. "Freiheit" in den Briefen des
           Apostels Paulus (Göttingen 1987) 110, 118-124, 136, 139f., 147A3, 155A88,
           217A44.

7:4-14   PAGELS, E. H. The Gnostic Paul. Gnostic Exegesis of the Pauline Letters
           (Philadelphia 1975) 31f.

7:4-13   BANDSTRA, A.J. The Law and the Elements of the World (1964) 125ff.

7:4-7   McDONALD, P. M. "Romans 5.1-11 as a Rhetorical Bridge," JSNT 40 (1990)
           81-96. SEGAL, A. F. Paul the Convert (New Haven/London 1990) 226.

7:4-6   STANLEY, D.M. Christ's Resurrection in Pauline Soteriology (1961) 186-89.
           DUNN, J.D.G. Baptism in the Holy Spirit (1970) 146f. MARTIN, B. L. Christ
           and the Law in Paul (Leiden 1989) 2, 16, 17, 19, 38, 80, 91, 101, 109f., 114,
           120, 131f., 134, 143, 156. SIBER, P. Mit Christus leben (Zürich 1971) 227ff.,
           235. DEIDUN, T. J. New Covenant Morality in Paul (Rome 1981) 195f.
           THEISSEN, G. Psychologische Aspekte paulinischer Theologie (Göttingen
           1983) 200, 229, 250. MOHRLANG, R. Matthew and Paul (Cambridge 1984)
           33, 115, 117. LAMPE, P. Die stadtrömischen Christen in den ersten beiden
           Jahrhunderten (Tübingen ²1989) 55f.

7:4   KENNEDY, H.A.A. St. Paul and the Mystery-Religions (1913) 226, 243.
           BEST, E. One Body in Christ (1955) 44, 45, 52ff., 56, 88, 170. SCHOEPS,
           H.–J. Paulus (1959) 201f. MINEAR, P.S. Images of the Church in the New
           Testament (1960) 174f. BORNKAMM-BARTH-HELD, Ueberlieferung und
           Auslegung im Matthäus-Evangelium (1961) 65. DELLING, G. Die Zueignung
           de Heils in der Taufe (1961) 74. SCHRAGE, W. Die konkreten Einzelgebote
           in der paulinischen Paränese (1961) 93, 95. BRAUMANN, G. Vorpaulinische
           christliche Taufverkündigung bei Paulus (1962) 12, 39, 45f, 73f., 76. SCHWEI-
           ZER, E. Erniedrigung und Erhöhung bei Jesus und seinen Nachfolgern (1962)
           §9e. DELLING, G. Die Taufe im Neuen Testament (1963) 129. HAHN, F.
           Christologische Hoheitstitel (1963) 204, 210. KRAMER, W. Christos Kyrios
           Gottessohn (1963) §§ 3d, 31b. GÜTTGEMANNS, E. Der leidende Apostel und
           sein Herr (1966) 256f. MERK, O. Handeln aus Glauben (1968) 5, 10, 12, 21,
           24, 30, 39, 138. SIBER, P. Mit Christus leben (Zürich 1971) 192, 196, 218,
           222ff., 234. BAUMERT, N. Täglich Sterben und Auferstehen. Der Literalsinn
           von 2 Kor 4, 12-5, 10 (München 1973) 57. KÜMMEL, W. G. Einleitung in das
           Neue Testament (Heidelberg 1973) 270f. GUNDRY, R. H. Soma in Biblical
           Theology with Emphasis on Pauline Anthropology (Cambridge 1976) 239f.
           SCHMITHALS, W. "Zur Herkunft der gnostischen Elemente in der Sprache des
           Paulus" in B. Aland et al., eds., Gnosis (FS H. Jonas; Göttingen 1978) 401f.
           FROITZHEIM, F. Christologie und Eschatologie bei Paulus (Würzburg 1979)
           118f., 243f. TISSOT, Y. "Encratisme et Actes apocryphes" in F. Bovon et al.,
           eds., Les Actes Apocryphes des Apotres (Geneva 1981) 110. BLANK, J.
           Paulus. Von Jesus zum Christentum (München 1982) 102. THEISSEN, G.
           Psychologische Aspekte paulinischer Theologie (Göttingen 1983) 84n35, 229,
           249f. MOHRLANG, R. Matthew and Paul (Cambridge 1984) 32, 47, 61, 81, 88,
           102, 115, 186. STAAB, K. Pauluskommentare aus der griechischen Kirche
           (Münster ²1984) 124:1-19 ThM. DIETZFELBINGER, C. Die Berufung des
           Paulus als Ursprung seiner Theologie (Neukirchen 1985) 98f., 117. MERK-
           LEIN, H. Studien zu Jesus und Paulus (Tübingen 1987) 13, 48f., 53, 321, 323,
           424n61. WEDDERBURN, A. J. M. Baptism and Resurrection (Tübingen 1987)

49, 65. MARTIN, B. L. Christ and the Law in Paul (Leiden 1989) 16, 20, 60, 75, 80, 82, 109-11, 113f., 119, 133, 147. OLIVEIRA, A. DE, Die Diakonie der Gerechtigkeit und der Versöhnung in der Apologie des 2. Korintherbriefes. Analyse und Auslegung von 2 Kor 2, 14-4, 6; 5, 11-6, 10 (Münster 1990) 352.

7:5-23 CERFAUX, L. The Christian in the Theology of St Paul (1967) 435-39.

7:5-6 LUZ, U. Das Geschichtsverständnis des Paulus (1968) 125f. SCHLATTER, T. "Tod für die Sünde, lebendig für Gott. Das Urteil des Paulus über seine Gemeinden," Jahrbuch der Theologischen Schule Bethel 3 (Bethel 1932) 19-58. CONZELMANN, H. and LINDEMANN, A. Arbeitsbuch zum Neuen Testament (Tübingen 1975) 115. RIDDERBOS, H. Paul. An Outline of His Theology (Grand Rapids 1975) 143-7. WILLIAMS, J. A. A Conceptual History of Deuteronomism in the Old Testament, Judaism, and the New Testament (Ph.D. diss. Southern Baptist Theological Seminary; Louisville KY 1976) 281. BAMMEL, C. P. H. "Philocalia IX, Jerome, Epistle 121, and Origen's Exposition of Romans VII," JThS 32 (1981) 56, 58. CONZELMANN, H. and LINDEMANN, A. Interpreting the New Testament (Peabody MA 1988) 101.

7:5 DELLING, G. Die Taufe im Neuen Testament (1963) 148. SCHWEIZER, E. "Die Sünde in den Gliedern": Abraham unser Vater (1963). BANDSTRA, A.J. The Law and the Elements of the World (1964) 130ff. STROBEL, A. Erkenntnis und Bekenntnis der Sünde in neutestamentlicher Zeit (1968) 53. VAN DÜLMEN, A. Die Theologie des Gesetzes bei Paulus (1968) 42, 105, 106, 107, 157, 158, 181, 182. BAUMERT, N. Täglich Sterben und Auferstehen. Der Literalsinn von 2 Kor 4, 12-5, 10 (München 1973) 271-3, 283. LADD, G. E. A Theology of the New Testament (Grand Rapids 1974) 469, 471, 484, 568. RÄISÄNEN, H. Paul and the Law (Tübingen 1983) 25, 112, 141-3, 148. THEISSEN, G. Psychologische Aspekte paulinischer Theologie (Göttingen 1983) 184, 189, 203, 221, 226n72, 227, 258f., 265. STAAB, K. Pauluskommentare aus der griechischen Kirche (Münster ²1984) 86:29-87:4 Diod; 124:20-125:33 ThM; 219:8-16 Sev; 369:4-23 Genn; 657:20 Areth. MARTIN, B. L. Christ and the Law in Paul (Leiden 1989) 16, 32, 38, 40, 42, 69f., 72, 74, 77, 80-3, 92, 97, 101, 104-6, 110, 112, 133, 156. OLIVEIRA, A. DE, Die Diakonie der Gerechtigkeit und der Versöhnung in der Apologie des 2. Korintherbriefes. Analyse und Auslegung von 2 Kor 2, 14-4, 6; 5, 11-6, 10 (Münster 1990) 162. ZIESLER, J. Pauline Christianity (Oxford 1990) 80, 96, 112-4. LONGENECKER, B. W. Eschatology and the Covenant. A Comparison of 4 Ezra and Romans 1-11 (Sheffield 1991) 229-31, 241f., 243.

7:6ff. SCHLIER, H. "Über die christliche Freiheit," GuL 50 (1977) 178-93. VIELHAUER, P. "Gesetzesdienst und Stoicheiadienst im Galaterbrief" in Oikodome [G. Klein, ed.] (München 1979) 193f.

7:6-7 VIA, D. O. Kerygma and Comedy in the New Testament (Philadelphia 1975) 52, 54f.

7:6 FEINE, D. P. Das gesetzesfreie Evangelium des Paulus (1899) 158-61. ELLIS, E. E. Paul's Use of the Old Testament (1957) 26f. HARRISVILLE, R.A. The Concept of Newness in the New Testament (1960) 3, 68ff, 70, 71. SCHRAGE, W. Die konkreten Einzelgebote in der paulinischen Paränese (1961) 49, 72, 83. DELLING, G. Die Taufe im Neuen Testament (1963) 98. BANDSTRA, A.J. The Law and the Elements of the World (1964) 131ff. KÄSEMANN, E. Exegetische Versuche und Besinnungen II (1964) 277. KERTELGE, K. "Rechtfertigung" bei Paulus (1967) 202. METZGER, B.M. "Explicit references in the works of Origen to variant readings in New Testament manuscripts" Historical and Literary Studies (1968) 98. VAN DÜLMEN, A. Die Theologie des Gesetzes bei Paulus (1968) 33, 104, 105f., 113, 134, 145. KÄSEMANN, E. "Geist und Buchstabe" Paulinische Perspektiven (1969) 237-85. SIBER, P. Mit Christus leben (Zürich 1971) 192, 196, 218, 222ff. LADD, G. E. A Theology of the New Testament (Grand Rapids 1974) 503, 506, 517f. DUNN, J. D. G. Jesus and the Spirit. A Study of the Religious and Charismatic Experience of Jesus and the First Christians as Reflected in the New Testament (London 1975) 201, 223, 241, 260. RIDDERBOS, H. Paul. An Outline of His Theology (Grand Rapids 1975) 279. MIRANDA, J. P. Marx and the Bible. A Critique of the Philosophy of Oppression (London 1977) 189-91. HÜBNER, H. Das Gesetz bei Paulus. Ein Beitrag zum Werden der paulinischen Theologie (Göttingen 1978) 128f. SCHMITHALS, W. "Zur Herkunft der gnostischen Elemente in der Sprache des Paulus" in B. Aland et al., eds., Gnosis (FS H. Jonas; Göttingen 1978) 388-90. DEIDUN, T. J. New Covenant Morality in Paul (Rome 1981) 203-7. PROVENCE, T. E. "Who is Sufficient for These Things? An Exegesis of 2 Corinthians ii 15–iii 18," NovT 24 (1982) 64. RÄISÄNEN, H. Paul and the Law (Tübingen 1983) 44f., 141, 153, 178, 205, 233. THEISSEN, G. Psychologische Aspekte paulinischer Theologie (Göttingen 1983) 148, 151, 186f., 203, 212, 227, 258. MOHRLANG, R. Matthew and Paul (Cambridge 1984) 30, 32, 47, 116, 120. STAAB, K. Pauluskommentare aus der griechischen Kirche (Münster ²1984) 125:34-126:6 ThM; 369:24-31 Genn. THOMPSON, S. The Apocalypse and Semitic Syntax (Cambridge 1985) 100. EHLER, B. Die Herrschaft des Gekreuzigten (Berlin/New York 1986) 86-9. RÄISÄNEN, H. The Torah and Christ (Helsinki 1986) 33. MERKLEIN, H. Studien zu Jesus und Paulus (Tübingen 1987) 48, 85, 88f., 444n132. WEDDERBURN, A. J. M. Baptism and Resurrection (Tübingen 1987) 49, 69. MARTIN, B. L. Christ and the Law in Paul (Leiden 1989) 14, 16, 20, 32, 60, 65, 75, 80, 82f., 99, 105f., 109-11, 119, 133. VOLLENWEIDER, S. Freiheit als neue Schöpfung (Göttingen 1989) 335n., 401. OLIVEIRA, A. DE, Die Diakonie der Gerechtigkeit und der Versöhnung in der Apologie des 2. Korintherbriefes. Analyse und Auslegung von 2 Kor 2, 14-4, 6; 5, 11-6, 10 (Münster 1990) 162, 165-9. SEGAL, A. F. Paul the Convert (New Haven/London 1990) 139, 252, 334n.25.

7:7-8:17   OLIVEIRA, A. DE, Die Diakonie der Gerechtigkeit und der Versöhnung in der Apologie des 2. Korintherbriefes. Analyse und Auslegung von 2 Kor 2, 14-4, 6; 5, 11-6, 10 (Münster 1990) 162, 165-9.

7:7–8:4   CAMBLIER, J. "Péchè des Hommes et Péchè d 'Adam en Rom. V.12" NTS 11 (1964-65) 233f. BENOIT, P. "Gesetz und Kreuz nach Paulus (Röm. 7, 7-8, 4)" Exegese und Theologie (1965) 221-45. VOLKWEIN, B. "La Ley y la Cruz en San Pablo" RevBi 27 (4, '65) 213-20. BENOIT, P. Jesus and the Gospel, Vol 2 (London 1974) 11-39. ROBINSON, J. A. T. Wrestling with Romans (London 1979) 81-95. RÄISÄNEN, H. The Torah and Christ (Helsinki 1986) 39, 117. WEBER, R. "Die Geschichte des Gesetzes und des Ich in Römer 7, 7-8, 4. Einige Überlegungen zum Zusammenhang von Heilsgeschichte und Anthropologie im Blick auf die theologische Grundstellung des paulinischen Denkens," NZSTh [Berlin] 29 (1987) 147-79. LONGENECKER, B. W. Eschatology and the Covenant. A Comparison of 4 Ezra and Romans 1-11 (Sheffield 1991) 170, 203, 224f., 230, 235-7, 246, 249f.

7:7–8:3   CAMBIER, J. "Péchè des Hommes et Péchè d'Adam en Rom, V.12" NTS 11 (1964-65) 222f.

7:7ff.   WINDISCH, H. Paulus und das Judentum (1935) 47f. BULTMANN, R. Theologie des Neuen Testaments (1965) 248ff., 265f. HAHN, F. Das Verständnis der Mission im Neuen Testament (1965) 86. STROBEL, A. Erkenntnis und

Bekenntnis der Sünde in neutestamentlicher Zeit (1968) 50. LUZ, U. Das Geschichtsverständnis des Paulus (1968) 158-68. WEDDERBURN, A. J. M. "Adam in Paul's Letter to the Romans" in E. A. Livingstone, ed., Studia Biblica 1978 III (Sheffield 1980) 413-30. KLEIN, G. "Gesetz III" in TRE 13 (1984) 67, 70. OSTEN-SACKEN, P. VON DER, Evangelium und Tora: Aufsätze zu Paulus (München 1987) 177f. THEISSEN, G. Psychological Aspects of Pauline Theology (Edinburgh 1987) 148f., 183f., 190f., 194-7, 201-4, 206, 226, 253, 255, 261, 318. BECKER, J. Paulus. Der Apostel der Völker (Tübingen 1989) 410, 413, 420ff. HOFIUS, O. Paulusstudien (Tübingen 1989) 57-60, 68, 85, 126, 163, 171.

7:7-25 FEINE, D.P. Das gesetzesfreie Evangelium des Paulus (1899) 132-68. SCHWEITZER, A. Die Mystik des Apostels Paulus (1954) 125, 189, 208, 288, 295. DAVIES, W.D. Paul and Rabbinic Judaism (1955) 19, 24f., 32, 34, 256. BRAUN, H. "Römer 7, 2-25 und das Selbstverständnis des Qumranfrommen" ZThK 56 (1, '59) 1-18. STANLEY, D.M. "Paul's Interest in the Early Chapters of Genesis" Studiorum Paulinorum Congressus Internationalis Catholicus 1961 (1963) I 248-49. BRAUN, H. "Römer 7, 2-25 und das Selbstverständnis des Qumran-Frommen" Gesammelte Studien Zum Neuen Testament und Seiner Umwelt (1962) 100-20. BANDSTRA, A.J. The Law and the Elements of the World (1964) 134ff. LONGENECKER, R.N. Paul Apostle of Liberty (1964) 87, 90, 91, 92, 110, 123. MODALSLI, ThZ 21 (1, '65) 22-37. BRAUN, H. Qumran und NT II (1966) 108, 127-29, 146, 167-69, 171, 254, 256. BLANK, J. "Der gespaltene Mensch. Zur Exegese von Röm 7, 7-25" BuL 9 (1, '68) 10-20. STROBEL, A. Erkenntnis und Bekenntnis der Sünde in neutestamentlicher Zeit (1968) 50, 28. BLANK, J. Schriftauslegung in Theorie und Praxis (1969) 158-73. KERTELGE, K. "Exegetische Ueberlegungen zum Verständnis der paulinischen Anthropologie Ueberlegungen zum Verständnis der paulinischen Anthropologie nach Römer 7" ZNW 62 (1-2, '71) 105-14. BRANDENBURGER, E. Adam und Christus (Neukirchen-Vluyn 1962) 166, 206, 248, 262f., 266. FEUILLET, A. "Les attaches bibliques des antithèses pauliniennes dans la première partie de l'Epitre aux Romains (1-8)" in A. Descamps and A. de Halleux, eds., Mélanges Bibliques en hommage au R. P. Béda Rigaux (Gembloux 1970) 340f., 342f. WATSON, N. M. "The Interpretation of Romans VII," AusBR 21 (1973) 27-39. LAMBRECHT, J. "Man Before and Without Christ. Rom 7 and Pauline Anthropology," LSt 5 (1974) 18-33. CONZELMANN, H. and LINDEMANN, A. Arbeitsbuch zum Neuen Testament (Tübingen 1975) 115, 214. DUNN, J. D. G. Jesus and the Spirit. A Study of the Religious and Charismatic Experience of Jesus and the First Christians as Reflected in the New Testament (London 1975) 313-6. ROMANIUK, K. "Zagadnienie podmiotu w Rz 7:7-25 [Le sujet dans Rom 7:7-25]," RBL 30 (1977) 189-94. FRIEDRICH, G. "Das Gesetz Glaubens Römer 3, 27" in Auf das Wort kommt es an. Gesammelte Aufsätze (Göttingen 1978) 116. BYRNE, B. "Sons of God"—"Seed of Abraham" (Rome 1979) 86f., 92. NICKLE, K. F. "Romans 7:7-25," Interp 33 (1979) 181-7. CAMPBELL, D. H. "The Identity of ἐγώ in Romans 7:7-25" in E. A. Livingstone, ed., Studia Biblica 1978 III (Sheffield 1980) 57-64. GUNDRY, R. H. "The Moral Frustration of Paul before his Conversion. Sexual Lust in Romans 7:7-25" in D. A. Hagner and M. J. Harris, eds., Pauline Studies (FS F. F. Bruce; Exeter 1980) 228-45. THISELTON, A. C. The Two Horizons (Grand Rapids 1980) 265. BAMMEL, C. P. H. "Philocalia IX, Jerome, Epistle 121, and Origen's Exposition of Romans VII," JThS 32 (1981) 51, 53, 56, 60, 63, 76f., 79. BYRNE, B. "Living out the

Righteousness of God. The Contribution of Rom 6:1-8:13 to an Understanding of Paul's Ethical Presuppositions," CBQ 43 (1981) 565-7. KIM, S. The Origin of Paul's Gospel (Tübingen 1981) 52-5. NEWMAN, B. M. "Once Again—The Question of 'I' in Romans 7, 7-25," BTr 34 (1983) 124-35. PATTE, D. Paul's Faith and the Power of the Gospel (Philadelphia 1983) 263-77. MERKEL, H. "Gesetz IV" in TRE 13 (1984) 80. BERGMEIER, R. "Röm 7, 7-25a (8, 2). Der Mensch-das Gesetz-Gott-Paulus-die Exegese im Widerspruch?" KuD 31 (1985) 162-72. DIETZFELBINGER, C. Die Berufung des Paulus als Ursprung seiner Theologie (Neukirchen 1985) 83ff. HEYMEL, M. "Lehre als Erfahrung—Was der Jude Paulus uns Heiden über das Gesetz zu lernen aufgibt" in G. Freund und E. Stegemann, eds., Theologische Brosamen für Lothar Steiger (DBAT 5; Heidelberg 1985) 183-201. SANDERS, E. P. Paul, the Law, and the Jewish People (London 1985) 73-81. LÜBKING, H.-M. Paulus und Israel im Römerbrief (Frankfurt/Bern/New York 1986) 44-8. PERKINS, P. "Pauline Anthropology in Light of Nag Hammadi," CBQ 48 (1986) 512-22. RÄISÄNEN, H. The Torah and Christ (Helsinki 1986) 34. HÜBNER, H. "Paulusforschung seit 1945. Ein kritischer Literaturbericht" in ANRW II.25.4 (1987) 2668-76. WEDDERBURN, A. J. M. The Reasons for Romans (Edinburgh 1988) 133-5, 138. HOFIUS, O. Paulusstudien (Tübingen 1989) 57-60, 84. LIMBECK, M. Mit Paulus Christ sein. Sachbuch zur Person und Theologie des Apostels Paulus (Stuttgart 1989) 76-8. MARTIN, B. L. Christ and the Law in Paul (Leiden 1989) 2, 16, 31, 38f., 75, 79f., 84, 93, 156. MEYER, P. W. "The Worm at the Core of the Apple. Exegetical Reflections on Romans 7" in R. T. Fortna and B. R. Gaventa, eds., The Conversation Continues. Studies in Paul and John (FS J. L. Martyn; Nashville 1990) 62-84. LONGENECKER, B. W. Eschatology and the Covenant. A Comparison of 4 Ezra and Romans 1-11 (Sheffield 1991) 180, 225-7, 229-34, 234n.2, 235-7, 240, 248.

7:7-25a   LUCK, U. "Das Gute und das Böse in Römer 7" in H. Merklein, ed., Neues Testament und Ethik (FS R. Schnackenburg; Freiburg/Basel/ Wien 1989) 220-37.

7:7-24   OSTEN-SACKEN, P. VON DER, Römer 8 als Beispiel paulinischer Soteriologie (Göttingen 1975) 194ff. BRANDENBURGER, E. Das Böse (Zürich 1986) 33, 94f., 96, 98f.n.239. OSTEN-SACKEN, P. VON DER, Evangelium und Tora: Aufsätze zu Paulus (München 1987) 13, 26, 69, 93. THEOBALD, M. "Glaube und Vernunft. Zur Argumentation des Paulus im Römerbrief," ThQ 169 (1989) 287-301. VOLLENWEIDER, S. Freiheit als neue Schöpfung (Göttingen 1989) 345. GEORGI, D. Theocracy in Paul's Praxis and Theology (Minneapolis 1991) 89n.19, 90-3, 100n.46.

7:7-23   THEISSEN, G. Psychologische Aspekte paulinischer Theologie (Göttingen 1983) 151f., 181-268, 318. BERGER, K. und COLPE, C., eds., Religionsgeschichtliches Textbuch zum Neuen Testament (Göttingen/Zürich 1987) 213f. THEISSEN, G. Psychological Aspects of Pauline Theology (Edinburgh 1987) 177-9, 184-9, 234-42, 260f.

7:7-22   EICHHOLZ, G. Die Theologie des Paulus im Umriss (1972) 251ff., 261.

7:7-16   KLAAS, W. in:G. Eichholz, ed. Herr, tue meine Lippen auf, Bd. 4 (1965) 122ff. SCHMITHALS, W. "Zur Herkunft der gnostischen Elemente in der Sprache des Paulus" in B. Aland et al., eds., Gnosis (FS H. Jonas; Göttingen 1978) 393.

7:7-13   FEINE, D.P. Das gesetzesfreie Evangelium des Paulus (1899) 132f, 140-50, 156f., 158f., 162f. LYONNET, S. "Quaestiones ad Rom 7, 7-13" VerbDom 40 (4, '62) 163-83. BANDSTRA, A.J. The Law and the Elements of the World

(1964) 136ff. BRANDENBURGER, E. Adam und Christus (Neukirchen 1962) 165f., 205-219, 248ff. RIDDERBOS, H. Paul. An Outline of His Theology (Grand Rapids 1975) 143-7. SCHNACKENBURG, R. "Römer 7 im Zusammenhang des Römerbriefes" in E. Ellis und E. Grässer, eds., Jesus und Paulus (FS W. G. Kümmel; Göttingen 1975) 285, 291ff. HÜBNER, H. Das Gesetz bei Paulus. Ein Beitrag zum Werden der paulinischen Theologie (Göttingen 1978) 63-71. BAMMEL, C. P. H. "Philocalia IX, Jerome, Epistle 121, and Origen's Exposition of Romans VII," JThS 32 (1981) 55, 58, 63, 66. DEIDUN, T. J. New Covenant Morality in Paul (Rome 1981) 196-8. RÄISÄNEN, H. Paul and the Law (Tübingen 1983) 68, 141f., 230. THEISSEN, G. Psychologische Aspekte paulinischer Theologie (Göttingen 1983) 187, 188n.12, 204-13, 223n.68, 233, 266. HEILIGENTHAL, R. "Gebot" in TRE 12 (1984) 125. DIETZFELBINGER, C. Die Berufung des Paulus als Ursprung seiner Theologie (Neukirchen 1985) 109ff. MAILLOT, A. "Notule sur Romains 7/7-8 ss," FV 84 (6, 1985) 17-23. SANDERS, E. P. Paul, the Law, and the Jewish People (London 1985) 71, 73-5, 93, 137, 144. KARLBERG, M. W. "Israel's History Personified. Romans 7:7-13 in Relation to Paul's Teaching on the 'Old Man'," Trinity Journal 7 (1986) 65-74. RÄISÄNEN, H. The Torah and Christ (Helsinki 1986) 19. SNYMAN, A. H. "Stilistiese tegnieke in Romeine 7:7-13 [Stylistic techniques in Romans 7:7-13]," NGTT 27 (1986) 23-8. RÖHSER, G. Metaphorik und Personifikation der Sünde (Tübingen 1987) 4, 8f., 14, 100, 116ff., 124, 126f., 137, 141f., 148, 150, 158, 160f., 165ff., 180f. THEISSEN, G. Psychological Aspects of Pauline Theology (Edinburgh 1987) 185f., 202-10, 264. MARTIN, B. L. Christ and the Law in Paul (Leiden 1989) 28, 44, 75-77, 81, 84. VOLLENWEIDER, S. Freiheit als neue Schöpfung (Göttingen 1989) 349. HAMERTON-KELLY, R. "Sacred Violence and Sinful Desire. Paul's Interpretation of Adam's Sin in the Letter to the Romans" in R. T. Fortna and B. R. Gaventa, eds., The Conversation Continues. Studies in Paul and John (FS J. L. Martyn; Nashville 1990) 35-54, esp.47-50. LONGENECKER, B. W. Eschatology and the Covenant. A Comparison of 4 Ezra and Romans 1-11 (Sheffield 1991) 237, 239, 239nn.2.3. SEIFRID, M. A. Justification by Faith (Leiden/New York/Köln 1992) 146-52.

7:7-12,21-23 FUCHS, D.E. "Existentiale Interpretation von Röm 7, 2-12 und 21-23" Glaube und Erfahrung (1965) 364-401.

7:7-12 FUCHS, E. "Existentiale Interpretation von Römer 7, 7-12 und 21-23" ZThK 59 (3, '62) 285-314. LUZ, U. Das Geschichtsverständnis des Paulus (1968) 158ff., 188, 206. MAUSER, U. Gottesbild und Menschwerdung (1971) 154-62, 164-66, 182. SCROGGS, R. Paul for a New Day (Philadelphia 1977) 9-12. SANDERS, E. P. "On the Question of Fulfilling the Law in Paul and Rabbinic Judaism" in E. Bammel et al., eds., Donum Gentilicium (FS D. Daube; Oxford 1978) 107. SCHMITHALS, W. Die theologische Anthropologie des Paulus (Stuttgart 1980) 25-30. MILNE, D. J. W. "Romans 7:7-12, Paul's Pre-conversion Experience," RThR 43 (1984) 9-17. MOO, D. J. "Israel and Paul in Romans 7.7-12," NTS 32 (1986) 122-35. SCHNACKENBURG, R. Die sittliche Botschaft des Neuen Testaments, Band 1 (Freiburg/Basel/Wien 1986) 194. LINDARS, B. "Paul and the Law in Romans 5-8. An Actantial Analysis" in B. Lindars, ed., Law and Religion (Cambridge 1988) 134f. MEYER, P. W. "The Worm at the Core of the Apple. Exegetical Reflections on Romans 7" in R. T. Fortna and B. R. Gaventa, eds., The Conversation Continues. Studies in Paul and John (FS J. L. Martyn; Nashville 1990) 62-84, esp.73f.

7:7-11   DUNN, J. D. G. Christology in the Making (London 1980) 103f., 116, 120.
                RÄISÄNEN, H. Paul and the Law (Tübingen 1983) 25, 141-3, 147-9.
                RÄISÄNEN, H. The Torah and Christ (Helsinki 1986) 149ff. DOWNING, F.
                G. Christ and the Cynics (Sheffield 1988) 154. ZIESLER, J. Pauline Christiani-
                ty (Oxford 1990) 57, 112f.
7:7b-10   LAYTON, B. The Gnostic Scriptures (Garden City NY 1987) 441n101Ab.
7:7-9   DELLING, G. Die Taufe im Neuen Testament (1963) 142. DIETZFELBIN-
                GER, C. Die Berufung des Paulus als Ursprung seiner Theologie (Neukirchen
                1985) 85f.
7:7-8   SCHRAGE, W. Die konkreten Einzelgebote in der paulinischen Paränese (1961)
                65f., 231, 270. STROBEL, A. Erkenntnis und Bekenntnis der Sünde in neutesta-
                mentlicher Zeit (1968) 53. RÄISÄNEN, H. "Zum Gebrauch von EPITHYMIA
                und EPITHYMEIN bei Paulus," StTh 33 (1989) 85-99. BAMMEL, C. P. H.
                "Philocalia IX, Jerome, Epistle 121, and Origen's Exposition of Romans VII,"
                JThS 32 (1981) 59f. RÄISÄNEN, H. Paul and the Law (Tübingen 1983) 111f.,
                148, 157, 230. STAAB, K. Pauluskommentare aus der griechischen Kirche
                (Münster ²1984) 219:17-30 Sev. RÄISÄNEN, H. The Torah and Christ (Hel-
                sinki 1986) 149, 154ff., 167. BERGER, K. und COLPE, C., eds., Religionsge-
                schichtliches Textbuch zum Neuen Testament (Göttingen/Zürich 1987) 214.
                MORRIS, T. F. "Law and the Cause of Sin in the Epistle to the Romans," HeyJ
                28 (3, 1987) 285-91.
7:7   FEINE, D.P. Das gesetzesfreie Evangelium des Paulus (1899) 134f., 149f., 225f.
                BRUNNER, E. Dogmatik II (1950) 139. ELLIS, E.E. Paul's Use of the Old
                Testament (1957) 21ff., 158. LYONNET, S. "'Tu ne convoiteras pas' (Rom. vii
                7)" in Neotestamentica et Patristica, Festschrift f. O. Cullmann (1962) 157-65.
                JÜNGEL, E. Paulus und Jesus (1966) 52. MCNAMARA, M. The New Testa-
                ment and the Palestinian Targum to the Pentateuch (1966) 32 fn.157. VAN
                DÜLMEN, A. Die Theologie des Gesetzes bei Paulus (1968) 20, 42, 62, 83,
                106ff., 169. BLANK, J. Schriftauslegung in Theorie und Praxis (1969) 161.
                LADD, G. E. A Theology of the New Testament (Grand Rapids 1974) 503,
                507f. SCHMITHALS, W. Der Römerbrief als historisches Problem (Gütersloh
                1975) 89. SCHNACKENBURG, R. "Römer 7 im Zusammenhang des Römer-
                briefes" in E. Ellis und E. Grässer, eds., Jesus und Paulus (FS W. G. Kümmel;
                Göttingen 1975) 291-3. HÜBNER, H. Das Gesetz bei Paulus. Ein Beitrag zum
                Werden der paulinischen Theologie (Göttingen 1978) 115. BAMMEL, C. P. H.
                "Philocalia IX, Jerome, Epistle 121, and Origen's Exposition of Romans VII,"
                JThS 32 (1981) 50, 52-61, 65. RHYNE, C. T. Faith establishes the Law (Chico
                CA 1981) 4b. STRELAN, J. G. "A Note on the Old Testament Background of
                Romans 7:7," LThJ 15 (1981) 23-5. PATTE, D. Paul's Faith and the Power of
                the Gospel (Philadelphia 1983) 46, 54, 75, 263, 272, 286. THEISSEN, G.
                Psychologische Aspekte paulinischer Theologie (Göttingen 1983) 183, 183n.5,
                187, 188f., 195-8, 200, 213, 225, 232. MOHRLANG, R. Matthew and Paul
                (Cambridge 1984) 28, 34, 38. STAAB, K. Pauluskommentare aus der griech-
                ischen Kirche (Münster ²1984) 63:20-65:12 Apoll; 87:5-20 Diod; 126:7-32
                ThM; 369:32-370:3 Genn; 503:24-8 Phot. CHARLESWORTH, J. H. The Old
                Testament Pseudepigrapha and the New Testament (Cambridge 1985) 78. LAY-
                TON, B. The Gnostic Scriptures (Garden City NY 1987) 440. NIEBUHR, K.-
                W. Gesetz und Paränese (Tübingen 1987) 63. SCHMELLER, TH. Paulus und
                die "Diatribe" (Münster 1987) 327. LAMPE, P. Die stadtrömischen Christen in
                den ersten beiden Jahrhunderten (Tübingen ²1989) 55. MARTIN, B. L. Christ
                and the Law in Paul (Leiden 1989) 13, 16, 19, 22, 28, 47, 75-80, 82, 143.

OLIVEIRA, A. DE, Die Diakonie der Gerechtigkeit und der Versöhnung in der Apologie des 2. Korintherbriefes. Analyse und Auslegung von 2 Kor 2, 14-4, 6; 5, 11-6, 10 (Münster 1990) 387.

7:8-24   MALINA B. J. Christian Origins and Cultural Anthropology (Atlanta 1986) 137.

7:8-11   THEISSEN, G. Psychologische Aspekte paulinischer Theologie (Göttingen 1983) 198, 232. STAAB, K. Pauluskommentare aus der griechischen Kirche (Münster ²1984) 370:13-371:4 Genn; 504:1-34 Phot. BRANDENBURGER, E. Das Böse (Zürich 1986) 79f.n.175, 254.

7:8-10   BAMMEL, C. P. H. "Philocalia IX, Jerome, Epistle 121, and Origen's Exposition of Romans VII," JThS 32 (1981) 61.

7:8-9   THEISSEN, G. Psychologische Aspekte paulinischer Theologie (Göttingen 1983) 189, 209, 230.

7:8   FEINE, D.P. Das gesetzesfreie Evangelium des Paulus (1899) 142-44, 145f. JEUNGEL, E. Paulus und Jesus (1966) 51, 58. STROBEL, A. Erkenntnis und Bekenntnis der Sünde in neutestamentlicher Zeit (1968) 50. VAN DÜLMEN, A. Die Theologie des Gesetzes bei Paulus (1968) 85, 99, 105, 108f, 158, 162, 224, 169. RÄISÄNEN, H. Paul and the Law (Tübingen 1983) 142, 147, 150. THEISSEN, G. Psychologische Aspekte paulinischer Theologie (Göttingen 1983) 143n.38, 188, 188n.12, 189f., 203, 207, 207n.47, 210, 213, 224, 226, 257. STAAB, K. Pauluskommentare aus der griechischen Kirche (Münster ²1984) 65:13-19 Apoll; 87:21-88:4 Diod; 126:33-127:37 ThM; 370:4-12 Genn.

7:8b-10   HOFIUS, O. Paulusstudien (Tübingen 1989) 58f.

7:9-15   ROBINSON, J. A. Pelagius's Exposition of Thirteen Epistles of St. Paul (Cambridge 1922) 48ff., 134, 228.

7:9-11   BERGER, K. Exegese des Neuen Testaments (Heidelberg 1977) 182. MILNE, D. J. W. "Genesis 3 in the Letter to Romans," RThR 39 (1980) 10-8. STAAB, K. Pauluskommentare aus der griechischen Kirche (Münster ²1984) 88:5-16 Diod; 128:1-18 ThM.

7:9-10   FEINE, D.P. Das gesetzesfreie Evangelium des Paulus (1899) 135-39. MAGNUSSON, M. Der Begriff "Verstehen" in Exegetischem Zusammenhang (1960) 170f., 175-81. LUZ, U. Das Geschichtsverständnis des Paulus (1968) 163ff. THEISSEN, G. Psychologische Aspekte paulinischer Theologie (Göttingen 1983) 29, 209, 212.

7:9   JÜNGEL, Paulus und Jesus (1966) 56, 58. ORBE, A. "S. Metodio y la exégese de Rom. 7:92: Ego autem vivebam sine lege aliquando" Gregorianum 50 (1, '69) 93-139. BURCHARD, C. Untersuchungen zu Joseph and Aseneth (Tübingen 1965) 149. FRIEDRICH, G. "'Αμαρτία οὐκ ἐλλογεῖται Rom 5, 13" in Auf das Wort kommt es an. Gesammelte Aufsätze (Göttingen 1978) 130. DAVIES, S. L. The Gospel of Thomas and Christian Wisdom (New York 1983) 119. THEISSEN, G. Psychologische Aspekte paulinischer Theologie (Göttingen 1983) 181, 188, 195f., 200, 202, 204, 209, 212, 226, 253, 256, 256n.110. STAAB, K. Pauluskommentare aus der griechischen Kirche (Münster ²1984) 54:1-10 AkazC. LAYTON, B. The Gnostic Scriptures (Garden City NY 1987) 432, 441. NIEBUHR, K.-W. Gesetz und Paränese (Tübingen 1987) 219. MARTIN, B. L. Christ and the Law in Paul (Leiden 1989) 16, 61, 70, 75f., 78, 97f.

7:10   FEINE, D. P. Das gesetzesfreie Evangelium des Paulus (1899) 146f, 210f. JÜNGEL, Paulus und Jesus (1966) 56, 59, 61, 172, 207. VAN DÜLMEN, A. Die Theologie des Gesetzes bei Paulus (1968) 83, 110, 116, 119, 122, 133, 139, 140, 181, 183, 195. PALLIS, A. Notes on St.John and the Apocalypse (London 1928) 53. RÄISÄNEN, H. Paul and the Law (Tübingen 1983) 152f., 154.

THEISSEN, G. Psychologische Aspekte paulinischer Theologie (Göttingen 1983) 18, 189n.14, 211, 233n.81, 235. KLEIN, G. "Gesetz III" in TRE XIII (1984) 71. STAAB, K. Pauluskommentare aus der griechischen Kirche (Münster ²1984) 65:20-31 Apoll. RÄISÄNEN, H. The Torah and Christ (Helsinki 1986) 8. SNODGRASS, K. "Spheres of Influence. A Possible Solution to the Problem of Paul and the Law," JSNT 32 (1988) 93-113. HOFIUS, O. Paulusstudien (Tübingen 1989) 58f. MARTIN, B. L. Christ and the Law in Paul (Leiden 1989) 16, 31, 37, 40, 44, 52, 72, 74-6, 78, 81f., 85, 97.

7:11-12   BAMMEL, C. P. H. "Philocalia IX, Jerome, Epistle 121, and Origen's Exposition of Romans VII," JThS 32 (1981) 63, 65.

7:11   ROBINSON, J.A.T. The Body (1952) 36f. JÜNGEL, E. Paulus und Jesus (1966) 58. VAN DÜLMEN, A. Die Theologie des Gesetzes bei Paulus (1968) 42, 99, 108, 110, 114, 163, 180, 183. THEISSEN, G. Psychologische Aspekte paulinischer Theologie (Göttingen 1983) 143n.38, 189, 189n.14, 190, 192, 208n.51, 210-3, 221, 226, 227n.72, 232n.80, 233n.81, 234, 247, 257. BERGER, K. und COLPE, C., eds., Religionsgeschichtliches Textbuch zum Neuen Testament (Göttingen/Zürich 1987) 214. SEGAL, A. F. Paul the Convert (New Haven/London 1990) 242.

7:12-13   FEINE, D. P. Das gesetzesfreie Evangelium des Paulus (1899) 147, 189f.

7:12,14   VOLLENWEIDER, S. Freiheit als neue Schöpfung (Göttingen 1989) 274.

7:12   BRUNNER, E. Dogmatik II (1950) 263. SCHRAGE, W. Die konkreten Einzelgebote in der paulinischen Paränese (1961) 94f., 229, 232. HAHN, F. Das Verständnis der Mission im Neuen Testament (1965) 87. JÜNGEL, E. Paulus und Jesus (1966) 56, 59. NICKELS, P. Targum and New Testament (1967) 69. VAN DÜLMEN, A. Die Theologie des Gesetzes bei Paulus (1968) 44, 102, 110, 111, 113, 116, 122, 130, 131, 212. LADD, G. E. A Theology of the New Testament (Grand Rapids 1974) 363, 405, 544. LOHSE, E. Grundriss der neutestamentlichen Theologie (Stuttgart 1974) 93f. KÖBERLE, A. "Christentum" in TRE 8 (1981) 15. PROVENCE, T. E. "'Who is Sufficient for These Things?' An Exegesis of 2 Corinthians ii 15–iii 18," NovT 24 (1982) 64f. RÄISÄNEN, H. Paul and the Law (Tübingen 1983) 7, 128, 139, 152, 206, 222, 225. THEISSEN, G. Psychologische Aspekte paulinischer Theologie (Göttingen 1983) 84n35, 189, 221. MOHRLANG, R. Matthew and Paul (Cambridge 1984) 26, 28, 34, 38, 152. STAAB, K. Pauluskommentare aus der griechischen Kirche (Münster ²1984) 129:19-30 ThM; 219:31-220:2 Sev; 371:5-14 Genn; 504:35-505:11 Phot. LAYTON, B. The Gnostic Scriptures (Garden City NY 1987) 313. OSTEN-SACKEN, P. VON DER, Evangelium und Tora: Aufsätze zu Paulus (München 1987) 20, 181, 202, 243. OLIVEIRA, A. DE, Die Diakonie der Gerechtigkeit und der Versöhnung in der Apologie des 2. Korintherbriefes. Analyse und Auslegung von 2 Kor 2, 14-4, 6; 5, 11-6, 10 (Münster 1990) 169n.442.

7:13ff.   THEISSEN, G. Psychologische Aspekte paulinischer Theologie (Göttingen 1983) 187n.10, 189n.14, 233n.81, 236. BETZ, H. D. "Hellenismus III" in TRE 15 (1986) 29.

7:13-25   GAVENTA, B. R. From Darkness to Light. Aspects of Conversion in the New Testament (Philadelphia 1986) 33-6.

7:13-24   MEYER, P. W. "The Worm at the Core of the Apple. Exegetical Reflections on Romans 7" in R. T. Fortna and B. R. Gaventa, eds., The Conversation Continues. Studies in Paul and John (FS J. L. Martyn; Nashville 1990) 62-84, esp. 74-79.

7:13-16   SCHMITHALS, W. "Zur Herkunft der gnostischen Elemente in der Sprache des Paulus" in B. Aland et al., eds., Gnosis (FS H. Jonas; Göttingen 1978) 393. SCHMITHALS, W. Die theologische Anthropologie des Paulus (Stuttgart 1980) 30-4.

7:13   JÜNGEL, E. Paulus und Jesus (1966) 58, 60. STROBEL, A. Erkenntnis und Bekenntnis der Sünde in neutestamentlicher Zeit (1968) 50. VAN DÜLMEN, A. Die Theologie des Gesetzes bei Paulus (1968) 20, 42, 84, 103, 119, 162, 163, 169, 180, 184, 212. EICHHOLZ, G. Die Theologie des Paulus im Umriss (1972) 257f. ROBINSON, J. A. Pelagius's Exposition of Thirteen Epistles of St. Paul (Cambridge 1922) 260, 309-15. BAUMERT, N. Täglich Sterben und Auferstehen. Der Literalsinn von 2 Kor 4, 12-5, 10 (München 1973) 346. PAGELS, E. H. The Johannine Gospel in Gnostic Exegesis (Nashville/New York 1973) 84f. MIRANDA, J. P. Marx and the Bible. A Critique of the Philosophy of Oppression (London 1977) 187-90. BAMMEL, C. P. H. "Philocalia IX, Jerome, Epistle 121, and Origen's Exposition of Romans VII," JThS 32 (1981) 63. RHYNE, C. T. Faith establishes the Law (Chico CA 1981) 47. THEISSEN, G. Psychologische Aspekte paulinischer Theologie (Göttingen 1983) 186, 189, 196-8, 200, 204n.39, 213, 221, 226n.72, 227n.72, 233, 233n.81. STAAB, K. Pauluskommentare aus der griechischen Kirche (Münster ²1984) 88:17-22 Diod; 129:1-130:33 ThM; 371:15-28 Genn; 505:12-34 Phot. SCHMELLER, TH. Paulus und die "Diatribe" (Münster 1987) 327. LINDARS, B. "Paul and the Law in Romans 5-8. An Actantial Analysis" in B. Lindars, ed., Law and Religion (Cambridge 1988) 135.

7:14-8:8   SANDERS, E. P. Paul, the Law, and the Jewish People (London 1985) 74f., 146f.

7:14ff.   BONHOEFFER, A. Epiktet und das Neue Testament (1911) 17, 60, 316. BRUNNER, E. Dogmatik I (1946) 206. ALTHAUS, P. "Zur Auslegung von Röm. 7, 14ff. Antwork an Anders Nygren" ThLZ 77 (1952) 475-80. SCHRAGE, W. Die konkreten Einzelgebote in der paulinischen Paränese (1961) 194-96. BULTMANN, R. Theologie des Neuen Testaments (1965) 201f., 248f. KÜMMEL, W. G. Römer 7 und das Bild des Menschen im Neuen Testament (München 1974) 184-92. RIDDERBOS, H. Paul. An Outline of His Theology (Grand Rapids 1975) 114-8, 126-30. GERSTENBERGER, G. und SCHRAGE, W. Leiden (Stuttgart 1977) 132f. [ET: J. E. Steely (trans.) Suffering (Nashville 1980) 154f.]. THEISSEN, G. Psychologische Aspekte paulinischer Theologie (Göttingen 1983) 186-190n.15, 195, 202, 213, 221, 223, 225, 232n.80, 233n.81, 236n.85, 265. SCHULZ, S. Neutestamentliche Ethik (Zürich 1987) 388. VOLLENWEIDER, S. Freiheit als neue Schöpfung (Göttingen 1989) 350, 352.

7:14-25   FEINE, D.P. Das gesetzesfreie Evangelium des Paulus (1899) 150-66, 215f. KUSS, O. Der Brief an die Römer (1940) 67f. BORNKAMM, G. GPM 8 (1954) 265-69. MAGNUSSON, M. Der Begriff "Verstehen" in Exegetischem Zusammenhang (1954) 151-54, 157-160, 179-86, 192-99. DINKLER, E. GPM 12 (1957/58) 265-71. BANDSTRA, A.J. The Law and the Elements of the World (1964) 138ff. SOUCEK, J.B. GPM 18 (1964) 357-64. LUZ, U. Das Geschichtsverständnis des Paulus (1968) 168. MULLER-SCHWEFE, H.R. GPM 24 (1969/70) 410-15. DUNN, J. D. G. "Rom. 7, 14-25 in the Theology of Paul," ThZ 31 (1975) 257-73. PAGELS, E. H. The Gnostic Paul. Gnostic Exegesis of the Pauline Letters (Philadelphia 1975) 32f. SCHNACKENBURG, R. "Römer 7 im Zusammenhang des Römerbriefes" in E. Ellis und E. Grässer, eds., Jesus und Paulus (FS W. G. Kümmel; Göttingen 1975) 285ff., 295ff. RÄISÄNEN, H. "'Myyty synnin alaisuuten'. Kuvaako Rm 7:14-25 kristittyä?"

TAik 81 (5, 1976) 426-41. FUNG, Y. K. "The Impotence of the Law" in Scripture, Tradition, and Interpretation (FS. E. F. Harrison; Grand Rapids 1978) 34-48. DEUSER, H. "Glaubenserfahrung und Anthropologie. Röm 7:14-25 und Luthers These: totum genus humanum carnem esse," EvTh 39 (5, 1979) 409-31. LEESTE, T. Ego i Rom. 7:14-25 (Abo, Finland 1980). WENHAM, D. "The Christian Life: a Life of Tension. A Consideration of the Nature of Christian Experience in Paul" in D. A. Hagner and M. J. Harris, eds., Pauline Studies (FS F. F. Bruce; Exeter 1980) 83-94. BAMMEL, C. P. H. "Philocalia IX, Jerome, Epistle 121, and Origen's Exposition of Romans VII," JThS 32 (1981) 67f., 74-6. DOCKERY, D. S. "Romans 7:14-25. Pauline Tension in the Christian Life," GThJ 2 (1981) 239-57. MARTIN, B. L. "Some Reflections on the Identity of *ego* in Rom. 7:14-25," SJTh 34 (1981) 39-47. RÄISÄNEN, H. Paul and the Law (Tübingen 1983) 109-13, 114, 132f., 149, 230f. MOHRLANG, R. Matthew and Paul (Cambridge 1984) 32f., 44, 115f., 188f. VARO, F. "La lucha del hombre contra el pecado. Exégesis de Rom 17, 14-25," ScrTh 16 (1984) 9-53. BELD, A. VAN DEN. "Romeinen 7:14-25 en het probleem van de akrasia [Romans 7:14-25 and the problem of weakness of will]," Bijdr 46 (1985) 39-58. BELD, A. VAN DEN. "Romans 7:14-25 and the Problem of *Akrasia*," RSt 21 (4, 1985) 495-515. HÄRING, H. Das Problem des Bösen in der Theologie (Darmstadt 1985) 93. SANDERS, E. P. Paul, the Law, and the Jewish People (London 1985) 74-81, 86, 89n.32, 98f., 124f., 149, 163n.11. RÄISÄNEN, H. The Torah and Christ (Helsinki 1986) 16ff., 148. SEGUNDO, J. L. The Humanist Christology of Paul (Maryknoll NY and London 1986) 113-25. SCHMIDT, H. in GPM 42 (1987/88) 432-8. GEBAUER, R. Das Gebet bei Paulus (Giessen/Basel 1989) 131ff., 294, 296. MARTIN, B. L. Christ and the Law in Paul (Leiden 1989) 38, 41, 76-81, 83-5, 91, 106, 107, 137. GARLINGTON, D. B. "Romans 7:14-25 and the Creation Theology of Paul," TJ 11 (2, 1990) 197-235. ROSENAU, H. "Der Mensch zwischen Wollen und Können. Theologische Reflexionen im Anschluss an Röm 7, 14-25," ThPh 65 (1990) 1-30. LONGE-NECKER, B. W. Eschatology and the Covenant. A Comparison of 4 Ezra and Romans 1-11 (Sheffield 1991) 225, 227, 239, 239n.2, 245, 249. KREITZER, L. "R. L. Stevenson's *Strange Case of Dr. Jekyll and Mr. Hyde* and Romans 7:14-25: Images of the Moral Duality of Human Nature," Journal for Literature and Theology 6 (1992) 125-44. SEIFRID, M. A. Justification by Faith (Leiden/New York/Köln 1992) 226-44. SEIFRID, M. A. "The Subject of Rom 7:14-25," NovT 34 (1992) 313-33. WINGER, M. By What Law? The Meaning of *Nomos* in the Letters of Paul (Atlanta GA 1992) passim.

7:14-24   THISELTON, A. C. The Two Horizons (Grand Rapids 1980) 278. PATTE, D. Paul's Faith and the Power of the Gospel (Philadelphia 1983) 275-7. MALINA B. J. Christian Origins and Cultural Anthropology (Atlanta 1986) 137.

7:14-20   LINDARS, B. "Paul and the Law in Romans 5-8. An Actantial Analysis" in B. Lindars, ed., Law and Religion (Cambridge 1988) 135f.

7:14-15   BAMMEL, C. P. H. "Philocalia IX, Jerome, Epistle 121, and Origen's Exposition of Romans VII," JThS 32 (1981) 69-71.

7:14   FEINE, D.P. Das gesetzesfreie Evangelium des Paulus (1899) 150-52. BOUSSET, W. Die Religion des Judentums im Späthellenistischen Zeitalter (1966 =1926) 121. LIETZMANN, H. An die Römer (1933) 75-77. JOHNSON, G. "Paul's Certainties: IV The Validity of Moral Standards and the Sinfulness of Man" ET 69 (8, '58) 240-43. SCHRAGE, W. Die konkreten Einzelgebote in der paulinsichen Paränese (1961) 50, 73, 95, 98, 232, 247. JÜNGEL, E. Paulus und Jesus (1966) 57-59, 68. STROBEL, A. Erkenntnis und Bekenntnis der

Sünde in neutestamentlicher Zeit (1968) 49, 51. VAN DÜLMEN, A. Die Theologie des Gesetzes bei Paulus (1968) 44, 112f., 115, 116, 117, 118, 138f., 162, 172, 193, 212. KEUCK, W. "Das 'Geistliche Gesetz'. Röm 7:14a in der Auslegung der griechischen Väter" in Wort Gottes in der Zeit (FS K. H. Schelkle; Düsseldorf 1973) 215-35. KÜMMEL, W. G. Römer 7 und das Bild des Menschen im Neuen Testament (München 1974) 180, 189, 194, 220. LADD, G. E. A Theology of the New Testament (Grand Rapids 1974) 363, 405, 503. DUNN, J. D. G. Jesus and the Spirit. A Study of the Religious and Charismatic Experience of Jesus and the First Christians as Reflected in the New Testament (London 1975) 208, 314. SCHNACKENBURG, R. "Römer 7 im Zusammenhang des Römerbriefes" in E. Ellis und E. Grässer, eds., Jesus und Paulus (FS W. G. Kümmel; Göttingen 1975) 294ff. HÜBNER, H. Das Gesetz bei Paulus. Ein Beitrag zum Werden der paulinischen Theologie (Göttingen 1978) 125f. BAMMEL, C. P. H. "Philocalia IX, Jerome, Epistle 121, and Origen's Exposition of Romans VII," JThS 32 (1981) 67f., 70. PROVENCE, T. E. "'Who is Sufficient for These Things?' An Exegesis of 2 Corinthians ii 15–iii 18," NovT 24 (1982) 64f. MEHL, R. "Freiheit" in TRE 11 (1983) 519. THEISSEN, G. Psychologische Aspekte paulinischer Theologie (Göttingen 1983) 186, 188, 190, 223n.68, 232n.78, 233, 258. STAAB, K. Pauluskommentare aus der griechischen Kirche (Münster ²1984) 88:23-29 Diod; 130:34-131:9 ThM; 372:1-15 Genn; 426:15-16 Oek; 506:1-7 Phot. BRANDENBURGER, E. Das Böse (Zürich 1986) 53, 66, 94n.129, 131, 189. PHILONENKO, M. "Sur l'expression 'vendu au péché' dans l'"épitre aux Romains'," RHR 203 (1986) 41-52. BERGER, K. und COLPE, C., eds., Religionsgeschichtliches Textbuch zum Neuen Testament (Göttingen/Zürich 1987) 215. LAYTON, B. The Gnostic Scriptures (Garden City NY 1987) 352. MERKLEIN, H. Studien zu Jesus und Paulus (Tübingen 1987) 10, 74n.183, 86-8. MARTIN, B. L. Christ and the Law in Paul (Leiden 1989) 14, 16, 19, 25, 27, 19, 31, 47, 52, 60, 67, 69, 70, 72, 75, 80-2, 92, 100, 104, 145, 147, 148. LONGENECKER, B. W. Eschatology and the Covenant. A Comparison of 4 Ezra and Romans 1-11 (Sheffield 1991) 226f., 236, 239, 239n.2, 240-5, 272.

7:15ff.   JÜNGEL, E. Paulus und Jesus (1966) 69.

7:15-21   LAFON, F. "Un moi sans oeuvre," RechSR 78 (2, 1990) 165-74.

7:15-20   STAAB, K. Pauluskommentare aus der griechischen Kirche (Münster ²1984) 506:8-507:10 Phot. MALHERBE, A. J. Moral Exhortation. A Greco-Roman Sourcebook (Philadelphia 1986) 62. RÄISÄNEN, H. The Torah and Christ (Helsinki 1986) 34, 148f.

7:15-18   MEHL, R. "Freiheit" in TRE 11 (1983) 518.

7:15-17   SEGAL, A. F. Paul the Convert (New Haven/London 1990) 244.

7:15   KÜMMEL, W. G. Römer 7 und das Bild des Menschen im Neuen Testament (München 1974) 187f., 190. THEISSEN, G. Psychologische Aspekte paulinischer Theologie (Göttingen 1983) 188, 190, 195, 213-23, 232-4. HÜBNER, H. Gottes Ich und Israel (Göttingen 1984) 75f. STAAB, K. Pauluskommentare aus der griechischen Kirche (Münster ²1984) 89:1-8 Diod; 372:16-373:3 Genn. RICHES, J. "Heiligung" in TRE 14 (1985) 730. BERGER, K. und COLPE, C., eds., Religionsgeschichtliches Textbuch zum Neuen Testament (Göttingen/Zürich 1987) 215f. HUGGINS, R. V. "Alleged Classical Parallels to Paul's 'What I want to do I do not do, but what I hate, that I do' (Röm 7:15)," WThJ 54 (1992) 153-61.

7:16-20   BAUMERT, N. Täglich Sterben und Auferstehen. Der Literalsinn von 2 Kor 4, 12-5, 10 (München 1973) 201.

7:16-17   BAMMEL, C. P. H. "Philocalia IX, Jerome, Epistle 121, and Origen's Exposition of Romans VII," JThS 32 (1981) 69.
7:16   THEISSEN, G. Psychologische Aspekte paulinischer Theologie (Göttingen 1983) 188, 190, 191, 196, 210, 221, 233, 234. STAAB, K. Pauluskommentare aus der griechischen Kirche (Münster ²1984) 373:4-7 Genn.
7:17-8:39 SCHMITHALS, W. Der Römerbrief als historisches Problem (Gütersloh 1975) 18ff., 22, 25. SCHMITHALS, W. "Zur Herkunft der gnostischen Elemente in der Sprache des Paulus" in B. Aland et al., eds., Gnosis (FS H. Jonas; Göttingen 1978) 393, 407f. SCHMITHALS, W. Die theologische Anthropologie des Paulus. Auslegung von Röm 7, 17-8, 39 (Stuttgart/Berlin/Cologne/Mainz 1980).
7:17ff.   SCHMITHALS, W. "Zur Herkunft der gnostischen Elemente in der Sprache des Paulus" in B. Aland et al., eds., Gnosis (FS H. Jonas; Göttingen 1978) 388-90, 393.
7:17-20   BRANDENBURGER, E. Adam und Christus (Neukirchen-Vluyn 1962) 160, 215f. SCHMITHALS, W. Die theologische Anthropologie des Paulus (Stuttgart 1980) 34-61. STAAB, K. Pauluskommentare aus der griechischen Kirche (Münster ²1984) 373:8-19 Genn.
7:17-18   SCHRAGE, W. Die konkreten Einzelgebote in der paulinischen Paränese (1961) 50, 64. STAAB, K. Pauluskommentare aus der griechischen Kirche (Münster ²1984) 131:10-22 ThM. BERGER, K. und COLPE, C., eds., Religionsgeschichtliches Textbuch zum Neuen Testament (Göttingen/Zürich 1987) 215. RÖHSER, G. Metaphorik und Personifikation der Sünde (Tübingen 1987) 119ff., 123f., 126f., 141f., 150, 156ff., 161f., 175.
7:17   DU TOIT, A. B. "Hyperbolical contrasts: a neglected aspect of Paul's style" in J. H. Petzer and P. J. Hartin, eds., A South African Perspective on the New Testament (FS B. M. Metzger; Leiden 1986) 184. YAGI, S. "'I' in the Words of Jesus" in J. Hick and P. F. Knitter, eds., The Myth of Christian Uniqueness. Toward a Pluralistic Theology of Religions (Maryknoll NY 1987) 117-34, esp.120.
7:18ff.   STROBEL, A. Erkenntnis und Bekenntnis der Sünde in neutestamentlicher Zeit (1968) 51.
7:18-19   BROWNING, W. "Studies in Texts Rm vii, 18f." Theology LII, 343 (1949) 22-25. WILSON, R. McL. "The New Testament in the Nag Hammadi Gospel of Philip" NTS 9 (1962-63) 292f. LUCK, U. "Das Gute und das Böse in Römer 7" in H. Merklein, ed., Neues Testament und Ethik (FS R. Schnackenburg; Freiburg/Basel/Wien 1989) 220-37.
7:18   KÜMMEL, W. G. Römer 7 und das Bild des Menschen im Neuen Testament (München 1974) 187f. THEISSEN, G. Psychologische Aspekte paulinischer Theologie (Göttingen 1983) 186, 188, 190n.15, 191, 193, 210, 210n.53, 213, 218n.64, 233, 247, 257, 263. STAAB, K. Pauluskommentare aus der griechischen Kirche (Münster ²1984) 426:17-427:11 Oek.
7:19-21   BERGER, K. und COLPE, C., eds., Religionsgeschichtliches Textbuch zum Neuen Testament (Göttingen/Zürich 1987) 215f.
7:19-20   TILLICH, P. Das Ewig im Jetzt (1964) 41-50. STAAB, K. Pauluskommentare aus der griechischen Kirche (Münster ²1984) 131:23-132:11 ThM.
7:19   BRUNNER, E. Dogmatik II (1950) 144. KÜMMEL, W. G. Römer 7 und das Bild des Menschen im Neuen Testament (München 1974) 187f., 190. THISELTON, A. C. The Two Horizons (Grand Rapids 1980) 318. THEISSEN, G. Psychologische Aspekte paulinischer Theologie (Göttingen 1983) 190, 195,

210, 213-23, 234. THEISSEN, G. Psychological Aspects of Pauline Theology (Edinburgh 1987) 211-21.

7:20 SCHRAGE, W. Die konkreten Einzelgebote in der paulinischen Paränese (1961) 64. THEISSEN, G. Psychologische Aspekte paulinischer Theologie (Göttingen 1983) 189, 190n.15, 196, 210n.53, 213, 221, 223n.68, 263. DU TOIT, A. B. "Hyperbolical contrasts: a neglected aspect of Paul's style" in J. H. Petzer and P. J. Hartin, eds., A South African Perspective on the New Testament (FS B. M. Metzger; Leiden 1986) 184. BERGER, K. und COLPE, C., eds., Religionsgeschichtliches Textbuch zum Neuen Testament (Göttingen/Zürich 1987) 215. RÖHSER, G. Metaphorik und Personifikation der Sünde (Tübingen 1987) 114, 119ff., 124, 126f., 141f., 150, 156ff., 161f., 175.

7:21-8:7 SNODGRASS, K. "Spheres of Influence. A Possible Solution to the Problem of Paul and the Law," JSNT 32 (1988) 93-113.

7:21-8:2 VOLLENWEIDER, S. Freiheit als neue Schöpfung (Göttingen 1989) 358.

7:21-8:1 CLARK, K. W. "The Meaning of APA" in The Gentile Bias and other Essays [selected by J. L Sharpe III] (Leiden 1980) 201.

7:21ff. GOGARTEN, F. Die Wirklichkeit des Glaubens (1957) 164ff.

7:21-25 RÄISÄNEN, H. Paul and the Law (Tübingen 1983) 52f., 67. RÄISÄNEN, H. The Torah and Christ (Helsinki 1986) 96f., 103, 113. LINDARS, B. "Paul and the Law in Romans 5-8. An Actantial Analysis" in B. Lindars, ed., Law and Religion (Cambridge 1988) 136. MARTIN, B. L. Christ and the Law in Paul (Leiden 1989) 26-8, 30.

7:21-24 DEIDUN, T. J. New Covenant Morality in Paul (Rome 1981) 199-201.

7:21-23 FUCHS, E. "Existentiale Interpretation von Römer 7, 7-12 und 21-23" ZThK 59 (3, '62) 285-314. FRIEDRICH, G. "Das Gesetz des Glaubens Römer 3, 27" in Auf das Wort kommt es an. Gesammelte Aufsätze (Göttingen 1978) 109, 110. SCHMITHALS, W. "Zur Herkunft der gnostischen Elemente in der Sprache des Paulus" in B. Aland et al., eds., Gnosis (FS H. Jonas; Göttingen 1978) 393. SCHMITHALS, W. Die theologische Anthropologie des Paulus (Stuttgart 1980) 61-72. THEISSEN, G. Psychologische Aspekte paulinischer Theologie (Göttingen 1983) 190n.15, 234, 259n.112. MERKLEIN, H. Studien zu Jesus und Paulus (Tübingen 1987) 85-9. VOLLENWEIDER, S. Freiheit als neue Schöpfung (Göttingen 1989) 266. MEYER, P. W. "The Worm at the Core of the Apple. Exegetical Reflections on Romans 7" in R. T. Fortna and B. R. Gaventa, eds., The Conversation Continues. Studies in Paul and John (FS J. L. Martyn; Nashville 1990) 62-84, esp.78f.

7:21 KÜMMEL, W. G. Römer 7 und das Bild des Menschen im Neuen Testament (München 1974) 187f., 190. THEISSEN, G. Psychologische Aspekte paulinischer Theologie (Göttingen 1983) 188, 191, 221, 234, 235. STAAB, K. Pauluskommentare aus der griechischen Kirche (Münster ²1984) 89:9-14 Diod; 132:12-20 ThM; 373:20-22 Genn; 507:11-508:18 Phot. RÄISÄNEN, H. The Torah and Christ (Helsinki 1986) 142.

7:22-8:3 MUELLER, F. "Zwei Marginalien im Brief des Paulus an die Römer" ZNW 40 (1941) 249-252. SAAKE, H. "Konstitutionsprobleme in Römer 7, 22-8, 3" SO XLVIII (1973) 109-14.

7:22-25 MOHRLANG, R. Matthew and Paul (Cambridge 1984) 188f.

7:22-23 STAAB, K. Pauluskommentare aus der griechischen Kirche (Münster ²1984) 89:15-23 Diod; 123:21-133:7 ThM; 373:23-374:19 Genn; 508:19-509:3 Phot. THEISSEN, G. Psychological Aspects of Pauline Theology (Edinburgh 1987) 255-7.

7:22   BONHOEFFER, A. Epiktet und das Neue Testament (1911) 115ff. JERVELL,
            J. Imago Dei (1960) 242f, 246. VAN DÜLMEN, A. Die Theologie des
            Gesetzes bei Paulus (1968) 44, 115-18, 131, 154. KÜMMEL, W. G. Römer 7
            und das Bild des Menschen im Neuen Testament (München 1974) 181, 187,
            189. RÜGER, H. P. "Hieronymus, die Rabbinen und Paulus. Zur Vorgeschichte
            des Begriffspaars 'innerer und äusserer Mensch'," ZNW 68 (1977) 132-7.
            KLEINKNECHT, K. T. Der leidende Gerechtfertigte (Tübingen 1984) 262.
            BERGER, K. und COLPE, C., eds., Religionsgeschichtliches Textbuch zum
            Neuen Testament (Göttingen/Zürich 1987) 216f. HECKEL, T. K. Der Innere
            Mensch. Die paulinische Verarbeitung eines platonischen Motivs (Tübingen
            1993) passim.
7:23-24   CAVALLIN, H. C. C. Life After Death. Paul's Argument for the Resurrection
            of the Dead in I Cor 15. Part I: An Enquiry into the Jewish Background (Lund
            1974) 3, 10n.17. STAAB, K. Pauluskommentare aus der griechischen Kirche
            (Münster ²1984) 427:12-15 Oek.
7:23   SCHRAGE, W. Die konkreten Einzelgebote in der paulinischen Paränese (1961)
            64. SCHWEIZER, E. "Die Sünde in den Gliedern": Aberham unser Vater,
            Festschr. f. Otto Michel (1963). JÜNGEL, E. Paulus und Jesus (1966) 57, 59,
            61. VAN DÜLMEN, A. Die Theologie des Gesetzes bei Paulus (1968) 115-18,
            131, 149, 159, 162. GIBBS, J.G. Creation and Redemption (1971) 35, 146f.
            KÜMMEL, W. G. Römer 7 und das Bild des Menschen im Neuen Testament
            (München 1974) 182, 188, 190. LADD, G. E. A Theology of the New Testa-
            ment (Grand Rapids 1974) 476, 504, 506. RIDDERBOS, H. Paul. An Outline
            of His Theology (Grand Rapids 1975) 114-8. BÖHLIG, A. Die Gnosis III: Der
            Manichäismus (Zürich/München 1980) 329n.17. BAMMEL, C. P. H. "Philo-
            calia IX, Jerome, Epistle 121, and Origen's Exposition of Romans VII," JThS
            32 (1981) 56, 64, 70. THEISSEN, G. Psychologische Aspekte paulinischer The-
            ologie (Göttingen 1983) 186, 191, 221, 247, 250, 257-9. RÄISÄNEN, H. The
            Torah and Christ (Helsinki 1986) 142f. RÖHSER, G. Metaphorik und Personifi-
            kation der Sünde (Tübingen 1987) 109, 114, 124, 126, 141, 166f. MARTIN, B.
            L. Christ and the Law in Paul (Leiden 1989) 17, 19, 26-8, 31, 38, 60, 75, 81f.,
            85, 92, 99.
7:24-8:9   LANDAU, R. "Komm, Heiliger Geist, du Tröster wert . . . " EvTh 41 (1981)
            189-93.
7:24-25   SMITH, E.W. "The Form and Religious Background of Rmans VII 24-25a"
            NovTest 13 (2, '71) 127-35. EICHHOLZ, G. Die Theologie des Paulus im
            Umriss (1972) 257ff. ENSLIN, M. S. Reapproaching Paul (Philadelphia 1972)
            52f. JÜNGEL, E. und RÖSSLER, D. Gefangenes Ich—befreiender Geist. Zwei
            Tübinger Römerbrief-Auslegungen (München 1976). SCHMITHALS, W. Die
            theologische Anthropologie des Paulus (Stuttgart 1980) 73-81. AMELUNG, E.
            "Gericht Gottes" in TRE 12 (1984) 496. STAAB, K. Pauluskommentare aus der
            griechischen Kirche (Münster ²1984) 220:3-13 Sev; 374:20-375:3 Genn.
            SELLIN, G. Der Streit um die Auferstehung der Toten (Göttingen 1986) 228f.
            GEBAUER, R. Das Gebet bei Paulus (Giessen/Basel 1989) 131-43.
7:24   BRUNNER, E., Dogmatik II (1950) 147. BEST, E. One Body in Christ (1955)
            217. KNOX, W.L. The Sources of the Synoptic Gospels II (1957) 116.
            MINEAR, P.S. Images of the Church in the New Testament (1960) 174f.
            ROBINSON, J.M. Kerygma und historischer Jesus (1960) 137, 140. SEVEN-
            STER, J.N. Paul and Seneca (1961) 82, 83. KRAMER, W. Christos Kyrios
            Gottessohn (1963) § 17e. JÜNGEL, E. Paulus und Jesus (1966) 57, 59, 61.
            STROBEL, A. Erkenntnis und Bekenntnis der Sünde in neutestamentlicher Zeit

(1968) 51. VAN DÜLMEN, A. Die Theologie des Gesetzes bei Paulus (1968) 44, 116, 118, 119, 131, 149, 154, 156, 182. DUNN, J. D. G. Jesus and the Spirit. A Study of the Religious and Charismatic Experience of Jesus and the First Christians as Reflected in the New Testament (London 1975) 241, 312, 314, 316, 326, 338. RIDDERBOS, H. Paul. An Outline of His Theology (Grand Rapids 1975) 127-30. BISER, E. Der Zeuge (Graz/Wien/Köln 1981) 60, 72, 110, 169. THEISSEN, G. Psychologische Aspekte paulinischer Theologie (Göttingen 1983) 182, 189n.14, 204n.39, 258. STAAB, K. Pauluskommentare aus der griechischen Kirche (Münster ²1984) 90:1-3 Diod. BERGER, K. und COLPE, C., eds., Religionsgeschichtliches Textbuch zum Neuen Testament (Göttingen/Zürich 1987) 217f. OSTEN-SACKEN, P. VON DER. "'Ich elender Mensch . . . ': Tod und Leben als Zentrum paulinischer Theologie" in Evangelium und Tora: Aufsätze zu Paulus (München 1987) 80-102. MERKLEIN, H. Studien zu Jesus und Paulus (Tübingen 1987) 86f. VOORWINDE, S. "Who is the 'Wretched Man' in Romans 7:24?" VR 54 (1990) 11-26.

7:25-8:2   STAAB, K. Pauluskommentare aus der griechischen Kirche (Münster ²1984) 375:4-13 Genn.

7:25-8:1   STAAB, K. Pauluskommentare aus der griechischen Kirche (Münster ²1984) 90:4-13 Apoll.

7:25   DELLING, G. Die Zueignung des Heils in der Taufe (1961) 53. KEUCK, W. "Dienst des Geistes und des Fleisches. Zur Auslegungsgeschichte und Auslegung von Rm 7, 25b" ThQ 141 (3, '61) 257-80. KRAMER, W. Christos Kyrios Gottessohn (1963) § 19 c. KÜRZINGER, J. "Der Schuüssel zum Verständnis von Röm 7" BZ 7 (2, '63) 270-74. LONGENECKER, R.N. Paul Apostle of Liberty (1964) 96, 97, 110, 111-13, 172. STROBEL, A. Erkenntnis und Bekenntnis der Sünde in neutestamentlicher Zeit (1968) 51. VAN DÜLMEN, A. Die Theologie des Gesetzes bei Paulus (1968) 44, 99, 118, 119, 131, 141, 149. KÜMMEL, W. G. Römer 7 und das Bild des Menschen im Neuen Testament (München 1974) 182, 188-90. LADD, G. E. A Theology of the New Testament (Grand Rapids 1974) 469, 476, 503f. PAULSEN, H. Überlieferung und Auslegung von Römer 8 (Neukirchen-Vluyn 1974) 25-76. DUNN, J. D. G. Jesus and the Spirit. A Study of the Religious and Charismatic Experience of Jesus and the First Christians as Reflected in the New Testament (London 1975) 239, 314f., 316, 336, 338, 355, 444. SCHMITHALS, W. Der Römerbrief als historisches Problem (Gütersloh 1975) 206. BYSKOV, M. "Simul Iustus et Peccator. A Note on Romans vii. 25b" StTh 30 (1976) 75-87. SCHULZ, S. Die Mitte der Schrift (Stuttgart 1976) 127. BANKS, R. "Romans 7.25a: An Eschatological Thanksgiving?" AusBR 26 (1978) 34-42. FRIEDRICH, G. "Das Gesetz Glaubens Römer 3, 27" in Auf das Wort kommt es an. Gesammelte Aufsätze (Göttingen 1978) 113. GRUNDMANN, W. Wandlungen im Verständnis des Heils (Berlin, DDR 1980) 25-46. SCHMITHALS, W. Die theologische Anthropologie des Paulus (Stuttgart 1980) 81-3. STAAB, K. Pauluskommentare aus der griechischen Kirche (Münster ²1984) 133:8-16 ThM. SCHNABEL, E. J. Law and Wisdom from Ben Sira to Paul (Tübingen 1985) 288, 295, 330. SCHNACKENBURG, R. Die sittliche Botschaft des Neuen Testaments, Band 1 (Freiburg/Basel/Wien 1986) 20. RÖHSER, G. Metaphorik und Personifikation der Sünde (Tübingen 1987) 127, 141, 166f. MERKLEIN, H. Studien zu Jesus und Paulus (Tübingen 1987) 87f. GEBAUER, R. Das Gebet bei Paulus (Giessen/Basel 1989) 131, 134f., 136-9, 141f., 144, 162, 204, 207, 209f., 218, 224, 294, 300f., 304f., 321, 346. MARTIN, B. L. Christ and the Law in Paul (Leiden 1989) 14, 17, 19, 26-8, 30f., 35, 38, 40, 46, 52, 60, 75,

7:25a

7:25b

8-11

8

78-82, 85, 92, 99, 104, 106, 107, 142. SIMONIS, W. Der gefangene Paulus. Die Entstehung des sogenannten Römerbriefs und anderer urchristlicher Schriften in Rom (Frankfurt/Bern/New York/Paris 1990) 46f. OLIVEIRA, A. DE, Die Diakonie der Gerechtigkeit und der Versöhnung in der Apologie des 2. Korintherbriefes. Analyse und Auslegung von 2 Kor 2, 14-4, 6; 5, 11-6, 10 (Münster 1990) 28. MEYER, P. W. "The Worm at the Core of the Apple. Exegetical Reflections on Romans 7" in R. T. Fortna and B. R. Gaventa, eds., The Conversation Continues. Studies in Paul and John (FS J. L. Martyn; Nashville 1990) 62-84, esp. 79.

MAYER, B. "Trotz allem in der Gewissheit des Heils. Zur Frage der göttlichen Vorherbestimmung bei Paulus," BuK 35 (1980) 13-6. SCHRAGE, E. Die konkreten Einzelgebote in der paulinischen Paränese (1961) 73, 89f. KÄSEMANN, E. "Der gottesdienstliche Schrei nach der Leben. Eine Auslgeung von Römer 8 (1965). HOFFMAN, P. Die Toten in Christus (1966) 308. SCHNACKENBURG, R. "Leben auf Hoffnung hin. Christliche Existenz nach Röm. 8" BuLit 39 (6, '66) 316-19. LOANE, M.L. The Hope of Glory. An Exposition of the Eighth Chapter in the Epistle to the Romans (1968). LUZ, U. Das Geschichtsverständnis des Paulus (1968) 19ff. CAMBIER, J. "La Chair et L'Esprit en I Cor. V.5" NTS 15 (1968-69) 228ff. DINKLER, E. "Die Taufaussagen des Neuen Testaments. New untersucht im Hinblick auf Karl Barths Tauflehre": Zu Karl Barths Lehre von der Taufe (1971) 79-84. GIBBS, J.G. Creation and Redemption (1971) 34-39, 154. GRAYSTON, K. "Das Heil bei Paulus nach Römer 8" in P. A. Potter, ed., Das Heil der Welt heute (Stuttgart 1973) 75-82. KÜMMEL, W. G. Römer 7 und das Bild des Menschen im Neuen Testament (München 1974) 11f., 66, 97, 110, 117, 219. PAULSEN, H. Überlieferung und Auslegung in Römer 8 (Neukirchen-Vluyn 1974). WILES, G. P. Paul's Intercessory Prayers (London 1974) 76, 87, 255, 267. FUCHS, E. "Der Anteil des Geistes am Glauben des Paulus. Ein Beitrag zum Verständnis von Römer 8," ZThK 72 (1975) 293-302. OSTEN-SACKEN, P. VON DER, Römer 8 als Beispiel paulinischer Soteriologie (Göttingen 1975). SCHNACKENBURG, R. "Römer 7 im Zusammenhang des Römerbriefes" in E. Ellis und E. Grässer, eds., Jesus und Paulus (FS W. G. Kümmel; Göttingen 1975) 286ff., 294. PATHRAPANKAL, J. "The Spirit of Sonship in Romans Chapter 8," Biblebhashyam 2 (1976) 181-95. VELLANICKAL, N. The Divine Sonship of Christians in the Johannine Writings (Rome 1977) 80-7. FRIEDRICH, G. "Die Fürbitte im Neuen Testament" in Auf das Wort kommt es an. Gesammelte Aufsätze (Göttingen 1978) 442-4. BYRNE, B. "Sons of God"—"Seed of Abraham" (Rome 1979) 92-5, 152, 181, 184. LIEBSCHNER, S. "Der eschatologische Charakter des Geistwirkens am Beispiel der 'neuen Kreatur'. Eine Studie zu Römer 8" in W. Popkes, ed., Theologisches Gespräch (FS R. Thaut; Kassel 1979) 45-50. KEHNSCHERPER, J. "Romans 8:19. On Pauline Belief and Creation" in E. A. Livingstone, ed., Studia Biblica 1978, Vol. 3: Papers on Paul and Other New Testament Authors (Sheffield 1980) 233-43. PEDERSEN, S. "Agape—der eschatologische Hauptbegriff bei Paulus" in S. Pedersen, ed., Die Paulinische Literatur und Theologie (Arhus/Göttingen 1980) 184f. WENHAM, D. "The Christian Life: a Life of Tension. A Consideration of the Nature of Christian Experience in Paul" in D. A. Hagner and M. J. Harris, eds., Pauline Studies (FS F. F. Bruce; Exeter 1980) 84f., 92f. MINEAR, P. S. New Testament Apocalyptic (Nashville 1981) 102-14. NIJENHUIS, W. "Calvin" in TRE

7 (1981) 586. RENSBURG, J. J. J. VAN. "The Children of God in Romans 8,"
Neotestamentica 15 (1981) 139-79. SAUTER, G. "Geist und Freiheit.
Geistvorstellungen und die Erwartung des Geistes," EvTh 41 (1981) 215f., 219,
223. BLANK, J. Paulus. Von Jesus zum Christentum (München 1982) 101-23.
HAYS, R. B. The Faith of Jesus Christ (Chico CA 1983) 263. THEISSEN, G.
Psychologische Aspekte paulinischer Theologie (Göttingen 1983) 119, 185-7,
223, 252, 263-8, 317, 321, 332-40, 381. TOIT, A. B. DU. "Freude" in TRE 11
(1983) 585. HELDERMANN, J. Die Anapausis im Evangelium Veritatis
(Leiden 1984) 269n.672. PERKINS, P. Resurrection. New Testament Witness
and Contemporary Reflection (London 1984) 269, 273, 308. FÄSSLER, M.
"Lecture de Romains 8," BCPE 37 (1985) 5-42. RICHES, J. "Heiligung" in
TRE 14 (1985) 721. SEGUNDO, J. L. The Humanist Christology of Paul
(Maryknoll NY and London 1986) 126-44. BYRNE, B. "Prophecy Now. The
Tug into the Future," Way 27 (1987) 106-16. HERMAN, Z. I. "Saggio
esegetico sul 'gia e non ancora' escatologico in Rm 8," Anton. 62 (1987) 26-84.
HÜBNER, H. "Paulusforschung seit 1945. Ein kritischer Literaturbericht" in
ANRW II.25.4 (1987) 2796ff. OSTEN-SACKEN, P. VON DER, Evangelium
und Tora: Aufsätze zu Paulus (München 1987) 9, 13, 19, 22f., 31, 63, 65ff., 82,
87, 92, 99, 171, 179, 181, 197, 206, 220. THEISSEN, G. Psychological Aspects
of Pauline Theology (Edinburgh 1987) 182-4. THOMAS, C. "Spirit Activity in
the Church. A view from Romans 8," BiTod 25 (1987) 160-2. WERBICK, J.
"Die Soteriologie zwischen 'christologischem Triumphalismus' und apokalyptischem Radikalismus" in I. Broer und J. Werbick, eds., "Auf Hoffnung hin sind
wir erlöst" (Röm 8, 14) (Stuttgart 1987) 157-60. CONZELMANN, H. and
LINDEMANN, A. Interpreting the New Testament (Peabody MA 1988) 196.
HOOKER, M. D. From Adam to Christ. Essays on Paul (Cambridge 1990) 5,
18f., 31-3, 39, 45, 57-60, 62f., 84, 130, 136, 168. SEGAL, A. F. Paul the
Convert (New Haven/London 1990) 63, 227, 247. VLEDDER, E. J. and
AARDE, A. D. VAN. "A holistic view of the Holy Spirit as agent of ethical
responsibility. This view experienced as exciting in Romans 8, but alarming in
1 Corinthians 12," HTS 47 (1991) 503-25. WAY, D. The Lordship of Christ.
Ernst Käsemann's Interpretation of Paul's Theology (Oxford 1991) 150-4.

8:1ff.   BANDSTRA, A.J. The Law and the Elements of the World (1964) 147ff.
BRANDENBURGER, E. Adam und Christus (Neukirchen 1962) 164, 166,
236f., 239, 255, 259, 261ff. KÜMMEL, W. G. Römer 7 und das Bild des
Menschen im Neuen Testament (München 1974) 11f., 70, 73f., 90, 104, 107,
110, 134. THEISSEN, G. Psychologische Aspekte paulinischer Theologie
(Göttingen 1983) 186f., 258, 332, 338. MOHRLANG, R. Matthew and Paul
(Cambridge 1984) 33, 61, 88. JONES, F. S. "Freiheit" in den Briefen des
Apostels Paulus (Göttingen 1987) 122f. GEBAUER, R. Das Gebet bei Paulus
(Giessen/Basel 1989) 132, 135, 137f., 142ff., 162, 207, 301f., 304f., 307.
VOLLENWEIDER, S. Freiheit als neue Schöpfung (Göttingen 1989) 196, 331,
346ff., 362ff., 402, 405.

8:1-39   GIBLIN, C.H. In Hope of God's Glory (1970) 388-98.

8:1-30   COETZER, W. C. "The Holy Spirit and the Eschatological View in Romans 8,"
Neotestamentica 15 (1981) 180-98. DUNN, J. D. G. "Paul's Epistle to the
Romans: An Analysis of Structure and Argument" in ANRW II.25.4 (1987)
2863-2865.

8:1-27   DUNN, J.D.G. Baptism in the Holy Spirit (1970) 147ff., 151.

8:1-17   TAYLOR, T.M. "'Abba, Father' and Baptism" SJTh 11 ('58) 65ff. GORDAY,
P. Principles of Patristic Exegesis: Romans 9-11 in Origen, John Chrysostom,

134 An Exegetical Bibliography of the New Testament

and Augustine (New York/Toronto 1983) 73, 119f., 164f. KLEINKNECHT, K.
T. Der leidende Gerechtfertigte (Tübingen 1984) 333f., 337. GARMUS, L., ed.,
Leitura da Bíblia a partir das condições reais da vida, Estudos Bíblicos 7
(Petrópolis, Brazil 1985).

8:1-14 DEIDUN, T. J. New Covenant Morality in Paul (Rome 1981) 69-80.

8:1-13 MONTAGUE, G. T. The Holy Spirit (New York 1976) 206-8. BYRNE, B.
"Sons of God"—"Seed of Abraham" (Rome 1979) 91-7. NIELSEN, H. K. Heilung und Verkündigung (Leiden 1987) 206.

8:1-12 DAHINTEN, G. in GPM 30 (1976) 247-53.

8:1-11 PFISTER, W. Das Leben im Geist nach Paulus (1963) 32-48. BINKLER, E.
GPM 18 (1964) 200-6. ZEISS, K. "Befreites Leben" Kleine Predigt-Typologie
III, ed. Schmidt (1965) 352-57. VOIGT, G. Der zerrissene Vorhang I (1969)
239-45. MARQUARDT, F.-W. GPM 24 (1970/71) 249-56. MARQUARDT, F.-
W. Die Juden im Römerbrief (Zürich 1971) 49-57. SIBER, P. Mit Christus
leben (Zürich 1971) 80-4. PAULSEN, H. Überlieferung und Auslegung von
Römer 8 (Neukirchen-Vluyn 1974) 25-76. SCHNACKENBURG, R. "Römer 7
im Zusammenhang des Römerbriefes" in E. Ellis und E. Grässer, eds., Jesus
und Paulus (FS W. G. Kümmel; Göttingen 1975) 286ff., 295. HOLZE, H. in P.
Krusche et al., eds., Predigtstudien für das Kirchenjahr 1976. Perikopenreihe
IV/2 (Stuttgart 1976) 84-7. FROITZHEIM, F. Christologie und Eschatologie bei
Paulus (Würzburg 1979) 125f. BYRNE, B. "Living out the Righteousness of
God. The Contribution of Rom 6:1-8:13 to an Understanding of Paul's Ethical
Presuppositions," CBQ 43 (1981) 567-71, 576. LANG, F. "Römer 8:1-11 in der
Revision des Luthertextes von 1975," ZThK 78 (1981) 20-31. GRÄSSER, E.
in GPM 38 (1983/84) 259-66. PERKINS, P. Resurrection. New Testament Wit-
ness and Contemporary Reflection (London 1984) 269f. REINMUTH, E. Geist
und Gesetz (Berlin, DDR 1985) 66-73. FROEHLICH, K. "Romans 8:1-11.
Pauline Theology in Medieval Interpretation" in J. T. Carroll et al., eds., Faith
and History (FS P. W. Meyer; Atlanta 1991) 239ff.

8:1-10 SCHWEIZER, E. Heiliger Geist (Berlin 1978) 120f.

8:1-9 KLAAS, W. in G. Eichholz, ed., Herr, tue meine Lippen auf Bd. 4 (1965)
131ff.

8:1-4 SOKOLOWSKI, E. Die Begriffe Geist und Leben bei Paulus (1903) 14ff., 45ff.,
47f., 121ff. GOGARTEN, F. Die Wirklichkeit des Glaubens (1957) 119ff.
PAGELS, E. H. The Gnostic Paul. Gnostic Exegesis of the Pauline Letters
(Philadelphia 1975) 33f. KECK, L. E. "The Law and 'The Law of Sin and
Death' (Rom 8:1-4). Reflections on the Spirit and Ethics in Paul" in J. L. Cren-
shaw et al., eds., The Divine Helmsman. Studies on God's Control of Human
Events (FS L. H. Silberman; New York 1980) 41-57. PATTE, D. Paul's Faith
and the Power of the Gospel (Philadelphia 1983) 277, 287-90. SANDERS, E.
P. Paul, the Law, and the Jewish People (London 1985) 98f., 103. LIMBECK,
M. Mit Paulus Christ sein. Sachbuch zur Person und Theologie des Apostels
Paulus (Stuttgart 1989) 127. LONGENECKER, B. W. Eschatology and the
Covenant. A Comparison of 4 Ezra and Romans 1-11 (Sheffield 1991) 240,
243, 245-50.

8:1-3 MARTIN, B. L. Christ and the Law in Paul (Leiden 1989) 111.

8:1-2 BRUNNER, E. Dogmatik II (1950) 334. BEST, E. One Body in Christ (1955)
10, 18. MÜLLER-SCHWEFE, H.R. GPM 24 (1969) 410-15. SCHNACKEN-
BURG, R. Die sittliche Botschaft des Neuen Testaments, Band 1 (Freiburg/Bas-
el/Wien 1986) 110, 194. LINDARS, B. "Paul and the Law in Romans 5-8. An

	Actantial Analysis" in B. Lindars, ed., Law and Religion (Cambridge 1988) 136f.
8:1	BEST, E. One Body in Christ (1955) 1, 2. MATTERN, L. Das Verständnis des Gerichtes bei Paulus (1966) 63, 91ff., 110, 213. KÜMMEL, W. G. Römer 7 und das Bild des Menschen im Neuen Testament (München 1974) 10, 65, 67, 70, 92f., 126. LADD, G. E. A Theology of the New Testament (Grand Rapids 1974) 409, 443, 566. SCHMITHALS, W. Der Römerbrief als historisches Problem (Gütersloh 1975) 206f. SCHMITHALS, W. "Zur Herkunft der gnostischen Elemente in der Sprache des Paulus" in B. Aland et al., eds., Gnosis (FS H. Jonas; Göttingen 1978) 388-90. GRUNDMANN, W. Wandlungen im Verständnis des Heils (Berlin, DDR 1980) 25-46. SCHMITHALS, W. Die theologische Anthropologie des Paulus (Stuttgart 1980) 81-3. THEISSEN, G. Psychologische Aspekte paulinischer Theologie (Göttingen 1983) 210n.53, 228, 338. MARTIN, B. L. Christ and the Law in Paul (Leiden 1989) 19, 31, 55, 59, 80, 98, 99, 107, 111, 112, 127, 133. OLIVEIRA, A. DE, Die Diakonie der Gerechtigkeit und der Versöhnung in der Apologie des 2. Korintherbriefes. Analyse und Auslegung von 2 Kor 2, 14-4, 6; 5, 11-6, 10 (Münster 1990) 189. ZIESLER, J. Pauline Christianity (Oxford 1990) 48-50, 80.
8:2ff.	RIDDERBOS, H. Paul. An Outline of His Theology (Grand Rapids 1975) 63-9, 221f. MOHRLANG, R. Matthew and Paul (Cambridge 1984) 33f., 118, 120f., 127. VOLLENWEIDER, S. Freiheit als neue Schöpfung (Göttingen 1989) 370, 404.
8:2-11	DAVIES, W.D. Paul and Rabbinic Judaism (1955) 19, 24, 36, 91, 177f., 181f., 186, 274, 318. ROBINSON, J.M. Kerygma und historischer Jesus (1960) 179. SCHMITHALS, W. "Zur Herkunft der gnostischen Elemente in der Sprache des Paulus" in B. Aland et al., eds., Gnosis (FS H. Jonas; Göttingen 1978) 388-90. SCHMITHALS, W. Die theologische Anthropologie des Paulus (Stuttgart 1980) 83-117.
8:2-10	MINDE, H. J. VAN DER. "Theologia crucis und Pneumaaussagen bei Paulus," Catholia 34 (1980) 141.
8:2-5	STALDER, K. Das Werk des Geistes in der Heiligung bei Paulus (1962) passim.
8:2-4	LYONNET, S. "Le Nouveau Testament à la lumière de l'Ancien A propos de Rom 8, 2-4" NRTh 87 (6, '65) 561-87. KERTELGE, K. "Rechtfertigung" bei Paulus (1967) 212-19, 224. HÜBNER, H. Das Gesetz bei Paulus. Ein Beitrag zum Werden der paulinischen Theologie (Göttingen 1978) 124-7, 129. BONSACK, B. K. A. "Philologische und hermeneutische Exegese" in H. F. Geisser and W. Mostert, eds., Wirkungen hermeneutischer Theologie (FS G. Ebeling; Zürich 1983) 65-79. MERKLEIN, H. Studien zu Jesus und Paulus (Tübingen 1987) 85-92, 94. OSTEN-SACKEN, P. VON DER, Die Heiligkeit der Tora (München 1989) 19-23. VOLLENWEIDER, S. Freiheit als neue Schöpfung (Göttingen 1989) 315.
8:2-3	ROBINSON, J.A.T. The Body (1952) 44-46. SCHRAGE, W. Die konkreten Einzelgebote in der paulinischen Paränese (1961) 98f. THEISSEN, G. Psychologische Aspekte paulinischer Theologie (Göttingen 1983) 250, 269, 332.
8:2	BRUNNER, E. Dogmatik I (1946) 223; Mensch im Widerspruch (1937) 150. BEST, E. One Body in Christ (1955) 5, 24. BANDSTRA, A.J. The Law and the Elements of the World (1964) 108ff. JÜNGEL, E. Paulus und Jesus (1966) 52, 54f., 57, 59, 61f., 270. KERTELGE, K. "Rechtfertigung" bei Paulus (1967) 204, 223f. VAN DÜLMEN, A. Die Theologie des Gesetzes bei Paulus (1968) 25, 115, 119f., 123, 193, 204, 207, 219. LOHSE, E. "ὁ νόμος τοῦ πνεύμα-

τος τῆς ζωῆς. Exegetische Anmerkungen zu Röm 8, 2" in H. D. Betz and L. Schottroff, eds., Neues Testament und Christliche Existenz (FS H. Braun; Tübingen 1973) 279-87. KÜMMEL, W. G. Römer 7 und das Bild des Menschen im Neuen Testament (München 1974) 55, 61, 64f., 68, 109, 125, 190. LADD, G. E. A Theology of the New Testament (Grand Rapids 1974) 469, 492, 504, 518. DUNN, J. D. G. Jesus and the Spirit. A Study of the Religious and Charismatic Experience of Jesus and the First Christians as Reflected in the New Testament (London 1975) 201, 223, 241, 315, 322, 337. JÜNGEL, E. und RÖSSLER, D. Gefangenes Ich—befreiender Geist. Zwei Tübinger Römerbrief-Auslegungen (München 1976). FRIEDRICH, G. "Das Gesetz des Glaubens Römer 3, 27" in Auf das Wort kommt es an. Gesammelte Aufsätze (Göttingen 1978) 109, 111-3. GRUNDMANN, W. "Das Gesetz des Geistes und das Gesetz der Sünde" in Wandlungen im Verständnis des Heils (Berlin, DDR 1980) 25-46. RÄISÄNEN, H. "Das 'Gesetz des Glaubens' (Röm 3:27) und das 'Gesetz des Geistes' (Röm 8:2)," NTS 26 (1980) 101-17. SCHMITHALS, W. Die theologische Anthropologie des Paulus (Stuttgart 1980) 91f. DEIDUN, T. J. New Covenant Morality in Paul (Rome 1981) 193-203. CRANFIELD, C. E. B. "Changes of Person and Number in Paul's Epistles" in M. D. Hooker and S. G. Wilson, eds., Paul and Paulinism (FS C. K. Barrett; London 1982) 283. LOHSE, E. "Röm. 8, 2" in Die Vielfalt des Neuen Testaments. Exegetische Studien zur Theologie des Neuen Testaments (Göttingen 1982) 128-36. RÄISÄNEN, H. Paul and the Law (Tübingen 1983) 42, 50-3, 67, 78, 80, 150, 240f. THEISSEN, G. Psychologische Aspekte paulinischer Theologie (Göttingen 1983) 186, 204n.39, 227, 229, 251, 258, 259. MOHRLANG, R. Matthew and Paul (Cambridge 1984) 32, 116, 150, 152. STAAB, K. Pauluskommentare aus der griechischen Kirche (Münster ²1984) 90:14-15 Apoll; 133:17-31 ThM; 509:4-5 Phot. GRÄSSER, E. Der Alte Bund im Neuen (Tübingen 1985) 66, 80, 83, 85. SCHNABEL, E. J. Law and Wisdom from Ben Sira to Paul (Tübingen 1985) 266, 268, 270, 278, 286, 288-90, 293f., 314, 340f. RÄISÄNEN, H. The Torah and Christ (Helsinki 1986) 13, 95-118, 119-21, 144-7, 363. GERHARDSSON, B. "Eleutheria (Freedom) in the Bible" in B. P. Thompson, ed., Scripture: Meaning and Method (FS A. T. Hanson; Hull 1987) 15f., 23n.19. JONES, F. S. "Freiheit" in den Briefen des Apostels Paulus (Göttingen 1987) 52, 63, 66, 110, 122-6, 127-9, 135, 136, 139, 145, 147n.3, 198n.45, 219f.n.66, 221n.72. MERKLEIN, H. Studien zu Jesus und Paulus (Tübingen 1987) 85f., 88-90, 91, 104. OSTEN-SACKEN, P. VON DER, Evangelium und Tora: Aufsätze zu Paulus (München 1987) 87, 181, 198, 203f. BROWN, C. E. "'The Last Enemy Is Death'. Paul and the Pastoral Task," Interp 43 (4, 1989) 380-92. MARTIN, B. L. Christ and the Law in Paul (Leiden 1989) 14, 17, 26, 28-31, 52, 60, 67, 82, 92, 107, 109, 112, 114, 120, 143. OSTEN-SACKEN, P. VON DER, Die Heiligkeit der Tora (München 1989) 13-9. OLIVEIRA, A. DE, Die Diakonie der Gerechtigkeit und der Versöhnung in der Apologie des 2. Korintherbriefes. Analyse und Auslegung von 2 Kor 2, 14-4, 6; 5, 11-6, 10 (Münster 1990) 187n.506. LONGENECKER, B. W. Eschatology and the Covenant. A Comparison of 4 Ezra and Romans 1-11 (Sheffield 1991) 231-3, 235f., 243, 243n.3, 244, 244n.3, 272.

8:3ff.   HAYS, R. B. The Faith of Jesus Christ (Chico CA 1983) 123, 127.

8:3-8   DIBELIUS, M. Die Geisterwelt im Glauben des Paulus (1909) 110ff. BRAUN, H. Qumran und NT II (1966) 123, 160, 168, 170, 248, 256. ROBINSON, J. A. Pelagius's Exposition of Thirteen Epistles of St. Paul (Cambridge 1922) 48ff., 134. 8:3-4 BYRNE, B. "Sons of God"—"Seed of Abraham" (Rome 1979) 92-5.

KIM, S. The Origin of Paul's Gospel (Tübingen 1981) 131f. SCHWEIZER, E. "Paul's Christology and Gnosticism" in M. D. Hooker and S. G. Wilson, eds., Paul and Paulinism (FS C. K. Barrett; London 1982) 118f. STUHLMACHER, P. "Sühne oder Versöhnung? Randbemerkungen zu Gerhard Friedrichs Studie: 'Die Verkündigung des Todes Jesu im Neuen Testament'" in U. Luz und H. Weder, eds., Die Mitte des Neuen Testaments (FS E. Schweizer; Göttingen 1983) 298f. HELDERMANN, J. Die Anapausis im Evangelium Veritatis (Leiden 1984) 197. STAAB, K. Pauluskommentare aus der griechischen Kirche (Münster ²1984) 90:16-91:24 Apoll; 134:1-14ThM; 375:14-34 Genn. SCHNACKENBURG, R. Die sittliche Botschaft des Neuen Testaments, Band 1 (Freiburg/Basel/Wien 1986) 163. MERKLEIN, H. Studien zu Jesus und Paulus (Tübingen 1987) 32, 52, 73, 81, 84, 94, 248, 257, 268. LINDARS, B. "Paul and the Law in Romans 5-8. An Actantial Analysis" in B. Lindars, ed., Law and Religion (Cambridge 1988) 137. BREYTENBACH, C. Versöhnung (Neukirchen-Vluyn 1989) 159-65, 171. HOFIUS, O. Paulusstudien (Tübingen 1989) 68f., 120, 126. SCHWEIZER, E. Theologische Einleitung in das Neue Testament (Göttingen 1989) ß 5.6. MULLER, E. C. Trinity and Marriage in Paul (New York/Bern/Frankfurt/Paris 1990) 56f., 72f. LIPS, H. VON. "Christus als Sophia? Weisheitliche Traditionen in der urchristlichen Christologie" in C. Breytenbach und H. Paulsen, eds., Anfänge der Christologie (FS F. Hahn; Göttingen 1991) 75-95, esp.89f.

8:3-4   BRUNNER, E. Dogmatik I (1946) 304. JÜNGEL, E. Paulus und Jesus (1966) 60. DUNN, J.D.G. Baptism in the Holy Spirit (1970) 148. SCHWEIZER, E. Beiträge zur Theologie des Neuen Testaments (1970) 83-95. EICHHOLZ, G. Die Theologie des Paulus im Umriss (1972) 155ff.

8:3   BRUNNER, E. Dogmatik I (1946) 333, II (1950) 378, 415. LEIVESTAD, R. Christ the Conqueror (1954) 116ff., 119f. SEIDENSTICKER, Ph. Lebendiges Opfer (1954) 190ff., 197f. ROBINSON, J.M. Kerygma und historischer Jesus (1960) 107. ROMANIUK, K. L'Amour du Pere et du Fils dans la Soteriologie de Saint Paul (1961) 4, 20, 32, 45, 55, 116-17, 130, 191, 243. SCHWEIZER, E. Erniedrigung und Erhöhung bei Jesus und seinen Nachfolgern (1962) §9d. DELLING, G. Die Taufe im Neuen Testament (1963) 130. HAHN, F. Christologische Hoheitstitel (1963) 315f. KRAMER, W. Christos Kyrios Gottessohn (1963) §§ 25c, 55b. KÄSEMANN, E. Exegetische Versuche und Besinnungen I (1964) 75. LJUNGMAN, H. Pistis (1964) 73f. WHITELEY, D.E.H. "Hard Sayings—VIII. ROMANS 8.3" Theology 67 (525, '64) 114-16. HAHN, F. Das Verständnis der Mission im Neuen Testament (1965) 140. LORIMER, W.L. "Romans xiii.3, Hebrews iii.13" NTS 12 (12 4, '66) 389-91. KERTELGE, K. "Rechtfertigung" bei Paulus (1967) 102f., 135, 205, 256. STROBEL, A. Erkenntnis und Bekenntnis der Sünde in neutestamentlicher Zeit (1968) 57. VAN DÜLMEN, A. Die Theologie des Gesetzes bei Paulus (1968) 67, 117, 120ff., 138, 149, 163, 221, 250. GIAVINE, G. "'Damnavit peccatum in carne': Rom. 8, 3 nel sue contesto" RivB 17 (3, '69) 233-48. MAUSER, U. Gottesbild und Menschwerdung (1971) 141f., 163, 167-74, 176, 178, 181. JEWETT, R. Paul's Anthropological Terms (1971) 150-152. THORNTON, T.C.G. "The Meaning of *kai peri hamartias* in Romans viii.3" JThS 22 (2, '71) 515-17. ROBINSON, J. A. Pelagius's Exposition of Thirteen Epistles of St. Paul (Cambridge 1922) 122, 309, 315f. SCHELKLE, K. H. Die Passion Jesu in der Verkündigung des Neuen Testament (Heidelberg 1949) 155f. JOHNSON, H. The Humanity of the Saviour (London 1962) 107-10. DALTON, W. J. Christ's Proclamation to the Spirits. A Study of 1 Peter 3:18-4:6 (Rome 1965) 247. SHIMADA, K. The

Formulary Material in First Peter. A Study According to the Method of Traditionsgeschichte (Ann Arbor MI 1966) 320-4, 341. SCHILLE, G. "Die Liebe Gottes in Christus," ZNW 59 (1968) 230-44. MIRANDA, J. P. Der Vater, der mich gesandt hat (Bern/Frankfurt 1972) 28. KÜMMEL, W. G. Römer 7 und das Bild des Menschen im Neuen Testament (München 1974) 17f., 19, 50, 64, 71f. LADD, G. E. A Theology of the New Testament (Grand Rapids 1974) 161, 418f., 421, 424f., 506. LOHSE, E. Grundriss der neutestamentlichen Theologie (Stuttgart 1974) 55, 82, 92f. RIDDERBOS, H. Paul. An Outline of His Theology (Grand Rapids 1975) 168f. BÜHNER, J. A. Der Gesandte und sein Weg im 4. Evangelium (Tübingen 1977) 94f. DUNN, J. D. G. Unity and Diversity in the New Testament. An Inquiry into the Character of Earliest Christianity (London 1977) 295. VANNI, U. "Homoiōma in Paolo (Rm 1, 23; 5, 14; 6, 5; 8, 3; Fil 2, 7). Un'interpretazione esegetico-teologica alla luce dell'uso dei LXX—Ia Parte," Gregorianum 58 (1977) 321-45. DALY, R. J. Christian Sacrifice (Washington 1978) 238f. SCHMITHALS, W. "Zur Herkunft der gnostischen Elemente in der Sprache des Paulus" in B. Aland et al., eds., Gnosis (FS H. Jonas; Göttingen 1978) 403, 405. BYRNE, B. "Sons of God"—"Seed of Abraham" (Rome 1979) 6, 92f., 96, 122, 179, 199, 205, 207f., 214. FROITZHEIM, F. Christologie und Eschatologie bei Paulus (Würzburg 1979) 40f. DEMAREST, B. A. "Process Theology and the Pauline Doctrine of the Incarnation" in D. A. Hagner and M. J. Harris, eds., Pauline Studies (FS F. F. Bruce; Exeter 1980) 132f. DUNN, J. D. G. Christology in the Making (London 1980) 38, 42-6, 56, 64, 111f., 117f., 126f., 166, 285n.173, 328n.49, 347n.104. SCHMITHALS, W. Die theologische Anthropologie des Paulus (Stuttgart 1980) 93-101. WRIGHT, N. T. "The Meaning of περὶ ἁμαρτίας in Romans 8:3" in E. A. Livingstone, ed., Studia Biblica 1978, Vol. III: Papers on Paul and Other New Testament Authors (Sheffield 1980) 453-9. KIM, S. The Origin of Paul's Gospel (Tübingen 1981) 275-7. HAYS, R. B. The Faith of Jesus Christ (Chico CA 1983) 128, 136, 221. RÄISÄNEN, H. Paul and the Law (Tübingen 1983) 7, 53, 60, 67, 110, 118, 143, 152, 209, 240. SCHNACKENBURG, R. "Paulinische und johanneische Christologie, Ein Vergleich" in U. Luz und H. Weder, eds., Die Mitte des Neuen Testaments (FS E. Schweizer; Göttingen 1983) 222. KLEINKNECHT, K. T. Der leidende Gerechtfertigte (Tübingen 1984) 216. STAAB, K. Pauluskommentare aus der griechischen Kirche (Münster ²1984) 509:6-18 Phot. ADINOLFI, M. "L'invio del Figlio in Rom 8, 3," RivB 33 (3, 1985) 291-317. GRÄSSER, E. Der Alte Bund im Neuen (Tübingen 1985) 68, 70, 83, 132. SCHIMANOWSKI, G. Weisheit und Messias (Tübingen 1985) 327, 335. CRANFIELD, C. E. B. "Some Comments on Professor J. D. G. Dunn's *Christology in the Making* with Special Reference to the Evidence of the Epistle to the Romans" in L. D. Hurst and N. T. Wright, eds., The Glory of Christ in the New Testament (FS G. B. Caird; Oxford 1987) 270-2. GILLMAN, F. M. "Another Look at Romans 8:3. 'In the Likeness of Sinful Flesh'," CBQ 49 (4, 1987) 597-604. LAYTON, B. The Gnostic Scriptures (Garden City NY 1987) 259. SCHWEIZER, E. Jesus Christ. The Man from Nazareth and the Exalted Lord (Macon GA 1987) 19, 78. WERBICK, J. "Die Soteriologie zwischen 'christologischem Triumphalismus' und apokalyptischem Radikalismus" in I. Broer und J. Werbick, eds., "Auf Hoffnung hin sind wir erlöst" (Röm 8, 14) (Stuttgart 1987) 161f. MERKLEIN, H. Studien zu Jesus und Paulus (Tübingen 1987) 34, 39, 89-91, 92, 94, 187, 191, 258n.66. JONGE, M. DE, Christology in Context. The Earliest Christian Response to Jesus (Philadelphia 1988) 114, 118, 121, 191. BREYTENBACH, C. "Oor die vertaling van

. . . in Romeine 8:3 (On the translation of . . . in Romans 8:3)," HTS 45 (1989) 30-3. BREYTENBACH, C. Versöhnung (Neukirchen-Vluyn 1989) 34, 127, 138, 140f., 159, 161-5, 169f., 170n., 171, 181, 195, 197, 201-3, 211, 213f. HOFIUS, O. Paulusstudien (Tübingen 1989) 55, 63, 68, 113, 159. MARTIN, B. L. Christ and the Law in Paul (Leiden 1989) 17, 19, 31, 38, 40, 43, 53, 70, 72, 82, 85, 92, 95f., 104f., 108, 111f., 134f., 156. VOLLENWEIDER, S. Freiheit als neue Schöpfung (Göttingen 1989) 302, 307n., 357. HOOKER, M. D. From Adam to Christ. Essays on Paul (Cambridge 1990) 3, 19, 22, 27. MULLER, E. C. Trinity and Marriage in Paul (New York/Bern/Frankfurt/Paris 1990) 55, 90, 101, 412f. OLIVEIRA, A. DE, Die Diakonie der Gerechtigkeit und der Versöhnung im Apologie des 2. Korintherbriefes. Analyse und Auslegung von 2 Kor 2, 14-4, 6; 5, 11-6, 10 (Münster 1990) 392. GREENE, M. D. "A Note on Romans 8:3" BZ 35 (1991) 103-6. KRAUS, W. Der Tod Jesu als Heiligtumsweihe. Eine Untersuchung zum Umfeld der Sühnevorstellung in Römer 3, 25-26a (Neukirchen-Vluyn 1991) 42n., 43n., 169n., 170, 190ff., 193, 277n. SCHWEIZER, E. "What Do We Really Mean When We Say 'God sent his son . . . ' ?" in J. T. Carroll et al., eds., Faith and History (FS P. W. Meyer; Atlanta 1991) 298-312.

8:4ff. DUNN, J. D. G. Jesus and the Spirit. A Study of the Religious and Charismatic Experience of Jesus and the First Christians as Reflected in the New Testament (London 1975) 315.

8:4ff.   MINEAR, P.S. Images of the Church in the New Testament (1960) 143f.

8:4-13   ROBINSON, J.M. Kerygma und historischer Jesus (1960) 107.

8:4-9   MARTIN, B. L. Christ and the Law in Paul (Leiden 1989) 31, 107, 112, 124, 127, 134, 156.

8:4-7   BANDSTRA, A.J. The Law and the Elements of the World (1964) 132ff.

8:4-5   SCHRAGE, W. Die konkreten Einzelgebote in der paulinischen Paränese (1961) 50, 73f., 76, 98, 167, 232. JÜNGEL, E. Paulus und Jesus (1966) 63.

8:4   DENNEY, J. The Death of Christ (1956) 109. FAHY, T. "Romans 8:3-4" IThQ 25 (4'58) 387. SCHARLEMANN, M.H. "'In the Likeness of Sinful Flesh'" CThM 32 (3, '61) 133-38. SEVENSTER, J.M. Paul and Seneca (1961) 79, 81. STANLEY, D.M. Christ's Resurrection in Pauline Soteriology (1961) 189-92. DELLING, G. Die Taufe im Neuen Testament (1963) 122. BANDSTRA, A.J. The Law and the Elements of the World (1964) 106ff. BLANK, J. Paulus und Jesus (1968) 279f., 287-94. LAUB, F. Eschatologische Verkündigung und Lebensgestaltung nach Paulus (Regensburg 1973) 51, 62, 93, 199. KÜMMEL, W. G. Römer 7 und das Bild des Menschen im Neuen Testament (München 1974) 10, 25, 72, 110, 180, 189, 191. LOHSE, E. Grundriss der neutestamentlichen Theologie (Stuttgart 1974) 97f. RIDDERBOS, H. Paul. An Outline of His Theology (Grand Rapids 1975) 279-81. GUNDRY, R. H. Soma in Biblical Theology with Emphasis on Pauline Anthropology (Cambridge 1976) 138f. SANDT, H. W. M. VAN DE. "Research into Rom. 8, 4a: The Legal Claim of the Law," Bijdr 37 (1976) 252-69. SANDT, H. W. M. VAN DE. "An Explanation of Rom. 8, 4a," Bijdr 37 (1976) 361-78. BYRNE, B. "Sons of God"— "Seed of Abraham" (Rome 1979) 93-5. SCHMITHALS, W. Die theologische Anthropologie des Paulus (Stuttgart 1980) (Stuttgart 1980) 101-4. RÄISÄNEN, H. Paul and the Law (Tübingen 1983) 28, 63f., 65-7, 70, 104f., 113-5, 139, 240-42. SANDERS, E. P. Paul, the Law, and the Jewish People (London 1985) 55n.44, 83, 89n.32, 93f.100, 103f., 116n.16, 161. SCHNABEL, E. J. Law and Wisdom from Ben Sira to Paul (Tübingen 1985) 280, 290, 294, 305, 327. RÄISÄNEN, H. The Torah and Christ (Helsinki 1986) 8, 12, 20. THOMPSON, R. W. "How is the Law Fulfilled in Us? An Interpretation of Rom 8:4," LSt 11

(1986) 31-40. MERKLEIN, H. Studien zu Jesus und Paulus (Tübingen 1987) 33, 90f., 94, 103. SCHULZ, S. "Neutestamentliche Ethik (Zürich 1987) 148. ZIESLER, J. A. "The Just Requirement of the Law (Romans 8:4)," AusBR 35 (1987) 77-82. MARTIN, B. L. Christ and the Law in Paul (Leiden 1989) 2, 14, 17, 19, 29, 30-2, 34, 60, 82f., 90f., 105, 108, 112, 120, 128, 132, 135, 137, 143, 148f., 152. THIELMAN, F. From Plight to Solution (Leiden 1989) 88-90, 100, 102. DUNN, J. D. G. Jesus, Paul and the Law (London 1990) 106, 209, 212, 224, 240. HOOKER, M. D. From Adam to Christ. Essays on Paul (Cambridge 1990) 60f. LONGENECKER, B. W. Eschatology and the Covenant. A Comparison of 4 Ezra and Romans 1-11 (Sheffield 1991) 185f., 227, 233, 233n.1, 234-6, 240f., 244n.1, 245, 247, 271.

8:5-13   ROBINSON, J. A. T. Wrestling with Romans (London 1979) 96-9.

8:5-11   IWAND, H.-J. Predigt-Meditationen (1964) 605-9.

8:5-10   RUDOLPH, K. Die Gnosis (Göttingen 1978) 320.

8:5-8   LINDARS, B. "Paul and the Law in Romans 5-8. An Actantial Analysis" in B. Lindars, ed., Law and Religion (Cambridge 1988) 137. THISELTON, A. C. The Two Horizons (Grand Rapids 1980) 278.

8:5-6   SCHMITHALS, W. Die theologische Anthropologie des Paulus (Stuttgart 1980) 104f.

8:5   JEWETT, R. Paul's Anthropological Terms (1971) 156-57. BAUMERT, N. Täglich Sterben und Auferstehen. Der Literalsinn von 2 Kor 4, 12-5, 10 (München 1973) 408.

8:6-7   KÜMMEL, W. G. Römer 7 und das Bild des Menschen im Neuen Testament (München 1974) 193f. DELLING, G. "Frieden" in TRE 11 (1983) 616.

8:6   STACEY, W.D. The Pauline View of Man (1956) 162f. KERTELGE, K. "Rechtfertigung" bei Paulus (1967) 214, 265. NICKELS, P. Targum and New Testament (1967) 69 STROBEL, A. Erkenntnis und Bekenntnis der Sünde in neutestamentlicher Zeit (1968) 51. SCHNEIDER, N. Die rhetorische Eigenart der paulinischen Antithese (1970) 93-95. LADD, G. E. A Theology of the New Testament (Grand Rapids 1974) 469, 473, 568.

8:7-8   SCHMITHALS, W. Die theologische Anthropologie des Paulus (Stuttgart 1980) 106f. STAAB, K. Pauluskommentare aus der griechischen Kirche (Münster ²1984) 376:8-14 Genn. LIEBERS, R. Das Gesetz als Evangelium (Zürich 1989) 182-6.

8:6   LADD, G. E. A Theology of the New Testament (Grand Rapids 1974) 469, 473, 568.

8:7-8   SCHMITHALS, W. Die theologische Anthropologie des Paulus (Stuttgart 1980) 106f. STAAB, K. Pauluskommentare aus der griechischen Kirche (Münster ²1984) 376:8-14 Genn. LIEBERS, R. Das Gesetz als Evangelium (Zürich 1989) 182-6.

8:7   BRUNNER, E. Dogmatik I (1946) 197, II (1950) 105, 107. Mensch im Widerspruch (1937) 127. STALDER, K. Das Werk des Geistes in der Heiligung bei Paulus (1962) 419f., 421f. KÜMMEL, W. G. Römer 7 und das Bild des Menschen im Neuen Testament (München 1974) 18f., 20, 61. LADD, G. E. A Theology of the New Testament (Grand Rapids 1974) 454, 495, 504. THISELTON, A. C. The Two Horizons (Grand Rapids 1980) 394f., 410. STAAB, K. Pauluskommentare aus der griechischen Kirche (Münster ²1984) 509:19-27 Phot. OSTEN-SACKEN, P. VON DER, Evangelium und Tora: Aufsätze zu Paulus (München 1987) 18f., 99. SNODGRASS, K. "Spheres of Influence. A Possible Solution to the Problem of Paul and the Law," JSNT 32 (1988) 93-

113. MARTIN, B. L. Christ and the Law in Paul (Leiden 1989) 17, 19, 31, 35, 46, 52, 104, 107, 107, 137, 142.

8:8-11 WIKENHAUSER, A. Die Christusmystik des Apostels Paulus (1956) 5, 20, 37f., 166.

8:8-9 DELLING, G. Die Taufe im Neuen Testament (1963) 122.

8:8 SCHRAGE, W. Die konkreten Einzelgebote in der paulinischen Paränese (1961) 85. BAUMERT, N. Täglich Sterben und Auferstehen. Der Literalsinn von 2 Kor 4, 12-5, 10 (München 1973) 408. JEWETT, P. K. Infant Baptism and the Covenant of Grace (Grand Rapids 1978) 223. THISELTON, A. C. The Two Horizons (Grand Rapids 1980) 394f., 410.

8:9ff. FEINE, P. Der Apostel Paulus (1927) 590f. MINEAR, P.S. Images of the Church in the New Testament (1960) 175f. RÖHSER, G. Metaphorik und Personifikation der Sünde (Tübingen 1987) 119f., 125f.

8:9-39 Paul's Literary Style. A Stylistic and Historical Comparison of II Corinthians 11:16-12:13, Romans 8:9-39, and Philippians 3:2-4:13

8:9-17 CRANFIELD, C. E. B. "Changes of Person and Number in Paul's Epistles" in M. D. Hooker and S. G. Wilson, eds., Paul and Paulinism (FS C. K. Barrett; London 1982) 284.

8:9-16 DAVIES, S. L. The Gospel of Thomas and Christian Wisdom (New York 1983) 48.

8:9-15 EICHHOLZ, G. Die Theologie des Paulus im Umriss (1972) 263, 274f., 275f.

8:9-14 LAMBRECHT, J. "Christus muss König sein," IKZ/Communio 13 (1984) 18-26.

8:9,11-13 BAULÈS, R. "Vivre selon l'esprit. Rm 8, 9.11-13," AssS 45 (1974) 10-5.

8:9-11 SOKOLOWSKI, E. Die Begriffe Geist und Leben bei Paulus (1903) 48ff., 54ff. SCHWEITZER, A. Die Mystik des Apostels Paulus (1954) 4f., 120, 122f., 143, 165f. CERFAUX, L. Christ in the Theology of St. Paul (1959)288, 386, 291, 322, 65, 492. PFAMMATTER, J. Die Kirche als Bau (1960) 67f. HERMANN, I. Kyrios und Pneuma (1961) 65-66, 110. THUESING, W. Per Christum in Deum (1965) 152f., 156f. GÜTTGEMANNS, E. Der leidende Apostel und sein Herr (1966) 271-79. DUNN, J. D. G. Jesus and the Spirit. A Study of the Religious and Charismatic Experience of Jesus and the First Christians as Reflected in the New Testament (London 1975) 323. GAFFIN, R. B. The Centrality of the Resurrection (Grand Rapids 1978) 66-8. FROITZHEIM, F. Christologie und Eschatologie bei Paulus (Würzburg 1979) 219f. SCHMITHALS, W. Die theologische Anthropologie des Paulus (Stuttgart 1980) 107-17. BYRNE, B. "Living out the Righteousness of God. The Contribution of Rom 6:1-8:13 to an Understanding of Paul's Ethical Presuppositions," CBQ 43 (1981) 570-80. MOULE, C. F. D. "Jesus of Nazareth and the Church's Lord" in U. Luz und H. Weder, eds., Die Mitte des Neuen Testaments (FS E. Schweizer; Göttingen 1983) 181. CRANFIELD, C. E. B. "Some Comments on Professor J. D. G. Dunn's *Christology in the Making* with Special Reference to the Evidence of the Epistle to the Romans" in L. D. Hurst and N. T. Wright, eds., The Glory of Christ in the New Testament (FS G. B. Caird; Oxford 1987) 272. WEDDERBURN, A. J. M. Baptism and Resurrection (Tübingen 1987) 267f. LINDARS, B. "Paul and the Law in Romans 5-8. An Actantial Analysis" in B. Lindars, ed., Law and Religion (Cambridge 1988) 137f.

8:9-10 RIDDERBOS, H. Paul. An Outline of His Theology (Grand Rapids 1975) 66-8. SCHMITHALS, W. "Zur Herkunft der gnostischen Elemente in der Sprache des Paulus" in B. Aland et al., eds., Gnosis (FS H. Jonas; Göttingen 1978) 388-90. STAAB, K. Pauluskommentare aus der griechischen Kirche (Münster ²1984)

376:23-377:5 Genn; 509:28-510:4 Phot. PARROTT, D. M. "First Jesus Is Present, Then the Spirit. An Early Christian Dogma and Its Effects" in J. E. Goehring et al., eds., Gospel Origins & Christian Beginnings (FS J. M. Robinson; Sonoma CA 1990) 119-33, esp.127.

8:9,10 KENNEDY, H.A.A. St. Paul and the Mystery-Religions (1913) 136, 289. STACEY, W.D. The Pauline View of Man (1956) 130f., 164, 179, 135f., 187. DELLING, G. Die Taufe im Neuen Testament (1963) 58, 132.

8:9 BRUNNER, E. Dogmatik I (1946) 38. BEST, E. One Body in Christ (1955) II nn., 12n. SANDMEL, S. The Genius of Paul (1958) 83-84. SCHWEIZER, E. Gemeinde und Gemeinde-Ordnung (1959) §7k. SCHRAGE, W. Die konkreten Einzelgebote in der paulinsichen Paränese (1961) 15, 71, 73f. STALDER, K. Das Werk des Geistes in der Heiligung bei Paulus (1962) 418f., 429f., 435f. KÄSEMANN, E. Exegetische Versuche und Besinnungen (1964) I 154. DUNN, J. D. G. Baptism in the Holy Spirit (1970)47, 55, 86, 88n, 115n, 148f., 150, 170. BOHREN, R. Predigtlehre (München 1971) 124. KÜMMEL, W. G. Römer 7 und das Bild des Menschen im Neuen Testament (München 1974) 18, 28, 32, 104. LADD, G. E. A Theology of the New Testament (Grand Rapids 1974) 452, 461, 471, 473, 483f. LOHSE, E. Grundriss der neutestamentlichen Theologie (Stuttgart 1974) 96f. DUNN, J. D. G. Jesus and the Spirit. A Study of the Religious and Charismatic Experience of Jesus and the First Christians as Reflected in the New Testament (London 1975) 142, 201f., 260, 287, 312, 318, 336. FRIEDRICH, G. "Die Kirche zu Korinth" in Auf das Wort kommt es an. Gesammelte Aufsätze (Göttingen 1978) 143. SAUTER, G. "Geist und Freiheit. Geistvorstellungen und die Erwartung des Geistes," EvTh 41 (1981) 217. CRANFIELD, C. E. B. "Changes of Person and Number in Paul's Epistles" in M. D. Hooker and S. G. Wilson, eds., Paul and Paulinism (FS C. K. Barrett; London 1982) 281f. HAYS, R. B. The Faith of Jesus Christ (Chico CA 1983) 107. MOHRLANG, R. Matthew and Paul (Cambridge 1984) 61, 115, 117. STAAB, K. Pauluskommentare aus der griechischen Kirche (Münster ²1984) 91:25-31 Diod; 135:10-30 ThM; 220:14 Sev; 376:15-22 Genn; 427:16 Oek. ELLIS, E. E. Pauline Theology (Grand Rapids/Exeter 1989) 3, 8, 30ff., 56.

8:10ff.
8:10-11 BRUNNER, E. Dogmatik I (1946) 226. NÖTSCHER, F. Altorientalischer und alttestamentlicher Auferstehungsglaube (Darmstadt 1970=1926) 304, 311. SCHELKLE, K. H. Die Passion Jesu in der Verkündigung des Neuen Testament (Heidelberg 1949) 259, 262f., 266. RICHTER, H.-F. Auferstehung und Wirklichkeit (Berlin 1969) 77f. PAGELS, E. H. The Gnostic Paul. Gnostic Exegesis of the Pauline Letters (Philadelphia 1975) 34. GUNDRY, R. H. Soma in Biblical Theology with Emphasis on Pauline Anthropology (Cambridge 1976) 37-46. FROITZHEIM, F. Christologie und Eschatologie bei Paulus (Würzburg 1979) 242ff. LANDAU, R. "Komm, Heiliger Geist, du Tröster wert . . . " EvTh 41 (1981) 193-9. HARRIS, M. J. Raised Immortal (London 1986) 145f.

8:10,11 BEST, E. One Body in Christ (1955) 9n, 10, 218. BAUER, K.-A. Leiblichkeit das Ende aller Werke Gottes (1971) 161-66. SPOERLEIN, B. Die Leugnung der Auferstehung (1971) 160-64. SCHRAGE, W. Die konkreten Einzelgebote in der paulinischen Paränese (1961) 15, 51, 80.

8:10 FORTNA, R.T. "Romans 8:10 and Paul's Doctrine of the Spirit" AThR 41 (2, '59) 77-84. JÜNGEL, E. Paulus und Jesus (1966) 32, 39, 41, 42, 61. KERTEL-GE, K. "Rechtfertigung" bei Paulus (1967) 128, 155-57. DUNN, J.D.G. Baptism in the Holy Spirit (1970) 107, 148, 149, 150, 156, 161. SIBER, P. Mit Christus leben (Zürich 1971) 81-3. DUNN, J. D. G. "I Corinthians 15:45—Last

Adam, Life-giving Spirit" in B. Lindars and S. S. Smalley, eds., Christ and the Spirit in the New Testament (FS C. F. D. Moule; Cambridge 1973) 132, 134, 136. KÜMMEL, W. G. Römer 7 und das Bild des Menschen im Neuen Testament (München 1974) 23, 31f. LADD, G. E. A Theology of the New Testament (Grand Rapids 1974) 369, 461, 463, 493, 525, 551. DUNN, J. D. G. Jesus and the Spirit. A Study of the Religious and Charismatic Experience of Jesus and the First Christians as Reflected in the New Testament (London 1975) 108, 314, 315f., 326, 338, 354. BYRNE, B. "Sons of God"—"Seed of Abraham" (Rome 1979) 90n., 92, 94, 96. FULLER, R. H. "Jesus Christ as Savior in the New Testament," Interp 35 (1981) 152. BERGER, K. und COLPE, C., eds., Religionsgeschichtliches Textbuch zum Neuen Testament (Göttingen/Zürich 1987) 218.

8:11-16   SCHWEIZER, E. Heiliger Geist (Berlin 1978) 155.
8:11-14   SCHNACKENBURG, R. Baptism in the Thought of St. Paul (1964) 38, 112, 166, 189, 198, 201, 163f. DUPONT, J. Essais sur la christologie de saint Jean (Bruges 1951 68f.
8:11-12   STALDER, K. Das Werk des Geistes in der Heiligung bei Paulus (1962) passim.
8:11   KUSS, O. Der Römerbrief (1957) 506-40, 540-95. HAHN, F. Christologische Hoheitstitel (1963) 204, 208, 210. KOCH, R. "L'aspect Eschatologiques de l'Esprit du Seigneur d'apres Saint Paul" Studiorum Paulinorum Congressus Internationalis Catholicus 1961 (1963) I 137-38. BRAUMANN, G. Vorpaulinische christliche Taufverkündigung bei Paulus (1962) 53f. KRAMER, W. Christos Kyrios Gottessohn (1963) §§ 3c, 62g, 3c, , 62g. MUSSNER, F. Die Auferstehung Jesu (1969) 114f. DUNN, J.D.G. Baptism in the Holy Spirit (1970) 143, 148, 150. MAUSER, U. Gottesbild und Menschwerdung (1971) 126, 133f., 142. SIBER, P. Mit Christus Leben (1972) 80-86. BOHREN, R. Wiedergeburt des Wunders (1972) 108-15. DALTON, W. J. Christ's Proclamation to the Spirits. A Study of 1 Peter 3:18-4:6 (Rome 1965) 126, 129. ELLIS, E. E. "Christ and Spirit in I Corinthians" in B. Lindars and S. S. Smalley, eds., Christ and the Spirit in the New Testament (FS C. F. D. Moule; Cambridge 1973) 269f., 275. CAVALLIN, H. C. C. Life After Death. Paul's Argument for the Resurrection of the Dead in I Cor 15. Part I: An Enquiry into the Jewish Background (Lund 1974) In.9, 4, In.31, 4, 9n.II. LADD, G. E. A Theology of the New Testament (Grand Rapids 1974) 409, 463, 488, 563f. SCHMITHALS, W. Der Römerbrief als historisches Problem (Gütersloh 1975) 200. GUNDRY, R. H. Soma in Biblical Theology with Emphasis on Pauline Anthropology (Cambridge 1976) 78f., 220f. SCHWEIZER, E. Heiliger Geist (Berlin 1978) 151. FRIEDRICH, G. "Die Bedeutung der Auferweckung Jesu nach Aussagen des Neuen Testaments" in Auf das Wort kommt es an. Gesammelte Aufsätze (Göttingen 1978) 357. GAFFIN, R. B. The Centrality of the Resurrection (Grand Rapids 1978) 66-8. FROITZHEIM, F. Christologie und Eschatologie bei Paulus (Würzburg 1979) 79ff. HOFFMANN, P. "Auferstehung" in TRE 4 (1979) 479. DUNN, J. D. G. Christology in the Making (London 1980) 139, 143-5. SÄNGER, D. Antikes Judentum und die Mysterien (Tübingen 1980) 153. MÜNCHOW, C. Ethik und Eschatologie (Göttingen 1981) 153f., 170. ROCHAIS, G. Les récits de résurrection des morts dans le Nouveau Testament (Cambridge 1981) 188. SAUTER, G. "Geist und Freiheit. Geistvorstellungen und die Erwartung des Geistes," EvTh 41 (1981) 215. BERGER, K. "Geist" in TRE 12 (1984) 189. STAAB, K. Pauluskommentare aus der griechischen Kirche (Münster ²1984) 92:1-8 Diod; 377:6-9 Genn. SCHIMANOWSKI, G.

Weisheit und Messias (Tübingen 1985) 260. SCHNACKENBURG, R. Die
sittliche Botschaft des Neuen Testaments, Band 1 (Freiburg/Basel/Wien 1986)
164. SELLIN, G. Der Streit um die Auferstehung der Toten (Göttingen 1986)
29, 38n., 47n., 80f., 229. OSTEN-SACKEN, P. VON DER, Evangelium und
Tora: Aufsätze zu Paulus (München 1987) 62f., 84, 86f.

8:12ff.   WETTER, G.P. Der Vergeltungsgedanke bei Paulus (1912) 100ff. STROBEL,
             A. Erkenntnis und Bekenntnis der Sünde in neutestamentlicher Zeit (1968) 51.
             BERGER, K. "Geist" in TRE 12 (1984) 195.

8:12-30   GEORGI, D. Theocracy in Paul's Praxis and Theology (Minneapolis 1991)
             100f. ALSUP, J. "Translation as Interpretation and Communication," Insights
             108 (1993) 15-23.

8:12-22   BERGER, K. Exegese des Neuen Testaments. Neue Wege vom Text zur
             Auslegung (Heidelberg 1977) 55-7.

8:12-17   STECK, K.G. GPM 5 (1951) 166-69. SEVENSTER, J.N. Paul and Seneca
             (1961) 35, 51, 60, 80, 159. SURKAU, H.W. GPM 16 (1962) 257-61. FRICK,
             R. GPM 10 (1956) 187-92. PFISTER, W. Das Leben im Geist nach Paulus
             (1963) 70-87. NIESEL, W. in Herr, tue meine Lippen auf (1966) 388-93.
             DORENE, M. Die alten Episteln (1967) 180-84. TRAUB, H. GPM 22
             (1967/68) 330-37. VOEGTLE, A. Das Neuen Testament und die Zukunft des
             Kosmos (1970) 190f. PAULSEN, H. Ueberlieferung und Auslegung von Römer
             8 (Neukirchen-Vluyn 1974) 77-106. SCHMITHALS, W. Die theologische
             Anthropologie des Paulus (Stuttgart 1980) 117-37. LANDAU, R. "Komm,
             Heiliger Geist, du Tröster wert . . . " EvTh 41 (1981) 199-202. LYALL, F.
             "Legal Metaphors in the Epistles," TB 32 (1981) 81-95. CAMBIER, J.-M. "La
             Liberté du Spirituel dans Rom. 8.12-17" in M. D. Hooker and S. G. Wilson,
             eds., Paul and Paulinism (FS C. K. Barrett; London 1982) 205-20. BINDE-
             MANN, W. Die Hoffnung der Schöpfung (Neukirchen 1983) 33-42. PERKINS,
             P. Resurrection. New Testament Witness and Contemporary Reflection (London
             1984) 270.

8:12-15   PAGELS, E. H. The Gnostic Paul. Gnostic Exegesis of the Pauline Letters
             (Philadelphia 1975) 34f.

8:12-14   STALDER, K. Das Werk des Geistes in der Heiligung bei Paulus (1962)
             passim.

8:12-13   SCHRAGE, W. Die konkreten Einzelgebote in der paulinischen Paränese (1961)
             32, 74. DELLING, G. Die Taufe im Neuen Testament (1963) 122, 148.
             KÜMMEL, W. G. Römer 7 und das Bild des Menschen im Neuen Testament
             (München 1974) 11, 18, 104. DUNN, J. D. G. Jesus and the Spirit. A Study of
             the Religious and Charismatic Experience of Jesus and the First Christians as
             Reflected in the New Testament (London 1975) 315. SCHMITHALS, W. Die
             theologische Anthropologie des Paulus (Stuttgart 1980) 118-25. BYRNE, B.
             "Living out the Righteousness of God. The Contribution of Rom 6:1-8:13 to an
             Understanding of Paul's Ethical Presuppositions," CBQ 43 (1981) 580.
             CAMBIER, J.-M. "La Liberté du Spirituel dans Rom. 8.12-17" in M. D.
             Hooker and S. G. Wilson, eds., Paul and Paulinism (FS C. K. Barrett; London
             1982) 206-8. STAAB, K. Pauluskommentare aus der griechischen Kirche (Mün-
             ster ²1984) 377:10-20 Genn. BERGER, K. und COLPE, C., eds., Religions-
             geschichtliches Textbuch zum Neuen Testament (Göttingen/Zürich 1987) 218.

8:12   DIBELIUS, M. "Vier Worte des Römerbriefs" in Symbolae Biblicae Up-
             salienses 3 (Uppsala 1944) 3-17. THISELTON, A. C. The Two Horizons
             (Grand Rapids 1980) 278. SCHNACKENBURG, R. Die sittliche Botschaft des
             Neuen Testaments, Band 1 (Freiburg/Basel/Wien 1986) 163.

8:13-17　　LINDARS, B. "Paul and the Law in Romans 5-8. An Actantial Analysis" in B. Lindars, ed., Law and Religion (Cambridge 1988) 138f. SCHWEIZER, E. Heiliger Geist (Berlin 1978) 116f.

8:13　　FEINE, P. Der Apostel Paulus (1927) 581f. BEST, E. One Body in Christ (1955) 217f., 218. JÜNGEL, E. Paulus und Jesus (1966) 57, 63. KERTELGE, K. "Rechtfertigung" bei Paulus (1967) 150f. STROBEL, A. Erkenntnis und Bekenntnis der Sünde in neutestamentlicher Zeit (1968) 66. SIBER, P. Mit Christus leben (Zürich 1971) 183. HAINZ, J. Ekklesia (Regensburg 1972) 327f. KÜMMEL, W. G. Römer 7 und das Bild des Menschen im Neuen Testament (München 1974) 18, 23, 25, 52, 78, 104, 193. LADD, G. E. A Theology of the New Testament (Grand Rapids 1974) 456, 474, 493, 525. THISELTON, A. C. The Two Horizons (Grand Rapids 1980) 394f., 410. BINDEMANN, W. Die Hoffnung der Schöpfung (Neukirchen 1983) 34. MOHRLANG, R. Matthew and Paul (Cambridge 1984) 60, 84, 117, 120.

8:14-11:36　　ELLIOT, N. The Rhetoric of Romans (Sheffield 1990) 253-70, 272.

8:14ff.　　DUNN, J. D. G. Jesus and the Spirit. A Study of the Religious and Charismatic Experience of Jesus and the First Christians as Reflected in the New Testament (London 1975) 319f., 321.

8:14-39　　HELEWA, G. "'Fedele è Dio'. Una lettura di Rom 8, 14-39," Teresianum 37 (1986) 3-36; 38 (1987) 3-49. VOLF, J. M. G. Paul and Perseverance (Tübingen 1990) 161, 161nn.1-7.

8:14-25　　BOISMARD, M.E. Quatre Hymnes Baptismales (1961) 47-53. MOUNCE, W. D. The Origin of the New Testament Metaphor of Rebirth (Ph.D. diss. University of Aberdeen 1981) 221f.

8:14-23　　THUESLING, W. Per Christum in Deum (1965) 119ff. MIRANDA, J. P. Marx and the Bible. A Critique of the Philosophy of Oppression (London 1977) 274-7.

8:14-17　　STALDER, K. Das Werk des Geistes in der Heiligung bei Paulus (1962) 469-87. LUZ, U. Das Geschichtsverständnis des Paulus (1968) 374f. DUNN, J.D.G. Baptism in the Holy Spirit (1970) 149f. BAULES, R. "Fils et héritiers de Dieu dans l'Esprit. Rm 8, 14-17," AssS 31 (1973) 22-7. MONTAGUE, G. T. The Holy Spirit (New York 1976) 208f. BYRNE, B. "Sons of God"—"Seed of Abraham" (Rome 1979) 97-103. ROBINSON, J. A. T. Wrestling with Romans (London 1979) 99f. DUNN, J. D. G. Christology in the Making (London 1980) 44, 58, 145. GENEST, H. and WALTER, N. in GPM 34 (1980) 353-60. WREGE, H.-T. und CHRISTIANSEN, R. in P. Krusche et al., eds., Predigtstudien für das Kirchenjahr 1980. Perikopenreihe II/2 (Stuttgart 1980) 198-205. SCHMITHALS, W. Die theologische Anthropologie des Paulus (Stuttgart 1980) 125-37. COFFEY, D. "The 'Incarnation' of the Holy Spirit in Christ," ThSt 45 (1984) 466-80, esp.475f. HELDERMANN, J. Die Anapausis im Evangelium Veritatis (Leiden 1984) 197. HASSELAAR, J. M. in GPM 40 (1985/86) 410-6. SCHÄFER, K. Gemeinde als "Bruderschaft" (Frankfurt/Bern/New York/Paris 1989) 41-80. VOLLENWEIDER, S. Freiheit als neue Schöpfung (Göttingen 1989) 303.

8:14-15　　JÜNGEL, E. Paulus und Jesus (1966) 64. BLANK, J. Paulus und Jesus (1968) 258ff.

8:14-16　　THISELTON, A. C. The Two Horizons (Grand Rapids 1980) 90, 395. CAMBIER, J.-M. "La Liberté du Spirituel dans Rom. 8:12-17" in M. D. Hooker and S. G. Wilson, eds., Paul and Paulinism (FS C. K. Barrett; London 1982) 209-13.

8:14   CAMILLERI, N. "Teologia pneumatica della prudenza cristiana" Studioirum Paulinorum Congressus Internationalis Catholicus 1961 I (1963) 175-85. SCHRAGE, W. Die konkreten Einzelgebote in der paulinischen Paränese (1961) 15, 71. HAINZ, J. Ekklesia (Regensburg 1972) 327f. LADD, G. E. A Theology of the New Testament (Grand Rapids 1974) 160, 461, 488, 519. HOFIUS, O. "Agrapha" in TRE 2 (1978) 106. SAUTER, G. "Geist und Freiheit. Geistvorstellungen und die Erwartung des Geistes," EvTh 41 (1981) 215. BINDEMANN, W. Die Hoffnung der Schöpfung (Neukirchen 1983) 34f. THEISSEN, G. Psychologische Aspekte paulinischer Theologie (Göttingen 1983) 276, 307, 318. HELDERMANN, J. Die Anapausis im Evangelium Veritatis (Leiden 1984) 270n.673. STAAB, K. Pauluskommentare aus der griechischen Kirche (Münster ²1984) 135:31-32 ThM; 377:21-29 Genn. NICOL, W. "Hoe direk lei die Gees? 'n Dogmatiese en eksegetiese ondersoek rondom Romeine 8:14" [How directly does the Spirit lead? A systematic and exegetical investigation of Romans 8:14], Skrif en Kerk (2, 1986) 173-97. I. Broer und J. Werbick, eds., "Auf Hoffnung hin sind wir erlöst" (Röm 8, 14) (Stuttgart 1987). GEBAUER, R. Das Gebet bei Paulus (Giessen/Basel 1989) 144ff., 152, 154, 158, 161, 218, 307, 316.

8:15-30   SIBER, P. Mit Christus leben (Zürich 1971) 135-68. CULLMANN. "La prière selon les Epitres pauliniennes," Tantur Yearbook (Jerusalem 1977/78) 67-82.

8:15-26   BEINTKER, H. "Gott VII" in TRE 13 (1984) 663.

8:15-23   DAVIES, W.D. Paul and Rabbinic Judaism (1955) 36-38, 40, 58, 88, 139, 185, 318f.

8:15-17   DELLING, G. Die Taufe im Neuen Testament (1963) 120, 144, 152. SIBER, P. Mit Christus leben (Zürich 1971) 135-8, 160. DELLING, G. "Die 'Söhne (Kinder) Gottes' im Neuen Testament" in R. Schnackenburg et al., eds., Die Kirche des Anfangs (FS H. Schürmann; Freiburg/Basel/Wien 1978) 616-8. STAAB, K. Pauluskommentare aus der griechischen Kirche (Münster ²1984) 510:5-23 Phot. MacDONALD, M. Y. The Pauline Churches (Cambridge 1988) 38.

8:15-16   DUNN, J. D. G. Jesus and the Spirit. A Study of the Religious and Charismatic Experience of Jesus and the First Christians as Reflected in the New Testament (London 1975) 239, 240f., 326. RAYAN, S. The Holy Spirit: Heart of the Gospel and Christian Hope (Maryknoll/New York 1978) 120f. BYRNE, B. "Sons of God"—"Seed of Abraham" (Rome 1979) 2, 98, 184, 232. DUNN, J. D. G. Christology in the Making (London 1980) 26f., 145. THEISSEN, G. Psychologische Aspekte paulinischer Theologie (Göttingen 1983) 332, 337. GEBAUER, R. Das Gebet bei Paulus (Giessen/Basel 1989) 144-63.

8:15,16   SOKOLOWSKI, E. Die Begriffe Geist und Leben bei Paulus (1903) 91ff., 148ff. BRAUN, H. Qumran und NT II (1966) 28, 29, 154, 169, 252-54, 259, 265, 288, 293.

8:15   BRUNNER, E. Dogmatik I (1946) 35, 216, 226, 334. TAYLOR, T.M. "'Abba, Father' and Baptism" SJTh 11 (1, '58) 62-71. ROBINSON, J.M. Kerygma und historischer Jesus (1960) 140. KNOX, W.L. St. Paul and the Church of the Gentiles (1961) 104ff. ROMANIUK, K. "Spiritus clamans (Gal 4, 6; Rom 8, 15)" VerbDom 40 (4, '62) 190-98. HAHN, F. Christologische Hoheitstitel (1963) 320. JÜNGEL, E. Paulus und Jesus (1966) 69. SEEBERT, A. Der Katechismus der Urchristenheit (1966) 225, 240-43. BECKER, J. "Quid locuto palin eis phobon in Rom 8, 15 proprie valeat" VerbDom 45 (3, '67) 162-67. SCHNEIDER, N. Die rhetorische Eigenart der paulinischen Antithese (1970) 112-14. FEINE, D. P. und BEHM, D. J. Einleitung in das Neue Testament (Heidelberg 1950) 168f. ADLER, N. Taufe und Handauflegung. Eine exege-

tisch-theologische Untersuchung von Apg 8, 14-17 (Münster 1951) 94f.
ECKART, K.-G. "Das Apokryphon Ezechiel," JSHRZ 5 (1974) 53n.3c.
KÜMMEL, W. G. Römer 7 und das Bild des Menschen im Neuen Testament
(München 1974) 30, 32, 34. LADD, G. E. A Theology of the New Testament
(Grand Rapids 1974) 87, 488, 521. DUNN, J. D. G. Jesus and the Spirit. A
Study of the Religious and Charismatic Experience of Jesus and the First Chris-
tians as Reflected in the New Testament (London 1975) 21f., 23, 25, 187f., 201,
245, 260, 310, 332. SCHMITHALS, W. Der Römerbrief als historisches
Problem (Gütersloh 1975) 88. RÜLER, H. P. "Aramäisch" in TRE 3 (1978)
602. BYRNE, B. "Sons of God"—"Seed of Abraham" (Rome 1979) 1, 80, 98-
100, 111, 119, 127, 184, 203, 215n., 222f. GUNKEL, H. The Influence of the
Holy Spirit (Philadelphia 1979) 79f., 83. MINDE, H. J. VAN DER. "Theologia
crucis und Pneumaaussagen bei Paulus," Catholia 34 (1980) 145. SCHELBERT,
G. "Sprachgeschichtliches zu 'Abba'" in P. Casetti et al., eds., Mélanges
Dominique Barthélemy (Fribourg/Göttingen 1981) 395-447, esp.408. DEICH-
GRÄBER, R. "Formeln, Liturgische" in TRE 11 (1983) 257. HAYS, R. B. The
Faith of Jesus Christ (Chico CA 1983) 107. THEISSEN, G. Psychologische
Aspekte paulinischer Theologie (Göttingen 1983) 186, 264, 318. KLEIN-
KNECHT, K. T. Der leidende Gerechtfertigte (Tübingen 1984) 245, 349f., 352.
MOHRLANG, R. Matthew and Paul (Cambridge 1984) 32, 61, 83, 91. STAAB,
K. Pauluskommentare aus der griechischen Kirche (Münster ²1984) 92:9-16
Diod; 136:1-28 ThM; 220:15-22 Sev; 378:1-11 Genn; 427:17-20 Oek. HAHN,
F. "Gottesdienst III" in TRE 14 (1985) 31, 34. HARRIS, M. J. Raised Immortal
(London 1986) 261. MALINA B. J. Christian Origins and Cultural Anthro-
pology (Atlanta 1986) 137. MacDONALD, M. Y. The Pauline Churches
(Cambridge 1988) 66. OBENG, E. A. "Abba, Father: The Prayer of the Sons
of God," ET 99 (12, 1988) 363-6. LAMPE, P. Die stadtrömischen Christen in
den ersten beiden Jahrhunderten (Tübingen ²1989) 55. VOLLENWEIDER, S.
Freiheit als neue Schöpfung (Göttingen 1989) 324. WALTER, N. "Paul and the
Early Christian Jesus-Tradition" in A. J. M. Wedderburn, ed., Paul and Jesus.
Collected Essays (Sheffield 1989) 51-80, esp.59.

8:16-25   FACY, T. "St. Paul, Romans 8, 16-25" IThQ XXIII/2 ('56) 178-81.

8:16-18   MacDONALD, M. Y. The Pauline Churches (Cambridge 1988) 66.

8:16-17   STAAB, K. Pauluskommentare aus der griechischen Kirche (Münster ²1984)
136:29-137:5 ThM; 378:12-379:7 Genn.

8:16   BRUNNER, E. Dogmatik I (1946) 35, 227, II (1950)74. STACEY, W.D. The
Pauline View of Man (1956) 132-4, 143. SCHRAGE, W. Die konkreten Einzelgebote in der paulinischen Paränese (19-61) 83. BEUTLER, J. Martyria (Frankfurt a.M. 1972) 175, 204, 299. VAWTER, B. This Man Jesus (New York 1973)
80ff. LADD, G. E. A Theology of the New Testament (Grand Rapids 1974)
461f., 488. TRITES, A. A. The New Testament Concept of Witness (Cambridge
1977) 201f. THEISSEN, G. Psychologische Aspekte paulinischer Theologie
(Göttingen 1983) 330, 333, 369n.39. SLENCZKA, R. "Glaube VI" in TRE 13
(1984) 340. STAAB, K. Pauluskommentare aus der griechischen Kirche
(Münster ²1984) 92:17-93:3 Diod. OLIVEIRA, A. DE, Die Diakonie der
Gerechtigkeit und der Versöhnung in der Apologie des 2. Korintherbriefes.
Analyse und Auslegung von 2 Kor 2, 14-4, 6; 5, 11-6, 10 (Münster 1990) 226.

8:17ff.   STROBEL, A. "Apokalyptik" in TRE 3 (1978) 252. KLAIBER, W. Rechtfertigung und Gemeinde (Göttingen 1982) 134-6.

8:17-39   COUSAR, C. B. A Theology of the Cross (Minneapolis 1990) 172-5.

8:17-30   SIBER, P. Mit Christus Leben (1971) 135-68.

8:17-26   EICHHOLZ, G. Die Theologie des Paulus im Umriss (1972) passim.
8:17-18   SCHELKLE, K. H. Die Passion Jesu in der Verkündigung des Neuen Testament
           (Heidelberg 1949) 74, 260, 265f. MÄHLUM, H. Die Vollmacht des Timotheus
           nach den Pastoralbriefen (Basel 1969) 63. SCHMITHALS, W. Der Römerbrief
           als historisches Problem (Gütersloh 1975) 199f. STAAB, K. Pauluskommentare
           aus der griechischen Kirche (Münster ²1984) 94:4-25 Diod; 379:8-21 Genn.
8:17   BEST, E. One Body in Christ (1955) 45, 49, 132. KUSS, O. Der Römerbrief
           (1957) 608-18. QUESNELL, Q. This Good News (1964) 67f. HOFFMANN, P.
           Die Toten in Christus (1966) 308. TANNEHILL, R.C. Dying and Rising With
           Christ (1966) 112-14. VOEGTLE, A. Das Neue Testament und die Zukunft des
           Kosmos (1970) 191f., 205f. SIBER, P. Mit Christus Leben (1971) 135-44, 182-
           88. BURCHARD, C. Untersuchungen zu Joseph and Aseneth (Tübingen 1965)
           150. CAVALLIN, H. C. C. Life After Death. Paul's Argument for the
           Resurrection of the Dead in I Cor 15. Part I: An Enquiry into the Jewish Back-
           ground (Lund 1974) 4, 3n.21. PEEL, M. L. Gnosis und Auferstehung (Neukir-
           chen 1974) 30, 36, 79, 143. DUNN, J. D. G. Jesus and the Spirit. A Study of
           the Religious and Charismatic Experience of Jesus and the First Christians as
           Reflected in the New Testament (London 1975) 25, 36, 328, 332. BYRNE, B.
           "Sons of God"—"Seed of Abraham" (Rome 1979) 98, 101-3, 118n., 160, 172,
           214. FROITZHEIM, F. Christologie und Eschatologie bei Paulus (Würzburg
           1979) 206f., 246. MINDE, H. J. VAN DER. "Theologia crucis und Pneumaaus-
           sagen bei Paulus," Catholia 34 (1980) 145. CAMBIER, J.-M. "La Liberté du
           Spirituel dans Rom. 8, 12-17" in M. D. Hooker and S. G. Wilson, eds., Paul
           and Paulinism (FS C. K. Barrett; London 1982) 214f. HAYS, R. B. The Faith
           of Jesus Christ (Chico CA 1983) 225, 244. POBEE, J. S. Persecution and
           Martyrdom in the Theology of Paul (Sheffield 1985) 111f. LAYTON, B. The
           Gnostic Scriptures (Garden City NY 1987) 321n.45i. HELEWA, G. "'Soffer-
           enza' e 'speranza della gloria' in Rom 8, 17," Teresianum 39 (1988) 233-73.
           BREYTENBACH, C. Versöhnung (Neukirchen-Vluyn 1989) 212. HELEWA,
           G. "Un ministero paolino: consolare gli afflitti," Teresianum 44 (1993) 3-51.
8:18ff.   SCHRAGE, W. Die konkreten Einzelgebote in derpaulinischen Paränese (1961)
           16. KÄSEMANN, E. Exegetische Versuche und Besinnungen (1964) II 130.
           GERBER, U. "Röm.viii 18ff. als exegetisches Problem der Dogmatik" NovTest
           8 (1, '66) 58-81. VOEGTLE, A. Das Neue Testament und die Zukunft des
           Kosmos (1970) 14, 24, 29-32, 90, 166f., 170-72, 174f., 183-208, 216f. HERR,
           T. Naturrechtaus der Kritischen Sicht des Neues Testaments (München 1976)
           200. GERSTENBERGER, G. und SCHRAGE, W. Leiden (Stuttgart 1977) 140f.
           [ET: J. E. Steely (trans.) Suffering (Nashville 1980) 163f.] SCHMITHALS, W.
           "Zur Herkunft der gnostischen Elemente in der Sprache des Paulus" in B. Aland
           et al., eds., Gnosis (FS H. Jonas; Göttingen 1978) 390-3. SCHADE, H.-H.
           Apokalyptische Christologie bei Paulus (Göttingen 1981) 102-4. NEBE, G.
           'Hoffnung' bei Paulus (Göttingen 1983) 93, 138, 149, 155, 181, 295f., 315, 336.
           THEISSEN, G. Psychologische Aspekte paulinischer Theologie (Göttingen
           1983) 117, 187, 265, 266, 270, 314-20, 321, 332-40. LAMPE, P. Die stadt-
           römischen Christen in den ersten beiden Jahrhunderten (Tübingen ²1989) 274.
           VOLLENWEIDER, S. Freiheit als neue Schöpfung (Göttingen 1989) 101,
           375ff., 405.
8:18-39   LEWIS, E. "A Christian Theodicy. An Exposition of Romans 8:18-39" Interpre-
           tation 11 (4, '57) 405-20. LUZ, U. Das Geschichtsverständnis des Paulus (1968)
           369-84, 397. BLAZ, H.R. Heilsvertrauen und Welterfahrung (1971). GIBBS,
           J.G. Creation and Redemption (1971) 34-47, 57f., 91f., 142, 153. FROITZ-

HEIM, F. Christologie und Eschatologie bei Paulus (Würzburg 1979) 246f. GORDAY, P. Principles of Patristic Exegesis: Romans 9-11 in Origen, John Chrysostom, and Augustine (New York/Toronto 1983) 74-6, 120f., 165-7. KLEINKNECHT, K. T. Der leidende Gerechtfertigte (Tübingen 1984) 182, 324f., 333-47, 350-6, 378f., 385. WATSON, F. Paul, Judaism and the Gentiles (Cambridge 1986) 158f. VOLLENWEIDER, S. Freiheit als neue Schöpfung (Göttingen 1989) 375.

8:18-38   HAYS, R. B. Echoes of Scripture in the Letters of Paul (New Haven/London 1989) 57-63.

8:18-30   SCHLIER, H. Das Ende der Zeit (1971) 250-70. BOHREN, R. Predigtlehre (München 1971) 206. BAUMGARTEN, J. Paulus und die Apokalyptik (Neukirchen-Vluyn 1975) 170-8. KIEFER, O. "Im Hoffen sind wir gerettet (Röm 8:24). Die Eigenart christlicher Hoffnung nach Röm 8:18-30," Dienender Glaube 52 (12, 1976) 333-8. LAMBRECHT, J. "Present World and Christian Hope. A Consideration of Rom. 8:18-30," Jeevadhara 8 (43, 1978) 29-39. BYRNE, B. "Sons of God"—"Seed of Abraham" (Rome 1979) 102, 103-122, 126. MENEZES, F. "Christian Hope of Glory. Rom 8:18-30," Biblebhashyam 5 (1979) 208-25. SCHMITHALS, W. Die theologische Anthropologie des Paulus (Stuttgart 1980) 137-75. PERKINS, P. Resurrection. New Testament Witness and Contemporary Reflection (London 1984) 270-2. WAINWRIGHT, G. "Gottesdienst IX" in TRE 14 (1985) 91. MOORE, B. "Suffering. A Study on Romans 8:18-30" in N. M. de S. Cameron and S. B. Ferguson, eds., Pulpit & People (FS W. Still; Edinburgh 1986) 141-8. THEISSEN, G. Psychological Aspects of Pauline Theology (Edinburgh 1987) 315-20, 332-40. LAMBRECHT, J. "The Groaning Creation. A Study of Rom 8:18-30," LSt 15 (1990) 3-18.

8:18-27   KRECK, W. in Herr, tue meine Lippen auf (1966) 362-67. BOHREN, R. Predigtlehre (München 1971) 335. PAULSEN, H. Überlieferung und Auslegung von Römer 8 (Neukirchen-Vluyn 1974) 107-32. MONTAGUE, G. T. The Holy Spirit (New York 1976) 209-13. BINDEMANN, W. Die Hoffnung der Schöpfung. Römer 8, 18-27 und die Frage einer Theologie der Befreiung von Mensch und Natur (Neukirchen-Vluyn 1983). FINDEIS, H.-J. Versöhnung-Apostolat-Kirche (Würzburg 1983) 286ff. FORDE, G. O. "Romans 8:18-27," Interp 38 (1984) 281-5. CHRISTOFFERSSON, O. "Pa jakt efter den rätta bakgrunden till Rom 8:18ff" [Stalking the Real Background to Rom 8:18ff], SEA 50 (1985) 135-43. RIMBACH, J. A. "'All Creation Groans.' Theology/Ecology in St. Paul," AsiaJT 1 (2, 1987) 379-91. THEISSEN, G. Psychological Aspects of Pauline Theology (Edinburgh 1987) 263f. CHRISTOFFERSSON, O. The Earnest Expectation of the Creature. The Flood-Tradition as Matrix of Romans 8:18-27 (Stockholm 1990).

8:18-25   HOFFMANN, P. Die Toten in Christus (1966) 334-45. VÖGTLE, A. "Röm 8:19-22: Eine schöpfungstheologische oder anthropologisch-soteriologische Aussage?" in A. Descamps and A. Halleux, eds., Mélanges Bibliques en hommage au R. P. Béda Rigaux (Gembloux 1970) 352-4, 362-5. SCHELLONG, D. in GPM 29 (1975) 303-8. SCHNATH, G. und LEUDESDORFF, R. in P. Krusche et al., eds., Predigtstudien für das Kirchenjahr 1975. Perikopenreihe III/2 (Stuttgart 1975) 114-22. ROBINSON, J. A. T. Wrestling with Romans (London 1979) 101-3. MAY, J. "Religious Symbolisations of Nature in Ethical Argumentation. A 'Pragmasemantic' Analysis of Romans 8:18-25 and a Buddhist Comparison," LiBi 48 (1980) 19-48. NEBE, G. 'Hoffnung' bei Paulus (Göttingen 1983) 81ff., 136, 269. HARRIS, M. J. Raised Immortal (London 1986) 166f. ROLLINS, W. G. "Greco-Roman Slave Terminology and Pauline

Metaphors for Salvation" in K. H. Richards, ed., Society of Biblical Literature 1987 Seminar Papers (Atlanta GA 1987) 100-10. ROSSI, B. "Struttura letteraria e teologia della creazione in Rm 8, 18-25," SBFLA 41 (1991) 87-124.

8:18-24   MUSSNER, F. Die Auferstehung Jesu (1969) 163-65.

8:18-23   DINKLER, E. GPM 5 (1951) 150-52. JERVELL, J. Imago Dei (1960) 264, 275, 277, 279, 282ff. SEVENSTER, J.N. Paul and Seneca (1961) passiim. BORN-KAMM, G. GPM 16 (1961/62) 240-44. THUESLING, W. Per Christum in Deum (1965) 120f., 130f., 249f. DOERNE, M. Die alten Episteln (1967) 165-69. WINTER, F. GPM 22 (1967/68) 303-9. BLANK, J. Schriftauslegung in Theorie und Praxis (1969) 237-47. SCHNEIDER, G. Neuschöpfung oder Wiederkehr (1961) 83-6. LYONNET, S. "Redemptio cosmica secundum," VD 44 (1966) 225-42. DUBARLE, A.-M. "Lois de l'univers et vie chrétienne. Rm 8, 18-23," AssS 46 (1974) 11-6. PAGELS, E. H. The Gnostic Paul. Gnostic Exegesis of the Pauline Letters (Philadelphia 1975) 35f. HASENSTAB, R. Modelle paulinischer Ethik (Mainz 1977) 170. NOERENBERG, K.-D. und HEUE, R. in P. Krusche et al., eds., Predigtstudien für das Kirchenjahr 1980. Perikopenreihe II/2 (Stuttgart 1980) 271-8. RUTHSATZ, R. in GPM 34 (1980) 426-9. BINDEMANN, W. Die Hoffnung der Schöpfung (Neukirchen 1983) 67-76. KIM, S. "The 'Son of Man'" as the Son of God (Tübingen 1983) 93f. HEIDENFELD, K. H. VON, in GPM 40 (1985/86) 495-500.

8:18-19   LÜHRMANN, D. Das Offenbarungsverständnis bei Paulus und in Paulinischen Gemeinden (1965) 105f. KLEIN, G. "Eschatologie" in TRE 10 (1982) 284.

8:18,28-30 BALZ, H.R. Heilsvertrauen und Welterfahrung (1971) 93-115.

8:18   BRUNNER, E. Dogmatik I (1946) 312. STÄHELIN, E. Die Verkündigung desReiches Gottes in der Kirche Jesu Christi I (1951) 25, 327, 350. BEST, E. One Body in Christ (1955) 132n. BOUSSET, W. Die Religion des Judentums im Späthellenistischen Zeitalter (1966) 245. KERTELGE, K. "Rechtfertigung" bei Paulus (1967) 79, 134, 141, 155. SIBER, P. Mit Christus Leben (1971) 143-45. SCHWANTES, H. Schöpfung der Endzeit (1962). BERKOUWER, G. C. The Return of Christ (Grand Rapids 1972) 110, 115, 314, 448. LADD, G. E. A Theology of the New Testament (Grand Rapids 1974) 46, 275, 563. KLIJN, A. F. J. "Die syrische Baruch-Apokalypse" in JSHRZ V/2 (1976) 133. ARRINGTON, F. L. New Testament Exegesis: Examples (Washington 1977) 3-5. GERSTENBERGER, G. und SCHRAGE, W. Leiden (Stuttgart 1977) 177. [ET: J. E. Steely (trans.) Suffering (Nashville 1980) 205.] BYRNE, B. "Sons of God"—"Seed of Abraham" (Rome 1979) 102, 103f., 108, 111, 113, 119, 121, 122, 128, 164n., 214. FROITZHEIM, F. Christologie und Eschatologie bei Paulus (Würzburg 1979) 246f. GEORGI, D. "Weisheit Salomos" in JSHRZ III/4 (1980) 3n.5b. NEBE, G. 'Hoffnung' bei Paulus (Göttingen 1983) 54f., 71, 84, 92, 148, 330. STAAB, K. Pauluskommentare aus der griechischen Kirche (Münster ²1984) 137:6-8 ThM. LÉON-DUFOUR, X. Life and Death in the New Testament (San Francisco 1986) 231, 232.

8:19-11:36 KUSS, O. Der Römerbrief. Übersetzt und erklärt. Dritte Lieferung (Röm 8, 19 bis 11, 36) (Regensburg 1978).

8:19ff.   STÄHELIN, E. Die Verkündigung des Reiches Gottes in der Kirche Jesu Christi I (1951) 25, 139, 212, 250, 280, 299. SCHRAGE, W. Die konkreten Einzelgebote in der paulinischen Paränese (1961) 15, 210, 214. RISSI, M. Studien zum zweiten Korintherbrief (1969) 83f., 85, 91, 217. GRASS, H. Osterge-schehen und Osterberichte (1970) 167ff. RATSCHOW, C. H. "Eschatologie" in TRE 10 (1982) 355. NEBE, G. 'Hoffnung' bei Paulus

(Göttingen 1983) 17, 30, 34, 55, 57ff., 63, 67, 70, 72, 172, 254, 337. LARS-
SON, E. "Heil und Erlösung III" in TRE 14 (1985) 620.

8:19-27 ROAMNIUK, K. "Perspektywy 'kosmiczne' w soteriologii sw. Pawla (Rz 8,
19-27) Perspectives 'cosmiques dans la sotériologie de S. Paul (Rom.
8, 19-27)" RTK 13 (1, '66) 81-94.

8:19-23 MAGNUSSSON, M. Der Begriff "Verstehen" in Exegetischem Zusammenhang
(1954) 211f. STANLEY, D.M. Christ's Resurrection in Pauline Soteriology
(1961) 192-95. BRAUN, H. Qumran und NT II (1966) 170, 266, 282.
LYONNET, S. "Redemptio 'cosmica' secundum Rom 8, 19-23" VerbDom 44
(5-6, '66) 225-42. GIBBS, J.G. Creation and Redemption (1971) 142-45.
HOFFMANN, P. Die Toten in Christus (1966) 271. ZEILINGER, F. Der Erstgeborene der Schöpfung (Wien 1974) 184-6, 189f.

8:19-22 DUBARLE, A.M. "Le gémissement des créatures dans l'ordre divin du cosmos
(Röm. 8, 19-22) RSPhTh 38 ('54) 445-65. BRINKMAN, B.R. "'Creation' and
'creature' II Texts and tendencies in the Epistle to the Romans" Bijdragen 18
(4, '57) 358-74. PETRAUSCH, J. "An Analysis of Romans viii, 19-22"
IrEcclRec (105) 5, '66 314-23. NICKELS, P. Targum and New Testament
(1967) 69. BALZ, H.R. Heislvertrauen und Welterfahrung (1974) 36-54.
SIBER, P. Mit Christus Leben (1971) 145-52. VÖGTLE, A. "Röm 8:19-22:
Eine schöpfungstheologische oder anthropologisch-soteriologische Aussage?"
in A. Descamps and A. Halleux, eds., Mélanges Bibliques en hommage au R.
P. Béda Rigaux (Gembloux 1970) 351-66. ARRINGTON, F. L. New Testament
Exegesis: Examples (Washington 1977) 1-20. FRANCIS, D. "Terrestrial Reali-
ties: their Liberation," Jeevadhara 8 (44, 1978) 148-58. BYRNE, B. "Sons of
God"—"Seed of Abraham" (Rome 1979) 104-8, 110f. FROITZHEIM, F. Chris-
tologie und Eschatologie bei Paulus (Würzburg 1979) 247ff., 254. DUNN, J. D.
G. Christology in the Making (London 1980) 104. MILNE, D. J. W. "Genesis
3 in the Letter to Romans," RThR 39 (1980) 10-8. SCHMITHALS, W. Die the-
ologische Anthropologie des Paulus (Stuttgart 1980) 142-6. BARTH. M. "Christ
and All Things" in M. D. Hooker and S. G. Wilson, eds., Paul and Paulinism
(FS C. K. Barrett; London 1982) 160-72. BINDEMANN, W. Die Hoffnung der
Schöpfung (Neukirchen 1983) 15-7, 29-31, 41f., 82-95. NEBE, G. 'Hoffnung'
bei Paulus (Göttingen 1983) 53, 69, 82, 85, 89, 177, 260f. VOEGTLE, A.
"'Dann sah ich einen neuen Himmel und eine neue Erde . . . ' (Apk 21, 1)" in
E. Grässer und O. Merk, eds., Glaube und Eschatologie (FS W. G. Kümmel;
Tübingen 1985) 309ff. COLLISON, J. G. F. "Biblical Perspectives on Steward-
ship of Earth's Resources," BangalTheolFor 18 (4, 1986) 153-60. LEON-DU-
FOUR, X. Life and Death in the New Testament (San Francisco 1986) 231,
234. PÖHLMANN, H. G. "Himmelfahrt Christi" in TRE 15 (1986) 340. LAM-
BRECHT, J. "De kreunende schepping. Een lezing van Rom. 8, 19-22," Colla-
tiones 19 (1989) 292-310. Schöpfung und Neuschöpfung, JBTh 5 (Neukirchen-
Vluyn 1990).

8:19-21 PATTE, D. Preaching Paul (Philadelphia 1984) 52f. CRANFIELD, C. E. B.
"The Creation's Promised Liberation. Some Observations on Romans 8, 19-21,"
The Bible and Christian Life (Edinburgh 1985) 94-104.

8:19 BRUNNER, E. Dogmatik II (1950) 218. DUDDINGTON, J.W. "Firstfruits of
a Cosmic Redemption" ChrTo 3 (25, '59) 6-8. PEEL, M. L. Gnosis and Auferstehung (Neukirchen 1974) 75, 97, 101. ARRINGTON, F. L. New Testament
Exegesis: Examples (Washington 1977) 3-8. BARTNICKI, R. "Wspólczesna a
patrystyczna interpretacja Rz 8, 19 [The Contemporary and Patristic Interpretation of Ro 8, 19]," SThV 16 (1978) 49-65. BYRNE, B. "Sons of God"—"Seed

of Abraham" (Rome 1979) 100n., 104f., 106, 109n., 119, 127, 214, 218n. KEHNSCHERPER, G. "Theologische und homiletische Aspekte von Röm 8:19," ThLZ 104 (1979) 411-24. KEHNSCHERPER, G. "Romans 8:19. On Pauline Belief and Creation" in E. A. Livingstone, ed., Studia Biblica 1978, Vol. III: Papers on Paul and Other New Testament Authors (Sheffield 1980) 233-43. DENTON, D. R. "Apokaradokia," ZNW 73 (1982) 138-40. NEBE, G. 'Hoffnung' bei Paulus (Göttingen 1983) 25ff., 32ff., 52f., 55, 66, 87, 247, 312, 321, 326. STAAB, K. Pauluskommentare aus der griechischen Kirche (Münster ²1984) 93:26-94:14 Diod; 137:9-138:37 ThM; 220:23-26 Sev; 379:22-380:16 Genn.

8:20-21   BRUNNER, E. Dogmatik II (1950) 149. HILL, E. "The Construction of Three Passages from St. Paul" CBQ 23 (3, '61) 296-301. STAAB, K. Pauluskommentare aus der griechischen Kirche (Münster ²1984) 94:15-95:4 Diod.

8:20   ARRINGTON, F. L. New Testament Exegesis: Examples (Washington 1977) 8-12. BYRNE, B. "Sons of God"—"Seed of Abraham" (Rome 1979) 41n., 105-7, 214. THEISSEN, G. Psychologische Aspekte paulinischer Theologie (Göttingen 1983) 117f., 318, 334n.111. STAAB, K. Pauluskommentare aus der griechischen Kirche (Münster ²1984) 65:32-68:8 Apoll; 139:1-6 ThM; 380:17-381:2 Genn.

8:21-22   FARICY, R. Praying for Inner Healing (London 1979) 72.

8:21   BEST, E. One Body in Christ (1955) 116. STÄHELIN, E. Die Verkündigung des Reiches Gottes in der Kirche Jesu Christi I (1951) 189, 191, 387. KERTELGE, K. "Rechtfertigung" bei Paulus (1967) 134. BÖHLIG, A. "Griechische und orientalische Einflüsse im Urchristentum" in Mysterion und Wahrheit. Gesammelte Beiträge zur spätantiken Religionsgeschichte (Leiden 1968) 52f. BERKOUWER, G. C. The Return of Christ (Grand Rapids 1972) 111, 222f., 450. LADD, G. E. A Theology of the New Testament (Grand Rapids 1974) 365, 369, 397, 480. ARRINGTON, F. L. New Testament Exegesis: Examples (Washington 1977) 12-6. JEWETT, P. K. Infant Baptism and the Covenant of Grace (Grand Rapids 1978) 233. BYRNE, B. "Sons of God"— "Seed of Abraham" (Rome 1979) 106-8, 124, 128, 188n. ROTTENBERG, I. C. The Promise and the Presence. Toward a Theology of the Kingdom of God (Grand Rapids 1980) 47. MEHL, R. "Freiheit" in TRE 11 (1983) 523. MEEKS, W. A. The First Urban Christians (New Haven/London 1983) 87, 169, 185. NEBE, G. 'Hoffnung' bei Paulus (Göttingen 1983) 51ff., 83. THEISSEN, G. Psychologische Aspekte paulinischer Theologie (Göttingen 1983) 186, 228, 332, 335. STAAB, K. Pauluskommentare aus der griechischen Kirche (Münster ²1984) 139:7-10 ThM; 381:3-12 Genn; 427:21-428:3 Oek. JONES, F. S. "Freiheit" in den Briefen des Apostels Paulus (Göttingen 1987) 64, 66, 90f., 96, 99, 108, 110, 114, 129-35, 136f., 139, 141-3, 147n.3, 225n.121. VOLLENWEIDER, S. Freiheit als neue Schöpfung (Göttingen 1989) 347, 398.

8:22-27   SCHWEIZER, E. Heiliger Geist (Berlin 1978) 150.

8:22-23   STACEY, W.D. "Paul's Certainties: II. God's Purpose in Creation-Romans viii. 22-23" ET 69 (6, '58) 178-81. BLAIR, H. A. "Rm 8:22f and some Pagan African Intuitions" in Studia Evangelica IV (TU 102; 1968) 377-81.

8:22   NICOLAU, M. "'Toda la creación gime y está con dolores de parto hasta el presente' (Rom 8, 22)," Salmanticensis 20 (3, 1973) 643-54. ARRINGTON, F. L. New Testament Exegesis: Examples (Washington 1977) 16-9. BYRNE, B. "Sons of God"—"Seed of Abraham" (Rome 1979) 108. THEISSEN, G. Psychologische Aspekte paulinischer Theologie (Göttingen 1983) 186, 333, 335. STAAB, K. Pauluskommentare aus der griechischen Kirche (Münster ²1984)

139:11-19 ThM; 381:13-15 Genn. MacRAE, G. W. Studies in the New Testament and Gnosticism (Wilmington/Delaware 1987) 67f.

8:23ff.   THEISSEN, G. Psychologische Aspekte paulinischer Theologie (Göttingen 1983) 315.

8:23-27   STAAB, K. Pauluskommentare aus der griechischen Kirche (Münster ²1984) 510:24-511:34 Phot.

8:23-25   SCHRAGE, W. Die konkreten Einzelgebote in der paulinischen Paränese (1961) 15. BALZ, H.R. Heilsvertrauen und Welterfahrung (1971) 54-69. BYRNE, B. "Sons of God"—"Seed of Abraham" (Rome 1979) 104, 108-11. SCHMITHALS, W. Die theologische Anthropologie des Paulus (Stuttgart 1980) 146-52.

8:23-24   GOPPELT, L. Christologie und Ethik (1968) 265f. SANDERS, J. T. Ethics in the New Testament (Philadelphia 1975) 54. HELDERMANN, J. Die Anapausis im Evangelium Veritatis (Leiden 1984) 270n.673. STAAB, K. Pauluskommentare aus der griechischen Kirche (Münster ²1984) 381:16-27 Genn.

8:23   BRUNNER, E. Dogmatik I (1946) 223. FLEW, R.N. Jesus and His Church (1956) 152. STACEY, W.D. The Pauline View of Man (1956) 133, 187. OKE, C.C. "A Suggestion With Regard to Romans 8:23" Interpretation II (4, '57) 455-60. ROBINSON, J.M. Kerygma und historischer Jesus (1960) 163. DELLING, G. Die Taufe im Neuen Testament (1963) 106, 144. JÜNGEL, E. Paulus und Jesus (1966) 185. KERTELGE, K. "Rechtfertigung" bei Paulus (1967) 54, 141, 149, 155, 257. SWETNAM, J. "On Romans 8, 23 and the 'Expectation of Sonship'" Biblica 48 (1, '67) 102-8. MERK, O. Handeln aus Glauben (19-68) 12, 18f., 38, 40. VAN DÜLMEN, A. Die Theologie des Gesetzes bei Paulus (1968) 193, 194, 195, 196, 198. MUSSNER, F. Die Auferstehung Jesu (1969) 116f. DUNN, J.D.G. Baptism in the Holy Spirit (1970) 150. DE LA CALLE, F. "La 'huiothesian' de Rom 8, 23" EstBi 30 (1, '71) 77-98. SIBER, P. Mit Christus Leben (1971) 159-61. BERKOUWER, G. C. The Return of Christ (Grand Rapids 1972) 10, 47, 112, 114, 115, 191, 370. BENOIT, P. Jesus and the Gospel, Vol 2 (London 1974) 40-50. LADD, G. E. A Theology of the New Testament (Grand Rapids 1974) 370, 433, 465f., 488, 492, 563f. DUNN, J. D. G. Jesus and the Spirit. A Study of the Religious and Charismatic Experience of Jesus and the First Christians as Reflected in the New Testament (London 1975) 159, 242, 245, 260, 309, 310f., 312, 332. LINDEMANN, A. Die Aufhebung der Zeit. Geschichtsverständnis und Eschatologie im Epheserbrief (Gütersloh 1975) 92, 196f., 232. SCHMITHALS, W. Der Römerbrief als historisches Problem (Gütersloh 1975) 200. BYRNE, B. "Sons of God"—"Seed of Abraham" (Rome 1979) 2, 4, 80, 100, 104, 105n., 108-11, 114n., 126f., 156, 214f. FROITZHEIM, F. Christologie und Eschatologie bei Paulus (Würzburg 1979) 240, 249f. MINDE, H. J. VAN DER. "Theologia crucis und Pneumaaussagen bei Paulus," Catholica 34 (1980) 143f. NEBE, G. 'Hoffnung' bei Paulus (Göttingen 1983) 25f., 32, 55, 63, 65f., 69, 83, 90, 92, 245, 253. THEISSEN, G. Psychologische Aspekte paulinischer Theologie (Göttingen 1983) 264, 337, 369n.39. HELDERMANN, J. Die Anapausis im Evangelium Veritatis (Leiden 1984) 197. MÖLLER, C. "Gemeinde" in TRE 12 (1984) 334. STAAB, K. Pauluskommentare aus der griechischen Kirche (Münster ²1984) 95:5-10 Diod; 428:4 Oek. HARRIS, M. J. Raised Immortal (London 1986) 139, 149, 261. LEON-DUFOUR, X. Life and Death in the New Testament (San Francisco 1986) 231, 237. GUNTON, C. "Christ the Sacrifice. Aspects of the Language and Imagery of the Bible" in L. D. Hurst and N. T. Wright, eds., The Glory of Christ in the New Testament (FS G. B. Caird;

	Oxford 1987) 229-38, esp.238. NIELSEN, H. K. Heilung und Verkündigung (Leiden 1987) 170, 205f., 208. OSTEN-SACKEN, P. VON DER, Evangelium und Tora: Aufsätze zu Paulus (München 1987) 62, 170, 206, 280, 303. OLIVEIRA, A. DE, Die Diakonie der Gerechtigkeit und der Versöhnung in der Apologie des 2. Korintherbriefes. Analyse und Auslegung von 2 Kor 2, 14-4, 6; 5, 11-6, 10 (Münster 1990) 223. VOLF, J. M. G. Paul and Perseverance (Tübingen 1990) 11, 27-9, 50f., 61, 174, 283.
8:23b	DAUTZENBERG, G. "Reich Gottes und Erlösung" in I. Broer und J. Werbick, eds., "Auf Hoffnung hin sind wir erlöst" (Röm 8, 14) (Stuttgart 1987) 61-4.
8:24-32	KLAAS, W. in G. Eichholz, ed. Herr, tue meine Lippen auf 4 (1965) 74ff.
8:24-30	STECK, K.G. GPM 12 (1957) 41-47, 18 (1963) 62-68. KOCSIS, E. GPM 24 (1968/69) 65-70. VOIGT, G. Der zerrissene Vorhang (1969) 64-70. KLEIN, G. in GPM 30 (1975) 59-66. LUZ, U. und MÜLLER, H. M. in P. Krusche et al., eds., Predigtstudien für das Kirchenjahr 1975/76. Perikopenreihe IV/1 (Stuttgart 1975) 85-91.
8:24-25	HOFFMANN, P. Die Toten in Christus (1966) 283. LUZ, U. Das Geschichtsverständnis des Paulus (1968) 324, 375. SIBER, P. Mit Christus leben (Zürich 1971) 161f. SCHMITHALS, W. Der Römerbrief als historisches Problem (Gütersloh 1975) 199. BYRNE, B. "Sons of God"—"Seed of Abraham" (Rome 1979) 104, 110, 112. LEON-DUFOUR, X. Life and Death in the New Testament (San Francisco 1986) 231, 238.
8:24	DELLING, G. Die Taufe im Neuen Testament (1963) 114. KERTELGE, K. "Rechtfertigung" bei Paulus (1967) 87, 149, 157. BERGMEIER, R. Glaube als Gabe nach Johannes (Stuttgart 1980) 232. THISELTON, A. C. The Two Horizons (Grand Rapids 1980) 389, 401. KLEIN, G. "Eschatologie" in TRE 10 (1982) 282. RATSCHOW, C. H. "Eschatologie" in TRE 10 (1982) 350. BINDEMANN, W. Die Hoffnung der Schöpfung (Neukirchen 1983) 31. NEBE, G. 'Hoffnung' bei Paulus (Göttingen 1983) 22, 31, 34, 65, 66, 72, 73, 76, 80f., 90, 255, 267, 268, 294f., 312. STAAB, K. Pauluskommentare aus der griechischen Kirche (Münster ²1984) 139:20-22 ThM. SAUTER, G. "Hoffnung III" in TRE 15 (1986) 493, 494. WEDER, H. "Hoffnung II" in TRE 15 (1986) 486, 490. BROER, I. und WERBICK, J., eds., "Auf Hoffnung hin sind wir erlöst" (Röm 8, 24) (Stuttgart 1987).
8:25	BYRNE, B. "Sons of God"—"Seed of Abraham" (Rome 1979) 85, 104, 109n., 110. DENTON, D. R. "Hope and Perseverance," SJTh 34 (1981) 313-20. NEBE, G. 'Hoffnung' bei Paulus (Göttingen 1983) 25f., 32, 65, 71, 73f., 90, 92, 268.
8:26ff.	DUNN, J. D. G. Jesus and the Spirit. A Study of the Religious and Charismatic Experience of Jesus and the First Christians as Reflected in the New Testament (London 1975) 245. BYRNE, B. "Sons of God"—"Seed of Abraham" (Rome 1979) 111-5.
8:26-30	ROBINSON, J. A. T. Wrestling with Romans (London 1979) 103-6. RATHKE, H. in GPM 38 (1983/84) 254-9. LEON-DUFOUR, X. Life and Death in the New Testament (San Francisco 1986) 172, 231, 239.
8:26-28	BERGER, K. "Gebet" in TRE 12 (1984) 50.
8:26-27	BOYD, R.F. "The Work of the Holy Spirit in Prayer. An Exposition of Romans 8, 26-27" Interpretation VIII ('54) 35-42. TILLICH, P. Das Neue Sein (1959) 128-31. SCHRAGE, W. Die konkreten Einzelgebote in der paulinischen Paränese (1961) 71, 92. STALDER, K. Das Werk des Geistes in der Heiligung bei Paulus (1962) 22, 45, 62f. NIEDERWIMMER, K. "Das Gebet des Geistes Röm. 8, 26f" ThZ 20 (4, '65) 252-65. LUZ, U. Das Geschichtsverständnis des

Paulus (1968) 380f. KÄSEMANN, E. "Der gottesdienstliche Schrei nach der Freiheit (1969) 211-36. BALZ, H.R. Heilsvertrauen und Welterfahrung (1971) 69-92. SIBER, P. Mit Christus Leben (1971) 162-67. SCHNIEWIND, J. Nachgelassenen Reden und Aufsätze (Berlin 1952) 81-104. GOEDT, M. DE. "The Intercession of the Spirit in Christian Prayer (Rom. 8, 26-27)," Concilium 79 (1972) 26-38. WILES, G. P. Paul's Intercessory Prayers (London 1974) 5n., 76, 90, 268n., 280n. DUNN, J. D. G. Jesus and the Spirit. A Study of the Religious and Charismatic Experience of Jesus and the First Christians as Reflected in the New Testament (London 1975) 239-42, 259, 268. STENDAHL, K. "Glossolalia and the Charismatic Movement" in J. Jervell and W. A. Meeks, eds., God's Christ and His People (FS N. A. Dahl; 1977) 123. TRITES, A. A. The New Testament Concept of Witness (Cambridge 1977) 202. RAYAN, S. The Holy Spirit: Heart of the Gospel and Christian Hope (Maryknoll/New York 1978) 119f. FROITZHEIM, F. Christologie und Eschatologie bei Paulus (Würzburg 1979) 250. VALLAURI, E. "I gemiti dello Spirito Santo (Rom. 8, 26 s.)," RivB 27 (1979) 95-113. MacRAE, G. W. "A Note on Romans 8:26-27," HThR 73 (1980) 227-30. SCHMITHALS, W. Die theologische Anthropologie des Paulus (Stuttgart 1980) 152-62. BISER, E. Der Zeuge (Graz/Wien/Köln 1981) 95, 121, 212, 230, 237. MITCHELL, C. C. "The Holy Spirit's Intercessory Ministry," BiblSa 139 (555, 1982) 230-42. BINDEMANN, W. Die Hoffnung der Schöpfung (Neukirchen 1983) 76-81. THEISSEN, G. Psychologische Aspekte paulinischer Theologie (Göttingen 1983) 117, 118, 269, 274, 287, 315, 337. BERGER, K. "Gebet" in TRE 12 (1984) 50. BERGER, K. "Geist" in TRE 12 (1984) 181. OBENG, E. A. "The Reconciliation of Rom. 8, 26f. to New Testament Writings and Themes," SJTh 39 (2, 1986) 165-74. MacRAE, G. W. Studies in the New Testament and Gnosticism (Wilmington/Delaware 1987) 65-71. O'BRIEN, P. T. "Romans 8:26, 27. A Revolutionary Approach to Prayer?" RThR 46 (3, 1987) 65-73. THEISSEN, G. Psychological Aspects of Pauline Theology (Edinburgh 1987) 111f. GEBAUER, R. Das Gebet bei Paulus (Giessen/Basel 1989) 164-71. WAY, D. The Lordship of Christ. Ernst Käsemann's Interpretation of Paul's Theology (Oxford 1991) 269-71.

8:26 BRUNNER, E. Dogmatik I (1946) 227. GALE, H.M. The Use of Analogy in the Letter of Paul (1964) 77f. SWEET, J.P.M. "A Sign for Unbelievers: Paul's attitude to Glossolalia" NTS 13 (1966-67) 247ff. DUNN, J. D. G. Jesus and the Spirit. A Study of the Religious and Charismatic Experience of Jesus and the First Christians as Reflected in the New Testament (London 1975) 86, 245, 260, 328. WEDDERBURN, A. J. M. "Romans 8:26—Towards a Theology of Glossolalia?" SJTh 28 (4, 1975) 369-77. RICKARDS, R. R. "The translation of *tē astheneia hēmōn* ('in our weakness') in Romans 8, 26," BTr 28 (2, 1977) 247f. OTT, H. Das Reden vom Unsagbaren. Die Frage nach Gott in unseren Zeit (Stuttgart 1978) 130-6. BYRNE, B. "Sons of God"—"Seed of Abraham" (Rome 1979) 111-4. GUNKEL, H. The Influence of the Holy Spirit (Philadelphia 1979) 80f. ARMOGATHE, J. R. "Gemitibus inenarrabilibus. Note sur Rom 8, 26," Augustinianum 20 (1980) 19-22. THEISSEN, G. Psychologische Aspekte paulinischer Theologie (Göttingen 1983) 186, 263, 315, 317, 318, 330, 333, 334n.113, 338, 369n.39. BLOTH, P. C. "Gebet" in TRE 12 (1984) 96. MÜLLER, G. "Gebet" in TRE 12 (1984) 88. OBENG, E. A. "The Spirit Intercession Motif in Paul," ET 95 (12, 1984) 360-4. STAAB, K. Pauluskommentare aus der griechischen Kirche (Münster ²1984) 140:1-141:3 ThM; 381:28-382:15 Genn; 428:5-7 Oek. OBENG, E. A. "The Origins of the Spirit Intercession Motif in Romans 8, 26," NTS 32 (4, 1986) 621-32. OBENG, E. A. "An Exe-

	getical Study of Rom. 8:26 and its Implication for the Church in Africa," DBM 18 (2, 1989) 88-98.
8:27	SCHRAGE, W. Die konkreten Einzelgebote in der paulinsichen Paränese (1961) 85. MONTAGUE, G. "'The Spirit Who Pleads for the Saints . . . " Rom 8, 27" Bible Today 1 (19, '65) 1241-47.THEISSEN, G. Psychologische Aspekte paulinischer Theologie (Göttingen 1983) 94n.57, 317, 334n.113, 335, 376. BERGER, K. "Geist" in TRE 12 (1984) 188. STAAB, K. Pauluskommentare aus der griechischen Kirche (Münster ²1984) 141:4-25 ThM; 382:16-28 Genn.
8:28–9:24	FARRELLY, M.J. "Predestination and the Christian in Saint Paul" ABR 14 (4, '63) 572-89.
8:28ff.	KNOX, W.L. St. Paul and the Church of the Gentiles (1961) 105ff. SCHMITHALS, W. "Zur Herkunft der gnostischen Elemente in der Sprache des Paulus" in B. Aland et al., eds., Gnosis (FS H. Jonas; Göttingen 1978) 390-3. LÜBKING, H.-M. Paulus und Israel im Römerbrief (Frankfurt/Bern/New York 1986) 48-50.
8:28-39	THUESING, W. Per Christum in Deum (1965) 121-29f., 132ff., 141f., 145f., 174ff., 219-22, 247f. PAULSEN, H. Ueberlieferung und Auslegung von Römer 8 (Neukirchen-Vluyn 1974) 133-77.
8:28-30	GOLLWITZER, H. GPM 8 (1953) 35-39. WIEDERKEHR, D. Die Theologie der Berufung in den Paulusbriefen (1963) 153-68. GRAYSTON, K. "The Doctrine of Election in Romans 8, 28-30" in Studia Evangelica II, ed. F.L. Cross (1964) 574-83. HAHN, F. Das Verständnis der Mission im Neuen Testament (1965) 89. LUZ, U. Das Geschichtsverständnis des Paulus (1968) 250ff., 263, 373f. SIBER, P. Mit Christus leben (Zürich 1971) 152ff. HAMERTON-KELLY, R. G. Pre-Existence, Wisdom, and The Son of Man (London 1973) 154, 180-2. MAYER, B. Unter Gottes Heilsratschluss. Prädestinationsaussagen bei Paulus (Würzburg 1974) 136-66. STUIBER, A. "Ambrosiaster" in TRE 2 (1978) 360. SCHMITHALS, W. Die theologische Anthropologie des Paulus (Stuttgart 1980) 162-72. LANDAU, R. "Komm, Heiliger Geist, du Tröster wert . . . " EvTh 41 (1981) 202-6. SCHADE, H.-H. Apokalyptische Christologie bei Paulus (Göttingen 1981) 51-3.
8:28-29	BRUNNER, E. Dogmatik I (1946) 354. PAGELS, E. H. The Gnostic Paul. Gnostic Exegesis of the Pauline Letters (Philadelphia 1975) 36f. SCHÄFER, K. Gemeinde als "Bruderschaft" (Frankfurt/Bern/New York/Paris 1989) 41-80. HIEBERT, D. E. "Romans 8:28-29 and the Assurance of the Believer," BiblSa 148 (590, 1991) 170-83. PETERSON, R. A. "'Though All Hell Should Endeavor to Shake'. God's Preservation of His Saints," Presbyterion 17 (1, 1991) 40-57.
8:28	BRUNNER, E. Dogmatik II (1950) 184, 218. WOOD, H.G. "Paul's Certainties: VI. God's Providential Care and Continual Help-Romans viii.28" ET 69 (10'58) 292-95. BAUER, J.B. "' . . . TOIS AGAPOSIN TON THEON' Rm 8, 28 (I Cor. 2:9, I Cor 8:3)" ZNW 50 (1-2, '59) 106-12. SCHRAGE, W. Die konkreten Einzelgebote in der paulinischen Paränese (1961) 51, 195. BLACK, M. "The interpretation of Romans viii 28" in Neotestamentica et Patristica, Festschrift O. Cullmann (1962) 166-72. STRECKER, G. Der Weg der Gerechtigkeit (1962) 219. CRANFIELD, C.E.B. "Romans 8.28" SJTh 19 (2, '66) 204-15. BAUER, J. B. Scholia Biblica et Patristica (Graz 1972) 92-4, 97. BAUMERT, N. Täglich Sterben und Auferstehen. Der Literalsinn von 2 Kor 4, 12-5, 10 (München 1973) 254. COLEMAN, W. L. "The Use and Abuse of Romans 8, 28," Eternity 26 (1975) 23f. DUNN, J. D. G. Jesus and the Spirit. A Study of the Religious and Charismatic Experience of Jesus and the First Christians as Reflected in the

New Testament (London 1975) 242, 321. ROSS, J. M. "Pánta synergeî, Rom. VIII.28," ThZ 34 (2, 1978) 82-5. BYRNE, B. "Sons of God"—"Seed of Abraham" (Rome 1979) 113f., 115n.118., 126, 128, 134, 214. PACK, F. "A Study of Romans 8:28," RestQ 22 (1979) 44-53. CLARK, K. W. "The Making of the Twentieth Century New Testament" in The Gentile Bias and other Essays [selected by J. L. Sharpe III] (Leiden 1980) 154. CLARK, K. W. "Textual Criticism and Doctrine" in The Gentile Bias and other Essays [selected by J. L. Sharpe III] (Leiden 1980) 95. DEIDUN, T. J. New Covenant Morality in Paul (Rome 1981) 138f. KOCH, T. "Erwählung" in TRE 10 (1982) 202. OSBURN, C. D. "The Interpretation of Romans 8:28," WThJ 44 (1982) 99-109. BINDEMANN, W. Die Hoffnung der Schöpfung (Neukirchen 1983) 42-4. THEISSEN, G. Psychologische Aspekte paulinischer Theologie (Göttingen 1983) 186, 333. STAAB, K. Pauluskommentare aus der griechischen Kirche (Münster ²1984) 141:26-142:11 ThM; 383:1-6 Genn; 512:1-2 Phot. HOMMEL, H. "Denen, die Gott lieben . . . Erwägungen zu Römer 8, 28," ZNW 80 (1989) 126-9. SÖDING, T. "Gottesliebe bei Paulus," ThG 79 (3, 1989) 219-42. VOLF, J. M. G. Paul and Perseverance (Tübingen 1990) 9, 13n.29, 58-62, 165, 188n.173.

8:29ff.   STUHLMACHER, P. Gerechtigkeit Gottes bei Paulus (1965) 185ff.

8:29-39   BINDEMANN, W. Die Hoffnung der Schöpfung (Neukirchen 1983) 42-53.

8:29-30   VOLZ, P. Eschatologie der jüdischen Gemeinde (1934) 109. JERVELL, J. Imago Dei (1960) 174, 183, 187, 189, 271-81, 287f, 334. KÄSEMANN, E. Exegetische Versuche und Besinnungen (1964) I 19, 41, 118. WHITELEY, D.E.H. The Theology of St. Paul (1964) 93f. SCHILLE, G. Frühchristliche Hymnen (1965) 90. HAHN, F. "Taufe und Rechtfertigung" in J. Friedrich et al., eds., Rechtfertigung (FS E. Käsemann; Tübingen/Göttingen 1976) 104, 110, 115f. STRECKER, G. "Befreiung und Rechtfertigung" in J. Friedrich et al., eds., Rechtfertigung (FS E. Käsemann; Tübingen/Göttingen 1976) 504. BYRNE, B. "Sons of God"—"Seed of Abraham" (Rome 1979) 114, 115-22, 116n. FROITZHEIM, F. Christologie und Eschatologie bei Paulus (Würzburg 1979) 254ff. BERGMEIER, R. Glaube als Gabe nach Johannes (Stuttgart 1980) 178. KIM, S. The Origin of Paul's Gospel (Tübingen 1981) 156-9, 267, 318-20. STAAB, K. Pauluskommentare aus der griechischen Kirche (Münster ²1984) 95:11-19 Diod. VOLF, J. M. G. Paul and Perseverance (Tübingen 1990) 9-14, 15, 16n.41, 49, 67, 126, 283.

8:29   KENNEDY, H.A.A. St. Paul and the Mystery-Religions (1913) 180, 190 BRUNNER, E. Dogmatik I (1946) 223, 335, 365; II (1950) 68, 91; Mensch im Widerspruch (1937) 67ff. KÜRZINGER, J. "Symmorphous tes eiko nos tou tyiou autou (Röm. 8, 29" BZ 2 (2, '58) 294-99. ELLIS, E.E. Paul and his recent interpreters (1961) 37ff. SCHRAGE, W. Die konkreten Einzelgebote in der paulinischen Paränese (1961) 164, 214. STANLEY, D.M. "Paul's Interest in the Early Chapters of Genesis" Studiorum Paulinorum Congressus Internationalis Caltholicus 1961 (1963) I 247-48. BARRETT, C.K. From First Adam to Last (1962) 97f. STALDER, K. Das Werk des Geistes in der Heiligung bei Paulus (1962) 63, 147f. HAHN, F. Christologische Hoheitstitel (1963) 107, 311. KRAMER, W. Christos Kyrios Gottessohn (1963) §54b. HENNECKE, E., SCHNEEMELCHER, W. Neutestamentliche Apokryphen (1964) II 328, 333. KÄSEMANN, E. Exegetische Versuche und Besinnungen (1964) II 191. LEANEY, A.R.C. "Conformed to the Image of His Son' (Rom. viii.29)" NTS 10 (4, '64) 470-79. SCROGGS, R. The Last Adam (1966) 103f. NICKELS, P. Targum and New Testament (1967) 69. BLANK, J. Paulus und Jesus 91968) 258ff. KÄSEMANN, E. New Testament Questions of Today (1969) 179.

LORENZMEIER, T. "Der Erstgeborene unter vielen Brüdern" in Weihnachten heute gesagt (1970) 78-83. LINDESKOG, G. Studien zum Neutestamentlichen Schöpfungsgedanken I (1952) 226, 229, 242. SIBER, P. Mit Christus leben (Zürich 1971) 10, 220. GREER, R. A. The Captain of Our Salvation. A Study in the Patristic Exegesis of Hebrews (Tübingen 1973) 92f., 117f., 138, 142. POTVIN, T. R. The Theology of the Primacy of Christ According to St. Thomas and Its Scriptural Foundations (Fribourg 1973) 35, 46n.3, 48, 59, 66, 68f., 151, 188n.1, 216, 266f. DUNN, J. D. G. Jesus and the Spirit. A Study of the Religious and Charismatic Experience of Jesus and the First Christians as Reflected in the New Testament (London 1975) 216, 321f. FRIEDRICH, G. "Die Bedeutung der Auferweckung Jesu nach Aussagen des Neuen Testaments" in Auf das Wort kommt es an. Gesammelte Aufsätze (Göttingen 1978) 371. BYRNE, B. "Sons of God"—"Seed of Abraham" (Rome 1979) 4, 104n., 115-21, 126, 128, 136, 197, 201n., 207f., 214. FROITZHEIM, F. Christologie und Eschatologie bei Paulus (Würzburg 1979) 251ff. JERVELL, J. "Bild Gottes" in TRE 6 (1980) 496f. DUNN, J. D. G. Christology in the Making (London 1980) 37, 41, 58, 103, 106, 108, 145, 189. KIM, S. The Origin of Paul's Gospel (Tübingen 1981) 196-8, 318f. BINDEMANN, W. Die Hoffnung der Schöpfung (Neukirchen 1983) 44-6. HAYS, R. B. The Faith of Jesus Christ (Chico CA 1983) 267. THEISSEN, G. Psychologische Aspekte paulinischer Theologie (Göttingen 1983) 155, 264, 266, 333. HELDERMANN, J. Die Anapausis im Evangelium Veritatis (Leiden 1984) 198. MOHRLANG, R. Matthew and Paul (Cambridge 1984) 86f. STAAB, K. Pauluskommentare aus der griechischen Kirche (Münster ²1984) 221:1-5 Sev; 383:7-12 Genn. SCHIMANOWSKI, G. Weisheit und Messias (Tübingen 1985) 338f. LAYTON, B. The Gnostic Scriptures (Garden City NY 1987) 255, 322. LIMBECK, M. Mit Paulus Christ sein. Sachbuch zur Person und Theologie des Apostels Paulus (Stuttgart 1989) 118. OLIVEIRA, A. DE, Die Diakonie der Gerechtigkeit und der Versöhnung in der Apologie des 2. Korintherbriefes. Analyse und Auslegung von 2 Kor 2, 14-4, 6; 5, 11-6, 10 (Münster 1990) 222n.652. SEGAL, A. F. Paul the Convert (New Haven/London 1990) 10f., 59.

8:30-33   STAAB, K. Pauluskommentare aus der griechischen Kirche (Münster ²1984) 512:3-513:5 Phot.

8:30   KÄSEMANN, E. Exegetische Versuche und Besinnungen (1964) II 184. BRAUN, H. Qumran und NT II (1966) 168. KERTELGE, K. "Rechtfertigung" bei Paulus (1967) 124f., 128, 154. KÄSEMANN, E. New Testament Questions of Today (1969) 171. SCHMITHALS, W. Der Römerbrief als historisches Problem (Gütersloh 1975) 200. BYRNE, B. "Sons of God"—"Seed of Abraham" (Rome 1979) 119-22, 128, 136f. HÜBNER, H. Gottes Ich und Israel (Göttingen 1984) 25, 31. SCHENKE, G. Die Dreigestaltige Protennoia (Berlin 1984) 135. BETZ, O. "Rechtfertigung in Qumran" in Jesus. Der Messias Israels (Tübingen 1987) 58. WOLTER, M. Die Pastoralbriefe als Paulustradition (Göttingen 1988) 85.

8:31ff.   RUDOLPH, K. Die Mandäer I (1960) 106, 5. POPKES, W. Christus Traditus (1967) 114, 195, 249, 276. STROBEL, A. "Apokalyptik" in TRE 3 (1978) 252. SCHMITHALS, W. "Zur Herkunft der gnostischen Elemente in der Sprache des Paulus" in B. Aland et al., eds., Gnosis (FS H. Jonas; Göttingen 1978) 391-3. FROITZHEIM, F. Christologie und Eschatologie bei Paulus (Würzburg 1979) 64f., 253f. THEISSEN, G. Psychologische Aspekte paulinischer Theologie (Göttingen 1983) 263f., 333, 281.

8:31-39   WEBER, O. GPM 7 (1952/3) 30-33. SCHWEITZER, A. Die Mystik des Apostels Paulus (1954) 11, 65, 126, 142, 298. SEITZ, M. GPM 22 (1967/68) 56-62. HOFFMANN, P. Die Toten in Christus (1966) 340. WEBER, O. Predigtmeditationen (1967) 191-94. SCHILLE, G. "Die Liebe Gottes in Christus. Beobachtungen zu Rm 8:31-39" ZNW 59 (3-4), '68) 230-44. BALZ, H.R. Heilsvertrauen und Welterfahrung (1971) 116-123. BÖHMER, U. et al. in E. Lange, ed., Predigtstudien für das Kirchenjahr 1973/74 (1973) 95-100. HAY, D. M. Glory at the Right Hand (Nashville/New York 1973) 59f., 126f., 131. HEROLD, G. Zorn und Gerechtigkeit Gottes bei Paulus. Eine Untersuchung zu Röm. 1, 16-18 (Bern/Frankfurt 1973) 330-6. FRAIKIN, D. "Romains 8:31-39. La position des églises de la Gentilité," HThR 68 (1975) 392. FIEDLER, P. "Röm 8:31-39 als Brennpunkt paulinischer Frohbotschaft," ZNW 68 (1977) 23-34. SYNOFZIK, E. Die Gerichts- und Vergeltungsaussagen bei Paulus (Göttingen 1977) 101-4. ADLOFF, K. in GPM 34 (1979) 50-8. BYRNE, B. "Sons of God"—"Seed of Abraham" (Rome 1979) 85, 99n., 122, 232. DELLING, G. "Die Entfaltung des 'Deus pro nobis' in Röm 8, 31-39," Studien zum Neuen Testament und seiner Umwelt 4 (1979) 76-96. ROBINSON, J. A. T. Wrestling with Romans (London 1979) 106-8. STUHLMANN, R. und DEMBEK, J. in P. Krusche et al., eds., Predigtstudien für das Kirchenjahr 1979/80. Perikopenreihe II/1 (Stuttgart 1979) 77-84. GRUNDMANN, W. Wandlungen im Verständnis des Heils (Berlin, DDR 1980) 38. SCHMITHALS, W. Die theologische Anthropologie des Paulus (Stuttgart 1980) 175-200. LANDAU, R. "Komm, Heiliger Geist, du Tröster wert . . . " EvTh 41 (1981) 206-11. FINDEIS, H.-J. Versöhnung-Apostolat-Kirche (Würzburg 1983) 286ff., 292-4. SCHNURR, G. "Furcht" in TRE 11 (1983) 763. PERKINS, P. Resurrection. New Testament Witness and Contemporary Reflection (London 1984) 220, 272. SNYMAN, A. H. "Style and meaning in Romans 8:31-39," Neotestamentica 18 (1984) 94-103. HÄGGLUND, B. "Heilsgewissheit" in TRE 14 (1985) 762. TRAUB, H. in GPM 40 (1985/86) 74-9. FRAIKIN, D. "The Rhetorical Function of the Jews in Romans" in P. Richardson, ed., Anti-Judaism in Early Christianity, Vol.1: Paul and the Gospels (Waterloo/Ont. 1986) 100. DUNN, J. D. G. "Paul's Epistle to the Romans: An Analysis of Structure and Argument" in ANRW II.25.4 (1987) 2865f. SCHMELLER, TH. Paulus und die "Diatribe" (Münster 1987) 389-406, 421. SNYMAN, A. H. "Style and the Rhetorical Situation of Romans 8, 31-39," NTS 34 (2, 1988) 218-31. VOLLENWEIDER, S. Freiheit als neue Schöpfung (Göttingen 1989) 376, 389n. PARLIER, I. "La folle justice de Dieu: Romains 8, 31-39," FV 91 (5, 1992) 103-10.

8:31-37   WINK, W. Naming the Powers (Philadelphia 1984) 48-50.

8:31-34   BAULES, R. "L'amour souverain de Dieu. Rm 8, 31b-34," AssS 15 (1973) 31-6. BINDEMANN, W. Die Hoffnung der Schöpfung (Neukirchen 1983) 46-9. VOLF, J. M. G. Paul and Perseverance (Tübingen 1990) 65-9.

8:31-32   GERSTENBERGER, G. und SCHRAGE, W. Leiden (Stuttgart 1977) 191. [ET: J. E. Steely (trans.) Suffering (Nashville 1980) 221.] SCHMITHALS, W. Die theologische Anthropologie des Paulus (Stuttgart 1980) 180-3. STAAB, K. Pauluskommentare aus der griechischen Kirche (Münster ²1984) 96:1-12 Diod; 383:13-22 Genn.

8:31   KERTELGE, K. "Rechtfertigung" bei Paulus (1967) 124f. THEISSEN, G. Psychologische Aspekte paulinischer Theologie (Göttingen 1983) 333.

8:32-33   ROMANIUK, K. L'Amour du Pere et du Fils dans la Soteriologie de Saint Paul (1961) 20, 21, 42, 88-89, 170-71.

8:32   BRUNNER, E. Dogmatik I (1946) 215, 223, 224. BEST, E. One Body in Christ
            (1955) 44. DENNEY, J. The Death of Christ (1956) 104. SCHRAGE, W. Die
            konkreten Einzelgebote in der paulinischen Paränese (1961) 51. SPEYART
            VAN WOERDEN, I. "The Iconography of the Sacrifice of Abraham" VigChr
            15 (4, '61) 214-55. WULF, F. "'Er hat seinen eigenen Sohn nicht geschont'
            (Röm. 8, 32) Zeitgemässe Gedanken zum Weichnachtsgeheimnis" GuL 34 (6,
            '61) 407-9. BARRETT, C.K. From First Adam to Last (1962) 28f. HAHN, F.
            Christologische Hoheitstitel (1963) 62, 63, 202, 210, 316. KRAMER, W.
            Christos Kyrios Gottessohn (1963) §§ 26a, 55c. TOEDT, H.E. Der Menschen-
            sohn in der synoptischen Ueberlieferung (1963) 145-47, 149f. HOFFMANN, P.
            Die Toten in Christus (1966) 303. MCNAMARA, M. The New Testament and
            the Palestinian Targum to the Pentateuch (1966) 164. NICKELS, P. Targum and
            New Testament (1967) 69. POPKES, W. Christus Traditus (1967) 195f., 200ff.,
            208, 223, 236f., 247, 249ff., 253, 261, 275f., 286, 291. BLANK, J. Paulus und
            Jesus (1968) 279f., 294-98. MERK, O. Handeln aus Glauben (1968) 5f., 152,
            211. LUZ, U. Das Geschichtsverständnis desPaulus (1968) 370ff. WOOD, J.E.
            "The Isaac Typology in the New Testament" NTS 14 (1968) 583-89. DAHL,
            N.A. "The Atonement—an Adequate Reward for the Akedah? (Ro 8:32)"
            Neotestamentica et Semitica, ed. E.Ellis and M. Wilcox (1969) 15-29. LOHSE,
            E. and others, eds., Der Ruf Jesu und die Antwort der Gemeinde (1970) 204-12.
            LERCH, D. Isaaks Opferung christlich gedeutet (Tübingen 1950) 134f.
            DAVIES, W. D. The Sermon on the Mount (Cambridge 1966) 119. SIBER, P.
            Mit Christus leben (Zürich 1971) 29. DELLING, G. Der Kreuzestod Jesu in der
            urchristlichen Verkündigung (Göttingen 1972) 18-20. HANSON, A. T. Studies
            in Paul's Technique and Theology (London 1974) 38, 81-3, 86, 282. SCHMI-
            THALS, W. "Zur Herkunft der gnostischen Elemente in der Sprache des
            Paulus" in B. Aland et al., eds., Gnosis (FS H. Jonas; Göttingen 1978) 391-3.
            FROITZHEIM, F. Christologie und Eschatologie bei Paulus (Würzburg 1979)
            33ff., 203ff. RICHARDSON, P. and HURD, J. C., eds., From Jesus to Paul (FS
            F. W. Beare; Waterloo 1984) 71, 177f. WENGST, K. "Glaubensbekenntnis(se)
            IV" in TRE 13 (1984) 394. PENNA, R. "Il motivo della 'aqedah sullo sfondo
            di Rom. 8, 32," RivB 33 (4, 1985) 425-60. SCHMELLER, TH. Paulus und die
            "Diatribe" (Münster 1987) 241n.39. JONGE, M. DE, Christology in Context.
            The Earliest Christian Response to Jesus (Philadelphia 1988) 40, 114, 180,
            240n.36. JONGE, M. DE. "Jesus' death for others and the death of the
            Maccabean martyrs" in T. Baarda et al., eds., Text and Testimony (FS A. F. J.
            Klijn; Kampen 1988) 142-51, esp.145. BREYTENBACH, C. Versöhnung
            (Neukirchen-Vluyn 1989) 126, 137, 159, 164, 171, 172n., 181f., 197f., 208,
            210. MELL, U. Neue Schöpfung (Berlin/New York 1989) 358. OLIVEIRA, A.
            DE, Die Diakonie der Gerechtigkeit und der Versöhnung in der Apologie des
            2. Korintherbriefes. Analyse und Auslegung von 2 Kor 2, 14-4, 6; 5, 11-6, 10
            (Münster 1990) 224n.663.

8:33-39   QUERVAIN de, A. in G. Eichholz, ed., Herr, tue meine Lippen auf 4 (1965)
            417ff.

8:33-37   SCHMITHALS, W. Die theologische Anthropologie des Paulus (Stuttgart 1980)
            183-91. KOCH, T. "Erwählung" in TRE 10 (1982) 203.

8:33-36   ECKERT, J. "Erwählung" in TRE 10 (1982) 194.

8:33-35   TRITES, A. A. The New Testament Concept of Witness (Cambridge 1977) 202.

8:33-34   MATTERN, L. Das Verständnis des Gerichtes bei Paulus (1966) 91ff. LOHSE,
            E. Grundriss der neutestamentlichen Theologie (Stuttgart 1974) 111. STAAB,

K. Pauluskommentare aus der griechischen Kirche (Münster [2]1984) 66:9-20 Apoll; 384:1-8 Genn.

8:33   STRECKER, G. Der Weg der Gerechtigkeit (1962) 217. JÜNGEL, E. Paulus und Jesus (1966) 49. KERTELGE, K. "Rechtfertigung" bei Paulus (1967) 124f. BAUMERT, N. Täglich Sterben und Auferstehen. Der Literalsinn von 2 Kor 4, 12-5, 10 (München 1973) 90, 405. SÄNGER, D. Antikes Judentum und die Mysterien (Tübingen 1980) 192. SCHMITHALS, W. Die theologische Anthropologie des Paulus (Stuttgart 1980) 184f. HULTGREN, A. J. Paul's Gospel and Mission (Philadelphia 1985) 83. LAMPE, P. Die stadtrömischen Christen in den ersten beiden Jahrhunderten (Tübingen [2]1989) 132f.

8:34-39   BISER, E. Der Zeuge (Graz/Wien/Köln 1981) 103, 120, 194, 300.

8:34   BEST, E. One Body in Christ (1955) 9. WORDEN, T. "Christ Jesus Who Died or rather Who has been Raised Up (Rom8:34)" Scripture 10 (10, '58) 33-43; 11 (14, '50) 51-59. SCHWEIZER, E. Erniedrigung und Erhöhung bei Jesus und seinen Nachfolgern (1962) §9b. HAHN, F. Christologische Hoheitstitel (1963) 130, 204, 233f. KRAMER, W. Christol Kyrios Gottessohn (1963) §§ 5b, 55c. JÜNGEL, E. Paulus und Jesus (1966) 49. BLANK, J. Paulus und Jesus (1968) 256f. LUZ, U. Das Geschichtsverständnis des Paulus (1968) 370f. LOHFINK, G. Die Himmelfahrt Jesus (1971) 84f. MAUSER, U. Gottesbild und Menschwerdung (1971) 134, 141f., 180. DALTON, W. J. Christ's Proclamation to the Spirits. A Study of 1 Peter 3:18-4:6 (Rome 1965) 126. SHIMADA, K. The Formulary Material in First Peter. A Study According to the Method of Traditionsgeschichte (Ann Arbor MI 1966) 376-9, 391-3. HARMAN, A. M. Paul's Use of the Psalms (Ann Arbor MI 1968) 185f. SIBER, P. Mit Christus leben (Zürich 1971) 24, 33. LADD, G. E. A Theology of the New Testament (Grand Rapids 1974) 411, 446, 523, 614. GOPPELT, L. Theologie des Neuen Testaments I: Jesu Wirken in seiner theologischen Bedeutung [J. Roloff, ed.] (Göttingen 1975) 280f. DUNN, J. D. G. Unity and Diversity in the New Testament. An Inquiry into the Character of Earliest Christianity (London 1977) 219. FRIEDRICH, G. "Die Fürbitte im Neuen Testament" in Auf das Wort kommt es an. Gesammelte Aufsätze (Göttingen 1978) 439. HOFFMANN, P. "Auferstehung" in TRE 4 (1979) 482, 488. FROITZHEIM, F. Christologie und Eschatologie bei Paulus (Würzburg 1979) 91, 127. BAIRD, W. "Ascension and Resurrection. An Intersection of Luke and Paul" in W. E. March, ed., Texts and Testaments (FS S. D. Currie; San Antonio 1980) 11. HENGEL, M. "Hymnus und Christologie" in W. Haubeck und M. Backmann, eds., Wort in der Zeit (FS K. H. Rengstorf; Leiden 1980) 10-3. SCHMITHALS, W. Die theologische Anthropologie des Paulus (Stuttgart 1980) 185-7. SCHÜRMANN, H. "Christliche Weltverantwortung im Lichte des Neuen Testaments," Catholica 34 (1980) 103. SEGAL, A. F. "Heavenly Ascent in Hellenistic Judaism. Early Christianity and their Environment" in ANRW II.23.2 (1980) 1374. LOADER, W. R. G. Sohn und Hoherpriester. Eine traditionsgeschichtliche Untersuchung zur Christologie des Hebräerbriefes (Neukirchen-Vluyn 1981) 154f., 158f. HENGEL, M. "Hymns and Christology" in Between Jesus and Paul (Philadelphia 1983) 86f. THEISSEN, G. Psychologische Aspekte paulinischer Theologie (Göttingen 1983) 117f., 228, 263, 333. BERGER, K. "Geist" in TRE 12 (1984) 188. MÜLLER, G. "Gebet" in TRE 12 (1984) 88. PERKINS, P. Resurrection. New Testament Witness and Contemporary Reflection (London 1984) 217, 220. STAAB, K. Pauluskommentare aus der griechischen Kirche (Münster [2]1984) 221:6-25 Sev; 384:19-385:5 Genn; 428:8-16 Oek; 513:5-16 Phot. DIETZFEL-BINGER, C. Die Berufung des Paulus als Ursprung seiner Theologie (Neukirchen 1985) 32, 129, 132. STUHLMACHER, P. "Jesus von Nazareth und die neutestamentliche Christologie im Lichte der Heiligen Schrift" in M. Klopfenstein et al., eds., Mitte der Schrift? Ein jüdisch-christliches Gespräch. Texte des Berner Symposions vom 6.-12. Januar 1985 (Bern etc. 1987) 93. HENGEL, M. "Psalm 110 und die Erhöhung des Auferstandenen zur Rechten Gottes" in C. Breytenbach und H. Paulsen, eds., Anfänge der Christologie (FS F. Hahn; Göttingen 1991) 43-73. LOHSE, E. Die Entstehung des Neuen Testaments (Stuttgart/ Berlin/Köln ⁵1991) 20.

8:35-39   EICHHOLZ, G. Die Theologie des Paulus im Umriss (1972) 169f. ZMIJEWSKI, J. Der Stil der paulinischen 'Narrenrede'. Analyse der Sprachgestaltung in 2 Kor 11, 1-12, 10 (Köln/Bonn 1978) 317-9. KLEIN, G. "Eschatologie" in TRE 10 (1982) 283. SCHNACKENBURG, R. Die sittliche Botschaft des Neuen Testaments, Band 1 (Freiburg/Basel/Wien 1986) 217. OLIVEIRA, A. DE, Die Diakonie der Gerechtigkeit und der Versöhnung in der Apologie des 2. Korintherbriefes. Analyse und Auslegung von 2 Kor 2, 14-4, 6; 5, 11-6, 10 (Münster 1990) 346. VOLF, J. M. G. Paul and Perseverance (Tübingen 1990) 16, 56-65.

8:35-37   SCHMITHALS, W. Der Römerbrief als historisches Problem (Gütersloh 1975) 199. SCHMITHALS, W. Die theologische Anthropologie des Paulus (Stuttgart 1980) 187-91.

8:35-36   MÜNDERLEIN, G. "Interpretation einer Tradition. Bemerkungen zu Röm. 8, 35f" KuD 11 (2, '65) 136-42.

8:35   SCHRAGE, W. Die konkreten Einzelgebote in der paulinischen Paränese (1961) 81. THEISSEN, G. Psychologische Aspekte paulinischer Theologie (Göttingen 1983) 119, 333, 370. STAAB, K. Pauluskommentare aus der griechischen Kirche (Münster ²1984) 385:6-9 Genn; 513:17-24 Phot. POBEE, J. S. Persecution and Martyrdom in the Theology of Paul (Sheffield 1985) 5, 91, 96, 112. KOCH, D.-A. Die Schrift als Zeuge des Evangeliums (Tübingen 1986) 263f.

8:36-37   STAAB, K. Pauluskommentare aus der griechischen Kirche (Münster ²1984) 385:10-18 Genn.

8:36   ELLIS, E.E. Paul's Use of the Old Testament (1957) 32, 116, 138, 150, 160. SCHWEIZER, E. Gemeinde und Gemeinde-Ordnung im Neuen Testament (1959) §7f. LUZ, U. Das Geschichtsverständnis des Paulus (1968) 376. HARMAN, A. M. Paul's Use of the Psalms (Ann Arbor MI 1968) 88-93. SIBER, P. Mit Christus leben (Zürich 1971) 113. GERSTENBERGER, G. und SCHRAGE, W. Leiden (Stuttgart 1977) 127f; ET: J. E. Steely (trans.) Suffering (Nashville 1980) 148f. METZGER, B. M. The Early Versions of the New Testament. Their Origin Transmission, and Limitations (Oxford 1977) 150. KOCH, D.-A. Die Schrift als Zeuge des Evangeliums (Tübingen 1986) 263f.

8:37.39   WERBICK, J. "Die Soteriologie zwischen 'christologischem Triumphalismus' und apokalyptischem Radikalismus" in I. Broer und J. Werbick, eds., "Auf Hoffnung hin sind wir erlöst" (Röm 8, 14) (Stuttgart 1987) 181f.

8:37   DELLING, G. Die Zueignung des Heils in der Tauge (1961) 62. SCHRAGE, W. Die konkreten Einzelgebote in der paulinischen Paränese (1961) 249. STAAB, K. Pauluskommentare aus der griechischen Kirche (Münster ²1984) 142:12-16 ThM; 221:26-29 Sev. MOULE, C. F. D. "Reflections on So-called 'Triumphalism'" in L. D. Hurst and N. T. Wright, eds., The Glory of Christ in the New Testament (FS G. B. Caird; Oxford 1987) 219-27, esp.222.

8:38ff.   BÖCHER, O. "Engel" in TRE 9 (1982) 598.

8:38-39   TILLICH, P. Das Neue Sein (1959) 56-64. JEFFREY, G.J. "Paul's Certainties: VIII. The Love of God in Christ—Romans vii, 38, 39" ET 69 (12, '58) 359-61. KÄSEMANN, E.Exegetische Versuche und Besinnungen (1964) I 86. HOFFMANN, P. Die Toten in Christus (1966) 6, 7, 17, 342f. LUZ, U. Das Geschichtsverständnis des Paulus (1968) 376. GIBBS, J.G. Creation and Redepmtion (1971) 46, 62, 69, 75, 106, 134f., 145. SCHMITHALS, W. Der Römerbrief als historisches Problem (Gütersloh 1975) 200. GERSTENBER-GER, G. und SCHRAGE, W. Leiden (Stuttgart 1977) 185; ET: J. E. Steely (trans.) Suffering (Nashville 1980) 214. KRUIJF, T. C. DE. "Antisemitismus" in TRE 3 (1978) 125. SCHMITHALS, W. Die theologische Anthropologie des Paulus (Stuttgart 1980) 191-200. BISER, E. Der Zeuge (Graz/Wien/Köln 1981) 73, 120, 228, 237. CARR, W. Angels and Principalities (Cambridge 1981) 112-4. BLACK, M. "πᾶσαι ἐξουσίαι αὐτῷ ὑποταγήσονται" in M. D. Hooker and S. G. Wilson, eds., Paul and Paulinism (FS C. K. Barrett; London 1982) 76-9. BINDEMANN, W. Die Hoffnung der Schöpfung (Neukirchen 1983) 52. STAAB, K. Pauluskommentare aus der griechischen Kirche (Münster ²1984) 142:17-143:8 ThM; 385:19-386:10 Genn. WINK, W. Naming the Powers (Philadelphia 1984) 47-50. BERGER, K. und COLPE, C., eds., Religionsge-schichtliches Textbuch zum Neuen Testament (Göttingen/Zürich 1987) 219. BECKER, J. Paulus. Der Apostel der Völker (Tübingen 1989) 404, 407, 428, 440. LIMBECK, M. Mit Paulus Christ sein. Sachbuch zur Person und Theologie des Apostels Paulus (Stuttgart 1989) 137.

8:38   BAUER, J. B. Scholia Biblica et Patristica (Graz 1972) 177f. LADD, G. E. A Theology of the New Testament (Grand Rapids 1974) 400, 401, 464, 553, 568. MANN, U. "Engel" in TRE 9 (1982) 611.

8:39   BRUNNER, E. Dogmatik I (1946) 207. BEST.E. One Body in Christ (1955) 6n, 11n. SCHRAGE, W. Die konkreten Einzelgebote in der paulinischen Paränese (1961) 81, 249. KRAMER, W. Christos Kyrios Gottessohn (1963) § 19c. KÄSEMANN, E. Exegetische Versuche und Besinnungen (1964) II 187. NICKELS, P. Targum and New Testament (1967) 69. KÄSEMANN, E. New Testament Questions of Today (1969) 174. ROON, A. VAN, The Authenticity of Ephesians (Leiden 1974) 265.

9ff.   ELLIS, E. E. Prophecy and Hermeneutic in Early Christianity (Tübingen 1978) 150, 159, 218, 221.

9-14   WESTHELLE, V. "Paul's Reconstruction of Theology: Romans 9-14 in Context," Word and World 4 (1984) 307-319.

9-11   GORE, C. "The argument of Romans IX-XI" Studia biblica et ecclesiastica III (1891) 37-34. BEYSCHLAG, W. Die paulinische Theodizee, Römer IX.XI [1868] (1896). KUEHL, E. "Zur paulinischen Theodizee" Theologische Studien (FS B. Weiss) (1897) 52-94. WEBER, E. Das Problem der Heilsgeschichte nach Röm. 9-11 (1911). HOPPE, T. Die Idee der Heilsgeschichte bei Paulus mit besonderer Berücksichtigung des Römerbriefes (1926). PUUKKO, Paulus und das Judentum (1928). MAIER, F.W. Israel in der Heislgeschichte / nach Röm. 9-11. (1929). PETERSON, E. Die Kirche aus Juden und Heiden (1951). WIN-DISCH, H. Paulus und das Judentum (1935). WENDLAND, H.D., Geschichts-anschauung und Geschichtsbe-wusstsein im Neuen Testament (1938). DELLING, G. Das Zeitverständnis des Neuen Testaments (1940) 64ff. DAHL, N.A. Das Volk Gottes (1941-1963). BRUETSCH, C. La question juive à la lumère de l'Epître aux Romains ch. 9-11 (1943). SCHMIDT, K.L. Die Judenfrage im Lichte der Kapitel 9-11 des Römerbriefes (1943). SCHRENK,

G. Der göttliche Sinn in Israels Geschick (1943). CULLMANN, O. Christus und die Zeit (1946); Christ and Time (1962). DAVIDSON, F. Pauline Predestination (1946). BULTMANN, R. "Heilsgeschichte und Geschichte—Zu Oscar Cullmann, Christus und die Zeit": Exegetica (1947) 356-68. FEUILLET, A. "Le plan salvifique de Dieu" RB 57 (1950) 336-87, 489-529. OEPKE, A. Das neue Gottesvolk (1950). VISCHER, W. "Das Geheimnis Israels. Eine Erklärung der Kapitel 9-11 des Römerbriefes" Judaica VI (1950) 81-132. FICHTNER, J. "Zum Problem Glaube und Geschichte in der israelitisch-jüdischen Weisheitsliteratur" ThLZ 76 (1951) 145-50. QUISPEL, G. "Zeit und Geschichte im antiken Christentum" ErJB (1951) 115-40, esp. 115-18. SCHRENK, G. Die Weissagung über Israel, im Neuen Testament (1951). MARSCH, J. The Fulness of Time (1952). SCHELKLE, K.H. "Kirche und Synagoge in der frühen Auslegung des Römerbriefes" ThQ 134 ('54) 290-318. MUNCK, J. Paulus und die Heilsgeschichte (1954) = Paul and the Salvation of Mankind (1960). SCHRENK, G. Die Geschichtsanschauung des Paulus (1954) 49-80. BULTMANN, R. "History and Eschatology in the New Testament" NTS I (1954/55) 5-16. RIDDERBOS, H. "Israel in het Nieuwe Testament in het bijzonder volgens Romeinen, 9-11" in G.C. Aalders—H. Ridderbos, Israel (1955). SCHLIER, H. "Das Mysterium Israels" in Die Zeit der Kirche (1955) 232-44. GRAHAM, H.H. "Continuity and Discontinuity in the Thought of Paul" ATR 38 ('56) 137-46. KUSS, O. "Zur Geschichtstheologie der paulinischen Hauptbriefe" TG 46 ('56) 241-60. MUNCK, J. Christus und Israel (1956). DINKLER, E. "The Historical and the Eschatological Israel in Romans, Chapter 9-11: A Contribution to the Problem of Predestination and Individual Responsibility" JR 36 ('56) 109-27. PLOEG, J. van der, The Church and Israel (1956). SCHELKLE, K.H. Paulus Lehrer der Väter (1956). BULTMANN, R. History and Eschatology (1957) 40-47. CAIRD, G.B. "Predestination—Romans ix-xi" ET (1957) 324-27. ELLIS, E.E. Paul's Use of the Old Testament (1957) 11, 72, 114, 120ff. KUSS, O. "Die Heilsgeschichte" Der Römerbrief (1957) 275-91. SMITH, M. "Pauline Problems. Apropos of J. Munck, 'Paulus und die Heilsgeschichte'" HThR 50 (2, '57) 107-131. DINKLER, E. "Geschichtsver-ständnis, das christliche" RGG³ II ('58) cols 1476-82. EVANS, D.D. "The Mystery of Israel: A reply to E. Flessmannvan Leer and David W. Hay" CJTh 5 (1, '58) 30-36. GOEDT, M. de "La destinée d'Israel dans le mystère du salut d'après l'epître aux Romains, IX-XI" SuppVie Spir 47 ('58) 443-61. KNIGHT, G.A.F. "Israel—A Theological Problem" RThR 17 (2, '58) 33-43. LEONARD, W. "The Jewish Enigma in the Epistle to the Romans" ACR 35 (3, 58) 202-11. SCHEDL, C. "Bund und Erwählung ZKTh 80 (v, '58) 493-515. TREMEL, Y.-B. "Le Mystère d' Israel" LuVie 37 (7, '58) 71-90. ARMSTRONG, C.B. "History in Pauline Thought" HibJourn 58 (1, '59) 36-41. DEUILLET, A. "La Citation d'Abacuc II.4 et les huit premiers Chapitres de l'Epître aux Romains" NTS 6 (1959-60) 70f. MULLER-DUVERNOY, C. "L'apôtre Paul et le problème juif" Judaica 15 (1959) 65-91. MUNCK, J. Paul and the Salvation of Mankind (1949) 42-44. SCHOEPS, H.-J. Paulus (1959) 248-59. SCHWEIZER, E. Gemeinde und Gemeindeordnung im Neuen Testament (1959) §72, 18a. STECK, K.G. Die Idee der Heilsgeschichte, ThSt 56 (1959). LOHSE, E. Israel und die Christenheit (1960). BULTMANN, R. "Das Verständnis der Geschichte im Griechentum und im Christentum" in Der Sin der Geschichte (1961) 50-65. JOURNEL, C. "La dialectique paulinienne des Juifs et des Gentils" NV 36 (2, '61) 107-29. LINDESKOG, G. "Israel in the NT—Some few remarks on a great problem" SEA 26 (1961) 57-92. MARTIN SANCHEZ, B. "El destino de Israel

(Cap. IX-XI)" CultBib 18 (177, '61) 79-96. THIEME, K. "Neue christliche Sicht des "Israel nach dem Fleisch'" Catholica 16 (4, '62) 271-92. GOPPELT, L. "Israel und die Kirche, heute und bei Paulus" LR 13 (4, '63) 429-52. JOURNET, C. "L'économie de la loi maisaique" RevThom 63 (1, '63) 5-36; (2, '63) 193-224; (4, '63)515-547. LOVSKY, F. "Remarques sur la notion de rejet par rapport au mystère d'Israel et à l'unité de l'Eglise" RHPhR 43 (1, '63) 32-47). OSTERREICHER, J.M. "Israel's Misstep and her rise" Studiorum Paulinorum Congressus Internationalis Catholicus 1961 (1963) I 317-27. SCHWANTES, H. Schöpfung der Endzeit (1963) 18ff. AAGAARD, J. "Die Kirche und die Juden in der Eschatologie" LR 14/3 (1964). ANON, "Two Branches of the People of God. A Jewish-Christian Conference in the Netherlands" HerCorr 1 (9-10, '64) 264-65. BEAUCHAMP, P. "L'Eglise et le peuple juif" Etudes 321 (9, '64) 249-68. GILBERT, A. "Die Sendung des jüdischen Volkes in der Geschichte und in der modernen Welt" LR 14 ('64) 377-94. LADD, G.E. "Israel and the Church" EQ 36 (4, '64) 206-13. KÄSE-MANN, E. Exegetische Versuche und Besinnungen I 146, II 24, 191, 196. LINDESKOG, G. "Christianity as Realized Judaism" Pistis kai Erga (1964) 15-36. MULLER, C. Gottes Gerechtigkeit und Gottes Volk. Eine Untersuchung zu Römer 9-11 (1964). BOLEWSKI, H. "Geschichtliche Schuld und geschichtliche Hoffnung" LR 14 (3, '64) 333-36. ANON, "Die Kirche und das jüdische Volk. Bericht über eine Konsultation" LR 14 (3, '64) 337-44. RENGSTORF, K.H. "Der Platzdes Juden in der Theologie der christlichen Mission" LR 14 (3, '64) 356-76. PFISTERER, R. "Das Judentum in der Verkündigung und im Unterricht der Kirche" LR 14 (3, '64) 395-412. HARDER, G. "Das christlich-jüdische Gespräch" LR 14 (3, '64) 427-52. MINETTE DE TILLESSE, G. "Le mystére du peuple juif" Irénikon 37 (1, '64) 7-49. MINETTE DE TILLESSE, G. "El misterio del pueblo judio" Selecteol 4 (14, '64) 135-44. RICHARDS, J. "Vatikan II and the Jews" ClR 49 (9, '64) 552-61. WHITELEY, D.E.H. The Theology of St. Paul (1964) 95- 97. BEA, A. "Das jüdische Volk undder göttliche Heilsplan" StZ 176 (15, '65) 641-59. "The Jewish People in the Divine Plan of Salvation" Thought 41 (160, '66) 9-32. HUSSAR, B. "Réflex-ions sur le mystère d'Israel" BibTerre Sainte 79 (1966) 6-7. SCHUBERT, K. "Die Erklärung des 2. Vatikan-ischen Konzils über die Juden" BuLit 39 (1, '66) 16-22. BEA, A. "Il popolo ebraico nel piano divino della salvezza" CivCatt 116/4 ('65) 209-29. BLACKMAN, E.E. "Divine Sovereignty and Missionary Strategy in Romans 9-11" Can JTh 11 (2, '65) 124-34. CARLI, L.M. "La questione giudaica davanti al Concilio Vaticano II" PaCl 44 ('65) 185-203. CULLMANN, O. Heil als Geschichte (1965) 97, 100, 106, 241, 286. DIETZ-FELBINGER, Chr. Heilsges-chichte bei Paulus (1965). HAHN, F. Das Verständnis der Mission im Neuen Testament (1965). THEYSSEN, G.W. "Unbelief" in the New Testament (1965) 11ff. ALTHAUS, P. "Rückblick auf Kap. 9-11" und "Israels Schicksal und die Christenheit" Der Brief an die Römer (1966) 120-23. CARLI, L.M. "Chiesa e Sinagoga" PaCl 45 ('66). JÜNGEL, E. Paulus und Jesus (1966) 26. LICHTENBERG, J.P. "Contenu et portée de la Déclaration conciliaire sur les Juifs" NRTh 88 (3, '66) 225-48. GOPPELT.L. "Paulus und die Heilsgeschichte" NTS 13 (1966/67) 31-42. RICHARDS, J.R. "Romans and I Corinthians: Their Chronological Relationship and Comparative Dates" NTS 13 (1966/67) 18ff. MUNCK, J. Christ and Israel. An Interpretation of Romans 9-11 (1967). FITZMYER, J. "The Father's Plan of Salvation History" Pauline Theology (1967) 23. ROBINSON, D.W.B. "The Salvation of Israel in Romans 9-11" RThR 26 (3, '67) 81-96. STUHLMACHER, P.

"Gegenwart und Zukunft in der paulinischen Eschatologie" ZThK 64 (1967) 423-50. BARTH, M. "Jews and Gentiles: The Social Character of Justification in Paul" JES 5 (1968) 241-67. HESTER, J.D. Paul's Concept of Inheritance (1968). KÄSEMANN, E. "Paulus und Israel" (1961): Exegetische Versuche und Besinnungen II (1968) 194-97. LUZ, U. Das Geschichtsverständnis des Paulus (1968) 20ff., 400ff. LUZ, U. Das Geschichtsverständnis, Rev. J. Cambier, "L'histoire et le salut dans Rm 9-11" Biblica 51 (2, '70) 241-52. ZERWICK, M. "Drama populi Israel secundum Rom 9-11" VerbDom 46 (6, '68) 321-38. PLAG, C. Israel's Wege zum Heil. Eine Untersuchung zu Römer 9 bis 11 (1969). RICHARDSON, P. Israel in the Apostolic Church (1969) 70-158, 126-127, 132-35, 138f; Rev. K. Kruby, Judaica 28 (1, '72) 30-40; Lebram, J.C.H. VigChr 26 (2, '72) 148-52. GIBLIN, C.H. In Hope of God's Glory (1970) 264-310. GÜTTGEMANNS, E. "Heilsgeschichte bei Paulus oder Dynamik des Evangeliums? Zur Strukturellen Relevanz von Röm 9-11 für die Theologie des Römerbriefes" Studia linguistica neotestamentica (1971) 34-58. HESSE, F. Abschied von der Heilsgeschichte (1971). MAIER, G. Mensch und Freier Wille (1971) 351-400. MINEAR, P.S. The Obedience of Faith (1971) 72-81. EICHHOLZ, G. Die Theologie des Paulus im Umriss (1972) 43, 84, 95, 124, 284ff. SHEPARD, J. W. The Life and Letters of St. Paul (Grand Rapids 1950) 414-430. ENSLIN, M. S. The Literature of the Christian Movement (New York 1956) 269f. BAUM, G. The Jews and the Gospel (London 1961) 208-18. BERKHOF, H. Der Sinn der Geschichte: Christus (Göttingen 1962) 158-64, 180, 241. OESTERREICHER, J. "Israel's Misstep and her Rise. The Dialectic of God's Saving Design in Romans 9-11," AnBib 17-18/I (1963) 317-27. REICHRATH, H. "Ein Stiefkind christlicher Theologie," Jud 23/3 (1967) 160-81. PLAG, C. Israels Wege zum Heil. Eine Untersuchung zu Römer 9 bis 11 (Stuttgart 1969). O'NEILL, J. C. The Theology of Acts in its historical setting (London 1970) 96, 133f. KUSS, O. Paulus (Regensburg 1971) 183f., 188, 307, 362, 382, 383-85, 408, 431. MARQUARDT, F.-W. "Die Juden im Römerbrief" in Theologische Studien 107 (Zürich 1971) 3-48. SELBY, D. J. Introduction to the New Testament (New York 1971) 388, 400-2. CORSANI, B. "I capitoli 9-11 della lettera ai Romani," BiOr 14 (1, 1972) 31-47. LAYMAN, F. D. Paul's Use of Abraham. An Approach to Paul's Understanding of History (diss. University of Iowa; Ann Arbor MI 1972) 84-100, 163-78, 220-23, 240-92. PIKAZA, J. La Biblia y la Teología de la Historia. Tierra y promesa de Dios (Madrid 1972) passim. CORSANI, B. "Passato presente e futuro di Israele in Rom 9-11. Rassegne," Protest. 28 (1973) 88-92. WILSON, S. G. The Gentiles and the Gentile Mission in Luke-Acts (London/Cambridge 1973) 115, 155, 169, 250. ZELLER, D. "Israel unter dem Ruf Gottes (Röm 9-11)," IKZ 2 (1973) 289-301. DAVIES, W. D. The Gospel and the Land. Early Christianity and Jewish Territorial Doctrine (London 1974) 173n.19, 183, 183n.38, 185, 196, 201-8, 216, 218, 399, 399n.24. LADD, G. E. A Theology of the New Testament (Grand Rapids 1974) 333, 394, 537. MAYER, B. Unter Gottes Heilsratschluss. Prädestinationsaussagen bei Paulus (Würzburg 1974) 167-313. WILES, G. P. Paul's Intercessory Prayers (London 1974) 75, 76, 84, 87, 132, 133, 254, 265. CONZELMANN, H. and LINDENMANN, A. Arbeitsbuch zum Neuen Testament (Tübingen 1975) 215, 218. GASQUE, W. A History of the Criticism of the Acts of the Apostles (Tübingen 1975) 30, 38, 196f., 242f., 271f., 272. LINDEMANN, A. Die Aufhebung der Zeit. Geschichtsverständnis und Eschatologie im Epheserbrief (Gütersloh 1975) 26-30, 39, 253. LYONNET, S. Quaestiones in epistulam ad Romanos. Rom 9-11, De praedestinatione Esrael et theologia historiae (Rome 1975) SCHMITHALS, W. Der Römerbrief als historisches Problem (Gütersloh 1975) 10f., 20ff., 26, 28, 37, 46, 56, 84, 153, 158, 160f. BEASLEY-MURRAY, G. R. "The Righteousness of God in the History of Israel and the Nations: Romans 9-11," RevEx 73 (1976) 437-50. CORLEY, B. "The Jews, the Future, and God (Romans 9-11)," SouJTh 19 (1976) 42-56. GOPPELT, L. Theologie des Neuen Testaments II: Vielfalt und Einheit des apostolischen Christuszeugnisses (Göttingen 1976) 460ff. BARTH, M. "Das Volk Gottes. Juden und Christen in der Botschaft des Paulus" in M. Barth et al. Paulus—Apostat oder Apostel? (Regensburg 1977) 75-96. DUGANDZIC, I. Das "Ja" Gottes in Christus (Würzburg 1977) 272-310. OSTEN-SACKEN, P. VON DER. "Israel als Anfrage an die Christliche Theologie. Beobachtungen und Erwägungen aus dem Bereich neutestamentlicher Schriftauslegung" in Treue zur Thora (FS. G. Harder; Berlin 1977) 72-83. WORGUL G. S. "Romans 9-11 and Ecclesiology," BThB 7 (1977) 99-109. KRUIJF, T. C. DE "Antisemitismus" in TRE 3 (1978) 125. BETZ, O. "Die heilsgeschichtliche Rolle Israels bei Paulus," Theol Beitr 9 (1978) 1-21. BLOCH, R. "Midrash" in W. S. Green, ed., Approaches to Ancient Judaism: Theory and Practice (Missoula 1978) 48. ECKERT, J. "Paulus und Israel. Zu den Strukturen paulinischer Rede und Argumentation," TThZ 87 (1978) 1-13. HÜBNER, H. Das Gesetz bei Paulus. Ein Beitrag zum Werden der paulinischen Theologie (Göttingen 1978) 50-3. SCHMITHALS, W. "Zur Herkunft der gnostischen Elemente in der Sprache des Paulus" in B. Aland et al., eds., Gnosis (FS. H. Jonas; Göttingen 1978) 392-3. RICHARDSON, P. Paul's Ethic of Freedom (Philadelphia 1979) 33-7. ROBINSON, J. A. T. Wrestling with Romans (London 1979) 108-10. ROLOFF. J. Neues Testament (Neukirchen-Vluyn 1979) 176-178. CAMPBELL, W. S. "Salvation for Jews and Gentiles: Krister Stendahl and Paul's Letter to the Romans" in E. A. Livingstone (ed). Studia Biblica 1978. III. Papers on Paul and Other New Testament Authors (Sheffield 1980) 65-72. DINKLER, E. "Die ekklesiologischen Aussagen des Paulus im kritischen Rückblick auf Barmen III" in A. Burgsmüller, ed., Kirche als 'Gemeinde von Brüdern' (Gütersloh 1980) 121-3. FISCHER, J. A. "Dissent Within a Religious Community: Romans 9-11," BThB 10 (1980) 105-10. HARRINGTON, D. J. God's People in Christ (Philadelphia 1980) 57-66. JERVELL, J. "Der unbekannte Paulus" in S. Pedersen, ed., Die Paulinische Literatur und Theologie (Arhus/Göttingen 1980) 46-8. McDONALD, J. I. H. Kerygma and Didache (Cambridge 1980) 58-9. MOXNES, H. Theology in Conflict (Leiden 1980) 28-30, 32-55, 88, 92, 267, 273, 275, 276. OKEKE, G. E. "I Thessalonians 2:13-16: The Fate of the Unbelieving Jews," NTS 27 (1980) 127-36, esp. 132-5. SCHILLEBEECKX, E. Christ: the Christian Experience in the Modern World (London 1980) 603-6; GT: Christus und die Christen (Freiburg/Basel/Wien 1977) 583-7. STEIGER, L. "Schutzrede für Israel. Römer 9-11" in Fides pro mundi vita (FS. H.-W. Gensichen; Fütersloh 1980) 44-58. THISELTON, A. C. The Two Horizons (Grand Rapids 1980) 290, 318. VICENT, R. "Derash homilético en Romanos 9-11," Sal. 42 (1980) 751-88. CAMPBELL, W. S. "The Freedom and Faithfulness of God in Relation to Israel," JSNT 13 (1981) 27-45. HAGEN, K. Hebrews Commenting from Erasmus to Bèze 1516-98 (Tübingen 1981) 68. HÜBNER, H. "Der 'Messias Israels' und der Christus des Neuen Testaments," Kud 27 (1981) 234-5. LOSADA, D. A. "La cuestión de Israel en Rom. 9-11," RevBi 43 (2, 1981) 65-80. VILLIERS, J. L. DE "The Salvation of Israel according to Romans 9-11," Neotestamentica 15 (1981) 199-221. BASSLER, J. M. Divine Impartiality (Chico/CA 1982) 160-2. ECKERT, J.

"Erwählung" in TRE 10 (1982) 194f. FEUILLET, A. "Les privilèges et l'incrédulité d'Israël, d'après les chapitres 9-11 de l'épître aux Romains. Quelques suggestions pour un dialogue fructueux entre Juifs et Chrétiens," EsVie 92 (37, 1982) 481-93, (38, 1982) 497-506. KEANE, H. "The Church and the Jewish people: Another look at the problem," ThEv 15 (1982) 37-47. KLAIBER, W. Rechtfertigung und Gemeinde (Göttingen 1982) 170-4. MAILLOT, A. "Essai sur les citations vétérotestamentaires contenues dans Romains 9 à 11, ou comment se servir de le Torah pour montrer que le 'Christ est la fin de la Torah'," EThR 57 (1, 1982) 55-73. STENDAHL, K. "Ancient Scripture in the Modern World" in F. E. Greenspahn, ed., Scripture in the Jewish and Christian Traditions (Nashville 1982) 214. FEUILLET, A. "La situación privilegiada de Israel en su rechazo de Cristo, según la Epístola a los Romanos (capítulos 9-11)," ScrTh 15 (1983) 31-81. GORDAY, P. Principlles of Patristic Exegesis. Romans 9-11 in Origen, John Chrysostom, and Augustine (New York/Toronto 1983) MAYER, G. "La réponse juive à la thèse paulinienne de la caducité de la loi mosaïque en Romains IX-XI," CahCER 31 (132, 1983) 135-41. MEEKS, W. A. The First Urban Christians (New Haven/London 1983) 85, 168, 187. NEBE, G. 'Hoffnung' bei Paulus (Göttingen 1983) 181, 190, 192, 286, 289, 318, 332. SCHNEIDER, P. "The Meaning of 'Israel' in the Writings of St. Paul," Face to Face [New York] 10 (1983) 12-6. DAVIES, W. D. Jewish and Pauline Studies (Philadelphia 1984) 130-52. DAVIES, W. D. "Paul and the People of Israel" in Jewish and Pauline Studies (Philadelphia 1984) 123-52, 341-56. EVANS, C. A. "Paul and the Hermeneutics of 'True Prophecy': A Study of Romans 9-11," Biblica 65 (1984) 560-570. LUZ, U. "Geschichte" in TRE 12 (1984) 601. HÜBNER, H. Gottes Ich und Israel. Zum Schriftgebrauch des Paulus in Römer 9-11 (Göttingen 1984) KLEIN, R. W. "Anti-Semitism as Christian Legacy: The Origin and Nature of our Estrangement from the Jews," CThMi 11 (5, 1984) 285-301. SCHMITT, R. Gottesgerechtigkeit—Heilsge-schichte—Israel in der Theologie des Paulus (Frankfurt/Bern/New York/Nancy 1984) 67-116. STENDAHL, K. "Judaism and Christianity: Then and Now" in Meanings (Philadelphia 1984) 213. VANGEMEREN, W. A. "Israel as the Hermeneutical Crux in the Interpretation of Prophecy (II)," WThJ 46 (1984) 254-97, esp.288-94. WALTER, N. "Zur Interpretation von Römer 9-11," ZThK 81 (2, 1984) 172-95. BADENAS, R. Christ the End of the Law (Sheffield 1985) 81-96. GRÄSSER, E. Der Alte Bund im Neuen (Tübingen 1985) 12, 17, 19, 23f., 28, 31, 54, 220, 227f., 243, 259, 279, 281-6. KLUMBIES, P.-G. "Israels Vorzüge und das Evangelium von der Gottesgerechtigkeit in Römer 9-11," WuD 18 (1985) 135-57. RADERMAKERS, J. and SONNET, J.-P. "Israël et l'Eglise," NRTh 107 (5, 1985) 675-97. SANDERS, E. P. Paul, the Law, and the Jewish People (London 1985) 29-32, 46, 50n.8, 57n.64, 58n.75, 62n.121, 77f., 158, 162, 185, 188, 192, 197, 199, 205nn.80-4, 206n.96. SIEGERT, F. Argumentation bei Paulus gezeigt an Röm 9-11 (Tübingen 1985) AAGESON, J. W. "Scripture and Structure in the Development of the Argument in Romans 9-11," CBQ 48 (1986) 265-89. BEKER, J. C. "The Faithfulness of God and the Priority of Israel in Paul's Letter to the Romans" in G. W. E. Nickelsburg and G. W. MacRae, eds., Christians among Jews and Gentiles (FS. Krister Stendahl; Philadelphia 1986) 11-6. FABRIS, R. "La 'gelosia' nella Lettera ai Romani (9-11). Per un nouvo rapporto tra ebrei e cristiani," RT 27 (1, 1986), 15-33. FRAIKIN, D. "The Rhetorical Function of the Jews in Romans" in P. Richard-son, ed., Anti-Judaism in Early Christianity, Vol.I: Paul and the Gospels (Waterloo Ont. 1986) 100-2. HOFIUS, O. "Das Evangelium und Israel.

Erwägungen zu Römer 9-11," ZThK 83 (3, 1986) 297-324. KOCH, D.-A. Die
Schrift als Zeuge des Evangeliums (Tübingen 1986) 288f., 300f. LÜBKING,
H.-M. Paulus und Israel im Römerbrief. Eine Untersuchung zu Römer 9-11
(Frankfurt/Bern/New York 1986) MALINA B. J. Christian Origins and Cultural
Anthropology (Atlanta 1986) 136. PENNA, R. "L'évolution de l'attitude de
Paul envers les Juifs" in A. Vanhoye, ed., L'Apôtre Paul (Leuven 1986) 390-
421. RÄISÄNEN, H. The Torah and Christ (Helsinki 1986) 62, 202.
SCHMIDT, L. "Hermeneutik" in TRE XV (1986) 139. SCHWARZ, R. "Israel
und die nichtjüdischen Christen im Römerbrief (Kapitel 9-11)," BuL 59 (3,
1986) 161-4. SNEEN, D. "The Root, the Remnant, and the Branches,"
WordWorld 6 (4, 1986) 398-409. WATSON, F. Paul, Judaism and the Gentiles
(Cambridge 1986) 160-74. WINKEL, J. "Argumentationsanalyse von Röm 9-
11," LiB 58 (1986) 65-79. AAGESON, J. W. "Typology, Correspondence, and
the Application of Scripture in Romans 9-11," JSNT 31 (1987) 51-72. DUNN,
J. D. G. "Paul's Epistle to the Romans. An Analysis of Structure and Argument" in ANRW II.25.4 (1987) 2866f. GETTY, M. A. "Paul on the Covenants
and the Future of Israel," BThB 17 (3, 1987) 92-9. HÜBNER, H. "Paulusforschung seit 1945. Ein kritischer Literaturbericht" in ANRW II.25.4 (1987)
2696ff. LINDARS, B. "The Old Testament and Universalism in Paul," BJRL
62 (2, 1987) 511-27. MERKLEIN, H. Studien zu Jesus und Paulus (Tübingen
1987) 16, 212n.13, 315n.101, 316n.104. MUSSNER, F. Die Kraft der Wurzel.
Judentum-Jesus-Kirche (Freiburg/ Basel/Vienna 1987) OSTEN-SACKEN, P.
VON DER, Evangelium und Tora: Aufsätze zu Paulus (München 1987) 27,
29f., 54, 67f., 70, 151, 183, 191-4, 206, 240-2, 244-50, 270f., 287, 294, 296,
299f., 304f., 308, 310f., 313. OSTEN-SACKEN, P. VON DER. "Römer 9-11
als Schibbolet christlicher Theologie" in Evangelium und Tora. Aufsätze zu
Paulus (München 1987) 294-314. RÄISÄNEN, H. "Römer 9-11. Analyse eines
geistigen Ringens" in ANRW II.25.4 (1987) 2891-939. REFOULÉ, F. "Unité
de l'Épître aux Romains et histoire du salut," RSPhTh 71 (2, 1987) 219-42.
SCHMELLER, TH. Paulus und die "Diatribe" (Münster 1987) 286-8, 316n.98,
326f., 418. THEOBALD, M. "Kirche und Israel nach Röm 9-11," Kairos 29
(1987) 1-22. WIESER, F. E. Die Abrahamvorstellungen im Neuen Testament
(Bern/Frankfurt/ New York/Paris 1987) 68-79, 81-3. BEKER, J. C. "Paul's
Theology: Consistent or Inconsistent?" NTS 34 (1988) 375-7. CONZELMANN,
H. and LINDENMANN, A. Interpreting the New Testament (Peabody MA
1988) 164, 196. GETTY, M. A. "Paul and the Salvation of Israel: A Perspective
on Romans 9-11," CBQ 50 (1988) 456-69. HAHN, F. "Die Verwurzelung des
Christentums im Judentum," KuD 34 (1988) 193-209. MacDONALD, M. Y.
The Pauline Churches (Cambridge 1988) 37-8, 75. SCHMIDT, J. M. "Zum
christlichen Verständnis der gemeinsamen Bibel" in E. Brocke and J. Seim,
eds., Gottes Augapfel. Beiträge zur Erneuerung des Verhältnisses von Christen
und Juden (Neukirchen-Vluyn ²1988) 86f. WAGNER, G. "The Future of Israel:
Reflections on Romans 9-11" in W. H. Gloer, ed., Eschatology and the New
Testament (FS. G. R. Beasley-Murray; Peabody MA 1988) 77-112. WEDDER-
BURN, A. J. M. The Reasons for Romans (Edinburgh 1988) 4, 7, 87-91, 112-3,
127, 130, 136-8, 148. BECKER, J. Paulus. Der Apostel der Völker (Tübingen
1989) 366f., 486-502. DEMSON, D. E. "Israel as the Paradigm of Divine
Judgment. An Examination of a Theme in the Theology of Karl Barth," JES 26
(4, 1989) 611-27. HOFIUS, O. Paulusstudien (Tübingen 1989) 64, 106, 118,
173, 174, 175-202. JOHNSON, E. E. The Function of Apocalyptic and Wisdom
Traditions in Romans 9-11 (Atlanta GA 1989) JOURNET, C. "Sur la con-

version d'Israël (A propos de saint Paul, Rm 9-11)," NV 64 (2, 1989) 146-51. LAMPE, P. Die stadtrömischen Christen in den ersten beiden Jahrhunderten (Tübingen ²1989) 54-56, 58, 126, 132, 134. LOHFINK, N. Der niemals gekündigte Bund (Freiburg 1989). LONGENECKER, B. W. "Different Answers to Different Issues. Israel, the Gentiles and Salvation History in Romans 9-11," JSNT 36 (1989) 95-123. LIMBECK, M. Mit Paulus Christ sein. Sachbuch zur Person und Theologie des Apostels Paulus (Stuttgart 1989) 139-42. MARTIN, B. L. Christ and the Law in Paul (Leiden 1989) 11-4, 46, 134, 135. MARTIN, R. P. Reconciliation. A Study of Paul's Theology (Grand Rapids 1989) 131-5. RESE, M. "Israels Unwissen und Ungehorsam und die Verkündigung des Glaubens durch Paulus in Römer 10" in D.-A. Koch et al., eds., Jesu Rede von Gott und ihre Nachgeschichte im frühen Christentum (FS. Willi Marxsen; Fütersloh 1989) 252-66, esp.252-5, 265f. SCHNELLE, U. Wandlungen im paulinischen Denken (Stuttgart 1989) 81-5. BEKER, J. C. "Romans 9-11 in the Context of the Early Church," PSB suppl. 1 (1990) 40-55. BUREN, P. M. VAN. "The Church and Israel: Romans 9-11," PSB suppl. 1 (1990) 5-18. DIPROSE, R. Passato, presente e futuro nell'opera di Dio (Rome 1990). ELLIOT, N. The Rhetoric of Romans (Sheffield 1990) 13, 32, 38, 41n., 42, 51f., 65n., 67, 69, 165, 200n., 220f., 223, 225, 237n., 253-8, 260, 263f., 270-3, 277f., 280, 283n., 290, 292, 296. GUERRA, A. J. "Romans. Paul's Purpose and Audience with Special Attention to Romans 9-11," RevBi 97 (2, 1990) 219-37. HOFIUS, O. "'All Israel Will be Saved'. Divine Salvation and Israel's Deliverance in Romans 9-11," PSB suppl. 1 (1990) 19-39. RESE, M. "Church and Israel in the Deuteropauline Letters," SJTh 43 (1, 1990) 19-32. SATRAN, D. "Paul Among the Rabbis and the Fathers. Exegetical Reflections," PSB suppl. 1 (1990) 90-105. SEGAL, A. F. "Paul's Experience and Romans 9-11," PSB suppl. 1 (1990) 56-70. SEGAL, A. F. Paul the Convert (New Haven/London 1990) 65, 262, 276. TROCMÉ, E. "Comment le Dieu d'Abraham, d'Isaac et de Jacob peut-il être à la fois fidèle et libre? (Epître aux Romains, chap. 9 à 11)," FV 89 (1, 1990) 7-10. WELKER, M. "Righteousness and God's Righteousness," PSB suppl. 1 (1990) 124-39. WISSE, F. W. "Textual Limits to Redactional Theory in the Pauline Corpus" in J. E. Goehring et al., eds., Gospel Origins & Christian Beginnings (FS J. M. Robinson; Sonoma CA 1990) 167-78, esp.171. ZIESLER, J. Pauline Christianity (Oxford 1990) 9, 11, 12, 27, 68-70, 91. ALETTI, J.-N. Comment Dieu est-il juste? Clefs pour interpréter l'épitre aux Romains (Paris 1991). FREDRIKSEN, P. "Judaism, the Circumcision of Gentiles, and Apocalyptic Hope. Another Look at Galatians 1 and 2," JThS 42 (1991) 532-64. GASTON, L. "Israel's Misstep in the Eyes of Paul" in K. P. Donfried, ed., The Romans Debate. Revised and Expanded Edition (Peabody MA 1991) 309-26. LONGENECKER, B. W. Eschatology and the Covenant. A Comparison of 4 Ezra and Romans 1-11 (Sheffield 1991) 251f., 254, 257, 265. MEEKS, W. A. "Om tilltron till en oförutsägbar Gud. En hermeneutisk meditation över Rom 9-11," SEA 56 (1991) 101-17. MEEKS, W. A. "On Trusting an Unpredictable God: A Hermeneutical Meditation on Romans 9-11" in J. T. Carroll et al., eds., Faith and History (FS P. W. Meyer; Atlanta 1991) 105ff. PINTO, C. O. "As citaçoes de Isaías em Romanos 9-11: Um teste para as técnicas hermenêuticas paulinas," VoxScript 1 (1991) 19-32. REFOULÉ, F. "Cohérence ou incohérence de Paul en Romains 9-11?" RevBi 98 (1, 1991) 51-79. SANDERS, E. P. Paul (Oxford/New York 1991) 117-28. SANDNES, K. O. Paul—One of the Prophets? (Tübingen 1991) 155, 175-80. BANON, D. "L'alliance irrevocable," BCPE 44 (1992) 17-21. BOVON, F.

"Paul aux côtes d'Israël et des nations (Rm 9-11)," BCPE 44 (1992) 6-16. CAMPBELL, W. S. Paul's Gospel in an Intercultural Context: Jew and Gentile in the Letter to the Romans (Frankfurt/ Berlin/ Bern etc. 1992) 43-59, 75-77. FÄSSLER, M. "La racine et la greffe," BCPE 44 (1992) 22-26. KELLENBERGER, E. "Heil und Verstockung. Zu Jes 6, 9f. bei Jesaja und im Neuen Testament," ThZ 48 (1992) 268-75. MOORE, W. E. "'Outside' and 'Inside': Paul and Mark," ET 103 (1992) 331-36. CARBONE, S. "Israele nella Lettera ai Romani," RivB 41 (1993) 139-70. SCOTT, J. M. "Paul's Use of Deuteronomic Tradition," JBL 112 (1993) 645-65, esp. 659-65. TAMEZ, E. "God's Election, Exclusion and Mercy: A Bible Study of Romans 9-11," IRM 82 (1993) 29-37.

9:1-11:36   HAYS, R. B. Echoes of Scripture in the Letters of Paul (New Haven/London 1989) 61-70, 188, 223n.12.

9-10   SANDERS, E. P. Paul, the Law, and the Jewish People (London 1985) 42f., 46, 62n.121, 78.

9   WEBER, V. Kritische Geschichte der Exegese des 9. Kap. resp. der Verse 14-23 des Römerbriefes bis auf Chrysostomos (1889). LEKKERKERKER, A.F.N. Römer 7 und Römer 9 bis Augustin (1942). PEDERSEN, F. "Röm. 9. Eine Studie über paulinische Prädestinationsverkündigung" (dän.) DTT XVII ('54) 138-72. LYONNET, S. "De doctrina praedestinationis et reprobationis in Rom. 9" VD 34-35 ('56) 193-201 & 257-71. MUNCK, J. Christ & Israel (1967). KÄSEMANN, E. New Testament Questions of Today (1969) 183. GIBLIN, C.H. In Hope of God's Glory (1970) 266-82. LAYMAN, F. D. Paul's Use of Abraham. An Approach to Paul's Understanding of History (diss. Ann Arbor MI 1972) 85-90, 148f. RIDDERBOS, H. Paul. An Outline of His Theology (Grand Rapids 1975) 341-354. BYRNE, B. "Sons of God"—"Seed of Abraham" (Rome 1979) 1, 5f., 84, 127-40, 174, 188, 216. CLARK, K. W. "The Israel of God" in The Gentile Bias and other Essays [selected by J. L. Sharpe III] (Leiden 1980) 23, 25, 28. WILLIAMS, S. K. "'The Righteousness of God' in Romans," JBL 99 (1980) 280f. HAGEN, K. Hebrews Commenting from Erasmus to Bèze 1516-1598 (Tübingen 1981) 52. DOOREN, J. P. VAN. "Dordrechter Synode" in TRE 9 (1982) 140. THEOBALD, M. Die überströmende Gnade (Würzburg 1982) 142-50. HÜBNER, H. Gottes Ich und Israel (Göttingen 1984) 25f., 34-6, 38, 43, 98, 101f., 105, 117, 126. BRANDENBURGER, E. "Paulinische Schriftauslegung in der Kontroverse um das Verheissungswort Gottes (Röm 9)," ZThK 82 (1985) 1-47. SIEGERT, F. Argumentation bei Paulus (Tübingen 1985) 119-44. RESE, M. "Israel und Kirche in Römer 9," NTS 34 (1988) 208-17. JOHNSON, E. E. The Function of Apocalyptic and Wisdom Traditions in Romans 9-11 (Atlanta GA 1989) 122, 127, 143, 196f. PARMENTIER, M. "Greek Church Fathers on Romans 9," Bijdragen 50 (1989) 139-54. PARMENTIER, M. "Greek Church Fathers on Romans 9. Part II," Bijdragen 51 (1990) 2-20. HARRISVILLE, R. A. The Figure of Abraham in the Epistles of St. Paul. In the Footsteps of Abraham (San Francisco 1992) passim. SCHREINER, T. R. "Does Romans 9 Teach Individual Election unto Salvation? Some Exegetical and Theological Reflections," JEThS 36 (1993) 25-40.

9:1ff.   BOUSSET, W. Die Religion des Judentums im Späthellenis-tischen Zeitalter (1926=1966) 197. HENGEL, M. Judentum und Hellenismus (Tübingen 1969) 561; ET: Judaism and Hellenism II (London 1974) 204. J. FRIEDRICH et al., eds., Rechtfertigung (FS. E. Käsemann; Tübingen/Göttingen 1976) 237f.

9:1-33   GORDAY, P. Principles of Patristic Exegesis: Romans 9-11 in Origen, John Chrysostom, and Augustine (New York/Toronto 1983) 76-9, 121-3, 167-70, 172-4.

9:1-29   HARRINGTON, D. J. God's People in Christ (Philadelphia 1980) 59-61.
            CAMPBELL, W. S. "The Freedom and Faithfulness of God in Relation to
            Israel," JSNT 13 (1981) 28-34. SCHMITT, R. Gottesgerechtigkeit—Heilsge-
            schichte—Israel in der Theologie des Paulus (Frankfurt/ Bern/New York/Nancy
            1984) 71-88. BADENAS, R. Christ the End of the Law (Sheffield 1985) 99-
            101. JOHNSON, E. E. The Function of Apocalyptic and Wisdom Traditions in
            Romans 9-11 (Atlanta GA 1989) 147-50.
9:1-23   PIPER, J. The Justification of God. An Exegetical and Theological Study of
            Romans 9:1-23 (Grand Rapids 1983)
9:1-18   FACY, T. "A Note on Romans 9:1-18" IThQ 32 (3, '65) 261-62.
9:1-13   BARRETT, C.K. From First Adam to Last (1962) 42f.
9:1-11   FRANSEN, I. "Le Dieu de toute consolation. Romains 9, 1-11, 36" BVieC 49
            ('63) 27-32.
9:1-5,31–10:4 STEGEMANN, E. in GPM 42 (1987/88) 346-53.
9:1-5   MICHEL, O. "Opferbereitschaft für Israel" In Memoraim E. Lohmeyer, ed. W.
            Schmauch (1951) 94-100. DAVIES, W.D. Paul and Rabbinic Judaism (1955)
            75f., 272. HAAR, GPM 16 (1961/62) 264ff. SEVENSTER, J.N. Paul and
            Seneca (1961) 81, 96, 99, 100, 102. SCHMITHALS, W. Paulus und Jakobus
            (1963) 42f. KÄSEMANN, E. Exegetische Versuche und Besinnungen (1964)
            II 194. MARQUARDT, F. GPM 22 (1967/68) 343-49. LUZ, U. Das Ge-
            schichtsverständnis des Paulus (1968) 26f. PLAG, C. Israels Wege zum Heil
            (1969) 13f. ZELLER, D. Juden und Heiden in der Mission des Paulus. Studien
            zum Römerbrief (Stuttgart 1973) 109ff., 285. BERNARD, J. "Le mystère de la
            foi. Rm 9, 1-5," AssS 50 (1974) 16-21. LYONNET, S. Quaestiones in
            epistulam ad Romanos (Rome 1975) 20-5. PAGELS, E. H. The Gnostic Paul.
            Gnostic Exegesis of the Pauline Letters (Philadelphia 1975) 37. LAYMAN, F.
            D. Paul's Use of Abraham. An Approach to Paul's Understanding of History
            (diss. Ann Arbor MI 1978) 245-7. ROBINSON, J. A. T. Wrestling with
            Romans (London 1979) 110-2. MOXNES, H. Theology in Conflict (Leiden
            1980) 48, 50, 220-1. KÜNKEL, K. in GPM 36 (1981/82) 343-57. LAPIDE, P.
            und GERLACH, W. in P. Krusche et al., eds., Predigtstudien für das Kirchen-
            jahr 1981/1982. IV/2 (Stuttgart 1982) 173-81. GABRIS, K. "Das Gewis-
            sen—normiert durch den Heiligen Geist. Bibelarbeit über Röm. 9, 1-5," CV 27
            (1984) 19-32. HÜBNER, H. Gottes Ich und Israel (Göttingen 1984) 15f., 21f.,
            27, 133. SCHMITT, R. Gottesgerechtigkeit—Heilsgeschichte—Israel in der
            Theologie des Paulus (Frankfurt/Bern/New York/Nancy 1984) 72-76. STAAB,
            K. Pauluskommentare aus der griechischen Kirche (Münster ²1984) 66:21-67:7
            Apoll; 96:13-28 Diod; 143:9-18 ThM; 386:11-388:39 Genn; 513:26-516:5 Phst.
            GRANFIELD, C. E. B. "Light from St Paul on Christian-Jewish Relations" in
            The Bible and Christian Life (Edinburgh 1985) 34-47. SIEGERT, F. Argumen-
            tation bei Paulus (Tübingen 1985) 119-123. EPP, E. J. "Jewish-Gentile Continu-
            ity in Paul: Torah and/or Faith? (Romans 9:1-5)," HThR 79 (1-3, 1986) 80-90.
            LÜBKING, H.-M. Paulus und Israel im Römerbrief (Frankfurt/Bern/New York
            1986) 53-9, 138. DUNN, J. D. G. "Paul's Epistle to the Romans: An Analysis
            of Structure and Argument" in ANRW II.25.4 (1987) 2868f. OSTEN-SACKEN,
            P. VON DER, Evangelium und Tora: Aufsätze zu Paulus (München 1987) 29,
            257, 299f. RÄISÄNEN, H. "Römer 9-11: Analyse eines geistigen Ringens" in
            ANRW II.25.4. (1987) 2895f. CONZELMANN, H. and LINDEMANN, A.
            Interpreting the New Testament (Peabody MA 1988) 30. WAGNER, G. "The
            Future of Israel: Reflections on Romans 9-11" in W. H. Gloer, ed., Eschatology
            and the New Testament (FS. G. R. Beasley-Murray; Peabody MA 1988) 77-81.

JOHNSON, E. E. The Function of Apocalyptic and Wisdom Traditions in Romans 9-11 (Atlanta GA 1989) 111, 121, 141, 147, 173.

9:1-3   BURCHARD, C. "Erfahrungen multikulturellen Zusammenlebens im Neuen Testament" in J. Micksch, ed., Multikulturelles Zusammenleben (Frankfurt 1983) 33. LÜBKING, H.-M. Paulus und Israel im Römerbrief (Frankfurt/Bern/New York 1986) 57-59.

9:1   BEST, E. One Body in Christ (1955) 3n, 11nn, 16, 28. STACEY, W.D. The Pauline View of Man (1956) 209f. SCHRAGE, W. Die konkreten Einzelgebote in der paulinischen Paränese (1961) 153. BEUTLER, J. Martyria (Frankfurt a.M. 1972) 174f., 182, 199, 299, 301. SCHMITHALS, W. Der Römerbrief als historisches Problem (Gütersloh 1975) 89. TRITES, A. A. The New Testament Concept of Witness (Cambridge 1977) 200f. THISELTON, A. C. The Two Horizons (Grand Rapids 1980) 318. BAMMEL, C. P. H. "Philocalia IX, Jerome, Epistle 121, and Origen's Expostion of Romans VII," JThS 32 (1981) 80. ECKSTEIN, H.-J. Der Begriff Syneidesis bei Paulus (Tübingen 1983) 179-190, 311ff. RICHARDSON, P. and HURD, J. C., eds., From Jesus to Paul (FS. F. W. Beare; Waterloo 1984) 166f. WOLTER, M. Die Pastoralbriefe als Paulustradition (Göttingen 1988) 78. JOHNSON, E. E. The Function of Apocalyptic and Wisdom Traditions in Romans 9-11 (Atlanta GA 1989) 110, 121, 141f.

9:2   JEREMIAS, J. Abba (1966) 277. UNNIK, W. C. VAN. "Jesus: Anathema or Kyrios (I Cor. 12:3)" in B. Lindars and S. S. Smalley, eds., Christ and the Spirit in the New Testament (FS. C. F. D. Moule; Cambridge 1973) 115ff., 119f. G. FREUND und E. STEGEMANN, eds., Theologische Brosamen für Lothar Steiger (DBAT 5; Heidelberg 1985) 7.

9:3-5   CERFAUX, L. Christ in the Theology of St. Paul (1959) 482, 497, 161, 212, 482, 517, 518. LORIMER, W.L. "Romans IX 3-5" NTS 13 (1966-67) 385f. JOHNSON, E. E. The Function of Apocalyptic and Wisdom Traditions in Romans 9-11 (Atlanta GA 1989) 193.

9:3-4   SCHMITHALS, W. Der Römerbrief als historisches Problem (Gütersloh 1975) 10. SÄNGER, D. Antikes Judentum und die Mysterien (Tübingen 1980) 17. BECKER, J. Paulus. Der Apostel der Völker (Tübingen 1989) 34, 47, 403.

9:3   SCHRAGE, W. Die konkreten Einzelgebote in der paulinischen Paränese (1961) 253. BRATSIOTIS, P. "Eine exegetische Notiz zu Röm. ix 3 und x 1" NovTest 5 (4, '62) 299-300. LUZ, U. Das Geschichtsverständnis des Paulus (1968) 21. VOIGT, S. "Paulo deseja ser Anátema por seus Irmaos Judeus (Rom 9, 3). Proposta de uma Interpretaçao Diferente," REB 33 (1973) 298-323. KÜMMEL, W. G. Römer 7 und das Bild des Menschen im Neuen Testament (München 1974) 16, 46, 66. WILES, G. P. Paul's Intercessory Prayers (London 1974) 19, 128n., 156n., 158, 164, 166n., 181n., 247n., 253, 255. LYONNET, S. Quaestiones in epistulam ad Romanos (Rome 1975) 21f. KRUIJF, T. C. DE. "Antisemitismus" in TRE 3 (1978) 125. STUPPERICH, R. "Bruderschaften" in TRE 7 (1981) 196, 202. GORDO, A. P. "Participación del apóstol en la función redentora de Cristo," Burg. 22 (1981) 45-92. HAGEN, K. Hebrews Commenting from Erasmus to Bèze 1516-1598 (Tübingen 1981) 48. KLEINKNECHT, K. T. Der leidende Gerechtfertigte (Tübingen 1984) 333. STAAB, K. Pauluskommentare aus der griechischen Kirche (Münster ^{2}1984) 657:21-27 Areth.

9:4-8   DELLING, G. "Die 'Söhne (Kinder) Gottes' im Neuen Testament" in R. Schnackenburg et al., eds., Die Kirche des Anfangs (FS. H. Schürmann; Wien 1978) 618f.

9:4-5   KÄSEMANN, E. Exegetische Versuche und Besinnungen 1964 II 192.
         ZELLER, D. Juden und Heiden in der Mission des Paulus. Studien zum Römer-
         brief (Stuttgart 1973) 85f., 261. RESE, M. "Die Vorzüge Israels in Röm. 9, 4f.
         und Eph. 2, 12. Exegetische Anmerkungen zum Thema Kirche und Israel," ThZ
         31 (1975) 211-22. MUSSNER, F. "Eine christliche Theologie des Judentums"
         in P. Lapide, F. Mussner und U. Wilckens, Was Juden und Christen vonein-
         ander denken [H. Küng und J. Moltmann, eds.] (Freiburg 1978) 47f. BYRNE,
         B. "Sons of God"—"Seed of Abraham" (Rome 1979) 79, 81-4, 129n.131, 139f.,
         195. MINEAR, P. S. "To Ask and to Receive. Some Clues to Johannine
         Ontology" in D. Y. Hadidian, ed., Intergerini Parietis Septvm (Eph. 2:14) (FS.
         M. Barth; Pittsburgh/PA 1981) 241. HÜBNER, H. Gottes Ich und Israel
         (Göttingen 1984) 14, 16, 19-21, 109. GRÄSSER, E. Der Alte Bund im Neuen
         (Tübingen 1985) 26, 28f., 128, 159, 279, 284. LÜBKING, H.-M. Paulus und
         Israel im Römerbrief (Frankfurt/Bern/ New York 1986) 53-7. RÄISÄNEN, H.
         The Torah and Christ (Helsinki 1986) 73f., 169, 180. OSTEN-SACKEN, P.
         VON DER, Evangelium und Tora: Aufsätze zu Paulus (München 1987) 193,
         244f., 286. OKURE, T. The Johannine Approach to Mission (Tübingen 1988)
         117f. JOHNSON, E. E. The Function of Apocalyptic and Wisdom Traditions
         in Romans 9-11 (Atlanta GA 1989) 139, 194, 201.

9:4   BOUSSET, W. Die Religion des Judentums im Späthellenistischen Zeitalter
         (1966 =1926) 362. SCHOENBERG, M.W. "Huiothesia: The Adoptive Sonship
         of the Israelites" AER 143 (4, '60) 261-73. SCHLIER, H. "Doxa bei Paulus als
         heilsgeschichtlicher Begriff" in Studiorum Paulinorum Congressus Internation-
         alis Catholicus I (1963) 45-56. GALE, H.M. The Use of Analogy in the Letter
         of Paul (1964) 58f. LUZ, U. Das Geschichtsverständnis des Paulus (1968) 269-
         74. VAN DÜLMEN, A. Die Theologie des Gesetzes bei Paulus (1968) 20, 44,
         79, 124, 133, 141, 194, 212, 216, 217, 220. KÄSEMANN, E. New Testament
         Questions of Today (1969) 180. ROETZEL, C. "Diathékai in Romans 9, 4"
         Biblica 51 (3, '70) 377-90. LYONNET, S. Quaestiones in epistulam ad
         Romanos (Rome 1975) 22-5. KUTSCH, E. Neues Testament—Neuer Bund?
         (Neukirchen-Vluyn 1978) 153-6. BYRNE, B. "Sons of God"—"Seed of Abra-
         ham" (Rome 1979) 5, 7, 79-83, 127, 131f., 178, 215f. HÜBNER, H. Gottes Ich
         und Israel (Göttingen 1984) 14-6, 19. GRÄSSER, E. Der Alte Bund im Neuen
         (Tübingen 1985) 8, 15f., 17ff., 23f., 55, 62, 220, 288. OSTEN-SACKEN, P.
         VON DER, Evangelium und Tora: Aufsätze zu Paulus (München 1987) 28, 71,
         242, 244, 300, 311. MARTIN, B. L. Christ and the Law in Paul (Leiden 1989)
         19, 46, 52, 69, 100, 142. BOCKMUEHL, M. N. A. Revelation and Mystery
         (Tübingen 1990) 148, 151. McDADE, J. "The Continuing Validity of the Jew-
         ish Covenant. A Christian Perspective," SIDIC [Rome] 23 (3, 1990) 20-5.

9:5   BEST, E. One Body in Christ (1955) 207. ROBINSON, J.M. Keryma und his-
         torischer Jesus (1960) 107, 177, 179. HAHN, F. Christologische Hoheitstitel
         (1963) 253. KRAMER, W. Christos Kyrios Gottessohn (1963) 62e. BARTSCH,
         H.-W. "Röm. 9, 5 und 1 Clem 32, 4. Eine notwendige Konjektur im Römer-
         brief" ThZ 21 (5, '65) 401-9. THUESING, W. Per Christum in Deum (1965)
         147-50. SCHENK, W. Der Segen im Neuen Testament (1967) 97. LUZ, U. Das
         Geschichtsverständnis des Paulus (1968) 27. STRÖMMAN, C. "Zu Röm 9, 5,"
         ZNW 8 (1907) 319f. PREUSCHEN, E. "Nochmals Rö 9, 5," ZNW 9 (1908) 80.
         WAINWRIGHT, A. W. The Trinity in the New Testament (1962) 54-8.
         METZGER, B. M. "The Punctuation of Rom. 9:5" in B. Lindars and S. S.
         Smalley, eds., Christ and the Spirit in the New Testament (FS C. F. D. Moule;
         Cambridge 1973) LYONNET, S. Quaestiones in epistulam ad Romanos (Rome

1975) 25-30. SKILTON, J. H. "Romans 9:5 in Modern English Versions" in J. H. Skilton, ed., The New Testament Student, Vol 2: The New Testament Student at Work (n.p., Presbyterian & Reformed Pub. Co. 1975) 104-30. KUSS, O. "Zu Römer 9:5" in J. Friedrich et al., eds., Rechtfertigung (FS E. Käsemann; Tübingen/Göttingen 1976) 291-303. DEICHGRÄBER, R. "Benediktionen" in TRE 5 (1980) 562. DUNN, J. D. Christology in the Making (London 1980) 45. METZGER, B. M. "The Punctuation of Rom. 9:5" in New Testament Studies: Philological, Versional, and Patristic (Leiden 1980) 57-74. DEICHGRÄBER, R. "Formeln, Liturgische" in TRE 11 (1983) 258. GRÄSSER, E. Der Alte Bund im Neuen (Tübingen 1985) 19, 220, 243. AUNE, D. E. The New Testament in Its Literary Environment (Philadelphia 1987) 193. GRANFIELD, C. E. B. "Some Comments on Professor J. D. G. Dunn's *Christology in the Making* with Special Reference to the Evidence of the Epistle to the Romans" in L. D. Hurst and N. T. Wright, eds., The Glory of Christ in the New Testament (FS G. B. Caird; Oxford 1987) 272f. JONGE, M. DE, Christology in Context. The Earliest Christian Response to Jesus (Philadelphia 1988) 49, 114, 122, 129, 226n.4, 231n.26. MELL, U. Neue Schöpfung (Berlin/ New York 1989) 352, 379. DETTORI, L. "La divinità di Gesú Christo," Lux Biblica [Rome] (2, 1990) 81-5. SIMONIS, W. Der gefangene Paulus. Die Entstehung des sogenannten Römerbriefs und anderer urchristlicher Schriften in Rom (Frankfurt/Bern/New York/Paris 1990) 47f. LOHSE, E. Die Entstehung des Neuen Testaments (Stuttgart/Berlin/Köln ⁵1991) 25, 146.

9:6-11:10   HOFIUS, O. Paulusstudien (Tübingen 1989) 178-82. LONGENECKER, B. W. Eschatology and the Covenant. A Comparison of 4 Ezra and Romans 1-11 (Sheffield 1991) 255-7.

9:6ff.   HÜBNER, H. Gottes Ich und Israel (Göttingen 1984) 14, 16, 19, 21-3, 28, 34, 60, 70f., 100f., 109, 122f. RÄISÄNEN, H. The Torah and Christ (Helsinki 1986) 74.

9:6-33   BETZ, 0. "Rechtfertigung im Qumran" in Jesus. Der Messias Israels (Tübingen 1987) 58.

9:6-29   LUZ, U. Das Geschichtsverständnis des Paulus (1968) 401. ZELLER, D. Juden und Heiden in der Mission des Paulus. Studien zum Römerbrief (Stuttgart 1973) 113ff. DUGANDZIC, I. Das "Ja" Gottes in Christus (Würzburg 1977) 281-5. ELLIS, E. E. Prophecy and Hermeneutic in Early Christianity (Tübingen 1978) 155, 218f. BYRNE, B. "Sons of God"—"Seed of Abraham" (Rome 1979) 129-139. HÜBNER, H. Gottes Ich und Israel (Göttingen 1984) 25, 29, 36f., 44, 46, 48f., 52f., 55, 57-60, 69f., 92, 98f., 102f., 117, 122, 124. STEGNER, W. R. "Romans 9.6-29—A Midrash," JSNT 22 (1984) 37-52. KOCH, D.-A. Die Schrift als Zeuge des Evangeliums (Tübingen 1986) 173f. LÜBKING, H.-M. Paulus und Israel im Römerbrief (Frankfurt/Bern/New York 1986) 61-8, 70-8, 138-40. WATSON, F. Paul, Judaism and the Gentiles (Cambridge 1986) 162-4. ALETTI, J.-N. "L'argumentation paulinienne en Rm 9," Biblica 68 (1987) 41-56. DUNN, J. D. G. "Paul's Epistle to the Romans: An Analysis of Structure and Argument" in ANRW II.25.4 (1987) 286f. GASTON, L. Paul and the Torah (Vancouver 1987) 80-99. RÄISÄNEN, H. "Römer 9-11: Analyse eines geistigen Ringes" in ANRW II.25.4 (1987) 2906, 2909-11, 2930ff. WAGNER, G. "The Future of Israel: Reflections on Romans 9-11" in W. H. Gloer, ed., Eschatology and the New Testament (FS G. R. Beasley-Murray; Peabody MA 1988) 81-5. HAYS, R. B. Echoes of Scripture in the Letters of Paul (New Haven/London 1989) 65-8. JOHNSON, E. E. The Function of Apocalyptic and Wisdom

Traditions in Romans 9-11 (Atlanta GA 1989) 121, 140, 141, 143, 145, 147, 154, 174, 194, 208.

9:6-18 PLAG, Chr. Israels Weg zum Heil (1969) 14f. HÜBNER, H. Gottes Ich und Israel (Göttingen 1984) 37, 44-46, 48. KOCH, D.-A. Die Schrift als Zeuge des Evangeliums (Tübingen 1986) 302-5.

9:6-13 SCHOEPS, H.-J—Paulus (1959) 251f. LUZ, U. Das Geschich-tsverständnis des Paulus (1968) 64-66, 28, 185, 274, 280f. EICHHOLZ, G. Die Theologie des Paulus im Umriss (1972) 290f., 293. ZELLER, D. Juden und Heiden in der Mission des Paulus. Studien zum Römerbrief (Stuttgart 1973) 119f. LYONNET, S. Quaestiones in epistulam ad Romanos (Rome 1975) 30-8. LAYMAN, F. D. Paul's Use of Abraham. An Approach to Paul's Understanding of History (diss. Ann Arbor MI 1978) 163-5. ROBINSON, J. A. T. Wrestling with Romans (London 1979) 113f. FRICKEL, J. "Die Zöllner, Vorbild der Demut und wahrer Gottesverehrung" in E. Dassmann und K. S. Frank, eds., Pietas (FS B. Kötting; JAC, Erg. 8; Münster 1980) 370. MOXNES, H. Theology in Conflict (Leiden 1980) 34, 45-8, 82, 96, 112, 221f., 228, 254, 271. GUEURET, A. "Epître de Paul aux Romains. Analyse des contenus du ch. 9, 6-13," SémiotBib 34 (1984) 15-28. HÜBNER, H. Gottes Ich und Israel (Göttingen 1984) 16, 27-9, 31, 36, 121. SIEGERT, F. Argumentation bei Paulus (Tübingen 1985) 123-7. LÜBKING, H.-M. Paulus und Israel im Römerbrief (Frankfurt/Bern/ New York 1986) 61-8. RÄISÄNEN, H. "Römer 9-11: Analyse eines geistigen Ringens" in ANRW II.25.4 (1987) 2897-902. JOHNSON, E. E. The Function of Apocalyptic and Wisdom Traditions in Romans 9-11 (Atlanta GA 1989) 139f., 148, 193.

9:6b-13 SCHMITT, R. Gottesgerechtigkeit—Heilsgeschichte—Israel in der Theologie des Paulus (Frankfurt/Bern/New York/Nancy 1984) 79-83. SIEGERT, F. Argumentation bei Paulus (Tübingen 1985) 182-5.

9:6-9 LUZ, U. Das Geschichtsverständnis des Paulus (1968) 64ff. MÜLLER, H. Die Auslegung alttestamentlichen Geschichtsstoffs bei Paulus (diss. Halle/Wittenberg 1960) 140-3. STAAB, K. Pauluskommentare aus der griechischen Kirche (Münster ²1984) 96:29-97:17 Diod; 389:1-30 Genn.

9:6-8 OSWALD, E. "Gebet Manasses" in JSHRZ IV/1 (1974) 23n.1e. PAGELS, E. H. The Gnostic Paul. Gnostic Exegesis of the Pauline Letters (Philadelphia 1975) 37f. LONA, H. E. Abraham in Johannes 8 (Bern/FLrankfurt 1976) 272-3.

9:6-7 SNODGRASS, K. The Parable of the Wicked Tenants (Tübingen 1983) 92n.84. STAAB, K. Pauluskommentare aus der griechischen Kirche (Münster ²1984) 516:6-14 Phot.

9:6 LUZ, U. Das Geschichtsverständnis des Paulus (1968) 25, 28, 35f., 70. SCHRAGE, W. Die konkreten Einzelgebote in der paulinischen Paränese (1961) 229. HAHN, F. Das Verständnis der Mission im Neuen Testament (1965) 91. BLANK, J. Paulus und Jesus (1968) 258ff. BORSE, U. Der Standort des Galaterbriefes (Köln 1972) 128, 134f. LYONNET, S. Quaestiones in epistulam ad Romanos (Rome 1975) 31f. KOTANSKY, R. D. "A Note on Romans 9:6. 'ho logos tou theou' as the proclamation of the Gospel," SBTh VII/1 (1977) 24-30. JEWETT, P. K. Infant Baptism and the Covenant of Grace (Grand Rapids 1978) 103. BYRNE, B. "Sons of God"—"Seed of Abraham" (Rome 1979) 129-31, 138f. BERGMEIER, R. Glaube als Gabe nach Johannes (Stuttgart 1980) 222. MOXNES, H. Theology in Conflict (Leiden 1980) 28, 56f., 59, 219. HÜBNER, H. Gottes Ich und Israel (Göttingen 1984) 15f., 21, 26, 28, 30f., 37, 44, 46, 52f., 95, 97, 99-102, 123f. STAAB, K. Pauluskommentare aus der griechischen Kirche (Münster ²1984) 657:28-658:14 Areth. MacDONALD, M.

Y. The Pauline Churches (Cambridge 1988) 32, 95. WAGNER, G. "The Future of Israel: Reflections on Romans 9-11" in W. H. Gloer, ed., Eschatology and the New Testament (FS G. R. Beasley-Murray; Peabody MA 1988) 81f., 97f. WOLTER, M. Die Pastoralbriefe als Paulustradition (Göttingen 1988) 88. JOHNSON, E. E. The Function of Apocalyptic and Wisdom Traditions in Romans 9-11 (Atlanta GA 1989) 139f., 143-5, 148, 150, 175, 193-5. SCHNELLE, U. Wandlungen im paulinischen Denken (Stuttgart 1989) 82. VOLF, J. M. G. Paul and Perseverance (Tübingen 1990) 162-5, 167, 171, 175, 175n.75, 181nn.124.126, 195.

9:6a   DUGANDZIC, I. Das "Ja" Gottes in Christus (Würzburg 1977) 277-80. SCHMITT, R. Gottesgerechtigkeit—Heilsgeschichte—Israel in der Theologie des Paulus (Frankfurt/Bern/New York/Nancy 1984) 76-9.

9:7-10:21   VOLF, J. M. G. Paul and Perseverance (Tübingen 1990) 164-7.

9:7-13   BERGER, K. und COLPE, C., eds., Religionsgeschichtliches Textbuch zum Neuen Testament (Göttingen/Zürich 1987) 219-20.

9:7-11   NICKELS, P. Targum and New Testament (1967) 70.

9:7,10   McNAMARA, M. The New Testament and the Palestinian Targum to the Pentateuch (1966) 164.

9:7-8   BRUCE, F. F. The Time is Fulfilled (Exeter 1978) 68.

9:7   ELLIS, E.E. Paul's Use of the Old Testament (1957) 16, 95, 116, 125, 150, 160, 187. LUZ, U. Das Geschichtsver-ständnid des Paulus (1968) 101. JEWETT, P. K. Infant Baptism and the Covenant of Grace (Grand Rapids 1978) 159, 235, 241. BYRNE, B. "Sons of God"—"Seed of Abraham" (Rome 1979) 128, 130f., 133, 138, 188. HÜBNER, H. Gottes Ich und Israel (Göttingen 1984) 18f., 24f., 31, 42, 56, 110. JOHNSON, E. E. The Function of Apocalyptic and Wisdom Traditions in Romans 9-11 (Atlanta GA 1989) 150, 172, 195, 201.

9:8   KERTELGE, K. "Rechtfertigung" bei Paulus (1967) 140, 185. SCHNEIDER, N. Die rhetorische Eigenart der paulinischen Antithese (1970) 100-2. JEWETT, R. Paul's Anthropological Terms; a study of their use in conflict settings (1971) 160-3. JANSSEN, E. "Testament Abrahams" in JSHRZ III/2 (1975) 217. LYONNET, S. Quaestiones in epistulam ad Romanos (Rome 1975) 33. BYRNE, B. "Sons of God"—"Seed of Abraham" (Rome 1979) 2, 8, 128, 130-2, 188, 219. HELDERMANN, J. Die Anapausis im Evangelium Veritatis (Leiden 1984) 325n.61. JOHNSON, E. E. The Function of Apocalyptic and Wisdom Traditions in Romans 9-11 (Atlanta GA 1989) 130, 139-41, 195.

9:9-13   STAAB, K. Pauluskommentare aus der griechischen Kirche (Münster ²1984) 143:19-144:8 ThM.

9:9   ELLIS, E.E. Paul's Use of the Old Testament (1957) 22, 125, 150, 160. LYONNET, S. Quaestiones in epistulam ad Romanos (Rome 1975) 33. KOCH, D.-A. Die Schrift als Zeuge des Evangeliums (Tübingen 1986) 141f., 171f. WOLTER, M. Die Pastoralbriefe als Paulustradition (Göttingen 1988) 88.

9:10-10:4   KÜNKEL, K. in GPM 36 (1981/82) 343-57.

9:10ff.   ELLIS, E.E. Paul's Use of the Old Testament (1957) 116.

9:10-18   PAGELS, E. H. The Gnostic Paul. Gnostic Exegesis of the Pauline Letters (Philadelphia 1975) 34f.

9:10-13   LUZ, U. Des Geschichtsverständnis des Paulus (1968) 70ff. MÜLLER, H. Die Auslegung alttestamentlichen Geschichtsstoffs bei Paulus (diss. Halle/Wittenberg 1960) 143-6. LYONNET, S. Quaestiones in epistulam ad Romanos (Rome 1975) 33f. LAYMAN, F. D. Paul's Use of Abraham. An Approach to Paul's Understanding of History (diss. Ann Arbor MI 1978) 249f. HÜBNER, H.

Gottes Ich und Israel (Göttingen 1984) 24, 28, 44f. STAAB, K. Pauluskommentare aus der griechischen Kirche (Münster [2]1984) 389:31-390:25 Genn.

9:10   DINKLER, E. Eirene. Der urchristliche Friedensgedanke (Heidelberg 1973) 32-5.

9:11-15   STAAB, K. Pauluskommentare aus der griechischen Kirche (Münster [2]1984) 516:15-517:27 Phot.

9:11-14   STAAB, K. Pauluskommentare aus der griechischen Kirche (Münster [2]1984) 54:11-30 Akazc.

9:11-12   JÜNGEL, E. Paulus und Jesus (1966) 48. WOLTER, M. Die Pastoralbriefe als Paulustradition (Göttingen 1988) 66.

9:11   ROMANIUK, K. L'Amour du Pere et du Fils dans la Soteriologie de Saint Paul (1961) 161, 164, 169-70, 173, 297. SCHRAGE, W. Die konkreten Einzelgebote in der paulinischen Paränese (1961) 53, 195. EBOROWICZ, W. "Ad Rm 9:11 et la critique augustinienne de la . . ." Studia Evangelica V (1968) 272-6. BERKOUWER, G. C. The Return of Christ (Grand Rapids 1972) 325, 329, 331f., 335, 339, 344. KÜMMEL, W. G. Römer 7 und das Bild des Menschen im Neuen Testament (München 1974) 5f. LYONNET, S. Quaestiones in epistulam ad Romanos (Rome 1975) 34-5. RIDDERBOS, H. Paul. An Outline of His Theology (Grand Rapids 1975) 344-9. METZGER, B. M. The Early Versions of the New Testament. Their Origin Transmission, and Limitations (Oxford 1977) 242. BYRNE, B. "Sons of God"—"Seed of Abraham" (Rome 1979) 115f., 128, 1313, 133f., 136. STAAB, K. Pauluskommentare aus der griechischen Kirche (Münster [2]1984) 98:1-12 Diod. JOHNSON, E. E. The Function of Apocalyptic and Wisdom Traditions in Romans 9-11 (Atlanta GA 1989) 139, 155, 172.

9:12-13   ELLIS, E.E. Paul's Use of the Old Testament (1957) 12, 125, 150, 160, 186. SCHOEPS, H.-J. Paulus (1959) 252f. LYONNET, S. Quaestiones in epistulam ad Romanos (Rome 1975) 35-8.

9:12   WIDERKEHR, D. Die Theologie der Berufung in den Paulus-briefen (1963) 168-74. HÄRING, H. Das Problem des Bösen in der Theologie (Darmstadt 1985) 97. JOHNSON, E. E. The Function of Apocalyptic and Wisdom Traditions in Romans 9-11 (Atlanta GA 1989) 121, 141, 154f., 174, 201. LIEBERS, R. Das Gesetz als Evangelium (Zürich 1989) 26f. DAVIES, G. N. Faith and Obedience in Romans. A Study in Romans 1-4 (Sheffield 1990) 122f.

9:13   ELLIS, E.E. Paul's Use of the Old Testament (1957) 120, 130, 150, 160. ELLIS, E. E. Prophecy and Hermeneutic in Early Christianity (Tübingen 1978) 155, 159, 218. HÜBNER, H. Gottes Ich und Israel (Göttingen 1984) 26-30, 36, 43, 46f., 56, 59, 121. KOCH, D.-A. Die Schrift als Zeuge des Evangeliums (Tübingen 1986) 107f. JOHNSON, E. E. The Function of Apocalyptic and Wisdom Traditions in Romans 9-11 (Atlanta GA 1989) 141, 162, 197.

9:14ff.   ELLIS, E.E. Paul's Use of the Old Testament (1957) 122. EICHHOLZ, G. Die Theologie des Paulus im Umriss (1972) 293f.

9:14-29   DALMER, J. "Zur paulinischen Erwählungslehre" in Greifswalder Studien, Festschrift H. Cremer (1895) 183-206. LIECHTEN-HAHN, R. Die göttliche Vorherbestimmung bei Paulus und in der Posidonianischen Philosophie (1922). SCHELKLE, K.H. "Erwählung und Freiheit im Römerbrief nach der Auslegung der Väter" ThQ 131 (1951) 189-207. DOBSCHUETZ, E.v. Prädestination, ThSt Kr 106 (1934/35) 9-19. DAVIDSON, F. Pauline Predestination (1946). HESSE, F. Das Verstockungsproblem im Alten Testament (1955). DINKLER, E. "Prädestination bei Paulus (1957) 81-102. DION, H.M. "Predestination in St. Paul" Theology Digest 15 (1967) 144-49; digest of "La pré-destination chez saint Paul" RechSR 53 (1965) 5-43. RICHARDSON, P. Israel in the Apostolic Church (1969) 132f. ROBINSON, J. A. T. Wrestling with Romans (London 1979) 114-20. SCHMITT, R. Gottesgerechtigkeit—Heilsgeschichte—Israel in der Theologie des Paulus (Frankfurt/Bern/New York/Nancy 1984) 83. LÜBKING, H.-M. Paulus und Israel im Römerbrief (Frankfurt/Bern/New York 1986) 70-8.

9:14-24   SOUCEK, J.B. GPM 14 (1959) 83-88. HAAR, J. GPM 20 (1965/66) 99-104. LUZ, U. Das Geschichtsverständnis des Paulus (1968) 28f. DANTINE, W, GPM 26 (1971) 93-98. KLAUS, B. und ÖFFNER, E. "Septuagesimae: Römer 9, 14-24" in P. Krusche et al., eds., Predigtstudien für das Kirchenjahr 1977/78. Perikopenreihe VI/1 (Stuttgart 1977) 88-99. SCHRAGE, W. in GPM 32 (1977/78) 82-91. LAYMAN, F. D. Paul's Use of Abraham. An Approach to Paul's Understanding of History (diss. Ann Arbor MI 1978) 165-8. KUHN, H.-W. "Predigt über Röm 9:14-24" in W. Haubeck und M. Beckmann, eds., Wort in der Zeit. Neutestamentliche Studien (FS K. H. Rengstorf; Leiden 1980) 288-93. THISELTON, A. C. The Two Horizons (Grand Rapids 1980) 394. HOFIUS, O. in GPM 38 (1983/84) 121-30. FREUND, G. und STEGEMANN, E., eds., Theologische Brosamen für Lothar Steiger (DBAT 5; Heidelberg 1985) 261.

9:14-21   STAAB, K. Pauluskommentare aus der griechischen Kirche (Münster ²1984) 67:8-68:39 Apoll; 98:13-100:12 Diod; 144:9-147:6 ThM; 390:26-393:16 Genn.

9:14-18   SCHMIDT, K.L. "Die Verstockung des Menschen durch Gott" ThZ 1 ('45) 1-17. LUZ, U. Das Geschichtsverständnis des Paulus (1968) 72-78, 235ff. LYONNET, S. Quaestiones in epistulam ad Romanos (Rome 1975) 38-43. MOXNES, H. Theology in Conflict (Leiden 1980) 34, 47-9, 82, 96. HÜBNER, H. Gottes Ich und Israel (Göttingen 1984) 36, 38f., 44f. SIEGERT, F. Argumentation bei Paulus (Tübingen 1985) 127-31. RÄISÄNEN, H. "Römer 9-11: Analyse eines geistigen Ringens" in ANRW II.25.4 (1987) 2902f. LIMBECK, M. Mit Paulus Christ sein. Sachbuch zur Person und Theologie des Apostels Paulus (Stuttgart 1989) 116. OLIVEIRA, A. DE, Die Diakonie der Gerechtigkeit und der Versöhnung in der Apologie des 2. Korintherbriefes. Analyse und Auslegung von 2 Kor 2, 14-4, 6; 5, 11-6, 10 (Münster 1990) 229.

9:14-15   PIPER, J. "Prolegomena to Understanding Romans 9:14-15. An Interpretation of Exodus 33:19," JETS 22 (3, 1979) 203-16.

9:14   SCHMITHALS, W. Der Römerbrief als historisches Problem (Gütersloh 1975) 89. RHYNE, C. T. Faith establishes the Law (Chico CA 1981) 48f. HÜBNER, H. Gottes Ich und Israel (Göttingen 1984) 36-9, 45f. RÄISÄNEN, H. The Torah and Christ (Helsinki 1986) 196f. SCHMELLER, TH. Paulus und die "Diatribe" (Münster 1987) 327. JOHNSON, E. E. The Function of Apocalyptic and Wisdom Traditions in Romans 9-11 (Atlanta GA 1989) 119, 144.

9:15-23   KAMLAH, E. "Barmherzigkeit" in TRE 5 (1980) 226.

9:15-21   VANNESTE, A. "Saint Paul et La Doctrine Augustinienne du Peche Originel" in Studiorum Paulinorum Congressus Internationalis Catholicus 1961 (1963) II 514-7.

9:15-16   LYONNET, S. Quaestiones in epistulam ad Romanos (Rome 1975) 40f.

9:15   ELLIS, E.E. Paul's Use of the Old Testament (1957) 34ff., 116, 125, 150, 160. HANSON, A. T. Studies in Paul's Technique and Theology (London 1974) 148f., 157, 180, 250. JEWETT, P. K. Infant Baptism and the Covenant of Grace (Grand Rapids 1978) 158n.104. STUIBER, A. "Ambrosiaster" in TRE 2 (1978) 360. KAMLAH, E. "Barmherzigkeit" in TRE 5 (1980) 227. HÜBNER, H. Gottes Ich und Israel (Göttingen 1984) 40, 42f., 53, 56.

9:16-21   STAAB, K. Pauluskommentare aus der griechischen Kirche (Münster ²1984)
           517:28-519:13 Phot.
9:16   SCHRAGE, W. Die konkreten Einzelgebote in der paulinischen Paränese (1961)
           73. PFITZNER, V.C. Paul and the Agon Motif (1967) 7, 51, 76, 89, 135f., 138.
           LUZ, U. Das Geschichtsverständnis des Paulus (1968) 90. NOACK, B. "Celui
           qui court. Rom IX, 16" StTh 24 (2, '70) 113-116. ROBINSON, J. A. Pelagius's
           Exposition of Thirteen Epistles of St. Paul (Cambridge 1922) 35, 37, 39f. HÜB-
           NER, H. Gottes Ich und Israel (Göttingen 1984) 39f., 53. JOHNSON, E. E. The
           Function of Apocalyptic and Wisdom Traditions in Romans 9-11 (Atlanta GA
           1989) 139, 154f., 201.
9:17-24   LUZ, U, Das Geschichtsverständnis des Paulus (1968) 233.
9:17-23   LYSCHIK, J. "El endurecimiento del Faraon (Rom. 9, 17-23)" RevBi 25 (109-
           10, '63) 173-80.
9:17-18   LYONNET, S. Quaestiones in epistulam ad Romanos (Rome 1975) 41-3.
           BEALE, G. K. "An Exegetical and Theological Consideration of the Hardening
           of Pharaoh's Heart in Exodus 4-14 and Romans 9," TrinJourn 5 (2, 1984) 129-
           54.
9:17   ELLIS, E.E. Paul's Use of the Old Testament (1957) 14, 21, 23, 116, 160.
           LUZ, U. Das Geschichtsverständnis des Paulus (1968) 90. MÜLLER, H. Die
           Auslegung alttestamentlichen Geschichtsstoffs bei Paulus (diss. Halle/Witten-
           berg 1960) 146f. ZELLER, D. Juden und Heiden in der Mission des Paulus.
           Studien zum Römerbrief (Stuttgart 1973) 206. STUIBER, A. "Ambrosiaster" in
           TRE 2 (1978) 359. HÜBNER, H. Gottes Ich und Israel (Göttingen 1984) 39f.,
           42-4, 47, 53, 59, 101, 110. STAAB, K. Pauluskommentare aus der griechischen
           Kirche (Münster ²1984) 428:17-20 Oek. KOCH, D.-A. Die Schrift als Zeuge des
           Evangeliums (Tübingen 1986) 112, 141, 150f. LÖFSTEDT, B. "Notes on St
           Paul's Letter to the Romans," FilolNeot 1 (2, 1988) 209-10. JOHNSON, E. E.
           The Function of Apocalyptic and Wisdom Traditions in Romans 9-11 (Atlanta
           GA 1989) 130, 195, 197.
9:18-21   CROUZEL, H. "Theological Construction and Research: Origen on Free Will"
           in R. Bauckham and B. Drewery, eds., Scripture, Tradition and Reason (FS R.
           P. C. Hanson; Edinburgh 1988) 259-63.
9:18.22   FURNISH, V. P. "Der 'Wille Gottes' in paulinischer Sicht" in D.-A. Koch et
           al., eds., Jesu Rede von Gott und ihre Nachgeschichte im frühen Christentum
           (FS Willi Marxsen; Gütersloh 1989) 208-21, esp.211f.
9:18-19   BAMMEL, C. P. H. "Philocalia IX, Jerome, Epistle 121, and Origen's
           Exposition of Romans VII," JThS 32 (1981) 80.
9:18   BAMMEL, C. P. H. "Philocalia IX, Jerome, Epistle 121, and Origen's Expo-
           sition of Romans VII," JThS 32 (1981) 79f. HÜBNER, H. Gottes Ich und Israel
           (Göttingen 1984) 37, 39-41, 46, 53, 103. JOHNSON, E. E. The Function of
           Apocalyptic and Wisdom Traditions in Romans 9-11 (Atlanta GA 1989) 139,
           141, 155, 162.
9:19ff   THACKERAY, H.St.J. The Relation of St. Paul to Contemporary Jewish
           Thought (1900) 226ff. FROITZHEIM, F. Christologie und Eschatologie bei
           Paulus (Würzburg 1979) 173. HÜBNER, H. Gottes Ich und Israel (Göttingen
           1984) 47f.
9:19-29   HÜBNER, H. Gottes Ich und Israel (Göttingen 1984) 36f., 46. SIEGERT, F.
           Argumentation bei Paulus (Tübingen 1985) 131-40.
9:19-26   PAGELS, E. H. The Gnostic Paul. Gnostic Exegesis of the Pauline Letters
           (Philadelphia 1975) 38f.

9:19-24   LUZ, U. Das Geschichtsverständnis des Paulus (1968) 235-50. EICHHOLZ, G. Die Theologie des Paulus im Umriss (1972) 295f. MALHERBE, A. J. Moral Exhortation. A Greco-Roman Sourcebook (Philadelphia 1986) 130.

9:19-23   LYONNET, S. Quaestiones in epistulam ad Romanos (Rome 1975) 48-70. GEORGI, D. "Weisheit Salomos" in JSHRZ III/4 (1980) 12n.12a. RÄISÄNEN, H. "Römer 9-11: Analyse eines geistigen Ringens" in ANRW II.25.4 (1987) 2903f.

9:19-21   LUZ, U. Das Geschichtsverständnis des Paulus (1968) 237-41. PLAG, Chr. Israels Wege zum Heil (1969) 15. DONFRIED, K. P. The Setting of Second Clement in Early Christianity (Leiden 1974) 85. STOWERS, S. K. The Diatribe and Paul's Letter to the Romans (Chico CA 1981) 80, 98f., 113f. WAGNER, G. "The Future of Israel: Reflections on Romans 9-11" in W. H. Gloer, ed., Eschatology and the New Testament (FS G. R. Beasley-Murray; Peabody MA 1988) 85f.

9:19-20   RÄISÄNEN, H. The Torah and Christ (Helsinki 1986) 196.

9:19   BAUMERT, N. Täglich Sterben und Auferstehen. Der Literalsinn von 2 Kor 4, 12-5, 10 (München 1973) 304ff. SCHMITHALS, W. Der Römerbrief als historisches Problem (Gütersloh 1975) 89. KLIJN, A. F. J. "Die syrische Baruch-Apokalypse" in JSHRZ V/2 (1976) 124. BERGMEIER, R. Glaube als Gabe nach Johannes (Stuttgart 1980) 93n.132. KLEINKNECHT, K. T. Der leidende Gerechtfertigte (Tübingen 1984) 385. MALHERBE, A. J. Moral Exhortation. A Greco-Roman Sourcebook (Philadelphia 1986) 129. BERGER, K. und COLPE, C., eds., Religionsgeschichtliches Textbuch zum Neuen Testament (Göttingen/Zürich 1987) 221. SCHMELLER, TH. Paulus und die "Diatribe" (Münster 1987) 328n.129. JOHNSON, E. E. The Function of Apocalyptic and Wisdom Traditions in Romans 9-11 (Atlanta GA 1989) 119, 144, 195.

9:19b   HÜBNER, H. Gottes Ich und Israel (Göttingen 1984) 47f.

9:20-23   SIEGERT, F. Argumentation bei Paulus (Tübingen 1985) 186-90. JOHNSON, E. E. The Function of Apocalyptic and Wisdom Traditions in Romans 9-11 (Atlanta GA 1989) 2, 131, 149, 175.

9:20-21   ROMANIUK, C. "Le Livre de la Sagresse dans le Nouveau Testament" NTS 14 (1967-68) 507f. STAAB, K. Pauluskommentare aus der griechischen Kirche (Münster ²1984) 222:1-14 Sev. HÄRING, H. Das Problem des Bösen in der Theologie (Darmstadt 1985) 96.

9:20   BRUNNER, E. Dogmatik I (1946) 197. SCHRAGE, W. Die konkreten Einzelgebote in der paulinischen Paränese (1961) 112, 210. LYONNET, S. Quaestiones in epistulam ad Romanos (Rome 1975) 48f. HÜBNER, H. Gottes Ich und Israel (Göttingen 1984) 46f., 49. KOCH, D.-A. Die Schrift als Zeuge des Evangeliums (Tübingen 1986) 144. MALHERBE, A. J. Moral Exhortation. A Greco-Roman Sourcebook (Philadelphia 1986) 130. JOHNSON, E. E. The Function of Apocalyptic and Wisdom Traditions in Romans 9-11 (Atlanta GA 1989) 131f., 155, 157.

9:20b   HÜBNER, H. Gottes Ich und Israel (Göttingen 1984) 47f.

9:21-23   LYONNET, S. Quaestiones in epistulam ad Romanos (Rome 1975) 50-70.

9:21   BRUNNER, E. Dogmatik I (1946) 355. LYONNET, S. Quaestiones in epistulam ad Romanos (Rome 1975) 49f. BERGMEIER, R. Glaube als Gabe nach Johannes (Stuttgart 1980) 89. GEORGI, D. "Weisheit Salomos" in JSHRZ III/4 (1980) 15n.7b.

9:22ff.   ELLINGWORTH, P. "Translation and Exegesis: A Case Study (Rom 9, 22ff.)," Biblica 59 (3, 1978) 396-402. THEOBALD, M. Die überströmende Gnade (Würzburg 1982) 143-7.

9:22-29   PLAG, Chr. Israels Wege zum Heil (1969) 15f. MOXNES, H. Theology in
           Conflict (Leiden 1980) 251-3. WAGNER, G. "The Future of Israel: Reflections
           on Romans 9-11" in W. H. Gloer, ed., Eschatology and the New Testament (FS
           G. R. Beasley-Murray; Peabody MA 1988) 86-8.
9:22-28   STAAB, K. Pauluskommentare aus der griechischen Kirche (Münster ²1984)
           393:17-394:27 Genn.
9:22-26   WINGREN, G. "Barmherzigkeit" in TRE 5 (1980) 233.
9:22-24   BORNKAMM, G. "Paulinische Anakoluthe": Das Ende des Gesetzes (1952) 76-
           92. MANSUS, H. The Wrath of God in the Pauline Homologoumena (1969) 58-
           63. HEROLD, G. Zorn und Gerechtigkeit Gottes bei Paulus. Eine Untersuchung
           zu Röm. 1, 16-18 (Bern/Frankfurt 1973) 212-9. ZELLER, D. Juden und Heiden
           in der Mission des Paulus. Studien zum Römerbrief (Stuttgart 1973) 203ff.
           ELLINGWORTH, P. "Translation and Exegesis: A Case Study (Rom 9:22ff.),"
           Biblica 59 (3, 1978) 396-402. LAYMAN, F. D. Paul's Use of Abraham. An
           Approach to Paul's Understanding of History (diss. Ann Arbor MI 1978) 258-
           61. MOXNES, H. Theology in Conflict (Leiden 1980) 82f. STAAB, K. Paulus-
           kommentare aus der griechischen Kirche (Münster ²1984) 147:7-148:19 ThM.
9:22-23   BAUMERT, N. Täglich Sterben und Auferstehen. Der Literalsinn von 2 Kor 4,
           12-5, 10 (München 1973) 306. GEORGI, D. "Weisheit Salomos" in JSHRZ
           III/4 (1980) 12n.20a. CAMPBELL, W. S. "The Freedom and Faithfulness of
           God in Relation to Israel," JSNT 13 (1981) 31-3. HANSON, A. T. "Vessels of
           Wrath or Instruments of Wrath? Romans IX.22-3," JThS 32 (2, 1981) 433-43.
           HÜBNER, H. Gottes Ich und Israel (Göttingen 1984) 47, 52f., 55, 58, 70, 121.
           STAAB, K. Pauluskommentare aus der griechischen Kirche (Münster ²1984)
           54:31-55:12 Akazc; 519:14-520:32 Phot. BAYER, H. "Hartmann von Aue" in
           TRE XIV (1985) 463. SIEGERT, F. Argumentation bei Paulus (Tübingen 1985)
           182-5.
9:22f.   LUZ, U. Das Geschichtsverständnis des Paulus (1968) 241-50.
9:22   BRUNNER, E. Dogmatik I (1946) 296; II (1950) 182. LYONNET, S.
           Quaestiones in epistulam ad Romanos (Rome 1975) 57-66. KLIJN, A. F. J.
           "Die syrische Baruch-Apokalypse" in JSHRZ V/2 (1976) 139. BAMMEL, C.
           P. H. "Philocalia IX, Jerome, Epistle 121, and Origen's Exposition of Romans
           VII," JThS 32 (1981) 80. THEOBALD, M. Die überströmende Gnade (Würz-
           burg 1982) 147f. STAAB, K. Pauluskommentare aus der griechischen Kirche
           (Münster ²1984) 222:15-22 Sev; 429:1-3 Oek; 658:15 Areth. JOHNSON, E. E.
           The Function of Apocalyptic and Wisdom Traditions in Romans 9-11 (Atlanta
           GA 1989) 126f., 149, 155, 197.
9:23f   REICKE, B. The Disobedient Spirits and Christian Baptism (1946) 168f.
9:23   BURCHARD, C. Untersuchungen zu Joseph and Aseneth (Tübingen 1965) 150.
           LYONNET, S. Quaestiones in epistulam ad Romanos (Rome 1975) 66-70.
           BYRNE, B. "Sons of God"—"Seed of Abraham" (Rome 1979) 112, 128, 135f.,
           140, 150f. THEOBALD, M. Die überströmende Gnade (Würzburg 1982) 148-
           50. JOHNSON, E. E. The Function of Apocalyptic and Wisdom Traditions in
           Romans 9-11 (Atlanta GA 1989) 127f., 139, 171. OLIVEIRA, A. DE, Die
           Diakonie der Gerechtigkeit und der Versöhnung in der Apologie des 2.
           Korintherbriefes. Analyse und Auslegung von 2 Kor 2, 14-4, 6; 5, 11-6, 10
           (Münster 1990) 229.
9:24-10:13 RÄISÄNEN, H. The Torah and Christ (Helsinki 1986) 73-6.
9:24-32   LYONNET, S. Quaestiones in epistulam ad Romanos (Rome 1975) 70-85.
9:24-29   JEREMIAS, J. Abba (1966) 283. RÄISÄNEN, H. "Römer 9-11: Analyse eines
           geistigen Ringens" in ANRW II.25.4 (1987) 2904f.

9:24-25   WIEDERKEHR, D. Die Theologie der Berufung in den Paulusbriefen (1963) 174-83.

9:24   LUZ, U. Das Geschichtsverständnis des Paulus (1968) 29. SCHMITHALS, W. "Zur Herkunft der gnostischen Elemente in der Sprache des Paulus" in B. Aland et al., eds., Gnosis (FS H. Jonas; Göttingen 1978) 390-3. MOXNES, H. Theology in Conflict (Leiden 1980) 23, 48f., 78, 89. HÜBNER, H. Gottes Ich und Israel (Göttingen 1984) 15, 46, 51, 53, 55-7. STAAB, K. Pauluskommentare aus der griechischen Kirche (Münster ²1984) 658:16 Areth. SANDERS, E. P. Paul, the Law, and the Jewish People (London 1985) 43, 174f. JOHNSON, E. E. The Function of Apocalyptic and Wisdom Traditions in Romans 9-11 (Atlanta GA 1989) 118, 139-41, 143, 147f., 155, 162, 195-7.

9:25ff.   BYRNE, B. "Sons of God"—"Seed of Abraham" (Rome 1979) 136-8.

9:25-33   ELLIS, E.E. Paul's Use of the Old Testament (1957) passim.

9:25-30   LAYMAN, F. D. Paul's Use of Abraham. An Approach to Paul's Understanding of History (diss. Ann Arbor MI 1978) 261f.

9:25-29   LUZ, U. Das Geschichtsverständnis des Paulus (1968) 29f., 85, 98. RICHARDSON, P. Israel in the Apostolic Church (1969) 214f. ELLIS, E. E. Paul's Use of the Old Testament (Edinburgh 1957) 11f., 20, 73f., 101f., 122f., 151, 162, 186. KOCH, D.-A. Die Schrift als Zeuge des Evangeliums (Tübingen 1986) 279f.

9:25-26   DAVIES, W. D. The Gospel and the Land (London 1974) 195f. BATTLE, J. A. "Paul's Use of the Old Testament in Romans 9:25-26," GraceTheolJourn 2 (1, 1981) 115-29. STAAB, K. Pauluskommentare aus der griechischen Kirche (Münster ²1984) 148:20-8 ThM. KOCH, D.-A. Die Schrift als Zeuge des Evangeliums (Tübingen 1986) 166f., 173f., 302f.

9:25f.   LUZ, U. Das Geschichtsverständnis des Paulus (1968) 90.

9:25   STÄHELIN, E. Die Verkündigung des Reiches Gottes in der Kirche Jesus Christi I (1951) 130, 282. LUZ, U. Das Geschichtsverständnis des Paulus (1968) 98. LYONNET, S. Quaestiones in epistulam ad Romanos (Rome 1975) 71-3. BYRNE, B. "Sons of God"—"Seed of Abraham" (Rome 1979) 120f., 128, 131, 137, 140. BURCHARD, C. "Römer 9:25 en to Hosee," ZNW 76 (1985) 131. KOCH, D.-A. Die Schrift als Zeuge des Evangeliums (Tübingen 1986) 104f. LAYTON, B. The Gnostic Scriptures (Garden City NY 1987) 243.

9:26   BLANK, J. Paulus und Jesus (1968) 258ff. ZELLER, D. Juden und Heiden in der Mission des Paulus. Studien zum Römerbrief (Stuttgart 1973) 284. DELLING, G. "Die 'Söhne (Kinder) Gottes' im Neuen Testament" in R. Schnackenburg et al., eds., Die Kirche des Anfangs (FS H. Schürmann; Freiburg/Basel/Wien 1978) 619. BYRNE, B. "Sons of God"—"Seed of Abraham" (Rome 1979) 2, 71f., 128, 131, 137, 139. DINKLER, E. "Die ekklesiologischen Aussagen des Paulus im kritischen Rückblick auf Barmen III" in A. Burgsmüller, ed., Kirche als 'Gemeinde von Brüdern' (Gütersloh 1980) 120f.

9:27-32   LYONNET, S. Quaestiones in epistulam ad Romanos (Rome 1975) 79-84. PAGELS, E. H. The Gnostic Paul. Gnostic Exegesis of the Pauline Letters (Philadelphia 1975) 39.

9:27-29   ZELLER, D. Juden und Heiden in der Mission des Paulus. Studien zum Römerbrief (Stuttgart 1973) 120f. LAYMAN, F. D. Paul's Use of Abraham. An Approach to Paul's Understanding of History (diss. Ann Arbor MI 1978) 168. HÜBNER, H. Gottes Ich und Israel (Göttingen 1984) 59, 101f. STAAB, K. Pauluskommentare aus der griechischen Kirche (Münster ²1984) 148:29-149:3 ThM.

9:27-28   LYONNET, S. Quaestiones in epistulam ad Romanos (Rome 1975) 73f.
             HÜBNER, H. Gottes Ich und Israel (Göttingen 1984) 57f. STAAB, K. Paulus-
             kommentare aus der griechischen Kirche (Münster ²1984) 100:13-29 Diod;
             520:33-522:3 Phot. KOCH, D.-A. Die Schrift als Zeuge des Evangeliums
             (Tübingen 1986) 82f., 145-9.
9:27   HÜBNER, H. Gottes Ich und Israel (Göttingen 1984) 57f., 102, 113, 117, 122.
             KOCH, D.-A. Die Schrift als Zeuge des Evangeliums (Tübingen 1986) 167f.
             WATTS, J. W. "The Remnant Theme: A Survey of New Testament Research,
             1921-1987," PRSt 15 (2, 1988) 109-29. JOHNSON, E. E. The Function of
             Apocalyptic and Wisdom Traditions in Romans 9-11 (Atlanta GA 1989) 128,
             130, 140, 150, 199.
9:28   STAAB, K. Pauluskommentare aus der griechischen Kirche (Münster ²1984)
             429:4-23 Oek.
9:29-31   STAAB, K. Pauluskommentare aus der griechischen Kirche (Münster ²1984)
             100:30-101:4 Diod; 394:28-395:2 Genn.
9:29-30   STAAB, K. Pauluskommentare aus der griechischen Kirche (Münster ²1984)
             522:4-523:6 Phot.
9:29   STAAB, K. Pauluskommentare aus der griechischen Kirche (Münster ²1984)
             429:25-5 Oek. OLIVEIRA, A. DE, Die Diakonie der Gerechtigkeit und der Ver-
             söhnung in der Apologie des 2. Korintherbriefes. Analyse und Auslegung von
             2 Kor 2, 14-4, 6; 5, 11-6, 10 (Münster 1990) 224n.664.
9:30-10:23   LAYMAN, F. D. Paul's Use of Abraham. An Approach to Paul's Understand-
             ing of History (diss. Ann Arbor MI 1978) 262-72.
9:30-10:21   LJUNGMAN, H. Pistis (1964) 80-105. WREGE, H.-T. Die Ueberliefer-
             ungsgeschichte der Bergpredigt (Tübingen 1968) 174f. ZELLER, D. Juden und
             Heiden in der Mission des Paulus. Studien zum Römerbrief (Stuttgart 1973)
             122ff., 209. VIA, D. O. "A Structuralist Approach to Paul's Old Testament
             Hermeneutic," Interp 28 (1974) 201-20. VIA, D. O. Kerygma and Comedy in
             the New Testament (Philadelphia 1975) 49-66. DUGANDZIC, I. Das "Ja"
             Gottes in Christus (Würzburg 1977) 286-90. ROBINSON, J. A. T. Wrestling
             with Romans (London 1979) 120-6. HARRINGTON, D. J. God's People in
             Christ (Philadelphia 1980) 61-3. RHYNE, C. T. Faith establishes the Law
             (Chico CA 1981) 98-112. BARRETT, C. K. "Romans 9:30-10:21. Fall and
             Responsibility of Israel" in Essays on Paul (London 1982) 132-53. HAYS, R.
             B. The Faith of Jesus Christ (Chico CA 1983) 69. HÜBNER, H. Gottes Ich und
             Israel (Göttingen 1984) 26, 60, 70, 94f., 97f., 102, 117, 122. SCHMITT, R.
             Gottesgerechtigkeit—Heilsgeschichte—Israel in der Theologie des Paulus
             (Frankfurt/Bern/New York/Nancy 1984) 88-97. BADENAS, R. Christ the End
             of the Law (Sheffield 1985) 97-137, 148-50. LÜBKING, H.-M. Paulus und
             Israel im Römerbrief (Frankfurt/Bern/New York 1986) 79-92, 141-3. WATSON,
             F. Paul, Judaism and the Gentiles (Cambridge 1986) 164-8. DUNN, J. D. G.
             "Paul's Epistle to the Romans: An Analysis of Structure and Argument" in
             ANRW II.25.4 (1987) 2870f. GASTON, L. Paul and the Torah (Vancouver
             1987) 126-33, 141. RÄISÄNEN, H. "Römer 9-11: Analyse eines geistigen
             Ringens" in ANRW II.25.4 (1987) 2906-11. WAGNER, G. "The Future of
             Israel: Reflections on Romans 9-11" in W. H. Gloer, ed., Eschatology and the
             New Testament (FS G. R. Beasley-Murray; Peabody MA 1988) 88-91. HAYS,
             R. B. Echoes of Scripture in the Letters of Paul (New Haven/London 1989) 74f.
             JOHNSON, E. E. The Function of Apocalyptic and Wisdom Traditions in
             Romans 9-11 (Atlanta GA 1989) 121, 141, 143, 145, 147, 150-9, 174, 198, 208.
             SEIFRID, M. A. Justification by Faith (Leiden/New York/Köln 1992) 244-49.

9:30–10:13   STALDER, K. Das Werk des Geistes in der Heiligung bei Paulus (1962) 349-59. LUZ, U. Das Geschichtsverständnis des Paulus (1968) 31, 188, 202f. VAN DÜLMEN, A. Die Theologie des Gesetzes bei Paulus (1968) 123-27. SCHWEIZER, E. et al, eds., Evangelisch-Katholischer Kommentar zum Neuen Testament (1969) 67-72. WILCKENS, U. "Was heisst bei Paulus: 'Aus Werken des Gesetzes wird dein Mensch gerecht'?" EKK I (1969) 51-77. BRING, R. "Paul and the Old Testament. A Study of the Ideas of Election, Faith and Law in Paul, with special reference to Roamns 9:30-10:13" StTh 25 (1, '71) 21-60. TOEWS, J. E. The Law in Paul's Letter to the Romans. A Study of Rom 9.30-10.13 (diss. Northwestern University 1977) SANDERS, E. P. Paul, the Law, and the Jewish People (London 1985) 30, 34-43, 53n.22, 61n.116, 78, 97, 140, 154f., 164n.25, 166n.40. KOCH, D.-A. Die Schrift als Zeuge des Evangeliums (Tübingen 1986) 291-6. DAVIES, G. N. Faith and Obedience in Romans. A Study in Romans 1-4 (Sheffield 1990) 177. LONGENECKER, B. W. Eschatology and the Covenant. A Comparison of 4 Ezra and Romans 1-11 (Sheffield 1991) 170, 203, 215, 224, 229, 246, 254.

9:30-10:8   THIELMAN, F. From Plight to Solution (Leiden 1989) 91, 87, 111-5, 129.

9:30-10:4   VAN DER MINDE, H.-J. Schrift und Tradition bei Paulus (München/Paderborn/Wien 1976) 107. LAYMAN, F. D. Paul's Use of Abraham. An Approach to Paul's Understanding of History (diss. Ann Arbor MI 1978) 169f. CRANFIELD, C. E. B. "Romans 9:30-10:4," Interp 34 (1980) 70-4. LÜBKING, H.-M. Paulus und Israel im Römerbrief (Frankfurt/Bern/New York 1986) 80-4.

9:30-10:3   MARTIN, B. L. Christ and the Law in Paul (Leiden 1989) 94, 135. SCHREINER, T. "Israel's Failure to Attain Righteousness in Romans 9:30-10:3," Trinity Journal 12 (1991) 209-20.

9:30ff.   JÜNGEL, E. Paulus und Jesus (1966) 17. CONZELMANN, H. Theologie als Schriftauslegung (München 1974) 197, 201f. MUSSNER, F. "Das Toraleben im jüdischen Verständnis" in K. Kertelge, ed., Das Gesetz im Neuen Testament (Freiburg/Basel/Wien 1986) 41.

9:30-33   HROMADKA, J.L. GPM 14 (1960) 259-62. BRAUN, H. GPM 29 (1965-66) 322-26. PLAG, Chr. Israels Wege zum Heil (1969) 17f. BORN, W./MUELLER, D. Predigtstudien (1972) ed. E.Lange 160-5. STECK, K.G. GPM 26 (1972) 333-41. SCHELKLE, K. H. Die Passion Jesu in der Verkündigung des Neuen Testament (Heidelberg 1949) 173, 203f. CRANFIELD, C. E. B. "Some Notes on Romans 9:30-33" in E. E. Ellis und E. Grässer, eds., Jesus und Paulus (FS W. G. Kümmel; Göttingen 1975) 35-43. RHYNE, C. T. Faith establishes the Law (Chico CA 1981) 98-102. HÜBNER, H. Gottes Ich und Israel (Göttingen 1984) 60, 69, 71, 84f., 98f. SCHMITT, R. Gottesgerechtigkeit—Heilsgeschichte—Israel in der Theologie des Paulus (Frankfurt/Bern/New York/Nancy 1984) 88. BADENAS, R. Christ the End of the Law (Sheffield 1985) 101-8. REFOULÉ, F. "Note sur Romains IX, 30-33," RB 92 (1985) 161-86. SIEGERT, F. Argumentation bei Paulus (Tübingen 1985) 140-4. SCHMELLER, TH. Paulus und die "Diatribe" (Münster 1987) 288n.8. SCHNELLE, U. Wandlungen im paulinischen Denken (Stuttgart 1989) 70.

9:30-32   FULLER, D. P. Gospel and Law. Contrast or Continuum? (Grand Rapids 1980) 71-85. THISELTON, A. C. The Two Horizons (Grand Rapids 1980) 419, 422. KOCH, D.-A. Die Schrift als Zeuge des Evangeliums (Tübingen 1986) 161f., 292f. MERKLEIN, H. Studien zu Jesus und Paulus (Tübingen 1987) 44-46. JOHNSON, E. E. The Function of Apocalyptic and Wisdom Traditions in Romans 9-11 (Atlanta GA 1989) 144f. BEKER, J. C. "The New Testament

View of Judaism" in J. H. Charlesworth, ed., Jews and Christians. Exploring the Past, Present, and Future (New York 1990) 60-9, esp.68f.

9:30-31   HÜBNER, H. Gottes Ich und Israel (Göttingen 1984) 37, 40, 60f., 64f., 103. STAAB, K. Pauluskommentare aus der griechischen Kirche (Münster [2]1984) 149:4-28 ThM. SIEGERT, F. Argumentation bei Paulus (Tübingen 1985) 182-5. JOHNSON, E. E. The Function of Apocalyptic and Wisdom Traditions in Romans 9-11 (Atlanta GA 1989) 118, 150f., 159, 195. MARTIN, B. L. Christ and the Law in Paul (Leiden 1989) 64, 125, 136-8, 140f.

9:30   BONHOEFFER, A. Epiktet und das Neue Testament (1911) 152, 166. JÜNGEL, E. Paulus und Jesus (1966) 28. KERTELGE, K. "Rechtgertigung" bei Paulus (1967) 128, 161. SCHMITHALS, W. Der Römerbrief als historisches Problem (Gütersloh 1975) 89. GONZALEZ FAUS, J. I. et al. La justicia que brota de la fe (Rom 9, 30) (Santander 1982) HÜBNER, H. Gottes Ich und Israel (Göttingen 1984) 37, 59-61, 65, 71, 78, 98, 103. JOHNSON, E. E. The Function of Apocalyptic and Wisdom Traditions in Romans 9-11 (Atlanta GA 1989) 119, 143, 148, 153, 159, 163, 198. MARTIN, B. L. Christ and the Law in Paul (Leiden 1989) 64, 125, 136-8, 140f.

9:30b-33   BARTH, G. "Romans 9:30b-33," GPM 32 (1978) 324-30.

9:31-10:4   LAPIDE, P. und GERLACH, W. in P. Krusche et al., eds., Predigtstudien für das Kirchenjahr 1981/1982. IV/2 (Stuttgart 1982) 173-81.

9:31-32a   CRANFIELD, C. E. B. "Some Notes on Romans 9:30-33" in E. E. Ellis und E. Grässer, eds., Jesus und Paulus (FS W. G. Kümmel; Göttingen 1975) 36ff.

9:31f.   JÜNGEL, E. Paulus und Jesus (1966) 51.

9:31   JÜNGEL, E. Paulus und Jesus (1966) 59. VAN DÜLMEN, A. Die Theologie des Gesetzes bei Paulus (1968) 72, 101, 124, 125, 131, 141, 177, 127, 255. HÜBNER, H. Gottes Ich und Israel (Göttingen 1984) 14, 60-2, 65f., 77, 83-5, 97, 103. KLEINKNECHT, K. T. Der leidende Gerechtfertigte (Tübingen 1984) 333. SANDERS, E. P. Paul, the Law, and the Jewish People (London 1985) 62f.nn.129, 130;174. LIEBERS, R. Das Gesetz als Evangelium (Zürich 1989) 85-8, 226-8. MARTIN, B. L. Christ and the Law in Paul (Leiden 1989) 17, 64f., 95, 125, 131, 136-8.

9:32-33   ELLIS, E.E. Paul's Use of the Old Testament (1957)150f., 164f., 186. JÜNGEL, E. Paulus und Jesus (1966) 51. ZELLER, D. Juden und Heiden in der Mission des Paulus. Studien zum Römerbrief (Stuttgart 1973) 189ff. RÄISÄNEN, H. Paul and the Law (Tübingen 1983) 174f. SNODGRASS, K. The Parable of the Wicked Tenants (Tübingen 1983) 110. STAAB, K. Pauluskommentare aus der griechischen Kirche (Münster [2]1984) 149:29-150:27 ThM; 395:3-6 Genn. JOHNSON, E. E. The Function of Apocalyptic and Wisdom Traditions in Romans 9-11 (Atlanta GA 1989) 198.

9:32   SCHRAGE, W. Die konkreten Einzelgebote in der paulinischen Paränese (1961) 196. OESTERREICHER, J.M. "Israel's Misstep and her Rise" Studiorum Paulinorum Congressus Internationalis Catholicus 1961 (1963) I 320-21. THEYSSEN, G.W. "Unbelief" in the New Testament (Rüschlikon 1965) 13-17. LYONNET, S. Quaestiones in epistulam ad Romanos (Rome 1975) 82-5. HÜBNER, H. Gottes Ich und Israel (Göttingen 1984) 61, 65f., 73, 81f., 85, 92. JOHNSON, E. E. The Function of Apocalyptic and Wisdom Traditions in Romans 9-11 (Atlanta GA 1989) 121, 154, 158, 184. LIEBERS, R. Das Gesetz als Evangelium (Zürich 1989) 27-9. MARTIN, B. L. Christ and the Law in Paul (Leiden 1989) 25, 62-4, 66, 137f., 141. DAVIES, G. N. Faith and Obedience in Romans. A Study in Romans 1-4 (Sheffield 1990) 123f. GORDON, T. D.

"Why Israel Did Not Obtain Torah-Righteousness: A Translation Note on Rom 9:32," WThJ 54 (1992) 163-66.

9:32b-33 CRANFIELD, C. E. B. "Some Notes on Romans 9:30-33" in E. E. Ellis und E. Grässer, eds., Jesus und Paulus (FS W. G. Kümmel; Göttingen 1975) 41ff.

9:33 FLEW, R.N. Jesus and His Church (1956) 67n, LINDARS, B. New Testament Apologetic (1961) 164, 175, 177-183, 241, 244. BRAUN, H. Qumran und NT II (1966) 172, 210, 304, 313-14. KERTELGE, K. "Rechtfertigung" bei Paulus (1967) 151, 169. LUZ, U. Das Geschichtsverständnis des Paulus (1968) 96ff. MUELLER, K.H. Anstoss und Gericht (1969) 71-83. ROBINSON, J. A. Pelagius's Exposition of Thirteen Epistles of St. Paul (Cambridge 1922) 309, 315f. WAINWRIGHT, A. W. The Trinity in the New Testament (London 1962) 101f. HEROLD, G. Zorn und Gerechtigkeit Gottes bei Paulus. Eine Untersuchung zu Röm. 1, 16-18 (Bern/ Frankfurt 1973) 131f. HANSON, A. T. Studies in Paul's Technique and Theology (London 1974) 146, 192f. ELLIS, E. E. Prophecy and Hermeneutic in Early Christianity (Tübingen 1978) 149, 174, 196. KOCH, D.-A. "Beobachtungen zum christologischen Schriftgebrauch in den vorpaulinischen Gemeinden," ZNW 71 (1980) 174-91. RÄISÄNEN, H. Paul and the Law (Tübingen 1983) 53f., 56. HÜBNER, H. Gottes Ich und Israel (Göttingen 1984) 43, 60f., 66-70, 91f. STAAB, K. Pauluskommentare aus der griechischen Kirche (Münster ²1984) 69:1-12 Apoll. FREUND, G. und STEGEMANN, E., eds., Theologische Brosamen für Lothar Steiger (DBAT 5; Heidelberg 1985) 225, 228. KOCH, D.-A. Die Schrift als Zeuge des Evangeliums (Tübingen 1986) 58-60, 69-71, 161f., 241f., 249f., 287f., 346f. KREITZER, L. J. Jesus and God in Paul's Eschatology (Sheffield 1987) 124, 224n.71. JOHNSON, E. E. The Function of Apocalyptic and Wisdom Traditions in Romans 9-11 (Atlanta GA 1989) 127f., 151, 153f., 161, 198, 205. MARTIN, B. L. Christ and the Law in Paul (Leiden 1989) 62, 66, 118, 132, 135f., 141, 144. OSS, D. A. "The Interpretation of the 'Stone' Passages by Peter and Paul. A Comparative Study," JEThS 32 (1989) 181-200.

9:36 FRANSEN, I. "Le Dieu de toute consolation. Romains 9, 1-11, 36" BVieC ('63) 27-32.

10-14 VAN DER MINDE, H.-J. Schrift und Tradition bei Paulus (München/Paderborn/Wien 1976) 111f.

10 McNAMARA, M. The New Testament and the Palestinian Targum to the Pentateuch (1966) 70. MUNCK, J. Christ & Israel (1967) 75-104. LUZ, U. Das Geschichtsverständnis des Paulus (1968) 30ff, 208. GIBLIN, C.H. In Hope of God's Glory (1970) 282-91. EGGER, W. Frohbotschaft und Lehre. Die Sammelberichte des Wirkens Jesu im Markusevangelium (Frankfurt a.M. 1976) 48-50. VAN DER MINDE, H.-J. Schrift und Tradition bei Paulus (München/ Paderborn/Wien 1976) 107-19. LAYMAN, F. D. Paul's Use of Abraham. An Approach to Paul's Understanding of History (diss. Ann Arbor MI 1978) 90-93. WILLIAMS, S. K. "The 'Righteousness of God' in Romans," JBL 99 (1980) 281-84. RHYNE, C. T. Faith establishes the Law (Chico CA 1981) 102-12. THEOBALD, M. Die überströmende Gnade (Würzburg 1982) 150-54. GORDAY, P. Principles of Patristic Exegesis: Romans 9-11 in Origen, John Chrysostom, and Augustine (New York/Toronto 1983) 79, 123f., 170f. HÜBNER, H. Gottes Ich und Israel (Göttingen 1984) 25f., 34, 59f., 69, 76, 98f., 102, 105, 117, 126. SIEGERT, F. Argumentation bei Paulus (Tübingen 1985) 148-56. JOHNSON, E. E. The Function of Apocalyptic and Wisdom Traditions in Romans 9-11 (Atlanta GA 1989) 36, 41, 133, 136. RESE, M. "Israels Unwissen

188   *An Exegetical Bibliography of the New Testament*

und Ungehorsam und die Verkündigung des Glaubens durch Paulus in Römer 10" in D.-A. Koch et al., eds., Jesu Rede von Gott und ihre Nachgeschichte im frühen Christentum (FS Willi Marxsen; Gütersloh 1989) 252-66.

10:1ff.   BRAUMANN, G. Vorpaulinische christliche Taufverkündigung bei Paulus (1962) 15, 18ff., 68. JÜNGEL, E. Paulus und Jesus (1966) 50f.

10:1-15   NIESEL, W. in:G. Eichholz ed. Herr, tue meine Lippen auf 4 (1965) 359ff.

10:1-13   STROBEL, A. Untersuchungen zum Eschatologischen Verzögerungsproblem (1961) 189-91. KERTELGE, K. "Rechtfertigung" bei Paulus (1967) 78, 98. PAGELS, E. H. The Gnostic Paul. Gnostic Exegesis of the Pauline Letters (Philadelphia 1975) 39f. LANGEVIN, P.-É. "Sur la Christologie de Romains 10, 1-13," LThPh 35 (1979) 35-54. KIM, S. The Origin of Paul's Gospel (Tübingen 1981) 129-31, 298-300. DUPONT, J. "'Le Seigneur de tous' (Ac 10:36; Rm 10:12). Arrière-fond scripturaire d'une formule christologigue" in G. F. Hawthorne and O. Betz, eds., Tradition and Interpretation in the New Testament (FS E. E. Ellis; Grand Rapids/Tübingen 1987) 229f.

10:1-10   DUNN, J. D. G. "'Righteousness from the Law' and 'Righteousness from Faith'. Paul's Interpretation of Scripture in Romans 10:1-10" in G. F. Hawthorne and O. Betz, eds., Tradition and Interpretation in the New Testament (FS E. E. Ellis; Grand Rapids/Tübingen 1987) 216-26.

10:1-6a,8-9   HAYS, R. B. Echoes of Scripture in the Letters of Paul (New Haven/London 1989) 76f.

10:1-5   SIEGERT, F. Argumentation bei Paulus (Tübingen 1985) 149f.

10:1-4   WILCKENS, U. "Statements on the Development of Paul's View of the Law" in M. D. Hooker and S. G. Wilson, eds., Paul and Paulinism (FS C. K. Barrett; London 1982) 18f. STAAB, K. Pauluskommentare aus der griechischen Kirche (Münster ²1984) 150:28–151:10 ThM. MARXSEN, W. "Christliche" und christliche Ethik im Neuen Testament (Gütersloh 1989) 144f.

10:1-3   PLAG, Chr. Israels Wege zum Heil (1969) 18f. OLLROG, W.-H. Paulus und seine Mitarbeiter (Neukirchen-Vluyn 1979) 214. STAAB, K. Pauluskommentare aus der griechischen Kirche (Münster ²1984) 101:5-13 Diod; 395:7-17 Genn; 523:7-14 Phot. BADENAS, R. Christ the End of the Law (Sheffield 1985) 108-12. RESE, M. "Israels Unwissen und Ungehorsam und die Verkündigung des Glaubens durch Paulus in Römer 10" in D.-A. Koch et al., eds., Jesu Rede von Gott und ihre Nachgeschichte im frühen Christentum (FS Willi Marxsen; Gütersloh 1989) 259f., 263.

10:1-2   KERTELGE, K. "Rechtfertigung" bei Paulus (1967) 95. LYONNET, S. Quaestiones in epistulam ad Romanos (Rome 1975) 87f. SCHMITHALS, W. Der Römerbrief als historisches Problem (Gütersloh 1975) 10. CRANFIELD, C. E. B. "Light from St Paul on Christian-Jewish Relations" in The Bible and Christian Life (Edinburgh 1985) 36ff.

10:1   BRATSIOTIS, "Eine exegetische Notiz zu Röm. ix 3 und x 1, NovTest 5 (4, '62) 299-300. WILES, G. P. Paul's Intercessory Prayers (London 1974) 20, 76, 132, 156f., 158, 164, 166f., 174, 181f., 253, 255-57, 277f. MÜLLER, U. B. Prophetie und Predigt im Neuen Testament. Formgeschichtliche Untersuchungen zur urchristlichen Prophetie (Gütersloh 1975) 229ff., 237. SCHMITT, R. Gottesgerechtigkeit—Heilsgeschichte—Israel in der Theologie des Paulus (Frankfurt/ Bern/New York/Nancy 1984) 90f. SCHMELLER, TH. Paulus und die "Diatribe" (Münster 1987) 288n.8.

10:2-13   SIEGERT, F. Argumentation bei Paulus (Tübingen 1985) 182-5.

10:2-4   KÄSEMANN, E. Exegetische Versuche und Besinnungen (1964) II 195. KIM,
           S. The Origin of Paul's Gospel (Tübingen 1981) 3f. SEGAL, A. F. Paul the
           Convert (New Haven/London 1990) 2.
10:2-3   SCHMITT, R. Gottesgerechtigkeit—Heilsgeschichte—Israel in der Theologie
           des Paulus (Frankfurt/Bern/New York/Nancy 1984) 91f.
10:2   McNAMARA, M. The New Testament and the Palestianian Targum to the
           Pentateuch (1966) 70. BEUTLER, J. Martyria (Frankfurt a.M. 1972) 173, 216,
           221. HÜBNER, H. Gottes Ich und Israel (Göttingen 1984) 64, 70, 73, 75, 80,
           119. JOHNSON, E. E. The Function of Apocalyptic and Wisdom Traditions in
           Romans 9-11 (Atlanta GA 1989) 154f., 159.
10:3ff.   KÄSEMANN, E. Exegetische Versuche und Besinnungen (1964) II 182.
           KÄSEMANN, E. New Testament Questions of Today (1969) 169.
10:3,13   CAMBIER, J. L'Evangile de Dieu selon L'Epître aux Romains I (1967) 184-93.
10:3-6   LÜHRMANN, D. "Gerechtigkeit" in TRE 12 (1984) 417.
10:3-4   SCHRAGE, W. Die konkreten Einzelgebote in der paulinischen Paränese (1961)
           96. LYONNET, S. Quaestiones in epistulam ad Romanos (Rome 1975) 88-90.
           HÖDL, L. "Gerechtigkeit" in TRE 12 (1984) 430. SANDERS, E. P. Paul, the
           Law, and the Jewish People (London 1985) 140, 156, 163n.11.
10:3   BRUNNER, Dogmatik I (1946) 298. BULTMANN, R. Glaube und Verstehen
           II (1952) 32-58. MAGNUSSON, M. Der Begriff "Verstehen" im Exegetischen
           Zusammenahang (1954) 71-74. ROBINSON, J.M. Kerygma und historischer
           Jesus (1960) 58. KÄSEMANN, E. Exegetische Versuche und Besinnungen
           (1964) II 186. LJUNGMAN, H. Pistis (1964) 38f, 102-4. MUELLER, C. Gottes
           Gerechtigkeit und Gottes Volk (1964) 72ff. STUHLMACHER, P. Gerechtigkeit
           Gottes bei Paulus (1965) 13-16, 24-27, 29f., 41f., 57f., 60-69, 91-99. JÜNGEL,
           Paulus und Jesus (1966) 33, 43, 51, 53, 276. KERTELGE, K. "Rechtfertigung"
           bei Paulus (1967) 95-99, 174, 208. NICKELS, P. Targum and New Testament
           (1967) 70. MERK, O. Handeln aus Glauben (1968) 9, 13, 31, 38. KÄSE-
           MANN, E. New Testament Questions of Today (1969) 173. EICHHOLZ, G.
           Die Theologie des Paulus im Umriss (1972) 246f. ZIESLER, J.A. The Meaning
           of Righteousness in Paul (1972) 205f. ZELLER, D. Juden und Heiden in der
           Mission des Paulus. Studien zum Römerbrief (Stuttgart 1973) 191. SCROGGS,
           R. Paul for a New Day (Philadelphia 1977) 27. HAYS, R. B. "Psalm 143 and
           the Logic of Romans 3," JBL 99 (1980) 107. WILLIAMS, S. K. "The 'Righ-
           teousness of God' in Romans," JBL 99 (1980) 259, 282-84. RÄISÄNEN, H.
           Paul and the Law (Tübingen 1983) 70, 163, 174, 175f. HÜBNER, H. Gottes Ich
           und Israel (Göttingen 1984) 66, 72f., 75, 92f., 103. KLEIN, G. "Gesetz III" in
           TRE 13 (1984) 69. HULTGREN, A. J. Paul's Gospel and Mission (Philadelphia
           1985) 12f., 15, 22, 30, 32f. RÄISÄNEN, H. The Torah and Christ (Helsinki
           1986) 36. MERKLEIN, H. Studien zu Jesus und Paulus (Tübingen 1987) 34,
           37f., 96. JOHNSON, E. E. The Function of Apocalyptic and Wisdom Traditions
           in Romans 9-11 (Atlanta GA 1989) 139, 151, 153f., 156. LIEBERS, R. Das Ge-
           setz als Evangelium (Zürich 1989) 55-58. MARTIN, B. L. Christ and the Law
           in Paul (Leiden 1989) 17, 61f., 93-95, 124-26, 136, 138, 141. MARXSEN, W.
           "Christliche" und christliche Ethik im Neuen Testament (Gütersloh 1989) 209.
           SCHNELLE, U. Wandlungen im paulinischen Denken (Stuttgart 1989) 63, 70.
10:4ff.   BANDSTRA, A.J. The Law and the Elements of the World (1964) 101ff.,
           183ff. SEEBERG, A. Der Katechismus der Urchristenheit (1966) 159-62.
           HOWARD, G.E. "Christ the End of the Law: The Meaning of Romans 10:4ff"
           JBL 88 (3, '69) 331-37.

10:4-15   BAARDA, T. "Het einde van de wet is Christus. Rom. 10:4-15, een Midrasj van Paulus over Deut. 30:11-14," [Christ is the End of the Law. Rom 10:4-15, a Midrash of Paul on Deut 30:11-14] GThT 88 (1988) 208-48.

10:4-13   KÄSEMANN, E "Geist und Buchstabe": Paulinische Perspektiven (1969) 237-85. PLAG, Chr. Israels Wege zum Heil (1969) 19ff. RESE, M. "Israels Unwissen und Ungehorsam und die Verkündigung des Glaubens durch Paulus in Römer 10" in D.-A. Koch et al., eds., Jesu Rede von Gott und ihre Nachgeschichte im frühen Christentum (FS W. Marxsen; Gütersloh 1989) 260-62, 264f. ZELLER, D. Juden und Heiden in der Mission des Paulus. Studien zum Römerbrief (Stuttgart 1973) 193ff. DUGANDZIC, I. Das "Ja" Gottes in Christus (Würzburg 1977) 57-87.

10:4-12   DOBBELER, A. VON, Glaube als Teilhabe (Tübingen 1987) 151f.

10:4-5   KAISER, W.J. "Leviticus 18:5 and Paul: Do This and You Shall Live (Eternally?)" JournEvangTheolSoc 14 (1, '71) 19-28. STAAB, K. Pauluskommentare aus der griechischen Kirche (Münster ²1984) 101:14-6 Diod. SCHREINER, T. R. "Paul's View of the Law in Romans 10:4-5," WTh 55 (1993) 113-35.

10:4   FUCHS, E. "Christus das Ende der Geschichte" (1949): Zur Frage nach dem Historischen Jesus (1960) 79-99. BRUNNER, Dogmatik II (1950) 139. BULTMANN, R. "Chritus des Gesetzes Ende": Glauben und Verstehen II (1952) 32-58. FLÜCKIGER, F. "Christus des Gesetzes *telos*" ThZ 11 ('55) 153-57. SCHOEPS, H.-J. Paulus (1959) 178ff. BORNKAMM-Barth-Held, Ueberlieferung und Auslegung im Matthäus-Evangelium (1961) 65, 150. GRZYBEK, S. "'Finis Legis Christus' (Rom. 10, 4)" RuchBibLit (RBL) 14 (5, '61) 181-89. SCHRAGE, W. Die konkreten Einzelgebote in der paulinischen Paränese (1961) 93-95, 99, 117, 230. SCHNEIDER, E.E. "Finis legis Christus, Röm. 10, 4" ThZ 20 (6, '64) 410-22. HAHN, F. Das Verständnis der Mission im Neuen Testament (1965) 86. BRING, R. "Das Gesetz und die Gerechtigkeit Gottes. Eine Studie zur Frage nach der Bedeutung des Ausdruckes telos nomou in Röm. 10:4-" StTh 20 (1, '66) 1-36. JÜNGEL, E. Paulus und Jesus (1966) 50, 54f. GÜNTHOR, A. "'Endziel des Gesetzes ist Christus' (Röm 10, 4). Zur heutigen innerkirchlichen Gesetzeskrise" ErbeAuf 43 (3, '67) 192-205. KERTELGE, K. "Rechtfertigung" bei Paulus (1967) 109, 135, 202, 207. LUZ, U. Das Geschichtsverständnis des Paulus (1968) 139ff., 156ff., 167, 218. MERK, O. Handeln aus Glauben (1968) 7-10. VAN DÜLMEN, A. Die Theologie des Gesetzes bei Paulus (1968) 67, 93, 107, 124, 126f., 133, 171, 177, 191, 237. BRING, R. Christus und das Gesetz (1969) 35-72. SAND, A. "Gesetz und Freiheit. Vom Sinn des Pauluswortes: Christus, des Gesetzes Ende" ThuG, 61 (1, '71) 1-14. EICHHOLZ, G. Die Theologie des Paulus im Umriss (1972) 203f., 245f., 297. DAVIES, W. D. Torah in the Messianic Age and/or the Age to come (Philadelphia 1952) 83. LADD, G. E. A Theology of the New Testament (Grand Rapids 1974) 369, 502, 512, 517. CONZELMANN, H. and LINDEMANN, A. Arbeitsbuch zum Neuen Testament (Tübingen 1975) 158f. GETTY, M. A. Christ Is the End of the Law. Rom 10.4 in its Context (diss. Katholieke Universiteit Leuven 1975) LINDEMANN, A. Die Aufhebung der Zeit. Geschichtsverständnis und Eschatologie im Epheserbrief (Gütersloh 1975) 28f., 174, 245. OSTEN-SACKEN, P. VON DER, Römer 8 als Beispiel paulinischer Soteriologie (Göttingen 1975) 250ff. METZGER, B. M. The Early Versions of the New Testament. Their Origin Transmission, and Limitations (Oxford 1977) 81. MUSSNER, F. "'Christus (ist) des Gesetzes Ende zur Gerechtigkeit für jeden, der glaubt' (Röm 10, 4)" in M. Barth et al. Paulus—Apostat oder Apostel? (Regensburg 1977) 31-44. KRUIJF, T. C. DE,

"Antisemitismus" in TRE 3 (1978) 125. STROBEL, A. "Apokalyptik" in TRE 3 (1978) 252. ALAND, K. Neutestamentliche Entwürfe (München 1979) 17. OLLROG, W.-H. Paulus und seine Mitarbeiter (Neukirchen-Vluyn 1979) 135, 212. BARTH, G. "Bergpredigt" in TRE 5 (1980) 610. CAMPBELL, W. S. "Christ the End of the Law: Romans 10:4" in E. A. Livingstone, ed., Studia Biblica 1978 III. Papers on Paul and Other New Testament Authors (Sheffield 1980) 73-81. COLLANGE, J.-F. De Jésus à Paul: l'éthique du Nouveau Testament (Genève 1980) 249-54. FULLER, D. P. Gospel and Law. Contrast or Continuum? (Grand Rapids 1980) 84f. MEYER, P. W. "Romans 10:4 and the End of the Law" in J. L. Crenshaw and S. Sandmel, eds., The Divine Helmsman: Studies on God's Control of Human Events (FS L. H. Silberman; New York 1980) 59-78. RHYNE, C. T. Faith establishes the Law (Chico CA 1981) 95-116. SCHADE, H.-H. Apokalyptische Christologie bei Paulus (Göttingen 1981) 92. SMEND, R. and LUZ, U. Gesetz (Stuttgart/Berlin/Köln/Mainz 1981) 93f. COURT, J. M. "Paul and the Apocalyptic Pattern" in M. D. Hooker and S. G. Wilson, eds., Paul and Paulinism (FS C. K. Barrett; London 1982) 65. GETTY, M. A. "An Apocalyptic Perspective on Rom 10:4," HBTh 4 (1982)/5 (1983) 79-131. RÄISÄNEN, H. Paul and the Law (Tübingen 1983) 17, 50, 53-6, 65, 175. SCHULZ, S. "Zur Gesetzestheologie des Paulus im Blick auf Gerhard Ebelings Galaterbrief-Auslegung" in H. F. Geisser und W. Mostert, eds., Wirkungen hermeneutischer Theologie (FS G. Ebeling; Zürich 1983) 96f. HÜBNER, H. Gottes Ich und Israel (Göttingen 1984) 62, 76-8, 80-5, 94. KLEIN, G. "Gesetz III" in TRE 13 (1984) 65f. KLEINKNECHT, K. T. Der leidende Gerechtfertigte (Tübingen 1984) 320. LAPIDE, P. "The Rabbi from Tarsus" in Lapide P. and Stuhlmacher P. Paul: Rabbi and Apostle (Minneapolis 1984) 36-43. MOHRLANG, R. Matthew and Paul (Cambridge 1984) 26f., 102. REFOULÉ, F. "Romains, X, 4. Encore une fois," RB 91 (1984) 321-50. SCHMITT, R. Gottesgerechtigkeit—Heilsgeschichte—Israel in der Theologie des Paulus (Frankfurt/Bern/New York/Nancy 1984) 92f. STAAB, K. Pauluskommentare aus der griechischen Kirche (Münster [2]1984) 69:13-23 Apoll; 222:23-7 Sev; 395:18-9 Genn; 523:15-7 Phot. BEDENAS, R. Christ the End of the Law. Romans 10.4 in Pauline Perspective (Sheffield 1985) DIETZFELBINGER, C. Die Berufung des Paulus als Ursprung seiner Theologie (Neukirchen 1985) 101, 105f., 109, 113, 117ff., 121, 123. FREUND, G. und STEGEMANN, E., eds., Theologische Brosamen für Lothar Steiger (DBAT 5; Heidelberg 1985) 104. GRÄSSER, E. Der Alte Bund im Neuen (Tübingen 1985) 68, 91, 93, 229f., 283. HULTGREN, A. J. Paul's Gospel and Mission (Philadelphia 1985) 28f. RHYNE, C. T. "Nomos Dikaiosynes and the Meaning of Romans 10:4," CBQ 47 (1985) 486-99. SANDERS, E. P. Paul, the Law, and the Jewish People (London 1985) 32, 60n.98, 61n.114, 83, 91n.51, 193. SCHNABEL, E. J. Law and Wisdom from Ben Sira to Paul (Tübingen 1985) 284, 290, 293, 297. DAUTZENBERG, G. "Gesetzeskritik und Gesetzesgehorsam in der Jesustradition" in K. Kertelge, ed., Das Gesetz im Neuen Testament (Freiburg/Basel/Wien 1986) 47. EHLER, B. Die Herrschaft des Gekreuzigten (Berlin/New York 1986) 102. MARQUARDT, F.-W. Die Juden und ihr Land (Gütersloh [3]1986) 78. RÄISÄNEN, H. The Torah and Christ (Helsinki 1986) 11, 100f. DUNN, J. D. G. "'A Light to the Gentiles': the Significance of the Damascus Road Christophany for Paul" in L. D. Hurst and N. T. Wright, eds., The Glory of Christ in the New Testament (FS G. B. Caird; Oxford 1987) 255, 257. GASTON, L. Paul and the Torah (Vancouver 1987) 17f., 118, 198, 219. HÜBNER, H. "Paulusforschung seit 1945. Ein kritischer Literaturbericht" in ANRW

II.25.4 (1987) 2678, 2684f., 2689f. MERKLEIN, H. Studien zu Jesus und Paulus (Tübingen 1987) 12f., 14, 42, 93-6, 266, 270, 443n.132. BRUCE, F. F. "Paul and the Law in Recent Research" in B. Lindars, ed., Law and Religion (Cambridge 1988) 117, 122. CONZELMANN, H. and LINDEMANN, A. Interpreting the New Testament (Peabody, Mass. 1988) 139. LINSS, W. C. "Exegesis of telos in Romans 10:4," BR 33 (1988) 5-12. HAYS, R. B. Echoes of Scripture in the Letters of Paul (New Haven/London 1989) 75f., 137, 219n.49. HOFIUS, O. Paulusstudien (Tübingen 1989) 64f., 66, 110f., 118, 120, 157, 159, 172. JOHNSON, E. E. The Function of Apocalyptic and Wisdom Traditions in Romans 9-11 (Atlanta GA 1989) 21, 41, 112, 136, 151f., 154-8, 208. MARTIN, B. L. Christ and the Law in Paul (Leiden 1989) 2, 17, 52, 56f., 59.68, 125, 128-35, 138-42, 144, 154. MARXSEN, W. "Christliche" und christliche Ethik im Neuen Testament (Gütersloh 1989) 147, 149. OSTEN-SACKEN, P. VON DER, Die Heiligkeit der Tora (München 1989) 33-40, 164. SCHNELLE, U. Wandlungen im paulinischen Denken (Stuttgart 1989) 21, 69f. VOLLENWEIDER, S. Freiheit als neue Schöpfung (Göttingen 1989) 313n. BOCKMUEHL, M. N. A. Revelation and Mystery (Tübingen 1990) 151ff. DAVIES, G. N. Faith and Obedience in Romans. A Study in Romans 1-4 (Sheffield 1990) 185-9. DUNN, J. D. G. Jesus, Paul and the Law (London 1990) 52n.1, 53n.9, 92f., 99, 186, 215, 233n.32. LOHSE, E. Die Entstehung des Neuen Testaments (Stuttgart/Berlin/Köln ⁵1991) 12. CAMPBELL, W. S. Paul's Gospel in an Intercultural Context: Jew and Gentile in the Letter to the Romans (Frankfurt/Berlin/Bert etc. 1992) 60-67.

10:5ff.   HÜBNER, H. Gottes Ich und Israel (Göttingen 1984) 72, 78, 80, 85f., 88, 94. SCHMITT, R. Gottesgerechtigkeit—Heilsgeschichte—Israel in der Theologie des Paulus (Frankfurt/Bern/New York/Nancy 1984) 94f.

10:5-21   SCHLIER, H. "'Evangelium' im Römerbrief" in V. Kubina und K. Lehmann, eds., Der Geist und die Kirche (FS H. Schlier; Freiburg/Basel/Wien 1980) 74-83.

10:5-13   LUZ, U. Das Geschichtsverständnis des Paulus (1968) 31f. KÄSEMANN, E. "Geist und Buchstabe": Paulinische Perspektiven (1969) 237-85. LYONNET, S. Quaestiones in epistulam ad Romanos (Rome 1975) 90-106. LAYMAN, F. D. Paul's Use of Abraham. An Approach to Paul's understanding of History (diss. Ann Arbor MI 1978) 169f. EHLER, B. Die Herrschaft des Gekreuzigten (Berlin/New York 1986) 97-107. LÜBKING, H.-M. Paulus und Israel im Römerbrief (Frankfurt/Bern/New York 1986) 84-8.

10:5-11   LUZ, U. "Paulinische Theologie als Biblische Theologie" in M. Klopfenstein et al., eds., Mitte der Schrift? Ein jüdisch-christliches Gespräch. Texte des Berner Symposions vom 6.-12. Januar 1985 (Bern etc. 1987) 119-47, esp.122n.9, 129f.

10:5-10   VAN DER MINDE, H.-J. Schrift und Tradition bei Paulus (München/ Paderborn/Wien 1976) 107f. DAVIES, S. L. The Gospel of Thomas and Christian Wisdom (New York 1983) 40, 43. GRANT, R. M. "Paul and the Old Testament" in D. K. McKim, ed., The Authoritative Word (Grand Rapids 1983) 34f. MILLER, D. G. "The Bible" in D. K. McKim, ed., The Authoritative Word (Grand Rapids 1983) 34f. HAYS, R. B. Echoes of Scripture in the Letters of Paul (New Haven/London 1989) 2-5, 73-83, 167. VOS, J. S. "Die hermeneutische Antinomie bei Paulus (Galater 3.11-12; Römer 10.5-10)," NTS 38 (1992) 254-70.

10:5-9   BRAUN, H. Qumran und NT II (1966) 172, 307.

10:5-8	ZORN, R.O. "The Apostle Paul's Use of the Old Testament in Romans 10:5-8" Gordon Review 5 (1, '59) 29-34. SAITO, T. Die Mosevorstellungen im Neuen Testament (Bern 1977) 24, 145-7. VIELHAUER, P. "Paulus und das Alte Testament" in Oikodome [G. Klein, ed.] (München 1979) 214-6. FULLER, D. P. Gospel and Law. Contrast or Continuum? (Grand Rapids 1980) 66-88. RÄISÄNEN, H. Paul and the Law (Tübingen 1983) 54f., 62, 70, 72, 175. KOCH, D.-A. Die Schrift als Zeuge des Evangeliums (Tübingen 1986) 130f., 291-6. JOHNSON, E. E. The Function of Apocalyptic and Wisdom Traditions in Romans 9-11 (Atlanta GA 1989) 130, 152, 155. BOCKMUEHL, M. N. A. Revelation and Mystery (Tübingen 1990) 150, 152, 154. DAVIES, G. N. Faith and Obedience in Romans. A Study in Romans 1-4 (Sheffield 1990) 191-203.
10:5-6	SCHRAGE, W. Die konkreten Einzelgebote in der paulinischen Paränese (1961) 230, 237. JÜNGEL, E. Paulus und Jesus (1966) 17. MERKLEIN, H. Studien zu Jesus und Paulus (Tübingen 1987) 12, 44-6.
10:5	ELLIS, E.E. Paul's Use of the Old Testament (1957) 11, 13, 22, 30, 73f, 87f, 118, 181. JERVELL, J. Imago Dei (1960) 180f, 280. JÜNGEL, E. Paulus und Jesus (1966) 55, 57. McNAMARA, M. The New Testament and the Palestinian Targum to the Pentateuch (1966) 70. KERTELGE, K. "Rechtfertigung" bei Paulus (1967) 150. VAN DÜLMEN, A. Die Theologie des Gesetzes bei Paulus (1968) 34, 76, 110, 127, 133, 134, 135, 139, 214. KLIJN, A. F. J. "Die syrische Baruch-Apokalypse" in JSHRZ V/2 (1976) 168. VAN DER MINDE, H.-J. Schrift und Tradition bei Paulus (München/Paderborn/Wien 1976) 109. LINDE-MANN, A. "Die Gerechtigkeit aus dem Gesetz. Erwägungen zur Auslegung und zur Textgeschichte von Römer 10:5," ZNW 73 (1982) 231-50. HÜBNER, H. Gottes Ich und Israel (Göttingen 1984) 62f., 65, 78-85, 87, 94. STAAB, K. Pauluskommentare aus der griechischen Kirche (Münster ²1984) 395:20-2 Genn. BADENAS, R. Christ the End of the Law (Sheffield 1985) 118-25. FREUND, G. und STEGEMANN, E., eds., Theologische Brosamen für Lothar Steiger (DBAT 5; Heidelberg 1985) 185. MERKLEIN, H. Studien zu Jesus und Paulus (Tübingen 1987) 2, 14, 40f., 48, 94. HOFIUS, O. Paulusstudien (Tübingen 1989) 53, 60, 76, 111, 127, 177. JOHNSON, E. E. The Function of Apocalyptic and Wisdom Traditions in Romans 9-11 (Atlanta GA 1989) 134, 156f. LIEBERS, R. Das Gesetz als Evangelium (Zürich 1989) 88-91. MARTIN, B. L. Christ and the Law in Paul (Leiden 1989) 17, 20, 60-3, 65, 85, 125, 127, 133, 137-41, 146.
10:6ff.	DAVIES, W.D. Paul and Rabbinic Judaism (1955) 153. KÄSEMANN, E. Exegetische Versuche und Besinnungen (1964) II 189. LJUNGMAN, H. Pistis (1964) 83f, 102-105. McNAMARA, M. The New Testament and the Palestinian Targum to the Pentateuch (1966). KÄSEMANN, E. New Testament Questions of Today (1969) 177. HÜBNER, H. Gottes Ich und Israel (Göttingen 1984) 80, 85f., 90f.
10:6-17	HOFIUS, O. Paulusstudien (Tübingen 1989) 157, 159f. BUZZARD, A. "Paul's Apocalyptic Gospel as a Challenge to Contemporary Christianity: A Commentary on Romans 10.6-17," Journal from the Radical Reformation 2 (1993) 27-40.
10:6-14	BAUMERT, N. Täglich Sterben und Auferstehen. Der Literalsinn von 2 Kor 4, 12-5, 10 (München 1973) 86f.
10:6-11	SIEGERT, F. Argumentation bei Paulus (Tübingen 1985) 150f.
10:6-10	GLASSON, T.F. "The Gospel of Thomas, Saying 3, and Deuteronomy xxx.11-14" ET 78 (5, '67) 151-52. SUGGS, M.J. "The Word is Near You: Romans 10:6-10, within the Purpose of the Letter" Christian History and Interpretation:

Studies presented to John Knox, ed. W.R. Farmer, C.F.D. Moule and R.R.
Niebuhr (1967) 289-312. LYONNET, S. Quaestiones in epistulam ad Romanos
(Rome 1975) 91-3. DUNN, J. D. G. Christology in the Making (London 1980)
184-7, 342n.56. BLANK, J. Paulus. Von Jesus zum Christentum (München
1982) 212-4. STAAB, K. Pauluskommentare aus der griechischen Kirche
(Münster ²1984) 101:17-9 Diod; 396:1-23 Genn. CRANFIELD, C. E. B. "Some
Comments on Professor J. D. G. Dunn's *Christology in the Making* with Special
Reference to the Evidence of the Epistle to the Romans" in L. D. Hurst and
N. T. Wright, eds., The Glory of Christ in the New Testament (FS G. B. Caird;
Oxford 1987) 273f. MARTIN, B. L. Christ and the Law in Paul (Leiden 1989)
60, 62, 123, 138.

10:6-9   ELLIS, E.E. Paul's Use of the Old Testament (1957) 2, 10, 123, 150f.
ROBINSON, J.M. Kerygma und historischer Jesus (1960) 68. RÄISÄNEN, H.
"Der Bruch des Paulus mit Israels Bund" in T. Veijola, ed., The Law in the
Bible and in Its Environment (Helsinki/Göttingen 1990) 156-72, esp.156f.

10:6-8   LJUNGMAN, H. Pistis (1964) 84f. FEUILLET, A. Le Christ sagesse de Dieu
(1966) 321-27. JÜNGEL, E. Paulus und Jesus (19-66) 275. McNAMARA, M.
The New Testament and the Palestinian Targum to the Pentateuch (1966) 36,
70ff., 75, 77, 80f., 156, 254. NICKELS, P. Targum and New Testament (1967)
70. LUZ, U. Das Geschichtsverständnis des Paulus (1968) 91ff. HANSON, A.
T. Studies in Paul's Technique and Theology (London 1974) 146-48, 152,
154f., 167, 171, 192, 194, 208, 294. LONGENECKER, R. N. Biblical Exegesis
in the Apostolic Period (Grand Rapids 1975) 108, 114, 121-3. LYONNET, S.
Quaestiones in epistulam ad Romanos (Rome 1975) 94-106. FRIEDRICH, G.
"Das Gesetz Glaubens Römer 3, 27" in Auf das Wort kommt es an. Gesam-
melte Aufsätze (Göttingen 1978) 119. HANSON, A. T. The New Testament
Interpretation of Scripture (London 1980) 135-41. BADENAS, R. Christ the
End of the Law (Sheffield 1985) 121-33. SEIFRID, M. A. "Paul's Approach to
the Old Testament in Rom 10:6-8," TrinJourn 6 (1985) 3-37. KOCH, D.-A. Die
Schrift als Zeuge des Evangeliums (Tübingen 1986) 129-32, 153-60, 185f.,
197f., 229f. WEDER, H. Neutestamentliche Hermeneutik (Zürich 1986) 256f.
JOHNSON, E. E. The Function of Apocalyptic and Wisdom Traditions in
Romans 9-11 (Atlanta GA 1989) 2, 22, 130f., 133f., 136f., 156, 175, 208.
LIEBERS, R. Das Gesetz als Evangelium (Zürich 1989) 156-81. LIPS, H.
VON, Weisheitliche Traditionen im Neuen Testament (Neukirchen-Vluyn 1990)
350, 444.

10:6-7   CAMBIER, J. "La Signification Christologique D'Eph. IV, 7-10" NTS 9
(1962063) 269f. JÜNGEL, E. Paulus und Jesus (1966) 63. GOLDBERG, A.M.
"Torah aus der Unterwelt? Eine Bemerkung zu Röm 10, 6-7" BZ 14 (1, '70)
127-31. DAVIES, W. D. Torah in the Messianic Age and/or the Age to come
(Philadelphia 1952) 87. HELLER, J. "Himmel- und Höllenfahrt nach Römer 10,
6-7," EvTh 32 (1972) 478-86. KIM, S. The Origin of Paul's Gospel (Tübingen
1981) 117. SCHWEIZER, E. "Paul's Christology and Gnosticism" in M. D.
Hooker and S. G. Wilson, eds., Paul and Paulinism (FS C. K. Barrett; London
1982) 115f. BARRETT, C. K. "The Interpretation of the Old in the New" in D.
K. McKim, ed., The Authoritative Word (Grand Rapids 1983) 39f. SCHNA-
BEL, E. J. Law and Wisdom from Ben Sira to Paul (Tübingen 1985) 247f.,
261, 263, 292. GRUDEM, W. "He Did Not Descend into Hell. A Plea for
Following Scripture instead of the Apostles' Creed," JEThS 34 (1991) 103-113.

10:6   SCHWEIZER, E. Erniedrigung und Erhöhung bei Jesus und seinen Nachfolgern
(1962) §8m, 9d. KÄSEMANN, E. Exegetische Versuche und Besinnungen

(1964) II 185. JÜNGEL, E. Paulus und Jesus (1966) 43. KÄSEMANN, E. New Testament Questions of Today (1969) 173. LINDEMANN, A. Die Aufhebung der Zeit. Geschichtsverständnis und Eschatologie im Epheserbrief (Gütersloh 1975) 74, 206, 218, 225. HÜBNER, H. Gottes Ich und Israel (Göttingen 1984) 80, 83, 89f., 94. JOHNSON, E. E. The Function of Apocalyptic and Wisdom Traditions in Romans 9-11 (Atlanta GA 1989) 24, 152f., 156.

10:7   BIEDER, W. Die Vorstellung von der Höllenfahrt Jesu Christi (1949) 71ff. HOFFMANN, P. Die Toten in Christus (1966) 176-180, 184. JÜNGEL, E. Paulus und Jesus (1966) 43.

10:8-18   PETERS, G. W. A Biblical Theology of Missions (Chicago 1972) 70, 133, 149, 269f.

10:8-17   HOFIUS, O. Paulusstudien (Tübingen 1989) 153.

10:8-13   LANGEVIN, P.-É. "Le salut par la foi. Rm 10, 8-13," AssS 14 (1973) 47-53.

10:8-9   BARRETT, C. K. "Proclamation and Response" in G. F. Hawthorne and O. Betz, eds., Tradition and Interpretation in the New Testament (FS E. E. Ellis; Grand Rapids/Tübingen 1987) 9f. HAYS, R. B. Echoes of Scripture in the Letters of Paul (New Haven/London 1989) 81f.

10:8ff.   BUTLER, D.C. "The Object of Faith according to St. Paul's Epistles" Studiorum Paulinorum Congressus Internationalis Catholicus 1961 (1963) I 18-19.

10:8-17   KRAUSE, O. GPM 21 (1966/67) 245-51.

10:8-9   JÜNGEL, E. Paulus und Jesus (1966) 275. SEEBERG, A. Der Katechismus der Urchristenheit (1966) 179.

10:8   KRAMER, W. Christos Kyrios Gottessohn (1963) §11a. LUZ, U. Das Geschichtsverständnis des Paulus (1968) 90. MUSSNER, F. Die Auferstehung Jesu (1969) 197f. DUNN, J.D.G. Baptism in the Holy Spirit (1970) 164f. SCHLIER, H. "'Evangelium' im Römerbrief" in V. Kubina und K. Lehmann, eds., Der Geist und die Kirche (FS H. Schlier; Freiburg/Basel/Wien 1980) 72-4. SCHRÖER, H. "Glaubensbekenntnis(se) X" in TRE 13 (1984) 441. KOCH, D.-A. Die Schrift als Zeuge des Evangeliums (Tübingen 1986) 107. DOBBELER, A. VON, Glaube als Teilhabe (Tübingen 1987) 20, 22. ECKSTEIN, H.-J. "'Nahe ist dir das Wort.' Exegetische Erwägungen zu Röm 10:8," ZNW 79 (1988) 204-20. JOHNSON, E. E. The Function of Apocalyptic and Wisdom Traditions in Romans 9-11 (Atlanta GA 1989) 152, 154, 157f., 208.

10:9-21   BADENAS, R. Christ the End of the Law (Sheffield 1985) 133-7.

10:9-17   FÜRST, W. in GPM 34 (1980) 376-80. STECK, W. in P. Krusche et al., eds., Predigtstudien für das Kirchenjahr 1980. Perikopenreihe II/2 (Stuttgart 1980) 220-7. MERKEL, F. in GPM 40 (1985/1986) 431-6.

10:9-15   FRIEDRICH, G. "Die Auferweckung Jesu, eine Tat Gottes oder ein Interpretament der Jünger" in Auf das Wort kommt es an. Gesammelte Aufsätze (Göttingen 1978) 323f., 367.

10:9-13   SCHWEIZER, E. Jesus Christ. The Man from Nazareth and the Exalted Lord (Macon GA 1987) 15.

10:9,13   LANGEVIN, P.E. Jésus Seigneur et l'Eschatologie (1967).

10:9-10   GILMORE, A. Christian Baptism (1959) 128ff., 148, 149. WILCKENS, U. Die Missionsreden der Apostelgeschichte (1961) 18, 137, 184. BRAUMANN, G. Vorpaulinische christlichte Taufverkündigung bei Paulus (1962) 33, 36, 53. JEREMIAS, J. Abba (1966) 281. RIDDERBOS, H. Paul. An Outline of His Theology (Grand Rapids 1975) 237-9. VAN DER MINDE, H.-J. Schrift und Tradition bei Paulus (München/Paderborn/ Wien 1976) 112-5. TRITES, A. A. The New Testament Concept of Witness (Cambridge 1977) 203.

10:9   HAHN, F. Das Verständnis der Mission im Neuen Testament (1965) 85. LIETZMANN, H. "Jesus der Herr" An die Römer (1933) 97-101. BEST, E. One Body in Christ (1955) 16, 66. FLEW, R.N. Jesus and His Church (1956) 152. CERFAUX, L. Christ in the Theology of St. Paul (1959) 20, 73, 76, 343, 369. RENGSTORF, K.H. Die Auferstheung Jesu (1960) 11, 25, 66, 70. SCHRAGE, W. Die konkreten Einzelgebote in der paulinischen Paränese (1961) 239. STANLEY, D.M. Christ's Resurrection in Pauline Soteriology (1961) 195-97. DELLING, G. Die Taufe im Neuen Testament (1963) 78. HAHN, F. Christologische Hoheitstitel (1963) 119, 204, 209f. KRAMER, W. Christos Kyrios Gottessohn (1963) §§ 15a, 16a, 3af, 6b. SCHWEIZER, E. Erniedrigung und Erhöhung bei Jesus und seinen Nachfolgern (1962) §9b, 15f. BULTMANN, R. Theologie des Neuen Testaments (1965) 83, 128, 313, 318. STUHLMACH-ER, P. Gerechtigkeit Gottes bei Paulus (1965) 81f. JÜNGEL, E. Paulus und Jesus (1966) 275. McNAMARA, M. The New Testament and the Palestinian Targum to the Pentateuch (19-66) 77. SEEBERG, A. Der Katechismus der Urchristenheit (1966) 56, 121, 156, 179f., 181, 182, 186. KERTELGE, K. "Rechtfertigung" bei Paulus (1967) 161, 175, 179, 231, 302. LANGEVIN, P.E. Jésus Seigneur et l'Eschatologie (1967) 19-20, 31, 32, 33-35, 105-6, 307, 314, 315. LEHMANN, K. Auferweckt am Dritten Tag nach der Schrift (1968) 35a, 44, 47-54, 61, 74, 145. SCHREINER, J. Gestalt und Anspruch des Neuen Testaments (1969) 44f., 58. DUNN, J.D.G. Baptism in the Holy Spirit (1970) 49f., 150, 164f. GÜTTGEMANNS, E. Offene Fragen zur Formgeschichte des Evangeliums (1970) 85, 208n141, 209. MAUSER, U. Gottesbild und Menschwerdung (1971) 131, 134, 142. MIKALSEN, T. "The Traditio-Historical Place of the Christology of 1 Peter in Light of 1:18-21" (Rüschlikon 1971) 84-86. BAUMERT, N. Täglich Sterben und Auferstehen. Der Literalsinn von 2 Kor 4, 12-5, 10 (München 1973) 160. CONZELMANN, H. Theologie als Schriftauslegung (München 1974) 48, 103, 109, 112, 121, 124, 125n.19, 129n.27, 133n.14, 143n.3, 178. LADD, G. E. A Theology of the New Testament (Grand Rapids 1974) 171, 244, 339, 415, 417, 544f., 555. CONZELMANN, H. and LINDENMANN, A. Arbeitsbuch zum Neuen Testament (Tübingen 1975) 107, 421. GOPPELT, L. Theologie des Neuen Testaments I: Jesu Wirken in seiner theologischen Bedeutung [J. Roloff, ed.] (Göttingen 1975) 200, 280f. GOPPELT, L. Theologie des Neuen Testaments II: Vielfalt und Einheit des apostolischen Christuszeugnisses (Göttingen 1976) 459. DUNN, J. D. G. Unity and Diversity in the New Testament. An Inquiry into the Character of Earliest Christianity (London 1977) 55. FRIEDRICH, G. "Die Bedeutung der Auferweckung Jesu nach Aussagen des Neuen Testaments" in Auf das Wort kommt es an. Gesammelte Aufsätze (Göttingen 1978) 357, 362f. JEWETT, P. K. Infant Baptism and the Covenant of Grace (Grand Rapids 1978) 228. SCHMITHALS, W. "Zur Herkunft der gnostischen Elemente in der Sprache des Paulus" in B. Aland et al., eds., Gnosis (FS H. Jonas; Göttingen 1978) 403. FROITZHEIM, F. Christologie und Eschatologie bei Paulus (Würzburg 1979) 79ff., 104f. HOFFMANN, P. "Auferstehung" in TRE 4 (1979) 480, 488. THISELTON, A. C. The Two Horizons (Grand Rapids 1980) 409. POKORNY, P. "Christologie et Baptème à l'Epoque du Christianisme Primitif," NTS 27 (1980/1981) 368. BISER, E. Der Zeuge (Graz/Wien/Köln 1981) 93, 117, 121, 123, 130, 142. MUELLER, P.-G. Der Traditionsprozess im Neuen Testament (Freiburg 1982) 227. DEICHGRÄBER, R. "Formeln, Liturgische" in TRE 11 (1983) 259. DEMKE, C. "Gott IV" in TRE 13 (1984) 647. PERKINS, P. Resurrection. New Testament Witness and Contemporary Reflection (London 1984) 197, 216f.

RITTER, A. M. "Glaubensbekenntnis(se) V" in TRE 13 (1984) 401. WENGST, K. "Glaubensbekenntnis(se) IV" in TRE 13 (1984) 396. HÄRING, H. Das Problem des Bösen in der Theologie (Darmstadt 1985) 36. POKORNY, P. Die Entstehung der Christologie (Berlin 1985) 60, 70, 74, 77, 80. FÜHRER, W. "'Herr ist Jesus.' Die Rezeption der urchristlichen Kyrios-Akklamation durch Paulus Römer 10, 9," KuD 33 (1987) 137-49. HÜBNER, H. "Paulusforschung seit 1945. Ein kritischer Literaturbericht" in ANRW II.25.4 (1987) 2738. MERKLEIN, H. Studien zu Jesus und Paulus (Tübingen 1987) 43, 46, 51, 222, 425n.62, 426n.63. CONZELMANN, H. and LINDEMANN, A. Interpreting the New Testament (Peabody, Mass. 1988) 93, 370. MARSHALL, I. H. "Jesus as Lord. The Development of the Concept" in W. H. Gloer, ed., Eschatology and the New Testament (Peabody, Mass. 1988) 129ff. STUHLMACHER, P. Jesus von Nazareth—Christus des Glaubens (Stuttgart 1988) 38. JOHNSON, E. E. The Function of Apocalyptic and Wisdom Traditions in Romans 9-11 (Atlanta GA 1989) 128, 152, 156, 199. SCHWEIZER, E. Theologische Einleitung in das Neue Testament (Göttingen 1989) ß 5.2. LOHSE, E. Die Entstehung des Neuen Testaments (Stuttgart/Berlin/Köln ^{5}1991) 20.

10:10   LJUNGMAN, H. Pistis (1964) 86f., 89f., 101-3. JÜNGEL, E. Paulus und Jesus (1966) 39, 276. WIRSCHING, J. "Bekenntnisschriften" in TRE 5 (1980) 487. STAAB, K. Pauluskommentare aus der griechischen Kirche (Münster ^{2}1984) 55:13-24 Akazc. SANDERS, E. P. Paul, the Law, and the Jewish People (London 1985) 39f., 46.

10:11-15   SIEGERT, F. Argumentation bei Paulus (Tübingen 1985) 151-3.

10:11-13   VAN DER MINDE, H.-J. Schrift und Tradition bei Paulus (München/ Paderborn/Wien 1976) 108, 116-8. MOXNES, H. Theology in Conflict (Leiden 1980) 52, 83-5, 89, 97. STAAB, K. Pauluskommentare aus der griechischen Kirche (Münster ^{2}1984) 101:20-7 Diod.

10:11,13   KÄSEMANN, E. New Testament Questions of Today (1969) 76.

10:11   VOLZ, P. Die Eschatologie der jüdischen Gemeinde (1934) 301. ELLIS, E.E. Paul's Use of the Old Testament (1957) 15, 21f., 164f. KÄSEMANN, E. Exegetische Versuche und Besinnungen (1964) II 78. LUZ, U. Das Geschichtsverständnis des Paulus (1968) 90. REIM, G. Studien zum Alttestamentlichen Hintergrund des Johannesevangeliums (Cambridge 1974) 78f. ELLIS, E. E. Prophecy and Hermeneutic in Early Christianity (Tübingen 1978) 152, 174, 196. KOCH, D.-A. Die Schrift als Zeuge des Evangeliums (Tübingen 1986) 93ff., 133f. GASTON, L. Paul and the Torah (Vancouver 1987) 118. JOHNSON, E. E. The Function of Apocalyptic and Wisdom Traditions in Romans 9-11 (Atlanta GA 1989) 127, 130, 153f., 156, 198.

10:12-17   STUHLMACHER, P. "Jesus von Nazareth und die neutestamentliche Christologie im Lichte der Heiligen Schrift" in M. Klopfenstein et al., eds., Mitte der Schrift? Ein jüdisch-christliches Gespräch. Texte des Berner Symposions vom 6.-12. Januar 1985 (Bern etc. 1987) 92.

10:12-15   STAAB, K. Pauluskommentare aus der griechischen Kirche (Münster ^{2}1984) 523:18-29 Phot. LIMBECK, M. Mit Paulus Christ sein. Sachbuch zur Person und Theologie des Apostels Paulus (Stuttgart 1989) 72.

10:12-13   JOHNSON, E. E. The Function of Apocalyptic and Wisdom Traditions in Romans 9-11 (Atlanta GA 1989) 153, 156, 199, 209. SEGAL, A. F. Paul the Convert (New Haven/London 1990) 137, 181, 280.

10:12   HAHN, F. Christologische Hoheitstitel (1963) 110, 118. HAHN, F. Das Verständnis der Mission im Neuen Testament (1965) 92. OLLROG, W.-H. Paulus und seine Mitarbeiter (Neukirchen-Vluyn 1979) 143. SWIDLER, L.

Biblical Affirmations of Woman (Philadelphia 1979) 323. DEMKE, C. "Gott IV" in TRE 13 (1984) 646. DIETZFELBINGER, C. Die Berufung des Paulus als Ursprung seiner Theologie (Neukirchen 1985) 46, 141f., 144. MALINA B. J. Christian Origins and Cultural Anthropology (Atlanta 1986) 138. DUPONT, J. "'Le Seigneur de tous' (Ac 10:36; Rm 10:12). Arrière-fond scripturaire d'une formule christologique" in G. F. Hawthorne and O. Betz, eds., Tradition and Interpretation in the New Testament (FS E. E. Ellis; Grand Rapids/Tübingen 1987) 229-36. JOHNSON, E. E. The Function of Apocalyptic and Wisdom Traditions in Romans 9-11 (Atlanta GA 1989) 118, 128, 153f., 157, 171.

10:13ff.	LUZ, U. Das Geschichtsverständnis des Paulus (1968) 99.
10:13-21	POPE, H. "A Possible View of Romans X 13-21" JThS, (1903) 273-79.
10:13-17	BLANK, J. Schriftauslegung in Theorie und Praxis (1969) 62, 64.
10:13-16	ZELLER, D. Juden und Heiden in der Mission des Paulus. Studien zum Römerbrief (Stuttgart 1973) 49.
10:13,14	DUNN, J.D.G. Baptism in the Holy Spirit (1970) 74, 150f.
10:13	ELLIS, E.E. Paul's Use of the Old Testament (1957) 94, 106, 108, 151, 164, 187. HAHN, F. Christologische Hoheitstitel (1963) 110, 118. KRAMER, W. Christos Kyrios Gottessohn (1963) §§ 17d, 43b. KÄSEMANN, E. Exegetische Versuche und Besinnungen (1964) II 78. LJUNGMAN, H. Pistis (1964) 86-88. KERTELGE, K. "Rechtfertigung" bei Paulus (1967) 151. LANGEVIN, P.E. Jésus Seigneur et l'Eschatologie (1967) 38, 57, 86, 88, 93, 117, 315. LUZ, U. Das Geschichtsverständnis des Paulus (1968) 101. METZGER, B. M. The Early Versions of the New Testament. Their Origin Transmission, and Limitations (Oxford 1977) 242. KREITZER, L. J. Jesus and God in Paul's Eschatology (Sheffield 1987) 114, 124.
10:14-11:10	PATTE, D. Preaching Paul (Philadelphia 1984) 21-2.
10:14ff	LJUNGMAN, H. Pistis (1964) 89-92, 95f.
10:14-21	MUNCK, J. Paul and the Salvation of Mankind (1959) 53, 112, 223, 235, 256f., 277. LUZ, U. Das Geschichtsverständnis des Paulus (1968) 32f. SKERRY, D.P. "Faith Born of Preaching" AER 158 (5, '68) 299-318. PLAG, Chr. Israels Wege zum Heil (1969) 28ff. LYONNET, S. Quaestiones in epistulam ad Romanos (Rome 1975) 106-14. LAYMAN, F. D. Paul's Use of Abraham. An Approach to Paul's Understanding of History (diss. Ann Arbor MI 1978) 170. RESE, M. "Israels Unwissen und Ungehorsam und die Verkündigung des Glaubens durch Paulus in Römer 10" in D.-A. Koch et al., eds., Jesu Rede von Gott und ihre Nachgeschichte im frühen Christentum (FS W. Marxsen; Gütersloh 1989) 262, 264. WAY, D. The Lordship of Christ. Ernst Käsemann's Interpretation of Paul's Theology (Oxford 1991) 139.
10:14-18	PAGELS, E. H. The Gnostic Paul. Gnostic Exegesis of the Pauline Letters (Philadelphia 1975) 40. DOBBELER, A. VON, Glaube als Teilhabe (Tübingen 1987) 10-25. SANDNES, K. O. Paul—One of the Prophets? (Tübingen 1991) 154-71.
10:14-17	ROLOFF, J. "Apostel" in TRE 3 (1978) 438. SIEGERT, F. Argumentation bei Paulus (Tübingen 1985) 191-5. GEWALT, D. "Die 'fides ex auditu' und die Taubstummen. Zur Auslegungsgeschichte von Gal. 3, 2 und Röm. 10:14-17," LiBi 58 (1986) 45-64. LÜBKING, H.-M. Paulus und Israel im Römerbrief (Frankfurt/ Bern/New York 1986) 88-90.
10:14-16	KRAMER, W. Christos Kyrios Gottessohn (1963) § 11a.
10:14-15	BAUER, J. B. Scholia Biblica et Patristica (Graz 1972) 33, 38f. LYONNET, S. Quaestiones in epistulam ad Romanos (Rome 1975) 107-109. WELLS, P. "L'église: messager de l'évangile de paix (Rom 10, 14.15)," EtEv 35 (1975) 44-

6. STAAB, K. Pauluskommentare aus der griechischen Kirche (Münster ²1984) 69:24-71:28 Apoll, 151:11-152:13 ThM; 396:24-397:5 Genn. SIEGERT, F. Argumentation bei Paulus (Tübingen 1985) 153-6. JOHNSON, E. E. The Function of Apocalyptic and Wisdom Traditions in Romans 9-11 (Atlanta GA 1989) 144, 158. SANDNES, K. O. Paul—One of the Prophets? (Tübingen 1991) 157-61.

10:14   LJUNGMAN, H. Pistis (1964) 91f., 95f. KERTELGE, K. "Rechtfertigung" bei Paulus (1967) 175, 179. THISELTON, A. C. The Two Horizons (Grand Rapids 1980) 361. BLOTH, P. C. "Gebet" in TRE 12 (1984) 100. MUSSNER, F. Die Kraft der Wurzel (Freiburg/Basel/Wien 1987) 41f.

10:15-18   MUELLER, F. "Zwei Marginalien im Brief des Paulus an die Römer" ZNW 40 (1941) 252-54.

10:15-16   SCHRAGE, W. Die konkreten Einzelgebote in der paulinischen Paränese (1961) 90, 195. MERKLEIN, H. Studien zu Jesus und Paulus (Tübingen 1987) 288.

10:15   LUZ, U. Das Geschichtsverständnis des Paulus (1968) 101. HEROLD, G. Zorn und Gerechtigkeit Gottes bei Paulus. Eine Untersuchung zu Röm. 1, 16-18 (Bern/Frankfurt 1973) 235ff. ZELLER, D. Juden und Heiden in der Mission des Paulus. Studien zum Römerbrief (Stuttgart 1973) 200. SCHÜTZ, J. H. Paul and the Anatomy of Apostolic Authority (Cambridge 1975) 36f., 39, 69. MÜHLEN, K.-H. ZUR, "Affekt" in TRE 1 (1977) 608. KOCH, D.-A. Die Schrift als Zeuge des Evangeliums (Tübingen 1986) 66-9, 81f., 113f., 122.

10:16ff   HAHN, F. Das Verständnis der Mission im Neuen Testament (1965) 91.

10:16-18   SANDNES, K. O. Paul—One of the Prophets? (Tübingen 1991) 161-4.

10:16-17   BRAUMANN, G. Vorpaulinische christliche Taufverkündigung bei Paulus (1962) 27ff. SCHLIER, H. "'Evangelium' im Römerbrief" in V. Kubina und K. Lehmann, eds., Der Geist und die Kirche (FS H. Schlier; Freiburg/Basel/ Wien 1980) 72-4. HAYS, R. B. The Faith of Jesus Christ (Chico CA 1983) 145-7, 181. STAAB, K. Pauluskommentare aus der griechischen Kirche (Münster ²1984) 152:14-30 ThM; 397:6-15 Genn.

10:16   ELLIS, E.E. Paul's Use of the Old Testament (1957) 22, 48, 87, 187. SCHRAGE, W. Die konkreten Einzelgebote in der paulinischen Paränese (1961) 79, 118. HAHN, F. Christologische Hoheitstitel (1963) 73. THEYSSEN, G.W. "Unbelief" in the New Testament (1965) 73. KERTELGE, K. "Rechtfertigung" bei Paulus (1967) 174. NICKELS, P. Targum and New Testament (1967) 70. REIM, G. Studien zum Alttestamentlichen Hintergrund des Johannesevangeliums (Cambridge 1974) 34-6. BERGMEIER, R. Glaube als Gabe nach Johannes (Stuttgart 1980) 230. HÜBNER, H. Gottes Ich und Israel (Göttingen 1984) 95f., 99f. KOCH, D.-A. Die Schrift als Zeuge des Evangeliums (Tübingen 1986) 243. JOHNSON, E. E. The Function of Apocalyptic and Wisdom Traditions in Romans 9-11 (Atlanta GA 1989) 153, 158, 199.

10:17   MUELLER, Fr. "Zwei Marginalien im Brief des Paulus an die Römer" ZNW 40, (1941) 249-54. JÜNGEL, E. Paulus und Jesus (1966) 43. LUZ, U. Das Geschichtsverständnis des Paulus (1968) 101. SCHMITHALS, W. Der Römerbrief als historisches Problem (Gütersloh 1975) 207. RICKARDS, R. R. "The translation of *dia rhematos Christou* ('through the word of Christ') in Romans 10.17," BTr 27 (1976) 447-8. CLARK, K. W. "The Meaning of APA" in The Gentile Bias and other Essays [J. L. Sharpe III, ed.] (Leiden 1980) 201. SCHÜRMANN, H. "Christliche Weltverantvortung im Lichte des Neuen Testaments," Catholica 34 (1980) 110. BISER, E. Der Zeuge (Graz/Wien/Köln 1981) 117f., 144. HAYS, R. B. The Faith of Jesus Christ (Chico CA 1983) 146-8, 181. HÜBNER, H. Gottes Ich und Israel (Göttingen 1984) 95f. SLENCZKA, R. "Glaube VI" in TRE 13 (1984) 321. FREUND, G. und STEGEMANN, E.,

eds., Theologische Brosamen für Lothar Steiger (DBAT 5; Heidelberg 1985)
466. SANDERS, E. P. Paul, the Law, and the Jewish People (London 1985)
41f., 157, 207n.88. BARRETT, C. K. "Proclamation and Response" in G. F.
Hawthorne and O. Betz, eds., Tradition and Interpretation in the New Testament
(FS E. E. Ellis; Grand Rapids/Tübingen 1987) 3-15. JOHNSON, E. E. The
Function of Apocalyptic and Wisdom Traditions in Romans 9-11 (Atlanta GA
1989) 136, 154, 158f., 168. SIMONIS, W. Der gefangene Paulus. Die
Entstehung des sogenannten Römerbriefs und anderer urchristlicher Schriften
in Rom (Frankfurt/Bern/New York/Paris 1990) 48.

10:18ff.   SCHMITT, R. Gottesgerechtigkeit—Heilsgeschichte—Israel in der Theologie
des Paulus (Frankfurt/Bern/New York/Nancy 1984) 95-7.

10:18-21   LYONNET, S. Quaestiones in epistulam ad Romanos (Rome 1975) 109-14.
KOCH, D.-A. Die Schrift als Zeuge des Evangeliums (Tübingen 1986) 280f.
LÜBKING, H.-M. Paulus und Israel im Römerbrief (Frankfurt/Bern/New York
1986) 91f.

10:18   LUZ, U. Das Geschichtsverständnis des Paulus (1968) 390. HARMAN, A. M.
Paul's Use of the Psalms. (Ann Arbor MI 1968) 93-104. WAGNER, F.
"Berufung" in TRE 5 (1980) 697. STAAB, K. Pauluskommentare aus der
griechischen Kirche (Münster ²1984) 71:28-72:3 Apoll; 153:1-7 ThM; 397:16-24
Genn. KOCH, D.-A. Die Schrift als Zeuge des Evangeliums (Tübingen 1986)
13f. JOHNSON, E. E. The Function of Apocalyptic and Wisdom Traditions in
Romans 9-11 (Atlanta GA 1989) 119, 139, 143f., 199, 209.

10:19-21   ELLIS, E.E. Paul's Use of the Old Testament (1957) passim. LUZ, U. Das
Geschichtsverständnis des Paulus (1968) 390. HÜBNER, H. Gottes Ich und
Israel (Göttingen 1984) 97f. STAAB, K. Pauluskommentare aus der griech-
ischen Kirche (Münster ²1984) 397:22-398:2 Genn.

10:19   HAGE, W. "Die griechische Baruch-Apokalypse" in JSHRZ V/1 (1974) 34n.2a.
KÖLICHEN, J.-C. VON, "Die Zitate aus dem Moselied Deut 32 im Römerbrief
des Paulus" ThV 5 (1975) 53-69. STAAB, K. Pauluskommentare aus der
griechischen Kirche (Münster ²1984) 72:4-14 Apoll; 153:8-16 ThM. KOCH, D.-
A. Die Schrift als Zeuge des Evangeliums (Tübingen 1986) 110. JOHNSON,
E. E. The Function of Apocalyptic and Wisdom Traditions in Romans 9-11
(Atlanta GA 1989) 119, 144, 159, 161, 198f.

10:20-21   McNAMARA, M. The New Testament and the Palestinian Targum to the
Pentateuch (1966) 124. LUZ, U. Das Geschichtsverständnis des Paulus (1968)
91. STAAB, K. Pauluskommentare aus der griechischen Kirche (Münster ²1984)
524:1-3 Phot. LUZ, U. "Paulinische Theologie als Biblische Theologie" in M.
Klopfenstein et al., eds., Mitte der Schrift? Ein jüdisch-christliches Gespräch.
Texte des Berner Symposions vom 6.-12. Januar 1985 (Bern etc. 1987) 119-47,
esp.129.

10:20   KOCH, D.-A. Die Schrift als Zeuge des Evangeliums (Tübingen 1986) 50f.,
317f. SCHUTTER, W. L. "Philo's Psychology of Prophetic Inspiration and
Romans 10:20" in Society of Biblical Literature 1989 Seminar Papers (Atlanta
1989) 624-33.

10:21   THEYSSEN, G.W. "Unbelief" in the New Testament (1965) 13-17. GOPPELT,
L. Christologie und Ethik (1968) 182f. BERKOUWER, G. C. The Return of
Christ (Grand Rapids 1972) 331, 336, 338, 348, 411. HÜBNER, H. Gottes Ich
und Israel (Göttingen 1984) 71, 92, 99f., 124. STAAB, K. Pauluskommentare
aus der griechischen Kirche (Münster ²1984) 102:1-3 Diod. KOCH, D.-A. Die
Schrift als Zeuge des Evangeliums (Tübingen 1986) 105f. HOFIUS, O. Paulusstudien (Tübingen 1989) 156, 176, 179, 194.

10:23-25   BOOTH, R. P. Jesus and the Laws of Purity. Tradition History and Legal History in Mark 7 (Sheffield 1986) 82.
10:23   BOOTH, R. P. Jesus and the Laws of Purity. Tradition History and Legal History in Mark 7 (Sheffield 1986) 107.
10:29   KUHN, H.-J. Christologie und Wunder. Untersuchungen zu Joh 1, 35-51 (Regensburg 1988) 147, 361, 374-6, 384, 388.
11   BRUNNER, E. Dogmatik I (1946) 358. ROBINSON, J. A. T. The Body (1952) 79f. FARRER, A. St Matthew and St Mark (1954) 69. MUNCK, J. Paul and the Salvation of Mankind (1959) 120f, 300, 303, 307. RICHARDS, J.R. "Romans and I Cor. Their Chronological Relationship and Comparative Dates" NTS 13 (1966/67) 15f. MUNCK, J. Christ and Israel (1967) 105-43. LUZ, U. Das Geschichtsverständnis des Paulus (1968) 33ff. RICHARSON, P. Israel in the Apostolic Church (1969) passim. GIBLIN, C.H. In Hope of God's Glory (1970) 292-310. EICHHOLZ, G. Die Theologie des Paulus im Umriss (1972) passim. KÜNZI, M. Das Naherwartungslogion Matthäus 10, 23. Geschichte seiner Auslegung (Tübingen 1970) 32, 52, 69, 72, 75, 126, 155. BERKOUWER, G. C. The Return of Christ (Grand Rapids 1972) 339, 341f., 346, 349f., 352, 356. RIDDERBOS, H. Paul. An Outline of His Theology (Grand Rapids 1975) 354-61. BERGOZ, K. "Abraham" in TRE 1 (1977) 376, 379. DUGANDZIC, I. Das "Ja" Gottes in Christus (Würzburg 1977) 291-6. LAYMAN, F. D. Paul's Use of Abraham. An Approach to Paul's Understanding of History (diss. Ann Arbor MI 1978) 93-100, 170-7. MUSSNER, F. "Reflexionen eines Neutestamentlers über das Heil Israels," KatBl 104 (12, 1979) 974-6. ROBINSON, J. A. T. Wrestling with Romans (London 1979) 126-33. FULLER, D. P. Gospel and Law. Contrast or Continuum? (Grand Rapids 1980) 189-97. HARRINGTON, D. J. God's People in Christ (Philadelphia 1980) 63-5. HOOKER, M. D. "Beyond the Things that are Written? St. Paul's Use of Scripture," NTS 27 (1980/1981) 300. PAINTER, J. "The Farewell Discourses and the History of Johannine Christianity," NTS 27 (1980/1981) 536. HAGEN, K. Hebrews Commenting from Erasmus to Bèze 1516-1598 (Tübingen 1981) 52. THEOBALD, M. Die überströmende Gnade (Würzburg 1982) 154-65. GORDAY, P. Principles of Patristic Exegesis: Romans 9-11 in Origen, John Chrysostom, and Augustine (New York/Toronto 1983) 80-2, 124f., 171f. STUHLMANN, R. Das eschatologische Mass im Neuen Testament (Göttingen 1983) 164-88, 194, 225f. ZERBE, G. "Jews and Gentiles as People of the Covenant: The Background and Message of Romans 11," Direction 12 (3, 1983) 20-8. HÜBNER, H. Gottes Ich und Israel (Göttingen 1984) 28f., 53, 58f., 97, 101f., 108f., 115, 126, 129f., 134. JOHNSON, D. G. "The Structure and Meaning of Romans 11," CBQ 46 (1984) 91-103. SCHMITT, R. Gottesgerechtigkeit—Heilsgeschichte—Israel in der Theologie des Paulus (Frankfurt/Bern/New York/Nancy 1984) 97-116. GRÄSSER, E. Der Alte Bund im Neuen (Tübingen 1985) 223, 229, 280, 314. HUGUET, M.-T. "Mise à l'écart d'Israël? Une approche au sujet de la spécificité théologique de la 'maison d'Israël' et de sa relation à l'église," NV 60 (2, 1985) 103-20. SIEGERT, F. Argumentation bei Paulus (Tübingen 1985) 164-76. RESE, M. "Die Rettung der Juden nach Römer 11" in A. Vanhoye, ed., L'Apôtre Paul. Personalité, style et conception du ministère (Leuven 1986) 422-30. WATSON, F. Paul, Judaism and the Gentiles (Cambridge 1986) 168-74. GASTON, L. Paul and the Torah (Vancouver 1987) 13, 33f., 123, 129, 132, 139-50, 232. OSTEN-SACKEN, P. VON DER, Evangelium und Tora: Aufsätze zu Paulus (München 1987) 29, 67f., 71, 191, 247, 300ff., 304f., 307. MacDONALD, M. Y. The Pauline Churches (Cambridge 1988) 33. JOHNSON, E. E. The

Function of Apocalyptic and Wisdom Traditions in Romans 9-11 (Atlanta GA 1989) 49, 129, 192, 196, 198. HARRISVILLE, R. A. The Figure of Abraham in the Epistles of St. Paul. In the Footsteps of Abraham (San Francisco 1992).

11:1ff HAHN, F. Das Verständnis der Mission im Neuen Testament (1965) 91, 93. OSTEN-SACKEN, P. VON DER, Evangelium und Tora: Aufsätze zu Paulus (München 1987) 277, 286, 299, 302. 11:1-36 WAGNER, G. "The Future of Israel: Reflections on Romans 9-11" in W. H. Gloer, ed., Eschatology and the New Testament (FS G. R. Beasley-Murray; Peabody, Mass. 1988) 91-7. HAYS, R. B. Echoes of Scripture in the Letters of Paul (New Haven/London 1989) 68-73.

11:1-32 DUNN, J. D. G. "Paul's Epistle to the Romans: An Analysis of Structure and Argument" in ANRW II.25.4 (1987) 2871-3. JOHNSON, E. E. The Function of Apocalyptic and Wisdom Traditions in Romans 9-11 (Atlanta GA 1989) 121, 141, 143, 147, 160-3, 175.

11:1-24 SNODGRASS, K. The Parable of the Wicked Tenants (Tübingen 1983) 92n.84. SCHMELLER, TH. Paulus und die "Diatribe" (Münster 1987) 286-332, 359, 389-406, 418.

11:1-15 WÜLLNER, W. "Paul's Rhetoric of Argumentation in Romans. An Alternative to the Donfried-Karris Debate over Romans" in K. P. Donfried, ed., The Romans Debate (Minneapolis 1977) 157-61.

11:1-12 HÜBNER, H. Gottes Ich und Israel (Göttingen 1984) 107f.

11:1-10 JEREMIAS, J. "Der Gedanke des 'Heiligen Restes' im Spätjudentum und in der Verkündigung Jesu" (1949): Abba (1966) 121-32. BECKER, J. Das Heil Gottes. Heils- und Sündenbegriffe in den Qumrantexten und im Neuen Testament (1964) 62ff. PLAG, Chr Israels Wege zum Heil (1969) 32f. ZELLER, D. Juden und Heiden in der Mission des Paulus. Studien zum Römerbrief (Stuttgart 1973) 126ff., 273. LYONNET, S. Quaestiones in epistulam ad Romanos (Rome 1975) 115-20. PAGELS, E. H. The Gnostic Paul. Gnostic Exegesis of the Pauline Letters (Philadelphia 1975) 40. LÜBKING, H.-M. Paulus und Israel im Römerbrief (Frankfurt/Bern/New York 1986) 99-104, 143. OSTEN-SACKEN, P. VON DER, Evangelium und Tora: Aufsätze zu Paulus (München 1987) 67, 247, 301. RÄISÄNEN, H. "Römer 9-11: Analyse eines geistigen Ringens" in ANRW II.25.4 (1987) 2911f. VOLF, J. M. G. Paul and Perseverance (Tübingen 1990) 167-71.

11:1-6 COMISKEY, J. P. "A Remnant Will Return" BibToday 1 (18, '65) 1210-15. MOXNES, H. Theology in Conflict (Leiden 1980) 34, 49-50. HÜBNER, H. Gottes Ich und Israel (Göttingen 1984) 102f.

11:1-3 ELLIS, E. E. Paul's Use of the Old Testament (1957) passim.

11:1-2 HARMAN, A. M. Paul's Use of the Psalms. (Ann Arbor MI 1968) 186-8. STAAB, K. Pauluskommentare aus der griechischen Kirche (Münster ²1984) 102:4-10 Diod; 398:3-9 Genn.

11:1 GOPPELT, L. Christologie und Ethik (1968) 183f. LUZ, U. Das Geschichtsverständnis des Paulus (1968) 34. RENGSTORF, K. H. "Paulus und die älteste römische Christenheit," StEv 2 (1963) 447-64. BAUMERT, N. Täglich Sterben und Auferstehen. Der Literalsinn von 2 Kor 4, 12-5, 10 (München 1973) 351. LADD, G. E. A Theology of the New Testament (Grand Rapids MI 1974) 360, 400, 537. MOXNES, H. Theology in Conflict (Leiden 1980) 28, 34, 49, 56f., 59, 62, 93, 219, 225. RHYNE, C. T. Faith establishes the Law (Chico CA 1981) 49-50. HÜBNER, H. Gottes Ich und Israel (Göttingen 1984) 15f., 100f., 105f., 117, 122, 134. STAAB, K. Pauluskommentare aus der griechischen Kirche (Münster ²1984) 153:17-154:3 ThM. CZAJKOWSKI, M. "'Czyz Bóg odrzucil lud swój?' (Rz 11, 1). Rola Izraela w historii zbawienia dzisiaj ['Hat Gott sein Volk verstossen? (Röm 11, 1). Die Rolle Israels in der Heilsoekonomie heute]," SThV 23 (2, 1985) 45-54. STEGEMANN, E. "'Das Gesetz ist nicht wider die Verheissungen!' Thesen zu Galater 3, 15-29" in FREUND, G. und STEGEMANN, E., eds., Theologische Brosamen für Lothar Steiger (DBAT 5; Heidelberg 1985) 391. RÄISÄNEN, H. The Torah and Christ (Helsinki 1986) 194. HOFIUS, O. Paulusstudien (Tübingen 1989) 179, 185, 198. JOHNSON, E. E. The Function of Apocalyptic and Wisdom Traditions in Romans 9-11 (Atlanta GA 1989) 119, 124, 139, 144f., 148, 159-61, 193, 199. COHEN, K. I. "Paul the Benjaminite. Mystery, Motives and Midrash," Center for Hermeneutical Studies Protocol Series (Berkeley/CA) 60 (1990) 21-8.

11:2-6   LUZ, U. Das Geschichtsverständnis des Paulus (1968) 80-83. LAYMAN, F. D. Paul's Use of Abraham. An Approach to Paul's Understanding of History (diss. Ann Arbor MI 1978) 171f. SIEGERT, F. Argumentation bei Paulus (Tübingen 1985) 186-90. KOCH, D.-A. Die Schrift als Zeuge des Evangeliums (Tübingen 1986) 305-7. WATTS, J. W. "The Remnant Theme. A Survey of New Testament Research, 1921-1987," PRSt 15 (2, 1988) 109-29.

11:2-5   MÜLLER, H. Die Auslegung alttestamentlichen Geschichtsstoffs bei Paulus (diss. Halle/Wittenberg 1960) 147-51. STAAB, K. Pauluskommentare aus der griechischen Kirche (Münster ²1984) 154:4-17 ThM.

11:2-4   SCHMITT, R. Gottesgerechtigkeit—Heilsgeschichte—Israel in der Theologie des Paulus (Frankfurt/Bern/ New York/Nancy 1984) 99.

11:2-3   STAAB, K. Pauluskommentare aus der griechischen Kirche (Münster ²1984) 398:10-12 Genn.

11:2   HÜBNER, H. Gottes Ich und Israel (Göttingen 1984) 29, 100f. BURCHARD, C. "Röm 9, 25 " in FREUND, G. und STEGEMANN, E., eds., Theologische Brosamen für Lothar Steiger (DBAT 5; Heidelberg 1985) 53. KOCH, D.-A. Die Schrift als Zeuge des Evangeliums (Tübingen 1986) 18.

11:3-5   STAAB, K. Pauluskommentare aus der griechischen Kirche (Münster ²1984) 102:11-15 Diod.

11:3-4   STANLEY, C. D. "The Significance of Romans 11:3-4 for the Text History of the LXX Book of Kingdoms," JBL 112 (1993) 43-54.

11:3   GERSTENBERGER, G. und SCHRAGE, W. Leiden (Stuttgart 1977) 128 [ET: J. E. Steely (trans.) Suffering (Nashville 1980) 149]. KOCH, D.-A. Die Schrift als Zeuge des Evangeliums (Tübingen 1986) 74f.

11:4-7   MINEAR, P. S. Images of the Church in the New Testament (1960) 80f.

11:4-5   STAAB, K. Pauluskommentare aus der griechischen Kirche (Münster ²1984) 398:13-18 Genn.

11:4   ELLIS, E. E. Paul's Use of the Old Testament (1957) 22ff., 151, 168. LUZ, U. Das Geschichtsverständnis des Paulus (1968) 80, 90. HANSON, A. T. "The Oracle in Romans xi.4," NTS 19 (3, 1973) 300-2. KOCH, D.-A. Die Schrift als Zeuge des Evangeliums (Tübingen 1986) 75-7. JOHNSON, E. E. The Function of Apocalyptic and Wisdom Traditions in Romans 9-11 (Atlanta GA 1989) 130, 139, 160.

11:5   CLEMENTS, R. E. "A Remnant Chosen by Grace (Romans 11:5). The Old Testament Background and Origin of the Remnant Concept" in D. A. Hagner and M. J. Harris, eds., Pauline Studies (FS F. F. Bruce; Exeter 1980) 106-21. HÜBNER, H. Gottes Ich und Israel (Göttingen 1984) 99, 102, 113, 124. JOHNSON, E. E. The Function of Apocalyptic and Wisdom Traditions in Romans 9-11 (Atlanta GA 1989) 140, 145, 160, 172, 199. OLIVEIRA, A. DE, Die Diakonie der Gerechtigkeit und der Versöhnung in der Apologie des 2. Korinther-

	briefes. Analyse und Auslegung von 2 Kor 2, 14-4, 6; 5, 11-6, 10 (Münster 1990) 367.
11:6	SCHRAGE, W. Die konkreten Einzelgebote in der paulinischen Paränese (1961) 94. BONHOEFFER, D. Gesammelte Schriften, Band 5 (München 1972) 417ff. THISELTON, A. C. The Two Horizons (Grand Rapids 1980) 389. STAAB, K. Pauluskommentare aus der griechischen Kirche (Münster ²1984) 102:16-19 Diod; 398:19-22 Genn; 524:4-29 Phot. LIEBERS, R. Das Gesetz als Evangelium (Zürich 1989) 29-31. DAVIES, G. N. Faith and Obedience in Romans. A Study in Romans 1-4 (Sheffield 1990) 124-6.
11:7-11	DEXINGER, F. "Erwählung" in TRE 10 (1982) 190.
11:7-10	SCHMITT, R. Gottesgerechtigkeit—Heilsgeschichte—Israel in der Theologie des Paulus (Frankfurt/Bern/ New York/Nancy 1984) 100f. BUCHANAN, G. W. "Paul and the Jews (II Corinthians 3:4-4:6 and Romans 11:7-10) in J. J. Petuchowski, ed., When Jews and Christians Meet (New York 1988) 141-62. COOK, M. J. "The Ties that Blind: A Exposition of II Corinthians 3:12-4:6 and Romans 11:7-10" in J. J. Petuchowski, ed., When Jews and Christians Meet (New York 1988) 125-139.
11:7-9	ELLIS, E. E. Paul's Use of the Old Testament (1957) passim.
11:7-8	ZELLER, D. Juden und Heiden in der Mission des Paulus. Studien zum Römerbrief (Stuttgart 1973) 252.
11:7	HÜBNER, H. Gottes Ich und Israel (Göttingen 1984) 103, 105f., 113, 124. STAAB, K. Pauluskommentare aus der griechischen Kirche (Münster ²1984) 102:20-4 Diod; 154:18-155:9 ThM; 399:1-7 Genn. SIEGERT, F. Argumentation bei Paulus (Tübingen 1985) 182-5. JOHNSON, E. E. The Function of Apocalyptic and Wisdom Traditions in Romans 9-11 (Atlanta GA 1989) 119, 139, 160, 162, 172, 205.
11:8-9	HÜBNER, H. Gottes Ich und Israel (Göttingen 1984) 103f.
11:8	BRUNNER, E. Dogmatik I (1946) 354. BEST, E. One Body in Christ (1955) 207. HESSE, F. Das Verstockungsproblem im Alten Testament (Berlin 1955)4f., 23, 64, 66. STAAB, K. Pauluskommentare aus der griechischen Kirche (Münster ²1984) 72:15-73:4 Apoll; 103:1-8 Diod; 399:8-11 Genn. KOCH, D.-A. Die Schrift als Zeuge des Evangeliums (Tübingen 1986) 111, 121, 170f. STOCKHAUSEN, C.K. Moses' Veil and the Glory of the New Covenant (Roma 1989) 141-3.
11:9-10	LUZ, U. Das Geschichtsverständnis des Paulus (1968) 85. HARMAN, A. M. Paul's Use of the Psalms. (Ann Arbor MI 1968) 104-11. STAAB, K. Pauluskommentare aus der griechischen Kirche (Münster ²1984) 155:10-6 ThM; 430:1-5 Oek.
11:9	MUELLER, K. Anstoss und Gericht (1969) 13-31. KOCH, D.-A. Die Schrift als Zeuge des Evangeliums (Tübingen 1986) 106, 137f. MUSSNER, F. Die Kraft der Wurzel (Freiburg/Basel/Wien 1987) 42-6.
11:10	CRANFIELD, C. E. B. "The Significance of διὰ παντός in Romans 11, 10" Studia Evangelica II, ed. F.L. Cross (1964) 546-50. CRANFIELD, C. E. B. "The Significance of dià pantós in Romans 11.10" in The Bible and Christian Life (Edinburgh 1985) 197-202.
11:11ff.	LUZ, U. Das Geschichtsverständnis des Paulus (1968) 34, 392ff., 402. OLLROG, W.-H. Paulus und seine Mitarbeiter (Neukirchen-Vluyn 1979) 147. SIEGERT, F. Argumentation bei Paulus (Tübingen 1985) 165. RÄISÄNEN, H. The Torah and Christ (Helsinki 1986) 169.

11:11-36   ZELLER, D. Juden und Heiden in der Mission des Paulus. Studien zum Römer-
            brief (Stuttgart 1973) 129f. RÄISÄNEN, H. "Römer 9-11: Analyse eines
            geistigen Ringens" in ANRW II.25.4 (1987) 2930ff.
11:11-32   PLAG, Chr. Israels Wege zum Heil (1969) 33ff. STUHLMANN, R. Das
            eschatologische Mass im Neuen Testament (Göttingen 1983) 181-5. LÜBKING,
            H.-M. Paulus und Israel im Römerbrief (Frankfurt/Bern/New York 1986) 105-
            18. HOFIUS, O. Paulusstudien (Tübingen 1989) 184-200. SCHWEIZER, E.
            Theologische Einleitung in das Neue Testament (Göttingen 1989) ß 23.7.
            LONGENECKER, B. W. Eschatology and the Covenant. A Comparison of 4
            Ezra and Romans 1-11 (Sheffield 1991) 249f., 252, 254, 275f.
11:11-27   LÜBKING, H.-M. Paulus und Israel im Römerbrief (Frankfurt/Bern/ New York
            1986) 143-5. JOHNSON, E. E. The Function of Apocalyptic and Wisdom
            Traditions in Romans 9-11 (Atlanta GA 1989) 141, 145.
11:11-24   LINDNER, S. Das Propfen mit wilden Oelzweigen (1930). GALE, H.M. The
            Use of Analogy in the Letters of Paul (1964) 212-15. LYONNET, S. Quaestio-
            nes in epistulam ad Romanos (Rome 1975) 120-33. MUSSNER, F. Die Kraft
            der Wurzel (Freiburg/Basel/Wien 1987) 153-9.
11:11-16   CONGAR, Y. M. J. "The State of Israel in Biblical Perspective" Blackfriars 38
            (447, '57) 244-49. PAGELS, E. H. The Gnostic Paul. Gnostic Exegesis of the
            Pauline Letters (Philadelphia 1975) 41. RÄISÄNEN, H. "Römer 9-11: Analyse
            eines geistigen Ringens" in ANRW II.25.4 (1987) 2913f.
11:11-15   ZELLER, D. Juden und Heiden in der Mission des Paulus. Studien zum Römer-
            brief (Stuttgart 1973) 238ff., 256, 288f. ALLISON, D. C. "Romans 11:11-15.
            A Suggestion," PRSt 12 (1985) 23-30. LÜBKING, H.-M. Paulus und Israel im
            Römerbrief (Frankfurt/Bern/New York 1986) 108-12. OSTEN-SACKEN, P.
            VON DER, Evangelium und Tora: Aufsätze zu Paulus (München 1987) 303f.
            JOHNSON, E. E. The Function of Apocalyptic and Wisdom Traditions in
            Romans 9-11 (Atlanta GA 1989) 125f., 161. VOLF, J. M. G. Paul and
            Perseverance (Tübingen 1990) 171-4. JEGHER-BUCHER, V. "Erwählung und
            Verwerfung im Römerbrief? Eine Untersuchung von Röm 11, 11-15," ThZ 47
            (1991) 326-36.
11:11-12   STAUDINGER, J. Die Bergpredigt (Wien 1957) 289-90. HÜBNER, H. Gottes
            Ich und Israel (Göttingen 1984) 107f., 134. SCHMITT, R. Gottesgerechtig-
            keit—Heilsgeschichte—Israel in der Theologie des Paulus (Frankfurt/Bern/New
            York/Nancy 1984) 101-3.
11:11   MUNCK, J. Paul and the Salvation of Mankind (1959) 44-46. SCHWEIZER,
            E. Gemeinde und Gemeindeordnung im Neuen Testament (1959) §11h.
            EICHHOLZ, G. Die Theologie des Paulus im Umriss (1972) 298f. ZELLER,
            D. Juden und Heiden in der Mission des Paulus. Studien zum Römerbrief
            (Stuttgart 1973) 209ff., 251f., 286. LYONNET, S. Quaestiones in epistulam ad
            Romanos (Rome 1975) 120-1. WILLIAMS, S. K. "'The Righteousness of God'
            in Romans," JBL 99 (1980) 248. RHYNE, C. T. Faith establishes the Law
            (Chico CA 1981) 50. HÜBNER, H. Gottes Ich und Israel (Göttingen 1984) 100,
            105f., 107f., 111, 113, 121, 125. STAAB, K. Pauluskommentare aus der
            griechischen Kirche (Münster ²1984) 73:5-74:6 Apoll; 103:9-20 Diod; 155:17-
            156:6 ThM; 399:12-22 Genn. BREYTENBACH, C. Versöhnung (Neukirchen-
            Vluyn 1989) 174f., 176. JOHNSON, E. E. The Function of Apocalyptic and
            Wisdom Traditions in Romans 9-11 (Atlanta GA 1989) 118f., 128, 139, 140,
            144, 161, 184, 200.
11:11a   HOFIUS, O. Paulusstudien (Tübingen 1989) 184f.
11:11b-15   HOFIUS, O. Paulusstudien (Tübingen 1989) 185f.

11:12-16   MINEAR, P. S. Images of the Church in the New Testament (1960) 45f.
11:12,15   ZELLER, D. Juden und Heiden in der Mission des Paulus. Studien zum
             Römerbrief (Stuttgart 1973) 240ff., 260, 274f., 278.
11:12   BERKHOF, H. Der Sinn der Geschichte: Christus (Göttingen 1959) 160f., 242.
             ROON, A. VAN, The Authenticity of Ephesians (Leiden 1974) 248f. LYON-
             NET, S. Quaestiones in epistulam ad Romanos (Rome 1975) 122-3. VIEL-
             HAUER, P. "Paulus und das Alte Testament" in Oikodome [G. Klein, ed.]
             (München 1979) 199. THEOBALD, M. Die überströmende Gnade (Würzburg
             1982) 154-8. STUHLMANN, R. Das eschatologische Mass im Neuen Testa-
             ment (Göttingen 1983) 2, 185-7, 164, 181, 183f. STAAB, K. Pauluskommentare
             aus der griechischen Kirche (Münster [2]1984) 103:21-104:6 Diod; 156:7-10
             ThM; 399:23-8 Genn; 658:17-8 Areth. SIEGERT, F. Argumentation bei Paulus
             (Tübingen 1985) 190-1. OSTEN-SACKEN, P. VON DER, Evangelium und
             Tora: Aufsätze zu Paulus (München 1987) 302f. JOHNSON, E. E. The Function
             of Apocalyptic and Wisdom Traditions in Romans 9-11 (Atlanta GA 1989) 124,
             128, 139, 140, 171. MUSSNER, F. "Fehl- und Falschübersetzungen von Röm
             11 in der 'Einheitsübersetzung'," ThQ 170 (2, 1990) 137-9. DONALDSON, T.
             L. "'Riches for the Gentiles' (Rom 11:12): Israel's Rejection and Paul's Gentile
             Mission," JBL 112 (1993) 81-98.
11:13ff.   KÄSEMANN, E. Exegetische Versuche und Besinnunges (1964) II 244; New
             Testament Questions of Today (1969) 241. FEINE, D. P. und BEHM, D. J.
             Einleitung in das Neue Testament (Heidelberg 1950) 84f.
11:13,25,28, CRANFIELD, C. E. B. "Changes of Person and Number in Paul's Epistles" in
30-31   M. D. Hooker and S. G. Wilson, eds., Paul and Paulinism (FS C. K. Barrett;
             London 1982) 280.
11:13.25   PETERS, G. W. A Biblical Theology of Missions (Chicago 1972) 149, 154-6.
11:13-24   HAHN, F. "Zum Verständnis von Römer 11.26a: ' . . . und so wird ganz Israel
             gerettet werden'" in M. D. Hooker and S. G. Wilson, eds., Paul and Paulinism
             (FS C. K. Barrett; London 1982) 225f. DAVIES, W. D. "Paul and the Gentiles.
             A Suggestion concerning Romans 11:13-24" in Jewish and Pauline Studies
             (Philadelphia 1984) 153-63. DAVIES, W. D. "Reflections on a Pauline Allegory
             in a French Context" in W. C. Weinreich, ed., The New Testament Age (FS B.
             Reicke; Macon GA 1984) 107-25. HÜBNER, H. Gottes Ich und Israel
             (Göttingen 1984) 108f.
11:13-15   KRUNF, T. C. DE, "Antisemitismus" in TRE 3 (1978) 125. WAY, D. The
             Lordship of Christ. Ernst Käsemann's Interpretation of Paul's Theology (Oxford
             1991) 139f.
11:13-14   SCHMITHALS, W. Paulus und Jakobus (1963) 43, 45f. ZELLER, D. Juden und
             Heiden in der Mission des Paulus. Studien zum Römerbrief (Stuttgart 1973)
             270, 275ff. WILLIAMS, S. K. "'The Righteousness of God' in Romans," JBL
             99 (1980) 248. HAGEN, K. Hebrews Commenting from Erasmus to Bèze 1516-
             1598 (Tübingen 1981) 48, 52. PATTE, D. Paul's Faith and the Power of the
             Gospel (Philadelphia 1983) 291-3, 315. PATTE, D. Preaching Paul (Philadel-
             phia 1984) 43. SCHMITT, R. Gottesgerechtigkeit-Heilsgeschichte-Israel in der
             Theologie des Paulus (Frankfurt/Bern/New York/Nancy 1984) 103. STAAB, K.
             Pauluskommentare aus der griechischen Kirche (Münster [2]1984) 400:1-7 Genn.
11:13   MUNCK, J. Paul and the Salvation of Mankind (1959) 201f. ROLOFF, J. Apos-
             tolat-Verkündigung-Kirche (1965) 128f. MERKLEIN, H. Das Kirchliche Amt
             nach dem Epheserbrief (München 1973) 82, 290, 293, 302. ROLOFF, J. "Amt"
             in TRE 2 (1978) 522. OLLROG, W.-H. Paulus und seine Mitarbeiter (Neu-
             kirchen-Vluyn 1979) 17, 74. DIETZFELBINGER, C. Die Berufung des Paulus

als Ursprung seiner Theologie (Neukirchen 1985) 44, 49, 138, 142. HULT-GREN, A. J. Paul's Gospel and Mission (Philadelphia 1985) 125ff. DUNN, J. D. G. "'A Light to the Gentiles': the Significance of the Damascus Road Christophany for Paul" in L. D. Hurst and N. T. Wright, eds., The Glory of Christ in the New Testament (FS G. B. Caird; Oxford 1987) 251-66, esp. 252. JOHNSON, E. E. The Function of Apocalyptic and Wisdom Traditions in Romans 9-11 (Atlanta GA 1989) 118, 163, 179, 199, 210. COLLINS, J. N. Diakonia (New York/Oxford 1990) 13, 37, 211-3, 215, 228, 230, 233, 326nn.1,2, 327nn.5,6, 328n.5. SEIFRID, M. A. Justification by Faith (Leiden/New York/Köln 1992) 190.

11:14   BAUMERT, N. Täglich Sterben und Auferstehen. Der Literalsinn von 2 Kor 4, 12-5, 10 (München 1973) 392, 394. CAVALLIN, H. C. C. Life After Death. Paul's Argument for the Resurrection of the Dead in I Cor 15. Part I: An Enquiry into the Jewish Background (Lund 1974) 7, 2n.27. SCHÜRMANN, H. "Christlich Weltverantwortung im Licht des Neuen Testaments," Catholica 34 (1980) 98. JOHNSON, E. E. The Function of Apocalyptic and Wisdom Traditions in Romans 9-11 (Atlanta GA 1989) 128, 161f.

11:15-32   RIDDERBOS, H. Paul. An Outline of His Theology (Grand Rapids 1975) 358-61.

11:15-28   DAVIES, W. D. Paul and Rabbinic Judaism (1955) 272, 293, 297f., 322.

11:15   STANLEY, D.M. Christ's Resurrection in Pauline Soteriology (1961) 197-98. HOFFMANN, P. Die Toten in Christus (1966) 182, 184f. LUZ, U. Das Geschichts-verständnis des Paulus (1968) 294, 392f. KUENZI, M. Das Naherwartungslogion Matthäus 10, 23 (1970) 128f, 132. LYONNET, S. Quaestiones in epistulam ad Romanos (Rome 1975) 123-6. PAGELS, E. H. The Gnostic Paul. Gnostic Exegesis of the Pauline Letters (Philadelphia 1975) 41-2. FINDEIS, H.-J. Versöhnung-Apostolat-Kirche (Würzburg 1983) 295-323, 331f., 507ff., 540. KLEINKNECHT, K. T. Der leidende Gerechtfertigte (Tübingen 1984) 279. SCHMITT, R. Gottesgerechtigkeit—Heilsgeschichte—Israel in der Theologie des Paulus (Frankfurt/Bern/New York/Nancy 1984) 103f. STAAB, K. Pauluskommentare aus der griechischen Kirche (Münster ²1984) 156:11-157:41 ThM; 430:6-8 Oek; 526:6-23 Phot. SIEGERT, F. Argumentation bei Paulus (Tübingen 1985) 190-1. BREYTENBACH, C. "Probleme rondom die interpretasie van die 'versoeningsuitsprake' by Paulus," HTS 42 (1986) 696-704. OSTEN-SACKEN, P. VON DER, Evangelium und Tora: Aufsätze zu Paulus (München 1987) 29f., 67, 302f. BREYTENBACH, C. Versöhnung (Neukirchen-Vluyn 1989) 12, 29f., 43, 79, 118f., 142, 143f., 172f., 176f., 178, 183, 187, 222f. HOFIUS, O. Paulusstudien (Tübingen 1989) 1, 9f., 185f., 195. JOHNSON, E. E. The Function of Apocalyptic and Wisdom Traditions in Romans 9-11 (Atlanta GA 1989) 128, 140.

11:16ff.   LUZ, U. Das Geschichtsverständnis des Paulus (1968) 34f., 274-79. RENGS-TORF, K. H. "Das Ölbaum-Gleichnis in Röm 11:16ff. Versuch einer weiter-führenden Deutung" in E. Bammel et al., eds., Donum Gentilicium (FS D. Daube; Oxford 1978) 127-164.

11:16-24   EICHHOLZ, G. Die Theologie des Paulus im Umriss (1972) 298f. ZELLER, D. Juden und Heiden in der Mission des Paulus. Studien zum Römerbrief (Stuttgart 1973) 215ff. STEWART, R. A. "Engrafting. A Study in New Testament Symbolism and Baptismal Application," EQ 50 (1978) 8-22. MOXNES, H. Theology in Conflict (Leiden 1980) 50-1. LÜBKING, H.-M. Paulus und Israel im Römerbrief (Frankfurt/Bern/New York 1986) 112-6. HOFIUS, O.

Paulusstudien (Tübingen 1989) 175, 186-8. VOLF, J. M. G. Paul and Perseverance (Tübingen 1990) 174-7.

11:16-23 LAYMAN, F. D. Paul's Use of Abraham. An Approach to Paul's Understanding of History (diss. Ann Arbor MI 1978) 284-6.

11:16 BOUSSET, W. Die Religion des Judentums (1966 =1926) 102. CAVALLIN, H. C. C. Life After Death. Paul's Argument for the Resurrection of the Dead in I Cor 15. Part I: An Enquiry into the Jewish Background (Lund 1974) 7, 2n.28. LADD, G. E. A Theology of the New Testament (Grand Rapids MI 1974) 519, 538f. LYONNET, S. Quaestiones in epistulam ad Romanos (Rome 1975) 126-7. LAYMAN, F. D. Paul's Use of Abraham. An Approach to Paul's Understanding of History (diss. Ann Arbor MI 1978) 173. SCHMITT, R. Gottesgerechtigkeit—Heilsgeschichte—Israel in der Theologie des Paulus (Frankfurt/Bern/New York/Nancy 1984) 104f. STAAB, K. Pauluskommentare aus der griechischen Kirche (Münster ²1984) 74:7-19 Apoll; 104:7-8 Diod; 158:1-10 ThM; 400:8-11 Genn; 430:9-10 Oek; 526:24-7 Phot; 658:19-21 Areth. LAYTON, B. The Gnostic Scriptures (Garden City NY 1987) 299f. OSTEN-SACKEN, P. VON DER, Evangelium und Tora: Aufsätze zu Paulus (München 1987) 246, 280, 299, 303. KLAUCK, H.-J. Gemeinde, Amt, Sakrament (Würzburg 1989) 352. VOLF, J. M. G. Paul and Perseverance (Tübingen 1990) 28, 185-8, 199.

11:17ff. RUDOLPH, K. Die Mandäer II (1961) 245, 1. STRECKER, G. Der Wed der Gerechtigkeit (1962) 239. KÄSEMANN, E. Exedetische Versuche und Besinnungen (1964) I 281.

11:17-34 BEST, E. One Body in Christ (1955) 99.

11:17-26 PAGELS, E. H. The Gnostic Paul. Gnostic Exegesis of the Pauline Letters (Philadelphia 1975) 41-2.

11:17-24 MINEAR, P.S. Images of the Church in the New Testament (1960) 45f. STOWERS, S. K. The Diatribe and Paul's Letter to the Romans (Chico CA 1981) 80, 99f., 114f. SCHMITT, R. Gottesgerechtigkeit—Heilsgeschichte—Israel in der Theologie des Paulus (Frankfurt/Bern/New York/Nancy 1984) 104-9. BAXTER, A. G. and ZIESLER, J. A. "Paul and Arboriculture: Romans 11, 17-24," JSNT 24 (1985) 25-32. DOBBELER, A. VON, Glaube als Teilhabe (Tübingen 1987) 248-51. RÄISÄNEN, H. "Römer 9-11: Analyse eines geistigen Ringens" in ANRW II.25.4 (1987) 2914-6. BREYTENBACH, C. Versöhnung (Neukirchen-Vluyn 1989) 175. KRUIJF, T. C. DE, "Der Ölbaum und seine Frucht in der Kultur und im Kult des Altertums," Bijdragen 51 (3, 1990) 246-56. VOLF, J. M. G. Paul and Perseverance (Tübingen 1990) 196-201, 226f., 285.

11:17-21 RIGGANS, W. "Romans 11:17-21," ET 98 (7, 1987) 205-6.

11:17 SCHRAGE, W. Die konkreten Einzelgebote in der paulineschen Paränese (1961) 228. ROBINSON, J. A. Pelagius's Exposition of Thirteen Epistles of St. Paul (Cambridge 1922) 127, 265f. LYONNET, S. Quaestiones in epistulam ad Romanos (Rome 1975) 127-8. HAINZ, J. Koinonia (Regensburg 1982) 122. GRÄSSER, E. Der Alte Bund im Neuen (Tübingen 1985) 23, 221f. MUSSNER, F. Die Kraft der Wurzel (Freiburg/Basel/Wien 1987) 155-9. OSTEN-SACKEN, P. VON DER, Evangelium und Tora: Aufsätze zu Paulus (München 1987) 241, 246f., 303.

11:18 LYONNET, S. Quaestiones in epistulam ad Romanos (Rome 1975) 128-30.

11:19-26 ELLIS, E. E. Paul's Use of the Old Testament (1957) 137f, 140, 168, 186.

11:19-21 STAAB, K. Pauluskommentare aus der griechischen Kirche (Münster ²1984) 158:11-7 ThM; 400:12-15 Genn.

11:20-26 SCHWEIZER, E. Gemeinde und Gemeindeordnung im Neuen Testament (1959) § 7f.

11:20,23 THEYSSEN, G.W. "Unbelief" in the New Testament (Rüchlikon 1965) 13-17.

11:20-22 AONO, T. Die Entwicklung des paulinischen Gerichtsgedankens bei den Apostolischen Vätern (Bern/Frankfurt/Las Vegas 1979) 4ff.

11:20-21 STAAB, K. Pauluskommentare aus der griechischen Kirche (Münster [2]1984) 74:20-28 Apoll.

11:20 SCHRAGE, W. Die konkreten Einzelgebote in der paulinischen Paränese (1961) 31. SIEGERT, F. Argumentation bei Paulus (Tübingen 1985) 182-5. DOBBELER, A. VON, Glaube als Teilhabe (Tübingen 1987) 184-6. MUSSNER, F. "Fehl- und Falschübersetzungen von Röm 11 in der 'Einheitsübersetzung'," ThQ 170 (2, 1990) 137-9.

11:21 KÜMMEL, W. G., ed., Jüdische Schriften aus hellenistisch-römischer Zeit, Band V: Apokalypsen (Lieferung 2) (Gütersloh 1976) 131. SIEGERT, F. Argumentation bei Paulus (Tübingen 1985) 190-1.

11:22-26 RICHARDSON, P. Israel in the Apostolic Church (1969) 128ff., 145f.

11:22-23 STAAB, K. Pauluskommentare aus der griechischen Kirche (Münster [2]1984) 400:16-23 Genn.

11:22 JEREMIAS, J. Abba (1966) 283, 279. HANSON, A. T. Studies in Paul's Technique and Theology (London 1974) 263-4. LYONNET, S. Quaestiones in epistulam ad Romanos (Rome 1975) 131-2. STAAB, K. Pauluskommentare aus der griechischen Kirche (Münster [2]1984) 158:18-26 ThM. SIEGERT, F. Argumentation bei Paulus (Tübingen 1985) 182-5.

11:23-24 ZELLER, D. Juden und Heiden in der Mission des Paulus. Studien zum Römerbrief (Stuttgart 1973) 244f. SCHMITT, R. Gottesgerechtigkeit—Heilsgeschichte—Israel in der Theologie des Paulus (Frankfurt/Bern/New York/Nancy 1984) 107f.

11:23 BRUNNER, E. Dogmatik I (1946) 354. BERKOUWER, G. C. The Return of Christ (Grand Rapids 1972) 339f., 343, 347. GRÄSSER, E. Der Alte Bund im Neuen (Tübingen 1985) 227f., 279, 289. RÄISÄNEN, H. The Torah and Christ (Helsinki 1986) 194. SCHNELLE, U. Wandlungen im paulinischen Denken (Stuttgart 1989) 83f.

11:24ff. WAGNER, G. "The Future of Israel: Reflections on Romans 9-11" in W. H. Gloer, ed., Eschatology and the New Testament (FS G. R. Beasley-Murray; Peabody, Mass. 1988) 103ff.

11:24 ROBINSON, J. A. Pelagius's Exposition of Thirteen Epistles of St. Paul (Cambridge 1922) 265f. VIELHAUER, P. "Paulus und das Alte Testament" in Oikodome [G. Klein, ed.] (München 1979) 199. THEOBALD, M. Die überströmende Gnade (Würzburg 1982) 159-61. STAAB, K. Pauluskommentare aus der griechischen Kirche (Münster [2]1984) 74:29-32 Apoll.; 223:1-6 Sev. SIEGERT, F. Argumentation bei Paulus (Tübingen 1985) 190-1. OSTEN-SACKEN, P. VON DER, Evangelium und Tora: Aufsätze zu Paulus (München 1987) 303f.

11:25ff. STÄHELIN, E. Die Verkündigung des Reiches Gottes in der Kirche Jesu Christi I (1951) 27, 338, 339. RIGAUX, B. "Révélation des Mysteres et perfection à Qumran et dans le Nouveau Testament" NTS 4 (1957/58) 237-62. STRECKER, G. Der Weg der Gerechtigkeit (1962) 239. GLOMBITZA, O. "Apostolische Sorge" NovTest 7 (1964/65) 312-18. KÄSEMANN, E. Exegetische Versuche und Besinnungen (1964) II 87f. LUZ, U. Das Geschichtsverständnis des Paulus (1968) 286-300. KÄSEMANN, E. New Testament Questions of Today (1969) 88. HÜBNER, H. Gottes Ich und Israel (Göttingen 1984) 108, 112, 119f. OSTEN-SACKEN, P. VON DER, Evangelium und Tora:

Aufsätze zu Paulus (München 1987) 67, 244f., 308. SCHMELLER, TH. Paulus und die "Diatribe" (Münster 1987) 286.

11:25-36   GRIFFITH, G.O. "The Apokalyptik Note in Romans" ET 56 (1944/45) 153ff. HÜBNER, H. Gottes Ich und Israel (Göttingen 1984) 111, 113-5. RÄISÄNEN, H. "Römer 9-11: Analyse eines geistigen Ringens" in ANRW II.25.4 (1987) 2916-23. SANDNES, K. O. Paul—One of the Prophets? (Tübingen 1991) 172-82.

11:25-32   GOLLWITZER, H. GPM 18 (1964) 274-83. BATEY, R. "'So All Israel Will Be Saved'. An Interpretation of Romans 11:25-32" Interpretation 20 (2, '66) 218-28. LUZ, U. Das Geschichtsverständnis des Paulus (1968) 23, 35f, 81, 268f., 286ff., 394, 401f. SCHOTT, E. GPM 24 (1970/71) 331-37. STUHL-MACHER, P. "Zur Interpretation von Römer 11:25-32" in Probleme biblischer Theologie, hrsg. H.W. Wolff (1971) 555-70. WENDLAND, G. und STÖHR, M. in P. Krusche et al., eds., Predigtstudien für das Kirchenjahr 1976. Perikopen-reihe IV/2 (Stuttgart 1976) 168-74. CELADA, B. "Llamada permanente a la consciencia cristiana respecto a Israel, en la carta de S. Pablo a los Romanos (11:25-32). Un trabajo de Eliseo Rodriguez," CuBi 269 (1977) 279-93. LAYMAN, F. D. Paul's Use of Abraham. An Approach to Paul's Understanding of History (diss. Ann Arbor MI 1978) 286-92. GOETZMANN, J. und KOESTER, R. in P. Krusche et al. Predigtstudien für das Kirchenjahr 1980. Perikopenreihe II/2 (Stuttgart 1980) 171-7. MOXNES, H. Theology in Conflict (Leiden 1980) 34, 51-2, 224, 285. SCHUNACK, G. in GPM 34 (1980) 321-6. GUTHRIE, S. C. "Romans 11:25-32," Interp 38 (1984) 286-91. HÜBNER, H. Gottes Ich und Israel (Göttingen 1984) 110-2, 114. REFOURLÉ, F. ' . . . et ainsi tout Israël sera sauvé'. Romains 11, 25-32, Lectio Divina 117 (Paris 1984) KRAUS, H.-J. in GPM 40 (1985/1986) 385-91. LÜBKING, H.-M. Paulus und Israel im Römerbrief (Frankfurt/Bern/New York 1986) 116-8. BREYTEN-BACH, C. Versöhnung (Neukirchen-Vluyn 1989) 174f. HOFIUS, O. Paulus-studien (Tübingen 1989) 122, 188f. OLIVEIRA, A. DE, Die Diakonie der Gerechtigkeit und der Versöhnung in der Apologie des 2. Korintherbriefes. Analyse und Auslegung von 2 Kor 2, 14-4, 6; 5, 11-6, 10 (Münster 1990) 208f. GLANCY, J. "Israel vs. Israel in Romans 11:25-32," USQR 45 (1991) 191-203.

11:25-29   LYONNET, S. Quaestiones in epistulam ad Romanos (Rome 1975) 133-9.

11:25-28   MUSSNER, F. "Fehl- und Falschübersetzungen von Röm 11 in der 'Einheits-übersetzung'," ThQ 170 (2, 1990) 137-9.

11:25-27   PLAG, Chr. Israels Wege zum Heil (1969) 36f. REFOULÉ, F. "' . . . et ainsi tout Israël sera sauvé'," Tantur Yearbook (1983/1984) 39-57. SÄNGER, D. "Rettung der Heiden und Erwählung Israels. Einige vorläufige Erwägungen zu Römer 11, 25-27," KuD 32 (1986) 99-119. WAGNER, G. "The Future of Israel: Reflections on Romans 9-11" in W. H. Gloer, ed., Eschatology and the New Testament (FS G. R. Beasley-Murray; Peabody, Mass. 1988) 103-10. JOHNSON, E. E. The Function of Apocalyptic and Wisdom Traditions in Romans 9-11 (Atlanta GA 1989) 137, 173, 175, 209. BOCKMUEHL, M. N. A. Revelation and Mystery (Tübingen 1990) 170, 173f., 186, 202, 204. HVALVIK, R. "A 'Sonderweg' for Israel. A Critical Examination of a Current Interpretation of Romans 11.25-27," JSNT 38 (1990) 87-107. SANDNES, K. O. Paul—One of the Prophets? (Tübingen 1991) 172-5. SEIFRID, M. A. Justification by Faith (Leiden/New York/Köln 1992) 190. VANLANINGHAM, M. G. "Romans 11:25-27 and the Future of Israel in Paul's Thought," Master's Seminary Journal 3 (1992) 141-74.

11:25-26 SCHOEPS, H.-J. Paulus (1959) 256f. BARRETT, C.K. From First Adam to Last (1962) 113ff. STRECKER, G. Der Weg der Gerechtigkeit (1962) 114. GOPPELT, L. Christologie und Ethik (1968) 170f., 185f. LUZ, U. Das Geschichtsverständnis des Paulus (1968) 288ff. KÜNZI, M. Das Naherwartungslogion Matthäus 10, 23. Geschichte seiner Auslegung (Tübingen 1970) 32, 111, 114. ZELLER, D. Juden und Heiden in der Mission des Paulus. Studien zum Römerbrief (Stuttgart 1973) 245ff., 277f. MÜLLER, U. B. Prophetie und Predigt im Neuen Testament. Formgeschichtliche Untersuchungen zur urchristlichen Prophetie (Gütersloh 1975) 131, 225ff., 232f., 237. COOPER, C. "Romans 11:25, 26," RestQ 21 (1978) 84-94. SCHMITHALS, W. "Zur Herkunft der gnostischen Elemente in der Sprache des Paulus" in B. Aland et al., eds., Gnosis (FS H. Jonas; Göttingen 1978) 398. HILL, D. New Testament Prophecy (Atlanta 1979) 131, 166. KARDP, H. "Bibel" in TRE 6 (1980) 72. MOXNES, H. Theology in Conflict (Leiden 1980) 78, 83, 85f., 89, 92f., 251. KIM, S. The Origin of Paul's Gospel (Tübingen 1981) 83-99. ASENDORF, U. "Eschatologie" in TRE 10 (1982) 319. STUHLMANN, R. Das eschatologische Mass im Neuen Testament (Göttingen 1983) 2, 53A, 65, 164-81, 186. HÜBNER, H. Gottes Ich und Israel (Göttingen 1984) 107, 111, 113f., 128-30, 134. STAAB, K. Pauluskommentare aus der griechischen Kirche (Münster [2]1984) 104:9-14 Diod. GRÄSSER, E. Der Alte Bund im Neuen (Tübingen 1985) 41, 54, 221, 314. SANDERS, E. P. Paul, the Law, and the Jewish People (London 1985) 189f., 193-5, 205n.89. LÜBKING, H.-M. Paulus und Israel im Römerbrief (Frankfurt/Bern/New York 1986) 122-8. RÄISÄNEN, H. The Torah and Christ (Helsinki 1986) 56, 65, 202. BARRETT, C. K. "Proclamation and Response" in G. F. Hawthorne and O. Betz, eds., Tradition and Interpretation in the New Testament (FS E. E. Ellis; Grand Rapids/Tübingen 1987) 13. HARRINGTON, D. J. "Israel's Salvation according to Paul," BiTod 26 (5, 1988) 304-8. GASTON, L. "Israel's Misstep in the Eyes of Paul" in K. P. Donfried, ed., The Romans Debate. Revised and Expanded Edition (Peabody, MA 1991) 309-26, esp.319.

11:25-26a SCHMITT, R. Gottesgerechtigkeit—Heilsgeschichte—Israel in der Theologie des Paulus (Frankfurt/Bern/ New York/Nancy 1984) 108-11. SANDERS, E. P. Paul, the Law, and the Jewish People (London 1985) 193f.

11:25 KENNEDY, H.A.A. St Paul and the Mystery-Religions (1913) 124, 128. MOULE, C.F.D. "'Fulness' and 'Fill' in the NT" SJTh 4 (1951) 79-86. GROSHEIDE, F.W. "Romeinen 11, 25" GThT 53 (1953) 49-52. MOLIN, G. "Mysterion Israel" Judaica 10 ('54) 231-43. WIKENHAUSER, A. Die Christusmystik des Apostels Paulus (1956) 4, 148. BROWN, R.E. "The Semitic Background of the N.T. Mysterion" Biblica 39 (1958) 426-48, 40 (1959) 70-87. COPPENS, J. "Le 'mystère' dans la théologie paulinienne et ses parallèles qumrâniens": Littérature et Théologie Pauliniennes, ed. A. Descamps (1960) 142-65. BENOIT, P. "Qumran et le Nouveau Testament" NTS 7 (1960/61) 290f. GIBLIN, C.H. The Threat of Faith(1967) 219-20. KUENZI, M. Das Naherwartungslogion Matthäus 10, 23 (1970) 111f., 115, 134. BERKHOF, H. Der Sinn der Geschichte: Christus (Göttingen 1959) 160ff., 163. BERKOUWER, G. C. The Return of Christ (Grand Rapids 1972) 326, 342-5, 357. ZMIJEWSKI, J. Die Eschatologiereden des Lukas-Evangeliums (Bonn 1972) 37, 145, 190, 217-9, 568. BAUMERT, N. Täglich Sterben und Auferstehen. Der Literalsinn von 2 Kor 4, 12-5, 10 (München 1973) 201. ROON, A. VAN, The Authenticity of Ephesians (Leiden 1974) 249f. LYONNET, S. Quaestiones in epistulam ad Romanos (Rome 1975) 133-6. KLIJN, A. F. J. "Die syrische Baruch-Apokalypse" in KÜMMEL, W. G., ed., JSRHZ V/2 (1976) 139. SCHMITHALS, W. "Zur Herkunft der gnostischen Elemente in der Sprache des Paulus" in B. Aland et al., eds., Gnosis (FS H. Jonas; Göttingen 1978) 390-3. SEEBASS, G. "Apokalyptik" in TRE 3 (1978) 283. AUS, R. D. "Paul's Travel Plans to Spain and the 'Full Number of the Gentiles' of Rom. xi 25," NovT 21 (3, 1979) 232-62. BERGMEIER, R. Glaube als Gabe nach Johannes (Stuttgart 1980) 60. STENDAHL, K. "Ancient Scripture in the Modern World" in F. E. Greenspahn, ed., Scripture in the Jewish and Christian Traditions (Nashville 1982) 214. HÜBNER, H. Gottes Ich und Israel (Göttingen 1984) 107-13, 115f., 119, 121f., 127f., 133, 135. KLEINKNECHT, K. T. Der leidende Gerechtfertigte (Tübingen 1984) 235. STAAB, K. Pauluskommentare aus der griechischen Kirche (Münster [2]1984) 75:1-5 Apoll; 159:1-11 ThM; 400:24-410:8 Genn. WENHAM, D. "Paul's Use of the Jesus Tradition: Three Samples" in D. Wenham, ed., Gospel Perspectives: The Jesus Tradition Outside the Gospels, Vol 5 (Sheffield 1984) 15. GRÄSSER, E. Der Alte Bund im Neuen (Tübingen 1985) 31, 228, 280, 282, 286, 314. DUNN, J. D. G. "'A Light to the Gentiles': the Significance of the Damascus Road Christophany for Paul" in L. D. Hurst and N. T. Wright, eds., The Glory of Christ in the New Testament (FS G. B. Caird; Oxford 1987) 251-66. OSTEN-SACKEN, P. VON DER, Evangelium und Tora: Aufsätze zu Paulus (München 1987) 34, 183, 250, 307, 313. BARRETT, C. K. "The Gentile Mission as an Eschatological Phenomenon" in W. H. Gloer, ed., Eschatology and the New Testament (FS G. R. Beasley-Murray; Peabody, Mass. 1988) 69f. JOHNSON, E. E. The Function of Apocalyptic and Wisdom Traditions in Romans 9-11 (Atlanta GA 1989) 2, 16, 38, 112, 118, 121, 123f., 130f., 139f., 142, 148f., 163, 192f. BOCKMUEHL, M. N. A. Revelation and Mystery (Tübingen 1990) 172, 175, 182, 197, 226, 229. BORING, M. E. The Continuing Voice of Jesus (Louisville 1991) 30, 171, 174.

11:25a	HOFIUS, O. Paulusstudien (Tübingen 1989) 188f.
11:25b-27	HOFIUS, O. Paulusstudien (Tübingen 1989) 174, 189-98, 200.
11:25b	HOFIUS, O. Paulusstudien (Tübingen 1989) 190-4.
11:26-32	BEKER, J. C. "The Faithfulness of God and the Priority of Israel in Paul's Letter to the Romans" in G. W. E. Nickelsburg and G. W. MacRae, eds., Christians among Jews and Gentiles (FS K. Stendahl; Philadelphia 1986) 14.
11:26-27	ZELLER, D. Juden und Heiden in der Mission des Paulus. Studien zum Römerbrief (Stuttgart 1973) 258ff. DAVIES, W. D. The Gospel and the Land (London 1974) 195. LYONNET, S. Quaestiones in epistulam ad Romanos (Rome 1975) 137-9. KUTSCH, E. Neues Testament—Neuer Bund? (Neukirchen-Vluyn 1978) 155-6. KOCH, D.-A. "Beobachtungen zum christologischen Schriftgebrauch in den vorpaulinischen Gemeinden," ZNW 71 (1980) 174-191. SANDERS, E. P. Paul, the Law, and the Jewish People (London 1985) 195f. KOCH, D.-A. Die Schrift als Zeuge des Evangeliums (Tübingen 1986) 175-7, 241f. HOFIUS, O. Paulusstudien (Tübingen 1989) 188, 192-7, 201. LOHFINK, N. Der niemals gekündigte Bund (Freiburg 1989).
11:26	WINDISCH, H. Paulus und das Judentum (1935) 32f. ITURBE, F.J.C " . . . et sic omnis Israel salvus fieret" Studiorum Paulinorum Congressus Internationalis Catholicus 1961 I (1963) 329-340; EstBi 21 (2, '62) 127-150. BERKHOF, H. Der Sinn der Geschichte: Christus (Göttingen 1959) 160f., 163. ITURBE, J. D. "Et sic omnis Israel salvus fieret," AnBib 17/18 (1963) 329-40. BERKOUWER, G. C. The Return of Christ (Grand Rapids 1972) 327, 343-8, 351f., 354. CAVALLIN, H. C. C. Life After Death. Paul's Argument for the Resurrection of the Dead in I Cor 15. Part I: An Enquiry into the Jewish Background (Lund

1974) 2, 4-7. DAVIES, W. D. The Gospel and the Land (London 1974) 195-8, 207, 209. HYLDAHL, N. "*kai houtōs* i Rom 11, 26. Note til Kresten Drejergaards fortolkning [*kai houtōs* in Rom 11:26. A Note on Kresten Drejergaard's Interpretation]," DTT 37 (3, 1974) 231-4. MUSSNER, "'Ganz Israel wird gerettet werden' (Röm 11, 26). Versuch einer Auslegung," Kairos 18 (4, 1976) 241-55. HORNE, C. M. "The Meaning of the Phrase 'And Thus All Israel Will Be Saved' (Romans 11:26)," JEThS 21 (4, 1978) 329-34. LAPIDE, P., MUSSNER, F. und WILCKENS, U. Was Juden und Christen voneinander denken [H. Küng und J. Moltmann, eds.] (Freiburg 1978) 52-5. DUPONT, D. J. The Salvation of the Gentiles (New York 1979) 144. FEUILLET, A. "L'espérance de la 'conversion' d'Israël en Rm 11, 25-32. L'interprétation des vv.26 et 31" in M. Carrez et al., eds., De le Tôrah au Messie (FS H. Cazelles; Paris 1979) 483-94. KLAIBER, W. Rechtfertigung und Gemeinde (Göttingen 1982) 142n.374. PONSOT, H. "Et ainsi tout Israël sera sauvé: Rom., XI, 26a," RB 89 (3, 1982) 406-17. HÜBNER, H. Gottes Ich und Israel (Göttingen 1984) 23, 57, 102, 107-9, 111, 113f., 116-8, 120, 123. STAAB, K. Pauluskommentare aus der griechischen Kirche (Münster ²1984) 401:9-10 Genn. GRÄSSER, E. Der Alte Bund im Neuen (Tübingen 1985) 21, 223, 227f., 280. SIEGERT, F. Argumentation bei Paulus (Tübingen 1985) 173. RESE, M. "Die Rettung der Juden nach Römer 11" in A. Vanhoye, ed., L'Apôtre Paul. Personalité, style et conception du ministère (Leuven 1986) 422-30. BERGER, K. und COLPE, C., eds., Religionsgeschichtliches Textbuch zum Neuen Testament (Göttingen/Zürich 1987) 221-2. KREITZER, L. J. Jesus and God in Paul's Eschatology (Sheffield 1987) 125, 127. MUSSNER, F. Die Kraft der Wurzel (Freiburg/ Basel/Wien 1987) 48-54, 62-4. OSTEN-SACKEN, P. VON DER, Evangelium und Tora: Aufsätze zu Paulus (München 1987) 116, 268, 277, 280, 285f., 288, 300, 302ff. BLOESCH, D. G. "'All Israel Will Be Saved'. Supersessionism and the Biblical Witness," Interp 43 (1989) 130-42. JOHNSON, E. E. The Function of Apocalyptic and Wisdom Traditions in Romans 9-11 (Atlanta GA 1989) 128, 139, 142, 158, 200, 208. SCHNELLE, U. Wandlungen im paulinischen Denken (Stuttgart 1989) 83-5. SIMPSON, J. W. "The Problems Posed by 1 Thessalonians 2:15-16 and a Solution," HBTh 12 (1, 1990) 42-72.

11:26a   HAHN, F. "Zum Verständnis von Römer 11.26a: '. . . und so wird ganz Israel gerrettet werden'" in M. D. Hooker and S. G. Wilson, eds., Paul and Paulinism (FS C. K. Barrett; London 1982) 221-36. HÜBNER, H. Gottes Ich und Israel (Göttingen 1984) 109-11, 113, 116-8, 121f. OSBORNE, W. L. "The Old Testament Background of Paul's 'All Israel' in Romans 11:26a," AsiaJT 2 (2, 1988) 282-93. HOFIUS, O. Paulusstudien (Tübingen 1989) 192-7.

11:26-27   MINEAR, P.S. Images of the Church in the New Testament (1960) 46f., 80f.

11:26b-27   SCHMITT, R. Gottesgerechtigkeit—Heilsgeschichte—Israel in der Theologie des Paulus (Frankfurt/Bern/ New York/Nancy 1984) 111. HOFIUS, O. Paulusstudien (Tübingen 1989) 189, 192, 196f.

11:26b   HÜBNER, H. Gottes Ich und Israel (Göttingen 1984) 111, 117, 121f.

11:27   STROBEL, A. Erkenntnis und Bekenntnis der Sünde in neutestamentlicher Zeit (1968) 54. HÜBNER, H. Gottes Ich und Israel (Göttingen 1984) 111, 118f., 121f. KLEINKNECHT, K. T. Der leidende Gerechtfertigte (Tübingen 1984) 333. GRÄSSER, E. Der Alte Bund im Neuen (Tübingen 1985) 8, 16, 18, 20-22, 24, 55. KOCH, D.-A. Die Schrift als Zeuge des Evangeliums (Tübingen 1986) 109, 113. OSTEN-SACKEN, P. VON DER, Evangelium und Tora: Aufsätze zu Paulus (München 1987) 241f.

11:28ff.   LÜBKING, H.-M. Paulus und Israel im Römerbrief (Frankfurt/Bern/ New York
            1986) 128-34, 146.
11:28-34   RICHARDSON, P. Israel in the Apostolic Church (1969) 127-30.
11:28-32   LUZ, U. Das Geschichtsverständnis des Paulus (1968) 295ff. PLAG, Chr.
            Israels Wege zum Heil (1969) 37ff. LAYMAN, F. D. Paul's Use of Abraham.
            An Approach to Paul's Understanding of History (diss. Ann Arbor MI 1978)
            176f. SCHMITT, R. Gottesgerechtigkeit—Heilsgeschichte—Israel in der
            Theologie des Paulus (Frankfurt/Bern/New York/Nancy 1984) 111-6. LÜB-
            KING, H.-M. Paulus und Israel im Römerbrief (Frankfurt/Bern/New York 1986)
            146. HOFIUS, O. Paulusstudien (Tübingen 1989) 198-200. JOHNSON, E. E.
            The Function of Apocalyptic and Wisdom Traditions in Romans 9-11 (Atlanta
            GA 1989) 122, 138, 140, 146, 163, 172-4, 200, 208. VOLF, J. M. G. Paul and
            Perseverance (Tübingen 1990) 185-95.
11:28-29   ZELLER, D. Juden und Heiden in der Mission des Paulus. Studien zum Römer-
            brief (Stuttgart 1973) 130ff., 261, 265f. MOXNES, H. Theology in Conflict
            (Leiden 1980) 51f., 251. STAAB, K. Pauluskommentare aus der griechischen
            Kirche (Münster ²1984) 223:7-14 Sev; 401:11-3 Genn; 430:11-5 Oek. HOFIUS,
            O. Paulusstudien (Tübingen 1989) 198f.
11:28   REICKE, B. "Um der Väter Willen Röm. 11, 28" Judaica 14 ('58) 106-14.
            NICKELS, P. Targum and New Testament (1967) 70. GOPPELT, L. Christolo-
            gie und Ethik (1968) 187f. BERKOUWER, G. C. The Return of Christ (Grand
            Rapids 1972) 289, 327, 332, 340, 345. BAUMERT, N. Täglich Sterben und
            Auferstehen. Der Literalsinn von 2 Kor 4, 12-5, 10 (München 1973) 101f.
            CAVALLIN, H. C. C. Life After Death. Paul's Argument for the Resurrection
            of the Dead in I Cor 15. Part I: An Enquiry into the Jewish Background (Lund
            1974) 2f., 6f. KÜMMEL, W. G., ed., Jüdische Schriften aus hellenistisch-
            römischer Zeit, Band V: Apokalypsen (Lieferung 2) (Gütersloh 1976) 152.
            BERGER, K. "Abraham" in TRE 1 (1977) 376. STAAB, K. Pauluskommentare
            aus der griechischen Kirche (Münster ²1984) 75:6-11 Apoll; 159:12-22 ThM;
            526:28-527:23 Phot. FREUND, G. und STEGEMANN, E., eds., Theologische
            Brosamen für Lothar Steiger (DBAT 5; Heidelberg 1985) 8. SIEGERT, F.
            Argumentation bei Paulus (Tübingen 1985) 182-5. OSTEN-SACKEN, P. VON
            DER, Evangelium und Tora: Aufsätze zu Paulus (München 1987) 153, 193,
            246, 288, 306, 308, 311.
11:29   SPICQ, C. "Ἀμεταμέλητος dnas Rom. XI, 29" RB 67 (1960) 210-19.
            WIEDERKEHR, D. Die Theologie der Berufung in den Paulusbriefen (1963)
            183-87. KÄSEMANN, E. Exegetische Versuche und Besinnungen (1964) I 111.
            VAN DÜLMEN, A. Die Theologie des Gesetzes bei Paulus (1968) 124, 216,
            217. 220, 223. KÄSEMANN, E. New Testament Questions of Today (1969)
            193. ZELLER, D. Juden und Heiden in der Mission des Paulus. Studien zum
            Römerbrief (Stuttgart 1973) 106. DUNN, J. D. G. Jesus and the Spirit. A Study
            of the Religious and Charismatic Experience of Jesus and the First Christians
            as Reflected in the New Testament (London 1975) 207. WAGNER, F.
            "Berufung" in TRE 5 (1980) 686. SCHÜTZ, J. H. "Charisma" in TRE 7 (1981)
            689. OSTEN-SACKEN, P. VON DER, Evangelium und Tora: Aufsätze zu
            Paulus (München 1987) 11f., 28, 71, 155, 244, 246, 286. SCHATZMANN, S.
            S. A Pauline Theology of Charismata (Peabody, MA 1987) 4f., 18f.
11:30-53   SEVENSTER, J.N. Paul and Seneca (1961) 27, 140, 165, 208.
11:30-32   LUZ, U. Das Geschichtsverständnis des Paulus (1968) 297ff. ZELLER, D.
            Juden und Heiden in der Mission des Paulus. Studien zum Römerbrief (Stuttgart
            1973) 213ff., 262ff., 286. LYONNET, S. Quaestiones in epistulam ad Romanos

(Rome 1975) 140-6. KAMLAH, E. "Barmherzigkeit" in TRE 5 (1980) 226. THEOBALD, M. Die überströmende Gnade (Würzburg 1982) 139-70. STAAB, K. Pauluskommentare aus der griechischen Kirche (Münster ²1984) 104:15-105:17 Diod; 401:14-402:12 Genn; 527:24-528:37 Phot.

11:30-31   DIBELIUS, M. "Vier Worte des Römerbriefs" in Symbolae Biblicae Upsalienses 3 (Uppsala 1944) 3-17. HOFIUS, O. Paulusstudien (Tübingen 1989) 198, 199f.

11:30   THEYSSEN, G.W. "Unbelief" in the New Testament (Rüschlikon 1965) 92. SIEGERT, F. Argumentation bei Paulus (Tübingen 1985) 174.

11:31   FEUILLET, A. "L'espérance de la 'conversion' d'Israël en Rm 11, 25-32. L'interprétation des vv.26 et 31" in M. Carrez et al., eds., De le Tôrah au Messie (FS H. Cazelles; Paris 1979) JUDANT, D. "A propos de la destinée d'Israel. Remarques concernant un verset de l'épître aux Romains XI, 31," Div. 23 (1979) 108-25. KLAIBER, W. Rechtfertigung und Gemeinde (Göttingen 1982) 142. FREUND, G. und STEGEMANN, E., eds., Theologische Brosamen für Lothar Steiger (DBAT 5; Heidelberg 1985) 7. OSTEN-SACKEN, P. VON DER, Evangelium und Tora: Aufsätze zu Paulus (München 1987) 30, 71, 307.

11:32-34   DAVIES, W. D. Paul and Rabbinic Judaism (1955) 58, 181, 194.

11:32   KÄSEMANN, E. Exegetische Versuche und Besinnungen (1964) II 191, 197. LUZ, U. Das Geschichtsverständnis des Paulus (1968) 192, 298f. KÄSEMANN, E. New Testament Questions of Today (1969) 179, 187. SCHMITHALS, W. Der Römerbrief als historisches Problem (Gütersloh 1975) 161. HÜBNER, H. Das Gesetz bei Paulus. Ein Beitrag zum Werden der paulinischen Theologie (Göttingen 1978) 74f. WAGNER, F. "Berufung" in TRE 5 (1980) 706. HAYS, R. B. The Faith of Jesus Christ (Chico CA 1983) 136. HÜBNER, H. Gottes Ich und Israel (Göttingen 1984) 47, 119, 124, 126. GRÄSSER, E. Der Alte Bund im Neuen (Tübingen 1985) 20, 227, 280, 314. HULTGREN, A. J. Paul's Gospel and Mission (Philadelphia 1985) 85. SIEGERT, F. Argumentation bei Paulus (Tübingen 1985) 175. BARRETT, C. K. "Proclamation and Response" in G. F. Hawthorne and O. Betz, eds., Tradition and Interpretation in the New Testament (FS E. E. Ellis; Grand Rapids/Tübingen 1987) 13. OSTEN-SACKEN, P. VON DER, Evangelium und Tora: Aufsätze zu Paulus (München 1987) 97, 250, 301. RÄISÄNEN, H. "Römer 9-11: Analyse eines geistigen Ringens" in ANRW II.25.4 (1987) 2928. JOHNSON, E. E. The Function of Apocalyptic and Wisdom Traditions in Romans 9-11 (Atlanta GA 1989) 123, 163, 175, 201f., 208.

11:33ff.   LIPS, H. VON, Weisheitliche Traditionen im Neuen Testament (Neukirchen-Vluyn 1990) 123, 151ff., 167, 299f., 339, 341, 444.

11:33-35   ELLIS, E. E. Paul's Use of the Old Testament (1957) 124, 144, 151, 170, 175. JEREMIAS, J. Abba (1966) 284.

11:33-36   STÄHELIN, E. Die Verkündigung des Reiches Gottes in der Kirche Jesu Christi I (1951) 27. EHRENBERG, GPM 5 (1951) 135-138. BORNKAMM, G. "Der Lobpreis Gottes (Röm. 11, 33-36)": Das Ende des Gesetzes (Gesammelte Aufsätze) I 70-75; GPM 10 (1955/56) 155-59. NORDEN, E. Agnostos Theos (1956) 191, 240ff., 243, 296. SCHOEPS, H.-J. Paulus (1959) 257f. DOBIAS, F.M. GPM 16 (1961/62) 219ff. KRECK, W. in Herr, tue meine Lippen auf, II, ed, G. Eichholz (1966) 342-46. DEICH-GRÄBER, R. "Römer 11, 33-36' in Gotteshymnus und Christushymnus in der frühen Christenheit (1967) 61-64. DOERNE, M. Die alten Episteln (1967) 150-53. MEZGER, M. GPM 22 (1967/68) 277-84. LUZ, U. Das Geschichtsverständnis des Paulus ('68) 26, 299f. PLAG, Chr. Israels Wege zum Heil (1969) 40f. ZELLER, D. Juden und

Heiden in der Mission des Paulus. Studien zum Römerbrief (Stuttgart 1973) 267ff. BONNARD, P.-É. "Les trésors de la miséricorde. Rm 11, 33-36," AssS 52 (1974) 9-14. LYONNET, S. Quaestiones in epistulam ad Romanos (Rome 1975) 146-51. SCHMITHALS, W. Der Römerbrief als historisches Problem (Gütersloh 1975) 161. ELLIS, E. E. Prophecy and Hermeneutic in Early Christianity (Tübingen 1978) 59. KRUIJF, T. C. DE, "Antisemitismus" in TRE 3 (1978) 125. LAYMAN, F. D. Paul's Use of Abraham. An Approach to Paul's Understanding of History (diss. Ann Arbor MI 1978) 177. BECKER, J. und SCHMIDT, H. in P. Krusche et al., eds., Predigtstudien für das Kirchenjahr 1980. Perikopenreihe II/2 (Stuttgart 1980) 99-106. HANSON, A. T. The New Testament Interpretation of Scripture (London 1980) 78-93. OVERHOFF, F. in GPM 34 (1980) 257-62. BISER, E. Der Zeuge (Graz/Wien/Köln 1981) 144f., 228f., 237. HÜBNER, H. Gottes Ich und Israel (Göttingen 1984) 124, 127. LAPIDE, P. "The Rabbi from Tarsus" in Lapide P. and Stuhlmacher P. Paul: Rabbi and Apostle (Minneapolis 1984) 51f. SCHMITT, R. Gottesgerechtig-keit—Heilsgeschichte—Israel in der Theologie des Paulus (Frankfurt/Bern/New York/Nancy 1984) 115f. STAAB, K. Pauluskommentare aus der griechischen Kirche (Münster ²1984) 75:12-29 Apoll; 402:13-31 Genn. BARTH, M. "Theologie—ein Gebet (Röm 11:33-36)," ThZ 41 (3, 1985) 330-48. RUH-BACH, G. in GPM 40 (1985/1986) 316-23. BEKER, J. C. "The Faithfulness of God and the Priority of Israel in Paul's Letter to the Romans" in G. W. E. Nickelsburg and G. W. MacRae, eds., Christians among Jews and Gentiles (FS K. Stendahl; Philadelphia 1986) 13. KOCH, D.-A. Die Schrift als Zeuge des Evangeliums (Tübingen 1986) 178f. LÜBKING, H.-M. Paulus und Israel im Römerbrief (Frankfurt/Bern/New York 1986) 146. DUNN, J. D. G. "Paul's Epistle to the Romans: An Analysis of Structure and Argument" in ANRW II.25.4 (1987) 2873f. OSTEN-SACKEN, P. VON DER, Evangelium und Tora: Aufsätze zu Paulus (München 1987) 30, 59, 300. JOHNSON, E. E. The Func-tion of Apocalyptic and Wisdom Traditions in Romans 9-11 (Atlanta GA 1989) 2, 22, 119, 121, 123, 138, 162, 163-75, 209.

11:33   BRUNNER, E. Dogmatik I (1946) 307, 309. KNOX, W.L. St. Paul and the Church of the Gentiles (1961) 191ff. LYONNET, S. Quaestiones in epistulam ad Romanos (Rome 1975) 146-9. KÜMMEL, W. G., ed., Jüdische Schriften aus hellenistisch-römischer Zeit, Band V: Apokalypsen (Lieferung 2) (Gütersloh 1976) 132. ROLOFF, J. "Amt" in TRE 2 (1978) 522. SEGERT, S. "Semitic Poetic Structures in the New Testament" in ANRW II.25.2 (1984) 1443. JOHN-SON, E. E. The Function of Apocalyptic and Wisdom Traditions in Romans 9-11 (Atlanta GA 1989) 129, 164, 166, 171f.

11:33b   LIEBERS, R. Das Gesetz als Evangelium (Zürich 1989) 127-37.

11:34-35   KÜMMEL, W. G., ed., Jüdische Schriften aus hellenistisch-römischer Zeit, Band V: Apokalypsen (Lieferung 2) (Gütersloh 1976) 132. HELDERMANN, J. Die Anapausis im Evangelium Veritatis (Leiden 1984) 268n.650. KOCH, D.-A. Die Schrift als Zeuge des Evangeliums (Tübingen 1986) 178f. JOHNSON, E. E. The Function of Apocalyptic and Wisdom Traditions in Romans 9-11 (Atlanta GA 1989) 48, 157, 164, 167, 170.

11:34   KÄSEMANN, E. Exegetische Versuche und Besinnungen (1964) I 275. KLEIN-KNECHT, K. T. Der leidende Gerechtfertigte (Tübingen 1984) 385. KOCH, D.-A. Die Schrift als Zeuge des Evangeliums (Tübingen 1986) 14, 166, 270. LIEBERS, R. Das Gesetz als Evangelium (Zürich 1989) 137-40.

11:35   SCHALLER, B. "Zum Textcharakter der Hiobzitate im paulinischen Schrift-tum," ZNW 71 (1980) 21-6. KOCH, D.-A. Die Schrift als Zeuge des Evangeliums (Tübingen 1986) 72f., 111, 188f. LIEBERS, R. Das Gesetz als Evangelium (Zürich 1989) 140-5.

11:36 SCHRAGE, W. Die konkreten Einzelgebote in der paulinischen Paränese (1961) 210. KRAMER, W. Christos Kyrios Gottessohn (1963) §22f. THUESING, W. Per Christum in Deum (1965) 229ff. ELTESTER, W. "Schoepfungsoffenbarung und Natürliche Theologie im Frühen Christentum" NTS 3 (1956/57) 98f. LANG-KAMMER, P.H. "Literarische und Theologische Einzelstücke in I Kor, viii.6" NTS 17 (1970/71) 194f. PETZKE, G. Die Traditionen über Apollonius von Tyana und das Neue Testament (1970) 45, 109, 204. VOEGTLE, A. Das Neue Testament und die Zukunft des Kosmos (1970) 24, 167f., 171. GÄRTNER, B. The Areopagus Speech and Natural Revelation (Uppsala 1955) 200f. POTVIN, T. R. The Theology of the Primacy of Christ According to St. Thomas and Its Scriptural Foundations (Fribourg 1973) 70n.3, 74, 93, 158, 263. LYONNET, S. Quaestiones in epistulam ad Romanos (Rome 1975) 150-1. SCHMITHALS, W. Der Römerbrief als historisches Problem (Gütersloh 1975) 160f. DOIGNON, J. "'Ipsius enim genus sumus' (Actes 17, 28b) chez Hilaire de Poitiers," JAC 23 (1980) 59-61. ALETTI, J.-N. Colossiens 1, 15-20. Genre et exégese du texte Fonction de la thématique sapientielle (Rome 1981) 30, 56, 68f., 118, 146, 148, 173, 186. KERN, U. "Eckart" in TRE 9 (1982) 261. SEGERT, S. "Semitic Poetic Structures in the New Testament" in ANRW II.25.2 (1984) 1443. SCHIMANOWSKI, G. Weisheit und Messias (Tübingen 1985) 340. SCHNA-BEL, E. J. Law and Wisdom from Ben Sira to Paul (Tübingen 1985) 250, 260-2. AUNE, D. E. The New Testament in Its Literary Environment (Philadelphia 1987) 193. BERGER, K. und COLPE, C., eds., Religionsgeschichtliches Textbuch zum Neuen Testament (Göttingen/Zürich 1987) 222-3. LAYTON, B. The Gnostic Scriptures (Garden City NY 1987) 287, 287n.1, 3, 4g. JOHNSON, E. E. The Function of Apocalyptic and Wisdom Traditions in Romans 9-11 (Atlanta GA 1989) 127, 164, 170-3. LIEBERS, R. Das Gesetz als Evangelium (Zürich 1989) 145-50. MULLER, E. C. Trinity and Marriage in Paul (New York/Bern/Frankfurt/Paris 1990) 50, 213f., 253, 254, 397, 454f. SIMONIS, W. Der gefangene Paulus. Die Entstehung des sogenannten Römerbriefs und anderer urchristlicher Schriften in Rom (Frankfurt/Bern/ New York/Paris 1990) 48f.

12–16 GIBLIN, C. H. In Hope of God's Glory (1970) 221-37. ADAMAS, B. E. "Responsible Living in Community Setting (Romans 12-16)," SouJTh 19 (1976) 57-69.

12–15 KÄSEMANN, E. Exegetische Versuche und Besinnungen (1964) I 117. JÜNGEL, E. Paulus und Jesus (1966) 26.

12–14 KÄSEMANN, E. Exegetische Versuche und Besinnungen (1964) II 184, 287.

12–13 SCHRAGE, W. Die konkreten Einzelgebote in der paulinischen Paränese (1961) 21, 42, 46, 199. DELLING, G. Römer 13, 1-7 innerhalb der Briefe des Neuen Testaments (1962) 15, 67f. CRANFIELD, C. E. B. A Commentary on Romans 12–13 (1965). FURNISH, V. P. The Love Command in the New Testament (1972) 102-11.

12:1–16:23 FRAIKIN, D. "The Rhetorical Function of the Jews in Romans" in P. Richardson, ed., Anti-Judaism in Early Christianity, Vol 1: Paul and the Gospels (Waterloo, Ont. 1986) 102.

12–15 McARTHUR, H. K. Understanding the Sermon on the Mount (New York 1960) 63, 70f., 170. SELBY, D. J. Introduction to the New Testament (New York 1971) 402-4. FORELL, G. W. The Christian Lifestyle. Reflections on Romans

12-15 (Philadelphia 1975) SCHMITHALS, W. Der Römerbrief als historisches Problem (Gütersloh 1975) 152ff., 162ff., 172, 177ff., 182f. CULPEPPER, R. A. "God's Righteousness in the Life of His People. Romans 12-15," RevEx 73 (4, 1976) 451-63. DUGANDZIC, I. Das "Ja" Gottes in Christus (Würzburg 1977) 311-3. KARRIS, R. J. "Romans 14:1-15:13 and the Occasion of Romans" in K. P. Donfried, ed., The Romans Debate (Minneapolis 1977) 95-8. JANKOWSKI, G. "Ermutigungen. Paulus an die Römer Kapitel 12-15," Texte und Kontexte 2 (1978) 11-27. RAMAZZOTTI, B. "Etica cristiana e peccati nelle lettere ai Romani e ai Galati," ScuC 106 (3/4, 1978) 290-342. BINDEMANN, W. Die Hoffnung der Schöpfung (Neukirchen 1983) 56-9. VERNER, D. C. The Household of God (Chico CA 1983) 116-8. ROETZEL, C. J. "Sacrifice in Romans 12-15," WaW 6 (4, 1986) 410-9. VOUGA, F. "L'épître aux Romains, comme document ecclésiologique (Rm 12-15)," EThR 61 (4, 1986) 485-95. SCHMELLER, TH. Paulus und die "Diatribe" (Münster 1987) 226. CONZEL-MANN, H. and LINDEMANN, A. Interpreting the New Testament (Peabody, Mass. 1988) 196. ELLIOT, N. The Rhetoric of Romans (Sheffield 1990) 59, 67, 91f., 98, 105, 225, 258, 272, 277f., 291. LIPS, H. VON, Weisheitliche Traditionen im Neuen Testament (Neukirchen-Vluyn 1990) 378ff., 400., 412, 444. MOISER, J. "Rethinking Romans 12-15," NTS 36 (1990) 571-82.

12:1-15:33
12:1-15:13   RICHARDS, E. R. The Secretary in the Letters of Paul (Tübingen 1991) 177. FLENDER, H. "Weisung statt Ermahnung. Einführung in die Bibelarbeit über Römer 12," BuK 28 (3, 1973) 81-4. SEGALLA, G. "Kerigma e parenesi come critica alla prassi in Rm. 12, 1-15, 13," Teol. 6 (4, 1981) 307-29. DUNN, J. D. G. "Paul's Epistle to the Romans: An Analysis of Structure and Argument" in ANRW II.25.4 (1987) 2874-81. WEDDERBURN, A. J. M. The Reasons for Romans (Edinburgh 1988) 87, 105. ELLIOT, N. The Rhetoric of Romans (Sheffield 1990) 58, 97, 263.

12:1-15:7   SANDERS, J. T. Ethics in the New Testament. Change and Development (Philadelphia 1975) 57-63, 65.

12:1-15:3   AUNE, D. E. The New Testament in Its Literary Environment (Philadelphia 1987) 220.

12–13   SHEPARD, J. W. The Life and Letters of St. Paul (Grand Rapids 1950) 430-9. MINEAR, P. S. The Obedience of Faith (London 1971) 82-90. VEERKAMP, T. "Ermutigungen. Paulus an die Römer—eine Übersetzung (Röm 12-13, 14)," TK 2 (1978) 5-11. DE LORENZI, L., ed., Dimensions de la vie chrétienne (Rm 12-13) (Rome 1979) BARRETT, C. K. "Ethics and Eschatology: a Résumé" in L. De Lorenzi, ed., Dimensions de la vie chrétienne (Rm 12-13) (Rome 1979) 221-35. BOSCH, J. S. "Le Corps du Christ et les charismes dans l'épître aux Romains" in L. De Lorenzi, ed., Dimensions de la vie chrétienne (Rm 12-13) (Rome 1979) 51-72. FESTORAZZI, F. "Originalità della morale cristiana secondo San Paolo" in L. De Lorenzi, ed., Dimensions de la vie chrétienne (Rm 12-13) (Rome 1979) 237-56. ORTKEMPER, F.-J. Leben aus dem Glauben. Christliche Grundhaltungen nach Römer 12-13 (Münster 1980) BINDEMANN, W. Die Hoffnung der Schöpfung (Neukirchen 1983) 97-99, 115-7. MUNRO, W. Authority in Paul and Peter (Cambridge 1983) 56-67. SCHEGGET, G. H. TER, Het moreel van de gemeente. Essays over de ethiek van Paulus volgens Romeinen 12 en 13 (Baarn 1985) LIPS, H. VON, Weisheitliche Traditionen im Neuen Testament (Neukirchen-Vluyn 1990) 358, 377f., 385ff., 400ff.

12:1–13:14   GIBLIN, C. H. In Hope of God's Glory (1970) 224-31. MINEAR, P. S. The Obedience of Faith (1971) 82-90.

12:1–13:10   DABECK, F. "Der Text Röm. 12:1–13:10 als Symbol des Pneuma" Studiorum
Paulinorum Congressus Internationalis Catholicus 1961 (1963) II 585-
90.DABECK, F. "Der Text Röm 12, 1-13, 10 als Symbol des Pneuma," AnBib
17-18 (2, 1963) 585-90. SANDERS, J. T. Ethics in the New Testament. Change
and Development (Philadelphia 1975) 61.
12   KÄSEMANN, E. "Gottesdienst im Alltag der Welt (zu Rm 12)" Judentum,
Urchristentum, Kirche (1960) 165-71. MINEAR, P. S. Images of the Church in
the New Testament (1960) 194f. KÄSEMANN, E. Exegetische Versuche und
Besinnungen (1964) II 198ff., 206, 257. New Testament Questions of Today
(1969) 189. MERK, O. Handeln aus Glauben (1968) 157, 159f., 164, 166f.,
234, 236. THIEME, K. "Die ταπεινοφροσύνη und Römer 12," ZNW 8
(1907) 9-33. HAINZ, J. Ekklesia (Regenburg 1972) 79f. SCHELKLE, K. H.
"Der Christ in der Gemeinde. Eine Auslegung von Röm 12," BuK 28 (3, 1973)
74-81. BROCKHAUS, U. Charisma und Amt. Die paulinische Charismenlehre
auf dem Hintergrund der frühchristlichen Gemeindefunktionen (Wuppertal
²1975) 27f., 30, 38, 60, 66, 71, 79, 87, 92f., 95, 129, 137, 139, 141, 189, 193f.,
196, 209, 213f., 217f., 220f., 223f., 226, 231, 235, 238. ROHDE, J. Urchristliche und frühkatholische Amter (Berlin 1976) 45-9. DUNN, J. D. G. Unity and
Diversity in the New Testament. An Inquiry into the Character of Earliest
Christianity (London 1977) 109-11. RIESNER, R. Handeln aus dem Geist.
Zwölf Thesen zu Römer 12 (Giessen/Basel 1977) BETZ, O. "Rechtfertigung
und Heiligung" in G. Müller, ed., Rechtfertigung Realismus Universalismus in
Biblischer Sicht. (FS A. Köberle; Darmstadt 1978) 39, 42. PIPER, J. 'Love your
enemies' (Cambridge 1979) 8f., 103f., 109, 191n.141, 211n.14, 212n.15.
ROBINSON, J. A. T. Wrestling with Romans (London 1979) 133-5. KLAS-
SEN, W. "A Child of Peace (Lk. 10:6) in First Century Context," NTS 27
(1980/1981) 498. SCHÖTZ, J. H. "Charisma" in TRE 7 (1981) 690. KLAIBER,
W. Rechtfertigung und Gemeinde (Göttingen 1982) 214-28. HAMANN, H. P.
"The Christian Life According to Romans 12," LThJ 19 (2, 1985) 73-9.
MALHERBE, A. J. Moral Exhortation. A Greco-Roman Sourcebook (Philadel-
phia 1986) 125. HAYTER, M. The New Eve in Christ (Grand Rapids 1987)
152. OSTEN-SACKEN, P. VON DER, Evangelium und Tora: Aufsätze zu
Paulus (München 1987) 107f. VOSS, G. "In Christus Gemeinschaft bilden. Eine
Auslegung des 12. Kapitels des Römerbriefes," US 43 (4, 1988) 277-83, 342.
LAMPE, P. Die stadtrömischen Christen in den ersten beiden Jahrhunderten
(Tübingen ²1989) 63f., 78, 131, 179, 336. HOOKER, M. D. From Adam to
Christ. Essays on Paul (Cambridge 1990) 54-7. SEGAL, A. F. Paul the Convert
(New Haven/London 1990) 252. DAWN, M. J. The Hilarity of Community.
Romans 12 and How to Be the Church (Grand Rapids 1992). RIDGWAY, J.
K. "'By the Mercies of God . . . '—Mercy and Peace in Romans 12," IrBS 14
(1992) 170-91.
12:1ff.   SEIDENSTICKER, Ph. Lebendiges Opfer (1954) 256ff. KÄSEMANN, E.
Exegetische Versuche und Besinnungen (1964) I 113, 122, 276. DUNN, J. D.
G. Jesus and the Spirit. A Study of the Religious and Charismatic Experience
of Jesus and the First Christians as Reflected in the New Testament (London
1975) 257. MÜNCHOW, C. Ehik und Eschatologie (Göttingen 1981) 154, 163f.
WEDDERBURN, A. J. M. The Reasons for Romans (Edinburgh 1988) 75-87.
12:1-21   SIMONIS, W. Der gefangene Paulus. Die Entstehung des sogenannten
Römerbriefs und anderer urchristlicher Schriften in Rom (Frankfurt/Bern/New
York/Paris 1990) 49-58.
12:1-17   BOISMARD, M.-E. Quatre Hymnes Baptismales (1961) 168-72.

12:1-8   RICHTER, A. "Die Gnadengaben in Röm. 12:1-8": Die Bedeutung der Gnadengaben für die Gemeinde Jesu Christi, ed. K. Hutten (1964) 98-107. BARTH, C. "Bible Study VI. 'Each According to the Gifts' Romans 12:1-8" SEAJTh 6 (4, '65) and 7 (1, '66) 22-25. DOERNE, M. Die alten Episteln (196) 45-49. FISCHER, K. M. in GPM 34 (1979) 77-83. HARRINGTON, D. J. "Freed for Life in the Spirit—Together. Romans 12:1-8. A Meditation," RR 45 (6, 1986) 831-5.

12:1-7   CRANFIELD, C. E. B. "Some Observations on Romans XII.1-7" NTS 6 (1959-60) 241f. RICHARDSON, P. Paul's Ethic of Freedom (Philadelphia 1979) 143. WINK, W. Naming the Powers (Philadelphia 1984) 45-7.

12:1-6   WEBER, O. GPM 10 (1955) 44-47. BRAUN, GPM 16 (1961/62) 80ff. KÄSEMANN, E. Exegetische Versuche und Besinnungen (1964) II 212. WEBER, O. Predigtmeditationen (1967) 231-34. HAHN, F. GPM 22 (1967/68) 75-85.

12:1-5   KLAIBER, W. Rechtfertigung und Gemeinde (Göttingen 1982) 110.

12:1-4   DAVIES, W.D. Paul and Rabbinic Judaism (1955) 56, 122, 133, 178, 239.

12:1-3   BONHOEFFER, A. Epiktet und das Neue Testament (1911) 133, 158, 177, 89, 299. THUESING, W. Per Christum in Deum (1965) 94f., 128f.171. BAUMERT, N. Täglich Sterben und Auferstehen. Der Literalsinn von 2 Kor 4, 12-5, 10 (München 1973) 231, 257f. WENDLAND, G. und STÖHR, M. in P. Krusche et al., Predigtstudien für das Kirchenjahr 1979/80. Perikopenreihe II/1 (1979) 99-105. BAYER, O. in GPM 40 (1985/86) 105-113. MOISER, J. "Rethinking Romans 12-15," NTS 36 (1990) 571-82. SEIFRID, M. A. Justification by Faith (Leiden/New York/Köln 1992) 190-93.

12:1-2   SCHLIER, H. Die Zeit der Kirche (1956) 74-89. SCHRAGE, W. Die konkreten Einzelgebote in der paulinischen Paränese (1961) 19, 24, 67, 117, 165, 188, 214, 224. BRAUMANN, G. Vorpaulinische christliche Taufverkündigung bei Paulus (1962) 11f., 70. STALDER, K. Das Werk des Geistes in der Heiligung bei Paulus (1962) 232-38, 250. STOESSEL, H.E. "Notes on Romans 12:1-2. The Renewal of the Mind and Internalizing the Truth" Interpretation 17 (2, '63) 161-75. KÄSEMANN, E. Exegetische Versuche und Besinnungen (1964) II 206f., 218, 248. SCHLIER, H. "Der Christ und die Welt" GuL 38 (6, '65) 416-28. BJERKELUND, C. J. Parakalo (1967) 12, 14, 18, 26, 113, 114, 116, 128, 138, 156, 158, 162, 164-5, 167-73, 185-86, 190. GRABNER-HAIDER, A. "Der weltliche Gottesdienst des Christen" GuL 40 (3, '67) 170-76; Paraklese und Eschatologie bei Paulus (1968) 116-18. MERK, O. Handeln aus Glauben (1968) 45, 158, 164, 166, 234, 240, 243. BLANK, J. Schriftauslegung in Theorie und Praxis (1969) 57, 138, 144, 174. KÄSEMANN, E. New Testament Questions of Today (1969) 189, 199, 246. RICHARDSON, P. Israel in the Apostolic Church (1969) 144f. KLINZING, G. Die Umdeutung des Kultus in der Qumrangemeinde und im Neuen Testament (1971) 214-18, 184, 194, 195, 221-22, 224. SCHLIER, H. Das Ende der Zeit (1971) 234-49. PEISKER, C. H. in GPM 28 (1973) 87-95. ROESSLER, R. in E. Lange, ed., Predigtstudien für das Kirchenjahr 1973/74 (1973) 118-23. LADD, G. E. A Theology of the New Testament (Grand Rapids 1974) 371, 524, 551. FORELL, G. W. The Christian Lifestyle. Reflections on Romans 12-15 (Philadelphia 1975) 4-7. PAGELS, E. H. The Gnostic Paul. Gnostic Exegesis of the Pauline Letters (Philadelphia 1975) 42f. SCHMITHALS, W. Der Römerbrief als historisches Problem (Gütersloh 1975) 183. FRIEDRICH, J. et al., eds., Rechtfertigung (FS E. Käsemann; Tübingen/Göttingen 1976) 397, 456f., 518. DALY, R. J. Christian Sacrifice (Washington 1978) 243f., 246, 251-5, 303. EVANS, C. "Romans 12:1-2. The True Worship" in L. De Lorenzi, ed., Dimensions de la vie chrétienne (Rm 12-

13) (Rome 1979) 7-33. FURNISH, V. P. The Moral Teaching of Paul (Nashville 1979) 23f., 116, 123, 125f., 138. FERGURSON, E. "Spiritual Sacrifice in Early Christianity and its Environment" in ANRW II.23.2 (1980) 1165. LOHSE, E. "Kirche im Alltag . . . " in D. Lührman und G. Strecker, eds., Kirche (FS G. Bornkamm; Tübingen 1980) 409. ORTKEMPER, F.-J. Leben aus dem Glauben (Münster 1980) 19. RIEKKINEN, V. Römer 13 (Helsinki 1980) 121-30, 219, 227. DEIDUN, T. J. New Covenant Morality in Paul (Rome 1981) 97-101. BLANK, J. Paulus. Von Jesus zum Christentum (München 1982) 169-91. LAUB, F. Die Begegnung des frühen Christentums mit der antiken Sklaverei (Stuttgart 1982) 77. BINDEMANN, W. Die Hoffnung der Schöpfung (Neukirchen 1983) 99-105. MEHL, R. "Freiheit" in TRE 11 (1983) 526. PATTE, D. Preaching Paul (Philadelphia 1984) 45-7. STAAB, K. Pauluskommentare aus der griechischen Kirche (Münster ²1984) 430:16-20 Oek. HAHN, F. "Gottesdienst III" in TRE 14 (1985) 37. NEWTON, M. The concept of purity at Qumran and in the letters of Paul (Cambridge 1985) 70-4. SCHNABEL, E. J. Law and Wisdom from Ben Sira to Paul (Tübingen 1985) 303, 330. WAINWRIGHT, G. "Gottesdienst IX" in TRE 14 (1985) 88. TANBERG, K. A. "Romerbrevet 12, 1-2 og parenesebegrepet i nytestamentlig forskning [Romans 12:1-2 and the concept of paraenesis in New Testament research]," TsTK 57 (1986) 81-91. DUNN, J. D. G. "Paul's Epistle to the Romans: An Analysis of Structure and Argument" in ANRW II.25.4 (1987) 2875f. SCHULZ, S. "Neutestamentliche Ethik (Zürich 1987) 156ff. BETZ, H. D. "Das Problem der Grundlagen der paulinischen Ethik (Röm 12, 1-2)," ZThK 85 (2, 1988) 199-218. DOWNING, F. G. Christ and the Cynics (Sheffield 1988) 188. FULLER, R. H. "Scripture, Tradition and Priesthood" in R. Bauckham and B. Drewery, eds., Scripture, Tradition and Reason (FS R. P. C. Hanson; Edinburgh 1988) 104f. WEDDERBURN, A. J. M. The Reasons for Romans (Edinburgh 1988) 67, 69f., 75f. BECKER, J. Paulus. Der Apostel der Völker (Tübingen 1989) 227, 339, 408, 418, 445, 463, 558. LIMBECK, M. Mit Paulus Christ sein. Sachbuch zur Person und Theologie des Apostels Paulus (Stuttgart 1989) 126ff. MARXSEN, W. "Christliche" und christliche Ethik im Neuen Testament (Gütersloh 1989) 198f., 234. ELLIOT, N. The Rhetoric of Romans (Sheffield 1990) 58, 66, 92f., 97f., 117, 225, 272, 277, 291. LIPS, H. VON, Weisheitliche Traditionen im Neuen Testament (Neukirchen-Vluyn 1990) 385, 387, 400f. REBELL, W. Zum neuen Leben berufen (München 1990) 96-9. SMIGA, G. "Romans 12:1-2 and 15:30-32 and the Occasion of the Letter to the Romans," CBQ 53 (2, 1991) 257-73.

12:1   BRUNNER, E. Dogmatik II (1950) 355; Mensch im Widerspruch (1937) 101. ROBINSON, J. A. T. The Body (1952) 28f. BEST, E. One Body in Christ (1955) 216. DELLING, G. Die Zueignung des Heils in der Taufe (1961) 54f. SCHRAGE, W. Die konkreten Einzelgebote in der paulinischen Paränese (1961) 49-51, 53, 104, 106, 108, 240. GÄRTNER, B. The Temple and the Community in Qumran and the New Testament (1965) 73, 75, 85f. JÜNGEL, E. Paulus und Jesus (1966) 57. MERK, O. Handeln aus Glauben (1968) 29, 45, 58, 155, 157f., 161, 235. KÄSEMANN, E. New Testament Questions of Today (1969) 198. BARRETT, C. K. The New Testament Background. Selected Documents (London 1956) 90. CONZELMANN, H. Theologie als Schriftauslegung (München 1974) 122f. LADD, G. E. A Theology of the New Testament (Grand Rapids 1974) 466, 470, 519. SANDERS, J. T. Ethics in the New Testament. Change and Development (Philadelphia 1975) 57. SCHMITHALS, W. Der Römerbrief als historisches Problem (Gütersloh 1975) 163f. GUNDRY, R. H. Sōma in

Biblical Theology with Emphasis on Pauline Anthropology (Cambridge 1976) 220f. KRETSCHMAR, G. "Abendmahl" in TRE 1 (1977) 71, 83. KÜHN, U. "Abendmahl" in TRE 1 (1977) 169. ROLOFF, J. "Amt" in TRE 2 (1978) 522. BUTTE, A. "Loi et Sagesse du sacrifice perpétuel," Hokhma 10 (1979) 11-7. PIPER, J. 'Love your enemies' (Cambridge 1979) 24, 102-5, 119, 121, 212nn.15, 19, 22. GEORGI, D. "Weisheit Salomos," JSHRZ 3 (4, 1980) 3n.6b. KAMLAH, E. "Barmherzigkeit" in TRE 5 (1980) 227. ORTKEMPER, F.-J. Leben aus dem Glauben (Münster 1980) 19-34, 168-73. PREUSS, H. D. "Barmherzigkeit" in TRE 5 (1980) 220. THISELTON, A. C. The Two Horizons (Grand Rapids 1980) 278. BERGER, K. "Das Buch der Jubiläen," JSHRZ 2 (3, 1981) 330n.22b. KLEIN, G. "Eschatologie" in TRE 10 (1982) 282. STAAB, K. Pauluskommentare aus der griechischen Kirche (Münster ²1984) 159:23-160:30 ThM; 402:32-403:9 Genn; 529:120 Phot. SCHNABEL, E. J. Law and Wisdom from Ben Sira to Paul (Tübingen 1985) 295, 305f. RÄISÄNEN, H. The Torah and Christ (Helsinki 1986) 293. SCHNACKENBURG, R. Die sittliche Botschaft des Neuen Testaments, Band 1 (Freiburg/Basel/Wien 1986) 235, 258. MAHER, M. "Christian Life and Liturgy," ReligiousLifeReview [Dublin] 26 (124, 1987) 46-52. COOK, J. E. "Ezra's Confession. Appeal to a Merciful God," JSP 3 (1988) 89-100. WEDDERBURN, A. J. M. The Reasons for Romans (Edinburgh 1988) 75, 88. KLAUCK, H.-J. Gemeinde, Amt, Sakrament (Würzburg 1989) 353f. LIMBECK, M. Mit Paulus Christ sein. Sachbuch zur Person und Theologie des Apostels Paulus (Stuttgart 1989) 130.

12:2-8
12:2-3
12:2
BAUMERT, N. "Zur 'Unterscheidung der Geister'," ZKTh 111 (1989) 183-95. WEDDERBURN, A. J. M. The Reasons for Romans (Edinburgh 1988) 77. KENNEDY, H.A.A. St. Paul and the Mystery-Religions (1913) 139, 182. BOUSSET, W. Die Religion des Judentums (1966 =1926) 245. STACEY, W.D. The Pauline View of Man (1956) 196, 199, 201, 208. WIKENHAUSER, A. Die Christusmystik des Apostels Paulus (1956) 154f. ROBINSON, J.M. Kerygma und historischer Jesus (1960) 57. SCHRAGE, W. Die konkreten Einzelgebote in der paulinischen Paränese (1961) 49f., 113, 164, 168-70, 187f, . HAHN, F. Christologische Hoheitstitel (1963) 311. KÄSEMANN, E. Exegetische Versuche und Besinnungen (1964) I 19. TILLICH, P. Das Ewige im Jetzt (1964) 131-39. MOULE, C.F.D. "St. Paul and Dualism: The Pauline Conception of Resurrection" NTS 12 (1965/66) 108f. BRAUN, H. Qumran und NT II (1966) 184, 248, 299, 326. KERTELGE, K. "Rechtfertigung" bei Paulus (1967) 141. MERK, O. Handeln aus Glauben (1968) 37, 50, 91, 95, 157, 161, 166f., 206, 241. KÄSEMANN, E. New Testament Questions of Today (1969) 190. RISSI, M. Studien zum zweiten Korintherbrief (1969) 67f. KÜMMEL, W. G. Römer 7 und das Bild des Menschen im Neuen Testament (München 1974) 25, 27, 181. LADD, G. E. A Theology of the New Testament (Grand Rapids 1974) 48, 464, 476, 480, 493. DUNN, J. D. G. Jesus and the Spirit. A Study of the Religious and Charismatic Experience of Jesus and the First Christians as Reflected in the New Testament (London 1975) 216, 223f., 315, 340, 405. RIDDERBOS, H. Paul. An Outline of His Theology (Grand Rapids 1975) 286f. PIPER, J. 'Love your enemies' (Cambridge 1979) 24, 39, 103-6, 122, 128, 133, 212n.16. ORTKEMPER, F.-J. Leben aus dem Glauben (Münster 1980) 34-40, 173-8, 237f. GRÜNDEL, J. "Consilia Evangelica" in TRE 8 (1981) 193. SCHRAGE, W. "Ethik" in TRE 10 (1982) 446f. ECKSTEIN, H.-J. Der Begriff Syneidesis bei Paulus (Tübingen 1983) 314f. LOHFINK, G. Jesus and Community. The Social Dimension of the Christian Faith (Philadelphia 1984) 127. MOHRLANG, R. Matthew and Paul (Cambridge 1984) 82, 118f., 121f., 154, 188. STAAB, K.

Pauluskommentare aus der griechischen Kirche (Münster [2]1984) 55:25-56:9
Akazc; 75:30-76:28 Apoll; 223:15-8 Sev; 403:10-6 Genn; 529:21-36 Phot.
SCHNABEL, E. J. Law and Wisdom from Ben Sira to Paul (Tübingen 1985)
304, 306, 326, 330, 331f. MALHERBE, A. J. Moral Exhortation. A Greco-
Roman Sourcebook (Philadelphia 1986) 33, 64. SCHNACKENBURG, R. Die
sittliche Botschaft des Neuen Testaments, Band 1 (Freiburg/Basel/Wien 1986)
20, 181, 225, 241. GUBLER, M.-L. "'Passt euch nicht den Massstäben dieser
Welt an!' (Röm 12, 2). Von der Zivilcourage biblischer Frauen," Diakonia 18
(5, 1987) 305-16. LOHFINK, G. Wem gilt die Bergpredigt? Beiträge zu einer
christlichen Ethik (Freiburg 1988) 140. STUHLMACHER, P. Jesus von Nazareth—Christus des Glaubens (Stuttgart 1988) 17. WEDDERBURN, A. J. M.
The Reasons for Romans (Edinburgh 1988) 75-7, 79, 87, 148. FURNISH, V.
P. "Der 'Wille Gottes' in paulinischer Sicht" in D.-A. Koch et al., eds., Jesu
Rede von Gott und ihre Nachgeschichte im frühen Christentum (FS W.
Marxsen; Gütersloh 1989) 208-21, esp.215-7. LIMBECK, M. Mit Paulus Christ
sein. Sachbuch zur Person und Theologie des Apostels Paulus (Stuttgart 1989)
125. VOLLENWEIDER, S. Freiheit als neue Schöpfung (Göttingen 1989) 371.

12:3-13:7 PIPER, J. 'Love your enemies' (Cambridge 1979) 103, 105.

12:3ff.   SCHWEIZER, E. Gemeinde und Gemeindeordnung im Neuen Testament (1959)
§71 21g, 22c, 24k, 27ab. SCHRAGE, W. Die konkreten Einzelgebote in der
paulinischen Paränese (1961) 71, 122, 179f. KÄSEMANN, E. Exegetische
Versuche und Besinnungen (1964) I 114, 119f. BJERKELUND, C.J. Parakalô
(1967) 160, 169, 170, 185, 186. RIDDERBOS, H. Paul. An Outline of His
Theology (Grand Rapids 1975) 369-76. REBELL, W. Gehorsam und Unabhängigkeit (München 1986) 113f., 122.

12:3-21   GOPPELT, L. Christologie und Ethik (1968) 128f. MERK, O. Handeln aus
Glauben (1968) 158. MALHERBE, A. J. Moral Exhortation. A Greco-Roman
Sourcebook (Philadelphia 1986) 93.

12:3-16   BINDEMANN, W. Die Hoffnung der Schöpfung (Neukirchen 1983) 105-10.
LIPS, H. VON, Weisheitliche Traditionen im Neuen Testament (Neukirchen-
Vluyn 1990) 168, 387f., 395, 412ff., 422.

12:3-16b   MERKEL, F. in GPM 28 (1, 1973) 95-102.

12:3-13   DRANE, J. W. "Why did Paul write Romans?" in D. A. Hagner and M. J.
Harris, eds., Pauline Studies (FS F. F. Bruce; Exeter 1980) 221. REBELL, W.
Zum neuen Leben berufen (München 1990) 100-3.

12:3-8   KÄSEMANN, E. New Testament Questions of Today (1969) 194. TALBERT,
C. H. "Tradition and Redaction in Romans XII, 9-21" NTS 16 (1969-70) 85f.
HAINZ, J. Ekklesia (Regensburg 1972) 181f., 192f., 335-7. DUNN, J. D. G.
Jesus and the Spirit. A Study of the Religious and Charismatic Experience of
Jesus and the First Christians as Reflected in the New Testament (London
1975) 203f., 263ff. SANDERS, J. T. Ethics in the New Testament. Change and
Development (Philadelphia 1975) 58. SCHMITHALS, W. Der Römerbrief als
historisches Problem (Gütersloh 1975) 184f. STAGG, E. and F. Women in the
World of Jesus (Philadelphia 1978) 165f. BOSCH, J. S. "Le Corps du Christ
et les charismes dans l'épitre aux Romains," Série Monographique de
"Benedictina." Section Biblio-Oecuménique 4 (1979) 51-83. PIPER, J. 'Love
your enemies' (Cambridge 1979) 5, 103. ORTKEMPER, F.-J. Leben aus dem
Glauben (Münster 1980) 41-85, 189f., 239. SCHRAGE, W. "Vielfalt in Gaben
und Aufgaben. Predigt über Römer 12, 3-8" in H. Schröer and G. Müller, ed.,
Vom Amt des Laien in Kirche und Theologie (FS G. Krause; Berlin/New York
1982) 92-100. MALHERBE, A. J. Moral Exhortation. A Greco-Roman

Sourcebook (Philadelphia 1986) 149. BROCKHAUS, U. Charisma und Amt (Wuppertal 1987) passim. DUNN, J. D. G. "Paul's Epistle to the Romans: An Analysis of Structure and Argument" in ANRW II.25.4 (1987) 2876f. SCHMELLER, TH. Paulus und die "Diatribe" (Münster 1987) 424, 426. CRUZ, H. Christological Motives and Motivated Actions in Pauline Paraenesis (Frankfurt/Bern/New York/Paris 1990) 136, 147. LIPS, H. VON, Weisheitliche Traditionen im Neuen Testament (Neukirchen-Vluyn 1990) 385, 401. ROHDE, J. "Charismen und Dienste in der Gemeinde. Von Paulus zu den Pastoralbriefen" in G. K. Schäfer and T. Strohm, eds., Diakonie—biblische Grundlagen und Orientierungen (Heidelberg 1990) 202-21, esp.210-3.

12:3-6   NIEDER, L. Die Motive der Religiös-Sittlichen Paränese in den Paulinischen Gemeinde-Briefen (1956) 91-93, 78. KÄSEMANN, E. Exegetische Versuche und Besinnungen (1964) II 207. PAGELS, E. H. The Gnostic Paul. Gnostic Exegesis of the Pauline Letters (Philadelphia 1975) 43.

12:3-5   KÄSEMANN, E. New Testament Questions of Today (1969) 192. FORELL, G. W. The Christian Lifestyle. Reflections on Romans 12-15 (Philadelphia 1975) 8-11.

12:3-4   BRAUMANN, G. Vorpaulinische christliche Taufverkündigung bei Paulus (1962) 33, 74.

12:3   SCHRAGE, W. Die konkreten Einzelgebote in der paulinischen Paränese (1961) 105f., 113, 119, 164, 167, 175. CRANFIELD, C. E. B. "Μέτρον πίστεως in Romans XII.3" NTS 8 (1961-62) 345f. BIRDSALL, J. N. "EMERISEN in Rom. XII, 3" JThSt 14 (1, '63) 103-4. SATAKE, A. "Apostolat und Gnade bei Paulus" NTS 15 (1968/69) 98-99. KÄSEMANN, E. New Testament Questions of Today (1969) 192, 194. BIRDSALL, J. "Belegt die Lesart in Rm 12:3," JThS 14 (1963) 103f. HAINZ, J. Ekklesia (Regensburg 1972) 182, 314-6, 335f. DUNN, J. D. G. Jesus and the Spirit. A Study of the Religious and Charismatic Experience of Jesus and the First Christians as Reflected in the New Testament (London 1975) 203f., 211, 223, 264, 269, 299, 347, 412. MAGASS, W. "Die Paradigmatik einer Paränese am Beispiel von Röm 12, 3: 'er soll nicht höher von sich denken, als er denken darf.' Ein Beitrag zum Häresieverdacht als Terma-Verdacht," LiBi 35 (1975) 1-26. SCHMITHALS, W. Der Römerbrief als historisches Problem (Gütersloh 1975) 166. FRIEDRICH, G. "Das Amt im Neuen Testament" in Auf das Wort kommt es an. Gesammelte Aufsätze (Göttingen 1978) 423f. OLLROG, W.-H. Paulus und seine Mitarbeiter (Neukirchen-Vluyn 1979) 176, 218. ORTKEMPER, F.-J. Leben aus dem Glauben (Münster 1980) 213-7, 248-50. SCHWARZ, H. "Glaubensbekenntnis(se) VII" in TRE 13 (1984) 327. STAAB, K. Pauluskommentare aus der griechischen Kirche (Münster ²1984) 76:29-30 Apoll; 105:18-25, 26-27 Diod; 160:31-38 ThM; 161:1-8 ThM; 403:17-28 Genn; 404:1-4 Genn; 530:1-11, 12-20 Phot. CRANFIELD, C. E. B. "Μέτρον πίστεως in Romans 12.3" in The Bible and Christian Life (Edinburgh 1985) 203-14. BAUMERT, N. Ehelosigkeit und Ehe im Herrn (Würzburg ²1986) 99f., 104, 482. DOBBELER, A. VON, Glaube als Teilhabe (Tübingen 1987) 238f. MARSHALL, P. Enmity in Corinth. Social Conventions in Paul's Relations with the Corinthians (Tübingen 1987) 199, 369. OSTEN-SACKEN, P. VON DER, Evangelium und Tora: Aufsätze zu Paulus (München 1987) 107f. WEDDERBURN, A. J. M. The Reasons for Romans (Edinburgh 1988) 76, 78, 82.

12:4-13:14 MUNRO, W. Authority in Paul and Peter (Cambridge 1983) 62f.
12:4ff.   BONHOEFFER, D. Gesammelte Schriften, Band 5 (München 1972) 250f. EBERTZ, M. N. Das Charisma des Gekreuzigten. Zur Soziologie der Jesus-

bewegung (Tübingen 1987) 17. MacDONALD, M. Y. The Pauline Churches (Cambridge 1988) 74. SANDNES, K. O. "'Legemet og lemmene' hos Paulus. Belyst ved antikke tekster om Philadelphia ('Body and Members' in St. Paul and Antique Texts of Philadelphia)," TsTK 62 (1, 1991) 17-26.

12:4-16   SCHARFENBERG, J. und SEILER, D. in P. Krusche et al., eds., Predigtstudien für das Kirchenjahr 1979/80. Perikopenreihe II/1 (1979) 106-13.

12:4-9   STAAB, K. Pauluskommentare aus der griechischen Kirche (Münster ²1984) 404:5-21 Genn.

12:4-8   FLEW, R. N. Jesus and His Church (1956) 142, 183. SOIRON, T. Die Kirche als der Leib Christi (Düsseldorf 1951) 95ff. STAAB, K. Pauluskommentare aus der griechischen Kirche (Münster ²1984) 223:19-29 Sev; 530:21-531:30 Phot.

12:4-6   HILL, D. New Testament Prophecy (Atlanta 1979) 119. SEGAL, A. F. Paul the Convert (New Haven/London 1990) 251.

12:4-5   BEST, E. One Body in Christ (1955) 84, 105f, 123, 149, 151. WIKENHAUSER, A. Die Christusmystik des Apostels Paulus (1956) 76. MUSSNER, F. Christus das All und die Kirche (1968) 125, 131, 134. GOLDSTEIN, H. Paulinische Gemeinde im Ersten Petrusbrief (Stuttgart 1975) 40. ROLOFF, J. "Amt" in TRE 2 (1978) 519. RUDOLPH, K. Die Gnosis (Göttingen 1978) 320. OLLROG, W.-H. Paulus und seine Mitarbeiter (Neukirchen-Vluyn 1979) 141-4, 146. ORTKEMPER, F.-J. Leben aus dem Glauben (Münster 1980) 47-59. HAHN, F. "Gottesdienst III" in TRE 14 (1985) 38. MERKLEIN, H. Studien zu Jesus und Paulus (Tübingen 1987) 323, 340f., 342n.87. WEDDERBURN, A. J. M. The Reasons for Romans (Edinburgh 1988) 78. CRUZ, H. Christological Motives and Motivated Actions in Pauline Paraenesis (Frankfurt/ Bern/New York/Paris 1990) 138-40. SÖDING, T. "'Ihr aber seid der Leib Christi' (1 Kor 12, 27). Exegetische Beobachtungen an einem zentralen Motiv paulinischer Ekklesiologie," Catholica 45 (2, 1991) 135-62.

12:5   BEST, E. One Body in Christ (1955) 6, 11n, 20, 29, 93, 110, 156, 167. HAINZ, J. Ekklesia (Regensburg 1972) 183f., 190-3, 337f. KRETSCHMAR, G. "Abendmahl" in TRE 1 (1977) 83. SCHMITHALS, W. "Zur Herkunft der gnostischen Elemente in der Sprache des Paulus" in B. Aland et al., eds., Gnosis (FS H. Jonas; Göttingen 1978) 388-90. SCHNELLE, U. Gerechtigkeit und Christusgegenwart (Göttingen 1983) 142f., 145. HÄRING, H. Das Problem des Bösen in der Theologie (Darmstadt 1985) 97.

12:6ff.   SATAKE, A. "Apostolat und Gnade bei Paulus" NTS 15 (1968/69) 101-3. MERKLEIN, H. Das Kirchliche Amt nach dem Epheserbrief (München 1973) 225f., 308, 315. SCHMIDT, K. L. "Das Amt und die Ämter in der Kirche des Neuen Testaments" in G. Sauter, ed., Neues Testament, Judentum, Kirche (München 1981) 201f.

12:6-16   SURKAU, H.W. GPM 10 (1955) 47-51. NAUCK, W. in Herr, tue meine Lippen auf (1966) 110-22. GROO, G. GPM 22 (1967/68) 85-91. (SCHWEIZER, E. GPM 16 (1961/62) 83ff.). SISTI, A. "Carismi e carità," BiblOr 12 (1, 1970) 127-31.

12:6-16b   KIMMEL, K.-H. und KÖKE, H.-H. in E. Lange, ed., Predigtstudien für das Kirchenjahr 1973/74 (1973) 124-30.

12:6-8   SCHRAGE, W. Die konkreten Einzelgebote in der paulinischen Paränese (1961) 136, 142, 185. DELLING, G. Die Taufe im Neuen Testament (1963) 151. KÄSEMANN, E. Exegetische Versuche und Besinnungen (1964) I 124. ROLOFF, J. Apostolat-Verkündigung-Kirche (1965) 127f. CHEVALLIER, M.-A. Esprit de Dieu, Paroles D'Hommes (1966) 146-48, 166-71. KÄSEMANN, E. New Testament Questions of Today (1969) 195. KÜNG, H. Die Kirche (Freiburg 1967) 221f., 225, 446; ET: The Church (London 1967) 182, 184f., 187, 395, 398. HAINZ, J. Ekklesia (Regensburg 1972) 185-7, 191, 337-9, 343f. FORELL, G. W. The Christian Lifestyle. Reflections on Romans 12-15 (Philadelphia 1975) 12-15. RIDDERBOS, H. Paul. An Outline of His Theology (Grand Rapids 1975) 440-58. SCHMITHALS, W. Der Römerbrief als historisches Problem (Gütersloh 1975) 176. MONTAGUE, G. T. The Holy Spirit (New York 1976) 213f. PRAST, F. Presbyter und Evangelium in nachapostolischer Zeit (Stuttgart 1979) 368. ORTKEMPER, F.-J. Leben aus dem Glauben (Münster 1980) 59-85, 185-9. SCHWARZ, R. Bürgerliches Christentum im Neuen Testament (Klosterneuburg 1983) 142. STAAB, K. Pauluskommentare aus der griechischen Kirche (Münster ²1984) 105:28-106:16 Diod. MAL-HERBE, A. J. Moral Exhortation. A Greco-Roman Sourcebook (Philadelphia 1986) 130. SCHATZMANN, S. S. A Pauline Theology of Charismata (Peabody, MA 1987) 19-26, 50f. MacDONALD, M. Y. The Pauline Churches (Cambridge 1988) 57. WEDDERBURN, A. J. M. The Reasons for Romans (Edinburgh 1988) 79-81. SCHWEIZER, E. "Die diakonische Struktur der neutestamentlichen Gemeinde" in G. K. Schäfer and T. Strohm, eds., Diakonie— biblische Grundlagen und Orientierungen (Heidelberg 1990) 159-85, esp.168f. SCIPPA, V. "I carismi per la vitalità della Chiesa. Studio esegetico su 1 Cor 12-14; Rm 12, 6-8; Ef 4, 11-13; 1 Pt 4, 10-11," Asprenas [Naples] 38 (1991) 5-25.

12:6   BRUNNER, E. Dogmatik II (1950) 31. BEST, E. One Body in Christ (1955) 163. KÄSEMANN, E. Exegetische Versuche und Besinnungen (1964) I 114, 120. HAINZ, J. Ekklesia (Regensburg 1972) 184, 192-4, 337f. DUNN, J. D. G. Jesus and the Spirit. A Study of the Religious and Charismatic Experience of Jesus and the First Christians as Reflected in the New Testament (London 1975) 203, 208, 211f., 227-33, 254f., 280f., 283, 412. ELLIS, E. E. Prophecy and Hermeneutic in Early Christianity (Tübingen 1978) 24f., 47, 214. TRACK, J. "Analogie" in TRE 2 (1978) 633. HILL, D. New Testament Prophecy (Atlanta 1979) 127, 130. OLLROG, W.-H. Paulus und seine Mitarbeiter (Neukirchen-Vluyn 1979) 85, 176. ORTKEMPER, F.-J. Leben aus dem Glauben (Münster 1980) 60f. STAAB, K. Pauluskommentare aus der griechischen Kirche (Münster ²1984) 76:31-77:12 Apoll; 161:9-13 ThM. BLOCHER, H. "L'analogie de la foi dans l'étude de l'Ecriture Sainte," Hokhma 36 (1987) 1-20. BORING, M. E. The Continuing Voice of Jesus (Louisville 1991) 42, 93, 96, 103, 106, 150.

12:6a   BROCKHAUS, U. Charisma und Amt. Die paulinische Charismenlehre auf dem Hintergrund der frühchristlichen Gemeindefunktionen (Wuppertal ²1975) 129, 200ff.

12:7-8   STUIBER, A. "Ambrosiaster" in TRE 2 (1978) 360.

12:7   DELLING, G. Die Taufe im Neuen Testament (1963) 79. DUNN, J. D. G. Jesus and the Spirit. A Study of the Religious and Charismatic Experience of Jesus and the First Christians as Reflected in the New Testament (London 1975) 236ff., 249f., 283, 285f. ZIMMERMANN, A. F. Die urchristlichen Lehrer (Tübingen 1984) 60, 64, 110, 217.

12:8.13   HAUSCHILD, W.-D. "Armenfürsorge" in TRE 4 (1979) 17.

12:8-9   STAAB, K. Pauluskommentare aus der griechischen Kirche (Münster ²1984) 77:13-78:4 Apoll.

12:8   BOUSSET, W. Die Religion des Judentums im Späthellenistischen Zeitalter (1966=1926) 419. KÄSEMANN, E. Exegetische Versuche und Besinnungen (1964) I 114. HAINZ, J. Ekklesia (Regensburg 1972) 38-40. LAUB, F. Eschatologische Verkündigung und Lebensgestaltung nach Paulus (Regensburg 1973)

72, 87f. MERKLEIN, H. Das Kirchliche Amt nach dem Epheserbrief (München 1973) 312, 323-7, 363. DUNN, J. D. G. Jesus and the Spirit. A Study of the Religious and Charismatic Experience of Jesus and the First Christians as Reflected in the New Testament (London 1975) 229, 250ff., 289. HILL, D. New Testament Prophecy (Atlanta 1979) 128. PRAST, F. Presbyter und Evangelium in nachapostolischer Zeit (Stuttgart 1979) 336. KAMLAH, E. "Barmherzigkeit" in TRE 5 (1980) 225. ORTKEMPER, F.-J. Leben aus dem Glauben (Münster 1980) 211-3. STAAB, K. Pauluskommentare aus der griechischen Kirche (Münster ²1984) 161:14-21 ThM; 531:31-532:3 Phot. MacDON-ALD, M. Y. The Pauline Churches (Cambridge 1988) 58. WEDDERBURN, A. J. M. The Reasons for Romans (Edinburgh 1988) 80f., 88. KLAUCK, H.-J. Gemeinde, Amt, Sakrament (Würzburg 1989) 50f., 223, 226f., 234.

12:9-13:10   SANDERS, J. T. Ethics in the New Testament. Change and Development (Philadelphia 1975) 58-62.

12:9ff.   KÄSEMANN, E. New Testament Questions of Today (1969) 194, 195. SCHULZ, S. "Neutestamentliche Ethik (Zürich 1987) 153ff. WEDDERBURN, A. J. M. The Reasons for Romans (Edinburgh 1988) 84. LIPS, H. VON, Weisheitliche Traditionen im Neuen Testament (Neukirchen-Vluyn 1990) 380ff., 394ff., 401ff.

12:9-21   DAVIES, W.D. Paul and Rabbinic Judaism (1955) 130, 138, 202, 327. TALBERT, C. H. "Tradition and Redation in Romans xii 9-21" NTS 16 (1, '69) 83-94. GOLLWITZER, H. Veränderung im Diesseits (München 1973) 130. ROON, A. VAN, The Authenticity of Ephesians (Leiden 1974) 152f., 156ff. PIPER, J. 'Love your enemies' (Cambridge 1979) 5, 8, 103, 176n.1, 212n.21. ORTKEMPER, F.-J. Leben aus dem Glauben (Münster 1980) 85-125. HAINZ, J. Koinonia (Regensburg 1982) 115f. KANJUPARAMBIL, P. "Imperatival Participles in Rom 12:9-21," JBL 102 (2, 1983) 285-8. DUNN, J. D. G. "Paul's Epistle to the Romans: An Analysis of Structure and Argument" in ANRW II.25.4 (1987) 2877. BLACK, D. A. "The Pauline Love Command. Structure, Style, and Ethics in Romans 12:9-21," Filol Neot 2 (1989) 3-22. LIMBECK, M. Mit Paulus Christ sein. Sachbuch zur Person und Theologie des Apostels Paulus (Stuttgart 1989) 119f. WALTER, N. "Paul and the Early Christian Jesus-Tradition" in A. J. M. Wedderburn, ed., Paul and Jesus. Collected Essays (Sheffield 1989) 51-80, esp.56. PAFFENROTH, K. "Romans 12:9-21—A Brief Summary of the Problems of Translation and Interpretation," IrBS 14 (1992) 89-99.

12:9-16   GEENSE, A. in GPM 34 (1979) 83-9. WEDDERBURN, A. J. M. The Reasons for Romans (Edinburgh 1988) 81f.

12:9-13   FORELL, G. W. The Christian Lifestyle. Reflections on Romans 12-15 (Philadelphia 1975) 16-9. PIPER, J. 'Love your enemies' (Cambridge 1979) 8, 132, 211n.13. MUNRO, W. Authority in Paul and Peter (Cambridge 1983) 59-61. SCHÄFER, K. Gemeinde als "Bruderschaft" (Frankfurt/Bern/New York/Paris 1989) 163-74.

12:9-10   STAAB, K. Pauluskommentare aus der griechischen Kirche (Münster ²1984) 532:4-12 Phot.

12:9   SCHRAGE, W. Die konkreten Einzelgebote in der paulinischen Paränese (1961) 195, 232, 251, 262, 267. BRAUN, H. Qumran und NT II (1966) 290, 298. KÄSEMANN, E. New Testament Questions of Today (1969) 189. METZGER, B. M. The Early Versions of the New Testament. Their Origin Transmission, and Limitations (Oxford 1977) 173. PIPER, J. 'Love your enemies' (Cambridge 1979) 11, 15, 34, 104f., 129f., 180n.24, 188 n.109, 212nn.16, 21. ORTKEM-

PER, F.-J. Leben aus dem Glauben (Münster 1980) 85-7. STAAB, K. Pauluskommentare aus der griechischen Kirche (Münster ²1984) 404:22-25 Genn.

12:10-20   SANDERS, J. T. Ethics in the New Testament. Change and Development
            (Philadelphia 1975) 58f.

12:10-13   ORTKEMPER, F.-J. Leben aus dem Glauben (Münster 1980) 88-101.

12:10   SCHRAGE, W. Die konkreten Einzelgebote in der paulinischen Paränese (1961)
            40, 252. SPICQ, C. "φιλόστοργος (A Propos de Rom. XII, 10)" RB 4 ('55)
            497-510. KÄSEMANN, E. Exegetische Versuche und Besinnungen (1964) I
            121. ORTKEMPER, F.-J. Leben aus dem Glauben (Münster 1980) 213-7, 248-
            50. MOHRLANG, R. Matthew and Paul (Cambridge 1984) 103-5. STAAB, K.
            Pauluskommentare aus der griechischen Kirche (Münster ²1984) 161:22-30
            ThM; 404:26-28 Genn. SEGAL, A. F. Paul the Convert (New Haven/London
            1990) 251.

12:11-14   SCHMITHALS, W. "Zur Herkunft der gnostischen Elemente in der Sprache des
            Paulus" in B. Aland et al., eds., Gnosis (FS H. Jonas; Göttingen 1978) 390-3.

12:11-12   STAAB, K. Pauluskommentare aus der griechischen Kirche (Münster ²1984)
            405:1-6 Genn.

12:11   DELLING, G. Die Taufe im Neuen Testament (1963) 68. KÄSEMANNE, E.
            Exegetische Versuche und Besinnungen (1964) I 164. PALLIS, A. Notes on
            St.John and the Apocalypse (London 1928) 54. BONHOEFFER, D. Gesammelte
            Schriften, Band 5 (München 1972) 463ff. HAINZ, J. Ekklesia (Regensburg
            1972) 327f. METZGER, B. M. "St.Jerome's explicit references to variant
            readings in manuscripts of the New Testament" in E. Best and R. McL. Wilson,
            eds., Text and Interpretation. Studies in the New Testament presented to
            Matthew Black (Cambridge 1979) 184. KRAUSE, G. "Bonhoeffer" in TRE 7
            (1981) 57. STAAB, K. Pauluskommentare aus der griechischen Kirche (Münster
            ²1984) 658:21-24 Areth.

12:12-14   WILES, G. P. Paul's Intercessory Prayers (London 1974) 44, 95, 166, 265, 289.

12:12   JÜNGEL, E. Paulus und Jesus (1966) 69. ROBINSON, J. A. Pelagius's
            Exposition of Thirteen Epistles of St. Paul (Cambridge 1922) 128, 143, 261.
            WILES, G. P. Paul's Intercessory Prayers (London 1974) 19, 80, 168, 181f.,
            192f. ORTKEMPER, F.-J. Leben aus dem Glauben (Münster 1980) 200-8.
            DENTON, D. R. "Hope and Perseverance," SouJTh 34 (1981) 313-20. NEBE,
            G. 'Hoffnung' bei Paulus (Göttingen 1983) 19, 23, 35f., 64f., 70, 73f. TOIT, A.
            B. DU, "Freude" in TRE 11 (1983) 585f. BLOTH, P. C. "Gebet" in TRE 12
            (1984) 97. WEDER, H. "Hoffnung II" in TRE 15 (1986) 486.

12:13-21   SCHNACKENBURG, R. Die sittliche Botschaft des Neuen Testaments, Band
            1 (Freiburg/Basel/Wien 1986) 215.

12:13-14   SCHRAGE, W. Die konkreten Einzelgebote in der paulinischen Paränese (1961)
            142, 263, 243, 252. STAAB, K. Pauluskommentare aus der griechischen Kirche
            (Münster ²1984) 405:7-11 Genn.

12:13   BRAUMANN, G. Vorpaulinische christliche Taufverkündigung bei Paulus
            (1962) 15, 26ff. HOOGT, M. J. VAN DE, "Wat zegt de Schrift van de
            verzorging der hulpbehoevenden?" GThT 1 (1900) 138-41, 150f., 170-85.
            ORTKEMPER, F.-J. Leben aus dem Glauben (Münster 1980) 208-10, 247.
            HAINZ, J. Koinonia (Regensburg 1982) 62, 77, 115f., 164, 168, 180, 187.
            STAAB, K. Pauluskommentare aus der griechischen Kirche (Münster ²1984)
            106:17-22 Diod; 162:1-4 ThM; 532:13-17 Phot. SEGAL, A. F. Paul the Convert
            (New Haven/London 1990) 251.

12:14-14:23 MOISER, J. "Rethinking Romans 12-15," NTS 36 (1990) 571-82, esp.575-9.

12:14-13:8   ELLER, V. "Romans 13 (Actually Romans 12:14-13:8) Reexamined," TSF Bulletin [Madison, WI] 10 (3, 1987) 7-10.

12:14ff.   Eschatologie und Jenseitserwartung im hellenistischen Diasporajudentum (Berlin 1978) 39.

12:14-21   LIPPERT, P. Leben als Zeugnis (1968) 11, 83, 98, 127, 170, 172. FORELL, G. W. The Christian Lifestyle. Reflections on Romans 12-15 (Philadelphia 1975) 10-23. PIPER, J. 'Love your enemies' (Cambridge 1979) 14f., 179n.23, 211n.13. RIEKKINEN, V. Römer 13 (Helsinki 1980) 44ff., 107. BRAATEN, C. E. "Romans 12:14-21," Interp 38 (1984) 291-5. MARSHALL, P. Enmity in Corinth. Social Conventions in Paul's Relations with the Corinthians (Tübingen 1987) 151. WALTER, N. "Paul and the Early Christian Jesus-Tradition" in A. J. M. Wedderburn, ed., Paul and Jesus. Collected Essays (Sheffield 1989) 51-80, esp.68.

12:14-17   PIPER, J. 'Love your enemies' (Cambridge 1979) 16.

12:14-16   LOHFINK, G. Studien zum Neuen Testament (Stuttgart 1989) 14.

12:14   DAVIES, W. D. The Sermon on the Mount (Cambridge 1966) 97. WESTER-MANN, C. Blessing in the Bible and the Life of the Church (Philadelphia 1978) 91-3, 98-101. PIPER, J. 'Love your enemies' (Cambridge 1979) 4-7, 15-7, 25, 41, 57, 63, 102-4, 114, 116-8, 121, 129, 132, 171f., 190nn.123, 126, 195n.174, 215n.47. ORTKEMPER, F.-J. Leben aus dem Glauben (Münster 1980) 101-3, 217-25. MÜLLER, U. B. "Zur Rezeption Gesetzeskritischer Jesusüberlieferung im frühen Christentum," NTS 27 (1981) 158. WENHAM, D. "Paul's Use of the Jesus Tradition. Three Samples" in D. Wenham, ed., Gospel Perspectives. The Jesus Tradition Outside the Gospels, Vol 5 (Sheffield 1984) 15-17.

12:15-16   PIPER, J. 'Love your enemies' (Cambridge 1979) 132, 211n.13. ORTKEMPER, F.-J. Leben aus dem Glauben (Münster 1980) 103-6. STAAB, K. Pauluskommentare aus der griechischen Kirche (Münster ²1984) 405:12-21 Genn.

12:15   BONHOEFFER, A. Epiktet und das Neue Testament (1911) 302, 331. BOUSSET, W. Die Religion des Judentums (1966 =1926) 417. GERSTEN-BERGER, G. und SCHRAGE, W. Leiden (Stuttgart 1977) 222; ET: J. E. Steely (trans.) Suffering (Nashville 1980) 256. FRIEDRICH, G. "Der Brief eines Gefangenen. Bemerkungen zum Philipperbrief" in Auf das Wort kommt es an. Gesammelte Aufsätze (Göttingen 1978) 234. MERKEL, F. "Bestattung" in TRE 5 (1980) 749. BEWRATH, G. A. "Busse" in TRE 7 (1981) 454. MAR-QUARDT, F.-W. Die Juden und ihr Land (Gütersloh ³1986) 80.

12:16-13:8a   KRUIJF, T. C. DE "The Literary Unity of Rom 12, 16-13, 8a. A Network of Inclusions," Bijdr. 48 (3, 1987) 319-26.

12:16-17   STAAB, K. Pauluskommentare aus der griechischen Kirche (Münster ²1984) 162:5-11 ThM.

12:16   SCHRAGE, W. Die konkret en Einzelgebote in der paulinischen Paränese (1961) 121, 195f, 233. PIPER, J. 'Love your enemies' (Cambridge 1979) 8, 13, 15f., 24, 211n.13. ORTKEMPER, F.-J. Leben aus dem Glauben (Münster 1980) 213-7, 248-50. MÜHLEN, K. H. ZUR, "Demut" in TRE 8 (1981) 475, 477. STAAB, K. Pauluskommentare aus der griechischen Kirche (Münster ²1984) 659:1 Areth. WENGST, K. " ' . . . einander durch Demut für vorzüglicher halten. . . . ' Zum Begriff 'Demut' bei Paulus und in paulinischer Tradition" in W. Schrage, ed., Studien zum Text und zur Ethik des Neuen Testaments (Berlin/New York 1986) 432. WEDDERBURN, A. J. M. The Reasons for Romans (Edinburgh 1988) 76, 78, 81. SEGAL, A. F. Paul the Convert (New Haven/London 1990) 251.

12:16c-21	HAAR, GPM 16 (1961/62) 87ff. NAUCK, W. in Herr, tue mei ne Lippen auf II ed. G. Eichholz (1966) 123-42. SOUCEK, J. GPM 22 (1967/68) 91-96. ADAM, I. und H.-M. in E. Lange, ed., Predigtstudien für das Kirchenjahr 1973/74 (1973) 131-7. KRUSE, M. in GPM 28 (1, 1973) 102-8.
12:17-13:7	BINDEMANN, W. Die Hoffnung der Schöpfung (Neukirchen 1983) 110-3.
12:17ff.	SCHLIER, H. "Der Friede nach dem Apostel Paulus" in V. Kubina und K. Lehmann, eds., Der Geist und die Kirche (FS H. Schlier; Freiburg/ Basel/Wien 1980) 131-3.
12:17-21	DOERNE, M. Die alten Episteln (1967) 52-56. WEBER, O. Predigtmeditationen (1967) 155-58. PIPER, J. 'Love your enemies' (Cambridge 1979) 16f., 102f., 132, 211n.13. ORTKEMPER, F.-J. Leben aus dem Glauben (Münster 1980) 106-25, 217-25. LAUFF, W. in GPM 38 (1983/84) 294-302. KLEINKNECHT, K. T. Der leidende Gerechtfertigte (Tübingen 1984) 230, 235. MALHERBE, A. J. Moral Exhortation. A Greco-Roman Sourcebook (Philadelphia 1986) 157. DOWNING, F. G. Christ and the Cynics (Sheffield 1988) 188. WEDDER-BURN, A. J. M. The Reasons for Romans (Edinburgh 1988) 82f. LIPS, H. VON, Weisheitliche Traditionen im Neuen Testament (Neukirchen-Vluyn 1990) 387ff., 404ff.
12:17-20	PIPER, J. 'Love your enemies' (Cambridge 1979) 4, 111f., 114, 171. WEN-HAM, D. "Paul's Use of the Jesus Tradition. Three Samples" in D. Wenham, ed., Gospel Perspectives. The Jesus Tradition Outside the Gospels, Vol 5 (Sheffield 1984) 17-23.
12:17-19	ORTKEMPER, F.-J. Leben aus dem Glauben (Münster 1980) 112-9.
12:17-18	SEGAL, A. F. Paul the Convert (New Haven/London 1990) 251.
12:17	SCHRAGE, W. Die konkreten Einzelgebote in der paulinischen Paränese (1961) 195, 232f., 243, 252, 267. BURCHARD, C. Untersuchungen zu Joseph und Aseneth (Tübingen 1965) 102, 150. DAVIES, W. D. The Sermon on the Mount (Cambridge 1966) 97. PIPER, J. 'Love your enemies' (Cambridge 1979) 5-9, 11, 13-7, 27, 34, 38f., 49, 53, 57, 64, 112f., 132, 178n.7, 178n.8, 182n.20, 184n.46, 212n.16. SÄNGER, D. Antikes Judentum und die Mysterien (Tübingen 1980) 203. MÜLLER, U. B. "Zur Rezeption Gesetzeskritischer Jesusüberlieferung im frühen Christentum," NTS 27 (1981) 158. STAAB, K. Pauluskommentare aus der griechischen Kirche (Münster ²1984) 405:21-406:3 Genn. VERHEY, A. The Great Reversal (Grand Rapids 1984) 66f. HÄRING, H. Das Problem des Bösen in der Theologie (Darmstadt 1985) 32. KOCH, D.-A. Die Schrift als Zeuge des Evangeliums (Tübingen 1986) 18. WEDDERBURN, A. J. M. The Reasons for Romans (Edinburgh 1988) 76f.
12:17b	PIPER, J. 'Love your enemies' (Cambridge 1979) 13, 15, 27, 112, 114, 179n.23. PIPER, J. 'Love your enemies' (Cambridge 1979) 7, 9, 13, 15, 17, 64, 112, 180nn.24, 26. STAAB, K. Pauluskommentare aus der griechischen Kirche (Münster ²1984) 106:23-5 Diod; 406:4-7 Genn.
12:18-21	LOHFINK, G. Jesus and Community. The Social Dimension of the Christian Faith (Philadelphia 1984) 112f.
12:19-21	NIEDER, L. Die Motive der Religiös-Sittlichen Paränese in den Paulinischen Gemeindle-Briefen (1956) 70-71. STENDAHL, K. "Hate, Non-Retaliation, and Love. 1 QS x, 17-20 and Rom. 12:19-21" HThR 55 (4, '62) 343-55. STEN-DHAL, I. "Hate, Nonretaliation, and Love. Coals of Fire" in Meanings (Philadelphia 1984) 137-49. BERGER, K. und COLPE, C., eds., Religionsgeschichtliches Textbuch zum Neuen Testament (Göttingen/Zürich 1987) 223. DUN-GAN, D. L. "Jesus and Violence" in E. P. Sanders, ed., Jesus, the Gospels, and the Church (Macon GA 1987) 143.

12:19-20   ELLIS, E.E. Paul's Use of the Old Testament (1957) 14f., 107f., 170, 187.
            BURCHARD, C. Untersuchungen zu Joseph and Aseneth (Tübingen 1965) 102.
            PIPER, J. 'Love your enemies' (Cambridge 1979) 15, 114, 116, 118, 127.
            DEIDUN, T. J. New Covenant Morality in Paul (Rome 1981) 158f.
12:19   HENNECKE, E./SCHNEEMELCHER, W. Neutestamentlche Apokryphen
            (1964) I 341. BRAUN, H. Qumran und NT II (1966) 290, 298. KÖLISCHEN,
            J.-C. VON, "Die Zitate aus dem Moselied Deut 32 im Römerbrief des Paulus,"
            ThViat 5 (1975) 53-69. ELLIS, E. E. Prophecy and Hermeneutic in Early
            Christianity (Tübingen 1978) 137, 174, 178, 180, 182f., 225. AONO, T. Die
            Entwicklung des paulinischen Gerichtsgedankens bei den Apostolischen Vätern
            (Bern/Frankfurt/Las Vegas 1979) 4ff. HILL, D. New Testament Prophecy
            (Atlanta 1979) 170. PIPER, J. 'Love your enemies' (Cambridge 1979) 6, 8, 34,
            36, 46, 59, 62, 112f., 115, 117, 194nn.172f. STAAB, K. Pauluskommentare aus
            der griechischen Kirche (Münster ²1984) 106:26-107:3 Diod; 406:8-11 Genn;
            532:18-29 Phot. HÄRING, H. Das Problem des Bösen in der Theologie
            (Darmstadt 1985) 20. KOCH, D.-A. Die Schrift als Zeuge des Evangeliums
            (Tübingen 1986) 17f.
12:19b   PIPER, J. 'Love your enemies' (Cambridge 1979) 27, 112, 115.
12:20-21   SCHRAGE, W. Die konkreten Einzelgebote in der paulinischen Paränese (1961)
            45, 53, 195, 232, 233, 234, 252, 267. KÄSEMANN, E. Exegetische Versuche
            und Besinnungen (1964) II 207. New Testament Questions of Today (1969)
            199. ORTKEMPER, F.-J. Leben aus dem Glauben (Münster 1980) 119-24.
            STAAB, K. Pauluskommentare aus der griechischen Kirche (Münster ²1984)
            107:4-15 Diod; 406:12-32 Genn; 533:1-4 Phot.
12:20   MORENZ, S. "Feurige Kohlen auf dem Haupt" ThLZ 78 ('53) 187-92.
            DAHOOD, M.J. "Two Pauline Quotations from the Old Testament" CBQ
            XVII/1 (1955) 19-24. VATTIONO, F. "Rom 12:20 E Prov. 25, 21-22"
            Studiorum Paulinorum Congressus Internationalis Catholicus 1961 (1963) I 341-
            45. KLASSEN, W. Coals of Fire: Sign of Repentance or Revenge? NTS 9
            (1962/63) 337f. GALE, H.M. The Use of Analogy in the Letters of Paul (1964)
            251f. RICHARDS, J.R. "Romans and I Corinthians: Their Chronological
            Relationship and Comparative Dates" NTS 13 (1966/67) 17ff. RAMARDSON,
            L. "'Charbons ardents': 'sur la tête' ou 'Pour le feu'? (Pr 25, 22a—Rm 12,
            20b)" Biblica 51 (2, '70) 230-34. BARTINA, S. "Carbones encendidos, sobre
            la cabeza o sobre el veneno? (Prov 25, 21-22; Rom 12, 20)," EstBi 31 (2, 1972)
            201f. PIPER, J. 'Love your enemies' (Cambridge 1979) 27, 30, 34, 61, 112,
            114-8, 129, 132, 194 n.173, 215n.52. KOCH, D.-A. Die Schrift als Zeuge des
            Evangeliums (Tübingen 1986) 14, 270f.
12:21   PIPER, J. 'Love your enemies' (Cambridge 1979) 15, 212n.16, 224n.38.
            HYGEN, J. B. "Böse" in TRE 7 (1981) 15. MÜLLER, U. B. "Zur Rezeption
            Gesetzeskritischer Jesusüberlieferung im frühen Christentum," NTS 27 (1981)
            158. HÄRING, H. Das Problem des Bösen in der Theologie (Darmstadt 1985)
            32, 165. MALHERBE, A. J. Moral Exhortation. A Greco-Roman Sourcebook
            (Philadelphia 1986) 93.

13-15   WEDDERBURN, A. J. M. The Reasons for Romans (Edinburgh 1988) 59-65.
13-14   FRIEDRICH, G. "Die Bedeutung der Auferweckung Jesu nach Aussagen des
            Neuen Testaments" in Auf das Wort kommt es an. Gesammelte Aufsätze
            (Göttingen 1978) 360, 362, 371.
13   KOCH-MEHRLIN, J. "Die Stellung des Christen zum Staat nach Röm. 13 und
            Apok. 13" EvTh 1948, 378-401. CAMPENHAUSEN, V. H. "Zur Auslegung

von Röm- 13: Die dämonistische Deutung des Ἐξουσία-Begriffs" in Festschrift A. Bertholet. ed. W. Baumgärtner, O. Eissfeldt, K. Elliger, L. Rost (1950) 97-113. REICKE, B. Diakonie, Festfreude und Zelos (1951) 296f. GOPPELT, L. "Der Staat in der Sicht des Neuen Testaments" in Macht und Recht (1956) 9-21, 13ff. STROBEL, A. "Zum Verständnis von Rm 13" ZNW 47 ('56) 67-93. MEINHOLD, P. Römer 13. Obrigkeit—Widerstand—Revolution—Krieg (1960). MORRISON, C. The Powers that be (1960) 25ff., 104ff., 107-9. SCHRAGE, W. Die konkreten Einzelgebote in der paulinischen Paränese (1961) 18f, 20. WOLF, E. "Politischer Gottesdienst" Ecclesia und Res Publica, Festschrift K. Dietrich (1961) 51-63. BOELD, W. Obrigkeit von Gott? Studien zum staatstheologischen Aspekt des Neuen Testaments (1962). DIBELIUS, O. Obrigkeit (1963). HILLERDAL, G. "Römer 13 und Luthers Lehre von den zwei Regimenten" LR 13 (1, '63) 17-34. KÄSEMANN, E. Exegetische Versuche und Besinnungen (1964) II 204ff. BAUER, W. "Jedermann sei untertan der Obrigkeit (Auslegungsgeschichte des Neuen Testaments)" in Aufsätze und Kleine Schriften, ed. G. Strecker (1967) 263-84. MERK, O. Handeln aus Glauben (1968) 157, 164, 166f., 234, 236. KÄSEMANN, E. New Testament Questions of Today (1969) 206, 207, 216. MOLNAR, A. "Romains 13 dans l'interprétation de la première Réforme" EThR 46 (3, '71) 231-40. LÖVESTAM, E. Spiritual Wakefulness in the New Testament (Lund 1963) 50f. BORG, M. "A New Context for Romans xiii," NTS 19 (2, 1973) 205-18. CONZELMANN, H. and LINDENMANN, A. Arbeitsbuch zum Neuen Testament (Tübingen 1975) 419. FRIEDRICH, G. "Das Problem der Autorität im Neuen Testament" in Auf das Wort kommt es an. Gesammelte Aufsätze (Göttingen 1978) 405, 407-10. MARTIN, R. P. New Testament Foundations II: Acts—Revelation (Exeter 1978) 308f. PIPER, J. 'Love your enemies' (Cambridge 1979) 103, 211n.14, 212n.15, 214n.39. ROBINSON, J. A. T. Wrestling with Romans (London 1979) 135-140. RIEKKINEN, V. Römer 13. Aufzeichnung und Weiterführung der exegetischen Diskussion (Helsinki 1980). PETERS, A. "Elert" in TRE 9 (1982) 497. ASENDORF, U. "Eschatologie" in TRE 10 (1982) 316. BAMMEL, E. "Romans 13" in E. Bammel and C. F. D. Moule, eds., Jesus and the Politics of His Day (Cambridge 1984) 365-83. POHLE, L. Die Christen und der Staat nach Römer 13 (Mainz 1984) MALHERBE, A. J. Moral Exhortation. A Greco-Roman Sourcebook (Philadelphia 1986) 125. NÜRNBERGER, K. "Theses on Romans 13," Scriptura 22 (1987) 40-7. LAMPE, P. Die stadtrömischen Christen in den ersten beiden Jahrhunderten (Tübingen ²1989) 54, 178.

13:1ff.　　BONHOEFFER, D. Nachfolge (1950) 182ff. BRUNNER, E. Dogmatik I (1946) 248, II (1950) 373. REICKE, B. Diakonie, Festfreude und Zelos (1951) 357f. WEITHAAS, A. "Kirche und Staat in paulinischer Sicht" ThuG 45 ('55) 433-41. CULLMANN, O. The State in the New Testament (1956) 56ff. SCHMIDT, L. "Unser Staat" in Kleine Predigt-Typologie III, ed. L. Schmidt (1965) 57ff. MERK, O. Handeln aus Glauben (1968) 94, 103, 164, 196-198, 222f, 228, 231. MAU, R. "Gesetz V" in TRE 13 (1984) 85. SCHULZ, S. "Neutestamentliche Ethik (Zürich 1987) 173f., 392, 402ff. BECKER, J. Paulus. Der Apostel der Völker (Tübingen 1989) 405, 462, 464.

13:1-10　　BEATRICE, P. F. "Il giudizio secondo le opere della legge e l'amore compimento della legge. Contributo all'esegesi di Rm 13, 1-10," StPa 20 (1973) 491-545. THISELTON, A. C. The Two Horizons (Grand Rapids 1980) 391.

13:1-8　　DEHN, G GPM 7 (1953) 180-85. DUESBERG, H. "La soumission aux autorités (Romains 13, 1-8)" BVieC 73 ('67) 15-26. JOSUTTIS, M. GPM 24 (1969/70) 425-31.

13:1-7   SCHELKLE, K.H. "Staat und Kirche in der patristischen Auslegung von Rm 13, 1-7" ZNW 44 (1952/53) 223-36. CULLMANN, O. "Zur neuesten Diskussion über die ἐξουσίαι in Röm 13, 1" ThZ 10 (1954) 321-36. SCHWEITZER, A. Die Mystik des Apostels Paulus (1954) 72, 171, 295, 306. DAVIES, W.D. Paul and Rabbinic Judaism (1955) 138, 141, 328. KUSS, O. "Paulus über die staatliche Gewalt" ThuG 45 (1955) 321-34. MICHEL, O. "Die göttliche Setzung der staatlichen Gewalt" Der Brief an die Römer (1955) 283f.; "Zur Eigenart der Tradition Röm. 13:1-7" 281f. AFFELDT, W. Die Auslegung von Röm. 13:1-7 bei Karl Barth" Antword, Festschrift K. Barth (1956) 114-23. NIEDER, L. Die Motive der Religiös-Sittlichen Paränese in den Paulinisden Gemeindel-Briefen (1956) 93-96. KÄSEMANN, E. "Römer 13, 1-7 in unserer Generation" ZThK 56 (3, '59) 316-76. CRANFIELD, C. E. B. "Some Observations on Romans xiii.1-7" NTS 6 (3, '60) 241-49. KÄHLER, E. Die Frau in Den Paulinischen Briefen (1960) 172-83. MORRISON, C. D. The Powers That Be. Earthly Rulers and Demonic Powers in Romand 13:1-7 (1960). BARNIKOL, E. Römer 13- Der nichtpaulinsche Ursprung der absoluten Obigkeitsbejahung von Römer 13, 1-7" Studien zum Neuen Testament und zur Patristik (Festschrift f. E. Klostermann 1961) 65-135. SCHRAGE, W. Die konkreten Einzelgebote in der paulinischen Paränese (1961) 112, 126, 128, 222-26, 243, 261, 263f. DELLING, G. Römer 13, 1-7 innerhalb der Briefe des Neuen Testaments (1962) passim. NEUGEBAUER, F. "Zur Auslegung von Röm. 13, 1-7" KUD 8 (3, '62) 151-72. KOSNETTER, J. "Röm. 13, 1-7: zeitbedingte Vorsichtsmassregel oder grundsätzliche Einstellung?" Studiorum Paulinorum Congressus Internationalis Catholicus 1961 (1963) I 347-55. KUSS, O. "Paulus über die staatliche Gewalt" Auslegung und Verkündigung I (1963) 246-59. STECK, GPM 18 (1963/64) 370ff. KALLAS, J. "Romans XIII 1-7: An Interpolation" NTS 11 (1964/65) 365f. ZSIFKOVITS, V. Der Staatsgedanke nach Paulus in Rom. 13:1-7 (1964). SCHELKLE, K. "Staat und Kirche in der patristischen Auslegung von Rom 13:1-7" Wort und Schrift (1966) 227-38. WALKER, R. Studie zu Römer 13, 1-7 (1966). BULNES ALDUNATE, J. "The Three Submissions und Continual Renewal" Concilium 39 ('68) 45-68. GOPPELT, L. Christologie und Ethik (1968) 127f., 196ff., 204f., 208f. DENIEL, R. "Omnis potestas a Deo. L'origine du pouvoir civil et sa relation à l'Eglise" RechSR 56 (1, '68) 43-85. MERK, O. Handeln aus Glauben (1968) 161-65, 167, 243f. AFFELDT, W. Die weltliche Gewalt in der Paulus-Exegese. Röm. 13, 1-7 in den Römerbriefkommentaren der lateinischen Kirche bis zum Ende des 13.Jahrhunderts (1969). BLANK, J. Schriftauslegung in Theorie und Praxis (1969) 174-80. KÄSEMANN, E. New Testament Questions of Today (1969) 212. KÄSEMANN, E. "Principles of the Interpretation of Romans 13": New Testament Questions of Today (1969) 196-216. DERRETT, J.D.M. Law in the New Testament (1970) 320n.1, 337n3. HUTCHINSON, S. "The Political Implications of Romans 13:1-7" BTh 21 (3, '71) 49-59. NEUFELDT, K.H. "Das Gewissen. Ein Deutungsversuch im Anschluss an Röm 13, 1-7" BuL 12 (1, '71) 32-45. RINIKER, H. "Römer 13 zwischen Militärjustiz und Theologiestudenten" KirchRefSchweiz 127 (10, '71) 146-52. KEIENBURG, F. Die Geschichte der Auslegung von Römer 13:1-7 (Gelsenkirchen 1952) BERGMEIER, R. "Loyalität als Gegenstand Paulinischer Paraklese. Eine religionsgeschichtliche Untersuchung zu Röm 13, 1ff und Jos. B.J. 2, 140," Theok 1/1967-1969 (1970) 51-63. KUSS, O. Paulus (Regensburg 1971) 426-8. ABINENO, J. L. C. "The State, According to Romans Thirteen," SEAJTh 14 (1972) 23-7. GOLDSTEIN, H. "Die politischen Paränesen in 1 Petr 2 und Röm 13," BiLe

14 (2, 1973) 88-104. LOHSE, E. Die Einheit des Neuen Testaments (Göttingen 1973) 312f. REESE, T. J. "Pauline Politics: Rom 13:1-7," BThB 3 (3, 1973) 323-31. RICHARDSON, A. The Political Christ (London 1973) 96-9. CUSS, D. Imperial Cult and Honorary Terms in the New Testament (Fribourg 1974) 39ff. RIDDERBOS, H. Paul. An Outline of His Theology (Grand Rapids 1975) 320-6. SANDERS, J. T. Ethics in the New Testament. Change and Development (Philadelphia 1975) 59f. SCHMITHALS, W. Der Römerbrief als historisches Problem (Gütersloh 1975) 63, 185ff., 191ff. FRIEDRICH, J., PÖHLMANN, W. and STUHLMACHER, P. "Zur historischen Situation and Intention von Röm 13, 1-7," ZThK 73 (2, 1976) 131-66. GARRETT, J. L. JR. "The Dialectic of Romans 13:1-7 and Revelation 13: Part One," JChS 18 (3, 1976) 433-42. HULTGREN, A. J. "Reflections of Romans 13:1-7: Submission to Governing Authorities," Dialog 15 (4, 1976) 263-9. WELLS, P. "Dieu Créateur et Politique," RevR 27 (1976) 30-44. FUCHS, E. "Romains 13, 1-7," BCPE 29 (3-4, 1977) 58-62. GARRETT, J. L. "The Dialectic of Romans 13, 1-7 and Revelation 13: Part Two," JChS 19 (1977) 5-20. MOULDER, J. "Romans 13 and Conscientious Disobedience," JTSA 21 (1977) 13-23. SCHILLEBEECKX, E. Christus und die Christen (Freiburg/Basel/Wien 1977) 553-7; Christ: the Christian Experience in the Modern World (London 1980) 572-5. SCROGGS, R. Paul for a New Day (Philadelphia 1977) 53-5. BEST, E. From Text to Sermon (Atlanta 1978) 18-20. BLANK, J. "Spolecenstvi viry v pohanskem svete. K prehistorii R 13:1-7 (Die Glaubensgemeinschaft in der heidnischen Welt. Zur Vorgeschichte von Röm 13:1-7) KrR 45 (1978) 9-14. GEIGER, M. "Theologie, Kirche und Todesstrafe" in M. Geiger et al. Nein zur Todesstrafe (Basel 1978) 19-22. KAYE, B. "The New Testament and Social Order" in B. Kaye and G. Wenham, eds., Law, Morality and the Bible (Downers Grove IL 1978) 104-8. OGLE, A. B. "What is Left for Caesar? A Look at Mark 12:13-17 and Romans 13:1-7," ThT 35 (1978) 254-64. ALAND, K. "Das Verhältnis von Kirche und Staat in der Frühzeit" in ANRW II.23.1 (1979) 174-86, 239-46. ALAND, K. Neutestamentliche Entwürfe (München 1979) 38-50, 110-6. FURNISH, V. P. The Moral Teaching of Paul (Nashville 1979) 115, 117-39. LAUB, F. "Der Christ und die Staatliche Gewalt—Zum Verständnis der 'Politischen' Paränese Röm 13, 1-7 in der gegenwärtigen Diskussion," MThZ 30 (4, 1979) 257-265. MOXNES, H. and BINDEMANN, W. Romans 13 (Geneva 1979) PANGRITZ, A. "Weder von Gott noch vom Teufel. Anmerkungen zum Gewalt-Verständnis des Paulus," Texte und Kontexte 4 (1979) 34-47. PIPER, J. 'Love your enemies' (Cambridge 1979) 5, 103, 132, 210n.124. ROMANIUK, K. "Il Cristiano e l'autorità civile in Romani 13, 1-7," RivB 27 (3-4, 1979) 261-9. WILCKENS, U. "Der Gehorsam gegen die Behörden des Staates im Tun des Guten. Zu Römer 13:1-7" in L. De Lorenzi, ed., Dimensions de la vie chrétienne (Rm 12-13) (Rome 1979) 85-130. LÜHRMANN, D. "Neutestamentliche Haustafeln und Antike Ökonomie," NTS 27 (1980) 94. MCDONALD, J. I. H. Kerygma and Didache (Cambridge 1980) 92. RIEKKINEN, V. Römer 13 (Helsinki 1980) ABBING, P. J. R. "Diakonie" in TRE 8 (1981) 653. CARR, W. Angels and Principalities (Cambridge 1981) 115-8. PICCA, J. V. Romanos 13, 1-7. Un texto discutido. Prolegómenos para su interpretación (Biblioteca di Scienze Religiose 34; Rome 1981) SCHMIDT, K. L. "Das Gegenüber von Kirche und Staat in der Gemeinde des Neuen Testaments" in Neues Testament, Judentum, Kirche [G. Sauter, ed.] (München 1981) 167-91. TÖDT, H. E. "Demokratie" in TRE 8 (1981) 434f., 443. WEBSTER, A. F. C. "St. Paul's Political Advice to the Haughty Gentile Christians in Rome.

An Exegesis of Romans 13:1-7," SVThQ 25 (4, 1981) 259-82. BOLOGNESI, P. "La situazione del cristiano davanti all'autorità secondo Romani 13," RBR 17 (1982) 9-23. SCHRAGE, W. "Ethik" in TRE 10 (1982) 450. LAUB, F. Die Begegnung des frühen Christentums mit der antiken Sklaverei (Stuttgart 1982) 76-9, 97. ECKSTEIN, H.-J. Der Begriff Syneidesis bei Paulus (Tübingen 1983) 276-300, 314. HEILIGENTAHL, R. "Strategien konformer Ethik im Neuen Testament am Beispiel von Röm 13, 1-7," NTS 29 (1983) 55-61. HEILIGEN-THAL, R. Werke als Zeichen (Tübingen 1983) 93-114. MEEKS, W. A. The First Urban Christians (New Haven/London 1983) 106, 170, 208n.192. MUNRO, W. Authority in Paul and Peter (Cambridge 1983) 56-67. PATTE, D. Paul's Faith and the Power of the Gospel (Philadelphia 1983) 290f. BAMMEL, E. "Romans 13" in E. BLammel and C. F. D. Moule, eds., Jesus and the Politics of His Day (Cambridge 1984) 365-83. BRUCE, F. F. "Paul and 'The Powers That Be'," BJRL 66 (2, 1984) 78-96. FREY, C. "Gesellschaft/Gesellschaft und Christentum VII" in TRE 13 (1984) 21. KLEINKNECHT, K. T. Der leidende Gerechtfertigte (Tübingen 1984) 177. POHLE, L. Die Christen und der Staat nach Römer 13. Eine typologische Untersuchung der neueren deutschsprachigen Schriftauslegung (Mainz 1984) passim. VONCK, P. "All Authority Comes from God: Romans 13:1-7—a tricky text about obedience to political power," AfrER 26 (6, 1984) 338-47. BARRACLOUGH, R. "Romans 13:1-7. Application in Context," Colloquium 17 (2, 1985) 16-22. CRANFIELD, C. E. B. "The Christian's Political Responsibility According to the New Testament" in The Bible and Christian Life (Edinburgh 1985) 48ff. DYCK, H. J. "The Christian and the Authorities in Romans 13:1-7," Direction 14 (1985) 44-50. EMSLIE, B. L. "The methodology of proceeding from exegesis to an ethical decision," Neotestamentica 19 (1985) 87-91. JÜNGEL, E., HERZOG, R. and SIMON, H. Evangelische Christen in unserer Demokratie. Beiträge aus des Synode der Evangelischen Kirche in Deutschland (Gütersloh 1986) passim. MALHERBE, A. J. Moral Exhortation. A Greco-Roman Sourcebook (Philadelphia 1986) 88. MALINA B. J. Christian Origins and Cultural Anthropology (Atlanta 1986) 136. PÖHLMANN, W. "Herrscherkult II" in TRE 15 (1986) 249. SCHNACKENBURG, R. Die sittliche Botschaft des Neuen Testaments, Band 1 (Freiburg/Basel/Wien 1986) 256-60. AUNE, D. E. The New Testament in Its Literary Environment (Philadelphia 1987) 196. BERGER, K. und COLPE, C., eds., Religionsgeschichtliches Textbuch zum Neuen Testament (Göttingen/Zürich 1987) 224. BIELECKI, S. "Rz 13, 1-7 w kontekście historii zbawienia (Röm 13, 1-7 im Kontext der Heilsgeschichte)," RTK 34 (1987) 47-56. BOYER, S. "Exegesis of Romans 13:1-7," BLT 32 (4, 1987) 208-16. DUNN, J. D. G. "Paul's Epistle to the Romans: An Analysis of Structure and Argument" in ANRW II.25.4 (1987) 2878. MCDONALD, J. I. H. "Romans 13.1-7 and Christian Social Ethics Today," MCh 29 (2, 1987) 19-25. REBELL, W. Gemeinde als Gegenwelt (Frankfurt am Main/ Bern/New York/Paris 1987) 122n.4. CONZELMANN, H. and LINDEMANN, A. Interpreting the New Testament (Peabody, Mass. 1988) 196f., 368. DRAPER, J. A. "'Humble Submission to Almighty God' and its Biblical Foundation. Contextual Exegesis of Romans 13:1-7," JTSA 63 (1988) 30-8. LÉGASSE, S. "La soumission aux autorités d'après 1 Pierre 2.13-17. Version spécifique d'une parénèse traditionelle," NTS 34 (1988) 390-3. MacDONALD, M. Y. The Pauline Churches (Cambridge 1988) 42. VENETZ, H.-J. "Zwischen Unterwerfung und Verweigerung. Widersprüchliches im Neuen Testament? Zu Röm 13 und Offb 13," BuK 43 (4, 1988) 153-63. WEDDERBURN, A. J. M. The Reasons for Romans

(Edinburgh 1988) 62f., 83. BECKER, J. Paulus. Der Apostel der Völker (Tübingen 1989) 59, 263, 360, 456, 468. LIMBECK, M. Mit Paulus Christ sein. Sachbuch zur Person und Theologie des Apostels Paulus (Stuttgart 1989) 32. MARXSEN, W. "Christliche" und christliche Ethik im Neuen Testament (Gütersloh 1989) 166, 233. McDONALD, J. I. H. "Romans 13.1-7: a Test Case for New Testament Interpretation," NTS 35 (4, 1989) 540-9. MERKLEIN, H. "Sinn und Zweck von Römer 13, 1-7. Zur semantischen und pragmatischen Struktur eines umstrittenen Textes" in H. Merklein, ed., Neues Testament und Ethik (FS R. Schnackenburg; Freiburg/Basel/Wien 1989) 238-70. STEIN, R. H. "The Argument of Romans 13:1-7," NovT 31 (4, 1989) 325-43. VOLLENWEI-DER, S. Freiheit als neue Schöpfung (Göttingen 1989) 357n. GIELEN, M. Tradition und Theologie neutestamentlicher Haustafelethik (Frankfurt 1990) 435-74. LIPS, H. VON, Weisheitliche Traditionen im Neuen Testament (Neukirchen-Vluyn 1990) 385ff., 394, 405. MUNRO, W. "Romans 13:1-7. Apartheid's Last Biblical Refuge," BThB 20 (4, 1990) 161-8. PORTER, S. E. "Romans 13:1-7 as Pauline Political Rhetoric," FilolNeot 3 (2, 1990) 115-39. SIMONIS, W. Der gefangene Paulus. Die Entstehung des sogenannten Römer-briefs und anderer urchristlicher Schriften in Rom (Frankfurt/ Bern/New York/Paris 1990) 78-82. ZIESLER, J. Pauline Christianity (Oxford 1990) 20, 124f. LOHSE, E. Die Entstehung des Neuen Testaments (Stuttgart/ Berlin/Köln ⁵1991) 27. WAY, D. The Lordship of Christ. Ernst Käsemann's Interpretation of Paul's Theology (Oxford 1991) 266-9. BOTHA, J. "Creation of New Meaning: Rhetorical Situations and the Reception of Romans 13:1-7," JTSA 79 (1992) 24-37. CUVILLIER, E. "Soumission aux autorités et liberté chrétienne. Exégèse de Romains 13, 1-7," Hokhma 50 (1992) 29-47. DENOVA, R. I. "Paul's Letter to the Romans, 13:1-7: The Gentile-Christian Response to Civil Authority," Encounter 53 (1992) 201-29. RACINE, J.-F. "Romains 13, 1-7: Simple préservation de l'ordre social?" EstBi 51 (1993) 187-205.

13:1-6   MULLINS, Y. "Topos as a NT Form," JBL 99 (1980) 543. BERGER, K. und COLPE, C., eds., Religionsgeschichtliches Textbuch zum Neuen Testament (Göttingen/Zürich 1987) 223f.

13:1-5   CAIRD, G.B. Principalities and Powers (1956) 22ff. STAAB, K. Pauluskom-mentare aus der griechischen Kirche (Münster ²1984) 533:15-37 Phot.

13:1-3   DELLING, G. Römer 13, 1-7 innerhalb der Briefe des Neuen Testaments (1962) 22-26.

13:1-2   FORELL, G. W. The Christian Lifestyle (Philadelphia 1975) 24-7. MAU, R. "Autorität" in TRE 5 (1980) 33. GERSTNER, J. H. "A Protestant View of Biblical Authority" in F. E. Greenspahn, ed., Scripture in the Jewish and Christian Traditions (Nashville 1982) 60. TOWNER, Ph. H. The Goal of Our Instruction. The Structure of Theology and Ethics in the Pastoral Epistles (Sheffield 1989) 14, 202f., 214, 216, 301n.2, 309n.8.

13:1   SCHRAGE, W. Die konkreten Einzelgebote in der paulinischen Paränese (1961) 97, 112, 119, 121, 227. SEVENSTER, J.N. Paul and Seneca (1961) 77, 94. MERK, O. Handeln aus Glauben (1968) 162f. ROON, A. VAN, The Authentic-ity of Ephesians (Leiden 1974) 257f. GEORGI, D. "Weisheit Salomos," JSHRZ 3 (4, 1980) 6n.3a. RIEKKINEN, V. Römer 13 (Helsinki 1980) 54-7, 134-70, 203-6. POHLE, L. Die Christen und der Staat nach Römer 13 (Mainz 1984) 88-119. SCHREY, H. H. "Gewalt/Gewaltlosigkeit I" in TRE 13 (1984) 170. STAAB, K. Pauluskommentare aus der griechischen Kirche (Münster ²1984) 56:10-23 Akazc; 78:5-19 Apoll; 107:16-35 Diod; 224:1-17 Sev; 407:1-29 Genn; 408:1-2 Genn. SCHARFFENORTH, E.-A. "Die Barmer Theologische Erklärung" in FREUND, G. und STEGEMANN, E., eds., Theologische Brosamen für Lothar Steiger (DBAT 5; Heidelberg 1985) 374. BOONE, K. C. The Bible Tells Them So. The Discourse of Protestant Fundamentalism (London 1990) 85. ELLUL, J. "Petite note complémentaire sur Romains 13, 1," FV 79 (6, 1990) 81-3.

13:1a GIELEN, M. Tradition und Theologie neutestamentlicher Haustafelethik (Frankfurt 1990) 441f., 457-9.

13:1b-2 GIELEN, M. Tradition und Theologie neutestamentlicher Haustafelethik (Frankfurt 1990) 442-4, 459-62.

13:2-3 STAAB, K. Pauluskommentare aus der griechischen Kirche (Münster ²1984) 408:3-5 Genn.

13:2 RIEKKINEN, V. Römer 13 (Helsinki 1980) 205-7. STAAB, K. Pauluskommentare aus der griechischen Kirche (Münster ²1984) 108:1-3 Diod. WINTER, B. W. "The Public Honouring of Christian Benefactors. Romans 13.3-4 and 1 Peter 2.14-15," JSNT 34 (1988) 87-103.

13:3-4 SCHRAGE, W. Die konkreten Einzelgebote in der paulinischen Paränese (1961) 53, 195. FORELL, G. W. The Christian Lifestyle. Reflections on Romans 12-15 (Philadelphia 1975) 28-37. UNNIK, W. D. VAN "Lob und Strafe durch die Obrigkeit. Hellenistisches zu Röm. 13:3-4" in E. E. Elis und E. Grässer, eds., Jesus und Paulus (FS W. G. Kümmel; Göttingen 1975) 334-43. RIEKKINEN, V. Römer 13 (Helsinki 1980) 207-11. FRITZSCHE, H.-G. "Dekalog" in TRE 8 (1981) 419. BERGER, K. und COLPE, C., eds., Religionsgeschichtliches Textbuch zum Neuen Testament (Göttingen/Zürich 1987) 224f. GIELEN, M. Tradition und Theologie neutestamentlicher Haustafelethik (Frankfurt 1990) 445-8, 462-4.

13:3 BRUNNER, E. Dogmatik II (1950) 129. LORIMER, W.L. "Romans XIII 3" NTS 12 (1965/66) 389f. STUIBER, A. "Ambrosiaster" in TRE 2 (1978) 361. PIPER, J. 'Love your enemies' (Cambridge 1979) 63, 180n.25, 191n.132, 212n.16. HYGEN, J. B. "Böse" in TRE 7 (1981) 9. ROMANIUK, K. "Furcht" in TRE 11 (1983) 758.

13:4ff. ROTTENBERG, I. C. The Promise and the Presence. Toward a Theology of the Kingdom of God (Grand Rapids 1980) 99.

13:4-6 KÄSEMANN, E. New Testament Questions of Today (1969) 213.

13:4-5 SCHRAGE, W. Die konkreten Einzelgebote in der paulinischen Paränese (1961) 47, 53, 96f., 11f., 113, 153, 227, 228. STAAB, K. Pauluskommentare aus der griechischen Kirche (Münster ²1984) 408:6-14 Genn.

13:4 BOUSSET, W. Die Religion des Judentums im Späthellenistischen Zeitalter (1926-1966) 431. CULLMANN, O. The State in the New Testament (1956) 57f. POHLE, L. Die Christen und der Staat nach Römer 13 (Mainz 1984) 120-38.

13:5-7 FORELL, G. W. The Christian Lifestyle. Reflections on Romans 12-15 (Philadelphia 1975) 33-5.

13:5-6 GIELEN, M. Tradition und Theologie neutestamentlicher Haustafelethik (Frankfurt 1990) 448-53, 466.

13:5 THRALL, M. "The Pauline Use of συνείδησις" NTS 14 (1967/68) 119f. SCHMITHALS, W. Der Römerbrief als historisches Problem (Gütersloh 1975) 207. SCHULZ, S. Die Mitte der Schrift (Stuttgart 1976) 129. RIEKKINEN, V. Römer 13 (Helsinki 1980) 30-3, 211. STAAB, K. Pauluskommentare aus der griechischen Kirche (Münster ²1984) 108:4-8 Diod; 162:12-26 ThM; 534:1-10 Phot. WOLTER, M. "Gewissen II" in TRE 13 (1984) 216f. SCHNABEL, E. J. Law and Wisdom from Ben Sira to Paul (Tübingen 1985) 312, 333-5. LEE, P.

"'Conscience' In Romans 13:5," Faith and Mission [Wake Forest, NC] 8 (1, 1990) 85-93.

13:6-7   MULLINS, T. Y. "Topos as a NT Form," JBL 99 (1980) 543. RIEKKINEN, V. Römer 13 (Helsinki 1980) 34-9, 91, 94, 116. WEDDERBURN, A. J. M. The Reasons for Romans (Edinburgh 1988) 62f., 78, 83. LAMPE, P. Die stadtrömischen Christen in den ersten beiden Jahrhunderten (Tübingen ²1989) 63. WALTER, N. "Paul and the Early Christian Jesus-Tradition" in A. J. M. Wedderburn, ed., Paul and Jesus. Collected Essays (Sheffield 1989) 51-80, esp.58n.15.

13:6-8   RIEKKINEN, V. Römer 13 (Helsinki 1980) 215f.

13:6   RIEKKINEN, V. Römer 13 (Helsinki 1980) 214f. STAAB, K. Pauluskommentare aus der griechischen Kirche (Münster ²1984) 108:9-11 Diod; 408:15-22 Genn.

13:7-8   ROON, A. VAN, The Authenticity of Ephesians (Leiden 1974) 167. LOHFINK, G. Jesus and Community. The Social Dimension of the Christian Faith (Philadelphia 1984) 113. STAAB, K. Pauluskommentare aus der griechischen Kirche (Münster ²1984) 408:23-409:10 Genn.

13:7   SCHRAGE, W. Die konkreten Einzelgebote in der paulinischen Paränese (1961) 97. STROBEL, A. "Furcht, wem Furcht gebührt. Zum profangriechischen Hintergrund von Rm 13:7" ZNW 55 (1-2, '64) 58-62. DAVIES, W. D. The Sermon on the Mount (Cambridge 1966) 97f. RIEKKINEN, V. Römer 13 (Helsinki 1980) 34f., 217. ALLISON, D. C. "The Pauline Epistles and the Synoptic Gospels: The Pattern of the Parallels," NTS 28 (1982) 16f. THIELICKE, H. "Ehre" in TRE 9 (1982) 365. ROMANIUK, K. "Furcht" in TRE 11 (1983) 758. STAAB, K. Pauluskommentare aus der griechischen Kirche (Münster ²1984) 162:27-28 ThM. SCHNACKENBURG, R. Die sittliche Botschaft des Neuen Testaments, Band 1 (Freiburg/Basel/Wien 1986) 253. GIELEN, M. Tradition und Theologie neutestamentlicher Haustafelethik (Frankfurt 1990) 453-6, 466, 468.

13:8ff.   KÄHLER, E. Die Frau in den Paulinischen Briefen (1960) 183-86. HAHN, F. Das Verständnis der Mission im Neuen Testament (1965) 87. MÜNCHOW, C. Ehik und Eschatologie (Göttingen 1981) 157, 164f. SCHULZ, S. "Neutestamentliche Ethik (Zürich 1987) 158f.

13:8-14   FROITZHEIM, F. Christologie und Eschatologie bei Paulus (Würzburg 1979) 13. FURNISH, V. P. The Moral Teaching of Paul (Nashville 1979) 23f., 123, 125. ORTKEMPER, F.-J. Leben aus dem Glauben (Münster 1980) 125-48.

13:8-12   STECK, K. G. in GPM 34 (1979) 2-8. WIESE, W. und MEYER-ROSCHER, W. in P. Krusche et al., eds., Predigtstudien für das Kirchenjahr 1979/80. Perikopenreihe II/1 (1979) 16-23. SEIM, J. in GPM 40 (1985/86) 8-14.

13:8-10   BERGER, K. Die Gesetzesauslegung Jesu (1972) 50-55. BEST, E. One Body in Christ (1955) 144. NIEDER, L. Die Motive der Religiös-Sittlichen Paränese in den Paulinischen Gemeinde-Briefen (1956) 42-43, 44, 45, 107, 144. SCHRAGE, W. Die konkreten Einzelgebote in der paulinischen Paränese (1961) 99, 121, 208, 230, 232, 237, 243, 252, 255, 263f. FUCHS, GPM 16 (19-61/62) 92ff. BANDSTRA, A.J. The Law and the Elements of the World (1964) 110f. QUESNELL, Q. This Good News (1964) 85f. SISTI, A. "La legge dell'amore (Rom.13, 8-10)" BiblOr 8 (2, '66) 60-70. DOERNE, M. Die alten Episteln (1967) 56-60. TRAUB, H. GPM 22 (1967/68) 96-103. GOPPELT, L. Christologie und Ethik (1968) 131f., 203f. MERK, O. Handeln aus Glauben (1968) 70, 161, 164f., 234, 244. VAN DÜLMEN, A. Die Theologie des Gesetzes bei Paulus (1968) 60, 133, 173, 198, 226, 229. KÄSEMANN, E. New Testament

Questions of Today (1969) 199. DAVIES, W. D. The Sermon on the Mount (Cambridge 1966) 98, 116f. ECKERT, J. Die Urchristliche Verkündigung im Streit zwischen Paulus und seinen Gegnern nach dem Galaterbrief (Regensburg 1971) 160f. BORSE, U. Der Standort des Galaterbriefes (Köln 1972) 129f. BENCZE, A. L. "An Analysis of Romans xiii. 8-10," NTS 20 (1973) 90-2. RANNENBERG, W. und MÜLLER, H. M. in E. Lange, ed., Predigtstudien für das Kirchenjahr 1973/74 (1973) 138-44. SCHMITHALS, W. in GPM 28 (1973) 108-14. FORELL, G. W. The Christian Lifestyle. Reflections on Romans 12-15 (Philadelphia 1975) 36-9. OSTEN-SACKEN, P. VON DER, Römer 8 als Beispiel paulinischer Soteriologie (Göttingen 1975) 256ff. PAGELS, E. H. The Gnostic Paul. Gnostic Exegesis of the Pauline Letters (Philadelphia 1975) 44. RIDDERBOS, H. Paul. An Outline of His Theology (Grand Rapids 1975) 279-82. SANDERS, J. T. Ethics in the New Testament. Change and Development (Philadelphia 1975) 60. HÜBNER, H. Das Gesetz bei Paulus. Ein Beitrag zum Werden der paulinischen Theologie (Göttingen 1978) 76-80. LYONNET, S. "La Charité Plénitude de la loi (Rm 13, 8-10)" in L. De Lorenzi, ed., Dimensions de la vie chrétienne (Rm 12-13) (Rome 1979) 151-63. PIPER, J. 'Love your enemies' (Cambridge 1979) 114, 131, 211n.14. LOHSE, E. "Kirche im Alltag" in D. Lührmann und G. Strecker, eds., Kirche (FS Günther Bornkamm; Tübingen 1980) 402. MULLINS, T. Y. "Topos as a NT Form," JBL 99 (1980) 543. ORTKEMPER, F.-J. Leben aus dem Glauben (Münster 1980) 126-32, 178-85. RIEKKINEN, V. Römer 13 (Helsinki 1980) 131, 133. DEIDUN, T. J. New Covenant Morality in Paul (Rome 1981) 157ff. HÜBNER, H. "Dekalog" in TRE 8 (1981) 416f. BINDEMANN, W. Die Hoffnung der Schöpfung (Neukirchen 1983) 113-5. RÄISÄNEN, H. Paul and the Law (Tübingen 1983) 7, 26f., 33-5, 63, 64-6, 68, 70, 78, 113, 139, 246. LÜHRMANN, D. "Gerechtigkeit" in TRE 12 (1984) 418. MOHRLANG, R. Matthew and Paul (Cambridge 1984) 34, 101, 150, 156. STAAB, K. Pauluskommentare aus der griechischen Kirche (Münster ²1984) 534:11-33 Phot. SCHNABEL, E. J. Law and Wisdom from Ben Sira to Paul (Tübingen 1985) 274f., 280, 294, 328, 341. MALINA B. J. Christian Origins and Cultural Anthropology (Atlanta 1986) 135. RÄISÄNEN, H. The Torah and Christ (Helsinki 1986) 5, 11f., 20, 292. WISCHMEYER, O. "Das Gebot der Nächstenliebe bei Paulus. Eine traditionsgeschichtliche Untersuchung," BZ 30 (2, 1986) 161-87. DUNN, J. D. G. "Paul's Epistle to the Romans: An Analysis of Structure and Argument" in ANRW II.25.4 (1987) 2878f. OSTEN-SACKEN, P. VON DER, Evangelium und Tora: Aufsätze zu Paulus (München 1987) 17, 25, 54, 183. DOWNING, F. G. Christ and the Cynics (Sheffield 1988) 188. MARTIN, F. Narrative Parallels to the New Testament (Atlanta 1988) R68. MARXSEN, W. "Christliche" und christliche Ethik im Neuen Testament (Gütersloh 1989) 167f. TRILLING, W. Studien zur Jesusüberlieferung (Stuttgart 1988) 150, 259f. WEDDERBURN, A. J. M. The Reasons for Romans (Edinburgh 1988) 23, 76, 83f. HOFIUS, O. Paulusstudien (Tübingen 1989) 69, 120. MARTIN, B. L. Christ and the Law in Paul (Leiden 1989) 2, 19, 32, 48, 54f., 60, 66f., 142, 148-52, 155. OSTEN-SACKEN, P. VON DER, Die Heiligkeit der Tora (München 1989) 40-3, 47. SCHÄFER, K. Gemeinde als "Bruderschaft" (Frankfurt/Bern/New York/Paris 1989) 179-85. SCHNELLE, U. Wandlungen im paulinischen Denken (Stuttgart 1989) 67f. THIELMAN, F. From Plight to Solution (Leiden 1989) 88-90, 100. VOLLEN-WEIDER, S. Freiheit als neue Schöpfung (Göttingen 1989) 306, 312, 370, 400, 403. WALTER, N. "Paul and the Early Christian Jesus-Tradition" in A. J. M. Wedderburn, ed., Paul and Jesus. Collected Essays (Sheffield 1989) 51-80, esp.57f., 72-4. CRUZ, H. Christological Motives and Motivated Actions in Pauline Paraenesis (Frankfurt/Bern/New York/Paris 1990) 56-61. DUNN, J. D. G. Jesus, Paul and the Law (London 1990) 99, 106, 215, 225, 240. SIMONIS, W. Der gefangene Paulus. Die Entstehung des sogenannten Römerbriefs und anderer urchristlicher Schriften in Rom (Frankfurt/Bern/New York/Paris 1990) 59.

13:8-9   SANDERS, J. T. Ethics in the New Testament. Change and Development (Philadelphia 1975) 51f.

13:8   MARXSEN, W. "Der ἕτερος νόμος Röm 13, 8" ThZ 11 ('55) 230-37. SCHRAGE, W. Die konkreten Einzelgebote in der paulinischen Paränese (1961) 97, 128, 156, 250. JÜNGEL, E. Paulus und Jesus (1966) 57, 68. KERTELGE, K. "Rechtfertigung" bei Paulus (1967) 202, 227, 312. WALTHER, J. A. "A Translator's Dilemma. An Exegetical Note on Romans 13:8," Perspective 13 (3, 1972) 243-6. FRIEDRICH, G. "Das Gesetz des Glaubens Römer 3, 27" in Auf das Wort kommt es an. Gesammelte Aufsätze (Göttingen 1978) 112. PIPER, J. 'Love your enemies' (Cambridge 1979) 13. BROER, I. Freiheit vom Gesetz und Radikalisierung des Gesetzes (Stuttgart 1980) 26. RIEKKINEN, V. Römer 13 (Helsinki 1980) 38f., 48, 50. SCHMITHALS, W. "Bultmann" in TRE 7 (1981) 394. KLEINKNECHT, K. T. Der leidende Gerechtfertigte (Tübingen 1984) 361. STAAB, K. Pauluskommentare aus der griechischen Kirche (Münster ²1984) 163:1-2 ThM. OSTEN-SACKEN, P. VON DER, Evangelium und Tora: Aufsätze zu Paulus (München 1987) 33, 102, 209. MARTIN, B. L. Christ and the Law in Paul (Leiden 1989) 17, 21, 51, 91, 142, 148.

13:9-10   MÜLLER, U. B. "Zur Rezeption Gesetzeskritischer Jesusüberlieferung im Frühen Christentum" NTS 27 (1981) 159. YARBROUGH, O. L. Not like the Gentiles: Marriage Rules in the Letters of Paul (Atlanta 1985) 79f.

13:9   ELLIS, E.E. Paul's Use of the Old Testament (1957) 12, 73, 93, 116, 151, 159, 183, 187. SCHRAGE, W. Die konkreten Einzelgebote in der paulinsichen Paränese (1961) 127f., 208, 233, 253, 269. BORSE, U. Der Standort des Galaterbriefes (Köln 1972) 129f. SANDERS, J. T. Ethics in the New Testament. Change and Development (Philadelphia 1975) 42. METZGER, B. M. The Early Versions of the New Testament. Their Origin Transmission, and Limitations (Oxford 1977) 244. PIPER, J. 'Love your enemies' (Cambridge 1979) 214n.39. BARTH, G. "Bergpredigt" in TRE 5 (1980) 611. SCHRAGE, W. "Ethik" in TRE 10 (1982) 448. SMEND, R. "Ethik" in TRE 10 (1982) 432. HEILIGENTHAL, R. "Gebot" in TRE 12 (1984) 124. MOHRLANG, R. Matthew and Paul (Cambridge 1984) 34, 42, 92, 157, 183. STAAB, K. Pauluskommentare aus der griechischen Kirche (Münster ²1984) 224:18-21 Sev. KOCH, D.-A. Die Schrift als Zeuge des Evangeliums (Tübingen 1986) 34, 116f. RÄISÄNEN, H. The Torah and Christ (Helsinki 1986) 154, 163, 255. NIEBUHR, K.-W. Gesetz und Paränese (Tübingen 1987) 16, 63. JEFFORD, C. N. The Sayings of Jesus in the Teaching of the Twelve Apostles (Leiden 1989) 32, 34, 160. MARTIN, B. L. Christ and the Law in Paul (Leiden 1989) 17, 22, 42, 44, 76, 148, 151. SEGAL, A. F. Paul the Convert (New Haven/London 1990) 169, 333n.12, 347n.26.

13:10   BRUNNER, E. Mensch im Widerspruch (1937) 97. SCHRAGE, W. Die konkreten Einzelgebote in der paulinischen Paränese (1961) 53, 232, 251, 262, 267, 269. JÜNGEL, E. Paulus und Jesus (1966) 68. PIPER, J. 'Love your enemies' (Cambridge 1979) 211n.16, 219n.98. SCHREY, H. H. "Goldene Regel III" in TRE 13 (1984) 576. STAAB, K. Pauluskommentare aus der griechischen Kirche (Münster ²1984) 163:3-12 ThM. SCHNABEL, E. J. Law and Wisdom from Ben Sira to Paul (Tübingen 1985) 276, 290, 328. SANDERS, E. P. Jewish Law from Jesus to the Mishnah (London/Philadelphia 1990) 71.

13:11ff. SCHRAGE, W. Die konkreten Einzelgebote in der paulinische Paränese (1961) 16, 21, 189, 215, 224, 226, 264. MERKO. Handeln aus Glauben (1968) 56, 121, 164. KÄSEMANN, E. New Testament Questions of Today (1969) 199. LÖVESTAM, E. Spiritual Wakefulness in the New Testament (Lund 1963) 41f. MÜLLER, U. B. Prophetie und Predigt im Neuen Testament (Gütersloh 1975) 142ff., 158, 162ff. MÜNCHOW, C. Ehik und Eschatologie (Göttingen 1981) 157, 161. SCHRAGE, W. "Ethik" in TRE 10 (1982) 446. KÖSTER, H. "Formgeschichte" in TRE 11 (1983) 289.

13:11-17 VÖGTLE, A. "Röm. 13:11-14 und die 'Nah'-Erwartung" in J. Friedrich, W. Pöhlmann und P. Stuhlmacher, eds., Rechtfertigung (FS E. Käsemann; Tübingen/ Göttingen 1976) 557-73.

13:11-14 FRICK, R. GPM 10 (1955) 2-6. LOCHMAN, GPM 16 (1961/62) 3ff. ROMANIUK, K. "Repentez-Vous, Car Le Royaume des Cieux est Tour Proche (Matt. IV. 17 par)" NTS 12 (1965-66) 259f., 268f. MARXSEN, W. Predigten (1968) 131-140. IWAND, H.-J. in Herr, tue meine Lippen auf II ed. G. Eichholz (1966) 1-15. BRANDENBURGER-BALTZER-MERKEL GPM 22 (1967/68) 8-11. DOERNE, M. Die alten Episteln (1967) 13ff. LOHSE, E. Das Aergernis des Kreuzes (1969) 7-11. LAFONT, G. "En état d'urgence," AssS 3 (1963) 29-38. LOVESTAM, E. Spiritual Wakefulness in the New Testament (Lund 1963) 25-45. SCHULZ, A. "Der Christ lebt situationsgerecht," Am Tisch des Wortes 6 (1965) 18-26. KREYSSIG, P. und STAMMLER, E. in E. Lange, ed., Predigtstudien für das Kirchenjahr 1973/74 (1973) 34-40. LAUB, F. Eschatologische Verkündigung und Lebensgestaltung nach Paulus (Regensburg 1973) 160, 162, 173, 183. SCHRAGE, W. in GPM 28 1973 2-12. DAUTZENBERG, G. "Was bleibt von der Naherwartung? Zu Röm 13, 11-14" in Biblische Randbemerkungen (FS R. Schnackenburg; Würzburg 1974) 361-74. BAUMGARTEN, J. Paulus und die Apokalyptik (Neukirchen-Vluyn 1975) 209-13. FORELL, G. W. The Christian Lifestyle. Reflections on Romans 12-15 (Philadelphia 1975) 40-3. SCHMITHALS, W. Der Römerbrief als historisches Problem (Gütersloh 1975) 187ff., 190f. HERR, T. Naturrecht aus der kritischen Sicht des Neuen Testaments (München 1976) 112. VÖGTLE, A. "Röm 13, 11-14 und die 'Nah'-Erwartung" in J. Friedrich et al., eds., Rechtfertigung (FS E. Käsemann; Tübingen 1976) 557-73. FRIEDRICH, G. "I Thessalonicher 5, 1-11, der apologetische Einschub eines Späteren" in Auf das Wort kommt es an. Gesammelte Aufsätze (Göttingen 1978) 268-70. FROITZHEIM, F. Christologie und Eschatologie bei Paulus (Würzburg 1979) 11ff. PIPER, J. 'Love your enemies' (Cambridge 1979) 211n.14. VÖGTLE, A. "Paraklese und Eschatologie nach Röm 13, 11-14" in L. De Lorenzi, ed., Dimensions de la vie chrétienne (Rm 12-13) (Rome 1979) 179-94. MULLINS, T. Y. "Topos as a NT Form," JBL 99 (1980) 543. ORTKEMPER, F.-J. Leben aus dem Glauben (Münster 1980) 132-48. SCHADE, H.-H. Apokalyptische Christologie bei Paulus (Göttingen 1981) 99f., 142. CRANFIELD, C. E. B. "Changes of Person and Number in Paul's Epistles" in M. D. Hooker and S. G. Wilson, eds., Paul and Paulinism (FS C. K. Barrett; London 1982) 284f. LAUB, F. Die Begegnung des frühen Christentums mit der antiken Sklaverei (Stuttgart 1982) 76f. BINDEMANN, W. Die Hoffnung der Schöpfung (Neukirchen 1983) 113-5. WENHAM, D. "Paul's Use of the Jesus Tradition. Three Samples" in D. Wenham, ed., Gospel Perspectives. The Jesus Tradition Outside the Gospels, Vol 5 (Sheffield 1984) 15. VÖGTLE, A. "Paraklese und Eschatologie nach Röm 13, 11-14" in

Offenbarungsgeschehen und Wirkungsgeschichte. Neutestamentliche Beiträge (Freiburg/Basel/Wien 1985) 205-17. VÖGTLE, A. "Röm 13, 11-14 und die 'Nah'-Erwartung" in Offenbarungsgeschehen und Wirkungsgeschichte. Neutestamentliche Beiträge (Freiburg/Basel/Wien 1985) 221-79. DUNN, J. D. G. "Paul's Epistle to the Romans: An Analysis of Structure and Argument" in ANRW II.25.4 (1987) 2879. CRUZ, H. Christological Motives and Motivated Actions in Pauline Paraenesis (Frankfurt/Bern/New York/Paris 1990) 274ff. SIMONIS, W. Der gefangene Paulus. Die Entstehung des sogenannten Römerbriefs und anderer urchristlicher Schriften in Rom (Frankfurt/Bern/New York/Paris 1990) 59-61.

13:11-13   SCHELKLE, K. "Biblische und patristische Eschatologie nach Rom 13:11-13" in Wort und Schrift (1966) 239-250. SCHELKLE, K. H. "Biblische und patristische Eschatologie nach Rom. XIII, 11-13" in J. Coppens, A. Descamps and É. Massaux, eds., Sacra Pagina. Miscellanea biblica congressus internationalis catholici de re biblica, Vol. 2 (Gembloux 1959) 357-72. PAGELS, E. H. The Gnostic Paul. Gnostic Exegesis of the Pauline Letters (Philadelphia 1975) 44. RUDOLPH, K. Die Gnosis (Göttingen 1978) 320. RIEKKINEN, V. Römer 13 (Helsinki 1980) 118-21, 131ff. SCHNACKENBURG, R. Die sittliche Botschaft des Neuen Testaments, Band 1 (Freiburg/Basel/Wien 1986) 181. LOVESTAM, E. Spiritual Wakefulness in the New Testament (Lund 1963) 34f. FRIEDRICH, G. "Die Kirche zu Korinth" in Auf das Wort kommt es an. Gesammelte Aufsätze (Göttingen 1978) 138. BERGMEIER, R. Glaube als Gabe nach Johannes (Stuttgart 1980) 204, 238n.32. ORTKEMPER, F.-J. Leben aus dem Glauben (Münster 1980) 132-42. STAAB, K. Pauluskommentare aus der griechischen Kirche (Münster ²1984) 535:1-27 Phot. MALMEDE, H. H. Die Lichtsymbolik im Neuen Testament (Wiesbaden 1986) 123f. DOWNING, F. G. Christ and the Cynics (Sheffield 1988) 156.

13:11,12   DAVIES, W.D. Paul and Rabbinic Judaism (1955) 130, 319.
13:11   JÜNGEL, E. Paulus und Jesus (1966) 29. KERTELGE, K. "Rechtfertigung" bei Paulus (1967) 138, 141, 143. MERK, O. Handeln aus Glauben (1968) 11, 20, 166, 176, 195. BERKOUWER, G. C. The Return of Christ (Grand Rapids 1972) 29, 94, 252, 347. KLEIN, G. "Eschatologie" in TRE 10 (1982) 280. STAAB, K. Pauluskommentare aus der griechischen Kirche (Münster ²1984) 108:12-23 Diod; 163:13-18 ThM; 224:23-28 Sev; 409:11-14 Genn; 659:2-4 Areth. DAUTZENBERG, G. "Reich Gottes und Erlösung" in I. Broer und J. Werbick, eds., 'Auf Hoffnung hin sind wir erlöst' (Röm 8, 14) (Stuttgart 1987) 64-6. SCHNELLE, U. Wandlungen im paulinischen Denken (Stuttgart 1989) 45.

13:12ff.   McDONALD, J. I. H. Kerygma and Didache (Cambridge 1980) 95f.
13:12-14   SEVENSTER, J.N. Paul and Seneca (1961) 34, 162, 140, 141. KAMHAH, E. Die Form der katalogischen Paränese im Neuen Testament (1964) 31-34. BRAUN, H. Qumran und NT II (1966) 174, 177, 228, 290, 298. LAUB, F. Eschatologische Verkündigung und Lebensgestaltung nach Paulus. (Regensburg 1973) 12f., 180, 198. MALHERBE, A. J. Moral Exhortation. A Greco-Roman Sourcebook (Philadelphia 1986) 160. BERGER, K. und COLPE, C., eds., Religionsgeschichtliches Textbuch zum Neuen Testament (Göttingen/Zürich 1987) 225. CRUZ, H. Christological Motives and Motivated Actions in Pauline Paraenesis (Frankfurt/Bern/New York/Paris 1990) 291-7.

13:12-13   KÜMMEL, W. G. Römer 7 und das Bild des Menschen im Neuen Testament (München 1974) 101, 104, 121.

13:12   SCHRAGE, W. Die konkreten Einzelgebote in der paulinischen Paränese (1961) 31, 54, 82. DELLING, G. Die Taufe im Neuen Testament (1963) 85.

KAMLAH, E. Die Form der katalogischen Paränese im Neuen Testament (1964) 33, 34, 35, 36, 181, 189. BERKOUWER, G. C. The Return of Christ (Grand Rapids 1972) 82, 94, 164, 253. BAUMERT, N. Täglich Sterben und Auferstehen. Der Literalsinn von 2 Kor 4, 12-5, 10 (München 1973) 28. LAUB, F. Eschatologische Verkündigung und Lebensgestaltung nach Paulus. (Regensburg 1973) 161, 181, 183, 198. STAAB, K. Pauluskommentare aus der griechischen Kirche (Münster ²1984) 108:24-109:6 Diod; 163:19-26 ThM; 409:15-18 Genn; 659:5 Areth. LAYTON, B. The Gnostic Scriptures (Garden City NY 1987) 321. DAVIES, G. N. Faith and Obedience in Romans. A Study in Romans 1-4 (Sheffield 1990) 126f.

13:13-14   ORTKEMPER, F.-J. Leben aus dem Glauben (Münster 1980) 142-7.

13:13   BOUSSET, W. Die Religion des Judentums (1966=1926) 426. WIBBING, S. Die Tugend- und Lasterkataloge im Neuen Testament (1959) 113ff. SCHRAGE, W. Die konkreten Einzelgebote in der paulinschen Paränese (1961) 63, 66, 197, 215f. BORSE, U. Der Standort des Galaterbriefes (Köln 1972) 103f., 132. LAUB, F. Eschatologische Verkündigung und Lebensgestaltung nach Paulus. (Regensburg 1973) 11, 51, 162, 183. ROON, A. VAN, The Authenticity of Ephesians (Leiden 1974) 167. SCHWEIZER, E. "Gottesgerechtigkeit und Lasterkataloge bei Paulus (inkl. Kol und Eph)" in J. Friedrich, W. Pöhlmann und P. Stuhlmacher, eds., Rechtfertigung (FS E. Käsemann; Tübingen/Göttingen 1976) 468f. SCHWEIZER, E. "Traditional ethical patterns in the Pauline and post-Pauline letters and their development (list of vices and house-tables)" in E. Best and R. McL. Wilson, eds., Text and Interpretation (FS M. Black; 1979) 198f., 201f. TISSOT, Y. "Les Actes apocryphes de Thomas: exemple de recueil composite" in F. Bovon et al., eds., Les Actes Apocryphes des Apôtres (Geneva 1981) 228n.17. LAUB, F. Die Begegnung des frühen Christentums mit der antiken Sklaverei (Stuttgart 1982) 97. STAAB, K. Pauluskommentare aus der griechischen Kirche (Münster ²1984) 535:28-34 Phot. REINMUTH, E. Geist und Gesetz (Berlin/DDR 1985) 17f.

13:14   BEST, E. One Body in Christ (1955) 67ff. HAHN, F. Christologische Hoheitstitel (1963) 122. KAMLAH, E. Die Form der katalogischen Paränese im Neuen Testament (1964) 31, 36, 183, 193, 205. NICKELS, P. Targum and New Testament (1967) 70. BÜCHSEL, D. F. Der Geist Gottes im Neuen Testament (Gütersloh 1926) 289-93. KÜMMEL, W. G. Römer 7 und das Bild des Menschen im Neuen Testament (München 1974) 17f. HELDERMANN, J. Die Anapausis im Evangelium Veritatis (Leiden 1984) 172. MOHRLANG, R. Matthew and Paul (Cambridge 1984) 84f., 117f. STAAB, K. Pauluskommentare aus der griechischen Kirche (Münster ²1984) 109:7-12 Diod; 163:27-164:23 ThM. RÄISÄNEN, H. The Torah and Christ (Helsinki 1986) 163f. OLIVEIRA, A. DE, Die Diakonie der Gerechtigkeit und der Versöhnung in der Apologie des 2. Korintherbriefes. Analyse und Auslegung von 2 Kor 2, 14-4, 6; 5, 11-6, 10 (Münster 1990) 155n.387.

14-16   MINEAR, P. S. The Obedience of Faith (London 1971) 1-35.

14:1-16:27   MINEAR, P. S. The Obedience of Faith (1971) 1-35.

14-15   SCHRAGE, W. Die konkreten Einzelgebote in der paulinsichen Paränese (1961) 42, 69, 121, 125, 150-54, 256-58. FURNISH, V. P. The Love Command in the New Testament (1972) 115-18. DRANE, J. W. "Why did Paul write Romans?" in D. A. Hagner and M. J. Harris, eds., Pauline Studies (FS F. F. Bruce; Exeter 1980) 221. MOXNES, H. Theology in Conflict (Leiden 1980) 86f. LORENZI, L. DE, ed., Freedom and Love. The Guide for Christian Life (1 Co 8.10; Rm

14-15) (Rome 1981) passim. BASSLER, J. M. Divine Impartiality (Chico CA 1982) 162-4. KLAIBER, W. Rechtfertigung und Gemeinde (Göttingen 1982) 251-4. KLAUCK, H.-J. Herrenmahl und hellenistischer Kult (Münster 1982) 281f. DOBBELER, A. VON, Glaube als Teilhabe (Tübingen 1987) 239-42. CONZELMANN, H. and LINDEMANN, A. Interpreting the New Testament (Peabody, Mass. 1988) 160. WEDDERBURN, A. J. M. The Reasons for Romans (Edinburgh 1988) 1, 31, 44. BECKER, J. Paulus. Der Apostel der Völker (Tübingen 1989) 357f., 464. LAMPE, P. Die stadtrömischen Christen in den ersten beiden Jahrhunderten (Tübingen ^{2}1989) 56f. MARCUS, J. "The Circumcision and the Uncircumcision in Rome," NTS 35 (1989) 67-81, esp.68ff. LIPS, H. VON, Weisheitliche Traditionen im Neuen Testament (Neu-kirchen-Vluyn 1990) 385, 400, 406f. PROBST, H. Paulus und der Brief (Tübingen 1991)

14:1–15:13   DUPONT, D.J. "Appel aux faibles et aux forts dans la communauté Romaine (Rom 14, 1-15, 13)" Studiorum Paulinorum Congressus Internationalis Catholicus 1961 I (1963) 357-66. MERK, O. Handeln aus Glauben (1968) 167-73, 234, 236, 239f. GIBLIN, C. H. In Hope of God's Glory (1970) 231-36. SHEPARD, J. W. The Life and Letters of St. Paul (Grand Rapids MI 1950) 439-45. HARADA, M. Paul's Weakness. A Study in Pauline Polemics (II Cor 10-13) (University Microfilms, Inc. Ann Arbor MI 1968) 52-78. KARRIS, R. J. "Rom 14:1-15:13 and the Occasion of Romans," CBQ 35 (2, 1973) 155-78. CRANFIELD, C. E. B. "Some Observations on the Interpretation of Romans 14, 1-15, 13," CV 17 (4, 1975) 193-204. SCHMITHALS, W. Der Römerbrief als historisches Problem (Gütersloh 1975) 48f., 95ff., 157. DONFRIED, K. P. "False Presuppositions in the Study of Romans" in K. P. Donfried, ed., The Romans Debate (Minneapolis 1977) 127-9. KARRIS, R. J. "Romans 14:1-15:13 and the Occasion of Romans" in K. P. Donfried, ed., The Romans Debate (Minneapolis 1977) 75-99. DAUTZENBERG, G. "Gesetzeskritik und Gesetzesgehorsam in der Jesustradition" in K. Kertelge, ed., Das Gesetz im Neuen Testament (Freiburg/Basel/Wien 1986) 48. WATSON, F. Paul, Judaism and the Gentiles (Cambridge 1986) 94-8. DOBBELER, A. VON, Glaube als Teilhabe (Tübingen 1987) 217-21. MEEKS, W. A. "Judgment and the Brother: Romans 14:1-15:13" in G. F. Hawthorne and O. Betz, eds., Tradition and Inter-pretation in the New Testament (FS E. E. Ellis; Grand Rapids/Tübingen 1987) 290-300. OSTEN-SACKEN, P. VON DER, Evangelium und Tora: Aufsätze zu Paulus (München 1987) 127f. SCHMELLER, TH. Paulus und die "Diatribe" (Münster 1987) 225-8. MEEKS, W. A. "The Polyphonic Ethics of the Apostle Paul," Annual of the Society of Christian Ethics (1988) 17-29. BECKER, J. Paulus. Der Apostel der Völker (Tübingen 1989) 360f. MARCUS, J. "The Circumcision and the Uncircumcision in Rome," NTS 35 (1989) 67-81, esp.68ff. SCHÄFER, K. Gemeinde als "Bruderschaft" (Frankfurt/Bern/New York/Paris 1989) 225-48. SCHNELLE, U. Wandlungen im paulinischen Denken (Stuttgart 1989) 72f. SIMONIS, W. Der gefangene Paulus. Die Entstehung des sogenannten Römerbriefs und anderer urchristlicher Schriften in Rom (Frank-furt/Bern/New York/Paris 1990) 61-8. TOMSON, P. J. Paul and the Jewish Law (Assen/Maastricht; Minneapolis 1990) 64, 236-54. WATSON, F. "The Two Roman Congregations: Romans 14:1-15:13" in K. P. Donfried, ed., The Romans Debate. Revised and Expanded Edition (Peabody, MA 1991) 203-15.

14:1–15:7   NIEDER, L. Die Motive der Religiös-Sittlichen Paränese in den Paulinischen Gemeinde-briefen (1956) 71-77. LAUB, F. Eschatologische Verkündigung und Lebensgestaltung nach Paulus. (Regensburg 1973) 90f.

14:1–15:6   AUSTGEN, R. J. Natural Motivation in the Pauline Epistles (1966) 98-101. SCHMITHALS, W. Der Römerbrief als historisches Problem (Gütersloh 1975) 60, 87, 95ff., 172, 178, 184f. ROBINSON, J. A. T. Wrestling with Romans (London 1979) 141-3. DUNN, J. D. G. "Paul's Epistle to the Romans: An Analysis of Structure and Argument" in ANRW II.25.4 (1987) 2879-81. LAMPE, P. Die stadtrömischen Christen in den ersten beiden Jahrhunderten (Tübingen ²1989) 9.

14:1-15:3   OUTKA, G. "On Harming Others," Interp 34 (1980) 384-7.

14:1-15:1   PAGELS, E. H. The Gnostic Paul. Gnostic Exegesis of the Pauline Letters (Philadelphia 1975) 44f.

14   MINEAR, P.S. Images of the Church in the New Testament (1960) 141f. KÄSEMANN, E. Exegetische Versuche und Besinnungen (1964) I 116f. FEINE, D. P. und BEHM, D. J. Einleitung in das Neue Testament (Heidelberg 1950) 174f. GREENLEE, J. H. Nine Uncial Palimpsests of the Greek New Testament (Salt Lake City 1968) 96f. GOULDER, M. D. Midrash and Lection in Matthew (London 1974) 159f. DUNN, J. D. G. Jesus and the Spirit. A Study of the Religious and Charismatic Experience of Jesus and the First Christians as Reflected in the New Testament (London 1975) 205, 236, 268. RIDDER-BOS, H. Paul. An Outline of His Theology (Grand Rapids 1975) 289-306. SANDERS, J. T. Ethics in the New Testament. Change and Development (Philadelphia 1975) 62. SYNOFZIK, E. Die Gerichts- und Vergeltungsaussagen bei Paulus (Göttingen 1977) 45-8. RAYAN, S. The Holy Spirit: Heart of the Gospel and Christian Hope (Maryknoll/New York 1978) 91f. RICHARDSON, P. Paul's Ethic of Freedom (Philadelphia 1979) 133f. SCHADE, H.-H. Apokalyptische Christologie bei Paulus (Göttingen 1981) 58f. KLAIBER, W. Rechtfertigung und Gemeinde (Göttingen 1982) 251-5. BINDEMANN, W. Die Hoffnung der Schöpfung (Neukirchen 1983) 56. ECKSTEIN, H.-J. Der Begriff Syneidesis bei Paulus (Tübingen 1983) 256, 266, 271f., 276. KLEINKNECHT, K. T. Der leidende Gerechtfertigte (Tübingen 1984) 356, 361, 363f. KARRER, M. Die Johannesoffenbarung als Brief (Göttingen 1986) 201. MacDONALD, M. Y. The Pauline Churches (Cambridge 1988) 68. WEDDERBURN, A. J. M. The Reasons for Romans (Edinburgh 1988) 31, 45, 48f., 59, 61, 79, 85. DUNN, J. D. G. Jesus, Paul and the Law (London 1990) 12, 39, 49, 50, 52, 175, 177, 179. SANDERS, E. P. Jewish Law from Jesus to the Mishnah (London/Philadelphia 1990) 96, 283f.

14:1ff.   LOEWENICH, W. VON "Bilder" in TRE 6 (1980) 546. MOHRLANG, R. Matthew and Paul (Cambridge 1984) 30f. SLENCZKA, R. "Glaube VI" in TRE 13 (1984) 363.

14:1-23   VOLF, J. M. G. Paul and Perseverance (Tübingen 1990) 85-97, 155, 241n.50, 285.

14:1-12   KRAMER, W. Christos Kyrios Gottessohn (1963) §§ 47c, 57d. MATTERN, L. Das Verständnis des Gerichtes bei Paulus (1966) 158ff. MERK, O. Handeln aus Glauben (1968) 167-69. CRUZ, H. Christological Motives and Motivated Actions in Pauline Paraenesis (Frankfurt/Bern/New York/Paris 1990) 89-98.

14:1-9   STECK, K.G. in G. Eichholz ed., Herr, tue meine Lippen auf, 4 (1965) 486ff.

14:1-6   SANDERS, E. P. Paul, the Law, and the Jewish People (London 1985) 112, 143, 149, 161, 177, 204n.67. MacDONALD, M. Y. The Pauline Churches (Cambridge 1988) 33.

14:1-5   STAAB, K. Pauluskommentare aus der griechischen Kirche (Münster ²1984) 536:1-30 Phot.

14:1-4   FORELL, G. W. The Christian Lifestyle. Reflections on Romans 12-5 (Philadelphia 1975) 44-7. STAAB, K. Pauluskommentare aus der griechischen Kirche (Münster ²1984) 409:19-410:32.

14:1-3   STAAB, K. Pauluskommentare aus der griechischen Kirche (Münster ²1984) 78:20-79:7 Apoll.

14:1   HARADA, M. Paul's Weakness. A Study in Pauline Polemics (II Cor 10-13) (University Microfilms, Inc. Ann Arbor MI 1968) 55-62. SCHMITHALS, W. Der Römerbrief als historisches Problem (Gütersloh 1975) 189. MUELLER, P.-G. Der Traditionsprozess im Neuen Testament (Freiburg 1982) 228. KOCH, D.-A. Die Schrift als Zeuge des Evangeliums (Tübingen 1986) 281-4. SCHÄFER, K. Gemeinde als "Bruderschaft" (Frankfurt/Bern/New York/Paris 1989) 232f.

14:2   HARADA, M. Paul's Weakness. A Study in Pauline Polemics (II Cor 10-13) (University Microfilms, Inc. Ann Arbor MI 1968) 63-7. SCHMITHALS, W. Der Römerbrief als historisches Problem (Gütersloh 1975) 97, 101. MARCUS, J. "The Circumcision and the Uncircumcision in Rome," NTS 35 (1989) 67-81, esp. 71f. SCHÄFER, K. Gemeinde als "Bruderschaft" (Frankfurt/Bern/New York/Paris 1989) 225ff.

14:3ff.   CRUZ, H. Christological Motives and Motivated Actions in Pauline Paraenesis (Frankfurt/Bern/New York/Paris 1990) 136.

14:3-12   SCHÄFER, K. Gemeinde als "Bruderschaft" (Frankfurt/ Bern/New York/Paris 1989) 233-5.

14:3-10   DUPONT, D.J. "Appel aux Faibles et aux Forts dans la Communauté Raomaine (Rom. 14, 1-15, 13)" Studiorum Paulinorum Congressus Internationalis Catholicus 1961 (1963) I359-60.

14:3   HARADA, M. Paul's Weakness. A Study in Pauline Polemics (II Cor 10-13) (University Microfilms, Inc. Ann Arbor MI 1968) 62f.

14:3a.6   CRUZ, H. Christological Motives and Motivated Actions in Pauline Paraenesis (Frankfurt/Bern/New York/Paris 1990) 92-6.

14:4ff.   KÄSEMANN, E. Exegetische Versuche und Besinnungen (1964) I 116.

14:4-13   THUESING, W. Per Christum in Deum (1965) 30-38, 56f.

14:4-12   HERMANN, I. Kyrios und Pneuma (1961) 89-91.

14:4   AONO, T. Die Entwicklung des paulinischen Gerichtsgedankens bei den Apostolischen Vätern (Bern/Frankfurt/Las Vegas 1979) 4ff. STAAB, K. Pauluskommentare aus der griechischen Kirche (Münster ²1984) 109:13-15 Diod; 224:29-31 Sev.

14:5-9   HARADA, M. Paul's Weakness. A Study in Pauline Polemics (II Cor 10-13) (University Microfilms, Inc. Ann Arbor MI 1968) 67-73. FORELL, G. W. The Christian Lifestyle. Reflections on Romans 12-15 (Philadelphia 1975) 48-59.

14:5-6   DEDEREN, R. "On Esteeming One Day Better Than Another" AUSS 9 (1, '71) 16-35. SCHMITHALS, W. Der Römerbrief als historisches Problem (Gütersloh 1975) 97, 99, 101. DAUTZENBERG, G. "Gesetzeskritik und Gesetzesgehorsam in der Jesustradition" in Kertelge, K., ed., Das Gesetz im Neuen Testament (Freiburg/Basel/Wien 1986) 48.

14:5   BECKER, J. "Quid plerophoreisthai in Rom 14, 5 significet" VerbDom 45 (1, '67) 11-18. BECKER, J. "Zu *plērophoreisthai* in Rom 14, 5," Biblica 65 (3, 1984) 364. STAAB, K. Pauluskommentare aus der griechischen Kirche (Münster ²1984) 164:24-34 ThM; 431:1-2 Oek. WEDDERBURN, A. J. M. The Reasons for Romans (Edinburgh 1988) 20, 32f. SCHÄFER, K. Gemeinde als "Bruderschaft" (Frankfurt/Bern/New York/Paris 1989) 226ff. CRUZ, H. Christological Motives and Motivated Actions in Pauline Paraenesis (Frankfurt/Bern/New York/Paris 1990) 97f.

14:6ff.　　SCHRAGE, W. Die konkreten Einzelgebote in der paulinischen Paränese (1961) 79, 155. HAHN, F. Das Verständnis der Mission im Neuen Testament (1965) 92.

14:6-17　　QUESNELL, Q. This Good News (1964) 98f.

14:6-13　　STAAB, K. Pauluskommentare aus der griechischen Kirche (Münster ²1984) 536:31-538:5 Phot.

14:6-7　　SCHRAGE, W. Die konkreten Einzelgebote in der paulinischen Paränese (1961) 43, 158.

14:6　　BOUSSET, W. Die Religion des Judentums im Späthellenistischen Zeitalter (1966=1926) 178. MERK, O. Handeln aus Glauben (1968) 168-70. BAUMERT, N. Täglich Sterben und Auferstehen. Der Literalsinn von 2 Kor 4, 12-5, 10 (München 1973) 379. KLAUCK, H.-J. Herrenmahl und hellenistischer Kult (Münster 1982) 278, 281f. STAAB, K. Pauluskommentare aus der griechischen Kirche (Münster ²1984) 109:16-27 Diod; 410:33-411:2 Genn. BERGER, K. und COLPE, C., eds., Religionsgeschichtliches Textbuch zum Neuen Testament (Göttingen/Zürich 1987) 226. VOLLENWEIDER, S. Freiheit als neue Schöpfung (Göttingen 1989) 230. SANDERS, E. P. Jewish Law from Jesus to the Mishnah (London/Philadelphia 1990) 27.

14:7-13　　SOUCEK, J.B. GPM 14 (1960) 221-28. HARDER, G. GPM 20 (1965/66) 278-87. KABITZ, U. "Sonntag nach Trinitatis" in Predigtstudien (1971-72), ed. E.Lange 118-22. SURKAU, H.-W. GPM 26 (1972) 281-89. STECK, J. G. "Romans 14:7-13 (14-19)" in GPM 32 (1978) 273-80.

14:7-12　　BRAUN, H. GPM 8 (1954) 278-83. DOERNE, M. Die alten Episteln (1967) 258-61. BAUMGARTEN, J. Paulus und die Apokalyptik (Neukirchen-Vluyn 1975) 82-5.

14:7-9　　STANLEY, D.M. Christ's Resurrection in Pauline Soteriology (1961) 198-200. HOFFMANN, P. Die Toten in Christus (1966) 342f, 347. JEREMIAS, J. Abba (1966) 280. WEBER, O. Predigtmeditationen (1967) 66-69. BAULES, R. "Le chrétien appartient au Seigneur. Rm 14, 7-9," AssS 55 (1974) 10-5. SCHMITHALS, W. "Zur Herkunft der gnostischen Elemente in der Sprache des Paulus" in B. Aland et al., eds., Gnosis (FS H. Jonas; Göttingen 1978) 391-3. FROITZHEIM, F. Christologie und Eschatologie bei Paulus (Würzburg 1979) 119f. SCHOLZ, F. und BERTHOLD-SCHOLZ, C. in P. Krusche et al., eds., Predigtstudien für das Kirchenjahr 1980. Perikopenreihe II/2 (Stuttgart 1980) 264-71. VOIGT, G. in GPM 34 (1980) 420-5. KLEIN, G. "Eschatologie" in TRE 10 (1982) 280, 285. STAAB, K. Pauluskommentare aus der griechischen Kirche (Münster ²1984) 109:28-110:10 Diod; 164:35-165:12 ThM. LINK, C. in GPM 40 (1985/86) 486-95. SCHNELLE, U. Wandlungen im paulinischen Denken (Stuttgart 1989) 44. VOLLENWEIDER, S. Freiheit als neue Schöpfung (Göttingen 1989) 58. CRUZ, H. Christological Motives and Motivated Actions in Pauline Paraenesis (Frankfurt/Bern/New York/Paris 1990) 89-92.

14:7-8　　SEVENSTER, J.N. Paul and Seneca (1961) 60, 159. BULTMANN, R. Theologie des Neuen Testaments (1965) 332f., 353. MERK, O. Handeln aus Glauben (1968) 69, 98, 171, 235. FRIEDRICH, G. "Freiheit und Liebe im ersten Korintherbrief" in Auf das Wort kommt es an. Gesammelte Aufsätze (Göttingen 1978) 182. BISER, E. Der Zeuge (Graz/Wien/Köln 1981) 94, 141f. JEZIERSKA, E. J. "'Żyjemy dla Pana, umieramy dla Pana . . . ' Św. Pawel o proegzystencji chrześcijanina w 2 Kor 5, 15 i Rz 14, 7-8 ('Nous vivons pour le Seigneur, nous mourons pour le Seigneur . . . ' St Paul et la proéxistence du chrétien dans le 2 Cor 5, 15 et le R 14, 7-8)," CoTh 59 (3, 1989) 27-33. CRUZ,

H. Christological Motives and Motivated Actions in Pauline Paraenesis (Frankfurt/Bern/New York/Paris 1990) 130-3.

14:7   BOLDREY, R. and J. Chauvinist Or Feminist? Paul's View of Women (Grand Rapids 1976) 51f. THISELTON, A. C. The Two Horizons (Grand Rapids 1980) 268. HUBER, W. "Frieden" in TRE 11 (1983) 636. MALHERBE, A. J. Moral Exhortation. A Greco-Roman Sourcebook (Philadelphia 1986) 130.

14:8-9   HOFFMANN, P. Die Toten in Christus (1966) 7. SIBER, P. Mit Christus leben (Zürich 1971) 63.

14:8   BAUMERT, N. Täglich Sterben und Auferstehen. Der Literalsinn von 2 Kor 4, 12-5, 10 (München 1973) 240. ROON, A. VAN, The Authenticity of Ephesians (Leiden 1974) 167. FISCHER, U. Eschatologie und Jenseitserwartung im hellenistischen Diasporajudentum (Berlin 1978) 96. THISELTON, A. C. The Two Horizons (Grand Rapids 1980) 268. ROCHAIS, G. Les récits de résurrection des morts dans le Nouveau Testament (Cambridge 1981) 197, 201, 204. SCHNACKENBURG, R. Die sittliche Botschaft des Neuen Testaments, Band 1 (Freiburg/Basel/Wien 1986) 227.

14:9-11.   CERFAUX, L. Christ in the Theology of St. Paul (1959) 28, 57, 96, 491, 380.

14:9   BIEDER, W. Die Vorstellung von der Höllenfahrt Jesu Christi (1949) 75f. ROBINSON, J.M. Kerygma und historischer Jesus (1960) 179 SCHWEIZER, E. Erniedrigung und Erhöhung bei Jesus und seinen Nachfolgern (1962) §9b. HAHN, F. Christologische Hoheitstitel (1963) 200, 216. MERK, O. Handeln aus Glauben (1968) 168f, 171f., 232, 237. LUZ, U. Das Geschichtsverständnis des Paulus (1968) 325f. DALTON, W. J. Christ's Proclamation to the Spirits. A Study of 1 Peter 3:18—4:6 (Rome 1965) 188. SIBER, P. Mit Christus leben (Zürich 1971) 24, 33. CONZELMANN, H. Theologie als Schriftauslegung (München 1974) 75, 135A25, 136A42, 178. GOPPELT, L. Theologie des Neuen Testaments I: Jesu Wirken in seiner theologischen Bedeutung [J. Roloff, ed.] (Göttingen 1975) 280f. FRIEDRICH, G. "Die Auferweckung Jesu, eine Tat Gottes oder ein Interpretament der Jünger" in Auf das Wort kommt es an. Gesammelte Aufsätze (Göttingen 1978) 348f. HOFFMANN, P. "Auferstehung" in TRE 4 (1979) 483. FROITZHEIM, F. Christologie und Eschatologie bei Paulus (Würzburg 1979) 91. SUBILIA, V. "Il Signore dei Morti e dei viventi (Rom 14, 9)," Protest. 35 (1980) 1-12. STAAB, K. Pauluskommentare aus der griechischen Kirche (Münster ²1984) 411:3-4 Genn. STUHLMACHER, P. Jesus von Nazareth—Christus des Glaubens (Stuttgart 1988) 56. CRUZ, H. Christological Motives and Motivated Actions in Pauline Paraenesis (Frankfurt/Bern/New York/Paris 1990) 82-8. LOHSE, E. Die Entstehung des Neuen Testaments (Stuttgart/Berlin/Köln ⁵1991) 20.

14:10-13   DAVIES, W.D. Paul and Rabbinic Judaism (1955) 138, 289. FÜRST, W. in GPM 34 (1980) 281-5. SCHMIDT, H. P. und KERN, H. in P. Krusche et al., eds., Predigtstudien für das Kirchenjahr 1980. Perikopenreihe II/2 (Stuttgart 1980) 127-34. SCHELLONG, D. in GPM 40 (1985/86) 348-54.

14:10-12   HAHN, F. Das Verständnis der Mission im Neuen Testament (1965) 87. DAVIES, W. D. The Sermon on the Mount (Cambridge 1966) 96. FORELL, G. W. The Christian Lifestyle. Reflections on Romans 12-15 (Philadelphia 1975) 52-5. AONO, T. Die Entwicklung des paulinischen Gerichtsgedankens bei den Apostolischen Vätern (Bern/Frankfurt/Las Vegas 1979) 4ff.

14:10-11   STAAB, K. Pauluskommentare aus der griechischen Kirche (Münster ²1984) 165:13-39 ThM; 411:5-28 Genn. BECKER, J. Paulus. Der Apostel der Völker (Tübingen 1989) 296f., 346, 460.

14:10   MATTERN, L. Das Verstándnis des Gerichtes bei Paulus (1966) 158ff., 166, 186, 559. MERK, O. Handeln aus Glauben (1968) 55, 150, 168, 201, 238. ROETZEL, C.J. Judgement in the Community (1972) 134-36. DAVIES, W. D. The Sermon on the Mount (Cambridge 1966) 99. BAUMERT, N. Täglich Sterben und Auferstehen. Der Literalsinn von 2 Kor 4, 12-5, 10 (München 1973) 245f., 287. FROITZHEIM, F. Christologie und Eschatologie bei Paulus (Würzburg 1979) 179. STOWERS, S. K. The Diatribe and Paul's Letter to the Romans (Chico CA 1981) 81, 115. KLAUCK, H.-J. Herrenmahl und hellenist- ischer Kult (Münster 1982) 247, 281. THEISSEN, G. Psychologische Aspekte paulinischer Theologie (Göttingen 1983) 108f., 112. STAAB, K. Pauluskom- mentare aus der griechischen Kirche (Münster ²1984) 79:8-80:13 Apoll. KREIT- ZER, L. J. Jesus and God in Paul's Eschatology (Sheffield 1987) 99, 107-9, 111, 114, 156f., 221n.45, 223n.56. REISER, M. Die Gerichtspredigt Jesu (Münster 1990) 73, 89.

14:11-12   STAAB, K. Pauluskommentare aus der griechischen Kirche (Münster ²1984) 431:3-6 Oek.

14:11   BRUNNER, E. Dogmatik I (1946) 168. ELLIS, E.E. Paul's Use of the Old Testament (19570 107f, 124f, 150f. LUZ, U. Das Geschichtsverständnis des Paulus (1968) 101. BAARDA, T. "Jes. 45, 23 in het Nieuwe Testament (Rm 14, 11; Flp 2, 10v.)" GThT 71 (3, '71) 137-79. ELLIS, E. E. Prophecy and Hermeneutic in Early Christianity (Tübingen 1978) 137, 178, 182f. SCHIMAN- OWSKI, G. Weisheit und Messias (Tübingen 1985) 334. KOCH, D.-A. Die Schrift als Zeuge des Evangeliums (Tübingen 1986) 108, 184f., 246f. KREITZER, L. J. Jesus and God in Paul's Eschatology (Sheffield 1987) 107-9, 227n.89.

14:12-13   STAAB, K. Pauluskommentare aus der griechischen Kirche (Münster ²1984) 411:29-412:5 Genn.

14:12   REISER, M. Die Gerichtspredigt Jesu (Münster 1990) 291.

14:13ff.   KNOX, W.L. The Sources of the Synoptic Gospels II (1957) 102. MINEAR, P.S. Images of the Church in the New Testament (1960) 142f.

14:13-23   DUPONT, D.J. "Appel aux Faibles et aux Forts dans la Communauté Romaine (Rom. 14, 13-15, 13)" Studiorum Paulinorum Congressus Internationalis Catholicus 1961 (1963) I 361-2. MERK, O. Handeln aus Glauben (1968) 169- 71, 237. KITZBERGER, I. Bau der Gemeinde (Würzburg 1986) 34-45. SCHÄFER, K. Gemeinde als "Bruderschaft" (Frankfurt/Bern/New York/Paris 1989) 235-42.

14:13-16   FORELL, G. W. The Christian Lifestyle. Reflections on Romans 12-15 (Phila- delphia 1975) 56-9.

14:13-15   RIDDERBOS, H. Paul. An Outline of His Theology (Grand Rapids 1975) 291- 5. MULLINS, T. Y. "Topos as a NT Form," JBL 99 (1980) 546.

14:13   MUELLER, K. Anstoss und Gericht (1969) 32-45. PALLIS, A. Notes on St.John and the Apocalypse (London 1928) 55. DAVIES, W. D. The Sermon on the Mount (Cambridge 1966) 99. BAUMERT, N. Täglich Sterben und Auferstehen. Der Literalsinn von 2 Kor 4, 12-5, 10 (München 1973) 28. ROON, A. VAN, The Authenticity of Ephesians (Leiden 1974) 167. STAAB, K. Paulus- kommentare aus der griechischen Kirche (Münster ²1984) 166:1-16 ThM. WEN- HAM, D. "Paul's Use of the Jesus Tradition. Three Samples" in D. Wenham, ed., Gospel Perspectives. The Jesus Tradition Outside the Gospels, Vol 5 (Sheffield 1984) 15. OLIVEIRA, A. DE, Die Diakonie der Gerechtigkeit und der Versöhnung in der Apologie des 2. Korintherbriefes. Analyse und Aus- legung von 2 Kor 2, 14-4, 6; 5, 11-6, 10 (Münster 1990) 404.

14:14-20	HÜBNER, H. Das Gesetz bei Paulus. Ein Beitrag zum Werden der paulinischen Theologie (Göttingen 1978) 77-80.
14:14f.,20	PASCHEN, W. Rein und Unrein (1970) 170f.
14:14-15	STAAB, K. Pauluskommentare aus der griechischen Kirche (Münster ²1984) 166:17-27 ThM. VOLLENWEIDER, S. Freiheit als neue Schöpfung (Göttingen 1989) 215, 240n., 400.
14:14	BEST, E. One Body in Christ (1955) 3n, 31, 33. EVANS, O.E. "Paul's Certainties. III. What God Requires of Man—Rom. xiv.14" ET 69 (7, '58) 199-202. SCHRAGE, W. Die konkreten Einzelgebote in der paulinsichen Paränese (1961) 104, 154, 214, 231, 241, 243. KRAMER, W. Christos Kyrios Gottessohn (1963) §51a. KÄSEMANN, E. Exegetische Versuche und Besinnungesn (1964) I 117. KÄSEMANN, E. New Testament Questions of Today (1969) 192. SCHMITHALS, W. Der Römerbrief als historisches Problem (Gütersloh 1975) 99f., 103. HILL, D. New Testament Prophecy (Atlanta 1979) 177. SCHREY, H.-H. "Egoismus" in TRE 9 (1982) 305. RÄISÄNEN, H. Paul and the Law (Tübingen 1983) 24, 48, 78f., 246-8, 258. STAAB, K. Pauluskommentare aus der griechischen Kirche (Münster ²1984) 80:14-8 Apoll; 110:11-3 Diod; 225:1 Sev; 412:6-9 Genn; 538:6-11 Phot. WENHAM, D. "Paul's Use of the Jesus Tradition. Three Samples" in D. Wenham, ed., Gospel Perspectives. The Jesus Tradition Outside the Gospels, Vol 5 (Sheffield 1984) 15. BOOTH, R. P. Jesus and the Laws of Purity. Tradition History and Legal History in Mark 7 (Sheffield 1986) 82, 87, 99f., 107. DAUTZENBERG, G. "Gesetzeskritik und Gesetzesgehorsam in der Jesustradition" in K. Kertelge, ed., Das Gesetz im Neuen Testament (Freiburg/Basel/Wien 1986) 49. RÄISÄNEN, H. The Torah and Christ (Helsinki 1986) 214f., 234ff., 238. BERGER, K. und COLPE, C., eds., Religionsgeschichtliches Textbuch zum Neuen Testament (Göttingen/Zürich 1987) 226. GARCÍA MARTÍNEZ, F. "Les limites de la communauté: pureté et impureté à Qumrân et dans I e Nouveau Testament" in T. Baarda et al., eds., Text and Testimony (FS A. F. J. Klijn; Kampen 1988) 121. LINDARS, B. "All Foods Clean: Thoughts on Jesus and the Law" in B. Lindars, ed., Law and Religion (Cambridge 1988) 61ff. WEDDERBURN, A. J. M. The Reasons for Romans (Edinburgh 1988) 20, 32. WALTER, N. "Paul and the Early Christian Jesus-Tradition" in A. J. M. Wedderburn, ed., Paul and Jesus. Collected Essays (Sheffield 1989) 51-80, esp.57, 71f., 75. DUNN, J. D. G. Jesus, Paul and the Law (London 1990) 39, 41, 50f., 58n.72, 80.
14:14a	BOOTH, R. P. Jesus and the Laws of Purity. Tradition History and Legal History in Mark 7 (Sheffield 1986) 120.
14:15-17	STAAB, K. Pauluskommentare aus der griechischen Kirche (Münster ²1984) 80:19-32 Apoll; 412:10-25 Genn.
14:15	SCHRAGE, W. Die konkreten Einzelgebote in der paulinischen Paränese (1961) 47. DELLING, D. Die Taufe im Neuen Testament (1963) 117. HAHN, F. Christologische Hoheitstitel (1962) 202, 210. KRAMER, W. Christos Kyrios Gottessohn (1963) §4b. MATTERN, L. Das Verständnis des Gerichtes bei Paulus (1966) 62, 111, 115ff., 232. LEHMANN, K. Auferweckt am Dritten Tag nach der Schrift (1968) 34-35, 49, 93, 121, 128A. MERK, O. Handeln aus Glauben (1968) 5, 123, 126, 171-73, 237. DELLING, G. Der Kreuzestod Jesu in der urchristlichen Verkündigung (Göttingen 1972) 40-2. CONZELMANN, H. and LINDENMANN, A. Arbeitsbuch zum Neuen Testament (Tübingen 1975) 181, 218. AONO, T. Die Entwicklung des paulinischen Gerichtsgedankens bei den Apostolischen Vätern (Bern/Frankfurt/Las Vegas 1979) 4ff. FROITZHEIM, F. Christologie und Eschatologie bei Paulus (Würzburg 1979)

31ff. OUTKA, G. "On Harming Others," Interp 34 (1980) 386. KLAUCK, H.-J. Herrenmahl und hellenistischer Kult (Münster 1982) 281f., 307. STAAB, K. Pauluskommentare aus der griechischen Kirche (Münster ²1984) 431:7-9 Oek. SCHNACKENBURG, R. Die sittliche Botschaft des Neuen Testaments, Band 1 (Freiburg/Basel/Wien 1986) 216. JONGE, M. DE "Jesus' death for others and the death of the Maccabean martyrs" in T. Baarda et al., eds., Text and Testimony (FS A. F. J. Klijn; Kampen 1988) 142-51, esp.145. CRUZ, H. Christological Motives and Motivated Actions in Pauline Paraenesis (Frankfurt/Bern/ New York/Paris 1990) 76-81.

14:16-17 STAAB, K. Pauluskommentare aus der griechischen Kirche (Münster ²1984) 538:12-34 Phot.

14:16 VOLLENWEIDER, S. Freiheit als neue Schöpfung (Göttingen 1989) 224.

14:17ff. FEINE, P. Der Apostel Paulus (1927) 411f.

14:17-19 FRICK, R GPM 7 (1953) 157-161. IWAND, H.-J. Predigt-Meditationen (1964) 134-37.

14:17-19 BIEDER, W. Die Verheissung der Taufe im Neuen Testament (Zürich 1966) 285f. FORELL, G. W. The Christian Lifestyle. Reflections on Romans 12-15 (Philadelphia 1975) 60-3. KREYSSIG, P. und ASKANI, T. in P. Krusche et al., eds., Predigtstudien für das Kirchenjahr 1980. Perikopenreihe II/2 (Stuttgart 1980) 227-34. FALKENROTH, A. in GPM 40 (1985/86) 436-42.

14:17-18 BAUMGARTEN, J. Paulus und die Apokalyptik (Neukirchen-Vluyn 1975) 89-91.

14:17 BOUSSET, W. Die Religion des Judentums im Späthellenistischen Zeitalter (1966=1926) 214, 277. FEINE, P. Der Apostel Paulus (1927) 582f. STÄHELIN, E. Die Verkündigung des Reiches Gottes in der Kirche Jesu Christi I (1951) 28, 278, 376. BEST, E. One Body in Christ (1955) 11n. KNOX, W.L. The Sources of the Synoptic Gospels II (1957) 108. ROBINSON, J.M. Kerygma und Historischer Jesus (1960) 140. DELLING, G. Die Taufe im Neuen Testament (1963) 135. JÜNGEL, E. Paulus und Jesus (1966) 26, 267. KERTELGE, K. "Rechtfertigung" bei Paulus (1967) 298. GOPPELT, L. Christolgie und Ethik (1968) 163f. MERK, O. Handeln aus Glauben (1968) 108f, 169-171, 173. HAINZ, J. Ekklesia (Regensburg 1972) 327f. LADD, G. E. A Theology of the New Testament (Grand Rapids 1974) 411, 413, 481, 484, 491, 518, 541, 630. MÜNCHOW, C. Ehik und Eschatologie (Göttingen 1981) 165ff. KLEIN, G. "Eschatologie" in TRE 10 (1982) 296. DELLING, G. "Frieden" in TRE 11 (1983) 615, 617. TOIT, A. B. DU "Freude" in TRE 11 (1983) 585. GRÄSSER, E. "Rechtfertigung des Einzelnen—Rechtfertigung der Welt: Neutestamentliche Erwägungen" in W. C. Weinreich, ed., The New Testament Age (FS B. Reicke; Macon GA 1984) I, 233. JOHNSTON, G. "'Kingdom of God' Sayings in Paul's Letters" in P. Richardson and J. C. Hurd, eds., From Jesus to Paul (FS F. W. Beare; Waterloo 1984) 144, 152-5. STAAB, K. Pauluskommentare aus der griechischen Kirche (Münster ²1984) 166:25-31 ThM. HÄRING, H. Das Problem des Bösen in der Theologie (Darmstadt 1985) 34. RICHES, J. "Heiligung" in TRE 14 (1985) 733. WALTHER, C. "Herrschaft Gottes/Reich Gottes VII" in TRE 15 (1986) 240. DONFRIED, K. P. "The Kingdom of God in Paul" in W. Willis, ed., The Kingdom of God in 20th-Century Interpretation (Peabody, Ma 1987) 178f. KREITZER, L. J. Jesus and God in Paul's Eschatology (Sheffield 1987) 110, 132f. BECKER, J. Paulus. Der Apostel der Völker (Tübingen 1989) 103, 111, 302f.

14:18-20 STAAB, K. Pauluskommentare aus der griechischen Kirche (Münster ²1984) 412:26-28 Genn.

14:18   SCHRAGE, W. Die kondreten Einzelgebote in der paulinischen Paränese (1961)
               78f, 83, 216. KRAMER, W. Christos Kyrios Gottessohn (1963) 62c. STAAB,
               K. Pauluskommentare aus der griechischen Kirche (Münster [2]1984) 539:1-4
               Phot.
14:19-15:2   VIELHAUER, P. Oikodome [G. Klein, ed.] (München 1979) 93-5.
14:19-20   PFAMMATTER, J. Die Kirche als Bau (1960) 57ff.
14:19   CLARK, K. W. "The Meaning of (KATA)KYRIEYEIN" in The Gentile Bias
               and other Essays [selected by J. L. Sharpe III] (Leiden 1980) 207-12.
               DELLING, G. "Frieden" in TRE 11 (1983) 615, 617. HAHN, F. "Gottesdienst
               III" in TRE 14 (1985) 35.
14:20-23   FORELL, G. W. The Christian Lifestyle. Reflections on Romans 12-15
               (Philadelphia 1975) 64-7.
14:20-21   CRUZ, H. Christological Motives and Motivated Actions in Pauline Paraenesis
               (Frankfurt/Bern/New York/Paris 1990) 82-8.
14:20   SCHRAGE, W. Die konkreten Einzelgebote in der paulinsichen Paränese (1961)
               214, 231, 243. BAUMERT, N. Täglich Sterben und Auferstehen. Der Literal-
               sinn von 2 Kor 4, 12-5, 10 (München 1973) 230f. SCHMITHALS, W. Der
               Römerbrief als historisches Problem (Gütersloh 1975) 101, 103. STAAB, K.
               Pauluskommentare aus der griechischen Kirche (Münster [2]1984) 167:1-17 ThM;
               431:10-11 Oek. RÄISÄNEN, H. The Torah and Christ (Helsinki 1986) 238,
               256. LOHFINK, G. Studien zum Neuen Testament (Stuttgart 1989) 280-3.
14:21-22   STAAB, K. Pauluskommentare aus der griechischen Kirche (Münster [2]1984)
               413:1-8 Genn.
14:21   SCHMITHALS, W. Der Römerbrief als historisches Problem (Gütersloh 1975)
               97, 105. KLAUCK, H.-J. Herrenmahl und hellenistischer Kult (Münster 1982)
               249, 281f. STAAB, K. Pauluskommentare aus der griechischen Kirche (Münster
               [2]1984) 110:14-17. BERGER, K. und COLPE, C., eds., Religionsgeschichtliches
               Textbuch zum Neuen Testament (Göttingen/Zürich 1987) 226. OLIVEIRA, A.
               DE, Die Diakonie der Gerechtigkeit und der Versöhnung in der Apologie des
               2. Korintherbriefes. Analyse und Auslegung von 2 Kor 2, 14-4, 6; 5, 11-6, 10
               (Münster 1990) 404.
14:22-23   DUNN, J. D. G. Jesus and the Spirit. A Study of the Religious and Charismatic
               Experience of Jesus and the First Christians as Peflected in the New Testament
               (London 1975) 212, 223. METZGER, B. M. Manuscripts of the Greek Bible
               (Oxford 1981) 134. KLAUCK, H.-J. Herrenmahl und hellenistischer Kult (Mün-
               ster 1982) 281f., 325. STAAB, K. Pauluskommentare aus der griechischen
               Kirche (Münster [2]1984) 110:18-22 Diod; 167:18-168:7 ThM; 413:9-12 Genn;
               539:5-17 Phot.
14:22   SCHRAGE, W. Die konkreten Einzelgebote in der paulinsichen Paränese (1961)
               47, 56, 85. KÄSEMANN, E. Exegetische Versuche und Besinnungen (1964) I
               116.
14:23   METZGER, B. M. "Explicit references in the works of Origen to variant
               readings in New Testament manuscripts": Historical and Literary Studies (1968)
               98f. FEINE, D. P. und BEHM, D. J. Einleitung in das Neue Testament (Heidel-
               berg 1950) 174f. KÜMMEL, W. G. Einleitung in das Neue Testament (Heidel-
               berg 1973) 275-7. SCHMITHALS, W. Der Römerbrief als historisches Problem
               (Gütersloh 1975) 108ff., 152. GAMBLE, H. The Textual History of the Letter
               to the Romans (Grand Rapids 1977) 16-29, 36. ALAND, K. "Der Schluss des
               Römerbriefes" in Neutestamentliche Entwürfe (München 1979) 284-301.
               KRÜGER, F. "Gewissen III" in TRE 13 (1984) 221. DOBBELER, A. VON,

Glaube als Teilhabe (Tübingen 1987) 219-21, 228-30. CLABEAUX, J. J. The Lost Edition of the Letters of Paul (CBQ.MS; Washington 1989) 3.

15-16   MANSON, T. W. "St.Paul's Letter to the Romans—and Others" in K. P. Donfried, ed., The Romans Debate (Minneapolis 1977) 6-15. CLABEAUX, J. J. The Lost Edition of the Letters of Paul (CBQ.MS; Washington 1989) 37.

15:1-16:24   GAMBLE, H. The Textual History of the Letter to the Romans (Grand Rapids 1977) 141, passim.

15:1-16:23   GAMBLE, H. The Textual History of the Letter to the Romans (Grand Rapids 1977) 141, passim. ALAND, K. "Der Schluss des Römerbriefes" in Neutestamentliche Entwürfe (München 1979) 284-301.

15   MARCHEL, W. Abba, Père! La Prière du Christ et des Crétiens (1963) 181-91, 213-43. MUNCK, J. Paul and the Salvation of Mankind (1959) 197f. EICHHOLZ, G. Die Theologie des Paulus im Umriss (1972) 20, 23ff. BECKER, J. Auferstehung der Toten im Urchristentum (Stuttgart 1976) 66-105. WILLIAMS, S. K. "The 'Righteousness of God' in Romans," JBL 99 (1980) 285-9. OSTENSACKEN, P. VON DER, Evangelium und Tora: Aufsätze zu Paulus (München 1987) 125-7, 129. MacDONALD, M. Y. The Pauline Churches (Cambridge 1988) 49. WEDDERBURN, A. J. M. The Reasons for Romans (Edinburgh 1988) 22f., 26f., 29, 74, 97f. BECKER, J. Paulus. Der Apostel der Völker (Tübingen 1989) 127, 130, 265, 461. LAMPE, P. Die stadtrömischen Christen in den ersten beiden Jahrhunderten (Tübingen ²1989) 125-7, 131.

15:1ff.   MINEAR, P.S. Images of the Church in the New Testament (1960) 141f.

15:1-13   THUESING, W. Per Christum in Deum (1965) 39-43, 49-50, 180f. SCHWEIZER, E. GPM 22 (1967/68) 11-16. MERK, O, Handeln aus Glauben (1968) 171-73. SCHWEIZER, E. Gott Versöhnt: 6 Reded in Nairobi (1971) 45-55. FROITZHEIM, F. Christologie und Eschatologie bei Paulus (Würzburg 1979) 47ff., 58ff. KITZBERGER, I. Bau der Gemeinde (Würzburg 1986) 46-58. WEDDERBURN, A. J. M. The Reasons for Romans (Edinburgh 1988) 84-7. MOISER, J. "Rethinking Romans 12-15," NTS 36 (1990) 571-82, esp.579f.

15:1-7   DE BOER, W.P. The Imitation of Paul (1962) 158f. LIMBECK, M. Mit Paulus Christ sein. Sachbuch zur Person und Theologie des Apostels Paulus (Stuttgart 1989) 124.

15:1-6   GEORGE, A. "Les Ecritures, Source d'Espérance (Romains 15, 1-6)" BVieC 22 ('58) 53-57. SANDERS, J. T. Ethics in the New Testament. Change and Development (Philadelphia 1975) 62. PEDERSEN, S. "Agape—der eschatologische Hauptbegriff bei Paulus" in S. Pedersen, ed., Die Paulinische Literatur und Theologie (Arhus/Göttingen 1980) 171f. KLEINKNECHT, K. T. Der leidende Gerechtfertigte (Tübingen 1984) 213, 274, 324, 356-64, 367. MALINA B. J. Christian Origins and Cultural Anthropology (Atlanta 1986) 135. SCHÄFER, K. Gemeinde als "Bruderschaft" (Frankfurt/Bern/New York/Paris 1989) 242-6.

15:1-3   SCHULZ, A. Nachfolge und Nachahmen (1962) 278ff. DUPONT, D.J. "Appel aux Faibles et aux Forts dans is Communauté Romaine (Rom. 14, 1-15, 13)" Studiorum Paulinorum Congressus Internationalis Catholicus 1961 (1963) I 362-63. FORELL, G. W. The Christian Lifestyle. Reflections on Romans 12-15 (Philadelphia 1975) 68-71. STAAB, K. Pauluskommentare aus der griechischen Kirche (Münster ²1984) 81:1-23 Apoll.

15:1-2   ROBINSON, J.M. Kerygma und historischer Jesus (1960) 178. SCHRAGE, W. Die konkreten Einzelgebote in der paulinsichen Paränese (1961) 97, 145, 232, 250, 252, 267. FRIEDRICH, G. "Freiheit und Liebe im ersten Korintherbrief" in Auf das Wort kommt es an. Gesammelte Aufsätze (Göttingen 1978) 182. METZGER, B. M. Manuscripts of the Greek Bible (Oxford 1981) 134. STAAB, K. Pauluskommentare aus der griechischen Kirche (Münster ²1984) 413:13-16 Genn. CRUZ, H. Christological Motives and Motivated Actions in Pauline Paraenesis (Frankfurt/Bern/New York/Paris 1990) 406-8.

15:1   KLAUCK, H.-J. Herrenmahl und hellenistischer Kult (Münster 1982) 272, 281f. STAAB, K. Pauluskommentare aus der griechischen Kirche (Münster ²1984) 168:8-14 ThM. CRUZ, H. Christological Motives and Motivated Actions in Pauline Paraenesis (Frankfurt/Bern/New York/ Paris 1990) 403-406.

15:2-3   KRAMER, W. Christos Kyrios Gottessohn (1963) §34a. MOHRLANG, R. Matthew and Paul (Cambridge 1984) 102f.

15:2   PFAMMATTER, J. Die Kirche als Bau (1960) 60f, 174.

15:3,7   SCHLIER H. "Ueber die christliche Freiheit," GuL 50 (1977) 178-93.

15:3,4   ELLIS, E. E. Paul's Use of the Old Testament (1957) 97, 116, 125, 139, 151, 172. SCHRAGE, W. Die konkreten Einzelgebote in der paulinischen Paränese (1961) 229, 236, 240.

15:3   ROBINSON, J.M. Kerygma und historischer Jesus (1960) 178. LJUNGMAN, H. Pistis (1964) 49-52. HAHN, F. Das Verständnis der Mission im Neuen Testament (1965) 92. MERK, O. Handeln aus Glauben (1968) 171, 173, 235, 238. MAUSER, U. Gottesbild und Menschwerdung (1971) 140, 174.176f., 181. HARMAN, A. M. Paul's Use of the Psalms (Ann Arbor MI 1968) 111-6. BAUMERT, N. Täglich Sterben und Auferstehen. Der Literalsinn von 2 Kor 4, 12-5, 10 (München 1973) 351. HANSON, A. T. Studies in Paul's Technique and Theology (London 1974) 15f., 36, 77, 158, 171, 181, 195, 213, 242. WORLEY, D. "'He Was Willing'," RestQ 18 (1975) 1-11. GERSTENBER-GER, G. und SCHRAGE, W. Leiden (Stuttgart 1977) 159; ET: J. E. Steely (trans.) Suffering (Nashville 1980) 184f. GRANT, R. M. "Paul and the Old Testament" in D. K. McKim, ed., The Authoritative Word (Grand Rapids 1983) 33. RICHARDSON, P. and HURD, J. C., eds., From Jesus to Paul (FS F. W. Beare; Waterloo 1984) 120-8. STAAB, K. Pauluskommentare aus der griechischen Kirche (Münster ²1984) 110:23-111:8 Diod; 413:17-25 Genn. POBEE, J. S. Persecution and Martyrdom in the Theology of Paul (Sheffield 1985) 49, 53, 64, 66, 70, 73. KOCH, D.-A. Die Schrift als Zeuge des Evangeliums (Tübingen 1986) 324ff. BREYTENBACH, C. Versöhnung (Neukirchen-Vluyn 1989) 125, 137, 158, 160, 197f., 201f., 208-10, 214. CRUZ, H. Christological Motives and Motivated Actions in Pauline Paraenesis (Frankfurt/ Bern/New York/Paris 1990) 399-403.

15:4-13   TRAUB, H. GPM 10 (1955) 6-10. STECK, K.G. in Herr, tue meine Lippen auf II, ed. G. Eichholz (1966) 15-25. DOERNE, M. Die alten Episteln (1967) 15-18. GATTWINKEL, K.-W. und BÜHLER, K.-W. in E. Lange, ed., Predigtstudien für das Kirchenjahr 1973/74 (Stuttgart 1973) 41-6. STECK, K. G. in GPM 28 (1973) 12-9. RIESS, H. und STAMMLER, E. in P. Krusche et al., eds., Predigtstudien für das Kirchenjahr 1981/82. Perikopenreihe IV/1 (Stuttgart 1981) 23-30. STUHLMANN, R. in GPM 36 (1981) 15-21. HOFIUS, O. in GPM 42 (1987/88) 23-9.

15:4-6   FORELL, G. W. The Christian Lifestyle. Reflections on Romans 12-15 (Philadelphia 1975) 72-5.

15:4-5   LUZ, U. Das Geschichtsverständnis des Paulus (1968) 110-13.

15:4   FITZMYER, J.A. NTS 7 (1960'61) 310. SIBER, P. Mit Christus leben (Zürich 1971) 162. MERKLEIN, H. Das Kirchliche Amt nach dem Epheserbrief (München 1973) 107, 163, 294, 316. DUGANDZIC, I. Das "Ja" Gottes in

Christus (Würzburg 1977) 234-9. JEWETT, P. K. Infant Baptism and the Covenant of Grace (Grand Rapids 1978) 154. VIELHAUER, P. "Paulus und das Alte Testament" in Oikodome [G. Klein, ed.] (München 1979) 197. KARPP, H. "Bibel" in TRE 6 (1980) 68. PLÜMACHER, E. "Bibel" in TRE 6 (1980) 17. LORENZI, L. DE "L' 'istruzione' che ci viene da Dio (Rom 15:4b)," PSV 1 (1980) 141-57. DENTON, D. R. "Hope and Perseverance," SouJTh 34 (1981) 313-20. HAYS, R. B. The Faith of Jesus Christ (Chico CA 1983) 237. NEBE, G. 'Hoffnung' bei Paulus (Göttingen 1983) 19, 23, 35f., 64f., 70, 73f., 233, 257. STAAB, K. Pauluskommentare aus der griechischen Kirche (Münster ²1984) 414:1-5 Genn. KOCH, D.-A. Die Schrift als Zeuge des Evangeliums (Tübingen 1986) 324ff. MALHERBE, A. J. Moral Exhortation. A Greco-Roman Sourcebook (Philadelphia 1986) 65. MÜLLER, H. M. "Homiletik" in TRE 15 (1986) 534. KECK, L. E. "Romans 15:4: An Interpolation?" in J. T. Carroll et al., eds., Faith and History (FS P. W. Meyer; Atlanta 1991) 125ff. BOCKMUEHL, M. N. A. Revelation and Mystery (Tübingen 1990) 154. ELLIS, E. E. The Old Testament in Early Christianity (Tübingen 1991) 70, 82, 107, 149.

15:5-6 MONTAGUE, G. T. Growth in Christ (Kirkwood/Mo. 1961) 64ff. WILES, G. P. Paul's Intercessory Prayers (London 1974) 29, 72, 77, 79, 86f., 96, 266, 270. SCHMITHALS, W. Der Römerbrief als historisches Problem (Gütersloh 1975) 126, 154ff., 157ff. GAMBLE, H. The Textual History of the Letter to the Romans (Grand Rapids 1977) 69. STAAB, K. Pauluskommentare aus der griechischen Kirche (Münster ²1984) 414:6-25 Genn.

15:5 SCHRAGE, W. Die konkreten Einzelgebote in der paulinischen Paränese (1961) 175, 177. WILES, G. P. Paul's Intercessory Prayers (London 1974) 30-2, 38, 81, 166f. SCHREY, H.-H. "Geduld" in TRE 12 (1984) 141. STAAB, K. Pauluskommentare aus der griechischen Kirche (Münster ²1984) 168:15-20.

15:6 HAHN, F. Christologische Hoheitstitel (1963) 110. WILES, G. P. Paul's Intercessory Prayers (London 1974) 81f., 213f., 267, 274f. WAINWRIGHT, G. "Gottesdienst IX" in TRE 14 (1985) 87.

15:7ff. LUZ, U. Das Geschichtsverständnis des Paulus (1968) 390.

15:7-33 HAHN, F. Das Verständnis der Mission im Neuen Testament (1965) 92f.

15:7-13 MINEAR, P.S. Images of the Church in the New Testament (1960) 71f., 73f., 142f. RICHARDSON, P. Israel in the Apostolic Church (1969) 144f. BIEDER, W. Die Verheissung der Taufe im Neuen Testament (Zürich 1966) 239-41. ZELLER, D. Juden und Heiden in der Mission des Paulus. Studien zum Römerbrief (Stuttgart 1973) 218ff., 264f. FORELL, G. W. The Christian Lifestyle. Reflections on Romans 12-15 (Philadelphia 1975) 76-9. SCHMITHALS, W. Der Römerbrief als historisches Problem (Gütersloh 1975) 46, 95ff., 157ff., 177. RICHARDSON, P. Paul's Ethic of Freedom (Philadelphia 1979) 134f. ROBINSON, J. A. T. Wrestling with Romans (London 1979) 143-5. MOXNES, H. Theology in Conflict (Leiden 1980) 86f., 217-9. KLEIN-KNECHT, K. T. Der leidende Gerechtfertigte (Tübingen 1984) 357, 360. DUNN, J. D. G. "Paul's Epistle to the Romans: An Analysis of Structure and Argument" in ANRW II.25.4 (1987) 2881. GASTON, L. Paul and the Torah (Vancouver 1987) 133f. SCHÄFER, K. Gemeinde als "Bruderschaft" (Frankfurt/Bern/New York/Paris 1989) 229-32. KECK, L. E. "Christology, Soteriology, and the Praise of God (Romans 15:7-13)" in R. T. Fortna and B. R. Gaventa, eds., The Conversation Continues. Studies in Paul and John (FS J. L. Martyn; Nashville 1990) 85-97. REICHRATH, H. L "Juden und Christen—Eine Frage von 'Ökumene'? Was uns Römer 15, 7-13 dazu lehrt," Judaica [Basel] 47 (1-2, 1991) 22-30.

15:7-12   DUPONT, D.J. "Appel aux Faibles et aux Forts dans la Commuaute Romaine (Rom. 14, 1-15, 13)" Studiorum Paulinorum Congressus Internationalis Catholicus 1961 (1963) I 362-64. KOCH, D.-A. Die Schrift als Zeuge des Evangeliums (Tübingen 1986) 281-4.

15:7-9   KLAIBER, W. Rechtfertigung und Gemeinde (Göttingen 1982) 255f. CRUZ, H. Christological Motives and Motivated Actions in Pauline Paraenesis (Frankfurt/Bern/New York/Paris 1990) 408-15.

15:7   SCHULZ, A. Nachfolgen und Nachahmen (1962) 280ff. HAHN, F. Christologische Hoheitstitel (1963) 202. KRAMER, W. Christos Kyrios Gottessohn (1963) §34a, 62e. LJUNGMAN, H. Pistis (1964) 48-50. MERK, O. Handeln aus Glauben (1968) 167, 172f., 226, 235, 237f. SANDERS, J. T. Ethics in the New Testament. Change and Development (Philadelphia 1975) 63. SCHMITHALS, W. Der Römerbrief als historisches Problem (Gütersloh 1975) 157ff. SCHRÖER, H. "Beratung" in TRE 5 (1980) 593. BLANK, J. Paulus. Von Jesus zum Christentum (München 1982) 119. MOHRLANG, R. Matthew and Paul (Cambridge 1984) 85, 102, 175. STAAB, K. Pauluskommentare aus der griechischen Kirche (Münster ²1984) 168:21-27 ThM; 414:26-28 Genn. WEDDERBURN, A. J. M. The Reasons for Romans (Edinburgh 1988) 25, 32, 87, 148f.

15:8-9   LJUNGMAN, H. Pistis (1964) 48-54. SCHMITHALS, W. Der Römerbrief als historisches Problem (Gütersloh 1975) 95, 161. MOXNES, H. Theology in Conflict (Leiden 1980) 83, 86f., 89, 222. WILLIAMS, S. K. "The 'Righteousness of God' in Romans," JBL 99 (1980) 286-9. STAAB, K. Pauluskommentare aus der griechischen Kirche (Münster ²1984) 415:1-13 Genn. DAUTZENBERG, G. "Gesetzeskritik und Gesetzesgehorsam in der Jesustradition" in K. Kertelge, ed., Das Gesetz im Neuen Testament (Feiburg/Basel/Wien 1986) 49, 52-4. OLIVEIRA, A. DE, Die Diakonie der Gerechtigkeit und der Versöhnung in der Apologie des 2. Korintherbriefes. Analyse und Auslegung von 2 Kor 2, 14-4, 6; 5, 11-6, 10 (Münster 1990) 229.

15:8   MAUSER, U. Gottesbild und Menschwerdung (1971) 142, 174, 176f., 181f. ZELLER, D. Juden und Heiden in der Mission des Paulus. Studien zum Römerbrief (Stuttgart 1973) 84f., 261. BETZ, O. "Beschneidung" in TRE 5 (1980) 719. MOXNES, H. Theology in Conflict (Leiden 1980) 78, 207, 216f., 220f. HAYS, R. B. The Faith of Jesus Christ (Chico CA 1983) 173. RICHARDSON, P. and HURD, J. C., eds., From Jesus to Paul (FS F. W. Beare; Waterloo 1984) 48, 120, 122, 162. SCHMIDT, W. H. "Gott II" in TRE 13 (1984) 610. STAAB, K. Pauluskommentare aus der griechischen Kirche (Münster ²1984) 111:9-14 Diod; 168:28-169:37 ThM; 431:12-15 Oek; 539:18-540:15 Phot; 659:6-12 Areth. WEDDERBURN, A. J. M. The Reasons for Romans (Edinburgh 1988) 17, 80, 87, 89f. WOLTER, M. Die Pastoralbriefe als Paulustradition (Göttingen 1988) 89. COLLINS, J. N. Diakonia (New York/Oxford 1990) 227f. OLIVEIRA, A. DE, Die Diakonie der Gerechtigkeit und der Versöhnung in der Apologie des 2. Korintherbriefes. Analyse und Auslegung von 2 Kor 2, 14-4, 6; 5, 11-6, 10 (Münster 1990) 156n.388.

15:9-12   ELLIS, E. E. Paul's Use of the Old Testament (1957) passim. LUZ, U. Das Geschichtsverständnis des Paulus (1968) 99, 390. VIELHAUER, P. "Paulus und das Alte Testament" in Oikodome [G. Klein, ed.] (München 1979) 204. STAAB, K. Pauluskommentare aus der griechischen Kirche (Münster ²1984) 169:38-170:3 ThM. KOCH, D.-A. Die Schrift als Zeuge des Evangeliums (Tübingen 1986) 281-4.

15:9,11   HARMAN, A. M. Paul's Use of the Psalms (Ann Arbor MI 1968) 116-22.

15:9   LJUNGMAN, H. Pistis (1964) 48f. HENSS, W. Das Verhältnis zwischen Dia-
          tessaron, Christlicher Gnosis und 'Western Text' (Berlin 1967) 27f.+n.20.
          KOCH, D.-A. Die Schrift als Zeuge des Evangeliums (Tübingen 1986) 34f.,
          121.

15:10   KÖLISCHEN J.-C. VON, Die Zitate aus dem Moselied Deut 32 im Römerbrief
          des Paulus," ThV 5 (1975) 53-69.

15:11   HAHN, F. Das Verständnis der Mission im Neuen Testament (1965) 60.
          KOCH, D.-A. Die Schrift als Zeuge des Evangeliums (Tübingen 1986) 109.
          GASTON, L. Paul and the Torah (Vancouver 1987) 118.

15:12-22 HERMANN, I. Kyrios und Pneuma (1961) 114, 115, 116, 117.

15:12-13 WEDER, H. "Hoffnung II" in TRE 15 (1986) 488.

15:12   HAHN, F. Christologische Hoheitstitel (1963) 249. SIBER, P. Mit Christus
          leben (Zürich 1971) 24. ZELLER, D. Juden und Heiden in der Mission des
          Paulus. Studien zum Römerbrief (Stuttgart 1973) 261. LINDEMANN, A. Die
          Aufhebung der Zeit. Geschichtsverständnis und Eschatologie im Epheserbrief
          (Gütersloh 1975) 180f. KOCH, D.-A. "Beobachtungen zum christologischen
          Schriftgebrauch in den vorpaulinischen Gemeinden," ZNW 71 (1980) 174-91.
          FRID, B. "Jesaja och Paulus versus Bibelkommissionen i Rom. 15.12," [Isaiah
          and Paul versus the Bible Commission on Rom 15:12] SvTK 58 (1982) 11-6.
          FRID, B. "Jesaja und Paulus in Röm 15, 12," BZ 27 (1983) 237-41. NEBE, G.
          'Hoffnung' bei Paulus (Göttingen 1983) 19, 20, 30f., 33, 35, 42f., 66, 143,
          164f., 168, 173, 233, 237, 244, 285, 325, 327. KOCH, D.-A. Die Schrift als
          Zeuge des Evangeliums (Tübingen 1986) 241f.

15:13-33 ROON, A. VAN, The Authenticity of Ephesians (Leiden 1974) 199.

15:13   JÜNGEL, E. Paulus und Jesus (1966) 69. THUESING, W. "Der Gott der
          Hoffnung (Rom. 1513)" Erwartung-Verheissung-Erfüllung, ed. W.Heinen und
          J. Schreiner (1969) 63-85. MONTAGUE, G. T. Growth in Christ (Kirk-
          wood/Mo. 1961) 66f. WILES, G. P. Paul's Intercessory Prayers (London 1974)
          22, 29f., 30-32, 38, 41f., 72, 77, 84, 85f., 88, 113f., 131f., 166f., 187, 270, 280f.
          SCHMITHALS, W. Der Römerbrief als historisches Problem (Gütersloh 1975)
          126, 154ff., 160. GAMBLE, H. The Textual History of the Letter to the
          Romans (Grand Rapids 1977) 69. FRIEDRICH, G. "Der Brief eines Gefangen-
          en. Bamerkungen zum Philipperbrief" in Auf das Wort kommt es an. Gesam-
          melte Aufsätze (Göttingen 1978) 235. NEBE, G. 'Hoffnung' bei Paulus
          (Göttingen 1983) 19, 35f., 43, 51f., 64ff., 73ff., 76, 80, 138, 173, 233, 327.
          STAAB, K. Pauluskommentare aus der griechischen Kirche (Münster ²1984)
          415:14-30 Genn; 540:16-22 Phot. DOBBELER, A. VON, Glaube als Teilhabe
          (Tübingen 1987) 205f. BEKER, J. C. "Paul's Theology: Consistent or
          Inconsistent?" NTS 34 (1988) 372f.

15:14–16:27 GIBLIN, C.H. In Hope of God's Glory (1970) 236-37. SHEPARD, J. W. The
          Life and Letters of St. Paul (Grand Rapids MI 1950) 446-53. DUNN, J. D. G.
          "Paul's Epistle to the Romans: An Analysis of Structure and Argument" in
          ANRW II.25.4 (1987) 2881-4.

15:14-16:23 WUELLNER, W. "Paul's Rhetoric of Argumentation in Romans. An Alterna-
          tive to the Donfried-Karris Debate over Romans" in K. P. Donfried, ed., The
          Romans Debate (Minneapolis 1977) 162-8. ROBINSON, J. A. T. Wrestling
          with Romans (London 1979) 145-7. JEWETT, R. "Romans as an Ambassadori-
          al Letter," Interp 36 (1982) 7, 15-8.

15:14ff. BJERKELUND, C.J. Parakalo (1967) 157, 159, 160, 172, 173. CONZEL-
          MANN, H. and LINDENMANN, A. Arbeitsbuch zum Neuen Testament
          (Tübingen 1975) 217. OLLROG, W.-H. Paulus und seine Mitarbeiter (Neukir-

chen-Vluyn 1979) 17, 52, 54, 117, 176f., 179. CONZELMANN, H. and LINDEMANN, A. Interpreting the New Testament (Peabody, Mass. 1988) 198. SCHÄFER, K. Gemeinde als "Bruderschaft" (Frankfurt/Bern/New York/Paris 1989) 350f.

15:14-33   KNOX, J. "Romans 15:14-33 and Paul's Conception of His Apostolic Mission" JBL 83 (1, '64) 1-11. Christian History and Interpretation: Studies presented to John Knox, ed. W. R. Farmer, C. F. D. Moule, and R. R. Niebuhr (1967) 250, 251-3, 290nl. ZELLER, D. Juden und Heiden in der Mission des Paulus. Studien zum Römerbrief (Stuttgart 1973) 64ff., 283. MANSON, T. W. "St. Paul's Letter to the Romans—and Others" in K. P. Donfried, ed., The Romans Debate (Minneapolis 1977) 1-2. MOSHER, C. S. "Romans 15:14-33 and Paul's Eschatological World-Wide Mission: A Key to Understanding Romans," DissAb 40 (7, 1980) 4098f. MOXNES, H. Theology in Conflict (Leiden 1980) 88, 217-9. WATSON, F. Paul, Judaism and the Gentiles (Cambridge 1986) 102-5. ZMIJEWSKI, J. Paulus—Knecht und Apostel Christi (Stuttgart 1986) 35, 130ff. DUNN, J. D. G. "Paul's Epistle to the Romans: An Analysis of Structure and Argument" in ANRW II.25.4 (1987) 2882f. OSTEN-SACKEN, P. VON DER, Evangelium und Tora: Aufsätze zu Paulus (München 1987) 118, 123, 128f. MÜLLER, P. "Grundlinien paulinischer Theologie (Röm 15, 14-33)," KuD 35 (3, 1989) 212-35. MOISER, J. "Rethinking Romans 12-15," NTS 36 (1990) 571-82, esp.580f. SIMONIS, W. Der gefangene Paulus. Die Entstehung des sogenannten Römerbriefs und anderer urchristlicher Schriften in Rom (Frankfurt/Bern/New York/Paris 1990) 69-75. JERVIS, L. A. The Purpose of Romans (Sheffield 1991) 27, 53, 105, 110, 112, 123f.

15:14-32   ELLIOT, N. The Rhetoric of Romans (Sheffield 1990) 10, 20, 24, 66, 86-93, 94n., 105, 281. JERVIS, L. A. The Purpose of Romans (Sheffield 1991) 19, 26, 120, 127.

15:14-29   SCHMITHALS, W. Der Römerbrief als historisches Problem (Gütersloh 1975) 10, 53, 55, 67, 126, 129, 165, 167ff., 171. HULTGREN, A. J. Paul's Gospel and Mission (Philadelphia 1985) 131ff.

15:14-21   MARTYRIA, Leiturgia, Diakonia, Festschrift für Hermann Volk ed. O. Semmelroth et al (1969). SCHLIER, H. Das Ende der Zeit (1971) 169-83. FORELL, G. W. The Christian Lifestyle. Reflections on Romans 12-15 (Philadelphia 1975) 80-3. SCHLIER, H. "'Evangelium' im Römerbrief" in V. Kubina und K. Lehmann, eds., Der Geist und die Kirche (FS H. Schlier; Freiburg/Basel/Wien 1980) 74-83. KITZBERGER, I. Bau der Gemeinde (Würzburg 1986) 59-63. ZMIJEWSKI, J. Paulus—Knecht und Apostel Christi (Stuttgart 1986) 129-38, 185.

15:14-19   ROLOFF, J. Apostolat-Verkündigung-Kirche (1965) 94-96.

15:14-16   ROOSEN, A. "Le genre littéraire de l'Epître aux Romains" in Studia Evangelica 2 (1963) 465-70. PORTER, C. L. "'For the sake of the grace given me'," Encounter 52 (3, 1991) 251-62.

15:14–15   SCHRAGE, W. Die konkreten Einzelgebote in der paulinischen Paränese (1961) 34, 108, 119, 137, 164, 174. SCHMITHALS, W. Der Römerbrief als historisches Problem (Gütersloh 1975) 28, 62, 165f., 170, 174.

15:14   ZELLER, D. Juden und Heiden in der Mission des Paulus. Studien zum Römerbrief (Stuttgart 1973) 54, 65f. ROON, A. VAN, The Authenticity of Ephesians (Leiden 1974) 167. STAAB, K. Pauluskommentare aus der griechischen Kirche (Münster ²1984) 170:4-17 ThM. SCHNABEL, E. J. Law and Wisdom from Ben Sira to Paul (Tübingen 1985) 330, 332, 337. MALHERBE, A. J. Moral Exhortation. A Greco-Roman Sourcebook (Philadelphia 1986) 48. SCHMEL-

LER, TH. Paulus und die "Diatribe" (Münster 1987) 231. LAMPE, P. Die stadtrömischen Christen in den ersten beiden Jahrhunderten (Tübingen ²1989) 55, 131.

15:15ff.   HAINZ, J. Ekklesia (Regensburg 1972) 175f., 269f.

15:15-21   JOSEPH, M. J. "The Self Understanding of Paul," Biblebhashyam 5 (3, 1979) 165-86.

15:15-19   PETERS, G. W. A Biblical Theology of Missions (Chicago 1972) 150, 154f., 272. SCHMELLER, TH. Paulus und die "Diatribe" (Münster 1987) 231.

15:15-16   GÄRTNER, B. The Tempel and the Community in Qumran and the New Testament (1965) 86. HAHN, F. Das Verständnis der Mission im Neuen Testament (1965) 83. KASTING, H. Die Anfänge der Urchristlichen Mission (1969) 56f., 77. HAINZ, J. Ekklesia (Regensburg 1972) 177f., 269f. SCHÜTZ, J. H. Paul and the Anatomy of Apostolic Authority (Cambridge 1975) 212f. DALY, R. J. Christian Sacrifice (Washington/D.C. 1978) 246-8, 304. SCHMITHALS, W. "Zur Herkunft der gnostischen Elemente in der Sprache des Paulus" in B. Aland et al., eds., Gnosis (FS H. Jonas; Göttingen 1978) 400. STAAB, K. Pauluskommentare aus der griechischen Kirche (Münster ²1984) 415:31-416:6 Genn; 540:23-541:20 Phot. DUNN, J. D. G. "'A Light to the Gentiles': the Significance of the Damascus Road Christophany for Paul" in L. D. Hurst and N. T. Wright, eds., The Glory of Christ in the New Testament (FS G. B. Caird; Oxford 1987) 251-66, esp.252. SEIFRID, M. A. Justification by Faith (Leiden/New York/Köln 1992) 193.

15:15   HAINZ, J. Ekklesia (Regensburg 1972) 175, 177f. ZELLER, D. Juden und Heiden in der Mission des Paulus. Studien zum Römerbrief (Stuttgart 1973) 66f. STAAB, K. Pauluskommentare aus der griechischen Kirche (Münster ²1984) 170:18-37 ThM. OSTEN-SACKEN, P. VON DER, Evangelium und Tora: Aufsätze zu Paulus (München 1987) 124f. WEDDERBURN, A. J. M. The Reasons for Romans (Edinburgh 1988) 27, 98-100. BYRNE, B. "'Rather Boldly' (Rom 15, 15). Paul's Prophetic Bid to Win the Allegiance of the Christians in Rome," Biblica 74 (1993) 83-96.

15:16-23   WAY, D. The Lordship of Christ. Ernst Käsemann's Interpretation of Paul's Theology (Oxford 1991) 140.

15:16-19   CERFAUX, L. Christ in the Theology of St. Paul (1959) 146, 308, 492, 504.

15:16,18   HULTGREN, A. J. Paul's Gospel and Mission (Philadelphia 1985) 125ff.

15:16   SEIDENSTICKER, Ph. Lebendiges Opfer (1954) 225ff. BEST, E. One Body in Christ (1955) 11n. SCHWEIZER, E. Gemeinde und Gemeindeordnung im Neuen Testament (1959) § 21a. WIENER, C. "'Ιεφουργεῖν (Rm 15, 16)" Studiorum Paulinorum Congressus Internationalis Catholicus 1961 II (1963) 399-404. KÄSEMANN, E. Exegetische Versuche und Besinnungen (1964) I 297. COOPER, R.M. "Leitourgos Christou Iesou. Toward a Theology of Christian Prayer" AThR 47 (3, '65) 263-75. LUZ, U. Das Geschichtsverständnis de Paulus (1968) 391f. ZELLER, D. Juden und Heiden in der Mission des Paulus. Studien zum Römerbrief (Stuttgart 1973) 222f., 277, 282f. LADD, G. E. A Theology of the New Testament (Grand Rapids 1974) 381, 484, 519. SCHÜTZ, J. H. Paul and the Anatomy of Apostolic Authority (Cambridge 1975) 45-7, 213. FRIEDRICH, G. "Das Amt im Neuen Testament" in Auf das Wort kommt es an. Gesammelte Aufsätze (Göttingen 1978) 421. CLARK, K. W. "The Israel of God" in The Gentile Bias and other Essays [selected by J. L. Sharpe III] (Leiden 1980) 27. FERGUSON, E. "Spiritual Sacrifice in Early Christianity and its Environment" in ANRW II.23.2 (1980) 1164. KLAIBER, W. Rechtfertigung und Gemeinde (Göttingen 1982) 140. MOHRLANG, R.

Matthew and Paul (Cambridge 1984) 82, 115, 187. DIETZFELBINGER, C. Die Berufung des Paulus als Ursprung seiner Theologie (Neukirchen 1985) 44, 138, 142. SANDERS, E. P. Paul, the Law, and the Jewish People (London 1985) 171, 179, 181, 198, 207. PONTHOT, J. "L'expression cultuelle du ministère paulinien selon Rom 15, 16" in Vanhoye, A., ed., L'Apôtre Paul (Leuven 1986) 254-62. ZMIJEWSKI, J. Paulus—Knecht und Apostel Christi (Stuttgart 1986) 45f., 49, 140, 185, 188. FULLER, R. H. "Scripture, Tradition and Priesthood" in R. Bauckham and B. Drewery, eds., Scripture, Tradition and Reason (FS R. P. C. Hanson; Edinburgh 1988) 105n.15. KLAUCK, H.-J. Gemeinde, Amt, Sakrament (Würzburg 1989) 354-6. JERVIS, L. A. The Purpose of Romans (Sheffield 1991) 121f., 129f., 161.

15:17ff. KLAIBER, W. Rechtfertigung und Gemeinde (Göttingen 1982) 130.
15:17-19 STAAB, K. Pauluskommentare aus der griechischen Kirche (Münster ²1984) 416:7-12 Genn; 541:21-34 Phot. 15:17-18 HAINZ, J. Ekklesia (Regensburg 1972) 177.
15:17 BEST, E. One Body in Christ (1955) 3. SCHÜTZ, J. H. Paul and the Anatomy of Apostolic Authority (Cambridge 1975) 212-4, 233.
15:18-21 ZELLER, D. Juden und Heiden in der Mission des Paulus. Studien zum Römerbrief (Stuttgart 1973) 49, 67f.
15:18-20 SCHÜTZ, J. H. Paul and the Anatomy of Apostolic Authority (Cambridge 1975) 212f.
15:18-19 ELLIS, E. E. Prophecy and Hermeneutic in Early Christianity (Tübingen 1978) 64, 73. GATZWEILER, K. "Der Paulinische Wunderbegriff" in A. Suhl, ed., Der Wunderbegriff im Neuen Testament (Darmstadt 1980) 400-2, 413f. NIELSEN, H. K. "Paulus' Verwendung des Begriffes Dunamis. Eine Replik zur Kreuztheologie" in S. Pedersen, ed., Die Paulinische Literatur und Theologie (Arhus/Göttingen 1980) 151f. MARQUARDT, F.-W. Die Juden und ihr Land (Gütersloh ³1986) 92. NIELSEN, H. K. Heilung und Verkündigung (Leiden 1987) 19, 188f., 196-9, 201, 203, 206, 208f., 213, 290. BECKER, J. Paulus. Der Apostel der Völker (Tübingen 1989) 78, 96, 135, 187, 253, 438. REBELL, W. Alles ist möglich dem, der glaubt (München 1989) 110ff.
15:18 BOUSSET, W. Die Religion des Judentums im Späthellenistischen Zeitalter (1966=1926) 375. SCHRAGE, W. Die konkreten Einzelgebote in der paulinischen Paränese (1961) 105, 113f., 195. HAINZ, J. Ekklesia (Regensburg 1972) 176, 178. MALHERBE, A. J. Moral Exhortation. A Greco-Roman Sourcebook (Philadelphia 1986) 38. YAGI, S. "'I' in the Words of Jesus" in J. Hick and P. F. Knitter, eds., The Myth of Christian Uniqueness. Toward a Pluralistic Theology of Religions (Maryknoll NY 1987) 117-34, esp.119.
15:19-23 OLLROG, W.-H. Paulus und seine Mitarbeiter (Neukirchen-Vluyn 1979) 120, 159.
15:19-22 STAAB, K. Pauluskommentare aus der griechischen Kirche (Münster ²1984) 416:13-25 Genn.
15:19-21 SCHMITHALS, W. Paulus und Jakobus (1963) 41.
15:19 FLEW, R.N. Jesus and His Church (1956) 156. MUNCK, J. Paul and the Salvation of Mankind (1959) 50-52, 54, 301. GEYSER, A.S. "Un Essai d'Explication de Rom XV.19" NTS 6 (1959/60) 156f. BORNKAMM-BARTH-HELD, Ueberlieferung und Auslegung im Matthäus-Evangelium (1961) 258. HENNECKE, E./SCHNEEMELCHER, W. Neutestamentliche Apokryphen (1964) II 118. BUJARD, W. Stilanalytische Untersuchungen zum Kolosserbrief (Göttingen 1973) 184f., 195. ZELLER, D. Juden und Heiden in der Mission des Paulus. Studien zum Römerbrief (Stuttgart 1973) 224ff., 278. LADD, G. E. A

Theology of the New Testament (Grand Rapids 1974) 382, 386, 412. DUNN, J. D. G. Jesus and the Spirit. A Study of the Religious and Charismatic Experience of Jesus and the First Christians as Reflected in the New Testament (London 1975) 163, 167, 210, 411. HENGEL, M. Zur urchristlichen Geschichtsschreibung (Stuttgart 1979) 75f.; ET: Acts and the History of Earliest Christianity [trans. J. Bowden] (London 1979) 87. OLLROG, W.-H. Paulus und seine Mitarbeiter (Neukirchen-Vluyn 1979) 17, 56, 79, 121, 128f., 161, 177, 222, 225. JUNOD, E. "Origène, Eusèbe et la tradition sur la réparttion des champs de mission des apotres (Eusèbe, HE III, 1:1-3)" in F. Bovon et al., eds., Les Actes Apocryphes des Apotres (Geneva 1981) 234, 237, 239. MEEKS, W. A. The First Urban Christians (New Haven/London 1983) 9, 40, 138, 198n.3. SANDERS, E. P. Paul, the Law, and the Jewish People (London 1985) 186f., 189, 203n.55, 204n.70. BOWERS, P. "Fulfilling the Gospel: The Scope of the Pauline Mission," JEThS 30 (2, 1987) 185-98. DOWNING, F. G. Christ and the Cynics (Sheffield 1988) 3. WOLTER, M. Die Pastoralbriefe als Paulustradition (Göttingen 1988) 32, 35. BLACKBURN, B. Theios Aner and the Markan Miracle Traditions (Tübingen 1991) 252, 256f.

15:20-21   HAHN, F. Das Verständnis der Mission im Neuen Testament (19-65) 81. SCHMITHALS, W. Der Römerbrief als historisches Problem (Gütersloh 1975) 59, 64, 88, 169ff., 172ff., 176f. OSTEN-SACKEN, P. VON DER, Evangelium und Tora: Aufsätze zu Paulus (München 1987) 121f.

15:20   BEST, E. One Body in Christ (1955) 162, 164. PFAMMATTER, J. Die Kirche als Bau (1960) 61f, 142, 180. KRAMER, W. Christos Kyrios Gottessohn (1963) §12d. HAINZ, J. Ekklesia (Regensburg 1972) 269-71, 311f. ZELLER, D. Juden und Heiden in der Mission des Paulus. Studien zum Römerbrief (Stuttgart 1973) 55, 57, 69, 270, 274. SCHÜTZ, J. H. Paul and the Anatomy of Apostolic Authority (Cambridge 1975) 37f., 47, 164, 213, 225. OLLROG, W.-H. Paulus und seine Mitarbeiter (Neukirchen-Vluyn 1979) 94, 140, 176. VIELHAUER, P. "Oikodome. Das Bild vom Bau in der christlichen Literatur vom Neuen Testament bis Clemens Alexandrinus" in Oikodome [G. Klein, ed.] (München 1979) 82f. STAAB, K. Pauluskommentare aus der griechischen Kirche (Münster ²1984) 111:15-19 Diod; 225:2-4 Sev. OSTEN-SACKEN, P. VON DER, Evangelium und Tora: Aufsätze zu Paulus (München 1987) 119-23. SCHMELLER, TH. Paulus und die "Diatribe" (Münster 1987) 231. WOLTER, M. Die Pastoralbriefe als Paulustradition (Göttingen 1988) 248. KLAUCK, H.-J. Gemeinde, Amt, Sakrament (Würzburg 1989) 45.

15:21   ELLIS, E. E. Paul's Use of the Old Testament (1957) 20, 121, 125, 143, 151, 172. ROBINSON, J. A. Pelagius's Exposition of Thirteen Epistles of St. Paul (Cambridge 1922) 241, 261, 263.

15:22ff.   WAGENMANN, J. Die Stellung des Apostles Paulus neben den Zwölf (1926) 40f. HAHN, F. Das Verständnis der Mission im Neuen Testament (1965) 81. SCHÄFER, K. Gemeinde als "Bruderschaft" (Frankfurt/Bern/New York/Paris 1989) 352.

15:22-30   PANIKULAM, G. Koinonia in the New Testament: A Dynamic Expression of Christian Life (Rome 1979) 34.

15:22-29   AUNE, D. E. The New Testament in Its Literary Environment (Philadelphia 1987) 219f.

15:22-25   LOHSE, E. Die Entstehung des Neuen Testaments (Stuttgart/Berlin/Köln ⁵1991) 47.

15:22-24   OLLROG, W.-H. Paulus und seine Mitarbeiter (Neukirchen-Vluyn 1979) 55.

15:22-23   LAMPE, P. Die stadtrömischen Christen in den ersten beiden Jahrhunderten
            (Tübingen ²1989) 7, 127f.
15:22   STAAB, K. Pauluskommentare aus der griechischen Kirche (Münster ²1984)
            171:1-4 ThM. OSTEN-SACKEN, P. VON DER, Evangelium und Tora:
            Aufsätze zu Paulus (München 1987) 121ff.
15:23-32   STOLLE, V. Der Zeuge als Angeklagter. Untersuchungen zum Paulus-Bild des
            Lukas (Stuttgart 1973) 268-70. REBELL, W. Zum neuen Leben berufen
            (München 1990) 65ff.
15:23-29   DOCKX, S. "Chronologie paulinienne de l'année de la grande collecte," RB 81
            (1974) 183-95. DOWNING, F. G. Christ and the Cynics (Sheffield 1988) 188.
15:23-28   JERVIS, L. A. The Purpose of Romans (Sheffield 1991) 160.
15:23-27   STAAB, K. Pauluskommentare aus der griechischen Kirche (Münster ²1984)
            416:26-30 Genn.
15:23-24   SEIFRID, M. A. Justification by Faith (Leiden/New York/Köln 1992) 193f.
15:23   OLLROG, W.-H. Paulus und seine Mitarbeiter (Neukirchen-Vluyn 1979) 32,
            56, 79, 148, 177. OSTEN-SACKEN, P. VON DER, Evangelium und Tora:
            Aufsätze zu Paulus (München 1987) 122f., 126, 307.
15:24-31   NICKLE, K.F. The Collection (1966) 68, 14f., 106, 69, 124, 67, 71.
15:24-28   BOWERS, W. P. "Jewish Communities in Spain in the Time of Paul the
            Apostle," JThS 26 (1975) 395-402. FISCHER, K. M. Das Urchristentum
            (Berlin, DDR 1985) 65, 117, 120, 126.
15:24,28   THORNTON, T. C. G. "St. Paul's Missionary Intentions in Spain," ET 86 (4,
            1975) 120. MEINARDUS, O. F. A. "Paul's Missionary Journey to Spain
            Tradition and Folklore," BA 41 (2, 1978) 61-3. SCHWEIZER, E. Theologische
            Einleitung in das Neue Testament (Göttingen 1989) ß 9.2; 14.2.
15:24   BEYSCHLAG, K. Clemens Romanus un der Frühkatholizismus (1966) 298.
            SCHMITHALS, W. Der Römerbrief als historisches Problem (Gütersloh 1975)
            28, 170. OLLROG, W.-H. Paulus und seine Mitarbeiter (Neukirchen-Vluyn
            1979) 124. WILLIAMS, S. K. "The 'Righteousness of God' in Romans," JBL
            99 (1980) 249. NEBE, G. 'Hoffnung' bei Paulus (Göttingen 1983) 19f., 32f.,
            35, 43, 65, 73. STAAB, K. Pauluskommentare aus der griechischen Kirche
            (Münster ²1984) 81:24-25 Apoll; 171:5-6 ThM. AUNE, D. E. The New
            Testament in Its Literary Environment (Philadelphia 1987) 219. OSTEN-
            SACKEN, P. VON DER, Evangelium und Tora: Aufsätze zu Paulus (München
            1987) 122, 128, 306. SCHMELLER, TH. Paulus und die "Diatribe" (Münster
            1987) 229, 231. DOWNING, F. G. Christ and the Cynics (Sheffield 1988) 3.
            LAMPE, P. Die stadtrömischen Christen in den ersten beiden Jahrhunderten
            (Tübingen ²1989) 9, 55, 63f., 131. JERVIS, L. A. The Purpose of Romans
            (Sheffield 1991) 19, 124f., 160.
15:25ff.   HAINZ, J. Ekklesia (Regensburg 1972) 241f., 244-6. ZELLER, D. Juden und
            Heiden in der Mission des Paulus. Studien zum Römerbrief (Stuttgart 1973)
            229ff., 279ff. OLLROG, W.-H. Paulus und seine Mitarbeiter (Neukirchen-Vluyn
            1979) 35, 55, 73. HAINZ, J. Koinonia (Regensburg 1982) 146, 150, 157f.
            MARQUARDT, F.-W. Die Juden und ihr Land (Gütersloh ³1986) 94.
            WATSON, F. Paul, Judaism and the Gentiles (Cambridge 1986) 174-6.
15:25-32   DALY, R. J. Christian Sacrifice (Washington 1978) 242.
15:25-28   HAINZ, J. Koinonia (Regensburg 1982) 145-51.
15:25-27   ACHTEMEIER, P. J. The Quest for Unity in the New Testament Church
            (Philadelphia 1987) 26, 34. SCHNELLE, U. Wandlungen im paulinischen
            Denken (Stuttgart 1989) 22.

15:25-26   LÜDEMANN, G. Paulus, der Heidenapostel, Band II (Göttingen 1983) 92n.99, 94f. BECKER, J. Paulus. Der Apostel der Völker (Tübingen 1989) 273, 358, 479.

15:25   O'ROURKE, J.J. "The Participle in Rom. 15, 25" CBQ 29 (1, '67) 116-18. O'ROURKE, J. "The Participle in Rm 15:25," CBQ 29 (1967) 116-8. COLLINS, J. N. Diakonia (New York/Oxford 1990) 64, 94, 220f., 222, 224, 229, 327n.1, 328n.2, 332n.11.

15:26ff.   HAINZ, J. Koinonia (Regensburg 1982) 133, 138, 152. SCHÄFER, K. Gemeinde als "Bruderschaft" (Frankfurt/Bern/New York/Paris 1989) 220-5.

15:26-27   HAHN, F. Das Verständnis der Mission im Neuen Testament (19-65) 93. ECKERT, J. Die Urchristliche Verkündigung im Streit zwischen Paulus und seinen Gegnern nach dem Galaterbrief (Regensburg 1971) 191f. HAINZ, J. Ekklesia (Regensburg 1972) 101f., 245f. LIERMANN, H. "Abgaben" in TRE 1 (1977) 329. SCHNACKENBURG, R. Die sittliche Botschaft des Neuen Testaments, Band 1 (Freiburg/Basel/Wien 1986) 203. WOLTER, M. Die Pastoralbriefe als Paulustradition (Göttingen 1988) 249.

15:26   FLEW, R.N. Jesus and His Church (1956) 109. MUNCK, J. Paul and the Salvation of Mankind (1959) 287, 292f. RUDOLPH, K. Die Mandäer I (1960) 117.2. BAUMERT, N. Täglich Sterben und Auferstehen. Der Literalsinn von 2 Kor 4, 12-5, 10 (München 1973) 234. SCHÜTZ, J. H. Paul and the Anatomy of Apostolic Authority (Cambridge 1975) 48f. KECK, L. E. "Armut" in TRE 4 (1979) 79. HANSCHILD, H.-D. "Armenfürsorge" in TRE 4 (1979) 17. HAINZ, J. Koinonia (Regensburg 1982) 78, 88, 111-3, 115f., 131, 138, 145-7, 149, 151-3, 155, 159, 164, 168, 181, 187. THORNTON, C.-J. Der Zeuge des Zeugen. Lukas als Historiker der Paulusreisen (Tübingen 1991) 230, 256, 259, 310, 348f.

15:27-28   SCHRAGE, W. Die konkreten Einzelgebote in der paulinischen Paränese (1961) 60, 97, 111, 250.

15:27   BORSE, U. Der Standort des Galaterbriefes (Köln 1972) 37, 135, 138, 145. HAINZ, J. Ekklesia (Regensburg 1972) 245f., 287f. BAUMERT, N. Täglich Sterben und Auferstehen. Der Literalsinn von 2 Kor 4, 12-5, 10 (München 1973) 359, 361. DUNN, J. D. G. Jesus and the Spirit. A Study of the Religious and Charismatic Experience of Jesus and the First Christians as Reflected in the New Testament (London 1975) 208, 285. ELLIS, E. E.Prophecy and Hermeneutic in Early Christianity (Tübingen 1978) 8, 10, 20, 24. HOLMBERG, B. Paul and Power (Lund 1978) 51f. HAINZ, J. Koinonia (Regensburg 1982) 76, 78, 82, 87f., 111-6, 131, 145, 148-51, 153, 155, 174.

15:28-29   STAAB, K. Pauluskommentare aus der griechischen Kirche (Münster ²1984) 417:1-10 Genn.

15:28   DOELGER, Sphragis (1911) 11. BRAUMANN, G. Vorpaulinische christliche Taufverkündigung bei Paulus (1962) 46f. DELLING, G. Die Taufe im Neuen Testament (1963) 105. RADERMACHER, L. "Rm 15:28," ZNW 32 (1933) 87. BARTSCH, H.-W. " . . . wenn ich ihnen diese Frucht versiegelt habe. Röm 15:28. Ein Beitrag zum Verständnis der paulinischen Mission," ZNW 63 (1972) 95-107. STAAB, K. Pauluskommentare aus der griechischen Kirche (Münster ²1984) 171:7-14 ThM. SCHMELLER, TH. Paulus und die "Diatribe" (Münster 1987) 229, 231. CONZELMANN, H. and LINDEMANN, A. Interpreting the New Testament (Peabody, Mass. 1988) 365. LAMPE, P. Die stadtrömischen Christen in den ersten beiden Jahrhunderten (Tübingen ²1989) 63f.

15:29   SCHENK, W. Der Segen im Neuen Testament (1967) 48-49. ZELLER, D. Juden und Heiden in der Mission des Paulus. Studien zum Römerbrief (Stuttgart

1973) 73, 234. ROON, A. VAN, The Authenticity of Ephesians (Leiden 1974) 249-51. WESTERMANN, C. Blessing. In the Bible and the Life of the Church (Philadelphia 1978) 70, 81f., 98-101. STAAB, K. Pauluskommentare aus der griechischen Kirche (Münster [2]1984) 171:15-18 ThM; 431:16-18 Oek. SCHMELLER, TH. Paulus und die "Diatribe" (Münster 1987) 231. ECKERT, J. Die Urchristliche Verkündigung im Streit zwischen Paulus und seinen Gegnern nach dem Galaterbrief (Regensburg 1971) 192f.

15:30-33　　ZELLER, D. Juden und Heiden in der Mission des Paulus. Studien zum Römerbrief (Stuttgart 1973) 73f., 281. SCHMITHALS, W. Der Römerbrief als historisches Problem (Gütersloh 1975) 33f., 127, 163, 170. STAAB, K. Pauluskommentare aus der griechischen Kirche (Münster [2]1984) 171:18-23 ThM. GEBAUER, R. Das Gebet bei Paulus (Giessen/Basel 1989) 172-83. SEIFRID, M. A. Justification by Faith (Leiden/New York/Köln 1992) 194-97.

15:30-32　　BJERKELUND, C.J. Parakalo (1967), 14, 18, 42, 54, 114, 116, 157, 158, 160, 163, 164, 167, 173. ENSLIN, M. S. Reapproaching Paul (Philadelphia 1972) 111f. WILES, G. P. Paul's Intercessory Prayers (London 1974) 16f., 77, 91, 96, 146f., 192, 259f., 260, 263f., 290, 292.STAAB, K. Pauluskommentare aus der griechischen Kirche (Münster [2]1984) 417:11-17 Genn. LIMBECK, M. Mit Paulus Christ sein. Sachbuch zur Person und Theologie des Apostels Paulus (Stuttgart 1989) 97. SCHÄFER, K. Gemeinde als "Bruderschaft" (Frankfurt/Bern/New York/Paris 1989) 351f. CRUZ, H. Christological Motives and Motivated Actions in Pauline Paraenesis (Frankfurt/Bern/New York/Paris 1990) 240-2. SMIGA, G. "Romans 12:1-2 and 15:30-32 and the Occasion of the Letter to the Romans," CBQ 53 (2, 1991) 257-73.

15:30-31　　SCHMITHALS, W. Paulus und Jakobus (1963) 65-70. ACHTEMEIER, P. J. The Quest for Unity in the New Testament Church (Philadelphia 1987) 26. SCHMELLER, TH. Paulus und die "Diatribe" (Münster 1987) 229. BECKER, J. Paulus. Der Apostel der Völker (Tübingen 1989) 275, 282, 479. LAMPE, P. Die stadtrömischen Christen in den ersten beiden Jahrhunderten (Tübingen [2]1989) 55, 131.

15:30　　　HERMANN, I. Kyrios und Pneuma (1961) 92, 93f. SCHRAGE, W. Die konkreten Einzelgebote in der paulinischen Paränese (1961) 104, 106, 113, 249. HAHN, F. Christologische Hoheitstitel (1963) 110. KRAMER, W. Christos Kyrios Gottessohn (1963) § 17e. PFITZNER, V.C. Paul and the Agon Motif (1967) 6, 77, 109, 117, 120ff., 125, 130. BAUMERT, N. Täglich Sterben und Auferstehen. Der Literalsinn von 2 Kor 4, 12-5, 10 (München 1973) 251, 274. WILES, G. P. Paul's Intercessory Prayers (London 1974)19f., 185, 266-8, 274f., 280f., 292. MOHRLANG, R. Matthew and Paul (Cambridge 1984) 102, 115, 120. SCHMELLER, TH. Paulus und die "Diatribe" (Münster 1987) 230. CRUZ, H. Christological Motives and Motivated Actions in Pauline Paraenesis (Frankfurt/Bern/New York/Paris 1990) 225-9.

15:31　　　KECK, L. E. "Armut" in TRE 4 (1979) 79. OLLROG, W.-H. Paulus und seine Mitarbeiter (Neukirchen-Vluyn 1979) 36, 73. HAINZ, J. Koinonia (Regensburg 1982) 145-51, 156, 160. RICHARDSON, P. and HURD, J. C., eds., From Jesus to Paul (FS F. W. Beare; Waterloo 1984) 64f. MARQUARDT, F.-W. Die Juden und ihr Land (Gütersloh [3]1986) 94. SCHMELLER, TH. Paulus und die "Diatribe" (Münster 1987) 230. COLLINS, J. N. Diakonia (New York/Oxford 1990) 13, 220f., 230, 326n.2, 327n.1. THORNTON, C.-J. Der Zeuge des Zeugen. Lukas als Historiker der Paulusreisen (Tübingen 1991) 229, 279, 310f., 349.

15:32　　　SCHRAGE, W. Die konkreten Einzelgebote in der paulinischen Paränese (1961) 168. STAAB, K. Pauluskommentare aus der griechischen Kirche (Münster

²1984) 542:1-3 Phot. FURNISH, V. P. "Der 'Wille Gottes' in paulinischer Sicht" in D.-A. Koch et al., eds., Jesu Rede von Gott und ihre Nachgeschichte im frühen Christentum (FS Willi Marxen; Gütersloh 1989) 208-21, esp.218. JERVIS, L. A. The Purpose of Romans (Sheffield 1991) 112, 124, 129f.

15:33;   16:16a.20b CUMING, G. J. "Service-Endings in the Epistles," NTS 22 (1975) 110-3.

15:33   KÜMMEL, W. G. Einleitung in das Neue Testament (Heidelberg 1973) 276-80. WILES, G. P. Paul's Intercessory Prayers (London 1974) 23f., 29, 31, 38f., 41f., 60f., 66f., 72f., 77, 90, 96, 102, 114f., 131, f., 166f. ELLIS, E. E. und GRÄSSER, E., eds., Jesus und Paulus (FS W. G. Kümmel; Göttingen 1975) 76, 78ff. SCHMITHALS, W. Der Römerbrief als historisches Problem (Gütersloh 1975) 116, 118, 125ff., 156. GAMBLE, H. The Textual History of the Letter to the Romans (Grand Rapids 1977) 68. DEICHGRÄBER, R. "Benediktionen" in TRE 5 (1980) 563. KLAUCK, H.-J. Hausgemeinde und Hauskirche im frühen Christentum (Stuttgart 1981) 24. AUNE, D. E. The New Testament in Its Literary Environment (Philadelphia 1987) 192. CONZELMANN, H. and LINDEMANN, A. Interpreting the New Testament (Peabody, Mass. 1988) 29. JERVIS, L. A. The Purpose of Romans (Sheffield 1991) 1, 26, 11, 135-7, 139, 141, 150, 155.

16   DEISSMANN, A. Licht vom Osten (1923) 137, 172, 199f. REICKE, B. Diakonie, Festfreude und Zelos (1951) 296f. MUNCK, J. Paul and the Salvation of Mankind (1959) 197f. MARCHEL, W. Abba, Père! La Prière du Christ et des Chrétiens (1963) 240-43. McDONALD, J. I. H. "Was Romans XVI a Separate Letter?" NTS 16 (1969-70) 369-72. DONFRIED, K. P. "A Short Note on Romans 16" JBL 89 (4, '70) 441-49. FEINE, D. P. und BEHM, D. J. Einleitung in das Neue Testament (Heidelberg 1950) 174ff. ENSLIN, M. S. The Literature of the Christian Movement (New York 1956) 263ff., 267f. HARRISON, P. N. Paulines and Pastorals (London 1964) 86-91. GEORGI, D. Die Geschichte der Kollekte des Paulus für Jerusalem (Hamburg 1965) 79f. SELBY, D. J. Introduction to the New Testament (New York 1971) 379, 390-2. BORSE, U. Der Standort des Galaterbriefes (Köln 1972) 9-11. HAINZ, J. Ekklesia (Regensburg 1972) 172, 193. KÜMMEL, W. G. Einleitung in das Neue Testament (Heidelberg 1973) 277-80. ADINOLFI, M. "Le collaboratrici ministeriali di Paolo nelle lettere ai Romani e ai Filippesi," BeO 17 (1975) 21-32. CONZELMANN, H. and LINDEMANN, A. Arbeitsbuch zum Neuen Testament (Tübingen 1975) 216. KAYE, B. N. "'To the Romans and Others' Revisited," NovT 18 (1976) 37-77. BRUCE, F. F. Paul: Apostle of the Free Spirit (Exeter 1977) 385-9. DONFRIED, K. P. "A Short Note on Romans 16" in K. P. Donfried, ed., The Romans Debate (Minneapolis 1977) 50-60. GAMBLE, H. The Textual History of the Letter to the Romans (Grand Rapids 1977) 37-55, 84-95. STAGG, E. and F. Women in the World of Jesus (Philadelphia 1978) 180f. OLLROG, W.-H. Paulus und seine Mitarbeiter (Neukirchen-Vluyn 1979) 23, 26. GERSTENBERGER, E. S. und SCHRAGE, W. Frau und Mann (Stuttgart 1980) 133, 141f. OLLROG, W.-H. "Die Abfassungsverhältnisse von Röm 16" in D. Lührmann und G. Strecker, eds., Kirche (FS G. Bornkamm; Tübingen 1980) 221-44. ADINOLFI, M. Il femminismo della Bibbia (Rome 1981) 193-204. MEEKS, W. A. The First Urban Christians (New Haven/London 1983) 16, 56, 143, 201n.41, 212n.264, 215n.26, 221n.7. SHAW, G. The Cost of Authority (Philadelphia 1983) 178-80. WATSON, F. Paul, Judaism and the Gentiles (Cambridge 1986) 98-102.

SCHMELLER, TH. Paulus und die "Diatribe" (Münster 1987) 225. CONZELMANN, H. and LINDEMANN, A. Interpreting the New Testament (Peabody, Mass. 1988) 197. WEDDERBURN, A. J. M. The Reasons for Romans (Edinburgh 1988) 12-8, 45-7, 50, 56. LAMPE, P. Die stadtrömischen Christen in den ersten beiden Jahrhunderten (Tübingen ²1989) 58, 124-54, 161, 238, 297, 301f., 305, 319, 335, 341. FURNISH, P. "Pauline Studies" in E. J. Epp and G. W. MacRae, eds., The New Testament and Its Modern Interpreters (Atlanta 1989) 321-50, esp.325. LAMPE, P. "The Roman Christians of Romans 16" in K. P. Donfried, ed., The Romans Debate. Revised and Expanded Edition (Peabody, MA 1991) 216-30. LOHSE, E. Die Entstehung des Neuen Testaments (Stuttgart/ Berlin/Köln ⁵1991) 48f. RICHARDS, E. R. The Secretary in the Letters of Paul (Tübingen 1991) 177, 190. SEIFRID, M. A. Justification by Faith (Leiden/New York/Köln 1992) 249-54.

16:1-23 KLAUCK, H.-J. Hausgemeinde und Hauskirche im frühen Christentum (Stuttgart 1981) 25. DUNN, J. D. G. "Paul's Epistle to the Romans: An Analysis of Structure and Argument" in ANRW II.25.4 (1987) 2883f. JERVIS, L. A. The Purpose of Romans (Sheffield 1991) 135-8.

16:1-20 HAHN, F. Das Verständnis der Mission im Neuen Testament (1965) 92. HAHN, F. Das Verständnis der Mission im Neuen Testament (Neukirchen ²1965) 92. SCHMITHALS, W. Der Römerbrief als historisches Problem (Gütersloh 1975) 125ff., 153.

16:1-16 SEVENSTER, J.N. "Waarom spreekt Pau us nooit van vrienden en vriendschap? (naar aanleiding van Rom 16, 1-16)" NedThT 9/6 (1954/55) 356-63. SCHELKLE, K. H. The Spirit and the Bride. Woman in the Bible (Collegeville 1979) 157-60. SCHOLER, D. M. "Paul's Women Co-Workers in the Ministry of the Church," Daughters of Sarah [Chicago] 6 (1980) 3-6. SCHNACKENBURG, R. Die sittliche Botschaft des Neuen Testaments, Band 1 (Freiburg/Basel/Wien 1986) 248. MARCUS, J. "The Circumcision and the Uncircumcision in Rome," NTS 35 (1989) 67-81, esp.70. SCHNELLE, U. Wandlungen im paulinischen Denken (Stuttgart 1989) 30. TRAITLER, R. "Eine Kirche der Frauen?" in E. R. Schmidt et al., eds., Feministisch gelesen, Band 2 (Stuttgart 1989) 215-22. SIMONIS, W. Der gefangene Paulus. Die Entstehung des sogenannten Römerbriefs und anderer urchristlicher Schriften in Rom (Frankfurt/Bern/New York/Paris 1990) 82-8. TREBILCO, P. "Women as Co-Workers and Leaders in Paul's Letters," Journal of the Christian Brethren Research Fellowship [Wellington, New Zealand] 122 (1990) 27-36.

16:1-12 BYRNE, B. Paul and the Christian Woman (Homebush NSW 1988) passim. DOWNING, F. G. Christ and the Cynics (Sheffield 1988) 4.

16:1-7 CLARK, S. B. Man and Woman in Christ (Ann Arbor MI 1980) 115.

16:1-4 WITHERINGTON, B. Women in the Ministry of Jesus (Cambridge 1984) 129.

16:1-2 SCHRAGE, W. Die konkreten Einzelgebote in der paulinischen Paränese (1961) 206. KÄSEMANN, E. Exegetische Versuche und Besinnungen (1964) I 124. FEINE, D. P. und BEHM, D. J. Einleitung in das Neue Testament (Heidelberg 1950) 175f. HAINZ, J. Ekklesia (Regensburg 1972) 87, 193. FURNISH, V. P. The Moral Teaching of Paul (Nashville 1979) 108-10. OLLROG, W.-H. Paulus und seine Mitarbeiter (Neukirchen-Vluyn 1979) 26, 31, 61, 74, 84, 129, 191, 223. SWIDLER, L. Biblical Affirmations of Woman (Philadelphia 1979) 295f., 314. CLARK, S. B. Man and Woman in Christ (Ann Arbor MI 1980) 118f. ADINOLFI, M. Il femminismo della Bibbia (Rome 1981) 195-200. KLAUCK, H.-J. Hausgemeinde und Hauskirche im frühen Christentum (Stuttgart 1981) 25, 30f., 33. MEEKS, W. A. The First Urban Christians (New Haven/London 1983)

49, 60, 230n.169. MALHERBE, A. J. Moral Exhortation. A Greco-Roman Sourcebook (Philadelphia 1986) 80. FINGER, R. H. "Phoebe: Role Model for Leaders," Daughters of Sarah [Chicago] 14 (1988) 5-7. MacDONALD, M. Y. The Pauline Churches (Cambridge 1988) 58. NUERNBERG, R. "'Non decet neque necessarium est, ut mulieres doceant'. Ueberlegungen zum altkirchlichen Lehrverbot für Frauen" in JAC 31 (1988) 57-73, esp.58f. KLAUCK, H.-J. Gemeinde, Amt, Sakrament (Würzburg 1989) 15, 40, 211, 223, 235. SCHOT-TROFF, L. "Dienerlnnen der Heiligen. Der Diakonat der Frauen im Neuen Testament" in G. K. Schäfer and T. Strohm, eds., Diakonie— biblische Grundlagen und Orientierungen (Heidelberg 1990) 222-42, esp.222, 224, 238f. JERVIS, L. A. The Purpose of Romans (Sheffield 1991) 136, 138, 150f., 155. WHELAN, C. F. "Amica Pauli: The Role of Phoebe in the Early Church," JSNT 49 (1993) 67-85.

16:1   BARRETT, C. K. The New Testament Background. Selected Documents (London 1956) 29. HAINZ, J. Ekklesia (Regensburg 1972) 193f. SCHMI-THALS, W. Der Römerbrief als historisches Problem (Gütersloh 1975) 129. ROLOFF, J. "Amt" in TRE 2 (1978) 520. MICKELSEN, B. and A. "Does Male Dominance Tarnish Our Translations?" ChrTo 22 (1979) 1313-18. SWIDLER, L. Biblical Affirmations of Woman (Philadelphia 1979) 310. THEISSEN, G. The Social Setting of Pauline Christianity (Edinburgh 1982) 88. MEEKS, W. A. The First Urban Christians (New Haven/London 1983) 41, 79, 229n.159. HEINE, S. Women and Early Christianity (London 1987) 88. ARICHEA, D. C. "Who Was Phoebe? Translating diakonos in Romans 16.1," BTr 39 (4, 1988) 401-9. MacDONALD, M. Y. The Pauline Churches (Cambridge 1988) 58. PAUL, C. "A Plethora of Phoebes," Faith and Culture [Sydney] 15 (1989) 75-86. COLLINS, J. N. Diakonia (New York/ Oxford 1990) 224f., 226, 287n.8, 328n.3. ROMANIUK, K. "Was Phoebe in Romans 16, 1 a Deaconess?" ZNW 81 (1990) 132-4. LOHSE, E. Die Entstehung des Neuen Testaments (Stuttgart/Berlin/Köln ⁵1991) 48. SEIFRID, M. A. Justification by Faith (Leiden/New York/Köln 1992) 197f.

16:2   BEST, E. One Body in Christ (1955) 2, 3, 29. HAINZ, J. Ekklesia (Regensburg 1972) 193. BAUMERT, N. Täglich Sterben und Auferstehen. Der Literalsinn von 2 Kor 4, 12-5, 10 (München 1973) 351. SWIDLER, L. Biblical Affirmations of Woman (Philadelphia 1979) 311. MEEKS, W. A. The First Urban Christians (New Haven/London 1983) 27, 79, 85. RINGELING, H. "Frau" in TRE 11 (1983) 432. HEINE, S. Women and Early Christianity (London 1987) 44, 89, 94. ZAPPELLA, M. "A proposito di Febe ΠΡΟΣΤΑΤΙΣ (Rm 16, 2)," RivB 37 (1989) 167-71. SCHULZ, R. R. "A Case for 'President' Phoebe in Romans 16:2," LThJ 24 (3, 1990) 124-7.

16:3ff.   MICHAELIS, W. Paulusstudien (1925) 85ff, 95ff. SCHMITHALS, W. Der Römerbrief als historisches Problem (Gütersloh 1975) 141f.

16:3-16, 21-23   SCHNIDER, F. und STENGER, W. Studien zum neutestamentlichen Briefformular (Leiden 1987) 108 and passim.

16:3-16   FURNISH, V. P. The Moral Teaching of Paul (Nashville 1979) 110. OLLROG, W.-H. "Die Abfassungsverhältnisse von Röm 16" in D. Lührmann und G. Strecker, eds., Kirche (FS G. Bornkamm; Tübingen 1980) 235-42. AUNE, D. E. The New Testament in Its Literary Environment (Philadelphia 1987) 187. REFOULÉ, F. "A contre-courant. Romains 16, 3-16," RHPR 70 (4, 1990) 409-20.

16:3-15   ERBES, K. "Zeit und Ziel der Grüsse Röm.16, 3-15 und der Mitteilungen 2 Tim.4, 9-21," ZNW 10 (1909) 128-47, 195-218.

16:3-5.23   SCHWEIZER, E. Theologische Einleitung in das Neue Testament (Göttingen 1989) ß 15.3.

16:3-5   HAINZ, J. Ekklesia (Regensburg 1972) 295f. FURNISH, V. P. The Moral Teaching of Paul (Nashville 1979) 106f. OLLROG, W.-H. Paulus und seine Mitarbeiter (Neukirchen-Vluyn 1979) 25f., 94, 192, 194. SWIDLER, L. Biblical Affirmations of Woman (Philadelphia 1979) 297f. MARSHALL, P. Enmity in Corinth. Social Conventions in Paul's Relations with the Corinthians (Tübingen 1987) 142. KLAUCK, H.-J. Gemeinde, Amt, Sakrament (Würzburg 1989) 14, 38, 223, 234f. LAMPE, P. Die stadtrömischen Christen in den ersten beiden Jahrhunderten (Tübingen ²1989) 7, 9, 11, 53, 58, 127, 160f., 301, 305, 314.

16:3-4   ADINOLFI, M. Il femminismo della Bibbia (Rome 1981) 200f. KLAUCK, H.-J. Hausgemeinde und Hauskirche im frühen Christentum (Stuttgart 1981) 26.

16:3,5a   KLAUCK, H.-J. Hausgemeinde und Hauskirche im frühen Christentum (Stuttgart 1981) 24.

16:3   HARNACK, A. von, Studien zur Geschichte des Neuen Testaments und der Alten Kirche (1931) 54ff. BEST, E. One Body in Christ (1955) 3, 31. SCHRAGE, W. Die konkreten Einzelgebote in der paulinsichen Paränese (1961) 205f. HAINZ, J. Ekklesia (Regensburg 1972) 194. SWIDLER, L. Biblical Affirmations of Woman (Philadelphia 1979) 294, 297. KLAUCK, H.-J. Hausgemeinde und Hauskirche im frühen Christentum (Stuttgart 1981) 43. STAAB, K. Pauluskommentare aus der griechischen Kirche (Münster ²1984) 172:1-3 ThM. BIERITZ, K.-H. and KÄHLER, C. "Haus III" in TRE 14 (1985) 484. HEINE, S. Women and Early Christianity (London 1987) 43. NUERNBERG, R. "'Non decet neque necessarium est, ut mulieres doceant'. Ueberlegungen zum altkirchlichen Lehrverbot für Frauen" in JAC 31 (1988) 57-73, esp.58.

16:4-6   SEVENSTER, J.N. Paul and Seneca (1961) 7, 77, 95, 178.

16:4-5   MacDONALD, M. Y. The Pauline Churches (Cambridge 1988) 56.

16:4   HAINZ, J. Ekklesia (Regensburg 1972) 195. OLLROG, W.-H. Paulus und seine Mitarbeiter (Neukirchen-Vluyn 1979) 9, 240.

16:5-6   OLLROG, W.-H. Paulus und seine Mitarbeiter (Neukirchen-Vluyn 1979) 25, 38, 55, 75, 79, 120. KLAUCK, H.-J. Hausgemeinde und Hauskirche im frühen Christentum (Stuttgart 1981) 23.

16:5   BEST, E. One Body in Christ (1955) 65n. DELLING, G. Die Zueignung des Heils in der Taufe (1961) 83. Die Taufe im Neuen Testament (1963) 72. KÄSEMANN, E. Exegetische Versuche und Besinnungen (1964) I 114. LADD, G. E. A Theology of the New Testament (Grand Rapids 1974) 349, 437, 532. SCHMITHALS, W. Der Römerbrief als historisches Problem (Gütersloh 1975) 143. LAUB, F. Die Begegnung des frühen Christentums mit der antiken Sklaverei (Stuttgart 1982) 50. MEEKS, W. A. The First Urban Christians (New Haven/London 1983) 16, 27, 42, 57, 221n.2, 229n.160. MURPHY-O'CONNOR, J. St. Paul's Corinth. Texts and Archaeology (Wilmington DE 1983) 158. DOWNING, F. G. Christ and the Cynics (Sheffield 1988) 155.

16:6-12   SCHILLE, G. Die urchristliche Kollegialmission (1967) 50ff. MARSHALL, P. Enmity in Corinth. Social Conventions in Paul's Relations with the Corinthians (Tübingen 1987) 133, 260.

16:6,12   SWIDLER, L. Biblical Affirmations of Woman (Philadelphia 1979) 294. NUERNBERG, R. "'Non decet neque necessarium est, ut mulieres doceant'. Ueberlegungen zum altkirchlichen Lehrverbot für Frauen" in JAC 31 (1988) 57-73, esp.58. 16:6-8 SWIDLER, L. Biblical Affirmations of Woman (Philadelphia 1979) 295, 299.

16:6-7   WITHERINGTON, B. Women in the Ministry of Jesus (Cambridge 1984) 129. LAMPE, P. Die stadtrömischen Christen in den ersten beiden Jahrhunderten (Tübingen ²1989) 53, 58, 127.
16:6   SCHMITHALS, W. Der Römerbrief als historisches Problem (Gütersloh 1975) 143. ROLOFF, J. "Amt" in TRE 2 (1978) 520. ADINOLFI, M. Il femminismo della Bibbia (Rome 1981) 201f.
16:7,9   BEST, E. One Body in Christ (1955) 3, 8, 26, 31, 164.
16:7   SCHRAGE, W. Die konkreten Einzelgebote in der paulinsichen Paränese (1961) 81. DA CASTEL S. PIETRO, T. "Συναιχμάλωτος: Compagno di Prigionia o Conquistato Assieme?" Studiorum Paulinorum Congressus Internationalis Catholicus 1961 II (1963) 417-28. ROLOFF, J. Apostolat-Verkündigung-Kirche ('65) [60f. KÜNG, H. Die Kirche (Freiburg 1967) 223, 274, 410, 412; ET.: The Church (London 1967) 186, 229, 347. HAINZ, J. Ekklesia (Regensburg 1972) 196, 197f. ROLOFF, J. "Apostel" in TRE 3 (1978) 434. BROOTEN, B. "'Junia . . . Outstanding among the Apostles' (Romans 16:7)" in L. Swidler and A. Swidler, eds., Women Priests. A Catholic Commentary on the Vatican Declaration (New York/Toronto 1977) 141-4; GT: "Junia . . . hervorragend unter den Aposteln" in E. Moltmann-Wendel, ed., Frauenbefreiung. Biblische und theologische Argumente (München/Mainz 1978) 148-51. SCHMITHALS, W. "Zur Herkunft der gnostischen Elemente in der Sprache des Paulus" in B. Aland et al., eds., Gnosis (FS H. Jonas; Göttingen 1978) 388-90. OLLROG, W.-H. Paulus und seine Mitarbeiter (Neukirchen-Vluyn 1979) 13, 51, 77, 82. ADINOLFI, M. Il femminismo della Bibbia (Rome 1981) 202f. KLAUCK, H.-J. Hausgemeinde und Hauskirche im frühen Christentum (Stuttgart 1981) 29f. STENDAHL, K. "Ancient Scripture in the Modern World" in F. E. Greenspahn, ed., Scripture in the Jewish and Christian Traditions (Nashville 1982) 206. LOHFINK, G. Jesus and Community. The Social Dimension of the Christian Faith (Philadelphia 1984) 97. FABREGA, V. "War Junia(s), der hervorragende Apostel (Röm. 16, 7), eine Frau?" JAC 27/28 (1984/1985) 47-64. LAMPE, P. "Iunia/Iunias: Sklavenherkunft im Kreise der vorpaulinischen Apostel (Röm 16:7)," ZNW 76 (1985) 132-4. HEINE, S. Women and Early Christianity (London 1987) 42, 44. NUERNBERG, R. "'Non decet neque necessarium est, ut mulieres doceant'. Ueberlegungen zum altkirchlichen Lehrverbot für Frauen," JAC 31 (1988) 58f.n12, 69. SCHULZ, R. R. "Romans 16:7. Junia or Junias?" ET 98 (1987) 108-110. MacDONALD, M. Y. The Pauline Churches (Cambridge 1988) 56. KLAUCK, H.-J. Gemeinde, Amt, Sakrament (Würzburg 1989) 223, 236f.
16:8-15   STAAB, K. Pauluskommentare aus der griechischen Kirche (Münster ²1984) 81:26-82:9 Apoll.
16:8   FURNISH, V. P. The Moral Teaching of Paul (Nashville 1979) 109. OLLROG, W.-H. Paulus und seine Mitarbeiter (Neukirchen-Vluyn 1979) 51, 77.
16:9   SCHMITHALS, W. Der Römerbrief als historisches Problem (Gütersloh 1975) 143, 150. OLLROG, W.-H. Paulus und seine Mitarbeiter (Neukirchen-Vluyn 1979) 9, 51. STAAB, K. Pauluskommentare aus der griechischen Kirche (Münster ²1984) 542:4-5 Phot.
16:10ff.   SCHRAGE, W. Die konkreten Einzelgebote in der paulinsichen Paränese (1961) 206.
16:10-11   BEST, E. One Body in Christ (1955) ln.4, 26. KLAUCK, H.-J. Hausgemeinde und Hauskirche im frühen Christentum (Stuttgart 1981) 28. MEEKS, W. A. The First Urban Christians (New Haven/London 1983) 75f., 217n.54. KLAUCK, H.-J. Gemeinde, Amt, Sakrament (Würzburg 1989) 15.

16:11   KRAMER, W. Christos Kyrios Gottessohn (1963) §50b. OLLROG, W.-H. Paulus und seine Mitarbeiter (Neukirchen-Vluyn 1979) 77.

16:12-13   BEST, E. One Body in Christ (1955) 3n, 4, 16, 26. WITHERINGTON, B. Women in the Ministry of Jesus (Cambridge 1984) 129.

16:12   SCHRAGE, W. Die konkreten Einzelgebote in der paulinischen Paränese (1961) 82. ROLOFF, J. "Amt" in TRE 2 (1978) 520. OLLROG, W.-H. Paulus und seine Mitarbeiter (Neukirchen-Vluyn 1979) 75, 77. ADINOLFI, M. Il femminismo della Bibbia (Rome 1981) 201f. KLAUCK, H.-J. Gemeinde, Amt, Sakrament (Würzburg 1989) 236.

16:13   SCHMITHALS, W. Der Römerbrief als historisches Problem (Gütersloh 1975) 143. OLLROG, W.-H. Paulus und seine Mitarbeiter (Neukirchen-Vluyn 1979) 26, 51. SWIDLER, L. Biblical Affirmations of Woman (Philadelphia 1979) 294. ECKERT, J. "Erwählung" in TRE 10 (1982) 193.

16:14-15   KLAUCK, H.-J. Hausgemeinde und Hauskirche im frühen Christentum (Stuttgart 1981) 27f. KLAUCK, H.-J. Gemeinde, Amt, Sakrament (Würzburg 1989) 14, 236.

16:14   METZGER, B. M. The Early Versions of the New Testament. Their Origin Transmission, and Limitations (Oxford 1977) 172. CLARK, S. B. Man and Woman in Christ (Ann Arbor MI 1980) 36. LAUB, F. Die Begegnung des frühen Christentums mit der antiken Sklaverei (Stuttgart 1982) 50f. MEEKS, W. A. The First Urban Christians (New Haven/London 1983) 56, 75f.

16:15   ROLOFF, J. "Amt" in TRE 2 (1978) 520. SWIDLER, L. Biblical Affirmations of Woman (Philadelphia 1979) 294. KLAUCK, H.-J. Hausgemeinde und Hauskirche im frühen Christentum (Stuttgart 1981) 71. LAUB, F. Die Begegnung des frühen Christentums mit der antiken Sklaverei (Stuttgart 1982) 50f. MEEKS, W. A. The First Urban Christians (New Haven/London 1983) 56, 75f. STAAB, K. Pauluskommentare aus der griechischen Kirche (Münster ²1984) 542:6-7 Phot. FINGER, R. H. "Was Julia a Racist? Cultural Diversity in the Book of Romans," Daughters of Sarah 19 (1993) 36-39.

16:16   RUDOLPH, K. Die Mandäer II (1961) 209, 5. THRAEDE, K. "Ursprünge und Foremen des Heiligen Kusses" in Jahrbuch für Antike und Christentum, ed. F. J. Dölger-Institut (1970) 124-80. GAMBLE, H. The Textual History of the Letter to the Romans (Grand Rapids 1977) 75f. KRETSCHMAR, G. "Abendmahlsfeier" in TRE 1 (1977) 245. RUDOLPH, K. Die Gnosis (Göttingen 1978) 256f. SCMIDT-LAUBER, H. C. "Gesten/Gebärden, Liturgische" in TRE 13 (1984) 154.

16:16b   OLLROG, W.-H. "Die Abfassungsverhältnisse von Röm 16" in D. Lührmann und G. Strecker, eds., Kirche (FS G. Bornkamm; Tübingen 1980) 228, 234f.

16:17ff.   HAHN, F. Christologische Hoheitstitel (1963) 103. SEEBERG, A. Der Katechismus der Urchristenheit (1966) 1, 35f, 12, 41, 50. MÜLLER, U. B. Prophetie und Predigt im Neuen Testament (Gütersloh 1975) 185ff., 211f., 236.

16:17-20   REICKE, B. Diakonie, Festfreude und Zelos (1951) 296f. BORSE, U. Der Standort des Galaterbriefes (Köln 1972) 173, A46, 448, 561. KÜMMEL, W. G. Einleitung in das Neue Testament (Heidelberg 1973) 278f. ZELLER, D. Juden und Heiden in der Mission des Paulus. Studien zum Römerbrief (Stuttgart 1973) 41. WILES, G. P. Paul's Intercessory Prayers (London 1974) 74f., 91, 93f., 196f., 265. SCHMITHALS, W. Der Römerbrief als historisches Problem (Gütersloh 1975) 25, 43, 132f., 148f. OLLROG, W.-H. "Die Abfassungsverhältnisse von Rom 16" in D. Lührmann und G. Strecker, eds., Kirche (FS G. Bornkamm; Tübingen 1980) 229-234, 243. FRANZMANN, M. H. "Exegesis on Romans 16:17ff.," ConcJ 7 (1981) 13-20. STAAB, K. Pauluskommentare aus der griechischen Kirche (Münster [2]1984) 417:18-31 Genn. MALINA B. J. Christian Origins and Cultural Anthropology (Atlanta 1986) 138. WEDDER-BURN, A. J. M. The Reasons for Romans (Edinburgh 1988) 15. BECKER, J. Paulus. Der Apostel der Völker (Tübingen 1989) 177, 196, 277, 359. SCHNELLE, U. Wandlungen im paulinischen Denken (Stuttgart 1989) 30. SIMONIS, W. Der gefangene Paulus. Die Entstehung des sogenannten Römerbriefs und anderer urchristlicher Schriften in Rom (Frankfurt/Bern/New York/Paris 1990) 78-82. JERVIS, L. A. The Purpose of Romans (Sheffield 1991) 136f., 162. SEIFRID, M. A. Justification by Faith (Leiden/New York/Köln 1992) 198-201.

16:17-18   MARSHALL, P. Enmity in Corinth. Social Conventions in Paul's Relations with the Corinthians (Tübingen 1987) 218, 342. LOHFINK, G. Studien zum Neuen Testament (Stuttgart 1989) 324-7, 340, 351.

16:17   SCHRAGE, W. Die konkreten Einzelgebote in der paulinischen Paränese (1961) 106, 108, 122, 132, 138, 159. BJERKELUND, C. J. Parakalo (1967) 14, 18, 116, 128, 157, 159, 160, 167. MUELLER, K. Anstoss und Gericht (1969) 46-67.

16:18   SCHRAGE, W. Die konkreten Einzelgebote in der paulinischen Paränese (1961) 78f, 83. SCHENK, W. Der Segen im Neuen Testament (1967) 36f. TREVI-JANO, R. "Eulogia in St. Paul and the Text of Rom 16, 18" in Studia Evangelica VI (1973) 537-40. ROLOFF, J. "Amt" in TRE 2 (1978) 513. HÜNZINGER, C.-H. "Bann" in TRE 5 (1980) 165. SCHRAGE, W. "Die Elia-Apokalypse" in JSHRZ V/3 (1980) 235. STAAB, K. Pauluskommentare aus der griechischen Kirche (Münster [2]1984) 172:4-12 ThM.

16:19,26   BOUSSET, W. Die Religion des Judentums (1966=1926) 375.

16:19   SCHRAGE, W. Die konkreten Einzelgebote in der paulinischen Paränese (1961) 106, 180, 195, 243. KRAMER, W. Christos Kyrios Gottessohn (1963) §50b. FRIEDRICH, G. "Der Brief eines Gefangenen. Bemerkungen zum Philipper-brief" in Auf das Wort kommt es an. Gesammelte Aufsätze (Göttingen 1978) 234. THISELTON, A. C. The Two Horizons (Grand Rapids 1980) 408. STAAB, K. Pauluskommentare aus der griechischen Kirche (Münster [2]1984) 111:20-26 Diod; 225:5-6 Sev. SCHNABEL, E. J. Law and Wisdom from Ben Sira to Paul (Tübingen 1985) 303, 317, 325f., 336. LIPS, H. VON, Weisheit-liche Traditionen im Neuen Testament (Neukirchen-Vluyn 1990) 125.

16:20   DIBELIUS, M. Die Geisterwelt im Glauben des Paulus (1909) 55f. CERFAUX, L. Christ in the Theology of St. Paul (1959) 6, 66, 107, 501, 515. HAHN, F. Christologische Hoheitstitel (1963) 110. HENNECKE, E./SCHNEEMELCHER, W. Nautestamentliche Apokryphen (1964) II 329. WILES, G. P. Paul's Intercessory Prayers (London 1974) 23f., 29-33, 35f., 41f., 44, 66f., 72, 90-3, 97, 102, 166f. BAUMGARTEN, J. Paulus und die Apokalyptik (Neukirchen-Vluyn 1975) 213-6. SCHMITHALS, W. Der Römerbrief als historisches Problem (Gütersloh 1975) 118f., 125f., 133, 156. GAMBLE, H. The Textual History of the Letter to the Romans (Grand Rapids 1977) 66, 68. SYNOFZIK, E. Die Gerichts- und Vergeltungsaussagen bei Paulus (Göttingen 1977) 25. SCHMITHALS, W. "Zur Herkunft der gnostischen Elemente in der Sprache des Paulus" in B. Aland et al., eds., Gnosis (FS H. Jonas; Göttingen 1978) 390-3. STROBEL, A. "Apokalyptik" in TRE 3 (1978) 252. JERVIS, L. A. The Purpose of Romans (Sheffield 1991) 54, 138f., 154f.

16:21-24   SIMONIS, W. Der gefangene Paulus. Die Entstehung des sogenannten Römerbriefs und anderer urchristlicher Schriften in Rom (Frankfurt/Bern/New York/Paris 1990) 76f.

16:21-23   SCHILLER, G. Die urchristliche Kollegialmission (1967) 47ff, 92f. SCHMI-
            THALS, W. Der Römerbrief als historisches Problem (Gütersloh 1975) 125,
            127f., 167. OLLROG, W.-H. Paulus und seine Mitarbeiter (Neukirchen-Vluyn
            1979) 124. MacDONALD, M. Y. The Pauline Churches (Cambridge 1988) 129.
            JERVIS, L. A. The Purpose of Romans (Sheffield 1991) 139, 151f., 155.
16:21   SEVENSTER, J. N. Paul and Seneca (1961) 178, 197. HAINZ, J. Ekklesia
            (Regensburg 1972) 297f. OLLROG, W.-H. Paulus und seine Mitarbeiter
            (Neukirchen-Vluyn 1979) 9, 21, 23, 37, 45, 50f., 58. THORNTON, C.-J. Der
            Zeuge des Zeugen. Lukas als Historiker der Paulusreisen (Tübingen 1991) 258f.
16:22   BEST, E. One Body in Christ (1955) 3n., 29. BUJARD, W. Stilanalytische
            Untersuchungen zum Kolosserbrief (Göttingen 1973) 165f. ROON, A. VAN,
            The Authenticity of Ephesians (Leiden 1974) 91-3. KLAUCK, H.-J. Hausge-
            meinde und Hauskirche im frühen Christentum (Stuttgart 1981) 33. MAL-
            HERBE, A. J. Moral Exhortation. A Greco-Roman Sourcebook (Philadelphia
            1986) 68. AUNE, D. E. The New Testament in Its Literary Environment (Phila-
            delphia 1987) 18. LOHSE, E. Die Entstehung des Neuen Testaments (Stutt-
            gart/Berlin/Köln ⁵1991) 29. RICHARDS, E. R. The Secretary in the Letters of
            Paul (Tübingen 1991) 170, 190.
16:23-27   MEEKS, W. A. The First Urban Christians (New Haven/London 1983) 48, 56f.,
            75f., 119, 143, 218n.75.
16:23   MICHAELIS, W. Paulusstudien (1925) 58f. BRUNNER, E. Dogmatik I (1946)
            223. DELLING, G. Die Taufe im Neuen Testament (1963) 118. HARRISON,
            P. N. Paulines and Pastorals (London 1964) 100-5. HAINZ, J. Ekklesia
            (Regensburg 1972) 195. ELLIGER, W. Paulus in Griechenland (Stuttgart 1978)
            230. KLAUCK, H.-J. Hausgemeinde und Hauskirche im frühen Christentum
            (Stuttgart 1981) 32, 34, 36. METZGER, B. M. Manuscripts of the Greek Bible
            (Oxford 1981) 64. LAUB, F. Die Begegnung des frühen Christentums mit der
            antiken Sklaverei (Stuttgart 1982) 51. THEISSEN, G. The Social Setting of
            Pauline Christianity (Edinburgh 1982) 75-83. MURPHY-O'CONNOR, J. St.
            Paul's Corinth. Texts and Archaeology (Wilmington DE 1983) 156, 158.
            STAAB, K. Pauluskommentare aus der griechischen Kirche (Münster ²1984)
            172:13-15 ThM. MARSHALL, P. Enmity in Corinth. Social Conventions in
            Paul's Relations with the Corinthians (Tübingen 1987) 135, 137, 147, 345.
            MacDONALD, M. Y. The Pauline Churches (Cambridge 1988) 58. GILL, D.
            W. "Erastus the Aedile," TB 40 (1989) 293-301. KLAUCK, H.-J. Gemeinde,
            Amt, Sakrament (Würzburg 1989) 15, 38f. LAMPE, P. Die stadtrömischen
            Christen in den ersten beiden Jahrhunderten (Tübingen ²1989) 161, 301.
            CLARKE, A. D. "Another Corinthian Erastus Inscription," TB 42 (1991) 146-
            51. THORNTON, C.-J. Der Zeuge des Zeugen. Lukas als Historiker der Paulus-
            reisen (Tübingen 1991) 225, 259f.
16:24-27   ALAND, K. Neutestamentliche Entwürfe (München 1979) 284-301. ELLIOT,
            J. K. "The Language and Style of the Concluding Doxology to the Epistle to
            the Romans," ZNW 72 (1981) 124-30.
16:24   SCHMITHALS, W. Der Römerbrief als historisches Problem (Gütersloh 1975)
            108, 116, 118f. GAMBLE, H. The Textual History of the Letter to the Romans
            (Grand Rapids 1977) 66. ALAND, K. Neutestamentliche Entwürfe (München
            1979) 284-301. ALAND, K. Der Text des Neuen Testaments (Stuttgart 1982)
            303, 312. NEIRYNCK, F. Evangelica (Leuven 1982) 970f. JERVIS, L. A. The
            Purpose of Romans (Sheffield 1991) 135, 138f., 154f.

16:25ff.   KÜMMEL, W. G. Einleitung in das Neue Testament (Heidelberg 1973) 275-7. LIPS, H. VON, Weisheitliche Traditionen im Neuen Testament (Neukirchen-Vluyn 1990) 153, 170, 351f.

16:25-27   HARNACK, A. von Studien zur Geschichte des Neuen Testaments und der Alten Kirche (1931) 184ff. LIETZMANN, H. An die Römer (1933) 130f. KAMLAH, E. Traditionsgeschichtliche Untersuchungen zur Schlussdoxologie des Römerbriefes (diss. Tübingen, 1955). FAHY, T. "Epistle to the Romans 16:25-27" IThQ 28 (3, '61) 238-41. SCHMIDT, H.W. Der Brief des Paulus an die Römer (1962) 265f. HAHN, F. Das Verständnis der Mission im Neuen Testament (1965) 92, 128, 130f. FEINE, D. P. und BEHM, D. J. Einleitung in das Neue Testament (Heidelberg 1950) 175f. BORSE, U. Der Standort des Galaterbriefes (Köln 1972) 9-11, A50. GATZWEILER, K. "Gloire au Dieu sauveur. Rm 16, 25-27," AssS 8 (1972) 34-8. MERKLEIN, H. Das Kirchliche Amt nach dem Epheserbrief (München 1973) 23, 72, 164, 167-9, 194, 209. WILES, G. P. Paul's Intercessory Prayers (London 1974) 72f., 77f., 97f., 264f. ZEILINGER, F. Der Erstgeborene der Schöpfung. Untersuchungen zur Formalstruktur und Theologie des Kolosserbriefes (Wien 1974) 101f. SCHMITHALS, W. Der Römerbrief als historisches Problem (Gütersloh 1975) 108ff. SCHULZ, S. Die Mitte der Schrift (Stuttgart 1976) 128. GAMBLE, H. The Textual History of the Letter to the Romans (Grand Rapids 1977) 16-29, 141, passim. MANSON, T. W. "St. Paul's Letter to the Romans—and Others" in K. P. Donfried, ed., The Romans Debate (Minneapolis 1977) 7-15. METZGER, B. M. "St. Jerome's explicit references to variant readings in manuscripts of the New Testament" in E. Best and R. McL. Wilson, eds., Text and Interpretation (FS M. Black; Cambridge 1979) 184. ROBINSON, J. A. T. Wrestling with Romans (London 1979) 147f. OLLROG, W.-H. "Die Abfassungsverhältnisse von Röm 16" in D. Lührmann und G. Strecker, eds., Kirche (FS G. Bornkamm; Tübingen 1980) 227, 243. ELLIOTT, J. K. "The Language and Style of the Concluding Doxology to the Epistle to the Romans," ZNW 72 (1981) 124-30. HURTADO, L. W. "The Doxology at the End of Romans" in E. J. Epp and G. D. Fee, eds., New Testament Textual Criticism (FS B. M. Metzger; Oxford 1981) 185-99. KLAUCK, H.-J. Hausgemeinde und Hauskirche im frühen Christentum (Stuttgart 1981) 25. METZGER, B. M. Manuscripts of the Greek Bible (Oxford 1981) 134. ALAND, K. Der Text des Neuen Testaments (Stuttgart 1982) 312. STAAB, K. Pauluskommentare aus der griechischen Kirche (Münster ²1984) 111:27-112:18 Diod; 418:1-6 Genn; 542:8-543:39 Phot. AUNE, D. E. The New Testament in Its Literary Environment (Philadelphia 1987) 221. SCHMELLER, TH. Paulus und die "Diatribe" (Münster 1987) 408n.1. WALKENHORST, K.-H. "The Concluding Doxology of the Letter to the Romans and its Theology," [in Japanese] Katorikku Kenkyu [Tokyo] 27 (53, 1988) 99-132. CLABEAUX, J. J. The Lost Edition of the Letters of Paul (CBQ.MS; Washington 1989) 4n.12. FURNISH, P. "Pauline Studies" in E. J. Epp and G. W. MacRae, eds., The New Testament and Its Modern Interpreters (Atlanta 1989) 321-50. SCHNELLE, U. Wandlungen im paulinischen Denken (Stuttgart 1989) 30. SCHWEIZER, E. Theologische Einleitung in das Neue Testament (Göttingen 1989) ß 5.7. BOCKMUEHL, M. N. A. Revelation and Mystery (Tübingen 1990) 199f., 206. MUNRO, W. "Interpolation in the Epistles. Weighing Probability," NTS 36 (3, 1990) 431-43. SIMONIS, W. Der gefangene Paulus. Die Entstehung des sogenannten Römerbriefs und anderer urchristlicher Schriften in Rom (Frankfurt/Bern/New York/Paris 1990) 76.

16:25-26 SCHOEPS, H.-J. Paulus (1959) 68f. ROBINSON, J.M. Kerygma und historischer Jesus (1960) 68, 176. STALDER, K. Das Werk des Geistes in der Heiligung bei Paulus (1962) 173f. BRAUN, H. Qumran und NT II (1966) 174, 240, 274. HEROLD, G. Zorn und Gerechtigkeit Gottes bei Paulus. Eine Untersuchung zu Röm. 1, 16-18 (Bern/Frankfurt 1973) 266f. LADD, G. E. A Theology of the New Testament (Grand Rapids 1974) 94, 383, 387, 392. RIDDERBOS, H. Paul. An Outline of His Theology (Grand Rapids 1975) 46f. STAAB, K. Pauluskommentare aus der griechischen Kirche (Münster ²1984) 432:1-4 Oek. BADENAS, R. Christ the End of the Law (Sheffield 1985) 138. DUNN, J. D. G. "'A Light to the Gentiles'. The Significance of the Damascus Road Christophany for Paul" in L. D. Hurst and N. T. Wright, eds., The Glory of Christ in the New Testament (FS G. B. Caird; Oxford 1987) 251-66, esp.252. WOLTER, M. "Verborgene Weisheit und Heil für die Heiden. Zur Traditionsgeschichte und Intention des 'Revelationsschemas'," ZThK 84 (1987) 297-319.

16:25 RUDOLPH, K. Die Mandäer II (1961) 221, 4. SCHRAGE, W. Die konkreten Einzelgebote in der paulinischen Paränese (1961) 79. KRAMER, W. Christos Kyrios Gottessohn (1963) § 11b. DEWAILLY, L.-M. "Den 'förtegade' hemligheten. Rom. 16:25" SEA 31 ('66) 114-121; "Mystère et silence dans Rom xvi 25" NTS 14 (1, '67) 111-18. DRIESSEN, E. "'Secundum Evangelium meum' (Rom 2, 16; 16, 25; 2 Tim 2, 8)," VD 24 (1944) 25-32. MERKLEIN, H. Das Kirchliche Amt nach dem Epheserbrief (München 1973) 203, 207, 294, 312. SCHÜTZ, J. H. Paul and the Anatomy of Apostolic Authority (Cambridge 1975) 69, 71f., 77. ROLOFF, J. "Apostel" in TRE 3 (1978) 438. HILL, D. New Testament Prophecy (Atlanta 1979) 106. HELDERMANN, J. Die Anapausis im Evangelium Veritatis (Leiden 1984) 112. BOCKMUEHL, M. N. A. Revelation and Mystery (Tübingen 1990) 191, 208f., 213.

16:26 PORUBCAN, S. "The Pauline Message and the Prophets" Studiorum Paulinorum Congressus Internationalis Catholicus 1961 I (1963) 257f. SCHRAGE, W. Die konkreten Einzelgebote in der paulinischen Paränese (1961) 229. KERTELGE, K. "Rechtfertigung" bei Paulus (1967) 169, 174. SEGALLA, G. "L''obbedienza di fede' (Rm 1, 5; 16, 26) tema della Lettera ai Romani?" RivB 36 (1988) 329-42. WOLTER, M. Die Pastoralbriefe als Paulustradition (Göttingen 1988) 47, 152. GARLINGTON, D. B. "The Obedience of Faith in the Letter to the Romans. Part I: The Meaning of ὑπακοὴ πίστεως (Rom 1:5; 16:26)," WThJ 52 (2, 1990) 201-24. ELLIS, E. E. The Old Testament in Early Christianity (Tübingen 1991) 4, 50, 118, 153.

16:27 DEICHGRÄBER, R. "Formeln, Liturgische" in TRE 11 (1983) 258. STAAB, K. Pauluskommentare aus der griechischen Kirche (Münster ²1984) 544:1-5 Phot.

16:28 GAMBLE, H. The Textual History of the Letter to the Romans (Grand Rapids 1977) 35, 141.

* * * * *

Galatians

ΠΡΟΣ ΓΑΛΑΤΑΣ

1ff.   NEBE, G. "Hoffnung" bei Paulus (Göttingen 1983) 339. MALINA B. J. Christian Origins and Cultural Anthropology (Atlanta 1986) 136. LAMPE, P. Die stadtrömischen Christen in den ersten beiden Jahrhunderten (Tübinger. ²1989) 55.

1–4   RAMAZZOTTI, B. "Etica cristiana e peccati nelle lettere ai Romani e ai Galati, " ScuC 106 (1978) 290-342. RICHARDS, E. R. The Secretary in the Letters of Paul (Tübingen 1991) 177.

1:1–4:11   HANSEN, G. W. Abraham in Galatians (Sheffield 1989) 97-99.

1:1–2:14   GOFFINET, A. "La prédication de l'évangile et de la croix dans l'Epfftre aux Galates" EphT 41 (1965) 395-450. ECKERT, J. Die Urchristliche Verkündigung im Streit zwischen Paulus und seinen Gergnern nach dem Galaterbrief (1971) 233-36. BYRNE, B. "Sons of God"—"Seed of Abraham" (Rome 1979) 141-43.

1–2   LINTON, O. "En dementi och dess öde. Gal 1 och 2—Apg. 9 och 15" SEA 12 (1947) 203-19. SCHLIER, H. "Galater Kapitel 1 und 2 und die Apostelgeschichte" in Der Brief and die Galater (1949) 66-78. LINTON, O. "The Third Aspect. A Neglected Point of View. A Study in Gal I-II and Acts IX and XV" StTh 4 (1952) 79–95. SANDERS, J.N. "Peter and Paul in Acts" NTS 2 (1955/56) 133-43. FRANZMANN, M. "The Inclusiveness and the Exclusiveness of the Gospel as Seen in the Apostolate of Paul" CThM 27 (1956) 337-51. HEUSSI, K. "Petrus und die deiden Jakobus in Galater 1-2" Wissenschaftliche Zeitschrift der Friedrich–Schiller–Universität 6 (1956-57) 147-52. MUNCK.J. Paul and the Salvation of Mankind (1959) 79-80. SANDERS, J.N. "Paul's "Autobiographical' Statements in Galatians 1-2" JBL 85 (1966) 335-43. VAN DÜLMEN, A. Die Theologie des Gesetzes bei Paulus (1968) 12-27. KASTING, H. Die Anfänge der Urchristlichen Mission (1969) 121-22. BURCHARD, C. Der Dreizehnte Zeuge (1970) 159-60, 171-72. SELBY, D. Introduction to the New Testament (1971) 332-35. ASHCRAFT, M. "Paul Defends His Apostleship. Galatians 1 and 2" RevEx 69 (1972) 459-69. BORSE, U. Der Standort des Galaterbriefes (1972) 165-67. VOEGTLE, A. "Zum Problem der Herkunft von 'Mt 16, 17-19'" in Orientierung an Jesus, edited by Hoffmann, P. (1973) 373-76. STROBEL, A. "Das Aposteldekret in Galatien: Zur Situation von Gal I und II" NTS 20 (1974) 177-90. GASQUE, W. A History of the Criticism of the Acts of the Apostles (1975) 177-78. SCHÜTZ, J.H. Paul and the Anatomy of Apostolic Authority (1975) 81-82, 114ff. JEWETT, R. A Chronology of Paul's Life (Philadelphia 1979) 52-54. KECK, L. E. "Armut" in TRE 4 (1979) 80. KIM, S. The Origin of Paul's Gospel (Tübingen 1981) 270-73. DUNN, J. D. G. "The Relationship between Paul and Jerusalem according to Galatians 1 and 2, " NTS 28 (1982) 461-78. WENHAM, D. "Paul's Use of the Jesus Tradition. Three Samples" in D. Wenham, ed., Gospel Perspectives. The Jesus Tradition Outside the Gospels, Vol 5 (Sheffield 1984) 24-28. DIETZFELBINGER, C. Die Berufung des Paulus als Ursprung seiner Theologie (Neukirchen 1985) 45ff. LYONS, G. Pauline Autobiography (Atlanta 1985) 75-176. SMIT, J. "Paulus, de galaten en het judaisme. Een narratieve analyse van Galaten 1–2 (Paul, Galatians and Judaism: A Narrative Analysis of Gal. 1–2), " TvTh 25 (1985) 337-62. GAVENTA, B. R. "Galatians 1 and 2: Autobiography as Paradigm, " NovT 28 (1986) 309-26. KARRER, M. Die Johannesoffenbarung als Brief (Göttingen 1986) 303. ZMIJEWSKI, J. Paulus—Knecht und Apostel Christi (Stuttgart 1986) 16-122. ALLAZ, J. et al. Chrétiens en conflit. L'Épître de Paul aux Galates. Dossier pour l'animation biblique (Geneva 1987) passim. COSGROVE, C. H. The Cross and the Spirit. A Study in the Argument and Theology of Galatians (Macon GA 1988) 120n., 144-46. MacDONALD, M. Y. The Pauline Churches (Cambridge 1988) 48f. LAMPE, P. Die stadtrömischen Christen in den ersten beiden Jahrhunderten (Tübingen ²1989) 216. OSTEN-SACKEN, P. VON DER, Die Heiligkeit der Tora (München 1989) 116-60. DUNN, J. D. G. Jesus, Paul and the Law (London 1990) 2-3, 30n.7, 98, 106, 108-109, 118-19, 125n.53, 126n.60, 131, 159, 175, 260n.33, 263n.54. HANSEN, G. W. "The Basis of Authority (Galatians 1 and 2), " Trinity Theological Journal [Singapore] 2 (1990) 42-54. STOCK-HAUSEN, C. K. "Paul the Exegete, " BiTod 28 (1990) 196-202. FREDRIKSEN, P. "Judaism, the Circumcision of Gentiles, and Apocalyptic Hope: Another Look at Galatians 1 and 2, " JThS 42 (1991) 532-64. HALL, R. G. "Historical Inference and Rhetorical Effect: Another Look at Galatians 1 and 2" in D. F. Watson, ed., Persuasive Artistry (FS G.A. Kennedy; Sheffield 1991) 308-20. MARTYN, J. L. "Events in Galatia. Modified Covenantal Nomism versus God's Invasion of the Cosmos in the Singular Gospel: A Response to J. D. G. Dunn and B. R. Gaventa" in J. M. Bassler, ed., Pauline Theology, Volume 1: Thessalonians, Philippians, Galatians, Philemon (Minneapolis MN 1991) 163-66. SCHOON-JANSSEN, J. Umstrittene "Apologien" in den Paulusbriefen. Studien zur rhetorischen Situation des 1. Thessalonicherbriefes, des Galaterbriefes und des Philipperbriefes (Göttingen 1991) passim. SCHWARZ, G. "Zum Wechsel von 'Kephas' zu 'Petros' in Gal 1 und 2, " Biblische Notizen 62 (1992) 46-50. TEMPLETON, E. "Reflecting on Acts, " One in Christ 28 (1992) 97-105. VERSEPUT, D. J. "Paul's Gentile Mission and the Jewish Christian Community. A Study of the Narrative in Galatians 1 and 2, " NTS 39 (1993) 36-58.

1:1–2:10 GARNET, P. "Qumran Light on Pauline Soteriology" in D. A. Hagner and M. J. Harris, eds., Pauline Studies (FS F. F. Bruce; Exeter 1980) 24-27.

1   FRIDRICHSEN, A. "Die Apologie des Paulus-Gal 1" in Paulus und die Urgemeinde (1921) 53-76. FEINE, P. Der Apostel Paulus (1927) 404ff. OEPKE, A. "Weshalb und in welchem Sinne behauptet Pls in Gl 1 seine Selbständigkeit?" in Der Brief des Paulus an die Galater (1957) 41f. WEGENAST, K. Das Verständnis der Tradition dei Paulus und in den Deuteropaulinen (1962) 34-49. KÄSEMANN, E. Exegetische Versuche und Besinnungen (1964) I 220. SCHILLE, G. Anfänge der Kirche (1966) 138ff. GUTBROD, K. Die Apostelgeschichte (1968) 48f. DAMERAU, R. Der Galaterbrief-kommentar des Nikolaus Dinkelsbühl (1970) 3–34. HAINZ, J. Ekklesia (1972) 247-49. KÜMMEL, W.G. Römer 7 und das Bild des Menschen im Neuen Testament (1974) 150f. HOFFMANN, P. "Auferstehung" in TRE 4 (1979) 496. HAGEN, K. Hebrews Commenting from Erasmus to Bèze 1516–1598 (Tübingen 1981) 1, 9, 11, 24, 28, 45. MALINA B. J. Christian Origins and Cultural Anthropology (Atlanta 1986) 167. SEGAL, A. F. Paul the Convert (New Haven/London 1990) 15, 20, 35, 70, 227, 314n.10.

1:1ff.   MAEHLUM, H. Die Vollmacht des Timotheus nach den Pastoralbriefen (Basel 1969) 43-45.

1:1–17   MOSKE, E. "Gal. 1, 1-17 und die Ananiasepisode" ThQ 92 (1910) 531-37. HAYS, R. B. The Faith of Jesus Christ (Chico CA 1983) 81.

1:1-16   KAHL, B. Traditionsbruch und Kirchengemeinschaft bei Paulus (Stuttgart 1977) 12ff.

1:1-12   SUHL, A. "Die Galater und der Geist. Kritische Erwägungen zur Situation in Galatien" in D.-A. Koch et al., eds., Jesu Rede von Gott und ihre Nachgeschichte im frühen Christentum (FS Willi Marxen; Gütersloh 1989) 273-77.

1:1–10   SHEPARD, J.W. The Life and Letters of St. Paul (1950) 332-34. ECKERT, J. Urchristliche Verkündigung im Streit zwischen Paulus und seinen Gegnern nach dem Galaterbrief (1971) 163-73. PANIER, L. "Parcours: Pour lire l'épître aux Galates. lère série, " Sémiotique et Bible 42 (1986) 40-46.

1:1-2,6-10 ZEDDA, S. "Le courage de la fidélité au Christ. Ga 1, 1–2, 6-10" AssS 40 (1972) 62-65.

1:1-9   LIMBECK, M. Mit Paulus Christ sein. Sachbuch zur Person und Theologie des Apostels Paulus (Stuttgart 1989) 11. PAULSEN, H. "Von der Unbestimmtheit des Anfangs. Zur Entstehung von Theologie im Urchristentum" in C. Breytenbach und H. Paulsen, eds., Anfänge der Christologie (FS F. Hahn; Göttingen 1991) 25-41, esp. 41.

1:1-6   OLLROG, W.-H. Paulus und seine Mitarbeiter (Neukirchen/Vluyn 1979) 78, 185-86.

1:1-5   STANLEY, D.M. Christ's Resurrection in Pauline Soteriology (1961) 147-50. GRUNDMANN, W. "Überlieferung und im eschatologischen Denken des Apostels Paulus" NTS 8 (1961/62) 12f. GIBLIN, C.H. In Hope of God's Glory (1970) 51f. PAGELS, E.H. The Gnostic Paul (1975) 101. FRIEDRICH, G. "Lohmeyers These über das paulinische Briefpräskript kritisch beleuchtet" in Auf das Wort kommt es an. Gesammelte Aufsätze (Göttingen 1978) 103-106. KIRCHSCHLÄGER, W. "Von Christus geprägt. Das Paulinische Selbstverständnis als Zeugnis des Osterglaubens, " BuK 36 (1981) 165-70. BRINSMEAD, B. H. Galatians—Dialogical Response to Opponents (Chico CA 1982) 58-63, 189. HAYS, R. B. The Faith of Jesus Christ (Chico CA 1983) 222. LYONS, G. Pauline Autobiography (Atlanta 1985) 124f. ZMIJEWSKI, J. Paulus—Knecht und Apostel Christi (Stuttgart 1986) 33, 80. EGGER, W. Methodenlehre zum Neuen Testament (Freiburg/Basel/ Wien 1987) 105-107. LULL, D. J. "Deliverance From an Evil Age" in W. A: Beardslee et al., eds., Biblical Preaching on the Death of Jesus (Nashville 1989) 200-205. OSTEN-SACKEN, P. VON DER, Die Heiligkeit der Tora (München 1989) 121f. BUS-CEMI, A. M. "Gal 1, 1-5: struttura e linea di pensiero, " SBFLA 40 (1990) 71-103. COOK, D. "The Prescript as Programme in Galatians, " JThS 43 (1992) 511-19. HONG, I.-G. The Law in Galatians (Sheffield 1993) 26f.

1:1-2   HAINZ, J. Ekklesia (1972) 104, 109. ROLOFF, J. "Amt" in TRE 2 (1978) 520. ZMIJEWSKI, J. Paulus—Knecht und Apostel Christi (Stuttgart 1986) 80-89.

1:1   FRIEDRICH, G. "Die Bedeutung der Auferweckung Jesu nach Aussagen des Neuen Testaments" in Auf das Wort kommt es an. Gesammelte Aufsätze (Göttingen 1978) 367. FRIEDRICH, G. "Freiheit und Liebe im ersten Korintherbrief" in Auf das Wort kommt es an. Gesammelte Aufsätze (Göttingen 1978) 181. FRIEDRICH, G. "Das Problem der Autorität im Neuen Testament" in Auf das Wort kommt es an. Gesammelte Aufsätze (Göttingen 1978) 392. ROLOFF, J. "Amt" in TRE 2 (1978) 513. ROLOFF, J. "Apostel" in TRE 3 (1978) 437. SCHMITHALS, W. "Zur Herkunft der gnostischen Elemente in der Sprache des Paulus" in B. Aland et al., eds., Gnosis (FS H. Jonas; Göttingen 1978) 393ff. FROITZHEIM, F. Christologie und Eschatologie bei Paulus (Würzburg 1979) 79ff., 120. HOFFMANN, P. "Auferstehung" in TRE 4 (1979) 479, 494. BERGER, K. "Das Buch der Jubiläen" in JSHRZ II/3 (1981) 477n.13b. HAGEN, K. Hebrews Commenting from Erasmus to Bèze 1516–1598 (Tübingen 1981) 9. HAYS, R. B. The Faith of Jesus Christ (Chico CA 1983) 118. LÜDEMANN, G. Paulus, der Heidenapostel, Band II (Göttingen 1983) 145f. MEEKS, W. A. The First Urban Christians (New Haven/London 1983) 116, 131, 176, 180. PERKINS, P. Resurrection. New Testament Witness and Contemporary Reflection (London 1984) 197-98, 216. ZMIJEWSKI, J. Paulus—Knecht und Apostel Christi (Stuttgart 1986) 33, 78, 91, 94, 99, 120, 123. AUNE, D. E. The New Testament in Its Literary Environment (Philadelphia 1987) 207. BERGER, K. und COLPE, C., eds., Religionsgeschichtliches Textbuch zum Neuen Testament (Göttingen/Zürich 1987) 268. SUHL, A. "Der Galaterbrief—Situation und Argumentation" in ANRW II.25.4 (1987) 3088f. BAARDA, T. "Marcion's Text of Gal 1:1. Concerning the Reconstruction of the First Verse of the Marcionite Corpus Paulinum, " VigChr 42 (1988) 236-56. CONZELMANN, H. and LINDEMANN, A. Interpreting the New Testament (Peabody MA 1988) 21. WOLTER, M.

Die Pastoralbriefe als Paulus-tradition (Göttingen 1988) 84. CLABEAUX, J. J. The Lost Edition of the Letters of Paul (CBQ.MS; Washington 1989) 120, 162. BECKER, J. Paulus. Der Apostel der Völker (Tübingen 1989) 74, 77, 85. VARGHA, Th. "'Paulus Apostolus non ab hominibus neque per hominem'" VD 8 (1928) 147-51. SCHRAGE, W. Die konkreten Einzelgebote in der paulinischen Paränese (1961) 102. HAHN, F. Christologische Hoheitstitel (1963) 204, 210. KRAMER, W. Christos Kyrios Gottessohn (1963) §§ 3c, 13e, 37. HENNECKE, E./SCHNEEMELCHER, W. Neutestamentliche Apokryphen (1964) II 83. ROLOFF, J. Apostola-Verkündigung-Kirche (1965) 41f. THÜSING, W. Per Christum in Deum (1965) 168-69. DELLING, G. Studien zum Neuen Testament und hellenistischen Judentum (1970) 418-22. ECKERT, J. Die Urchristliche Verkündigung im Streit zwischen Paulus und seinen Gegnern nach dem Galaterbrief (1971) 205-10. BORSE, U. Der Standort des Galaterbriefes (1972) 120-121, 167-168. HAINZ, J. Ekklesia (1972) 111-13. O'NEILL, J.C. The Recovery of Paul's Letter to the Galatians (1972) 19. WILSON, S.G. The Gentiles and the Gentile Mission in Luke—Acts (1973) 162-63. CONZELMANN, H./LINDEMANN, A. Arbeitsbuch zum Neuen Testament (1975) 24. DUNN, J.D.G. Jesus and the Spirit (1975) 110-11.

1:1-2   SCHNIDER, F. und STENGER, W. Studien zum neutestamentlichen Briefformular (Leiden 1987) 5 and passim.

1:2-6   BAUMERT, N. Täglich Sterben und Auferstehen. Der Literalisinn von 2 Kor 4, 12–5, 10 (1973) 27.

1:2   SCHRAGE, W. Die kondreten Einzelgebote in der paulinischen Paränese (1961) 41. BORSE, U. Der Standort des Galaterbriefes (1972) 40-44. HAINZ, J. Ekklesia (1972) 236-37. CONZELMANN, H./LINDEMANN, A. Arbeitsbuch zum Neuen Testament (1975) 387. MEEKS, W. A. The First Urban Christians (New Haven/London 1983) 42, 108, 235n.16.

1:3-5   AUNE, D. E. The New Testament in Its Literary Environment (Philadelphia 1987) 185.

1:3   KRAMER, W. Christos Kyrios Gottessohn (1963) § 42b, e. HENNECKE, E./SCHNEEMELCHER, W. Neutestamentliche Apokryphen (1964) II 83.

1:4-5   SYNOFZIK, E. Die Gerichts- und Vergeltungsaussagen bei Paulus (Göttingen 1977) 26-28. CONZELMANN, H. and LINDEMANN, A. Interpreting the New Testament (Peabody MA 1988) 29, 169. CONZELMANN, H./LINDEMANN, A. Arbeitsbuch zum Neuen Testament (1975) 33.

1:4   DALTON, W. J. Christ's Proclamation to the Spirits. A Study of 1 Peter 3:18–4:6 (Rome 1965) 118. RIDDERBOS, H. Paul. An Outline of His Theology (Grand Rapids 1975) 91-99. SANDERS, J. T. Ethics in the New Testament. Change and Development (Philadelphia 1975) 52. WINGREN, G. "Abendmahl" in TRE 1 (1977) 54. FRIEDRICH, G. "Die Kirche zu Korinth" in Auf das Wort kommt es an. Gesammelte Aufsätze (Göttingen 1978) 138. STROBEL, A. "Apokalyptik" in TRE 3 (1978) 252. FROITZHEIM, F. Christologie und Eschatologie bei Paulus (Würzburg 1979) 33ff., 120. HENGEL, M. The Atonement (London 1981) 26, 35f. HYGEN, J. B. "Böse" in TRE 7 (1981) 9. SCHRAGE, W. "Die Elia-Apokalypse" in JSHRZ V/3 (1980) 231n.19i. BRINSMEAD, B. H. Galatians—Dialogical Response to Opponents (Chico CA 1982) 59f., 62. HAYS, R. B. The Faith of Jesus Christ (Chico CA 1983) 118, 128, 188, 248. MEEKS, W. A. The First Urban Christians (New Haven/London 1983) 96, 175, 183, 227n.112, 239n.78. KLEINKNECHT, K. T. Der leidende Gerechtfertigte (Tübingen 1984) 182. POBEE, J. S. Persecution and Martyrdom in the Theology of Paul (Sheffield 1985) 48, 53, 87. KIRCHSCHLÄGER, W. "Zu Herkunft und Aussage von Gal 1, 4" in A. Vanhoye, ed., L'Apôtre Paul (Leuven 1986) 332-39. PASTOR-RAMOS, F. "'Murió por nuestros pecados'

(1 Cor 15:3, Gal 1:4). Observaciones sobre el origen de esta fórmula en Is 53, " EstEc 61 (239, 1986) 358-93. MERKLEIN, H. Studien zu Jesus und Paulus (Tübingen 1987) 8, 24, 43, 51n.129, 187, 293. COSGROVE, C. H. The Cross and the Spirit. A Study in the Argument and Theology of Galatians (Macon GA 1988) 35, 69, 79n., 139, 141, 173n., 176n., 177-79, 182f. JONGE, M. DE, Christology in Context. The Earliest Christian Response to Jesus (Philadelphia 1988) 37, 40. BREYTENBACH, C. Versöhnung (Neukirchen/Vluyn 1989) 126, 164, 197-98, 201-202, 209, 213n. FURNISH, V. P. "Der 'Wille Gottes' in paulinischer Sicht" in D.-A. Koch et al., eds., Jesu Rede von Gott und ihre Nachgeschichte im frühen Christentum (FS Willi Marxsen; Gütersloh 1989) 208-21, esp. 211-12. HAYS, R. B. "'The Righteous One' as Eschatological Deliverer: A Case Study in Paul's Apocalyptic Hermeneutics" in J. Marcus and M. L. Soards, eds., Apocalyptic and the New Testament (FS J. L. Martyn; Sheffield 1989) 191-215, esp. 199. OLIVEIRA, A. DE, Die Diakonie der Gerechtigkeit und der Versöhnung in der Apologie des 2. Korintherbriefes. Analyse und Auslegung von 2 Kor 2, 14–4, 6; 5, 11–6, 10 (Münster 1990) 350. DIBELIUS, M. Die Geisterwelt im Glauben des Paulus (1909) 109-110. BOUSSET, W. Die Religion des Judentums im Spät-hellenistischen Zeitalter (1966=1926) 245. ROBINSON, J.M. Kerygma und historischer Jesus (1960) 109. ROMANIUK, K. L'Amour du Pere et du Fils dans la Soteriologie de Saint Paul (1961) 54-58, 69-70, 73-76, 157-58. SCHRAGE, W. Die konkreten Einzelgebote in der paulinischen Paränese (1961) 15f., 112f. GIBLIN, C.H. The Threat to Faith (1967) 126-27. KERTELGE, K. "Rechtfertigung" bei Paulus (1967) 36, 134. NICKELS, P. Targum and the New Testament (1967) 73. POPKES, W. Christus Traditus (1967) 196f., 248, 274f. VAN DÜLMEN, A. Die Theologie des Gestzes bei Paulus (1968) 48f., 157-60, 204-5. STROBEL, A. Erkenntnis und Bekenntnis der Sünde in neutestamentlicher Zeit (1968) 54, 57. DELLING, G. Studien zum Neuen Testament und zum helle-nistischen Judentum (1970) 173f., 337-39. LOHSE, E. (editor) Der Ruf Jesu und die Antwort der Gemeinde (1970) 204-12. EICHHOLZ, G. Die Theologie des Paulus im Umriss (1972) 107f. O'NEILL, J.C. The Recovery of Paul's Letter to the Galatians (1972) 19f. LAUB, F. Eschatologische Verkündigung und Lebens-gestaltung nach Paulus (1973) 35, 52, 138, 165, 172. ZELLER, D. Juden und Heiden in der Mission des Paulus (1973) 46. LADD, G.E. A Theology of the New Testament (1974) 48, 354, 371, 480, 551. BAUMGARTEN, J. Paulus und die Apokalyptik (1975) 183.

1:4a   HAHN, F. Christologische Hoheitstitel (1963) 202, 210.

1:5-6   ROBERTS, J. H. "Transitional techniques to the letter body in the Corpus Paulinum" in J. H. Petzer and P. J. Hartin, eds., A South African Perspective on the New Testament (FS B. M. Metzger; Leiden 1986) 195, 198.

1:5   KARRER, M. Die Johannesoffenbarung als Brief (Göttingen 1986) 71. LAMPE, P. Die stadtrömischen Christen in den ersten beiden Jahrhunderten (Tübingen ²1989) 126.

1:6–5:1 SANDMEL, S. The Genius of Paul (1958) 37f.

1:6–2:14 LÜDEMANN, G. Paulus, der Heidenapostel, Band I (Göttingen 1980) 58-110. LÜDEMANN, G. Paul: Apostle to the Gentiles (London 1984) 44-80, 196-200.

1:6–2:10 GIBLIN, C.H. In Hope of God's Glory (1970) 52-62.

1:6ff. FREUND, G. und STEGEMANN, E., eds., Theologische Brosamen für Lothar Steiger (DBAT 5; Heidelberg 1985) 389.

1:6-16 SCHMITHALS, W. "Zur Herkunft der gnostischen Elemente in der Sprache des Paulus" in B. Aland et al., eds., Gnosis (FS H. Jonas; Göttingen 1978) 399.

1:6-11 HAYS, R. B. The Faith of Jesus Christ (Chico CA 1983) 222.

1:6-10   HONG, I.-G. The Law in Galatians (Sheffield 1993) 28-29, 100-03. GRÄSSER, E.
         "Das Eine Evangelium. Hermeneutische Erwägungen zu Gal 1, 6-10" ZThK 66 (3,
         1969) 306-44.
1:6-9   DUNN, J. D. G. Unity and Diversity in the New Testament. An Inquiry into the
         Character of Earliest Christianity (London 1977) 23. LÜDEMANN, G. Paulus, der
         Heidenapostel, Band I (Göttingen 1980) 65-68. BRINSMEAD, B. H. Gala-
         tians—Dialogical Response to Opponents (Chico CA 1982) 49, 67, 190. KLAIBER,
         W. Rechtfertigung und Gemeinde (Göttingen 1982) 145-48. LÜDEMANN, G.
         Paulus, der Heidenapostel, Band II (Göttingen 1983) 138f. GASTON, L. "Paul and
         Jerusalem" in P. Richardson and J. C. Hurd, eds., From Jesus to Paul (FS F. W.
         Beare; Waterloo 1984) 65. GRANT, R. M. "Marcion and the Critical Method" in P.
         Richardson and J. C. Hurd, eds., From Jesus to Paul (FS F. W. Beare; Waterloo
         1984) 208, 212. LÜDEMANN, G. Paul: Apostle to the Gentiles (London 1984) 48,
         53f., 85. LYONS, G. Pauline Autobiography (Atlanta 1985) 125. ZMIJEWSKI, J.
         Paulus—Knecht und Apostel Christi (Stuttgart 1986) 89f. MARTYN, J. L. "A Law-
         Observant Mission to Gentiles: The Background of Galatians" in M. P. O'Connor
         and D. N. Freedman, eds., Backgrounds for the Bible (Winona Lake/Indiana 1987)
         199-214, esp. 204ff. OSTEN-SACKEN, P. VON DER, Evangelium und Tora:
         Aufsätze zu Paulus (München 1987) 177f. SUHL, A. "Der Galaterbrief—Situation
         und Argumentation" in ANRW II.25.4 (1987) 3089f. OSTEN-SACKEN, P. VON
         DER, Die Heiligkeit der Tora (München 1989) 122-24. LOHSE, E. Die Entstehung
         des Neuen Testaments (Stuttgart/ Berlin/Köln ⁵1991) 73. SANDNES, K. O.
         Paul—One of the Prophets? (Tübingen 1991) 70-73. ARZT, P. Bedrohtes Christsein.
         Zu Eigenart und Funktion eschatologisch bedrohlicher Propositionen in den echten
         Paulusbriefen (Frankfurt/Berlin/Bern 1992) passim. BRUCE, F.F. "Galatian
         Problems. 3. The 'Other' Gospel" BJRL 53 (1970-71) 253-71. BORSE, U. Der
         Standort des Galater-briefes (1972) 41f., 84-91. MACGORMAN, J.W. "Problem
         Passages in Galatians" SouJTh 15 (1, 1972) 35-51. MÜLLER, U.B. Prophetie und
         Predigt im Neuen Testament (1975) 197ff. SCHÜTZ, J.H. Paul and the Anatomy of
         Apostolic Authority (1975) 116-23.
1:6-8   PAGELS, E.H. The Gnostic Paul (1975) 102.
1:6-7   METZGER, B. M. The Early Versions of the New Testament. Their Origin,
         Transmission, and Limitations (Oxford 1977) 179. ROLOFF, J. "Apostel" in TRE
         3 (1978) 438. CRONJÉ, J. VAN W. "Defamiliarization in the Letter to the
         Galatians" in J. H. Petzer and P. J. Hartin, eds., A South African Perspective on the
         New Testament (FS B. M. Metzger; Leiden 1986) 222. RAMSAY, W.M. "On the
         Interpretation of Two Passages in the Epistle to the Galatians" Exp 5th series 2
         (1895) 103-18. LAMBERT, J.C. "'Another Gospel that is not Another'— Galatians
         1:6, 7" ET 12 (1900-1901) 89-93. HAINZ, J. Ekklesia (1972) 307f. SCHÜTZ, J.H.
         Paul and the Anatomy of Apostolic Authority (1975) 41f.
1:6   KAHL, B. Traditionsbruch und Kirchengemeinschaft bei Paulus (Stuttgart 1977).
         ELLIS, E. E. Prophecy and Hermeneutic in Early Christianity (Tübingen 1978) 95,
         97-98, 110, 121. OLLROG, W.-H. Paulus und seine Mitarbeiter (Neukirchen/Vluyn
         1979) 33, 169, 177, 185, 200. MUELLER, P.-G. Der Traditionsprozess im Neuen
         Testament (Freiburg 1982) 222f. HAYS, R. B. The Faith of Jesus Christ (Chico CA
         1983) 28, 135. MOHRLANG, R. Matthew and Paul (Cambridge 1984) 87, 166, 176.
         BAUMERT, N. Ehelosigkeit und Ehe im Herrn (Würzburg ²1986) 415-16, 558.
         REBELL, W. Gehorsam und Unabhängigkeit (München 1986) 120, 141, 144.
         WOLTER, M. Die Pastoralbriefe als Paulustradition (Göttingen 1988) 212.
         CLABEAUX, J. J. The Lost Edition of the Letters of Paul (CBQ.MS; Washington
         1989) 24-25, 83-84, 150. OLIVEIRA, A. DE, Die Diakonie der Gerechtigkeit und

der Versöhnung in der Apologie des 2. Korintherbriefes. Analyse und Auslegung von 2 Kor 2, 14–4, 6; 5, 11–6, 10 (Münster 1990) 33. ROBERTS, J. H. "Paul's Expression of Perplexity in Galatians 1:6. The Force of Emotive Argumentation, " Neotestamentica 26 (1992) 329-38. FEINE, P. & BEHM, J. Einleitung in das Neue Testament (1950) 144f. WIEDERKEHR, D. Die Theologie der Berufung in den Paulusbriefen (1963) 75-81. BORSE, U. Der Standort des Galaterbriefes (1972) 45-47, 84-91. O'NEILL, J.C. The Recovery of Paul's Letter to the Galatians (1972) 20f.

1:7ff. BISER, E. Der Zeuge (Graz/Wien/Köln 1981) 14, 42, 132, 24.

1:7-9   KRAMER, W. Christos Kyrios Gottessohn (1963) § 12d.

1:7   WOLTER, M. Die Pastoralbriefe als Paulustradition (Göttingen 1988) 103. FREUND, G. und STEGEMANN, E., eds., Theologische Brosamen für Lothar Steiger (DBAT 5; Heidelberg 1985) 389. ZMIJEWSKI, J. Paulus—Knecht und Apostel Christi (Stuttgart 1986) 90, 92, 136. JEWETT, R. "Agitators and the Galatian Congregation" NTS 17 (1970-71) 198-212. BORSE, U. Der Standort des Galaterbriefes (1972) 85-91. HAINZ, J. Ekklesia (1972) 113. O'NEILL, J.C. The Recovery of Paul's Letter to the Galatians (1972) 22f.

1:8ff. FRIEDRICH, G. "Das Problem der Autorität im Neuen Testament" in Auf das Wort kommt es an. Gesammelte Aufsätze (Göttingen 1978) 396.

1:8-9   BEYER, H.W., ALTHAUS, P. "Anathema" in:Der Brief an die Galater (1962) 8. HAINZ, J. Ekklesia (1972) 109, 284f. WILES, G.P. Paul's Intercessory Prayers (1974) 126-29. SCHÜTZ, J.H. Paul and the Anatomy of Apostolic Authority (1975) 37-38. FRIEDRICH, G. "Das Problem der Autorität im Neuen Testament" in Auf das Wort kommt es an. Gesammelte Aufsätze (Göttingen 1978) 392f. HUNZINGER, C.-H. "Bann" in TRE 5 (1980) 165. COOK, R. B. "Paul . . . Preacher or Evangelist?" BTr 32 (1981) 441-44. HALL, S. G. "Formeln, Liturgische" in TRE 11 (1983) 265. CRONJÉ, J. VAN W. "Defamiliarization in the Letter to the Galatians" in J. H. Petzer and P. J. Hartin, eds., A South African Perspective on the New Testament (FS B. M. Metzger; Leiden 1986) 225-26.

1:8   ELLIS, E. E. Prophecy and Hermeneutic in Early Christianity (Tübingen 1978) 36, 42, 71, 110-11, 232. OLLROG, W.-H. Paulus und seine Mitarbeiter (Neukirchen/ Vluyn 1979) 177. DUNN, J. D. G. Christology in the Making (London 1980) 132, 155-56. CLABEAUX, J. J. The Lost Edition of the Letters of Paul (CBQMS; Washington 1989) 18, 24-25, 107-108, 150, 162. SCHRAGE, W. Die konkreten Einzelgebote in der paulinischen Paränese (1961) 115, 122. BORSE, U. Der Standort des Galaterbriefes (1972) 85f., 101f. HAINZ, J. Ekklesia (1972) 110f.

1:9   SANDERS, J. T. Ethics in the New Testament. Change and Development (Philadelphia 1975) 47. KLAIBER, W. Rechtfertigung und Gemeinde (Göttingen 1982) 241n.209. BEHNISCH, M. "Fluch und Evangelium. Galater 1, 9 als ein Aspekt paulinischer Theologie, " Berliner Theologische Zeitschrift 1 (1984) 241-53. GRANT, R. M. "'Holy Law' in Paul and Ignatius" in D. E. Groh and R. Jewett, eds., The Living Text (FS E. W. Saunders; Lanham/London/ New York 1985) 66. SATO, M. Q und Prophetie (Tübingen 1988) 265, 274. FEINE, P. & BEHM, J. Einleitung in das Neue Testament (1950) 143f. SCHRAGE, W. Die konkreten Einzelgebote in der paulinischen Paränese (1961) 47, 106. HAHN, F. Christologische Hoheitstitel (1963) 93. KÄSEMANN, E. Exegetische Versuche und Besinnungen (1964) II 72; New Testament Questions of Today (1969) 70. BORSE, U. Der Standort des Galaterbriefes (1972) 85f. HAINZ, J. Ekklesia (1972) 111, 113. SCHÜTZ, J.H. Paul and the Anatomy of Apostolic Authority (1975) 37-38.

1:10–2:21 FREUND, G. und STEGEMANN, E., eds., Theologische Brosamen für Lothar Steiger (DBAT 5; Heidelberg 1985) 389. LYONS, G. Pauline Autobiography (Atlanta 1985) 130ff. AUNE, D. E. The New Testament in Its Literary Environment

(Philadelphia 1987) 189f. KERTELGE, K. "The Assertion of Revealed Truth as Compelling Argument in Galatians 1:10–2:21, " Neotestamentica 26 (1992) 339-50. DRANE, J.W. Paul: Libertine or Legalist? (1975) 12-23. KLOSTERMANN, E. "Zur Apologie des Paulus, Gal 1, 10–2, 21" in Gottes ist der Orient. Festschrift für Otto Eissfeldt (1959) 84-87.

1:10ff.   HÜBNER, H. "Galaterbrief" in TRE 12 (1984) 6. DIETZFELBINGER, C. Die Berufung des Paulus als Ursprung seiner Theologie (Neukirchen 1985) 5.

1:10-24   CONZELMANN, H. and LINDEMANN, A. Interpreting the New Testament (Peabody MA 1988) 169. OSTEN-SACKEN, P. VON DER, Die Heiligkeit der Tora (München 1989) 124-28. GIBLET, J. "Apologia SPauli de apostolatu suo in Gal 1, 10–24" Collectanea Mechliniensia 26 (1956) 472-74. ROLOFF, J. Apostolat–Verkündigung–Kirche (1965) 64-68.

1:10-13   LYONS, G. Pauline Autobiography (Atlanta 1985) 136-38.

1:10-12   JEREMIAS, J. Abba (1966) 285-86. BALZ, H.R. Methodische Probleme der neutestamentlichen Christologie (1967) 194f. SCHÜTZ, J.H. Paul and the Anatomy of Apostolic Authority (1975) 128-31. KIM, S. The Origin of Paul's Gospel (Tübingen 1981) 67-74.

1:10-11   OLIVEIRA, A. DE, Die Diakonie der Gerechtigkeit und der Versöhnung in der Apologie des 2. Korintherbriefes. Analyse und Auslegung von 2 Kor 2, 14–4, 6; 5, 11–6, 10 (Münster 1990) 324.

1:10   FRIEDRICH, G. "Freiheit und Liebe im ersten Korintherbrief" in Auf das Wort kommt es an. Gesammelte Aufsätze (Göttingen 1978) 181. LÜDEMANN, G. Paulus, der Heidenapostel, Band I (Göttingen 1980) 68-73. BORGEN, P. "Paul Preaches Circumcision and Pleases Men" in M. D. Hooker and S. G. Wilson, eds., Paul and Paulinism (FS C. K. Barrett; London 1982) 41-44. SARACINO, F. "Come si persuade Dio. Su Gal 1, 10a, " Biblica 63 (1982) 84-89. MUNRO, W. Authority in Paul and Peter (Cambridge 1983) 28f. KLEINKNECHT, K. T. Der leidende Gerechtfertigte (Tübingen 1984) 201f. LÜDEMANN, G. Paul: Apostle to the Gentiles (London 1984) 50-53, 114n.32, 116nn.40, 41. SIEGERT, F. Argumentation bei Paulus (Tübingen 1985) 214, 249-51. LYONS, G. Pauline Autobiography (Atlanta 1985) 138-52. ZMIJEWSKI, J. Paulus—Knecht und Apostel Christi (Stuttgart 1986) 39, 61, 92, 120. MARSHALL, P. Enmity in Corinth: Social Conventions in Paul's Relations with the Corinthians (Tübingen 1987) 133, 154, 306-307, 316. SUHL, A. "Der Galaterbrief—Situation und Argumentation" in ANRW II.25.4 (1987) 3090-92. DOWNING, F. G. Christ and the Cynics (Sheffield 1988) 190. SEGAL, A. F. Paul the Convert (New Haven/London) 1990 144, 213, 240. GRAEBE, P. J. "Paul's Assertion of Obedience as a Function of Persuasion, " Neotestamentica 26 (1992) 351-58. FEINE, P. Das Gesetfreie Evangelium des Paulus (1899) 48-50. ZEYDNER, H. "Galatians 1:10" Theologische Studien 18 (1900) 363–64. FEUILLET, A. "'Chercher à persuader Dieu' (Gal I 10a). Le début de l'Epître aux Galates et la scéne matthéenne de Césarée de Philippe" NovT 12 (4, 1970) 350-60. HAINZ, J. Ekklesia (1972) 112-13. O'NEILL, J.C. The Recovery of Paul's Letter to the Galatians (1972) 23-24.

1:11–2:21 DIETERLÉ, C. "Être juste ou vivre (Galates 1, 11–2, 21), " FV 84 (1985) 5-18. PANIER, L. "Parcours pour lire l'épître aux Galates, " Sémiotique et Bible 43 (1986) 23-29. COSGROVE, C. H. The Cross and the Spirit. A Study in the Argument and Theology of Galatians (Macon GA 1988) 3n., 14, 27-28, 31, 34, 119-20, 123, 124n. BELSER, J. Die Selbstverteidigung des hl. Paulus im Galaterbrief (1, 11–2, 21) (1896). SHEPARD, J.W. The Life and Letters of St. Paul (1950) 334-42.

1:11–2:14 HESTER, J. D. "The Rhetorical Structure of Galatians 1:11–2:14, " JBL 103 (1984) 223-33. COSGROVE, C. H. The Cross and the Spirit. A Study in the

Argument and Theology of Galatians (Macon GA 1988) 25, 120-21, 126. STENG-ER, W. "Biographisches und Idealbiographisches in Gal 1, 11–2, 14" in Strukturale Beobachtungen zum Neuen Testament (Leiden 1990) 292-309. FERET, H.-M. Pierre et Paul à Antioche et à Jerusalem. Le 'conflict' des deux apôtres (1955). ECKERT, J. "Paulus und die Jerusalemer Autoritäten nach dem Galaterbrief und der Apostelgeschichte" in Schriftauslegung, hrsg. von Josef Ernst (1972) 283-304. BRUCE, F.F. "Further Thoughts on Paul's Autobiography (Gal. 1:11–2:14)" in Jesus und Paulus. Festschrift für W.G. Kümmel. Hrsg. von E.E. Ellis und E. Grässer (1975) 21-29.

1:11–2:10 SUNDBERG, A. C., Jr. "Paul: A Christian Jonah?" in D. E. Groh and R. Jewett (eds.) The Living Text (FS E. W. Saunders; Lanham/London/New York 1985) 45-58.

1:11ff. BOCKMUEHL, M. N. A. Revelation and Mystery (Tübingen 1990) 136.

1:11-24 PLÜMACHER, E. "Apostelgeschichte" in TRE 3 (1978) 519. BENRATH, G. A. "Autobiographie" in TRE 4 (1979) 773. MALINA B. J. Christian Origins and Cultural Anthropology (Atlanta 1986) 134. MARQUARDT, F.-W. Die Juden und ihr Land (Gütersloh ³1986) 91. LOWRY, E. L. How to Preach a Parable. Designs for Narrative Sermons (Nashville 1989) 142-70. ECKERT, J. Die Urchristliche Verkündigung im Streit zwischen Paulus und seinen Gegnern nach dem Galaterbrief (1971) 173-83.

1:11-20 BRUCE, F. F. "'All Things to All Men'. Diversity in Unity and Other Pauline Tensions" in R. A. Guelich, ed., Unity and Diversity in New Testament Theology (FS G. E. Ladd; Grand Rapids 1978) 82-99. SEEBERG, A. Der Katechismus der Urchristenheit (1966) 189-92.

1:11-18 EICHHOLZ, G. Die Theologie des Paulus im Umriss (1972) 17-20.

1:11-17 SABUGAL, S. "El primer autotestimonio de Pablo sobre su conversión: Gál 1, 1.11-17 (Damasco [1, 17]: ciudad de Siria o región de Qumrán?)" Augustinianum 15 (1975) 429-43. FUNG, R. Y. K. "Revelation and Tradition: the Origins of Paul's Gospel, " EQ 57 (1985) 23-41. FUNG, R. Y. K. "Révélation et tradition: les origines de l'Evangile de Paul, " Hokma 32 (1986) 53-70. GAVENTA, B. R. From Darkness to Light. Aspects of Conversion in the New Testament (Philadelphia 1986) 22-28. MALHERBE, A. J. Moral Exhortation. A Greco-Roman Sourcebook (Philadelphia 1986) 37. RÄISÄNEN, H. The Torah and Christ (Helsinki 1986) 63-67, 72, 84. RÄISÄNEN, H. "Paul's Conversion and the Development of his View of the Law, " NTS 33 (1987) 404-19. CRAFFERT, P. F. "Paul's Damascus Experience as Reflected in Galatians 1: Call or Conversion?" Scriptura 29 (1989) 36-47. WIKEN-HAUSER, A. Die Christusmystik des Apostels Paulus (1956) 87-90. BAIRD, W. "What is the Kerygma? A Study of 1 Cor. 15:3-8 and Gal. 1:1-17" JBL 76 (1957) 181-91. DAVIES, W.D. Invitation to the New Testament (1966) 254-65. PAGELS, E.H. The Gnostic Paul (1975) 102-3.

1:11-16 KERR, F. "Paul's Experience: Sighting or Theophany?" New Blackfriars 58 (686, 1977) 304-13. SWIDLER, L. Biblical Affirmations of Woman (Philadelphia 1979) 223. KLEINKNECHT, K. T. Der leidende Gerechtfertigte (Tübingen 1984) 269. WOLTER, M. Die Pastoralbriefe als Paulustradition (Göttingen 1988) 92. BLANK, J. Paulus und Jesus (1968) 208-30. LANGEVIN, P.-E. "Saint Paul, prophéte des Gentils" LThPh 26 (1970) 3-16.

1:11-12 DUNN, J. D. G. Unity and Diversity in the New Testament. An Inquiry into the Character of Earliest Christianity (London 1977) 66. SCHMITHALS, W. "Zur Herkunft der gnostischen Elemente in der Sprache des Paulus" in B. Aland et al., eds., Gnosis (FS H. Jonas; Göttingen 1978) 398f. LÜDEMANN, G. Paulus, der Heidenapostel, Band I (Göttingen 1980) 73f. BISER, E. Der Zeuge (Graz/Wien/Köln 1981) 21, 42-43, 45, 147, 181. GRUENLER, R. G. New Approaches to Jesus and the Gospels (Grand Rapids 1982) 83. LÜDEMANN, G. Paul: Apostle to the Gentiles (London 1984) 53f. PERKINS, P. Resurrection. New Testament Witness and Contemporary Reflection (London 1984) 88f. DIETZFELBINGER, C. Die Berufung des Paulus als Ursprung seiner Theologie (Neukirchen 1985) 44, 60f. LYONS, G. Pauline Autobiography (Atlanta 1985) 152-58. ZMIJEWSKI, J. Paulus—Knecht und Apostel Christi (Stuttgart 1986) 89-98. AUNE, D. E. The New Testament in Its Literary Environment (Philadelphia 1987) 207. SUHL, A. "Der Galaterbrief—Situation und Argumentation" in ANRW II.25.4 (1987) 3092-94. LATEGAN, B. "Is Paul Defending his Apostleship in Galatians? The Function of Galatians 1.11-12 and 2.19-20 in the Development of Paul's Argument, " NTS 34 (1988) 411-30. DUNN, J. D. G. Jesus, Paul and the Law (London 1990) 89, 101n.3, 106, 110, 112. HONG, I.-G. The Law in Galatians (Sheffield 1993) 29-30. SQUILLACI, D. "La Rivelazione e San Paolo" PaCl 40 (1961) 625-30. ECKERT, J. Die Urchristliche Verkündigung im Streit zwischen Paulus und seinen Gergnern nach dem Galaterbrief (1971) 201-3, 209. HAINZ, J. Ekklesia (1972) 113. WILSON, S.G. The Gentiles and the Gentile Mission in Luke—Acts (1973) 144, 154, 164, 168. DRANE, J.W. Paul Libertine or Legalist? (1975) 17-22. DUNN, J.D.G. Jesus and the Spirit (1975) 110-11. SUHL, A. Paulus und seine Briefe (1975) 35-38. GOPPELT, L. Theologie des Neuen Testaments II (1976) 365.

1:11   HAYS, R. B. The Faith of Jesus Christ (Chico CA 1983) 19. ZMIJEWSKI, J. Paulus—Knecht und Apostel Christi (Stuttgart 1986) 78, 151, 154. SCHRAGE, W. Die konkreten Einzelgebote in der paulinischen Paränese (1961) 74. BORMANN, P. Die Heilswirksamkeit der Verkündigung nach dem Apostel Paulus (1964) 21-23. HAINZ, J. Ekklesia (1972) 112. BAUMERT, N. Täglich Sterben und Auferstehen. Der Literalsinn von 2 Kor 4, 12–5, 10 (1973) 361. BUJARD, W. Stilanalytische Untersuchungen zum Kolosserbrief (1973) 157f., 190. SCHÜTZ, J.H. Paul and the Anatomy of Apostolic Authority (1975).

1:12–2:14 BRINSMEAD, B. H. Galatians—Dialogical Response to Opponents (Chico CA 1982) 49-51. HAYS, R. B. The Faith of Jesus Christ (Chico CA 1983) 30, 222.

1:12ff.   LÜHRMANN, D. Das Offenbarungsverständnis bei Paulus und in paulinischen Gemeinden (1965) 73–79, 107f., 157f.

1:12–22   FAHY, T. "The Council of Jerusalem" IThQ 30 (1963) 232-61.

1:12-16   SCHNELLE, U. Wandlungen im paulinischen Denken (Stuttgart 1989) 15-16, 17. OLIVEIRA, A. DE, Die Diakonie der Gerechtigkeit und der Versöhnung in der Apologie des 2. Korintherbriefes. Analyse und Auslegung von 2 Kor 2, 14–4, 6; 5, 11–6, 10 (Münster 1990) 256ff. ROLOFF, J. Apostolat—Verkündigung—Kirche (1965) 41-45. STRECKER, G. "Befreiung und Rechtfertigung: Zur Stellung der Rechtfertigungslehre in der Theologie des Paulus" in Rechtfertigung, ed. J. Friedrich, W. Pöhlmann, P. Stuhlmacher (1976) 485–86.

1:12-15   DUNN, J. D. G. Unity and Diversity in the New Testament. An Inquiry into the Character of Earliest Christianity (London 1977) 288f.

1:12   ROLOFF, J. "Apostel" in TRE 3 (1978) 438. BERGER, K. "Das Buch der Jubiläen" in JSHRZ II/3 (1981) 477n.13b. GRUENLER, R. G. New Approaches to Jesus and the Gospels (Grand Rapids 1982) 234. GRANT, R. M. "Marcion and the Critical Method" in P. Richardson and J. C. Hurd, eds., From Jesus to Paul (FS F. W. Beare; Waterloo 1984) 208, 212. PRZYBYLSKI, B. "The Spirit. Paul's Journey to Jesus and Beyond" in P. Richardson and J. C. Hurd, eds., From Jesus to Paul (FS F. W. Beare; Waterloo 1984) 160. ZMIJEWSKI, J. Paulus—Knecht und Apostel Christi (Stuttgart 1986) 86, 120-21, 127. AUNE, D. E. The New Testament in Its Literary Environment (Philadelphia 1987) 226. MacDONALD, M. Y. The Pauline Churches (Cambridge 1988) 79. TRILLING, W. Studien zur Jesusüberlieferung (Stuttgart

1988) 324. WOLTER, M. Die Pastoralbriefe als Paulustradition (Göttingen 1988) 102. DUNN, J. D. G. Jesus, Paul and the Law (London 1990) 90, 103n.37, 110, 118, 132, 257. KOLLMANN, B. Ursprung und Gestalten der frühchristlichen Mahlfeier (Göttingen 1990) 45n.34. OLIVEIRA, A. DE, Die Diakonie der Gerechtigkeit und der Versöhnung in der Apologie des 2. Korintherbriefes. Analyse und Auslegung von 2 Kor 2, 14–4, 6; 5, 11–6, 10 (Münster 1990) 257. SEGAL, A. F. Paul the Convert (New Haven/London 1990) 36, 159, 161. FEINE, P. Der Apostel Paulus (1927) 221ff. SCHRAGE, W. Die konkreten Einzelgebote in der paulinischen Paränese (1961) 129f. HAHN, F. Christologicshe Hoheitstitel (1963) 93. RICHTER, H.-F. Auferstehung und Wirklichkeit (1960) 79-80. BORSE, U. Der Standort des Galaterbriefes (1972) 167f. HAINZ, J. Ekklesia (1972) 108, 112. MERKLEIN, H. Das kirchliche Amt nach dem Epheserbrief (1973) 193-200. WILSON, S.G. The Gentiles and the Gentile Mission in Luke—Acts (1973) 162-63, 170. ZELLER, D. Juden und Heiden in der Mission des Paulus (1973) 225. KERTELGE, K. "Apokalypsis Jesou Christou (Gal 1, 12)" in Neues Testament und Kirche, ed. J. Gnilka (1974) 266-81. LADD, G.E. A Theology of the New Testament (1974) 367, 386, 392. DUNN, J.D.G. Jesus and the Spirit (1975) 105f., 108. SCHÜTZ, J.H. Paul and the Anatomy of Apostolic Authority (1975) 131-33.

1:13–2:21 SUHL, A. "Die Galater und der Geist. Kritische Erwägungen zur Situation in Galatien" in D.-A. Koch et al., eds., Jesu Rede von Gott und ihre Nachgeschichte im frühen Christentum (FS Willi Marxen; Gütersloh 1989) 277-84. HESTER, J. D. "Placing the Blame. The Presence of Epideictic in Galatians 1 and 2" in D. F. Watson, ed., Persuasive Artistry (FS G. A. Kennedy; Sheffield 1991) 281-307.

1:13–2:14 HOWARD, G. Paul. Crisis in Galatia (Cambridge 1979) 20-45. JEWETT, R. A Chronology of Paul's Life (Philadelphia 1979) 23. LÜDEMANN, G. Paulus, der Heidenapostel , Band I (Göttingen 1980) 74f. MUELLER, P.-G. Der Traditionsprozess im Neuen Testament (Freiburg 1982) 231. KILPATRICK, G. D. "Peter, Jerusalem and Galatians 1:13–2:14, " NovT 25 (1983) 318-26. LÜDEMANN, G. Paul: Apostle to the Gentiles (London 1984) 50, 53-60, 116n.40. KOPTAK, P. E. "Rhetorical Identification in Paul's Autobiographical Narrative. Galatians 1.13–2.14, " JSNT 40 (1990) 97-113. SUHL, A. Paulus and seine Briefe (1975) 26-76.

1:13–2:1 HURD, J.C. The Origin of 1 Corinthians (1965) 19-22.

1:13ff. MacDONALD, M. Y. The Pauline Churches (Cambridge 1988) 81. ROBINSON, J.M. Kerygma und historischer Jesus (1960) 178.

1:13-24 SCHNELLE, U. Wandlungen im paulinischen Denken (Stuttgart 1989) 54f. HONG, I.-G. The Law in Galatians (Sheffield 1993) 30-33, 68-70.

1:13, 14, 22-24 O'NEILL, J.C. The Recovery of Paul's Letter to the Galatians (1972) 24.

1:13-23 MENOUD, P. "Le sens du verbe porthein" in Jésus-Christ et la foi (Neuchatel-Paris 1975) 40-47. SUHL, A. "Der Galaterbrief—Situation und Argumentation" in ANRW II.25.4 (1987) 3069. MENOUD, P. "Le sens du verbe πορθεῖν (Gal. 1, 13-23 and Acts 9, 21)" in Apophoreta, ed. W. Eltester (1964) 178-86.

1:13-17 DOWNING, F. G. Christ and the Cynics (Sheffield 1988) 190. SEGAL, A. F. Paul the Convert (New Haven/London 1990) 12. SCHÜTZ, J.H. Paul and the Anatomy of Apostolic Authority (1975) 133-35.

1:13-16 LOHFINK, G. Studien zum Neuen Testament (Stuttgart 1989) 283-86. OLIVEIRA, A. DE, Die Diakonie der Gerechtigkeit und der Versöhnung in der Apologie des 2. Korintherbriefes. Analyse und Auslegung von 2 Kor 2, 14–4, 6; 5, 11–6, 10 (Münster 1990) 173.

1:13-16a HAHN, F. Das Verständnis der Mission im Neuen Testament (1965) 82.

1:13-15 ACHTEMEIER, P. J. The Quest for Unity in the New Testament Church (Philadelphia 1987) 29. DOEVE, J.W. "Paulus der Pharisäer und Galater i 13-15" NovT 6 (1963) 170-81.

1:13-14 KÜMMEL, W. G. Römer 7 und das Bild des Menschen im Neuen Testament (München 1974) 111, 144, 154. RIVKIN, E. A Hidden Revolution (Nashville 1978) 78. OLLROG, W.-H. Paulus und seine Mitarbeiter (Neukirchen/Vluyn 1979) 151. THEISSEN, G. Psychologische Aspekte paulinischer Theologie (Göttingen 1983) 236, 239, 243, 247. DIETZFELBINGER, C. Die Berufung des Paulus als Ursprung seiner Theologie (Neukirchen 1985) 11, 12, 23, 45, 96, 101. MALINA B. J. Christian Origins and Cultural Anthropology (Atlanta 1986) 131. SUHL, A. "Der Galaterbrief—Situation und Argumentation" in ANRW II.25.4 (1987) 3095. THEISSEN, G. Psychological Aspects of Pauline Theology (Edinburgh 1987) 234, 237-38, 241, 245. BECKER, J. Paulus. Der Apostel der Völker (Tübingen 1989) 34, 38, 48, 70f. LIMBECK, M. Mit Paulus Christ sein. Sachbuch zur Person und Theologie des Apostels Paulus (Stuttgart 1989) 41. DUNN, J. D. G. Jesus, Paul and the Law (London 1990) 57n.66, 67, 80, 82n.30, 105, 256. OLIVEIRA, A. DE, Die Diakonie der Gerechtigkeit und der Versöhnung in der Apologie des 2. Korintherbriefes. Analyse und Auslegung von 2 Kor 2, 14–4, 6; 5, 11–6, 10 (Münster 1990) 231. HENGEL, M. Judentum und Hellenismus (1969) 194; Judaism and Hellenism (1974) I: 105, II:71. ENSLIN, M.S. Reapproaching Paul (1972) 51-52. LOENING, K. Die Saulustradition in der Apostelgeschichte (1973) 54ff. STOLLE, V. Der Zeuge als Angeklagter (1973) 200, 204.

1:13 RIDDERBOS, H. Paul. An Outline of His Theology (Grand Rapids 1975) 328-30. MENOUD, P. H. Jesus Christ and the Faith (Pittsburg 1978) 47-60. KIM, S. The Origin of Paul's Gospel (Tübingen 1981) 49-50. DIETZFELBINGER, C. Die Berufung des Paulus als Ursprung seiner Theologie (Neukirchen 1985) 6-8, 11, 13, 44. GRAESSER, E. Der Alte Bund im Neuen (Tübingen 1985) 222, 254, 285. MERKLEIN, H. Studien zu Jesus und Paulus (Tübingen 1987) 300n.25, 301-303, 308, 311. LIMBECK, M. Mit Paulus Christ sein. Sachbuch zur Person und Theologie des Apostels Paulus (Stuttgart 1989) 61. MUNCK, J. Paul and the Salvation of Mankind (1959) 13-14. GÄRTNER, B. The Temple and the Community in Qumran and the New Testament (1965) 67. STUHLMACHER, P. Gerechtigkeit Gottes bei Paulus (1965) 210-11. BLANK, J. Paulus und Jesus (1968) 238-42. HAINZ, J. Ekklesia (1972) 106f. BAUMERT, N. Täglich Sterben und Auferstehen. Der Literalsinn von 2 Kor 4, 12-5, 10 (1973) 361. WILSON, S.G. The Gentiles and the Gentile Mission in Luke—Acts (1973) 143, 157, 158. HULTGREN, A.J. "On Translating and Interpreting Galatians 1.13" BTr 26 (1975) 146-48.

1:14 MÜLLER, U. B. "Zur Rezeption Gesetzeskritischer Jesusüberlieferung im frühen Christentum," NTS 27 (1981) 168. MUELLER, P.-G. Der Traditionsprozess im Neuen Testament (Freiburg 1982) 221f. THEISSEN, G. Psychologische Aspekte paulinischer Theologie (Göttingen 1983) 104, 148, 239-40, 299. DIETZFELBINGER, C. Die Berufung des Paulus als Ursprung seiner Theologie (Neukirchen 1985) 6, 9, 10, 13, 26, 84. FREUND, G. und STEGEMANN, E., eds., Theologische Brosamen für Lothar Steiger (DBAT 5; Heidelberg 1985) 391. LIMBECK, M. Mit Paulus Christ sein. Sachbuch zur Person und Theologie des Apostels Paulus (Stuttgart 1989) 37, 40, 52. DUNN, J. D. G. Jesus, Paul and the Law (London 1990) 46, 68, 71, 92, 140, 153, 165n.28, 169n.80, 227, 264n.59. SANDERS, E. P. Jewish Law from Jesus to the Mishnah (London/Philadelphia 1990) 109. STACEY, W.D. The Pauline View of Man (1956) 5, 7, 14. MUNCK, J. Paul and the Salvation of Mankind (1959) 14f. MCNAMARA, M. The New Testament and the Palestinian Targum to the Pentateuch (1966) 254. BLANK, J. Schriftauslegung in Theorie und Praxis (1969)

161. RICHTER, H.-F. Auferstehung und Wirklichkeit (1969) 90f. CAVALLIN, H.C.C. Life After Death (1974) §5·n·5· LADD, G.E. A Theology of the New Testament (1974) 300, 364, 500.

1:15–2:10 KLEIN, G. Die Zwölf Apostel (1961) 44ff.

1:15ff. SCHMITHALS, W. "Zur Herkunft der gnostischen Elemente in der Sprache des Paulus" in B. Aland et al., eds., Gnosis (FS H. Jonas; Göttingen 1978) 397, 399. MINDE, H. J. VAN DER, "Theologia crucis und Pneumaussagen bei Paulus, " Catholica 34 (1980) 133. TUCKETT, C. M. "Deuteronomy 21, 23 and Paul's Conversion" in A. Vanhoye, ed., L'Apôtre Paul (Leuven 1986) 345-50. ZMIJEWSKI, J. Paulus—Knecht und Apostel Christi (Stuttgart 1986) 89, 97-105. MEINERTZ, M. "Zur Bekehrung des hl. Paulus" ThQ 93 (1911) 223-29.

1:15-17 ACHTEMEIER, P. J. The Quest for Unity in the New Testament Church (Philadelphia 1987) 20-21. PRENTICE, W. "St. Paul's Journey to Damascus" ZNW 64 (1956) 250-55. DENIS, A.M. "L'élection et la vocation de Paul, faveurs célestes" RThom 57 (1957) 405-28. SABUGAL, S. "La conversión de S. Pablo en Damasco: ¿ciudad de Siria o región de Qumrân?" Augustinianum 15 (1975) 213-24.

1:15-16 KRUIJF, T. C. DE, "Antisemitismus" in TRE 3 (1978) 125. ROLOFF, J. "Apostel" in TRE 3 (1978) 437. SCHMITHALS, W. "Zur Herkunft der gnostischen Elemente in der Sprache des Paulus" in B. Aland et al., eds., Gnosis (FS H. Jonas; Göttingen 1978) 397. BYRNE, B. "Sons of God"—"Seed of Abraham" (Rome 1979) 206, 206n. FROITZHEIM, F. Christologie und Eschatologie bei Paulus (Würzburg 1979) 79. HENGEL, M. "Zur urchristlichen Geschichtsschreibung (Stuttgart 1979) 70-78, 85; ET: [J. Bowden (trans.)] Acts and the History of Earliest Christianity (London 1979) 81-91, 100. HILL, D. New Testament Prophecy (Atlanta 1979) 111ff. HOFFMANN, P. "Auferstehung" in TRE 4 (1979) 494. SCHILLEBEECKX, E. Christ: the Christian Experience in the Modern World (London 1980) 118f.; GT: Christus und die Christen (Freiburg/Basel/Wien 1977) 108f. BISER, E. Der Zeuge (Graz/Wien/-Köln 1981) 21, 35, 80, 147, 150, 152, 171, 231, 253, 259, 286, 309, 320. BOVON, F. "La vie des apôtres: tradtions bibliques et narrations apocryphes" in F. Bovon et al., eds., Les Actes Apocryphes des Apôtres (Geneva 1981) 145. KIM, S. The Origin of Paul's Gospel (Tübingen 1981) 59f. GRUENLER, R. G. New Approaches to Jesus and the Gospels (Grand Rapids 1982) 234. BERGER, K. "Geist" in TRE 12 (1984) 181. GASTON, L. "Paul and Jerusalem" in P. Richardson and J. C. Hurd, eds., From Jesus to Paul (FS F. W. Beare; Waterloo 1984) 72. SCOBIE, C. H. H. "Jesus or Paul? The Origin of the Universal Mission of the Christian Church" in P. Richardson and J. C. Hurd, eds., From Jesus to Paul (FS F. W. Beare; Waterloo 1984) 47f. STANLEY, D. "Imitation in Paul's Letters. Its Significance for His Relationship to Jesus and to His Own Christian Foundations" in P. Richardson and J. C. Hurd, eds., From Jesus to Paul (FS F. W. Beare; Waterloo 1984) 131. DIETZFEL-BINGER, C. Die Berufung des Paulus als Ursprung seiner Theologie (Neukirchen 1985) 44, 45ff., 50f., 60ff., 72, 104, 137, 141. HULTGREN, A. J. Paul's Gospel and Mission (Philadelphia 1985) 128ff. NICKELSBURG, G. W. E. "An *Ektroma*, Though Appointed from the Womb. Paul's Apostolic Self-Description in 1 Corinthians 15 and Galatians 1" in G. W. E. Nickelsburg and G. W. MacRae, eds., Christians among Jews and Gentiles (FS K. Stendahl; Philadelphia 1986) 198-205. RÄISÄNEN, H. The Torah and Christ (Helsinki 1986) 282. REBELL, W. Gehorsam und Unabhängigkeit (München 1986) 47, 99, 140. ZMIJEWSKI, J. Paulus—Knecht und Apostel Christi (Stuttgart 1986) 59, 111, 126. DUNN, J. D. G. "'A Light to the Gentiles': the Significance of the Damascus Road Christophany for Paul" in L. D. Hurst and N. T. Wright, eds., The Glory of Christ in the New Testament (FS G. B. Caird; Oxford 1987) 251-66. McCAUGHEY, J. D. "The Glory of God in the Face of Jesus Christ, " AusBR 35 (1987) 95-98. MEYER, B. F. "The World Mission and the Emergent Realization of Christian Identity" in E. P. Sanders, ed., Jesus, the Gospels, and the Church (Macon GA 1987) 243-63, esp. 248ff. SUHL, A. "Der Galaterbrief—Situation und Argumentation" in ANRW II.25.4 (1987) 3095. TRILLING, W. Studien zur Jesusüberlieferung (Stuttgart 1988) 324. BECKER, J. Paulus. Der Apostel der Völker (Tübingen 1989) 8, 77, 81, 178, 399. KLAUCK, H.-J. Gemeinde, Amt, Sakrament (Würzburg 1989) 270f., 415f. LIMBECK, M. Mit Paulus Christ sein. Sachbuch zur Person und Theologie des Apostels Paulus (Stuttgart 1989) 62, 85. DUNN, J. D. G. Jesus, Paul and the Law (London 1990) 89, 110, 230, 232, 248-49, 256. OLIVEIRA, A. DE, Die Diakonie der Gerechtigkeit und der Versöhnung in der Apologie des 2. Korintherbriefes. Analyse und Auslegung von 2 Kor 2, 14–4, 6; 5, 11–6, 10 (Münster 1990) 250f. STENGER, W. "Biographisches und Idealbiographisches in Gal 1, 11–2, 14" in Strukturale Beobachtungen zum Neuen Testament (Leiden 1990) 292-309, esp. 301-309. SANDNES, K. O. Paul— One of the Prophets? (Tübingen 1991) 48-76, 240. REFOULÉ, F. "Le parallèle Matthieu 16/16-17—Galates 1/15-16 réexaminé, " EThR 67 (1992) 161-75. STALDER, K. Das Werk des Geistes in der Heiligung bei Paulus (1962) 376f. KRAMER, W. Christos Kyrios Gottessohn (1963) §§ 53, 54b. KÄSEMANN, E. Exegetische Versuche und Besinnungen (1964) II 45; New Testament Questions of Today (1969) 38. HAHN, F. Das Verständnis der Mission im Neuen Testament (²1965) 82. KASTING, H. Die Anfänge der Urchristlichen Mission (1969) 56f., 107. BORSE, U. Der Standort des Galaterbriefes (1972) 121f. LANGE, J. Das Erscheinen des Auferstandenen im Evangelium nach Matthäus (1973) 495-99. MERKLEIN, H. Das kirchliche Amt nach dem Epheserbrief (1973) 193-200. ZELLER, D. Juden und Heiden in der Mission des Paulus (1973) 270f.

1:15   HASENSTAB, R. Modelle paulinischer Ethik (Mainz 1977) 157, 166, 168, 176. WAGNER, F. "Berufung" in TRE 5 (1980) 686. DIETZFELBINGER, C. Die Berufung des Paulus als Ursprung seiner Theologie (Neukirchen 1985) 71ff. MAL-HERBE, A. J. Moral Exhortation. A Greco-Roman Sourcebook (Philadelphia 1986) 36. ZMIJEWSKI, J. Paulus—Knecht und Apostel Christi (Stuttgart 1986) 44, 51, 55, 120, 122, 127, 142, 183. KNOX, J. "On the Meaning of Galatians 1:15, " JBL 106 (1987) 301-304. OLIVEIRA, A. DE, Die Diakonie der Gerechtigkeit und der Versöhnung in der Apologie des 2. Korintherbriefes. Analyse und Auslegung von 2 Kor 2, 14–4, 6; 5, 11–6, 10 (Münster 1990) 257, 373. DENIS, A.-M. "L'élection et la vocation de Paul faveurs célestes. Etude thématique de Gal. 1, 15" RThom 57 (1957) 405-28. HAHN, F. Christologische Hoheitstitel (1963) 307. WIEDERKEHR, D. Die Theologie der Berufung in den Paulusbriefen (1963) 82-90.

1:16ff. EHRHARDT, A. The Acts of the Apostles (1969) 62f.

1:16-24 FISCHER, U. Das Urchristentum (Berlin, DDR 1985) 39, 88f., 90f.

1:16-18 LIMBECK, M. Mit Paulus Christ sein. Sachbuch zur Person und Theologie des Apostels Paulus (Stuttgart 1989) 82. ENSLIN, M.S. Reapproaching Paul (1972) 71f.

1:16-17 HOLMBERG, B. Paul and Power (Lund 1978) 15f. OLLROG, W.-H. Paulus und seine Mitarbeiter (Neukirchen/Vluyn 1979) 9f., 17. BISER, E. Der Zeuge (Graz/Wien/Köln 1981) 37, 93, 103, 112, 147, 178, 221, 244, 291, 306. COGGAN, D. Paul. Portrait of a Revolutionary (New York 1984) 49-57. DUNN, J. D. G. Jesus, Paul and the Law (London 1990) 89, 106, 112, 132.

1:16   FRIEDRICH, G. "Die Auferweckung Jesu, eine Tat Gottes oder ein Interpretament der Jünger" in Auf das Wort kommt es an. Gesammelte Aufsätze (Göttingen 1978) 324. FRIEDRICH, G. "Die Bedeutung der Auferweckung Jesu nach Aussagen des Neuen Testaments" in Auf das Wort kommt es an. Gesammelte Aufsätze (Göttingen 1978) 367. ROLOFF, J. "Amt" in TRE 2 (1978) 518. ROLOFF, J. "Apostel" in TRE

3 (1978) 437. SCHMITHALS, W. "Zur Herkunft der gnostischen Elemente in der Sprache des Paulus" in B. Aland et al., eds., Gnosis (FS H. Jonas; Göttingen 1978) 392f. THISELTON, A. C. The Two Horizons (Grand Rapids 1980) 277, 420. KIM, S. The Origin of Paul's Gospel (Tübingen 1981) 58-59, 251-52, 256-57. MÜLLER, U. B. "Zur Rezeption gesetzeskritischer Jesusüberlieferung im frühen Christentum, " NTS 27 (1981) 168. MUSSNER, F. "Epheserbrief" in TRE 9 (1982) 743. HAYS, R. B. The Faith of Jesus Christ (Chico CA 1983) 231. GASTON, L. "Paul and Jerusalem" in P. Richardson and J. C. Hurd, eds., From Jesus to Paul (FS F. W. Beare; Waterloo 1984) 65. GRANT, R. M. "Marcion and the Critical Method" in P. Richardson and J. C. Hurd, eds., From Jesus to Paul (FS F. W. Beare; Waterloo 1984) 208, 212. STANLEY, D. "Imitation in Paul's Letters. Its Significance for His Relationship to Jesus and to His Own Christian Foundations" in P. Richardson and J. C. Hurd, eds., From Jesus to Paul (FS F. W. Beare; Waterloo 1984) 127. DIETZ-FELBINGER, C. Die Berufung des Paulus als Ursprung seiner Theologie (Neukirchen 1985) 44, 64, 72, 81, 137. SCHIMANOWSKI, G. Weisheit und Messias (Tübingen 1985) 326. BROER, I. "'Der Herr ist wahrhaftig auferstanden' (Lk 24, 34). Auferstehung Jesu und historisch-kritische Methode. Erwägungen zur Entstehung des Osterglaubens" in L. Oberlinner, ed., Auferstehung Jesu—Auferstehung der Christen (Freiburg/Basel/Wien 1986) 59ff. MARQUARDT, F.-W. Die Juden und ihr Land (Gütersloh ³1986) 91. RÄISÄNEN, H. The Torah and Christ (Helsinki 1986) 251. ZMIJEWSKI, J. Paulus—Knecht und Apostel Christi (Stuttgart 1986) 96, 120ff., 127, 140. JONGE, M. DE, Christology in Context. The Earliest Christian Response to Jesus (Philadelphia 1988) 33, 39ff., 114. MacDONALD, M. Y. The Pauline Churches (Cambridge 1988) 79. MARXSEN, W. "Christliche" und christliche Ethik im Neuen Testament (Gütersloh 1989) 136, 143-44. DUNN, J. D. G. Jesus, Paul and the Law (London 1990) 90, 94, 96, 98, 101n.3, 103nn.35, 37, 109-10, 116, 118-19, 127, 132. OLIVEIRA, A. DE, Die Diakonie der Gerechtigkeit und der Versöhnung in der Apologie des 2. Korintherbriefes. Analyse und Auslegung von 2 Kor 2, 14–4, 6; 5, 11–6, 10 (Münster 1990) 177, 224, 256-57, 380. SEGAL, A. F. Paul the Convert (New Haven/London 1990 4, 70, 161. ROBINSON, J.A.T. The Body (1952) 18f. DENIS, A.M. "L'investiture de la fonction apostolique par 'Apocalypse.' Etude thématique de Gal., I, 16" RevBi 64 (1957) 335-62; 481–515. DUPONT, J. "La Révélation du Fils de Dieu en faveur de Pierre (Mt. 16, 17) et de Paul (Gal. 1, 16)" RechSr 52 (1964) 411-20. ROLOFF, J. Apostolat— Verkündigung— Kirche (1965) 91f. WILSON, S.G. The Gentiles and the Gentile Mission in Luke—Acts (1973) 163, 168, 170, 250. DUNN, J.D.G. Jesus and the Spirit (1975) 105f. SCHÜTZ, J.H. Paul and the Anatomy of Apostolic Authority (1975) 37-38, 131-132, 135-136.

1:16a   MUSSNER, F. "Theologische 'Wiedergutmachung'" FrR 26 (1974)7-11.

1:17–2:2   BORSE, U. Der Standort des Galaterbriefes (1972) 92-100.

1:17ff.   ROLOFF, J. "Apostel" in TRE 3 (1978) 433. SCHWEIZER, E. Theologische Einleitung in das Neue Testament (Göttingen 1989) §§8.3, 7; 27.1. HAHN, F. Das Verständnis der Mission im Neuen Testament (1965) 50, 69, 78. ZELLER, D. Juden und Heiden in der Mission des Paulus (1973) 225.

1:17-24   DIETZFELBINGER, C. Die Berufung des Paulus als Ursprung seiner Theologie (Neukirchen 1985) 45.

1:17-23   OLLROG, W.-H. Paulus und seine Mitarbeiter (Neukirchen/Vluyn 1979) 11, 55, 116, 151, 156.

1:17-19   SELLIN, G. Der Streit um die Auferstehung der Toten (Göttingen 1986) 240f. ROLOFF, J. Apostolat—Verkündigung—Kirche (1965) 59f. KASTING, H. Die

Anfänge der Urchristlichen Mission (1969) 68f., 97f. BORSE, U. Der Standort des Galaterbriefes (1972) 167f.

1:17-21 NORRIS, F. W. "Antiochien," in TRE 3 (1978) 102.

1:17-18 BRAUN, H. Qumran und das Neue Testament II (1966) 163, 180.

1:17 & WILLIAMS, A.L. The Epistle of Paul the Apostle to the
4:25 Galatians (1914=1910) 144.

1:17 ROLOFF, J. "Amt" in TRE 2 (1978) 513. ROLOFF, J. "Apostel" in TRE 3 (1978) 430. SCHMITHALS, W. "Zur Herkunft der gnostischen Elemente in der Sprache des Paulus" in B. Aland et al., eds., Gnosis (FS H. Jonas; Göttingen 1978) 392. LÜDEMANN, G. Paulus, der Heidenapostel, Band II (Göttingen 1983) 71-72, 145, 148. DIETZFELBINGER, C. Die Berufung des Paulus als Ursprung seiner Theologie (Neukirchen 1985) 16, 22, 75, 144-45. MARQUARDT, F.-W. Die Juden und ihr Land (Gütersloh ³1986) 91. ZMIJEWSKI, J. Paulus— Knecht und Apostel Christi (Stuttgart 1986) 84f. CLABEAUX, J. J. The Lost Edition of the Letters of Paul (CBQ.MS; Washington 1989) 120. LIMBECK, M. Mit Paulus Christ sein. Sachbuch zur Person und Theologie des Apostels Paulus (Stuttgart 1989) 61. SCHMITHALS, W. "Paulus als Heidenmissionar und das Problem seiner theologischen Entwicklung" in D.-A. Koch et al., eds., Jesu Rede von Gott und ihre Nachgeschichte im frühen Christentum (FS Willi Marxen; Gütersloh 1989) 235-51, esp. 241f. SIMCOX, G.A. "Brevia—Secret History of St. Paul" Exp 4 (1886) 156-58. FRIES, D.S.A. "Was meint Paulus mit Ἀραβία in Gal 1, 17?" ZNW 2 (1901) 150f. KNOX, W.L. The Sources of the Synoptic Gospels II (1957) 116. MUNCK, J. Paul and the Salvation of Mankind (1959) 101, 212f. KRAMER, W. Christos Kyrios Gottessohn (1963) §13c. OSBORNE, R.E. "Did Paul go to Qumran?" Canadian Theological Journal 10 (1964) 15-24. EHRHARDT, A. The Acts of the Apostles (1969) 63f. KASTING, H. Die Anfänge der Urchristlichen Mission (1969) 66, 68f.106. ECKERT, J. Die Urchristliche Verkündigung im Streit zwischen Paulus und seinen Gegnern nach dem Galaterbrief (1971) 206f. BORSE, U. Der Standort des Galaterbriefes (1972) 52, 92, 95, 99, 134f. HAINZ, J. Ekklesia (1972) 154f. WILSON, S.G. The Gentiles and the Gentile Mission in Luke—Acts (1973) 110, 115, 144, 165.

1:18–2:14 ORCHARD, B. "A New Solution of the Galatian Problem" BJRL 28 (1944) 154-74.

1:18–2:10 TALBERT, C.H. "Again Paul's Visits to Jerusalem" NovT 9 (1967) 26-40. SCHÜTZ, J.H. Paul and the Anatomy of Apostolic Authority (1975) 136–50.

1:18–2:1 CONZELMANN, H. and LINDEMANN, A. Interpreting the New Testament (Peabody MA 1988) 340. GIET, S. "Les trois premiers voyages de Saint Paul à Jérusalem" RechSr 41 (1953) 321-47. DUPONT, J. "Les trois premiers voyages de Saint Paul à Jérusalem" in Etudes sur les Actes des Apôtres (1967) 167-71.

1:18-21 ACHTEMEIER, P. J. The Quest for Unity in the New Testament Church (Philadelphia 1987) 47f.

1:18-20 BAUERNFEIND, O. "Tradition und Komposition in dem Apokatastasisspruch Apostelgeschichte 3, 20f" in Kommentar und Studien zur Apostelgeschichte (Tübingen 1980) 464-72. LYONS, G. Pauline Autobiography (Atlanta 1985) 158-64. SUHL, A. "Der Galaterbrief—Situation und Argumentation" in ANRW II.25.4 (1987) 3095. BAUERNFEIND, O. "Die Begegnung zwischen Paulus und Kephas, Gal 1:18-20" ZNW 47 (1956) 268-76.

1:18-19 BROWN, R. E. et al., eds., Peter in the New Testament (Minneapolis 1973) 27, 30. ROLOFF, J. "Amt" in TRE 2 (1978) 512. OLLROG, W.-H. Paulus und seine Mitarbeiter (Neukirchen/Vluyn 1979) 9, 14. REBELL, W. Gehorsam und Unabhängigkeit (München 1986) 45-47, 64. PRATSCHER, W. Der Herrenbruder Jakobus und die Jakobustradition (Göttingen 1987) 45n.77, 49, 52-53, 55-59.

1:18 HOLMBERG, B. Paul and Power (Lund 1978) 16f. RÜGER, H. P. "Aramäisch" in TRE 3 (1978) 606. FITZMYER, J. A. "Aramaic Kepha' and Peter's name in the New Testament" in E. Best and R. McL. Wilson, eds., Text and Interpretation (FS M. Black; Cambridge 1979) 124-30. CRAGG, K. Paul and Peter (London 1980) passim. FARMER, W. R. "Peter and Paul. A Constitutive Relationship for Catholic Christianity" in W. E. March, ed., Texts and Testaments (FS S. D. Currie; San Antonio 1980) 219-36. LÜDEMANN, G. Paulus, der Heidenapostel, Band I (Göttingen 1980) 83-86. MURPHY-O'CONNOR, J. St. Paul's Corinth. Texts and Archaeology (Wilmington/Del. 1983) 129. HOFIUS, O. "Gal 1:18: historēsai Kēphan, " ZNW 75 (1984) 73-85. LÜDEMANN, G. Paul: Apostle to the Gentiles (London 1984) 4, 20, 31n.10, 56, 59, 61-63, 64, 172, 197. DUNN, J. D. G. "Once More— Gal 1:18: historēsai Kēphan. In Reply to Otfried Hofius, " ZNW 76 (1985) 138f. REBELL, W. Gehorsam und Unabhängigkeit (München 1986) 20, 32, 47. COSGROVE, C. H. The Cross and the Spirit. A Study in the Argument and Theology of Galatians (Macon GA 1988) 121, 126, 127n. HEMER, C. J. The Book of Acts in the Setting of Hellenistic History [C. H. Gempf, ed.] (Tübingen 1989) 261, 263, 279, 356. HOFIUS, O. "Gal 1, 18: *historēsai Kēphan*" in Paulusstudien (Tübingen 1989) 255-67. WALTER, N. "Paul and the Early Christian Jesus-Tradition" in A. J. M. Wedderburn, ed., Paul and Jesus. Collected Essays (Sheffield 1989) 51-80, esp. 64-66. DUNN, J. D. G. Jesus, Paul and the Law (London 1990) 3, 12, 101n.3, 109, 111-12, 116, 118-19, 123nn.20-22, 126-27, 132. ULRICHS, K. F. "Grave verbum, ut de re magna. Nochmals Gal 1, 18: *historēsai Kēphan*, " ZNW 81 (1990) 262-69. LOHSE, E. Die Entstehung des Neuen Testaments (Stuttgart/Berlin/Köln [5]1991) 31, 100. ROBERTSON, A.T. Luke the Historian in the Light of Research (1920) 171f. FEINE, P. & BEHM, J. Einleitung in das Neue Testament (1950) 126f. BAUERNFEIND, O. "Die erste Begegnung zwischen Paulus und Kephas Gal. 1, 18" tHlz 81 (1956) 343-344. KILPATRICK, G.D. "Galatians 1:18 ἱστορῆσαι Κηφᾶν," in New Testament Essays in Memory of T.W. Manson, ed. by A.J.B. Higgins (1959) 144-49. GOULDER, M.D. Type and History in Acts (1964) 193f., 197f. HAHN, F. Das Verständnis der Mission im Neuen Testament ([2]1965) 39, 73, 78. BORSE, U. Der Standort des Galaterbriefes (1972) 68f. ENSLIN, M.S. Reapproaching Paul (1972) 77f. HAINZ, J. Ekklesia (1972) 107, 122-24, 248f.

1:19 HOWARD, G. "Was James an Apostle? A Reflection on a New Proposal for Gal. i. 19, " NovT 19 (1977) 63f. ROLOFF, J. "Apostel" in TRE 3 (1978) 430. BÖHLIG, A. Die Gnosis III: Der Manichäismus (Zürich/München 1980) 343n.48. LÜDEMANN, G. Paulus, der Heidenapostel, Band II (Göttingen 1983) 71f. PRATSCHER, W. Der Herrenbruder Jakobus und die Jakobustradition (Göttingen 1987) 10, 33n.26, 34, 35n.32, 56, 56n.33, 57, 75n.107, 114, 186, 197, 204. PURTON, J.S. "A Biblical Note" Exp 1st series 10 (1879' 162-64. LEISEGANG, H. "Der Bruder des Erlösers" Angelos 1 (1925) 24-33. KOCH, H. "Zur Jakobusfrage" ZNW 33 (1934) 204-9. KRETZMANN, P.E. "Zur Jakobusfrage, Gal. 1, 19" CThM 6 (1935) 378. SCHOEPS, H.-J. "Jacobus Ο ΔΙΚΑΙΟΣ ΚΑΙ ΩΒΛΙΑΣ. Neuer Lösungsvorschlag in einer schwierigen Frage" Biblica 24 (1943) 398-403. MUNCK, J. Paul and the Salvation of Mankind (1959) 92f. HAHN, F. Christologische Hoheitstitel (1963) 91f. KRAMER, W. Christos Kyrios Gottessohn (1963) § 13c. BLINZLER, J. Die Brüder und Schwestern Jesu (1967) 121, 132f. RICHTER, H.-F. Auferstehung und Wirklichkeit (1969) 44, 52, 80. BORSE, U. Der Standort des Galaterbriefes (1972) 68f. HAINZ, J. Ekklesia (1972) 108, 122-24, 154-56. LADD, G.E. A Theology of the New Testament (1974) 353, 380, 589. SCHÜTZ, J.H. Paul and the Anatomy of Apostolic Authority (1975) 140-41. TRUDINGER, L.P. "HETERON DE TōN APOSTOLōN OUK EIDON, EI MĒ IAKōBON. A Note on Galatians i 19" NovT 17 (3,

       1975) 200-2. YOUNG, J.E. "'That Some Should Be Apostles'" EQ 48 (2, 1976) 96-104.

1:20   SAMPLEY, J. P. "'Before God, I do not lie' (Gal. i. 20). Paul's Self-Defence in the Light of Roman Legal Praxis, " NTS 23 (1977) 477-82. HOLMBERG, B. Paul and Power (Lund 1978) 14. COSGROVE, C. H. The Cross and the Spirit. A Study in the Argument and Theology of Galatians (Macon GA 1988) 34n., 126-27, 129.

1:21-24 BORSE, U. Der Standort des Galaterbriefes (1972) 94f. ENSLIN, M.S. Reapproaching Paul (1972) 79f.

1:21-22 SCHMITHALS, W. Paulus und Jokobus (1963) 24.

1:21   SCHMITHALS, W. "Zur Herkunft der gnostischen Elemente in der Sprache des Paulus" in B. Aland et al., eds., Gnosis (FS H. Jonas; Göttingen 1978) 392. LÜDEMANN, G. Paulus, der Heidenapostel, Band I (Göttingen 1980) 79-83. LÜDEMANN, G. Paul: Apostle to the Gentiles (London 1984) 4, 14, 20, 56, 59-61, 63-64, 118n.53, 119n.62, 180n.2, 291. PRATSCHER, W. Der Herrenbruder Jakobus und die Jakobustradition (Göttingen 1987) 51, 51nn.8.10, 53, 53n.21. HEMER, C. J. The Book of Acts in the Setting of Hellenistic History [C. H. Gempf, ed.] (Tübingen 1989) 182-83, 191, 290, 381. LOHSE, E. Die Entstehung des Neuen Testaments (Stuttgart/Berlin/Köln ⁵1991) 36. FEINE, P. & BEHM, J. Einleitung in das Neue Testament (1950) 141f. GREEN, E.M.B. "Syria and Cilicia — A Note" ET 71 (1959-60) 52-53. HAHN, F. Das Verständnis der Mission im Neuen Testament (²1965) 50. ROLLINS, W.G. "The New Testament and Apocalyptic" NTS 17 (1970–71) 470f.

1:22-24 BECKER, J. Paulus. Der Apostel der Völker (Tübingen 1989) 13, 40, 60, 95. SCHMITHALS, W. "Paulus als Heidenmissionar und das Problem seiner theologischen Entwicklung" in D.-A. Koch et al., eds., Jesu Rede von Gott und ihre Nachgeschichte im frühen Christentum (FS Willi Marxen; Gütersloh 1989) 235-51, esp. 242ff. KRAMER, W. Christos Kyrios Gottessohn (1963) § 12d. ENSLIN, M.S. Reapproaching Paul (1972) 41f.

1:22-23 DIETZFELBINGER, C. Die Berufung des Paulus als Ursprung seiner Theologie (Neukirchen 1985) 6f. FEINE, P. Der Apostel Paulus (1927) 420f.

1:22   SCHMITHALS, W. "Zur Herkunft der gnostischen Elemente in der Sprache des Paulus" in B. Aland et al., eds., Gnosis (FS H. Jonas; Göttingen 1978) 388-90. KIM, S. The Origin of Paul's Gospel (Tübingen 1981) 33f. DIETZFELBINGER, C. Die Berufung des Paulus als Ursprung seiner Theologie (Neukirchen 1985) 8, 15-16, 21. MARQUARDT, F.-W. Die Juden und ihr Land (Gütersloh ³1986) 91. CLABEAUX, J. J. The Lost Edition of the Letters of Paul (CBQ.MS; Washington 1989) 106n.60. SCHWEIZER, E. Theologische Einleitung in das Neue Testament (Göttingen 1989) § 9.2. HAINZ, J. Ekklesia (1972) 108, 238-40.

1:23-24 SCHMITHALS, W. Paulus und Jakobus (1963) 16. LOENING, K. Die Saulustradition in der Apostelgeschichte (1973) 49ff.

1:23   MENOUD, P. H. Jesus Christ and the Faith (Pittsburg 1978) 47-60. STOCKMEIER, P. "Christlicher Glaube und antike Religiosität" in ANRW II.23.2 (1980) 892f. THISELTON, A. C. The Two Horizons (Grand Rapids 1980) 409. COOK, R. B. "Paul . . . Preacher or Evangelist?" BTr 32 (1981) 441-44. HAYS, R. B. The Faith of Jesus Christ (Chico CA 1983) 144-45, 149, 174, 187. DIETZFELBINGER, C. Die Berufung des Paulus als Ursprung seiner Theologie (Neukirchen 1985) 6-7, 8-9, 11, 13, 43, 58, 82, 144. SCHNELLE, U. Wandlungen im paulinischen Denken (Stuttgart 1989) 15. SEGAL, A. F. Paul the Convert (New Haven/London 1990) 117. BAMMEL, E. "Galater 1:23" ZNW 59 (1-2, 1968) 108-12. BLANK, J. Paulus und Jesus (1968) 238-42. BURCHARD, C. Der dreizehnte Zeuge (1970) 49, 126f., 143, 152, 171. STOLLE, V. Der Zeuge als Angeklagter (1973) 200-4.

1:24   DIETZFELBINGER, C. Die Berufung des Paulus als Ursprung seiner Theologie (Neukirchen 1985) 7.

2–3   JÜNGEL, E. Paulus und Jesus (1966) 32. FULLER, D. P. "Paul and the Works of the Law" WThJ 38 (1975-76) 28-42. GASTON, L. "Paul and the Law in Galatians 2-3" in P. Richardson, ed., Anti-Judaism in Early Christianity, Vol. 1: Paul and the Gospels (Waterloo, Ont. 1986) 37-57. GASTON, L. Paul and the Torah (Vancouver 1987) 64-79.

2   BLOM, A. H. "Jacobus en Petrus. Bijdrag tot verklaring van Gal. II" TT 4 (1870) 465-86. GROSHEIDE, F. W. "De Synode der Apostelen" GThT 11 (1910) 1-16. BRUN, L. "Apostelkonzil und Aposteldekret" in Paulus und die Urgemeinde (1921) 1-52. WAGENMANN, J. Die Stellung des Apostels Paulus neben den Zwölf (1926) 36f. FOERSTER, W. "Die δοκοῦντες in Gal 2" ZNW 36 (1937) 286-92. DUPONT, J.P. Les Problémes du Livre des Actes (1950) 53, 57, 61. FEINE, P., & J. BEHM. Einleitung in das Neue Testament (1950) 82f. HEUSSI, K. "Galater 2 und der Lebensausgang der jerusalemitischen Urapostel" ThLZ 77 (1952) 67-72. BARRETT, C. K. "Paul and the 'Pillar' Apostles (Gal 2)" in Studia Paulina. In honorem Johannis de Zwaan septuagenarii (1953) 1-19. SANDERS, J.N. "Peter and Paul in the Acts" NTS 2 (1955) 133-41. SANDMEL, S. The Genius of Paul (1958) 144-45. SCHRAGE, W. Die konkreten Einzelgebote in der paulinischen Paränese (1961) 266f. GOULDER, M.D. Type and History in Acts (1964) 197-202. KÄSEMANN, E. Exegetische Versuche und Besinnungen (1964) I 128. BLINZLER, J. "Petrus und Paulus—Über iene angebliche Folge des Tages von Antiochien (Gal 2)" in Aus der Welt und Umwelt des Neuen Testaments. Gesammelte Aufsätze 1 (1969) 147-57. BARRETT, C.K. "Titus" in Neotestamentica et Semitica. Studies in Honour of Matthew Black, ed. by E.E. Ellis & M. Wilcox (1969) 3-6. DAMERAU, R. Der Galaterbriefkommentar des Nikolaus Dinkelsbühl (1970) 34-67. BORSE, U. Der Standort des Galaterbriefes (1972) 1f. HAINZ, J. Ekklesia (1972) 247-49. KLIJN, A.F.J.& REININK, G.J. Patristic Evidence for Jewish—Christian Sects (1973) 50. KÜMMEL, W.G. Einleitung in das Neue Testament (1973 ?) 262-64. HOLTZ, T. "Die Bedeutung des Apostelkonzils für Paulus" NovT 16 (1974) 110-48. CONZEL-MANN, H. & LINDEMANN, A. Arbeitsbuch zum Neuen Testament (1975) 409-13. GASQUE, W. A History of the Criticism of the Acts of the Apostles (1975) 38, 59, 88. DESCHNER, J. "Visible Unity as Conciliar Fellowship" ER 28 (1976) 22-27. BURCHARD, C. Untersuchungen zu Joseph and Aseneth (Tübingen 1965) 131. KUSS, O. Paulus (Regensburg 1971) 33, 57-59, 116f. DUNN, J. D. G. Unity and Diversity in the New Testament. An Inquiry into the Character of Earliest Christianity (London 1977) 252-54. HÜBNER, H. Das Gesetz bei Paulus. Ein Beitrag zum Werden der paulinischen Theologie (Göttingen 1978) 21-25, 53-58. ROLOFF, J. "Amt" in TRE 2 (1978) 513. BASSLER, J. M. Divine Impartiality (Chico CA 1982) 171-74. CORLEY, B., ed., Colloquy on New Testament Studies (Macon GA 1983) 164, 169. HAYS, R. B. The Faith of Jesus Christ (Chico CA 1983) 216. HEILIGENTHAL, R. Werke als Zeichen (Tübingen 1983) 133f. LÜDEMANN, G. Paulus, der Heidenapostel, Band II (Göttingen 1983) 28, 32, 38, 49, 62n.12, 92n.98. ACHTEMEIER, P. J. The Quest for Unity in the New Testament Church (Philadelphia 1987) 5, 23f. CONZELMANN, H. and LINDEMANN, A. Interpreting the New Testament (Peabody MA 1988) 5, 170, 337f., 360f. HEMER, C. J. The Book of Acts in the Setting of Hellenistic History [C. H. Gempf, ed.] (Tübingen 1989) 8, 10, 185, 247f., 261, 263, 267, 278, 288, 313, 359, 413. SCHWEIZER, E. Theologische Einleitung in das Neue Testament (Göttingen 1989) § 9.1; 16.2 (cf.16.3). DUNN, J. D. G. Jesus, Paul and the Law (London 1990) 98,

121, 129, 130, 159, 163nn.4.6, 177, 217, 230f., 233n.33. FUCHS, O. Zwischen Wahrhaftigkeit und Macht. Pluralismus in der Kirche? (Frankfurt 1990) passim. HALLBÄCK, G. "Jerusalem og Antiokia i Gal. 2. En historisk hypotese" [Jerusalem and Antioch in Gal. 2. A Historical Hypothesis], DTT 53 (1990) 300-16. SANDERS, E. P. Jewish Law from Jesus to the Mishnah (London/Philadelphia 1990) 96.

2:1ff.   OLLROG, W.-H. Paulus und seine Mitarbeiter (Neukirchen/Vluyn 1979) 14f., 34f., 156, 206, 208. KLEIN, G. "Gesetz III" in TRE 13 (1984) 63. PRATSCHER, W. Der Herrenbruder Jakobus und die Jakobustradition (Göttingen 1987) 49, 54n.23, 59-74, 86n.143, 88, 114, 115n.40, 187n.20, 196. BECKER, J. Paulus. Der Apostel der Völker (Tübingen 1989) 92ff., 106. SUHL, A. "Die Galater und der Geist. Kritische Erwägungen zur Situation in Galatien" in D.-A. Koch et al., eds., Jesu Rede von Gott und ihre Nachgeschichte im frühen Christentum (FS Willi Marxsen; Gütersloh 1989) 278ff.

2:1-14 REICKE, B. "Der geschichtliche Hintergrund des Apostelkonzils und der Antiochia-Episode, Gal. 2, 1-14" in Studia Paulina. In honorem Johannis de Zwaan septuagenarii (1953) 172-87. NICKLE, K.F. The Collection (1966) 40-73. BRUCE, F. F. Paul: Apostle of the Free Spirit (Exeter 1977) 175-78. HESTER, J. D. "The Use and Influence of Rhetoric in Galatians 2:1-14," ThZ 42 (1986) 386-408. SCHNELLE, U. Wandlungen im paulinischen Denken (Stuttgart 1989) 54f. VOLLENWEIDER, S. Freiheit als neue Schöpfung (Göttingen 1989) 400. BURGOS NÚÑEZ, M. DE, "Asamblea de Jerusalén (Hch XV) y Gal 2, 1-14 en la obra Les Actes de Deux Apôtres de M.-É. Boismard y A. Lamouille," Communio 23 (1990) 405-28. SANCHEZ BOSCH, J. "La chronologie de la première aux Thessaloniciens et les relations de Paul avec d'autres églises," NTS 37 (1991) 336-47.

2:1-13 KENNEDY, G. A. Classical Rhetoric and Its Christian and Secular Tradition from Ancient to Modern Times (London 1980) 131f.

2:1-10 RAMSAY, W.M. "On the Interpretation of Two Passages in the Epistle to the Galatians" Exp 5th series 2 (1895) 103-18. MACKINTOSH, R. "The Tone of Galatians 2:1-10" ET 21 (1909-10) 327-28. WILLIAMS, A.L. "Gal. ii.1-10 in relation to Ac. xv.4-29" in The Epistle of Paul the Apostle to the Galatians (1914=1910) 145-47. KISSANE, E.J. "The Visit in Gal. 2, 1-10," IThQ 14 (1919) 373ff. BOYLAN, P. "The Visit of Paul to Jerusalem in Galatians 2:1-10" IThQ 17 (1922) 293-304. DIBELIUS, M. Aufsätze zur Apostelgeschichte (1951) 84-90. FERET, H.-M. Pierre et Paul à Antioche et à Jérusalem (1955). DIBELIUS, M. Studies in the Acts of the Apostles (1956) 93-101. OEPKE, A. "Die Apostelzusammenkunft in Jerusalem" in Der Brief an die Galater (1957) 51-55. MUNCK, J. Paul and the Salvation of Mankind (1959) 102f. SCHOEPS, H.-J. Paulus (1959) 57ff. HOERBER, R.G. "Galatians 2:1-10 and the Acts of the Apostles" CThM 31 (1960) 482-91. HAENCHEN, E. NTS 7 (1960-61) 192f. MANCERO, V. "Gal. II, 1-10 y Act. XV. Estado actual de la cuestion" EstBi 22 (3-4, 1963) 315-50. SCHMITHALS, W. Paulus und Jakobus (1963) 29-51. TOUSSAINT, S.D. "The Chronological Problem of Galatians 2:1-10" BiblSa 120 (480, 1963) 334-40.KLOSTERMANN, E. "Noch einmal über Paulus zum Apostelkonvent" Wissenschaftliche Zeitschrift der Martin—Luther—Universität 12 (3, 1964) 149-50. ROBINSON, D.W.B. "The Circumcision of Titus, and Paul's Liberty" AusBR 12 (1-4, 1964) 24-42. HAHN, F. Das Verständnis der Mission im Neuen Testament (²1965) 66-70, 73f. HURD, J.C. The Origin of 1 Corinthians (1965) 265-69. ROLOFF, J. Apostolat—Verkündigung—irche (1965) 68-73. CER-FAUX, L. The Christian in the Theology of St. Paul (1967) 377f. DIETZFELBINGER, C. Was ist Irrlehre? (1967) 12-16. PARKER, P. "Once More Acts and Galatians" JBL 86 (1967) 175-82. GUTBROD, K. Die Apostelgeschichte (1968) 49f. KASTING, H. Die Angänge der urchristlichen Mission

(1969) 76f., 98f., 116-20. ECKERT, J. Die urchristliche Verkündigung im Streit zwischen Paulus und seinen Gegnern nach dem Galaterbrief (1971) 183-93, 219-24. HAINZ, J. Ekkiesia (1972) 113, 116f. VAN BRUGGEN, J. 'Na veertein jaren'. De datering van het in Galaten 2 genoemde overleg te Jeruzalem (1973). WILSON, S.G. The Gentiles and the Gentile Mission in Luke—Acts (1973) 179-87. ZELLER, D. Juden und Heiden in der Mission des Paulus (1973) 226f. GOULDER, M.D. Midrash and Lection in Matthew (1974) 139f. STEIN, R.H. "The Relationship of Galatians 2:1-10 and Acts 15:1-35: Two Neglected Arguments" JEThS 17 (4, 1974) 239-42. BROWN, R. E. et al., eds., Peter in the New Testament (Minneapolis 1973) 25-29, 51. BRUCE, F. F. Paul: Apostle of the Free Spirit (Exeter 1977) 148-59. CATCH-POLE, D. R. "Paul, James and the Apostolic Decree," NTS 28 (1977) 428-44. KAHL, B. Traditionsbruch und Kirchengemeinschaft bei Paulus (Stuttgart 1977) 17-19. SAMPLEY, J. P. "Societas Christi: Roman Law and Paul's Conception of the Christian Community" in J. Jervell and W. A. Meeks, eds., God's Christ and His People (FS N. A. Dahl; New York 1977) 164-66. HOLMBERG, B. Paul and Power (Lund 1978) 18-32. NORRIS, F. W. "Antiochien" in TRE 3 (1978) 101. SCHMI-THALS, W. "Zur Herkunft der gnostischen Elemente in der Sprache des Paulus" in B. Aland et al., eds., Gnosis (FS H. Jonas; Göttingen 1978) 400f. FERRARESE, G. Il concilio di Gerusalemme in Ireneo di Lione. Ricerche sulla storia dell'esegesi di Atti 15, 1-29 (e Galati 2, 1-10) nel II secolo (Brescia 1979) passim. HENGEL, M. Zur urchristlichen Geschichtsschreibung (Stuttgart 1979) 93-105; ET: Acts and the History of Earliest Christianity [trans. J. Bowden] (London 1979) 111-26. HOWARD, G. Paul. Crisis in Galatia (Cambridge 1979) 21-34. HURTADO, L. W. "The Jerusalem Collection and the Book of Galatians," JSNT 5 (1979) 46-62. JEW-ETT, R. A Chronology of Paul's Life (Philadelphia 1979) 64-75, 78-87, 89-93. PANI-KULAM, G. Koinōnia in the New Testament: A Dynamic Expression of Christian Life (Rome 1979) 34. ROLOFF, J. Neues Testament (Neukirchen-Vluyn 1979) 47-62. LÜHRMANN, D. "Abendmahlsgemeinschaft? Gal 2, 11ff" in D. Lührmann und G. Strecker, eds., Kirche (FS Günther Bornkamm; Tübingen 1980) 275-77. MÜLLER, U. B. "Zur Rezeption gesetzeskritischer Jesusüberlieferung im frühen Christentum," NTS 27 (1981) 159. HAINZ, J. Koinonia (Regensburg 1982) 124, 130, 140, 158. GASTON, L. "Paul and Jerusalem" in P. Richardson and J. C. Hurd, eds., From Jesus to Paul (FS F. W. Beare; Waterloo 1984) 65f., 71. HÜBNER, H. "Galaterbrief" in TRE 12 (1984) 9. BETZ, H. D. "Häresie I" in TRE 14 (1985) 315. DIETZFELBINGER, C. Die Berufung des Paulus als Ursprung seiner Theologie (Neukirchen 1985) 45f., 144. BETZ, H. D. "Hellenismus III" in TRE 15 (1986) 27. BRUCE, F. F. "The Conference in Jerusalem. Galatians 2:1-10" in P. T. O'Brian and D. G. Peterson, eds., God Who Is Rich In Mercy (FS D. B. Knox; Homebush West NSW, Australia 1986) 195-212. FIEDLER, P. "Die Tora bei Jesus und in der Jesus-überlieferung" in K. Kertelge, ed., Das Gesetz im Neuen Testament (Freiburg/ Basel/Wien 1986) 82. HAHN, F. "Die Bedeutung des Apostelkonvents für die Einheit der Christenheit" in Exegetische Beiträge zum ökumenischen Gespräch [Ges. Aufs., I] (Göttingen 1986) 95-115. REBELL, W. Gehorsam und Unabhängigkeit (München 1986) 13, 20, 33, 35, 38, 41-43, 47, 48, 65, 73, 77n.122, 167. SCHNACKENBURG, R. Die sittliche Botschaft des Neuen Testaments, Band 1 (Freiburg/Basel/Wien 1986) 191. ACHTEMEIER, P. J. The Quest for Unity in the New Testament Church (Philadelphia 1987) 6, 8, 21f., 27, 33, 44, 48-51, 53, 89. OSTEN-SACKEN, P. VON DER, Evangelium und Tora: Aufsätze zu Paulus (München 1987) 294, 297. SUHL, A. "Der Galaterbrief—Situation und Argumentation" in ANRW II.25.4 (1987) 3096. WEDDERBURN, A. J. M. The Reasons for Romans (Edinburgh 1988) 37f. HEMER, C. J. The Book of Acts in the Setting of Hellenistic History [C. H. Gempf, ed.] (Tübingen 1989) 257, 288. KLAUCK, H.-J. Gemeinde, Amt, Sakrament (Würzburg 1989) 340f. MARXSEN, W. "Christliche" und christliche Ethik im Neuen Testament (Gütersloh 1989) 139, 143. OSTEN-SACKEN, P. VON DER, Die Heiligkeit der Tora (München 1989) 128-35. SCHMITHALS, W. "Paulus als Heidenmissionar und das Problem seiner theologischen Entwicklung" in D.-A. Koch et al., eds., Jesu Rede von Gott und ihre Nachgeschichte im frühen Christentum (FS Willi Marxen; Gütersloh 1989) 235-51, esp. 246-50. DUNN, J. D. G. Jesus, Paul and the Law (London 1990) 92, 98, 101, 126n.63, 129, 152f., 159f., 163n.4, 170n.96, 171n.111, 173n.124, 181, 189, 227, 245, 251, 254f., 257. HOWARD, G. Paul. Crisis in Galatia (Cambridge ²1990) ix, 10, 21, 28-34, 80. SCHMIDT, A. "Das historische Datum des Apostelkonzils," ZNW 81 (1990) 122-31. SUHL, A. "Ein Konfliktlösungsmodell der Urkirche und seine Geschichte," BuK 45 (1990) 80-86. HONG, I.-G. The Law in Galatians (Sheffield 1993) 33f., 68-70.

2:1-6   ORCHARD, B. "The Problem of Acts and Galatians" CBQ 7 (1945) 377-97.

2:1-5   PAGELS, E.H. The Gnostic Paul (1975) 103-4. WALKER, W. O. "Why Paul Went to Jerusalem: The Interpretation of Galatians 2:1-5," CBQ 54 (1992) 503-10.

2:1-2   ENSLIN, M.S. Reapproaching Paul (1972) 80f., 88-93. BOOTH, R. P. Jesus and the Laws of Purity. Tradition History and Legal History in Mark 7 (Sheffield 1986) 82f. KLAUCK, H.-J. Gemeinde, Amt, Sakrament (Würzburg 1989) 241, 416.

2:1   KNOX, J. "Fourteen Years Later" JR 16 (1936) 341-49. DIEU, L. "Quatorze ans ou. . . quatre ans? A propos de Gal. 2, 1" EphT 14 (1937) 308-17. SCHMITHALS, W. Paulus und Jakobus (1963) 33. HURD, J.C. The Origin of 1 Corinthians (1965) 15-18. BARRETT, C.K. "Titus" in Neotestamentica et Semitica. Studies in Honour of Matthew Black, ed. by E.E. Ellis & M. Wilcox (1969) 2f., 5f. BORSE, U. Der Standort des Galaterbriefes (1972) 92-97. KLEIN, P. "Zum Verständnis von Gal 2:1. Zugleich ein Beitrag zur Chronologie des Urchristentums," ZNW 70 (1979) 250f. LÜDEMANN, G. Paulus, der Heidenapostel, Band I (Göttingen 1980) 83-86. LÜDEMANN, G. Paul: Apostle to the Gentiles (London 1984) 4, 20, 30n., 5, 53, 56, 59, 61-64, 78, 106, 119n.62, 172, 180n.2, 193n.106, 197. REBELL, W. Gehorsam und Unabhängigkeit (München 1986) 20, 64f., 81. HEMER, C. J. The Book of Acts in the Setting of Hellenistic History [C. H. Gempf, ed.] (Tübingen 1989) 20, 182f., 253, 261, 263, 279. SEGAL, A. F. Paul the Convert (New Haven/London 1990) 187f. LOHSE, E. Die Entstehung des Neuen Testaments (Stuttgart/ Berlin/Köln ⁵1991) 31, 100.

2:2ff.   FRIEDRICH, G. "Das Problem der Autorität im Neuen Testament" in Auf das Wort kommt es an. Gesammelte Aufsätze (Göttingen 1978) 396.

2:2-9   BLOMMERDE, A.C.M. "Is There an Ellipsis between Galatians 2, 3 and 2, 4?" Biblica 56 (1, 1975) 100-2.

2:2   SCHMITHALS, W. Paulus und Jakobus (1963) 30-33. QUESNELL, Q. This Good News (1964) 104f. LÜHRMANN, D. Das Offenbarungs–verständnis bei Paulus und in paulinischen Gemeinden (1965) 41f. PFITZNER, V.C. Paul and the Agon Motif (1967) 99ff. WEISS, B. "Die Sorge, vergebens zu laufen" GuL 44 (1971) 85-92. BORSE, U. Der Standort des Galaterbriefes (1972) 95, 97, 99. O'NEILL, J.C. The Recovery of Paul's Letter to the Galatians (1972) 27-30. HAINZ, J. Ekklesia (1972) 118. WILSON, S.G. The Gentiles and the Gentile Mission in Luke—Acts (1973) 182f. DUNN, J.D.G. Jesus and the Spirit (1975) 217, 222. SCHÜTZ, J.H. Paul and the Anatomy of Apostolic Authority (1975) 71-72. BJERKELUND, C. J. "'Vergeblich' als Missionsergebnis bei Paulus" in J. Jervell and W. A. Meeks, eds., God's Christ and His People (FS N. A. Dahl; New York 1977) 175-91. HOLMBERG, B. Paul and Power (Lund 1978) 22. ROLOFF, J. "Amt" in TRE 2 (1978) 513, 518. ROLOFF, J. "Apostel" in TRE 3 (1978) 436. HILL, D. New Testament Prophecy

(Atlanta 1979) 177. MÜLLER, U. B. "Zur Rezeption gesetzeskritischer Jesusüber-lieferung im frühen Christentum," NTS 27 (1981) 167. HAINZ, J. Koinonia (Regensburg 1982) 125-27. KÄSEMANN, E. "Urchristliche Konflikte um die Freiheit der Gemeinde" in Kirchliche Konflikte, Band 1 (Göttingen 1982) 40. DIETZFELBINGER, C. Die Berufung des Paulus als Ursprung seiner Theologie (Neukirchen 1985) 44, 51, 60, 131. MARQUARDT, F.-W. Die Juden und ihr Land (Gütersloh ³1986) 91. REBELL, W. Gehorsam und Unabhängigkeit (München 1986) 36, 43, 48, 78. JONES, F. S. "Freiheit" in den Briefen des Apostels Paulus (Göttingen 1987) 72, 74, 194n.10, 196n.24. BOCKMUEHL, M. N. A. Revelation and Mystery (Tübingen 1990) 144, 188. DUNN, J. D. G. Jesus, Paul and the Law (London 1990) 108-10, 112-16, 119, 121, 123n.27, 124n.38, 132, 157, 173n.124, 177, 254. HOWARD, G. Paul. Crisis in Galatia (Cambridge ²1990) 21, 30f., 38. OLIVEIRA, A. DE, Die Diakonie der Gerechtigkeit und der Versöhnung in der Apologie des 2. Korintherbriefes. Analyse und Auslegung von 2 Kor 2, 14-4, 6; 5, 11-6, 10 (Münster 1990) 398, 400. SEGAL, A. F. Paul the Convert (New Haven/London 1990 36, 161, 188. VOLF, J. M. G. Paul and Perseverance (Tübingen 1990) 239n.39, 245n.69, 261-63, 266n.31, 267, 281, 285.

2:3-8   WARNER, D. "Galatians 2:3-8: as an Interpolation" ET 62 (1950-51) 380. FUNG, R. Y. K. "A Note on Galatians 2:3-8," JEThS 25 (1982) 49-52.

2:3-6   TAG, P. "Zur Exegese von Luk. 18, 7 und Gal. 2, 3-6" ThSK 57 (1884) 167-72.

2:3-5   BRUCE, A.B. "Was Titus Circumcised?" Exp 1st series 11 (1880) 201-5. LAKE, K. "Galatians 2:3-5" Exp 7th series 1 (1906) 236-45. ORCHARD, B. "A Note on the Meaning of Galatians 2, 3-5" JThS 43 (1942) 173-77. ROBINSON, D.W.B. "The Circumcision of Titus and Paul's 'Liberty' (Gal 2:3-5)" AusBR 12 (1964) 24-42. RICHARDSON, P. Israel in the Apostolic Church (1969) 92-93. O'NEILL, J.C. The Theology of Acts in its Historical Setting (1970) 103-4). HOLMBERG, B. Paul and Power (Lund 1978) 23. WALKER, W. O. "The Timothy-Titus Problem Reconsidered," ET 92 (1981) 231-35. SCHÄFER, K. Gemeinde als "Bruderschaft" (Frankfurt/Bern/New York/ Paris 1989) 189ff. DUNN, J. D. G. Jesus, Paul and the Law (London 1990) 108, 117, 119, 122n.2.

2:3-4   ORCHARD, B. "The Ellipsis between Galatians 2, 3 and 2, 4" Biblica 54 (4, 1973) 469-81. BLOMMERDE, A.C.M. "Is There An Ellipsis Between Galatians 2, 3 and 2, 4" Biblica 56 (1975) 100-2. ORCHARD, J. B. "Once again the Ellipsis between Gal. 2, 3 and 2, 4," Biblica 57 (1976) 254f.

2:3   BORSE, U. Der Standort des Galaterbriefes (1972) 52f. O'NEILL, J.C. The Recovery of Paul's Letter to the Galatians (1972) 30f. OLLROG, W.-H. Paulus und seine Mitarbeiter (Neukirchen/Vluyn 1979) 36. LÜDEMANN, G. Paulus, der Heidenapostel, Band II (Göttingen 1983) 59f., 151n.147. COSGROVE, C. H. The Cross and the Spirit. A Study in the Argument and Theology of Galatians (Macon GA 1988) 31n., 123-25. SCHNELLE, U. Wandlungen im paulinischen Denken (Stuttgart 1989) 74. DUNN, J. D. G. Jesus, Paul and the Law (London 1990) 120, 124n.42, 156, 253f. LOHSE, E. Die Entstehung des Neuen Testaments (Stuttgart/-Berlin/ Köln ⁵1991) 99.

2:4-6   O'NEILL, J.C. The Recovery of Paul's Letter to the Galatians (1972) 31-37.

2:4-5   MUNCK, J. Paul and the Salvation of Mankind (1959) 93f., 96-98. SCHMITHALS, W. Paulus und Jakobus (1963) 89f. WATSON, F. Paul, Judaism and the Gentiles (Cambridge 1986) 50-53. PRATSCHER, W. Der Herrenbruder Jakobus und die Jakobustradition (Göttingen 1987) 71f., 91, 60n.47. CLABEAUX, J. J. The Lost Edition of the Letters of Paul (CBQ.MS; Washington 1989) 116.

2:4   MUNCK, J. Paul and the Salvation of Mankind (1959) 97f. STALDER, K. Das Werk des Geistes in der Heiligung bei Paulus (1962) 307f., 341f. BRAUN, H.

Qumran und das Neue Testament II (1966) 162, 213. HAINZ, J. Ekklesia (1972) 114. RAMOS, F. P. La libertad en la Carta a los Gálatas. Estudio exegético-teológico (Madrid 1977) passim. ELLIS, E. E. Prophecy and Hermeneutic in Early Christianity (Tübingen 1978) 111, 123, 230f. FREUND, G. und STEGEMANN, E., eds., Theologische Brosamen für Lothar Steiger (DBAT 5; Heidelberg 1985) 186. GERHARDSSON, B. "Eleutheria (Freedom) in the Bible" in B. P. Thompson, ed., Scripture. Meaning and Method (FS A. T. Hanson; Hull 1987) 13f., 23n.19. JONES, F. S. "Freiheit" in den Briefen des Apostels Paulus (Göttingen 1987) 14, 31, 44, 64, 70, 71-82, 85, 91f., 99, 103, 105-09, 130, 136, 139, 144f., 147n.3, 155n.88, 161n.15, 197n.43, 198n.45, 199n.48, 200n.61, 200f.n.81, 223n.91. BECKER, J. Paulus. Der Apostel der Völker (Tübingen 1989) 115, 224, 278. CLABEAUX, J. J. The Lost Edition of the Letters of Paul (CBQ.MS; Washington 1989) 23, 100, 106n.60, 110, 137, 150f. VOLLENWEIDER, S. Freiheit als neue Schöpfung (Göttingen 1989) 298ff.

2:5,14   BARTOLOMÉ, J. J. El evangelio y su verdad. La justificación por la fe y su vivencia en común. Un estudio exegético de Gal 2, 5.14 (Rome 1988) passim.

2:5   BACON, B.W. "The Reading ὅς οὐδέ in Gal. 2, 5" JBL 42 (1923) 69-80. LIGHTFOOT, J.B. "Various Readings in ii.5" in The Epistle of St. Paul to the Galatians (1957) 121-23. TAYLOR, V. The Text of the New Testament (1961) 103f. METZGER, B. M. "St. Jerome's explicit references to variant readings in manuscripts of the New Testament" in E. Best and R. McL Wilson, eds., Text and Interpretation (FS M. Black; Cambridge 1979) 185. THISELTON, A. C. The Two Horizons (Grand Rapids 1980) 413. KÄSEMANN, E. "Urchristliche Konflike um die Freiheit der Gemeinde" in Kirchliche Konflikte, Band 1 (Göttingen 1982) 37-45. JONES, F. S. "Freiheit" in den Briefen des Apostels Paulus (Göttingen 1987) 71f., 74, 78, 80, 194n.10, 195n.14, 196n.20. COSGROVE, C. H. The Cross and the Spirit. A Study in the Argument and Theology of Galatians (Macon GA 1988) 25n., 122-25, 145. CLABEAUX, J. J. The Lost Edition of the Letters of Paul (CBQ.MS; Washington 1989) 84f., 102, 106f., 113, 143, 151.

2:6ff.   ALAND, K. "Wann starb Petrus? Eine Bemerkung zu Gal. II.6" NTS 2 (1955-56) 267ff. LÜDEMANN, G. Paulus, der Heidenapostel, Band II (Göttingen 1983) 60, 64-66.

2:6-14   HOLL, K. "Der Streit zwischen Petrus und Paulus zu Antiochien in seiner Bedeutung für Luthers innere Entwicklung" ZKG 38 (1919) 23-40.

2:6-10   PAGELS, E.H. The Gnostic Paul (1975) 104-5. ZMIJEWSKI, J. Paulus—Knecht und Apostel Christi (Stuttgart 1986) 84, 89, 105-19, 121f., 125.

2:6-9   ANNAND, R. "A Note on the Three Pillars" ET 67 (1955-56) 178. KLEIN, G. "Galater 2, 6-9 und die Geschichte der Jerusalemer Urgemeinde" ZThK 57 (3, 1960) 275-95. FÜRST, H. "Paulus und die 'Säulen' der Jerusalemer Urgemeinde" in Studiorum Paulinorum Congressus Internationalis Catholicus 1961 II (1963) 3-10. KLEIN, G. "Galater 2, 6-9 und die Geschichte der Jerusalemer Urgemeinde" in Rekonstruktion und Interpretation (1969) 99-128. BORSE, U. Der Standort des Galaterbriefes (1972) 167f.

2:6-7   DE BEUS, C. "De positie van de gemeente te Jerusalem in de oudchristelijke kerk, in het licht van Gal 2, 6s' NedThT 7 (1952-53) 1-18.

2:6   BURK "Versuch einer Erklärung von Gal. 2, 6" ThSK 38 (1865) 734-40. MAERCKER, F. "Über Gal. 2, 6" ThSK 39 (1866) 532-44. BURK "Nochmals über Galater 2, 6" ThSK 41 (1868) 527-34. BRUNEC, M. "'Ἀπὸ δὲ δοκούντων (Gal. 2, 6)" VD 25 (1947) 280-88. DAVIES, W.D. Torah in the Messianic Age and/or the Age to Come (1952) 92. ALAND, K. "Wann Starb Petrus?" NTS 2 (1956) 267-75. HÄSLER, B. "Sprachlich-grammatische Bemerkungen zu Gal II 6" ThLZ 82 (1957)

393-94. MUNCK, J. Paul and the Salvation of Mankind (1959) 90f., 98f. SCHRAGE, W. Die konkreten Einzelgebote in der paulinischen Paränese (1961) 177. SCHMITHALS, W. Paulus und Jakobus (1963) 69, 82. ROLOFF, J. Apostolat—Verkündigung—Kirches (1965) 92f. HAY, D.M. "Paul's Indifference to Authority" JBL 88 (1969) 36-44. KASTING, H. Die Anfänge der Urchristlichen Mission (1969) 118-22. HAINZ, J. Ekklesia (1972) 116, 118f. SHIMADA, K. The Formulary Material in First Peter. A Study According to the Method of Traditionsgeschichte (Union Theological Seminary, NY; Th.D. diss. University Microfilms, Ann Arbor MI 1966) 206f., HOLMBERG, B. Paul and Power (Lund 1978) 24-26. ROLOFF, J. "Amt" in TRE 2 (1978) 513. LÜDEMANN, G. Paulus, der Heidenapostel, Band II (Göttingen 1983) 148f. MAVROFIDIS, S. "Gal 2, 6b: l'imperfetto e le sue conseguenze storiche," Biblica 64 (1983) 118-21. CRONJÉ, J. VAN W. "Defamiliarization in the letter to the Galatians" in J. H. Petzer and P. J. Hartin, eds., A South African Perspective on the New Testament (FS B. M. Metzger; Leiden 1986) 220f. ACHTEMEIER, P. J. The Quest for Unity in the New Testament Church (Philadelphia 1987) 89. PRATSCHER, W. Der Herrenbruder Jakobus und die Jakobustradition (Göttingen 1987) 62, 67, 67n.71, 72, 73, 73n.97, 74, 86, 91n.159. CLABEAUX, J. J. The Lost Edition of the Letters of Paul (CBQ.MS; Washington 1989) 120. MELL, U. Neue Schöpfung (Berlin/New York 1989) 287. DUNN, J. D. G. Jesus, Paul and the Law (London 1990) 109, 114, 116f., 119-21, 125n.44, 132, 155, 160, 177, 254f.

2:7ff.   SCHÜTZ, J.H. Paul and the Anatomy of Apostolic Authority (1975) 147-48. FARMER, W. R. "Peter and Paul. A Constitutive Relationship for Catholic Christianity" in W. E. March, ed., Texts and Testaments (FS S. D. Currie; San Antonio 1980) 219-36.

2:7-10   BARRETT, C.K. "Paul's Opponents in II Corinthians" NTS 17 (1970/71) 238f.

2:7-9   ALGER, B. "Cephas-Peter" Scripture 10 (1958) 57-58. MUNCK, J. Paul and the Salvation of Mankind (1959) 231f. SCHILLE, G. Die urchristliche Kollegialmission (1967) 59ff. HAINZ, J. Ekklesia (1972) 125f. OLLROG, W.-H. Paulus und seine Mitarbeiter (Neukirchen/Vluyn 1979) 17, 82, 208. KIM, S. The Origin of Paul's Gospel (Tübingen 1981) 292f. WENHAM, D. "Paul's Use of the Jesus Tradition. Three Samples" in D. Wenham, ed., Gospel Perspectives. The Jesus Tradition Outside the Gospels, Vol 5 (Sheffield 1984) 24f. WATSON, F. Paul, Judaism and the Gentiles (Cambridge 1986) 53ff. LIMBECK, M. Mit Paulus Christ sein. Sachbuch zur Person und Theologie des Apostels Paulus (Stuttgart 1989) 63, 82. McLEAN, B. H. "Galatians 2.7-9 and the Recognition of Paul's Apostolic Status at the Jerusalem Conference. A Critique of G. Luedemann's Solution," NTS 37 (1991) 67-76.

2:7-9a   HAHN, F. Das Verständnis der Mission im Neuen Testament (1965) 83.

2:7-8   MUNCK, J. Paul and the Salvation of Mankind (1959) 61-64. SCHMITHALS, W. Paulus und Jakobus (1963) 37.40. KASTING, H. Die Anfänge der Urchristlichen Mission (1969) 76-78. ECKERT, J. Die Urchristliche Verkündigung im Streit zwischen Paulus und seinen Gegnern nach dem Galaterbrief (1971) 206, 208, 210, 213. EICHHOLZ, G. Die Theologie des Paulus im Umriss (1972) 29f. O'NEILL, J.C. The Recovery of Paul's Letter to the Galatians (1972) 37. HOLMBERG, B. Paul and Power (Lund 1978) 31f. ROLOFF, J. "Apostel" in TRE 3 (1978) 436. LÜDEMANN, G. Paulus, der Heidenapostel, Band I (Göttingen 1980) 86-94. LÜDEMANN, G. Paul: Apostle to the Gentiles (London 1984) 64-71, 80, 120n.77, 120n.80, 197. EHRMAN, B. D. "Cephas and Peter," JBL 109 (1990) 463-74. SCHMIDT, A. "Das Missionsdekret in Galater 2.7-8 als Vereinbarung vom ersten Besuch Pauli in Jerusalem," NTS 38 (1992) 149-52.

2:7   MUNCK, J. Paul and the Salvation of Mankind (1959) 61f. ROLOFF, J. Apostolat—Verkündigung—Kirche (1965) 90-93. HAINZ, J. Ekklesia (1972) 115. MINDE,

H.-J. VAN DER, Schrift und Tradition bei Paulus (München/Paderborn/Wien 1976) 153f. ROLOFF, J. "Amt" in TRE 2 (1978) 518. ROLOFF, J. "Apostel" in TRE 3 (1978) 436, 438. SCHMITHALS, W. "Zur Herkunft der gnostischen Elemente in der Sprache des Paulus" in B. Aland et al., eds., Gnosis (FS H. Jonas; Göttingen 1978) 400. BAUMERT, N. Ehelosigkeit und Ehe im Herrn (Würzburg ²1986) 232ff., 559. RÄISÄNEN, H. The Torah and Christ (Helsinki 1986) 64.

2:8-9   FREUND, G. und STEGEMANN, E., eds., Theologische Brosamen für Lothar Steiger (DBAT 5; Heidelberg 1985) 389f. HULTGREN, A. J. Paul's Gospel and Mission (Philadelphia 1985) 125ff.

2:8   KÄSEMANN, E. Exegetische Versuche und Besinnungen (1964) I 293. HAHN, F. Das Verständnis der Mission im Neuen Testament (1965) 39, 43. OLLROG, W.-H. Paulus und seine Mitarbeiter (Neukirchen/Vluyn 1979) 117. RÄISÄNEN, H. The Torah and Christ (Helsinki 1986) 47.

2:9-14 HENZE, C.M. "Cephas seu Kephas non est Simon Petrus!" DiThom 61 (1958) 63-67. HERRERA, J. "Cephas seu Kephas est Simon Petrus" DiThom 61 (1958) 481-84.

2:9,11,14 FITZMYER, J. A. "Aramaic Kepha' and Peter's name in the New Testament" in: E. Best and R. McL. Wilson, eds., Text and Interpretation (FS M. Black; Cambridge 1979) 124-30.

2:9-10 OLLROG, W.-H. Paulus und seine Mitarbeiter (Neukirchen/Vluyn 1979) 17f., 36, 62, 176.

2:9   WAGENMANN, J. Die Stellung des Apostels Paulus neben den Zwölf (1962) 15, 18, 22, 25. EISLER, R. "The Meeting of Paul and the 'Pillars' in Galatians and in the Acts of the Apostles" Bulletin of the Bezan Club 12 (1937) 58-64. FEINE, P. & BEHM, J. Einleitung in das Neue Testament (1950) 241f. BARRETT, C.K. "Paul and the 'Pillar' Apostles" in Studia Paulina (1953) 1-19. ANNAND, R. "Notes on the Three Pillars: Galatians II, 9" ET 67 (1956) 178. SCHWEIZER, E. Gemeinde und Gemeinde—Ordnung im Neuen Testament (1959) § 24 b, i. PFAMMATTER, J. Die Kirche als Bau (1960) 9ff. SCHMITHALS, W. Paulus und Jakobus (1963) 35f. GÄRTNER, B. The Temple and the Community in Qumran and the New Testament (1965) 68. HAHN, F. Das Verständnis der Mission im Neuen Testament (1965) 83. BRAUN, H. Qumran und das Neue Testament II (1966) 154f., 327f. KÜNG, H. Die Kirche (1967) 135, 351, 412-13; The Church (1967) 11, 295, 347-48. NICKELS, P. Targum and New Testament (1967) 73. KASTING, H. Die Anfänge der urchristlichen Mission (1969) 56-58. MCKELVEY, R.J. The New Temple (1969) 135. RICHTER, H.-F. Auferstehung und Wirklichkeit (1969) 42, 44, 54, 93. GASTON, L. No Stone on Another (1970) 194-97. GRAYSTON, K. "The Signifance of the Word 'Hand' in the New Testament" in Mélanges Bibliques en hommage au R.P. Béda Rigaux, ed. A. Descamps and A. Halleux (1970) 483-388. ECKERT, J. Die urchristliche Verkündigung im Streit zwischen Paulus und seinen Gegnern nach dem Galaterbrief (1971) 195, 208, 221, 226. HAINZ, J. Ekklesia (1972) 114f. MERKLEIN, H. Das Kirchliche Amt nach dem Epheserbrief (1973) 242, 259, 261, 275. WILSON, S.G. The Gentiles and the Gentile Mission in Luke—Acts (1973) 110, 115, 185-87. ZELLER, D. Juden und Heiden in der Mission des Paulus (1973) 270f., 275. FRIEDRICH, G. "Das Amt im Neuen Testament" in Auf das Wort kommt es an. Gesammelte Aufsätze (Göttingen 1978) 423f. HOLMBERG, B. Paul and Power (Lund 1978) 29-31. ROLOFF, J. "Amt" in TRE 2 (1978) 513f. RÜGER, H. P. "Aramäisch" in TRE 3 (1978) 606. AUS, R. D. "Three Pillars and Three Patriarchs. A Proposal Concerning Gal 2:9," ZNW 70 (1979) 252-61. HENGEL, M. Zur urchristlichen Geschichtsschreibung (Stuttgart 1979) 82; ET: Acts and the History of Earliest Christianity [trans. J. Bowden] (London 1979) 96. LÜDEMANN,

G. Paulus, der Heidenapostel, Band I (Göttingen 1980) 94-101. McDONALD, J. I.
H. Kerygma and Didache (Cambridge 1980) 110. SÄNGER, D. Antikes Judentum
und die Mysterien (Tübingen 1980) 73. KRAFT, H. Die Entstehung des Christen-
tums (Darmstadt 1981) 124-34. LÜHRMANN, D. "Gal 2:9 und die katholischen
Briefe. Bemerkungen zum Kanon und zur regula fidei," ZNW 72 (1981) 65-87.
HAINZ, J. Koinonia (Regensburg 1982) 11f., 119, 123-34, 151f., 157-59, 164, 213.
LÜDEMANN, G. Paulus, der Heidenapostel, Band II (Göttingen 1983) 61f., 75f.,
113f., 148, 163. WILSON, S. G. Luke and the Law (Cambridge 1983) 64f.
LÜDEMANN, G. Paul: Apostle to the Gentiles (London 1984) 64, 69, 71-77, 80,
120nn.77.80, 124n.104, 193n.105, 197, 198. SUGGIT, J. "'The Right Hand of
Fellowship' (Galatians 2:9)," JTSA 49 (1984) 51-54. FISCHER, K. M. Das
Urchristentum (Berlin, DDR 1985) 40, 71, 95, 97. HENGEL, M. "Jakobus der
Herrenbruder— der erste 'Papst'?" in E. Grässer und O. Merk, eds., Glaube und
Eschatologie (FS W. G. Kümmel; Tübingen 1985) 71. MATTHEWS, R. J. H.
"'Pillars of the Church'," Prudentia [Auckland] 18 (1986) 55-59. REBELL, W.
Gehorsam und Unabhängigkeit (München 1986) 20, 32f., 36, 43, 48, 56, 63, 68.
ZMIJEWSKI, J. Paulus—Knecht und Apostel Christi (Stuttgart 1986) 51, 120, 128,
135, 208. BETZ, O. Jesus. Der Messias Israels (Tübingen 1987) 113, 116.
PRATSCHER, W. Der Herrenbruder Jakobus und die Jakobustradition (Göttingen
1987) 10, 35n.32, 52n.14, 60n.46, 62, 62n.51, 64, 66, 67, 67n.72, 69, 70n.81, 74, 91,
113, 180, 187n.20, 188, 189, 189n.24, 197n.40, 261. COSGROVE, C. H. The Cross
and the Spirit. A Study in the Argument and Theology of Galatians (Macon GA
1988) 121n., 122f., 128. SCHÄFER, K. Gemeinde als "Bruderschaft" (Frank-
furt/Bern/New York/Paris 1989) 212-16. DUNN, J. D. G. Jesus, Paul and the Law
(London 1990) 114, 117f., 120f., 126n.60, 157, 162, 171nn.107.111, 245, 254f.,
264n.56. SEGAL, A. F. Paul the Convert (New Haven/London 1990) 188f.
KLAUCK, H.-J. Die Johannesbriefe (Darmstadt 1991) 25.

2:10-21 CERFAUX, L. The Christian in the Theology of St. Paul (1967) 378-81.
2:10 WALKER, D. "Galatians 2:10" ET 11 (189901900) 190. FRIDRICHSEN, A.
"Quatre conjectures sur le texte du Nouveau Testament" RHPR 3 (1923) 439-42.
MUNCK, J. Paul and the Salvation of Mankind (1959) 99f. RUDOLPH, K. Die
Mandäer (1960) I 117. SCHMITHALS, W. Paulus und Jakobus (1963) 64-70.
HAHN, F. Das Verständnis der Mission im Neuen Testament (1965) 93. NICKLE,
K.F. The Collection (1966) 59-61, 90-93, 103f. KASTING, H. Die Anfänge der Ur-
christlichen Mission (1969) 77, 119. HALL, D.R. "St Paul and Famine Relief: A
Study in Galatians 2:10" ET 82 (1971) 309-11. BORSE, U. Der Standort des
Galaterbriefes (1972) 33-36, 144, 148, 176. ENSLIN, M.S. Reapproaching Paul
(1972) 93f. HAINZ, J. Ekklesia (1972) 115. ZELLER, D. Juden und Heiden in der
Mission des Paulus (1973) 229, 232f. DAVIES, W.D. The Gospel and the Land
(1974) 199-200, 214-16. BERGER, K. "Almosen für Israel. Zum historischen Kon-
text der paulinischen Kollekte," NTS 23 (1977) 180-204. HOLMBERG, B. Paul and
Power (Lund 1978) 35-43. JEWETT, R. A Chronology of Paul's Life (Philadelphia
1979) 34. KECK, L. E. "Armut" in TRE 4 (1979) 79. LÜDEMANN, G. Paulus, der
Heidenapostel, Band I (Göttingen 1980) 105-10. HAINZ, J. Koinonia (Regensburg
1982) 11, 123-35, 140, 145-48, 151f., 157-59. MEEKS, W. A. The First Urban
Christians (New Haven/London 1983) 110, 112, 234n.75. LÜDEMANN, G. Paul:
Apostle to the Gentiles (London 1984) 22, 77-80, 83-87, 130n.153, 198f. SCHI-
MANOWSKI, G. Weisheit und Messias (Tübingen 1985) 326. MAVROFIDIS, S.
"Gal 2, 10: *Apopseis tōn meletētōn kata ta etē* 1893-1979" [Gal. 2:10—Scholarly
Views during the Years 1893-1979], DBM 15 (1986) 20-34. PRATSCHER, W. Der
Herrenbruder Jakobus und die Jakobustradition (Göttingen 1987) 64n.59, 65, 73.

WEDDERBURN, A. J. M. The Reasons for Romans (Edinburgh 1988) 30, 37-39. SCHNELLE, U. Wandlungen im paulinischen Denken (Stuttgart 1989) 30. DUNN, J. D. G. Jesus, Paul and the Law (London 1990) 116-18, 121, 124n.35, 126n.62, 155, 171n.109, 251f., 254f. FERNÁNDEZ, V. M. "Santiago, la plenificación cristiana de la espiritualidad postexílica," RivB 53 (1991) 29-33.

2:11-3:4 BARRETT, C.K. "The Allegory of Abraham, Sarah, and Hagar in the Argument of Galatians" in Rechtfertigung, edited by J. Friedrich, W. Pöhlmann, P. Stuhlmacher (1976) 3.

2:11ff. OVERBECK, F. Über die Auffassung des Streits des Paulus mit Petrus in Antiochien (Gal 2, 11ff.) bei den Kirchenvätern (1968=1877). HARNACK, A. Studien zur Geschichte des Neuen Testaments und der Alten Kirche (1931) 20ff. DUPONT, J. "Pierre et Paul à Antioche et à Jérusalem" RechSr 45 (1957) 42-60;225-39. LIGHT-FOOT, J.B. "Patristic Accounts of the Collision at Antioch" in The Epistle of St. Paul to the Galatians (1957) 128-32. MUNCK, J. Paul and the Salvation of Mankind (1959) 100-2, 123f. SCHRAGE, W. Die konkreten Einzelgebote in der paulinischen Paränese (1961) 232. HAHN, F. Das Verständnis der Mission im Neuen Testament (1965) 71f. LOENNING, I. "Paulus und Petrus. Gal 2, 11ff. als kontrovers—theologisches Fundamentalproblem" StTh 24 (1970) 1-60. HAENDLER, G. "Cyprians Auslegung von Galater 2:11ff." ThLZ 97 (1972) 561-68. SCHMITHALS, W. "Zur Herkunft der gnostischen Elemente in der Sprache des Paulus" in B. Aland et al., eds., Gnosis (FS H. Jonas; Göttingen 1978) 400f. OLLROG, W.-H. Paulus und seine Mitarbeiter (Neukirchen/Vluyn 1979) 11, 16, 34, 36, 45, 47, 119, 151, 206-15, 232. FARMER, W. R. "Peter and Paul. A Constitutive Relationship for Catholic Christianity" in W. E. March, ed., Texts and Testaments (FS S. D. Currie; San Antonio 1980) 219-36. LÜDEMANN, G. Paulus, der Heidenapostel, Band I (Göttingen 1980) 101-05. LÜHRMANN, D. "Abendmahlsgemeinschaft? Gal 2, 11ff" in D. Lührmann und G. Strecker, eds., Kirche (FS G. Bornkamm; Tübingen 1980) 271-86. KLAIBER, W. Rechtfertigung und Gemeinde (Göttingen 1982) 145-49. LÜDEMANN, G. Paulus, der Heidenapostel, Band II (Göttingen 1983) 62, 76, 93, 142, 147n.130, 149n.1, 252. HÜBNER, H. "Galaterbrief" in TRE 12 (1984) 10, 12. MOHRLANG, R. Matthew and Paul (Cambridge 1984) 30f., 152. BARRETT, C. K. Freedom and Obligation (Philadelphia 1985) 18ff. DUNN, J. D. G. The Living Word (London 1987) 57f. HENGEL, M. "Der Jakobusbrief als antipaulinische Polemik" in G. F. Hawthorne and O. Betz, eds., Tradition and Interpretation in the New Testament (FS E. E. Ellis; Grand Rapids/Tübingen 1987) 253. PRATSCHER, W. Der Herrenbruder Jakobus und die Jakobustradition (Göttingen 1987) 49, 54n.23, 62n.52, 69, 72, 77-89, 90n.157, 113f., 141f., 187n.20, 207, 212. BECKER, J. Paulus. Der Apostel der Völker (Tübingen 1989) 90, 99, 106, 174ff., 267. MARXSEN, W. "Christliche" und christliche Ethik im Neuen Testament (Gütersloh 1989) 139, 143, 193. SCHÄFER, K. Gemeinde als "Bruderschaft" (Frankfurt/ Bern/New York/Paris 1989) 196ff.

2:11-4:7 GRAESSER, E. Der Alte Bund im Neuen (Tübingen 1985) 56f.

2:11-3:4 BARRETT, C. K. "The Allegory of Abraham, Sarah, and Hagar in the Argument of Galatians" in Essays on Paul (London 1982) 154-70.

2:11-21 FEINE, P. Das Gesetzesfreie Evangelium des Paulus (1899) 19-27. JACOBUS, M.W. "Paul and his Teaching in Galatians 2:11-21" BibW 24 (1904) 351-58. BOVER, J.M. "Pauli oratio ad Petrum (Gal. 2, 11-21)" VD 4 (1924) 48-55. MAAS, A.J. "St. Paul's Address to Peter (Gal. 2, 11-21)" Ecclesistical Review 71 (1924) 37-47. SHEPARD, J.W. The Life and Letters of St. Paul (1950) 124-28. OEPKE, A. "Die Beurteilung des antiochenischen Konflikts und seiner Folgen" in Der Brief des Paulus an die Galater (1957) 64-66. SWUILLACI, D. "La correzione di S.Paolo a

S.Pietro (Gal. 2, 11-21)" PaCl 40 (1961) 1025-30. LACKMANN, M. "Beiträge zum Amt des Petrus im Neuen Testament" Bausteine 3 (10, 1963) 1-7; (11, 1963) 1-6. SCHMITHALS, W. Paulus und Jakobus (1963) 51-64. ROLOFF, J. Apostolat—Verkündigung—Kirche (1965) 73-75. BARTH, M. "Justification. From Text to Sermon on Galatians 2:11-21" Interp 22 (1968) 147-57. GIBLIN, C.H. In Hope of God's Glory (1970) 62-66. MACGORMAN, J.W. "Problem Passages in Galatians" SouJTh 15 (1, 1972) 35-51. LOHSE, E. Die Einheit des Neuen Testaments (1973) 341f. HAMEL, J. GPM 30 (1, 1975) 113-19. SCHÜTZ, J.H. Paul and the Anatomy of Apostolic Authority (1975) 150-58. BROWN, R. E. et al., eds., Peter in the New Testament (Minneapolis 1973) 29-32, 51. SAMPLEY, J. P. "Societas Christi. Roman Law and Paul's Conception of the Christian Community" in J. Jervell and W. A. Meeks, eds., God's Christ and His People (FS N. A. Dahl; New York 1977) 162f. COLLANGE, J.-F. "De Jésus de Nazareth à Paul de Tarse," LuVie 27 (139, 1978) 87-95. GARNET, P. "Qumran Light on Pauline Soteriology" in D. A. Hagner and M. J. Harris, eds., Pauline Studies (FS F. F. Bruce; Exeter 1980) 27-31. KLAIBER, W. Rechtfertigung und Gemeinde (Göttingen 1982) 254f. NEITZEL, H. "Zur Interpretation von Galater 2, 11-21. Teil 1," ThQ 163 (1983) 15-39. NEITZEL, H. "Zur Interpretation von Galater 2, 11-21. Teil 2," ThQ 163 (1983) 131-49. FISCHER, K. M. Das Urchristentum (Berlin, DDR 1985) 41, 97, 114. SMIT, J. F. M. "'Hoe kun je de Heidenen verplichten als Joden te leven?' Paulus en de Torah in Galaten 2, 11-21," Bijdr. 46 (1985) 118-40. MUSSNER, F. Die Kraft der Wurzel (Freiburg/Basel/Wien 1987) 182. GARCÍA MARTÍNEZ, F. "Les limites de la communauté: pureté et impureté à Qumrân et dans l e Nouveau Testament" in T. Baarda et al., eds., Text and Testimony (FS A. F. J. Klijn; Kampen 1988) 121. LAMPE, P. "Der antiochenische Konflikt" in C. Link et al., eds., Sie aber hielten fest an der Gemeinschaft . . . (Zürich 1988) 85-87. LIMBECK, M. Mit Paulus Christ sein. Sachbuch zur Person und Theologie des Apostels Paulus (Stuttgart 1989) 90f. BÖTTGER, P. C. "Paulus und Petrus in Antiochien. Zum Verständnis von Galater 2.11-21," NTS 37 (1991) 77-100. HONG, I.-G. The Law in Galatians (Sheffield 1993) 35-38, 68-70.

2:11-20 SCHWEITZER, A. Die Mystik des Apostels Paulus (1954) 193-94.

2:11-18 WINGREN, G. "Abendmahl" in TRE 1 (1977) 214. DUNN, J. D. G. "The Incident at Antioch (Gal. 2:11-18)," JSNT 18 (1983) 3-57. COHN-SHERBOK, D. Rabbinic Perspectives on the New Testament (Lewiston/Queenston/Lampeter 1990) 87-95. DUNN, J. D. G. Jesus, Paul and the Law (London 1990) 2, 12, 16, 19f., 29n.4, 39, 99, 101, 122, 129-82, 227. SANDERS, E. P. Jewish Law from Jesus to the Mishnah (London/Philadelphia 1990) 360n.1. SEGAL, A. F. "Studying Judaism with Christian Sources," USQR 44 (1991) 267-86.

2:11-16 BLINZLER, J. Aus der Welt und Umwelt des Neuen Testaments. Gesammelte Aufsätze 1 (1969) 147-57. PAGELS, E.H. The Gnostic Paul (1975) 105. HEMER, C. J. The Book of Acts in the Setting of Hellenistic History [C. H. Gempf, ed.] (Tübingen 1989) 288. JEGHER-BUCHER, V. "Formgeschichtliche Betrachtung zu Galater 2, 11-16. Antwort an James D. Hester," ThZ 46 (1990) 305-21.

2:11-14 AUVRAY, P. "S.Jérôme et S.Augustin. La controverse au sujet de l'incident d'Antioche" RechSR 29 (1939) 594-610. GÄCHTER, P. "Petrus in Antiochia" ZKTh 72 (1950) 177-212. AUGUSTINE, JEROME, "Paul et Pierre, Jérôme et Augustin" BVieC 39 (1961) 13-22. RUIZ, J.M.G. "Pedro en Antioquia, Jefe de toda la Iglesia, sequn Gal. 2, 11-14" EstBi 21 (1962) 75-81; Studiorum Paulinorum Congressus Internationalis Catholicus 1961 (1963) II: 11-16. DUPONT, J. "Pierre et Paul à Antioche et à Jérusalem" in Etudes sur les Actes des Apôtres (1967) 185-215. KASTING, H. Die Anfänge der urchristlichen Mission (1969) 99, 121f. PASCHEN,

W. Rein und Unrein (1970) 170f. ECKERT, J. Die urchristliche Verkündigung im Streit zwischen Paulus und seinen Gegnern nach dem Galaterbrief (1971) 193-200, 203f., 220-22. SCHNEIDER, G. "Contestation in the New Testament" Concilium 68 (1971) 80-87. HAINZ, J. Ekklesia (1972) 119f. HOLMBERG, B. Paul and Power (Lund 1978) 32-34. NORRIS, F. W. "Antiochien" in TRE 3 (1978) 101. BRUCE, F. F. Men and Movements in the Primitive Church (Exeter 1979) 34-39. BYRNE, B. "Sons of God"-"Seed of Abraham" (Rome 1979) 142f. HOWARD, G. Paul. Crisis in Galatia (Cambridge 1979) 21-28, 34-35. RICHARDSON, P. Paul's Ethic of Freedom (Philadelphia 1979) 91-97. RICHARDSON, P. "Pauline Inconsistency: I Corinthians 9:19-23 and Galatians 2:11-14," NTS 26 (1980) 347-62. KLAUCK, H.-J. Hausgemeinde und Hauskirche im frühen Christentum (Stuttgart 1981) 40. BARTSCH, H.-W. "Freiheit" in TRE 11 (1983) 508. MEEKS, W. A. The First Urban Christians (New Haven/London 1983) 11, 81, 103, 133, 199n.8. RÄISÄNEN, H. Paul and the Law (Tübingen 1983) 10, 73, 75f., 216, 248, 258, 263. LÜDE-MANN, G. Paul: Apostle to the Gentiles (London 1984) 20, 33n., 18, 57-59, 75-77, 122n.97, 124n.102, 153, 291. BETZ, H. D. "Häresie I" in TRE 14 (1985) 315. SANDERS, E. P. Paul, the Law, and the Jewish People (London 1985) 20, 100, 101f., 165n.35, 177, 185, 203n.57. BETZ, H. D. "Hellenismus III" in TRE 15 (1986) 27. DAUTZENBERG, G. "Gesetzeskritik und Gesetzesgehorsam in der Jesustradi-tion" in K. Kertelge, ed., Das Gesetz im Neuen Testament (Freiburg/Basel/Wien 1986) 48. HOLTZ, T. "Der antiochenische Zwischenfall (Galater 2.11-14)," NTS 32 (1986) 344-61. RÄISÄNEN, H. The Torah and Christ (Helsinki 1986) 44, 48, 52. REBELL, W. Gehorsam und Unabhängigkeit (München 1986) 11, 19, 31, 39, 41, 49, 72. SCHNACKENBURG, R. Die sittliche Botschaft des Neuen Testaments, Band 1 (Freiburg/Basel/Wien 1986) 171, 191f. ACHTEMEIER, P. J. The Quest for Unity in the New Testament Church (Philadelphia 1987) 53, 56ff. KAHL, B. Armenevan-gelium und Heidenevangelium. "Sola scriptura" und die ökumenische Traditionsprob-lematik im Lichte von Väterkonflikt und Väterkonsens bei Lukas (Berlin 1987) 175. MARXSEN, W. "Sündige tapfer. Wer hat sich beim Streit in Antiochien richtig verhalten?" EvKomm 20 (1987) 81-84. SUHL, A. "Der Galaterbrief— Situation und Argumentation" in ANRW II.25.4 (1987) 3083ff., 3097f. DOWNING, F. G. Christ and the Cynics (Sheffield 1988) 190. LINDARS, B. "All Foods Clean. Thoughts on Jesus and the Law" in B. Lindars, ed., Law and Religion (Cambridge 1988) 61ff. MacDONALD, M. Y. The Pauline Churches (Cambridge 1988) 33f. CAMERON, P. S. "An Exercise in Translation: Galatians 2.11-14," BTr 40 (1989) 135-45. KLAUCK, H.-J. Gemeinde, Amt, Sakrament (Würzburg 1989) 341f. MÉHAT, A. "'Quand Kèphas vint à Antioche . . . ' Que s'est-il passé entre Pierre et Paul? LuVie 192 (1989) 29-43. OSTEN-SACKEN, P. VON DER, Die Heiligkeit der Tora (München 1989) 135-38. DUNN, J. D. G. Jesus, Paul and the Law (London 1990) 46, 47, 49, 71, 92, 179, 245, 251, 255. HOLMBERG, B. "Sociologiska perspektiv på Gal 2:11-14(21)," SEA 55 (1990) 71-92. KOLLMANN, B. Ursprung und Gestalten der frühchristlichen Mahlfeier (Göttingen 1990) 194, 235. REBELL, W. Zum neuen Leben berufen (München 1990) 59-61. SANDERS, E. P. "Jewish Associations with Gentiles and Galatians 2:11-14" in R. T. Fortna and B. R. Gaventa, eds., The Conversation Continues. Studies in Paul and John (FS J. L. Martyn; Nashville 1990) 170-88. SANDERS, E. P. Jewish Law from Jesus to the Mishnah (London/Philadelphia 1990) 258, 283, 360n.8. SMITH, D. E. and TAUSSIG, H. E. Many Tables. The Eucharist in the New Testament and Liturgy Today (London/Philadelphia 1990) 58-63, 69. TOMSON, P. J. Paul and the Jewish Law (Assen/Maastricht; Minneapolis 1990) 222-30.

2:11-13   BAUERNFEIND, O. "Der Schluss der Antiochenischen Paulusrede" in Kommentar und Studien zur Apostelgeschichte (Tübingen 1980) 450f., 457, 460f. [orig. in Theologie als Glaubenwagnis (FS K. Heim; Hamburg 1954) 64-78]. ACHTEMEIER, P. J. The Quest for Unity in the New Testament Church (Philadelphia 1987) 24, 41, 63f., 90. COSGROVE, C. H. The Cross and the Spirit. A Study in the Argument and Theology of Galatians (Macon GA 1988) 130f. BECKER, J. "Das Ethos Jesu und die Geltung des Gesetzes" in H. Merklein, ed., Neues Testament und Ethik (FS R. Schnackenburg; Freiburg/Basel/Wien 1989) 31-52, esp. 42.48.

2:11-12   GERDES, H. "Luther und Augustin über den Streit zwischen Petrus und Paulus zu Antiochien (Gal 2, 11f)" Luther—Jahrbuch 29 (1962) 9-24. DIETZFELBINGER, C. Die Berufung des Paulus als Ursprung seiner Theologie (Neukirchen 1985) 41, 46. SEGAL, A. F. Paul the Convert (New Haven/London 1990 230.

2:11a,12 HAHN, F. Das Verständnis der Mission im Neuen Testament (1965) 42.

2:11   PESCH, C. "Über die Person des Kephas, Gal. II, 11" ZKTh 7 (1883) 456-90. BLASS, F. Philosophy of the Gospels (1898) 26ff. DONOVAN, J. "Iota or Epsilon: A Suggested Reading in Galatians 2:11" IThQ 17 (1922) 324-34. GRUEN, W. "A proposito de *kata prosôpon* em Gal 2, 11" RCB 1 (1957) 141-59. HENNECKE, E./ SCHNEEMELCHER, W. Neutestamentliche Apokryphen (1964) II 34.

2:11b   BALJON, J.M.S. "Gal. 2:11b" Theologische Studien 5 (1887) 251-55.

2:12ff.   BOUSSET, W. Die Religion des Judentums im Späthellenistischen Zeitalter (1966=1926) 93. RICHTER, H.-F. Auferstehung und Wirklichkeit (1969) 39f., 44, 51.

2:12-21   BETZ, O. "Firmness in Faith: Hebrews 11:1 and Isaiah 28:16" in B. P. Thompson, ed., Scripture. Meaning and Method (FS A. T. Hanson; Hull 1987) 109f.

2:12-13   MINEAR, P.S. Images of the Church in the New Testament (1960) 73f. BARRETT, C. K. "Ψευδαπόστολοι (Cor 11, 13)" in Mélanges Bibliques en hommage au R.P. Béda Rigaux, ed. A. Descamps and A. Halleux (1970) 387-88.

2:12   MUNCK, J. Paul and the Salvation of Mankind (1959) 106f. SCHRAGE, W. Die kondreten Einzelgobote in der paulinischen Paränese (1961) 158. SCHMITHALS, W. Paulus und Jakobus (1963) 53-55. VAN DÜLMEN, A. Die Theologie des Gesetzes bei Paulus (1968) 13-14, 217-18. ECKERT, J. Die urchristliche Verkündigung im Streit zwischen Paulus und seinen Gegnern nach dem Galaterbrief (1971) 216-18. HAINZ, J. Ekklesia (1972) 123f. O'NEILL, J.C. The Recovery of Paul's Letter to the Galatians (1972) 37. ELLIS, E. E. Prophecy and Hermeneutic in Early Christianity (Tübingen 1978) 94, 102, 107, 110f., 116f., 124, 227, 230. ROLOFF, J. "Amt" in TRE 2 (1978) 513. BOOTH, R. P. Jesus and the Laws of Purity. Tradition History and Legal History in Mark 7 (Sheffield 1986) 81-83. BERGER, K. und COLPE, C., eds., Religionsgeschichtliches Textbuch zum Neuen Testament (Göttingen/Zürich 1987) 268f. PRATSCHER, W. Der Herrenbruder Jakobus und die Jakobustradition (Göttingen 1987) 10, 33n.26, 52n.14, 71, 75, 81n.131, 91. SCHMELLER, Th. Paulus und die "Diatribe" (Münster 1987) 325n.116. DUNN, J. D. G. Jesus, Paul and the Law (London 1990) 46, 130, 153f., 157, 164n.6, 169n.94, 178, 251, 262n.41, 264n.56. SANDERS, E. P. Jewish Law from Jesus to the Mishnah (London/Philadelphia 1990) 27.

2:13-14   FEINE, P. Der Apostel Paulus (1927) 417f. STUHLMACHER, P. Gerechtigkeit Gottes bei Paulus (1965) 207f.

2:13   SCHMITHALS, W. Paulus und Jakobus (1963) 59. OLLROG, W.-H. Paulus und seine Mitarbeiter (Neukirchen/Vluyn 1979) 16, 18, 204. HEILIGENTHAL, R. Werke als Zeichen (Tübingen 1983) 129-33. BERGER, K. und COLPE, C., eds., Religionsgeschichtliches Textbuch zum Neuen Testament (Göttingen/Zürich 1987) 269.

LAMPE, P. Die stadtrömischen Christen in den ersten beiden Jahrhunderten (Tübingen ²1989) 5.

2:14ff. BAUERNFEIND, D.O. "Der Schluss der Antiochenischen Paulusrede" in Theologie als Glaubenswagnis (1954) 64-78.

2:14-21 SCHMIDT, R. "Über Gal. 2, 14-51" ThSK 50 (1877) 638-705. WETZEL, L. "Versuch einer Erklärung der Stelle Gal. 2, 14-21" ThSK 53 (1880) 432-64. ZIMMER, F. "Paulus gegen Petrus; Gal. 2, 14-21 erläutert" Zeitschrift für wissenschaftliche Theologie 25 (1882) 129-88. KLOEPPER, A. "Zur Erläuterung von Gal. II, 14-21" Zeitschrift für wissenschaftliche Theologie 37 (1894) 373-95. LAMBRECHT, J. "The Line of Thought in Gal. 2.14b-21," NTS 24 (1978) 484-95. BAUERNFEIND, O. "Der Schluss der Antiochenischen Paulusrede" in Kommentar und Studien zur Apostelgeschichte (Tübingen 1980) 449-63 [orig. in Theologie als Glaubenswagnis (FS K. Heim; Hamburg 1954) 64-78]. BISER, E. Der Zeuge (Graz/Wien/Köln 1981) 215f., 289. BUSCEMI, A. M. "La struttura letteraria di Gal 2, 14b-21," SBFLA 31 (1981) 59-74. KIEFFER, R. Foi et justification à Antioche. Interprétation d'un conflit (Ga 2, 14-21) (Paris 1982) passim. PANIER, L. "Pour une approche sémiotique de l'épître aux Galates," FV 84 (5, 1985) 19-32. MALINA B. J. Christian Origins and Cultural Anthropology (Atlanta 1986) 131. BARTOLOMÉ, J. J. El evangelio y su verdad. La justificación por la fe y su vivencia en común. Un estudio exegético de Gal 2, 5.14 (Rome 1988) passim. GEORGI, D. Theocracy in Paul's Praxis and Theology (Minneapolis 1991) 35-38.

2:14-18 BOUWMAN, G. "'Christus Diener der Sünde.' Auslegung von Galater 2, 14b-18," Bijdr 40 (1979) 44-54. COSGROVE, C. H. The Cross and the Spirit. A Study in the Argument and Theology of Galatians (Macon GA 1988) 131f., 135, 138f., 145.

2:14-16 DUNN, J. D. G. "The Theology of Galatians. The Issue of Covenantal Nomism" in J. M. Bassler, ed., Pauline Theology, Vol. 1 (Minneapolis 1991) 139ff.

2:14 "Hieronymus und Augustinus im Streit über Gal. 2, 14" ThQ 6 (1824) 195-219. ROBERTS, C.H. "A Note on Galatians 2:14" JTS 40 (1939) 55-56. WINTER, J.G. "Another Instance of ὀρθοποδεῖν" HThR 34 (1941) 161-62. KILPATRICK, G.D. "Gal 2, 14 ὀρθοποδοῦσιν" in Neutestamentliche Studien für Rudolf Bultmann (1954) 269-74. MUNCK, J. Paul and the Salvation of Mankind (1959) 124f. SCHMITHALS, W. Paulus und Jakobus (1963) 56f. VAN DÜLMEN, A. Die Theologie des Gesetzes bei Paulus (1968) 19-21. ECKERT, J. Die urchristliche Verkündigung im Streit zwischen Paulus und seinen Gegnern nach dem Galaterbrief (1971) 25, 32, 41, 48, 227. O'NEILL, J.C. The Recovery of Paul's Letter to the Galatians (1972) 39-42. KLIJN, A.F.J. & REININK, G.J. Patristic Evidence for Jewish—Christian Sects (1973) 51. KÜMMEL, W.G. "'Individual—geschichte' und 'Weltgeschichte' in Gal. 2:15-21" in Christ and the Spirit in the New Testament, ed. by B. Lindars and S.S. Smalley (1973) 161f. BURCHARD, C. Untersuchungen zu Joseph and Aseneth (Tübingen 1965) 131. WINGREN, G. "Abendmahl" in TRE 1 (1977) 215. KRUIJF, T. C. DE, "Antisemitismus" in TRE 3 (1978) 123. RÜGER, H. P. "Aramäisch" in TRE 3 (1978) 606. CLARK, K. W. "The Israel of God" in The Gentile Bias and Other Essays [Selected by J. L. Sharpe III] (Leiden 1980) 24. KÄSEMANN, E. "Liebe, die sich der Wahrheit freut" in Kirchliche Konflikte, Band 1 (Göttingen 1982) 161f. MUELLER, P.-G. Der Traditionsprozess im Neuen Testament (Freiburg 1982) 222f. HAYS, R. B. The Faith of Jesus Christ (Chico CA 1983) 197. RÄISÄNEN, H. The Torah and Christ (Helsinki 1986) 65. DUNN, J. D. G. Jesus, Paul and the Law (London 1990) 120, 153, 158, 169n.85, 170n.102, 172n.117, 179, 180, 189, 202, 245, 252f. HOWARD, G. Paul. Crisis in Galatia (Cambridge ²1990) 15, 42, 67.

2:15–4:31 KLEIN, G. "Individualgeschichte und Weltgeschichte bei Paulus" EvTh 24 (1964) 126-65.

2:15-4:7 SCHMITT, R. Gottesgerechtigkeit—Heilsgeschichte—Israel in der Theologie des Paulus (Frankfurt/Bern/ New York/Nancy 1984) 38ff.

2:15-3:5 VOS, J. Traditionsgeschichtliche Untersuchungen zur paulinischen Pneumatologie (1973) 85-88.

2:15ff. FEINE, P. Der Apostel Paulus (1927) 256f. BANDSTRA, A.J. The Law and the Elements of the World (1964) 141ff. KLAIBER, W. Rechtfertigung und Gemeinde (Göttingen 1982) 150f. SUHL, A. "Die Galater und der Geist. Kritische Erwägungen zur Situation in Galatien" in D.-A. Koch et al., eds., Jesu Rede von Gott und ihre Nachgeschichte im frühen Christentum (FS Willi Marxsen; Gütersloh 1989) 281ff. BACHMANN, M. Sünder oder Übertreter. Studien zur Argumentation in Gal 2, 15ff. (Tübingen 1992) passim.

2:15-21 LIPSIUS, D. "Über Gal 2, 17f." Zeitschrift für wissenschaftliche Theolofie 4 (1861) 72-82. STALDER, K. Das Werk des Geistes in der Heiligung bei Paulus (1962) 311-17. LARSSEN, J.A. Law, Justification and Christ—Mysticism in Gal. 2:15-21 (B.D. Treatise, RÜschlikon 1968). HASLER, V. "Glaube und Existenz. Hermeneutische Erwägungen zu Gal 2, 15-21" ThZ 25 (1969) 241-51. KLEIN, G. "Individualgeschichte und Weltgeschichte bei Paulus" in Rekonstruktion und Interpretation (1969) 180-224. ECKERT, J. Die urchristliche Verkündigung im Streit zwischen Paulus und seinen Gegnern nach dem Galaterbrief (1971) 39, 72, 107, 202. STOGIANNOS, B.P. "He peri Nomou didaskalia tes pros Galatas epistoles tou Apostolou Paulou (The Teaching Concerning the Law in the Apostle Paul's Epistle to the Galatians)" DBM 1 (1972) 312-28. ZIESLER, J.A. The Meaning of Righteousness in Paul (1972) 172-74. FELD, H. "'Christus Diener der SÜnde.' Zum Ausgang des Streites zwischen Petrus und Paulus" ThQ 153 (1973) 119-31. KÜMMEL, W.G. "'Individual-geschichte' and 'Weltgeschichte in Gal. 2:15-21" in Christ and the Spirit in the New Testament, ed. B. Lindars and S.S. Smalley (1973) 157-73. BYRNE, B. "Sons of God"-"Seed of Abraham" (Rome 1979) 143-47. OLLROG, W.-H. Paulus und seine Mitarbeiter (Neukirchen/Vluyn 1979) 207-15. DEIDUN, T. J. New Covenant Morality in Paul (Rome 1981) 122-26. BRINSMEAD, B. H. Galatians—Dialogical Response to Opponents (Chico CA 1982) 51f., 69-78, 190, 201. KLAIBER, W. Rechtfertigung und Gemeinde (Göttingen 1982) 148f. HAYS, R. B. The Faith of Jesus Christ (Chico CA 1983) 141, 196, 222, 268. RÄISÄNEN, H. Paul and the Law (Tübingen 1983) 47f., 70, 179, 254, 259. GASTON, L. "Paul and the Law in Galatians 2-3" in P. Richardson, ed., Anti-Judaism in Early Christianity, Vol. 1: Paul and the Gospels (Waterloo Ont 1986) 38-57. KITZBERGER, I. Bau der Gemeinde (Würzburg 1986) 139-44. RÄISÄNEN, H. The Torah and Christ (Helsinki 1986) 10, 48, 67. GASTON, L. Paul and the Torah (Vancouver 1987) 14, 65-72, 73. RAMAROSON, L. "La justification par la foi du Christ Jésus," SciE 39 (1987) 81-92. SUHL, A. "Der Galaterbrief—Situation und Argumentation" in ANRW II.25.4 (1987) 3098-119. JONGE, M. DE, Christology in Context. The Earliest Christian Response to Jesus (Philadelphia 1988) 33, 41. HANSEN, G. W. Abraham in Galatians (Sheffield 1989) 100-08. OSTEN-SACKEN, P. VON DER, Die Heiligkeit der Tora (München 1989) 138-40. WINGER, M. By What Law? The Meaning of Nomos in the Letters of Paul (Atlanta GA 1992) passim.

2:15-18 SCHMITHALS, W. Paulus und Jakobus (1963) 60-64. BULTMANN, R. "Zur Auslegung von Galater 2, 15-18" in Exegetica, hrsg. E. Dinkler (1967) 394-400.

2:15-17 WILCKENS, U. "Was heisst bei Paulus: 'Aus Werken des Gesetzes wird kein Mensch gerecht'?" in Evangelisch—Katholischer Kommentar zum Neuen Testament (Vorarbeiten Heft I:1969) 57-65. BYRNE, B. "Sons of God"-"Seed of Abraham"

(Rome 1979) 143-46, 149, 156, 164, 189, 220, 231. SCHMITT, R. Gottesgerechtig-keit— Heilsgeschichte—Israel in der Theologie des Paulus (Frankfurt/Bern/ New York/Nancy 1984) 40-44. MERKLEIN, H. Studien zu Jesus und Paulus (Tübingen 1987) 44f. SUHL, A. "Der Galaterbrief—Situation und Argumentation" in ANRW II.25.4 (1987) 3098-111. JOHNSON, E. E. The Function of Apocalyptic and Wisdom Traditions in Romans 9-11 (Atlanta GA 1989) 189.

2:15-16   FEINE, P. Der Apostel Paulus (1927) 216f. TYSON, J.B. "'Works of Law' in Gal" JBL 92 (1973) 432-431. SCHMITHALS, W. "Zur Herkunft der gnostischen Elemente in der Sprache des Paulus" in B. Aland et al., eds., Gnosis (FS H. Jonas; Göttingen 1978) 391-93. PATTE, D. Paul's Faith and the Power of the Gospel (Philadelphia 1983) 77-81, 84. HÜBNER, H. "Was heisst bei Paulus 'Werke des Gesetzes'?" in E. Grässer und O. Merk, eds., Glaube und Eschatologie (FS W. G. Kümmel; Tübingen 1985) 126-33. SANDERS, E. P. Paul, the Law, and the Jewish People (London 1985) 29f., 46, 68, 77, 80, 148, 172. THIELMAN, F. From Plight to Solution (Leiden 1989) 45, 60-65, 86, 129f. DUNN, J. D. G. Jesus, Paul and the Law (London 1990) 7, 172n.119, 189, 208f.

2:15   SÄNGER, D. Antikes Judentum und die Mysterien (Tübingen 1980) 17. BERGER, K. "Das Buch der Jubiläen" in JSHRZ II/3 (1981) 444n.23b. MELL, U. Neue Schöpfung (Berlin/New York 1989) 274. SCHNELLE, U. Wandlungen im paulin-ischen Denken (Stuttgart 1989) 55. DUNN, J. D. G. Jesus, Paul and the Law (London 1990) 16, 19, 74, 136, 150f., 156, 169n.85, 172n.117, 205n.33, 214n.13, 248, 249, 253, 254.

2:16–3:29 LONGWORTH, A. "'Faith' in Galatians. A Study of Galatians 2, 16-3, 29" in Studia Evangelica II, ed. F.L. Cross (1964) 605-10.

2:16-21   BRAUN, H. GPM 8 (1953/54) 64-67. IWAND, H.-.J. "Predigt über Galater 2, 16-21" EvTh 14 (1954) 289-97. HAAR, J. GPM 24 (1968/69) 94-100. DUNN, J.D.G. Baptism in the Holy Spirit (1970) 106f. SPIJKERBOER, A. in GPM 36 (1981/82) 361-65. ADOLPHSEN, H. und KNUTH, H. C. in P. Krusche et al., eds., Predigtstu-dien für das Kirchenjahr 1981/82. Perikopenreihe IV/2 (Stuttgart 1982) 181-88. HARTMANN, G. in GPM 42 (1987/88) 354-60. SÖDING, T. "Kreuzestheologie und Rechtfertigungslehre. Zur Verbindung von Christologie und Soteriologie im Ersten Korintherbrief und im Galaterbrief," Catholica 46 (1992) 31-60.

2:16,   COTHENET, E. "La vie dans la foi au Christ (Gal 2, 16.
19-21   19-21) AssS 42 (1970) 73-79.

2:16-20   BRAUN, H. GPM 12 (1957/58) 61-64. KRUSCHE, W. GPM 18 (1963/64) 85ff. VOIGT, G. Der zerrissene Vorhang (1969) I 109-16. SCHULZ, H. und DOMAY, E. in P. Krusche et al., eds., Predigtstudien für das Kirchenjahr 1975/76. Perikopen-reihe IV/1 (Stuttgart 1975) 126-33. SCHLIER, H. "Fragment über die Taufe" in V. Kubina und K. Lehmann, eds., Der Geist und die Kirche (FS H. Schlier; Freiburg/-Basel/Wien 1980) 137. METZGER, B. M. Manuscripts of the Greek Bible (Oxford 1981) 126.

2:16,20   HOWARD, G. "The Faith of Christ" ET 85 (1974) 212-15. RAMAROSON, L. "Trois études récentes sur 'la foi de Jésus' dans saint Paul," SciE 40 (1988) 365-77.

2:16   GOODWIN, D.R. "Ἐὰν μή, Gal. ii. 16" JBL (June, 1886) 122-27. MUNCK, J. Paul and the Salvation of Mankind (1959) 127f. SCHRAGE, W. Die konkreten Ein-zelgebote in der paulinischen Paränese (1961) 94, 230. JÜNGEL, E. Paulus und Jesus (1966) 17, 57, 62. KERTELGE, K. "Rechtfertigung" bei Paulus (1967) 126-28, 147-49. BLIGH, J. "Did Jesus Live by Faith" HeyJ 9 (1968) 414-19. VAN DÜL-MEN, A. Die Theologie des Gesetzes bei Paulus (1968) 21-24. KERTELGE, K. "Zur Deutung des Rechtfertigungsbegriffs im Galaterbrief" BZ 12 (1968) 211-22. MERK, O. Handeln aus Glauben (1968) 6-9. BARTH, M. "'The Faith of the Messiah',"

HeyJ 10 (1969) 363-70. BLANK, J. "Warum sagt Paulus: 'Aus Werken des Gesetzes wird niemand gerecht'?" in Evangelisch—Katholischer Kommentar zum Neuen Testament (Vorarbeiten Heft I:1969) 79-95. BORSE, U. Der Standort des Galater-briefes (1972) 122f. LADD, G.E. A Theology of the New Testament (1974) 271, 441, 447, 506. HARMAN, A. M. Paul's Use of the Psalms (Ann Arbor MI 1968) 151f. MUSSNER, F. Petrus und Paulus—Pole der Einheit (Freiburg/Basel/Wien 1976) 86-89. HÜBNER, H. Das Gesetz bei Paulus. Ein Beitrag zum Werden der paulinischen Theologie (Göttingen 1978) 16. BYRNE, B. "Sons of God"-"Seed of Abraham" (Rome 1979) 143f., 146, 151, 171n., 176, 163n. VIELHAUER, P. "Paulus und das Alte Testament" in Oikodome [G. Klein, ed.] (München 1979) 214. LADARIA, L. F. "Espíritu y justificación. A propósito de Gál 2, 16; 3, 2.5," EstEc 55 (212, 1980) 111-15. MÜLLER, U. B. "Zur Rezeption gesetzeskritischer Jesus-überlieferung im frühen Christentum," NTS 27 (1981) 159. BLANK, J. Paulus. Von Jesus zum Christentum (München 1982) 42-68. DUNN, J. D. G. "The New Perspec-tive on Paul," BJRL 65 (1983) 103-22. HAYS, R. B. The Faith of Jesus Christ (Chico CA 1983) 140-42, 158-60, 163, 171, 175, 178, 185, 217, 249. HÜBNER, H. "Galaterbrief" in TRE 12 (1984) 8. FREUND, G. und STEGEMANN, E., eds., The-ologische Brosamen für Lothar Steiger (DBAT 5; Heidelberg 1985) 187. RÄISÄ-NEN, H. "Galatians 2.16 and Paul's Break with Judaism," NTS 31 (1985) 543-53, also in The Torah and Christ (Helsinki 1986) 168-84. GASTON, L. "Paul and the Law in Galatians 2-3" in P. Richardson, ed., Anti-Judaism in Early Christianity, Vol. 1: Paul and the Gospels (Waterloo/Ont. 1986) 38, 44-46. COSGROVE, C. H. "Justi-fication in Paul. A Linguistic and Theological Reflection," JBL 106 (1987) 653-70. GASTON, L. Paul and the Torah (Vancouver 1987) 13, 58, 65, 103f., 195, 210f., 223. HOFIUS, O. "'Rechtfertigung des Gottlosen' als Thema biblischer Theologie," JBTh 2 (1987) 79-105, esp. 85f. TRUMMER, P. "Wieso 'aus Werken des Gesetzes kein Mensch gerechtfertigt wird' (Gal 2, 16) und welche Konsequenzen dies für uns hat" in Aufsätze zum Neuen Testament (Graz 1987) 81-94. BRUCE, F. F. "Paul and the Law in Recent Research" in B. Lindars, ed., Law and Religion (Cambridge 1988) 117, 124f. COSGROVE, C. H. The Cross and the Spirit. A Study in the Argument and Theology of Galatians (Macon GA 1988) 31n., 32, 55f., 68, 133, 135, 137, 142n., 143. BECKER, J. Paulus. Der Apostel der Völker (Tübingen 1989) 101, 218, 302f. HOFIUS, O. Paulusstudien (Tübingen 1989) 68, 90, 127, 128, 154f., 156, 172, 173. HOOKER, M. D. "ΠΙΣΤΙΣ ΧΡΙΣΤΟΥ," NTS 35 (1989) 321-42. JOHN-SON, E. E. The Function of Apocalyptic and Wisdom Traditions in Romans 9-11 (Atlanta GA 1989) 187, 190. MARTIN, B. L. Christ and the Law in Paul (Leiden 1989) 5, 40, 87, 89, 105, 115-18, 127, 138, 146, 150. SCHNELLE, U. Wandlungen im paulinischen Denken (Stuttgart 1989) 56. THIELMAN, F. From Plight to Solution (Leiden 1989) 23, 59, 62, 63, 65, 67, 120. DUNN, J. D. G. Jesus, Paul and the Law (London 1990) 158, 160, 176, 188-214, 220, 225, 227, 235n.51, 238, 245, 248f., 253, 260n.16. HOOKER, M. D. From Adam to Christ. Essays on Paul (Cambridge 1990) 168. HOWARD, G. Paul. Crisis in Galatia (Cambridge [2]1990) 48, 57, 95. SEGAL, A. F. Paul the Convert (New Haven/London 1990 130-32, 211. CRANFIELD, C. E. B. "'The Works of the Law' in the Epistle to the Romans," JSNT 43 (1991) 89-101. WALTER, N. "Gottes Erbarmen mit 'allem Fleisch' (Röm 3, 20 / Gal 2, 16)—ein 'femininer' Zug im paulinischen Gottesbild?" BZ 35 (1991) 99-102.

2:16c   MUSSNER, F. "Theologische 'Wiedergutmachung'. Am Beispiel der Auslegung des Galaterbriefes" FrR 26 (1974) 7-11.

2:17-21   THÜSING, W. Per Christum in Deum (1965) 86f., 109-13.

2:17-20   THEISSEN, G. Psychological Aspects of Pauline Theology (Edinburgh 1987) 197f.

2:17-19   ARNDT, W. "On Gal. 2:17-19" CThM 27 (1956) 128-32.

2:17-18 MUNDLE, W. "Zur Auslegung von Gal 2, 17.18" ZNW 23 (1924) 152f. MOULE, C.F.D. "A Note on Galatians 2:17, 18" ET 56 (1944-45) 223. LAMBRECHT, J. "Once Again Gal 2, 17-18 and 3, 21," EphT 63 (1987) 148-53. SEGAL, A. F. Paul the Convert (New Haven/London 1990) 241.

2:17 FEINE, P. Das Gesetzesfreie Evangelium des Paulus (1899) 19-24. MUNCK, J. Paul and the Salvation of Mankind (1959) 127f. WAGNER, G. "Le repas du Seigneur et la justification par la foi. Exégèse de Galates 2:17" EThR 36 (1961) 245-54. KÄSEMANN, E. Exegetische Versuche und Besinnungen (1964) I 75. VAN DÜLMEN, A. Die Theologie des Gesetzes bei Paulus (1968) 160-62. O'NEILL, J.C. The Recovery of Paul's Letter to the Galatians (1972) 42-44. HANSON, A.T. Studies in Paul's Technique and Theology (1974) 28-29. BYRNE, B. "Sons of God"-"Seed of Abraham" (Rome 1979) 144nn., 145, 171, 176. CLARK, K. W. "The Meaning of APA" in The Gentile Bias and Other Essays [Selected by J. L. Sharpe III] (Leiden 1980) 200. RHYNE, C. T. Faith Establishes the Law (Chico CA 1981) 50-54. HAYS, R. B. The Faith of Jesus Christ (Chico CA 1983) 165, 250. RÄISÄNEN, H. Paul and the Law (Tübingen 1983) 76, 257. RÄISÄNEN, H. The Torah and Christ (Helsinki 1986) 47, 179. WATSON, F. Paul, Judaism and the Gentiles (Cambridge 1986) 68. RÖHSER, G. Metaphorik und Personifikation der Sünde (Tübingen 1987) 107, 133, 166f. SCHMELLER, Th. Paulus und die "Diatribe" (Münster 1987) 328. MELL, U. Neue Schöpfung (Berlin/New York 1989) 290. SOARDS, M. L. "Seeking (Zetein) and Sinning (Hamartolos & Hamartia) According to Galatians 2.17" in J. Marcus and M. L. Soards, eds., Apocalyptic and the New Testament (FS J. L. Martyn; Sheffield 1989) 237-54. DUNN, J. D. G. Jesus, Paul and the Law (London 1990) 101, 156, 158, 172nn.117.119, 208. HAMERTON-KELLY, R. G. "Sacred Violence and 'Works of Law.' 'Is Christ Then an Agent of Sin?' (Galatians 2:17)," CBQ 52 (1990) 55-75. OLIVEIRA, A. DE, Die Diakonie der Gerechtigkeit und der Versöhnung in der Apologie des 2. Korintherbriefes. Analyse und Auslegung von 2 Kor 2, 14-4, 6; 5, 11-6, 10 (Münster 1990) 156nn.388f.

2:18-3:1 MULLER, E. C. Trinity and Marriage in Paul (New York/Bern/Frankfurt/Paris 1990) 367, 418.

2:18ff. BYRNE, B. "Sons of God"-"Seed of Abraham" (Rome 1979) 145f., 171.

2:18-21 SCHMITT, R. Gottesgerechtigkeit—Heilsgeschichte—Israel in der Theologie des Paulus (Frankfurt/Bern/New York/Nancy 1984) 56-58. FREUND, G. und STEGEMANN, E., eds., Theologische Brosamen für Lothar Steiger (DBAT 5; Heidelberg 1985) 190. SUHL, A. "Der Galaterbrief—Situation und Argumentation" in ANRW II.25.4 (1987) 3111-19. LAMBRECHT, J. "Transgressor by Nullifying God's Grace. A Study of Gal 2, 18-21," Biblica 72 (1991) 217-36.

2:18 MUNCK, J. Paul and the Salvation of Mankind (1959) 128f. PFAMMATER, J. Die Kirche als Bau (1960) 12ff. ELLIS, E.E. "Christ and Spirit in I Cor" in Christ and Spirit in the New Testament. In Honour of C.F.D. Moule, ed. by B. Lindars and S.S. Smalley (1973) 276f. HOOKER, M.D. "Were There False Teachers in Colossae?" in Christ and the Spirit in the New Testament. In Honour of C.F.D. Moule, ed. by B. Lindars and S.S. Smalley (1973) 327f. VIELHAUER, P. "Oikodome. Das Bild vom Bau in der Christlichen Literatur vom Neuen Testament bis Clemens Alexandrinus" in Oikodome [G. Klein, ed.] (München 1979) 83-85. BROER, I. Freiheit vom Gesetz und Radikalisierung des Gesetzes (Stuttgart 1980) 25. RÄISÄNEN, H. Paul and the Law (Tübingen 1983) 13, 19, 47, 56, 58, 70, 76, 179, 258, 259f. THEISSEN, G. Psychologische Aspekte paulinischer Theologie (Göttingen 1983) 195, 198, 198n.24, 200ff. RÄISÄNEN, H. The Torah and Christ (Helsinki 1986) 179. DUNN, J. D. G. Jesus, Paul and the Law (London 1990) 153, 158, 172n.120. SEGAL, A. F. Paul the Convert (New Haven/London 1990) 130, 202.

2:19ff. FEINE, P. Der Apostel Paulus (1927) 575ff. THEISSEN, G. Psychologische Aspekte paulinischer Theologie (Göttingen 1983) 256n.110.

2:19-21 BÜCHSEL, F. Der Geist Gottes im Neuen Testament (1926) 295ff. SCHELKLE, K.H. Die Passion Jesu in der Verkündigung des Neuen Testaments (1949) 237f. STANLEY, D.M. Christ's Resurrection in Pauline Soteriology (1961) 150-52. MODALSLI, O. "Gal. 2, 19-21; 5, 16-18 und Röm. 7, 7-25" ThZ 21 (1965) 22-37. ORT-KEMPER, F.-J. Das Kreuz in der Verkündigung des Apostels Paulus (1967) 19-26. EICHHOLZ, G. Die Theologie des Paulus im Umriss (1972) 247f. BORSE, U. Der Standort des Galaterbriefes (1972) 71-75. PAGELS, E.H. The Gnostic Paul (1975) 105-6. FROITZHEIM, F. Christologie und Eschatologie bei Paulus (Würzburg 1979) 121. FARAHIAN, E. Le "je" paulinien. Etude pour mieux comprendre Gal. 2, 19-21 (Rome 1988) passim. MARTIN, B. L. Christ and the Law in Paul (Leiden 1989) 109, 113.

2:19-20 WIKENHAUSER, A. Die Christusmystik des Apostels Paulus (1956) 24f. SCHOEPS, H.-J. Paulus (1959) 201f. KNOX, W.L. St.Paul and the Church of the Gentiles (1961) 62f., 151f., 159f. LARSON, E. Christus als Vorbild (1962) 92-105. DELLING, G. Die Taufe im Neuen Testament (1963) 125. DOWNING, J.D.H. "Possible Baptismal References in Galatians" in Studia Evangelica II/1, ed. by F.L. Cross (1964) 551-56. TANNEHILL, R.C. Dying and Rising With Christ (1966) 55-61. BLANK, J. Paulus und Jesus (1968) 279f., 298-303. THYEN, H. Studien zur Sündenvergebung (1970) 190f., 198f., 203f. BORSE, U. Der Standort des Gal-ater-briefes (1972) 71f. DUNN, J.D.G. Jesus and the Spirit (1975) 331f. SIBER, P. Mit Christus leben (Zürich 1971) 192, 196, 218, 222ff., 227ff., 234f. ELLIS, E. E. Prophecy and Hermeneutic in Early Christianity (Tübingen 1978) 67, 77f. GAFFIN, R. B. The Centrality of the Resurrection (Grand Rapids 1978) 52f. STOLLBERG, D. und LÜHRMANN, D. "Tiefenpsychologische oder historisch-kritische Exegese? Identität und der Tod des Ich (Gal 2, 19-20)" in Y. Spiegel, ed., Doppeldeutlich. Tiefendimensionen biblischer Texte (München 1978) 215-36. KIM, S. The Origin of Paul's Gospel (Tübingen 1981) 302. WEDER, H. Das Kreuz Jesu bei Paulus (Göttingen 1981) 175-82. BRINSMEAD, B. H. Galatians—Dialogical Response to Opponents (Chico CA 1982) 141. SCHNELLE, U. Gerechtigkeit und Christusgegen-wart (Göttingen 1983) 54-56. THEISSEN, G. Psychologische Aspekte paulinischer Theologie (Göttingen 1983) 36, 201, 229. COFFEY, D. "The 'Incarnation' of the Holy Spirit in Christ," ThSt 45 (1984) 466-80, esp. 475f. WEDER, H. Neutestament-liche Hermeneutik (Zürich 1986) 397-99, 401-04. BERGER, K. und COLPE, C., eds., Religionsgeschichtliches Textbuch zum Neuen Testament (Göttingen/Zürich 1987) 270. MERKLEIN, H. Studien zu Jesus und Paulus (Tübingen 1987) 50, 53, 56-59, 98, 101, 104, 425n.62. RÖHSER, G. Metaphorik und Personifikation der Sünde (Tübingen 1987) 110, 119f., 122f., 141. THEISSEN, G. Psychological Aspects of Pauline Theology (Edinburgh 1987) 191, 199, 227f., 254n. WEDDERBURN, A. J. M. Baptism and Resurrection (Tübingen 1987) 5, 382. YAGI, S. "'I' in the Words of Jesus" in J. Hick and P. F. Knitter, eds., The Myth of Christian Uniqueness. Toward a Pluralistic Theology of Religions (Maryknoll NY 1987) 117-34, esp. 118f., 126, 130. COSGROVE, C. H. The Cross and the Spirit. A Study in the Argu-ment and Theology of Galatians (Macon GA 1988) 35, 79n., 131f., 140n., 141, 143, 145, 176f. LATEGAN, B. "Is Paul Defending His Apostleship in Galatians?" NTS 34 (1988) 411-30. BECKER, J. Paulus. Der Apostel der Völker (Tübingen 1989) 81f., 127, 364, 401, 441. VOLLENWEIDER, S. Freiheit als neue Schöpfung (Göttingen 1989) 303f., 366n. ZEDDA, S. "'Morto alla legge mediante la legge' (Gal 2, 19a). Testo autobiografico sulla conversione di san Paolo?" RivB 37 (1989) 81-95. VOLLENWEIDER, S. "Grosser Tod und grosses Leben. Ein Beitrag zum buddhistisch-christlichen Gespräch im Blick auf die Mystik des Paulus," EvTh 51 (1991) 365-82.

2:19   LEAL, J. "Christo confixus sum cruci (Gal. 2, 19)" VD 19 (1939) 76-80, 98-105. SCHNACKENBURG, R. Das Heils-geschehen bei der Taufe nach dem Apostel Paulus (1950) 57-62; Baptism in the Thought of St.Paul (1964) 62-67. SCHRAGE, W. Die konkreten Einzelgebote in der paulinischen Paränese (1961) 93f. SCHWEIZ- ER, E. Erniedrigung und Erhöhung bei Jesus und seinen Nachfolgern (1962) § 9d. DELLING, G. Die Taufe im Neuen Testament (1963) 132. JÜNGEL, E. Paulus und Jesus (1966) 54, 61. HOFFMANN, P. Die Toten in Christus (1966) 303. KER- TELGE, K. "Recht-fertigung" bei Paulus (1967) 239-42. VAN DÜLMEN, A. Die Theologie des Gesetzes bei Paulus (1968) 24ff. MOULE, C.F.D. "Death 'to Sin', 'to Law', and 'to the World': a Note on Certain Datives" in Mélanges Bibliques en hommage au R.P. Béda Rigaux, ed. by A. Descamps and A. de Halleux (1970) 372- 74. BORSE, U. Der STandort des Galaterbriefes (1972) 71f., 74f., 123f. SIBER, P. Mit Christus leben (Zürich 1971) 185f. KÜMMEL, W. G. Römer 7 und das Bild des Menschen im Neuen Testament (München 1974) 52, 123. FISCHER, U. Eschatologie und Jenseitserwartung im hellenistischen Diasporajudentum (Berlin 1978) 96. ORGE, M. "Gal 2, 19. El cristiano crucificado con Cristo," Claretianum [Rome] 18 (1978) 303-60. BYRNE, B. "Sons of God"-"Seed of Abraham" (Rome 1979) 92n., 95, 97, 146. YAGI, S. "Das Ich bei Paulus und Jesus—zum neutestamentlichen Denken," AJBI 5 (1979) 139, 142. SCHADE, H.-H. Apokalyptische Christologie bei Paulus (Göttingen 1981) 146. BLANK, J. Paulus. Von Jesus zum Christentum (München 1982) 102. HAYS, R. B. The Faith of Jesus Christ (Chico CA 1983) 168, 250. RÄISÄNEN, H. Paul and the Law (Tübingen 1983) 57f., 61, 143, 258. THEISSEN, G. Psychologische Aspekte paulinischer Theologie (Göttingen 1983) 195, 198, 198n.25, 200ff., 229. MOHRLANG, R. Matthew and Paul (Cambridge 1984) 27, 84, 116. DIETZFELBINGER, C. Die Berufung des Paulus als Ursprung seiner Theologie (Neukirchen 1985) 32, 33, 97ff., 117, 131. FREUND, G. und STEGEMANN, E., eds., Theologische Brosamen für Lothar Steiger (DBAT 5; Heidelberg 1985) 190. ZEDDA, S. "Christo confixus sum Cruci (Gal 2, 19)" in C. M. Martini, ed., Testi- monium Christi (FS J. Dupont; Brescia 1985) 481-92. RÄISÄNEN, H. The Torah and Christ (Helsinki 1986) 179. MERKLEIN, H. Studien zu Jesus und Paulus (Tübingen 1987) 13, 45n.119, 48f., 58, 75, 78, 343, 424n.61. WEDDERBURN, A. J. M. Baptism and Resurrection (Tübingen 1987) 49, 65, 345, 348, 350. COS- GROVE, C. H. The Cross and the Spirit. A Study in the Argument and Theology of Galatians (Macon GA 1988) 7, 119, 132, 137, 139-41, 173, 193. SCHNELLE, U. Wandlungen im paulinischen Denken (Stuttgart 1989) 57f. OLIVEIRA, A. DE, Die Diakonie der Gerechtigkeit und der Versöhnung in der Apologie des 2. Korinther- briefes. Analyse und Auslegung von 2 Kor 2, 14-4, 6; 5, 11-6, 10 (Münster 1990) 352f.

2:20-21   DENNEY, J. The Death of Christ (1956) 74f. CERFAUX, L. Christ in the Theology of St. Paul (1959) 325f. THEISSEN, G. Psychologische Aspekte paulinischer Theologie (Göttingen 1983) 201.

2:20   CARPUS "Heaven" Exp ist series 3 (1876) 62-73. MOULE, H.C.G. "A Study in the Connexion of Doctrines" Exp 3rd series 2 (1885) 447-44. SOKOLOW-SKI, E. Die Begriffe Geist und Leben bei Paulus (1903) 28ff., 120f. VAN DER HOOGT, M.J. "Het ware leven" GThT 6 (1905) 10-12, 48-53. CHRISTIE, F.W. "The Judicial and Mystic Idea of Religion: An Exposition of Rom. 3:24 and Gal. 2:20" BibW 31 (1908) 445-47. KENNEDY, H.A.A. St.Paul and the Mystery—Religions (1913) 146f., 222f. LATTEY, C. "These Paulinae: VII, De nova vita iusti: Secundum S. Paulum per iustificationem 'vivo iam non ego, vivit vero in me Christus' (Gal. 2,

20)" VD 4 (19240 196-200, 241-44. ROBINSON, J.A.T. The Body (1952) 21f. DAVIES, W.D. Paul and Rabbinic Judaism (1955) 87f. ROBINSON, J.M. Kerygma und historischer Jesus (1960) 107, 109. ROMANIUK, K. L'Armour du Pere et du Fils dans la Soteriologie de Saint Paul (1961) 58-59, 74-77. SEVENSTER, J.N. Paul and Seneca (1961) 81, 185. ROMANIUK, K. "Gal 2, 20 w soteriologii sw. Pawla' Ruch Biblijny i Liturgiczny 15 (1962) 73-82. DELLING, G. Die Taufe im Neuen Testament (1963) 117, 121. HAHN, F. Christologische Hoheitsitiel (1963) 62-63, 210. KRAMER, W. Christos Kyrois Gottessohn (1963) §§ 26b, 27e, 55d, h. BALAGUE, M. "'In fide vivo filii Dei' (Gal 2, 20)" Cultura Biblica 21 (1964) 264-70; "'In fide vivl Filii Dei' vivo en la fe del Hijo de Dios (Gal 2, 20)" RivB 26 (1964) 73-78. KÄSEMANN, E. Exegetische Versuche und Besinnungen (1964) I 266; II 64, 186, 248; New Testament Questions of Today (1969) 173, 230, 245. HOFFMANN, P. Die Toten in Christus (1966) 283. JÜNGEL, E. Paulus und Jesus (1966) 63. KERTELGE, K. "Rechtfertigung" bei Paulus (1967) 137, 180, 227. NICKELS, P. Targum and New Testament (1967) 73. POPKES, W. Christus Traditus (1967) 197f., 201ff. VAN DÜLMEN, A. Die Theologie des Gesetzes bei Paulus (1968) 192-98, 205-8. MERK, O. Handein aus Glauben (1968) 5, 12, 17, 36, 60, 69. LOHSE, E. et al. Der Ruf Jesu und die Antwort der Gemeinde (1970) 204-12. MAUSER, U. Gottesbild und Menschwerdung (1971) 180f. BORSE, U. Der Standort des Galaterbriefes (1972) 72-74. O'NEILL, J.C. The Recovery of Paul's Letter to the Galatians (1972) 44-46. FIORENZA, E.S. Priester für Gott (1972) 205f. SCHWEIZER, E. "Christus und Geist im Kolosserbrief" in Christ and the Spirit in the New Testament (1973) 305f. KÜMMEL, W.G. Römer 7 und das Bild des Menschen im Neuen Testament (1974) 16-18, 102f. LADD, G.E. A Theology of the New Testament (1974) 424-28, 469-74, 483-93. LOHSE, E. Grundriss der neutestamentlichen Theologie (1974) 96, 98f. BAKER, J. A. "The Myth of the Church. A Case Study in the Use of the Scripture for Christian Doctrine" in M. Hooker and C. Hickling, eds., What About the New Testament? (FS C. Evans; London 1975) 170. RIDDERBOS, H. Paul. An Outline of His Theology (Grand Rapids 1975) 230-33. WINGREN, G. "Abendmahl" in TRE 1 (1977) 54. DALY, R. J. Christian Sacrifice (Washington 1978) 241. FRIEDRICH, G. "Der Brief eines Gefangenen. Bemerkungen zum Philipperbrief" in Auf das Wort kommt es an. Gesammelte Aufsätze (Göttingen 1978) 226. SCHMITHALS, W. "Zur Herkunft der gnostischen Elemente in der Sprache des Paulus" in B. Aland et al., eds., Gnosis (FS H. Jonas; Göttingen 1978) 388-90. BYRNE, B. "Sons of God"-"Seed of Abraham" (Rome 1979) 6, 146f., 166, 169, 171, 171n., 199, 200, 204, 207f. FARICY, R. Praying for Inner Healing (London 1979) 50f. FROITZHEIM, F. Christologie und Eschatologie bei Paulus (Würzburg 1979) 33ff. PIPER, J. 'Love your enemies' (Cambridge 1979) 106, 133, 219n.95. YAGI, S. "Das Ich bei Paulus und Jesus—zum neutestamentlichen Denken," AJBI 5 (1979) 139, 142. FULLER, D. P. Gospel and Law. Contrast or Continuum? (Grand Rapids 1980) 113f. BISER, E. Der Zeuge (Graz/Wien/Köln 1981) 58, 107, 128, 136, 156, 168, 265f., 292. BRUENING, W. "Das Erbsündenverständis der Confessio Augustana: noch ungenützte Einsichten und Möglichkeiten?" Catholica 35 (1981) 129. MÜLLER, U. B. "Zur Rezeption gesetzeskritischer Jesusüberlieferung im frühen Christentum," NTS 27 (1981) 159. HAYS, R. B. The Faith of Jesus Christ (Chico CA 1983) 10, 118, 142, 153, 167, 169, 184, 201, 207, 217, 232, 249f., 262f. MUNRO, W. Authority in Paul and Peter (Cambridge 1983) 29. THEISSEN, G. Psychologische Aspekte paulinischer Theologie (Göttingen 1983) 194f., 200, 202, 229, 380. BERÉNYI, G. "Gal 2, 20: A Pre-Pauline or a Pauline Text?" Biblica 65 (1984) 490-537. GASTON, L. "Paul and Jerusalem" in P. Richardson and J. C. Hurd, eds., From Jesus to Paul (FS F. W. Beare; Waterloo

1984) 71. GRANT, R. M. "Marcion and the Critical Method" in P. Richardson and J. C. Hurd, eds., From Jesus to Paul (FS F. W. Beare; Waterloo 1984) 212. JOHNSTON, G. "'Kingdom of God' Sayings in Paul's Letters" in P. Richardson and J. C. Hurd, eds., From Jesus to Paul (FS F. W. Beare; Waterloo 1984) 147. KLEIN-KNECHT, K. T. Der leidende Gerechtfertigte (Tübingen 1984) 182. MOHRLANG, R. Matthew and Paul (Cambridge 1984) 82, 88, 102f., 116, 173. SCHELKLE, K. "Im Leib oder Ausser des Leibes: Paulus als Mystiker" in W. C. Weinreich, ed., The New Testament Age (FS B. Reicke; Macon GA 1984) II, 455. STANLEY, D. "Imitation in Paul's Letters. Its Significance for His Relationship to Jesus and to His Own Christian Foundations" in P. Richardson and J. C. Hurd, eds., From Jesus to Paul (FS F. W. Beare; Waterloo 1984) 129. POBEE, J. S. Persecution and Martyrdom in the Theology of Paul (Sheffield 1985) 48, 53, 91. BERÉNYI, G. "Gal 2, 20: A Pre-Pauline or a Pauline Text?" in A. Vanhoye, ed., L'Apôtre Paul. Personalité, style et conception du ministère (Leuven 1986) 340-44. MERKLEIN, H. Studien zu Jesus und Paulus (Tübingen 1987) 24, 29n.85, 43, 51n.129, 104, 187. OSTEN-SACKEN, P. VON DER, Evangelium und Tora: Aufsätze zu Paulus (München 1987) 16, 20, 64, 172, 174. SCHMELLER, Th. Paulus und die "Diatribe" (Münster 1987) 241n.39. SCHWEIZER, E. Jesus Christ. The Man from Nazareth and the Exalted Lord (Macon GA 1987) 18. COSGROVE, C. H. The Cross and the Spirit. A Study in the Argument and Theology of Galatians (Macon GA 1988) 35, 55, 57, 139, 141, 173, 176, 193f. JONGE, M. DE, Christology in Context. The Earliest Christian Response to Jesus (Philadelphia 1988) 40f., 88, 113f. KUHN, H.-J. Christologie und Wunder. Untersuchungen zu Joh 1, 35-51 (Regensburg 1988) 147, 356, 360-62, 375, 382, 388. BREYTENBACH, C. Versöhnung (Neukirchen/Vluyn 1989) 125n., 126, 197, 198, 213n. CLABEAUX, J. J. The Lost Edition of the Letters of Paul (CBQ.MS; Washington 1989) 169. HOOKER, M. D. "ΠΙΣΤΙΣ ΧΡΙΣΤΟΥ," NTS 35 (1989) 321-42. LAMPE, P. Die stadtrömischen Christen in den ersten beiden Jahrhunderten (Tübingen ²1989) 215. MARTIN, B. L. Christ and the Law in Paul (Leiden 1989) 53, 71, 80, 103-05, 109, 113f., 118f. HOOKER, M. D. From Adam to Christ. Essays on Paul (Cambridge 1990) 71, 168, 174, 180. OLIVEIRA, A. DE, Die Diakonie der Gerechtigkeit und der Versöhnung in der Apologie des 2. Korintherbriefes. Analyse und Auslegung von 2 Kor 2, 14-4, 6; 5, 11-6, 10 (Münster 1990) 224n.663, 346f.

2:20b   HAHN, F. Christologische Hoheitstitel (1963) 202, 210, 316.
2:21   BOUSSET, W. Die Religion des Judentums im Späthellenistischen Zeitalter (1966=1926) 119. STALDER, K. Das Werk des Geistes in der Heiligung bei Paulus (1962) 316f., 354, 356, 365f. KRAMER, W. Christos Kyrios Gottessohn (1963) §4b. JÜNGEL, E. Paulus und Jesus (1966) 17, 50. VAN DÜLMEN, Die Theologie des Gesetzes bei Paulus (1968) 19-23, 26f. ECKERT, J. Die urchristliche Verkündigung im Streit zwischen Paulus und seinen Gegner nach dem Galaterbrief (1971) 33, 36, 64, 107, 110. BORSE, U. Der Standort des Galaterbriefes (1972) 73f. LADD, G.E. A. Theology of the New Testament (1974) 423, 439, 448. BYRNE, B. "Sons of God"-"Seed of Abraham" (Rome 1979) 142, 147. HAYS, R. B. The Faith of Jesus Christ (Chico CA 1983) 118, 197, 206f., 228. DIETZFELBINGER, C. Die Berufung des Paulus als Ursprung seiner Theologie (Neukirchen 1985) 68, 106, 116, 120. SANDERS, E. P. Paul, the Law, and the Jewish People (London 1985) 27, 28, 76, 152, 159, 165n.34, 208. RÄISÄNEN, H. The Torah and Christ (Helsinki 1986) 16, 33. COSGROVE, C. H. The Cross and the Spirit. A Study in the Argument and Theology of Galatians (Macon GA 1988) 11, 13, 35, 41, 60, 79n., 132, 142, 171n., 177. MARTIN, B. L. Christ and the Law in Paul (Leiden 1989) 5, 19, 20, 37, 39, 49, 52-54, 89, 95f., 99, 103, 118, 123, 125, 127, 132. DUNN, J. D. G. Jesus, Paul

and the Law (London 1990) 172n.117, 230, 232, 238, 245, 261n.34. REINMUTH, E. "'Nicht vergeblich' bei Paulus und Pseudo-Philo, *Liber Antiquitatum Biblicarum*," NovT 33 (1991) 97-123.

3:1-6:10 FEUILLET, A. "Ressemblances structurales et doctrinales entre Ga 3, 1-6, 10 et Rm 1-8. La triple référence de l'épître aux Romains aux origines de l'histoire humaine," NV 57 (1982) 30-64. FEUILLET, A. "Structure de la section doctrinale de l'Épître aux Galates (III, I-VI, 10)," RThom 82 (1982) 5-39.

3:1-5:25 SUHL, A. "Der Galaterbrief—Situation und Argumentation" in ANRW II.25.4 (1987) 3127-32.

3:1-5:17 SCHMITHALS, W. "The Corpus Paulinum and Gnosis" in A. H. B. Logan and A. J. M. Wedderburn, eds., The New Testament and Gnosis (FS R. M. Wilson; Edinburgh 1983) 112f.

3:1-5:12 MERK, O. "Der Beginn der Paränese im Galaterbrief" ZNW 60 (1969) 83-104. SELBY, D.J. Introduction to the New Testament (1971) 335-37. BECKER, J. Paulus. Der Apostel der Völker (Tübingen 1989) 305ff., 342.

3:1-5:1 GIBLIN, C.H. In Hope of God's Glory (1974) 66-84.

3-4 MINDE, H.-J. VAN DER, Schrift und Tradition bei Paulus (München/Paderborn/ Wien 1976) 142-56. BLOCH, R. "Midrash" in W. S. Green, ed., Approaches to Ancient Judaism. Theory and Practice (Missoula 1978) 48. SCHMITHALS, W. "Zur Herkunft der gnostischen Elemente in der Sprache des Paulus" in B. Aland et al., eds., Gnosis (FS H. Jonas; Göttingen 1978) 392f. HOWARD, G. Paul. Crisis in Galatia (Cambridge 1979) 46-65. HARTMANN, L. "Bundesideologie in und hinter einigen paulinischen Texten" in S. Pedersen, ed., Die Paulinische Literatur und Theologie (Arhus/ Göttingen 1980) 109-12. BRINSMEAD, B. H. Galatians - Dialogical Response to Opponents (Chico CA 1982) 52f., 82-85, 192. HAYS, R. B. The Faith of Jesus Christ (Chico CA 1983) 30, 66, 141, 222f. VOUGA, F. "La construction de l'histoire en Galates 3-4," ZNW 75 (1984) 259-69. BARRETT, C. K. Freedom and Obligaion (Philadelphia 1985) 22-31. GRAESSER, E. Der Alte Bund im Neuen (Tübingen 1985) 55f., 62, 66, 68, 75, 89, 95. ALLAZ, J. et al., Chrétiens en conflit. L'Epître de Paul aux Galates (Geneva 1987) passim. FUNG, R. Y. K. "Justification, Sonship and the Gift of the Spirit. Their Mutual Relationships as Seen in Galatians 3-4," CGST Journal [Hong Kong] 3 (1987) 73-107. GASTON, L. Paul and the Torah (Vancouver 1987) 14, 73-76. MERKLEIN, H. Studien zu Jesus und Paulus (Tübingen 1987) 68-76. CONZELMANN, H. and LINDEMANN, A. Interpreting the New Testament (Peabody MA 1988) 173. COSGROVE, C. H. The Cross and the Spirit. A Study in the Argument and Theology of Galatians (Macon GA 1988) 7, 13, 19, 23n., 32, 39, 48, 51, 61, 85, 87, 144, 159f., 166. UKPONG, J. S. and ASAHU-EJERE, "The Letter to the Galatians and the Problem of Cultural Pluralism in Christianity," RATh 12 (23-24, 1988) 67-77. BECKER, J. Paulus. Der Apostel der Völker (Tübingen 1989) 390ff. HANSEN, G. W. Abraham in Galatians. Epistolary and Rhetorical Contexts (Sheffield 1989) passim. HAR-RINGTON, D. J. Paul on the Mystery of Israel (Collegeville MN 1992) passim. HARRISVILLE, R. A. The Figure of Abraham in the Epistles of St. Paul. In the Footsteps of Abraham (San Francisco 1992) passim.

3:1-4:31 THYEN, H. Studien zur Sündenvergebung (1970) 201f. ECKERT, J. Die urchristliche Verkündigung im Streit zwischen Paulus und seinen Gegnern nach dem Galaterbrief (1971) 231f. JONES, P.R. "Exegesis of Galatians 3 and 4" RevEx 69 (1972) 471-82.

3:1-4:11 HAYS, R. B. The Faith of Jesus Christ. An Investiga-tion of the Narrative Substructure of Galatians 3:1-4:11 (Chico CA 1983) passim, esp. 5f., 8, 28-30, 193-246, 247.

SMIT, J. "Naar een nieuwe benadering van Paulus' brieven. De historische bewijs-voering in Gal. 3, 1-4, 11," TvTh 24 (1984) 207-34. SUHL, A. "Die Galater und der Geist. Kritische Erwägungen zur Situation in Galatien" in D.-A. Koch et al., eds., Jesu Rede von Gott und ihre Nachgeschichte im frühen Christentum (FS Willi Marxsen; Gütersloh 1989) 286ff.

3:1–4:10 STALDER, K. Das Werk des Geistes in der Heiligung bei Paulus (1962) 317-41.

3:1–4:7 LUZ, U. Das Geschichtsverständnis des Paulus (1968) 146-56. KLAIBER, W. Rechtfertigung und Gemeinde (Göttingen 1982) 149-53.

3 LAURENTIUS, di F. "De semine Abrahae, promissionum herede, iuxta S. Paulum in Gal. 3" VD 21 (1941) 49-58. FEINE, P. & BEHM, J. Einleitung in das Neue Testament (1950) 145f. BERGER, K. "Abraham in den paulinischen Hauptbriefen (Gal 3; 4, 21-31; Röm 4; 9-11; 2 C 11, 22) MThZ 17 (1966) 47-89. LUZ, U. Das Geschichtsverständnis des Paulus (1968) 168-86. BRING, R.A. "Trosrättfärdighet och lagens fullgörande" Svensk Teologisk Kvartalskrift 45 (1969) 101-15. DAHL, N.A. "Motsigelser i Skriften, et gammelt hermeneutiskt problem" Svensk Teologisk Kvartalskrift 45 (1969) 22-36. DAMERAU, R. Der Galaterbriefkommentar des Nikolaus Dinkelsbühl (1970) 67-103. DAHL, N.A. "Widersprüche in der Bibel, ein hermeneutisches Problem" StTh 25 (1971) 1-19. PENTECOST, J.D. "The Purpose of the Law" BiblSa 128 (1971) 227-33. MÜLLER, H. Die Auslegung alttestament-lichen Geschichtsstoffs bei Paulus (diss. Halle/Wittenberg 1960) 116-27. LAYMAN, F. D. Paul's Use of Abraham. An Approach to Paul's Understanding of History (diss. Ann Arbor MI 1978) passim. BERGER, K. "Abraham II" in TRE 1 (1977) 374, 376. DUGANDZIC, I. Das "Ja" Gottes in Christus (Würzburg 1977) 198-221. MIRANDA, J. P. Marx and the Bible. A Critique of the Philosophy of Oppression (London 1977) 218. SEEBASS, H. "Zur Ermöglichung biblischer Theologie. Fragen an G. Klein zur 'zentralen urchristlichen Konstuktion des Glaubens'," EvTh 37 (6, 1977) 591-600. BRUCE, F. F. The Time is Fulfilled (Exeter 1978) 64-67. FRIED-RICH, G. "Das Gesetz des Glaubens Römer 3, 27" in Auf das Wort kommt es an. Gesammelte Aufsätze (Göttingen 1978) 116. HÜBNER, H. Das Gesetz bei Paulus. Ein Beitrag zum Werden der paulinischen Theologie (Göttingen 1978) 16-21, 25-37, 44-53. HOWARD, G. Paul. Crisis in Galatia (Cambridge 1979) 49-65. VIEL-HAUER, P. "Paulus und das Alte Testament" in Oikodome [G. Klein, ed.] (München 1979) 204, 209. CLARK, K. W. "The Israel of God" in The Gentile Bias and Other Essays [Selected by J. L. Sharpe III] (Leiden 1980) 22f., 25, 28. GASTON, L. "Abraham and the Righteousness of God," HBTh 2 (1980) 39-68. HARRINGTON, D. J. God's People in Christ (Phila-delphia 1980) 45-52. MOXNES, H. Theology in Conflict (Leiden 1980) 104, 119, 129, 207-16, 221f., 228f., 248, 263, 265, 271. WILLIAMS, S. K. "The 'Righteousness of God' in Romans," JBL 99 (1980) 263-65, 269, 274. HAYS, R. B. The Faith of Jesus Christ (Chico CA 1983) 142. PATTE, D. Paul's Faith and the Power of the Gospel (Philadelphia 1983) 190, 194, 208-14. THEISSEN, G. Psychologische Aspekte paulinischer Theologie (Göttingen 1983) 56, 211, 248. HÜBNER, H. Gottes Ich und Israel (Göttingen 1984) 35, 42, 71, 73. SAN-DERS, E. P. Paul, the Law, and the Jewish People (London 1985) 19-23, 25f., 28, 30, 46, 51n.18, 52n.21, 57n.64, 68, 78, 96, 102, 127, 137, 154, 159, 163nn.12.18, 174. DOBBELER, A. VON, Glaube als Teilhabe (Tübingen 1987) 145f. WIL-LIAMS, S. K. "Justification and the Spirit in Galatians," JSNT 29 (1987) 91-100. WILLIAMS, S. K. "The Hearing of Faith: AKOH ΠΙΣΤΕΩΣ in Galatians 3," NTS 35 (1989) 82-93. COUSAR, C. B. A Theology of the Cross (Minneapolis 1990) 111-21, 129. DIPROSE, R. Passato, presente e futuro nell'opera di Dio (Rome 1990) passim. HOOKER, M. D. From Adam to Christ. Essays on Paul (Cambridge 1990)

14, 16, 156, 159, 170, 173, 175, 177, 185. SANDERS, E. P. Jewish Law from Jesus to the Mishnah (London/Philadelphia 1990) 51.

3:1ff. RIDDERBOS, H. Paul. An Outline of His Theology (Grand Rapids 1975) 216f. FREUND, G. und STEGEMANN, E., eds., Theologische Brosamen für Lothar Steiger (DBAT 5; Heidelberg 1985) 389.

3:1-18 MINDE, H.-J. VAN DER, Schrift und Tradition bei Paulus (München/Paderborn/Wien 1976) 126-36. ROLOFF, J. Exegetische Verantwortung in der Kirche (Göttingen 1990) 237-43.

3:1-14 GIBLET, J. "De justifications per fidem Christi juxta Gal III, 1-14" Collectanea Mechliniensia 26 (1956) 597-600. VAN DÜLMEN, A. Die Theologie des Gesetzes bei Paulus (1968) 27-36. ECKERT, J. Die urchristliche Verkündigung im Streit zwischen Paulus und seinen Gegnern nach dem Galaterbrief (1971) 73-79. ACHTEMEIER, E. The Old Testament and the Proclamation of the Gospel (1973) 172ff. BERGER, K. Exegese des Neuen Testaments (Heidelberg 1977) 43-45. WILLIAMSON, L. Jr. "Translations and Interpretation: New Testament," Interpretation 32 (1978) 158-70. BYRNE, B. "Sons of God"-"Seed of Abraham" (Rome 1979) 147-57. MINDE, H. J. VAN DER, "Theologia crucis und Pneumaaussagen bei Paulus," Catholica 34 (1980) 137, 140. DEIDUN, T. J. New Covenant Morality in Paul (Rome 1981) 47-50. KLAIBER, W. Rechtfertigung und Gemeinde (Göttingen 1982) 151. HAYS, R. B. The Faith of Jesus Christ (Chico CA 1983) 196, 212, 234. DOBBELER, A. VON, Glaube als Teilhabe (Tübingen 1987) 57f., 145f., 148-51, 157-70. COSGROVE, C. H. The Cross and the Spirit. A Study in the Argument and Theology of Galatians (Macon GA 1988) 32, 38f., 51f., 59, 63, 119, 131, 143, 178f. HAYS, R. B. Echoes of Scripture in the Letters of Paul (New Haven/London 1989) 105-11. GEORGI, D. Theocracy in Paul's Praxis and Theology (Minneapolis 1991) 38-46. HONG, I.-G. The Law in Galatians (Sheffield 1993) 38-42, 70-75.

3:1-9 SCHMITT, R. Gottesgerechtigkeit—Heilsgeschichte—Israel in der Theologie des Paulus (Frankfurt/Bern/ New York/Nancy 1984) 44-47. AUNE, D. E. The New Testament in Its Literary Environment (Philadelphia 1987) 200.

3:1-8 ELLIS, E.E. Paul's Use of the Old Testament (1957) 21ff., 116ff., 124f.

3:1-6 LAMMER, H. R. "Mnemonic Reference to the Spirit as a Persuasive Tool. Galatians 3:1-6 within the argument, 3:1-4:11," Neotestamentica 26 (1992) 359-88.

3:1-5 SOKOLOWSKI, E. Die Begriffe Geist und Leben bei Paulus (1903) 79ff. LUZ, U. Das Geschichtsverständnis des Paulus (1968) 147f. DUNN, J.D.G. Baptism in the Spirit (1970) 107ff. JEWETT, R. "Agitators and the Galatian Congregation" NTS 17 (1970/71) 209f. PAGELS, E.H. The Gnostic Paul (1975) 106. MONTAGUE, G. T. The Holy Spirit (New York 1976) 193f. MINDE, H.-J. VAN DER, Schrift und Tradition bei Paulus (München/Paderborn/Wien 1976) 126f. LULL, D. J. The Spirit in Galatia (Chico CA 1980) 54-57. MOXNES, H. Theology in Conflict (Leiden 1980) 208f., 213, 223. BRINSMEAD, B. H. Galatians—Dialogical Response to Opponents (Chico CA 1982) 78-82, 141, 143f., 191. HILL, D. "Salvation Proclaimed. IV: Galatians 3:10-14: Freedom and Acceptance," ET 93 (7, 1982) 196. HAYS, R. B. The Faith of Jesus Christ (Chico CA 1983) 179, 196-98, 212, 222. CRONJÉ, J. VAN W. "Defamiliarization in the letter to the Galatians" in J. H. Petzer and P. J. Hartin, eds., A South African Perspective on the New Testament (FS B. M. Metzger; Leiden 1986) 218f. ARRONIZ, J. M. "Experiencia del espíritu y salvación (Gal 3, 1-5)," ScrVict 34 (1987) 67-101. COSGROVE, C. H. The Cross and the Spirit. A Study in the Argument and Theology of Galatians (Macon GA 1988) 2, 39f., 42n., 43, 48f., 186. BECKER, J. Paulus. Der Apostel der Völker (Tübingen 1989) 8, 171, 178, 241, 344, 396, 440f. HANSEN, G. W. Abraham in Galatians (Sheffield 1989) 109-12. SCHNELLE, U. Wandlungen im paulinischen

Denken (Stuttgart 1989) 57. SEGAL, A. F. Paul the Convert (New Haven/London 1990) 210. JOHNSON, J. F. "Paul's Argument from Experience. A Closer Look at Galatians 3:1-5," Conc 19 (1993) 234-37.

3:1-4,11 KLEIN, G. "Individualgeschichte und Weltgeschichte bei
21-31   Paulus" in Rekonstruktion und Interpretation (1969) 180-224.

3:1-2,5   MARTYN, J. L. "A Law-Observant Mission to Gentiles. The Background of Galatians" in M. P. O'Connor and D. N. Freedman, eds., Backgrounds for the Bible (Winona Lake/Indiana 1987) 199-214, esp. 204ff.

3:1,3   BETZ, H.D. Lukian von Samosata und Neue Testament (1961) 69, 125.

3:1-2   ORTKEMPER, F.-J. Das Kreuz in der Verkündigung des Apostels Paulus (1967) 26-28.

3:1   RETTIG, H.M. "Exegetische Analekten I" ThSK 3 (1830) 96-100. BURCH, V. "To Placard the Crucified (Gal. 3:1)" ET 30 (1918-1919) 232-33. BOVER, J.M. "'Quis vos fascinavit?' (Gal 3, 1)" VD 2 (1922) 240-42. SCHELKLE, K.H. Die Passion Jesu in der Verkündigung des Neuen Testaments (1949) 51f. GRANT, R.M. "Hellenistic Elements in Galatians" AThR 34 (1952) 223-26. BRETSCHER, P.G. "Light from Galatians 3:1 on Pauline Theology" CThM 34 (1963) 77-97. KRAMER, W. Christos Kyrios Gottessohn (1963) § 31a. JÜNGEL, E. Paulus und Jesus (1966) 275. ECKERT, J. Die urchristliche Verkündigung im Streit zwischen Paulus und seinen Gegnern nach dem Galaterbrief (1971) 10, 21, 44, 100. ELLIS, E. E. Prophecy and Hermeneutic in Early Christianity (Tübingen 1978) 72-79, 114. FRIEDRICH, G. "Die Bedeutung der Auferweckung Jesu nach Aussagen des Neuen Testaments" in Auf das Wort kommt es an. Gesammelte Aufsätze (Göttingen 1978) 359f. BYRNE, B. "Sons of God"-"Seed of Abraham" (Rome 1979) 142f., 147, 189. METZGER, B. M. "St. Jerome's explicit references to variant readings in manuscripts of the New Testament" in E. Best and R. McL. Wilson, eds., Text and Interpretation (FS M. Black; Cambridge 1979) 185. OLLROG, W.-H. Paulus und seine Mitarbeiter (Neukirchen/Vluyn 1979) 55, 207. BISER, E. Der Zeuge (Graz/Wien/Köln 1981) 47, 92, 133, 160, 165, 208, 258. MÜLLER, U. B. "Zur Rezeption gesetzeskritischer Jesusüberlieferung im frühen Christentum," NTS 27 (1981) 159. WEDER, H. Das Kreuz Jesu bei Paulus (Göttingen 1981) 182-86. HAYS, R. B. The Faith of Jesus Christ (Chico CA 1983) 7, 29, 118, 133, 143, 196-98, 237f. FREUND, G. und STEGEMANN, E., eds., Theologische Brosamen für Lothar Steiger (DBAT 5; Heidelberg 1985) 389. SCHIMANOWSKI, G. Weisheit und Messias (Tübingen 1985) 325. WALTER, N. "Paulus und die Gegner des Christusevangeliums in Galatien" in A. Vanhoye, ed., L'Apôtre Paul (Leuven 1986) 351-56. COSGROVE, C. H. The Cross and the Spirit. A Study in the Argument and Theology of Galatians (Macon GA 1988) 2, 3, 5f., 13, 27f., 35, 36n., 41, 79n., 149, 177f., 185. GREEN, J. B. The Death of Jesus (Tübingen 1988) 185f. NEYREY, J. H. "Bewitched in Galatia. Paul and Cultural Anthropology," CBQ 50 (1988) 72-100. SCHRAGE, W. " ' . . . den Juden ein Skandalon'? Der Anstoss des Kreuzes nach I Kor 1, 23" in E. Brocke and J. Seim, eds., Gottes Augapfel. Beiträge zur Erneuerung des Verhältnisses von Christen und Juden (Neukirchen-Vluyn ²1988) 61f. ELLIOT, J. H. "Paul, Galatians, and the Evil Eye," CThMi 17 (1990) 262-73. OLIVEIRA, A. DE, Die Diakonie der Gerechtigkeit und der Versöhnung in der Apologie des 2. Korinther-briefes. Analyse und Auslegung von 2 Kor 2, 14-4, 6; 5, 11-6, 10 (Münster 1990) 336.

3:2-5   KREMER, J. Pfingstbericht und Pfingstgeschehen. Eine exegetische Untersuchung zu Apg 2, 1-13 (Stuttgart 1973) 28-34. FULLER, D. P. Gospel and Law. Contrast or Continuum? (Grand Rapids 1980) 114-16. MINDE, H. J. VAN DER, "Theologia crucis und Pneumaaussagen bei Paulus," Catholica 34 (1980) 133. HAYS, R. B. The

Faith of Jesus Christ (Chico CA 1983) 108, 143-49, 211. RÄISÄNEN, H. The Torah and Christ (Helsinki 1986) 38. LIMBECK, M. Mit Paulus Christ sein. Sachbuch zur Person und Theologie des Apostels Paulus (Stuttgart 1989) 92. SEGAL, A. F. Paul the Convert (New Haven/London 1990) 211.

3:2,5   O'NEILL, J.C. The Recovery of Paul's Letter to the Galatians (1972) 46f.

3:2   JÜNGEL, E. Paulus und Jesus (1966) 57, 62. KERTELGE, K. "Rechtfertigung" bei Paulus (1967) 248, 298. VAN DÜLMEN.A. Die Theologie des Gesetzes bei Paulus (1968) 27-30, 190-93. ECKERT, J. Die urchristliche Verkündigung im Streit zwischen Paulus und seinen Gegnern nach dem Galaterbrief (1971) 152f. BORSE, U. Der Standort des Galaterbriefes (1972) 123f., 151. KÜMMEL, W.G. Einleitung in das Neue Testament (1973) 260f. TYSON, J.B. "'Works of Law' in Gal" JBL 92 (1973) 423-31. ZELLER, D. Juden und Heiden in der Mission des Paulus (1973) 94. BYRNE, B. "Sons of God"-"Seed of Abraham" (Rome 1979) 147, 148n., 150, 153n., 156. LADARIA, L. F. "Espíritu y justificación. A propósito de Gal 2, 16; 3, 2.5," EE 55 (1980) 111-15. DEIDUN, T. J. New Covenant Morality in Paul (Rome 1981) 46-49, 118f., 210f. MUELLER, P.-G. Der Traditionsprozess im Neuen Testament (Freiburg 1982) 223. HAYS, R. B. The Faith of Jesus Christ (Chico CA 1983) 109, 142, 179, 182, 198. GEWALT, D. "Die 'fides ex auditu' und die Taubstummen. Zur Aus-legungsgeschichte von Gal. 3, 2 und Röm. 10, 14-17," LiBi 58 (1986) 45-64. DOBBELER, A. VON, Glaube als Teilhabe (Tübingen 1987) 19-25. GASTON, L. Paul and the Torah (Vancouver 1987) 59, 69, 103f., 210. COSGROVE, C. H. The Cross and the Spirit. A Study in the Argument and Theology of Galatians (Macon GA 1988) 2, 32, 38f., 41f., 44, 46f., 52n., 114, 152, 175f. JOHNSON, E. E. The Function of Apocalyptic and Wisdom Traditions in Romans 9-11 (Atlanta GA 1989) 183, 187, 190. LIEBERS, R. Das Gesetz als Evangelium (Zürich 1989) 50-52. MARTIN, B. L. Christ and the Law in Paul (Leiden 1989) 5, 89, 116-18, 120, 127, 138, 146, 150. WILLIAMS, S. K. "The Hearing of Faith: ΑΚΟΗ ΠΙΣΤΕΩΣ in Galatians 3," NTS 35 (1989) 82-93. KOLLMANN, B. Ursprung und Gestalten der frühchristlichen Mahlfeier (Göttingen 1990) 119n.80.

3:3   STACEY, W.D. The Pauline View of Man (1956) 164f., 174-180. VAN DÜLMEN, A. Die Theologie des Gesetzes bei Paulus (1968) 195f. O'NEILL, J.C. The Recovery of Paul's Letter to the Galatians (1972) 47. KÜMMEL, W.G. Römer 7 uns das Bild des Menschen im Neuen Testament (1974) 17f. KÜMMEL, W. G. Römer 7 und das Bild des Menschen im Neuen Testament (München 1974) 17f., 30, 193. LULL, D. J. The Spirit in Galatia (Chico CA 1980) 103f. THISELTON, A. C. The Two Horizons (Grand Rapids 1980) 278f. HAYS, R. B. The Faith of Jesus Christ (Chico CA 1983) 154. DUNN, J. D. G. Jesus, Paul and the Law (London 1990) 175, 200, 202, 225, 245, 249.

3:4-18   CALLAN, T. "Pauline Midrash. The Exegetical Back-ground of Gal. 3:19b," JBL 99 (1980) 549.

3:4   BJERKELUND, C. J. "'Vergeblich' als Missionsergebnis bei Paulus" in J. Jervell and W. A. Meeks, eds., God's Christ and His People (FS N. A. Dahl; New York 1977) 175-91. BINDEMANN, W. Die Hoffnung der Schöpfung (Neukirchen 1983) 35, 37f. HAYS, R. B. The Faith of Jesus Christ (Chico CA 1983) 197.

3:5-13   WEDER, H. Neutestamentliche Hermeneutik (Zürich 1986) 357-83.

3:5   BORNKAMM/BARTH/HELD Überlieferung und Auslegung im Matthäus-Evangelium (1961) 258. SCHRAGE, W. Die konkreten Einzelgebote in der paulinischen Paränese (1961) 72, 90. DELLING, G. Taufe im Neuen Testament (1963) 119, 145. KÄSEMANN, E. Exegetische Versuche und Besinnungen (1964) I 293. PARRATT, J.K. "Romans i.11 and Galatians iii.5—Pauline Evidence for the Laying on of Hands?" ET 79 (1967/68) 151-52. VAN DÜLMEN, A. Die Theologie des Gesetzes bei Paulus (1968) 190-93. BORSE, U. Der Standort des Galaterbriefes (1972) 123f. BAUMERT, N. Täglich Sterben und Auferstehen. Der Literalsinn von 2 Kor 4, 12-5, 10 (1973) 277f., 318. KREMER, J. Pfingstbericht und Pfingstgeschehen. Eine exegetische Untersuchung zu Apg 2, 1-13 (Stuttgart 1973) 31f., 34. BYRNE, B. "Sons of God"-"Seed of Abraham" (Rome 1979) 147, 148n., 150, 153n. FULLER, D. P. Gospel and Law. Contrast or Continuum? (Grand Rapids 1980) 115f. GATZWEILER, K. "Der Paulinische Wunderbegriff" in A. Suhl, ed., Der Wunderbegriff im Neuen Testament (Darmstadt 1980) 318-84, 405f. LADARIA, L. F. "Espíritu y justificación. A propósito de Gál 2, 16; 3, 2.5," EstEc 55 (1980) 111-15. LULL, D. J. The Spirit in Galatia (Chico CA 1980) 69-71. NIELSEN, H. K. "Paulus' Verwendung des Begriffes Dynamis. Eine Replik zur Kreuztheologie" in S. Pedersen, ed., Die Paulinische Literatur und Theologie (Arhus/Göttingen 1980) 154f. HAYS, R. B. The Faith of Jesus Christ (Chico CA 1983) 179, 197-200, 238. DOBBELER, A. VON, Glaube als Teilhabe (Tübingen 1987) 19-25. GASTON, L. Paul and the Torah (Vancouver 1987) 59, 69, 103f., 210. NIELSEN, H. K. Heilung und Verkündigung (Leiden 1987) 2, 19, 189, 191, 197, 203f., 206, 209. COSGROVE, C. H. The Cross and the Spirit. A Study in the Argument and Theology of Galatians (Macon GA 1988) viii, 2, 32, 42, 44-48, 51, 60, 109, 118, 122, 152, 166, 173-76, 178. REBELL, W. Alles ist möglich dem, der glaubt (München 1989) 110, 120f. WILLIAMS, S. K. "The Hearing of Faith: ΑΚΟΗ ΠΙΣΤΕΩΣ in Galatians 3," NTS 35 (1989) 82-93.

3:6–4:31 SHEPARD, J.W. The Life and Letters of St.Paul (1950) 343-56. JEWETT, R. "Agitators and the Galatian Congregation" NTS 17 (1970-71) 209f.

3:6–4:20 LEON–DUFOUR, X. "Une lecture chrétienne de l'Ancien Testament: Galates 3:6 à 4:20" in L'Evangile hier et aujourd'hui (1968) 109-16.

3:6-4:11 BRINSMEAD, B. H. Galatians—Dialogical Response to Opponents (Chico CA 1982) 116ff.

3:6–4:7 DRANE, J. Paul: Libertine or Legalist? (1975) 24-38. SCHÜTZ, J.H. Paul and the Anatomy of Apostolic Authority (1975) 126-27. HAYS, R. B. The Faith of Jesus Christ (Chico CA 1983) 59f., 215. ALLAZ, J. et al., Chrétiens en conflit. L'Épître de Paul aux Galates (Geneva 1987) passim. HOFIUS, O. "'Rechtfertigung des Gottlosen' als Thema biblischer Theologie," JBTh 2 (1987) 79-105, esp. 88. COSGROVE, C. H. The Cross and the Spirit. A Study in the Argument and Theology of Galatians (Macon GA 1988) 15, 19f., 22. MARTYN, J. L. "Events in Galatia. Modified Covenantal Nomism versus God's Invasion of the Cosmos in the Singular Gospel: A Response to J. D. G. Dunn and B. R. Gaventa" in J. M. Bassler, ed., Pauline Theology, Volume 1: Thessalonians, Philippians, Galatians, Philemon (Minneapolis MN 1991) 166-74.

3:6ff. HAHN, F. Christologische Hoheitstitel (1963) 243. HAHN, F. Das Verständnis der Mission im Neuen Testament (1965) 88. JÜNGEL, E. Paulus und Jesus (1966) 52. NICKELS, P. Targum and the New Testament (1967) 74. GOPPELT, L. Christologie und Ethik (1968) 251ff. LUZ, U. Das Geschichtsverständnis des Paulus (1968) 149, 279ff. FREUND, G. und STEGEMANN, E., eds., Theologische Brosamen für Lothar Steiger (DBAT 5; Heidelberg 1985) 390. LUZ, U. "Paulinische Theologie als Biblische Theologie" in M. Klopfenstein et al., eds., Mitte der Schrift? Ein jüdisch-christliches Gespräch. Texte des Berner Symposions vom 6.-12. Januar 1985 (Bern etc. 1987) 119-47, esp. 136f. PETERSEN, N. R. Rediscovering Paul. Philemon and the Sociology of Paul's Narrative World (Philadelphia 1985) 223ff. SCHNELLE, U. Wandlungen im paulinischen Denken (Stuttgart 1989) 58f.

3:6-29 ELLIS, E. E. Prophecy and Hermeneutic in Early Christianity (Tübingen 1978) 74, 155, 162, 216f., 250. MOXNES, H. Theology in Conflict (Leiden 1980) 209-16.

HAYS, R. B. The Faith of Jesus Christ (Chico CA 1983) 195. PATTE, D. Preaching Paul (Philadelphia 1984) 25-27. MARTYN, J. L. "A Law-Observant Mission to Gentiles. The Background of Galatians," SJTh 38 (1985) 307-24. LEON-DUFOUR, X. Life and Death in the New Testament (San Francisco 1986) 181, 183. GASTON, L. Paul and the Torah (Vancouver 1987) 58-60, 88. WIESER, F. E. Die Abraham-vorstellungen im Neuen Testament (Bern/ Frankfurt/New York/Paris 1987) 40-50, 79-81. HANSEN, G. W. Abraham in Galatians (Sheffield 1989) 155f.

3:6-25   LULL, D. J. The Spirit in Galatia (Chico CA 1980) 153f. HAYS, R. B. The Faith of Jesus Christ (Chico CA 1983) 232.

3:6-24   ZIESLER, J.A. The Meaning of Righteousness in Paul (1972) 174-79.

3:6-18   BARRETT, C.K. From First Adam to Last (1962) 46f. HAYS, R. B. The Faith of Jesus Christ (Chico CA 1983) 154, 157. KOCH, D.-A. Die Schrift als Zeuge des Evangeliums (Tübingen 1986) 307-12.

3:6-14   JUNG, P. "Das paulinische Vokabular in Gal 3, 6-14" ZKTh 74 (1952) 439-49. VOS, J. Traditionsgeschichtliche Untersuchungen zur paulinischen Pneumatologie (1973) 88-93. ZELLER, D. Juden und Heiden in der Mission der Paulus (1973) 94f. MONTAGUE, G. T. The Holy Spirit (New York 1976) 194-96. MINDE, H. J. VAN DER, "Theologia crucis und Pneumaaussagen bei Paulus," Catholica 34 (1980) 138f. HAYS, R. B. The Faith of Jesus Christ (Chico CA 1983) 29, 222. HAACKER, K. "Glaube II" in TRE 13 (1984) 298. FREUND, G. und STEGEMANN, E., eds., Theolog-ische Brosamen für Lothar Steiger (DBAT 5; Heidelberg 1985) 392. KOCH, D.-A. Die Schrift als Zeuge des Evangeliums (Tübingen 1986) 224ff. BERGER, K. und COLPE, C., eds., Religionsgeschichtliches Textbuch zum Neuen Testament (Göttingen/Zürich 1987) 270. SEGAL, A. F. Paul the Convert (New Haven/London 1990) 118. PELSER, G. M. M. "The Opposition of Faith and Works as Persuasive Device in Galatians (3:6-14)," Neotestamentica 26 (1992) 389-405.

3:6-11   PAGELS, E.H. The Gnostic Paul (1975) 106-7.

3:6-9   BARRETT, C.K. From First Adam to Last (1962) 33f. MÜLLER, H. Die Auslegung alttestamentlichen Geschichtsstoffs bei Paulus (diss. Halle/Wittenberg 1960) 41f. DAVIES, W. D. The Gospel and the Land (London 1974) 176. MINDE, H.-J. VAN DER, Schrift und Tradition bei Paulus (München/Paderborn/Wien 1976) 127-30. HAYS, R. B. The Faith of Jesus Christ (Chico CA 1983) 194f., 198-206, 213, 237. JOHNSON, H. W. "The Paradigm of Abraham in Galatians 3:6-9," Trinity Journal 8 (1987) 179-99. HANSEN, G. W. Abraham in Galatians (Sheffield 1989) 112-16. ZIESLER, J. Pauline Christianity (Oxford 1990) 51, 66.

3:6-7   MUSSNER, F. "Theologische 'Wiedergutmachung.' AmBeispiel der Auslegung des Galaterbriefes" FrR 26 (1974) 7-11. BERGER, K. "Abraham" in TRE 1 (1977) 378. MUSSNER, F. Die Kraft der Wurzel (Freiburg/Basel/ Wien 1987) 59f.

3:6   MOORE, G.F. Judaism (1946) II 238. KÄSEMANN, E. Exegetische Versuche und Besinnungen (1964) II 183; New Testament Questions of Today (1969) 170. JÜNGEL, E. Paulus und Jesus (1966) 39. KERTELGE, K. "Rechtfertigung" bei Paulus (1967) 120, 122, 184, 192. BYRNE, B. "Sons of God"-"Seed of Abraham" (Rome 1979) 132, 147-50, 156, 160. HAYS, R. B. The Faith of Jesus Christ (Chico CA 1983) 165, 187, 199f. KOCH, D.-A. Die Schrift als Zeuge des Evangeliums (Tübingen 1986) 106, 243f. HANSEN, G. W. "Paul's Three-Dimensional Application of Genesis 15:6 in Galatians," Trinity Theological Journal [Singapore] 1 (1989) 59-77. DUNN, J. D. G. Jesus, Paul and the Law (London 1990) 68, 91, 140, 227, 256, 264n.59. HOWARD, G. Paul. Crisis in Galatia (Cambridge [2]1990) 54f., 57, 95. HONG, I.-G. The Law in Galatians (Sheffield 1993) 126-32.

3:7-9   HAYS, R. B. The Faith of Jesus Christ (Chico CA 1983) 201.

3:7   BLANK, J. Paulus und Jesus (1968) 258ff. JEWETT, P. K. Infant Baptism and the
           Covenant of Grace (Grand Rapids 1978) 236. BYRNE, B. "Sons of God"-"Seed of
           Abraham" (Rome 1979) 90n., 148-50. THISELTON, A. C. The Two Horizons
           (Grand Rapids 1980) 402. HAYS, R. B. The Faith of Jesus Christ (Chico CA 1983)
           150, 154, 198, 201-03, 206. FREUND, G. und STEGEMANN, E., eds., Theologische
           Brosamen für Lothar Steiger (DBAT 5; Heidelberg 1985) 389. GRAESSER, E. Der
           Alte Bund im Neuen (Tübingen 1985) 58, 69, 216, 222. HOWARD, G. Paul. Crisis
           in Galatia (Cambridge ²1990) 55-57. CHANCE, J. B. "The Seed of Abraham and the
           People of God. A Study of Two Pauls" in E. H. Lovering, ed., Society of Biblical
           Literature 1993 Seminar Papers (Atlanta 1993) 384-411.
3:8-9,14   SCHENK, W. Der Segen im Neuen Testament (1967) 42-46. WESTERMANN, C.
           Blessing (Philadelphia 1978) 70, 76-78, 98-101.
3:8-13   HAYS, R. B. The Faith of Jesus Christ (Chico CA 1983) 238.
3:8   HAHN, F. Christologische Hoheitstitel (1963) 385. JÜNGEL, E. Paulus und Jesus
           (1966) 56. KERTELGE, K. "Rechtfertigung" bei Paulus (1967) 124. GOPPELT, L.
           Christologie und Ethik (1968) 222-23. LUZ, U. Das Geschichtsverständnis des
           Paulus (1968) 111-12. BERGER, K. "Abraham" in TRE 1 (1977) 374. FRIEDRICH,
           G. "Das Gesetz des Glaubens Römer 3, 27" in Auf das Wort kommt es an.
           Gesammelte Aufsätze (Göttingen 1978) 119. BYRNE, B. "Sons of God"-"Seed of
           Abraham" (Rome 1979) 150, 153n., 155, 163, 186. WILLIAMS, S. K. "The
           'Righteousness of God' in Romans," JBL 99 (1980) 264f., 267. HAYS, R. B. The
           Faith of Jesus Christ (Chico CA 1983) 150, 158, 202-06, 209, 217, 238. KOCH, D.-
           A. Die Schrift als Zeuge des Evangeliums (Tübingen 1986) 124, 162f. JOHNSON,
           E. E. The Function of Apocalyptic and Wisdom Traditions in Romans 9-11 (Atlanta
           GA 1989) 189f. HOWARD, G. Paul. Crisis in Galatia (Cambridge ²1990) 54, 55, 57.
           ELLIS, E. E. The Old Testament in Early Christianity (Tübingen 1991) 3, 78, 90f.
3:9   BYRNE, B. "Sons of God"-"Seed of Abraham" (Rome 1979) 90n., 150, 150n.
           HAYS, R. B. The Faith of Jesus Christ (Chico CA 1983) 150, 154, 200-04, 206.
           COSGROVE, C. H. The Cross and the Spirit. A Study in the Argument and
           Theology of Galatians (Macon GA 1988) 2n., 32, 48-51, 60, 68, 85, 175. WOLTER,
           M. Die Pastoralbriefe als Paulustradition (Göttingen 1988) 38, 61.
3:10-25   HAYS, R. B. The Faith of Jesus Christ (Chico CA 1983) 219-21.
3:10-18   BARRETT, C.K. From First Adam to Last (1962) 34f., 40f. SCHMITT, R.
           Gottesgerechtigkeit—Heilsgeschichte—Israel in der Theologie des Paulus (Frank-
           furt/Bern/New York/Nancy 1984) 47-50.
3:10-14   SCHWEITZER, A. Die Mystik des Apostels Paulus (1954) 64, 124, 186, 204f., 207,
           216. ROBINSON, J.M. Kerygma und historischer Jesus (1960) 69, 178. WILLIAMS,
           J. A. A Conceptual History of Deuteronomism in the Old Testament, Judaism, and
           the New Testament (Ph.D. diss. Lousville 1976) 281. MOXNES, H. Theology in
           Conflict (Leiden 1980) 261, 263, 273. HILL, D. "Salvation Proclaimed: IV.
           Galatians 3:10-14: Freedom and Acceptance," ET 93 (7, 1982) 196-200. WILC-
           KENS, U. "Statements on the Development of Paul's View of the Law" in M. D.
           Hooker and S. G. Wilson, eds., Paul and Paulinism (FS C. K. Barrett; London 1982)
           21f. HAYS, R. B. The Faith of Jesus Christ (Chico CA 1983) 194f., 206-13.
           HAACKER, K. "Glaube II" in TRE 13 (1984) 298. DUNN, J. D. G. "Works of the
           Law and the Curse of the Law (Galatians 3.10-14)," NTS 31 (1985) 523-42.
           LAMBRECHT, J. "Gesetzes-verständnis bei Paulus" in K. Kertelge, ed., Das Gesetz
           im Neuen Testament (Freiburg/Basel/Wien 1986) 108-26.HANSEN, G. W. Abraham
           in Galatians (Sheffield 1989) 116-27. THIELMAN, F. From Plight to Solution
           (Leiden 1989) 11, 49, 60, 65-72, 86, 113. DUNN, J. D. G. Jesus, Paul and the Law
           (London 1990) 5, 215-41, 248, 249. STANLEY, C. D. "'Under a Curse'. A Fresh

Reading of Galatians 3.10-14," NTS 36 (1990) 481-511. LAMBRECHT, J. "Vloek en zegen. Een studie van Galaten 3, 10-14," Collationes 21 (1991) 133-57.

3:10-13   SCHOEPS, H.-J. Paulus (1959) 183-92. LONGENECKER, R.N. Paul Apostle of Liberty (1964) 120f., 123f., 147f. WILCKENS, U. "Was heisst bei Paulus: 'Aus Werken des Gesetzes wird kein Mensch gerecht'?" in Evangelisch—Katholischer Kommentar zum Neuen Testament (Vorarbeiten Heft I, 1969) 57-65. HÜBNER, H. Das Gesetz bei Paulus. Ein Beitrag zum Werden der paulinischen Theologie (Göttingen 1978) 39-43. KOCH, D.-A. Die Schrift als Zeuge des Evangeliums (Tübingen 1986) 120, 265-69. LUZ, U. "Paulinische Theologie als Biblische Theologie" in M. Klopfenstein et al., eds., Mitte der Schrift? Ein jüdisch-christliches Gespräch. Texte des Berner Symposions vom 6.-12. Januar 1985 (Bern etc. 1987) 119-47, esp. 130. MULLER, E. C. Trinity and Marriage in Paul (New York/Bern/Frankfurt/Paris 1990) 58f., 367. BRASWELL, J. P. "'The Blessing of Abraham' versus 'the Curse of the Law'. Another Look at Gal 3:10-13," WThJ 53 (1991) 73-91.

3:10-12   BRING, R. "Till frågan om Pauli syn på lagens förhållande till tron. En studie över Gal. 3:10-12 och Rom. 10:2-8" SvTK 21 (1945) 26-54. ELLIS, E.E. Paul's Use of the Old Testament (1957) 22, 124, 138, 152, 157, 180, 187. BANDSTRA, A.J. The Law and the Elements of the World (1964) 116ff. LUZ, U. Das Geschichtsverständnis des Paulus (1968) 149ff. FULLER, D.P. "Paul and the Works of the Law" WThJ 38 (1975) 28-42. MINDE, H.-J. VAN DER, Schrift und Tradition bei Paulus (München/Paderborn/Wien 1976) 130-32. VIELHAUER, P. "Paulus und das Alte Testament" in Oikodome [G. Klein, ed.] (München 1979) 205. FULLER, D. P. Gospel and Law. Contrast or Continuum? (Grand Rapids 1980) 88-105. SMEND, R. and LUZ, U. Gesetz (Stuttgart/Berlin/Köln/Mainz 1981) 94f. BRING, R. Paulus lagen och konsten att översätta Bibeln (Lund 1982) passim. HAYS, R. B. The Faith of Jesus Christ (Chico CA 1983) 219f. RÄISÄNEN, H. Paul and the Law (Tübingen 1983) 55, 94-96, 109, 177. KLEIN, G. "Gesetz III" in TRE 13 (1984) 68. SANDERS, E. P. Paul, the Law, and the Jewish People (London 1985) 20-24, 26, 52n.21, 53n.22, 184. RÄISÄNEN, H. The Torah and Christ (Helsinki 1986) 14. DOBBELER, A. VON, Glaube als Teilhabe (Tübingen 1987) 149f. COSGROVE, C. H. The Cross and the Spirit. A Study in the Argument and Theology of Galatians (Macon GA 1988) 52f., 60f. LIEBERS, R. Das Gesetz als Evangelium (Zürich 1989) 76-78.

3:10-11   SCHRAGE, W. Die konkreten Einzelgebote in der paulinischen Paränese (1961) 94. WILLIAMS, J. A. A Conceptual History of Deuteronomism in the Old Testament, Judaism, and the New Testament (Ph.D. diss. Lousville 1976) 276.

3:10   NOTH, M. "Die mit des Gesetzes Werken umgehen, die sind unter dem Fluch. Gal. 3, 10" in In piam memoriam Alexander von Bulmerincq (1938) 127-145. BULTMANN, R. Theologie des Neuen Testaments (1965) 263f. JÜNGEL, E. Paulus und Jesus (1966) 48. VAN DÜLMEN, A. Die Theologie des Gesetzes bei Paulus (1968) 32f. BUJARD, W. Stilanalytische Untersuchungen zum Kolosserbrief (1973) 180f. HÜBNER, H. "Gal 3, 10 und die Herkunft des Paulus" KuD 19 (3, 1973) 215-31. MUSSNER, F. "Theologische 'Wieder-gutmachung'. Am Beispiel der Auslegung des Galaterbriefes" FrR 26 (1974) 7-11. FRIEDRICH, G. "Das Gesetz des Glaubens Römer 3, 27" in Auf das Wort kommt es an. Gesammelte Aufsätze (Göttingen 1978) 117. SANDERS, E. P. "On the Qestion of Fulfilling the Law in Paul and Rabbinic Judaism" in E. Bammel, C. K. Barrett and W. D. Davies, eds., Donum Gentilicium (FS D. Daube; Oxford 1978) 105. BYRNE, B. "Sons of God"-"Seed of Abraham" (Rome 1979) 92n., 150f., 152, 154, 154n., 155n. FULLER, D. P. Gospel and Law. Contrast or Continuum? (Grand Rapids 1980) 89-104. HILL, D. "Salvation Proclaimed: IV. Galatians 3:10-14: Freedom and Acceptance," ET 93 (7, 1982) 197. HAYS, R. B. The Faith of Jesus Christ (Chico CA 1983) 177, 206. LÜDEMANN, G. Paulus, der Heidenapostel, Band II (Göttingen 1983) 196f. HEILIGENTHAL, R. "Gebot" in TRE 12 (1984) 126. KLEIN, G. "Gesetz III" in TRE 13 (1984) 66, 67. MOHRLANG, R. Matthew and Paul (Cambridge 1984) 28f., 184. SCHREINER, T. R. "Is Perfect Obedience to the Law Possible? A Re-examination of Galatians 3:10," JEThS 27 (1984) 151-60. HÜBNER, H. "Was heisst bei Paulus 'Werke des Gesetzes'?" in E. Grässer und O. Merk, eds., Glaube und Eschatologie (FS W. G. Kümmel; Tübingen 1985) 130f. SANDERS, E. P. Paul, the Law, and the Jewish People (London 1985) 25f., 27, 28f., 51n.17, 54n.35, 57n.64, 87n.6, 115n.6, 150, 161. KOCH, D.-A. Die Schrift als Zeuge des Evangeliums (Tübingen 1986) 120f., 163-65, 249ff. BERGER, K. und COLPE, C., eds., Religions-geschichtliches Textbuch zum Neuen Testament (Göttingen/Zürich 1987) 271f. BETZ, O. Jesus. Der Messias Israels (Tübingen 1987) 72, 331. GASTON, L. Paul and the Torah (Vancouver 1987) 30, 69, 103, 106, 210f. MUSSNER, F. Die Kraft der Wurzel (Freiburg/Basel/Wien 1987) 61f. COSGROVE, C. H. The Cross and the Spirit. A Study in the Argument and Theology of Galatians (Macon GA 1988) 48f., 52-54. HOFIUS, O. Paulusstudien (Tübingen 1989) 53, 60, 68, 80, 82f., 117, 127, 130. JOHNSON, E. E. The Function of Apocalyptic and Wisdom Traditions in Romans 9-11 (Atlanta GA 1989) 153, 183, 187f., 190. LIEBERS, R. Das Gesetz als Evangelium (Zürich 1989) 52-54. MARTIN, B. L. Christ and the Law in Paul (Leiden 1989) 5, 32, 52, 86-88, 91, 100, 102f., 112, 138, 146. DUNN, J. D. G. Jesus, Paul and the Law (London 1990) 205n.43, 215, 226f., 228f., 231, 234n.46, 235nn.48.51.53, 237, 249, 251, 261n.38, 262n. 44. HOWARD, G. Paul. Crisis in Galatia (Cambridge ²1990) 16, 54, 58-60, 62, 64. OLIVEIRA, A. DE, Die Diakonie der Gerechtigkeit und der Versöhnung in der Apologie des 2. Korintherbriefes. Analyse und Auslegung von 2 Kor 2, 14-4, 6; 5, 11-6, 10 (Münster 1990) 391n.664. GEORGI, D. Theocracy in Paul's Praxis and Theology (Minneapolis 1991) 36f., 39. SCOTT, J. M. "Paul's Use of Deuteronomic Tradition," JBL 112 (1993) 645-65, esp. 657-59.

3:11-13   LESQUIVIT, C. "Qui a la justice de la foi vivra" Témoignages 44 (1954) 3-14.
3:11-12   STROBEL, A. Untersuchungen sum eschatologischen Verzögerungsproblem (1961) 191-92. HERR, T. Naturrecht aus der kritischen Sicht des Neuen Testaments (München 1976) 112. SANDERS, E. P. "On the Qestion of Fulfilling the Law in Paul and Rabbinic Judaism" in E. Bammel, C. K. Barrett and W. D. Davies, eds., Donum Gentilicium (FS D. Daube; Oxford 1978) 106. HAYS, R. B. The Faith of Jesus Christ (Chico CA 1983) 216. BEKER, J. C. "Paul's Letter to the Romans as Model for a Biblical Theology. Some Preliminary Observations" in J. T. Butler et al., eds., Understanding the Word (FS B. W. Anderson; Sheffield 1985) 359-67, esp. 364f. DUNN, J. D. G. Jesus, Paul and the Law (London 1990) 215, 226, 227f., 231. VOS, J. S. "Die hermeneutische Antinomie bei Paulus (Galater 3.11-12; Römer 10.5-10)," NTS 38 (1992) 254-70.

3:11   CHADWICK, G.A. "The Just Shall Live by Faith" Exp 7th series (1906) 178-82. RUFFENACH, F. "'Iustus ex fide vivit' (Gal. 3, 11)" VD 3 (1923) 337-40. HANSE, H. "ΔΗΛΟΝ (zu Gal 3, 11)" ZNW 34 (1935) 299-303. MOORE, G.F. Judaism (1946) II 84. SCHRAGE, W. Die konkreten Einzelgebote in der paulinischen Paränese (1961) 85, 229. BRAUN, H. Qumran und das Neue Testament (1966) II 171, 308, 321-22. JÜNGEL, E. Paulus und Jesus (1966) 17, 39, 43, 61. KERTELGE, K. "Rechtfertigung" bei Paulus (1967) 90, 93, 115, 150. VAN DÜLMEN, A. Die Theologie des Gesetzes bei Paulus (1968) 32-34. LUZ, U. Das Geschichtsverständnis des Paulus (1968) 101. HEROLD, G. Zorn und Gerechtigkeit Gottes bei Paulus. Eine Untersuchung zu Röm. 1, 16-18 (1973) 170-84. ELLIS, E. E. Prophecy and

Hermeneutic in Early Christianity (Tübingen 1978) 193, 204, 217, 224. BYRNE, B. "Sons of God"-"Seed of Abraham" (Rome 1979) 93, 151f. VIELHAUER, P. "Paulus und das Alte Testament" in Oikodome [G. Klein, ed.] (München 1979) 213f. FULLER, D. P. Gospel and Law. Contrast or Continuum? (Grand Rapids 1980) 97f. STOCKMEIER, P. "Christlicher Glaube und antike Religiosität" in ANRW II.23.2 (1980) 883. HAYS, R. B. The Faith of Jesus Christ (Chico CA 1983) 142.150-58, 174, 182f., 201, 207, 209, 217, 239, 267. HÄRING, H. Das Problem des Bösen in der Theologie (Darmstadt 1985) 35. KOCH, D.-A. Die Schrift als Zeuge des Evangeliums (Tübingen 1986) 127ff. BERGER, K. und COLPE, C., eds., Religions-geschichtliches Textbuch zum Neuen Testament (Göttingen/Zürich 1987) 270f. DOBBELER, A. VON, Glaube als Teilhabe (Tübingen 1987) 152-54. LUZ, U. "Paulinische Theologie als Biblische Theologie" in M. Klopfenstein et al., eds., Mitte der Schrift? Ein jüdisch-christliches Gespräch. Texte des Berner Symposions vom 6.-12. Januar 1985 (Bern etc. 1987) 119-47, esp. 135f. COSGROVE, C. H. The Cross and the Spirit. A Study in the Argument and Theology of Galatians (Macon GA 1988) 32, 48, 54, 56f., 60, 68, 134, 153, 173, 175. HAYS, R. B. "'The Righteous One' as Eschatological Deliverer. A Case Study in Paul's Apocalyptic Hermeneutics" in J. Marcus and M. L. Soards, eds., Apocalyptic and the New Testament (FS J. L. Martyn; Sheffield 1989) 191-215, esp. 209-11. MARTIN, B. L. Christ and the Law in Paul (Leiden 1989) 5, 19f., 85, 87-89, 91, 117, 122, 127, 146. HOWARD, G. Paul. Crisis in Galatia (Cambridge [2]1990) 54, 58, 62f., 99.

3:12   KÄSEMANN, E. Exegetische Versuche und Besinnungen (1964) II 78; New Testament Questions of Today (1969) 76. VAN DÜLMEN, A. Die Theologie des Gesetzes bei Paulus (1968) 34f. RIDDERBOS, H. Paul. An Outline of His Theology (Grand Rapids 1975) 153-56. BYRNE, B. "Sons of God"-"Seed of Abraham" (Rome 1979) 93n., 94, 151nn., 152, 155, 162n. BERGMEIER, R. Glaube als Gabe nach Johannes (Stutt-gart 1980) 238n.33. FULLER, D. P. Gospel and Law. Contrast or Continuum? (Grand Rapids 1980) 98f., 120n.45. HILL, D. "Salvation Proclaimed: IV. Galatians 3:10-14: Freedom and Acceptance," ET 93 (7, 1982) 198. HAYS, R. B. The Faith of Jesus Christ (Chico CA 1983) 150f., 182, 207, 221. KOCH, D.-A. Die Schrift als Zeuge des Evangeliums (Tübingen 1986) 120. MERKLEIN, H. Studien zu Jesus und Paulus (Tübingen 1987) 2, 10, 14, 28, 41, 48, 72, 94. COSGROVE, C. H. The Cross and the Spirit. A Study in the Argument and Theology of Galatians (Macon GA 1988) 48, 54f., 59f., 90.

3:13-29   COSGROVE, C. H. "The Mosaic Law Preaches Faith. A Study in Galatians 3," WThJ 41 (1978) 146-164.

3:13, 16,   BLOM, A.H. "Handhaving mijner verklaring van Gal.
20   III:13, 16, 20. Antwoord aan Dr. J.J.Prins" TT 12 (1878) 614-25.

3:13-18   HAYS, R. B. The Faith of Jesus Christ (Chico CA 1983) 220f.

3:13-14   SCHWEIZER, A. "Die Lehre des Apostels Paulus vom erlösenden Tode Christi, von Galat. 3, 13 und 14 aus beleuchtet" ThSK 31 (1858) 425-73. FEINE, P. Das gesetz-freie Evangelium des Paulus (1899) 199-203. BURTON, E.DeW. "Redemption from the Curse of the Law (Exposition of Gal. 3:13-14)" American Journal of Theology II (1907) 624-46. STANLEY, D.M. Christ's Resurrection in Pauline Soteriology (1961) 152-54. THÜSING, W. Per Christum in Deum (1965) 85ff. WOLFF, H.W. Wegweisung (1965) 10, 92. BLANK, J. Paulus und Jesus (1968)262ff. LUZ, U. Das Geschichtsverständnis des Paulus (1968) 152. ECKERT, J. Die urchristliche Ver-kündigung im Streit zwischen Paulus und seinen Gegnern nach dem Galaterbrief (1971) 110f. PAGELS, E.H. The Gnostic Paul (1975) 107. MOXNES, H. "Fri fra loven. Jesu død og misjons-teologien i Galaterbrevet [Free from the Law. The Death of Jesus and the Theology of Mission in Galatians]," NTM 30 (1976) 235-45.

MINDE, H.-J. VAN DER, Schrift und Tradition bei Paulus (München/Pader-born/ Wien 1976) 132-34. BYRNE, B. "Sons of God"-"Seed of Abraham" (Rome 1979) 94, 152-57, 179, 189, 214. BRUCE, F. F. "The Curse of the Law" in M. D. Hooker and S. G. Wilson, eds., Paul and Paulinism (FS C. K. Barrett; London 1982) 27-36. HAYS, R. B. The Faith of Jesus Christ (Chico CA 1983) 29, 86-92, 110-21, 125, 127, 134, 139, 175, 201, 207f., 230, 237, 255. RÄISÄNEN, H. Paul and the Law (Tübingen 1983) 19f. DIETZFEL-BINGER, C. Die Berufung des Paulus als Ur-sprung seiner Theologie (Neukirchen 1985) 37f., 134, 136. DONALDSON, T. L. "The 'Curse of the Law' and the Inclusion of the Gentiles: Galatians 3.13-14," NTS 32 (1986) 94-112. MALINA B. J. Christian Origins and Cultural Anthropology (Atlanta 1986) 135. OSTEN-SACKEN, P. VON DER, Evangelium und Tora: Auf-sätze zu Paulus (München 1987) 19, 21, 26, 172. COSGROVE, C. H. The Cross and the Spirit. A Study in the Argument and Theology of Galatians (Macon GA 1988) 36, 61, 143, 177-79, 193. HOFIUS, O. Paulusstudien (Tübingen 1989) 63f., 73, 120, 126, 130, 149, 166. VOLLENWEIDER, S. Freiheit als neue Schöpfung (Göttingen 1989) 301, 402. DUNN, J. D. G. Jesus, Paul and the Law (London 1990) 5, 106, 228-30, 232, 233n.26, 236n.66, 237, 248, 257. HOOKER, M. D. From Adam to Christ. Essays on Paul (Cambridge 1990) 60f., 174. SÖDING, T. "Kreuzes-theologie und Rechtfertigungslehre. Zur Verbindung von Christologie und Soteriologie im Er-sten Korintherbrief und im Galaterbrief," Catholica 46 (1992) 31-60.

3:13   BÄHR, D. "Exegetische Erörterungen: II. Gal. 3, 13" ThSK 22 (1849) 917-35. HOLZMEISTER, U. "De Christi crucifixione quid e Deut 21, 22s. et Gal. 3, 13 con-sequatur" Biblica 27 (1946) 18-29. SCHELKLE, K.-H. Die Passion Jesu in der Ver-kündigung des Neuen Testaments (1949) 192f. DENNEY, J. The Death of Christ (1956) 91f. LIGHTFOOT, J.B. "The Interpretation of Deut. xxi. 23" in The Epistle of St. Paul to the Galatians (1957) 152-54. SANDMEL, S. The Genius of Paul (1958) 92-93. CERFAUX, L. Christ in the Theology of St.Paul (1959) 23f. SCHOEPS, H.-J. Paulus (1959) 186ff. LYONNET, S. "L'emploi paulinien de *exagorazein* au sens de 'redimere' est-il attesté dans la litterature grecque?" Biblica 42 (1, 1961) 86-89. FITZMYER, J.A. NTS 7 (1960-61) 324f. SABOURIN, L. "Le Christ fait 'péché' (2 Co 5 21) et 'malédiction' (Ga 3 13): Le sens de ces formules dans l'histoire de l'exégèse" in Rédemption sacrificielle. Une enquête (1961) 11-160. SCHWEIZER, E. Erniedrigung und Erhöhung bei Jesus und seinen Nachfolgern (1962) § 9ad. KRAMER, W. Christos Kyrois Gottessohn (1963) § 4b. MORRIS, L. The Apostolic Preaching of the Cross (1965) 62ff. KERTELGE, K. "Rechtfertigung" bei Paulus (1967) 209-12. NICKELS, P. Targum and the New Testament (1967) 74. ORTKEMPER, F.-J. Das Kreuz in der Verkündigung des Apostels Paulus (1967) 10-18. VAN DÜLMEN, A. Die Theologie des Gesetzes bei Paulus (1968) 35. HOOKER, M.D. "Interchange in Christ" JThS 22 (2, 1971) 349-61. MAUSER, U. Gottesbild und Menschwerdung (1971) 163-66, 171-74. BORSE, U. Der Standort des Galaterbriefes (1972) 60f., 75f. DELLING, G. Der Kreuzestod Jesu in der urchrist-lichen Verkündigung (1972) 20-22. EDWARDS, E.G. Christ, a Curse, and the Cross (diss. Princeton Theol. Seminary 1972). KRAENKL, E. Jesus der Knecht Gottes (1972) 111f. STRUYS, T. "Galaten 3, 13 en de Septuagint" GThT 72 (2, 1972) 86-99. VAN UNNIK, W.C. "Jesus: Anathema or Kyrois (1 Cor 12:3)" in Christ and the Spirit in the New Testament. In Honour of C.F.D. Moule (1973) 120f. RUPPERT, L. Jesus als der leidende Gerechte? (Stuttgart 1972) 59. RIDDERBOS, H. Paul. An Outline of His Theology (Grand Rapids 1975) 190-96. WILLIAMS, J. A. A Con-ceptual History of Deuteronomism in the Old Testament, Judaism, and the New Testament (Ph.D. diss. Lousville 1976) 275, 278. WILCOX, M. "'Upon the Tree'—Deut 21:22-23 in the New Testament," JBL 96 (1977) 85-99. DALY, R. J.

Christian Sacrifice (Washington 1978) 238f. FRIEDRICH, G. "Die Bedeutung der Auferweckung Jesu nach Aussagen des Neuen Testaments" in Auf das Wort kommt es an. Gesammelte Aufsätze (Göttingen 1978) 360. FRIEDRICH, G. "Freiheit und Liebe im ersten Korintherbrief" in Auf das Wort kommt es an. Gesammelte Aufsätze (Göttingen 1978) 180. BYRNE, B. "Sons of God"-"Seed of Abraham" (Rome 1979) 95, 147, 152-55, 182, 203, 214, 231. VIELHAUER, P. "Paulus und das Alte Testament" in Oikodome [G. Klein, ed.] (München 1979) 204. PLÜMACHER, E. "Bibel" in TRE 6 (1980) 17. THISELTON, A. C. The Two Horizons (Grand Rapids 1980) 270. BISER, E. Der Zeuge (Graz/Wien/ Köln 1981) 96, 98, 102, 108, 194, 265. KIM, S. The Origin of Paul's Gospel (Tübingen 1981) 46f., 275-77. MÜLLER, U. B. "Zur Rezeption gesetzeskritischer Jesusüberlieferung im frühen Christentum," NTS 27 (1981) 159. WEDER, H. Das Kreuz Jesu bei Paulus (Göttingen 1981) 186-93. BETZ, O. "Probleme des Prozesses Jesu" in ANRW II.25.1 (1982) 606-12. HAYS, R. B. The Faith of Jesus Christ (Chico CA 1983) 88-91, 112f., 115, 117, 120, 127f., 134, 188, 207f., 228, 230, 256, 262. RÄISÄNEN, H. Paul and the Law (Tübingen 1983) 9, 17, 21, 47, 58-61, 151, 158, 205, 249-51. STUHL-MACHER, P. "Sühne oder Versöhnung? Randbemerkungen zu Gerhard Friedrichs Studie: 'Die Verkündigung des Todes Jesu im Neuen Testament" in U. Luz und H. Weder, eds., Die Mitte des Neuen Testaments (FS E. Schweizer; Göttingen 1983) 304-07. THEISSEN, G. Psychologische Aspekte paulinischer Theologie (Göttingen 1983) 152, 229, 311. KLEIN, G. "Gesetz III" in TRE 13 (1984) 66. KLEINKNECHT, K. T. Der leidende Gerechtfertigte (Tübingen 1984) 320. LØNNING, I. "Gott VIII" in TRE 13 (1984) 701. SCHENKE, G. Die Dreigestaltige Protennoia (Berlin 1984) 162. DIETZFELBINGER, C. Die Berufung des Paulus als Ursprung seiner Theologie (Neukirchen 1985) 35, 37, 114, 131, 135. POBEE, J. S. Persecution and Martyrdom in the Theology of Paul (Sheffield 1985) 4, 48, 55, 56f., 77. RUBINKIEWICZ, R. "Ukrzyżowanie Jezusa w świetle 4QpNa 1 1-12 i Zwoju Świątyni 64, 6-13 [Die Kreuzigung Jesu im Lichte von 4QNah I, 1-12 und Tempelrolle 64, 6-13]," RTK 32 (1985) 63-73. SANDERS, E. P. Paul, the Law, and the Jewish People (London 1985) 25f., 47, 68f., 82, 88n.20. KOCH, D.-A. Die Schrift als Zeuge des Evangeliums (Tübingen 1986) 124ff., 165f., 249f., 287f. RÄISÄNEN, H. The Torah and Christ (Helsinki 1986) 9, 87ff. BERGER, K. und COLPE, C., eds., Religionsgeschichtliches Textbuch zum Neuen Testament (Göttingen/Zürich 1987) 271f. BETZ, O. Jesus. Der Messias Israels (Tübingen 1987) 69, 71, 331. DUNN, J. D. G. "'A Light to the Gentiles': the Significance of the Damascus Road Christophany for Paul" in L. D. Hurst and N. T. Wright, eds., The Glory of Christ in the New Testament (FS G. B. Caird; Oxford 1987) 256, 264f. MERKLEIN, H. Studien zu Jesus und Paulus (Tübingen 1987) 1, 7f., 10, 12f., 15, 23-25, 28f., 31-35, 39f., 50f., 54, 72f., 88-90, 93, 104, 187, 191, 231n.41, 258n.66, 380. OSTEN-SACKEN, P. VON DER, Evangelium und Tora: Aufsätze zu Paulus (München 1987) 15, 95f., 172. DOWNING, F. G. Christ and the Cynics (Sheffield 1988) 79. JONGE, M. DE, Christo-logy in Context. The Earliest Christian Response to Jesus (Philadelphia 1988) 37, 113, 118, 217n.8, 227n.13, 231n.37. SCHRAGE, W. " ' . . . den Juden ein Skandalon'? Der Anstoss des Kreuzes nach I Kor 1, 23" in E. Brocke and J. Seim, eds., Gottes Augapfel. Beiträge zur Erneuerung des Verhältnisses von Christen und Juden (Neukirchen/Vluyn ²1988) 61ff. BREYTENBACH, C. Versöhnung (Neukirchen/Vluyn 1989) 130, 139, 140f., 167, 170n., 211, 213n. CANEDAY, A. "'Redeemed From the Curse of the Law': The Use of Deut 21:22-23 in Gal 3:13," Trinity Journal 10 (1989) 185-209. LOHFINK, G. Studien zum Neuen Testament (Stuttgart 1989) 151. MARTIN, B. L. Christ and the Law in Paul (Leiden 1989) 2, 5, 19f., 37f., 41, 52f., 87-89, 97, 101-04, 109, 111-14, 118, 132, 134, 156. MELL,

U. Neue Schöpfung (Berlin/New York 1989) 295, 391. SCHNELLE, U. Wandlungen im paulinischen Denken (Stuttgart 1989) 21. DUNN, J. D. G. Jesus, Paul and the Law (London 1990) 93, 99, 235n.57, 236n.61, 237. HAMERTON-KELLY, R. G. "Sacred Violence and the Curse of the Law (Galatians 3.13): The Death of Christ as a Sacri-ficial Travesty," NTS 36 (1990) 98-118. HOOKER, M. D. From Adam to Christ. Essays on Paul (Cambridge 1990) 13f., 16f., 33, 42, 61, 92, 99. HOWARD, G. Paul. Crisis in Galatia (Cambridge ²1990) 48, 54, 58, 60f., 64. MULLER, E. C. Trinity and Marriage in Paul (New York/ Bern/Frankfurt/Paris 1990) 55f., 85-87, 413. OLIVEIRA, A. DE, Die Diakonie der Gerechtigkeit und der Ver-söhnung in der Apologie des 2. Korintherbriefes. Analyse und Auslegung von 2 Kor 2, 14-4, 6; 5, 11-6, 10 (Münster 1990) 390f. HONG, I.-G. The Law in Galatians (Sheffield 1993) 77-79.

3:14-22 CERFAUX, L. Christ in the Theology of St. Paul (1959) 224-26, 502-4.

3:14-18 SCHOEPS, H.-J. Paulus (1959) 186ff.

3:14,29 PITTA, A. "La funzione 'eufonica' dell 'articolo in Gv 8, 39b.c; Gal 3:14, 29," RivB 35 (1987) 321-25.

3:14   SOKOLOWSKI, E. Die Begriffe Geist und Leben bei Paulus (1903) 81ff. DELLING, G. Die Taufe im Neuen Testament (1963) 106, 119. DUNN, J.D.G. Baptism in the Holy Spirit (1970) 107ff. BORSE, U. Der Standort des Galaterbriefes (1972) 124f. WILLIAMS, J. A. A Conceptual History of Deuteronomism in the Old Testament, Judaism, and the New Testament (Ph.D. diss. Lousville 1976) 275, 277, 278. BYRNE, B. "Sons of God"-"Seed of Abraham" (Rome 1979) 147, 150, 153n., 155-57, 175, 182n., 183n. HAYS, R. B. The Faith of Jesus Christ (Chico CA 1983) 87, 113-15, 123, 140, 153, 158, 167, 170, 206, 208-12, 219, 225. COSGROVE, C. H. The Cross and the Spirit. A Study in the Argument and Theology of Galatians (Macon GA 1988) 2, 32, 38, 48-52, 59, 60, 63, 68, 85, 104, 105n., 152, 175. WILLIAMS, S. K. "Promise in Galatians. A Reading of Paul's Reading of Scripture," JBL 107 (1988) 709-720. CLABEAUX, J. J. The Lost Edition of the Letters of Paul (CBQ.MS; Washington 1989) 103-04, 111, 151. MARTIN, B. L. Christ and the Law in Paul (Leiden 1989) 87, 89, 101-03, 105, 118, 120, 134, 150. DUNN, J. D. G. Jesus, Paul and the Law (London 1990) 99, 235n.57, 248, 262n.45, 263n.53. HOWARD, G. Paul. Crisis in Galatia (Cambridge ²1990) 55, 61, 63, 64. MULLER, E. C. Trinity and Marriage in Paul (New York/Bern/ Frankfurt/Paris 1990) 113f.

3:15–4:11 VAN DÜLMEN, A. Die Theologie des Gesetzes bei Paulus (1968) 36-51.

3:15–4:7 CONRAT, M. "Das Erbrecht im Galaterbrief (3, 15-4, 7)" ZNW 5 (1904) 204-27. VOS, J.S. Traditionsgeschichtliche Untersuchungen zur Paulinischen Pneumatologie (1973) 93-102.

3:15ff. LUZ, U. Das Geschichtsverständnis des Paulus (1968) 182-86. HUGHES, J. J. "Hebrews ix 15ff and Galatians iii 15ff. A Study in Covenant Practice and Procedure," NovT 21 (1979) 27-96. HAYS, R. B. The Faith of Jesus Christ (Chico CA 1983) 234. STEGEMANN, E. "Das Gesetz ist nicht wider die Verheis-sungen—Thesen zu Gal 3, 15-29" in G. Freund und E. Stegemann, eds., Theologische Brosamen für Lothar Steiger (DBAT 5; Heidelberg 1985) 389-95. RÄISÄ-NEN, H. The Torah and Christ (Helsinki 1986) 364.

3:15-29 FINDEISEN, H. "Zu Galater 3:15-29" NKZ 9 (1898) 241-50. STOLLE, V. "Die Eins in Gal 3, 15-29" Theokratia 2 (1973) 204-13. ZELLER, D. Juden und Heiden in der Mission des Paulus (1973) 96ff. GIBLIN, C.H. "Three Monotheistic Texts in Paul" CBQ 37 (1975) 527-47.

3:15-26 BRING, R. Christus und das Gesetz (1969) 93-111. SANDERS, E. P. Paul, the Law, and the Jewish People (London 1985) 26f.

3:15-25 HAYS, R. B. The Faith of Jesus Christ (Chico CA 1983) 227. RÄISÄNEN, H. The Torah and Christ (Helsinki 1986) 10.

3:15-24 DRANE, J.W. Paul: Libertine or Legalist? (1975) 31-35. BYRNE, B. "Sons of God"-"Seed of Abraham" (Rome 1979) 158-65.

3:15-22 HAUCK.W. "Exegetischer Versuch über Galat. 3, 15-22" ThSK 35 (1862) 512-48. BARTH, M. GPM 5 (1950/51) 183-86. IWAND, H.-J. Predigt—Meditationen (1964) 509-16. DOERNE, M. Die alten Episteln (1967) 200-4. BRANDENBURGER—MERKEL, GPM 22 (1967/68) 368-73. GABRIS, K. "Zur Kraft der Verheissungen (Zum Gal 3, 15-22)" Communio Viatorum 11 (1968) 251-64. MOXNES, H. Theology in Conflict (Leiden 1980) 257f. KLAIBER, W. Rechtfertigung und Gemeinde (Göttingen 1982) 152. LIEBERS, R. Das Gesetz als Evangelium (Zürich 1989) 229-36. HONG, I.-G. The Law in Galatians (Sheffield 1993) 42-45.

3:15-20 RÄISÄNEN, H. Paul and the Law (Tübingen 1983) 21, 23, 43f., 45, 62, 128, 136-38, 230, 245. RÄISÄNEN, H. The Torah and Christ (Helsinki 1986) 9, 33.

3:15-19 HAYS, R. B. The Faith of Jesus Christ (Chico CA 1983) 225.

3:15-18 BANDSTRA.A.J. The Law and the Elements of the World (1964) 120f. ECKERT, J. Die urchristliche Verkündigung im Streit zwischen Paulus und seinen Gegnern nach dem Galaterbrief (1971) 79-81. PAGELS, E.H. The Gnostic Paul (1975) 107. MINDE, H.-J. VAN DER, Schrift und Tradition bei Paulus (München/Paderborn/Wien 1976) 134-36. KUTSCH, E. Neues Testament—Neuer Bund? (Neukirchen/Vluyn 1978) 136-42. BYRNE, B. "Sons of God"-"Seed of Abraham" (Rome 1979) 158-60. FRICKEL, J. "Die Zöllner, Vorbild der Demut und wahrer Gottesverehrung" in E. Dassmann und K. S. Frank, eds., Pietas (FS B. Kötting; Jahrbuch für Antike und Christentum, Ergänzungsband 8, Münster 1980) 370. HAYS, R. B. The Faith of Jesus Christ (Chico CA 1983) 104, 216, 217, 222, 225, 228. FREUND, G. und STEGEMANN, E., eds., Theologische Brosamen für Lothar Steiger (DBAT 5; Heidelberg 1985) 392. COSGROVE, C. H. "Arguing like a Mere Human Being: Galatians 3.15-18 in Rhetorical Perspective," NTS 34 (1988) 536-49. COSGROVE, C. H. The Cross and the Spirit. A Study in the Argument and Theology of Galatians (Macon GA 1988) 61, 63, 66, 85, 95. HANSEN, G. W. Abraham in Galatians (Sheffield 1989) 127-29.

3:15-17 BAMMEL, E. "Gottes *diatheke* (Gal. iii. 15-17) und das jüdische Rechtsdenken" NTS 6 (1960) 313-19. RÄISÄNEN, H. Paul and the Law (Tübingen 1983) 129f., 208.

3:15-16 MORRIS, L. The Apostolic Preaching of the Cross (1955) 85f.

3:15 JEREMIAS, J. "*HOMOS* (1 Cor 14, 7; Gal 3, 15)" ZNW 52 (1961) 127-28. SCHRAGE, W. Die konkreten Einzelgebote in der paulinischen Paränese (1961) 74. BAUMERT, N. Täglich Sterben und Auferstehen. Der Literalsinn von 2 Kor 4, 12-5, 10 (1973) 371. DRANE, J.W. Paul: Libertine or Legalist? (1975) 31-32. BYRNE, B. "Sons of God"-"Seed of Abraham" (Rome 1979) 82n., 153n., 158f., 175, 183n., 187n., 189. HAYS, R. B. The Faith of Jesus Christ (Chico CA 1983) 216, 225. GRAESSER, E. Der Alte Bund im Neuen (Tübingen 1985) 2, 3, 8, 9, 56-60, 63. BAUMERT, N. Ehelosigkeit und Ehe im Herrn (Würzburg ²1986) 539ff., 559.

3:16-4:11 HAYS, R. B. The Faith of Jesus Christ (Chico CA 1983) 213, 225-33.

3:16-29 HESTER, J. Paul's Concept of Inheritance (1968) 47-57. BETZ, O. "Beschneidung" in TRE 5 (1980) 720. HAYS, R. B. The Faith of Jesus Christ (Chico CA 1983) 194f., 202, 213.

3:16, 28-29 SCHWEIZER, E. Gemeinde und Gemeinde—Ordnung im Neuen Testament (1959) § 7c.

3:16-27 PATTE, D. Paul's Faith and the Power of the Gospel (Philadelphia 1983) 195-200.

3:16-22 LIESE, H. "Promissiones Abrahae factae complentur per fidem, non per legem (Gal 3, 16-22)" VD 13 (1933) 257-63. LACAN, M.-F. "L'éducation de la foi (Gal 3, 16-22)" AssS 67 (1965) 19-35. SISTI, A. "Le promesse Messianiche" BiblOr 11/3 (1969) 125-34.

3:16-19 HAYS, R. B. The Faith of Jesus Christ (Chico CA 1983) 194, 225.

3:16   GARDINER, F. "Note on Galatians 3:16" BiblSa 36 (1879) 23-27. BACON, B.W. "Notes on New Testament Passages" JBL 16 (1897) 136-42. COFFIN, C.P. "Seeds, or Seed, in Gal. 3:16" BibW 32 (1908) 267-68. BOVER, J.M. "'Et semini tuo qui est Christus' (Gal. 3:16)" VD 3 (1923) 365-66. BOUSSET, W. Die Religion des Judentums im Späthellenistischen Zeitalter (1966-1926) 161. A VALLISOLETO, X. "Et semini tuo qui est Christus" VD 12 (1932) 327-32. DI FONZO, L. "De semine Abrahae, promissionum herede, juxta S. Paulum in Gal. 3" VD 21 (1941) 49-58. DAUBE, D. "The Interpretation of a Generic Singular in Galatians 3, 16" Jewish Quarterly Review 35 (1945) 491-500. ELLIS, E.E. Paul's Use of the Old Testament (1957) 76f. SCHWEIZER, E. Erniedrigung und Erhöhung bei Jesus und seinen Nachfolgern (1962) § 5g. BRAUN, H. Qumran und das Neue Testament (1966) II 320. MCNARMARA, M. The New Testament and the Palestinian Targum to the Pentateuch (1966) 49 n32. NICKELS, P. Targum and the New Testament (1967) 74. WOOD, J.E. "Isaac Typology in the New Testament" NTS 14 (1968) 583-89. MÜLLER, H. Die Auslegung alttestamentlichen Geschichtsstoffs bei Paulus (diss. Halle/Wittenberg 1960) 24-30. WILLIAMS, J. A. A Conceptual History of Deuteronomism in the Old Testament, Judaism, and the New Testament (Ph.D. diss. Lousville 1976) 275. BYRNE, B. "Sons of God"-"Seed of Abraham" (Rome 1979) 159-62, 168n., 172, 175. DUNN, J. D. G. Unity and Diversity in the New Testament. An Inquiry into the Character of Earliest Christianity (London 1977) 92. LUCCHESI, E. "Nouveau Parallèle entre Saint Paul (Gal. iii 16) et Philon d'Alexandrie (Quaestiones in Genesim)?" NovT 21 (1979) 150-55. VIELHAUER, P. "Paulus und das Alte Testament" in Oikodome [G. Klein, ed.] (München 1979) 200. MUTIUS, H. G. VON, "Ein judaistischer Beitrag zu Galater 3, 16" BN 11 (1980) 35-37. THISELTON, A. C. The Two Horizons (Grand Rapids 1980) 402. GRANT, R. M. "Paul and the Old Testament" in D. K. McKim, ed., The Authoritative Word (Grand Rapids 1983) 30f.HAYS, R. B. The Faith of Jesus Christ (Chico CA 1983) 152-54, 183, 195, 198, 206, 209, 211. HELDERMANN, J. Die Anapausis im Evangelium Veritatis (Leiden 1984) 325n.61. NEWMAN, B. M. "Translating 'Seed' in Galatians 3.16, 19," BTr 35 (1984) 334-37. GRAESSER, E. Der Alte Bund im Neuen (Tübingen 1985) 18, 68, 159f. LUZ, U. "Paulinische Theologie als Biblische Theologie" in M. Klopfen-stein et al., eds., Mitte der Schrift? Ein jüdisch-christliches Gespräch. Texte des Berner Symposions vom 6.-12. Januar 1985 (Bern etc. 1987) 119-47, esp. 122, 136. MUSSNER, F. Die Kraft der Wurzel (Freiburg/ Basel/Wien 1987) 90f. COSGROVE, C. H. The Cross and the Spirit. A Study in the Argument and Theology of Galatians (Macon GA 1988) 32, 63, 66f., 72, 117, 178, 182. HOOKER, M. D. From Adam to Christ. Essays on Paul (Cambridge 1990) 173f.

3:17   KRETZMANN, P.E. "The Chronology of the Two Testaments" CThM 15 (1944) 767-71. SCHRAGE, W. Die konkreten Einzelgebote in der paulinischen Paränese (1961) 95, 106. JÜNGEL, E. Paulus und Jesus (1966) 55. KUTSCH, E. "Bund" in TRE 7 (1981) 408. GRAESSER, E. Der Alte Bund im Neuen (Tübingen 1985) 8, 56ff., 58-60, 75. RÄISÄNEN, H. The Torah and Christ (Helsinki 1986) 179f. LÜHRMANN, D. "Die 430 Jahre zwischen den Verheissungen und dem Gesetz (Gal 3, 17)," ZAW 100 (1988) 420-23. WOLTER, M. Die Pastoralbriefe als Paulustradition (Göttingen 1988) 55. HUGHES, J. Secrets of the Times. Myth and History in Biblical Chronology (Sheffield 1990) 258.

3:18   ZELLER, D. Juden und Heiden in der Mission des Paulus (1973) 106. DRANE, J.W. Paul: Libertine or Legalist? (1975) 31-32. BYRNE, B. "Sons of God"-"Seed of Abraham" (Rome 1979) 159f., 162, 162nn., 186, 206. FULLER, D. P. Gospel and Law. Contrast or Continuum? (Grand Rapids 1980) 199-204. THISELTON, A. C. The Two Horizons (Grand Rapids 1980) 391. HAYS, R. B. The Faith of Jesus Christ (Chico CA 1983) 227. JOHNSTON, G. "'Kingdom of God' Sayings in Paul's Letters" in P. Richardson and J. C. Hurd, eds., From Jesus to Paul (FS F. W. Beare; Waterloo 1984) 147f. GRAESSER, E. Der Alte Bund im Neuen (Tübingen 1985) 57, 61, 62, 70. HOWARD, G. Paul. Crisis in Galatia (Cambridge [2]1990) 64, 95, 97.

3:19-5:1   THIELMAN, F. From Plight to Solution (Leiden 1989) 72-86.

3:19-4:7   GIBLET, J. "De libertate filiorum dei juxta Gal III, 19-IV, 7" Collectanea Mechliniensia 26 (1956) 701-4. CALLAN, T. "Pauline Midrash: The Exegetical Background of Gal. 3:19b," JBL 99 (1980) 549. LONGENECKER, R. N. "The Pedagogical Nature of the Law in Galatians 3:19-4:7," JEThS 25 (1982) 53-61. SANDERS, E. P. Paul, the Law, and the Jewish People (London 1985) 65-70.

3:19-4:5   BERGER, K. und COLPE, C., eds., Religionsgeschicht-liches Textbuch zum Neuen Testament (Göttingen/Zürich 1987) 272.

3:19ff.   BRANDENBURGER, E. Adam und Christus (1962) 248ff. STALDER, K. Das Werk des Geistes in der Heiligung bei Paulus (1962) 322-25, 329-33. HAHN, F. Das Verständnis der Mission im Neuen Testament (1965) 86. LUZ, U. Das Geschichts-verständnis des Paulus (1968) 188ff. HENGEL, M. Judentum und Hellenismus (1969) 564; Judaism and Hellenism (1974) I 309. HÜBNER, H. Das Gesetz bei Paulus. Ein Beitrag zum Werden der paulinischen Theologie (Göttingen 1978) 27-37. FREUND, G. und STEGEMANN, E., eds., Theologische Brosamen für Lothar Steiger (DBAT 5; Heidelberg 1985) 392.

3:19-29   BARRETT, C.K. From First Adam to Last (1962) 60-63. MACGORMAN, J.W. "Problem Passages in Galatians" SouJTh 15 (1972) 35-51.

3:19-26   RAMAROSON, L. "La justification par la foi du Christ Jésus," SciE 39 (1987) 81-92.

3:19-25   BANDSTRA, A.J. The Law and the Elements of the World (1964) 122-23. ECKERT, J. Die urchristliche Verkündigung im Streit zwischen Paulus und seinen Gegnern nach dem Galaterbrief (1971) 81-86. DUNN, J. D. G. Unity and Diversity in the New Testament. An Inquiry into the Character of Earliest Christianity (London 1977) 98. BUSCEMI, A. M. "La funzione della Legge nel piano salvifico di Dio in Gal 3, 19-25," SBFLA 32 (1982) 109-32. SCHMITT, R. Gottesgerechtigkeit—Heils-geschichte—Israel in der Theologie des Paulus (Frankfurt/ Bern/New York/Nancy 1984) 50-54. SCHNABEL, E. J. Law and Wisdom from Ben Sira to Paul (Tübingen 1985) 271, 274, 293. LULL, D. J. "'The Law Was Our Pedagogue'. A Study in Galatians 3:19-25," JBL 105 (1986) 481-98. RÄISÄNEN, H. The Torah and Christ (Helsinki 1986) 180. ZIESLER, J. Pauline Christianity (Oxford 1990) 108-10.

3:19-24   BYRNE, B. "Sons of God"-"Seed of Abraham" (Rome 1979) 158, 161-65.

3:19-22   MOXNES, H. Theology in Conflict (Leiden 1980) 212f. FREUND, G. und STEGEMANN, E., eds., Theologische Brosamen für Lothar Steiger (DBAT 5; Heidelberg 1985) 392. AUNE, D. E. The New Testament in Its Literary Environment (Philadelphia 1987) 200. HANSEN, G. W. Abraham in Galatians (Sheffield 1989) 129-33. THIELMAN, F. From Plight to Solution (Leiden 1989) 73-77, 99, 101.

3:19-21   BANDSTRA, A.J. The Law and the Elements of the World (1964) 120f., 128f. BARRETT, C. K. Freedom and Obligation (Philadelphia 1985) 32-34.

3:19-20   DAVIDSON, W.L. "The Mediator—Argument of Galatians iii.19, 20" Exp 3rd series 7 (1888) 377-86. THACKERAY, H.St.J. The Relation of St.Paul to Contemporary Jewish Thought (1900) 67ff., 72ff. DIBELIUS, M. Die Geisterwelt im Glauben des

Paulus (1909) 23ff. BRING, R. "Några reflexioner till tolkningen av Gal. 3, 19f."
SEA 12 (1947) 51-66. BANDSTRA, A.J. The Law and the Elements of the World
(1964) 149ff. BRING, R. Christus und das Gesetz (1969) 73-111. PAGELS, E.H.
The Gnostic Paul (1975) 107. SAITO, T. Die Mosevorstellungen im Neuen
Testament (Bern 1977) 24-28, 147. VANHOYE, A. "Un médiateur des anges en Ga
3, 19-20," Biblica 59 (1978) 403-11. BYRNE, B. "Sons of God"-"Seed of Abraham"
(Rome 1979) 161f. RÄISÄNEN, H. Paul and the Law (Tübingen 1983) 22, 128-33,
134f., 139, 140f., 144f., 148, 256. HÜBNER, H. "Galaterbrief" in TRE 12 (1984)
8. RIESENFELD, H. "The Misinterpreted Mediator in Gal 3:19-20" in W. C.
Weinreich, ed., The New Testament Age (FS B. Reicke; Macon GA 1984) II, 405-
12. RÄISÄNEN, H. The Torah and Christ (Helsinki 1986) 362. SCHULZ, S.
Neutestamentliche Ethik (Zürich 1987) 194f. SCHNACKENBURG, R. Die sittliche
Botschaft des Neuen Testaments, Band 1 (Freiburg/Basel/Wien 1986) 194.
SCHNELLE, U. Wandlungen im paulinischen Denken (Stuttgart 1989) 59, 68, 74.
THIELMAN, F. From Plight to Solution (Leiden 1989) 73f. VOLLENWEIDER, S.
Freiheit als neue Schöpfung (Göttingen 1989) 267n., 304. WALLACE, D. B.
"Galatians 3:19-20: A crux interpretum for Paul's View of the Law," WThJ 52
(1990) 225-45.

3:19   FEINE, P. Das Gesetzesfreie Evangelium des Paulus (1899) 204-6. SCHOEPS, H.-J.
Paulus (1959) 190f. BOUSSET, W. Die Religion des Judentums im späthellenistischen Zeitalter (1966=1926) 120-329. VAN DÜLMEN, A. Die Theologie des
Gesetzes bei Paulus (1968) 41-45. LUZ, U. Das Geschichtsverständnis des Paulus
(1968) 186f. STROBEL, A. Erkenntnis und Bekenntnis der Sünde in neutestament-
licher Zeit (1968) 49. LADD, G.E. A Theology of the New Testament (1974) 400,
403. KÜMMEL, W.G. Jüdische Schriften aus hellenistisch—römischer Zeit (1976)
5: 69. MIRANDA, J. P. Marx and the Bible. A Critique of the Philosophy of
Oppression (London 1977) 182-84. BLOCH, R. "Midrash" in W. S. Green, ed.,
Approaches to Ancient Judaism. Theory and Practice (Missoula 1978) 49. HÜBNER,
H. Das Gesetz bei Paulus. Ein Beitrag zum Werden der paulinischen Theologie
(Göttingen 1978) 171-75. RUDOLPH, K. Die Gnosis (Göttingen 1978) 320. BYRNE,
B. "Sons of God"-"Seed of Abraham" (Rome 1979) 146n., 161f., 162n., 163, 177,
179. CALLAN, T. "Pauline Midrash: The Exegetical Background of Gal 3:19b," JBL
99 (1980) 549-67. DUNN, J. D. G. Christology in the Making (London 1980) 43,
155f. BERGER, K. "Das Buch der Jubiläen" in JSHRZ II/3 (1981) 319n.27b.
BÖCHER, O. "Engel" in TRE 9 (1982) 597, 598. GASTON, L. "Angels and
Gentiles in early Judaism and in Paul," StR/SciR 11 (1982) 65-75. HAYS, R. B. The
Faith of Jesus Christ (Chico CA 1983) 195, 211, 225, 227, 230f., 245. RÄISÄNEN,
H. Paul and the Law (Tübingen 1983) 9, 17, 24, 56, 59, 140, 151, 153f., 205, 209,
220, 227. HELDERMANN, J. Die Anapausis im Evangelium Veritatis (Leiden 1984)
325n.61. HÜBNER, H. "Galaterbrief" in TRE 12 (1984) 8. KLEIN, G. "Gesetz, III)
in TRE 13 (1984) 67. MOHRLANG, R. Matthew and Paul (Cambridge 1984) 28f.,
188. DIETZFELBINGER, C. Die Berufung des Paulus als Ursprung seiner Theologie
(Neukirchen 1985) 101, 107f. SCHNABEL, E. J. Law and Wisdom from Ben Sira
to Paul (Tübingen 1985) 210, 271-73, 296. GASTON, L. Paul and the Torah
(Vancouver 1987) 17, 35, 41, 89, 195, 198, 201f. MERKLEIN, H. Studien zu Jesus
und Paulus (Tübingen 1987) 69-71, 72, 74, 92, 99. COSGROVE, C. H. The Cross
and the Spirit. A Study in the Argument and Theology of Galatians (Macon GA
1988) 7, 21, 28, 32, 36, 63-65, 71f., 178, 182. BANDSTRA, A. J. "The Law and
Angels: Antiquities 15.136 and Galatians 3:19," CThJ 24 (1989) 223-40. HOFIUS,
O. Paulusstudien (Tübingen 1989) 52, 60, 62, 84, 95. MARTIN, B. L. Christ and the
Law in Paul (Leiden 1989) 6, 19, 35, 37, 39, 41, 43, 46, 52, 55, 57f., 61, 118, 134.

SUHL, A. "Die Galater und der Geist. Kritische Erwägungen zur Situation in Galatien" in D.-A. Koch et al., eds., Jesu Rede von Gott und ihre Nachgeschichte im frühen Christentum (FS Willi Marxsen; Gütersloh 1989) 289-92. DUNN, J. D. G. Jesus, Paul and the Law (London 1990) 158, 234 n.46, 249, 250, 261nn.38-40, 262nn.40-41. KRAUS, W. Der Tod Jesu als Heiligtumsweihe. Eine Untersuchung zum Umfeld der Sühnevorstellung in Römer 3, 25-26a (Neukirchen-Vluyn 1991) 108f., 111. HONG, I.-G. The Law in Galatians (Sheffield 1993) 150-53, 194-97.

3:19a   DRANE, J.W. Paul: Libertine or Legalist? (1975) 34-35.

3:19b   DRANE, J.W. Paul: Libertine or Legalist? (1975) 32-34, 112-13, 132-33.

3:20-21 SUHL, A. "Die Galater und der Geist. Kritische Erwägungen zur Situation in Galatien" in D.-A. Koch et al., eds., Jesu Rede von Gott und ihre Nachgeschichte im frühen Christentum (FS Willi Marxsen; Gütersloh 1989) 292-95.

3:20   LÜCKE, Fr. "Noch ein Versuch über Galat. 3:20" ThSK 1 (1828) 83-109. SCHNECKENBERGER, M. "Noch etwas über Galater 3, 20" ThSK 6 (1833) 121-43. RINCK, W.F. Über Gal. 3, 20" ThSK 7 (1834) 309-12. MACK, "Über Galat. 3, 20" ThQ 17 (1835) 453-92. VON SCHÜTZ, W. "Über Gal. 3, 20" ThQ 17 (1835) 623-45. GURLITT, T.F.K. "Noch ein Wort über Gal. 3, 20" ThSK 10 (1837) 805-29. REINHARDT, E.H.K. "Noch ein Wort über Gal. 3, 20" ThSK 15 (1842) 990-1011; ThSK 16 (1843) 715-21. VOGEL, A. "Zur Auslegung der Stelle Gal. 3, 20" ThSK 38 (1865) 524-38. HAUCK, W. "Ein Wort zur Auslegung der Stelle Gal. 3, 20 v. Prof. D. Vogel in Wien" ThSK 39 (1866) 699-701. BLOM, A.H. "Verklaring van Gal. III:20" TT 12 (1878) 216-27. PRINS, J.J. "Nog iets over Gal. III:20 en, in verband daarmede, over vs. 13 en 16. Open brief aan Dr. A.H. Blom" TT 12 (1878) 410-20. FORBES, J. "Brevia—Galatians 3:20" Exp 3rd series 4 (1886) 150-56. BLEIBTREU, W. "Das Wort vom Mittler im Galaterbriefe Kap. 3, 20" NKZ 6 (1895) 534-60. SIEBERT, W. "Exegetische—theologische Studie über Galater 3:20 und 4:4" NKZ 15 (1904) 699-733. WALTHER, F. "Miszellen. Gal. 3:20" NKZ 32 (1921) 706-9. ISAACS, W.H. "Galatians 3:20" ET 35 (1923-24) 565-67. CLARKE, W.K.L. "Studies in Texts: Gal. 3:20" Th 9 (1924) 215. CLARKE, W.K.L. New Testament Problems (1929) 153-56. TREMENHEERE, G.H. "Studies in Texts. Gal. 3:20" Th 22 (1931) 35. STEGMANN, A. "ὁ δὲ μεσίτης ἑνὸς οὐκ ἔστιν, Gal. 3, 20" BZ 22 (1934) 30-42. DANIELI, J. "Mediator autem unius non est" VD 33 (1955) 9-17. WAINWRIGHT, A.W. The Trinity in the New Testament (1962) 41-42. BANDSTRA, A.J. The Law and the Elements of the World (1964) 156f. BRING, R. "Der Mittler und das Gesetz. Eine Studie zu Gal. 3, 20" KuD 12 (1966) 292-309. MAUSER, U. "Galater iii.20: Die Universalität des Heils" NTS 13 (1967) 258-70. GIBLIN, C.H. "Three Monotheistic Texts in Paul" CBQ 37 (1975) 527-47. CALLAN, T. "Pauline Midrash: The Exegetical Background of Gal. 3:19b," JBL 99 (1980) 549f., 565-67. THISELTON, A. C. The Two Horizons (Grand Rapids 1980) 390, 401. ROMANIUK, K. "Exégèse du Nouveau Testament et ponctuation," NovT 23 (1981) 195-209. MAUSER, U. "*Heis theos* und *Monos theos* in Biblischer Theologie," JBTh 1 (1986) 80f. LACEY, D. R. DE, "Jesus as Mediator," JSNT 29 (1987) 101-21. GASTON, L. Paul and the Torah (Vancouver 1987) 29f. SCHMELLER, Th. Paulus und die "Diatribe" (Münster 1987) 328. COSGROVE, C. H. The Cross and the Spirit. A Study in the Argument and Theology of Galatians (Macon GA 1988) 65f. LOHSE, E. Die Entstehung des Neuen Testaments (Stuttgart/Berlin/Köln ⁵1991) 20.

3:21-4:11 BELLEVILLE, L. L. "'Under Law'. Structural Analysis and the Pauline Concept of Law in Galatians 3.21-4.11," JSNT 26 (1986) 53-78.

3:21ff. BULTMANN, R. Theologie des Neues Testaments (1965) 266f.

3:21-29 SEGAL, A. F. Paul the Convert (New Haven/London 1990) 212f.

3:21-25 ECKERT, J. Die urchristliche Verkündigung im Streit zwischen Paulus und seinen Gegnern nach dem Galaterbrief (1971) 109f.

3:21-24 LONGENECKER, R.N. Paul, Apostle of Liberty (1964) 150-52.

3:21 VAN DÜLMEN, A. Die Theologie des Gesetzes bei Paulus (1968) 45f. SANDERS, E. P. "On the Question of Fulfilling the Law in Paul and Rabbinic Judaism" in E. Bammel, C. K. Barrett and W. D. Davies, eds., Donum Gentilicium (FS D. Daube; Oxford 1978) 108. BYRNE, B. "Sons of God"-"Seed of Abraham" (Rome 1979) 93, 93n., 123, 145n., 155n., 162f., 163n. VIELHAUER, P. "Paulus und das Alte Testament" in Oikodome [G. Klein, ed.] (München 1979) 204. CALLAN, T. "Pauline Midrash. The Exegetical Background of Gal. 3:19b," JBL 99 (1980) 549. MOXNES, H. Theology in Conflict (Leiden 1980) 263f., 268, 272. RHYNE, C. T. Faith establishes the Law (Chico CA 1981) 54-56. BLANK, J. Paulus. Von Jesus zum Christentum (München 1982) 55. HAYS, R. B. The Faith of Jesus Christ (Chico CA 1983) 121-23, 136, 182, 207, 220f., 227. RÄISÄNEN, H. Paul and the Law (Tübingen 1983) 132, 151-54, 192, 208. BARRETT, C. K. Freedom and Obligation (Philadelphia 1985) 34-36. SCHNABEL, E. J. Law and Wisdom from Ben Sira to Paul (Tübingen 1985) 271, 273, 292, 296. WINGER, M. "Unreal Conditions in the Letters of Paul," JBL 105 (1986) 110-12. LAMBRECHT, J. "Once again Gal 2, 17-18 and 3, 21," EphT 63 (1987) 148-53. MERKLEIN, H. Studien zu Jesus und Paulus (Tübingen 1987) 3n.4, 40, 71-73, 86. COSGROVE, C. H. The Cross and the Spirit. A Study in the Argument and Theology of Galatians (Macon GA 1988) 11-13, 32, 36, 60, 64-66, 91, 102, 112, 142. HOFIUS, O. Paulusstudien (Tübingen 1989) 55, 84, 113, 124. MARTIN, B. L. Christ and the Law in Paul (Leiden 1989) 6, 19f., 35, 37f., 41, 52, 54, 85, 89, 95f., 116, 129, 123, 125, 127, 132, 143, 146. SEGAL, A. F. Paul the Convert (New Haven/London 1990) 131, 212.

3:22 BRANDENBURGER, E. Adam und Christus (1962) 168f. HOWARD, G. "The Faith of Christ" ET 85 (1974) 212-15. FRIEDRICH, G. "Das Gesetz des Glaubens Römer 3, 27" in Auf das Wort kommt es an. Gesammelte Aufsätze (Göttingen 1978) 117. BYRNE, B. "Sons of God"-"Seed of Abraham" (Rome 1979) 156, 162f., 163nn., 164n., 172, 179, 181, 182, 220. HAYS, R. B. The Faith of Jesus Christ (Chico CA 1983) 29, 123-25, 137, 139f., 142, 150, 157-71, 175, 188, 201f., 206, 217, 225, 231. RÄISÄNEN, H. The Torah and Christ (Helsinki 1986) 110f. BERGER, K. und COLPE, C., eds., Religionsgeschichtliches Textbuch zum Neuen Testament (Göttingen/Zürich 1987) 272f. COSGROVE, C. H. The Cross and the Spirit. A Study in the Argument and Theology of Galatians (Macon GA 1988) 2n., 55f., 64n., 68, 70-72, 102, 152n. HOFIUS, O. Paulusstudien (Tübingen 1989) 56, 63, 76, 84, 123, 154, 172, 197. LIMBECK, M. Mit Paulus Christ sein. Sachbuch zur Person und Theologie des Apostels Paulus (Stuttgart 1989) 74. MARTIN, B. L. Christ and the Law in Paul (Leiden 1989) 22, 39, 70, 80, 82, 100, 102, 103, 115f., 155. SCHNELLE, U. Wandlungen im paulinischen Denken (Stuttgart 1989) 56. HOOKER, M. D. From Adam to Christ. Essays on Paul (Cambridge 1990) 168, 172, 174.

3:22ff. SUHL, A. "Die Galater und der Geist. Kritische Erwägungen zur Situation in Galatien" in D.-A. Koch et al., eds., Jesu Rede von Gott und ihre Nachgeschichte im frühen Christentum (FS Willi Marxsen; Gütersloh 1989) 295f.

3:22-25 HAYS, R. B. The Faith of Jesus Christ (Chico CA 1983) 225.

3:22.24 SANDERS, E. P. Paul, the Law, and the Jewish People (London 1985) 39, 47, 64n.146, 70f., 73, 150.

3:22-23 RÖHSER, G. Metaphorik und Personifikation der Sünde (Tübingen 1987) 17f., 168, 173.

3:23–4:11 ATTFIELD, R. "On Translating Myth" The International Journal for the Philosophy of Religion 2 (1971) 228-45.

3:23–4:9 CERFAUX, L. "Le fils né de la femme" BVieC 4 (1953-54) 59-65. SANDERS, E. P. Paul, the Law, and the Jewish People (London 1985) 81f.

3:23–4:7 TAYLOR, T.M. "'Abba, Father' and Baptism" SJTh 11 (1958) 62-71. THIELMAN, F. From Plight to Solution (Leiden 1989) 77-80.

3:23ff. LUZ, U. Das Geschichtsverständnis des Paulus (1968) 191-93.

3:23-36 JOURNET, C. "L'économie de la loi mosaique" RThom 63 (1963) 5-36. RIDDERBOS, H. Paul. An Outline of His Theology (Grand Rapids 1975) 199-203. HAYS, R. B. The Faith of Jesus Christ (Chico CA 1983) 149, 229. RÄISÄNEN, H. Paul and the Law (Tübingen 1983) 20, 21, 23. TOLMIE, D. F. *"Ho nomos paidagōgos hēmon gegonen eis Christon.* The Persuasive Force of a Pauline Metaphor (Gl 3:23-26)," Neotestamentica 26 (1992) 407-16.

3:23-29 ROELS, E.D. God's Mission (1962) 131f. IWAND, H.-J. Predigt—Meditationen (1964) 477-84. GOLLWITZER, H. in Herr, tue meine Lippen suf. Bd. II, hrsg, von G. Eichholz (1966) 72-79. DOERNE, M. Die alten Episteln (1967) 34-37. VOIGT, M. GPM 22 (1967/68) 62-67. WILLIAMS, J. A. A Conceptual History of Deuteronomism in the Old Testament, Judaism, and the New Testament (Ph.D. diss. Lousville 1976) 278. CLARK, S. B. Man and Woman in Christ (Ann Arbor MI 1980) 139-42. HAYS, R. B. The Faith of Jesus Christ (Chico CA 1983) 229f., 245. KOLLMANN, B. Ursprung und Gestalten der frühchristlichen Mahlfeier (Göttingen 1990) 119n.80. HONG, I.-G. The Law in Galatians (Sheffield 1993) 45-47.

3:23-28 PAGELS, E.H. The Gnostic Paul (1975) 108. MINEAR, P. S. To Die and to Live. Christ's Resurrection and Christian Vocation (New York 1977) 73.

3:23-25 BYRNE, B. "Sons of God"-"Seed of Abraham" (Rome 1979) 163-65, 176. HAYS, R. B. The Faith of Jesus Christ (Chico CA 1983) 169f., 181, 194, 228, 230f. DIETZ-FELBINGER, C. Die Berufung des Paulus als Ursprung seiner Theologie (Neukirchen 1985) 101, 117, 142. CRONJÉ, J. VAN W. "Defamiliarization in the letter to the Galatians" in J. H. Petzer and P. J. Hartin, eds., A South African Perspective on the New Testament (FS B. M. Metzger; Leiden 1986) 220. HANSEN, G. W. Abraham in Galatians (Sheffield 1989) 133-36. LIMBECK, M. Mit Paulus Christ sein. Sachbuch zur Person und Theologie des Apostels Paulus (Stuttgart 1989) 78. MARXSEN, W. "Christliche" und christliche Ethik im Neuen Testament (Gütersloh 1989) 150.

3:23-24 BRANDENBURGER, E. Adam und Christus (1962) 252f. LUZ, U. Das Geschichtsverständnis des Paulus (1968) 153f. BORSE, U. Der Standort des Galaterbriefes (1972) 59f. CALLAN, T. "Pauline Midrash. The Exegetical Background of Gal 3:19b," JBL 99 (1980) 549. HAYS, R. B. The Faith of Jesus Christ (Chico CA 1983) 228, 230. VOLLENWEIDER, S. Freiheit als neue Schöpfung (Göttingen 1989) 344n., 362n. SEGAL, A. F. Paul the Convert (New Haven/London 1990) 130.

3:23,25 HAACKER, K. "Glaube II" in TRE 13 (1984) 278.

3:23 FEINE, P. Das gesetzfreie Evangelium des Paulus (1899) 99f., 204ff. BOISMARD, M.E. Quatre Hymnes Baptismales (1961) 53-56. LÜHRMANN, D. Das Offenbarungsverständnis bei Paulus und in paulinischen Gemeinden (1965) 79f. VAN DÜLMEN, A. Die Theologie des Gesetzes bei Paulus (1968) 46f. BYRNE, B. "Sons of God"-"Seed of Abraham" (Rome 1979) 163f., 179, 181. HAYS, R. B. The Faith of Jesus Christ (Chico CA 1983) 145, 228, 229, 231, 245. THEISSEN, G. Psychologische Aspekte paulinischer Theologie (Göttingen 1983) 258, 348n.13. JOHNSON, E. E. The Function of Apocalyptic and Wisdom Traditions in Romans 9-11 (Atlanta GA 1989) 187. MARTIN, B. L. Christ and the Law in Paul (Leiden 1989) 19, 21, 37-39, 60, 70, 72, 74, 80, 83, 87, 99, 100, 102-04, 134, 137, 142, 144, 155. HONG, I.-G. The Law in Galatians (Sheffield 1993) 156-58.

3:24-29 DINKLER, E. "Die Taufaussagen des Neuen Testaments. Neu untersucht im Hinblick auf Karl Barths Tauflehre" in Zu Karl Barths Lehre von der Taufe, hrsg. von F. Viering (1971) 84-87.
3:24,28 CALLAWAY, J.S. "Paul's Letter to the Galatians and Plato's Lysis" JBL 67 (1948) 353-55.
3:24-25 YOUNG, N. H. "*Paidagogos*. The Social Setting of a Pauline Metaphor," NovT 29 (1987) 150-76. GORDON, T. D. "A Note on *PAIDAGOGOS* in Galatians 3.24-25," NTS 35 (1989) 150-54. MULLER, E. C. Trinity and Marriage in Paul (New York/Bern/Frankfurt/Paris 1990) 405f. OLIVEIRA, A. DE, Die Diakonie der Gerechtigkeit und der Versöhnung in der Apologie des 2. Korintherbriefes. Analyse und Auslegung von 2 Kor 2, 14-4, 6; 5, 11-6, 10 (Münster 1990) 169n.442. YOUNG, N. H. "The Figure of the *Paidagōgos* in Art and Literature," BA 53 (1990) 80-86.
3:24 WOHLFEIL, L.T. "Gal. 3, 24" CThM 6 (1935) 192-96. STENDAHL, K. "Lagen som övervakare intill Kristus (Gal 3, 24)" SEA 18-19 (1953-54) 161-73. VAN DÜLMEN, A. Die Theologie des Gesetzes bei Paulus (1968) 47f. SCHOTT, E. "'lex paedagogus noster fuit in Christo Iesu' (Vulgata). Zu Luthers Auslegung von Gal 3, 24" ThLZ 95 (1970) 561-70. CONZELMANN, H. und LINDEMANN, A. Arbeitsbuch zum Neuen Testament (1975) 196. FRIEDRICH, G. "Das Gesetz des Glaubens Römer 3, 27" in Auf das Wort kommt es an. Gesammelte Aufsätze (Göttingen 1978) 115. HORN, H.-J. "Allegorese" in TRE 2 (1978) 280. THISELTON, A. C. The Two Horizons (Grand Rapids 1980) 318. FRITSCHE, H.-G. "Dekalog" in TRE 8 (1981) 426. HAYS, R. B. The Faith of Jesus Christ (Chico CA 1983) 150, 158, 230, 232, 245, 246. BERGER, K. und COLPE, C., eds., Religionsgeschicht-liches Textbuch zum Neuen Testament (Göttingen/Zürich 1987) 273. COSGROVE, C. H. The Cross and the Spirit. A Study in the Argument and Theology of Galatians (Macon GA 1988) 32, 70-72, 153. HANSON, A. T. "The Origin of Paul's Use of *PAIDAGOGOS* for the Law," JSNT 34 (1988) 71-76. MARTIN, B. L. Christ and the Law in Paul (Leiden 1989) 21, 38, 57, 60, 118, 132, 134, 142, 150, 155.
3:25-29 BYRNE, B. "Sons of God"-"Seed of Abraham" (Rome 1979) 165-74, 189.
3:25-26 HAYS, R. B. The Faith of Jesus Christ (Chico CA 1983) 169, 230.
3:25 BYRNE, B. "Sons of God"-"Seed of Abraham" (Rome 1979) 165f., 172f., 179, 181, 185, 218. FRITSCHE, H.-G. "Dekalog" in TRE 8 (1981) 426. HAYS, R. B. The Faith of Jesus Christ (Chico CA 1983) 50, 145, 230f., 246. MARTIN, B. L. Christ and the Law in Paul (Leiden 1989) 83, 100, 102, 134, 142, 155.
3:26-4:11 HAYS, R. B. The Faith of Jesus Christ (Chico CA 1983) 222.
3:26-4:7 GRAIL, A. "Le Baptême dans l'Epître aus Galates" RB 58 (1951) 503-20. HERMANN, I. Kyrois und Pneuma (1961) 94-97. SCHMITT, R. Gottesgerechtig-keit—Heilsgeschichte—Israel in der Theologie des Paulus (Frankfurt/Bern/New York/Nancy 1984) 54f. DOBBELER, A. VON, Glaube als Teilhabe (Tübingen 1987) 58-60. MacDONALD, M. Y. The Pauline Churches (Cambridge 1988) 38.
3:26ff. RICHARDSON, P. Paul's Ethic of Freedom (Philadelphia 1979) 15-78. FREUND, G. und STEGEMANN, E., eds., Theologische Brosamen für Lothar Steiger (DBAT 5; Heidelberg 1985) 392.
3:26-29 BOVER, J.M. "'In Christo Iesu' filii Dei omnes unus, semen Abrahae (Gal. 3, 26-29)" VD 4 (1924) 14-21. A VALLISOLETO, X. "In Christo Iesu" VD 12 (1932) 16-24; VD 13 (1933) 311-19. MOCSY, E. "De unione mystica cum Christo" VD 25 (1947) 270-79, 328-39. STANLEY, D.M. Christ's Resurrection in Pauline Soteriology (1961) 154-55. THÜSING, W. Per Christum in Deum (1965) 116-19. BLANK, J. Paulus und Jesus (1968) 258ff. BOUTTIER, M. "L'évangile paulinien

(Ga 3, 26-29)" AssS 43 (1969) 66-71. ECKERT, J. Die Urchristliche Verkündigung im Streit zwischen Paulus und seinen Gegnern nach dem Galaterbrief (1971) 86-88. BIEDER, W. Die Verheissung der Taufe im Neuen Testament (Zürich 1966) 250-57. BECKWITH, R. "The Bearing of Holy Spirit" in P. Moore, ed., Man, Woman, and Priesthood (London 1979) 56. BYRNE, B. "Sons of God"-"Seed of Abraham" (Rome 1979) 1, 165-72, 173, 173n., 174, 175n., 178, 186, 195, 217n. PAULSEN, H. "Einheit und Freiheit der Söhne Gottes—Gal 3:26-29," ZNW 71 (1980) 74-95. BARTH, G. Die Taufe in frühchristlicher Zeit (Neukirchen/Vluyn 1981) 18, 40, 104-06. KLAIBER, W. Rechtfertigung und Gemeinde (Göttingen 1982) 92-94, 184. DAVIES, S. L. The Gospel of Thomas and Christian Wisdom (New York 1983) 48, 127. HAYS, R. B. The Faith of Jesus Christ (Chico CA 1983) 198f., 202, 225, 232, 267. SCHWANKL, O. Die Sadduzäerfrage (Mk. 12, 18-27 parr) (Frankfurt a.M. 1987) 373-75. ELLIS, E. E. Pauline Theology (Grand Rapids/Exeter 1989) 79ff. HANSEN, G. W. Abraham in Galatians (Sheffield 1989) 136-39. BRUCE, F. F. "One in Christ Jesus. Thoughts on Galatians 3:26-29," Journal of the Christian Brethren Research Fellowship [Wellington, New Zealand] 122 (1990) 7-10. MULLER, E. C. Trinity and Marriage in Paul (New York/Bern/ Frankfurt/Paris 1990) 63, 152, 368, 413, 434. CAMPBELL, D. A. Paul's Gospel in an Intercultural Context. Jew and Gentile in the Letter to the Romans (Frankfurt/ Berlin/Bern etc. 1992) 106-10. PATTE, C. M. The Glory of Adam and the Afflictions of the Righteous. Pauline Suffering in Context (Lewiston NY 1993) passim.

3:26-28 BOUTTIER, M. "Complexio Oppositorum: sur les Formules de I Cor. xii.13; Gal. iii.26-28; Col. iii.10, 11," NTS 23 (1976) 1-19. GAYER, R. Die Stellung des Sklaven in den paulinischen Gemeinden und bei Paulus (Bern/Frankfurt 1976) 135-53, 169-71. FUNK, A. "Mann und Frau in den Briefen des hl. Paulus," US 32 (1977) 280-85. VELLANICKAL, M. The Divine Sonship of Christians in the Johannine Writings (Rome 1977) 74-77. SCHMITHALS, W. "Zur Herkunft der gnostischen Elemente in der Sprache des Paulus" in B. Aland et al., eds., Gnosis (FS H. Jonas; Göttingen 1978) 406. BYRNE, B. "Sons of God"-"Seed of Abraham" (Rome 1979) 146, 165-71, 166, 168n., 174, 190. SCHELKLE, K. H. The Spirit and the Bride. Woman in the Bible (Collegeville 1979) 164f. MÜLLER, U. B. "Zur Rezeption gesetzeskritischer Jesusüberlieferung im frühen Christentum," NTS 27 (1981) 159f., 171. KLEIN, G. "Eschatologie" in TRE 10 (1982) 278. LAUB, F. Die Begegnung des frühen Christentums mit der antiken Sklaverei (Stuttgart 1982) 63, 97. BURCHARD, C. "Erfahrungen multikulturellen Zusammenlebens im Neuen Testament" in J. Micksch, ed., Multikulturelles Zusammenleben (Frankfurt 1983) 28-30, 33, 39. HAYS, R. B. The Faith of Jesus Christ (Chico CA 1983) 29. SCHARFFENORTH, G. and REICHLE, E. "Frau" in TRE 11 (1983) 447, 464. SCHNELLE, U. Gerechtigkeit und Christusgegenwart (Göttingen 1983) 57-62, 109f. BARRETT, C. K. Freedom and Obligation (Philadelphia 1985) 36-40. FREUND, G. und STEGEMANN, E., eds., Theologische Brosamen für Lothar Steiger (DBAT 5; Heidelberg 1985) 390. CRONJÉ, J. VAN W. "Defamiliarization in the letter to the Galatians" in J. H. Petzer and P. J. Hartin, eds., A South African Perspective on the New Testament (FS B. M. Metzger; Leiden 1986) 223. MacDONALD, D. R. There Is No Male and Female (Philadelphia 1987) passim. MERKLEIN, H. Studien zu Jesus und Paulus (Tübingen 1987) 324-27, 336, 341, 433. JONGE, M. DE, Christology in Context. The Earliest Christian Response to Jesus (Philadelphia 1988) 41f., 218n.18, 226n.11. MacDONALD, M. Y. The Pauline Churches (Cambridge 1988) 66, 237. BECKER, J. Paulus. Der Apostel der Völker (Tübingen 1989) 110ff., 118, 142, 260, 269, 283, 344, 405, 449, 455. BÜHRIG, M. "Eine Gemeinschaft der Wechselseitigkeit" in E. R. Schmidt et al., eds., Feministisch gelesen, Band 2

(Stuttgart 1989) 231-37. MELL, U. Neue Schöpfung (Berlin/New York 1989) 303,
306ff., 316, 390, 392. SCHÄFER, K. Gemeinde als "Bruderschaft" (Frank-
furt/Bern/New York/Paris 1989) 80-110. SCHNELLE, U. Wandlungen im
paulinischen Denken (Stuttgart 1989) 58f., 73. VOLLENWEIDER, S. Freiheit als
neue Schöpfung (Göttingen 1989) 228n., 233, 239f., 303.

3:26-27   BEASLEY—MURRAY, G.R. Baptism in the New Testament (1962) 146ff.
WAGNER, G. Das religionsgeschichtliche Problem von Römer 6, 1-11 (1962) 60-62.
SEEBERG, A. Der Katechismus der Urchristenheit (1966) 176ff. SZYMANEK, E.
"Istota synostwa Bozego (3, 26-27)" RTK 16 (1969) 61-76. DUNN, J.D.G. Baptism
in the Holy Spirit (1970) 109ff. LEGASSE, S. "Foi et baptême chez saint Paul:
Etude de Galates 3, 26-27" BLE 74 (1973) 81-102. VENETZ, H.-J. "'Christus
anziehen.' Eine Exegese zu Gal 3, 26-27 als Beitrag zum paulinischen
Taufverständnis" FZPhTh 20 (1973) 3-36. DELLING, G. "Die 'Söhne (Kinder)
Gottes' im Neuen Testament" in R. Schnackenburg, ed., Die Kirche des Anfangs (FS
H. Schürmann; Freiburg/Basel/Wien 1978) 616. JEWETT, P. K. Infant Baptism and
the Covenant of Grace (Grand Rapids 1978) 88, 140. BYRNE, B. "Sons of God"-
"Seed of Abraham" (Rome 1979) 1, 2, 4, 165f., 171, 171n., 173, 173n., 175n., 186,
215. SCHLIER, H. "Fragment über die Taufe" in V. Kubina und K. Lehmann, eds.,
Der Geist und die Kirche (FS H. Schlier; Freiburg/Basel/Wien 1980) 137.
BINDEMANN, W. Die Hoffnung der Schöpfung (Neukirchen 1983) 35f. HAYS, R.
B. The Faith of Jesus Christ (Chico CA 1983) 142, 169f., 217, 243. FREUND, G.
und STEGEMANN, E., eds., Theologische Brosamen für Lothar Steiger (DBAT 5;
Heidelberg 1985) 389. CLABEAUX, J. J. The Lost Edition of the Letters of Paul
(CBQ.MS; Washington 1989) 19, 56, 126, 151. SCHÄFER, K. Gemeinde als
"Bruderschaft" (Frankfurt/Bern/New York/Paris 1989) 84-87.

3:26   KERTELGE, K. "Rechtfertigung" bei Paulus (1967) 236-39.

3:27-29   SOIRON, T. Die Kirche als der Leib Christi (1951) 101ff. WIKENHAUSER, A. Die
Christusmystik des Apostels Paulus (1956) 71-79. QUESNELL, Q. This Good News
(1964) 6f. DAVIES, W. D. The Gospel and the Land (Berkeley 1974) 177, 182.
BRINSMEAD, B. H. Galatians—Dialogical Response to Opponents (Chico CA
1982) 141ff., 146ff. HAYTER, M. The New Eve in Christ (Grand Rapids MI 1987)
133-39, 141, 147.

3:27-28   HANSON, S. The Unity of the Church in the New Testament (1946) 79-82.
ROBINSON, J.A.T. The Body (1952) 60ff. LINDEBOOM, A.M. "De kinderdoop
in de brief aan de Galaten? (II)" Homiletica en Biblica 21 (1962) 225. BRAUN, H.
Qumran und das Neue Testament (1966) II 153, 171, 287, 290. MERKLEIN, H. Das
kirchliche Amt nach dem Epheserbrief (1973) 60, 84, 86, 88. LONGSTAFF, T.R.
"The Ordination of Women: A Biblical Perspective" AThR 57 (1975) 316-27.
SMITH, D.C. "Paul and the Non-Eschatological Women" Ohio Journal of Religious
Studies 4 (1976) 11-18. SCHULZ, S. "Evangelium und Welt" in H. D. Betz and L.
Schottroff, eds., Neues Testament und christliche Existenz (FS H. Braun; Tübingen
1973) 490-94. SCROGGS, R. Paul for a New Day (Philadelphia 1977) 44.
MARXSEN, W. Christologie—praktisch (Gütersloh 1978) 88f. SCHMITHALS, W.
"Zur Herkunft der gnostischen Elemente in der Sprache des Paulus" in B. Aland et
al., eds., Gnosis (FS H. Jonas; Göttingen 1978) 388-90. FURNISH, V. P. The Moral
Teaching of Paul (Nashville 1979) 92-95, 101, 102, 111f. SWIDLER, L. Biblical
Affirmations of Woman (Philadelphia 1979) 323. MOXNES, H. Theology in Conflict
(Leiden 1980) 90f. KLAIBER, W. Rechtfertigung und Gemeinde (Göttingen 1982)
85. LAUB, F. Die Begegnung des frühen Christentums mit der antiken Sklaverei
(Stuttgart 1982) 66. MacDONALD, D. R. The Legend and the Apostle (Philadelphia
1983) 98. BERGER, K. "Gnosis/Gnostizismus I" in TRE 13 (1984) 529.

SCHNACKENBURG, R. Die sittliche Botschaft des Neuen Testaments, Band 1 (Freiburg/Basel/Wien 1986) 246f. MacDONALD, D. R. There is No Male and Female. The Fate of a Dominical Saying in Paul and Gnosticism (Philadelphia 1987) passim. SELLIN, G. "Hauptprobleme des Ersten Korintherbriefes" in ANRW II.25.4 (1987) 2961f. ANON, "Une lecture féministe des 'codes domestiques' par un groupe de femmes," FV 88 (5, 1989) 59-69. KLAUCK, H.-J. Gemeinde, Amt, Sakrament (Würzburg 1989) 26, 223, 232-34, 341, 357. LIMBECK, M. Mit Paulus Christ sein. Sachbuch zur Person und Theologie des Apostels Paulus (Stuttgart 1989) 95. OLIVEIRA, A. DE, Die Diakonie der Gerechtigkeit und der Versöhnung in der Apologie des 2. Korintherbriefes. Analyse und Auslegung von 2 Kor 2, 14-4, 6; 5, 11-6, 10 (Münster 1990) 361. WIRE, A. C. The Corinthian Women Prophets (Minneapolis 1990) 19, 123f., 131, 185, 221. WIRE, A. C. "Prophecy and Women Prophets in Corinth" in J. E. Goehring et al., eds., Gospel Origins and Christian Beginnings (FS J. M. Robinson; Sonoma CA 1990) 134-50, esp. 139. GEORGI, D. Theocracy in Paul's Praxis and Theology (Minneapolis 1991) 44f.

3:27   BÜCHSEL, D.F. Der Geist Gottes im Neuen Testament (1926) 282-83. SCHNACK-ENBURG, R. Das Heilsgeschehen bei der Taufe nach dem Apostel Paulus (1950) 18-23; Baptism in the Thought of St. Paul (1964) 21-26. BEST, E. One Body in Christ (1955) 67ff. DELLAGIACOMA, V. "Induere Christum" RevB 4 (1956) 114-42. GILMORE, A. Christian Baptism (1959) 138f., 148f. DELLING, G. Die Zueignung des Heils in der Taufe (1961) 75-77. SCHRAGE, W. Die konkreten Einzelgebote in der paulinischen Paränese (1961) 80-82. BRAUMANN, G. Vorpaulinische christliche Taufverkündigung bei Paulus (1962) 14, 24f., 64. DELLING, G. Die Taufe im Neuen Testament (1963) 119-122. MARCHEL, W. Abba, Père! La Prière du Christ et des Chrétiens (1963) 223-25. NICKELS, P. Targum and New Testament (1967) 74. MERK, O. Handeln aus Glauben (1968) 204-8. LINDEMANN, A. Die Aufhebung der Zeit. Geschichtsverständnis und Eschatologie im Epheserbrief (1975) 72f. BARTH, M. Die Taufe—ein Sakrament? (Zöllikon-Zürich 1951) 353ff. SIBER, P. Mit Christus leben (Zürich 1971) 206. LINDEMANN, A. Die Aufhebung der Zeit. Geschichtsverständnis und Eschatologie im Epheserbrief (Gütersloh 1975) 72f. JEWETT, P. K. Infant Baptism and the Covenant of Grace (Grand Rapids 1978) 140. BYRNE, B. "Sons of God"-"Seed of Abraham" (Rome 1979) 166, 168n., 171. BROOKS, O. S. "A Contextual Interpretation of Galatians 3:27" in E. A. Livingstone, ed., Studia Biblica 1978 III. Papers on Paul and Other New Testament Authors (Sheffield 1980) 47-56. LULL, D. J. The Spirit in Galatia (Chico CA 1980) 65f. BARTH, G. Die Taufe in frühchristlicher Zeit (Neukirchen/ Vluyn 1981) 44, 46, 54f., 75f., 92, 99. SCHMIDT-LAUBER, H.-C. "Epiphaniasfest" in TRE 9 (1982) 769. BARTSCH, H.-W. "Freiheit" in TRE 11 (1983) 508. HAYS, R. B. The Faith of Jesus Christ (Chico CA 1983) 231. HELDERMANN, J. Die Anapausis im Evangelium Veritatis (Leiden 1984) 172. MOHRLANG, R. Matthew and Paul (Cambridge 1984) 83f., 118. BURNISH, R. The Meaning of Baptism. A Comparison of the Teaching and Practice of the Fourth Century with the Present Day (London 1985) 7, 29, 97, 154, 157, 161. FORCK, G. Im Blickpunkt: Taufe (Berlin, DDR 1985) 43f. FREUND, G. und STEGEMANN, E., eds., Theologische Brosamen für Lothar Steiger (DBAT 5; Heidelberg 1985) 390. MALMEDE, H. H. Die Lichtsymbolik im Neuen Testament (Wiesbaden 1986) 163. BERGER, K. und COLPE, C., eds., Religionsgeschichtliches Textbuch zum Neuen Testament (Göttingen/Zürich 1987) 273. HAYTER, M. The New Eve in Christ (Grand Rapids MI 1987) 152. LAYTON, B. The Gnostic Scriptures (Garden City NY 1987) 347n.86d. ELLIS, E. E. Pauline Theology (Grand Rapids/Exeter 1989)

31f., 45, 79. SCHÄFER, K. Gemeinde als "Bruderschaft" (Frankfurt/Bern/New York/Paris 1989) 87f.

3:28-29 SCHRAGE, W. Die konkreten Einzelgebote in der paulinischen Paränese (1961) 82. SCHWEIZER, E. Erniedrigung und Erhöhung bei Jesus und seinen Nachfolgern (1962) §5g. THÜSING, W. Per Christum in Deum (1955) 116f. PORTER, S. E. "Wittgenstein's Classes of Utterances and Pauline Ethical Texts," JEThS 32 (1989) 85-97.

3:28 BONHOEFFER, A. Epiktet und das Neue Testament (1911) 166, 306.BOUSSET, W. Die Religion des Judentums im Späthellenistischen Zeitalter (1966=1926) 427. LOCHLET, L. "Autorité et amour dans la vie conjugale" L'Anneau d'Or 68 (1956) 108-21. SCHRAGE, W. Die konkreten Einzelgebote in der paulinischen Paränese (1961) 118, 178, 205. LINDEBOOM, A.M. "De kinderdoop in de brief aan de Galaten" Homiletica en Biblica 21 (1962) 127-28. DELLING, G. Die Taufe im Neuen Testament (1963) 119-120. KRAMER, W. Christos Kyrios Gottessohn (1963) §33b. BAIRD, W. The Corinthian Church — A Biblical Approach to Urban Culture (1964) 126-27. KÄSEMANN, E. Exegetische Versuche und Besinnungen (1964) I 115. HAHN, F. Das Verständnis der Mission im Neuen Testament (1965) 92. KÜNG, H. Die Kirche (1967) 252, 359, 361; The Church (1967) 210, 302, 304. MERK, O. Handeln aus Glauben (1968) 227-28. MUSSNER, F. Christus, das All und die Kirche (1968) 127. SUMMERS, R. The Secret Sayings of the Living Jesus (1968) 60. BOUCHER, M. "Some Unexplored Parallels to 1 Cor 11, 11-12 and Gal 3, 28: The NT on the Role of Women" CBQ 31 (1969) 50-58. CAVALLIN, H.C.C. "Demythologizing the Liberal Illusion" Churchman 83 (1969) 263-74. CREN, P.R. "'Il n'y a plus ni juif ni grec. . . (Gal 3, 28)" LuVit 18 (1969) 113-29. BARTCHY, S.S. First Century Slavery and I Corinthians (1973) 162-65. HALL, B. "Paul and Women" ThT 31 (1974) 50-55. LADD, G.E. A Theology of the New Testament (1974) 528, 530. VOLCKAERT, J. "Ordination of Women in Pauline Letters" Vidyajyoti 39 (1975) 394-400. GRAHAM, R.W. "Women in the Pauline Churches" LThQ 11 (1976) 25-34. STENDAHL, K. The Bible and the Role of Women (1966) 32-37. BOLDREY, R. and J., Chauvinist Or Feminist? Paul's View of Women (Grand Rapids 1976) 11, 24, 25 n.20, 32f., 35, 46ff., 50, 57, 70. DAVIS, J. J. "Some Reflections on Galatians 3:28, Sexual Roles, and Biblical Hermeneutics," JEThS 19 (1976) 201-08. BURRI, J. 'Als Mann und Frau schuf er sie.' Differenz der Geschlechter aus moral- und praktisch-theologischer Sicht (1977) passim. LA-MARCHE, P. "'Ni mâle, ni femelle' Galates 3, 28," Christus 24 (95, 1977) 349-55. PASTOR RAMOS, F. La libertad en la Carta a los Gálatas. Estudio exegético-teológico (Madrid 1977) passim. GALITIS, G. "Hoi anypotaktoi tēs Krētēs kai hē entolē tēs hypotages (The Disobedients of Crete and the Command for Obedience)," DBM 5 (1977/78) 196-208. FRIEDRICH, G. "Christus, Einheit und Norm der Christen. Das Grundmotiv des 1. Korintherbriefes" in Auf das Wort kommt es an. Gesammelte Aufsätze (Göttingen 1978) 153. FRIEDRICH, G. "Das Problem der Autorität im Neuen Testament" in Auf das Wort kommt es an. Gesammelte Aufsätze (Göttingen 1978) 397f. MERODE, M. DE, "Une théologie primitive de la femme?" RThL 9 (1978) 176-89. ROLOFF, J. "Amt" in TRE 2 (1978) 520. RUDOLPH, K. Die Gnosis (Göttingen 1978) 285-320. SCHMITHALS, W. "Zur Herkunft der gnostischen Elemente in der Sprache des Paulus" in B. Aland et al., eds., Gnosis (FS H. Jonas; Göttingen 1978) 388-90, 401. STAGG, E. and F. Women in the World of Jesus (Philadelphia 1978) 163-66. STENDAHL, K. "Die biblische Auffassung von Mann und Frau" in E. Moltmann-Wendel, ed., Frauenbefreiung. Biblische und theologische Argumente (München 1978) 126-29. VIVIANO, B. T. "Saint Paul and the Ministry of Women," Spirituality Today [Chicago] 30 (1978) 37-44. BYRNE,

B. "Sons of God"-"Seed of Abraham" (Rome 1979) 100n., 166f., 168nn., 171, 173, 194. LITFIN, A. D. "Evangelical Feminism: Why Traditionalists Reject It," BiblSa 136 (543, 1979) 258-71. CLARK, S. B. Man and Woman in Christ (Ann Arbor MI 1980) 32, 138-63, 219, 229, 237, 250, 264, 289, 361, 364. GERSTENBERGER, E. S. und SCHRAGE, W. Frau und Mann (Stuttgart 1980) 121-23. LÜHRMANN, D. "Abendmahlsgemeinschaft? Gal 2, 11ff" in D. Lührmann und G. Strecker, eds., Kirche (FS G. Bornkamm; Tübingen 1980) 282f., 285. LÜHRMANN, D. "Neutestamentliche Haustafeln und Antike Ökonomie," NTS 27 (1980) 92f. SARACINO, F. "Forma e funzione di una formula paolina: Gal 3, 28," RivB 28 (1980) 385-406. KLAUCK, H.-J. Hausgemeinde und Hauskirche im frühen Christentum (Stuttgart 1981) 100. LEGRAND, L. " 'There is neither Slave nor Free, neither Male nor Female': St Paul and Social Emancipation," IndTheol Stu 18 (1981) 135-63. WITHERINGTON, B. "Rite and Rights for Women—Galatians 3.28," NTS 27 (1981) 593-604. CASEY, M. "Chronology and the Development of Pauline Christology" in M. D. Hooker and S. G. Wilson, eds., Paul and Paulinism (FS C. K. Barrett; London 1982) 132f. DAUTZENBERG, G. "'Da ist nicht männlich und weiblich.' Zur Interpretation von Gal 3, 28," Kairos 24 (1982) 181-206. REICKE, B. "Ehe" in TRE 9 (1982) 322. SCHRAGE, W. "Ethik" in TRE 10 (1982) 449. STENDAHL, K. "Ancient Scripture in the Modern World" in F. E. Greenspahn, ed., Scripture in the Jewish and Christian Traditions (Nashville 1982) 208. THEISSEN, G. The Social Setting of Pauline Christianity (Edinburgh 1982) 109. BARRETT, C. K. "The Centre of the New Testament and the Canon" in U. Luz und H. Weder, eds., Die Mitte des Neuen Testaments (FS E. Schweizer; Göttingen 1983) 12. HAYS, R. B. The Faith of Jesus Christ (Chico CA 1983) 169, 232. LUDOLPHY, I. "Frau" in TRE 11 (1983) 442. RINGELING, H. "Frau" in TRE 11 (1983) 433, 434. SCHARFFENORTH, G. and REICHLE, E. "Frau" in TRE 11 (1983) 448, 450, 459, 460. SCHÜSSLER FIORENZA, E. In Memory of Her (London 1983) 50, 76, 78, 162, 199, 205-36, 251-53, 270, 272, 278f. THEISSEN, G. Psychologische Aspekte paulinischer Theologie (Göttingen 1983) 57, 161, 170f., 171n.29, 171n.31, 301. FREY, C. "Gesellschaft/Gesellschaft und Christentum VII" in TRE 13 (1984) 35. KLASSEN, W. "Musonius Rufus, Jesus, and Paul: Three First-Century Feminists" in P.Richardson and J. C. Hurd, eds., From Jesus to Paul (FS F. W. Beare; Waterloo 1984) 201-03. LONGENECKER, R. N. New Testament Social Ethics for Today (Grand Rapids 1984) 29-93. VERHEY, A. The Great Reversal (Grand Rapids 1984) 113-17. BIERITZ, K.-H. and KÄHLER, C. "Haus III" in TRE 14 (1985) 484. FREUND, G. und STEGEMANN, E., eds., Theologische Brosamen für Lothar Steiger (DBAT 5; Heidelberg 1985) 390. FULLER, D. P. "Paul and Galatians 3:28," TSFBulletin [Madison, WI] 9 (2, 1985) 9-13. HAHN, F. "Gottesdienst III" in TRE 14 (1985) 36. NEYREY, J. H. Christ is Community. The Christologies of the New Testament (Wilmington, DE 1985) 226, 249f., 253, 256. MALINA B. J. Christian Origins and Cultural Anthropology (Atlanta 1986) 138. RÄISÄNEN, H. The Torah and Christ (Helsinki 1986) 291. WIRE, A. C. "*Not* Male and Female," Pacific Theological Review [San Francisco CA] 19 (2, 1986) 37-43. BERGER, K. und COLPE, C., eds., Religionsgeschichtliches Textbuch zum Neuen Testament (Göttingen/Zürich 1987) 273-78. HAYTER, M. The New Eve in Christ (Grand Rapids 1987) 128f., 146, 164. HEINE, S. Women and Early Christianity (London 1987) 4, 9, 50, 53, 84f., 100, 146, 150-53. JONES, F. S. "Freiheit" in den Briefen des Apostels Paulus (Göttingen 1987) 21, 28, 52, 70, 76, 85, 138, 147n.3, 160n.9, 161n.18, 192n.1. MacDONALD, D. R. There Is No Male and Female (Philadelphia 1987) 88f. MERKLEIN, H. Studien zu Jesus und Paulus (Tübingen 1987) 60, 102, 293, 331n.55a, 334, 337-40, 342, 396, 407. OSTEN-SACKEN, P. VON DER,

Evangelium und Tora: Aufsätze zu Paulus (München 1987) 66, 71, 87, 236. BYRNE, B. Paul and the Christian Woman (Homebush, NSW 1988) 1-14. DOWNING, F. G. Christ and the Cynics (Sheffield 1988) 2. HOUSE, H. W. "A Biblical View of Women in the Ministry. Part 1 (of 5 parts): 'Neither . . . Male nor Female . . . in Christ Jesus'," BiblSa 145 (577, 1988) 47-56. JONGE, M. DE, Christology in Context. The Earliest Christian Response to Jesus (Philadelphia 1988) 41ff., 218n.21, 228n.4. MacDONALD, M. Y. The Pauline Churches (Cambridge 1988) 103. ELLIS, E. E. Pauline Theology (Grand Rapids/Exeter 1989) 46, 55f., 58, 64, 66, 78-85. MARXSEN, W. "Christliche" und christliche Ethik im Neuen Testament (Gütersloh 1989) 167. MOTYER, S. "The Relationship between Paul's Gospel of 'All One in Christ Jesus' (Galatians 3:28) and the 'Household Codes'," VE 19 (1989) 33-48. SCHÄFER, K. Gemeinde als "Bruderschaft" (Frankfurt/Bern/New York/Paris 1989) 88. TOWNER, Ph. H. The Goal of Our Instruction. The Structure of Theology and Ethics in the Pastoral Epistles (Sheffield 1989) 35f., 171f., 176, 209f., 212, 218-21, 248, 306n.89. WEDDERBURN, A. J. M. "Paul and the Story of Jesus" in A. J. M. Wedderburn, ed., Paul and Jesus. Collected Essays (Sheffield 1989) 161-89, esp. 161, 168ff. GIELEN, M. Tradition und Theologie neutestamentlicher Haustafelethik (Frankfurt 1990) 551f. MULLER, E. C. Trinity and Marriage in Paul (New York/Bern/Frankfurt/Paris 1990) 149-57, 168, 193, 428, 434, 435f., 441f. REBELL, W. Zum neuen Leben berufen (München 1990) 103-11, 206. SEGAL, A. F. Paul the Convert (New Haven/London 1990) 137, 146, 181. WIRE, A. C. The Corinthian Women Prophets (Minneapolis 1990) 62, 86, 138, 162, 185, 281n.2. HOPKO, T. "Galatians 3:28: An Orthodox Interpretation," SVThQ 35 (1991) 169-86. LOWE, S. D. "Rethinking the Female Status/Function Question. The Jew/Gentile Relationship as Paradigm," JEThS 34 (1991) 59-75. GRANT, R. M. "Neither Male Nor Female," BR 37 (1992) 5-14.

3:29-4:2 HAYS, R. B. The Faith of Jesus Christ (Chico CA 1983) 104.

3:29 ELLIS, E. E. Paul's Use of the Old Testament (1957) 70, 72, 130-31. SCHRAGE, W. Die konkreten Einzelgebote in der paulinischen Paränese (1961) 78. MINDE, H.-J. VAN DER, Schrift und Tradition bei Paulus (München/ Paderborn/Wien 1976) 137f. SCHMITHALS, W. "Zur Herkunft der gnostischen Elemente in der Sprache des Paulus" in B. Aland et al., eds., Gnosis (FS H. Jonas; Göttingen 1978) 388-90. BYRNE, B. "Sons of God"-"Seed of Abraham" (Rome 1979) 165, 168, 171f., 173, 175, 175n., 185, 190, 208. THISELTON, A. C. The Two Horizons (Grand Rapids 1980) 401. HAYS, R. B. The Faith of Jesus Christ (Chico CA 1983) 202, 206, 244. MÖLLER, C. "Gemeinde" in TRE 12 (1984) 318. COSGROVE, C. H. The Cross and the Spirit. A Study in the Argument and Theology of Galatians (Macon GA 1988) 2n., 32, 51f., 63, 73, 173, 175, 180. CHANCE, J. B. "The Seed of Abraham and the People of God. A Study of Two Pauls" in E. H. Lovering, ed., Society of Biblical Literature 1993 Seminar Papers (Atlanta 1993) 384-411. HONG, I.-G. The Law in Galatians (Sheffield 1993) 46-48.

4-5 JÜNGEL, E. Paulus und Jesus (1966) 32. KAYE, B. "Law and Morality in the Epistles of the New Testament" in B. Kaye and G. Wenham, eds., Law, Morality and the Bible (Downers Grove Ill. 1978) 81f. VOLLENWEIDER, S. Freiheit als neue Schöpfung (Göttingen 1989) 285ff.

4 KURZE, G. "Die στοιχεῖα τοῦ κόσμου, Gal 4 und Kol 2" BZ 15 (1918-1921) 335-37. HAHN, F. Christologische Hoheitstitel (1963) 316. SARGENT, R. "The Spirit of Sons in Galations 4" Bible Today 1 (1964) 656-59. HESTER, J.D. "The 'Heir' and Heilsgeschichte: A Study of Galatians 4:1ff." in Oikonomia, hrsg. von f. Christ (1967) 118-28. DAMERAU, R. Der Galaterbriefkommentar des Nikolaus

Dinkelsbühl (1970) 103-36. WELLS, G. The Jesus of the Early Christians (1971) 146-47. BÖHLIG, A. "Vom 'Knecht' zum 'Sohn'" in Mysterion und Wahrheit. Gesammelte Beiträge zur spätantiken Religionsgeschichte (1968) 64f. BRINSMEAD, B. H. Galatians—Dialogical Response to Opponents (Chico CA 1982) 107ff. HELDERMANN, J. Die Anapausis im Evangelium Veritatis (Leiden 1984) 269n.672. GRAESSER, E. Der Alte Bund im Neuen (Tübingen 1985) 55, 68, 69, 81, 89, 95. MUELLER-SCHWEFE, H.-R. Christus im Zeitalter der Oekumene (Göttingen 1986) 174-78. PANIER, L. "Parcours pour lire l'épître aux Galates. 4ème série: Ga 4," SémiotBib 53 (1989) 48-53. HOOKER, M. D. From Adam to Christ. Essays on Paul (Cambridge 1990) 16, 61, 158f., 168, 173, 185.

4:1ff.   THEISSEN, G. Psychologische Aspekte paulinischer Theologie (Göttingen 1983) 248. FREUND, G. und STEGEMANN, E., eds., Theologische Brosamen für Lothar Steiger (DBAT 5; Heidelberg 1985) 393.

4:1-20   BLACK, D. A. "Weakness Language in Galatians," GThJ 4 (1, 1983) 15-36. COSGROVE, C. H. The Cross and the Spirit. A Study in the Argument and Theology of Galatians (Macon GA 1988) 18, 75f.

4:1-11   REICKE, B. "Lagen och denna världen hos Paulus. Några tankar inför Gal. 4, 1-11" SEA 8 (1943) 49-70; "The Law and This World According to Paul" JBL 70 (1951) 259-76. SCHWEITZER, A. Die Mystik des Apostels Paulus (1954) 71f. CAIRD, G.B. Principalities and Powers (1956) 47ff. MÜLLER—BARDORFF, J. Paulus (1970) 169-80. MACGORMAN, J.W. "Problem Passages in Galatians" SouJTh 15 (1972) 35-51. BRINSMEAD, B. H. Galatians—Dialogical Response to Opponents (Chico CA 1982) 122-27. HAYS, R. B. The Faith of Jesus Christ (Chico CA 1983) 245. RÄISÄNEN, H. Paul and the Law (Tübingen 1983) 22f., 204.

4:1-10   CRAMER, A.W. Stoicheia Tou Kosmou (1961) 115-31. MINEAR, P. S. To Die and to Live. Christ's Resurrection and Christian Vocation (1977) 73. HOWARD, G. Paul. Crisis in Galatia (Cambridge 1979) 71-82. PATTE, D. Paul's Faith and the Power of the Gospel (Philadelphia 1983) 52-57.

4:1-9   ANTOINE, P. "Vous n'êtes plus esclaves mais fils" Christus 45 (1965) 56-70. MOORE-CRISPIN, D. R. "Galatians 4:1-9. The Use and Abuse of Parallels," EQ 61 (1989) 203-23.

4:1-7   CALDER, W.M. "Adoption and Inheritance in Galatia," JThS 31 (1929-30) 372-74. GEORGE, A. "De l'esclavage à la liberté" AssS 11 (1961) 19-28. SURKAU, H.-W. GPM 16 (1961/62) 56ff. BANDSTRA, A.J. The Law and the Elements of the World (1964) 59ff. SISTI, A. "L'adozione divina (Gal. 4, 1-7)" BiOr 6 (1964) 267-72. THÜSING, W. Per Christum in Deum (1965) 116-119. DE QUERVAIN, A. in Herr, tue meine Lippen auf II, hrsg. von G. Eichholz (1966) 65-72. DOERNE, M. Die alten Episteln (1967) 31-34. LUZ, U. Das Geschichtsverständnis des Paulus (1968) 155f., 282f. ECKERT, J. Die urchristliche Verkündigung im Streit zwischen Paulus un dseinen Gegnern nach dem Galaterbrief (1971) 88-91. GEORGI, D. GPM 28 (1973/74) 54-62. ROESSLER, D.u. SIMPFENDOERFER, in Predigtstudien für das Kirchenjahr 1973/74, hrsg. VON E. lANGE (1973) 90-94. DRANE, J.W. Paul: Libertine or Legalist? (1975) 36-38. VON DER OSTEN-SACKEN, P. Römer 8 als Beispiel paulinischer Soteriologie (1975) 129ff. PAGELS, E.H. The Gnostic Paul (1975) 108-9. FRIEDRICH, G. "Freiheit und Liebe im ersten Korintherbrief" in Auf das Wort kommt es an. Gesammelte Aufsätze (Göttingen 1978) 181. BYRNE, B. "Sons of God"-"Seed of Abraham" (Rome 1979) 173n., 174-86, 203. BUSCEMI, A. M. "Libertà e Huiothesia. Studio esegetico di Gal 4, 1-7," SBFLA 30 (1980) 93-136. KIM, S. The Origin of Paul's Gospel (Tübingen 1981) 316-18. KLAIBER, W. Rechtfertigung und Gemeinde (Göttingen 1982) 152. HAYS, R. B. The Faith of Jesus Christ (Chico CA 1983) 216f., 245. THEISSEN, G. Psychological Aspects of

Pauline Theology (Edinburgh 1987) 246f. COSGROVE, C. H. The Cross and the Spirit. A Study in the Argument and Theology of Galatians (Macon GA 1988) 51, 69f., 72f., 75. HONG, I.-G. The Law in Galatians (Sheffield 1993) 47f., 160f.

4:1-3   HAYS, R. B. The Faith of Jesus Christ (Chico CA 1983) 128.

4:1-2   CALLAWAY, J.S. "Paul's Letter to the Galatians and Plato's Lysis" JBL 67 (1948) 353-55. STUHLMANN, R. Das eschatologische Mass im Neuen Testament (Göttingen 1983) 68f., 78n.

4:1   SCHRAGE, W. Die konkreten Einzelgebote in der paulinischen Paränese (1961) 106. HAYS, R. B. The Faith of Jesus Christ (Chico CA 1983) 230.

4:2ff.   DEMKE, C. "Gott IV" in TRE 13 (1984) 646.

4:2   PFAMMATER, J. Die Kirche als Bau (1960) 69ff.

4:3ff   TACHAU, P. 'Einst' und 'Jetzt' im Neuen Testament (1972) 82-83.

4:3-11   WINK, W. Naming the Powers (Philadelphia 1984) 70-72. THIELMAN, F. From Plight to Solution (Leiden 1989) 80-83. THORNTON, T. C. G. "Jewish New Moon Festivals, Galatians 4:3-11 and Colossians 2:16," JThS 40 (1989) 97-100.

4:3,9   DIBELIUS, M. Die Geisterwelt im Glauben des Paulus (1909) 78ff., 199ff. KENNEDY, H.A.A. St.Paul and the Mystery-Religions (1913) 61, 169. HATCH, W.H.P. "τὰ στοιχεῖα in Paul and Bardaisān" JThS 28 (1926-27) 181-82. MACGREGOR, G.H.C. "Principalities and Powers: The cosmic Background of Paul's Thought" NTS 1 (1954-55) 21ff. CRAMER, A.W. Stoicheia Tou Kosmou (1961). BLINZLER, J. "Lexikalisches zu dem Terminus τὰ στοιχεῖα τοῦ κόσμου bei Paulus" in Studiorum Paulinorum Congressus Internationalis Catholicus 1961, Vol. II (1963) 429-43. BANDSTRA, A.J. The Law and the Elements of the World (1964). BOUSSET, W. Die Religion des Judentums im späthellenistischen Zeitalter (1966=1926) 323. KEHL, N. Der Christushymnus im Kolosserbrief (1967) 138-40. SCHWEIZER, E. "Die 'Elemente der Welt' Gal 4, 3.9; Kol 2, 8.20" in Beiträge zur Theologie des Neuen Testaments (1970) 147-63; in Verborum Veritas. Festschrift für G. Stählin, hrsg. von O. Böcher u. K. Haacker (1970) 245-59. VIELHAUER, P. "Gesetzesdienst und Stoicheiadienst im Galaterbrief" in Oikodome [G. Klein, ed.] (München 1979) 183-95.

4:3,8-10 SCHWEIZER, E. Erniedrigung und Erhöhung bei Jesus und seinen Nachfolgern (1962) §9c.

4:3,9-10 SCHNELLE, U. Wandlungen im paulinischen Denken (Stuttgart 1989) 54.

4:3,9   RUDOLPH, K. Die Gnosis (Göttingen 1978) 320. BÖCHER, O. Kirche in Zeit und Endzeit. Aufsätze zur Offenbarung des Johannes (Neukirchen 1983) 25. SCHWEIZER, E. Theologische Einleitung in das Neue Testament (Göttingen 1989) § 17.4. RUSAM, D. "Neue Belege zu den *stoicheia tou kosmou* (Gal 4, 3.9; Kol 2, 8.20)," ZNW 83 (1992) 119-25.

4:3-7   BINDEMANN, W. Die Hoffnung der Schöpfung (Neukirchen 1983) 36. HAYS, R. B. The Faith of Jesus Christ (Chico CA 1983) 229. LOHFINK, G. Studien zum Neuen Testament (Stuttgart 1989) 273-76.

4:3-6   HAYS, R. B. The Faith of Jesus Christ (Chico CA 1983) 29, 86-92, 104-11, 116-21, 123, 125, 127, 134, 227, 230.

4:3-5   WULF, F. "Einssein und Uneinssein met Gott — und mit den Mitmenschen" GuL 42 (1969) 311-14. VOLLENWEIDER, S. Freiheit als neue Schöpfung (Göttingen 1989) 218.

4:3   HINCKS, E.Y. "The Meaning of the Phrase τὰ στοιχεῖα τοῦ κόσμου in Gal. iv. 3 and Col. ii. 8" JBL 15 (1896) 183-92. THACKERAY, H.St.J. The Relation of St. Paul to Contemporary Jewish Thought (1900) 164ff. HUBY, J. "Στοιχεῖα dans Bardesane et dans Saint Paul" Biblica 15 (1934) 365-368. BURTON, E. "TA STOI-XEIA TOY KOSMOY" in The Epistle to the Galatians (1950=1921) 510-18.

DEWITT, N.W. St.Paul and Epicurus (1954) 63-64. CRAMER, A.W. Stoicheia Tou Kosmou (1961) 143-58. ADAM, A. "Die sprachliche Herkunft des Wortes Elementum" NovT 6 (1963) 229-32; in XAPI? KAI ?o?IA. Festschrift Karl Heinrich Rengstorf (1964) 229-32. KÄSEMANN, E. Exegetische Versuche und Besinnungen (1964) 229-32. KÄSEMANN, E. Exegetische Versuche und Besinnungen (1964) I 73. HAMERTON—KELLY, R.G. Pre-Existence, Wisdom, and the Son of Man (1973) 107-8. KERN, W. "Die Antizipierte Entideologisierung oder die 'Weltelemente' des Galater — und Kolosserbriefes heute" ZThK 96 (1974) 185-216. LADD, G.E. A Theology of the New Testament (1974) 398-99, 402-3. VIELHAUER, P. "Gesetzesdienst und Stoicheiadienst im Galaterbrief" in Rechtfertigung. Festschrift für Ernst Käsemann (1976) 543-55. CARL, K. J. "The Pauline View of Christian Freedom in Terms of the Enigmatic Phrase, the *Stoicheia tou Kosmou*, in the Epistle to the Galatians," BangalTheolFor 9 (1977) 28-46. BYRNE, B. "Sons of God"-"Seed of Abraham" (Rome 1979) 175-78, 176nn., 188n. HOWARD, G. Paul. Crisis in Galatia (Cambridge 1979) 66-82. VIELHAUER, P. "Gesetzesdienst und Stoicheiadienst im Galaterbrief" in Oikodome [G. Klein, ed.] (München 1979) 183-95. BRINSMEAD, B. H. Galatians— Dialogical Response to Opponents (Chico CA 1982) 120ff. HAYS, R. B. The Faith of Jesus Christ (Chico CA 1983) 104, 107, 108, 110, 123, 229. BARRETT, C. K. Freedom and Obligation (Philadelphia 1985) 39, 41f. SCHIMANOWSKI, G. Weisheit und Messias (Tübingen 1985) 328. MALMEDE, H. H. Die Lichtsymbolik im Neuen Testament (Wiesbaden 1986) 136f. WINK, W. Unmasking the Powers (Philadelphia 1986) 130, 145, 149. HÜBNER, H. "Paulusforschung seit 1945. Ein kritischer Literaturbericht" in ANRW II.25.4 (1987) 2691-94. SCHWEIZER, E. "Slaves of the Elements and Worshipers of Angels. Gal 4:3, 9 and Col 2:8, 18, 20," JBL 107 (1988) 455-68. LIMBECK, M. Mit Paulus Christ sein. Sachbuch zur Person und Theologie des Apostels Paulus (Stuttgart 1989) 74. HOWARD, G. Paul. Crisis in Galatia (Cambridge ²1990) 66-69, 98. BUNDRICK, D. R. "*Ta Stoicheia tou Kosmou* (Gal 4:3)," JEThS 34 (1991) 353-64.

4:4ff.   THEISSEN, G. Psychologische Aspekte paulinischer Theologie (Göttingen 1983) 56, 264f. RIDDERBOS, H. Paul. An Outline of His Theology (Grand Rapids 1975) 198-204.

4:4-7   STANLEY, D.M. Christ's Resurrection in Pauline Soteriology (1961) 155-58. BLANK, J. Paulus und Jesus (1968) 258ff. VELLANICKAL, M. The Divine Sonship of Christians in the Johannine Writings (Rome 1977) 78f. DELLING, G. "Die 'Söhne (Kinder) Gottes' im Neuen Testament" in R. Schnackenburg et al., eds., Die Kirche des Anfangs (FS H. Schürman; Freiburg/Basel/Wien 1978) 615f. CLARK, S. B. Man and Woman in Christ (Ann Arbor MI 1980) 144. STOEVESANDT, H. in GPM 38 (1983/84) 42-51. HELDERMANN, J. Die Anapausis im Evangelium Veritatis (Leiden 1984) 197.

4:4-6   SCHNACKENBURG, R. Das Heilsgeschehen bei der Taufe nach dem Apostel Paulus (1950) 80f.; Baptism in the Thought of St. Paul (1964) 86. TROADEC, H.-G. "La Bible et la Vierge. La famme, cause de notre adoption divine; le témoignage de saint Paul" Cahiers Evangiles 13 (1954) 8-10. LEGAULT, A. "Saint Paul a-t-il parlé de la maternité virginale de Marie?" Sciences Ecclésistiques 16 (1964) 481-93. OSTEN-SACKEN, P. VON DER, "Das paulinische Verständnis des Gesetzes im Spannungsfeld von Eschatologie und Geschichte. Erläuterungen zum Evangelium als Faktor von theologischem Antijudaismus," EvTh 37 (1977) 549-87. LULL, D. J. The Spirit in Galatia (Chico CA 1980) 154-57, 169-71. HAYS, R. B. The Faith of Jesus Christ (Chico CA 1983) 113, 114, 255. OSTEN-SACKEN, P. VON DER, Evangelium und Tora: Aufsätze zu Paulus (München 1987) 26, 161, 172. THEISSEN, G. Psychological Aspects of Pauline Theology (Edinburgh 1987) 47, 262f.

JONGE, M. DE, Christology in Context. The Earliest Christian Response to Jesus (Philadelphia 1988) 42, 114, 121, 190, 193. HOFIUS, O. Paulusstudien (Tübingen 1989) 149, 166. LIEBERS, R. Das Gesetz als Evangelium (Zürich 1989) 182-86. LIMBECK, M. Mit Paulus Christ sein. Sachbuch zur Person und Theologie des Apostels Paulus (Stuttgart 1989) 95. VOLLENWEIDER, S. Freiheit als neue Schöpfung (Göttingen 1989) 302f., 359.

4:4-5   BOVER, J.M. "Un texto de San Pablo (Gal. 4, 4-5) interpretado por San Ireneo" EstEc 17 (1943) 145-81. ROBINSON, J.M. Kerygma und historischer Jesus (1960) 175. ULRICH, U. "Historische Fragen zum Verhältnis Kyrios und Pneuma bei Paulus" ThLZ 85 (1960) 845-48. BRANDENBURGER, E. Adam und Christus (1962) 236f. BRAUMANN, G. Vorpaulinische christliche Taufverkündigung bei Paulus (1962) 73f. DELLING, G. Die Taufe im Neuen Testament (1963) 120. SCHILLE, G. Frühchristliche Hymnen (1965) 133. JÜNGEL, E. Paulus und Jesus (1966) 59f. SCHWEIZER, E. "Zum religionsgeschichtlichen Hintergrund der 'Sendungsformel' Gal 4:4f., Rm 8:3f., John 3:16f., 1 Joh 4:9" ZNW 57 (1966) 199-210; in Beiträge zur Theologie des Neuen Testaments (1970) 83-95. LUZ, U. Das Geschichtsverständnis des Paulus (1968) 282f. VOEGTLE, A. Das Evangelium und die die Evangelien (1971) 48-50. BORSE, U. Der Standort des Galaterbriefes (1972) 59-61. FULLER, R. H. "The Conception/Birth of Jesus as a Christological Moment," JSNT 1 (1978) 37-52. SCHMITHALS, W. "Zur Herkunft der gnostischen Elemente in der Sprache des Paulus" in B. Aland et al., eds., Gnosis (FS H. Jonas; Göttingen 1978) 403, 406. BYRNE, B. "Sons of God"-"Seed of Abraham" (Rome 1979) 6, 94, 94n., 152, 178-84, 185, 197, 199, 205, 207, 208, 214. FROITZHEIM, F. Christologie und Eschatologie bei Paulus (Würzburg 1979) 51ff. BERGMEIER, R. Glaube als Gabe nach Johannes (Stuttgart 1980) 210. DEMAREST, B. A. "Process Theology and the Pauline Doctrine of the Incarnation" in D. A. Hagner and M. J. Harris, eds., Pauline Studies (FS F. F. Bruce; Exeter 1980) 129f. BISER, E. Der Zeuge (Graz/Wien/Köln 1981) 34, 90, 100, 102, 187, 259, 265f. KIM, S. The Origin of Paul's Gospel (Tübingen 1981) 131-33, 277f. SCHWEIZER, E. "Paul's Christology and Gnosticism" in M. D. Hooker and S. G. Wilson, eds., Paul and Paulinism (FS C. K. Barrett; London 1982) 118f. HAYS, R. B. The Faith of Jesus Christ (Chico CA 1983) 86-91, 118f., 127, 129, 135, 256. RÄISÄNEN, H. Paul and the Law (Tübingen 1983) 54, 131, 248. SCHNACKENBURG, R. "Paulinische und johanneische Christologie. Ein Vergleich" in U. Luz und H. Weder, eds., Die Mitte des Neuen Testaments (FS E. Schweizer; Göttingen 1983) 222. DAUTZENBERG, G. "Gesetzeskritik und Gesetzesgehorsam in der Jesustradition" in K. Kertelge, ed., Das Gesetz im Neuen Testament (Freiburg/Basel/Wien 1986) 49-52. MUSSNER, F. Die Kraft der Wurzel (Freiburg/Basel/Wien 1987) 91. OSTEN-SACKEN, P. VON DER, Evangelium und Tora: Aufsätze zu Paulus (München 1987) 162, 168, 172. SCHULZ, S. Neutestamentliche Ethik (Zürich 1987) 187, 189f. SCHWEIZER, E. Jesus Christ. The Man from Nazareth and the Exalted Lord (Macon GA 1987) 19f., 78. BECKER, J. Paulus. Der Apostel der Völker (Tübingen 1989) 118, 126f., 398, 400, 424, 427. LIMBECK, M. Mit Paulus Christ sein. Sachbuch zur Person und Theologie des Apostels Paulus (Stuttgart 1989) 66. MARXSEN, W. "Christliche" und christliche Ethik im Neuen Testament (Gütersloh 1989) 52, 148, 157. DUNN, J. D. G. Jesus, Paul and the Law (London 1990) 229, 236n.61, 248, 250. HOOKER, M. D. From Adam to Christ. Essays on Paul (Cambridge 1990) 33, 59f. OLIVEIRA, A. DE, Die Diakonie der Gerechtigkeit und der Versöhnung in der Apologie des 2. Korintherbriefes. Analyse und Auslegung von 2 Kor 2, 14-4, 6; 5, 11-6, 10 (Münster 1990) 224n.663. LIPS, H. VON, "Christus als Sophia? Weisheitliche Traditionen in der urchristlichen Christologie" in C. Breytenbach und H. Paulsen, eds., Anfänge der

Christologie (FS F. Hahn; Göttingen 1991) 75-95, esp. 89f. SCHWEIZER, E. "What Do We Really Mean When We Say 'God sent his son . . . '?" in J. T. Carroll et al., eds., Faith and History (FS P. W. Meyer; Atlanta 1991) 298-312.

4:4   MITCHELL, A.W. "'The Fulness of Time' (Gal. 4:4)" ET 19 (1907-08) 237. ROBINSON, J.M. Kerygma und historischer Jesus (1960) 177f. SCHRAGE, W. Die konkreten Einzelgebote in der paulinischen Paränese (1961) 14f. SCHELKLE, K.-H. "Geworden aus dem Weibe — Geboren aus der Jungfrau" BiLe 3 (1962) 232-40. SCHWEIZER, E. Erniedrigung und Erhöhung bei Jesus und seinen Nachfolgern (1962) §9d. HAHN, F. Christologische Hoheitstitel (1963) 252, 315. KRAMER, W. Christos Kyrios Gottessohn (1963) §§ 25b, 55e, h. NEUENZEIT, P. "'Als die Fülle der Zeit gekommen war. . .' (Gal 4, 4). Gedanken zum biblischen Zeitverständnis" BiLe 4 (1963) 223-39. DE ROOVER, E. "La Maternite Virginale de Marie dans l'Interpretation de Gal 4, 4" in Studiorum Paulinorum Congressus Internationalis Catholicus 1961, Vol. II (1963) 17-37. STUHLMACHER, P. Gerechtigkeit Gottes bei Paulus (1965) 208f. GOGARTEN, F. Christ the Crisis (1967) 68f. VAN DÜLMEN, A. Die Theologie des Gesetzes bei Paulus (1968) 50f. MAUSER, U. Gottesbild und Menschwerdung (1971) 141f., 152f., 166f. BORSE, U. Der Standort des Galaterbriefes (1972) 60f. CAPALDI, G.I. "In the Fulness of Time (Gal 4, 4)" SJTh 25 (1972) 197-216. KLIJN, A.F.J. & REININK, G.J. Patristic Evidence for Jewish-Christian Sects (1973) 21. LINDEMANN, A. Die Aufhebung der Zeit (1975) 28f. KÜMMEL, W.G., ed., Jüdische Schriften aus hellenistisch—römischer Zeit, Band V: Apokalypsen (Lieferung 2) (1976) 142, 147. ROON, A. VAN, The Authenticity of Ephesians (Leiden 1974) 248. LINDEMANN, A. Die Aufhebung der Zeit. Geschichtsverständnis und Eschatologie im Epheserbrief (Gütersloh 1975) 28f., 32, 95. RIDDERBOS, H. Paul. An Outline of His Theology (Grand Rapids 1975) 44f. BÜHNER, J. A. Der Gesandte und sein Weg im 4. Evangelium (Tübingen 1977) 94f. STROBEL, A. "Apokalyptik" in TRE 3 (1978) 252. VANHOYE, A. "La Mère du Fils de Dieu selon Ga 4, 4," Marianum 40 (1978) 237-47. BYRNE, B. "Sons of God"-"Seed of Abraham" (Rome 1979) 133, 178-81, 180n., 189, 199n., 231. SWIDLER, L. Biblical Affirmations of Woman (Philadelphia 1979) 351. DUNN, J. D. G. Christology in the Making (London 1980) 38-44, 46, 56, 64, 111f., 121, 126f., 166, 284n., 160, 285n.173, 309n.58, 328n.49, 351n.1. KECK, L. E. "The Law and 'The Law of Sin and Death' (Rom 8:1-4). Reflections on the Spirit and Ethics in Paul" in J. L. Crenshaw et al., eds., The Divine Helmsman. Studies on God's Control of Human Events (FS L. H. Silberman; New York 1980) 44f. MERK, O. "Biblische Theologie" in TRE 6 (1980) 471. THISELTON, A. C. The Two Horizons (Grand Rapids 1980) 264. HAYS, R. B. The Faith of Jesus Christ (Chico CA 1983) 88, 91, 104, 105, 108, 112, 127, 128, 191, 230f. STUHLMANN, R. Das eschatologische Mass im Neuen Testament (Göttingen 1983) 2, 18, 62-69, 70, 70n., 71, 72. DIETZFELBINGER, C. Die Berufung des Paulus als Ursprung seiner Theologie (Neukirchen 1985) 121, 133, 134. SCHIMANOWSKI, G. Weisheit und Messias (Tübingen 1985) 84, 324-28, 335. SCHNABEL, E. J. Law and Wisdom from Ben Sira to Paul (Tübingen 1985) 240-42, 261f. THEISSEN, G. Psychologische Aspekte paulinischer Theologie (Göttingen 1983) 255, 349n.15, 380. OSTEN-SACKEN, P. VON DER, Evangelium und Tora: Aufsätze zu Paulus (München 1987) 62, 162-70, 182, 200. WERBICK, J. "Die Soteriologie zwischen 'christologischem Triumphalismus' und apokalyptischem Radikalismus" in I. Broer und J. Werbick, eds., "Auf Hoffnung hin sind wir erlöst" (Röm 8, 14) (Stuttgart 1987) 161f. JONGE, M. DE, Christology in Context. The Earliest Christian Response to Jesus (Philadelphia 1988) 43, 60, 190, 220n.5. JOHNSON, E. E. The Function of Apocalyptic and Wisdom

Traditions in Romans 9-11 (Atlanta GA 1989) 187f. MARTIN, B. L. Christ and the Law in Paul (Leiden 1989) 100f., 104, 111, 113f., 118, 122, 132, 134.

4:4a   CLEVES RENZA, I. Gal 4, 4a. Factum ex muliere. Disertacion historico—teologica (diss. P. Univ. Gregoriana 1959).

4:5-6   HAYS, R. B. The Faith of Jesus Christ (Chico CA 1983) 113. RÄISÄNEN, H. Paul and the Law (Tübingen 1983) 20f.

4:5   SCHRAGE, W. Die konkreten Einzelgebote in der paulinischen Paränese (1961) 94, 231. MARCHEL, W. Abba, Père! La Prière du Christ et des Chrétiens (1963) 217-22. SCHOENBERG, M.W. "Huiothesia: The Word and the Institution" Scripture 15 (1963) 115-23. SCHOENBERG, M.W. "St. Paul's Notion on the Adoptive Sonship of Christians" Thomist 28 (1964) 51-75. VAN DÜLMEN, A. Die Theologie des Gesetzes bei Paulus (1968) 50f. RIDDERBOS, H. Paul. An Outline of His Theology (Grand Rapids 1975) 193-99. SCHMITHALS, W. "Zur Herkunft der gnostischen Elemente in der Sprache des Paulus" in B. Aland et al., eds., Gnosis (FS H. Jonas; Göttingen 1978) 404. BYRNE, B. "Sons of God"-"Seed of Abraham" (Rome 1979) 80, 153, 153n., 176, 182-84. HAYS, R. B. The Faith of Jesus Christ (Chico CA 1983) 50, 88f., 106, 112, 117, 128, 228. HELDERMANN, J. Die Anapausis im Evangelium Veritatis (Leiden 1984) 197. JOHNSON, E. E. The Function of Apocalyptic and Wisdom Traditions in Romans 9-11 (Atlanta GA 1989) 187. MARTIN, B. L. Christ and the Law in Paul (Leiden 1989) 6, 19, 89, 100, 102-04, 112f., 118, 132, 134, 145.

4:6-9   DAVIES, S. L. The Gospel of Thomas and Christian Wisdom (New York 1983) 48, 123.

4:6-7   LUZ, U. Das Geschichtsverständnis des Paulus (1968) 282. DUNN, J.D.G. Baptism in the Holy Spirit (1970) 113ff. SIBER, P. Mit Christus leben (1971) 135-38. SIBER, P. Mit Christus leben (Zürich 1971) 135-38. MONTAGUE, G. T. The Holy Spirit (New York 1976) 196-98. BYRNE, B. "Sons of God"-"Seed of Abraham" (Rome 1979) 175n., 184-86. DUNN, J. D. G. Christology in the Making (London 1980) 27, 37, 112. HAYS, R. B. The Faith of Jesus Christ (Chico CA 1983) 244. COFFEY, D. "The Incarnation of the Holy Spirit in Christ," ThSt 45 (1984) 466-80, esp. 475f.

4:6   SOKOLOWSKI, E. Die Begriffe Geist und Leben bei Paulus (1903) 85ff. BENOIT, P. "Nous gémissons, attendant la délivrance de notre corps (Rom. 8, 23)" RechSR 39 (1951) 267-80. ZEDDA, S. L'adozione a Figli di Dio e lo Spirito Santo (1952) 23-190. MORRISON, R.J. and LAMPE, G.W.H. "Gal 4, 6" The Church Quarterly Review 156 (1955) 195-96. TAYLOR, T.M. "'Abba, Father' and Baptism" SJTh 11 (1958) 62-71. RENGSTORF, K.H. Die Auferstehung Jesu (1960) 149f. HERMANN, I. Kyrios und Pneuma (1961) 95-97. SEVENSTER, J.N. Paul and Seneca (1961) 51, 105. ROMANIUK, K. "Spiritus clamans (Gal 4, 6; Rom 8, 15)" VD 40 (1962) 190-98. WAINWRIGHT, A.W. The Trinity in the New Testament (1962) 256-57. DELLING, G. Die Taufe im Neuen Testament (1963) 58, 119. MARCHEL, W. Abba, Pére! La Prière du Christ et des Chrétiens (1963) 181-91, 213, 243. DOWNING, J.D.H. "Possible Baptismal References in Galatians" in Studia Evangelica II/1, ed. by F.L. Cross (1964) 551-56. DUPREZ, A. "Note sur le rôle de l'Esprit-Saint dans la filiation du chrétien. A propos de Gal. 4, 6" RechSR 52 (1964) 421-31. BRAUN, H. Qumran und das Neue Testament II (1966) 197, 254. SEEBERG, A. Der Katechismus der Urchristenheit (1966) 240-43. DUNN, J.D.G. "I Corinthians 15:45 — Last Adam, Life-giving Spirit" in Christ and the Spirit in the New Testament. In Honour of Charles Francis Digby Moule (1973) 132ff. KÜMMEL, W.G. Römer 7 und das Bild des Menschen im Neuen Testament (1974) 33f. DUNN, J.D.G. Jesus and the Spirit (1975) 21f., 187f., 240f. ECKART, K.-G.

"Das Apokryphon Ezechiel" in JSHRZ V/1 (1974) 53n.3c. KÜMMEL, W. G. Römer 7 und das Bild des Menschen im Neuen Testament (München 1974) 29, 33f. PENNA R. Lo Spirito di Christo. Christologia e pneumatologia secondo un'originale formulazione paolina (1976) passim. RÜGER, H. P. "Aramäisch" in TRE 3 (1978) 602. BYRNE, B. "Sons of God"-"Seed of Abraham" (Rome 1979) 1, 101, 147, 182n., 184f., 186, 215, 222, 223. DUPONT, D. J. The Salvation of the Gentiles (New York 1979) 44. GUNKEL, H. The Influence of the Holy Spirit (Philadelphia 1979) 79f., 83. DUNN, J. D. G. Christology in the Making (London 1980) 26, 35, 39, 41, 143. LULL, D. J. The Spirit in Galatia (Chico CA 1980) 66-69, 105-09. MINDE, H. J. VAN DER, "Theologia crucis und Pneumaaussagen bei Paulus," Catholica 34 (1980) 145. SCHELBERT, G. "Sprachgeschichtliches zu 'Abba'" in P. Casetti et al., eds., Mélanges Dominique Barthélemy (Fribourg/ Göttingen 1981) 395-447, esp. 408. HAYS, R. B. The Faith of Jesus Christ (Chico CA 1983) 87, 90, 106-09, 118, 211f. MEEKS, W. A. The First Urban Christians (New Haven/London 1983) 94, 121, 152. THEISSEN, G. Psychologische Aspekte paulinischer Theologie (Göttingen 1983) 135n.28, 322, 349n.15. KLEINKNECHT, K. T. Der leidende Gerechtfertigte (Tübingen 1984) 245. MOHRLANG, R. Matthew and Paul (Cambridge 1984) 115f., 119. SLENCZKA, R. "Glaube VI" in TRE 13 (1984) 322. HAHN, F. "Gottesdienst III" in TRE 14 (1985) 31, 34. JONGE, M. DE, Christology in Context. The Earliest Christian Response to Jesus (Philadelphia 1988) 169f., 234n.14. MacDONALD, M. Y. The Pauline Churches (Cambridge 1988) 66. CLABEAUX, J. J. The Lost Edition of the Letters of Paul (CBQ.MS; Washington 1989) 31, 40, 101. GEBAUER, R. Das Gebet bei Paulus (Giessen/Basel 1989) 20f., 32, 34, 37, 55, 65f., 70f., 73, 108, 146ff., 151, 153, 156, 162, 208, 210, 217, 220, 224, 226, 258ff., 262, 307ff., 312f., 350. BOCKMUEHL, M. N. A. Revelation and Mystery (Tübingen 1990) 136, 144f. OLIVEIRA, A. DE, Die Diakonie der Gerechtigkeit und der Versöhnung in der Apologie des 2. Korintherbriefes. Analyse und Auslegung von 2 Kor 2, 14-4, 6; 5, 11-6, 10 (Münster 1990) 172n.454.

4:7-16   JUNCKER, A. Die Ethik des Apostels Paulus (1919) 279-81, 297-99.

4:7   BOVER, J.M. "Heres 'per Deum' (Gal. 4, 7)" Biblica 5 (1924) 373-75. RAYAN, S. The Holy Spirit: Heart of the Gospel and Christian Hope (Maryknoll NY 1978) 121. BYRNE, B. "Sons of God"-"Seed of Abraham" (Rome 1979) 165, 172, 175, 175nn., 176, 185f., 190.

4:8ff.   FREUND, G. und STEGEMANN, E., eds., Theologische Brosamen für Lothar Steiger (DBAT 5; Heidelberg 1985) 390.

4:8-20   HONG, I.-G. The Law in Galatians (Sheffield 1993) 48-52.

4:8-11   BANDSTRA, A.J. The Law and the Elements of the World (1964) 62ff., 181ff. ECKERT, J. Die Urchristliche Verkündigung im Streit zwischen Paulus und seinen Gegnern nach deam Galaterbrief (1971) 91-93. PAGELS, E.H. The Gnostic Paul (1975) 109. VIELHAUER, P. "Gesetzesdienst und Stoicheiadienst im Galaterbrief" in Oikodome [G. Klein, ed.] (München 1979) 186. DEMKE, C. "Gott IV" in TRE 13 (1984) 646.

4:8-10   GIBBS, J.G. Creation and Redemption (1971) 63f., 146f. HAMERTON—KELLY, R.G. Pre-Existence, Wisdom, and the Son of Man (1973) 107-8. HAYS, R. B. The Faith of Jesus Christ (Chico CA 1983) 128. DUNN, J. D. G. Jesus, Paul and the Law (London 1990) 236n.58, 250, 261n.38.

4:8-9   THACKERAY, H.St.J. The Relation of St. Paul to Contemporary Jewish Thought (1900) 164ff. KENNEDY, H.A.A. St.Paul and the Mystery—Religions (1913) 24f. BULTMANN, R. Theologie des Neuen Testaments (1965) 70f.; Theology of the New Testament (1965) I 66f. BUSSMANN, C. Themen der paulinischen Missionspredigt auf dem Hintergrund der spätjüdisch—hellenistischen Missionsliteratur (1971)

57-74. SIBER, P. Mit Christus leben (Zürich 1971) 44. MEEKS, W. A. The First Urban Christians (New Haven/London 1983) 116, 166, 184, 226n.110. BEINTKER, H. "Gott VII" in TRE 13 (1984) 665. WINK, W. Unmasking the Powers (Philadelphia 1986) 131, 145, 149. BECKER, J. Paulus. Der Apostel der Völker (Tübingen 1989) 113, 284, 404. HOWARD, G. Paul. Crisis in Galatia (Cambridge ²1990) 66, 67, 77.

4:8   FEINE, P. & BEHM, J. Einleitung in das Neue Testament (1950) 142f. LINDARS, B. New Testament Apologetic (1961) 52-54. SCHRAGE, W. Die konkreten Einzelgebote in der paulinischen Paränese (1961) 212. SCHWEIZER, E. Erniedrigung und Erhöhung bei Jesus und seinen Nachfolgern (1962) §9b. CLABEAUX, J. J. The Lost Edition of the Letters of Paul (CBQ.MS; Washington 1989) 23, 162. LIMBECK, M. Mit Paulus Christ sein. Sachbuch zur Person und Theologie des Apostels Paulus (Stuttgart 1989) 74. HOWARD, G. Paul. Crisis in Galatia (Cambridge ²1990) 67-69.

4:9-10   SMITH, M. Tannaitic Parallels to the Gospels (1968) §3.11. ECKERT, J. Die Urchristliche Verkündigung im Streit zwischen Paulus und seinen Gegnern nach dem Galaterbrief (1971) 9f., 126f. KÜMMEL, W.G. Einleitung in das Neue Testament (1973) 260f. BERGER, K. und COLPE, C., eds., Religions-geschichtliches Textbuch zum Neuen Testament (Göttingen/Zürich 1987) 278. HÜBNER, H. "Paulusforschung seit 1945. Ein kritischer Literaturbericht" in ANRW II.25.4 (1987) 2691-94. LIMBECK, M. Mit Paulus Christ sein. Sachbuch zur Person und Theologie des Apostels Paulus (Stuttgart 1989) 90. CRONJE, J. VAN W. "The Strategem of the Rhetorical Question in Galatians 4:9-10 as a Means Toward Persuasion," Neotestamentica 26 (1992) 417-24.

4:9   CRAMER, A.W. Stoicheia Tou Kosmou (1961) 143-58. BANDSTRA, A.J. The Law and the Elements of the World (1964) 55f., 57ff., 173ff., BORNKAMM, G. Geschichte und Glaube II (1971) 195-98. ELLIS, E. E. Prophecy and Hermeneutic in Early Christianity (Tübingen 1978) 41, 74, 83, 85, 98, 111. FRIEDRICH, G. "Ein Taufhid hellenistischer Judenchristen I Thess 1, 9f" in Auf das Wort kommt es an. Gesammelte Aufsätze (Göttingen 1978) 237f. HOLTZ, T. "'Euer Glaube an Gott'. Zu Form und Inhalt von 1 Thess. 1:9f." in R. Schnackenburg et al., eds., Die Kirche des Anfangs (FS H. Schürmann; Freiburg/Basel/Wien 1978) 474-76. BRINSMEAD, B. H. Galatians—Dialogical Response to Opponents (Chico CA 1982) 120ff. HAYS, R. B. The Faith of Jesus Christ (Chico CA 1983) 249. THEISSEN, G. Psychologische Aspekte paulinischer Theologie (Göttingen 1983) 134, 213n.56. BRUCE, F. F. "'Called to Freedom.' A Study in Galatians" in W. C. Weinreich, ed., The New Testament Age (FS B. Reicke; Macon GA 1984) I, 65-67. MOHRLANG, R. Matthew and Paul (Cambridge 1984) 87, 118, 152, 188. MALMEDE, H. H. Die Lichtsymbolik im Neuen Testament (Wiesbaden 1986) 136f. BUNDRICK, D. R. "Ta Stoicheia tou Kosmou (Gal 4:3)," JEThS 34 (1991) 353-64. LOHSE, E. Die Entstehung des Neuen Testaments (Stuttgart/Berlin/ Köln ⁵1991) 37.

4:10-11 LIMBECK, M. Mit Paulus Christ sein. Sachbuch zur Person und Theologie des Apostels Paulus (Stuttgart 1989) 95.

4:10   BARTON, G.A. "The Exegesis of ἐνιαυτούς in Galatians 4:10 and its Bearing on the Date of the Epistle" JBL 33 (1914) 118-26. GRANT, R.M. "Hellenistic Elements in Galatians" AThR 34 (1952) 223-26. SCHRAGE, W. Die konkreten Einzelgebote in der paulinischen Paränese (1961) 154, 231f. BRAUN, H. Qumran und das Neue Testament II (1966) 174, 289, 296. ELLIS, E. E. Prophecy and Hermeneutic in Early Christianity (Tübingen 1978) 110, 124f. HÜBNER, H. Das Gesetz bei Paulus. Ein Beitrag zum Werden der paulinischen Theologie (Göttingen 1978) 26. VIELHAUER, P. "Gesetzesdienst und Stoicheiadienst im Galaterbrief" in Oikodome [G. Klein, ed.] (München 1979) 186-89. LÜHRMANN, D. "Tage, Monate, Jahreszeiten, Jahre (Gal 4, 10)" in R. Albertz et al., eds., Werden und Wirken des Alten Testaments (FS C. Westermann; Göttingen 1980) 428-45. FREUND, G. und STEGE-MANN, E., eds., Theologische Brosamen für Lothar Steiger (DBAT 5; Heidelberg 1985) 391. DAUTZENBERG, G. "Gesetzeskritik und Gesetzesgehorsam in der Jesustradition" in K. Kertelge, ed., Das Gesetz im Neuen Testament (Feiburg/Basel/Wien 1986) 48. CONZELMANN, H. and LINDEMANN, A. Interpreting the New Testament (Peabody MA 1988) 173. HOWARD, G. Paul. Crisis in Galatia (Cambridge ²1990) 72f., 76, 88.

4:11-39 BARRETT, C.K. "The Allegory of Abraham, Sarah, and Hagar in the Argument of Galatians" in Rechtfertigung. Festschrisft für Ernst Käsemann (1976) 4f.

4:11-20 JERVIS, L. A. The Purpose of Romans (Sheffield 1991) 112, 127.

4:11-19 JERVIS, L. A. The Purpose of Romans (Sheffield 1991) 119.

4:11-15 RETTIG, H.M. "Exegetische Analekten" ThSK 3 (1830) 108-14.

4:11 BJERKELUND, C. J. "'Vergeblich' als Missionsergebnis bei Paulus" in J. Jervell and W. A. Meeks, eds., God's Christ and His People (FS N. A. Dahl; New York 1977) 175-91. MARSHALL, P. Enmity in Corinth. Social Conventions in Paul's Relations with the Corinthians (Tübingen 1987) 154, 260. LAMPE, P. Die stadtrömischen Christen in den ersten beiden Jahrhunderten (Tübingen ²1989) 137. VOLF, J. M. G. Paul and Perseverance (Tübingen 1990) 261-63, 266f., 271n.55, 272n.57, 275, 281f., 285. REINMUTH, E. "'Nicht vergeblich' bei Paulus und Pseudo-Philo, *Liber Antiquitatum Biblicarum,*" NovT 33 (1991) 97-123.

4:12-6:18 SMIT, J. "Redactie in de brief aan de galaten. Retorische analyse van Gal. 4, 12-6, 18 (Redaction in the Letter to the Galatians. Rhetorical Analysis of Gal. 4, 12-6, 18)," TvTh 26 (1986) 113-44.

4:12-5:12 VAN DÜLMEN, A. Die Theologie des Gesetzes bei Paulus (1968) 51-58.

4:12-20 GÜTTGEMANS, E. Der leidende Apostel und sein Herr (1966) 170-94. HAYS, R. B. The Faith of Jesus Christ (Chico CA 1983) 222. BUSCEMI, A. M. "Gal 4, 12-20. Un argomento di amicizia," SBFLA 34 (1984) 67-108. BARRETT, C. K. Freedom and Obligation (Philadelphia 1985) 43ff. LYONS, G. Pauline Autobiography (Atlanta GA 1985) 164-68, 180. REBELL, W. Gehorsam und Unabhängigkeit (München 1986) 114, 140, 144. COSGROVE, C. H. The Cross and the Spirit. A Study in the Argument and Theology of Galatians (Macon GA 1988) 28, 34, 36, 77, 186. BECKER, J. Paulus. Der Apostel der Völker (Tübingen 1989) 85, 134, 178.

4:12-16 MARSHALL, P. Enmity in Corinth. Social Conventions in Paul's Relations with the Corinthians (Tübingen 1987) 153f.

4:12 DE BOER, W.P. The Imitation of Paul (1962) 188ff. BJERKE-LUND, C. Parakalo (1967) 13-18, 177f. LAUB, F. Die Begegnung des frühen Christentums mit der antiken Sklaverei (Stuttgart 1982) 73. MALHERBE, A. J. Moral Exhortation. A Greco-Roman Sourcebook (Philadelphia 1986) 144. REBELL, W. Gehorsam und Unabhängigkeit (München 1986) 114, 122, 130, 132. MARSHALL, P. Enmity in Corinth. Social Conventions in Paul's Relations with the Corinthians (Tübingen 1987) 156, 306. SEGAL, A. F. Paul the Convert (New Haven/London 1990) 200, 210.

4:13ff. BECKER, J. Paulus. Der Apostel der Völker (Tübingen 1989) 185ff.

4:13-16 MALHERBE, A. J. "A Physical Description of Paul" in G. W. E. Nickelsburg and G. W. MacRae, eds., Christians among Jews and Gentiles (FS K. Stendahl; Philadelphia 1986) 171.

4:13-15 BORSE, U. Der Standort des Galaterbriefes (1972) 47-49, 101-3. BINDER, H. "Die angebliche Krankheit des Paulus," ThZ 32 (1976) 1-13. SEYBOLD, K. und MÜLLER, U. Krankheit und Heilung (Stuttgart 1978) 148-50. REBELL, W. Alles ist möglich dem, der glaubt (München 1989) 129ff.

354					*An Exegetical Bibliography of the New Testament*

4:13-14 ENSLIN, M.S. Reapproaching Paul (1972) 100f. BISER, E. Der Zeuge (Graz/Wien/Köln 1981) 71f., 195, 197. KLEINKNECHT, K. T. Der leidende Gerechtfertigte (Tübingen 1984) 196, 233, 237. HECKEL, U. "Der Dorn im Fleisch. Die Krankheit des Paulus in 2 Kor 12, 7 und Gal 4, 13f." ZNW 84 (1993) 65-92.

4:13   BORSE, U. Der Standort des Galaterbriefes (1972) 47-49. KÜMMEL, W.G. Einleitung in das Neue Testament (1973) 263f. ZELLER, D. Juden und Heiden in der Mission des Paulus (1973) 56. SCHÜTZ, J.H. Paul and the Anatomy of Apostolic Authority (1975) 37-38. OLLROG, W.-H. Paulus und seine Mitarbeiter (Neukirchen/Vluyn 1979) 33, 56, 61. LÜDEMANN, G. Paulus, der Heidenapostel, Band I (Göttingen 1980) 124. LÜDEMANN, G. Paul. Apostle to the Gentiles (London 1984) 71, 90-92, 132n.168. HEMER, C. J. The Book of Acts in the Setting of Hellenistic History [C. H. Gempf, ed.] (Tübingen 1989) 183f., 247, 286, 305. LOHSE, E. Die Entstehung des Neuen Testaments (Stuttgart/Berlin/Köln ⁵1991) 36. WOODS, L. "Opposition to a Man and His Message. Paul's 'Thorn in the Flesh' (2 Cor 12:7)," AusBR 39 (1991) 44-53.

4:14-15 CRONJÉ, J. VAN W. "Defamiliarization in the letter to the Galatians" in J. H. Petzer and P. J. Hartin, eds., A South African Perspective on the New Testament (FS B. M. Metzger; Leiden 1986) 222.

4:14   DE ZWAAN, J. "Gal 4, 14 aus dem Neugriechischen erklärt" ZNW 10 (1909) 246-50. BETZ, H.D. Lukian von Samosata und das Neue Testament (1961) 102, 116, 132. KÄSEMANN, E. Exegetische Versuche und Besinnungen (1964) I 170. BORSE, U. Der Standort des Galaterbriefes (1972) 101f. DUNN, J. D. G. Christology in the Making (London 1980) 132, 155f. FREUND, G. und STEGEMANN, E., eds., Theologische Brosamen für Lothar Steiger (DBAT 5; Heidelberg 1985) 390.

4:15-17 LÜDEMANN, G. Paul: Apostle to the Gentiles (London 1984) 213, 220, 221-37.
4:15-16 BISER, E. Der Zeuge (Graz/Wien/Köln 1981) 160f., 195, 208.
4:15   DE WITT, N.W. St.Paul and Epicurus (1954) 68-69. BLIGH, J. "Comment on Gal 4:15" in Studia Evangelica IV (1968) 382-83. BAUMERT, N. Täglich sterben und auferstehen. Der Literalsinn von 2 Kor 4, 12-5, 10 (1973) 302. TRITES, A. A. The New Testament Concept of Witness (Cambridge 1977) 206. LÜDEMANN, G. Paul: Apostle to the Gentiles (London 1984) 210, 213, 221, 231f., 236f., 239.

4:16-17 LÜDEMANN, G. Paul: Apostle to the Gentiles (London 1984) 213, 218, 225-37.
4:16   MARSHALL, P. Enmity in Corinth. Social Conventions in Paul's Relations with the Corinthians (Tübingen 1987) 151f.

4:17   TRITES, A. A. The New Testament Concept of Witness (Cambridge 1977) 206. BRINSMEAD, B. H. Galatians—Dialogical Response to Opponents (Chico CA 1982) 98. MARTYN, J. L. "A Law-Observant Mission to Gentiles. The Background of Galatians" in M. P. O'Connor and D. N. Freedman, eds., Backgrounds for the Bible (Winona Lake/ Indiana 1987) 199-214, esp. 204ff. WOLTER, M. Die Pastoralbriefe als Paulustradition (Göttingen 1988) 250.

4:18-19 BISER, E. Der Zeuge (Graz/Wien/Köln 1981) 47, 75, 161, 183, 259, 273.
4:18   SCHRAGE, W. Die konkreten Einzelgebote in der paulinischen Paränese (1961) 146.
4:19-26 SCHWEITZER, A. Die Mystik des Apostels Paulus (1954) 123f., 206f.
4:19   HERMANN, R. "Über den Sinn des Μορφοῦσθαι Χριστὸν ἐν ὑμῖν in Gal 4, 19" ThLZ 80 (1955) 713-26. BARRETT, C.K. The New Testament Background: Selected Documents (1956) 100. KÄSEMANN, E. Exegetische Versuche und Besinnungen (1964) I 19. BRUPPACHER, H. "Kleine Beiträge zu einer kommenden Revision der Zürcher Bibel, XV" Kirchenblatt für die Reformierte Schweiz 127 (1971) 105-6. DUNN, J.D.G. Jesus and the Spirit (1975) 328f. ROON, A. VAN, The Authenticity of Ephesians (Leiden 1974) 324. SCHMITHALS, W. "Zur Herkunft der

gnostischen Elemente in der Sprache des Paulus" in B. Aland et al., eds., Gnosis (FS H. Jonas; Göttingen 1978) 388-90. OLLROG, W.-H. Paulus und seine Mitarbeiter (Neukirchen/Vluyn 1979) 77, 179f. SWIDLER, L. Biblical Affirmations of Woman (Philadelphia 1979) 322. LAUB, F. Die Begegnung des frühen Christentums mit der antiken Sklaverei (Stuttgart 1982) 73. CRONJÉ, J. VAN W. "Defamiliarization in the letter to the Galatians" in J. H. Petzer and P. J. Hartin, eds., A South African Perspective on the New Testament (FS B. M. Metzger; Leiden 1986) 220. WOLTER, M. Die Pastoralbriefe als Paulustradition (Göttingen 1988) 248. GAVENTA, B. R. "The Maternity of Paul. An Exegetical Study of Galatians 4:19" in R. T. Fortna and B. R. Gaventa, eds., The Conversation Continues. Studies in Paul and John (FS J. L. Martyn; Nashville 1990) 189-201. HOWARD, G. Paul. Crisis in Galatia (Cambridge [2]1990) 10, 49, 60. OLIVEIRA, A. DE, Die Diakonie der Gerechtigkeit und der Versöhnung in der Apologie des 2. Korintherbriefes. Analyse und Auslegung von 2 Kor 2, 14-4, 6; 5, 11-6, 10 (Münster 1990) 226, 249. SEGAL, A. F. Paul the Convert (New Haven/London 1990) 63, 150f.

4:20ff. MELL, U. Neue Schöpfung (Berlin/New York 1989) 288.
4:20 BORSE, U. Der Standort des Galaterbriefes (1972) 48-51. WILHELMI, G. "ἀλλάξαι τὴν φωνήν μου? (Galater 4:20)" ZNW 65 (1974) 151-54.
4:21–6:10 DRANE, J.W. Paul: Libertine or Legalist? (1975) 39-58.
4:21–5:1 DRANE, J.W. Paul: Libertine or Legalist? (1975) 39-45. PASTOR RAMOS, F. La libertad en la Carta a los Gálatas. Estudio exegético-teológico (Madrid 1977) passim. BYRNE, B. "Sons of God"-"Seed of Abraham" (Rome 1979) 186-89, 190. LINCOLN, A. T. Paradise Now and Not Yet (Cambridge 1981) 9-32. THIELMAN, F. From Plight to Solution (Leiden 1989) 83-86. ELLIS, E. E. The Old Testament in Early Christianity (Tübingen 1991) 86, 98, 110. MARTYN, J. L. "Events in Galatia. Modified Covenantal Nomism versus God's Invasion of the Cosmos in the Singular Gospel: A Response to J. D. G. Dunn and B. R. Gaventa" in J. M. Bassler, ed., Pauline Theology, Volume 1: Thessalonians, Philippians, Galatians, Philemon (Minneapolis MN 1991) 174-76. MALAN, F. S. "The Strategy of Two Opposing Covenants. Galatians 4:21-5:1," Neotestamentica 26 (1992) 425-40. PERRIMAN, A. C. "The Rhetorical Strategy of Galatians 4:21-5:1," EQ 65 (1993) 27-42.
4:21ff. THACKERAY, H.St.J. The Relation of St. Paul to Contemporary Jewish Thought (1900) 196ff., 212ff. SCHRAGE, W. Die konkreten Einzelgebote in der paulinischen Paränese (1961) 229. SCHLIER, H. "Über die christliche Freiheit," GuL 50 (1977) 178-93. FRIEDRICH, G. "Das Gesetz des Glaubens Römer 3, 27" in Auf das Wort kommt es an. Gesammelte Aufsätze (Göttingen 1978) 119f. SCHULZ, S. Neutestamentliche Ethik (Zürich 1987) 195f. SCHMIDT, J. M. "Zum christlichen Verständnis der gemeinsamen Bibel" in E. Brocke and J. Seim, eds., Gottes Augapfel. Beiträge zur Erneuerung des Verhältnisses von Christen und Juden (Neukirchen/Vluyn [2]1988) 85. SCHNELLE, U. Wandlungen im paulinischen Denken (Stuttgart 1989) 60.
4:21-31 OGARA, F. "Quae sunt per allegoriam dicta" VD 15 (1935) 67-76. VAN STEMPVOORT, P.A. De allegorie in Gal 4, 21-31 als hermeneutisch probleem (1953). BARRETT, C.K. From First Adam to Last (1962) 44f. HAHN, F. Das Verständnis der Mission im Neuen Testament (1965) 85, 93. BERGER, K. "Abraham in den paulinischen Hauptbriefen (Gal 3; 4, 21-31; Röm 4; 9-11; 2 Cor 11, 22)" MThZ 17 (1966) 47-89. LUZ, U. "Der alte und der neue Bund bei Paulus und im Hebräerbrief" EvTh 27 (1967) 318-36. NICKELS, P. Targum and New Testament (1967) 74. LUZ, U. Das Geschichtsverständnis des Paulus (1968) 283ff. SISTI, A. "Le duo alleanze" BiOr 11 (1969) 25-32. JEWETT, R. "The Agitators and the Galatian Congregation" NTS 17 (1970-71) 201f. ECKERT, J. Die urchristliche

Verkündigung im Streit zwischen Paulus und seinen Gegnern nach dem Galaterbrief (1971) 94-99. VOS.J.S. Traditionsgeschichtliche Untersuchungen zur paulinischen Pneumatologie (1973) 102-5. ZELLER, D. Juden und Heiden in der Mission des Paulus (1973) 95, 229. MUSSNER, F. "Theologische 'Wiedergutmachung'. Am Beispiel der Auslegung des Galaterbriefes" FrR 26 (1974) 7-11. CALLAWAY, M.C. "The Mistress and the Maid: Midrashic Traditions Behind Galatians 4:21-31" Radical Religion 2 (2-3, 1975) 94-101. LONGENECKER, R.N. Biblical Exegesis in the Apostolic Period (1975) 126-29. SCHÜTZ, J.H. Paul and the Anatomy of Apostolic Authority (1975) 126-27. BARRETT, C.K. "The Allegory of Abraham, Sarah, and Hagar in the Argument of Galatians" in Rechtfertigung. Festschrift für Ernst Käsemann (1976) 1-16. MÜLLER, H. Die Auslegung alttestamentlichen Geschichtsstoffs bei Paulus (diss. Halle/Wittenberg 1960) 127-39. BURCHARD, C. Untersuchungen zu Joseph and Aseneth (Tübingen 1965) 118, 121. PASTOR RAMOS, F. "Alegoría o tipología en Gal 4, 21-31," EstBi 34 (1975) 113-19. RIDDERBOS, H. Paul. An Outline of His Theology (Grand Rapids 1975) 217-19. MINDE, H.-J. VAN DER, Schrift und Tradition bei Paulus (München/Paderborn/Wien 1976) 138-42. SOARES PRABHU, G. M. The Formula Quotations in the Infancy Narrative of Matthew (Rome 1976) 113(18). BARTH, M. "Das Volk Gottes. Juden und Christen in der Botschaft des Paulus" in M. Barth et al., Paulus—Apostat oder Apostel? (Regensburg 1977) 96f. MINEAR, P. S. To Die and to Live. Christ's Resurrection and Christian Vocation (New York 1977) 72f. BRUCE, F. F. The Time is Fulfilled (Exeter 1978) 67f. KLAUCK, H.-J. Allegorie und Allegorese in Synoptischen Gleichnistexten (Münster 1978) 116-25. LIAO, P. S. H. "The Meaning of Galatians 4:21-31. A New Perspective," NEAJTh 22-23 (1979) 115-32. VIELHAUER, P. "Paulus und das Alte Testament" in Oikodome [G. Klein, ed.] (München 1979) 200f., 205, 209f. LULL, D. J. The Spirit in Galatia (Chico CA 1980) 110-13, 157-60. MINDE, H. J. VAN DER, "Theologia crucis und Pneumaaussagen bei Paulus," Catholica 34 (1980) 139. MOXNES, H. Theology in Conflict (Leiden 1980) 119, 211, 215f., 221, 227-29, 240, 254. BARRETT, C. K. "The Allegory of Abraham, Sarah, and Hagar in the Argument of Galatians" in Essays on Paul (London 1982) 154-70. GASTON, L. "Israel's Enemies in Pauline Theology," NTS 28 (1982) 400-23. KLAIBER, W. Rechtfertigung und Gemeinde (Göttingen 1982) 163-67. RÄISÄNEN, H. Paul and the Law (Tübingen 1983) 44, 62, 70, 72, 242. HÜBNER, H. Gottes Ich und Israel (Göttingen 1984) 20, 115, 118, 132. SCHMITT, R. Gottesgerechtigkeit—Heilsgeschichte—Israel in der Theologie des Paulus (Frankfurt/Bern/New York/Nancy 1984) 55f. GRAESSER, E. Der Alte Bund im Neuen (Tübingen 1985) 20, 22, 25, 68-70, 77, 84, 160, 285. KOCH, D.-A. Die Schrift als Zeuge des Evangeliums (Tübingen 1986) 204-11, 306f., 311f., 314. LÜBKING, H.-M. Paulus und Israel im Römerbrief (Frankfurt/Bern/New York 1986) 68-70. THOMAS, K. J. "Covenant in relation to Hagar and Ishmael in Galatians," BTr 37 (1986) 445f. BOUWMAN, G. "De Twee Testamenten. Een exegese van Gal 4, 21-31," Bijdragen 48 (1987) 259-76. BOUWMAN, G. "Die Hagar- und Sara-Perikope (Gal 4, 21-31). Exemplarische Interpretation zum Schriftbeweis bei Paulus" in ANRW II.25.4 (1987) 3135-55 (Lit. 3153-55). GASTON, L. Paul and the Torah (Vancouver 1987) 14, 80-82, 88-91, 97. JEWETT, P. K. "Children of Grace," ThT 44 (1987) 170-78. JONES, F. S. "Freiheit" in den Briefen des Apostels Paulus (Göttingen 1987) 14, 70, 82-92, 96f., 99, 105, 107f., 113, 115, 126f., 142, 145, 155n.88, 203n.126, 204n.128. LAYTON, B. The Gnostic Scriptures (Garden City NY 1987) 273. MERKLEIN, H. Studien zu Jesus und Paulus (Tübingen 1987) 62, 75f., 84. MUSSNER, F. Die Kraft der Wurzel (Freiburg/Basel/ Wien 1987) 60f. RÄISÄNEN, H. "Römer 9-11: Analyse eines geistigen Ringens" in ANRW II.25.4

(1987) 2925f. WIESER, F. E. Die Abrahamvorstellungen im Neuen Testament (Bern/ Frankfurt/New York/Paris 1987) 50-56, 81-83. COSGROVE, C. H. The Cross and the Spirit. A Study in the Argument and Theology of Galatians (Macon GA 1988) 15, 22, 28, 37, 51f., 71, 80. BECKER, J. Paulus. Der Apostel der Völker (Tübingen 1989) 59, 115, 419, 491ff. HANSEN, G. W. Abraham in Galatians (Sheffield 1989) 141-54, 156f. HAYS, R. B. Echoes of Scripture in the Letters of Paul (New Haven/London 1989) 86, 111-21, 169, 187f. JOHNSON, E. E. The Function of Apocalyptic and Wisdom Traditions in Romans 9-11 (Atlanta GA 1989) 139, 188. VOLLENWEIDER, S. Freiheit als neue Schöpfung (Göttingen 1989) 194, 253, 285, 291ff., 311, 319, 398f., 404. DUNN, J. D. G. Jesus, Paul and the Law (London 1990) 245, 249, 261nn.35.36. MULLER, E. C. Trinity and Marriage in Paul (New York/ Bern/Frankfurt/Paris 1990) 85, 114, 426, 428f. ZIESLER, J. Pauline Christianity (Oxford 1990) 19, 47, 66f., 78, 80, 106, 110. GLASSNER, G. Vision eines auf Verheissung gegründeten Jerusalem. Textanalytische Studien zu Jesaja 54 (Klosterneuburg 1991) passim. JANZEN, J. G. "Hagar in Paul's Eyes and in the Eyes of Yahweh (Genesis 16). A Study in Horizons," HBTh 13 (1991) 1-22. WAGNER, G. "Les enfants d'Abraham ou les chemins de la promesse et de la liberté. Exégèse de Galates 4, 21 à 31," RHPR 71 (1991) 285-95. HONG, I.-G. The Law in Galatians (Sheffield 1993) 52-55, 71-75, 100-02.

4:21-30 ELLIS, E.E. Paul's Use of the Old Testament (1957) 51-54. COSGROVE, C. H. "The Law has given Sarah No Children (Gal. 4:21-30)," NovT 29 (1987) 219-35.

4:21-28 KUTSCH, E. Neues Testament—Neuer Bund? (Neukirchen/Vluyn 1978) 142-45.

4:21-26 PAGELS, E.H. The Gnostic Paul (1975) 110.

4:21-22 JEWETT, P. K. Infant Baptism and the Covenant of Grace (Grand Rapids 1978) 99.

4:21 VAN DÜLMEN, A. Die Theologie des Gesetzes bei Paulus (1968) 54. FREUND, G. und STEGEMANN, E., eds., Theologische Brosamen für Lothar Steiger (DBAT 5; Heidelberg 1985) 389. JOHNSON, E. E. The Function of Apocalyptic and Wisdom Traditions in Romans 9-11 (Atlanta GA 1989) 187.

4:22—5:1 FRICK, R. GPM 22 (1967/68) 161-66. MARXSEN, W. Predigten (1968) 77-87.

4:22-31 BOUSSET, W. Die Religion des Judentums im späthellenistischen Zeitalter (1966=1926) 161. HAYS, R. B. The Faith of Jesus Christ (Chico CA 1983) 222.

4:22-26 GRANT, R. M. "Paul and the Old Testament" in D. K. McKim, ed., The Authoritative Word (Grand Rapids 1983) 29. CLABEAUX, J. J. The Lost Edition of the Letters of Paul (CBQ.MS; Washington 1989) 18, 55f.

4:22-24 BRAUN, H. Qumran und das Neue Testament II (1966) 270, 306, 309, 318.

4:22-23 MÜLLER, H. Die Auslegung alttestamentlichen Geschichtsstoffs bei Paulus (diss. Halle/ Wittenberg 1960) 127-30.

4:22 CLABEAUX, J. J. The Lost Edition of the Letters of Paul (CBQ.MS; Washington 1989) 23, 55.

4:23 SCHWEIZER, E. Heiliger Geist (Stuttgart 1978) 116. CLABEAUX, J. J. The Lost Edition of the Letters of Paul (CBQ.MS; Washington 1989) 86, 86n.13, 151.

4:24ff. KÄSEMANN, E. Exegetische Versuche und Besinnungen (1964) I 28.

4:24-31 WALLIS, W. B. "The Pauline Conception of the Old Covenant," Presbyterion 4 (2, 1978) 71-83.

4:24-27 MÜLLER, H. Die Auslegung alttestamentlichen Geschichtsstoffs bei Paulus (diss. Halle/ Wittenberg 1960) 130-39.

4:24-26 KEPPLE, R. J. "An Analysis of Antiochene Exegesis of Galatians 4:24-26," WThJ 39 (1977) 239-49. ALAND, K. "Das Verhältnis von Kirche und Staat in der Frühzeit" in ANRW II.23.1 (1979) 195f.

4:24-25 GRANT, R.M. "Hellenistic Elements in Galatians" AThR 34 (1952) 223-26.

4:24 SCHMID, R. "Exil" in TRE 10 (1982) 710. GRAESSER, E. Der Alte Bund im Neuen (Tübingen 1985) 8, 16, 18, 62, 69ff., 77, 223. MARQUARDT, F.-W. Die Juden und ihr Land (Gütersloh [3]1986) 95. BOUWMAN, G. "Die Hagar- und Sara-Perikope (Gal 4, 21-31). Exemplarische Interpretation zum Schriftbeweis bei Paulus" in ANRW II.25.4 (1987) 3143ff., 3151. JONES, F. S. "Freiheit" in den Briefen des Apostels Paulus (Göttingen 1987) 70, 86f., 89, 91, 94, 96, 100, 127, 203n.126. CLABEAUX, J. J. The Lost Edition of the Letters of Paul (CBQ.MS; Washington 1989) 54.

4:25-29 FRICKEL, J. "Die Zöllner, Vorbild der Demut und wahrer Gottesverehrung" in E. Dassmann und K. S. Frank, eds., Pietas (FS B. Kötting) JAC 8 (1980) 370.

4:25-26 BÖCHER, O. Kirche in Zeit und Endzeit. Aufsätze zur Offenbarung des Johannes (Neukirchen 1983) 127. MARQUARDT, F.-W. Die Juden und ihr Land (Gütersloh [3]1986) 94.

4:25 KRETZMANN, P.E. "Miscellanea" CThM 3 (1932) 457. LIGHTFOOT, J.B. "The meaning of Hagar in iv. 25" in the Epistle of St. Paul to the Galatians (1957) 192-200. GESE, H. "Τὸ δὲ Σινὰ ὄρος ἐστίν ἐν τῇ 'Αραβίᾳ (Gal. 4:25)" in Das ferne und nahe Wort. Festschrift Leonhard Rost (1967) 81-94. MONTAGNINI, F. "Il monte Sinai si trova in Arabia" BiOr 11 (1969) 33-37. BARRETT, C.K. "The Allegory of Abraham, Sarah, and Hagar in the Argument of Galatians" in Rechtfertigung. Festschrift für Ernst Käsemann (1976) 11f. MÜLLER, H. Die Auslegung alttestamentlichen Geschichtsstoffs bei Paulus (diss. Halle/ Wittenberg 1960) 30-37. McNAMARA, M. "'to de (Hagar) Sina oros estin en tê Arabia' (Gal. 4:25a). Paul and Petra," Milltown Studies 2 (1978) 24-41. VIELHAUER, P. "Paulus und das Alte Testament" in Oikodome [G. Klein, ed.] (München 1979) 200. LINCOLN, A. T. Paradise Now and Not Yet (Cambridge 1981) 14-16. MARQUARDT, F.-W. Die Juden und ihr Land (Gütersloh [3]1986) 92. BOUWMAN, G. "Die Hagar- und Sara-Perikope (Gal 4, 21-31). Exemplarische Interpretation zum Schriftbeweis bei Paulus" in ANRW II.25.4 (1987) 3136, 3140-42, 3150. JONES, F. S. "Freiheit" in den Briefen des Apostels Paulus (Göttingen 1987) 70, 87f., 205nn.136.137. HAACKER, K. "Elemente des heidnischen Antijudaismus im Neuen Testament," EvTh 48 (1988) 404-18. STEINHAUSER, M. G. "Gal 4, 25a. Evidence of Targumic Tradition in Gal 4, 21-31?" Biblica 70 (1989) 234-40.

4:25a. MUSSNER, F. "Hagar, Sinai, Jerusalem. Zum Text von Gal. 4, 25a" ThQ 1 (1955) 56-60. PASTOR, F. "A proposito de Gal. 4, 25a" EstBi 31 (1972) 205-10.

4:26ff. SCHMITHALS, W. "Zur Herkunft der gnostischen Elemente in der Sprache des Paulus" in B. Aland et al., eds., Gnosis (FS H. Jonas; Göttingen 1978) 405.

4:26-27 DAVIES, S. L. The Gospel of Thomas and Christian Wisdom (New York 1983) 124.

4:26 BETZ, P. "Die Geburt der Gemeinde durch den Lehrer" NTS 3 (1956/57) 322f. SCHWEIZER, E. Erniedrigung undErhöhung bei Jesus und seinen Nachfolgern (1962) §16e. KÄSEMANN, E. Exegetische Versuche und Besinnungen (1964) I 133. MCKELVEY, R.J. The New Temple (1969) 141-44. LINCOLN, A. T. Paradise Now and Not Yet (Cambridge 1981) 16-32. SCHADE, H.-H. Apokalyptische Christologie bei Paulus (Göttingen 1981) 91. SCHMIDT, K. L. "Jerusalem als Urbild und Abbild" in Neues Testament, Judentum, Kirche [G. Sauter, ed.] (München 1981) 267ff. BRINSMEAD, B. H. Galatians—Dialogical Response to Opponents (Chico CA 1982) 98f. HAYS, R. B. The Faith of Jesus Christ (Chico CA 1983) 43. MARQUARDT, F.-W. Die Juden und ihr Land (Gütersloh [3]1986) 74. JONES, F. S. "Freiheit" in den Briefen des Apostels Paulus (Göttingen 1987) 70, 87, 89, 96, 108, 130, 134f., 137, 139, 142f., 147n.3, 204n.133, 205n.137. CLABEAUX, J. J. The Lost Edition of the Letters of Paul (CBQ.MS; Washington 1989) 3, 23, 30n.29, 37, 100,

118f., 128, 143, 151. PATE, C. M. The Glory of Adam and the Afflictions of the Righteous. Pauline Suffering in Context (Lewiston NY 1993) passim.

4:27   PAGELS, E.H. The Gnostic Paul (1975) 110. PAVAN, V. "Is 54, 1 (*Laetare sterilis*) nella catechesi dei primi due secoli," VChr 18 (1981) 341-55. POWELL, D. "Clemensbrief, Zweiter" in TRE 8 (1981) 122. KOCH, D.-A. Die Schrift als Zeuge des Evangeliums (Tübingen 1986) 209.

4:28-31   NICKELS, P. Targum and New Testament (1967) 74. BARRETT, C.K. "The Allegory of Abraham, Sarah, and Hagar in the Argument of Galatians" in Rechtfertigung, edited by J. Friedrich, W. Pöhlmann, P. Stuhlmacher (1976) 12f. MÜLLER, H. Die Auslegung alttestamentlichen Geschichtsstoffs bei Paulus (diss. Halle/Wittenberg 1960) 127-30.

4:28-29   HANSON, A.T. Studies in Paul's Technique and Theology (1974) 97-98. KÜMMEL, W.G. Jüdische Schriften aus hellenisch—römischer Zeit III (1975) 217. LE DEAUT, R. "Traditions targumiques dans le corpus paulinien? (Hebr 11, 4 et 12, 24; Gal 4, 29s; 2C 3, 16)" Biblica 42 (1961) 28-48.

4:28   SCHRAGE, W. Die konkreten Einzelgebote in der paulinischen Paränese (1961) 229. MCNAMARA, M. The New Testament and the Palestinian Targum to the Pentateuch (1966) 164. JEWETT, P. K. Infant Baptism and the Covenant of Grace (Grand Rapids 1978) 95, 99.

4:29   SCHRAGE, W. Die konkreten Einzelgebote in der paulinischen Paränese (1961) 74. BEYSCHLAG, K. Clemens Romanus und der Frühkatholizmus (1966) 69. MCNAMARA, M. The New Testament and the Palestinian Targum to the Pentateuch (1966) 164. COSGROVE, C. H. The Cross and the Spirit. A Study in the Argument and Theology of Galatians (Macon GA 1988) 83f., 186, 188. MULLER, E. C. Trinity and Marriage in Paul (New York/Bern/Frankfurt/Paris 1990) 85f., 115, 119, 426.

4:30   JEWETT, P. K. Infant Baptism and the Covenant of Grace (Grand Rapids 1978) 99, 154, 234f. LINCOLN, A. T. Paradise Now and Not Yet (Cambridge 1981) 11-13. THOMPSON, S. The Apocalypse and Semitic Syntax (Cambridge 1985) 15. KOCH, D.-A. Die Schrift als Zeuge des Evangeliums (Tübingen 1986) 121, 149f., 211. JONES, F. S. "Freiheit" in den Briefen des Apostels Paulus (Göttingen 1987) 70, 83f., 86, 91, 147n.3, 204n.128.

4:31-5:12 COSGROVE, C. H. The Cross and the Spirit. A Study in the Argument and Theology of Galatians (Macon GA 1988) 31, 34f., 148.

4:31   JONES, F. S. "Freiheit" in den Briefen des Apostels Paulus (Göttingen 1987) 70, 84-86, 91, 147n.3, 204n. 128, 209n.170, 223n.91. COSGROVE, C. H. The Cross and the Spirit. A Study in the Argument and Theology of Galatians (Macon GA 1988) 29, 84f., 148, 160, 173. CLABEAUX, J. J. The Lost Edition of the Letters of Paul (CBQ.MS; Washington 1989) 100f., 152.

5-6   FRUNISH, V.P. The Love Command in the New Testament (1972) 96-102. STAGG, F. "Freedom and Moral Responsibility without License or Legalism" RevEx 69 (1972) 483-94. RAMAZZOTTI, B. "Etica cristiana e peccati nelle lettere ai Romani a ai Galati," ScuC 106 (3-4, 1978) 290-342. BRINSMEAD, B. H. Galatians—Dialogical Response to Opponents (Chico CA 1982) 182-86. BERGER, K. "Gnosis/Gnostizismus I" in TRE 13 (1984) 523. HARNISCH, W. "Einübung des neuen Seins. Paulinische Paränese am Beispiel des Galaterbriefs," ZThK 84 (1987) 279-96. MATERA, F. J. "The Culmination of Paul's Argument to the Galatians. Gal. 5.1-6.17," JSNT 32 (1988) 79-91. LIPS, H. VON, Weisheitliche Traditionen im Neuen Testament (Neukirchen/Vluyn 1990) 358, 364ff., 371f., 378, 380, 384, 396,

398f., 436. HONG, I.-G. "The law and Christian ethics in Galatians 5-6," Neotestamentica 26 (1992) 113-30.

5:1–6:10 SHEPARD, J.W. The Life and Letters of St. Paul (1950) 356-62. GIBLIN, C.H. In Hope of God's Glory (1970) 84-89. LULL, D. J. The Spirit in Galatia (Chico CA 1980) 113-29. BRINSMEAD, B. H. Galatians—Dialogical Response to Opponents (Chico CA 1982) 53f. HAYS, R. B. The Faith of Jesus Christ (Chico CA 1983) 222. ALLAZ, J. et al., Chrétiens en conflit. L'Épître de Paul aux Galates (Geneva 1987) passim.

5 STACEY, W.D. The Pauline View of Man (1956) 163f. SCHRAGE, W. Die konkreten Einzelgebote in der paulinischen Paränese (1961) 73. TOUSSAINT, S.D. "Contrast between the Spiritual Conflict in Romans 7 and Galatians 5" BiblSa 123 (1966) 310-14. DAMERAU, R. Der Galaterbriefkommentar des Nikolaus Dinkelsbühl (1970) 136-82. GRESO, J. "Sloboda v 5. kapitole Listu Galatskym" Krestamska Revue 38 (1971) 228-32. SCHWEIZER, E. Heiliger Geist (Stuttgart 1978) 117. HAYS, R. B. The Faith of Jesus Christ (Chico CA 1983) 109. PANIER, L. "Parcours pour lire l'épître aux Galates. 4ème série: Ga 5," Sémiotique et Bible 54 (1989) 36-41. VOLLENWEIDER, S. Freiheit als neue Schöpfung (Göttingen 1989) 309ff., 359. DUKE, P. D. "The Imperative of Freedom: Galatians 5," Faith and Mission 8 (1990) 94-100.

5:1-24 STALDER, K. Das Werk des Geistes in der Heiligung bei Paulus (1962) 455-63. PAGELS, E. The Gnostic Paul (1975) 110-11.

5:1,13-25 MADUKA—NGOMA, P. "Visions chrétienne de la Liberté selon S. Paul en Gal 5, 1.13-25 et 1 Cor 9, 19-23" RCIA 26 (1971) 231-43.

5:1,13-18 LACAN, M.-F. "Le choix fondamental: être asservi ou servir (Ga 5, 1.13-18)" AssS 44 (1969) 60-64.

5:1-17 MÜLLER—BARDORFF, J. Paulus (1970) 187-206.

5:1-15 GOLLWITZER, H. in Herr, tue meine Lipper auf, Bd II. hrsg. von G. Eichholz (1966) 510-17.

5:1-12 ECKERT, J. Die urchristliche Verkündigung im Streit zwischen Paulus und seinen Gegnern nach dem Galaterbrief (1971) 39-47. DEVRIES, C.E. "Paul's 'Cutting' Remarks about a Race: Galatians 5;1-12" in Current Issues in Biblical and Patristic Interpretation, ed. by G.F. Hawthorne (1975) 115-20. MACGORMAN, J.W. "Problem Passages in Galatians" SouJTh 15 (1972) 35-51. VOS, J. Traditionsgeschichtliche Untersuchungen zur paulinischen Pneumatologie (1973) 105-6. HONG, I.-G. The Law in Galatians (Sheffield 1993) 56-59, 70-75.

5:1-11 MEZGER, M. GPM 18 (1964) 364-69. STECK, K.G. GPM 24 (1969/70) 415-24. GÜNTER BADER et al. in Predigtstudien (1976) Perikopenreihe IV; Zweiter Halband, 247-254. MEZGER, M. in GPM 30/4 (1975/76) 424-28.

5:1-6 STALDER, K. Das Werk des Geistes in der Heiligung bei Paulus (1962) 341-46. LONGENECKER, R.N. Paul Apostle of Liberty (1964) 40-42. BALTENSWEILER, H. und OTT, H. in P. Krusche et al., eds., Predigtstudien für das Kirchenjahr 1981/82. Perikopenreihe IV/2 (Stuttgart 1982) 250-56. DOBBELER, A. VON, Glaube als Teilhabe (Tübingen 1987) 66-69. KLEIN, G. in GPM 42 (1987/88) 439-44. VOLLENWEIDER, S. Freiheit als neue Schöpfung (Göttingen 1989) 288.

5:1-5 SCHWEIZER, E. Gott Versöhnt: 6 Reden in Nairobi (1971) 33-43.

5:1-4 SANDERS, E. P. Jewish Law from Jesus to the Mishnah (London/Philadelphia 1990) 283. VOLF, J. M. G. Paul and Perseverance (Tübingen 1990) 203-16, 285.

5:1-2 LAMPE, P. Die stadtrömischen Christen in den ersten beiden Jahrhunderten (Tübingen ²1989) 55.

5:1.13 FREUND, G. und STEGEMANN, E., eds., Theologische Brosamen für Lothar Steiger (DBAT 5; Heidelberg 1985) 186.

5:1 RENGSTORF, K.H. "Zu Gal 5, 1" ThLZ 76 (1951) 659-62. SCHWEITZER, A. Die Mystik des Apostels Paulus (1954) 124f., 156f., 196. LIGHTFOOT, J.B. The Epistle of St. Paul to the Galatians (1957) 200-2. HERMANN, I. Kyrois und Pneuma (1961) 106f. HAHN, F. Das Verständnis der Mission im Neuen Testament (1965) 85. JÜNGEL, E. Paulus und Jesus (1966) 64. GNILKA, J. "Zur Liebe befreit" BiLe 8 (1967) 145-48. VAN DÜLMEN, A. Die Theologie des Gesetzes bei Paulus (1968) 55-57, 58-59. MÜLLER, K. aNSTOSS UND gERICHT (1969) 108-111. BORSE, U. Der Standort des Galaterbriefes (1972) 76-77, 129. BUJARD, W. Stilanalytische Untersuchungen zum Kolosserbrief (1973) 157f. SCHLIER, H. "Über die christliche Freiheit," GuL 50 (1977) 178-93. FRIEDRICH, G. "Freiheit und Liebe im ersten Korintherbrief" in Auf das Wort kommt es an. Gesammelte Aufsätze (Göttingen 1978) 180. THISELTON, A. C. The Two Horizons (Grand Rapids 1980) 390. LINCOLN, A. T. Paradise Now and Not Yet (Cambridge 1981) 25-27. BARTSCH, H. W. and MEHL, R. "Freiheit" in TRE 11 (1983) 509, 523. HAYS, R. B. The Faith of Jesus Christ (Chico CA 1983) 106, 233, 260. BRUCE, F. F. "'Called to Freedom'. A Study in Galatians" in W. C. Weinrich, ed., The New Testament Age (FS B. Reicke; Macon GA 1984) I, 61-71. MOHRLANG, R. Matthew and Paul (Cambridge 1984) 36, 39, 47, 88. BARRETT, C. K. Freedom and Obligation (Philadelphia 1985) 55-62. SCHNABEL, E. J. Law and Wisdom from Ben Sira to Paul (Tübingen 1985) 113, 340f. MALHERBE, A. J. Moral Exhortation. A Greco-Roman Sourcebook (Philadelphia 1986) 159. DOBBELER, A. VON, Glaube als Teilhabe (Tübingen 1987) 183f. GERHARDSSON, B. "Eleutheria (Freedom) in the Bible" in B. P. Thompson, ed., Scripture. Meaning and Method (FS A. T. Hanson; Hull 1987) 14, 17, 23n.19. JONES, F. S. "Freiheit" in den Briefen des Apostels Paulus (Göttingen 1987) 31, 44, 52, 64, 70, 85, 92, 96-102, 104f., 107f., 113f., 147n.3, 223n.91. MUSSNER, F. Die Kraft der Wurzel (Freiburg/Basel/Wien 1987) 182ff. OSTEN-SACKEN, P. VON DER, Evangelium und Tora: Aufsätze zu Paulus (München 1987) 200. CONZELMANN, H. and LINDEMANN, A. Interpreting the New Testament (Peabody MA 1988) 170. BLANK, J. "Zu welcher Freiheit hat uns Christus befreit? Die Theologische Dimension der Freiheit," StZ 207 (7, 1989) 460-72. CLABEAUX, J. J. The Lost Edition of the Letters of Paul (CBQ.MS; Washington 1989) 162. KERTELGE, K. "Freiheitsbotschaft und Liebesgebot im Galaterbrief" in H. Merklein, ed., Neues Testament und Ethik (FS R. Schnackenburg; Freiburg/Basel/ Wien 1989) 326-37. VOLLENWEIDER, S. Freiheit als neue Schöpfung (Göttingen 1989) 319. CRUZ, H. Christological Motives and Motivated Actions in Pauline Paraenesis (Frankfurt/Bern/New York/Paris 1990) 107-14. LACH, J. "'Dla wolnosce wyswobodzil nas Chrystus'(Ga 5, 1) ['For Freedom—Christ has set us free' (Ga 5, 1)]," SThV 29 (2, 1991) 33-46.

5:2-6:18 RICHARDS, E. R. The Secretary in the Letters of Paul (Tübingen 1991) 177.

5:2ff. HAHN, F. Das Verständnis der Mission im Neuen Testament (1965) 87. WATSON, F. Paul, Judaism and the Gentiles (Cambridge 1986) 69.

5:2-10 MÜLLER, K. Anstoss und Gericht (1969) 111-13.

5:2-4 FRIEDRICH, G. "Das Gesetz des Glaubens Römer 3, 27" in Auf das Wort kommt es an. Gesammelte Aufsätze (Göttingen 1978) 118. BRINSMEAD, B. H. Galatians—Dialogical Response to Opponents (Chico CA 1982) 139-41. MOHRLANG, R. Matthew and Paul (Cambridge 1984) 29, 60, 106, 166.

5:2-3 WILSON, S. G. Luke and the Law (Cambridge 1983) 64f. BARRETT, C. K. Freedom and Obligation (Philadelphia 1985) 62f. FREUND, G. und STEGEMANN, E., eds., Theologische Brosamen für Lothar Steiger (DBAT 5; Heidelberg 1985) 389. ZMIJEWSKI, J. Paulus—Knecht und Apostel Christi (Stuttgart 1986) 77f. DOWNING, F. G. Christ and the Cynics (Sheffield 1988) xiiin. LIMBECK, M. Mit

Paulus Christ sein. Sachbuch zur Person und Theologie des Apostels Paulus (Stuttgart 1989) 90f.

5:2   SCHRAGE, W. Die konkreten Einzelgebote in der paulinischen Paränese (1961) 106, 231. VAN DÜLMEN, A. Die Theologie des Gesetzes bei Paulus (1968) 55-57. ECKERT, J. Die urchristliche Verkündigung im Streit zwischen Paulus und seinen Gegnern nach dem Galaterbrief (1971) 8, 30, 36, 64.

5:3-4   HÜBNER, H. "Galaterbrief" in TRE 12 (1984) 9. HÜBNER, H. "Was heisst bei Paulus 'Werke des Gesetzes'?" in E. Grässer und O. Merk, eds., Glaube und Eschatologie (FS W. G. Kümmel; Tübingen 1985) 130f. ZIESLER, J. Pauline Christianity (Oxford 1990) 78, 106f.

5:3   MUNCK, J. Paul and the Salvation of Mankind (1959) 88-90. SCHRAGE, W. Die konkreten Einzelgebote in der paulinischen Paränese (1961) 94. JÜNGEL, E. Paulus und Jesus (1966) 57. DRANE, J.W. Paul: Libertine or Legalist? (1975) 46-51. VIELHAUER, P. "Gesetzesdienst und Stoicheiadienst im Galaterbrief" in Rechtfertigung. Festschrift für Ernst Käsemann. Hrsg. von J. Friedrich et al. (1976) 544-46. TRITES, A. A. The New Testament Concept of Witness (Cambridge 1977) 206. HÜBNER, H. Das Gesetz bei Paulus. Ein Beitrag zum Werden der paulinischen Theologie (Göttingen 1978) 24, 26. VIELHAUER, P. "Gesetzesdienst und Stoicheiadienst im Galaterbrief" in Oikodome [G. Klein, ed.] (München 1979) 185f. HILL, D. "Salvation Proclaimed. IV: Galatians 3:10-14," ET 93 (1982) 198f. LÜDEMANN, G. Paulus, der Heidenapostel, Band II (Göttingen 1983) 147, 150-52, 196f. RÄISÄNEN, H. Paul and the Law (Tübingen 1983) 27, 55, 63f., 95, 190, 261. HÜBNER, H. "Galaterbrief" in TRE 12 (1984) 6, 8. HÜBNER, H. "Der Galaterbrief und das Verhältnis von antiker Rhetorik und Epistolographie," ThLZ 109 (1984) 241-50, esp. 246f. SANDERS, E. P. Paul, the Law, and the Jewish People (London 1985) 20, 23, 27-29, 51n.17, 56nn.58.59, 96f., 150. MERKLEIN, H. Studien zu Jesus und Paulus (Tübingen 1987) 68n.167, 98, 100, 101, 104, 105n.242. DOWNING, F. G. Christ and the Cynics (Sheffield 1988) 161. LIEBERS, R. Das Gesetz als Evangelium (Zürich 1989) 78-80. MARTIN, B. L. Christ and the Law in Paul (Leiden 1989) 46, 53, 86, 88f., 145f., 149f. SCHNELLE, U. Wandlungen im paulinischen Denken (Stuttgart 1989) 54, 60, 74. HOWARD, G. Paul. Crisis in Galatia (Cambridge ²1990) 14-17, 18.

5:4-6   FROITZHEIM, F. Christologie und Eschatologie bei Paulus (Würzburg 1979) 188. BETZ, O. "Beschneidung" in TRE 5 (1980) 720. COSGROVE, C. H. The Cross and the Spirit. A Study in the Argument and Theology of Galatians (Macon GA 1988) 150, 152f., 182.

5:4-5   JÜNGEL, E. Paulus und Jesus (1966) 32. ZIESLER, J.A. The Meaning of Righteousness in Paul (1972) 179-80. BARRETT, C. K. Freedom and Obligation (Philadelphia 1985) 63-65.

5:4   KÄSEMANN, E. Exegetische Versuche und Besinnungen (1964) II 73; New Testament Questions of Today (1969) 71. ECKERT, J. Die urchristliche Verkündigung im Streit zwischen Paulus und seinen Gegnern nach dem Galaterbrief (1971) 12, 16, 42. HAYS, R. B. The Faith of Jesus Christ (Chico CA 1983) 206. MERKLEIN, H. Studien zu Jesus und Paulus (Tübingen 1987) 40f., 48, 76, 96, 100, 102, 104f. COSGROVE, C. H. The Cross and the Spirit. A Study in the Argument and Theology of Galatians (Macon GA 1988) 14, 149-52, 171n. DUNN, J. D. G. Jesus, Paul and the Law (London 1990) 208, 238, 245f., 248, 250.

5:5-6   MONTAGUE, G. T. The Holy Spirit (New York 1976) 198. DOBBELER, A. VON, Glaube als Teilhabe (Tübingen 1987) 207f. BECKER, J. Paulus. Der Apostel der Völker (Tübingen 1989) 110f., 283, 297, 304. MELL, U. Neue Schöpfung

(Berlin/New York 1989) 302, 302n.80, 390. MULLER, E. C. Trinity and Marriage in Paul (New York/Bern/Frankfurt/Paris 1990) 52, 122f.

5:5 KÄSEMANN, E. Exegetische Versuche und Besinnungen (1964) II 183, 190; New Testament Questions of Today (1969) 170, 178. JÜNGEL, E. Paulus und Jesus (1966) 61. KERTELGE, K. "Rechtfertigung" bei Paulus (1967) 147-50. MERK, O. Handeln aus Glauben (1968) 12-14. MIRANDA, J. P. Marx and the Bible. A Critique of the Philosophy of Oppression (London 1977) 241-45. FRIEDRICH, G. "Die Kirche zu Korinth" in Auf das Wort kommt es an. Gesammelte Aufsätze (Göttingen 1978) 138. LULL, D. J. The Spirit in Galatia (Chico CA 1980) 171f. THISELTON, A. C. The Two Horizons (Grand Rapids 1980) 419. DEIDUN, T. J. New Covenant Morality in Paul (Rome 1981) 46f. HAYS, R. B. The Faith of Jesus Christ (Chico CA 1983) 231. NEBE, G. 'Hoffnung' bei Paulus (Göttingen 1983) 19, 22, 25f., 32, 34ff., 55f., 64ff., 70, 72f., 75, 145, 164, 170, 240, 253, 295. KLEINKNECHT, K. T. Der leidende Gerechtfertigte (Tübingen 1984) 199. WEDER, H. "Hoffnung II" in TRE 15 (1986) 485, 487. DUNN, J. D. G. Jesus, Paul and the Law (London 1990) 162, 190, 207f., 246, 248. OLIVEIRA, A. DE, Die Diakonie der Gerechtigkeit und der Versöhnung in der Apologie des 2. Korintherbriefes. Analyse und Auslegung von 2 Kor 2, 14-4, 6; 5, 11-6, 10 (Münster 1990) 172n.453.

5:6-8 BARRETT, C. K. Freedom and Obligation (Philadelphia 1985) 66-68.

5:6 BURTON, E.DeW. "Religion and Ethics in the Thought of the Apostle Paul: Gal. 5:6" BibW 36 (1910) 307-15. SCHRAGE, W. Die konkreten Einzelgebote in der paulinischen Paränese (1961) 56, 100, 269. SCHMITHALS, W. Paulus und Jakobus (1963) 21. JÜNGEL, E. Paulus und Jesus (1966) 32, 65, 68. MULKA, A.L. 'Fides quae per Caritatem Operatur' (Gal 5, 6)" CBQ 28 (1966) 174-88. BORSE, U. Der Standort des Galaterbriefes (1972) 65-67. ZIESLER, J.A. The Meaning of Righteousness in Paul (1972) 179f. BAUMERT, N. Täglich sterben und auferstehen. Der Literalsinn von 2 Kor 4, 12-5, 10 (1973) 231, 273, 283. WILES, G.P. Paul's Intercessory Prayers (1974) 130. JEWETT, P. K. Infant Baptism and the Covenant of Grace (Grand Rapids 1978) 89. SCHMITHALS, W. "Zur Herkunft der gnostischen Elemente in der Sprache des Paulus" in B. Aland et al., eds., Gnosis (FS H. Jonas; Göttingen 1978) 400. FURNISH, V. P. The Moral Teaching of Paul (Nashville 1979) 22, 26. FULLER, D. P. Gospel and Law. Contrast or Continuum? (Grand Rapids 1980) 115f. DEIDUN, T. J. New Covenant Morality in Paul (Rome 1981) 119-22. MÜLLER, U. B. "Zur Rezeption gesetzeskritischer Jesusüberlieferung im frühen Christentum," NTS 27 (1981) 160. SCHMITHALS, W. "Bultmann" in TRE 7 (1981) 394. BRINSMEAD, B. H. Galatians—Dialogical Response to Opponents (Chico CA 1982) 168. HAYS, R. B. The Faith of Jesus Christ (Chico CA 1983) 262. RÄISÄNEN, H. Paul and the Law (Tübingen 1983) 67f., 139. MOHRLANG, R. Matthew and Paul (Cambridge 1984) 45, 101f., 105. GRAESSER, E. Der Alte Bund im Neuen (Tübingen 1985) 25, 226, 257, 284, 287. SCHNACKENBURG, R. Die sittliche Botschaft des Neuen Testaments, Band 1 (Freiburg/Basel/Wien 1986) 195, 198. MERKLEIN, H. Studien zu Jesus und Paulus (Tübingen 1987) 68n.167, 98, 100, 102, 104. HOFIUS, O. Paulusstudien (Tübingen 1989) 69. MELL, U. Neue Schöpfung (Berlin/New York 1989) 298f., 301, 304, 305n.88, 314, 389f. VOLLENWEIDER, S. Freiheit als neue Schöpfung (Göttingen 1989) 239, 312f. DUNN, J. D. G. Jesus, Paul and the Law (London 1990) 198, 240, 245, 248, 262n.45.

5:7-12 BORSE, U. Der Standort des Galaterbriefes (1972) 90f. MARTYN, J. L. "A Law-Observant Mission to Gentiles. The Background of Galatians" in M. P. O'Connor and D. N. Freedman, eds., Backgrounds for the Bible (Winona Lake/Indiana 1987) 199-214, esp. 204ff.

5:7   PFITZNER, V.C. Paul and the Agon Motif (1967) 136ff. BORSE, U. Der Standort
          des Galaterbriefes (1972) 90f. OLLROG, W.-H. Paulus und seine Mitarbeiter
          (Neukirchen/Vluyn 1979) 33.
5:8   BIRD, C. "Notes on Galatians 5:8" Exp 4th series 7 (1893) 471-72. WIEDERKEHR,
          D. Die Theologie der Berufung in den Paulusbriefen (1963) 90-93.
5:9-10   BARRETT, C. K. Freedom and Obligation (Philadelphia 1985) 68.
5:9   SCHOEN A. "Eine weitere metrische Stelle bei Paulus" Biblica 30 (1949) 510-13.
          GALE, H.M. The Use of Analogy in the Letters of Paul (1964) 95f. CLABEAUX,
          J. J. The Lost Edition of the Letters of Paul (CBQ.MS; Washington 1989) 86, 152.
5:10-12   TYSON, J.B. "'Works of Law' in Gal" JBL 92 (1973) 423-31.
5:10   BORSE, U. Der Standort des Galaterbriefes (1972) 90f. SYNOFZIK, E. Die
          Gerichts- und Vergeltungsaussagen bei Paulus (Göttingen 1977) 33. AONO, T. Die
          Entwicklung des paulinischen Gerichtsgedankens bei den Apostolischen Vätern
          (Bern/Frankfurt/Las Vegas 1979) 4ff. SCHADE, H.-H. Apokalyptische Christologie
          bei Paulus (Göttingen 1981) 53f. MUELLER, P.-G. Der Traditionsprozess im Neuen
          Testament (Freiburg 1982) 224. FREUND, G. und STEGEMANN, E., eds.,
          Theologische Brosamen für Lothar Steiger (DBAT 5; Heidelberg 1985) 389.
5:11-12   FEINE, P. & BEHM, J. Einleitung in das Neue Testament (1950) 144ff. BARRETT,
          C. K. Freedom and Obligation (Philadelphia 1985) 68-70. SCHNELLE, U.
          Wandlungen im paulinischen Denken (Stuttgart 1989) 54.
5:11   FEINE, P. Das gesetzesfreie Evangelium des Paulus (1899) 50-52. SCHELKLE,
          K.H. Die Passion Jesu in der Verkündigung des Neuen Testament (1949) 203f.
          MUNCK, J. Paul and the Salvation of Mankind (1959) 90f., 100. ORTKEMPER, F.-
          J. Das Kreuz in der Verkündigung des Apostels Paulus (1967) 28-31. MÜLLER, K.
          Anstoss und Gericht (1969) 113-21. BORSE, U. Der Standort des Galaterbriefes
          (1972) 62-65, 89-91. BAUMERT, N. Täglich sterben und auferstehen (1973) 304.
          MINEAR, P. S. To Die and to Live. Christ's Resurrection and Christian Vocation
          (New York 1977) 72. ELLIS, E. E. Prophecy and Hermeneutic in Early Christianity
          (Tübingen 1978) 74, 98f., 234. BORGEN, P. "Observations on the Theme 'Paul and
          Philo'. Paul's Preaching of Circumcision in Galatia (Gal. 5:11) and Debates on
          Circumcision in Philo" in S. Pedersen, ed., Die Paulinische Literatur und Theologie
          (Arhus/ Göttingen 1980) 85-102. KIM, S. The Origin of Paul's Gospel (Tübingen
          1981) 39f. WEDER, H. Das Kreuz Jesu bei Paulus (Göttingen 1981) 193-97.
          BORGEN, P. "Paul Preaches Circumcision and Pleases Men" in M. D. Hooker and
          S. G. Wilson, eds., Paul and Paulinism (FS C. K. Barrett; London 1982) 37-41.
          WILSON, S. G. Luke and the Law (Cambridge 1983) 64f. KLEINKNECHT, K. T.
          Der leidende Gerechtfertigte (Tübingen 1984) 196, 320. FREUND, G. und
          STEGEMANN, E., eds., Theologische Brosamen für Lothar Steiger (DBAT 5;
          Heidelberg 1985) 476. LAMBRECHT, J. "Unreal Conditions in the Letters of Paul.
          A Clarification," EphT 63 (1987) 153-56. COSGROVE, C. H. The Cross and the
          Spirit. A Study in the Argument and Theology of Galatians (Macon GA 1988) 35,
          37, 79, 177, 187f. HOWARD, G. Paul. Crisis in Galatia (Cambridge [2]1990) 8, 10,
          39, 44, 91f. DALTON, W. "Once More Paul among Jews and Gentiles," Pacifica 4
          (1991) 51-61. GEORGI, D. Theocracy in Paul's Praxis and Theology (Minneapolis
          1991) 46-51, 52n.63. BAARDA, T. "ti eti diōkomai in Gal. 5:11. Apodosis or
          Parenthesis?" NovT 34 (1992) 250-56.
5:12-15   BORGEN, P. "Observations on the Theme 'Paul and Philo'. Paul's Preaching of
          Circumcision in Galatia (Gal. 5:11) and Debates on Circumcision in Philo" in S.
          Pedersen, ed., Die Paulinische Literatur und Theologie (Arhus/Göttingen 1980) 92-
          97. BAARDA, T. "ti eti diōkomai in Gal. 5:11. Apodosis or Parenthesis?" NovT 34
          (1992) 250-56.

5:12   VON CAMPENHAUSEN, H. "Ein Witz des Apostels Paulus" in Neutestamentliche Studien für Rudolf Bultmann (1954) 189-93. KÜMMEL, W.G. Einleitung in das Neue Testament (1973) 260-62. JEWETT, P. K. Infant Baptism and the Covenant of Grace (Grand Rapids 1978) 234. REISER, M. Syntax and Stil des Markusevangeliums (Tübingen 1984) 151. MALHERBE, A. J. Moral Exhortation. A Greco-Roman Sourcebook (Philadelphia 1986) 130. RÄISÄNEN, H. The Torah and Christ (Helsinki 1986) 48. HAACKER, K. "Elemente des heidnischen Antijudaismus im Neuen Testament," EvTh 48 (1988) 404-18.

5:13–6:18 VAN DÜLMEN, A. Die Theologie des Gesetzes bei Paulus (1968) 58-71.

5:13–6:10 GIBLET, J. "De carne et spiritu secundum Gal V, 13–VI, 10" Collectanea Mechliniensia 27 (1957) 37-39. MERK, O. Handeln aus Glauben (1968) 68-80, 236f. JEWETT, R. "The Agitators and the Galatian Congregation" NTS 17 (1970-71) 209f. ECKERT, J. Die urchristliche Verkündigung im Streit zqischen Paulus und seinen Gegnern nach dem Galaterbrief (1971) 131f., 149ff., 232ff. DRANE, J.W. Paul: Libertine or Legalist? (1975) 52-58. HOWARD, G. Paul. Crisis in Galatia (Cambridge 1979) 11-14. VIELHAUER, P. "Gesetzesdienst und Stoicheiadienst im Galaterbrief" in Oikodome [G. Klein, ed.] (München 1979) 185. BORGEN, P. "Nomisme og libertinisme i Paulus' brev til galaterne," TsTK 51 (1980) 257-67. REINMUTH, E. Geist und Gesetz (Berlin, DDR 1985) 54-66. BERGER, K. und COLPE, C., eds., Religionsgeschichtliches Textbuch zum Neuen Testament (Göttingen/Zürich 1987) 274-76. BARCLAY, J. M. G. Obeying the Truth. A Study of Paul's Ethics in Galatians (Edinburgh 1988) passim. COSGROVE, C. H. The Cross and the Spirit. A Study in the Argument and Theology of Galatians (Macon GA 1988) 31, 148, 154, 158f., 173. PRETORIUS, E. A. C. "The Opposition *pneuma* and *sarx* as Persuasive Summons (Galatians 5:13-6:10)," Neotestamentica 26 (1992) 441-60. WESSELS, G. F. "The Call to Responsible Freedom in Paul's Persuasive Strategy. Galatians 5:13-6:10," Neotestamentica 26 (1992) 461-74.

5:13ff. SCHRAGE, W. Die konkreten Einzelgebote in der paulinischen Paränese (1961) 249f. SMITH, M. Clement of Alexandria and a Secret Gospel of Mark (1973) 259f. BRAUN, H. Qumran und das Neue Testament II (1966) 173f. PFISTER, W. Das Leben im Geist nach Paulus (1963) 49-65. HINZ, C. GPM 22 (1967/68) 374-82. DUNN, J.D.G. Jesus and the Spirit (1975) 312f. CONZELMANN, H. and LINDEMANN, A. Interpreting the New Testament (Peabody MA 1988) 173. VOLLENWEIDER, S. Freiheit als neue Schöpfung (Göttingen 1989) 312. VOLF, J. M. G. Paul and Perseverance (Tübingen 1990) 142-54.

5:13-26 MONTAGUE, G. T. The Holy Spirit (New York 1976) 198-202. GALANIS, I. "Gal. 5, 13-26 (Biblikē meletē)," DBM 5 (2-3, 1977/78) 189-95. THISELTON, A. C. The Two Horizons (Grand Rapids 1980) 280. HAYS, R. B. The Faith of Jesus Christ (Chico CA 1983) 261. SCHNABEL, E. J. Law and Wisdom from Ben Sira to Paul (Tübingen 1985) 278f., 305. DOBBELER, A. VON, Glaube als Teilhabe (Tübingen 1987) 66-69. GERHARDSSON, B. "Eleutheria (Freedom) in the Bible" in B. P. Thompson, ed., Scripture. Meaning and Method (FS A. T. Hanson; Hull 1987) 16f.

5:13-25 MIRANDA, J. P. Marx and the Bible. A Critique of the Philosophy of Oppression (London 1977) 225. MINDE, H. J. VAN DER, "Theologia crucis und Pneumaaussagen bei Paulus," Catholica 34 (1980) 141. PATTE, D. Paul's Faith and the Power of the Gospel (Philadelphia 1983) 332, 334-38. LOHFINK, G. Jesus and Community. The Social Dimension of the Christian Faith (Philadelphia 1984) 111f. BARRETT, C. K. Freedom and Obligation (Philadelphia 1985) 71-74. SUHL, A. "Der Galaterbrief—Situation und Argumentation" in ANRW II.25.4 (1987) 3119-27.

5:13-24 HONG, I.-G. The Law in Galatians (Sheffield 1993) 59-62, 70ff., 100ff.

5:13-15 FRICK, R. GPM 19 (1964/65) 270-77. ECKERT, J. Die urchristliche Verkündigung im Streit zwischen Paulus und seinen Gegnern nach dem Galaterbrief (1971) 132-36, 159f.
5:13-14 BEYER, W.-ALTHAUS, P. "Freiheit vom Gesetz und sittliche Freiheit" in Der Brief an die Galater (1949) 44-46. NIEDER, L. Die Motive der religiös–sittlichen Paränese in den paulinischen Gemeindebriefen (1956) 41-42. BORSE, U. Der Standort des Galaterbriefes (1972) 129f. HÜBNER, H. Das Gesetz bei Paulus. Ein Beitrag zum Werden der paulinischen Theologie (Göttingen 1978) 35-37. MATA, J. A. "Galatas 5, 13-14. El ser amados nos hace libres para amar," Estudios Teológicos 9 (17, 1982) 69-118. RÄISÄNEN, H. Paul and the Law (Tübingen 1983) 63f., 68. KERTELGE, K. "Freiheitsbotschaft und Liebesgebot im Galaterbrief" in H. Merklein, ed., Neues Testament und Ethik (FS R. Schnackenburg; Freiburg/Basel/ Wien 1989) 326-37, esp. 332ff.
5:13 MINEAR, P.S. Images of the Church in the New Testament (1960) 157f. SCHRAGE, W. Die konkreten Einzelgebote in der paulinischen Paränese (1961) 83f., 160f. WIEDERKEHR, D. Die Theologie der Berufung in den Paulusbriefen (1963) 93-99. SINT, J. "Dienet einander durch die Liebe (Gal 5, 13)" BuL 37 (1963-64) 213-16. JÜNGEL, E. Paulus und Jesus (1966) 65. VAN DÜLMEN, A. Die Theologie des Gestzes bei Paulus (1968) 58f. MERK, O. Handeln aus Glauben (1968) 68-70. BAUMERT, N. Täglich sterben und auferstehen. Der Literalsin von 2 Kor 4, 12-5, 10 (1973) 231, 274, 361. PASTOR RAMOS, F. La libertad en la Carta a los Gálatas. Estudio exegético-teológico (Madrid 1977) passim. ELLIS, E. E. Prophecy and Hermeneutic in Early Christianity (Tübingen 1978) 85, 90, 98, 231. HÜBNER, H. Das Gesetz bei Paulus. Ein Beitrag zum Werden der paulinischen Theologie (Göttingen 1978) 117. HAYS, R. B. The Faith of Jesus Christ (Chico CA 1983) 260. BRUCE, F. F. "'Called to Freedom'. A Study in Galatians" in W. C. Weinrich, ed., The New Testament Age (FS B. Reicke; Macon GA 1984) I, 61-71. MOHRLANG, R. Matthew and Paul (Cambridge 1984) 32, 103, 176. KOCH, D.-A. Die Schrift als Zeuge des Evangeliums (Tübingen 1986) 296f. MALHERBE, A. J. Moral Exhortation. A Greco-Roman Sourcebook (Philadelphia 1986) 158. GERHARDSSON, B. "Eleutheria (Freedom) in the Bible" in B. P. Thompson, ed., Scripture. Meaning and Method (FS A. T. Hanson; Hull 1987) 14f., 23n.19. JONES, F. S. "Freiheit" in den Briefen des Apostels Paulus (Göttingen 1987) 15, 44, 70, 102-07, 109, 114, 136, 139, 144f., 147n.3, 157n.4, 211n.213, 212n.228, 213n.236. OSTEN-SACKEN, P. VON DER, Evangelium und Tora: Aufsätze zu Paulus (München 1987) 202, 204. VOLLENWEIDER, S. Freiheit als neue Schöpfung (Göttingen 1989) 117n., 289, 319, 403f. ZIESLER, J. Pauline Christianity (Oxford 1990) 78.
5:14-6:2 MULLER, E. C. Trinity and Marriage in Paul (New York/Bern/Frankfurt/Paris 1990) 369, 426.
5:14 ELLIS, E.E. Paul's Use of the Old Testament (1957) 182, 187. KOSOWSKI, S. "Milosc blizniego w ujeciu sw. Pawla Apostola" Ruch Biblijny i Liturgiczny 10 (1957) 261-66. SCHRAGE, W. Die konkreten Einzelgebote in der paulinischen Paränese (1961) 230-32, 255. BANDSTRA, A.J. The Law and the Elements of the World (1964) 110f. ECKERT, J. Die urchristliche Verkündigung im Streit zwischen Paulus und seinen Gegnern nach dem Galaterbrief (1971) 159, 160. BORSE, U. Der Standort des Galaterbriefes (1972) 129f. HÜBNER, H. "Das ganze und das eine Gesetz. Zum Problemkreis Paulus und die Stoa" KuD (1975) 239-56. DAVIES, W. D. The Sermon on the Mount (Cambridge 1966) 117. RIDDERBOS, H. Paul. An Outline of His Theology (Grand Rapids 1975) 279-85. HÜBNER, H. Das Gesetz bei Paulus. Ein Beitrag zum Werden der paulinischen Theologie (Göttingen 1978) 37-39.

BARTH, G. "Bergpredigt" in TRE 5 (1980) 611. LOHSE, E. "Kirche im Alltag . . . " in D. Lührmann und G. Strecker, eds., Kirche (FS G. Bornkamm; Tübingen 1980) 401f. DEIDUN, T. J. New Covenant Morality in Paul (Rome 1981) 157ff. SMEND, R. "Ethik" in TRE 10 (1982) 432. HAYS, R. B. The Faith of Jesus Christ (Chico CA 1983) 260. PATHRAPANKAL, J. "The whole Law is Summed up in one Commandment: 'Love Your Neighbor as you Love Yourself' (Gal 5:14)," Jeevadhara 13 (74, 1983) 114-21. RÄISÄNEN, H. Paul and the Law (Tübingen 1983) 7, 9, 26f., 33f., 65f., 78, 80, 139, 222, 246. THEISSEN, G. Psychologische Aspekte paulinischer Theologie (Göttingen 1983) 229, 259, 367. HEILIGENTHAL, R. "Gebot" in TRE 12 (1984) 124. HÜBNER, H. "Galaterbrief" in TRE 12 (1984) 9. HÜBNER, H. "Der Galaterbrief und das Verhältnis von antiker Rhetorik und Epistolographie," ThLZ 109 (1984) 241-50, esp. 246f. LÜHRMANN, D. "Gerechtigkeit" in TRE 12 (1984) 418. MOHRLANG, R. Matthew and Paul (Cambridge 1984) 34, 101, 105, 150, 183. FREUND, G. und STEGEMANN, E., eds., Theologische Brosamen für Lothar Steiger (DBAT 5; Heidelberg 1985) 187. SANDERS, E. P. Paul, the Law, and the Jewish People (London 1985) 49n.6, 93, 94, 95, 96-100, 103, 112, 115nn.4.12, 149. SCHNABEL, E. J. Law and Wisdom from Ben Sira to Paul (Tübingen 1985) 274-78, 281, 294, 328, 341. KOCH, D.-A. Die Schrift als Zeuge des Evangeliums (Tübingen 1986) 296f. RÄISÄNEN, H. The Torah and Christ (Helsinki 1986) 5, 11, 255, 292. SCHNACKENBURG, R. Die sittliche Botschaft des Neuen Testaments, Band 1 (Freiburg/Basel/Wien 1986) 215. WESTERHOLM, S. "On Fulfilling the Whole Law (Gal. 5:14)," SEA 51-52 (1986/87) 229-37. MERKLEIN, H. Studien zu Jesus und Paulus (Tübingen 1987) 97f., 100, 103f., 105n.242, 268. OSTEN-SACKEN, P. VON DER, Evangelium und Tora: Aufsätze zu Paulus (München 1987) 17, 26, 54, 102, 183, 203, 206. MARTIN, F. Narrative Parallels to the New Testament (Atlanta 1988) 268. TRILLING, W. Studien zur Jesusüberlieferung (Stuttgart 1988) 150. BECKER, J. Paulus. Der Apostel der Völker (Tübingen 1989) 115-30, 265, 462. CLABEAUX, J. J. The Lost Edition of the Letters of Paul (CBQ.MS; Washington 1989) 26, 29, 91, 100, 101, 115f., 152. HOFIUS, O. Paulusstudien (Tübingen 1989) 69. JEFFORD, C. N. The Sayings of Jesus in the Teaching of the Twelve Apostles (Leiden 1989) 32, 160. MARTIN, B. L. Christ and the Law in Paul (Leiden 1989) 2, 19f., 48, 53f., 58, 66, 91, 142, 148-50, 152, 155. SCHNELLE, U. Wandlungen im paulinischen Denken (Stuttgart 1989) 60, 74. THIELMAN, F. From Plight to Solution (Leiden 1989) 19, 50-54, 59, 62, 65f., 77, 89. VOLLENWEIDER, S. Freiheit als neue Schöpfung (Göttingen 1989) 306, 370, 400, 403. WALTER, N. "Paul and the Early Christian Jesus-Tradition" in A. J. M. Wedderburn, ed., Paul and Jesus. Collected Essays (Sheffield 1989) 51-80, esp. 57f., 72f. DUNN, J. D. G. Jesus, Paul and the Law (London 1990) 99, 175, 200, 209, 226, 228, 240, 249, 262nn.44.45. ELLIS, E. E. The Old Testament in Early Christianity (Tübingen 1991) 81, 108, 138. HONG, I.-G. The Law in Galatians (Sheffield 1993) 60f., 123f., 170-73, 175-78, 181-83, 193-96.

5:15-24   LANGAN, M.F. "Der Weg der Freiheit" Am Tisch des Wortes 12 (1966) 14-27.

5:15   CRONJÉ, J. VAN W. "Defamiliarization in the letter to the Galatians" in J. H. Petzer and P. J. Hartin, eds., A South African Perspective on the New Testament (FS B. M. Metzger; Leiden 1986) 220. BERGER, K. und COLPE, C., eds., Religionsge- schicht-liches Textbuch zum Neuen Testament (Göttingen/Zürich 1987) 278f. LOHSE, E. Die Entstehung des Neuen Testaments (Stuttgart/Berlin/Köln ⁵1991) 37.

5:16-6:18 MARTYN, J. L. "Events in Galatia. Modified Covenantal Nomism versus God's Invasion of the Cosmos in the Singular Gospel: A Response to J. D. G. Dunn and B. R. Gaventa" in J. M. Bassler, ed., Pauline Theology, Volume 1: Thessalonians, Philippians, Galatians, Philemon (Minneapolis MN 1991) 176-79.

5:16-6:10 BORGEN, P. "Observations on the Theme 'Paul and Philo'. Paul's Preaching of Circumcision in Galatia (Gal. 5:11) and Debates on Circumcision in Philo" in S. Pedersen, ed., Die Paulinische Literatur und Theologie (Arhus/Göttingen 1980) 97-101.

5:16ff.   BANDSTRA, A.J. The Law and the Elements of the World (1964) 108ff., 132ff. SCHRAGE, W. "Ethik" in TRE 10 (1982) 446. HÜBNER, H. "Galaterbrief" in TRE 12 (1984) 8. VOLLENWEIDER, S. Freiheit als neue Schöpfung (Göttingen 1989) 316.

5:16-26   MALINA B. J. Christian Origins and Cultural Anthropology (Atlanta 1986) 135. MARTÍNEZ PEQUE, M. "Unidad de forma y contenido en Gál 5, 16-26," EstBi 45 (1-2, 1987) 105-24.

5:16-25   NIEDER, L. Die Motive der Religiös—Sittlichen Paränese in den paulinischen Gemeindebriefen (1956) 14-19. WIKENHAUSER, A. Die Christusmystik des Apostels Paulus (1956) 101, 166f. BOHREN, R. Predigtlehre (1971) 197f., 322. MOHRLANG, R. Matthew and Paul (Cambridge 1984) 115f.

5:16-24   OGARA, F. "'Spiritu ambulate' Gal. 5:16-24" VD 18 (1938) 257-61, 289-93. STECK, K.G. GPM 5 (1950/51) 186-89. SCHOTT, E. GPM 10 (1953/54) 216-18. KRECK, W. GPM 16 (1961/62) 282-85. LACAN, M.-F. "Le chemin de la liberté (Gal 5, 16-24)" AssS 68 (1964) 17-30; "Der Weg der Freiheit (Gal 5, 16-24)" Am Tisch des Wortes 12 (1966) 14-24. SISTI, A. "Carne, spirito e liberta (Gal 5, 16-24)" Bibbia e Oriente 6 (1964) 219-24. FAUSEL, H. in Herr, tue meine Lippen auf, Bd II, hrsg. G. Eichholz (1966) 421-26. DOERNE, M. Die alten Episteln (1967) 204-7. DREHER, B. "Der unerklärliche Christ" Am Tisch des Wortes 12 (1967) 70-74. ECKERT, J. Die urchristliche Verkündigung im Streit zwischen Paulus und seinen Gegnern nach dem Galaterbrief (1971) 136-42. MINEAR, P. S. To Die and to Live. Christ's Resurrection and Christian Vocation (New York 1977) 72. COVOLO, E. DAL, "Il kerygma come critica alla prassi nella parenesi di Gal. 5, 16-24," RivB 29 (1981) 379-91.

5:16-23   CONZELMANN, H. & LINDERMANN, A. Arbeitsbuch zum Neuen Testament (1975) 117. CONZELMANN, H. and LINDEMANN, A. Interpreting the New Testament (Peabody MA 1988) 102f.

5:16-21   SCHADE, H.-H. Apokalyptische Christologie bei Paulus (Göttingen 1981) 55.

5:16-18   BARRETT, C. K. Freedom and Obligation (Philadelphia 1985) 74-76. VOLLENWEIDER, S. Freiheit als neue Schöpfung (Göttingen 1989) 318n., 363n.

5:16-17   SHCRAGE, W. Die konkreten Einzelgebote in der paulinischen Paränese (1961) 63. DELLING, G. Die Taufe im Neuen Testament (1963) 148. SUHL, A. "Der Galaterbrief—Situation und Argumentation" in ANRW II.25.4 (1987) 3123-26.

5:16   SCHRAGE, W. SHCRAGE, W. Die konkreten Einzelgebote in der paulinischen Paränese (1961) 90. STROBEL, A. Erkenntnis und Bekenntnis der Sünde in neutestamentlicher Zeit (1968) 53. DUNN, J.D.G. Jesus and the Spirit (1975) 222f. HAYS, R. B. The Faith of Jesus Christ (Chico CA 1983) 260, 262. RÄISÄNEN, H. The Torah and Christ (Helsinki 1986) 165f.

5:17-23   HÜBNER, H. Das Gesetz bei Paulus. Ein Beitrag zum Werden der paulinischen Theologie (Göttingen 1978) 42.

5:17   MASSIE, J. "Professor Alexander Roberts on Galatians 5:17" ET 3 (1891/92) 219-20. ALTHAUS, P. ". . .Dass ihr nicht tut was ihr wollt" ThLZ 76 (1951) 15-18. JEREMIAS, J. Abba (1966) 279. BAUER, J.B. Scholia Biblica et Patristica (1972) 177-78. RIDDERBOS, H. Paul. An Outline of His Theology (Grand Rapids 1975) 269f. FROITZHEIM, F. Christologie und Eschatologie bei Paulus (Würzburg 1979) 183. BAMMEL, C. P. H. "Philocalia IX, Jerome, Epistle 121, and Origen's Exposition of Romans VII," JThS 32 (1981) 64. DEIDUN, T. J. New Covenant

Morality in Paul (Rome 1981) 37-40. MOHRLANG, R. Matthew and Paul (Cambridge 1984) 32f., 117. LUTJENS, R. "'You Do Not Do What You Want'. What Does Galatians 5:17 Really Mean?" Presbyterion 16 (2, 1990) 103-17.

5:18-25 SCHWEITZER, A. Die Mystik des Apostels Paulus (1954) 120-22, 166-67.

5:18-21 REICKE, B. Diakonie, Festfreude und Zelos (1951) 248ff.

5:18 SCHRAGE, W. Die konkreten Einzelgebote in der paulinischen Paränese (1961) 232. JÜNGEL, E. Paulus und Jesus (1966) 68. ECKERT, J. Die urchristliche Verkündigung im Streit zwischen Paulus und seinen Gegnern nach dem Galaterbrief (1971) 112, 131, 141, 149, 158. MERK, O. Handeln aus Glauben (1968) 72-74. DUPONT, D. J. The Salvation of the Gentiles (New York 1979) 45. DEIDUN, T. J. New Covenant Morality in Paul (Rome 1981) 251-54. MOHRLANG, R. Matthew and Paul (Cambridge 1984) 32f., 116. SCHNACKENBURG, R. Die sittliche Botschaft des Neuen Testaments, Band 1 (Freiburg/Basel/Wien 1986) 163, 232. JOHNSON, E. E. The Function of Apocalyptic and Wisdom Traditions in Romans 9-11 (Atlanta GA 1989) 187. SCHNELLE, U. Wandlungen im paulinischen Denken (Stuttgart 1989) 57.

5:19ff. MOHRLANG, R. Matthew and Paul (Cambridge 1984) 39, 60, 115. LIPS, H. VON, Weisheitliche Traditionen im Neuen Testament (Neukirchen/Vluyn 1990) 364ff., 436.

5:19-26 SCHADE, H.-H. Apokalyptische Christologie bei Paulus (Göttingen 1981) 142. HEILIGENTHAL, R. Werke als Zeichen (Tübingen 1983) 201-07.

5:19-24 VOS, J. Traditionsgeschichtliche Untersuchungen zur paulinsichen Pneumatologie (1973) 26-33.

5:19-23 BARCLAY, W. Flesh and Spirit. An Examination of Galatians 5:19-23 (1962) KAMLAH, E. Die Form der katalogischen Paränese im Neuen Testament (1964) 14-18. PETZKE, G. Die Traditionen über Apollonius von Tyana und das Neue Testament (1970) 225-27. HERR, T. Naturrecht aus der kritischen Sicht des Neuen Testaments (München 1976) 110f., 137-48. MINDE, H. J. VAN DER, "Theologia crucis und Pneumaaussagen bei Paulus," Catholica 34 (1980) 133. MALHERBE, A. J. Moral Exhortation. A Greco-Roman Sourcebook (Philadelphia 1986) 138, 141.

5:19-22 SCHWEIZER, E. "Gottesgerechtigkeit und Lasterkataloge bei Paulus (inkl. Kol und Eph)" in J. Friedrich et al., eds., Rechtfertigung (FS E. Käsemann; Tübingen/Göttingen 1976) 466. SCHWEIZER, E. "Traditional ethical patterns in the Pauline and post-Pauline letters and their development (lists of vices and house-tables)" in E. Best and R. McL. Wilson, eds., Text and Interpretation (FS M. Black; Cambridge 1979) 197f., 201.

5:19-21 JUNCKLER, A. Die Ethik des Apostles Paulus (1919) 116-78. WIBBING, S. Die Tugend- und Lasterkataloge im Neuen Testament (1959) 108ff. SCHRAGE, W. Die konkreten Einzelgebote in der paulinischen Paränese (1961) 21f., 54f. HAGE, W. "Die griechische Baruch-Apokalypse" in JSHRZ V/1 (1974) 27n.17d. SYNOFZIK, E. Die Gerichts- und Vergeltungsaussagen bei Paulus (Göttingen 1977) 65f. FISCHER, U. Eschatologie und Jenseitserwartung im hellenistischen Diasporajudentum (Berlin 1978) 74. McDONALD, J. I. H. Kerygma and Didache (Cambridge 1980) 97. SCHADE, H.-H. Apokalyptische Christologie bei Paulus (Göttingen 1981) 55. BARRETT, C. K. Freedom and Obligation (Philadelphia 1985) 76f. REINMUTH, E. Geist und Gesetz (Berlin, DDR 1985) 20. CLABEAUX, J. J. The Lost Edition of the Letters of Paul (CBQ.MS; Washington 1989) 18. JEFFORD, C. N. The Sayings of Jesus in the Teaching of the Twelve Apostles (Leiden 1989) 27, 84. MARTIN, B. L. Christ and the Law in Paul (Leiden 1989) 98, 105, 108, 147f. VOLF, J. M. G. Paul and Perseverance (Tübingen 1990) 131, 141-53, 284.

5:19 BOUSSET, W. Die Religion des Judentums im späthellenistischen Zeitalter (1966=1926) 425f. THISELTON, A. C. The Two Horizons (Grand Rapids 1980)

410. CLABEAUX, J. J. The Lost Edition of the Letters of Paul (CBQ.MS; Washington 1989) 162.

5:20-21   LAMPE, P. Die stadtrömischen Christen in den ersten beiden Jahrhunderten (Tübingen ²1989) 178.

5:20   BORSE, U. Der Standort des Galaterbriefes (1972) 103f., 131f. CRANFORD, L. "Encountering Heresy. Insight From the Pastoral Epistles," SouJTh 22 (1980) 24. THISELTON, A. C. The Two Horizons (Grand Rapids 1980) 410. REBELL, W. Gemeinde als Gegenwelt (Frankfurt am Main/Bern/New York/Paris 1987) 116. CLABEAUX, J. J. The Lost Edition of the Letters of Paul (CBQ.MS; Washington 1989) 163.

5:21   SCHRAGE, W. Die konkreten Einzelgebote in der paulinischen Paränese (1961) 127f. JÜNGEL, E. Paulus und Jesus (1966) 267. MERK, O. Handeln aus Glauben (1968) 73f. BAUMERT, N. Täglich sterben und auferstehen. Der Literalsinn von 2 Kor 4, 12-5, 10 (1973) 90. BEYER, W.-ALTHAUS, P. "Die Früchte des Geistes und der hellenistische Tugendbegriff" in Der Brief an die Galter (1949) 48f. AONO, T. Die Entwicklung des paulinischen Gerichtsgedankens bei den Apostolischen Vätern (Bern/Frankfurt/Las Vegas 1979) 4ff. TISSOT, Y. "Les Actes apocryphes de Thomas: ememple de recueil composite" in F. Bovon et al., eds., Les Actes Apocryphes des Apôtres (Geneva 1981) 228n.17. JOHNSTON, G. "'Kingdom of God' Sayings in Paul's Letters" in P. Richardson and J. C. Hurd, eds., From Jesus to Paul (FS F. W. Beare; Waterloo 1984) 147f. MALHERBE, A. J. Moral Exhortation. A Greco-Roman Sourcebook (Philadelphia 1986) 138. DONFRIED, K. P. "The Kingdom of God in Paul" in W. Willis, ed., The Kingdom of God in 20th-Century Interpretation (Peabody, MA 1987) 185f. CLABEAUX, J. J. The Lost Edition of the Letters of Paul (CBQ.MS; Washington 1989) 163. WILKIN, R. N. "Christians Who Lose Their Legacy: Galatians 5:21," Journal of the Grace Evangelical Society 4 (2, 1991) 23-37.

5:22-6:8   KIRK, J. A. "The Meaning of Wisdom in James. Examination of a Hypothesis," NTS 16 (1969/70) 26.

5:22ff.   DEIDUN, T. J. New Covenant Morality in Paul (Rome 1981) 80-83.

5:22-24   MINDE, H. J. VAN DER, "Theologia crucis und Pneumaaussagen bei Paulus," Catholica 34 (1980) 137, 141.

5:22-23   VIARD, A. "Le fruit de l'esprit (Gal 5, 22-23)" VieS (1953) 451-70. O'CALLAGHAN, D. "The Christian Life — XII. The Frutis of the Spirit" Furrow 12 (1961) 288-295. PAINTER, J. "The Fruit of the Spirit is Love. Galatians 5:22-23. An Exegetical note" Journal of Theology for Southern Africa 5 (1973) 57-59. DUNN, J.D.G. Jesus and the Spirit (1975) 295. SANDERS, J. T. Ethics in the New Testament (Philadelphia 1975) 55. RÄISÄNEN, H. Paul and the Law (Tübingen 1983) 66, 104, 114f., 124. COGGAN, D. Paul. Portrait of a Revolutionary (New York 1984) 183-91. MOHRLANG, R. Matthew and Paul (Cambridge 1984) 32, 105, 117, 120f., 183. BARRETT, C. K. Freedom and Obligation (Philadelphia 1985) 77f.

5:22   SCHRAGE, W. Die konkreten Einzelgebote in der paulinischen Paränese (1961) 44, 54-56. HAINZ, J. Ekklesia (1972) 327f. MOULE, C. F. D. The Holy Spirit (London 1978) 86f. STOCKTON, E. D. "Fruit of the Spirit," Studies in Faith and Culture 4 (1980) 61-67. BISER, E. Der Zeuge (Graz/Wien/Köln 1981) 124ff. DEIDUN, T. J. New Covenant Morality in Paul (Rome 1981) 118f. TOIT, A. B. DU and STEIGER, L. "Freude" in TRE 11 (1983) 585, 587, 589. MOHRLANG, R. Matthew and Paul (Cambridge 1984) 101f., 186. MARTIN, B. L. Christ and the Law in Paul (Leiden 1989) 6, 58, 108, 147f. OLIVEIRA, A. DE, Die Diakonie der Gerechtigkeit und der Versöhnung in der Apologie des 2. Korintherbriefes. Analyse und Auslegung von 2 Kor 2, 14-4, 6; 5, 11-6, 10 (Münster 1990) 412.

5:23 BAEUMLEIN, E. "Über Galat. 5, 23" ThSK 35 (1862) 551-53. ROBB, J.D. "Galatians 5:23. An Explanation" ET 56 (1944-45) 279-80. SCHRAGE, W. Die konkreten Einzelgebote in der paulinischen Paränese (1961) 234. MALHERBE, A. J. Moral Exhortation. A Greco-Roman Sourcebook (Philadelphia 1986) 138. MARTIN, B. L. Christ and the Law in Paul (Leiden 1989) 108, 147f., 153. VOLLENWEIDER, S. Freiheit als neue Schöpfung (Göttingen 1989) 308.

5:24-25 TANNEHILL, R. Dying and Rising With Christ (1966) 61-62.

5:24 SPENS, M. "Query on Galatians 5, 24" Th 30 (1935) 109-10. DENNEY, J. The Death of Christ (1956) 95. DOWNING, J.D.H. "Possible Baptismal References in Galatians" in Studia Evangelica II/1. Ed. by F.L. Cross (1964) 551-56. SCHNACK-ENBURG, R. Baptism in the Thought of St.Paul (1964) 62f. THÜSING, W. Per Christum in Deum (1965) 17f. ORTKEMPER, F.-J. Das Kreuz in der Verkündigung des Apostels Paulus (1967) 35-39. BAUMERT, N. Täglich sterben und auferstehen. Der Literalsinn von 2 Kor 4, 12-5, 10 (1973) 271f. SIBER, P. Mit Christus leben (Zürich 1971) 185f., 192, 196, 218, 222ff., 227ff. KÜMMEL, W. G. Römer 7 und das Bild des Menschen im Neuen Testament (München 1974) 17f., 25. SCHMITH-ALS, W. "Zur Herkunft der gnostischen Elemente in der Sprache des Paulus" in B. Aland et al., eds., Gnosis (FS H. Jonas; Göttingen 1978) 388-90. WEDER, H. Das Kreuz Jesu bei Paulus (Göttingen 1981) 198-201. MOHRLANG, R. Matthew and Paul (Cambridge 1984) 84, 93, 117f., 174. RÄISÄNEN, H. The Torah and Christ (Helsinki 1986) 166. BERGER, K. und COLPE, C., eds., Religionsgeschichtliches Textbuch zum Neuen Testament (Göttingen/Zürich 1987) 279. MERKLEIN, H. Studien zu Jesus und Paulus (Tübingen 1987) 49, 58, 98, 100, 343, 424n.61. JONGE, M. DE, Christology in Context. The Earliest Christian Response to Jesus (Philadelphia 1988) 41f., 217n.8. MARTIN, B. L. Christ and the Law in Paul (Leiden 1989) 105f., 108, 114, 127.

5:25–6:10 SCHLIER, H. GPM 5 (1950/51) 191-93. WILCKENS, U. GPM 16 (1961/62) 286 -90. WARNACH, V. "Communauté dans l'Espirit" AssS 69 (1964) 15-28. BÜK-MANN, O. in Herr, tue meine Lippen suf, Bd. II. Hrsg. von G. Eichholz (1966) 426-32. IWAND, H.-J. Predigt–Meditationen (1966) 516-22. STECK, K. GPM 22 (1967/68) 382-90. SISTI, A. "La practica della carita fraterna" BiOr 11 (1969) 189-96. ECKERT, J. Die urchristliche Verkündigung im Streit zwischen Paulus und seinen Gegnern nach dem Galaterbrief (1971) 142-48. HONG, I.-G. The Law in Galatians (Sheffield 1993) 62-65, 70, 73, 75, 86, 176.

5:25-26; 6:1-3,
7-10 MARQUARDT, F. in GPM 36 (1981/82) 381-89. MERKEL, F. in GPM 42 (1987/88) 387-92.

5:25–6:5 DOERNE, M. Die alten Episteln (1967) 207-11.

5:25-26 HERRMANN, W. und GREMMELS, C. in P. Krusche et al., eds., Predigtstudien für das Kirchenjahr 1981/82. Perikopenreihe IV/2 (Stuttgart 1982) 210-16. MAR-QUARDT, F.-W. in GPM 36 (1982) 381-89.

5:25 FEINE, P. & BEHM, J. Einleitung in das Neue Testament (1950) 146f. BULT-MANN, R. Theologie des Neuen Testaments (1965) 334f. JÜNGEL, E. Paulus und Jesus (1966) 63f. HAINZ, J. Ekklesia (1972) 327f. SCHWEIZER, E. "Christus und Geist im Kolosserbrief" in Christ and the Spirit in the New Tesatment. In Honour of C.F.D. Moule (1973) 302f. CONZELMANN, H. u. LINDEMANN, A. Arbeits-buch zum Neuen Testament (1975) 192. SANDERS, J. T. Ethics in the New Testament (Philadelphia 1975) 55f. MOULE, C. F. D. The Holy Spirit (London 1978) 28. KÖRTNER, U. H. J. "Rechtfertigung und Ethik bei Paulus. Bemerkungen zum Ansatz paulinischer Ethik," Wort und Dienst 16 (1981) 93-109. BRINSMEAD, B. H. Galatians—Dialogical Response to Opponents (Chico CA 1982) 168. HAINZ,

J. Koinonia (Regensburg 1982) 64f., 70, 73, 83. SCHRAGE, W. "Ethik" in TRE 10 (1982) 445. HAYS, R. B. The Faith of Jesus Christ (Chico CA 1983) 260. SCHNACKENBURG, R. Die sittliche Botschaft des Neuen Testaments, Band 1 (Freiburg/Basel/Wien 1986) 163. CONZELMANN, H. and LINDEMANN, A. Interpreting the New Testament (Peabody MA 1988) 170. COSGROVE, C. H. The Cross and the Spirit. A Study in the Argument and Theology of Galatians (Macon GA 1988) 14, 59, 147, 152n., 153, 156, 163-65, 173. MARXSEN, W. "Christliche" und christliche Ethik im Neuen Testament (Gütersloh 1989) 169f. MULLER, E. C. Trinity and Marriage in Paul (New York/Bern/ Frankfurt/Paris 1990) 93, 109-11, 122.

5:26-6:5   HAINZ, J. Koinonia (Regensburg 1982) 65f.

5:26ff.   SCHULZ, S. Neutestamentliche Ethik (Zürich 1987) 150ff.

5:26   DEWITT, N.W. St.Paul and Epicurus (1954) 71-72.

6   HIRSCH, E. "Zwei Fragen zu Galater 6" ZNW 29 (1930) 192-97. HOLTZMANN, O. "Zu Emanuel Hirsch, Zwei Fragen zu Galater 6" ZNW 30 (1931) 76-83. DAMERAU, R. Der Galaterbrief-kommentar des Nikolaus Dinkelsbühl (1970) 182-210. PANIER, L. "Parcours pour lire l'épître aux Galates. 6ᵉ série: Ga 6," Sémiotique et Bible 55 (1989) 29-33.

6:1-10   NIEDER, L. Die Motive der religiös—sittlichen Paränese in den paulinischen Gemeindebriefen (1956) 65-67. PFISTER, W. Das Leben im Geist nach Paulus (1963) 65-68.

6:1-5   MATHESON, G. "The Paradox of Christian Ethics" Exp 1st series 19 (1879) 81-98. PAGELS, E.H. The Gnostic Paul (1975) 111. SYNOFZIK, E. Die Gerichts- und Vergeltungsaussagen bei Paulus (Göttingen 1977) 43f. HÜBNER, H. Das Gesetz bei Paulus. Ein Beitrag zum Werden der paulinischen Theologie (Göttingen 1978) 82-88, 91. MARXSEN, W. Christologie—praktisch (Gütersloh 1978) 150-59. SCHADE, H.-H. Apokalyptische Christologie bei Paulus (Göttingen 1981) 58f. KLAIBER, W. Rechtfertigung und Gemeinde (Göttingen 1982) 249-51. KLEIN, G. "Werkruhm und Christusruhm im Galaterbrief und die Frage nach einer Entwicklung des Paulus. Ein hermeneutischer und exegetischer Zwischenruf" in W. Schrage, ed., Studien zum Text und zur Ethik des Neuen Testaments (Berlin/New York 1986) 202ff. MALHERBE, A. J. Moral Exhortation. A Greco-Roman Sourcebook (Philadelphia 1986) 28. GARLINGTON, D. B. "Burden Bearing and the Recovery of Offending Christians (Galatians 6:1-5)," Trinity Journal 12 (2, 1991) 151-83.

6:1-3   MARQUARDT, F.-W. in GPM 36 (1982) 381-89. HERRMANN, W. und GREMMELS, C. in P. Krusche et al., eds., Predigtstudien für das Kirchenjahr 1981/82. Perikopenreihe IV/2 (Stuttgart 1982) 210-16.

6:1   ROBB, J.D. "Galatians 6:1" ET 57 (1945-46) 222. SCHRAGE, W. Die konkreten Einzelgebote in der paulinischen Paränese (1961) 35f., 115, 243. BRAUN, H. Wumran und das Neue Testament II (1966) 248, 287, 290. KÜMMEL, W.G. Einleitung in das Neue Testament (1973) 261f. DUNN, J.D.G. Jesus and the Spirit (1975) 208, 287f. ELLIS, E. E. Prophecy and Hermeneutic in Early Christianity (Tübingen 1978) 26, 50, 98f. BARRETT, C. K. Freedom and Obligation (Philadelphia 1985) 79. MALHERBE, A. J. Moral Exhortation. A Greco-Roman Sourcebook (Philadelphia 1986) 48. SCHNELLE, U. Wandlungen im paulinischen Denken (Stuttgart 1989) 96. LOHSE, E. Die Entstehung des Neuen Testaments (Stuttgart/Berlin/Köln ⁵1991) 37.

6:2,5   HALL, B.G. "Φορτίον and βάρη (Gal. 6:2, 5)" ET 34 (1922-23) 563. JONES, A. "Βάρος and φορτίον" ET 34 (1922-23) 333. STOIKE, D.A. 'The Law of Christ': A Study of Paul's Use of the Expression in Gal 6:2 (diss. School of Theology at

Claremont, n.d.). BERLAGE, H.P. "De juiste verklaring van Gal. 6:2" TT 25 (1891) 47-61. VAN STEMPVOORT, P.A. "Gal. 6:2" THhT 7 (1952-53) 362-63. SCHRAGE, W. Die konkreten Einzelgebote in der paulinischen Paränese (1961) 99f. BAMMEL, E. "Νόμος Χριστοῦ" in Studia Evangelica III. Ed. by F.L. Cross (1964) 120-28. BANDSTRA.A.J. The Law and the Elements of the World (1964) 111ff. SCHÜRMANN, H. "'Das Gesetz des Christus' (Gal 6, 2)" in Neues Testament und Kirche. Für Rudolf Schnackenburg. Hrsg. von J. Gnilka (1974) 282-300. DRANE, J.W. Paul: Libertine or Legalist? (1975) 55-58. STRELAN, J.G. "Burden–Bearing and the Law of Christ: A Re–examination of Galatians 6:2" JBL 94 (1975) 266-76.

6:2   DAVIES, W. D. The Sermon on the Mount (Cambridge 1966) 101. MINEAR, P. S. To Die and to Live. Christ's Resurrection and Christian Vocation (New York 1977) 72. FRIEDRICH, G. "Das Gesetz des Glaubens Römer 3, 27" in Auf das Wort kommt es an. Gesammelte Aufsätze (Göttingen 1978) 112, 113f. FURNISH, V. P. The Moral Teaching of Paul (Nashville 1979) 13, 125. OUTKA, G. "On Harming Others," Interp 34 (1980) 384. HAINZ, J. Koinonia (Regensburg 1982) 65f., 69, 83. BLANK, J. Paulus. Von Jesus zum Christentum (München 1982) 119. SCHRAGE, W. "Ethik" in TRE 10 (1982) 448. HAYS, R. B. The Faith of Jesus Christ (Chico CA 1983) 260. RÄISÄNEN, H. Paul and the Law (Tübingen 1983) 16, 64f., 77-80, 238, 240. KLEINKNECHT, K. T. Der leidende Gerechtfertigte (Tübingen 1984) 360. MOHRLANG, R. Matthew and Paul (Cambridge 1984) 40, 101, 107, 150, 183. VERHEY, A. The Great Reversal (Grand Rapids 1984) 112f. BARRETT, C. K. Freedom and Obligation (Philadelphia 1985) 79f. FREUND, G. und STEGEMANN, E., eds., Theologische Brosamen für Lothar Steiger (DBAT 5; Heidelberg 1985) 407. SANDERS, E. P. Paul, the Law, and the Jewish People (London 1985) 49n.6, 94, 97f., 115n.11, 116n.12. SCHNABEL, E. J. Law and Wisdom from Ben Sira to Paul (Tübingen 1985) 266, 268f., 277-79, 281, 294, 296, 314, 341. RÄISÄNEN, H. The Torah and Christ (Helsinki 1986) 98, 100, 143, 277f., 363f. SCHNACKENBURG, R. Die sittliche Botschaft des Neuen Testaments, Band 1 (Freiburg/Basel/Wien 1986) 194. CLABEAUX, J. J. The Lost Edition of the Letters of Paul (CBQ.MS; Washington 1989) 52f. HOFIUS, O. "Das Gesetz des Mose und das Gesetz Christi" in Paulusstudien (Tübingen 1989) 50-74. MARTIN, B. L. Christ and the Law in Paul (Leiden 1989) 6, 91, 146, 151, 152. SCHNELLE, U. Wandlungen im paulinischen Denken (Stuttgart 1989) 60f. VOLLENWEIDER, S. Freiheit als neue Schöpfung (Göttingen 1989) 214, 306f., 313, 362n., 403. HONG, I.-G. The Law in Galatians (Sheffield 1993) 11, 114, 123, 154, 170f., 173-78, 182, 191, 194.

6:3   OUTKA, G. "On Harming Others," Interp 34 (1980) 387. THISELTON, A. C. The Two Horizons (Grand Rapids 1980) 391.

6:4-10   RÄISÄNEN, H. The Torah and Christ (Helsinki 1986) 326.

6:4-5   FABREGAS, I. R. I, "El 'Discerniment cristià' en la carta als Gàlates. Estudi de Ga 6, 4.5," Revista Catalana de Teología 13 (1, 1988) 1-22.

6:4   WETTER, G.P. Der Vergeltungsgedanke bei Paulus (1912) 118ff. ZEDDA, S. L'adowionea figli di Dio e lo Spirito Santo (1952) SCHRAGE, W. Die konkreten Einzelgebote in der paulinischen Paränese (1961) 54-56. HÜBNER, H. Das Gesetz bei Paulus. Ein Beitrag zum Werden der paulinischen Theologie (Göttingen 1978) 81, 82-88, 91. KLEIN, G. "Werkruhm und Christusruhm im Galaterbrief und die Frage nach einer Entwicklung des Paulus. Ein hermeneutischer und exegetischer Zwischenruf" in W. Schrage, ed., Studien zum Text und zur Ethik des Neuen Testaments (Berlin/New York 1986) 199ff.

6:5   REY, B. Créés dans le Christ Jesus (1966) 21-35. OUTKA, G. "On Harming Others," Interp 34 (1980) 384, 387. HAINZ, J. Koinonia (Regensburg 1982) 67, 69, 80, 83.

6:6-10 KOSOWSKI, S. "Dobre czyny w nauczaniu sw. duszpasterza w Galacjix" Ruch Biblijny i Liturgiczny 11 (1958) 38-42. BORSE, U. Der Standort des Galaterbriefes (1972) 37f. HURTADO, L. W. "The Jerusalem Collection and the Book of Galatians," JSNT 5 (1979) 46-62.

6:6   SEEBERT, A. Der Katechismus der Urchristenheit (1966) 268-70. DUNN, J.D.G. Jesus and the Spirit (1975) 282f. LIERMANN, H. "Abgaben" in TRE 1 (1977) 329. HOLMBERG, B. Paul and Power (Lund 1978) 112. HILL, D. New Testament Prophecy (Atlanta 1979) 127. OLLROG, W.-H. Paulus und seine Mitarbeiter (Neukirchen/Vluyn 1979) 74, 85, 94, 117. HAGEN, K. Hebrews Commenting from Erasmus to Bèze 1516-1598 (Tübingen 1981) 1. HAINZ, J. Koinonia (Regensburg 1982) 11, 62-89, 109-11, 113f., 116, 138, 148, 150, 158, 164, 167f., 180, 187. MacDONALD, M. Y. The Pauline Churches (Cambridge 1988) 57. WOLTER, M. Die Pastoralbriefe als Paulustradition (Göttingen 1988) 249. KLAUCK, H.-J. Gemeinde, Amt, Sakrament (Würzburg 1989) 94. LAMPE, P. Die stadtrömischen Christen in den ersten beiden Jahrhunderten (Tübingen ²1989) 62, 310. BEERNAERT, P. M. "Le verbe grec katêchein dans le N.T.," LuVit 44 (1989) 377-87.

6:7ff. WETTER, G.P. Der Vergeltungsgedanke bei Paulus (1912) 68ff.

6:7-10 SYNOFZIK, E. Die Gerichts- und Vergeltungsaussagen bei Paulus (Göttingen 1977) 72-74. MÜNCHOW, C. Ethik und Eschatologie (Göttingen 1981) 158, 161f. SCHADE, H.-H. Apokalyptische Christologie bei Paulus (Göttingen 1981) 55. HAINZ, J. Koinonia (Regensburg 1982) 66f., 69, 80, 84. HERRMANN, W. und GREMMELS, C. in P. Krusche et al., eds., Predigtstudien für das Kirchenjahr 1981/82. Perikopenreihe IV/2 (Stuttgart 1982) 210-16. MARQUARDT, F.-W. in GPM 36 (1982) 381-89. FROITZHEIM, F. Christologie und Eschatologie bei Paulus (Würzburg 1979) 183f. SNYMAN, A. H. "Modes of Persuasion in Galatians 6:7-10," Neotestamentica 26 (1992) 475-84.

6:7-9   PAGELS, E.H. The Gnostic Paul (1975) 111. AONO, T. Die Entwicklung des paulinischen Gerichtsgedankens bei den Apostolischen Vätern (Bern/Frankfurt/Las Vegas 1979) 4ff. HAINZ, J. Koinonia (Regensburg 1982) 68, 82, 84.

6:7   BAUMERT, N. Tänglich sterben und auferstehen. Der Literalsinn von 2 Kor 4, 12-5, 10 (1973) 160. BÖHLIG, A. Die Gnosis III: Der Manichäismus (Zürich/München 1980) 343n.20. HAINZ, J. Koinonia (Regensburg 1982) 66-68, 75f., 84f. HELDERMANN, J. Die Anapausis im Evangelium Veritatis (Leiden 1984) 82n.147. NORTH, J. L. "Sowing and Reaping (Galatians 6:7B): More Examples of a Classical Maxim," JThS 43 (1992) 523-27.

6:8   SCHRAGE, W. Die konkreten Einzelgebote in der paulinischen Paränese (1961) 20f. STROBEL, A. Erkenntnis und Bekenntnis der Sünde in neutestamentlicher Zeit (1968) 66. BAUMERT, N. Täglich sterben und auferstehen. Der Literalsinn von 2 Kor 4, 12-5, 10 (1973) 139f. KÜMMEL, W.G. Römer 7 und das Bild des Menschen im Neuen Testament (1974) 17f. KÜMMEL, W. G. Römer 7 und das Bild des Menschen im Neuen Testament (München 1974) 17f. MINEAR, P. S. To Die and to Live. Christ's Resurrection and Christian Vocation (New York 1977) 72. LULL, D. J. The Spirit in Galatia (Chico CA 1980) 173f. HAINZ, J. Koinonia (Regensburg 1982) 67, 76, 84f. HARRIS, M. J. Raised Immortal (London 1986) 146. MARTIN, B. L. Christ and the Law in Paul (Leiden 1989) 98, 105-07, 120, 150.

6:9   SMITH, H. "Galatians 6:9" ET 13 (1901-02) 139. BAUMERT, N Täglich sterben und auferstehen. Der Literalsinn von 2 Kor 4, 12-5, 10 (1973) 322f. MOULTON, H.K. "Tired of doing good?" BTr 26 (1975) 445. HAINZ, J. Koinonia (Regensburg

1982) 67f., 84f. CLABEAUX, J. J. The Lost Edition of the Letters of Paul (CBQ.MS; Washington 1989) 100, 152.

6:10 PFAMMATER, J. Die Kirche als Bau (1960) 17f. LIPPERT, P. Leben als Zeugnis (1968) 11. PIPER, J. 'Love your enemies' (Cambridge 1979) 42, 63, 179n.21, 191n.132, 219n.98. CLARK, K. W. "The Israel of God" in The Gentile Bias and Other Essays [Selected by J. L. Sharpe III] (Leiden 1980) 22. ABBING, P. J. R. "Diakonie" in TRE 8 (1981) 646. HAINZ, J. Koinonia (Regensburg 1982) 67f., 79, 83, 85. HAYS, R. B. The Faith of Jesus Christ (Chico CA 1983) 149. MALHERBE, A. J. Moral Exhortation. A Greco-Roman Sourcebook (Philadelphia 1986) 93. SCHNACKENBURG, R. Die sittliche Botschaft des Neuen Testaments, Band 1 (Freiburg/Basel/Wien 1986) 219. DOBBELER, A. VON, Glaube als Teilhabe (Tübingen 1987) 251-73.

6:11ff. BANDSTRA, A.J. The Law and the Elements of the World (1964) 54f.

6:11-18 SHEPARD, J.W. The Life and Letters of St.Paul (1950) 363-64. GIBLIN, C.H. In Hope of God's Glory (1970) 89-91. ECKERT, J. Die urchristliche Verkündigung im Streit zwischen Paulus und seinen Gegnern nach dem Galaterbrief (1971) 31-39. STOGIANNOS, B.P. "Hēhypo tou Paulou idiocheiros anakephalaiō tēs pros Galatas" DBM 1 (1971) 59-79. DRANE, J.W. Paul: Libertine or Legalist? (1975) 59. BUSCEMI, A. M. "Lo sviluppo strutturale e contenutistico in Gal 6, 11-18," SBFLA 33 (1983) 153-92. HAYS, R. B. The Faith of Jesus Christ (Chico CA 1983) 222. STOGIANNOS, V. "Die eigenhändige Zusammenfassung des Galaterbriefes des Paulus (Gal 6, 11-18)," DBM 14 (2, 1985) 11-23. MELL, U. Neue Schöpfung (Berlin/New York 1989) 262ff., 275ff., 280ff. COUSAR, C. B. A Theology of the Cross (Minneapolis 1990) 136, 137-48, 156f., 163. HOWARD, G. Paul. Crisis in Galatia (Cambridge ²1990) 46, 48, 49. HONG, I.-G. The Law in Galatians (Sheffield 1993) 65-67. WEIMA, J. A. D. "Gal 6:11-18. A Hermeneutical Key to the Galatian Letter," CThJ 28 (1993) 90-107.

6:11-17 LYONS, G. Pauline Autobiography (Atlanta GA 1985) 168-70.

6:11-16 MULLER, E. C. Trinity and Marriage in Paul (New York/Bern/ Frankfurt/Paris 1990) 121, 370.

6:11-14 HÜBNER, H. Das Gesetz bei Paulus. Ein Beitrag zum Werden der paulinischen Theologie (Göttingen 1978) 88-91.

6:11-12 BARRETT, C. K. Freedom and Obligation (Philadelphia 1985) 83-87.

6:11 CLEMENS, J.S. "St.Paul's Handwriting" ET 24 (1911-12) 380. CLARKE, W.K.L. "St.Paul's Large Letters" ET 24 (1912-13) 285. GAMBLE, H. The Textual History of the Letter to the Romans (Grand Rapids 1977) 76-80. OLLROG, W.-H. Paulus und seine Mitarbeiter (Neukirchen/Vluyn 1979) 185f., 242. MURPHY-O'CONNOR, J. St. Paul's Corinth. Texts and Archaeology (Wilmington, Del. 1983) 169. FREUND, G. und STEGEMANN, E., eds., Theologische Brosamen für Lothar Steiger (DBAT 5; Heidelberg 1985) 389. RICHARDS, E. R. The Secretary in the Letters of Paul (Tübingen 1991) 172, 174, 190.

6:12-18 BRINSMEAD, B. H. Galatians—Dialogical Response to Opponents (Chico CA 1982) 63-66, 189. RICHARDS, E. R. The Secretary in the Letters of Paul (Tübingen 1991) 190. PATTE, C. M. The Glory of Adam and the Afflictions of the Righteous. Pauline Suffering in Context (Lewiston NY 1993) passim.

6:12-15 ORTKEMPER, F.-J. Das Kreuz in der Verkündigung des Apostels Paulus (1967) 31-35.

6:12-14 SCHELKLE, K.H. Die Passion Jesu in der Verkündigung des Neuen Testament (1949) 237ff., 242f. WEDER, H. Neutestamentliche Hermeneutik (Zürich 1986) 387f. MARTYN, J. L. "A Law-Observant Mission to Gentiles. The Background of

Galatians" in M. P. O'Connor and D. N. Freedman, eds., Backgrounds for the Bible (Winona Lake/Indiana 1987) 199-214, esp. 204ff.

6:12-13   KENNEDY, H.A.A. "Galatians 6:12, 13" ET 22 (1910-11) 419-20. FEINE, P. & BEHM, J. Einleitung in das Neue Testament (1950) 142f. MUNCK, J. Paul and the Salvation of Mankind (1959) 89f. RICHARDSON, P. Israel in the Apostolic Church (1969)84-91, 96f. JEWETT, R. "The Agitators and the Galatian Congregation" NTS 17 (1970-71) 201-4. KÜMMEL, W.G. Einleitung in das Neue Testament (1973) 259f. MINEAR, P. S. To Die and to Live. Christ's Resurrection and Christian Vocation (New York 1977) 72. BORGEN, P. "Paul Preaches Circumcision and Pleases Men" in M. D. Hooker and S. G. Wilson, eds., Paul and Paulinism (FS C. K. Barrett; London 1982) 41-44. BRINSMEAD, B. H. Galatians—Dialogical Response to Opponents (Chico CA 1982) 64f. ZMIJEWSKI, J. Paulus—Knecht und Apostel Christi (Stuttgart 1986) 77f. BECKER, J. Paulus. Der Apostel der Völker (Tübingen 1989) 218, 278, 280, 343, 345. MELL, U. Neue Schöpfung (Berlin/New York 1989) 285ff., 323, 391. SCHNELLE, U. Wandlungen im paulinischen Denken (Stuttgart 1989) 54. HONG, I.-G. The Law in Galatians (Sheffield 1993) 88f., 101, 103, 110f., 115, 117, 119, 134, 180.

6:12   SCHOEPS, H.-J. Paulus (1959) 72f. SCHMITHALS, W. Paulus und Jakobus (1963) 17, 29. MINEAR, P. S. To Die and to Live. Christ's Resurrection and Christian Vocation (New York 1977) 72. WEDER, H. Das Kreuz Jesu bei Paulus (Göttingen 1981) 201-05. LÜDEMANN, G. Paulus, der Heidenapostel, Band II (Göttingen 1983) 144, 150f. HÜBNER, H. "Galaterbrief" in TRE 12 (1984) 6, 7. KLEIN-KNECHT, K. T. Der leidende Gerechtfertigte (Tübingen 1984) 196, 320, 387. HOWARD, G. Paul. Crisis in Galatia (Cambridge [2]1990) 13, 18, 88.

6:13-15   BARRETT, C. K. Freedom and Obligation (Philadelphia 1985) 87-89.

6:13-14   MINEAR, P. S. To Die and to Live. Christ's Resurrection and Christian Vocation (New York 1977) 72. HÜBNER, H. Das Gesetz bei Paulus. Ein Beitrag zum Werden der paulinischen Theologie (Göttingen 1978) 81, 88f.

6:13   MUNCK, J. Paul and the Salvation of Mankind (1959) 87-90. VAN DÜLMEN, A. Die Theologie des Gesetzes bei Paulus (1968) 70f. BORSE, U. Der Standort des Galaterbriefes (1972) 82f. KÜMMEL, W.G. Einleitung in das Neue Testament (1973) 260-62. VIELHAUER, P. "Gesetzesdienst und Stoicheiadienst im Galaterbrief" in Rechtfertigung. Festschrift für Ernst Käsemann (1976) 544-46. HÜBNER, H. Das Gesetz bei Paulus. Ein Beitrag zum Werden der paulinischen Theologie (Göttingen 1978) 26. HOWARD, G. Paul. Crisis in Galatia (Cambridge 1979) 17-19. VIELHAUER, P. "Gesetzesdienst und Stoicheiadienst im Galaterbrief" in Oikodome [G. Klein, ed.] (München 1979) 185f. THISELTON, A. C. The Two Horizons (Grand Rapids 1980) 269, 280, 410. LÜDEMANN, G. Paulus, der Heidenapostel, Band II (Göttingen 1983) 150-52. CLABEAUX, J. J. The Lost Edition of the Letters of Paul (CBQ.MS; Washington 1989) 163. LIEBERS, R. Das Gesetz als Evangelium (Zürich 1989) 73-75, 80-82. MELL, U. Neue Schöpfung (Berlin/New York 1989) 271ff. HOWARD, G. Paul. Crisis in Galatia (Cambridge [2]1990) 6, 11, 13-19. SEGAL, A. F. Paul the Convert (New Haven/London 1990) 146, 209.

6:14-17   BISER, E. Der Zeuge (Graz/Wien/Köln 1981) 26, 56, 74f., 173, 191, 196, 254.

6:14-16   PAGELS, E.H. The Gnostic Paul (1975) 111-12. BRINSMEAD, B. H. Galatians—Dialogical Response to Opponents (Chico CA 1982) 65-67.

6:14-15   STANLEY, D.M. Christ's Resurrection in Pauline Soteriology (1961) 158-60. TANNEHILL, R.C. Dying and Rising With Christ (1966) 62-65. BORSE, U. Der Standort des Galaterbriefes (1972) 64-67. MINEAR, P. S. To Die and to Live. Christ's Resurrection and Christian Vocation (New York 1977) 66-88. WOLTER, M. "Bekehrung" in TRE 5 (1980) 443. COSGROVE, C. H. The Cross and the Spirit.

A Study in the Argument and Theology of Galatians (Macon GA 1988) 77, 139, 179-82, 193. MELL, U. Neue Schöpfung (Berlin/New York 1989) 293ff., 316ff., 350, 354, 370, 383, 391. MULLER, E. C. Trinity and Marriage in Paul (New York/Bern/Frankfurt/Paris 1990) 52, 122. OLIVEIRA, A. DE, Die Diakonie der Gerechtigkeit und der Versöhnung in der Apologie des 2. Korintherbriefes. Analyse und Auslegung von 2 Kor 2, 14-4, 6; 5, 11-6, 10 (Münster 1990) 362.

6:14 BÜCHSEL, D.F. Der Geist Gottes im Neuen Testament (1926) 295ff. MCNEILE, A.H. "Studies in Texts" Th 19 (1929) 108f. DENNEY, J. The Death of Christ (1956) 95f. SCHWEIZER, E. Erniedrigung und Erhöhung bei Jesus und seinen Nachfolgern (1962) §9a. KRAMER, W. Christos Kyrios Gottessohn (1963) §31a. SCHNACKEN-BURG, R. Baptism in the Thought of St.Paul (1964) 62f. LADD, G.E. A Theology of the New Testament (1974) 399-400. DUNN, J.D.G. Jesus and the Spirit (1975) 331f. SIBER, P. Mit Christus leben (Zürich 1971) 185f., 192, 196, 218, 222ff., 227ff. BETZ, O. "Beschneidung" in TRE 5 (1980) 720. THISELTON, A. C. The Two Horizons (Grand Rapids 1980) 269, 280, 410. SCHADE, H.-H. Apokalyptische Christologie bei Paulus (Göttingen 1981) 91. WEDER, H. Das Kreuz Jesu bei Paulus (Göttingen 1981) 205-209. LAYTON, B. The Gnostic Scriptures (Garden City NY 1987) 288, 338. BECKER, J. Paulus. Der Apostel der Völker (Tübingen 1989) 82, 127, 218, 364. MELL, U. Neue Schöpfung (Berlin/New York 1989) 291.

6:15 THACKERAY, H.St.J. The Relation of St.Paul to Contemporary Jewish Thought (1900) 245ff. TILLICH, P. Das Neue Sein (1959) 23-32. SCHNEIDER, G. Neuschöpfung oder Wiederkehr (1961) 74-76. SCHRAGE, W. Die konkreten Einzelgebote in der paulinischen Paränese (1961) 100, 203f. SCHWANTES, H. Schöpfung der Endzeit (1962). BOYER, C. "ΚΑΙΝΗ ΚΤΙΣΙΣ (2 Cor 5, 17; Gal 6, 15)" in Studiorum Paulinorum Congressus Internationalis Catholicus 1961, Vol. I (1963) 487-90. NICKELS, P. Targum and New Testament (1967) 74. STUHL-MACHER, P. "Erwägungen zum ontologischen Charakter der kainē ktisis bei Paulus" EvTh 27 (1967) 1-35. VOEGTLE, A. Das Neue Testament und die Zukunft des Kosmos (1970) 178-83. BORSE, U. Der Standort des Galaterbriefes (1972) 65-67, 79f. SCHIMADA, K. The Formulary Material in First Peter. A Study According to the Method of Traditionsgeschichte (Th.D. diss., Union Theological Seminary New York; Ann Arbor MI 1966) 195, 196-98. SIBER, P. Mit Christus leben (Zürich 1971) 235. HASENSTAB, R. Modelle paulinischer Ethik (Mainz 1977) 167. MINEAR, P. S. To Die and to Live. Christ's Resurrection and Christian Vocation (New York 1977) 72. MIRANDA, J. P. Marx and the Bible. A Critique of the Philosophy of Oppression (London 1977) 255f. CHILTON, B. D. "Galatians 6:15. A Call to Freedom before God," ET 89 (10, 1978) 311-13. SCHMITHALS, W. "Zur Herkunft der gnostischen Elemente in der Sprache des Paulus" in B. Aland et al., eds., Gnosis (FS H. Jonas; Göttingen 1978) 400. MÜLLER, U. B. "Zur Rezeption gesetzeskritischer Jesusüberlieferung im frühen Christentum," NTS 27 (1981) 160. KLAIBER, W. Rechtfertigung und Gemeinde (Göttingen 1982) 95-101. BARTSCH, H.-W. "Freiheit" in TRE 11 (1983) 508. HAYS, R. B. The Faith of Jesus Christ (Chico CA 1983) 232, 250, 260. NEBE, G. 'Hoffnung' bei Paulus (Göttingen 1983) 47, 143, 172, 181, 269, 296, 316. RÄISÄNEN, H. Paul and the Law (Tübingen 1983) 67f., 139. LENTZEN-DEIS, W. "Jesus Christus, der 'neue Mensch'. Eine Hinführung zur Christologie im Ausgang von Erich Fromms 'Haben oder Sein'," TThZ 93 (1984) 100-17. FREUND, G. und STEGEMANN, E., eds., Theologische Brosamen für Lothar Steiger (DBAT 5; Heidelberg 1985) 390. GRAESSER, E. Der Alte Bund im Neuen (Tübingen 1985) 15, 25, 240, 248, 295. SANDERS, E. P. Paul, the Law, and the Jewish People (London 1985) 20, 100, 143, 149, 159, 174, 177, 200n.7, 201n.14, 204n.67. MERKLEIN, H. Studien zu Jesus und Paulus (Tübingen

1987) 60, 68n.167, 102, 293, 325n.34, 326, 444n.134. OSTEN-SACKEN, P. VON DER, Evangelium und Tora: Aufsätze zu Paulus (München 1987) 25, 62, 66. BECKER, J. Paulus. Der Apostel der Völker (Tübingen 1989) 110f., 302. MELL, U. Neue Schöpfung (Berlin/New York 1989) 284, 298ff., 305n.89, 306, 314, 316f., 324f., 350, 352f., 369f., 389f., 392. VOLLENWEIDER, S. Freiheit als neue Schöpfung (Göttingen 1989) 239f., 318, 320n. MULLER, E. C. Trinity and Marriage in Paul (New York/Bern/Frankfurt/Paris 1990) 33, 43f., 50, 93. OLIVEIRA, A. DE, Die Diakonie der Gerechtigkeit und der Versöhnung in der Apologie des 2. Korintherbriefes. Analyse und Auslegung von 2 Kor 2, 14-4, 6; 5, 11-6, 10 (Münster 1990) 363n.520. SANDERS, E. P. Jewish Law from Jesus to the Mishnah (London/Philadelphia 1990) 283. SEGAL, A. F. Paul the Convert (New Haven/London 1990) 137, 147, 181, 263.

6:16,21 MINEAR, P. S. To Die and to Live. Christ's Resurrection and Christian Vocation (New York 1977) 72.

6:16 SCHRENK, G. "Was bedeutet 'Israel Gottes'?" Judaica 5 (1949) 81-94. DAHL, N.A. "Der Name Israel. Zur Auslegung von Gal 6, 16" Judaica 6 (1950) 161-70. SCHRENK, G. "Der Segenswunsch nach der Kampfepistel (Antwort an N.A. Dahl)" Judaica 6 (1950) 170-90. RAURELL, F. Israel y la Iglesia: un problema de continuidad y discontinuidad" Estudios Franciscanos 66 (1965) 289-304. BRAUN, H. Qumran und das Neue Testament II (1966) 146, 326. O'CONNOR, D.J. "Is the Church the New Israel" IThQ 33 (1966) 161-64. LUZ, U. Das Geschichtsverständnis des Paulus (1968) 285f. RICHARDSON, P. Israel in the Apostolic Church (1969) 74-84, 100f. ZELLER, D. Juden und Heiden in der Mission des Paulus (1973) 98, 109, 115. WILES, G.P. Paul's Intercessory Prayers (1974) 129-35. ROON, A. VAN, The Authenticity of Ephesians (Leiden 1974) 94-98. GAMBLE, H. The Textual History of the Letter to the Romans (Grand Rapids 1977) 68. ECKERT, J. "Paulus und Israel. Zu den Strukturen paulinischer Rede und Argumentation," TThZ 87 (1978) 1-13. DINKLER, E. "Die ekklesiologischen Aussagen des Paulus im kritischen Rückblick auf Barmen III" in A. Burgsmüller, ed., Kirche als 'Gemeinde von Brüdern' (Gütersloh 1980) 121. FERGUSON, E. "Spiritual Sacrifice in Early Christianity and its Environment" in ANRW II.23.2 (1980) 1163. KAMLAH, E. "Barmherzigkeit" in TRE 5 (1980) 226. SCHNEEMELCHER, W. "Bibel" in TRE 6 (1980) 25f. GRAESSER, E. Der Alte Bund im Neuen (Tübingen 1985) 19, 222, 223, 288. SANDERS, E. P. Paul, the Law, and the Jewish People (London 1985) 54n.28, 173f. CRONJÉ, J. VAN W. "Defamiliarization in the letter to the Galatians" in J. H. Petzer and P. J. Hartin, eds., A South African Perspective on the New Testament (FS B. M. Metzger; Leiden 1986) 225. MacDONALD, M. Y. The Pauline Churches (Cambridge 1988) 32f., 95. WOLTER, M. Die Pastoralbriefe als Paulustradition (Göttingen 1988) 89. BECKER, J. Paulus. Der Apostel der Völker (Tübingen 1989) 338, 457, 492. LAMPE, P. Die stadtrömischen Christen in den ersten beiden Jahrhunderten (Tübingen ²1989) 126. MELL, U. Neue Schöpfung (Berlin/New York 1989) 317ff., 391ff. SCHNELLE, U. Wandlungen im paulinischen Denken (Stuttgart 1989) 80, 85. JERVIS, L. A. The Purpose of Romans (Sheffield 1991) 148, 149, 156. LOHSE, E. Die Entstehung des Neuen Testaments (Stuttgart/ Berlin/Köln ⁵1991) 12. CAMPBELL, W. S. Paul's Gospel in an Intercultural Context. Jew and Gentile in the Letter to the Romans (Frankfurt/Berlin/Bern etc. 1992) 74f.

6:17-18 MELL, U. Neue Schöpfung (Berlin/New York 1989) 268ff.

6:17 MOULTON, J.H. "The Marks of Jesus" ET 21 (1909-10) 283-84. KOUWENHOVEN, H.J. "Paulus' beroep op de litteekenen van den Heere Jezus in zijn lichaam" GThT 13 (1912) 105-15. PRIERO, G. "'Stigmata' in corport meo (Gal 6, 17)" PaCl 29 (1949) 138. WIKENHAUSER, A. Die Christusmystik des Apostels

Paulus (²1956) 103. ANDRIESSEN, P. "Les stigmates dé Jesus" Bijdragen 23 (1962) 139-154. WAGNER, G. Das religionsgeschichtliche Problem von Römer 6, 1-11 (1962) 303f. KÄSEMANN, E. Exegetische Versuche und Besinnungen (1964) I 126. LÜHRMANN, D. Das Offenbarungsverständnis bei Paulus und in paulinischen Gemeinden (1965) 69-71. GÜTTGEMANNS, E. Der leidende Apostel und sein Herr (1966) 126-135. BORSE, U. "Die Wundmale und der Todesbescheid" BZ 14 (1970) 88-111. KLASSEN, W. "Galatians 6:17" ET 81 (1970) 378. BAUER, K.-A. Leiblichkeit: das Ende aller Werke Gottes (1971) 69-70. BORSE, U. Der Standort des Galaterbriefes (1972) 54-55. DUNN, J.D.G. Jesus and the Spirit (1975) 449. MINEAR, P. S. To Die and to Live. Christ's Resurrection and Christian Vocation (New York 1977) 72. STOYANNOS, B. P. "'Ta stigmata tou Iesou' (Gal. 6, 17) ['The Marks of Jesus'(Gal. 6, 17)]," DBM 5 (1977) 37-69. FRIEDRICH, G. "Das Problem der Autorität im Neuen Testament" in Auf das Wort kommt es an. Gesammelte Aufsätze (Göttingen 1978) 394. ROLOFF, J. "Apostel" in TRE 3 (1978) 437. BETZ, O. "Beschneidung" in TRE 5 (1980) 720. KLEINKNECHT, K. T. Der leidende Gerechtfertigte (Tübingen 1984) 196, 246. BETZ, H. D. "Hellenismus III" in TRE 15 (1986) 27, 29. CLABEAUX, J. J. The Lost Edition of the Letters of Paul (CBQ.MS; Washington 1989) 169f. JERVIS, L. A. The Purpose of Romans (Sheffield 1991) 149, 150.

6:18 KÜMMEL, W. G. Römer 7 und das Bild des Menschen im Neuen Testament (1974) 32f. GAMBLE, H. The Textual History of the Letter to the Romans (Grand Rapids 1977) 66. AUNE, D. E. The New Testament in Its Literary Environment (Philadelphia 1987) 192. JERVIS, L. A. The Purpose of Romans (Sheffield 1991) 135, 150.

6:21 HEMER, C. J. The Book of Acts in the Setting of Hellenistic History [C. H. Gempf, ed.] (Tübingen 1989) 188f., 402.

* * * * *

An Exegetical Bibliography of the New Testament: Romans and Galatians
EBNT 4. Edited by Günter Wagner.

Mercer University Press, 6316 Peake Road, Macon, Georgia 31210-3960.
Isbn 0-86554-468-9. Catalog and warehouse pick number MUP/376.
Original design (1983): titles by Haywood Ellis (†);
        text by Edd Rowell and Janet Middlebrooks;
                redesigned 1996 by Edd Rowell.
Camera-ready pages and cover mechanicals composed on a Gateway 2000
        via WordPerfect (wp5.1 and wpwin5.1/5.2/6.0) and printed on a LaserMaster 1000.
Text font: TimesNewRomanPS. Main titles: ITC Souvenir.
Printed and bound by McNaughton & Gunn, Inc., Saline, Michigan 48176
        via offset lithography on 50# Natural Smooth paper;
        smyth sewn and cased in .088 binder boards,
                rounded and backed with matching headbands;
        cover cloth: Holliston Roxite C 57561 (linen finish), stamped on spine
                and covers 1 and 4 with matte pigment #418 (red) and S18 gold.
[May 1996]

LaVergne, TN USA
16 December 2010
209014LV00008B/53/A